REF
D
11
W65
1999

D1608841

The Wilson Calendar of World History

THE WILSON CALENDAR OF WORLD HISTORY

Edited by

John Paxton and Edward W. Knappman

Based on S. H. Steinberg's *Historical Tables*

Contributors:

Rodney Carlisle
Hilary D. Claggett
Ron Formica
Michael Golay
Paul T. Hellman
Lisa Paddock
Jan Rogozinski
Carl Rollyson
John D. Wright

THE H. W. WILSON COMPANY
NEW YORK AND DUBLIN

A New England Publishing Associates Book
1999

Copyright © 1999 by New England Publishing Associates, Inc., and John Paxton

All rights reserved. No part of this work may be reproduced or copied in any form or by any means, including, but not restricted to graphic, electronic, and mechanical—for example, photocopying, recording, taping, or information and retrieval systems—without the express written permission of the publisher except that a reviewer may quote and a magazine or newspaper may print brief passages as part of a review written specifically for inclusion in that magazine or newspaper.

Copy Editor: Barbara Jean DiMauro
Design and Page Composition: Ron Formica
Photo Researcher: Victoria Harlow
Editorial Administration: Ron Formica
Editorial Assistants: Victoria S. Chase, Dione Daffin, Susan Evensen, Reneé Ferrucci and Penny White
Indexer and Proofreader: Marlene London

To the knowledge of the editors and publisher, all photos and artwork that appear in this book were used by permission or are believed to be in the public domain. If you believe that any of the photos or artwork were used without permission or are not in the public domain, please contact the editors or publisher.

Library of Congress Cataloging–in–Publication Data
The Wilson calendar of world history: based on S.H. Steinberg's Historical tables / edited by John Paxton and Edward W. Knappman; contributors, Rodney Carlisle…[et al.].
p. cm.
"A New England Publishing Associates book."
Includes bibliographical references and index.
ISBN 0-8242-0937-0
1. Chronology, Historical. 2. Calendars.
I. Steinberg, S.H. (Sigfrid Henry), 1899–1969. Historical tables, 58 BC–AD 1990.
II. Paxton, John. III. Knappman, Edward W. IV. Carlisle, Rodney P.
D11.W65 1999
902' .02—dc21 98-50998
CIP

Henry and Christine Steinberg
mentors and friends

Contents

The material in this book is presented in a six-column format. The column categories change with each epoch to reflect the dynamics and events of the period.

Introduction by John Paxton ix
How to Use This Book xi

EPOCH	COLUMN STRUCTURE	PAGE
3500 B.C.–44 B.C.	Egypt & Africa Middle East, Asia, Pacific & Americas Greece & Asia Minor Rome & Europe Science, Invention & Technology Culture & Arts	2
43 B.C.–A.D 399	Roman Empire & Europe Africa, Asia & Pacific Americas Religion Science, Invention & Technology Culture & Arts	30
400–1453	British Isles & Western Europe Mediterranean Basin Africa, Asia & Pacific Americas Science, Invention & Technology Religion, Culture & Arts	58
1454–1774	British Isles & Europe Africa & Middle East Asia & Pacific Americas Science, Invention & Technology Religion, Culture & Arts	140
1775–August 31, 1939	British Isles & Europe U.S. & Canada Latin America Africa, Asia & Pacific Science, Invention & Technology Religion, Culture & Arts	222
September 1, 1939–1945	International Affairs; European, African, Mideast War Zone U.S. & Canadian Domestic Developments Asia & Pacific War Zone Latin America Science, Invention & Technology Religion, Culture & Arts	322
1946–1998	International Affairs Western & Eastern Europe U.S. & Canada Asia, Africa & Latin America Science, Invention & Technology Religion, Culture & Arts	336

Index 387

Introduction

The genealogy of this chronology stretches back to the very beginning of written history. In the simplest terms but in the truest sense, genealogy begat chronology—as the books of the Old Testament teach us. Religion and chronology march hand in hand through most of recorded history. In ancient Rome, the high priests inscribed the important religious and political events of the year on tablets preserved in the holiest temples. During the Middle Ages, year after year, monastic chroniclers patiently and dutifully recorded the passing of abbots, miraculous occurrences, great storms, the quantity and quality of annual harvests, and the visits and edicts of kings and great nobles. It was only after the secular Renaissance that narrative and interpretative histories displaced chronologies as the dominant historical form. Yet, historical analysis rests on a foundation of agreed-upon facts, and historical narration requires an established chronological sequence. Although interpretative historians may argue that the writing of chronology is mere record keeping, they always have and always will depend upon chronologies as essential tools, which underscores their usefulness and accounts for their durability as a reference genre over two millennia.

Although *The Wilson Calendar of World History* has a 2,000-year-long genealogy, its immediate origins go back to Germany in the early 1930s. S. H. Steinberg was a lecturer in history at Leipzig University from 1925 to 1933. There, he worked as joint editor with Walter Goetz on the *Propyläen-Weltgeschichte*, the German counterpart of the *Cambridge Ancient*, *Medieval* and *Modern Histories*. When Adolf Hitler came to power, Goetz was replaced by a Nazi, who dismissed Steinberg from the Institute of Cultural and Universal History. As a result, Steinberg emigrated from Germany to England to accept a research fellowship at the Courtauld Institute in London. In 1936, he signed a contract with Macmillan to produce *Historical Tables*, which was an extension and adaptation of the synchronistic tables he had conceived and produced for the *Propyläen-Weltgeschichte*. The first edition was lost in a bombing raid during World War II, but between then and 1990, there were 12 editions of that first comprehensive chronology of world history. Following Steinberg's death in 1969, I undertook the revision and expansion of the *Historical Tables*, helped until 1985 by Steinberg's widow, Christine. By the middle of the 1990s, it was apparent that a completely new edition with an expanded concept was needed. *Historical Tables* tended to be European-oriented. Indeed, Steinberg stated in the preface to the first edition, "*Historical Tables* will probably be used by the Anglo-Saxon students, [therefore] the history of the British Commonwealth and that of the United States of America have been given a slight predominance." Moreover, reflecting the times, *Historical Tables* focused intently on political, diplomatic and military events at the expense of other topics. Our primary goal for *The Wilson Calendar of World History* was to produce a chronology with a truly global perspective befitting today's world and answering the needs of today's students of history. We were also determined to pack in as many events as possible in a single, relatively compact volume that would be easy to use and easy on the eye.

We tried to improve on the several attempts made since World War II to publish chronologies that provide a universal and balanced picture of the world. An example is *Kulturfahrplan* (1946), compiled by Warner Stein and better known to English-speaking readers as *Timetables of History*, translated and adapted by Bernard Grun and published in 1975. Although it was a worthy effort, it suffered from several flaws, which we tried to learn from and rectify in planning and compiling our volume. The most obvious flaw was a design grid that resulted in a great deal of wasted space, which limited the number of events that could be reported. A second was that *Timetables of History* did not go very far in correcting the Eurocentric vision of the world; entries on events in Africa, Asia and Latin America were still few and far between. A third was a level of conciseness in the phrasing of entries that sometimes left readers clueless about the significance of events. Other works attempted to improve on the flaws of *Timetables of History*. One such attempt, *The Chronology of the Ancient, Medieval, Expanding and Modern World* (Helicon, 1996), is a further move toward the chronological ideal. However, its four volumes can hardly be described as concise or convenient as a desk reference.

Our goals were ambitious, perhaps impossibly so, and we must leave it to others to determine how well we have achieved them. With that bow to modesty, I think we can say that *The Wilson Calendar of World History* is the most balanced and universal chronology of world history yet published in a single volume. Yet, we have no doubt that future chroniclers will greatly improve upon our work, just as we have tried to improve upon the efforts of our predecessors.

John Paxton
Bruton, Somerset
England
November 1998

HOW TO USE THIS BOOK

Covering more than 25,000 distinct events, *The Wilson Calendar of World History* is the most comprehensive one-volume chronology of world history ever published in English—perhaps in any language.

It is also the most globally balanced in its coverage. Nearly all previous chronologies focused on events in Europe and North America, to the exclusion of occurrences in other parts of the world. (Indeed, since many of the chronologies originated in Britain or elsewhere in Europe, even North American events often received short shrift.) We have made a particular effort to include in-depth coverage of African, Asian and Latin American events. Our inclusive approach extends beyond just geography: There are more entries on women as well as on racial and ethnic minorities here than in any other general chronology.

Another distinguishing feature of the *Calendar* is its broad, modern view of history. Although wars, revolutions and the rise and fall of empires and kingdoms are all found here, so, too, are social, religious, cultural, artistic, scientific and economic milestones in human history. Our goal has been to record the significant events that shaped the lives of ordinary people as well as those of society's upper crust.

STRUCTURE

The organizational structure of the *Calendar* is easy to grasp. The reader can read down a vertical column to follow an unfolding series of related events, or can read across horizontally, to see what events were occurring in different areas during a specific time period.

Events are organized in six columns spread across facing pages. The headings for the columns change at seven points to reflect the pattern of events during major historical epochs:

3500 – 44 B.C.	**The Ancient World**
43 B.C. – A.D. 399	**The Roman Imperium**
400 – 1453	**The Middle Ages**
1454 – 1774	**The Renaissance & Enlightenment**
1775 – August 31, 1939	**The Industrial Age**
September 1, 1939 – 1945	**World War II**
1946 – 1998	**The Contemporary World**

Generally, four columns define geographic regions, and two are devoted to topics: *Science, Invention & Technology* and *Religion, Culture & Arts*. (The entire column structure can be seen at a glance in the table of contents.) Although the vast majority of events logically fall under one and only one of the six headings found at the top of each two-page spread, a minority relate to more than one heading. Some span two or more geographic regions, and others take place literally on the border between two regions. In such cases, events are categorized according to two principles: consistency and the reader's convenience. For example, the military conflicts between the Ottoman Empire and the Christian states of Europe during the 16th and 17th centuries stretched from

Central Asia through the Middle East to the gates of Vienna. Rather than appearing scattered over three columns, such entries are collected under the column headed *Africa & Middle East* so the reader can readily follow the thread of events. In a few cases, where the placement choice between two columns was purely discretionary, the availability of space determined placement.

The events in the six columns are aligned horizontally by time. For most of the book, all the events that occurred during a given year begin at the same vertical location on the page. In the earliest periods, when the dating of historical events is both less specific and less reliable, events are aligned by longer periods of time, such as centuries or decades.

Dating and Event Sequence

Within each year or time period, events that cannot be dated closer than the year are recorded first. (This is either because the specific season, month or day is not known or because an event had a longer duration.) Those events are followed by chronologically arranged events for which more specific dates are known. Unrelated events are separated by ellipses, and closely related events are separated by only a single period.

Events that took place over more than a single year, for example, 1947–1952, are recorded in the first year (1947), but separately and following a line space after the events that began and ended during that year.

Names and Dates

The first time a person is mentioned in *Calendar*, his or her full name along with the birth and death dates are provided. If the mention concerns the person's birth, only the death year is provided. Similarly, only the birth year is recorded if the mention concerns the person's death. Occasionally, a person's full name is repeated, either for the sake of clarity or if it has been several pages since the person was last mentioned.

The final column, *Religion, Culture & Arts*, includes many specific works of art (paintings, books, poems, movies, operas, symphonies, etc.) under the year of creation or public release. In most cases, the name of the work follows the name of the creator, separated by a colon. The first time an artist, composer or writer appears, his or her full name, birth and death years, and a brief identifying description (e.g., "British painter") are provided. In subsequent mention on the same page, only the last name is provided. When the artist is mentioned on a subsequent page, the first name but not the years or the description is given to avoid confusion.

Criteria

In selecting events for inclusion, we have been guided by several objectives. First and foremost, we wanted to include the maximum number of events. Second, as mentioned above, we strove for balance and historical inclusiveness. Third, we did our best to anticipate the events readers would actually need to look up in such a chronology. Last, but certainly not least, we weighed the historical importance of the event. Although no two historians will ever agree on the ten most significant events in human history—much less the 25,000 most significant—we've tried to ensure that no major historical development was left out by double-checking our judgments against those made by the compilers of many other chronologies. We apologize for any omissions and welcome suggestions from readers for events to include in future editions.

Sources

Several hundred sources have been consulted in the course of compiling this book. As everyone who has studied history knows, sources often contradict one another, even about the most elementary facts and dates. Whenever there was a doubt about a fact or date, we cross-checked it in several sources and adopted what appeared to us to be the most authoritative, either based on the internal evidence or the reputation of the source. Despite our best efforts, a few factual errors are inevitable in a work of this scope and detail. As with omissions, we will gladly rectify any demonstrable error called to our attention when we prepare the next edition.

Dating

The dating of events would seem to be a fairly straightforward matter. Today, at least for secular purposes, nearly everyone everywhere uses the Gregorian calendar, as do we in this book. Developed between 1580 and 1582 under the papacy of Gregory XIII, that calendar replaced the Julian calendar adopted by the Romans under Julius Caesar in 46 B.C., which had become ten days out of sync with the solar year by the 1580s.

Over the centuries, time has been measured in different ways by different peoples. Calendars have been compiled with the years containing different numbers of days and varying starting years so that the Muslim Era begins in A.D. 622; Coptic, in A.D. 284; Parsee, in A.D. 632; Japanese, in A.D. 600; and Chinese, in 2697 B.C., to mention a few.

Universal acceptance of the Gregorian system took nearly 400 years. It was adopted in Italy, France, Spain and Portugal in 1582; in Prussia, Switzerland, Holland, Flanders and most of the German Roman Catholic states in 1583, in Poland in 1586; in Hungary in 1587, and in Denmark and the German and Dutch Protestant states in 1700. In 1752, it was adopted by Great Britain; in 1753, by Sweden; in 1872, by Japan; in 1912, by China and Albania; in 1915, by Bulgaria; in 1917, by Turkey; and in 1923 by Greece. Russia did not adopt the Gregorian system until after the Bolshevik Revolution in 1917. According to the Gregorian system, the revolution began on November 6. According to the Julian calendar, this event took place on October 24, which explains why the Russian revolution is commonly referred to as the October Revolution.

Further complicating the problem of consistent dating, even the beginning and ending of the year varied from place to place and time to time—even within a single country. In England from the sixth century to 1066, both December 25 and March 25 were commonly used as the beginning of the year. Then January 1 was used until 1155. From 1155 to 1751, March 25 was again used to mark the beginning of the year. It wasn't until 1599 in Scotland and 1752 in England that January 1 was finally and permanently fixed as the first day of the new year. To use one example to illustrate the confusion this can cause, that means that as far as the Scots were concerned Charles I was executed on January 30, 1649 while the English said he lost his head on January 30, 1648.

In this book, we have followed the Gregorian calendar as consistently as possible in the modern era. Thus, we say the Bolshevik Revolution occurred in November 1917, and provide the Julian calendar dates in parentheses to demonstrate the origins of the term October Revolution. However, the traditional dates of most historical events prior to the widespread adaptation of the Gregorian calendar have never been recalculated, and we were not about to undertake such a Herculean task. Therefore, our policy for the periods prior to the modern era has been to use the dates traditionally given for an event rather than convert them. Since exact dates prior to the Renaissance are of questionable accuracy, we have given them very rarely and only when they seemed particularly germane.

Finding Information

Typically, there are two reasons to consult a chronology such as this: to find out when a specific event happened and to find out what happened in a specific time period. The first is most readily accomplished by consulting the index, which includes headings for all proper names, countries, and topics. The second is best accomplished by using the running heads at the top of each page; these indicate the years covered by each two-page spread.

When using the index, note that the entries refer not only to the page number but also to the column (A, B or C) on the page where the information sought is found.

Edward W. Knappman
November 1998

THE CALENDAR

Egypt & Africa

c. 3500 B.C. Egyptian trading routes are developed. ...Egyptian women stain their hands and feet with henna dyes to enhance their beauty.

c. 3200 B.C. Menes (fl. c. 3200 B.C.), first king of Egypt, founds Memphis as his capital and unifies Upper and Lower Egypt.

c. 3200–2770 B.C. Egypt experiences its early dynastic period.

c. 3000 B.C. Egyptian families breed dogs, cats and monkeys as pets.

c. 2800 B.C. Bee keeping becomes popular in Egypt.

c. 2700–2200 B.C. Old Kingdom of Egypt initiates a golden age.

c. 2600 B.C. Egyptians import timber from the eastern coast of the Mediterranean Sea (present-day Lebanon).

Middle East, Asia, Pacific & Americas

c. 3500 B.C. Sumerians establish the world's first major civilization between the Tigris and Euphrates Rivers in south Mesopotamia (present-day Iraq).

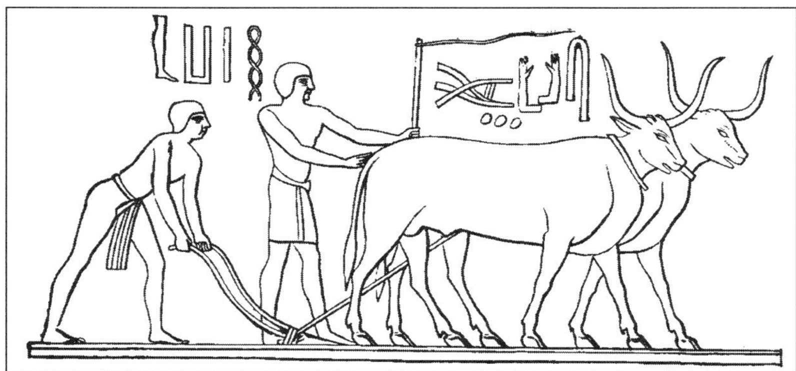

▲ ***This drawing, based on a contemporary bas-relief, depicts Egyptians plowing during the time of King Menes.***

c. 3100 B.C. Sumerians begin keeping official records on clay tablets.

c. 3000 B.C. Phoenicians inhabit the eastern coast of the Mediterranean (present-day Lebanon, Syria and Israel. ...Hunters from the North American plains move into the Arctic tundra (present-day Northwest Territories in Canada). ...Ur becomes the center of the Sumerian civilization in south Mesopotamia (present-day Iraq). ...Koreans turn to agriculture, cultivating millet. ...People of the Indus Valley (present-day Pakistan) cultivate cotton. ...The dog is introduced into Australia.

c. 3000–500 B.C. Chinese settlers displace the Melanesian people in Indonesia. ...The city of Mohenjo-Daro is founded in the Indus Valley.

c. 3000–2700 B.C. Details about temple administration are recorded on some 30,000 clay tablets in Lagash, Sumer.

c. 2800 B.C. Mesopotamia suffers a great flood; the population is decimated.

2690 B.C. Huang Ti (fl. 27th century B.C.), the Yellow Emperor, later revered by the Chinese as "prime ancestor," begins his reign.

Greece & Asia Minor

c. 3000 B.C. Minoan civilization begins on the island of Crete, initiating the Bronze Age.

c. 3000–2000 B.C. Mycenaeans migrate to Greece from the north, displacing the Neolithic culture.

▲ ***Huang Ti, the legendary Yellow Emperor.***

Rome & Europe

c. 3300 B.C. Decorative pottery and grooved ware are produced by Neolithic people in the British Isles.

c. 3000 B.C. Europeans domesticate wild horses. ...Stone circles are erected in the Hebrides islands off Scotland.

▲ *A 19th-century rendition of the Great Sphinx.*

Science, Invention & Technology

c. 3500 B.C. Bronze is used in southeast Asia (present-day northern Thailand), having been introduced there about 4000 B.C. ...The plow and wheel are invented in Mesopotamia (present-day Iraq). ...Egyptians divide daytime and nighttime into 12 hours each, so the length of hours changes with the seasons. ...Egyptians use first sail-powered boats.

c. 3200 B.C. Earth and stone dams are built at Jawa (present-day northern Jordan).

3114 B.C. Mayan civilization of Central America devises a 354-day calendar.

c. 3000 B.C. Bricks are first used in Assyrian and Egyptian buildings. ...Egyptian king Atothis (fl. 3000 B.C.) writes on anatomy. ...Ox-drawn carts and armor (of bronze) are invented in Mesopotamia (present-day Iraq). ...A copper culture is established near the upper Great Lakes of North America. ...Babylonians standardized the length of an hour. ...Australians develop stone tools with handles. ...Assyrians and Egyptians make the first reed boats.

c. 3000–2000 B.C. Hunters in North American Arctic (present-day Alaska) fashion small tools. ...Arches are used at Mohenjo-Daro in Indus Valley (present-day Pakistan).

c. 2690 B.C. Chinese emperor Huang Ti (fl. 27th century B.C.) invents boat oars and conducts first known fire drill.

c. 2600 B.C. Ropes are produced from hemp in China. ...Egyptians begin mummifying their dead.

Culture & Arts

c. 3500 B.C. Sumerians invent cuneiform script. ...A large stone circle is erected in present-day southern England (Avebury, Wiltshire).

3200 B.C. Egyptians begin performing ritual religious drama.

c. 3000 B.C. The first known hieroglyphic writings are produced in Egypt.

c. 2800 B.C. Construction of Stonehenge, the megalithic monument on Salisbury Plain in present-day Wiltshire, England, begins. ...Egyptians create artistic metalworks and relief carvings.

2700–2500 B.C. Pyramids are constructed in Egypt.

c. 2650 B.C. Zoser (fl. 27th century B.C.), king of Egypt, has the world's first known stone monument, the Step Pyramid, built at Saqqara.

c. 2550–2528 B.C. Khufu (Cheops) (fl. 26th century B.C.) supervises the building of the Great Pyramid at Giza.

2530 B.C. The Great Sphinx is built in Egypt under the supervision of the pharaoh Khafra (Chefren).

Egypt & Africa

c. 2500 B.C. The Sahara is created by a climate change. ...Egyptian women use oils pressed from plants and herbs for cosmetics.

c. 2200–1786 B.C. Middle Kingdom of Egypt sees great pyramids built and subjection of Nubia (roughly present-day Sudan).

c. 2180 B.C. Pepi II (b. 2287 B.C.) dies after reigning more than 90 years as king of Egypt.

c. 2100 B.C. Egyptian king Akhthoes (fl. 22nd century B.C.), known for his cruelty, leaves instructions on government to his descendents.

c. 2065 B.C. Egypt and Crete trade ivory and faience earthenware.

c. 2040 B.C. Nebhepetre Mentuhotep (fl. 2040 B.C.) becomes king of all Egypt after an unsettled era.

c. 1990 B.C. Amenemhet I (? –1970 B.C.) becomes king of Egypt and moves the capital from Thebes to Ith-tawi, 25 miles from Memphis.

c. 1980–1935 B.C. Sesostris I (?–1935 B.C.) rules Egypt, replacing the private army with a professional one.

c. 1900 B.C. Horses are used for transportation in Egypt.

c. 1887–1849 B.C. Sesostris III (?–1849 B.C.) rules Egypt, reducing nobility to status of royal officials.

c. 1810 B.C. Amenemhet III (?–1801 B.C.) of Egypt builds dams and irrigation systems.

Middle East, Asia, Pacific & Americas

c. 2500 B.C. Chinese towns specialize in products to trade. ...Mesopotamia (present-day Iraq) agriculture produces an annual surplus of grain.

c. 2500–1500 B.C. Indus Valley (present-day Pakistan) civilization flourishes.

c. 2370–2315 B.C. Trade develops between Indus people and Akkadians of north Babylonia.

c. 2334–2279 B.C. Sargon (c. 2340–2279 B.C.), king of Akkad in Mesopotamia, establishes the Akkadian kingdom during his 55-year-reign.

c. 2333 B.C. Tangun dynasty establishes the kingdom of Korea.

c. 2100 B.C. Impoverished Babylonian citizens begin selling themselves and their children as slaves. ...Ur-Nammu (fl. 2100 B.C.), king of Ur, produces the first known written laws.

c. 2000 B.C. Abraham (fl. 2000 B.C.), first called Abram, founds Judaism by leading his people from Sumer (present-day southern Iraq) to Canaan, or Palestine (parts of present-day Israel, Jordan and Egypt).

c. 2000 B.C. Indonesian peoples migrate to the Melanesian islands. ...Silver and grain are used to purchase goods in Mesopotamia.

c. 2000–1000 B.C. Corn is cultivated in southwestern North America (present-day United States).

c. 1792 B.C. Hammurabi (fl. c. 1800 B.C.) becomes ruler of Babylonia.

Greece & Asia Minor

c. 2500 B.C. The city of Knossos is founded on Crete. ...Spain begins trade with the Aegean peoples.

c. 2300 B.C. Greek-speaking people migrate to Crete.

▲ ***A granite statue of Egyptian King Sesostris III.***

c. 2000–1700 B.C. A volcano destroys early civilization on the Greek island of Thera.

c. 1900 B.C. Hittite people, possibly from Asia, migrate into Anatolia (present-day Turkey).

Rome & Europe

c. 2500 B.C. People from Anatolia (present-day Turkey) migrate into the south Balkans and later establish Macedonia.

c. 2300 B.C. Beaker people from southern Spain migrate to the British Isles.

Detailed wall panels from the Temple of Karnak in Thebes.

Science, Invention & Technology

c. 2500 B.C. First known use of iron in Middle East is a statue of a god for the king of Agade in Babylon. ...Indus Valley people build a dike system on Indus River. ...Papyrus is used as writing sheets in Egypt. ...Egyptians devise an accurate calendar.

c. 2300 B.C. Astronomers in China make systematic observations of the sky.

c. 2100–2005 B.C. Mesopotamians invent glass.

c. 2000 B.C. Eskimos in present-day Alaska and Canada use flint for knives, arrowheads and harpoons. ...Medical prescriptions are recorded on tablets by Sumerians. ...Vedic medicine in India uses numerous herbs. ...Babylonians build first known underwater tunnel, digging beneath the Euphrates River to connect their king's palace with a temple. ...Priests in Babylon keep astronomical records. ...Cave dwellers along the Njoro River in eastern Africa fashion tools from black volcanic glass.

c. 1900 B.C. Egyptians begin to use bronze.

c. 1800 B.C. Babylonians devise positional notation in mathematics and develop squares and square roots.

Culture & Arts

c. 2500 B.C. World's first known libraries are established in Mesopotamia (present-day Iraq). ...Gold is molded into everyday objects on the west coast of South America (present-day Peru).

c. 2500–2000 B.C. Beaker people of southern Spain make bell-shaped pots.

c. 2300 B.C. Enheduanna (fl. 24th century B.C.), high priestess of Sumer (present-day Iraq), writes world's first known poetry.

c. 2200 B.C. Wheel-thrown pottery is produced in north and northeastern China. ...An anonymous Semitic poet writes *Epic of Gilgamesh*, the world's oldest written story.

c. 2200–1500 B.C. Middle Minoan civilization on Crete produces hieroglyphic writing, great palaces and artistic works.

c. 2000 B.C. The Temple of Karnak to the god Amon is built in Thebes, capital of Egypt. ...Linear writing is devised by Minoans on Crete. ...Last stages of Stonehenge are built in England.

Egypt & Africa

c. 1720–1567 B.C. The Hyksos, a Semitic people, invade the Nile Delta, and their kings rule Egypt.

1570 B.C. Egyptians mine copper ore in the Sinai Peninsula. ...Ahmose I (fl. 16th century B.C.) defeats Hyksos and founds the New Kingdom of Egypt.

c. 1570–1087 B.C. New Kingdom of Egypt produces an expanded empire in the Levant. ...Egyptian capital moves from Memphis to Thebes. ...Pharaohs, including Tutankhamen, are buried at Valley of the Kings (near present-day Luxor).

1560 B.C. Egypt, under Ahmose I, conquers kingdom of Kush in Nubia (present-day Sudan).

1545–1525 B.C. Amenhotep I reigns in Egypt, conquering Memphis and invading Palestine.

1525–1492 B.C. Thutmose I reigns in Egypt.

c. 1500 B.C. Israelites migrate to Egypt to escape famine.

c. 1500–1000 B.C. A skilled worker's village exists at Deir el-Medina next to the Valley of the Kings.

1492 B.C. Thutmose I is the first pharaoh buried at the Valley of the Kings.

1480 B.C. Egypt has an active trade with Punt (south of the Red Sea), importing panther skins, monkeys, myrrh and incense wood.

c. 1475 –1447 B.C. Thutmose III (c. 1490–1436 B.C.) rules Egypt, conducting 17 invasions of Syria and Palestine.

Middle East, Asia, Pacific & Americas

c. 1766–1122 B.C. Shang dynasty rules China.

c. 1750 B.C. The first known code of laws is issued by Hammurabi. ...The first known regulation requiring women to wear veils is incorporated into the law code of the Middle Assyrian empire.

c. 1740 B.C. Mesopotamians use the horse for transportation and work.

c. 1700 B.C. Lapita people of Melanesia migrate to islands in the southwest Pacific.

c. 1595 B.C. Babylon is sacked by Mursilis (c. 1620–1570 B.C.), the king of the Hittite empire (present-day Turkey).

This bas-relief from the gateway of Hattusas (present-day Boghazkoy), the Hittite capital, portrays an armed god in a war chariot.

c. 1523–1027 B.C. Shang dynasty establishes the first great civilization of China.

c. 1500 B.C. Aryans of eastern Europe migrate into north India.

Greece & Asia Minor

c. 1650 B.C. Hittites choose Hattusas (present-day Boghazkoy) in north-central Anatolia as their capital.

c. 1627 B.C. Volcanic eruption destroys the city of Acrotiri on the island of Thera (present-day Santorini).

c. 1550 B.C. Mycenaeans occupy Crete.

c. 1500 B.C. The city of Knossos on Crete is destroyed by earthquakes.

Rome & Europe

▲ ***A wall painting depicting a woman of Crete about 1600 B.C.***

c. 1550 B.C. Celts clear the forests of England.

c. 1500 B.C. Use of bronze tools spreads throughout southern England.

Science, Invention & Technology

c. 1750 B.C. Babylonians formalize the study and practice of medicine.

c. 1730 B.C. Copper is used by people in the mountains of west central Africa (present-day Niger).

c. 1700 B.C. The Hyksos Semitic invaders introduce horse-drawn chariots to Egypt. ...Use of tin-bronze tools spreads throughout Europe.

1642–1626 BC. Babylonian astronomers record the rising and setting of Venus during the reign of Ammisaduga.

◀ ***During the Shang dynasty in China, this bronze tripod signified sovereignty.***

c. 1550 B.C. Egyptian physicians use practical methods that do not incorporate magic to attempt to cure diseases.

c. 1500 B.C. People in North America (in present-day Wisconsin and Minnesota) discuss metallurgy techniques. ...European farmers use bronze scythes. ...Celts replace stone axes with bronze ones. ...Ox-drawn carts are used in Greece.

Culture & Arts

c. 1766–1122 B.C. The Shang dynasty of China creates bronze vases, a pictograph language and the first Chinese calendar.

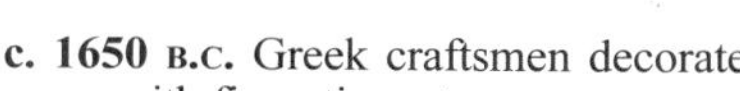

c. 1650 B.C. Greek craftsmen decorate vases with figurative art.

c. 1500 B.C. The first known phonetic alphabet, using symbols for consonants, is devised by Canaanites, or Phoenicians. ...The Punjab Rig-Veda, hymns and chants, is composed in India. ...Pictograph scripts are written on bones and turtle shells in China. ...Stone dolmen monuments are raised in northeast France (present-day Brittany).

Egypt & Africa

1473–1468 B.C. Queen Hatshepsut (?–1468 B.C.) rules Egypt during a peaceful and prosperous era.

c. 1450 B.C. Thutmose III takes children of conquered Nubia princes to be educated in Egypt. ...Egyptian society ignores Queen Hatshepsut's reign and accomplishments.

1450–1425 B.C. Amenhotep II (c. 1470–1425 B.C.) rules Egypt, capturing in one campaign seven Syrian kings, whom he executes.

c. 1411–1375 B.C. Amenhotep III (c. 1430–1375 B.C.) rules Egypt through a prosperous period of great construction.

c. 1370 B.C. Egypt's queen Nefertiti (c. 1400–1350 B.C.) paints her fingernails and toenails.

c. 1350 B.C. Tutankhamen (c. 1357–1338 B.C.) begins his reign as pharaoh of Egypt.

c. 1313 B.C. Seti I (c. 1330–1290 B.C.) reconquers land in Syria and Palestine for Egypt.

c. 1279–1213 B.C. Ramses II (c. 1290–1213 B.C.) reigns in Egypt, carrying out an extensive building program.

c. 1250 B.C. Moses (fl. 13th century B.C.) leads the Israelite exodus from Egypt to Canaan (Palestine). Moses receives the Ten Commandments at Mount Sinai on the Sinai Peninsula, according to the Bible.

c. 1184–1153 B.C. Ramses III (c. 1200–1153 B.C.) reigns in Egypt, building impressive monuments.

1175 B.C. Ramses III repulses land and sea invasions by Libyans, Greeks, Sicilians, and others.

1170 B.C. Ramses III survives a plot in his harem to assassinate him. ...History's first recorded strike occurs in Egyptian city of Thebes when laborers working on a new pyramid refuse to work when their pay is delayed.

Middle East, Asia, Pacific & Americas

Ramses II of Egypt dressed in a war costume.

c. 1300–400 B.C. Olmec culture flourishes in Mesoamerica (present-day Central America and Mexico).

1275 B.C. Egyptian and Hittite forces clash at the inconclusive battle of Qadesh in Syria, which becomes their border.

c. 1200 B.C. The walls of Jericho fall to the Israelite forces of Joshua, supposedly because of the blast of their trumpets. ...Chinese use cowry shells to pay for goods.

c. 1200–800 B.C: Phoenicians experience a golden age as sailors, traders and artisans.

c.1200–1000 B.C. Judges administer Israel.

1122 B.C. The Kija dynasty is established in Korea by a Chinese sage.

c. 1122–255 B.C. The Chou dynasty rules China, creating an artistic flowering during a turbulent era.

Greece & Asia Minor

c. 1400 B.C. The great palace of Knossos on Crete burns down, and Minoan civilization is virtually destroyed, probably by war. ...Trade routes are established by Greece throughout Mediterranean.

c. 1400–1200 B.C. Mycenaean civilization experiences its golden era.

1250 B.C. Greek invaders sack and burn Troy.

c. 1200 B.C. Hittite empire collapses after attacks by Mediterranean invaders.

c. 1200–700 B.C. Greece experiences a dark age between its Bronze Age and classical civilizations.

Rome & Europe

▲ ***Sculpted head of Queen Nefertiti of Egypt.***

c. 1300 B.C. Aurochs (wild cattle) become extinct in the British Isles.

c. 1200 B.C. Celtic tribes move through central Europe.

Science, Invention & Technology

c. 1400 B.C. Hittites of Anatolia (present-day Turkey) forge harder iron by adding carbon. ...Ironwork used in India and Asia.

c. 1300 B.C. Fertility tests exist in Egypt.

c. 1250 B.C. Europeans use bronze swords and armor.

c. 1200 B.C. Phoenicians build ships with keels and plank hulls.

c. 1150 B.C. Egyptians produce topographical maps.

Culture & Arts

c. 1460 B.C. Pharaoh Thutmose III (c. 1490–1436 B.C.) erects two obelisks at Heliopolis.

c. 1450 B.C. Mycenaean script is invented on Crete. ...Great temple of Deir el-Bahri is constructed near Thebes, Egypt.

c. 1370 B.C. Amenhotep IV (Ikhnaton) (fl. 14th century B.C.) initiates sun worship in Egypt.

c. 1360 B.C. The head of Nefertiti (1400–1350 B.C.), the Egyptian queen, is sculpted.

c. 1300 B.C. In the lower Amazon, people produce pots decorated with figures.

c. 1300–400 B.C. The Olmec culture in Mesoamerica (present-day Central America and Mexico) produces hieroglyphic writing and sculpted basalt heads.

c. 1250 B.C. Two temples are hewn out of the rock at Abu-Simbel in Egypt. (They will be raised in 1966 to avoid flooding caused by the Aswan Dam.) ...Europeans begin cremating the dead and placing ashes in urns.

c. 1122–255 B.C. The Chou dynasty of China creates a golden era for philosophers, including Confucius and Lao-tzu.

Egypt & Africa

1100 B.C. High priest Herihor seizes Egyptian throne.

1060 B.C. Egypt's economy suffers when Nubian gold reserves are depleted.

c. 1060–664 B.C. Egyptian central control breaks down.

c. 1000 B.C. Dogs are bred for hunting in the southern tip of Africa (present-day South Africa).

c. 945 B.C. Sheshonk (fl. 10th century B.C.) founds the XXII Egyptian dynasty of Libyan-origin kings.

c. 900 B.C. Kingdom of Nubia (parts of present-day Egypt and Sudan) gains independence from Egypt.

814 B.C. Phoenicians found Carthage in north Africa (present-day Tunisia).

c. 750–661 B.C. Nubian kings rule Egypt.

Middle East, Asia, Pacific & Americas

c. 1100–1000 B.C. Aramaic language is established throughout the Middle East. ...Phoenicia trades with the British Isles.

c. 1020 B.C. Saul (fl. 1000 B.C.) becomes the first king of Israel. ...Elephants and rhinoceroses are hunted in northern China.

c. 1012–961 B.C. King David (fl. 1000 B.C.) rules Israel as its second king.

c. 1000 B.C. David captures Jerusalem from the Jebusites and makes it his capital. ...Migration of Asian hunters across the Arctic tundra ends at the North Atlantic (present-day Canada and Greenland). ...Mayan civilization develops in the Yucatán Peninsula (present-day Mexico, Belize, and Guatemala). ...The Chinese city of Beijing is founded.

c. 961–922 B.C. King Solomon (fl. 950 B.C.) rules Israel, introducing taxation and foreign trade. He is visited by the queen of Sheba (present-day Ethiopia).

930 B.C. Solomon's temple is plundered by Egyptian invaders.

922 B.C. Solomon dies, and Judah separates from Israel.

c. 900 B.C. Chinese merchants trade silk with places as far away as Parthia (present-day northeastern Iran). ...Agricultural villages are established along the Amazon floodplain.

c. 880 B.C. Omni (fl. 880 B.C.), king of Israel, builds a new capital at Samaria (present-day Sebastiyeh, Jordan).

c. 870–850 B.C. Ahab (fl. 9th century B.C.) reigns as king of Israel.

c. 868 B.C. Phoenicia falls to Assyrian forces.

825–750 B.C. Assyrian nobility revolt against the emperors, demanding more power.

Greece & Asia Minor

c. 1100 B.C. Dorians, using iron weapons, invade Greece from the north and destroy the Mycenaean civilization. ...Minoan civilization, long in decline, comes to an end.

c. 1100–1000 B.C. Greek writing seems to disappear.

c. 1000 B.C. Last great Greek migrations begin with Athenian immigration to Ionia in western Asia Minor.

c. 900 B.C. Dorians of Crete institute state-run education.

c. 900–750 B.C. Greeks create city-states.

c. 850 B.C. Defensive walls are constructed around the city of Smyrna (present-day Izmir, Turkey).

c. 790 B.C. Some streets in Greek cities are paved with stones.

c 766 B.C. Milesians establish a trading post at Sinope on the Black Sea.

c. 750 B.C. Greek women use lead powder to whiten their skins. ...Greek farmers plow up pasturelands to grow crops.

Rome & Europe

c. 1100 B.C. Etruscans migrate to Italy from Lydia (present-day northwestern Turkey).

c. 1100–700 B.C. The culture of Villanova, founded by central Europeans, dominates north-central Italy.

c. 994 B.C. Teuton tribes from Jutland migrate to the Rhine.

884 B.C. Phoenicians establish the trading post of Gadir (present-day Cadiz, Spain).

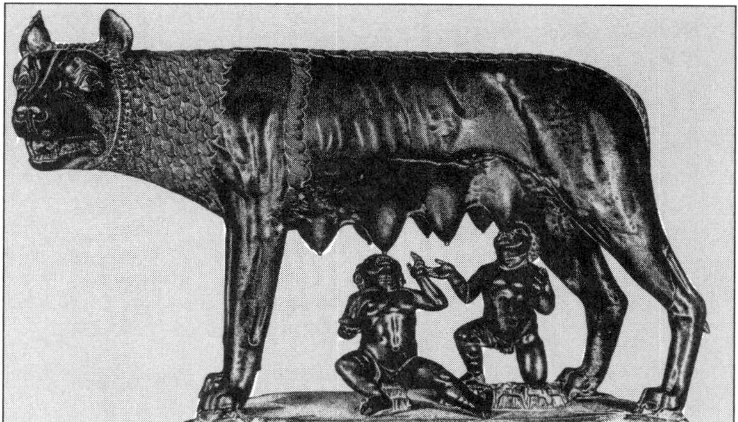

This bronze statue of the **Capitoline Wolf** *was created by an Etruscan artist in the 6th century B.C.; the twins Romulus and Remus were added in the 16th century A.D.*

753 B.C. Rome is founded by Romulus and Remus, according to legend.

Science, Invention & Technology

c. 1000 B.C. Iron is introduced in Greece. Methods of contraception are known in Egypt.

c. 900 B.C. The Upanishads, the mystical and speculative scriptures of Hinduism, begin being composed in India.

c. 750 B.C. The Celtic Hallstatt culture (present-day Austria) uses iron, developing such tools as scissors and saws.

Culture & Arts

c. 1100 B.C. The first dictionary is published in China.

1000 B.C. Pottery derived from Asia is made in Great Lakes region of North America. ...Troupes of secular dancers, many of them women, perform professionally and independently in the major cities of Egypt.

c. 950 B.C. Solomon (c. 985–933 B.C.) builds the Temple in Jerusalem.

c. 900 B.C. Nok culture in present-day central Nigeria creates pottery heads.

c. 860 B.C. Hebrew prophet Elijah (fl. 9th century B.C.) overturns pagan worship of Baal in Israel.

c. 800 B.C. Homer (fl. 8th century B.C.), the Greek poet, composes the *Iliad* and the *Odyssey*.

776 B.C. Olympic Games are first recorded in Greece.

c. 750 B.C. Book of Genesis is written. ...Greeks adapt the Phoenician alphabet first developed c. 1500 B.C.

Egypt & Africa

727 B.C. Egypt is reunified briefly by the Kushite king.

▲ ***Assyrian soldiers in combat.***

c. 670 B.C. Assyrians conquer Thebes and Memphis in Egypt.

664–610 B.C. Although installed as a puppet king by Assyrians, Psamtek I (700–609 B.C.) rules Egypt independently.

c. 660 B.C. The first Greek traders enter Egypt.

c. 630 B.C. Cyrene, the first Greek colony in Africa, is established in present-day Libya.

c. 620 B.C. Greeks establish a trading center at Naucratis in Egypt's Nile Delta.

Middle East, Asia, Pacific & Americas

745–727 B.C. Tiglath-Pileser III (fl. 8th century B.C.) reigns in Assyria and turns it into a military power and true empire.

732 B.C. Assyrians take Damascus and control Syria.

722 B.C. Assyrians conquer Israel and annex the northern kingdom.

c. 700–200 B.C. Chavín culture flourishes in the Peruvian Andes.

689 B.C. Assyrians destroy Babylon.

687 B.C. A spectacular meteor shower occurs in China.

c. 660 B.C. Jimmu (fl. 7th century B.C.) becomes the first emperor of Japan. ...The City of Byzantium (present-day Istanbul) is founded.

c. 620 B.C. The town of Azotos (present-day Ashdod, Israel) surrenders after a 29-year siege by Egyptians.

Greece & Asia Minor

c. 735 B.C. Greeks begin to colonize Sicily. ...The first Messenian War is fought, with Sparta defeating Messenia, its neighbor .

730–680 B.C. The cities of Chalcis and Eretria on the island of Euboea fight the last aristocratic Greek war (arrows and stones are banned) to an inconclusive end.

725 B.C. Direct trade is established between Greece and the Etruscans at Cumae in southwestern Italy.

720 B.C. Greeks begin to colonize southern Italy.

c. 700 B.C. Common Greek foot soldiers armed with long lances begin to replace cavalry of noblemen. ...Greeks first enter Black Sea. ...Cavalry of Thessalians becomes the best in Greece. ...Corinth becomes most powerful Greek city.

c. 700–500 B.C. Greece experiences its Archaic Age, developing modern thought and politics.

c. 700–675 B.C. Greek trading port of Al Mina in northern Syria is destroyed by Cilicians of southeastern Asia Minor.

669 B.C. Argos defeats Sparta at battle of Hysiae.

657 B.C. Cyselus (fl. 7th century B.C.) rules Corinth as a tyrant.

c 650 B.C. Greek colonies are established around the Black Sea. ...The second Messenian War is waged, with Sparta conquering Messenia.

c. 640–620 B.C. Theagenes (c. 650–620 B.C.), dictator of Megara in central Greece, seeks popularity by slaughtering the cattle of the rich.

631 B.C. Milesians colonize Sinope on the Black Sea.

621 B.C. Greek magistrate Draco (fl. 7th century B.C.) compiles Athens's first written code of laws. Its frequent death penalties give us the term *Draconian* for harsh justice.

Rome & Europe

c. 733 B.C. Syracuse is founded by Greeks in Sicily.

c. 700 B.C. Celtic tribes migrate to southern England in large numbers. ...Celts begin burying warriors under wagons in wooden vaults. ...Etruscans erect walls around their villages. ...Greek traders arrive in Rome. ...Etruscans wear false teeth (often carved from animal teeth).

c. 700–400 B.C. The Celtic Hallstatt culture flourishes in central Europe (present-day Austria).

c. 650 B.C. Southern Gaul (present-day southern France) emerges as a key European trading center.

Science, Invention & Technology

747 B.C. Babylonians devise a calendar.

This painting, on the bottom of a cup, portrays the Greek fabulist Aesop talking with a fox. ➤

c. 700 B.C. Ironworking spreads to the British Isles. ...Systematic records of eclipses and astronomical phenomena are recorded by Babylonians. ...Phoenicians and Egyptians invent galley warships.

c. 700–500 B.C. Phoenicians and Greeks add several levels of oars to their ships.

c. 680 B.C. Iron and copper smelting spreads to west-central and east Africa.

c. 650 B.C. China develops an iron technology.

c. 636 B.C. The first known Western philosopher, Thales, is born in Miletus, Greece. He will introduce geometry into Greece.

Culture & Arts

c. 700 B.C. Hesiod (fl. 8th century B.C.) writes the epic *Works and Days*. ...Etruscans introduce the tunic and toga to the Italians. ...Chavín culture (Peru) creates painted sculptures and textiles.

690 B.C. Paracas people on the Pacific coast of Peru mutilate their dead and preserve remains in underground vaults.

c. 650 B.C. Ashurbanipal (?–626 B.C.), ruler of Assyria, establishes a library of 25,000 clay tablets. ...Greek vases from Corinth are painted with three-dimensional perspectives.

c. 630 B.C. A library with medical texts is established at Sultan Tepe in Syria. ...Chinese poems are collected in the *Shih Ching* (*Book of Songs*).

c. 628 B.C. Prophet Jeremiah (fl. 7th century B.C.) begins preaching in Jerusalem.

627–605 B.C. Judah, the southern Hebrew kingdom in Palestine, is ruled by Egypt.

c. 620 B.C. Greek slave Aesop (fl. 7th century B.C.), the reputed author of *Aesop's Fables*, is said to have been born.

Egypt & Africa

c. 600 B.C. Meroe (near present-day Khartoum) is established as the capital of Nubia.

Nebuchadnezzar II and his advisers in a painting by Frans Francken the Younger, painted more than 2,000 years after Nebuchadnezzar's death.

569 B.C. Egyptian army rises against King Apries, who is replaced by Amasis II.

Middle East, Asia, Pacific & Americas

618 B.C. Zedekiah (fl 600 B.C.), last king of Judah, is born.

612 B.C. The Babylonians, Medes, and Scythians sack Nineveh.

608 B.C. Egyptian king Necho (fl. c. 610–595 B.C.) defeats and kills Josiah (649–608 B.C.), king of Judah, at battle of Megiddo (in present-day Israel).

605 B.C. Nebuchadnezzar II (c. 630–562 B.C.) defeats Assyrians at battle of Carchemish (present-day Karkamis, Turkey), ending their empire.

602 B.C. China's Yellow River changes course, flowing 100 miles to the east.

600 B.C. Chinese emperors become dependent on powerful land-owning princes. ...Elephants are used during battles in India.

587 B.C. Nebuchadnezzar II destroys Jerusalem and the Temple of Solomon, taking Jews captive to Babylon.

585 B.C. Nebuchadnezzar II destroys Tyre, the Phoenician seaport.

575 B.C. The caste system begins in India.

Greece & Asia Minor

c. 600 B.C. Sparta initiates strict military training. The severe regime gives rise to the adjective *Spartan*. ...The kingdom of Lydia uses the first coinage, made of metal. ...Greek symposium evolves as a men's social organization. ...Corinth begins relying on customs duties to raise funds.

595 B.C. A Phoenician fleet begins a three-year exploration from Egypt to the Indian Ocean.

c. 594 B.C. Solon reforms Athenian constitution and law, the first steps to democracy.

c. 590 B.C. Silver coins with a turtle design are issued on Greek island of Aegina.

c. 590–583 B.C. Athens helps Delphi defeat its harbor town of Cirrha in the Sacred War (fought over which could levy tolls on pilgrims).

585 B.C. An eclipse of the sun during a battle between Lydia (in present-day Turkey) and Media (in present-day Iran) frightens both sides into declaring peace.

c. 580 B.C. Sparta wages war under the pretext of liberating others from tyrants.

c. 576 B.C. Cleisthenes (fl. 6th century B.C.), dictator of Sicyon, invites Greeks to compete for his daughter's hand.

575 B.C. Athens adopts its first coinage.

Rome & Europe

c. 616–578 B.C. Lucius Tarquinius Priscus (fl. 6th century B.C.) reigns as king of Rome and constructs the Cloaca Maxima (Great Sewer).

c. 600 B.C. Etruscans have intensive trade with the Greeks.

Chinese philosopher Confucius.

c. 578–535 B.C. Servius Tullius (?–535 B.C.) reigns as king of Rome, creating the first legion.

575 B.C. The first Roman forum is created as a marketplace.

Science, Invention & Technology

c. 610 B.C. Greek philosopher Anaximander is born. A student of Thales, he will try to map the known world and devise crude theories of evolution and astronomy.

c. 600 B.C. Egyptians switch from bronze to hardened iron for tools and weapons. …Windmills are used in Persia (present-day Iran) to grind corn. …Corinthians invent a slideway for pulling ships across the isthmus. …Corinthians develop the 50-oar longboat. …Etruscans devise the arch.

c. 580 B.C. Greek mathematician Pythagoras, who will devise what will become known as the Pythagorean theorem, is born.

Culture & Arts

c. 604 B.C. Lao-tzu (believed to be the founder of Taoism) is born in China (d. 531 B.C.).

c. 600 B.C. Greek tragedy is born with choral performances. …Sappho of Lesbos, a Greek island, writes verses about love between women. …Romans adapt the Greek alphabet (from the Etruscans). …Circus Maximus is built in Rome. …The first known Latin inscriptions are written. …Persian prophet Zoroaster founds religion of Zoroastrianism.

594 B.C. Hanging Gardens of Babylon are built.

c. 580 B.C. Hebrew scriptures are collected into one body (later called the Old Testament).

c. 563 B.C. Siddhartha Gautama (d. 483 B.C.)is born in Nepal. He will become known as Buddha and found Buddhism.

c. 551 B.C. Confucius, who will devise a Chinese system of ethical wisdom, is born in China.

Egypt & Africa

c. 550 B.C. Amasis II (569–525 B.C.), king of Egypt, hires Greek mercenaries.

525 B.C. Persia, under King Cambyses (?–522 B.C.), conquers Egypt and deposes the last Egyptian king.

c. 500 B.C. Bantu-speaking peoples settle in East Africa. ...Hanno of Carthage (fl. 5th century B.C.) reports that he sailed to west coast of Africa (present-day Sierra Leone). ...Darius the Great (548–486 B.C.), Persian ruler of Egypt, plants extensive crops at oases.

In this seal cylinder, Darius the Great is portrayed hunting lions among palm trees. The vertical symbols on the left spell Darius's name in the Persian, Susian and Babylonian languages.

Middle East, Asia, Pacific & Americas

550–529 B.C. Cyrus the Great (600–529 B.C.) reigns, having founded the Persian empire in present-day Iran.

c. 542 B.C. Magadha kingdom is established in northeastern India (present-day Bihar).

539 B.C. Cyrus the Great recruits Babylonian priests as spies against their king, Belshazzar.

538 BC. Cyrus defeats Babylonia and ends Jewish captivity.

522 B.C. Darius the Great becomes king of Persia, introducing taxation and a legal system.

520 B.C. Persia builds paved roads with guard stations.

c. 500 B.C. Many Chinese cities separate the living areas of aristocracy from those of merchants and craftsmen.

Greece & Asia Minor

c. 550 B.C. Phalaris (?–550 B.C.), dictator of Acragas, is deposed. ....The Peloponnesian League is formed by Sparta and its allies.

c. 546 B.C. Pisistratus (c. 560–527 B.C.) becomes tyrant of Athens. ...Sparta and Argos choose 300 warriors each to decide a dispute about battle, but inconclusive result leads to a real battle won by Sparta.

540 B.C. In a war for trade, the Phoenicians and Etruscans expel the Phocaeans from Alalia (present-day Corsica).

524 B.C. The city of Cumae (near present-day Naples) defeats combined Etruscan forces arriving after a famous long march.

c. 520 B.C. Maeandrius (fl. 6th century B.C.), dictator of Samos, is first known ruler to declare and support equal rights. ...Athens produces silver coins depicting the head of Athena. ...Homosexuality is encouraged in Greece.

c. 510 B.C. Hippias, the Athenian tyrant, is deposed with the help of Sparta. ...Athens joins Sparta's Peloponnesian League.

508–507 B.C. A spartan garrison occupies Acropolis in Athens by invitation from opponents of reforms instituted by Greek statesman Cleisthenes.

c. 507 B.C. Cleisthenes establishes true democracy in Athens.

c. 500 B.C. Darius the Great of Persia builds a road to transport slaves between Lydia and his capital at Susa (in present-day Iran). ...Use of coins spreads throughout Greece, except in Sparta, where owning silver or gold is prohibited.

499 B.C. Ionian cities revolt against Persia.

499–449 B.C. Greek city-states and the Persian empire fight the Persian Wars.

495 B.C. The Persian fleet defeats the Ionian fleet at the battle of Lade.

494 B.C. Persians put down a five-year revolt by Ionian Greeks. ...Cleomenes I (c. 520–490 B.C.), king of Sparta, is believed to have killed 6,000 Argives by burning them alive in a forest.

493 B.C. Soldier-statesman Themistocles (c. 523–458 B.C.) persuades Athenians to build a great fleet. ...Athenians build a harbor at Piraeus.

Rome & Europe

c. 550 B.C. Etruscans, becoming powerful throughout Italy, rule Rome. ...Iron tools are made in southern England.

540 B.C. Etruscans and Phoenicians combine fleets to defeat the Phocaean navy.

c. 535 B.C. Sardinia is colonized by Carthage.

c. 530 B.C. Europeans increase imports of luxury goods, such as Greek bronzes and Italian pottery. ...Rome begins its first large-scale building program.

509 B.C. Rome becomes an independent republic. ...Rome records 132 patrician families.

508 B.C. Rome and Carthage sign a peace treaty.

c. 500 B.C. Etruscan trade reaches to the Celts of northern Europe. ...Carthaginian trading centers and colonies flourish in southern Spain.

499 B.C. Rome defeats neighboring Latin tribes at the battle of Lake Regillus.

493 B.C. Cassius Viscellinus (?–485 B.C.) negotiates a Roman treaty with the Latin League. ...Tribunes are created to represent ordinary Roman citizens.

Science, Invention & Technology

c. 550 B.C. Iron tools are used throughout west Africa.

c. 530 B.C. Pythagoras settles in Greek colony of Croton in southern Italy to study mathematics and astronomy. ...Eupalinus of Megara (fl. 6th century B.C.) builds a system of tunnels to convey water throughout the Greek island of Samos.

c. 520–500 B.C. Darius the Great (548–486 B.C.), king of Persia, has a canal completed between the Nile and the Red Sea.

c. 500 B.C. The use of iron tools spread throughout China. ...Celts develop uniform iron tools and weapons. ...Greeks and Carthaginians invent catapults for use in war. ...Greek philosopher Anaxagoras is born. He will discover the reason for eclipses.

Culture & Arts

550 B.C. Temple of Artemis is constructed at Ephesus in Asia Minor (present-day Turkey).

c. 540 B.C. Greek philosopher Heraclitus (d. c. 475 B.C.) is born. To describe the changing world, he will declare, "You cannot step in the same river twice."

525 B.C. Aeschylus (d. 456 B.C.), father of Greek tragedy, is born.

509 B.C. Romans establish cult of the god Jupiter.

c. 500 B.C. Eskimo cultures of the present-day Bering Sea region create pottery. ...Mahavira establishes religion of Jainism in India. ...Theano (fl. 6th century B.C.), believed to be the daughter of Pythagoras, contributes to the studies of mathematics, philosophy, and medicine.

▲ ***Roman soldiers dressed for combat.***

Egypt & Africa

A drawing of a bust of Greek ruler Pericles.

462–454 B.C. Egypt tries to overthrow Persian rule but fails.

454 B.C. Persians defeat an Athenian force in Egypt.

This image from a 7th-century Italian illuminated manuscript portrays the prophet Ezra at his work.

Middle East, Asia, Pacific & Americas

485 B.C. Xerxes (520–465 B.C.) becomes king of Persia. He soon invades Greece and burns Athens.

464–425 B.C. Artaxerxes I (?–425 B.C.) reigns as king of Persia, sanctioning the Jewish religion in Jerusalem.

c. 440 B.C. Ezra (fl. 450 B.C.) devises a legal code for the Jewish people.

c. 430 B.C. Hebrew leader Nehemiah rebuilds walls of Jerusalem.

Greece & Asia Minor

491 B.C. Representatives of Persia visit Greek cities to receive the symbols of submission, earth and water.

490 B.C. Athenians defeat Persians at the battle of Marathon, fought on the Greek plain of Marathon. ...Cleomenes I (b. c. 520 B.C.), king of Sparta, is assassinated; some believe he commits suicide.

487 B.C. Athenians introduce the punishment of ostracism.

482 B.C. Athenian coffers are filled by the city's new Laurium silver mines.

480 B.C. Persians sack Athens during the Persian Wars. ...The Greek navy defeats Persians off the Greek island of Salamis.

479 B.C. Athenians build a defensive wall around Piraeus, their port.

471 B.C. Athenian aristocrats ostracize the statesman Themistocles.

470 B.C. Greek island of Naxos tries to secede from Delian League but is forced to remain.

464 B.C. Helot slaves in Sparta revolt unsuccessfully following an earthquake.

462–429 B.C. Pericles (c. 480–429 B.C.) rules Athens, making it a wealthy, powerful and culturally rich city.

454 B.C. Athenians move the Delian League treasury from Delos to their city. ...Athens limits citizenship to those whose mother and father are citizens.

c. 450 B.C. Assembly becomes more powerful in Athens. ...Payment for Athenian jurors is introduced.

c. 449 B.C. Athens and Persia sign a peace treaty.

446 B.C. Athens and Sparta sign a 30-year peace treaty that lasts 14 years.

c. 445 B.C. Athens decrees that only Athenian weights, measures and coins can be used by Delian League states.

440 B.C. The Peloponnesian League votes down Sparta's request for war with Athens.

437 B.C. Athenians colonize Thrace (in present-day Greece and Bulgaria).

431–404 B.C. Athens and Sparta fight the Peloponnesian War.

430–426 B.C. A plague begins and kills a third of the population of Athens, including Pericles.

Rome & Europe

490 B.C. The Volsci tribe attacks Rome.

486 B.C. Cassius Viscellinus achieves land reform with Rome's first Agrarian Law.

471 B.C. In Rome, the patricians acknowledge plebeian institutions in the *Lex Publilia*.

c. 450 B.C. Rome codifies the Twelve Tables, which will last for 600 years. ...Roman trade with Europe is interrupted by Celtic migrations.

448 B.C. Plebeians conduct their second secession, and Rome reduces patrician power.

445 B.C. The *Lex Canuleia* allows intermarriage between Roman patricians and plebeians.

c. 443 B.C. Rome elects its first censor to take a census.

Science, Invention & Technology

c. 475–221 B.C. Chinese invent iron molds to produce axes, hoes and other tools.

c. 460 B.C. Greek physician Hippocrates (d. c. 370 B.C.), father of medicine, is born. He will note that climate, food and occupation can affect health. The Hippocratic oath recalls his ethical principles.

c. 450 B.C. Athenians begin scientific specializations, separating medicine from mathematics.

c. 440 B.C. Chinese devise a solar calendar. ...Greek scientists theorize that atoms exist.

Culture & Arts

◀ ***A bust of the Greek dramatist Euripides.***

c. 483 B.C. Siddhartha Gautama, the Buddha, founder of Buddhist religion, dies.

c. 480–330 B.C. Golden age of Greek culture flowers in art, drama and philosophy.

c. 479 B.C. Confucius dies. According to legend, he wrote, edited or compiled the *Wu Ching*, the five classics of Chinese literature, including the *I Ching* (*Book of Changes*).

470 B.C. Temple of Zeus, with its statue of Zeus, is constructed at Olympia.

469 B.C. Greek philosopher Socrates (d. 399 B.C.) is born in Athens.

c. 460 B.C. Myron (fl. 5th century B.C.) sculpts *Discus Thrower*.

450 B.C. Herodotus (c. 484–425 B.C.) writes a history of the Persian Wars.

447–438 B.C. Parthenon is constructed on Acropolis at Athens.

443 BC. Euripides (c. 485–406 B.C.) writes *Medea*.

442–441 B.C. Sophocles (c. 496–406 B.C.) writes *Antigone*.

c. 430 B.C. Sophocles' *Oedipus Rex* is first performed.

c. 428 B.C. Greek philosopher Plato (d. 347 B.C.) is born.

Egypt & Africa

404–399 B.C. Amyrtaios (?–399 B.C.) reigns as king of Egypt.

399–380 B.C. Nepherites (?–380 B.C.) reigns as king of Egypt.

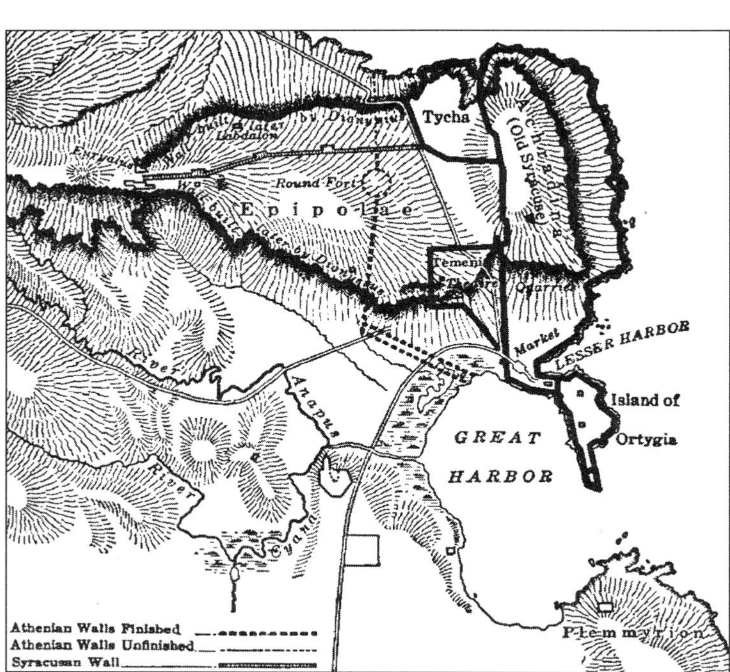

▲ *This map depicts the siege of Syracuse, a Greek city in southeastern Sicily, by the Athenians during the Peloponnesian War.*

Middle East, Asia, Pacific & Americas

423–404 B.C. Darius II (?–404 B.C.) reigns as king of Persia.

413 B.C. Darius II becomes Sparta's ally against Athens.

403–221 B.C. China splits into kingdoms in Age of Warring States.

Greece & Asia Minor

424 B.C. Spartan general Brasidas takes northern Athenian cities, including Amphipolis.

422 B.C. Generals Brasidas of Sparta (fl. 5th century B.C.) and Cleon of Athens (fl. 5th century B.C.) die at battle of Amphipolis.

c. 420 B.C. Athens puts down a revolt on Lesbos.

413 B.C. Athens loses 50,000 men and more than 200 ships trying to capture Syracuse.

411 B.C. Sparta and Persia sign a peace treaty.

405 B.C. Spartan fleet defeats Athenian navy at Aegospotami.

404 B.C. Athens surrenders to Sparta.

403 B.C. Athenians overthrow the "Thirty Tyrants" imposed by Sparta.

397 B.C. A revolt by lower classes in Sparta is suppressed.

c. 395 B.C. Athenians rebuild their long walls destroyed by Sparta.

395–387 B.C. Corinthian War is fought between Sparta and Persia. The peace treaty favors Sparta.

382 B.C. Philip II (382–336 B.C.) becomes king of Macedonia.

371 B.C. Greek city of Thebes defeats Sparta, which begins its decline.

369 B.C. Thebes frees its Helot slaves.

362 B.C. Epaminondas, the Theban general, is killed by Spartans at battle of Mantinea, ending Thebes's military power.

356 B.C. Alexander the Great (d. 323 B.C.) is born in Pella in northern Greece.

353 B.C. Mausolus, king of Caria (present-day southeast Turkey), dies.

352–341 B.C. The orator Demosthenes speaks against Philip II of Macedonia (382–336 B.C.).

Rome & Europe

409 B.C. Plebeians are allowed to become Roman quaestors (magistrates).

c. 400 B.C. Celtic tribes migrate into the Po Valley in northern Italy.

c. 400–15 B.C. The Celtic La Téne culture flourishes in Switzerland.

396 B.C. Rome conquers its rival, Etruscan Veii.

390 B.C. Gauls, led by Brennus, sack Rome.

386 B.C. Rome and the Etruscan Caere adopt joint citizenship.

367 B.C. Camillus (c. 415–365 B.C.) is elected Roman dictator for the fifth time. . . .The number of Rome's patrician families has declined from 132 in 509 B.C. to 81.

366 B.C. The judicial position of praetor is established in Rome. . . .A new Roman law requires one of the two consuls to be a plebeian.

Science, Invention & Technology

c. 414 B.C. Greek mathematician Theaetetus is born. He will identify the five regular solid figures.

408 B.C. Greek mathematician and astronomer Eudoxus is born. He will map the stars and correct the length of the solar year.

c. 400 B.C. Chinese invent the crossbow. Plato studies the mathematical motions of heavenly bodies.

c. 380 B.C. Babylonian astronomer Kidinnu (343 B.C.–?) calculates a lunar month to within one second.

c. 372 B.C. Theophrastus (d. 287 B.C.), the Greek philosopher, is born. He will write classic botanical works, distinguishing between monocotyledons and dicotyledons.

365 B.C. Observing without telescopes, Chinese astronomers discover the satellites of Jupiter.

c. 360 B.C. Chinese mass-produce crossbows.

Culture & Arts

423 B.C. *The Clouds*, a play by Aristophanes (c. 448–c. 380 B.C.), is first performed in Athens.

423–404 B.C. While in exile, Greek historian Thucydides (?–401 B.C.) writes *History of the Peloponnesian War.*

413 B.C. Euripides writes *Electra.*

c. 412 B.C. Greek philosopher Diogenes is born (d. 320 B.C.).

c. 400 B.C. Philosophic school of Cynicism is created in Greece by Antisthenes.

399 B.C. Socrates (b. 469 B.C.), tried and condemned to death, commits suicide by drinking hemlock.

c. 387 B.C. Plato founds the Academy, a school of philosophy.

384 B.C. Greek philosopher Aristotle (d. 322 B.C.) is born.

c. 371–367 B.C. Plato writes *The Republic*, *Apology*, *Phaedo* and *Symposium.*

An early 18th-century drawing depicting the Greek philosopher Theophrastus.

Egypt & Africa

332 B.C. Alexander the Great (356–323 B.C.) enters Egypt and is crowned pharaoh at Memphis.

331 B.C. According to legend, oracles of Amon at Siwah (present-day Libya) tell Alexander the Great that he is the son of Zeus.

305 B.C. Ptolemy I (367–284 B.C.) becomes king of Egypt, founding the Macedonian dynasty.

285 B.C. Ptolemy II (c. 308–246 B.C.) becomes king of Egypt and rules during Alexandria's golden era.

Middle East, Asia, Pacific & Americas

338 B.C. Artaxerxes III (b. 400 B.C.), king of Persia, is poisoned by his favorite eunuch.

332 B.C. Alexander the Great takes the new city of Tyre, ending Phoenicia's independence.

331 B.C. Alexander the Great defeats Darius III and overthrows his Persian empire.

326 B.C. Alexander the Great invades northern India and defeats King Porus (fl. 4th century B.C.).

325 B.C. Alexander the Great decrees his empire will enforce racial equality.

323 B.C. Alexander the Great dies of a fever in Babylon at the age of 33.

321–238 B.C. Most of India is unified by the Mauryan dynasty of Magadha.

312–64 B.C. Seleucid empire, founded by Seleucus I (c. 330–280 B.C.), expands as far as India.

301 B.C. Palestine is conquered by Egyptians.

c. 300 B.C. The city of Ur in Mesopotamia is abandoned. . . . Teotihuacán culture expands in present-day central Mexico.

Greece & Asia Minor

338 B.C. In the battle of Chaeronea, Macedonians under Philip II defeat Athens and Thebes.

336 B.C. Alexander the Great becomes king of Macedonia at the death of his father.

334 B.C. Alexander the Great defeats the Persians at the battle of Granicus in northwestern Asia Minor.

333 B.C. According to tradition, Alexander the Great cuts the Gordian knot with his sword after being unable to untie it.

324 B.C. Alexander the Great allows Greek exiles to return to their home cities.

322 B.C. Demosthenes takes poison to avoid capture by Macedonians.

320 B.C. Pytheas (fl. 4th century B.C.), according to legend, circumnavigates the British Isles and visits Thule (present-day Iceland).

305 B.C. Cassander (c. 358–297 B.C.) becomes king of Macedonia. Shortly thereafter, he murders the wife and mother of Alexander the Great.

280 B.C. Twelve Greek city-states establish the Achaean League to oppose Macedonia.

280–279 B.C. Pyrrhus defeats Romans at Heraclea and Ausculum, but loses many men, giving rise to the expression "a Pyrrhic victory" to denote a costly victory.

Rome & Europe

343–340 B.C. The Romans and the Samnite tribe of the Apennines engage in the First Samnite War.

c. 338 B.C. Rome becomes dominant in its local region, Latium.

326 B.C. Naples and Rome become allies.

326–304 B.C. Second Samnite War is fought between the Romans and the Samnites.

312 B.C. The Appian Way, a 132-mile stone road, is begun from Rome to Capua. ...Rome's first aqueduct, the Aqua Appia, is built underground.

304 B.C. Rome defeats the Aequi, a neighboring Latin tribe, and massacres prisoners.

298–290 B.C. Third Samnite War is fought between the Romans and Samnites (and their allies), leaving Rome the ruler of central Italy.

287 B.C. Plebeians mount their third secession in Rome. The plebeian assembly, the concilium plebis, is allowed to make laws.

275 B.C. Romans defeat Pyrrhus, king of Epirus, at Malventum.

269 B.C. Silver coinage is introduced in Rome.

Science, Invention & Technology

c. 350 B.C. Greek astronomer Heracleides Ponticus (c. 388–315 B.C.) proposes the theory that the earth turns on its axis.

c. 330 B.C. Euclid, the Greek mathematician, is born. His 13-volume *Elements* outlines basic geometry. ...Aristotle teaches that matter is continuous and that the universe is timeless. ...Greek astronomer Aristarchus of Samos is born. He is the first known person to propose that the earth revolves around the sun.

c. 300 B.C. The water clock and steam power are invented in Alexandria, Egypt. ...Japan begins iron and bronze production. ...Teotihuacán culture devises an extensive grid pattern of streets in present-day Mexico.

c. 287 B.C. Archimedes, Greek mathematician, is born.

c. 287–269 B.C. Strato (c. 310–269 B.C.), Greek philosopher, heads the Peripatetic School.

c. 270 B.C. Greek inventer Ctesibius (c. 300–250 B.C.) uses pressure to devise a pump with a plunger.

Culture & Arts

c. 350–150 B.C. Proverbs of the Bible are written.

c. 340 B.C. Timotheus of Miletus (450–360 B.C.) is criticized for introducing emotionalism to Greek music.

335 B.C. Aristotle establishes his Lyceum outside Athens.

331 B.C. School of Alexandria is founded in Egypt by scholars and writers.

325 B.C. Greek painter Apelles (fl. 4th century B.C.) paints portraits of Alexander the Great at his court.

323 B.C. A museum is established at Alexandria.

c. 300 B.C. Rome's plebeians are admitted to the colleges of priests. ...Valmiki (fl. 4th century B.C.) writes India's epic Hindu poem, the *Ramayana*. ...Greek philosophy of stoicism is founded by Zeno of Citium (c. 335–264 B.C.). ...Epicurus founds the Greek Epicurean school of philosophy.

292–280 B.C. Colossus of Rhodes is erected in the harbor of Rhodes.

c. 275 B.C. The Pharos of Alexandria (lighthouse) is erected.

270 B.C. Manetho (fl. 3rd century B.C.), an Egyptian priest, compiles a list of Egyptian dynasties.

Egypt & Africa

264 B.C. The city of Adulis on the Red Sea (in present-day Ethiopia) becomes a center for international trading.

222 B.C. Ptolemy IV (244–205 B.C.) commences his reign by killing his mother.

▲ *A 17th-century drawing of the first emperor of a unified China, Shih Huang Ti.*

Middle East, Asia, Pacific & Americas

c. 250 B.C. Rice growing is introduced to Japan from China.

c. 248 B.C. Arsacid empire is founded in Parthia southeast of Caspian Sea.

221 B.C. The Ch'in dynasty is established in China by Emperor Shih Huang Ti (259–210 B.C.), who unifies the country.

c. 220 B.C. China establishes nine ranks of Mandarin imperial officials.

214 B.C. Shih Huang Ti begins construction of the Great Wall of China.

210 B.C. Chinese emperor Shih Huang Ti (b. 259 B.C.) dies and is buried with 7,000 life-size clay soldiers.

206 B.C. Han dynasty is established in China by Liu Pang (fl. 2nd century B.C.).

c. 200 B.C. Mogollon farmers (in present-day New Mexico and Arizona) live in pit houses around a ceremonial building.

c. 200 B.C.–A.D. 600. Mochica culture flourishes on the Peruvian coast of western South America.

Greece & Asia Minor

279 B.C. Celts pillage Delphi but are defeated.

c. 267 B.C. In the Chremonidean War, Athens and Sparta rebel unsuccessfully against the Macedonians.

241 B.C. Agis IV, king of Sparta, is executed by those opposing his reforms.

229 B.C. Romans invade Greece.

227 B.C. Cleomenes III (?–219 B.C.), king of Sparta, frees Helot slaves to form a citizens' army.

222 B.C. The Achaean League, led by Antigonus Doson (fl. 3rd century B.C.), defeats Sparta.

215–205 B.C. The First Macedonian War is fought. Rome defeats Philip V of Macedonia, confining him to Macedonia.

c. 200 B.C. Several Greek cities provide free education and medicine to poor.

200–197 B.C. Second Macedonian War is fought.

196 B.C. Roman general Titus Quinctius Flamininus (228–174 B.C.) withdraws from Greece, granting independence.

Rome & Europe

266 B.C. Rome becomes the ruler of all Italy.

264–241 B.C. Rome and Carthage fight the First Punic War.

260 B.C. Roman and Carthaginian fleets clash for the first time.

250 B.C. Rome has alliances with more than 150 cities.

241 B.C. Number of Roman tribes reaches 35 (from the original 20). ...Rome takes Sicily from Carthage.

227 B.C. Sardinia becomes Rome's second province.

225 B.C. Roman army defeats invading Gauls at Telamon on the Etruscan coast.

220 B.C. Via Flaminia is built from Rome to Ariminum (Rimini) in northern Italy.

218 B.C. During the Second Punic War, Hannibal (c. 247–183 B.C.), the Carthaginian general, crosses the Alps with 57 elephants and defeats the Roman army.

216 B.C. Hannibal is victorious over the Romans at Cannae in southeastern Italy.

215–195 B.C. A wartime edict prohibits Roman women from owning luxuries.

212 B.C. Rome captures Syracuse.

206 B.C. Rome conquors Spain.

202 B.C. Hannibal is defeated by Romans at Zama (present-day Algeria).

c. 200 B.C. Gold Celtic coins are imported into the British Isles. ...Rome bans bacchanalian orgies.

184 BC. Cato the Elder (234–149 B.C.) becomes a Roman censor and fights corruption.

Science, Invention & Technology

c. 260 BC. Greek physician Herophilus (c. 300–250 B.C.) dissects the human body and writes first anatomy texts.

c. 250 BC. Eratosthenes (c. 275–195 B.C.), Greek astronomer, measures earth's circumference and determines sizes of the sun and moon and their distances from earth.

240 B.C. Chinese record the appearance of what will become known as Halley's comet.

c. 220 B.C. Chinese emperor Shih Huang Ti writes about internal medicine. ...Apollonius of Perga (247–205 B.C.) introduces the mathematical terms *ellipse*, *parabola* and *hyperbola*.

c. 200 B.C. Chinese introduce the horse collar and harness. ...Greek physician Erasistratus discovers that arteries and veins connect to the heart.

c. 190 B.C. Greek astronomer Hipparchus is born. He will develop trigonometry and make the first comprehensive star chart.

Culture & Arts

254 B.C. Roman comic dramatist Titus Maccius Plautus (d. 184 B.C.) is born.

c. 250 B.C. Latin literature begins with works of Roman poet and dramatist Livius Andronicus (c. 284–204 B.C.).

c. 240 B.C. Asoka (fl. 3rd century B.C.), emperor of India, converts to Buddhism.

239 B.C. Scholars in Chinese state of Ch'in compile *The Spring and Autumn Annals of Mr. Lu*.

This image, from a central Italian plate, depicts Hannibal and his troops crossing the Alps to confront the Romans in 218 B.C.

202 B.C. Roman general Quintus Fabius Pictor (fl. 3rd century B.C.) writes the first history of Rome (in Greek).

c. 200 B.C. Vyasa (fl. 3rd century B.C.) writes India's epic Hindu poem *Mahabharata*, the world's longest verse story. It contains the *Bhagavad-Gita* (*Song of the Blessed*).

196 B.C. Egyptian priests inscribe the Rosetta Stone (later used to decipher hieroglyphics).

186 B.C. Rome holds its first Greek-style athletic games.

Egypt & Africa	Middle East, Asia, Pacific & Americas	Greece & Asia Minor

180–164 B.C. Ptolemy VI reigns as king of Egypt.

167–141 B.C. Maccabean revolt against Seleucid empire restores independence to Palestine.

165 B.C. Judas Maccabeus (fl. 160 B.C.) takes Jerusalem and rededicates the Temple.

171–168 B.C. The Third Macedonian War is fought with Rome.

168 B.C. Macedonia becomes four states after Perseus is defeated by Romans.

166–69 B.C. The Greek island of Delos engages in the slave trade.

Maccabean rebel leader, Judas Maccabeus, as depicted in this painting by Peter Paul Rubens (1577–1640).

148 B.C. Macedonia becomes a Roman province.

146 B.C. The Roman army, under Caecilius Metellus, sacks Corinth. ...The Achaean League is defeated by the Romans, who annex Greece.

133 B.C. The Greek city of Pergamum (in present-day Turkey) becomes a Roman province.

c. 130 B.C. Aristonicus (fl. 2nd century B.C.) leads a revolt of slaves and the poor in the city of Pergamum.

c. 100 B.C. Nomads in the Sahara begin to use camels.

c. 100 B.C. China's Han dynasty establishes diplomatic relations with other states. ...Chinese civil servants are selected by written examinations.

c. 100–66 B.C. Pirates disrupt trading across the Mediterranean.

Rome & Europe

183 B.C. Hannibal, the Carthaginian general, commits suicide.

172 B.C. For the first time, both Roman consuls are plebeians.

167 B.C. Direct taxation of Romans is abolished.

c. 160 B.C. Roman women begin to take a more active role in public life.

c. 150 B.C. Roman consuls are banned from second terms. ...Roman women darken their eyelids with wood ash.

149–146 B.C. The Third Punic War is fought and ends with the Roman army destroying Carthage.

139 B.C. Secret ballots are allowed for Roman elections.

133 B.C. Roman senators murder the land reformer Tiberius Sempronius Gracchus (b. 168 B.C.). ...Besieged by the Roman army, the residents of Numantia (in present-day Spain) burn their city and commit mass suicide.

132 B.C. Slaves rebel in Sicily, and 20,000 are executed on crosses.

121 B.C. Rome conquers southern Gaul (present-day southern France).

120 B.C. Southern Gaul is annexed as the Roman province of Gallia Transalpina.

111–106 B.C. The Roman army, led by Marius (c. 157–87 B.C.), defeats Jugurtha (c. 156–104 B.C.), king of Numidia (roughly present-day Algeria).

102–101 B.C. Marius commands victories over the Teutones and the Cimbri, becoming a popular hero.

91–88 B.C. Rome battles Italian allies in the Social (meaning allies) War.

90 B.C. People of the Latin tribes are made citizens of Rome.

90–88 B.C. Italians rise up unsuccessfully against Rome in the Social War.

88 B.C. A civil war is waged in Rome.

82 B.C. Sulla (138–78 B.C.) becomes dictator of Rome after murdering his democratic opponents.

Science, Invention & Technology

c. 170 B.C. Tools are fashioned out of volcanic rock in Teotihuacán, in present-day Mexico.

c. 140 B.C. The first recorded observatory is built at Rhodes by Hipparchus.

c. 133 B.C. Romans develop concrete as a building material.

▲ ***This map shows the spread of Roman power through 133 B.C.***

c. 100 B.C. Greek physician Asclepiades (fl. 1st century B.C.) advocates diet and exercise as cures. ...Greeks import the water mill from China. ...Rome creates public baths and underfloor heating (hypocaust). ...Scribes of Greek city of Pergamum (in present-day Turkey) invent parchment to replace papyrus. ...Philo of Byzantium (present-day Istanbul) writes *Seven Wonders of the World* and a summary of technology. ...Chinese invent hinged boat rudder.

Culture & Arts

c. 166 B.C. Terence (c. 195–159 B.C.), the Roman dramatist, writes his first play, *Andria*.

c. 160 B.C. Pergamum (in present-day Turkey) has an artistic flowering, including construction of the great altar of Zeus.

c. 150 B.C. Essenes, members of a Jewish sect, begin writing documents later found (A.D. 1947–1956) in caves on Israel's West Bank and since called the Dead Sea Scrolls. ...Chinese poet Cho Wen-chun (c. 179–117 B.C.) sells her love poems to support herself and her husband.

c. 100 B.C. Roman men start a new fashion trend by shaving their beards.

c. 90 B.C. Golden Age of Latin literature begins; it lasts until A.D. 17.

Egypt & Africa

Sculpted head of Cleopatra VII, the last queen of Egypt.

51 B.C. Cleopatra VII (69–30 B.C.) begins reign as the last queen of Egypt.

48–47 B.C. Julius Caesar (100–44 B.C.) joins Cleopatra in Egypt.

47 B.C. Cleopatra and Caesar dispose of her brother and co-ruler.

46–44 B.C. Cleopatra lives in Rome as Caesar's mistress.

44 B.C. Roman trading centers appear on the east African coast. ...Cleopatra returns to Egypt to reign with her son.

Middle East, Asia, Pacific & Americas

64 B.C. Seleucid empire falls when Rome conquers Syria.

63 B.C. Jerusalem is occupied by the Romans.

57 B.C. The Period of the Three Kingdoms begins in Korea.

56 B.C. Orodes II (?–37 B.C.) begins his reign in Parthia.

53 B.C. Orodes II of Parthia defeats Romans at the city of Carrhae (in present-day Turkey).

Greece & Asia Minor

c. 60–40 B.C. Olympias of Thebes (fl. 1st century B.C.), a Greek midwife, writes on various medical topics.

A 19th-century engraving of Julius Caesar.

44 B.C. Caesar rebuilds the Greek city of Corinth.

Rome & Europe

75 B.C. Cicero (c. 102–43 **B.C.**) is the first quaestor elected without 10 years of military service.

73–71 B.C. Spartacus (fl. 73 B.C.) leads the unsuccessful revolt of gladiators and slaves against Rome.

60 B.C. Caesar (c. 100–44 B.C.), Pompey (106–48 B.C.), and Crassus (c. 100–53 B.C.) form the first Triumvirate.

59 B.C. Caesar's daughter Julia weds Pompey.

58–57 B.C. Caesar is briefly banished by the tribune Clodius (100–52 B.C.).

58–51 B.C. Caesar conquers all Gaul.

55 B.C. Caesar crosses the Rhine. ...Caesar invades Britain for the first time.

54 B.C. Caesar invades Britain again but cannot conquer the island.

53 B.C. Crassus is captured by Parthians and executed.

52 B.C. Caesar captures Celtic leader Vercingetorix (?–46 B.C.) at the battle of Alesia (in present-day France). ...Clodius is slain during a street fight.

49 B.C. Roman senate passes an emergency decree asking magistrates to defend the city against Caesar's possible attack. Caesar, stating "The die is cast," crosses the Rubicon, a river in north-central Iraly, to begin a civil war against Pompey.

48 B.C. Caesar defeats Pompey at the battle of Pharsalus (present-day Pharsala), a city in northern Greece. Pompey retreats to Egypt and is assassinated. Caesar becomes dictator of Rome.

47 B.C. Caesar defeats Pharnaces II (fl. 1st century B.C.) of Asia Minor and declares, *"Veni, vidi, vici"* ("I came, I saw, I conquered").

46 B.C. The Julian calendar is adopted by Julius Caesar, introducing the leap year.

44 B.C. Caesar is assassinated in the senate. Mark Antony (c. 83–30 B.C.) assumes power.

Science, Invention & Technology

c.60 B.C. Chinese develop the flash lock for transferring boats to different levels in their elaborate canal system. ...Roman medical practitioners make house calls. ...Romans develop iron-framed catapults and use metal bolts in place of stones for ammunition. ...Chinese use a gimbals perfume burner to scent their rooms. ...Romans invent the water organ, a musical instrument that uses air forced through pipes by pumped water. ...Windowpanes made of blown glass are installed in the Forum in Pompeii. ...A system of steam baths is developed by the citizens of Douro Valley (in present-day northern Portugal.)

Culture & Arts

59 B.C. Livy (Titus Livius), the Roman historian, is born. He will write a 142-book history of Rome.

54 B.C. Roman poet Catullus (b. 84 B.C.) dies. His love poems will influence later generations.

54–51 B.C. Cicero (c. 106–43 B.C.) writes *De Republica* (*The Republic*).

51 B.C. Caesar writes *De Bello Gallico* (*The Gallic Wars*)

Cicero, Roman statesman and orator, as imagined by a 19th-century artist.

Roman Empire & Europe

43 B.C. Mark Antony (83–30 B.C.) is defeated by Octavian (63 B.C.–A.D. 14). ...Rome's Second Triumvirate rules.

42 B.C. Antony and Octavian are victorious at the battle of Philippi. ...Tiberius (d. A.D. 37), future Roman emperor, is born.

41 B.C. The Roman Empire is divided: Octavian rules the West, Antony rules the East. ...The military forces of Antony and Octavian clash.

39 B.C. Sextus Pompeius (c. 80–38 B.C.), whose fleet has harassed Roman trade, signs a peace treaty with Antony and Octavian.

32 B.C. Octavian's soldiers and supporters swear an oath of allegiance to him. ...Octavian declares war on Antony.

31 B.C. Agrippa's (63–12 B.C.) fleet defeats Antony and Cleopatra at the battle of Actium off the coast of Greece.

30 B.C. Octavian becomes emperor of Roman Empire. ...Romans develop a banking system, with profits being derived solely from services.

28 B.C. Octavian reforms the senate and claims to have reestablished a republic.

27 B.C. Octavian accepts the Roman senate's title of Augustus. He creates a census for taxation purposes and establishes a civil service.

25 B.C. The Roman garrison town of Aosta is founded in northern Italy.

22 B.C. Augustus refuses the offer of lifetime consulship and dictatorship.

18 B.C. Rome encourages families to have children to offset a falling birthrate.

17 B.C. Augustus grants the title of Caesar to his two grandsons.

16 B.C. Augustus travels to the northern frontiers to inspire his defenses against invaders. ...Tiberius becomes praetor.

Africa, Asia & Pacific

41 B.C. Lepidus (?–13 B.C.) rules as emperor in the African Roman Empire.

40 B.C. The Parthians of Asia invade and occupy Judaea.

37 B.C. Cleopatra (c. 69–30 B.C.) marries Mark Antony (83–30 B.C.). ...The kingdom of Koguryo is established in north Korea. ...The Romans drive the Parthians from Judaea.

30 B.C. Antony and Cleopatra commit suicide. ...Egypt becomes a Roman province.

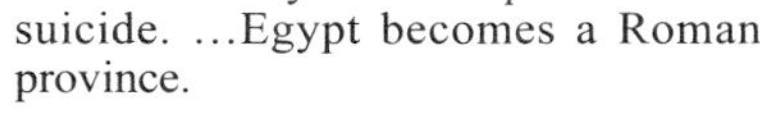

25 B.C. Romans strengthen the frontier between Egypt and Ethiopia.

c. 20 B.C. Korean men and women wear tight white clothes consisting of waist-length jackets and short trousers.

18 B.C. The kingdom of Paekche is formed in southeast Korea.

Americas

c. **40 B.C.** Teotihuacán culture dominates the Basin of Mexico. ...Simple Mesoamerican agricultural villages become complex settlements with sociopolitical organizations.

▲ ***Bust of Mark Antony, Roman emperor and philosopher.***

c. **20 B.C.–A.D. 300.** Trade develops over a wide area along the Mississippi River. ...Saladero culture spreads across Venezuelan coast to West Indies.

Religion

◄ *Roman emperor Augustus depicted on a bronze coin.*

34–33 B.C. Roman emperor Augustus recruits patricians for the priesthood.

29 B.C. Buddhist scriptures, which were for centuries transmitted only orally, are written for the first time in the Indian language of Pali.

27 B.C. The Pantheon is built in Rome to honor the gods.

17 B.C. Rome's ancient Sibylline Books, thought to be written by the priestess of Apollo, are recopied. ...Herod the Great (c.74–4 B.C.) rebuilds the Temple at Jerusalem.

Science, Invention & Technology

c. 40 B.C. Mirrors made of polished bronze are used by Romans to distribute light deep into mine shafts. ...Chinese dig the first known coal mines. ...Fulvius Lippinus (fl. 1st century B.C.) begins practice of farming snails. ...Chinese originate use of insecticides.

c. 35 B.C. A complex computing machine with 17 gears called the Antikythera, used to make celestial calculations, is part of shipwreck cargo off Crete. ...A four-mile crude railway with parallel grooves in rock is used to transfer boats across the Corinth Isthmus in Greece. ...Romans develop pearl culturing. ...Roman scientist Marcus Varro (116–27 B.C.) suggests that small organisms living in swamps are the source of diseases among people who live near the swamps.

c. 30 B.C. Chinese use thumbprints for identification. ...Maps of the Roman road system are created under Emperor Marcus Agrippa (63–12 B.C.). ...Celts create finely patterned handheld bronze mirrors. ...Chinese sailors use lodestones as crude navigational instruments. ...Romans use sophisticated central heating systems in their residences, baths and public buildings. ...Hindus of India use a variety of surgical instruments. ...Greeks develop a single-piston water pump. ...The first wheeled plows are in use in the valleys of Switzerland. ...Romans invent a barbed-spring iron padlock.

20 B.C. Marcus Vitruvius (fl. late 1st century B.C.) refers to water mills being used in the Roman Empire with a tympanum, a bucket fitted on a drum wheel for lifting water. ...Chinese invent the belt drive.

15 B.C. Extensive fish-farming operations are underway at Lapithos in northern Cyprus.

Culture & Arts

43 B.C. Cicero (b. 106 B.C.), Roman statesman and writer, dies.

c. 40 B.C. A marble frieze is carved for the Basilica Aemilia in Rome. ...Roman poets Virgil (c. 70–19 B.C.) and Horace (65– 8 B.C.) write during this period. ...Roman historian Livy writes *Ab urb condita,* a 142-volume history of Rome. ...Greek geographer Strabo (c. 63 B.C.–A.D. 21) presents *Geographica*, a compilation of the geography and history of the ancient world.

34 B.C. Sallust (b. c. 70 B.C.), Roman historian, dies. His writing drew upon Greek models. His histories included *Bellum Iugurthinum* about Rome's Jugurthine War.

31 B.C. Virgil's *Georgics* (*Art of Husbandry*), four books about animals and agriculture, are completed.

c. 30 B.C. Dionysius of Halicarnassus (c. 60–10 B.C.), Greek historian, moves to Rome and writes a history of Rome.

29 B.C. Augustus beautifies Rome with temples and public buildings. ...Horace completes his *Epodes*.

27 B.C. Vargo (b. c. 70 B.C.), a Roman author, dies. His *Imagines* is a series of 700 Greek and Roman biographies, each with a miniature picture.

26 B.C. Roman poet Cornelius Gallus (fl. 30 B.C.) commits suicide.

c. 22 B.C. The *fabulae salticae* seductive dances are introduced in Rome.

21 B.C. The first of the Roman *thermae* baths are built.

19 B.C. Horace produces three books of *Odes*. ...Tibullus (b. c. 55 B.C.), Roman elegiac poet, dies. ...Virgil dies.

17 B.C. Horace's *Carmen Seculare* is sung by a mixed choir at Rome's *Ludi Saeculares* (Secular Games).

16 B.C. Romans erect a temple at Nemausus (present-day Nîmes, France), the best preserved example of Roman temple architecture.

Roman Empire & Europe

12 B.C. Drusus begins campaign to subjugate Germany.

9 B.C. Drusus dies after falling from his horse.

8 B.C. A Roman census is taken.

2 B.C. Augustus forms the Praetorian Guard. ...Augustus banishes his daughter, Julia, because of her adulteries.

c. A.D. 1. Formation of a gothic kingdom on the lower Vistula begins.

3. Tiberius returns to Rome.

4. Augustus adopts Tiberius as his heir.

5. Cunobelinus (Cymbeline, ?–40) begins reign as king of the Catuvellauni in Britain.

6. Tiberius continues campaign to subjugate Germany.

9. Arminius (?–21) surprises and defeats three Roman legions in Teutoburg Forest.

12. Caligula (d. 41), future emperor of Rome, is born.

14. Augustus (b. 63 B.C.) dies. Tiberius becomes emperor. ...Campaign of Germanicus (15 B.C.–A.D. 19) begins in northern Germany.

25–30. Pontius Pilate (?–36) is procurator of Judaea.

27. Tiberius retires to Capreae.

29. Livia (b. c. 55 B.C.), wife of Augustus, dies.

31. Tiberius executes Sejanus for his ambitions to rule.

Africa, Asia & Pacific

10 B.C. Enrollment at the Imperial University at Loyang, China, reaches 3,000.

4 B.C. Herod the Great of Judaea dies.

c A.D. 1. The Asian kingdom of Parthia is recognized by Rome and renounces rights to Armenia. ...First Polynesians arrive in uninhabited Hawaii. ...First hospital is established by Emperor Wang Mang (45 B.C.–A.D. 24) of China.

9–23. Wang Mang establishes the Hsin dynasty in China.

17. An earthquake devastates the seaport of Ephesus (in present-day Turkey) and other parts of Asia Minor.

18. Roman soldier Germanicus (15 B.C.–A.D. 19) is given command over all rulers of the eastern Empire. ...Calpurnius Piso (fl. 1st century A.D.) becomes viceroy of Syria.

24. Mongolians invade China. ...Wang Mang (b. 45 B.C.), the Chinese ruler, is killed by his soldiers.

25–220. The Eastern Han dynasty reigns in China.

Americas

10 B.C.–A.D. 250. Ball games and courts are introduced into Mesoamerica. ...Intensive farming and irrigation develop around Teotihuacán. ...Maya are on the brink of their greatest development.

c. A.D. 1. Population of the Americas reaches 4.5 million, mostly in tropical zones. ...Beginning of the Hohokam culture in southern Arizona. ...Stela 10, Kamin- aljuyu, a precursor of the Maya calendar, is built in black basalt with four column text. ...Plateau Indians (living between Rocky and Cascade Mountains) begin developing hunting and gathering techniques and rudimentary technology. ...Beginning of Desert culture and basket making in present-day southwestern United States. ...Aztecs of present-day Mexico use hallucinogenic drugs in their religious ceremonies. ...Adena mound builders flourish in present-day southern Ohio.

c. 10. In the Mayan city of Tikal, in present-day Guatemala, an urban structure suggests foreign influence and evidence of trade with the Teotihuacán culture.

In this 16th-century painting by Quentin Massys, Pontius Pilate presents Jesus to be crucified.

Religion

12 B.C. Augustus revives Roman religious cults and restores temples. ...Jewish scholar Hillel (c. 30 B.C.–A.D. 10) begins interpreting scriptures.

c. 6 B.C. Jesus of Nazareth (d. c. A.D. 30) is born in Bethlehem, Palestine. He will become the founder of Christianity, which takes its name from the title Christ, meaning Messiah, or annointed. A spiritual teacher reputed to have healing powers, he will attract many followers, some of whom will claim to have seen him alive after his crucifixion. His purported resurrection will be perceived by Christians as a sign of his divinity.

c. 6. Jesus, at age 12, is believed to discuss the teachings of Judaism with Jewish scribes.

14. Upon his death, Emperor Augustus is deified with a temple.

c. 18. Jesus visits the Temple of Jerusalem.

18–36. Caiaphas (fl. 1st century) is high priest in Jerusalem.

25. For the first time, Buddha is represented as a human figure in Gandhara, India.

27. Jesus is baptized by John the Baptist (c. 3–29).

29. John the Baptist is executed on the order of Herod Antipas (?–39).

c. 30. Jesus is crucified on Pontius Pilate's (?–36) order.

31. Stephen (b. c. A.D. 1) is convicted of blasphemy in Jerusalem and stoned to death, becoming the first Christian martyr.

Science, Invention & Technology

c. 10 B.C. Roman horticulturists use propagation pots that have holes in the bottom. ...Chinese invent a deep-drill seeding device.

c. A.D. 1. Roman soldiers use iron helmets and face protectors. ...Chinese invent the sinan, a compass made of lodestone. ...The Great Wall of China is reinforced and observation towers are added. ...Hopewell culture of central North America makes smoking pipes carved into human and animal forms. ...Romans manufacture artificial gemstones. ...Chinese use soap beans as a detergent. ...Roman horticulturists develop numerous new plant species. ...Romans invent a writing fluid called *encaustum*.

20. Construction begins on six miles of underground tunnels chiseled into solid rock at Ellora, western India. ...Chinese invent a water-powered pounding machine. ...Romans install the first residential water-tap system.

c. 25. Chinese develop padlocks and chains for securing prisoners.

30. Aulus Cornelius Celsus (fl. 1st century) describes treatments for fractures.

31. Tu Shih (fl. 1st century) of China invents a water-powered metalworking machine.

Culture & Arts

c. 10 B.C. Augustus builds a theater in Rome.

9 B.C. King Natakamani (fl. 10 B.C.) of Kush (present-day Sudan) launches a building program.

8 B.C. Romans construct an aqueduct at Nemausus (present-day Nîmes, France). ...Roman poet Horace (b. 65 B.C.) dies, leaving *Ars Poetica* unfinished.

c. A.D. 1. Ovid (43 B.C.–A.D. 17), Roman poet, completes his 15-book *Ars Amatoria*. ...Romans use primitive methods of bookbinding. ...Greeks develop a form of musical script and notation. ...Romans incorporate the dome as the central feature in their architecture.

8. Ovid is banished by Augustus to Tomis on the Black Sea.

9–23. During his reign, Wang Mang of China builds a series of nine gigantic ancestral shrines.

17. Ovid (b. 43 B.C.) dies at Tomis. ...Roman historian Livy (b. 59 B.C.) dies.

20. Strabo, Greek geographer and author of the 47-volume *Historical Studies*, dies.

25. Vitruvius (fl. 1st century) completes *De Architectura*, the only surviving Roman treatise on architecture. ...Cremutius Cordus (b. 10 B.C.), Roman historian, commits suicide.

30. Romans popularize artistic glasswork. ...Velleius Paterculus (fl. 1st century), Roman writer, completes *Historiae Romanae*. ...A triumphal arch is dedicated to Emperor Tiberius at Arausio (present-day Orange in Provence, France).

Roman Empire & Europe

37. Tiberius (b. 42 B.C.) dies and Caligula becomes emperor.

39. Caligula leads his army to the English Channel for an invasion of Britain but decides against invading Britain.

40. Caligula bankrupts the Roman treasury. ...Cunobelinus's reign as "Britannorum Rex" ends.

41. Caligula (b. 12) is assassinated by two guards after declaring himself a god. ...Emperor Claudius, Caligula's uncle, begins reign.

43. Romans begin conquest of Britain. ...Romans defeat the Britons under Caractacus (?–54) at the battle of the Medway, a river in southeast England.

47. Romans begin constructing the Fosse Way from Lincoln to Exeter in Britain.

48. Claudius has his wife, Messalina, executed for her sexual affairs. Claudius marries Agrippina and adopts her son Nero (37–68).

50. Romans defeat Britons under Caractacus at the battle of Shropshire.

51. British leader Caractacus is captured by the Romans.

c. 54. Claudius dies, poisoned by his wife, Agrippina. Nero begins infamous reign as emperor of Rome.

60. Suetonius Paulinus (?–69) becomes governor of Britain. ...A large fire consumes much of Londinium (London). ...Spanish wine is exported throughout Europe.

61. Romans conquer Anglesey in Wales. ...Queen Boadicea (11 B.C.–A.D. 62) leads bloody but unsuccessful British rebellion against Rome.

64. The great fire devastates Rome.

Africa, Asia & Pacific

33–156. Taoism expands in China under Chang Tao-ling.

35. Kujula Kadphises (fl. 1st century) rules Bactria and Sogdiana in India.

41. Herod Agrippa I (10 B.C.–A.D. 44) becomes king of Judaea and Samaria.

42–562. The small kingdom of Karak exists in southeast Korea.

43. Chinese general Ma Yuan (14 B.C.–A.D. 49) reconquers Annam (present-day Vietnam) after its four-year revolt.

44. Herod Agrippa I dies, and Judaea is governed by Roman procurators. Roman forces conquer Mauretania (present-day Morocco).

48. China, under Emperor Guang Wudi (fl. 1st century), subdues and rules Inner Mongolia.

c. 50. The Ethiopian kingdom begins to expand. ...The sea between India and Egypt becomes a major trade route. ...Roman explorers discover the source of the Nile River.

57. The first Japanese envoy arrives at the Chinese court.

58–76. Emperor Ming Ti (fl. 1st century) introduces Buddhism to China.

60. India begins trading silk and spices with Rome.

61. The port of Adulis brings riches to the kingdom of Axum (present-day Ethiopia).

Americas

Bust of Nero, who succeeded his stepfather, Claudius, as emperor of Rome in A.D. 54.

c. 50–370. Teotihuacán is built and rebuilt after fires.

c. 50–290. Quetzalpapalotl Palace is built at Teotihuacán.

c. 60. Teotihuacán develops into the first important Mesoamerican urban center.

Religion

32. Saul of Tarsus (c. 10–65) converts to Christianity on the road to Damascus. He becomes known as Paul.

38. The first known pogrom occurs when mobs in Alexandria break into synagogues.

40. Philo Judaeus (20 B.C.–A.D. 40) of Alexandria makes Jewish scriptures compatible with the philosophy of Plato.

c. 42–54. Paul writes his letters to Christians.

44. Herod Agrippa has the apostle James (b. c. A.D. 1) executed and the apostle Peter (fl. 1st century A.D.) imprisoned.

49. An apostolic council in Jerusalem sends Paul as a missionary to the gentiles.

51–57. Paul begins more extensive missionary travels.

57. Paul is arrested by the Romans.

58. Paul is held in prison in Caesarea.

60. Paul is tried by Festus (c. 1–62), procurator of Judaea.

61. Paul is transferred to a Roman prison after claiming his rights as a Roman citizen. ...Roman legions suppress the Druid religion in England.

c. 63. Mary, mother of Jesus, dies.

64. Persecutions of Christians begin in the Roman Empire after Nero blames them for the great fire. ...Peter the apostle is martyred.

Science, Invention & Technology

38. A three-mile-long pontoon bridge is built across the Gulf of Baiae near Capreae by Roman emperor Caligula.

c. 40. The Farnese globe in Rome is the world's first celestial globe. ...Lighthouses are built at Ostia, Rome's port.

49. Romans begin mining lead from the Mendip Hills in southwest Britain.

c. 50. The vallus, an iron box-shaped cart with toothed edges used for reaping corn, is invented by the Romans. ...The first wool-processing factory is established in England by the Romans. ...The 25-mile-long Pont du Gard aqueduct is built by the Romans at Nîmes, France. ...White lead is used in the cosmetics of Roman women.

55. Greek Pedanius Dioscordius (fl. 1st century) writes about medicinal plants and animal by-products in *De Masteria Medica*.

c. 60. Flavored desserts are made from snow shipped from the mountains at the command of Roman emperor Nero. ...Sliding sash mirrors and novelty mirrors are invented by the Romans. ...Fish farming becomes a reliable source of income for lower-class Romans.

Culture & Arts

c. 40. Seneca the Elder (b. c. A.D. 1), the Roman historian and rhetorician, dies. ...The Arawak people of Mesoamerica use plant dyes for body paint.

c. 45. Philo Judaeus (b. 20 B.C.) of Alexandria, Jewish philosopher and writer, dies.

c. 50. Romans import cheap red and black Samian pottery from Gaul. ...Roman author Apicius (fl. 1st century) is credited with writing the world's first cookbook.

62. Lucan (39–65), Roman poet, publishes the first of his three-book series, *Pharsalia*, about the war between Caesar and Pompey.

64. Nero begins to act on the public stage and write poetry.

Roman Empire & Europe

68. Roman legions in Gaul and Spain revolt. ...Rome's Praetorian Guard rise against Nero and proclaims Galba (3 B.C.–A.D. 69) emperor. Nero commits suicide.

69. Four "emperors" claim the Roman throne. Otho (b. 32) has Galba assassinated and becomes emperor for three months. Vitellius's (b. 15) forces defeat those of Otho, who commits suicide. Vitellius is proclaimed emperor but is defeated and killed by Vespasian (9–79). ...Batavians, a German tribe near the Rhine River, begin unsuccessful uprising under Claudius Civilis (fl. 69–70).

71. Batavian uprising ends.

76. Hadrian (d. 138), future emperor of Rome, is born.

77–84. Roman forces conquer northern Britain.

78. Agricola (c. 40–93), Roman governor of Britain, begins campaign to subdue entire island.

79. Roman emperor Vespasian dies. Emperor Titus (39–81), son of Vespasian, begins reign. ...An eruption of Vesuvius destroys Pompeii, Herculaneum and Stabiae.

81. Emperor Titus dies. Domitian (51–96), Titus's brother, becomes emperor of Rome.

84. Agricola defeats the Caledonians at the battle of Mons Graupius.

85. Decebalus of Dacia (40–106) (present-day Romania) defeats the Romans. ...Agricola completes conquest of Britain as far as Clyde and Firth of Forth. Agricola is recalled to Rome.

Africa, Asia & Pacific

66. Judaea rises up against its Roman procurator Florus.

67. Roman soldier Vespasian quells a Judaean revolt.

70. Jerusalem is destroyed by Titus after a 139-day siege. The Jewish revolt against Rome collapses.

73. Roman forces capture the Jewish hill fortification of Masada after a siege of almost two years, and the last Zealots there commit suicide.

74. General Pan Chao (fl. 1st century) of China extends Han power into Turkistan.

Americas

c. 70. In Oaxaca, the Zapotec erect 15 stone monuments with glyphs celebrating their conquests. ...Terracing, canals and other forms of agricultural technology are introduced into Mesoamerica.

c. 85. Early Kachemak culture, hunter-gatherers, settle what will become known as Cook Inlet, Alaska.

Hadrian's Wall, built by Roman emperor Hadrian in A.D. 122–130 to strengthen Britain's northern boundary. The wall stretched for 73 miles.

Religion

c. 65. The Gospel of Mark is written.

c. 67. Paul (b. 10) the apostle is martyred. ...Buddhist missionaries begin to arrive in China.

69. Ignatius (c. 35–108) becomes Bishop of Antioch.

70. The Torah is completed by the addition of the oral laws of Moses. ...The Romans destroy the Temple at Jerusalem.

73. The Dead Sea Scrolls are hidden in caves by the Christian community of Qumran when Romans attack.

76. The Pharisee Johanan ben Zakkai (fl. 1st century) reestablishes the Sanhedrin, the supreme council of the Jews at Jabneh (in present-day Syria).

77. Buddhist missionaries are supported by Kanishka after he founds Kashmir.

c. 80. The Gospel of Luke is written.

c. 85. The Gospel of Matthew is written. ...The original Jewish branch of the Christian church in Jerusalem begins to decline.

Science, Invention & Technology

c. 70. Petroleum-fueled lamps are used by Romans. ...Goat fat is imported by Romans from Germany to make soap. ...Catheters, forceps and other instruments are used in Pompeii. ...Metal screws are used in Rome. ...A method of removing brands from the skin of slaves is developed by Romans.

77. Pliny the Elder (23–79), Roman natural history writer, completes his 37-volume encyclopedia *Historia naturalis*.

79. Pliny the Elder is killed by the fumes of Vesuvius when he comes close to see its eruption.

c. 80. Roman medical cures include using goat's dung sealed in old wine to heal fractured ribs.

Culture & Arts

c. 65. Nero builds his expensive Golden House in the middle of Rome. ...Roman poet Lucan (b. 39) commits suicide.

◂ ***In this 16th-century depiction, Paul is shown with the Gospels and a sword, a symbol of his martyrdom.***

70. Flavius Josephus (c. 37–100), Jewish historian, describes the horror of war in his *Bellum Judaicum* (*History of the Jewish War*). ...Iron Age pottery is produced in present-day Maputo, Mozambique. ...Construction is begun on Rome's Colosseum. ...Emperor Vespasian builds a temple of peace in Rome.

76. Pliny the Younger (c. 62–113), Roman writer, pens his first Greek tragedy at the age of 14.

79. China holds a conference on the true meanings of the classics.

80. The Colosseum in Rome is completed. ...The baths of Titus are completed.

81. Emperor Domitian (51–96) dedicates the triumphal arch in Rome begun by Titus after his victory over the Jews.

82. New public libraries are built in Rome.

85. Emperor Domitian completes a magnificent concrete palace on the Palatine, Rome's highest hill.

86–98. Martial (40–?), Roman poet and epigrammist, publishes his first satirical 12 books of *Epigrams*.

Roman Empire & Europe

93. Roman soldier and statesman Agricola (b. c. 40) dies.

96. In a plot led by his wife, Domitian (b. 51) is assassinated. ...Nerva (30–98) succeeds Domitian. ...Roman conquest of west and south Germany is completed by finishing the Limes, a fortified road.

98. Emperor Nerva dies. Trajan (c. 53–117), born in Spain, becomes first Roman emperor not born in Italy.

c. 100. Trajan expands agriculture and gives corn to the poor. ...African pottery is sold throughout the Roman Empire. ...Roman road system extends some 48,000 miles.

106. Emperor Trajan completes the subjection of Dacia (part of present-day Romania).

117. Trajan dies. Hadrian becomes emperor. ...Roman Empire reaches its peak, covering 2.5 million square miles.

118. Hadrian declares the Euphrates the Roman frontier.

120. Several Roman legions revolt in Britain.

128. Hadrian has the laws of Athens codified.

130. Lucius Verus (d. 169), future emperor of Rome, is born.

Africa, Asia & Pacific

91. The Chinese are victorious over the Huns of Mongolia.

100. The Near East enjoys the *Pax Romana*. ...First settlers arrive in what will become known as New Zealand, centuries ahead of the Maori.

106–132. Gotamiputa Sri Satakani (fl. 2nd century) rules Deccan in southern India.

114–116. Parthia conducts war against the Romans in present-day Iran.

115. Roman emperor Trajan (c. 53–117) suppresses a rebellion by Jews in Egypt and North Africa.

123. China's Han rulers join the Xianbei nomads of Mongolia to defeat the Xiongnu warrior nomads.

130. A new Egyptian capital is created at Antinopolis, founded by Hadrian in memory of Antinoüs (110–130), his lover.

Americas

c. 90 Tenanyecac culture begins 500 years of development in the central highlands of present-day Mexico.

c. 100. End of Tezoquipan period of civic-ceremonial architecture in valley of Teotihuacán. ...End of Okvik culture (present-day northern Alaska), builders of sedentary villages with round houses. ...Old Bering Sea culture in present-day northern Alaska produces rudimentary pottery. ...Dorset culture in present-day Hudson Bay builds small circular underground houses. ...Permanent habitations—domed shelters and log buildings—appear in present-day southeastern United States. ...Ipiutak culture near present-day Point Hope, Alaska, constructs several hundred houses, partially underground.

▲ ***Rubbings from tomb bricks depict Han dynasty officials in formal costumes, with pikes and shields.***

126. Stela 5, Abaj Takalik, Mayan calendar with figures, is constructed.

Religion

c. 90–95. The Gospel of John is written. ...The Book of Revelation is written.

98. Buddhism in India is reformed.

100. The canon of the Old Testament is approved by the Synod of Jamnia in Palestine. ...The Great Stupa Buddhist shrine is built in Sanchi, India.

101. Christians begin to use the catacombs near Rome to bury their dead.

108. Ignatius (b. c. 35), Bishop of Antioch, is martyred in Rome.

118. Roman emperor Hadrian begins to rebuild the Pantheon.

128. The first translation of Buddhist texts into Chinese is done by the monk An Shigao.

c. 130. Justin of Samaria (c. 100–165) is converted to Christianity. ...Mithraism, an ancient Persian religion, is revived and spreads.

Science, Invention & Technology

c. 90. Concrete develops as a major building material in Rome.

c. 95. Romans use wheeled iron plows.

100. Chang Hing (78–139) develops a grid system for Chinese maps. ...Romans use rock crystals as magnifying instruments. ...Romans construct two octagonal lighthouses at Dover on the English Channel. ...Persians are among first to use natural gas for fuel. ...Romans are first to use ball bearings, in turntables on ship decks. ...Romans invent an organ operated by bellows. ...Chinese doctors become aware of existence of hormones and succeed in isolating them. ...Dionysius of Alexandria (fl. 2nd century) invents a small rapid-fire catapult.

105. Tsai Lun of China (50–118) invents method of making paper from mulberry bark.

114. Roman alphabet is basically completed.

c. 117. Hadrian builds a 15-mile aqueduct in Athens. ...Roman cavalry and their horses wear coats of mail. ...Romans invent a type of telegraph system that uses torch signals from the tops of towers.

c. 120. Romans are first to build substantial apartment blocks.

125. Hadrian's Wall is completed in northern England; it includes signal stations one mile apart.

128. Romans develop several varieties of bread.

c. 130. Several North American cultures by now have built extensive irrigation systems.

Culture & Arts

c. 90. Plutarch (c. 46–120), Greek philosopher, completes *Parallel Lives*, 46 biographies. ...Flavius Josephus writes his *Autobiography*.

96. Roman epic poet Statius (b. 45) dies. ...Among his works are the occasional verses titled *Silvae*, the 12-book *Thebais*, and the unfinished epic *Achilleis*.

c. 96–118. *Agricola*, *Germania*, *Annales* and *Historiae* by Tacitus (55–117) are written.

c. 100. Quintilian (b. 35), Roman rhetorician, dies. ...Early Christian art appears in frescoes painted on walls of the Roman catacombs. ...Indian sculpture of the later Andhra period develops into a more delicate, creative art. ...Juvenal (fl. 2nd century), the Roman Stoic and satirist, writes his 16 satires of Roman times in verse.

103. Julius Frontinus (b. 50), Roman writer and governor of Britain, dies. Among his works is the four-volume *Strategematica* on war.

105. The arts of writing and painting change in China following the invention of a rag-and-bark paper by Tsai Lun.

107. The Roman emperor Trajan conducts 123 days of games with 10,000 men to celebrate the conquest of Dacia (part of present-day Romania).

113. Pliny the Younger (b. c. 62) dies. ...Rome's new Forum is completed by architect Apollodorus of Damascus (fl. 2nd century).

115. Chinese poet and historian Ban Zhao (b. c. 80) dies. Among her works is *Lessons for Women*, a book on morality.

118. The 130-foot Trajan's Column is completed in Rome's new Forum.

c. 120. Romans establish baths for workers at mining sites.

c. 125. Gaius Suetonius (69–140) completes *The Lives of the First Twelve Caesars*.

128. Emperor Hadrian builds a library and aqueduct in Athens.

129. Apollodorus of Damascus is executed for criticizing Emperor Hadrian's design for a temple.

Roman Empire & Europe

131. Hadrian has Roman law codified.

132–135. Simon Bar Kokba (?–135) leads unsuccessful Jewish uprising against Romans.

138. Emperor Hadrian (b. 76) dies. Antoninus (86–161) begins reign as emperor of Rome.

140. Construction of Antonine Wall begins in Britain.

142. Antonine Wall completed from Forth to Clyde.

145. Lucius Septimius Severus (d. 211), future emperor of Rome, is born.

c. 150. Goths migrate to the Black Sea. ...Antoninus forbids violence against slaves. ...Bandits roam the countryside of the eastern Roman Empire, so the rich keep valuables in strong rooms at the center of their villas.

152. Rome suffers a corn shortage when Egyptian farmers revolt.

154. Roman reinforcements from Germany land in the north of Britain to put down a revolt by the Brigantes.

161. Antoninus dies and his nephew, Marcus Aurelius (121–180) and Lucius Verus (130–169), begin joint reign as emperors of Rome.

165. The plague sweeps through Italy.

Africa, Asia & Pacific

132. Romans rename Jerusalem Aelia Capitolina and forbid Jews to enter.

▲ ***A world map based on the work of astronomer and geographer Ptolemy.***

c. 150. The Berber and Mandingo tribes rule the Niger Basin. ...Korea wins independence from China.

160. The Egyptian economy suffers from Rome's new agricultural taxes, which force workers into cities.

162. Parthian king Vologases III (?–192) attacks Armenia.

163. The Parthians are forced out of Armenia. ...A new Armenian capital is established at Valarshapat.

Americas

c. 150. Aztecs build large floating gardens (chinampas), in which vegetables and flowers are grown. ...Mochica culture in northern Peru develops first true cities and organized political states in South America. ...Pottery manufacture begins in present-day southeastern United States ...Construction of residential mounds and pyramids completed in present-day eastern El Salvador.

c. 150–200. Teotihuacán settlers conduct tomb construction in their Ahualolco colony.

c. 150–250. Teotihuacán achieves its maximum expansion, colonizing present-day central Mexico.

c. 150–250. Population in Oaxaca Valley moves into Teotihuacán.

162. The Tuxtla statuette, a Mayan jadeite carving with nine columns of glyphs, is built.

c. 164. The oldest surviving Mayan monuments are constructed in Mesoamerica.

Library, Nova Scotia Community College

Religion

c. 140. Justin of Samaria writes the *Apologies* to Roman emperor Aurelius, defending Christians as good Roman citizens.

▲ ***A bust of Roman emperor Hadrian.***

155. Polycarp (b. 70), Bishop of Smyrna, is martyred during a pagan festival.

156. Montanus (?–c. 180) of Phrygia declares he will bring the promised Kingdom of Heaven to Earth.

160. Oriental religions and the Egyptian cult of Isis become popular in western Europe.

162. Christians develop their "Feast of Love," an early form of the Mass. ...Mithraism becomes popular among Romans.

165. Christians are persecuted in Smyrna (present-day Izmir, Turkey).

Science, Invention & Technology

132. Chinese develop a crude seismograph consisting of delicately balanced tiger-head figures.

138. The Carthage Aqueduct is completed, extending 88 miles from Zaghouan Springs to present-day Djebe Djougar, Tunisia.

c. 140. The practice of reconstructive surgery is developed by doctors in Sicily.

c. 150. Ptolemy (fl. 2nd century), Alexandrian mathematician, astronomer and geographer, presents geocentric theory of the universe, in which the sun, moon and planets revolve around the earth. ...Roman Julius Maternus (fl. 2nd century) crosses the Sahara and explores present-day Chad. ...Chinese begin the practice of rubbing paper against stone ideographs to create crude prints. ...Germany becomes known for its large glass factories. ...Romans and other civilizations practice trepanation, the extremely painful—and often fatal—practice of drilling holes in a patients' skulls to cure headaches and "worms". ...Depletion of oyster beds in China inspires development of controlled oyster farming.

Culture & Arts

c. 130. Hadrian rebuilds Rome's Pantheon as a circular concrete building.

134. Hadrian completes a palatial villa at Tivoli in the Roman countryside to resemble famous buildings he has visited.

c. 135. Epictetus (b. c. 55), Greek Stoic philosopher, dies.

139. Rome's new imperial mausoleum is completed.

c. 140. Appian (fl. 2nd century), Roman historian, writes his 24 books of Roman military conquests. ...Romans build a theater at Verulamium (present-day St. Albans) in Britain.

c. 150. The Second Sophistic movement revives Greek oratory. ...The Nok culture of Nigeria produces quality terracotta sculpture.

160. The great Market Gate at Miletus (in present-day Turkey) is built.

161. Roman jurist Gaius (fl. 130–180) writes the voluminous legal text *Institutiones* (*Institutes*).

162. Herodes (c. 101–177), Greek orator, builds a large covered *odeon* (theater) in Athens.

164. Demetrius (fl. 2nd century), a "place painter" from Alexandria, visits Rome seeking to work for commissions.

c. 165. Lucian (fl. 2nd century), Greek satirist, creates the new form of humorous dialogue. ...Wangfu (fl. 2nd century), Chinese Confucian philosopher, dies.

Roman Empire & Europe

166. Marcus Aurelius recruits barbarian soldiers to stop incursions by northern tribes.

169. Lucius Verus dies, leaving Aurelius sole Roman Emperor. ...Rome at war with the Germanic tribes of the Marcomanni and Quadi.

174. Aurelius conquers the Quadi and other barbarians. ...Rome's boundary reaches the Carpathian Mountains.

175. Aurelius makes peace with the Germanic tribes.

177. Aurelius appoints his son, Commodus (161–192), as joint emperor.

178. Roman forces defeat the Marcomanni tribe in Germany.

180. Aurelius marches north to battle the Germanic tribes. ...Romans are defeated in Caledonia (present-day Scotland). ...Aurelius (b. 121) dies. Commodus becomes emperor.

185. Antonine Wall in northern Britain is abandoned.

188. Caracalla (d. 217), future emperor of Rome, is born.

192. Commodus (b. 161) is murdered.

193. Pertinax (b. 126) becomes Roman emperor. Praetorian Guard assassinates Pertinax and sells the Roman Empire to Didius Julianus, who is assassinated by a soldier after ruling for two months. Lucius Septimius Severus (146–211) begins reign as Roman emperor. Severus reorganizes the Praetorian Guard.

197. Clodius Albinus, Roman ruler of Britain and rival to Severus, is killed during the battle of Lyons.

199. Severus completes conquest of Mesopotamia.

Africa, Asia & Pacific

166. Syrian merchants arrive in China.

167. The plague spreads in Egypt and Asia Minor.

168. A struggle for power develops between the Han mandarins and eunuchs in China.

173–184. The plague sweeps through China.

180. The Goths migrate south to the Black Sea and the Crimean Peninsula.

184. China's "Yellow Turban" peasant forces rise up against the Han dynasty.

189–220. Hsien Ti (fl. 3rd century) reigns as the last Han emperor of China.

192. In China, a usurper imprisons Hsien Ti and kills his court eunuchs.

This porcelain vase was one of the first of its type created in China during the Han dynasty. ➤

Americas

c. 166. In El Trapiche, in present-day El Salvador, an eight-column Mayan calendar is built.

c. 170. Polychrome pottery begins to appear in parts of Mesoamerica.

c. 175. Tiahuanaco in the southern Andes (in present-day Bolivia) develops as a major urban complex.

c. 180. Arawak people settle in present-day Puerto Rico.

c. 190. Maya develop a hallucinogenic drug from peyote cactus.

Religion

166. The first Christian church in England is built at Glastonbury.

167. Romans make public vows to their gods and symbolically entertain them at meals, hoping to be saved from the plague.

172. The first Christian Council rejects Gnostic doctrines.

175. The new standardized version of Confucianism is promulgated in China.

177. Roman emperor Marcus Aurelius increases the persecution of Christians. ...Pothinus (b. 87), the Bishop of Lyons, is martyred.

c. 178. Celsus (fl. 2nd century) writes *True Discourse* against Jewish and Christian beliefs.

180. The first Africans who are Christians are martyred at Scillium.

190. Praxeas (fl. 2nd century) of Asia Minor teaches Monarchianism in Rome, proclaiming that God the Father is the only deity and that he suffered on the cross.

196. Tertullian of Carthage (c. 160 – 230) is converted to Christianity.

197. Tertullian, the father of Latin theology, writes his *Apology*, defending the Christians.

Science, Invention & Technology

Depicted here is a panel that was part of a memorial erected in honor of Roman emperor Marcus Aurelius. It shows him entering Rome, perhaps through a triumphal arch.

c. 190. Chinese invent porcelain.

191. A towering monument built in A.D. 46 in the harbor at Boulogne, France, by Emperor Caligula to honor himself is converted into a lighthouse.

Culture & Arts

168. Greek artist Metrodorus (fl. 2nd century) is employed by the Romans to paint a frieze of their victory at Macedonia for a triumphal celebration.

c. 170. Apuleius (b. 120), Roman rhetorician and satirist, dies. His novel *Metamorphoses* (*Golden Ass*), the only complete Latin novel to survive, recounts the vices of doctors and priests.

173. Pausanias (fl. 2nd century), Greek historian and geographer, completes *Pariegesis* (*Itinerary*), a guidebook to Greece.

c. 176. Marcus Cornelius Fronto (b.100), Rome's greatest orator of his day, dies.

c. 180. Shortly before his death this year, Emperor Aurelius writes his *Meditations*, recording his personal thoughts. ...Greek historian Arrian (fl. 2nd century) dies.

193. Rome's column honoring Marcus Aurelius is completed.

Roman Empire & Europe

c. 200. Goths settle on the shores of the Black Sea and the Danube Delta. ...Severus begins to depend too heavily on the prefect Plautianus (?–205).

205. Plautianus is assassinated on orders from Severus's son, Caracalla.

205–211. Roman armies suppress a series of invasions of Britain.

208. Severus rebuilds Hadrian's Wall in Britain.

211. Severus (b. 146) dies at York and his sons, Caracalla and Geta, become joint emperors to end the wars in Britain.

212. Geta is assassinated at the instigation of his brother, Caracalla.

217. Caracalla is murdered by a soldier. Macrinus (164–218), who ordered Caracalla killed, becomes emperor.

218. Macrinus is executed and Elagabalus (Heliogabalus) (c. 205–222) is proclaimed emperor.

220. Goths begin to threaten Balkans and Asia Minor.

c. 220. Defensive fort walls are built around Londinium (London).

222. The Praetorian Guard murders Emperor Elagabalus and his mother. Alexander Severus (208–235) begins reign as emperor of Rome.

225. Gordianus III (d. 244), future emperor of Rome, is born.

c. 232. Probus (d. 282), future emperor of Rome, is born.

Africa, Asia & Pacific

c. 200. Japanese forces invade Korea. ...The Iron Age Nok culture ends in Nigeria. ...Ghana gains power and riches from trading. ...Sailors from Indonesia become the first settlers of the island of Madagascar in the Indian Ocean.

204. North Africans begin to sell olive oil to the Roman Empire.

212. Egyptians may be among those excluded from the Edict of Caracalla, which grants Roman citizenship to free people living within the Roman Empire.

217. The Asian kingdom of Parthia makes peace with Rome.

220. China's emperor Hsien Ti is deposed, ending the Han dynasty. The Three Kingdoms in China become established.

220–265. The Wei dynasty rules part of China.

222–280. The Wu dynasty rules part of China.

225. Southern India divides into several kingdoms.

226. Ardashir I (c. 200–240) establishes the neo-Persian empire under the Sassanid dynasty.

230. Sujin (fl. 3rd century) becomes emperor and ruler of Japan.

232. Ardashir I is defeated by the Roman emperor Alexander Severus.

Americas

c. 200. Izapa 500-year dominance on Pacific slope of Mexico ends. ...Maya embark on 600 years of intellectual and artistic expansion. ...Anasazi culture is founded. ...Arenal phase in western Mexico ends; sites with architectural complexes are established.

200–900. Growth of the six dominant cultures in Mesoamerica—Teotihuacán, Maya, Oaxaca, Veracruz, Cotzumalhualpa, and western Mexico—begins.

c. 215. Teotihuacán introduces formal ceremonial centers, adobe brick architecture and pyramids to its surrounding areas.

c. 220. Teotihuacán comes into conflict with nomadic Chalchihuites.

▲ ***A bust depicting the Roman emperor Probus.***

Religion

c. 200. *Mishnah*, the first part of the *Talmud*, is compiled. ...Christians begin making extensive use of bookbinding for their religious works. ...Clement of Alexandria (fl. 3rd century), Christian theologian and teacher, teaches at the Alexandrian School.

202. Emperor Lucius Septimius Severus (146–211) declares that anyone who converts to Christianity will be killed.

203. Perpetua (b. c. 180) of Carthage is martyred, having written a diary of her Christian life.

207. Tertullian is chosen to lead the Montanist Christian sect in Carthage.

c. 215. The Egyptian Coptic Church spreads to Ethiopia.

218. Christian priest Hippolytus (c. 170–236) forms a separate church and is elected antipope.

218–222. Roman emperor Elagabalus introduces worship of the Syrian sun god.

222. Pope Calixtus (b. 180) is martyred. ...Christian persecution ceases under Roman emperor Alexander Severus.

c. 225. Origen (c.185–254) writes *De Principiis* to systematize Christianity.

230. Pope Urban I (b. c. 180) is martyred and Pope Fabian (200–250) begins his reign.

Science, Invention & Technology

c. 200. Claudius Ptolemy (fl. 2nd century) publishes his *Guide to Geography*. ...Chinese doctor Hua T'o (fl. 2nd century) describes a remedy called *mafeisan*, believed to be mandrakes dissolved in wine, used as knockout drops. ...Romans develop the first glass mirrors and begin manufacturing glassware. ...Miriam (fl. 2nd century) the Prophetess of Alexandria, an alchemist, invents a double boiler that holds a constant boiling point for her experiments. ...Romans' extensive survey system includes centuriation, small parcels of property similar to modern-day land units.

215–225. A Roman coin forger produces a series of bronze coins covered with a silver wash.

219. Chinese physician Zhang Zhongjing (fl. 3rd century) dies. He wrote a massive volume about diagnoses and cures.

c. 220. Roman emperor Elagabalus uses snow transported from the mountains to cool his palace.

This drawing, done soon after the Han dynasty, portrays the noted physician Hua T'o, performing surgery on a wounded soldier. To avoid thinking about the painful surgery, the patient plays a game called Go.

Culture & Arts

c. 200. Athenaeus (fl. 3rd century), Greek writer, completes *Deipnosophistae* (*Banquet of the Learned*). ...Restaurants become popular in China. ...Greeks play a forerunner of tennis called *a la phoeninde.*

c. 201. Greek physician Galen (b. 130) dies. He was a prolific writer on medicine and philosophy.

203. Emperor Lucius Septimius Severus completes his victory arch in Rome.

216. The baths of Caracalla are completed in Rome.

217. Julia Domna (b. c.170), aunt of Roman emperor Caracalla, dies. She gave great support to artists, philosophers, scholars and scientists.

c. 220. Chinese literature develops.

222. Roman jurist Ulpianus (fl. 3rd century) becomes chief adviser to Emperor Alexander Severus and a prolific writer.

c. 225. Indian painting and sculpture flourish.

Roman Empire & Europe

235. Emperor Alexander Severus is deposed by his army. Maximinus (? – 238) becomes emperor of Rome. Roman Empire begins to decline.

235–270. Rome has 37 emperors during this period—an average of more than one per year.

238. Goths begin to invade the eastern Roman Empire.

240. Franks in Germany consolidate their power.

244. Gordianus III (b. 225) is assassinated by his soldiers at the instigation of his deputy, Philip the Arabian (204–249). Philip becomes emperor of Rome.

249. Trajanus Decius (201?–251?) defeats and kills Philip at the battle of Verona. Decius begins reign as emperor of Rome.

251. Decius is defeated and killed by the Goths at Silistria (present-day Bulgaria). Gallus (?–253) becomes emperor of Rome and pays off the Goths.

253. Gallus is murdered by his troops to avoid a disastrous military engagement with the newly proclaimed Roman emperor Aemilian.

253–259. Italy is invaded by Franks, Goths, Marcomanni and Alamanni.

254. Valerian becomes emperor of the East and appoints his son, Gallienus emperor of the West.

257. Goths occupy Dacia (present-day Romania).

258 Postumus (?–269) takes the titles emperor and ruler of Gaul, but is recognized only by his soldiers.

Africa, Asia & Pacific

238. Gordianus I (b. 157) and his son, Gordianus II (b. 192), become joint emperors in Africa. Gordianus II is killed in a battle near Carthage, and Gordianus I commits suicide.

239. Empress Himiko (?–247) of Japan becomes an ally of China.

240. Rome's African colonies revolt.

241. Shapur I (c. 220–272) becomes king of Persia.

243. Persian forces under Shapur I are defeated by the Romans at the battle of Resaena.

245. Philip, the first Arab emperor of Rome, makes peace with Persia. . . .China sends its first envoys to Funan (present-day Cambodia).

247. Empress Iyo (fl. 3rd century) takes power in Japan as a priestess and empress.

c. 250. Odenathus (?–268) builds the Kingdom of Palmyra (in Syria) into a power. . . .In Japan, men wear crossed-front jackets over trousers and women wear crossed-front jackets over pleated skirts.

254. Persians break the peace with Rome.

Americas

c. 235. Volcanic eruption devastates several lowland Mayan cites.

c. 240. Lowland Mayan city of Dzibilichaltun begins resettlement and large-scale architectural construction.

c. 245. Temple building structure at Tikal is completed.

c. 250. Small-scale architecture and ceramics prevail in west Mexico. . . .Economic boom in Dzibilichaltun ends in bankruptcy. . . .Mining operations are conducted in Teotihuacán. . . .End of Mayan expansion in southern and northern Yucatán. . . .Hopewell culture complex in the Ohio River valley declines.

250–300. Development of Floral Park complex in lowland Mayan areas.

250–450. Population decreases in central valley near Monte Albán.

Religion

235. The antipope Hippolytus is excommunicated and dies after being forced to work in Roman mines in Sardinia.

241. Persian mystic, Manichaeus (or Mani) (c. 216–276), proclaims himself a messiah and founds Manichaeism.

245. Cyprian (c. 200–258) is converted to Christianity.

248. Cyprian becomes Bishop of Carthage. ...Origen writes *Contra Celsum*, a Christian defense against Celsus's anti-Christian *True Discourse*.

250. Roman Emperor Decius begins persecuting Christians. ...Christianity takes hold in Egypt and Asia Minor. ...Pope Fabian (b. 200) is martyred.

252. Cyprian writes *De Catholicae Ecclesia Unitate* to plead for Church unity. Cyprian brings together a council of bishops at Carthage.

254. Pope Stephen I (?–257) begins reign. ...Origen dies of torture suffered four years earlier under Emperor Decius.

257. Pope Stephen dies. Pope Sixtus II (?–258) begins reign.

258. Cyprian, originator of Catholic conception of the church, is beheaded in Carthage. ...Pope Sixtus II is martyred.

Science, Invention & Technology

c. 240. Romans develop mail binding, an early form of fabric.

248. Millenary (the one-thousand-year anniversary) of the founding of Rome is observed. A menagerie of exotic animals—the world's first zoo—is established in Rome.

c. 250. Romans fashion overlapping plates made of iron and brass to protect their horses in battle. ...The first cultures to inhabit present-day Malawi in southeast Africa develop a variety of iron implements.

Culture & Arts

239. Philostratus (fl. 3rd century), the Greek Sophist, writes *Lives of the Sophists*.

240. Herodian (b. c.170), Greek historian, dies. He wrote an eight-volume history of Roman emperors.

244–270. Plotinus (205–270) develops ideas behind Neoplatonism, a philosophy based on Plato's teachings that contain elements of Asian philosophy and mysticism.

c. 250. Roman architecture spreads throughout Europe. ...Syrian-born Greek writer Heliodorus of Emesa (fl. 3rd century) publishes the first romantic adventure novel, *Aethiopica*. ...Ethiopian king Aphilas erects grand obelisks. ...Roman sculpture becomes realistic, showing the subject's wrinkles and unattractive features.

▲ ***The influence of Roman architecture is clearly seen in this modern-day reconstruction of a villa in Mehring, Germany.***

Roman Empire & Europe

260. Alamanni settle between Limes Road and the Rhine. Franks advance towards the lower Rhine. ...Gallienus (c. 218–268) becomes joint emperor with Postumus.

c. 265. Gallienus creates a corps of armored horsemen.

268. Gallienus is assassinated by his generals from the Danube area. ...Claudius II begins reign as emperor of Rome. ...Goths sack Athens, Corinth, and Sparta. Claudius II gives Dacia to the Goths. Claudius II regains the Danube and Rhine from the Goths.

269. Claudius II defeats Goths at Nish (in present-day Serbia).

270. The plague kills Emperor Claudius II (b. 214). Lucius Domitius Aurelianus (c. 215–275), known as Aurelian, begins reign as emperor of Rome.

273. The Roman senate elects Tacitus emperor.

275. Aurelian is assassinated while on a military campaign in Persia.

276. Probus (232–282) begins reign as emperor of Rome.

276–282. Probus defeats the Vandals, Franks and Burgundians, German tribes along the Rhine River valley. Probus also defeats Alamanni, German tribe occupying present-day southwestern Germany.

282. Probus is murdered by his own soldiers. ...Carus (?–283) becomes emperor.

283. Carus dies, believed murdered, and his sons, Carinus (?–285) and Numerian (?–284), succeed him as joint emperors.

284. Numerian is assassinated by his Praetorian Guard Arrius Aper. Diocletian (245–313) begins reign as Roman emperor.

285. Carinus is assassinated by one of his officers. Diocletian divides the Roman Empire into Western and Eastern Empires. Diocletian moves his capital from Rome to Nicomedia (present-day Izmit, Turkey).

286. Diocletian appoints Maximian ruler of the Western Roman Empire. Maximian establishes his capital in Milan. ...An independent British kingdom is established under the rule of Carausius.

Africa, Asia & Pacific

260. Bantu tribes expand into southern Africa.

261. Odenathus (?–268), king of Palmyra (present-day Tadmur, Syria), defeats the forces of Shapur I.

265. China is united and controlled by the western Chin (Jin) dynasty.

268. Shapur I of Persia captures Roman emperor Valerian. ...Odenathus is murdered. ...Zenobia (?–272), widow of Odenathus, becomes queen of Palmyra. During her reign, she conquers Syria, Mesopotamia, and parts of Egypt.

272. Roman commander Probus (?–282) retakes Egypt from Zenobia.

273. Zenobia is captured by the Roman emperor Aurelian (c. 212–275), and Palmyra is conquered.

277. Roman emperor Probus crushes unrest in Egypt.

278. Emperor Wu Ti (fl. 3rd century) reunites China.

Americas

c. 260. Teotihuacán covers more than 74 acres; its population reaches 45,000.

c. 265. Maya begin to carve dates at ceremonial sites.

c. 270. Olmec culture declines. Zapotec culture begins to flourish.

c. 280. End of Yucuita as the political and economic capital of Nochixtlan Valley of the Oaxaca.

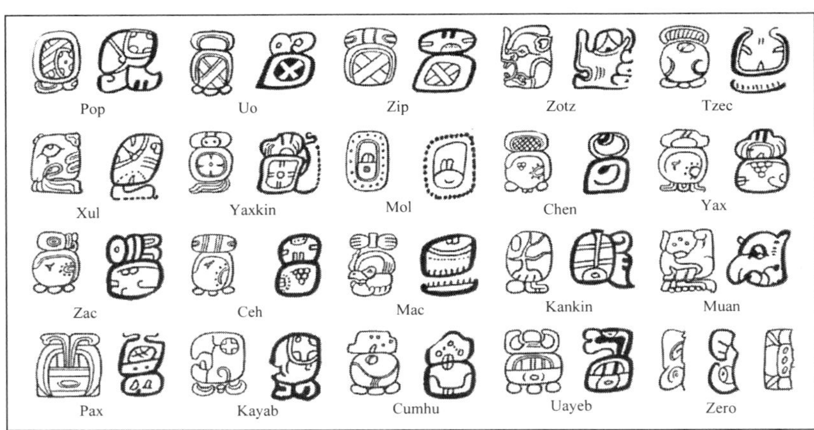

▲ ***The 19 signs of the months of the Mayan year; 18 months with 20 days each and 1 month (Uayeb, the 19th) with five days. The last three symbols were signs for zero.***

Religion

260. Pope Dionysius (?–268) begins reign. ...Paul of Samosata becomes Bishop of Antioch.

268. Synod of Antioch condemns heresy of Paul of Samosata.

c. 269. Valentine (fl. 3rd century), Roman priest, is martyred.

c. 270. Anthony of Thebes (c. 251–350) becomes a religious hermit in the desert. He will be canonized.

275. Dionysius converts the Parisians to Christianity.

276. Manichaeus (or Mani) (b. c. 216), founder of Manichaeism, is crucified by the Zoroastrians.

c. 280. Armenia is Christianized.

284. Roman emperor Diocletian proclaims himself a living god.

c. 285. Monastic life in Egypt begins. ...Confucianism reaches Japan.

Science, Invention & Technology

c. 260. Windows in Egypt are fitted with glass panes.

c. 265. Chinese use latitude and longitude on their maps and for navigation.

269. Greek designs on dies are used to produce new Roman coins.

274. Japanese construct a 100-foot ore-powered ship under the direction of Emperor Ojin.

276. National Academy of China is founded.

c. 280. The Greek mathematician Pappus of Alexandria (fl. 3rd century) publishes his *Mathematical Collection.*

Culture & Arts

c. 265. Roman philosopher Plotinus tries to found "Platonopolis," based on Plato's *Republic*, but is refused permission by Emperor Gallienus.

270. Roman military personnel wear *focales*, a form of the necktie.

◄ Greek styles on Roman coins became prevalent in the 3rd century. Pictured left is a coin depicting joint emperors Diocletian and Maximian.

Roman Empire & Europe

290. Carausius (?–293) in Britain is recognized by Diocletian and Maximian as a third emperor.

293. Carausius is assassinated in Britain.

296. Constantius I (250–306) puts down the British rebellion led by Allectus, who is killed.

298. Constantius I defeats the Alamanni in Gaul.

300. Lombards move south from Germany. ...Roman villas with heating systems, mosaics, courtyards and gardens, are popular in Britain.

305. Diocletian and Maximian abdicate. Constantius I and Galerius (?–311) become joint emperors.

306. Constantine (288–337) joins his father Constantius I, in Britain, and they win victories over the Picts. ...Constantius I dies in Britain. Constantine is dubbed Constantine the Great and is proclaimed emperor at York in Britain.

307. Rome has six joint emperors. ...Constantine defeats Alamanni and Franks in present-day Germany.

312. Constantine invades Italy and defeats and kills Maxentius at the Battle of Milvian Bridge in Rome.

313. Constantine and Licinius (250–325) agree to work together. ...Constantine defeats Licinius in Pannonia (present-day Austria, Hungary and Serbia). Constantine allows him to retain Thrace.

Africa, Asia & Pacific

296. Narses (fl. 3rd century) becomes king of Persia.

297. Narses invades Mesopotamia and defeats the Roman Galerius. ...An Egyptian revolt is crushed by Roman emperor Diocletian.

298. Narses is defeated by Galerius in Armenia and loses Mesopotamia and other territory to Rome.

300. Lolang, the last Chinese colony in Korea, is taken over by the Koguryo kingdom.

c. 300. Asian peoples settle eastern Polynesia. ...Marquesas Islands in the South Pacific are settled by Samoans, from the west.

304. Huns invade China.

304–439. The Sixteen Kingdoms rule China.

310. Shapur II (d. 379), future king of Persia, is born.

311. The Chinese capital of Loyang is captured by Xiongnu warriors from the north.

c. 313–399. Nintoku (fl. 4th century) rules in Japan.

314. Tiridates (fl. 4th century), the Christian king of Armenia, dies.

Americas

292. Emblem glyph on Stela 29 in Tikal identifies it as the earliest center of political power in Mesoamerica.

c. 300. End of Crucero period in Mesoamerica, begun c. 300 B.C., when large populations shift from riverine-estuary (coastal) areas to piedmont. ...Beginning of 200-year development of Frontenac culture (in present-day central New York State); hunter-gatherers organized in villages. ...Beginning of Laurentian culture (in present-day lower Ontario, Quebec, New York State, and upper New England); hunter-gatherers organized in villages. ...Cerros and El Mirador, early centers of Mayan civilization, decline. ...Work begins on the six-tiered Temple of Quetzacoatl in Teotihuacán. ...End of Mayan city Xolalpan (near Teotihuacán). ...Beginning of the Classic period in Mayan prehistory in the Yucatán peninsula (present-day Chiapas, Mexico, Guatemala, El Salvador and Honduras). End of chiefdoms in Mesoamerica, a period of rule that began c. 600 B.C. ...Eskimos incorporate representational and geometric designs in small-scale sculpture, such as burial masks and shaman figures.

c. 300–900. Zapotec culture flourishes in southwest Mexico, centered in the cities of Monte Albán and Mitla.

Religion	Science, Invention & Technology	Culture & Arts

293. Emperor Diocletian introduces gold coins.

296. Marcellinus (?–310) is elected pope.

297. Japanese begin the practice of decorative tattooing.

c. 300. Buddhism expands throughout China. ...Christians make up 10 percent of the Roman Empire's population. ...Hindu worship of images is established.

301. Gregory "the Illuminator" (c. 240–331) converts King Tiridates III (fl. 4th century) of Armenia to Christianity and is made patriarch of Armenia.

303. Rome destroys Christian churches and disperses their congregations.

304. Alban (fl. 3rd century) becomes the first British Christian martyr.

305. Anthony of Thebes founds the first community of Christian monks.

305–311. Persecution of Christians by Roman emperors Diocletian and Galerius.

310. Pope Marcellus is martyred. Constantine's mother, Helena (c. 248–328) converts to Christianity.

311. Constantine, Galerius, and Licinius issue Toleration Edict.

312. Constantine converts to Christianity after seeing a cross in the sky before winning the battle of Milvian Bridge in Rome.

313. Constantine and Licinius issue Edict of Milan, recognizing Christianity as a legal religion. ...Eusebius of Caesarea (263–339) becomes Bishop of Caesarea.

314. Pope Miltiades dies. Pope Silvester I (?–335) begins reign. ...Constantine hosts Christian leaders at the Council of Arles.

c. 300. Klismos chair, with curved legs, becomes popular in Greece. ...Hebrews adopt a seven-month calendar. ...Use of hieroglyphics is phased out in Egypt. ...Small handheld mirrors appear in Gaul. ...Romans develop the onager, a catapult-like device. ...Chinese invent a device used for measuring distance traveled, an odometer prototype. Chinese drill for natural gas, used for boiling salt out of brine; the gas and the brine are often taken from the same locality. ...Oil lamps hung from ropes provide street lighting for the city of Antioch, Syria. ...At Barbégal, France, the Romans build a complex of waterwheels, eight wheels on either side of a millhouse arranged in descending order.

c. 300. Mogollon people (in present-day southwestern United States) produce artistic pottery of coiled clay.

301. The Roman Edict of Prices lists the highest wages for various craftsmen, including scribes (25 denarii for one hundred lines of script).

c. 305. Porphyry (b. 232), Roman Neoplatonist, dies.

305. Diocletian builds a magnificent palace fortress on the Adriatic Sea that combines civil and military architecture.

▲ ***A carving of Roman emperor Constantine the Great and his wife, Fausta.***

Roman Empire & Europe	Africa, Asia & Pacific	Americas
	316. The Western Chin dynasty ends when the Xiongnu warriors capture Changan.	
	318. China is divided into northern and southern realms.	
	320. Chandragupta I (?–330) establishes Gupta Empire in India.	**320.** The so-called Leyden Plate, a Mayan jade plaque and calendar, is made.
321. Valentinian I (d. 375), future Roman emperor of the West, is born.		
323. Constantine defeats and overthrows Licinius, his coregent, and becomes sole ruler of the Roman Empire.		
	325. Ethiopia conquers Nubia.	**325.**Teotihuacán, the ancient Mexican city, is first mentioned in written documents.
326. Constantine has his wife, Fausta, and eldest son, Crispus, executed for treason.		
328. Valens (d. 378), future Byzantine emperor, is born.		**328.** The Mayan city of Uaxactún (in present-day Guatemala) is founded.
330. Constantine dedicates his new capital of Constantinople (present-day Istanbul) on the site of Byzantium and begins his reign as first Byzantine emperor.	**330.** Chandragupta I dies.	
	330–375. Samudragupta (?–380), son of Chandragupta I, reigns as emperor of India, extending his empire to the northwest.	
332. Constantine defeats the Goths. ...Julian (d. 363), future Byzantine emperor, is born.		
337. Constantine the Great dies.		
338. Constantine's sons, Constantius II (317–361), Constantine II (c. 315–340) and Constans (c. 320–350), divide the Roman Empire.		
340. Constantine II dies invading Constans's region.		
342. Scots and Picts unite and invade England.		
343. Constans travels to Britain, the last true Roman emperor to do so, and makes peace with the Scots and Picts.		
347. Theodosius I (d. 395), future Byzantine emperor, is born.		
	348. Shapur II's (310–379) Persian forces defeat the Romans at the battle of Singara.	

▲ ***The Pyramid of the Sun in the ancient Mexican city of Teotihuacán.***

Religion

315. Constantine makes Christianity the official religion of the Roman Empire.

319. Arius (c. 256–336), a Libyan theologian, founds Arianism (the belief that God is divine but Christ was not).

320. The first Christian monastery in Egypt is founded by Pachomius (fl. 4th century). ...The new Gupta dynasty in India revives Hindu religious thought. ...Arianism begins to spread throughout the Eastern Empire.

324. Constantine begins building program for Christian churches.

326. Athanasius (c. 293–373) is chosen Patriarch of Alexandria and Primate of Egypt. ...Constantine begins building (the old) St. Peter's Church in Rome.

330. Nicholas (fl. 4th century), Bishop of Myra in Lycia, in southwest Asia Minor, is at the height of his ministry.

331. Constantine confiscates treasures from pagan temples. ...Sopatrus (fl. 4th century), a Neoplatonist, is beheaded for practicing magic in Constantinople.

335. Pope Silvester I dies. ...Athanasius is deposed by the Synod of Tyre on charges made by the Arians.

336. Arius is readmitted into the church but dies shortly after.

337. Pope Julius I (?–352) begins reign. ...Constantine is baptized a Christian on his deathbed by Eusebius of Nicomedia (?–c. 342).

339. Eusebius of Nicomedia becomes patriarch of Constantinople.

341. Synod of Antioch deposes Athanasius who goes to Rome to introduce the monastic system. ...Christians are persecuted and killed in Seleucia, Mesopotamia.

343. Synod of Sardica confirms jurisdiction of Roman see.

348. Visigoths persecute Christians. ...Constantius II settles Visigothic Christians in the Balkans.

Science, Invention & Technology

⮝ ***Romans in combat with Goths.***

c. 340. Chinese use natural defenses against agricultural pests, including ants, praying mantises and frogs.

347. Chinese develop natural-gas pipelines made of bamboo.

Culture & Arts

315. Constantine's arch is erected in Rome.

326. Constantine has celebrations in Rome for his 20th year as emperor.

340. Eusebius of Caesarea (fl. 4th century), Palestinian bishop and historian, dies. His writings include *Chronicon*, a chronological history of the world to 325, and *De Vita Constantini*, a biography of Constantine.

c. 344. Ku K'ai-chih is born in China. He will become the major artist at the Chin court.

Roman Empire & Europe

350. The soldier Magnentius (303–353) leads an uprising against Constans. Constans flees to Spain but is assassinated. Magnentius, a former slave of Constantine the Great, becomes a breakaway emperor in the Western Empire. ...The Alamanni occupy Alsace.

351. Constantius II defeats Magnentius at the battle of Mursa Major in Pannonia.

353. Magnentius commits suicide and Constantius II becomes sole emperor. ...Saxons invade British coasts.

355. Julian (331–363) becomes caesar and governor of Gaul.

357. Julian defeats the Alamanni at Strasbourg.

358. Salian Franks settle in northern Brabant (present-day Belgium).

360–367. Picts, Irish and Saxons invade Britain.

361. Constantius II (b. 317) dies of a fever. Julian begins reign as emperor of Byzantium.

363. Emperor Julian (b. 331) dies invading Persia. Jovian (c. 330–364) becomes emperor of Byzantium.

364. Jovian dies. Valentinian I and Valens become joint emperors.

365. Procopius (326–366), a military commander, revolts against Valens.

366. Athanaric begins warfare against Visigoths.

367. Picts breach Hadrian's Wall in Britain.

368. Valentinian I defeats the Alamanni in the Black Forest and remains there six years, building fortifications on the Rhine.

369. Theodosius I drives the Scots and Picts from England. ...Romans repair Hadrian's Wall.

370. Huns, led by Balamir (fl. 4th century), arrive from Asia and terrorize Europe. ...Theodosius I rebuilds British cities.

Africa, Asia & Pacific

350. Huns invade India and Persia. ...Ethiopian forces destroy Meroe, the capital of Kush (present-day Sudan).

353–358. Shapur II of Persia conducts war against tribes in the east.

355. Huns move west into Russia.

359. Shapur II captures Amida.

360. Shapur II captures Singara and Bezabde.

363. Shapur II repels a Roman invasion and recovers Armenia. Persia wins a peace agreement from Jovian.

366. Valens defeats Procopius at Nacolea, Phrygia, in Asia Minor and has him executed.

369. Japanese forces attack Korea and establish a colony.

371. Persia's third war with Rome is indecisive.

Americas

c. 350. Interaction among communities around the Mississippi River declines. ...Fortifications around the Mayan temple at Tikal (in present-day Guatemala) are completed.

A statue of Julian, one of Rome's later emperors.

c. 370. Street of the Dead is constructed in Teotihuacán.

Religion

350. Christianity is introduced into Ethiopia.

352. Pope Julius I dies. Pope Liberius (?–366) begins reign.

353. The first Roman coin devoted to a Christian emblem is minted. Its letters *XP* stand for "Christos."

354. Aurelius Augustinus (d. 430) is born at Tagaste in Numidia (present-day Tunisia). He will become known as St. Augustine.

360. Martin (c. 316–397) founds the first monastery in France near Poitiers. ...Apollinaris the Younger (315–390) becomes Bishop of Laodicea; he founds Apollinarianism which denies the divine nature of Christ.

362. The Synod of Alexandria decides that the Holy Spirit is not an entity separate from Christ.

366. Pope Liberius dies. Pope Damasus I (c. 305–384) begins reign.

370. Basil the Great (330–379) becomes Bishop of Caesarea. ...Beginning of monastic life in the West.

c. 371. Gregory of Nyssa (c. 335–394) is consecrated Bishop of Nyssa by his brother, Basil the Great.

Science, Invention & Technology

c. 350. Chinese make candles from beeswax. ...First eating forks are made by the Byzantines.

361. Physicians in Constantinople are licensed.

c. 370. Romans develop paddle-wheel ships. ...The Egyptian mathematician Hypatia is born in Alexandria.

371. The city of Caesarea establishes gas streetlights.

Culture & Arts

c. 350. Vatsayana Mallagana (c. 325–400), an Indian sage, publishes the *Kama Sutra*, a guide to sexual pleasure. ...Chinese bucolic literature becomes popular. ...Early Roman Christian architecture is evident in the domed, round mausoleum of Constantia, Constantine's daughter. ...Wei Furen, who developed calligraphy in China, dies. ...Buddhist art flourishes in India.

360. Bound books begin to replace scrolls in the Roman Empire.

363. Emperor Julian (b. 331) dies, having been the most prolific author of all Roman emperors. His *Beard-Hater* is a satirical piece about those in Antioch who laughed at his old-fashioned beard.

▲ ***A reconstruction of a wagon used by the Huns in the 4th century. The Wagon was also used as a house by the Huns.***

Roman Empire & Europe

375. Valentinian dies (b. 321). Gratian (359–383) and Valentinian II (371– 392) become joint emperors of the West.

376. Pressed byHuns, Visigoths settle in Transylvania and Thrace.

380. Ostrogoths settle in Pannonia (present-day Austria, Hungary and Serbia).

382. Emperor Theodosius I resettles Visigoths in the empire.

383. Magnus Maximus revolts in Britain, invades Gaul and kills Gratian.

386. Roman forces defeat Ostrogoths on the Danube.

387. Maximus names his infant son, Flavius Victor, as fellow emperor. Maximus attacks Italy, and Valentinian II retreats to Theodosius I.

388. Theodosius I defeats Maximus and executes him and his son.

390. Theodosius I massacres 7,000 people at Thessalonica after a mob killed his master of soldiers.

392. Valentinian II (b. 371) is murdered on orders from Arbogast, master of soldiers. Arbogast supports Eugenius as new emperor of Rome.

394. Theodosius I defeats Eugenius and executes him. Arbogast commits suicide.

395. Theodosius I (b. 347) dies. The Roman Empire is permanently divided into Eastern (Byzantine) and Western Empires. ...Alaric becomes king of the Visigoths.

396–398. Roman forces in Britain win battles against Saxons, Scots and Picts.

397. Alaric is defeated by the Roman armies of the West.

399. Roman positions in Britain are secured.

Africa, Asia & Pacific

372. Balamir's Huns defeat Ostrogoths in the Ukraine, north of the Black Sea.

375. Indian emperor Samudragupta dies.

375–413. Chandragupta II (fl. 4th and 5th centuries) is emperor of India, conquering the city of Ujjain during his reign.

378. The Visigoths defeat the Byzantine emperor Valens (b. 328), who is killed at Adrianople (present-day Edirne, Turkey). ...Romans massacre Goths in Asia.

386–534. Wei dynasty reigns in northern China.

387. Byzantine emperor Theodosius I and Shapur III (?–388) of Persia partition Armenia.

388. Chandragupta II defeats the Shakas to control northwest India.

390. Japanese influence in Korea ends.

395. Arcadius (377–408) becomes Roman emperor of the East, or Byzantine emperor.

399. Tribigild leads a revolt of Ostrogoths in Asia Minor. ...The Japanese emperor is buried in one of the world's largest earthen tombs.

Americas

378. Curl Nose (fl. 4th and 5th centuries) marries into the Jaguar Paw dynasty at Tikal.

380. An intrusive elite begins 100-year rule in Tikal in northern Guatemala.

▲ ***Crown belonging to a Visigothic king, discovered in 1859 near Toledo, the capital of the Spanish Goths.***

Religion

372. Buddhism reaches Korea.

373. Athanasius (b. 293) dies.

375. Jerome (c. 342–420) sees a vision and renounces paganism.

379. Buddhism becomes China's state religion. ...Roman emperor Gratian (359–383) outlaws heresy in the West.

380. Emperor Theodosius I is baptized a Christian. Theodosius's edict on the Catholic faith is issued; he begins persecuting heretics.

381. Second General Council of the Church is held at Constantinople.

384. Pope Damasus I dies. Pope Siricius (c. 325–399) begins reign.

385. Priscillian (fl. 4th century), a Spanish bishop, becomes the first person executed by the Christian church for heresy.

390. Ambrose excommunicates Theodosius I until he does public penance for the massacre of 7,000 at Thessalonica.

394. Ninian (fl. 4th century) of Britain is consecrated as a bishop by the pope and sent to Scotland to convert the Picts. ...Eugenius is defeated by Emperor Theodosius I, and Christianity is permanently established.

396. Augustine is made Bishop of Hippo (in present-day Algeria).

397. The Third Council of Carthage recognizes the disputed Epistle of James, which becomes the first Catholic Epistle.

Science, Invention & Technology

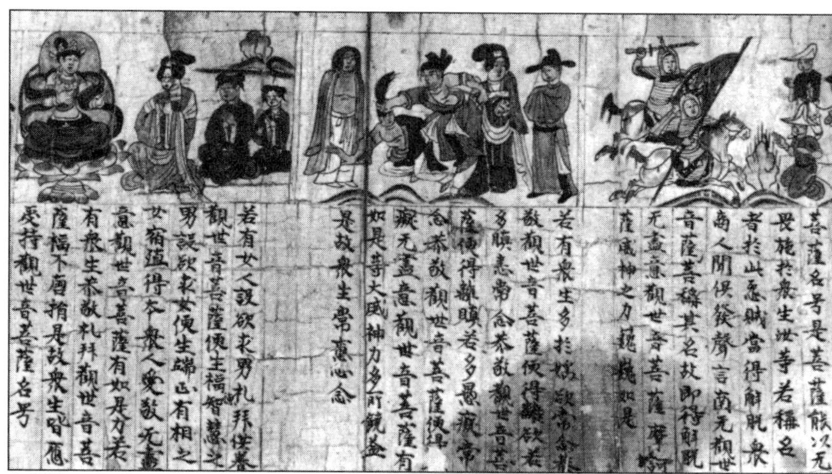

▲Silk painting, found in the caves at Tun-huang, depicts the origins of Buddhism in China.

382. Rome establishes plumbing codes, which restrict the diameter of pipes leading into residences and other structures, a response to depletion of the water supply.

c. 395. Romans have more than 30 lighthouses scattered along the Mediterranean and Atlantic coasts.

Culture & Arts

391. The Great Library of Alexandria is burned to the ground, one of the crucial events in the decay of classical civilization.

c. 395. Greek-born Roman historian Ammianus Marcellinus (b. c. 330) dies. Among his writings are 354 books on Roman history, beginning with the year 96.

British Isles & Western Europe

400. Huns reach the River Elbe.

401–403. Visigoths invade Italy.

402. Imperial residence of the Ostrogothic kingdom moves to Ravenna, Italy.

406. Burgundians found kingdom on the middle Rhine (capital, Worms).

408–410. Second Visigothic invasion of Italy.

410. Romans begin withdrawing legions from Britain to protect Italy.

415. Wallia establishes Visigothic kingdom of Toulouse.

420. Franks invade north of France and settle there.

⮝ ***Medallion depicting Attila the Hun.***

433–453. Attila (406–453) is ruler of the Huns.

436. Huns destroy Burgundian kingdom of Worms. ...Last Roman forces withdraw from England.

Mediterranean Basin

406. Stilicho checks Ostrogothic invasion at Fiesole.

406–428. Gunderic (fl. 5th century) reigns as the Vandal king.

408–450. Theodosius II (401–450) is Byzantine emperor.

409. Vandals, Alani and Suevi overrun Spain.

410. Alaric sacks Rome.

416–418. Visigoths conquer Vandal kingdom in Spain.

418–451. Theodoric I (?–451) is king of Visigoths.

422. An earthquake cracks the walls of the Colosseum in Rome.

425. Vandals capture Seville and Cartagena.

425–455. Valentinian III (419–455) is Roman emperor of the West.

428–477. Genseric (390–477) reigns as Vandal king.

429. Genseric founds Vandal kingdom in northern Africa. ...Suevi remain in northern Spain.

438. *Codex Theodosianus* legally separates Eastern and Western Roman Empires.

Africa, Asia & Pacific

c. 400. Region of Kalambo Falls (present-day Zambia, southern Africa) is settled. ...Khmer (present-day Cambodia) develop as a distinctive nation. ...Easter Island, in the eastern Pacific Ocean, is settled by Polynesians arriving in outrigger canoes from the Marquesas Islands to the west. ...Aksum kingdom at the mouth of the Red Sea (in present-day Eritrea and Ethiopia), flourishes as it provides a trade link between Egypt to the north and India to the east.

404–415. Liu Yu (fl. 5th century) leads Eastern Chin forces against the northern Chinese.

413–455. Kumaragupta I (fl. 5th century) reigns as Persia's Indian emperor.

413–490. Changsu (fl. 5th century) rules Korean kingdom of Koguryo from capital at Pyongyang.

c. 420. Abyssinia establishes trade links with India. ...Nanking becomes the power center of northern China.

420–439. Bahram V (c. 390–439) reigns in Persia and persecutes Christians. ...Persians are attacked by White Huns.

420–479. Sung dynasty dominates southern China.

422. Persia and Rome agree to a "100-year" peace.

428–633. Armenia is ruled by Persians.

440–457. Yazdagird II (c. 410–457) reigns as emperor of Persia.

Americas

c. 400–550. Teotihuacán reaches the peak of its influence and expansion.

c. 400. Sinagua develop their tradition in northernmost reaches of Hohokam culture in southern Arizona. ...Stela cult in Mesoamerica reaches its greatest geographical extent. ...Basin of Mexico develops an extensive trading network. ...Hopewell culture of central North America is at its peak, with earthen burial mounds and quarried pipestone for ceremonial pipes.

425. Curl Nose (b. late 4th century) dies.

426. Stormy Sky (fl. 5th century), Curl Nose's son, ascends to power in Tikal, in present-day Guatemala.

Science, Invention & Technology°

c. 400. Europeans cultivate apples, pears and other fruit trees. ....First paper in the Americas is produced from fig-tree bark at Teotihuacán, Mexico. ...Stone beaters are used to process bark into paper. ...Astrolabe and brass hydrometer are invented by Hypatia (c. 370–415) of Alexandria. ...Windmills are used as a source of power by the Persians. ...Chinese begin widespread use of ginger. ...Roman glassware industry continues in Italy, producing such features as stemmed cups and bronze accents. ...Glassware manufacturing becomes important industry in Belgium and Holland. ...Development of grain mills in Europe is the result of a sharp decline in labor supply caused by disease and war. ...Chinese develop the first practical umbrellas. ...Peoples of Central Asia develop wind-driven prayer wheels. ...Butter is introduced to Rome by the Vandals and other invaders from the north.

c. 410. Alchemy, the pseudoscience of converting base metals into gold, begins in Europe and the Arab world.

c. 415. Central Europeans begin brewing cider from apples and perry from pears.

◀ ***Biblical scenes from the* Augustine Gospels*, an Italian book of gospels used by the first Roman missionaries to England, allegedly including Augustine.***

Religion, Culture & Arts

c. 400–500. First written version of Bharata's *Natya Sastra*, a codification of the movements and expressions of Indian dance.

c. 400. Hieronymus (c. 347 – 420) translates Scriptures into Latin. ...Trousers are introduced to Roman areas by the Huns, replacing togas. ...Bishop of Rome establishes primacy of Rome in Christian church.

c. 400–750. Merovingian glass, found in Northern European pagan tombs of this period, include ribbed ware, drinking horns, and 'claw beakers'.

411–418. Pelagius (c. 355–?), British theologian, affirms freedom of will.

413–426. Augustine (354–430), who will be known as St. Augustine of Hippo, writes *Civitas Dei*.

422–432. Celestine I (?–432) is pope.

425. Constantinople University is founded.

431. Third Council of Ephesus condemns Pelagianism.

432–461. Patrick's (c. 385–461) mission in Ireland. He will be canonized.

440–461. Leo I (c. 400–461) is pope.

British Isles & Western Europe

443. Alamanni colonize Alsace and parts of Germany.

449. Angles, Saxons and Jutes begin the conquest of Britain.

456–472. The Teuton Ricimer is virtual ruler of the Western Roman Empire.

457. Anglo-Saxons defeat Britons at Crayford.

460. Franks capture Cologne on the Rhine.

470. Huns withdraw from Europe.

476. Odovacar (c. 435–493) deposes Romulus Augustulus, the last Roman Emperor of the West.

477. The kingdom of Sussex is founded.

481–511. Clovis (c. 466–511) reigns as king of Franks.

486. Franks establish their capital at Paris.

Mediterranean Basin

442. Genseric (c. 390–477), king of Vandals, takes last Roman possessions and establishes absolute monarchy.

450–457. Marcian (396–457) is Byzantine emperor.

451. Aëtius (c. 396–454) defeats the Huns under Attila on the Mauriac Plains near Châlons (in present-day France). ...Huns are supported by Ostrogoths and defied by Visigoths and Burgundians.

452. Attila invades northern Italy and is turned back by Pope Leo I (401–461). ...Refugees from Attila's Huns found Venice.

453–466. Theodoric II (426–466) is king of Visigoths.

c. 455. Romans adopt a barter economy because of a decline in the value of Roman money.

457–474. Leo I is Byzantine emperor.

460 and 468. Vandals destroy Roman fleets off Cartagena and Cape Bon.

466. Theodoric II is murdered by his brother, Euric (?–484).

471–526. Theodoric the Great (454–526) is king of Ostrogoths.

474–491. Zeno (440–491) is Byzantine emperor.

475. Rome recognizes Visigoths as sovereign in Spain.

477–484. Vandal king Hunneric (?–484) carries out persecutions of Christians.

484–507. Alaric II (450–507) is king of Visigoths.

489. Theodoric the Great defeats Odovacar on the Isonzo River near Verona.

491–518. Anastasius I (430–518) is Byzantine emperor.

Africa, Asia & Pacific

c. 450. Sung forces push south into Annam (Vietnam). ...Toba forces defeat Liu Sung and exact tribute. ...Polynesian chief Hawaii-Loa (fl. 5th century) reaches Hawaiian Islands after 2,400-mile voyage.

455–467. Skandagupta (c. 420–467) reigns as emperor of India.

459–483. Firuz (c. 420–483) reigns as emperor of Persia.

463. Sinhalese wrest control of Ceylon (present-day Sri Lanka) from Tamils.

c. 470. White Huns begin to break up the Gupta Empire.

471–499. Wen Ti (c. 450–499) rules as Toba emperor.

479–502. Southern China is ruled by Chi dynasty.

480. Hujr Akil al-Murai (fl. 5th century) is first al-Kindah ruler of central Arabia.

485. Chinese implement a lifetime land ownership system.

Americas

Science, Invention & Technology

Religion, Culture & Arts

444. Chinese invent the wheelbarrow.

450. Civilizations in Ecuador and the central Andes reach their peak of development. ...Mayan influences extend to the Gulf Coast cultures. ...Maya establish Chichén Itzá, one of their main governing cities, in the Yucatán Peninsula in Mexico.

c. 450. Irish are first to produce whiskey; traditionally, credit is given to St. Patrick.

c. 450–700. Monte Albán (Zapotec capital) reaches a population of 25,000. ...Ball game cult reaches its peak in Mesoamerica.

450–500. Moshica culture of the Chimic is established in Peru. ...Pre-Inca culture is established in Tiahuanaco, Peru. ...Shift from basket-maker period to modified basket-maker period in North America. ...Mississippi Valley culture is established in North America.

455. Stormy Sky, ruler of Tikal, dies.

Mausoleum of Theodoric the Great at Ravenna, Italy.

c. 470. Mayan city civilization is dominant in southern Mexico.

470. Greeks construct an efficient type of waterwheel at the Agora in Athens.

c. 476. Cave temples at Yun-Kang in northern China are decorated with figures of Buddha.

480–830. Tikal increases density of settlement, extending more than 120 square kilometers.

480–680. Middle Classic period at Tikal is characterized by political instability, fluctuating between one-man dynasties and divided rule.

484–519. First Schism between Western and Eastern Christian churches opens.

489. Heretical Christians, expelled from Athens, establish a large hospital at Shushtar in western Persia.

491. Armenian church secedes from Byzantium and Rome.

British Isles & Western Europe

495. Kingdom of Wessex is founded.

Mosaic, dated A.D. 547, showing the emperor Justinian in the center with a crown and halo. Justinian has gifts for the Church of San Vitale in Ravenna, Italy.

511. Frankish kingdom is divided between Clovis's sons, Childebert I (?–558), Clodomir (?–524), Theuderic I (?–534), and Clotaire I (?–561).

523–532. Godomar II (?–532) reigns as the last king of Burgundy.

531. Franks overthrow kingdom of Thuringia.

532–534. Franks overthrow kingdom of Burgundy.

Mediterranean Basin

493. Odovacar surrenders to Theodoric at Ravenna.

494–534. Ostrogoths rule in Malta.

496–523. Thrasamund (?–523) is king of Vandals.

510. Italian Ostrogoths overrun Provence.

513. New eruption of Mount Vesuvius drops more layers of lava and ash over Pompeii.

518–527. Justin I (c. 450–527) is Byzantine emperor.

523–530. Hilderic (fl. 6th century) is king of Vandals.

527–565. Emperor Justinian I (483–565) reunites the empire.

530–534. Gelimer (fl. 6th century) is last king of Vandals.

531. Frankish King Childebert (?–558) defeats Visigoths in Spain.

532. Belisarius (505–565) quells Nika uprising in Constantinople; 30,000–40,000 are killed.

Africa, Asia & Pacific

495. Wei dynasty in China establishes its capital at Loyang.

500–600. The Gujara settle the west coast of India. ...Sarnath Stupa, a late Gupta-period stupa (Buddhist sacred mound), is built near Benares, India.

c. 500. Trade links are formed between the Red Sea coast and the interior of Africa.

502–549. Wu Ti (c. 480–549) reigns as emperor of southern China.

503–513. Persians defeat White Huns.

c. 510–534. With Hun setbacks, India is divided into numerous small kingdoms.

c. 514–543. Caleb (?–543) reigns as king of Abyssinia.

523. Jews massacre Christians in Najran in southwest Arabia.

525. Abyssinia conquers Yemen.

526. An earthquake devastates city of Antioch in Asia Minor.

529. Ghassan ruler al-Harith II (fl. 6th century) is lord of the Syrian Arabs.

c. 530. Gokomere culture develops in Mashonaland in Africa.

531–579. Persia reaches its political and cultural prime under Chosroes I (c. 510–579).

Americas

495. First Mayan state develops in the lowlands.

c. 500. Basket making spreads from present-day Mexico and Arizona to the present-day upper southwestern United States. ...Mogollon culture develops in present-day southeastern Arizona and southwestern New Mexico.

c. 500–700. First phase (hunting, fishing food gathering) of human development in eastern North America ends.

c. 500–900. Second Laurentian culture (in present-day lower Ontario, Quebec, New York, upper New England) begins; hunter-gatherers develop pottery and more intricate tools. ...Adena culture (in present-day Ohio, Kentucky, Indiana, West Virginia), village dwellers, raise corn and manufacture small-scale pottery. ...Intermediate period in present-day Arkansas, Mississippi, Alabama, Tennessee, Kentucky, southern Missouri) sees introduction of agriculture, pottery making, and pipe smoking. ...Alexander culture (in present-day northern Alabama) engages in rudimentary agriculture and pottery manufacture. ...Poverty Point culture, hunter-gatherers in present-day northern Louisiana, dig large cache pits.

c. 500–1100. Pre-Koniag culture (in present-day Kodiak Island) builds rectangular houses with central oblong fireplaces. ...Teotihuacán architecture is displayed in the buildings of Tingambato (in present-day central Mexico). ...Middle Kachemak Bay culture (in present-day Alaska) builds underground houses from whalebone, stone and wood.

c. 500–1300. Indians from the east penetrate the Plains of present-day United States, establishing villages, farming and pottery production. ...Sterns Creek culture in present-day eastern Nebraska grows squash and gourds. ...Ozark Plateau Indians develop agriculture and pottery making.

Science, Invention & Technology

493. Imperial University at Loyang, China, specializing in medical science, is established.

c. 500. Chinese produce a form of brandy by heating wine. ...Chinese build an iron-chain suspension bridge. ...Wood carvings are used as first repeatable stamps in Europe. ...Various peoples of North America develop the bow and arrow. ...Silk-screen printing is developed in China and soon spreads to Japan. ...Axes are used in agriculture and for clearing forests in Europe. ...The Christian Church's harsh disapproval of nakedness, even in private, is partially to blame for a decline in bathing and cleanliness during the Dark Ages. ...Sugarcane is introduced to the Near East from India. ...Refuse mounds (terpen) are used as foundations for structures in Holland and Belgium.

525. Alexandrine explorer Cosmas Indicopleustes (fl. 6th century) explores the upper Nile River and the Indian Ocean as far east as Ceylon (present-day Sri Lanka). He writes *Topographia Christiane* upon his return.

529. Athenian Academy closes as social institutions continue to decline.

c. 530. First attempts to produce raw silk in Europe are made under Byzantine emperor Justinian I.

Religion, Culture & Arts

499. Synod of Rome issues first decree on papal election.

c. 500. Neoplatonic writings of so-called Dionysius the Areopagite....Nazca artists of Peru make polychrome pottery, gold funerary masks, jewellery and portrait vases. ...*Codex Bezae*, the New Testament in Greek and Latin, appears. ...Macedonian Johannes Stobaios (fl. 5th century) prepares an anthology of Greek literature. ...First plans of the Vatican palace are drawn. ...Cholula (now ruined), a solid earth, stepped, flat-topped pyramid, is built in Mexico. ...Japanese begin to translate and adapt the teachings of the Chinese on beautiful gardens.

c. 500–600. Emperor Justinian I closes mime theaters in Byzantium. ...Coptic art flourishes in Egypt.

513. Bosra (Syria) Cathedral is built on an experimental plan that combines a circular central tower within a square. It will serve as a prototype for the Byzantine churches at Constantinople and Ravenna.

517. Emperor Wu Ti (fl. 6th century) converts to Buddhism, which spreads throughout central China.

523. Sung Yüeh pagoda is built in Honan, China.

524. Roman scholar Boethius (b. 475) is accused of high treason and executed.

526. Church of San Vitale is built at Ravenna, Italy.

527. Church of the Nativity is built at Bethlehem, on the traditional site of the birthplace of Jesus.

c. 530. Mausoleum of Theodoric the Great is constructed in Ravenna, Italy.

532–537. Basilica of Santa Sophia in Constantinople is constructed.

British Isles & Western Europe

537. Arthur, legendary king of the Britons, is killed in the battle of Camlan, according to tradition.

544–565. Diarmait (?–565) is the first Christian high king of Ireland.

547. Kingdom of Bernicia is founded. ...An epidemic of the plague reaches Britain.

560–616. Ethelbert (c. 522–616) reigns as king of Kent.

567. The Frankish kingdom is partitioned into Austrasia, Neustria and Burgundy.

569–575. Langobards invade Gaul.

577. The English of Wessex defeat Welsh at Deorham, Glostershire.

584. The kingdom of Mercia is founded.

584–590. Authari (c. 550–590) reigns as the first king of Langobards.

Mediterranean Basin

533. Toledo becomes the capital of Visigothic Spain.

533–534. Belisarius (505–565) overthrows Vandal kingdom and makes northern Africa a Byzantine province.

540. Baduila (Totila) (?–553) reestablishes Gothic rule in Italy.

542. Syrian and Egyptian rats spread plague from Constantinople throughout southern Europe.

551. Byzantine fleet defeats Ostrogoths at sea.

552. Baduila is killed at Taginae.

552–553. Teia (?–553) is last king of Ostrogoths.

552–555. Narses destroys Gothic kingdom in Italy and makes Italy a Byzantine province.

559. Belisarius checks Hun army near Constantinople.

565–578. Justin II (?–578) is Byzantine emperor.

567–586. Leovigild (?–586) is king of Visigoths.

568. Langobards invade northern Italy.

578–582. Tiberius II (?–582) is Byzantine emperor.

582–602. Maurice (539–602) is Byzantine emperor.

585. Leovigild extends Visigothic rule to Spain.

Africa, Asia & Pacific

539. Persia goes to war with the Byzantine Empire.

540. Persian forces capture Antioch. ...Three Nubian kingdoms—Nobatia, Alodia and Mukurra—develop in northeast Africa.

550. Migration of Turks begins. ...Kao Yang (fl. 6th century) is founding emperor of northern Chi dynasty. ...Gupta Empire ends in India.

554–569. Ibn al-Hind is Lakhmid ruler.

557–580. Yu-wen family establishes northern Chu dynasty in China.

557–589. Chen dynasty rules in southern China.

562. Kingdom of Silla breaks Japanese power in Korea.

570. Smallpox destroys Abyssinian army as Persians invade Yemen.

572–591. War rages between Persia and Byzantium again.

575. Persians complete overthrow of Abyssinian rule over Yemen.

579–590. Hormuzd (c. 540–590) reigns as emperor of Persia.

581–618. The Sui dynasty reestablishes a centralized government in China.

Americas

534–593. Most construction in Mayan areas is suspended.

c. 550. Puebloid culture develops in northern Utah. ...Lamoka culture (in present-day New York State), organized as hunter-gatherers in villages, ends. ...Indian Knoll culture (in present-day Kentucky), village, cave, and rock-dwellers engaging in hunting and gathering, ends. ...Faulkner culture (in present-day southern Illinois), hunter-gatherers living in temporary shelters, ends. ...Archaic period for Plains Indians (hunting and gathering, but no farming or pottery manufacture) ends. ...Old Signal Butte culture in present-day western Nebraska, organized in skin-tent villages, ends. ...Archaic period in Ozark Plateau area, characterized by hunting, fishing and chipped-stone weapons, ends. ...Proto-Bluff Dwellers in present-day Missouri and Arkansas, communities in caves and rock shelters, making baskets and coarse textiles, ends. ...Archaic period in middle southern area, hunting and fishing, tool making in stone, bone and possibly wood, ends. ...Lauderdale culture (in present-day northern Alabama and southern Tennessee), dwellers in rock shelters and shell-mounds, hunter-gatherers, ends. ...Early Macon culture (in present-day Georgia), hunter-gatherers, ends. ...Tick Island culture (in present-day Savannah, Georgia), hunter-gathererers with tools made of stone, bone and shells, ends. ...Copell culture, hunter-gatherers in present-day coastal Louisiana, ends. ...Amargosa culture in present-day southern California ends. ...Early Aleut culture, builders of rectangular pit houses, ends. ...Pacific coastal Indians begin trading with Indians of the Plateau (between Rocky and Cascade Mountains). ...Mound builders spread over Costa Rica and Panama. ...Yaxchilan, Mayan lowland city, is built. ...Yarumela in the southern Yucatán is developed.

Science, Invention & Technology

536. Ship mills, corn mills on floating barges operated by paddle wheels, are placed in the Tiber River by Emperor Belisarius during the siege of Rome.

537. Handheld crossbows are first used during the siege of Rome.

c. 540. Toilet paper is invented and widely used by Chinese. ...A division of mounted archers becomes part of the Byzantine military strategy.

c. 550. Elaborate carpets, some scented or studded with gems, are produced by the Persians.

552. A wind-powered carriage, said to be capable of traveling hundreds of miles in one day, is described by Chinese emperor Luan (fl. 6th century). ...Silk industry in Europe is firmly established after China's silk production trade secrets are smuggled to Constantinople and China's monopoly on silk is broken.

577. Matches are invented in northern coastal China.

Religion, Culture & Arts

c. 534. Church of St. Apollinaire in Classe, Italy, is begun by Justinian I on the site of a temple of Apollo.

537–555. Vigilius (?–555) is pope.

550. David (c. 520–588), first abbot of Menevia (present-day Saint David, Wales), converts the Welsh to Christianity.

553–555. Fifth Council of Constantinople meets.

556–561. Pelagius I (?–561) is pope.

560. Emperor of the northern Chu Chinese dynasty commissions a 26-foot-high woven hanging as a Buddhist icon.

561–574. John III (?–574) is pope.

563. Irish abbot Columba begins his mission to the Picts (in present-day Scotland).

◄ ***This seventh-century drawing depicts Prince Shotoku, a leading proponent of Buddhism in Japan, with his two sons.***

c. 575. Introduction of Buddhism into Japan stimulates sculpture as missionaries bring craftsmen from Korea to make religious statues.

c. 588. Shitennoji, the earliest Buddhist monastery in Japan, is built at Osaka.

British Isles & Western Europe

590–616. Agilulf (?–616) reigns as king of Langobards.

c. 592–616. Ethelfrith (?–616) reigns as king of Bernicia.

c. 600 European candlemakers form guilds. ...Celts begin playing the stringed instrument known as the crwth (or crowd or chrotta), a plucked or bowed lyre.

616. Anglo-Saxons gain control of Britain with defeat of Britons at Chester.

617–685. Northumbria in northeast England is at peak of its influence.

▲ ***Signature of Harsha, ruler of northern India.***

Mediterranean Basin

590. Plague breaks out in Rome.

602–610. Phocas (?–610) is Byzantine emperor.

603. Langobards move south and take Cremona and Mantua.

610–638. Sergius (?–638) is Patriarch of Constantinople.

614. Persians take Damascus and Jerusalem.

616–626. Adalwald (602–626) reigns over the Langobards.

618–619. Persians conquer Egypt.

619. Persians reach the Hellespont, gateway to Constantinople.

Africa, Asia & Pacific

593–628. Empress Suiko (c. 560–628) reigns in Japan.

c. 600–700. Strong trade links are established between western and northern Africa.

601. Indian physicians compile the medical treatise known as the *Vaghbata*.

604. Japan adopts Constitution with 17 articles.

605. Chinese complete Grand Canal system to the capital at Loyang.

606–647. Harsha (c. 590–647) rules northern India.

607. First Japanese ambassadors arrive in China.

608–642. Pulakeshin II (c. 590–642) rules the Deccan region of India.

611. Persians invade Syria and take Antioch.

612. Harsha consolidates his rule over upper India. ...Korean kingdom of Koguryo repulses Chinese invasion.

615–618. Turk attacks weaken and finally destroy Sui dynasty in China.

618. Tang dynasty is established in China.

620. Pulakeshin II of the Deccan (in southern India) defeats Harsha of the north.

Americas

c. 600. Nasca in southern Peru produce ceramic vessels. ...Teotihuacán architectural elements make their appearance in Dzibilichaltun (lowland Maya site). ...Copán reaches its cultural peak. ...Great ceremonial centers of Mexico begin to decline. ...Hohokam build irrigation ditches and large ball courts in southern Arizona. ...First Pan-Andean empire is established.

c. 600–900. Mayan civilization reaches the height of its development.

▲ *Tang dynasty emperor Li Shih-min, known by his reign title, T'ai Tsung.*

615. Pacal (?–683) founds the first ruling dynasty at Palenque.

Science, Invention & Technology

c. 590. New lightweight plow opens wide areas for farming in northwest Europe.

c. 600. Glass mirrors fall out of use during the Dark Ages.... Persia's postal service is started by the Umayyad caliphs. ...Chinese begin using cast-iron drill bits. ...Sweat houses are used by the Maya of Mexico for physical therapy. ...Byzantine architects use metal sheets and braces to reinforce walls against earthquakes. ...People of northern Peru develop a system of irrigation canals. ...The stirrup is invented by the Chinese, added to the already invented saddle. ...Maya make false teeth from sea shell fragments. ...Compass is used by Arab sailors. ...Iron bindings are used to reinforce coffins in Lombardy. ...Turning lathes are used in northern Europe. ...Heat required by Islamic potters is regulated to conserve combustible fuel. ...Egyptians develop luster-painting, which yields an attractive metallic sheen. ...Paris's Hôtel-Dieu, one of the oldest hospitals in Europe, is established.

605. China's Emperor Yang Kuang's Imperial Library has more than 50,000 volumes.

c. 610. A segmental bridge is built in China by engineer Li Chhun (fl. 7th century). ...First section of China's Grand Canal is completed. ...A horse-drawn carriage with sails, claimed to be capable of transporting thousands of passengers at one time, is built for Chinese Emperor Yang Kuang.

c. 620. Papermaking methods spread to India from China. ...Damascus (in present-day Syria) is known for its variety of strong steel.

Religion, Culture & Arts

593. Construction of the Temple of the Four Heavenly Kings begins in Osaka, Japan.

594. Gregory of Tours (b. 538), author of *Historia Francorum*, dies.

c. 600. Aneirin (fl. 7th century), a Scottish poet, writes *The Gododdin*. ...Tantric school of Buddhism is developed in India. ...Maya complete building of Tikal, which has a number of towering pyramids and nine groups of courts and plazas.

c. 600–625. King Mahendra Varman (fl. 7th century) in Tamil Nadu (in India) commissions artists to paint frescoes in caves at Sittannavasal.

c. 600–700. Palenque, a group of Mayan-style vaulted temples with exterior relief sculpture, is built in Mexico.

602. Augustine establishes archiepiscopal see at Canterbury.

603. Lombards embrace Catholicism.

604. St. Paul's Church is founded in London. ...Augustine dies.

609. Pantheon in Rome is consecrated as Christian church.

614. *Edictum Chlotacharii II* defines rights of king, nobles and the church.

c. 620. Chinese begin to export porcelain to the Islamic world.

British Isles & Western Europe

629–638. Dagobert I (c. 612–639) rules a united Frankish kingdom.

633–641. Oswald (?–641) reigns as king of Northumbria and Bernicia.

636–652. Rothari (fl. 7th century) reigns as king of Langobards.

641–652. Chindaswinth (?–653) reigns as king of Visigoths.

641–670. Oswiu (612–670) reigns as king of Northumbria and Bernicia.

Mediterranean Basin

622. Heraclius (575–641) of Byzantium drives Persians out of Asia Minor.

625. Heraclius repulses a joint Persian and Avan assault on Constantinople.

627. Heraclius defeats Persians at Nineveh, lifting threat to Constantinople.

629. Visigoth Svinthila expels the Byzantines from Spain. ...Heraclius recovers Jerusalem.

634–644. Omar (581–644) reigns as caliph of Islam.

635. Omar takes Damascus.

636. Byzantines are defeated at Yarmuk; they lose Syria to Arabs.

638. Omar captures Jerusalem.

639–641. Omar conquers Mesopotamia.

640–642. Omar takes Egypt.

641. Fustat (present-day Old Cairo) is founded.

641–668. Constans II (630–668) is Byzantine emperor.

643. Muslims capture Tripoli.

644–656. Othman (574–656) reigns as caliph of Islam.

Africa, Asia & Pacific

623. China is united under the Tang dynasty.

624. Muslims under Muhammad (c. 570–632) defeat the Meccans at battle of Badr in Arabia.

629–630. Chinese forces destroy eastern Turkish invaders.

630. Muhammad occupies Mecca.

633. Arabs invade Persian empire.

635. Chalukyas of southern India check Harsha's invasion from the north. ...Basra is established as trade center on the Persian Gulf.

638. Muslim forces advance into Mesopotamia (present-day Iraq) and central Persia.

c. 639. Tibetans found Lhasa.

639–648. Chinese conquer Turkestan and Korea.

640. Abyssinians turn back Arab invasion fleet.

641. Arabs take Mosul on the River Tigris in Mesopotamia.

643. Muslims take Baluchistan in northwest India.

644. Major famine strikes Japan.

Americas

c. 630. Mochica on the south coast of Peru erect pyramidal temples. ...Maya devise a 260-day calendar and are accomplished astronomers.

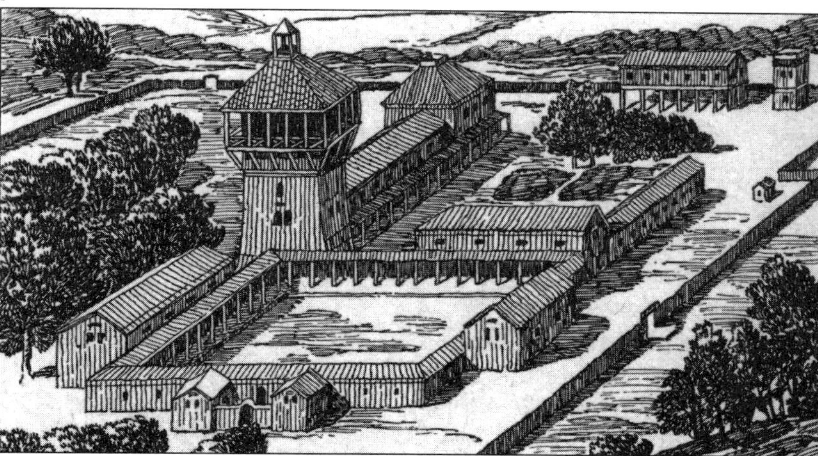

^ *Representation of a Frankish villa of the 600s.*

c. 640. Yucatán becomes a center for trade and cultural exchanges.

Science, Invention & Technology

621. An official bureau of porcelain manufacturing is established by the Chinese.

628. Sugarcane is brought to Constantinople from India by the Byzantines.

c. 630. A mail delivery system using pigeon is developed by the Muslims.

c. 640. Persian postal system consists of mounted couriers relaying intelligence among some 930 stations. ...Wooden ski boards are in use by tribes in the Lake Baikal region of Siberia. ...Chinese send a delegation to India to study sugar production methods.

Religion, Culture & Arts

622. In the Hegira, Muhammad flees from Mecca to Medina. This is year 1 in the Islamic calendar.

c. 624. Third part of the Koran is believed to be composed.

625. Abbey of St. Denis is founded near Paris. ...First Ise shrine opens in Japan. ...Building of Changan Temple commences in China.

625–638. Honorius I (?–638) is pope.

c. 630. Church of St. Agnese Fuori Le Mura, an example of an early Christian basilica, is built in Rome.

632. Christianization of East Anglia (in present-day England) begins. ...Muhammad (b. c. 570) dies.

635. Christianization of Wessex in present-day England begins.

636. Southern Irish church submits to papacy.

641–661. Armenian architecture flourishes under Patriarch Nerses III.

642. Work begins on Amr Mosque in present-day Old Cairo, Egypt.

c. 643. Dome of the Rock in Jerusalem is built over rocky outcrop where Muhammad is said to have ascended to heaven: it is the earliest surviving mosque.

c. 644. Wang Chi (b. 590), the first notable poet of the Chinese Tang period, dies.

British Isles & Western Europe

653–672. Recceswinth (612–672) reigns as king of Visigoths.

654. Penda (c. 580–654), heathen king of Mercia, is defeated and killed by Oswiu.

658–675. Wulfhere (fl. 7th century), Penda's son, reigns as king of Mercia.

664. Plague breaks out in Saxon England.

672–680. Wamba (?–c. 687) reigns as king of Visigoths.

673. Childeric II dies, and civil war breaks out in Frankish kingdom.

685. Picts defeat Northumbrians at Nechtansmere.

687–701. Egica (?–701) reigns as king of Visigoths.

690–725. Wihtred (fl. 7th century) reigns as king of Kent.

Mediterranean Basin

647. Arabs conquer Tripoli.

649. Arabs conquer Cyprus.

650. Arab caliphs inaugurate a news service.

652. Arabs raid Syracuse.

654–661. Arabs subdue Armenia.

655. Arab fleet defeats Byzantines in Battle of the Masts at Lycia.

656. Caliph Othman is murdered and is succeeded by Ali (c. 600–661).

658. Moawiya (c. 600–680) sets up Omayyad dynasty at Damascus.

661. Caliph Ali is murdered and is succeeded by Moawiya.

664. Arabs invade the Punjab.

668–685. Constantine IV (652–685) is Byzantine emperor.

669. Arabs besiege Constantinople.

670. Arabs begin conquest of North Africa.

674. Byzantines rain Greek "fire" missiles on Arabs at Constantinople.

680. Husain (b. 626), son of Ali, is killed fighting against Caliph Yezid I (fl. 7th century).

685–705. Abdalmalik (646–705) reigns as Caliph of Islam.

685–695. Justinian II (669–711) is Byzantine emperor.

690. Byzantines defeat Slavs in Macedonia.

Africa, Asia & Pacific

647. Harsha (b. c. 590) dies. His death hastens disintegration of the North Indian empire.

650–700. China's Tang rulers expand trade with central and western Asia.

650. Hindu empire flourishes in Sumatra (in present-day East Indies).

663. Tibetans repel Tukuhun Mongols.

664. Arabs take Kabul (in present-day Afghanistan).

668. Silla kingdom of Korea, with the help of Chinese allies, destroys Koguryo.

670–780. Silla kingdom is at the zenith of its power and culture.

674. Muslim forces raid Bukhara (present-day Transoxiana in central Asia).

683. Shrivijaya emerges as an East Indies power, with capital at Palembang in Sumatra.

Americas

647. Shield Jaguar, ruler of Yaxchilan (present-day Chiapas, Mexico), is born.

650–800. Dam is built at Copán.

c. 650. Teotihuacán culture begins to decline after suffering a devastating fire. ....Tenanyecac power in highlands of central Mexico ends. ...Texcalac culture establishes political power in central Mexico. ...Olmeca-Xicalanca take Cholula in Puebla Valley and establish their capital at Cacaxtla.

▲ ***This model presents an overview of the ceremonial center of Copán, Mexico; the Copán River runs alongside the center.***

c. 674. Maya abandon Chichén Itzá.

683. Pacal dies.

684. Lord Chan-Bahlum (b. middle 7th century) succeeds his father, Pacal.

687–756. Sixty percent of all Mayan monuments are erected.

Science, Invention & Technology

648. Paper made from cotton fiber is introduced to Greece.

c. 650. Saxons make crude crosses from grit-stone; other, more suitable materials are technologically within reach.

674. English begin using glass for windows and stone instead of timber in the construction of churches.

c. 685. Toltecs of Mesoamerica develop advanced methods of weaving.

Religion, Culture & Arts

647. Gupta period (begun 320), the great age of Indian dance and drama, ends.

649–655. Martin I (?–655) is pope.

650. Proverbs about love, life and resignation of Buddhist monk Bhartrihariá (fl. 7th century) appear.

c. 650. Chuguji style of sculpture, with realistic three-dimensional modeling and concern for surface texture, is developed in Japan.

650–750. British and Irish monasteries create ornamented manuscripts, using interlacing linear pattern.

657–672. Vitalian (?–672) is pope.

658. Caliph Othman edits the Koran.

662. A complex of temples is carved into rock at Mamallapuram, India.

664. Oswiu (c. 612–670) of Northumbria adopts Roman ritual.

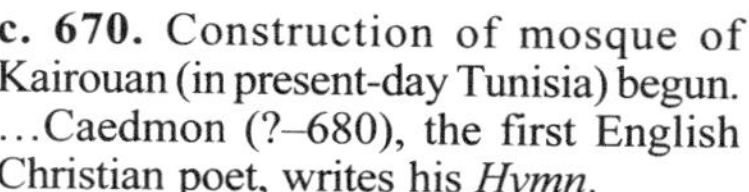

c. 670. Construction of mosque of Kairouan (in present-day Tunisia) begun. ...Caedmon (?–680), the first English Christian poet, writes his *Hymn*.

673. Yen Li Pen (fl. 7th century), court painter to the Tang Chinese emperor Li Shih-min (reign title T'ai Tsung), dies.

678. Wang Po (b. 650), poet and prose writer, who was one of the four masters of 7th century Chinese literature, dies.

685. *Ravenna Cosmography*, first gazetteer, is created in Italy.

686. Sussex, last heathen kingdom in England, is converted to Christianity.

British Isles & Western Europe

695. Wihtred's law code is established.

c. 700. Vikings venture over land to the Black Sea. ...Latin falls out of use in Gaul.

c. 700–799. Varangian Norsemen raid Russia and gradually colonize it.

▲ ***The first page from the manuscript of* Beowulf.**

716–757. Ethelbald of Mercia is virtual lord of all England except Northumbria.

717–741. Charles Martel (688–741) comes to power as mayor of the palace of Austrasia (parts of present-day France, Germany and Netherlands).

Mediterranean Basin

695–698. Leontius (?–705) is Byzantine emperor.

696. Paoluccio Anafesto (?–717) is first doge of Venice.

698–705. Tiberius III (?–705) is Byzantine emperor.

705–711. Justinian II is restored as Byzantine emperor.

708–715. Pope Constantine I (?–715) reigns and is the last pope to call on the emperor in Constantinople.

710. Moorish invaders cross from North Africa into Spain. ...Bulgarians march on Constantinople.

711–715. Moors overrun most of Spain.

711. Moors introduce rice, saffron, and sugar to Spain. ...Córdoba, founded by Carthaginians, will be under Moorish control until 1236.

711–717. Byzantium is governed successively by Philippicus, Anastasius II and Theodosius III.

716. Lisbon falls to Moors.

717–741. Leo III (680–741) is Byzantine emperor.

718. Battle of Covandonga temporarily checks Muslim advance in Spain.

724–743. Hisham (?–743) reigns as caliph in Islam and reforms taxation system.

725. Moors raid southern France.

Africa, Asia & Pacific

695. Shrivijaya and China exchange embassies and establish trade relations.

697. Arabs destroy Carthage, ending Byzantine rule in North Africa.

c. 700. Changan, the first of the large-scale planned cities in China, reaches its zenith. ...Arabs take Algiers.

c. 700–725. Muslims settle along the west coast of India.

701. Japanese codify law. ...Arab and Persian traders reach the Moluccas (Spice Islands).

708. Japanese strike first copper coins. ...Boiled tea drinking increases in popularity in China.

710. Nara becomes the capital of Japan.

c. 710. Khmer (Cambodia) dissolves into anarchy.

712. Arabs take central Asian trade center of Samarkand.

715. Damascus is the capital of a vast Muslim empire, stretching from the Iberian Peninsula to the frontiers of China.

717. Tibetans form alliance with Arabs against China. ...Caliph Omar II (fl. 8th century) exempts Muslim believers from taxes.

722. Annamites (Vietnamese) rise in rebellion against China.

725. China's capital, Changan, is the world's largest city.

Americas

c. 700 Major population increases make Dzibilichaltun the center of development in northern Yucatán. ...Siouan-speaking tribes spread northward along the present-day Mississippi River. ...Salado culture develops in present-day east-central Arizona. ...Old Copper culture in present-day Minnesota, Wisconsin, and upper Michigan ends. ...Savannah River culture ends. ...Monte Albán, the sacred capital of Zapotecs in southern Mexico, reaches a population of 20,000.

c. 700–775. Lambityeco (near Monte Albán) becomes a salt-mining center.

c. 700–800. Populations from northwestern frontier of Mexico move into central Mexico in the Prado phase. ...Anasazi influences pervade Mogollon culture.

c. 700–1100. Red Ocher culture in present-day central Illinois hunt, gather and engage in rudimentary farming. ...Candy Creek culture (in present-day eastern Tennessee) establish camps, rudimentary farming and pottery manufacturing. ...Early Coastal culture (in present-day New York, New Jersey, and Pennyslvania) develops.

725. Casa Grande, a fort and irrigation works, is built in present-day Arizona.

Science, Invention & Technology

695. First Arab coinage appears.

c. 700. Catalan forge is developed in Europe; forced air is used to sustain heat in blast furnaces. ...Wrought iron is used in Europe for balcony railings and other architectural embellishments. ...Vikings use sails and oars to propel their large warships. ...Japanese invent the folding fan. ...Waterwheels are in widespread use in England. ...Alchemy spreads in the Muslim world. ...Coin makers in Europe begin using punch dies instead of carved dies. ...Arabs introduce paper-making industry to Samarkand (in present-day Uzbekistan).

c. 710. Egyptians begin cultivating sugarcane. ...A river gauge, called a nilometer, is erected on Rhoda Island in the Nile River, Egypt.

◂ An early Arab coin (A.D. 698–699).

723. Chinese monk I-Hsing (fl. early 8th century) invents what he calls "water-driven spherical bird's eye view map of the heavens," a clockwork instrument.

Religion, Culture & Arts

695. Jews are persecuted in Spain.

697. Northern Irish Church submits to papacy.

c. 700. St. Jean's Church is built at Poitiers (France). It is a rare survivor of the Merovingian period. ...Caves I and II of the Buddhist rock-cut temple at Ajanta (in India) are painted. ...Wall-painting in elaborate floral and figurative designs reaches its peak in Buddhist temple-caves. ...Arabs hold organized horse racing events. ...Psalms are translated into Old English. ...Pagoda of Tsu-an Temple is built in Sian, China.

c. 700–730. *Beowulf*, the earliest extant Anglo-Saxon heroic epic, is written in Old English by an unknown poet.

704. Adamnan (b. 625), a historian, dies. He will be made a saint.

705. Ummayad mosque is built on the site of a Roman temple in Damascus.

708. Abbey at Mont-St.-Michel, one of earliest examples of Gothic architecture, is built on a small islet off the Brittany coast.

712. *Kojiki*, a historical chronicle and the earliest known book on Japan, is written in China.

715–731. Gregory II (c. 680–731) is pope.

716. Li Ssu-Hsun (b. 651), founder of the "blue-and-green" style of Chinese landscape painting, dies.

719–754. Boniface (c. 680–754) Christianizes central Germany. He will be made a saint.

725. Venerable Bede (625–735) writes *De Temporum Ratione.*

British Isles & Western Europe

729–737. Ceolwulf (?–760) reigns as king of Northumbria.

732. Charles Martel (c. 688–741) defeats Arabs at Poitiers.

735. Martel subdues Burgundy.

c. 745. Pepper is introduced to central Europe.

748–788. Tassilo (fl. 8th century) reigns as the last independent duke of Bavaria.

750. Childeric III is dethroned, ending Merovingian line in France. . . .Epidemics of St. Vitus's Dance break out in Germany.

752. Cuthred (?–754) of Wessex defeats Ethelbald (?–757) at Burford.

754–756. Pepin (c. 714–768) wages war against Langobards. . . .Aistulf becomes a Frankish vassal.

757–796. Offa (?–796) reigns as king of Mercia.

765. Franks establish their royal court at Aix-la-Chapelle.

768–814. Charlemagne (742?–814) reigns as king of Franks.

772–804. Charlemagne subdues Saxony.

774. Offa subdues Kent.

Mediterranean Basin

732–736. Plague spreads throughout southeastern Europe.

741–775. Constantine V (718–775) is Byzantine emperor.

742. Sijilmassa (Morocco) develops as center of trans-Sahara gold and salt trade.

744–750. Mervan II (?–750) reigns as the last Omayyad caliph in Arabia.

746–747. New plague epidemics ravage southeastern Europe.

750. Granada is founded in Andalusia, in southern Spain. It will become the Moorish capital.

751. Aistulf takes Ravenna, Italy, from Byzantium.

754–775. Abu Jafar al-Mansur (709–775) rules as caliph of Islam.

756–764. Moors extend conquest of Spain.

757–774. Desiderius (730–774) is last king of Langobards.

Africa, Asia & Pacific

726. Arab *Ecloga* codifies civil law and some criminal law.

730. China and Tibet make peace.

c. 732–820. Sanjaya dynasty rules in Java (present-day East Indies).

736. Tibetans conquer Kashmir in northwest India.

740. Earthquake causes widespread damage in Asia Minor.

743–789. Khri Srong Ide Tsan (c. 720–789) reigns as king of Tibet.

748. First printed newspaper circulates in China.

751. Arabs check Chinese forces at Samarkand and establish their dominance in central Asia.

760–775. Krishna I (fl. 8th century) is ruler of Rastrakuta in the Deccan in central India.

763. Baghdad (in present-day Iraq) replaces Damascus as capital of Arab caliphate.

765. Tibetans invade China.

767. Chinese at Tonkin (northern Vietnam) repel Javanese invasion.

c. 770. Wagudu drive Berbers from Ghana in present-day West Africa and establish a dynasty there.

770. Arab naval force from Basra clears out pirates of the Indus Delta in India.

Americas

c. 730. Cauac Sky (fl. early 8th century) is first ruler of Quirigua.

731. Jaguar Paw dynasty is reinstated in Mayan civilization.

735. Tikal is raided by rivals for Mayan rulers.

737. Quirigua and Copan fight a war, and Quirigua wins independence.

c. 750. Temple complex is built at Uaxactún (in present-day Guatemala). ...Nazca culture in southern coastal Peru declines. ...Santa Maria and Palo Blanco chiefdoms (in central and southern Mexico) end. ...City-states in central and southern Mexico rise. ...Olmeca-Xicalanca dynasty in Puebla area of Mexico begins. ...Pueblo period in southwestern part of North America begins. ...Teotihuacán culture ends.

756. Dispute arises over the succession of the fifth ruler at Piedras Negras (southern Mayan lowlands), and the ruler of nearby Yaxchilan intervenes.

770–900. Seibal in southern Mayan lowlands becomes a major population center.

Science, Invention & Technology

This copy of a 9th-century drawing depicts Frankish king Charlemagne (left) with his second son, Pepin, who became king of Italy.

c. 750. Woodcut stamps of Buddha are created in Turkistan, probably by Chinese prisoners. ...Arab alchemist Jabir ibn Hayyan (c. 721–815) develops a process for synthesizing nitric acid. ...Soap first used as a cleanser.

c. 760. A corn mill at a monastery east of Dover is the first built in England.

c. 765. A crop rotation system is adopted in Europe. ...Pictorial book printing develops in Japan.

Religion, Culture & Arts

726. Leo III (680–741), Byzantine emperor, orders all sacred images in human form destroyed.

731–741. Gregory III (c. 700–741) is pope.

741–752. Zacharias (?–752) is pope.

744. Monks of Fulda establish a singing school. ...Chinese poet Li Po (c. 700–762) is banished by Tang rulers; more than 1,000 of his poems will survive.

c. 750–800. Cynewulf (fl. late 8th century), English poet, writes *Elene, Fuliana, The Ascension, Fates of the Apostles.*

750. First records showing the existence of a Tamil language appear.

752–757. Stephen III (c.720–757) is pope.

757–767. Paul I (?–767), brother of Stephen III, is pope.

c. 760. Wu Tao-Tzu (b. 689), Chinese painter, dies. ...Kailasanatha Temple in Ellora, India, is cut out from rock as a complete building in the round.

c. 765. Yunus ibn Sulaiman Al-Katib (fl. 8th century), Arabian musical historian and editor, dies.

770. Euclid's *Elements* is translated into Arabic.

772–795. Hadrian I (?–795) is pope.

British Isles & Western Europe

777. Offa subdues Wessex.

778. Basques defeat Charlemagne at Roncesvalles.

782. Offa's Dyke is built in Mercia as outwork against the Welsh.

787. Charlemagne annexes Langobardian duchy of Beneventum.

789–820. Constantine I (c. 770–820) reigns as king of Scots.

792. Viking era begins in Britain.

793. Offa annexes East Anglia.

796–821. Cenwulf (c. 780–821) reigns as king of Mercia.

800. Franks invade Bohemia. ...Norsemen discover the Faroe Islands. ...Charlemagne is crowned emperor of the West by Pope Leo III (c. 750–816) at Rome, creating a schism between the Eastern and Western Empires.

Mediterranean Basin

775–785. Caliph Mahdi (750–785) institutes inquisition.

775–780. Leo IV (749–780) is Byzantine emperor.

780–797. Constantine VI (c. 770–820) is Byzantine emperor.

788. Idris I (?–791) establishes a Shiite kingdom in present-day Morocco.

788–796. Hisham I (760–796) is caliph of Córdoba.

791–828. Idris II (?–828) rules in Morocco. During his reign he founds the capital city of Fez.

796–822. Hakam I (760–822) is caliph of Córdoba.

797–802. Irene (752–803) is empress of Byzantium.

Africa, Asia & Pacific

775. Tibet and China reach a boundary agreement. ...Shrivijaya controls northern Malaya, with capital at Kedah.

c. 780–800. Panungulan (fl. 8th century) extends his Sanjaya kindom into central Java.

783. Chinese government attempts to make the tea trade a state monopoly.

786–809. Harun al-Rashid (c. 760–809) is caliph of the Muslim dominions.

793. China imposes a tax on tea.

794. Heian (later named Kyoto) becomes the capital of Japan.

c. 800. Tiloutane (fl. 9th century) founds a Berber empire in the western Sahara. ...Rajputs occupy Kana Uj in north India and rule from Bihar to the Sutlej River. ...Pyu kingdom in Burma collapses. ...Settlers from the Marquesas Islands (in present-day Polynesia) migrate northward to present-day Hawaii.

c. 800–850. Arabs establish tin trade with northern Malaya. ...Pandyans (from southern India) invade and subdue Ceylon (present-day Sri Lanka).

▲ ***St. Albans Abbey, England. King Offa of Mercia began its construction c. 790.***

Americas

784. Sky Xul (fl. late 8th century) begins 11-year rule in Quirigua.

795–800. Imix Dog and Scroll Sky rule briefly in Quirigua.

c. 800. Mochica culture in Peru declines. ...Metal is used on a large scale in Mesoamerica. ...Indians from present-day southern California push across the desert to the Colorado River. ...Mixtec culture develops in Mexico.

c. 800–900. Ceremonial centers and sites of occupation are enlarged in the Corral phase in Mesoamerica. ...Metal from northern Peru or Ecuador is introduced into Mesoamerica.

c. 800–1000. Morton culture (in present-day central Illinois) establishes temporary camps for hunting, gathering and possibly rudimentary farming. ...Glacial Kame culture (present-day southern Michigan, northwestern Ohio and northeastern Indiana) establishes hunting and gathering society. ...Maya of the northern lowlands trade with people in present-day southern Central America for gold and copper. ...Oxkintok in northern Mayan lowlands is established. ...Sayil in northern Mayan lowlands becomes a major urban center. ...Uxmal, a great Mayan architectural site in the lowlands, becomes a major city.

Science, Invention & Technology

780. Arabs bring the use of their decimal numbers system from India.

783. Paddleboats are described by Li Kao (fl. late 8th century) of China.

785. Floating magnetic compass is in use in China.

790. Irish monks discover Iceland. ...Scandinavians use blast furnaces in the manufacture of cast iron.

c. 800. Translucent porcelain is invented by the Chinese. ...An elaborate water clock is built for Emperor Charlemagne. ...Longships, with keel and steering oar, give Vikings the ability to cross open expanses of the sea. ...Chinese scholars accurately identify the origin of petrified wood. ...Chinese develop armor made of pleated paper that deflects arrows. ...Estonians develop the evaporation method of chilling water. ...Hungary becomes an important silver mining region. ...A system of lighthouses is built along the Indian Ocean coast by the Arabs and Indians. ...Corvey Abbey at Höxter, Germany, first introduces hops in the beer brewing process. ...Sycamore wood door locks are in use at Thebes, Greece. ...Potash is first used in glass making in Europe. ...Tin oxide is used in the manufacture of porcelain in Mesopotamia. ...Europe's first stoneware is produced in the Rhine River region. ...Celts use simple chip-carving in the production of wooden utensils and ware. ...Simple lamps consisting of saucers with wicks floating in oil are used in medieval Europe. ...Screw battering rams are used in Europe to knock down castle doors.

Religion, Culture & Arts

779. Arabian musician Ibrahim ibn al-Mahdi (d. 839) is born.

781. Nestorians establish Christian monasteries in China.

783. Bashshar ibn Burd (fl. 8th century), Arabic satiric poet, dies.

785. Widukind (?–c. 807), Saxon duke, is baptized.

786–809. Tomb of Zobeide, an eight-sided structure surmounted by a pyramidical roof, is built in Baghdad.

787. Seventh Council of Nicaea regulates image-worship.

790. Offa founds St. Albans Abbey. Schola Cantorum of Rome establishes church music schools at Paris, Cologne, Soissons and Metz.

792–805. Palatine Chapel at present-day Aix-la-Chapelle is built by Odo of Metz as Charlemagne's mausoleum, modeled on San Vitale, Ravenna.

795–816. Leo III (c. 750–816) is pope.

c. 800. Abu Nuwas (c. 760–814), the Arabic poet of courtly life, is active. ...Norwegians build wooden mast-churches, similar to inverted ships. ...Borobudur, one of the most impressive monuments in the Asiatic world, is built on Java.

800–822. Church of St. Boniface at Fulda in Germany is built.

c. 800–900. Byzantine figures of Christ crucified begin to show suffering, stressing Christ's painful death. ...Huge adobe brick Temple of the Sun is built at Moche, Peru. ...Shadow plays based on stories from the two ancient Hindu epics, the *Ramayana* and *Mahabharata*, are introduced into Indonesia from India. ...Khmer city of Angkor in present-day Cambodia emerges as a center of culture.

c. 800–1000. Lusterware pottery is further developed at Old Cairo and Baghdad by reducing silver and copper pigments on an already fused glaze.

British Isles & Western Europe

802–839. Egbert of Wessex (?–839) reigns as first "king of the English."

804. Charlemagne defeats Saxons and extends rule to the Elbe.

808. Jewish merchants in northern Italy begin Europe's first banking system.

809. Widespread famine afflicts Charlemagne's empire. ...Bulgars take Sofia, Bulgaria.

812. Charlemagne orders cultivation of anise, sage, fennel and other plants in Germany.

814–840. Louis I the Pious (c. 780–840), reigns as Roman emperor of the West.

821. Cenwulf of Mercia dies, ending era of Mercian supremacy.

825. Egbert of Wessex conquers Kent and defeats Beornwulf of Mercia at Ellendun.

829. Egbert of Wessex annexes Mercia. ...Eanred of Northumbria (fl. 9th century) pays homage to Egbert.

832–860. Kenneth MacAlpin (c. 800–860) reigns as king of Kintyre (Scotland).

839–858. Ethelwulf (?–858) reigns as king of England.

840–855. Emperor Lothair I (795–855) reigns as Roman emperor of the West.

841. Lothair I is defeated by his brothers at Fontenoy.

843. According to the Treaty of Verdun, Lothair I is granted northern Italy and Lorraine.

845. Norsemen sack Hamburg and invade Germany.

846. Prince Moimir (fl. 9th century) forms Slav federation in central Europe.

Mediterranean Basin

802–811. Nicephorus I (c. 780–811) rules as Byzantine emperor.

803. Byzantium recognizes Venetian independence.

811–813. Michael I Rhangabe (c. 770–814) rules as Byzantine emperor.

813–820. Leo V the Armenian (?–820) rules as Byzantine emperor.

818. Córdoba rises against Arabs.

820–829. Michael II (c. 800–829) rules as Byzantine emperor.

822–852. Abd ar-Rahman II (788–852) is caliph of Córdoba.

826. Arabs take Crete.

827. Arabs begin the conquest of Sicily.

829–842. Theophilus (c. 805–842) rules as Byzantine emperor and persecutes image worshippers.

838. Arabs sack Marseilles and settle in southern Italy.

842–867. Michael III (836–867) rules as Byzantine emperor.

846. Arabs pillage Rome. ...Arab fleet destroys Venetian fleet at sea.

Africa, Asia & Pacific

802. Khmer emerges as an independent kingdom in present-day Cambodia.

c. 810. Bengali king Dharmapala (fl. 9th century) deposes the king of Kanauj (fl. late 8th century) and establishes rule over much of northern India.

813–833. Al-Mamun (786–833) reigns as caliph in Baghdad.

815–877. Amoghavarsna reigns as Rastrakuta ruler, with his capital at Manyakheta (the Deccan, central India).

831. Arabs capture Tarsus.

c. 831–851. Pikatan (c. 820–851) reigns in Sanjaya (in Java).

840–890. Bhoja (c. 830–890) reigns as king of Kanauj.

842. Tibetan empire breaks up, and power passes to the Buddhist clergy.

Americas

805. Jade Sky (fl. 9th century) takes power in Quirigua.

810. The last Mayan palaces and temples are erected.

▲*In this 18th-century copy from an early mosaic, St. Peter (center) presents Pope Leo IV (left) with spiritual power and Charlemagne (right) with temporal power to equalize their positions.*

c. 830. Mayan site of Lubaantun (present-day Southern Belize) is abandoned.

830–1000. Dzibilichaltun dominates salt trade in central Mexico.

830–899. Barton Ramie begins to decline. ...Seibal (in southern Belize) undergoes massive construction.

Science, Invention & Technology

802. Chia Tun (fl. early 9th century) produces a large road map of China, complete with distances between locations.

805. Tea is first introduced to Japan as a medicine.

c. 810. Arabs develop tinglazing in the manufacture of opaque pottery. ...A windmill built in Afghanistan uses ducts to allow air to turn sails mounted inside a tower.

c. 820. Hop growing flourishes in Germany.

823. Lock gates are added to China's canal system.

c. 825. First rotary grindstone is used in Holland.

827. Spinach is brought to Sicily from Persia for the first time.

828. Arabs translate Ptolemy's great 2nd-century work on astronomy, *Megalé syntaxis tes astronomias*, as *Al magiste* (*The Greatest*); it will become known as *Almagest*.

Religion, Culture & Arts

802. First rose bushes are cultivated in England.

804. Alcuin (b. 735), who carried English traditions of learning to the Germans as counsellor to Charlemagne, dies.

805–832. Wulfred (c. 770–832) is Archbishop of Canterbury.

813. Mainz synod decrees a four-day Christmas festival.

814. Work begins on palace of the Venetian doges.

817. *Pactum Hludovicianum* confirms papal territory.

c. 820. *Vita Caroli Magni*, attributed to the cleric Einhard (770–840), is written.

821. Theodulf of Orleans (b. 760), Latin poet at the court of Charlemagne, dies.

827–844. Gregory IV (c. 790–844) is pope.

830. Caliph Mamun (786–833) establishes a translation school in Baghdad.

843. Methodius (826–865) restores icons as objects of veneration.

845. *Hamasa*, a collection of Arabian legends and proverbs, is written. ...Buddhists are persecuted in China.

847–855. Leo IV (?–855) is pope.

British Isles & Western Europe

850. Bulgarian empire flourishes along the Volga.

851. Danes take Canterbury and burn London before being defeated by Ethelwulf at Oakley.

855–875. Louis II (822–875) reigns as king of Italy and Holy Roman emperor.

856. Ethelbald (c. 810–860), son of Ethelwulf, leads rebellion and reigns.

860–866. Ethelbert (?–866) reigns as king of England.

861. Norsemen sack Paris, Cologne, Aix-la-Chapelle and Worms.

866–871. Ethelred I (?–871) reigns as king of England.

870. Treaty of Mersen divides Lotharingia between Germany and France.

871–899. Alfred the Great (849–899) reigns as king of England.

874. Norsemen settle Iceland.

875. Charles II (823–877) is crowned Roman emperor of the West.

876–887. Charles III (839–888), the Fat, reigns as king of Swabia.

877–879. Louis II (846–879) reigns as king of France.

878. Treaty of Wedmore gives Danes East Anglia, Essex and part of Mercia. ...Alfred recaptures London and defeats the Danes at Edington.

879–882. Louis III (863–882) reigns as king of northern France.

879–884. Carloman (fl. 9th century) reigns as king of southern France.

Mediterranean Basin

851. Earthquake damages Rome.

852-886. Mahomet I (816–886) is caliph of Córdoba.

858–859. Vikings sack Algeciras before being expelled by Muslims.

860. Russian fleet attacks Constantinople.

861–862. Turkish mercenaries murder Caliph Al-Mutawakkil (?–861), and Turks establish dominance over the caliphate.

867–886. Basil I (813–886) reigns as Byzantine emperor and recovers southern Italy from the Arabs.

868–905. Independent Tulunid dynasty rules in Egypt and Syria.

869. Arabs capture Malta.

870–892. Al-Mutamid (?–892) reigns as caliph of Islam.

878. Arabs establish Sicilian capital at Palermo.

880. Emperor Basil I evicts Arabs from Italy.

Africa, Asia & Pacific

c. 850. Settlers from present-day New Guinea begin slow migration southeast to present-day Cook Islands and New Zealand.

850–877. Jayavarman III (fl. 9th century) reigns as king of Khmer.

c. 850–900 Instability in northern Burma closes overland trade routes between India and China.

859–890. Ashot I (fl. 9th century) founds Bagratide dynasty of Armenia.

860. Famine provokes uprisings in Chekiang province, China. ...City of Angkor is founded in Khmer.

▲ ***A drawing based on the jewel of Alfred, king of England, now in the Ashmolean Museum, Oxford, England.***

874–999. Samanid dynasty rules in Persia.

874. Peasants revolt against Tang rulers in eastern China.

879. Huang Chao (fl. 9th century), merchant leader of the peasant insurgency in China, burns Canton. ...Nepal gains independence from Tibet.

Americas

850. Lowland Maya abandon ceremonial centers and with this their urban and ritual arts come to an end. ...Tlaxcalan consolidates its power in central Mexico.

c. 875. Anasazi traits seep into Big Bend culture (in present-day west Texas).

Science, Invention & Technology

c. 850. Cyril (827–869) and Methodius (826–884) of Macedonia develop the Cyrillic alphabet, later adopted by Russia and Slavic countries. ...Dutch invent a hand crank for turning grindstones. ...Caspian oil fields at Baku are extensively exploited. ...Chinese alchemists accidentally discover that a mixture of saltpeter, sulfur and carbon is explosive. ...English build a tangential flow water mill at Tamworth. ...Arabs perfect the astrolabe.

859. Bavarians begin brewing hopped beer.

861. Nilometer to measure Nile flood is installed near Fustat (Old Cairo).

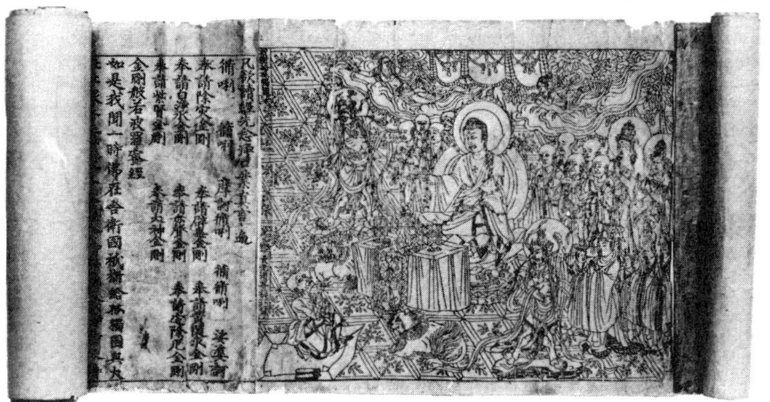

▲ ***The oldest printed book still in existence,* The Diamond Sutra *(868).***

870. English use calibrated candles to mark time.

875. A six-mile-long causeway is built into the Nile Delta, extending northwest from Fustat (Old Cairo), Egypt, in the direction of Alexandria.

Religion, Culture & Arts

850. Groups of Jewish settlers in Germany develop their own language, Yiddish. ...The acropolis of Zimbabwe (in southern Africa) is built. ...University of Salerno in Italy is established.

857. Wooden Temple of Ko Fuang is built at Shansi, China.

c. 860. Hiragana, a simplified Japanese alphabet, is developed. It becomes popular among women but is considered inferior among intellectuals.

863. Cyril and Methodius are appointed to lead a mission to the Moravian Slavs.

864. Prince Boris I (?–907) of Bulgaria converts to Christianity.

c. 865. Creative period of the poet Otfrid of Weissenburg (fl. 9th century), author of the earliest rhyming verse in German.

868. Beginning of the Tulunid Muslim dynasty in Egypt, where religious tolerance leads to a blurring of the distinction between Coptic and Islamic arts. ...Oldest known surviving printed book, *The Diamond Sutra*, is written.

882. Pope John VIII (b. c. 840) is murdered by Roman nobles.

875. St. Pietro at Agliote, the earliest known Italian church to incorporate distinctive Romanesque features (a barrel vault over the choir) is built.

British Isles & Western Europe

881. Charles III, the Fat, is crowned Roman emperor of the West. ...Louis III defeats Normans at Saucourt.

882. Normans sack Cologne, Aix-la-Chapelle and Prüm.

884. Emperor Charles III assumes control of France.

885–886. Normans besiege Paris.

886. Alfred the Great, king of England, rebuilds London.

889–900. Donald I (c. 850–900) reigns as king of Scots.

890. King Alfred establishes fairs and market centers in England.

891. Arnulf (850–899) defeats Normans at Louvain.

892. Lambert of Spoleto (fl. 9th and 10th centuries) is crowned emperor.

893–923. Charles III the Simple (879–929) reigns as king of France.

893–927. Reign of Simeon I (c. 863–927), who becomes the first tsar of Bulgaria in 925.

898. Emperor Lambert dies.

899–925. Edward the Elder (c. 850–925) reigns as king of England.

900–935. Gorm (c. 880–935), founder of the Danish kingdom, reigns.

900–942. Constantine III (c. 880–942) reigns as king of Scots.

907. Magyars crush Moravian empire and raid Germany and Italy.

Mediterranean Basin

886–912. Leo VI, the Wise (862–912), reigns as Byzantine emperor.

888. Arabs occupy Garde-Freinet on the coast of Provence.

888–912. Abdallah (868–912) is caliph of Córdoba.

888–924. Berengar of Friuli (860–924) is king of Italy.

891. Wido of Spoleto (fl. 9th century) is crowned emperor of Italy.

894. Arnulf marches into Italy.

896. Arnulf leads his second expedition into Italy, where he is crowned emperor.

c. 900. Christian reconquest of Spain begins.

902. Arabs take Taormina, last Byzantine city in Sicily.

904. Saracens seize Salonika in Greece. ...Russians renew their attack on Constantinople.

905. County of Navarre in Spain is made a kingdom.

907. Constantinople negotiates trade treaty with Kiev.

909–1171. Caliphate of the Fatimids is established in Tunisia and, in 969, in Egypt.

Africa, Asia & Pacific

881. Huang Chao captures Changan in China and proclaims himself emperor.

883–884. Sha-to Turks, allied with the Tang rulers, retake Changan and capture and kill Huang Chao.

885. Tang dynasty is restored to power. ...Ashot I of Armenia assumes title of king.

c. 887. Mogadishu in present-day Somalia in northeast Africa is established.

c. 890. Songhai kings of Kukia extend their rule to Gao on the Niger River in West Africa.

895. Governors of the Chinese provinces of Szechwan and Chekiang establish dynasties. ...Fujiwaras are the ruling family in Japan.

c. 900. Ogiso dynasty of Benin emerges. ...The Hausa dynasty of Daura, Nigeria, is founded. ...Kalomo culture develops in Zambezi Basin in southern Africa.

903. Weakening caliphate recognizes the local Samanid dynasty, with its capital at Bukhara in central Asia.

906. Annam (Vietnam) gains independence after 1,000 years of Chinese rule.

907. Tang dynasty ends with the murder of the emperor and his entourage.

907–960. Epoch of the five dynasties in China.

Americas

c. 889. Motul de San Jose and Seibal replace Palenque and Copán as Mayan capitals.

▲ ***Palenque's Pyramid of the Inscriptions.***

c. 900–1300. Third phase of Indian development in eastern North America. ...Southern Ohio Hopewell culture establishes villages and intricate earthworks. ...People of southern Illinois Lewis culture build log houses, hunt, fish, and farm. ...Hopewell culture builds mounds, villages, and possibly engages in rudimentary farming. ...Swift Creek culture in present-day northwestern Florida builds rectangular houses and engages in extensive farming and pottery manufacture for cooking. ...First signs of Anasazi culture in the present-day southwestern United States. ...Veracruz culture develops along Gulf of Mexico. ...Huastec cultures occupy northern coast of Gulf of Mexico. ...Cult of the Dead reaches its height in Mexico. ...Shoshonean and Salish peoples occupy the Great Basin north of the present-day southwestern United States. ...Ancient Mayan city of Palenque is abandoned.

Science, Invention & Technology

883. Irrigation schemes in the mountain valleys of Kashmir are promoted by King Avantivarman (fl. 9th century).

c. 900. Windmills come into general use throughout the Arab World. ...Large ship mills for grinding grain are built by the Arabs in the Tigris and Euphrates Rivers. ...First paper mill operates in Egypt. ...Arab Ibn al-Haytham (c. 965–1039) invents the first camera obscura. ...Lenses are first used in Europe to concentrate the sun's rays for starting fires. ...Irish build wooden milk churns and staved buckets. ...Simple furniture-making technology, such as the addition of drawers, is lost in most of Europe. ...The spoke reel and spool winder are invented by the Siamese for the manufacture of silk thread. ...Silk industry spreads into Spain. ...Technology needed for making Greek "fire missiles" is acquired by the Chinese, who add a bellows to the flamethrower. ...The Toltecs adopt sweat house therapy from the Maya. ...Distinction is made between smallpox and measles by Rhazes of Baghdad (fl. 10th century).... Plaster pottery molds are invented by the Arabs.

Religion, Culture & Arts

881. *Ludwigslied,* first historical ballad in German, is written in praise of Louis of Bavaria.

882. Marinus I (?–884) becomes first bishop elevated to pope.

889. Bukong Temple, a terraced stone pyramid, is built at Angkor, Khmer.

c. 890. *Cantilène de Sainte Eulalie*, the earliest extant French poem, is written.

891. First entry is made in the *Anglo-Saxon Chronicle*, which will provide a main source for English history until c. 1150.

893. Earliest Hebrew manuscript of the Old Testament is found.

894. Alfred, king of England, produces, with his scholars, a translation into English of Pope Gregory's *Cura Pastoralis*.

c. 900. *The Story of the Bamboo Gatherer*, the earliest known extant Japanese novel, is written by an unknown author. ...Art of landscape gardening is developed by the Japanese.

c. 900–930. Lara Jonggrang at Prambanam, Java, is constructed with 200 temples incorporated into the overall design.

c. 900–1100. St. Martial music school flourishes near Limoges in France.

c. 900–1200. Toltecs in Mexico make lead-containing pottery which vitrifies in firing.

c. 900–1300. Chi-chou pottery is in mode in China. It includes white porcelain, stoneware and mottled ware.

British Isles & Western Europe

910. The kingdom of Wessex defeats the Northumbrian Danes at Tettenhall.

911. Treaty of St. Clair-sur-Epte establishes the dukedom of Normandy.

911–918. Conrad I (c. 880–918), duke of Franconia, reigns as German king.

916. Danes renew attacks on Ireland.

917. Edward the Elder subdues Danes of East Anglia.

919–936. Henry I (c. 990–936), duke of Saxony, reigns as German king.

924–939. Aethelstan (c. 890–939) reigns as king of England.

927–968. Peter (c. 900–968) reigns as tsar of Bulgaria.

928–929. Henry I subdues Slavs on the Havel.

929. Wenceslas of Bohemia (b. c. 907) is murdered.

936–973. Otto I the Great (912–973) reigns as king of Germany.

936–986. Harold Bluetooth (c. 910–986) reigns as king of Denmark.

937. Aethelstan defeats Celts and Vikings at Brunanburh.

938–941. Rebellions against Otto I break out in Franconia, Bavaria and Lorraine.

Mediterranean Basin

910. Spanish kingdom of Asturias is renamed León.

911. Russia and Byzantium agree on treaty of commerce.

912–961. Abd ar-Rahman III (c. 900–961) reigns as caliph of Córdoba, marking zenith of Omayyad rule in Spain.

913–959. Constantine VII (905–959) reigns as Byzantine emperor.

915. Failure of wheat crop brings famine to the Iberian Peninsula.

916. Arabs are expelled from central Italy.

917. Byzantines defeat Cretan pirate Leo of Tripoli.

917–926. Arabs attack southern Italy.

919–944. Romanus I Lecapenus (c. 890–944) reigns as coregent with Constantine VII in Byzantium and extends empire to Euphrates and Tigris Rivers.

921–926. Hungarians raid northern Italy.

922. Córdoba becomes autonomous caliphate. ...Fatimids conquer most of Idrisi in Morocco.

924. Bulgarians ravage Greece and threaten Constantinople. ...Arabs destroy Navarran capital of Pamplona.

926–945. Hugh of Vienne is king of Italy.

927. Famine spreads throughout realm of Byzantines.

931. Abd ar-Rahman III takes Ceuta in North Africa from the Berbers.

932. Abd ar-Rahman III takes Toledo in Spain.

937. Navarre recognises Abd ar-Rahman III as suzerain.

Africa, Asia & Pacific

c. 916. Indra III (fl. 10th century) takes Kanauj in north India.

916. Malayan Kedah flourishes as a center for trade in aloes, brazilwood, camphor, ebony, ivory, spices and tin.

918. Korean state of Koryo is founded.

920–950. Ghana reaches its zenith as a West African empire.

923–936. Dynasty of Hou-Tang is established in China.

925. China bars foreign merchants.

c. 925. Maori are established along New Zealand coastline.

c. 930. East Java kingdom under Sindok emerges.

935. Wang Chien (fl. 10th century) establishes central monarchy in China. ...Koryo subdues Silla in Korea.

936. Mongols capture Yu-chow, the future site of Beijing. ...Koryo subdues Paekche, forming a united Korea.

937–1125. Liap (Khitan) dynasty reigns in Manchuria and north China.

Americas

c. 910. Classical period of Mesoamerican theocratic city-states ends. ...Maya abandon their settlements in lowlands of Mexico and immigrate to Yucatán Peninsula. ...Second Pueblo period in southwestern part of present-day United States constructs houses entirely above-ground. ...Bravo Valley culture develops in present-day west Texas. ...Thule culture in present-day Arctic Canada and Hudson Bay constructs underground houses with elevated platforms.

c. 920. Weedon Island culture develops along Gulf Coast in present-day Florida. ...Development of regional states in the Central Andes ends. ...Mixtecs fight their way into the Zapotec Valley, occupying Monte Albán.

c. 930. Seibal undergoes a decline.

935. Topiltzin (fl. 10th century), Toltec ruler, comes into conflict with followers of Tezcatlipoca, god of war, and is forced to flee.

Science, Invention & Technology

c. 910. Harnesses are developed for draft animals in Europe, allowing for efficient pulling of loads and plowing.

919. Chinese begin using gunpowder with their flamethrowers.

920. A medical school is founded at Córdoba, Spain.

922. First water mill in Bohemia is built.

c. 925. The island of Madagascar, off East Africa, is mentioned by Arab geographer al-Masudi.

931. Medical schools in Persia begin requiring entrance examinations.

c. 935. Chinese invent a game very similar to golf; it includes tees and flagged holes.

Religion, Culture & Arts

910. William of Aquitaine founds Cluny Abbey in Burgundy in France.

917. Bulgarian church separates from Rome and Constantinople.

c. 920. The Koryo period in Korea begins. It will witness technological and artistic advances in the creation of pottery and porcelain.

930. Hucbald of Belgium (c. 840–930) develops a system of musical scales. ...Ekkehart (900–973) writes his epic poem, *Walter of Aquitaine*.

938. Aethelstan of England establishes Milton Abbey in Dorset.

British Isles & Western Europe

939–946. Edmund I (921–946), half-brother to Aethelstan, reigns as king of England.

942–954. Malcolm I (?–954) rules as king of Scots.

945. Scots acquire Cumberland and Westmorland.

946. Otto I supports Louis IV (921–954) of France and advances to Rouen and Paris.

946–955. Edred (c. 920–955), brother to Edmund, reigns as king of England.

953–955. Rebellions against Otto I break out in Germany.

954–986. Lothair (c. 930–986) reigns as king of France.

955. Otto I defeats Magyars at Augsburg.

955–959. Edwy (?–959), son of Edmund I, reigns as king of England.

959–975. Edgar the Peaceable (943–975), brother to Edwy, reigns as king of England.

960–992. Mleszko I (c. 922–992) reigns as king of Poland.

962. Otto I is crowned the first Holy Roman emperor; the empire of the west is revived.

965. English invade Gwynedd in present-day North Wales.

967–971. Cuilean (fl. 10th century) reigns as king of Scots.

967–999. Boleslav II (c. 940–999) reigns as duke of Bohemia.

971. John Tzimisces subdues Bulgaria and defeats Sviatoslav of Russia.

971–995. Kenneth II (?–995) reigns as king of Scots.

972. Eastern Slav tribes in Russia unite.

Mediterranean Basin

c. 940. Population of Córdoba, the seat of Moorish power in Spain, reaches 500,000.

945–950. Lothair III (?–950) is king of Italy.

945-1055. Buyides rule over Baghdad.

950. Berengar (c. 900–960) and his son, Adalbert (c. 936–960), are crowned kings of Italy.

958. Fatimids control all of present-day Morocco.

959–963. Romanus II (939–963) reigns as Byzantine emperor.

961–976. Hakam II (913–976) rules Córdoba as caliph.

961. Byzantines reconquer Crete from the Arabs.

963. Otto I takes Berengar prisoner.

963–969. Nicephorus II Phocas (912–969) is Byzantine emperor.

965. Fatimid Arabs conquer Sicily.

966–972. Otto I leads a third expedition to Italy against Byzantines in Apulia.

969. Fatimid Arabs conquer Egypt. ...Nicephorus II Phocas is murdered by John Tzimisces (925–976), who succeeds him as Byzantine emperor.

Africa, Asia & Pacific

942–947. Mularaja (c. 900–947) reigns as Gujarat king in western India.

c. 945. Arabs establish trade links with Madagascar.

c. 950. Mogadishu clans unite to resist Somali pressures.

951–960. Dynasty of Hou-Chou is established in China.

960–1279. Sung dynasty is established in China.

962. Turkish principality at Ghazna (present-day Ghazni, Afghanistan) is founded.

964. Sung dynasty reforms Chinese administration and removes civil tasks from the military.

967–1068. Fujiwaras are at the zenith of their power in Japan.

Americas

c. 950. Itzas migrate north to what will become Chichén Itzá. ...Algonquian-speaking tribes dominate Northeastern and Great Lakes regions.

c. 950–1100. Late Woodland Indians occupy Dickson Mounds in present-day Fulton County, Illinois.

In this ivory panel from an altar, St. Peter and other saints surround Otto I (seated on an ivory wreath), who is offering a church to Christ.

964. New Mayan empire begins, during what archaeologists will refer to as the Post Classic period (900–1500) of Mayan civilization.

Science, Invention & Technology

942. Linen and woolen factories are well established in Flanders.

956. Persians build windmills in Sijistan province.

960. Abbé Gilbert of France (fl. 10th century) invents wheel clocks. ...A large dam is built on the Kur River in the Fars province of Persia.

963. First mention of a London bridge appears.

964. Germans mine silver and copper in the Harz Mountains.

968. A large silver ore deposit is discovered at Goslar, Germany.

970. A complete system of nurses, interns and pharmacists is in place at Baghdad's hospital.

Religion, Culture & Arts

c. 940. Abu Abdollah Ja'far Rudaki (fl. 10th century), first great Persian poet, dies.

942. Pilgrim (fl. 10th century), Bishop of Passau, begins Christianizing Hungary. ...Arabs introduce kettledrums and trumpets into European music.

c. 950. White-glazed, painted pottery, which has been made in Baghdad for some 50 years, spreads to Moorish Spain.

955. Al-Mutannabi (b. c. 915), regarded as the greatest Arab poet, dies in Syria.

959–988. Dunstan (930–988) is Archbishop of Canterbury.

960. Hi-Khio, the first Chinese plays with music, are staged.

961. St. Paul's Church in London is rebuilt after a fire. ...Emperor Li Yu (fl. 10th century) founds the Academy of Painting in Nanking, China.

963. First monastic institutions are established on Mount Athos in Greece. ...Roman synod deposes John XII.

963–965. Leo VIII (925–965) is pope.

965–967. Widukind of Corvey writes *Saxon History*.

965–972. John XIII (?–972) is pope.

c. 970. Hrosvitha of Gandersheim (fl. 10th century), a German nun, writes six plays, which are modeled on the comedies of Terence (c. 195–159 B.C.).

972. A university is founded in Cairo.

British Isles & Western Europe

973. Though officially the king of England since 959, Edgar is crowned at Bath in the first coronation ceremony in English history.

973–983. Otto II (955–983) reigns as Holy Roman emperor.

978. Lothair of France sacks Aix-la-Chapelle, but Germans advance to Paris. ...Edward the Martyr is murdered at Corfe castle. Ethelred II (965–1016) is crowned king of England at Kingston.

980. Vikings attack Chester, Southampton and Thanet.

980–1015. Vladimir (c. 960–1015) rules as grand prince of Kiev.

981–982. Vikings ravage Devonshire and South Wales.

983–1002. Otto III (980–1002) reigns as German king.

985. Quarrel begins between Ethelred II and the Witan.

985–1014. Svein (c. 960–1014) reigns as king of Denmark and (from 995) of Sweden.

986–987. Louis V (c. 967–987) reigns as king of France.

987. Hugh Capet (938–996) becomes king of France.

989. Carinthia reunites with Bavaria.

990–992. Poland submits to the Holy See.

991. After battle at Maldon, Essex, Ethelred buys off Vikings.

994. Olaf I Tryggveson of Norway (c. 963–1000) and Svein of Denmark besiege London.

996. German king Otto III is crowned Holy Roman emperor. ...Hugh Capet dies and is succeeded as king of France by Robert II (970–1031).

997–999. Vikings renew attacks on Dorset, Hampshire, Sussex and Kent.

Mediterranean Basin

973. Italy and Egypt establish trade relations.

975. William, Count of Arles, takes Garde-Freinet from Arabs.

976–1025. Basil II (958–1025) is Byzantine emperor.

977. Arabs renew attacks on southern Italy.

977–1002. Al-Mansur (960–1002) is virtual ruler of Córdoba.

981–983. Otto II wages war against Saracens in southern Italy.

982. Otto II is defeated by Saracens.

983. Venice and Genoa establish important trade links with Asia.

983–991. Empress Theophano (955–991) conducts government of Italy from Rome. She rules as coregent for her son, Otto III.

992. Byzantines grant Venice trading privileges throughout the empire.

996. Civil war flares briefly in Rome. ...Basil II of Byzantium ousts Bulgarians from Greece.

997–1027. Alfonso V (c. 994–1027) is king of León.

Africa, Asia & Pacific

973. Sung dynasty decrees protectorate over Annam (Vietnam) and extends influence into the East Indies. ...Second Chalukya dynasty ends with the removal of the last of the Rastrakuta (central India).

c. 980. Arabs and Persians push south along East African coast and settle there.

982–1029. Ceylonese king Mahinda (c. 960–1029) rules with the aid of south Indian mercenaries.

985–1014. Rajaraja I (c. 960–1014), ruler of the Cholas (southeast India), expands into Kerala, Ceylon (present-day Sri Lanka), and the Maldive Islands.

986. Sabuktagin (fl. 10th century), emir of Ghazna (present-day Ghazni), invades Punjab in northern India.

c. 990. Ghana takes Audaghost in West Africa from the Berbers and installs an African governor.

991–1006. East Java invades Shrivijaya and expands dominion to include Bali and the west coast of Borneo.

c. 993–994. Delhi in north India is founded.

997–1030. Mahmud (971–1030), son of Sabuktagin, rules as sultan of Ghazna.

Americas

⮝ ***Otto III was 14 years old when he became Holy Roman emperor.***

982. Eric the Red (fl. 10th century) begins exploration of Greenland.

985. Eric the Red establishes a Scandinavian settlement in Greenland.

987. Tula is established as the Toltec capital near present day Tula de Allende central Mexico. ...Kukulcan invades Mayan sites in southern Mexico.

Science, Invention & Technology

976. Chang Ssu-Hsun (fl. late 10th century) builds a mercury clock in China.

979. First mention of Billingsgate Wharf in London appears.

983. A fulling mill is built in Tuscany on the Serchio River.

984. Chinese build locks on their Grand Canal.

986. Arab doctor al-Tasrif (fl. 10th century) writes a surgical manual at Córdoba, Spain.

994. A medical encyclopedia is written in Persia.

Religion, Culture & Arts

973. Deccan sculpture and architecture are revived in India.

974–983. Benedict VII (c. 940–985) is pope.

976–1010. Abu'l Qasim Firdowsi (940–1010) writes poem *Shah-Nameh*. It will become Persia's national epic.

978. Chinese scholars begin 1,000-volume encyclopedia.

984–985. Second pontificate of Boniface VII.

985–996. John XV (c. 930–996) is pope.

988–989. Vladimir, grand prince of Kiev, adopts the Christian Orthodox faith as his country's religion and orders all pagan works of art destroyed.

c. 990–1020. Aelfric the Grammarian (c. 955–1020), abbot of Eynsham, writes *Homilies*, *Latin Grammar* and *Glossary*.

993. Christian church canonizes its first saints.

997. St. Martin's, with first known east end plan of apse ambulatory and radiating chapels, is built at Tours in France. It will become the blueprint for pilgrimage churches.

British Isles & Western Europe

1000. Ethelred II ravages Cumberland and Isle of Man. ...Vikings attack Normandy. ...Svein of Denmark conquers Norway and kills Olaf at Svold. ...Danegeld, a general tax, is introduced in England.

1002. Danes in England are murdered in the Massacre of St. Brice.

1002–1024. Henry II (973–1024), formerly duke of Bavaria, reigns as German king, and, from 1014, as Holy Roman emperor.

1004. Henry II defeats Ardoin. Henry II is crowned king of Lombardy at Pavia.

1005–1034. Malcolm II (c. 980–1034) reigns as king of Scotland.

1008. Ethelred II organizes English fleet.

1009. Danes attack London.

1011. Ethelred II invades South Wales. Danes take Canterbury.

1012. Danes murder Archbishop Elfheah, and are again paid off by Ethelred II.

1013. Danes conquer Northumbria, Wessex and London. Ethelred II flees to Normandy.

1014. Svein dies and is succeeded by Cnut (c. 995–1035). ...Ethelred II returns to England. ...Cnut withdraws to Denmark. ...Norse rule in Ireland ends at battle of Clontarf.

1016. Shortly before his death, Edmund Ironside divides England between himself and Cnut, who becomes king upon the former's death. ...Ethelred II dies.

Mediterranean Basin

c. 1000. Venice extends rule down Dalmatian coast.

c. 1000–1050. Caliphate in Spain gradually breaks up into 20 smaller states.

1002–1008. Muzaffar (c. 980–1008) is ruler of Córdoba.

1004. Arabs sack Pisa, Italy.

1009. Muhammadans profane Holy Sepulchre at Jerusalem.

1011. Arabs again sack Pisa.

1015. Arabs conquer the island of Sardinia.

1016. The Pope, Pisa and Genoa rescue Sardinia from Mujahid of Denia. ...Norman knights arrive in southern Italy.

Africa, Asia & Pacific

c. 1000. First Shonas settle Zimbabwe in southern Africa. ...Gao is the capital of the Songhai empire of West Africa. ...Chola ruler Rajaraja ransacks Chalukya lands and conquers Ceylon.

c. 1000–1100. Tungus seize part of Korea. ...Burmese ransack Thaton. ...Turks withdraw toward Russia from Central Asia.

1001. Mahmud of Ghazna (present-day Ghazni) defeats Jaipal (fl. 11th century), raja of the Punjab, and annexes his territory.

1001–1024. Mahmud of Ghazna leads Muslim drive into India.

c. 1004. Military spending accounts for one-quarter of China's budget.

1004. China becomes tributary of the Tungusic Khitans. ...Rule of Samanides is overthrown in Persia.

1006. Muhammadans settle in northwest India. ...Shrivijayans invade East Java and burn its capital.

1007. Chola conquer the Maldive Islands.

1008. Mahmud of Ghazna defeats Hindu league at Peshawar.

1009. Mahmud of Ghazna captures the Hindu stronghold of Kangra.

1010. Civil war breaks out in East Java.

1012–1042. Chola ruler Rajendra Choladeva absorbs southern Chalukya provinces (present-day Hyderabad) and launches new campaigns into Kerala, Ceylon (present-day Sri Lanka), and Shrivijaya.

1012. Drought-resistant rice is introduced into China from Champa (present-day southern Vietnam).

Americas

c. 1000. Chicle, a gum derivative of the sapodilla tree, is chewed by the Maya. ...Iroquois build longhouses in present-day upstate New York. ...Mitla is the capital of the Mixtecs in Mexico. ...Navajo and Apache begin to reach present-day southwestern United States. ...First signs of metalwork in Mesoamerica. ...Toltecs invade Yucatán Peninsula. ...Mayan city of Chichén Itzá becomes a Toltec colonial capital. ...Woodland people are succeeded by mound builders from east of Mississippi River. ...Siouan groups of Indians migrate from the Mississippi River valley to present-day northeastern Wisconsin. ...Leif Ericsson (fl. 11th century) discovers North America (Nova Scotia). ...Tiahuanaco culture spreads throughout Peru.

c. 1000–1300. Hamilton culture (in present-day eastern Tennessee) establishes base camps near rivers for fishing and rudimentary pottery manufacture. ...Wilmington culture (in present-day coastal Georgia) builds thatch-covered village huts and engages in subsistence farming.

c. 1000–1470. Chimú dominate northern Peru. ...Chimú establish imperial capital, Chan Chan.

1010–1013. Thorfinn Karlsevni (fl. 11th century), Icelandic trader, explores North American mainland with 160 men and three ships.

1014–1015. Freydis, Eric the Red's daughter, makes the last trip by a Viking to the North American mainland.

Science, Invention & Technology

c. 1000. Horse-drawn ambulances are used by the Crusaders in the Holy Land. ...Stronger armor-piercing swords are made in Europe. ...Inuit people of Arctic North America develop kayaks, umiaks, harpoons and parkas as they migrate eastward to inhabit the Arctic islands and coastline. ...Muslim surgeon Albucasis (fl. 11th century) of Spain advances use of cauterization and demonstrates various dental devices and procedures. ...Aleppo and Epiphania in Syria are important cotton trade centers. ...A dam is built on the Leck River at Augsburg, Germany. ...Germans develop glass painting. ...Abacus is reintroduced to Europe. ...The huo-pa'o, a type of catapult, is invented in China. ...There is large-scale porcelain manufacturing in the city of Ching-teo Chen, China. ...The first striking matches are invented in China. ...Wire drawing is begun in Europe. ...Crossbows are used in Italy, the technology having been brought from China. ...Copper smelters are built by the Inca of Peru. ...Cypriots develop gold-leaf thread. ...A type of toothpaste is made from soap bean powder by Chinese. ...Corinth, Greece, becomes noted for its glass manufacturing. ...A portable flamethrower, or fire lance, is invented by the Chinese. ...Byzantines use gasoline-filled grenades against the Crusaders. ...Arabs make bars of soft soap from olive oil and wood ash. ...Greeks at Corinth invent thimbles. ...Coal mining is widespread in China. ...Vikings invent equipment for ironing clothes. ...Late Kachemak Bay culture develops several stone tools.

Religion, Culture & Arts

c. 1000. Earliest existing Mesoamerican codices, long folded parchment strips with stories told in miniature paintings, are created. ...Earliest surviving translation of the Gospels into English is made. ...*Bamberg Apocalypse*, an illustrated manuscript exemplifying best of the Reichenau (Germany) school of illumination, is created. ...Italians are leaders in the craft of furniture making. ...Elaborate carvings are part of Hindu architecture in India. ...Kiev (Ukraine) becomes an important centre of *cloisonné* enamelling. ...Great Temple at Tanjore (India) is built on a traditional square plan from which rises a monumental, pyramidal structure with a high stupa. ...Guido d' Arezzo (?–1050) proposes that stave of four lines be used for writing plainsong. (After 1200 five lines became the norm).

c. 1000–1010. *Chanson de Roland*, the poetic cycle of legends celebrating Charlemagne and his court, is written.

c. 1000–1200. Ife terra-cotta sculpture of human forms flourishes in Nigeria.

c. 1000–1200. Mimbres pottery of Pueblo Indians (in present-day southwestern United States) reaches highest point of their abstract designs, based on plant, animal and human forms.

1012. First persecution of heretics in Germany.

▲ ***The cultural influence of the Toltecs from central Mexico is clearly seen on an altar at Uxmal in the Yucatán, showing the morbid design of a skull and crossbones.***

British Isles & Western Europe

1018. At the Assembly of Oxford, Danes and English agree to live under English laws.

1021. St. Vitus's Dance epidemic spreads throughout Europe.

1024–1039. Conrad II (c. 990–1039) reigns as king of Germany.

1026. Cnut is defeated by Swedes and Norwegians on Helge River.

1027. Treaty of succession between Conrad II and Rudolf III, king of Burgundy. ...Conrad II is crowned Holy Roman emperor.

1028. Cnut conquers Norway.

1031–1060. Henry I (1008–1060) reigns as king of France.

1032. Rudolf III of Burgundy dies, and Conrad unites Burgundy with the Holy Roman Empire.

1034. Malcolm II is murdered; he is succeeded by Duncan (1010–1040).

1035. Cnut dies, and his kingdom is divided between his three sons.

1036. Harold I (c. 1022–1040) defeats Alfred (fl. 11th century), son of Ethelred II.

1039. Conrad II (b. 990) dies; he is succeeded as Holy Roman emperor and king of Germany by Henry III (1017–1056).

1040. Harold I of England dies and is succeeded; he is succeeded by Hardacnut (1018–1042). ...Duncan is slain by Macbeth (c. 1005–1057), who becomes king of Scots.

1042. Hardacnut dies; he is succeeded by Edward the Confessor (?–1066), son of Ethelred II.

1043. Agnes of Poitou (fl. 11th century) marries Henry III.

Mediterranean Basin

1018. Byzantines defeat Lombards and Normans at Cannae. ...Byzantium regains Macedonia.

1020. Alfonso V (994–1027) issues the *fuero* (statutes) of León and charters in favor of the cities.

1025–1028. Constantine VIII (c. 1000–1028) is Byzantine emperor.

1027–1031. Hisham III (?–1031) is caliph of Córdoba.

1028–1034. Zoë (980–1050) and Romanus III (c. 968–1034) are joint Byzantine emperors.

1030. Normans settle at Aversa near Naples. ...Seljuks advance in Asia Minor.

1034–1042. Byzantine empress Zoë rules jointly with a succession of co-rulers.

1035. Sancho III of Spain dies and his kingdom is partitioned into Castile, Navarre and Aragon.

1035–1065. Ferdinand I (c. 1010 – 1065) reigns as king of Castile and conquers Portugal.

1037. Conrad II issues *Constitutio de feudis*, which makes fiefs of small holders (*valvassores*) hereditary in Italy.

1042–1055. Constantine IX (1020–1055) is Byzantine emperor, ruling with Zoë (until 1050) and Theodora (980–1056).

1043. George Maniakes (fl. 11th century), Byzantine commander, leads rebellion.

1045. Byzantines conquer Armenia.

Africa, Asia & Pacific

1019. Mahmud of Ghazna (present-day Ghazni) conquers Kanauj.

1023. Chola empire extends its rule northward to the Ganges River.

1025. Chola forces capture and loot Shrivijayan capital of Palembang.

1025–1026. Mahmud of Ghazna conquers Gujarat.

1031. Hsi-Hsia in north China is renamed Toba, after 5th-century Tatar empire.

1037. Seljuk Turks begin their conquests.

c. 1043. Mandingo people found empire of Jenne in the Upper Niger Valley in West Africa.

1044. Resurgent Hindus retake the fortress of Kangra in India.

Americas

c. 1020. Anasazi build a semicircular city in a valley of present-day northwest New Mexico consisting of apartments arranged in concentric, stair-stepped rings.

1040. Bronze, highly valued as a more useful metal than gold, is introduced in Peru.

Science, Invention & Technology

1020. Arab scientist Ibn al-Haytham (c. 965–1039) invents a parabolic mirror made of polished silver and iron.

1026. Wang Wei-I (fl. 11th century) of China writes a treatise describing acupuncture.

1027. A recording drum used to measure distance traveled is added to a carriage built by Lu Daolong (fl. 11th century) of China.

1040. Draft animals gain wide use in Europe. ...Helei province in China has large war factories that produce thousands of armor suits and millions of arrowheads.

1041. Pi Sheng (fl. 11th century) of China invents moveable type made from clay bricks.

1044. Kung-Liang (fl. 11th century) of China describes a formula for a glass-contained excrement bomb.

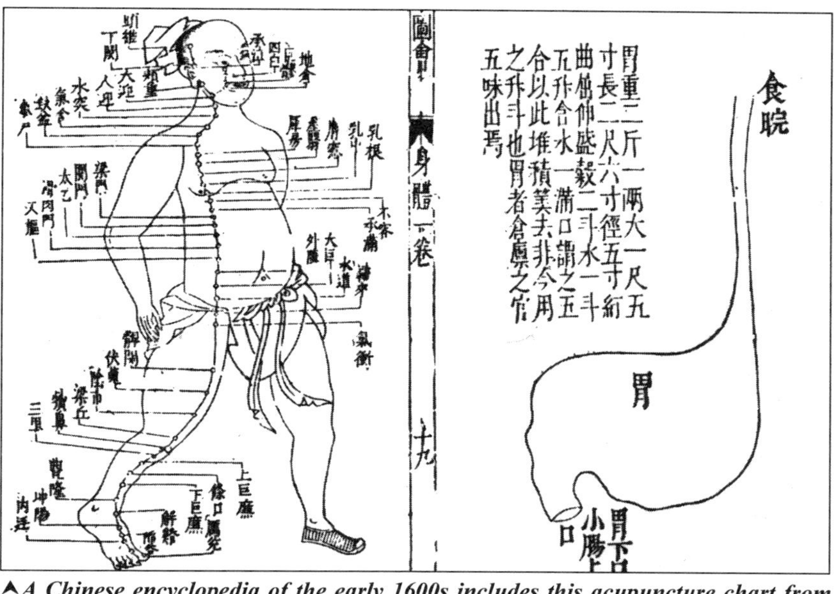

▲*A Chinese encyclopedia of the early 1600s includes this acupuncture chart from the* **Wei Chung,** *or* **Treatise on the Stomach.**

Religion, Culture & Arts

1019. Synod of Goslar decides against allowing priests to marry.

1020. Aelfric (b. 955), leading scholar of the Benedictine revival of learning in England, dies.

1022. Synod of Pavia insists on celibacy of higher clergy.

1024–1032. John XIX (980–1032) is pope.

1032. Mount Abu, the most important group of Jain temples, is built in India. ...Restoration of Bury St. Edmunds Abbey is completed.

1032–1045. Benedict IX (c. 990–1045) is pope.

1036. D'Arezzo (991?–1050) invents the modern scale of musical notes. ...Avicenna (b. c. 979), Arab philosopher, dies.

1040. Truce of God proclaimed in Aquitaine.

1042. Truce of God proclaimed in Normandy.

1042–1095. St. Mark's Cathedral in Venice is built on a Greek cross plan, with a central dome and four surrounding domes in the Byzantine style.

1045. Silvester III (?–1045) is elected antipope.

British Isles & Western Europe	Mediterranean Basin	Africa, Asia & Pacific
1047. William of Normandy (c. 1027–1987), also known as William the Conqueror, aided by Henry I of France, defeats rebellious nobles at Val-des-Dunes.		
1048. William of Normandy defeats Geoffrey of Anjou and takes Domfront and Alençon.		
1050. Normans infiltrate England.	**1050.** Military dictatorship rules Egypt....Seljuk Turks devastate Kars in eastern Anatolia.	
1051. William of Normandy visits Edward the Confessor and receives promise of succession to English throne.	**1052.** Pisa expels Arabs from Sardinia.	
1053. Godwin dies and Harold succeeds him as earl of Wessex. ...Normans defeat and capture Leo IX at Civitate.	**1053.** Robert Guiscard (1015–1085) establishes a Norman empire in southern Italy.	**1053.** Buddhist temple Byodoin is consecrated in Uji, Japan.
1054. William of Normandy defeats Henry I at Mortemer.	**1054.** Godfrey of Lorraine (1058–1100) marries Matilda (c. 1046–1115), marchioness of Tuscany.	**1054.** Almoravids begin Islamic conquest of West Africa.
	1055. Seljuks take Baghdad.	**1055–1110.** King Vijayabahu (c. 1040–1110) reigns in Ceylon.
1056. Henry III (b. 1017) dies; he is succeeded by Henry IV (1050–1106).	**1056–1082.** Muslim Almoravids conquer central Algeria and Morocco.	
1057. Malcolm III (1031–1093) kills Macbeth.	**1057–1059.** Isaac I Comnenus (1005–1061) is Byzantine emperor.	
1058. Malcolm becomes king of Scots. ...William of Normandy defeats Geoffrey of Anjou at Varaville.	**1059–1067.** Constantine X (1007–1067) is Byzantine emperor.	
1060. Henry I of France dies; he is succeeded by Philip I (?–1108).	**1061.** Normans conquer Messina in Sicily.	**1060.** Arabs and Berbers conquer the West African kingdom of Ghana.
1063. William of Normandy conquers Maine.	**1063–1072.** Alp-Arslan (c. 1040–1072) rules Seljuks.	
	1064. Seljuks conquer Armenia. ...Hungarians take Belgrade from Byzantines.	
	1065. Seljuks invade Asia Minor.	
1066. Edward the Confessor dies. ...Harold is crowned king of England. ...Harold defeats invaders at Stamford Bridge. ...William of Normandy lands at Pevensey. ...Harold is defeated and killed at battle of Hastings. ...William of Normandy is crowned king of England as William I.	**1065–1072.** Sancho II (c. 1040–1072) is king of Castile.	
	1065–1109. Alfonso VI (c. 1050–1109) is king of León and (from 1072) Castile.	
	1067–1078. Michael VII (1059–1078) is Byzantine emperor. His rule is interrupted (1068–1071) by Romanus IV (?–1071).	**c. 1067.** Kanem empire expands west to the River Niger and absorbs most of Hausaland in West Africa.
1068. William I conquers western and northern England.	**1068.** Moorish Seville absorbs Córdoba and becomes paramount Spanish-Arab kingdom.	**1068–1086.** Shen Tsung (fl. 11th century) rules as emperor of China. China is disrupted by state interference in economy.

Americas

c. 1050–1450. Communal pit houses and new styles of pottery are introduced in present-day northwestern Argentina.

c. 1065. Koniag culture builds underground houses with skylights and smoke holes.

Science, Invention & Technology

c. 1050. Chinese use explosive bombs launched from catapults. …Chinese invent a rapid-fire crossbow capable of shooting 2,000 arrows in 15 seconds. …Arabs invent complex mechanical calendars. …Anglo-Saxons invent double-bladed spades.

1054. A supernova explodes in the constellation Taurus.

Based on the Bayeux Tapestry, this image portrays William of Normandy conquering Dinan in northern France in 1064.

1063. Persia's noted postal system is disrupted.

1064. Chinese regulate their granary system.

1066. A fortress of prefabricated timbers is carried as part of the equipment of William of Normandy's navy. …English use floating casks as the world's first buoys.

1067. Castile province in Spain has world's first leper colony.

Religion, Culture & Arts

1046. Holy Roman Emperor Henry III deposes antipope Silvester III at Synod of Sutri. Clement II (?–1047) is elected pope at Synod of Rome.

1047. Pope Clement II dies. Damasus II (?–1048) is elected pope.

1049. Hugh of Semur (1024–1109) becomes abbot of Cluny.

1050. Welsh heroic poem *The Mabinogion* appears. …First bullfights are held in Spain.

1052. Construction begins on Westminster Abbey.

1053. Archbishop of Rouen excommunicates William of Normandy, who deposes him.

1054. Pope Leo IX and Michael Cerularius, patriarch of Constantinople, exchange anathemas of excommunication in the Schism of 1054.

1059. Lanfranc reconciles William of Normandy with the Church. Robert Guiscard (c.1015–1085), duke of Apulia, and Richard of Aversa become papal vassals. …Decree establishes papal election by cardinals only.

1063. Work begins on Pisa Cathedral. With the Baptistery, which will be altered in the 14th century, and the campanile, or "leaning tower," it forms the most magnificent complex of Romanesque architecture.

1066. Pope Alexander II supports William of Normandy's conquering of England.

British Isles & Western Europe

1069. William I subdues uprising in the North and expels Danish invaders.

1071. Philip I (1052–1108) of France attacks Robert I (1013?–1093), Count of Flanders, and is defeated at Cassel. ...William I suppresses the last risings in England.

1072. Malcolm III of Scotland (c. 1031–1093) acknowledges William I's suzerainty.

1080. Robert I invades Scotland and builds Newcastle-upon-Tyne. ...Henry IV is defeated and Rudolf, king of Germany, is killed at Pegau.

1083–1086. Maine rebels anew against William I.

1085. Denmark, Norway and Flanders prepare to invade England. ...Henry IV reconciles Saxony. ...**June 15:** Vratislav II (c. 1035–1092), duke of Bohemia, is crowned king.

1086. On the orders of William I, the Domesday Book (an inventory and assessment of landed property), is compiled, making all English vassals dependent on the king.

1087. Philip I's invasion of Normandy is repelled by William I. ...**September 9:** William I dies and is succeeded by his eldest son, Robert II (1054–1134), in Normandy and by his second surviving son, William II, known as William Rufus, in England (c. 1056–1100).

1089. Henry IV marries Praxedis (Adelaide) of Kiev.

1090–1112. Ingo I (fl. 12th century) is king of Sweden.

Mediterranean Basin

1070. Marrakesh (in Morocco) is founded.

1071. Normans conquer Bari and Brindisi, last Byzantine possessions in Italy. ...Seljuks take Jerusalem. ...Romanus IV (?–1071) is defeated and captured by Seljuks at Manzikert, Armenia.

1072. Normans conquer Palermo. ...Oghuz Turks capture Seljuk leader Alp Arslan (b. 1029); he dies while confined in an iron cage.

1073–1076. Normans take Amalfi and Salerno.

1075. Seljuks subdue Palestine.

1076. Seljuks conquer Damascus. ...Aragon and Castile divide Navarre.

1078–1081. Nicephorus III (c. 1060–1081) is Byzantine emperor. He will be succeeded by Alexius I Comnenus (1048–1118), who seizes the throne in 1081.

1080. An Armenian state is established in Cilicia (Armenia Minor). ...Autonomous consuls at Lucca in Italy are mentioned for the first time.

1081. Henry IV marches to Italy.

1083. Alexius I Comnenus defeats Normans at Larissa in Greece. ...**June 3:** Henry IV storms Rome.

1086. The Almoravids, a Berber dynasty, revive Muhammadan rule in Spain.

1088–1090. Patzinaks, Turkish tribes, settle between the Danube and the Balkans.

1090–1097. Henry IV wages war in Italy.

Africa, Asia & Pacific

1076. Chinese campaign in Tonkin in northern Vietnam. ...Almoravids sack Ghanaian capital at Kumbi.

1077. Almoravids overrun Ghana and depose Soninke dynasty.

c. 1080. Sosso kingdom of Kaniaga emerges.

1084–1112. Kyansittha (c. 1060–1112) rules as elected king of Pagan in Burma.

▲ ***After being dismissed by Pope Gregory VII, German king Henry IV (center), sought refuge in Canosa at the castle of Countess Matilda of Tuscany (right). This illumination was taken from an original manuscript,* Vita Mathildis, *written by the monk Denis in 1114.***

Americas

1073. Pueblo structures at Mesa Verde in present-day southwestern Colorado are in ruins.

c. 1075. The "sky city" of Acoma, considered to be the oldest continuously inhabited city in North America, is founded at an elevation of about 7,000 feet in present-day Valencia County, New Mexico.

c. 1090. Sinchi Roca culture is established in present-day Peru.

Science, Invention & Technology

c. 1070. Roquefort cheese is developed by the French.

1071. A two-pronged eating fork is introduced to Venice by the Greeks.

1075. Elliptical orbits of the planets are suggested by Arab astronomer Arzachel (fl. 11th century).

1078. Venetians build first tidal mills.

c. 1080. Chinese are first to recognize fossils as evidence of previous life forms and climatic periods.

1086. Shen Kua (fl. 11th century) of China invents a magnetic compass that points south when rubbed.

1090. Su Sung (1020–1101) of China builds his "cosmic engine," a clockwork device powered by a waterwheel.

Religion, Culture & Arts

1070. Avicebron (b. c. 1022), Spanish-born Jewish poet and philosopher, dies.

c. 1070. The Bayeux Tapestry, actually an embroidery, is embroidered in wool on linen. Its images chronicle the conquest of England by William of Normandy.

1073. George VII (c. 1020–1085) becomes pope and excommunicates the counselors of Henry IV of Germany.

1074. March 1: Pope Gregory VII announces a Crusade. ...**March 9:** Married priests are excommunicated.

1076. Roman ritual is introduced in Navarre and Castile. ...Pope Gregory VII excommunicates Henry IV.

1078. Construction begins on Cathedral of Santiago de Compostela, one of the earliest pilgrimage churches. ...Work begins on the Tower of London.

1080. Pope Gregory VII again excommunicates Henry IV. ...**June 25:** Synod of Brixen elects imperial antipope Clement III.

1085. Ssu-ma Kuang (1019–1086) publishes his chronological history of China. ...Pope Gregory VII (b. c. 1020) dies at Salerno.

1086. Bruno of Cologne (c. 1030–1101) founds the Carthusian Order.

A 17th-century engraving of the Tower of London by artist Wenzel Hollar (1607–1677) of Prague.

1088–1099. Urban II (c. 1042–1099) is pope.

1089. Construction begins on Gloucester Cathedral.

1089–1130. Abbey Church of Cluny is rebuilt.

British Isles & Western Europe

1091. Malcolm III invades England.

1092. William II conquers Cumberland and Westmorland.

1093. November 13: Malcolm III (b. c. 1031) is defeated and killed near Alnwick.

1096. Robert II mortgages Normandy to his brother William II.

1097. William II is at war with Philip I.

1098. Louis VI (1081–1137) is made co-regent with his father, Philip I of France.

1100. August 2: William II (b. c. 1056) is killed in New Forest and is succeeded by his brother Henry I (1068–1135) as king of England.

1101. July 19: Robert II of Normandy invades England and is bought off by the Treaty of Alton.

1103. Magnus III (b. c. 1073) of Norway invades Ireland and is killed.

1104. Henry V (1081–1125) deserts his father, Henry IV.

1105. War breaks out between Henry IV and Robert II in Normandy. Henry IV is captured by his son, Henry V, and abdicates.

1106. Henry IV (b. 1050) flees and dies. ...Henry I of England defeats Robert II and takes Normandy. ...Henry V succeeds Henry IV as Holy Roman emperor and king of Germany.

1108. Philip I of France dies and is succeeded by his son Louis VI.

1109–1113. The Anglo-French War is fought.

Mediterranean Basin

1091. Normans complete conquest of Sicily. ...Seljuks make Baghdad their capital.

1092. Malek Shah (b. 1055), Seljuk sultan, dies.

1095. Hungarians conquer Croatia and Dalmatia.

1096. Rodrigo Díaz de Vivar, known as El Cid (c. 1043–1099), conquers Valencia. ...Peter I (c. 1050–1104) of Aragon defeats Moors at Alcaraz.

1096–1099. First Crusade is organized following Pope Urban II's (c. 1042–1099) call at the Council of Clermont.

1099. The kingdom of Jerusalem is organized. ...After the death of El Cid (b. c. 1043), Moors recover Valencia. ... **July–August:** Crusaders take Jerusalem and defeat Egyptians at Ascalon.

1100. David III (1073–?) of Georgia expels Arabs from Tiflis.

1100–1118. Baldwin I (c. 1080–1118) is king of Jerusalem.

1104–1108. Bohemond (c. 1080–1120), prince of Antioch, wages war in Epirus against Byzantium.

1104–1134. Alfonso I (c. 1090–1134) is king of Aragon.

1109. Tripoli is made an independent principality under the Count of Toulouse.

1111. Matilda of Tuscany appoints Henry V her heir. ...Alexius I Comnenus grants commercial privileges to Pisa.

Africa, Asia & Pacific

1095–1130. Gijimasu (fl. 12th century) reigns as king of Kano in West Africa.

1098. China sets up a state agency to care for the aged.

c. 1100. Habe dynasty of Katsina is founded in West Africa.

1100–1150. Hoysala dynasty is established in South India, with its capital near present-day Mysore.

1100–1200. Timbuktu emerges as a prominent Tuareg oasis.

1102. China establishes a state health bureau.

1107. Toba (1103–1123) succeeds his father, Horikawa (1079–1107), as Japanese emperor.

Americas

c. 1100. Mayapan (in Yucatán) is founded. ...Cliff Palace is constructed at Mesa Verde in present-day Colorado. ...Inca move into the valley of Cuzco in Peru. ...Sinagua in present-day southern Arizona disappear. ...Tula is destroyed.

c. 1100–1200. Tiahuanaco is a ceremonial center in Bolivia and, like others, a station for making observations of the solar year. ...Middle Mississippian Indians from the south of present-day United States mingle with northern present-day Illinois groups. ...Chitimecs and other groups invade the central valley of Mexico, weakening Toltec power.

c. 1100–1250. Hopewell culture (in present-day New York), farmers and hunter-gatherers, develops pottery vessels and tools.

c. 1100–1300. Troyville culture (in present-day Texas, Arkansas, Mississippi, Alabama and Florida) builds villages and ceremonial centers. ...Pueblo culture reaches its peak.

c. 1100–1400. Intrusive Mount culture builds wigwams and probably engages in small-scale farming and pottery manufacture. ...Laurel culture (in present-day northern Minnesota) establishes summer villages and part-time farming.

Science, Invention & Technology

1094. *The Book of Roads and Kingdoms* is produced by Muslim geographer al-Bakri (1010–1094) of Spain.

1096. Sugarcane is introduced to the Holy Land by the Crusaders.

◄ Japanese artist Gengzhi Tu's* Pictures of Tilling and Weaving *depict silkworm culture. This plate shows how cocoons are selected for the quality of their silk.

c. 1100. Soft soaps, used mainly for washing fabrics, are made by the Scandinavians. ...Cotton is introduced to France and Italy. ...Italians begin silk production. ...Various styles of metal coats of mail are worn by European knights. ...Dutch build the first lift locks in their canals. ...Spanish sailors adopt use of the compass. ...Lighthouse construction resumes along the Mediterranean coast. ...Salerno Medical School makes bone-setting casts from eggs and flour. ...Paper is introduced in Europe by the Spanish Moors. ...Umbrellas are first used in Europe as part of ceremonial dress of Roman Catholic officials.... The trebuchet, a counterweighted throwing arm, is invented, a significant improvement of the catapult. ...Chinese use multicolor printing in the production of paper money. ...Sericulture, the technology of breeding silkworms, is widespread in China. ...French and British produce lead-glazed pottery. ...A seven-color printing process is developed by the Arabs. ...Central Europeans have water-driven hammer forges. ...Ballistae, large siege crossbows, are placed on fortress walls in Europe. ...Chinese accurately explain solar and lunar eclipses. ...A small zoological garden is opened at Woodstock, England, by King Henry I.

Religion, Culture & Arts

1092. Vladislav (1040–1095), king of Hungary, allows marriage of priests.

1093–1109. Anselm (c. 1033–1109), considered a founder of Scholasticism, is Archbishop of Canterbury.

1095. Clergymen are forbidden to take oath of fealty to laymen. ...Pope Urban II consecrates rebuilt Abbey Church of Cluny.

1097–1099. Westminster Hall is built in London.

1097–1100. Archbishop Anselm is in exile in Rome and Cluny.

1099–1118. Paschal II (c. 1060–1118) is pope.

c. 1100. Omar Khayyam (1050–1132), Persian poet and scientist, writes the *Rubáiyát*. ...The Indian love poem *Gitagovinda* appears. ...Work begins on St. Germain des Près, an early example of Gothic architecture, in Paris. ...Notre Dame du Port at Clermont-Ferrand in France, a typical example of the Auvergne school of Romanesque architecture, is built. ...The five windows in Augsburg (Germany) Cathedral, thought to be the oldest surviving stained-glass windows, are installed. ...Byzantine mosaic artists begin work on St. Mark's, in Venice. ...Paganica, a Roman game similar to golf, is popular in Scotland.

c. 1100–1200. Kelso Abbey, finest Romanesque church in Scotland, is built. ...Earliest motet, *Ex Semine Abrahae*, is written in England by an unknown composer. ...Angkor Wat, a funerary temple for the deified King Suryavarman II, is built in Khmer (Cambodia). It is a vast rectangle surrounded by a moat 2½ miles long, with stepped pyramids capped by a central conical tower. ...Ananda Temple is built in Burma. ...Fortifications for the town of Carcassonne (in France) are begun. ...Construction of the hilltown of San Gimignano, with 48 towers (13 survive), is begun.

c. 1100–1200. Iso-No-Zenji (fl. 12th century) performs dances wearing men's costumes. She will become known as the mother of Japanese drama.

British Isles & Western Europe

1112. Rebellion breaks out in eastern Normandy. Henry I imprisons Robert of Belesme (c. 1052–1134).

1114. January 7: Henry V marries Matilda (1102–1167), daughter of Henry I of England.

1119–1127. Charles the Good (1084–1127) reigns as count of Flanders.

1124. Henry V of Germany (and Holy Roman emperor) aids Henry I of England in his French campaign.

1125. May 23: Henry V (b. 1081) dies.

1125–1137. Lothair II (1075–1137) reigns as king of Germany and Holy Roman emperor.

1129–1155. Swerker I (c. 1100–1155) is king of Sweden.

1130–1133. Henry I gives a charter to London.

1132. Henry I grants charters to French towns to encourage commerce and manufacturing.

Mediterranean Basin

1113. Order of the Knights Hospitalers of St. John is founded in Jerusalem.

1113–1115. Pisa conquers Balearic Islands.

1115. Florence becomes a free republic.

1116. Henry V occupies Tuscany.

1118. Alfonso I (c. 1073–1134) of Aragon and Navarre takes Saragossa.

1118–1131. Baldwin II (c. 1090–1131) is king of Jerusalem.

1118–1143. John II Comnenus (1088–1143) is Byzantine emperor.

1122. Byzantines exterminate Patzinaks.

1124. Christians capture Tyre (in Lebanon).

1125. Almohades conquer Morocco.

1126. Venetian commercial privileges in Byzantine Empire renewed.

1126–1157. Alfonso VII (c. 1104–1157) is king of Castile and León.

1127–1146. Imadeddin Zengi (fl. 12th century) is ruler of Mosul (in Iraq).

1128–1130. Conrad reigns as king of Italy.

1128–1185. Afonso I (1109–1185) is the first king of Portugal.

1130. Anacletus II (?–1138) invests Roger II (1095–1154) with Sicily. . . . **December 25:** Roger II is crowned king.

1131–1143. Fulk of Anjou (1082–1143) is king of Jerusalem.

1133. Innocent II assigns Sardinia and half of Corsica to Pisa. The other half of Corsica is awarded to Genoa.

1134. September 7: Moors defeat and kill Alfonso I of Aragon at Fraga.

Africa, Asia & Pacific

1112–1167. Alaungsithu (fl. 12th century) reigns as king of Pagan.

c. 1113–1155. Suryavarman II (fl. 12th century) reigns as king of the Khmer empire (Cambodia).

1115. The state of Chin is established in northern China.

1123. The Jurchen (Chin dynasty) become suzerains of Korea.

1125. The Jurchen capture Beijing and end Liao dynasty.

1126–1129. Enforcement of strict Buddhist laws against killing animals causes unrest in Japan.

1131. Khmer (Cambodians) make Dai Viet a tributary state.

Americas

c. 1120. Third Pueblo period begins in southwestern part of North America. Apache settle in present-day southwestern United States.

This 12th-century mosaic portrays Roger II being crowned by Christ after Roger gained control of southern Italy in 1130.

c. 1130. Severe drought devastates Hopi in present-day northeastern Arizona.

Science, Invention & Technology

1118. Henricus (?–1162), Bishop of Greenland, produces a map depicting Vinland (northeastern North America).

1120. Degrees of latitude and longitude are first measured.

1121. Al-Khazini (fl. 12th century), an Arab, argues that the center of the earth is the source of gravity.

1124. Scots begin minting coins.

c. 1125. Chinese invent an iron-plated armored car as a defense against Mongol invaders. ...French build a tidal mill at the mouth of the Ardour River.

1128. English monks begin a program of swamp reclamation and agricultural reform. ...Arabs pass their technology for making smoking grenades to the Chinese. ...Chinese make the earliest known handguns.

Religion, Culture & Arts

1112. Synod of Vienne excommunicates Henry V.

1116. Pope Paschal II withdraws concessions to Henry V.

1120. Ari the Wise (fl. 12th century) writes the *Islandinbók*, the Icelandic saga.

1121. Synod of Soissons condemns Pierre Abélard's (1079–1144) philosophy.

1123. March: First Lateran Council confirms Worms Concordat and suppresses simony and marriage of priests.

1125–1135. Sculptor Gislebertus (fl. 12th century) decorates the whole of Autun Cathedral (France).

1126. French theologian Bernard of Clairvaux (1090–1153) writes *On the Love of God.*

1130–1143. Pope Innocent II (c. 1090–1143) is exiled from Rome by Roger II.

1132. Lothair conducts Pope Innocent II to Rome at Bernard of Clairvaux's instigation.

1134. The Pontifical University at Salamanca, Castile province, Spain, is established.

British Isles & Western Europe

1135. Henry I (b. 1068) dies and is succeeded as king of England by Stephen of Blois, his nephew (c. 1097–1154).

1136. February: By the Agreement of Durham, David I of Scotland acknowledges Stephen of Blois as king.

1137. Stephen of Blois launches a successful expedition against Geoffrey of Anjou (1113–1151). ...Louis VI (b. 1081) dies and is succeeded as king of France by Louis VII (1120–1180).

1138. March 7: Conrad III (1093–1152) is elected king of Germany. ...**August 22:** Stephen of Blois defeats David of Scotland at the battle of the Standard.

1139. Geoffrey of Anjou begins conquest of Normandy. ...**September 30:** Matilda lands at Arundel, and civil war breaks out.

1141. February 2: Stephen of Blois is captured at Lincoln. ...**March 3:** Matilda is proclaimed queen at Winchester. ...**December 25:** Stephen of Blois, exchanged for Robert of Gloucester, is crowned at Canterbury.

1147. Conrad III joins the Second Crusade.

1151. September 7: Geoffrey of Anjou (b. 1113) dies, and Henry (1133–1189) succeeds to Anjou and Touraine.

1152. Louis VII divorces Eleanor of Aquitaine (1122–1204). ...Henry of Anjou marries Eleanor and renews war against Stephen of Blois. ...Conrad III (b. 1093) dies. ...Frederick I Barbarossa (c. 1123–1190) becomes king of Germany and Holy Roman emperor.

Mediterranean Basin

1135. Alfonso VII of Castile assumes title of emperor of Castile.

1136–1137. Lothair launches second Italian expedition and conquers Apulia.

1137. Pisans sack Amalfi. ...Raymond of Antioch (fl. 12th century) becomes Byzantine vassal. ...John II defeats Armenians. ...**December 4:** Lothair (b. 1075) dies.

1139. Afonso I of Portugal becomes papal vassal. **July 25:** Portuguese defeat Moors at Alentejo.

1140. Navarre is made vassal of Aragon.

1143. Portugal is made a kingdom with papal consent. ...Roger II raids North African coast. ...Manuel I Comnenus (1122–1180) becomes Byzantine emperor and allies with Conrad III.

1144–1163. Baldwin III (1131–1162) is king of Jerusalem.

1146–1174. Nureddin (1118–1174) is sultan of Syria.

1147. Normans take Corfu and ransack Greek mainland. ...**October 25:** Afonso I of Portugal takes Lisbon.

1148. Raymond Berengar IV (c. 1110–1162) of Catalonia takes Tortosa. ...**July:** Normans subdue Tunis and Tripoli.

1149. Raymond Berengar IV takes Lerida (in Spain). ...Normans attack Byzantine Empire and lose Corfu.

1150–1153. Aragon extends its rule to all of Spain north of the Ebro River.

Africa, Asia & Pacific

▲ ***The great seal of Henry I, king of England.***

1143. Mongols turn back a Chinese military expedition.

c. 1150. Yusa finish work on the fortress of Kano (in West Africa). ...Sultan of Ghor, Alauddin Husain (fl. 12th century), destroys empire of Ghazna.

1151. Chinese forces use explosives in battle. ...Chinese retake Beijing from Mongols.

Americas

▲*This section of the 11th-century Bayeux Tapestry portrays Norman troops on horses preparing to fight Anglo-Saxon foot soldiers.*

1150. Hopi found Oraibi northeast of present-day Flagstaff, Arizona. (It is the oldest continuously occupied town in the United States.)

1150–1300. Point Peninsula culture (present-day New York State and lower Ontario) establishes villages and produces corn and perhaps other crops.

Science, Invention & Technology

c. 1135. Chinese build a military paddleboat, with 22 side paddle wheels (11 to a side) and a large stern wheel.

1136. A silver deposit is discovered at Freiburg, Saxony, Germany.

1137. A map of Sian in Shensi province, China, is produced on stone slabs. ...First windmills are built in England.

1140. A commercial trade route through the Alps is opened in southern Switzerland (present-day St. Gotthard Pass).

1143. China reorganizes its state hospital system.

1145. A bridge over the Danube at Ratisbon is completed.

1147. Normans attack Corinth and destroy its renowned glass manufacturing industry.

1148. Crusaders bring sugarcane from Syria to Cyprus and Sicily.

1149. Abu Mervan ibn Zuh (Avenzoar) (fl. 12th century), an Arab doctor, describes paralysis of the pharynx and other medical conditions in his treatise *Theisir (al-Taysir).*

c. 1150. Sword forging is a specialized craft in Milan, Italy, and Passau, Germany. ...Papermaking is introduced in Spain. ...Process of gold beating is invented at present-day Nuremberg, Germany. ...Chinese invent the "magnetic turtle," a turtle-shaped object balanced on a pivot that functions as a compass. ...A drainage system, complete with fish pond and herbarium, is installed at Canterbury Cathedral, England. ...Italians invent the stirrup crossbow.

Religion, Culture & Arts

1135. At the Council of Pisa, Bernard of Clairvaux successfully pleads the cause of Pope Innocent II.

1136. Pierre Abélard recounts his love for Héloïse in *Historia calamitatum mearum.*

1137–1144. The choir and west front of Saint-Denis Abbey are built by Abbé Suger (1081–1151).

1138–1161. Theobald (c. 1090–1161) is Archbishop of Canterbury.

1139. The Second Lateran Council ends schism. ...**July 22:** Pope Innocent II recognizes Norman kingdom in Sicily.

1141–1143. The Abbot of Cluny sponsors first Latin translation of the Koran.

1143. William of Malmesbury (b. c. 1090), author of *Gesta Pontificum Anglorum* and *Gesta Regum Anglorum*, dies.

1144. Stained-glass production begins at the Abbey of Saint-Denis (in France) under Abbé Suger.

1145–1153. Eugenius III (?–1153) is pope.

1147. Geoffrey of Monmouth (1100–1155) writes *Historia regum Britanniae.* It will provide source material for later stories about King Arthur.

1150. Construction of cathedral at Trondheim begins. ...University of Paris is founded.

British Isles & Western Europe

1153. David I of Scotland dies and is succeeded by his grandson, Malcolm IV (?–1165). ...In Treaty of Wallingford, English king Stephen recognizes Henry of Anjou as his successor.

1154. October 25: Stephen (b. c. 1097) dies. ...**December 19:** Henry of Anjou is crowned king of England, becoming Henry II.

1155. Pope Adrian IV (1100–1159) bestows Ireland on Henry II.

1157. Henry II leads successful expeditions against Owain (?–1170) and Malcolm IV, who cedes Northumberland, Cumberland and Westmorland.

1158. January 11: Frederick I makes Ladislaus II (?–1175) king of Bohemia.

1165. Great invasion of Wales by Henry II fails. ...**December 9:** Malcolm IV dies and is succeeded as king of Scotland by his brother, William the Lion (1143–1214).

1168. Frederick I reconciles Henry the Lion (c. 1130–1195) of Saxony and Albert I the Bear (1100–1170) of Brandenburg.

1169. Peace between Henry II of England and Louis VII of France. ...Norman nobles begin conquest of Ireland.

1173. Henry II's sons rebel against him in alliance with France and Scotland. ...Queen Eleanor is imprisoned.

1174. July 13: William the Lion is captured and pays homage to Henry II.

1175. In Treaty of Windsor, Rory O'Connor (1116–1198) acknowledges Henry II as lord of Ireland.

Mediterranean Basin

1153. Normans take Bona, Tunis. **March 23:** With Treaty of Constance, Frederick I (1125–1190) and Pope Eugenius III ally against Roger II and Arnold of Brescia (c. 1100–1155).

1154. Nureddin takes Damascus.

1154–1166. William I (c. 1130–1166) is king of Sicily.

1155. Arnold of Brescia (b. c. 1100) is hanged. ...Manuel I Comnenus attacks Normans in southern Italy.

1156. Normans take Brindisi. ...**September:** Hungary recognizes Byzantine overlordship.

1157. Castile and León are briefly separated after the death of Alfonso VII (b. c. 1104).

1158–1214. Alfonso VIII (1155–1214) is king of Castile.

1158. Arabs retake Tunisia.

1160. January: Frederick I captures Crema. ...Normans are expelled from North Africa.

1162. March: Frederick I destroys Milan and returns to Germany.

1162–1173. Amalric I (1140–1173) is king of Jerusalem.

1165. Byzantium allies with Venice against Frederick I.

1166. Frederick I leads fourth Italian expedition.

1166–1189. William II (?–1189) is king of Sicily.

1169. Nureddin of Damascus invades Egypt.

1169–1193. Saladin (1138–1193) rules in Damascus after taking it from Nureddin.

1173–1185. Baldwin IV (c. 1150–1185) is king of Jerusalem.

1174. Frederick I leads fifth Italian expedition. He buys Tuscany, Spoleto, Sardinia and Corsica from Guelph VI.

Africa, Asia & Pacific

1153–1186. Parakrama Bahu I (c. 1130–1186) reigns in Ceylon (present-day Sri Lanka).

c. 1156–1183. Taira family is paramount in Japan.

1158–1169. The caste system in Bengal (in northeast India and present-day Bangladesh) is reorganized.

1162. Genghis Khan (d. 1227) is born.

1167. Chinese government provides low-interest loans to the poor.

1170. First instance of a ritual warrior suicide is recorded in Japan.

1173–1210. Narapatisithu (c. 1160–1210) reigns as king of Pagan (in Burma).

Americas

Seal of Oxford University (c. 1300).

c. 1162. Mass human sacrifices are conducted in Toltec city of Teotenango.

c. 1168. Aztecs drift eastward into the Anahuac Valley of Mexico.

Science, Invention & Technology

1154. Al-Tifashi (fl. 12th century) writes a treatise on precious stones. ...Arab al-Idrisi (c. 1099–1154) mentions a noria, a water-raising wheel driven by the force of running water, built at Toledo, Spain.

1161. Chinese invent a teargas bomb composed of lime and sulfur.

1163. Council of Tours officially discourages dissection of human bodies.

1174. Monks at Engelburg, Switzerland, make wooden printing blocks.

Religion, Culture & Arts

1153. Bernard of Clairvaux (b. 1090), leading scholar of the Cistercian order, dies. ...Present-day Bucket Chicken House in Kaifeng, China, has its beginnings.

1154–1159. Pope Adrian IV renews quarrel with emperor.

1159–1181. Alexander III (c. 1110–1181) is pope.

1160. Celtic epic *Tristan et Iseult* appears. ...Benoît de Sainte Maure (fl. c. 1150) writes epic *Roman de Troie*.

1162–1170. Thomas à Becket (1118–1170) is Archbishop of Canterbury.

1165. Gautier d'Arras (1135–1198) writes the romance *Eracle*. ...Charlemagne is canonized.

1167–1168. Oxford University is founded.

1170. Alexander III establishes rules for canonization of saints. ...**July 22:** Henry II and Becket formally reconcile. ...**December 3:** Becket returns to Canterbury. ...**December 29:** Becket (b. 1118) is murdered by four Norman knights.

1172. Henry II is reconciled with papacy; right of appeal to Rome conceded.

1174. Choir of Canterbury Cathedral is built. ...Campanile of Pisa Cathedral (the "Leaning Tower of Pisa") is built .

1175. Ahmad al-Rifai (b. 1110), founder of the dervish order, dies.

British Isles & Western Europe

1176. Henry the Lion refuses to help Frederick I. **May 29:** Lombards defeat Frederick I at Legnano.

1177. Prince John is made lord of Ireland. ...Treaty of Ivry between Henry II and Louis VII.

1179. Grand Assize of Windsor checks feudal courts in favor of king's court.

1180. Henry the Lion is outlawed and loses his imperial fiefs. ...Louis VII (b. 1120) dies and is succeeded as king of France by Philip II Augustus (?–1223).

1181. Henry the Lion submits but keeps Brunswick. He is exiled for three years and goes to England.

1182–1202. Canute VI (1163–1202) is king of Denmark.

1183. June 11: Prince Henry, eldest son of Henry II, dies, ending the rebellion.

1185. Brothers Ivan (fl. 12th century) and Peter Asen (fl. 12th century) found second Bulgarian empire.

1186. Henry VI (1165–1197) marries Constance (1154–1198), heiress of Sicily, and assumes title of caesar.

1187. Richard (1157–1199) and John (1167–1216) rebel against their father, Henry II.

1188. August. Henry the Lion is exiled again. ...**November 18.** Richard allies with Philip II of France and pays homage to him for Aquitaine.

1189. Henry II loses Berry to Philip II. ...**July 6.** Henry II (b. 1133) dies and is succeeded by Richard I.... **December 5:** Richard I acknowledges independence of Scotland and sells Roxburgh and Berwick to William the Lion.

1190. June 10. Frederick I (b. c. 1123) drowns in river Saleph in Cilicia (in Turkey). ...**July:** Henry VI makes peace with Henry the Lion.

1191–1197. Henry VI is king of Germany and Holy Roman emperor.

1192. December 21: Richard I is captured by Leopold V (1157–1194), duke of Austria.

Mediterranean Basin

1176. Saladin conquers Syria.

1177. Henry II arbitrates between kings of Castile and Navarre.

1178. Henry II and Louis VII meet and arrange a Crusade.

1179. Venetian privileges in Eastern Empire are again confirmed.

1180–1183. Alexius II Comnenus (1168–1183) is Byzantine emperor.

1181. Crusade begins against Albigenses.

1183. Andronicus I Comnenus (1118–1185) becomes Byzantine emperor.

1184. Cyprus frees itself from Byzantium.

1185. Norman invasion of Byzantine Empire fails.

1185–1195. Isaac II Angelus (c. 1160–1204) is Byzantine emperor.

1186–1187. Guy of Lusignan (c. 1140–1194) is king of Jerusalem.

1187. July 4: Saladin defeats Christians at Hittin. ...**October 2:** Saladin takes Jerusalem.

1189. Florentines mint first silver florins. ...**May:** Frederick I sets out on Third Crusade. ...**November 18:** William II of Sicily dies.

1190. July 1: Richard I and Philip II start on the Third Crusade. **October 4:** Richard I storms Messina.

1191. April: Richard I conquers Cyprus and sells it to Templars. Expedition against Sicily fails. ...**July 12:** Crusaders take Acre.

1191–1192. Conrad of Montferrat (?–1192) is king of Jerusalem.

Africa, Asia & Pacific

1177–1181. Champa invades Khmer (Cambodia) and occupies capital at Angkor.

1180. Minamoto uprisings challenge Taira family power in Japan.

1183. Minamotos drive Tairas out of Kyoto.

1184–1212. Tamara (c. 1160–1212) reigns as queen of Georgia.

1185. Muhammad of Ghor (?–1206) attacks the Rajput states on the Ganges plain (in India). ...Minamoto clan completes its rise to power in Japan.

1187. Muhammad of Ghor conquers the Punjab.

1189. Genghis Khan becomes leader of the Mongols.

c. 1190. Kanem empire (in north central Africa) controls trade routes of the Sahara.

1191. Tea reaches Japan from China.

Americas

c. 1180. Nukleet culture is established along the western present-day Alaskan coast.

▲ ***A depiction of Genghis Khan (top left) with his wives and sons.***

c. 1190. Chimú culture is established in northern Peru.

Science, Invention & Technology

1176–1209. The stone version of the London Bridge is built over the Thames River. (It will stand until 1832.)

1177–1185. Pont St. Bénézet, the famous Pont d'Avignon (in France), is built by the guild of bridge builders.

1179. First section of Tuscany's Naviglio Grand Canal is opened.

c. 1180. Chinese begin developing rockets. ...A Cantonese robber tells of his escape from the law by safely parachuting from a tower using a large umbrella with the handle removed. ...A windmill is built at France's Abbey of St. Sauviére de Vicomte Normandy. ...First windmills with vertical sails are used in Normandy and France.

1184. Paris, France, begins paving its streets.

c. 1185. Vertical windmills for irrigation are built in England.

1187. Englishman Alexander Neckam describes two types of early compasses—a dry compass and a floating compass.

1189. A paper mill is built at Herault, France.

c. 1190. Paris begins laying lead pipes for first municipal water system in post-medieval Europe. ...Mining of coal begins near Liége, Belgium. The coal will be used to fuel the city's forges.

Religion, Culture & Arts

1176. Walter Map (c. 1140–1210) arranges the Arthurian legends in their familiar form. ...**November:** Preliminary peace of Anagni is arranged between Emperor Frederick I and Pope Alexander III.

1179. March: Third Lateran Council establishes procedures for elections of popes.

1181–1185. Lucius III (c. 1110–1185) is pope.

1182. Jews are expelled from France. ...St. Francis of Assisi (d. 1226) is born.

1184. Negotiations between Frederick I and Pope Lucius III at Verona fail.

1185. Quarrel between Frederick I and Pope Lucius III is renewed.

1186–1333. Kamakura period in Japan is marked by restoration of 8th century Buddhist monasteries of Nara.

c. 1190. Construction begins on Church of the Holy Apostles in Cologne.

1191–1204. First extant version of the *Nibelungenlied* is written. It is based on Germanic legends that probably originated in the 6th century.

British Isles & Western Europe

1193. Philip II attacks Normandy. ...**February 14:** Richard I surrenders to Henry VI and is imprisoned at Trifels.

1194. February 3: Richard I is released. ...**July 22:** Richard I defeats Philip at Fréteval.

1195. August 6: Henry the Lion (b. c. 1130) dies.

1196. April: Henry VI attempts to make the empire hereditary.

1197. A wall is constructed around the city of Vienna, Austria. ...**September 28:** Henry VI (b. 1165) dies.

1198. Otto IV of Brunswick (c. 1174–1218) and Philip of Swabia (1178–1208) both lay claim to Holy Roman Empire.

1199. Richard I dies and is succeeded as king of England by his brother, John.

1200. May 22: The Peace of Le Goulet between John of England and Philip II of France is signed.

1201. Rebellion in Poitou against John is supported by Philip II.

1202. War breaks out between John and Philip II. ...First trial of a peer (King John) is held in France.

1203. April 3: John of England murders Arthur of Brittany.

1204. Philip II conquers Normandy, Maine, Anjou and Touraine; Poitou submits to Philip II; Gascony remains faithful to John of England.

1206. July 27: Philip of Swabia defeats Otto IV at Wassenberg.

1208. Llywelyn (1173–1240) seizes Powys (Wales). ...**June 21:** Philip of Swabia (b. 1178) is murdered at Bamberg.

Mediterranean Basin

1193. March 4: Saladin (b. 1138) dies.

1194. December 25: Henry VI is crowned king of Sicily after conquering it.

1195. Armenia and Cyprus recognise Henry VI as their overlord.

1195–1203. Alexius III Angelus (?–1210) is Byzantine emperor.

1196–1213. Peter II (1174–1213) is king of Aragon.

1197. Henry VI's Crusaders take Beirut and put down a rebellion in Sicily.

1198. Venetian merchants are freed from customs duties in Byzantine Empire. ...**May 17:** Frederick II (1194–1250) is crowned king of Sicily under guardianship of Pope Innocent III (1161–1216).

c. 1200. Population of Constantinople approaches 1 million.

1202–1204. Fourth Crusade, against Constantinople, is directed by Venice.

1204. Crusaders take Constantinople and establish Latin empire.

1204–1222. Theodore I Lascaris (1175–1222) is Byzantine emperor.

1208. Theodore I Lascaris founds empire of Nicaea.

Africa, Asia & Pacific

1194. Muhammad of Ghor captures Kana Uj (in north India) and abolishes it as a kingdom.

1196. Muhammad of Ghor conquers Gwalior and Gujarat.

1197. Muhammad of Ghor takes Anhilwara.

1199. Pala dynasty in Bengal (in northeast India and Bangladesh) ends.

c. 1200. Hawaii is settled by Polynesians from Tahiti and the Marquesas Islands to the south.

1203. Muhammad of Ghor completes subjection of upper India. ...Soumangouroun conquers Ghana (in West Africa).

1204. Sultanates of Pate and Vumba are established in East Africa. ...Southern Sung campaign in northern China founders.

1206. March: Muhammad of Ghor is murdered.

1206–1227. Genghis Khan rules as emperor of the Mongols.

Americas

▲ ***A detailed image from one of the ornaments on an Aztec sacrificial stone.***

c. 1200. Aztecs develop human sacrifice as part of their religious ritual. ...Anasazi people of western North America begin construction of cliff-side dwellings as a defense against marauding Athapascans. ...Salt trade is dominated by the Maya. ...Tula falls to Chichimecs from the north. ...North American natives develop the longhouse. ...Salado culture takes on southern Anasazi character.

c. 1200–1300. Chan Chan, capital of the Chimú empire, is built over 15 square kilometers and divided into ten compounds. ...Paramonga, a massive brick fortress with corner bastions, is built by the Chimú in Peru. ...Mississippian influence (hamlets, support camps, work stations) spreads to present-day Illinois.

c. 1200–1400. Elaborate murals decorate the walls of Hopi and Zuni kivas (circular underground structures) in present-day southwestern United States. ...Promontory Indians settle in northern and central Utah. ...Crystal River culture (in lower Mississippi River area) farms and produces painted pottery.

c. 1200–1500. Mississippian culture (in present-day Tennessee) builds temple mounds and incised burial objects (shells and copper cutouts). ...Burial mounds in present-day Ohio are constructed in the shape of serpents for ceremonial functions.

Science, Invention & Technology

1193. English import indigo and brazil wood from India for use in dyeing.

1194. Spitsbergen, an island group north of mainland Norway, is discovered by Norsemen.

c. 1200. Europe adopts Arabic numerals. ...Wooden undershoes called pattens are worn in the muddy streets of Europe. ...European peasants exist on a steady diet of millet porridge and oatmeal. ...Floating boat mills are used in France and northern Italy....European potters develop the kickwheel, which frees both hands for shaping the clay. ...Koreans adopt movable type. ...Chinese propel arrows with black powder rockets. ...Italians build galleys with stern post rudders. ...Glass manufacturing is revived in England. ...Great Zimbabwe (Shona for "house of stone") is built as the capital of the Shona nation of south central Africa. ...Blast furnaces of the Harz Mountains of southern Germany are fueled by a form of gunpowder. ...Augsburg, Germany, develops a flourishing brewing industry. ...Wine production spreads into the Oder district of Germany. ...The screw press begins to replace the winch press in Europe. ...Incendiary warfare is developed by the Muslims, who use oil tapped from natural seepage combined with technology gained from the Greeks.

1206. Arab engineer Ismaeel al-Jazari (1181–1224) compiles *The Book of Knowledge of Ingenious Mechanical Devices*. It includes descriptions of clocks and automata.

Religion, Culture & Arts

1193. Zen order in Japan is founded.

1194. Earliest of the stained-glass windows in Chartres Cathedral are installed.

1196–1199. Château Gaillard in Les Andelys, France, is built.

1198. Averroës (b. 1126), Spanish-born Islamic philosopher, dies.

1198–1216. Innocent III (1161–1216) is pope.

c. 1200. Umar ibn al-Farid (1181–1235), regarded as among the greatest of Arab mystical poets, is active. ...The Sufi mystic poet Farid od-Din Attar (1142–1220) is active. ...Decorative gargoyles are added to European cathedrals to drain water off the immense roofs. ..."Classical period," during which Hindu styles dominated Indian art, ends. ...Chand Bardai (fl. 13th century) writes Hindi poem *Prithi Raj Raso*, celebrating the life of the Rajput (India) chief Prithi Raj. ...Islam spreads throughout India. ...Cambridge University is founded.

1203–1278. Lerida Cathedral is built in Spain.

1204. December 13: Moses ben Maimon (b. 1135) (Maimonides), Spanish-born Jewish philosopher, dies.

1206. *Shinkokinshu*, a collection of Japanese poems, is compiled on the order of Emperor Gotoba. ...**December:** Stephen Langton (c. 1155–1228) is elected archbishop of Canterbury.

1208. March 23: England and Wales are laid under interdict by Pope Innocent III.

British Isles & Western Europe

1209. Simon IV de Montfort-l'Amaury (c. 1160–1218) overruns Languedoc. ...John invades Scotland. ...Peace between John and William the Lion. ...Otto IV (1175–1218) is crowned emperor at Rome after the death of Philip of Swabia.

1211. May: War breaks out between John and Llywelyn.

1212. December 5: Frederick II is elected German king.

1213. Truce between John and Llywelyn is established. ...**August 4:** Council of St. Albans, precursor of British Parliament, meets. ...**September 28:** Queen Gertrude of Hungary is murdered by Magyar magnates.

1214. Philip II defeats Otto IV and the English at Bouvines. English barons make truce with Philip II. ...William the Lion (b. 1143) of Scotland dies and is succeeded by Alexander II (1198–1249).

1215. January 8: Council of Montpellier elects Simon de Montfort lord of Languedoc. John cedes Poitou, Anjou and Brittany to France, keeping Guienne and Gascony. ...**June 19:** John issues Magna Carta at Runnymede, granting feudal rights to England's barons. ...**August 24:** Pope Innocent III annuls Magna Carta in favor of John. ...**October:** Barons begin civil war.

1216. Prince Louis of France enters London. ...John dies at Newark. ...**October 28:** Henry III (1207–1272) is crowned king of England at Gloucester.

1217. May 20: French are defeated at Lincoln. ...**August 24:** French are defeated off Sandwich. ...**September 11:** Under Treaty of Lambeth, French leave England. ...**September 23:** Magna Carta is re-issued at Merton.

1218. Newgate Prison in London opens. ...**March:** Peace of Worcester between Henry III and Wales is signed. ...**May 19:** Otto IV (b. c. 1174) dies.

1220. November 22: Frederick II is crowned emperor at Rome.

1221–1288. Henry the Illustrious (?–1288) is margrave of Meissen (in Germany).

Mediterranean Basin

1209. Albigensian Crusade begins in southern France.

1210. Peter II (1174–1213) of Aragon rekindles war in Spain.

1212. Venice conquers Candia on Crete. ...**July 16:** Kings of Castile, Aragon, and Navarre defeat Moors at Navas de Tolosa.

1213. September 12: Albigenses are decisively defeated at Muret, but Peter II (b. 1174) of Aragon is killed.

1213–1276. James I (c. 1200–1276) is king of Aragon.

1214. Frederick II invests Wittelsbachs with a palatinate.

1217–1221. Crusade against Egypt fails.

1217–1252. Ferdinand III (c. 1200–1252) is king of Castile.

1218. Catalonia establishes a Cortes (a representative assembly).

Africa, Asia & Pacific

1209. Genghis Khan subdues Khitans.

1210–1234. Nadoungmya (c. 1190–1234) reigns as king of Pagan (in Burma).

1211–1215. Genghis Khan invades China.

1211–1236. Iltutmish (?–c. 1236) rules as sultan of Delhi.

1213. Genghis Khan destroys 100,000-strong Chinese army.

1214. Genghis Khan takes Beijing.

1215. South Indians invade Ceylon (present-day Sri Lanka). ...Thai migrants found Mogaung kingdom in northern Burma.

1217. Genghis Khan conquers Manchuria and Korea.

1218–1224. Genghis Khan conquers Khwarazm, Transoxiana and Samarkand.

1219. Genghis Khan captures Bukhara and advances into Persia. ...Hojo family is paramount in Japan.

c. 1220. Damdam invades Ethiopia and Nubia. ...Indraditya (fl. 13th century) becomes first Thai ruler of Sukhotai (in Siam) dynasty.

1221. Genghis Khan invades sultanate of Delhi and plunders Samarkand.

Americas

c. 1210. Toltecs abandon Chichén Itzá.

c. 1220. Matlazincas settle in Teotenango.

Science, Invention & Technology

1212. Tofu, made from bean curd, is introduced to Japan from China. ...London authorities make tile a compulsory roofing material as a fire safety measure.

A Chinese drawing of a mounted archer in the Mongol calvary of the 13th century.

1217. Crescent rolls are first baked in Vienna for departing Crusaders.

1220. First official soccer match is played between the towns of Derby and Chester in England. ...Catalan carpenters add the plane to their tool chests.

Religion, Culture & Arts

1209. Francis of Assisi issues first rule for his brotherhood.

1210. November 18: Pope Innocent III excommunicates Otto IV.

1211. Construction begins on Rheims Cathedral, the coronation church of France.

1212. Karl Jónsson, the Icelandic saga writer, author of the first part of *Sverris saga*, dies.

1213. Philip II submits to Pope Innocent III in his matrimonial dispute. ... **May 15:** John submits to Pope Innocent III, making England and Ireland papal fiefs.

1215. November: Fourth Lateran Council establishes doctrine of transubstantiation, regulates auricular confession and inquisition, and prohibits trial by ordeal.

1216–1227. Honorius III (c. 1170–1227) is pope.

1217. Dominicans (Black Friars) arrive in England. ...University of Salamanca, Spain, is established.

1220. Notre Dame Cathedral in Paris is completed according to the plan of 1163.

1220–1288. Amiens Cathedral in France is built with refinement of the high Gothic style started at Chartres.

British Isles & Western Europe

1223. Mongols invade Russia. ...**April:** Pope Honorius III declares Henry III competent to rule. ...**July 14:** Philip II Augustus (b. 1165) of France dies and is succeeded by Louis VIII (1187–1226).

1224. France declares war on England. Louis VIII conquers Poitou.

1225. February 25: The Magna Carta is reissued for the third time. This is the lasting form. ...**March:** English secure Gascony.

1226. Frederick II authorizes Teutonic Order to conquer Prussia. ...**November:** Louis VIII (b. 1187) dies and is succeeded as king of France by Louis IX (1214–1270).

1227. Henry III declares himself of age. ...A truce between France and England is declared. ...**July 22:** Valdemar (fl. 13th century) is defeated by Germans at Bornhöved.

1229. Treaty of Meaux brings district between Rhône and Narbonne under French crown.

1230. Campaign of Henry III in France. ...Ferdinand III (c. 1201–1252) unites León and Castile.

1231. England, France and Brittany agree on a three-year truce.

1234. Theobald of Champagne (?–1161) cedes Chartres, Blois and Sancerre to French crown.

1235. Rebellion of Henry VII (1211–1242), son of Frederick II, is subdued, and Henry is imprisoned until his death.

1236. Alexander Nevsky (c. 1210–1263) rules as grand duke of Novgorod. ...**April 25:** Louis IX comes of age.

1237. Mongols conquer Russia and occupy Muscovy (Moscow). ...**February:** Conrad IV (1228–1254) is elected king of Germany.

Mediterranean Basin

1223–1245. Sancho II (c. 1200–1245) is king of Portugal.

1224. Byzantine emperor John III Vatatzes (1193–1254) of Nicaea expels Latins from Asia Minor.

1226. Frederick II captures Ancona and Spoleto.

1228. Frederick II lands at Acre. ...Civil war between Saladin's heirs erupts.

1229. February 18: Treaty between Frederick II and the sultan of Egypt. ...**March 18:** Frederick II declares himself king of Jerusalem. ...**June 10:** Frederick II defeats papal troops.

1230. Frederick II makes peace with Pope Gregory IX at San Germano, and is absolved from excommunication.

1231–1288. Erthogrul (?–1299) reigns as first Ottoman sultan and converts to Islam.

1232–1272. Muhammad I (c. 1215–1272) founds Nasrid dynasty at Granada, Spain.

1235. Frederick II declares war on Lombard League.

1236. June 29: Ferdinand III of Castile and León conquers Córdoba.

1237. November 27: Frederick II defeats Lombard League at Cortenuova, Italy.

1237–1238. James I of Aragon annexes Valencia and Murcia.

Africa, Asia & Pacific

1223. Thais establish kingdom of Muong Nai.

c. 1224. Trading center of Walata (in West Africa) is established.

c. 1225. Khwarazm rulers regain control of Shiraz and other areas in Persia lost to Mongols. ...Great fire consumes many temples in Pagan (in Burma).

1226–1252. Jaya Paramesvaravarman (c. 1200–1252) reigns as king of Champa (present-day southern Vietnam).

1227. Genghis Khan destroys Hsi-Hsia state in northern China. ...Genghis Khan (b. 1162) dies. ...**August:** Ughetai (?–1241) succeeds Genghis Khan as emperor of Mongols.

1228. Mongols destroy Khwarazm army near Isfahan (in Persia).

1229. Ughetai is invested as great khan at Karakorum. ...Mongols raid India and gain control of western Punjab.

1231. Mongols subdue northern Persia, Iraq and Armenia.

1232. Mongols destroy 150,000-strong Chinese army at Kunchow.

1233. Southern Sung dynasty strikes an alliance with the Mongols.

1234–1250. Kyaswan (c. 1200–1254) reigns as king of Pagan (in Burma).

c. 1235. Iltutmish subdues Bengal and takes Malwa (in central India) and Sind. ...Malinke (Mandingo) leader Sundiata (fl. 13th century) founds Mali empire.

1237. Rulers of Kanem send a trading embassy to Tunis. ...Seljuk empire breaks up into a series of lesser states.

Americas	Science, Invention & Technology	Religion, Culture & Arts
		1222. Padua University in Italy is founded.
		1224. The Arab geographical encyclopedia *Mu'jam ul-Buldam* appears.
c. 1225. Mayapan, a new Mayan capital, is established in the Yucatán.	**1225.** Jordanus Nemorarius (fl. 13th century) establishes the law of the lever, the law of movement and other maxims. ...Manufacture of cotton fabric begins in Spain.	**1225.** Guillaume de Lorris (fl. 1230) writes *Roman de la Rose*.
		1226. October 3: Francis of Assisi (b. 1182) dies.
		1226–1270. Paris becomes a major center of painting and book illustration.
	1227. Porcelain industry is introduced to Japan from China.	**1227.** Pope Gregory IX (c. 1143–1241) excommunicates Frederick II.
	1228. Westphalia province in Germany becomes an important iron production area.	**1228. July 16:** Francis of Assisi is canonized.
		1229. Toulouse University is founded in France.
c. 1230. The Quiché, a Mayan warrior group, enter the highlands of present-day Guatemala from eastern lowlands.		
	1233. Coal production begins at Newcastle-upon-Tyne in northern England.	**1233.** Penitentiary movement (Great Hallelujah) in northern Italy begins.
		1234. Crusade against peasants in Stedingen near Bremen, Germany, begins.
	1235. Salerno Medical School begins the dissection of human cadavers for the study of anatomy.	**1235.** Umar ibn al-Farid (b. c. 1181), Arabian poet, dies.
	1236. English begin using lead piping in the distribution of their water supply. ...Friar Theodoric (fl. 13th century) of Lucca introduces narcotics as anesthetics.	
	1237. Distillation of alcoholic beverages is introduced to Asia from Europe by the Mongols.	

▲ ***Holy Roman Emperor Frederick II, portrayed in this 13th-century illumination, was devoted to the sport of falconry.***

British Isles & Western Europe

1241. Mongols invade present-day Poland and Hungary. ...**April 9:** Mongols defeat Germans at Liegnitz, Silesia.

1242. March–July: Campaign of Henry III in Poitou fails. He is defeated at Taillebourg and Saintes.

1243. April 7: England and France begin five-year truce. ...**September:** Henry II resigns claims to Poitou and cedes Isle of Rhé to France.

1245. July 17: Pope Innocent IV (c. 1200–1254) declares Frederick II and Conrad IV dethroned at Lyons Council.

1249. England and France renew truce.

1249–1286. Alexander III (1241–1286) is king of Scotland, succeeding his father, Alexander II (b. 1198).

1250. Gascony rebels against Simon de Montfort (1208–1265), the earl of Leicester and son of Simon IV de Montfort-l'Amaury. ...**December 13:** Frederick II (b. 1194) dies.

1251. May: Simon de Montfort subdues Gascony.

1253. Simon de Montfort secures Gascony for England. ...Anglo-French truce is renewed.

1253–1278. Otakar II (1230–1278) is king of Bohemia.

Mediterranean Basin

1238. Enzio (fl. 13th century), Frederick II's son, is made king of Sardinia. ...Christian kingdom is established in Granada, Spain.

1239. Mongols sack Ani, the capital of Armenia.

1244. Khwarazm Turks take Jerusalem from Crusaders. Persecution of Albigenses ends.

1245. Innocent IV declares Sancho II of Portugal dethroned and his brother Afonso III (1210–1279) his successor.

1246. John III Vatatzes of Nicaea conquers Salonika. ...Christian forces take Jaen in Spain.

1247. Georgia becomes Persian vassalage.

1248. Genoese take Greek island of Rhodes. ...Lombards defeat Frederick II at Parma. ...**November 22:** Ferdinand III of Castile conquers Seville.

1249. June 4: Louis IX of France invades Saracen, Egypt.

1250. Northern and central Italian cities enjoy economic boom. ...Saracens capture Louis IX, who restores Damietta (Egypt) to them. ...Mameluke rule in Egypt begins, after murder of the last Ayyubid.

1251. Afonso III of Portugal conquers Algarve from Moors.

1252–1284. Alfonso X (1221–1284), the Wise, is king of Castile and León.

1253. Pope Innocent IV offers Sicily to Richard (1209–1272) of Cornwall, who refuses.

Africa, Asia & Pacific

1238. Mogadishu (in Somalia) flourishes as a trading center. ...Mongols conquer Armenia.

1240. Empire of Ghana (in West Africa) is absorbed into Mali.

1241. Ughetai, khan of Mongols, dies.

1241–1242. Mongols take Lahore, ransack it and raid Sind (in northwest India).

1243. Mongols elect Guyuk (fl. 13th century) Great Khan. Mongols enter Seljuk lands and rout the Seljuks at Erzinjan.

1245–1389. Kurt dynasty reigns in Herat (in Afghanistan).

1246–1248. Mongols establish embassy in Tibet.

1246–1266. Nasiruddin Mahmud (c. 1210–1266) rules as sultan of Delhi.

1248–1268. Visnuvardhana (fl. 13th century) rules in Java.

1250. Maravi (Malawi) empire is established in southeastern Africa.

1250–1254. Uzana (c. 1230–1254) reigns as king of Burma.

1251–1259. Mongke (fl. 13th century) rules as Great Khan of the Mongols.

1252. Kublai Khan (1215–1294) attacks China through Szechwan and Yunnan.

1252–1258. Mongols advance south to Annamese frontier (in Vietnam).

1253. Ahom Shans establish a kingdom that becomes Assam (in northeast India). ...Kublai Khan takes eastern Tibet. ...Thais seize territory of Khmer to establish kingdom of Sukhotai (in Siam).

Americas

c.1240. Economy in northwestern Mexico is overextended and stagnates.

▲ *This image from the late 13th century depicts Kublai Khan on a hunting expedition.*

c. 1250. Anasazi build Sun Temple in Mesa Verde in present-day southwestern Colorado. ...Owasco culture in present-day New York, Vermont, New Jersey and Pennyslvania establishes semisedentary populations farming corn and beans. ...Shungopovi and Mishongnovi are founded by Tewa Indians and Hopi.

Science, Invention & Technology

c. 1240. Production of scythes becomes an important industry in Styria (in Austria).

c. 1241. Hanseatic League introduces the use of rudders and bowsprits in ships.

1242. Englishman Roger Bacon (c. 1214–1294) writes a formula for the manufacture of black powder.

c. 1250. Crusaders use two-masted vessels with lateen sails to cross the eastern Mediterranean Sea. ...Japanese use crude bombs and grenades. ...Chinese use a horizontal warping reel for making silk thread. ...Spinning wheel is introduced to Europe. It is opposed by the hand spinners' guilds. ...The writing quill and ink are invented in Europe. ...French invent a water-powered sawing machine. ...Glass mirrors are reintroduced to Europe.

1252. Florence coins first golden florins.

1253. Alfonso X the Wise, king of León and Castile, directs the production of astronomical tables. ...First linen is manufactured in England.

Religion, Culture & Arts

1240. Siena University in Italy is established. ...Castel del Monte (in Italy), with an octagonal plan and towers, is built as hunting lodge for Frederick II.

1243–1254. Innocent IV (c. 1200–1254) is pope.

1243–1248. St. Chapelle, designed to house relics brought from the Holy Land, is built in Paris.

1248. Cologne Cathedral introduces the French high Gothic style to Germany on a grand scale. ...The University of Piacenza in Italy is established.

c. 1250. Indians of what will become known as the Little Colorado Valley use lead glaze to decorate pottery in black, green, brown and purple. ...Mu Ch'i (fl. 13th century), a leading Chinese artist in the "ink-splash" style, flourishes. ...*The Harrowing of Hell*, earliest extant English play, is written and performed. ...Scandinavians use paint and gilding to brighten the interiors of their buildings.

1253. Sorbonne theological college is established at the University of Paris.

British Isles & Western Europe

1254. Treaty between Henry III of England and Alfonso X of León and Castile.

1256. January 28: William of Holland (b. 1228) is killed in skirmish against rebellious Frisians.

1257. January 13: Richard of Cornwall is elected king of the Romans. **May 17:** Richard of Cornwall is crowned at Aix-la-Chapelle.

1258. June 11: English barons, headed by Simon de Montfort, extort Provisions of Oxford (Mise of Amiens) from Henry III. The Provisions of Oxford call for a committee for political and economic affairs, three sessions of Parliaments every year, and for the expulsion of aliens from office.

1259. Provisions of Westminster complete the reforms promised in Provisions of Oxford.

1260. July 12: Otakar II (1230–1278) of Bohemia defeats Hungarians at Croissenbrunn.

1261. Pope Alexander IV (1191–1261) frees Henry III from Provisions of Oxford and Provisions of Westminster.

1262. Otakar II recognizes King Richard and is invested with Austria and Styria.

1263. October 2: Scots defeat and kill Haakon IV (b. 1204) of Norway at Largs. Norway cedes Hebrides.

1264. January 23: Louis IX arbitrates between Henry III and barons and annuls Provisions of Oxford. ...**May 14:** Simon de Montfort defeats Henry III at Lewes, England.

1265. January 20: Parliament, representing shires, cities and boroughs, is summoned by Simon de Montfort. ...**August 4:** Prince Edward (1239–1307) defeats Simon de Montfort (b. 1208), who is killed, at Evesham, England.

1266. In Treaty of Perth, Norway cedes Isle of Man to Scotland.

1267. September 29: Treaty of Shrewsbury (or Montgomery) between Henry III and Llywelyn is signed. Llywelyn is recognized as Prince of Wales.

Mediterranean Basin

1254. December 2: Manfred (c. 1232–1266), illegitimate son of Frederick II, keeps Sicily through his victory at Foggia.

1254–1258. Theodore II Lascaris (1222–1258) is Byzantine emperor.

1258. Manfred is crowned king of Sicily at Palermo. ...Pope Alexander IV cancels grant of Sicily to Prince Edmund (1245–1296). ...John IV Lascaris (1250–1261) is Byzantine emperor. ...**January 17:** Mongols take Baghdad and overthrow Caliphate. ...**May 11:** Treaty of Corbeil between Louis IX and James of Aragon (1208–1276) establishes Pyrenees frontier.

1259–1282. Michael VIII Palaeologus (1224–1282) is Nicaean emperor of Byzantium. For the first two years of his reign he rules with John IV Lascaris.

1260. September 3: Kotuz (fl. 13th century), sultan of Egypt, compels Mongols to retreat behind Euphrates. ...**September 4:** Florentine Ghibellines defeat Guelphs at Montaperti.

1260–1287. Baybars I (1223–1277) is Mameluke sultan of Egypt after assassinating Kotuz.

1264. Venetians defeat Genoese off Trapani. ...Pisa and Tunis negotiate a commercial treaty.

1265. June 21: Charles of Anjou (1226–1285) invested with Naples and Sicily by Pope Clement IV (?–1268).

1266. Febuary 26. Manfred (b. c. 1232) is defeated and killed by Charles of Anjou at Benevento.

1267. Portuguese annex Algarve.

Africa, Asia & Pacific

1254–1287. Narathihapat (c. 1220–1287) reigns as king of Pagan (in Burma).

1256. Mongols seize assassin strongholds in western Asia.

1257. Mongols subdue Yunnan (Sung China).

1258. Mongols under Hulagu Khan (1217–1265) besiege Baghdad. **February 10:** Baghdad surrenders; Mongols slaughter the populace and burn the city. ...Mongols sack Hanoi in Tonkin (in present-day northern Vietnam).

1260. Mongols proclaim Kublai Khan supreme Mongol khan. ...**September 3:** Mamelukes check Mongol forces at Ain Jaluta in Syria.

1260–1294. Kublai Khan founds Mongol Yüan dynasty in China.

1260–1304. Il-Khans of Persia rule from the Caucasus to the Indian Ocean, with their capital at Tabriz.

1263. Ceylon (present-day Sri Lanka) acknowledges Pandyans (in southern India) as suzerains.

1265. Mongols mount offensive toward Persia but are checked near Herat. ...Niccoló and Maffeo Polo (fl. 13th century), father and uncle, respectively, of Marco Polo (1254–1324), are first Europeans to reach China.

1266–1287. Balban (?–1287) rules as sultan of Delhi.

1266. July 23: Mameluke sultan of Egypt Baybars I captures Safad and executes 2,000 Knights Templar in violation of surrender pledge.

Americas	Science, Invention & Technology	Religion, Culture & Arts

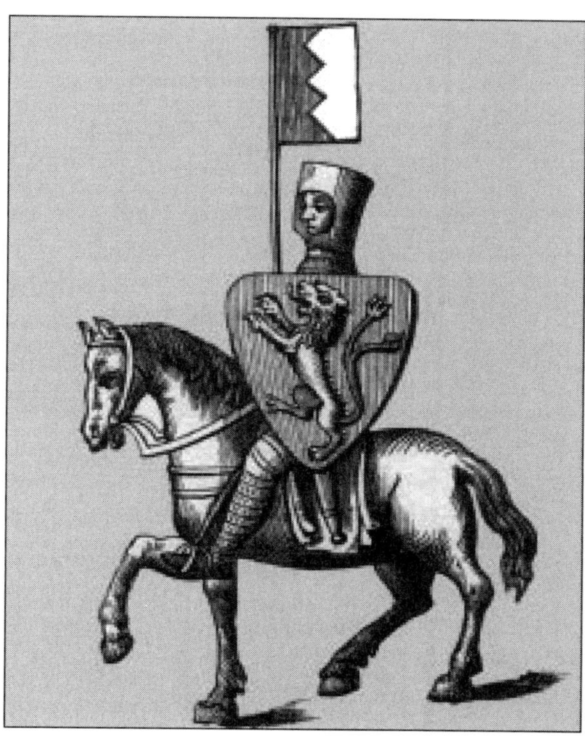

◄ ***This depiction of Simon de Montfort, earl of Leicester, is based on a stained-glass window in Chartres Cathedral (c. 1231).***

1257. Persian poet Saadi (c.1184–1292) writes *The Fruit Garden.*

1259. Matthew Paris (b. c. 1200), English chronicler, dies.

c. 1260. Pueblo culture expands into Verde Valley, Tonto Basin, upper Salt River Basin and present-day southeastern Arizona.

c. 1265. Plains Indians begin to develop large villages and farming.

c. 1260. English open the first toll roads.

1264. English bakers begin to identify their bread and other goods with bakers' marks, a precursor of trademarks.

c. 1266. On the death of Manfred, king of Sicily, the silk industry moves to Lucca, which becomes leading center of silk weaving in Italy.

1260. *Ars antiqua* (polyphony) is at its zenith in France, especially in Paris. ...**October 24:** Chartres Cathedral is consecrated.

1260–1261. First Flagellant movements in northern Italy and southern Germany begin.

1263. Pope Urban IV (c. 1200–1264) issues *Qui celum* on the right of electing the German king.

1264. Thomas Aquinas (1224–1274) writes poems on the Eucharist. ... Merton College, Oxford, is founded.

1266. Roger Bacon writes *Opus Maius.* ...Sanjusangendo Temple is built in Kyoto (in Japan).

1267. Brunetto Latini (1220–1294) completes *Trésor* and *Tesoretto.*

British Isles & Western Europe

1270. August 25: Louis IX (b. 1214) dies and is succeeded as king of France by Philip III (1245–1285).

1271. Toulouse and Poitou are united to French crown.

1272. Henry III (b. 1207) dies and is succeeded as king of England by Edward I (1239–1307).

1273. October 1: Rudolf I, count of Habsburg, is elected king of Germany and Holy Roman emperor.

1276. November: First Welsh War begins. ...**November 21:** Otakar II of Bohemia submits to Rudolf I and keeps only Bohemia and Moravia.

1277. Treaty of Conway reduces Llywelyn's power.

1278. August 26: Otakar II is defeated and killed by Rudolf I at Dürnkrut, Marchfeld.

1279. Edward I seizes Ponthieu. ...**May 23:** Philip III recognizes English claims to Ponthieu and Agenais.

1280–1299. Erik II Magnusson (1268–1299) is king of Norway.

1282. Second Welsh War begins. ...**December 27:** Rudolf I invests his sons, Albert (c. 1255–1308) and Rudolf (1271–1307), with Austria, Styria, and Carniola.

1283. Teutonic Order completes subjection of Prussia.

1284. Statute of Wales, issued at Rhuddlan, establishes English county administration.

1285. October 5: Philip III (b. 1245) dies and is succeeded as king of France by Philip IV the Fair (?–1314)

1286. Margaret (1283–1290), "Maid of Norway," becomes queen of Scots under six guardians.

Mediterranean Basin

1268. Conradin (b. 1252) is defeated by Charles of Anjou at Tagliacozzo and is beheaded at Naples.

1270. Louis IX (b. 1214) leads Seventh Crusade (and last) to Tunis, where he dies.

1271. Charles of Anjou conquers Albania.

1275. Ghilbellines defeat Charles of Anjou and drive him from the Piedmont.

1276–1285. Peter III (1239–1285) is king of Aragon.

1278. French counts of Foix recognize Pyrenean Andorra as an independent republic.

1279–1325. Diniz the Husbandman (1261–1325) is king of Portugal.

1281. Egypt and Byzantium ratify a trade treaty.

1283. October 3: Peter III of Aragon grants general privilege to estates.

1284. Genoese defeat Pisans off Meloria. ...Castile and Aragon divide Moorish North Africa. ...Alfonso X of Castile and León is deposed by his son, Sancho IV (c. 1257–1295).

1285–1291. Henry II (fl. 13th century) is last king of Jerusalem.

Africa, Asia & Pacific

1268. Earthquake in Cilicia (in Asia Minor) kills an estimated 60,000 people.

1270–1340. A succession of 21 lamas rules Tibet.

1271. Kublai Khan formally proclaims Mongol Yüan dynasty.

1271–1295. Marco Polo makes second long journey through Asia.

1274. Kublai Khan fails to conquer Japan. ...Mameluke sultan Baybars I destroys the last of the Assassins.

1275. Mongols invade northern Burma.

1275–1292. Marco Polo is in the service of Kublai Khan.

1276. Mongols capture Hangchow (in China) and take the empress and her son captive.

1277. Mongols defeat a powerful Burmese army in Koungai.

1278–1282. Thai raiders clash with Burmese forces.

1279. Mongol Yüan ruling class is forbidden to intermarry with the Chinese.

1279–1282. Balban, the sultan of Delhi, suppresses rebellion in Bengal.

1282–1388. Sultanate of Delhi governs Bengal.

1283. Mongols and their Thai allies attack Burma; Burmese king flees Pagan.

1284. Thais establish control over most of the Malay Peninsula. ...Mongols conquer Annam (Vietnam) and Khmer (Cambodia).

Americas

This illustration appeared in a 13th-century illuminated manuscript titled **La Somme le Roy,** *which was given to Philip III in 1279.*

c. 1276–1300. Severe drought disrupts Pueblo community in present-day Arizona.

c. 1280. Severe drought devastates Hopi community in present-day northeastern Arizona.

Science, Invention & Technology

1269. French scholar Petrus Peregrinus de Maricourt (fl. 13th century) discovers opposite poles in magnets and describes the navigational capabilities of the compass.

1272. Twisting mills for the manufacture of thread are built at Bologna, Italy.

c. 1275. First mechanical clocks are made in Europe. ...Mongols invent ox-drawn battle wagons. ...Turks adopt pigeon postal service after conquering Arab regions that had the service.

1277. Chinese use land mines and booby traps against invading Mongols.

1278. Frenchman Jean Pitard (fl. 13th century) establishes a fraternity of surgeons in Paris.

1279. Alfonso X of Castile and León writes about mining techniques in his work *Lapidaris.*

1280. Stucco is invented in Italy by Magaritone (fl. 13th century).

1283. Willem Beuckelszoon (fl. 13th century) of Holland invents process of salting herring. ...Italians make ravioli.

Religion, Culture & Arts

1268. Balliol College, Oxford, is founded.

1268–1271. The papacy is vacant.

1271–1276. Gregory X (c. 1230–1276) is pope.

1273. Jalal ad-Din ar-Rumi (b. 1207), Persian mystic poet and founder of Order of Whirling Dervishes, dies.

1274. Second Council of Lyons, regulates papal election (*Ubi periculum maius*) and carries out reunion with Orthodox Church. ...**March 7:** Thomas Aquinas (b. 1224) dies.

1278–1350. St. Maria Novella is built for the Dominicans in Florence.

1279. Pope Nicholas III (1225–1280) forbids controversy concerning apostolic poverty (*Exit qui seminat*).

1280. German scholar Albertus Magnus (b. 1206), a Scholastic philosopher, dies.

1282. Union of Eastern and Western Churches is repealed.

1283. Siamese script is developed.

1284–1298. Giovanni Pisano (1250–1314) creates sculptures on facade of Siena Cathedral.

1285. German epic poem *Lohengrin* appears.

British Isles & Western Europe

1287. July 15: Treaty of Oléron between Edward I of England and Alfonso III (1265–1291) of Aragon grants broad powers to nobles.

1289. November 6: Treaty of Salisbury between England, Scotland and Norway brings Scotland under English influence.

1290. September 26: Margaret of Scotland (b. 1283) dies.

1291. July 15: Rudolf I (b. 1218) dies.

1292. May 5: Adolf (1248–1298), count of Nassau, is elected German king. ...**June 24:** Adolf is crowned at Aix-la-Chapelle. ...**November 17:** Edward I awards the Scottish throne to John Baliol (1249–1315).

1294. Hanseatic cities acknowledge Lübeck as paramount. ...**June:** England declares war on France.

1295. January 22: Welsh are defeated at Conway. ...**November 27:** "Model Parliament" meets and grants money for French and Scottish wars.

1296. April 27: Edward I defeats Scots at Dunbar. ...**July 10:** John Baliol resigns his crown.

1297. April: Truce is declared between England and France, which keeps nearly all Gascony. ...**May:** Scots rebel under William Wallace (c. 1272–1305). ...**September 11:** Scots defeat English at Stirling Bridge.

1298. Anglo-French truce is signed at Tournai. ...**July 22:** Edward I defeats Wallace at Falkirk. ...**July 27:** Albert I of Austria is elected king.

1299. June 19: Anglo-French truce is signed at Montreuil. ...**November:** Scots take Stirling Castle.

Mediterranean Basin

1288–1326. Osman I (1259–1326), son of Erthogrul, founds Ottoman Empire.

1291. Crusaders abandon most of Syria, ending the era of the Crusades. ...**May 18:** Mamelukes conquer Acre, ending Christian rule in the East.

1291–1327. James II (c. 1260–1327) is king of Aragon.

1292. Sancho IV takes fortress of Tarifa on Straits of Gibraltar. ...Venice's population, spread over 112 islands in the Venetian Lagoon, reaches 200,000.

1294. Portugal concludes commercial treaty with England.

1295–1312. Ferdinand IV (1285–1312) reigns as king of Castile and León.

1296–1337. Frederick II (c. 1280–1337), brother of James II of Aragon, is king of Sicily.

1297. Genoese defeat Venetians off Curzola. ...Great Council of Venice is formed.

1299. Treaty between Venetians and Turks is signed. ...Mongols defeat Egyptian army at Homs (Syria).

Africa, Asia & Pacific

1287. Kublai Khan's forces complete their conquest of Pagan (in Burma).

1287. Hanoi falls to Mongols.

1287–1298. Kyawswar (c. 1260–1298) reigns as Pagan puppet king under Mongol supervision.

1287–1306. Burmese ruling dynasty of Hanthawaddy is founded at Pegu.

1290. Kaikobad (b. 1269), sultan of Delhi, is murdered and is succeeded by Jalaluddin (?–1296). ...Mongol Golden Horde elects Toqtai (fl. 13th century) khan. ...Earthquake at Chihli in China kills 100,000 people.

c. 1291–1339. Fumomadi the Great (c. 1270–1339) rules as Sultan of Pate, controlling East African coast from Pate to Mogadishu.

1292. Rama Kambeng (fl. 13th century) unites the Thais. ...Acting as Mongol ambassador, Marco Polo visits Sumatra and Java.

1294. Kublai Khan (b. 1215) dies, ending a 35-year reign.

1296. Thais raid Khmer lands in the Menam Basin. ...Mangray establishes the Thai kingdom of Lan Na, with capital at Chiang Mai. ...Mongols raid Delhi sultanate. ...**July:** Jalaluddin of Delhi is murdered and is succeeded by Alauddin Muhammad Khalji (?–1316).

1299. Shans burn Burmese capital of Pagan.

Americas

Science, Invention & Technology

Religion, Culture & Arts

1289. Printers at Ravenna use block techniques for printing, a first in Europe.

1289. Worcester College, Oxford, is founded. ...University of Montpellier in France is established.

c. 1290. Apache invade territory of the cliff dwellers in present-day southwestern United States.

This Genoese mosaic portrait of Marco Polo was made long after his death.

c. 1295. An agricultural economy is well established in the eastern woodlands of North America.

c. 1290. Chinese develop an early version of the gun. ...Oared galleys, called triremes, are in use in the Mediterranean.

1291. As a fire-safety measure, the glassmaking ovens of Venice are moved to the island of Murano.

1292. Venetians carry larger amounts of cargo over greater distances with their great galley ships. ...Bank notes are printed in Persia by occupying Mongols.

1294. English begin mining silver in Devonshire.

1290. Lisbon University is founded. ...University of Coimbra, Portugal, is established....**July:** Jews are expelled from England.

1292. Saadi (b. c. 1213), Persian poet, dies.

1292–1294. Dante Alighieri (1265–1321) writes *Vita Nuova.*

1293. Christian missionaries arrive in China.

1296. February 25: Papal bull *Clericis laicos* forbids ecclesiastics to pay taxes to temporal powers. Philip IV of France and Edward I of England oppose it.

1299–1344. Palazzo Vecchio in Florence, the best known of the great municipal palaces of Italy, is constructed.

British Isles & Western Europe

1300. Trade fairs open at Bruges, Antwerp, Lyons and Geneva. ...**July–August:** Edward I and the Scots under William Wallace are at war.

1301. January 20: Parliament of Lincoln rejects papal claims on Scotland.

1302. January: Anglo-Scots truce. ...**April 10:** First meeting of French Estates General. ...**December:** Bordeaux expels the French and calls in the English.

1303. May 20: Treaty of Paris restores Gascony to England. ...**June 13:** French Estates General support king against the pope. ...**September:** Edward I conquers Scotland again.

The Great Seal of Edward I of England. ➤

1304. Edward I retakes Stirling Castle and takes William Wallace prisoner.

1305. Wenceslas II (b. 1271) of Bohemia, Poland and Hungary, dies. ...Treaty of Athis between Philip IV and Flemings gives Philip Lille, Douai, Béthune Orchies. ...**August 23:** William Wallace (b. c. 1272) is executed at Smithfield.

1306. Wenceslas III (b. 1289) of Bohemia, last of Přemyslids, dies. ...Robert I (the Bruce) (1274–1329) is crowned king of Scotland. ...English defeat Robert I at Methuen and Dalry.

1307. Albert I of Austria invades Bohemia. ...Robert I defeats English in Ayrshire. ...Edward I (b. 1239) dies at Burgh-on-Sands and is succeeded as king of England by Edward II (1284–1327). ...Bohemians elect Henry (?–1335) of Carinthia king.

Mediterranean Basin

1301. Osman I defeats Byzantines at Baphaion.

1302. Crusaders are chased from their last stronghold in Syria. ...Venice and Egypt conclude a trade treaty. ...Guelphs rise to power in Florence.

1303. Andronicus II Palaeologus (1258–1332), Byzantine emperor, hires services of the Grand Catalan Company against Turks.

1305–1307. Grand Catalan Company lays siege to Constantinople.

1307–1313. Neapolitan Angevins subdue the Morea (in Greece).

Africa, Asia & Pacific

1300. Mongols occupy Damascus and northern Syria.

1300–1400. Kashmir (in northwest India) converts to Islam. ...Ibo move into present-day Nigeria. ...Kingdom of Kongo is established in Central Africa.

1302–1311. Malik Kafur (fl. 14th century), general of Alauddin Muhammad Khalji, conquers southern India.

1305. Sultanate of Delhi annexes Ujjain, Mandu, Dhar and Chanderi.

1306. Mongols withdraw raiding parties from India.

1307–1332. Empire of Mali reaches its zenith under Gongo Musa.

Americas

c. 1300–1400. Indian development and intensive agriculture and tool making are in the fourth phase. ...Pecos (in present-day New Mexico) becomes a center of pottery trade. ...Sun Temple in Mesa Verde is abandoned. ...Hopi town of Walpi is founded. ...Refugees from north move into Hopi country. ...Salado and Hohokam cultures overlap. ...Middle Mississippi culture in present-day Illinois establishes village-states, complete with mound-temple structures. ...Tampico people in present-day southern Illinois hunt, fish, farm and produce well-designed pottery. ...Fisher culture in present-day northeastern Illinois develops intensive farming. ...Aztalan culture of south-central Wisconsin establishes fortified villages, grows corn and squash and produces well-tempered pottery. ...Upper Republican culture in present-day Nebraska and Kansas establishes earthen lodges, gardens, and pottery for cooking. ...Top Layer culture of the Ozarks occupies bluff shelters, cultivates several crops and produces shell-tempered pottery. ...Savannah culture in present-day coastal Georgia builds fortified dwellings around a central mound. ...Macon Plateau culture in Georgia develops temple mounds and double- ditch moats. ...Coles Creek culture in present-day Louisiana and Mississippi builds pyramidal mounds with temples. ...Tenochtitlán (present-day Mexico City) is built in the middle of a lake as the Aztec capital. ...Tribes in present-day southeastern Missouri burn their villages, and begin to disperse to other areas.

Science, Invention & Technology

c. 1300–1400. Arabs invent some of the first guns and cannons. ...Gunpowder becomes widely used in Europe. ...Europeans make first crude grenades. ...Hourglasses are used as timepieces in Europe. ...Criss-crossing rhumb lines are added to portolans, navigation charts used by European sailors. Portolans give seafarers accurate guidance through the Mediterranean and Black Seas. ...Compartmentalized desks, cupboards and boxes are built by English craftsmen. ...Chinese develop wheeled flame-throwing batteries. ...Game of shuttlecock, a forerunner of badminton, is invented by the English. ...Techniques and designs in weaving show a mutual influence of the Chinese and the Muslims. ...Practice of alchemy is widespread in parts of southern Europe. ...The shaduf, a device consisting of a long hinged pole with a bucket tethered to the upper end used for lifting water from wells, developed in the Near East, is adopted in Flanders and Germany. ...Cotton replaces flax imported from Egypt as the fiber of choice in Europe. ...Europeans make liqueurs from distilled wine mixed with herbs and spices. ...Chinese invent the push-scythe, an early mechanical reaper. ...Frame-and-panel technique of furniture making becomes common in Europe. ...Chimú people of Peru build a system of canals and aqueducts. ...Montpellier Medical School in France produces the first brandy. ...Koreans invent metal-cast type. ...First weight-driven clocks are built in Europe. ...Blast furnaces gain widespread use in Europe as iron production increases. ...Medicinal wines are described by Catalan physician Arnau de Villanova (c. 1235–1312), who discovers that carbon monoxide and decayed meat are toxic.

1304. Arabs invent an early gun made of iron that shoots incendiary arrows.

▲ *Diego Rivera, Mexico's famous 20th-century muralist, painted this image of Tenochtitlán (present-day Mexico City) for the National Palace.*

Religion, Culture & Arts

c. 1300–1330. Ch'ing-pai, white Chinese porcelain with a transparent glaze that thickens and develops a blue tint, is made.

c. 1300–1400. Chester Cycle of mystery plays have their first performances in England. ...Madrigals are first performed. ...Doges' Palace, Venice, is begun (later rebuilt). ...Introduction of No theater stimulates a native Japanese school of decorative textiles. ...Buddhist priests introduce the art of suiboko, or ink painting, to Japan.

1303. September 7: William of Nogaret (fl. 14th century) takes Pope Boniface VIII prisoner at Anagni. ...**October 11:** Pope Boniface VIII (b. c. 1235) dies.

1304. Ypres Cloth Hall, the most impressive of the great Flemish halls, is built in Belgium.

1305. University of Orléans, France, is established. ...**June 5:** Bertrand de Got is elected Pope Clement V, but continues to reside in France.

c. 1306. *Alexandreis*, an epic by Walter Châtillon (1135–1184), is translated into Czech from the French.

1307–1314. Trial of Order of Templars is held at instigation of Philip IV of France.

1307–1321. Dante Alighieri writes *The Divine Comedy*.

British Isles & Western Europe

1308. May 1: Albert I (b. 1250) is murdered while advancing against Swiss League. ...**November 27:** Henry VII (1275–1313), count of Luxembourg, is elected German king and Holy Roman Emperor.

1311. Lord Ordainers in England issue ordinances, transferring government from king to barons.

1313. August 24: Henry VII (b. 1275) dies while advancing against Naples.

1314. Frederick of Austria (c. 1286–1330) is elected king of Germany but is opposed by Louis IV (c. 1283–1347), who also claims the throne of Germany and Holy Roman Empire. ...Robert I defeats Edward II at Bannockburn. ...Philip IV dies and is succeeded as king of France by Louis X (1289–1316).

1316. Louis X (b. 1289) dies and is succeeded as king of France by Philip V (1294–1322).

1317. Salic Law, excluding women from succession to throne, is adopted in France.

1318. Robert I captures Berwick. ...Treaty of Leek between Edward II and the factions of the barons is signed.

1320. Gedimin of Lithuania conquers Kiev. ...**August:** "Black Parliament" at Scone tries 70 persons for conspiracy against Robert I.

1322. Philip V (b. 1294) dies and is succeeded as king of France by Charles IV (1294–1328). ...Edward II defeats Thomas, earl of Lancaster at Boroughbridge. ...Thomas (b. c. 1278), earl of Lancaster, is executed. ...Robert I defeats Edward II at Byland. ...Louis IV takes Frederick of Austria prisoner at Mühldorf.

1326. September 24: Queen Isabella (1296–1358) and Roger de Mortimer (1287–1330) raise rebellion against Edward II. ...**November 16:** Edward II is captured by forces under Queen Isabella and Roger de Mortimer.

1327. Fire devastates Munich. ...**January 20:** Edward II resigns throne and is succeeded as king of England by Edward III (1312–1377). ...**June–August:** Scots invade England. ...**September 21:** Edward II (b. 1284) is murdered.

Mediterranean Basin

1309. Aragon and Valencia are united.

1309–1343. Robert of Anjou (1277–1343) is king of Naples.

1310. Expedition of Henry VII to Italy. ...Council of Ten established at Venice.

1312. Genoese discover Canary Islands.

1312–1350. Alfonso XI (1311–1350) is king of Castile and León.

1315. Golden Book of patrician families in Venice is closed.

1318–1346. George V (?–1346) is king of Georgia.

1319. Granada repels Castilian attacks.

1323. James II of Aragon takes Sardinia from Pisa.

1325–1357. Afonso IV (1291–1357) is king of Portugal.

1326. Orkhan (c. 1288–1360) succeeds his father, Osman I, as leader of the Ottoman Empire.

Africa, Asia & Pacific

1310. Delhi subdues Malwa. Muslims capture Dwarasamudra, capital of Mysore.

c. 1313. Mossi kingdom of Ourbri is established in the Volta River Basin of West Africa.

1315. Malik Kafur is murdered. ...Ala-uddin Muhammad Khalji of Delhi dies.

1316–1320. Mubarak (c. 1290–1320) rules Delhi as last of the Khalji rulers.

1318. Muhammadans defeat Harapala, ruler of west Deccan.

1320. Mubarak (b. c. 1290) is murdered.

c. 1325. Mossi raiders burn Sahara trading center of Timbuktu.

1325. Chinese rise in rebellion against Mongol overlords.

1325–1351. Muhammad Adil (c. 1300–1351) reigns as sultan of Delhi.

Americas

▲ *This 15th-century fresco by Domenico de Michelino depicts Dante Alighieri holding a manuscript of his* The Divine Comedy.

1325. Aztec capital of Tenochtitlán (present-day Mexico City) is founded.

Science, Invention & Technology

c. 1310. Maori of present-day New Zealand hunt the giant flightless moa bird to extinction.

1313. Water-powered bellows are used in Chinese ironworks.

1314. Scots build large hidden pits as a defense against invading cavalries.

1315. Lyons, France, becomes known for its silk industry, started by immigrant Italians.

1320. Arabs use artificial insemination in animal breeding. ...Mainz, Germany, a papermaking center, produces first European paper money.

1322. Crofting, the practice of bleaching cloth by laying it in a grassy meadow, is developed in Scotland and Ireland.

c. 1325. Steel crossbow is developed in Europe.

1327. Earliest known use of cannons in France, Italy and Britain.

Religion, Culture & Arts

1308. University of Perugia, Italy, is established. ...University of Lisbon is moved to Coimbra.

1311. Festival of Corpus Christi is established as traditional day for performance of mystery plays.

1312. March 22: Pope Clement V suppresses Order of Templars.

1314. Jacques de Molay (b. 1243), Grand Master of Templars, is burned at the stake in Paris. ...**April 14:** Pope Clement V (b. 1264) dies, and Holy See is left vacant for 27 months.

1315. Simone Martini (c. 1285–1344) paints *The Virgin in Majesty* in Siena, Italy.

1316–1334. John XXII (c. 1270–1334) is pope.

1317. Simone Martini paints an altarpiece for Robert of Anjou. Its composition is an early example of the use of perspective. ...Jean de Joinville (b. 1224), French chronicler, dies.

1319–1348. Italian painter Ambrogio Lorenzetti (c. 1290–1348) flourishes.

1321. University of Florence, Italy, is established. ...**September14:** Dante Alighieri (b. 1265), author of *The Divine Comedy*, dies.

1323. November 12: Papal bull *Cum inter nonnullos* declares Franciscan doctrine of Christ's poverty heretical.

1325. Francesco Landini (d. 1397), Italian poet and composer, is born. Although blind from childhood, he will become the most brilliant 14th-century Italian composer.

British Isles & Western Europe

1328. Ivan I (c. 1304–1341), the grand duke of Russia, chooses Muscovy (Moscow) as his capital. ...**February 1:** Charles IV (b. 1294), last of the Capets, dies and is succeeded as king of France by Philip VI (1293–1350) of Valois. ...**May 4:** In Treaty of Northampton between England and Scotland Robert I is recognized as king of Scotland.

1329. Robert I dies and is succeeded as king of Scotland by David II (1324–1371).

1330. January 13: Frederick (b. c. 1286) of Austria dies.

1332. First division of British Parliament into two Houses is recorded. ...Edward Baliol (c. 1203–1263) defeats David II's troops at Duplin Moor. ...**September 24:** Edward Baliol is crowned king of Scotland. ...**November 23:** In Treaty of Roxburgh, Edward Baliol recognizes Edward III of England as overlord. ...**December 16:** Edward Baliol flees to England.

1333. July 19: Edward III defeats Scots at Halidon Hill.

1333–1370. Casimir III (c. 1320–1370), the Great, is king of Poland.

1334. May 14: David II flees to France. ...**June 12:** In Treaty of Newcastle, Edward Baliol submits completely to Edward III and cedes Berwick.

1335. Edward III invades Scotland.

1336. Philip VI of France attacks Isle of Wight and Channel Islands.

1337. October: Edward III claims French crown. ...**November:** English defeat Count of Flanders, Philip VI's ally, at Cadsand. This action sparks the Hundred Years' War, 1337–1453.

1338. September 5: Louis IV and Edward III conclude alliance at Coblenz.

1339. October: Edward III invades France from Flanders.

1340. January 25: Edward assumes title of king of France at Ghent. ...**June 24:** English defeat French off Sluys. French occupy Guienne.

1341. April 30: John III (b. 1286) of Britanny dies, triggering the War of Breton Succession between John de Montfort (1293–1345) and Charles of Blois (1319–1364). ...Edward Baliol finally takes refuge in England.

Mediterranean Basin

1328. Louis Gonzaga (fl. 14th century) establishes his dynasty at Mantua in Italy.

1329. Battle between Andronicus III Palaeologus (1296–1341), Byzantine emperor, and Orkhan at Pelekanon is indecisive; Orkhan takes Nicaea.

1333. Moors recapture Gibraltar from Castile. ...Alauddin, brother of Orkhan and organizer of the Ottoman Empire, dies.

1333–1354. Yussuf I (fl. 14th century) is caliph of Granada.

1336–1387. Peter IV (1319–1387), the Ceremonious, is king of Aragon.

1337. Orkhan takes Nicomedia.

1339. Venice conquers Treviso, its first mainland possession.

1340. October 30: Alfonso XI of Castile and León defeats Moors at River Salado.

1341–1376. John V Palaeologus (1332–1391) is Byzantine emperor.

Africa, Asia & Pacific

1329. Famine is widespread in China, with an estimated 7 million affected.

1330. Port of Hormuz is founded at the head of Persian Gulf.

1331. Civil war breaks out over imperial succession in Japan.

1333. Death of the regent Takatoki ends Kamakura period in Japan.

1334. Pandyans (in south India) engineer a successful revolt against Delhi overlords.

1335. Songhai (in West Africa) becomes independent of Mali.

1336. Overthrow of Emperor Godaigo (1288–1339) inaugurates Muromachi period in Japan. ...**April 8:** Timur (d. 1405) (Tamerlane) is born at Kesh in the Transoxiana (in central Asia).

1339–1400. Rival shoguns are in intermittent conflict in Japan.

1340. Sultanate of Delhi reaches its zenith.

c. 1341–1360. Sulieman (c. 1320–1360) reigns as king of Mali.

Americas

1330–1521. **1330–1521.** Aztec empire dominates ancient Mexico.

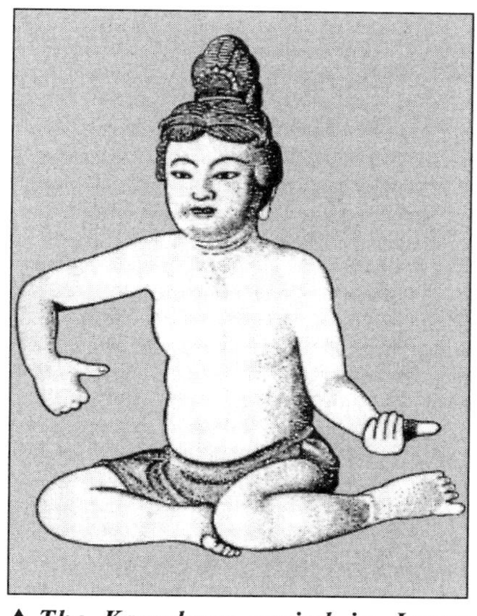

The Kamakura period in Japan celebrated many religious spirits. This is a drawing of a statue of Benzaiten, the goddess of music and good fortune; the statue was made for the Tsurugaoka Hachiman shrine in 1266.

c. 1340. Inuit (Eskimo) people from present-day Arctic Canada settle in Greenland.

Science, Invention & Technology

1328. The sawmill is invented.

c. 1330. The longbow is developed in Wales.

1335. Church of St. Gotthard in Milan, Italy, has first known mechanical striking clock in Europe. ...First compound crank is used in France.

1338. The swing plow comes is used in Europe; it includes a mallet for adjusting the components in the field. ...A trade route is built through Septimen Pass in the Swiss Alps.

1340. Coal mining begins at Marche-les-Dames, in eastern Belgium. ...Chinese pioneer two-color printing. ...Belgians build blast furnaces for their foundries.

Religion, Culture & Arts

1328. April 18: Louis IV declares Pope John XXII deposed for heresy and lèse-majesté.

1329–1336. Sculptor Andrea Pisano (c. 1270–1348) works on the bronze doors of the baptistry at Florence.

1333. *Annunciation* is painted by Simone Martini of Siena.

1333–1348. John Stratford (c. 1290–1348) is Archbishop of Canterbury.

1334. Work begins on the Palace of the Popes in Avignon.

1334–1342. Benedict XII (c. 1280–1342) is pope.

1338. Electoral princes at the Diet of Rense declare that the emperor, Louis IV, does not need papal confirmation. Louis annuls all papal verdicts against himself.

1340. Queen's College at Oxford University is established.

1341. April 8: Petrarch (1304–1374) is crowned poet laureate in Rome.

British Isles & Western Europe

1342. John de Montfort and the English defeat Charles of Blois at Morlaix.

1343. January 19: Truce of Malestroit between Edward III and Philip VI.

1344. Electors desert Louis IV in favor of Charles of Luxembourg (1316–1378).

1345. Louis IV obtains Holland, Zeeland, Frisia, and Hainaut.

1346. July 11: Charles of Luxembourg is elected German king. ...**August 26:** Edward III defeats French at Crécy.

1347. June 19: English defeat and capture Charles of Blois at La Roche. ...**August 3:** Calais surrenders to Edward III. ...**September 28:** Anglo-French truce is declared at Calais. ...**October 11:** Louis IV (b. c. 1283) dies.

1347–1351. Black Death (bubonic plague) devastates Europe.

1350. August 22: Philip VI (b. 1293) dies and is succeeded as king of France by John II (1319–1364). ...**August 29:** English defeat Spaniards at Winchelsea (in England).

1352. French are defeated in Brittany.

1355. April 5: Charles of Luxembourg is crowned Holy Roman Emperor as Charles IV.

1356. September 19: Edward the Black Prince (1330–1376) defeats French at Maupertuis; John II and his son, Philip, are taken prisoners.

Mediterranean Basin

1342–1349. Zealots rebel at Salonika.

1343–1344. Peter the Ceremonious gains control of Roussillon and the Balearics.

1344. Holy League evicts Turkish pirates from Greek islands. ...Alfonso XI of Castile and León takes Algiceras.

1346. Stephen Dušan (1308–1355), king of Serbia, crowns himself emperor of Serbs, Greeks, Bulgars and Albanians.

1347. Louis I of Hungary (1326–1382) invades Naples to avenge murder of King Andrew (?–1345), his brother. ...**April–December:** Cola di Rienzo (1313–1354), tribune of the people, rules Rome after leading a revolution.

1347–1354. John VI Cantacuzenus (c. 1292–1383), usurping emperor of Byzantium, is aided by Turks.

1348. Byzantines repulse Genoese naval attack in the Bosporus. ...Cola di Rienzo is expelled from Rome.

1348–1355. Plague outbreaks claim an estimated 900,000 in Egypt.

1349–1387. Charles II (1332–1387), the Bad, rules as king of Navarre.

1349. Stephen Dušan issues Serbian law code.

1350–1369. Peter the Cruel (1334–1369) is king of Castile and León.

1352. January 14: Peace between Louis I of Hungary and Joan I (1326–1382) of Naples is established.

1353. Turks begin to invade Europe by settling at Tzympe.

1354. Turks take Gallipoli. ...Cola di Rienzo (b. 1313) reestablishes his tyranny at Rome and is murdered shortly afterward.

1355. Conspiracy and execution of Marino Falieri at Venice.

Africa, Asia & Pacific

1344–1372. Saifa Harud (c. 1320–1372) reigns as king of Ethiopia.

1347. Hasan Bahmani establishes the Muslim kingdom of Kulbarga in the Deccan (in India).

1350. Refugees from Java resettle in the Moluccas (Spice Islands).

1351–1388. Firuz Shah Tughluq (c. 1308–1388) rules as sultan of Delhi.

1352. Chinese receive government appointments under Mongol rule for the first time.

1353–1359. Bengal successfully checks expansion of Delhi sultanate.

1353. Laotian kingdom of Lan Chang is founded.

1355–1368. Forces of Chu Yüan-chang (1328–1398) gradually drive Mongols from China.

1356. Koryo (Korea) revolts against the Mongols.

Americas

^This drawing, based on a 14th-century manuscript, depicts a 14th-century sea battle.

c. 1350. The 250-year fourth phase of development, also known as the militaristic stage, at Monte Albán ends. ...Old Iroquois culture in present-day northeastern United States builds houses, villages and fortifications. ...Aztecs build an agricultural canal system in the vicinity of Tenochtitlán, their new capital city.

c. 1350–1400. Salado people move into Chihuahua (on the border between present-day Arizona and Mexico).

Science, Invention & Technology

1342. First ring in Amsterdam's concentric canal system is built, originally for defensive purposes.

1346. August 26: English use longbows and cannons against the French in the battle of Crécy.

c. 1350. Pinned barrel organs linked to mechanical clocks are used in European churches. ...Rudolf of Nuremberg (fl. 14th century) makes improvements to wire drawing and introduces water power to the process. ...First gun-mounted ships are used in Europe. ...Flax breaker for processing flax stalks is invented in Holland.

1352. Eyeglasses are manufactured in Treviso, Italy.

1353. German monk Berthold Schwarz (fl. 14th century) invents one of first viable guns. ...Arabs invent a reinforced bamboo gun.

1356. Verona's Ponté del Castelvecchio over the Adige River in Italy is completed.

Religion, Culture & Arts

1342–1352. Clement VI (c. 1290–1352) is pope.

1344. German electors reject papal interference in electing German king.

1346. April 13: Pope Clement VI excommunicates and dethrones Louis IV.

1348. *Siete Partidas*, the encyclopedia of Spanish law, is published.

1348–1353. Giovanni Boccaccio (1313–1375) writes the *Decameron*.

1349. Jews in Germany are persecuted. ...**April 10:** William of Occam (b. c. 1300) dies. ...**October 20:** Pope Clement VI outlaws Flagellant movement.

1352. Corpus Christi College is established at Oxford University, England.

1353. Statute of *Praemunire* forbids appeals of English clergy to Holy See.

1354. Wu Chen (b. 1280), Chinese landscape painter, dies.

1356–1363. Hassan mosque is built in Cairo.

British Isles & Western Europe

1357. Étienne Marcel (c. 1316–1358) and Robert Le Coq lead revolution against the dauphin in Paris. ...Treaty of Berwick; David II is released from captivity.

1358. Rebellion of French peasants (Jacquerie) is subdued by the dauphin, as is Marcel and LeCoq's revolt in Paris; Marcel is killed.

1359. Edward III invades northern France, Champagne and Burgundy.

1361. The Black Death reappears in England.

1362–1389. Dmitri Donskoi (1350–1389) is grand duke of Muscovy (Moscow).

1363. Magnus II (?–1374) of Sweden is dethroned and is succeeded by Albert of Mecklenburg (c. 1350–1412).

1364. April 8: John II (b. 1319) of France dies and is succeeded by Charles V (1338–1380). ...**September 29:** French defeat Anglo-Breton army at Auray; Charles of Blois (b. 1319) is killed in battle.

1365. June 4: Charles IV (1316–1378) is crowned king of Burgundy at Arles. He allies with France and appoints the dauphin imperial vicar.

1366. Statute of Kilkenny forbids Anglo-Irish intermarriage and abolishes Irish laws and customs.

1369. Charles IV returns to Germany. ...**May 21:** Charles V of France declares war on England. ...**June 3:** Edward III resumes title of king of France.

1370. February 17: Teutonic Order defeats Lithuanians at Rudau. ...**September 19:** Edward the Black Prince sacks Limoges. ...**November 17:** Casimir III (b. c. 1320) dies, and Louis I of Hungary is elected king of Poland.

1371. English defeat Flemings off Bourgneuf.

1371–1390. Robert II (1316–1390), founder of the Stuart dynasty, is king of Scotland.

Mediterranean Basin

1357. Turks take Adrianople.

1357–1367. Peter I (1320–1367) is king of Portugal.

1358. Venetians, defeated by Genoese off Sapienza, cede Dalmatia to Hungary.

1360–1389. Murad I (c. 1326–1389) succeeds his father, Orkhan, as Ottoman sultan.

1362. Turks capture Adrianople, rename it Edirne, and make it their capital.

1363. Turks capture Philippopolis.

1364. Crete revolts against Venice. ...**May 16:** French defeat Charles II of Navarre at Cocherel.

1365. Peter I of Cyprus (?–1367) takes Alexandria but fails to keep it.

1366. French expel Peter the Cruel from Castile and install his half-brother Henry Trastámara (fl. 14th century) as king.

1367. February: Edward the Black Prince makes expedition to Spain to assist Peter the Cruel. ...**April 3:** Edward the Black Prince defeats Henry of Trastámara at Najara (in Spain) and restores Peter the Cruel.

1369. Venice repels Hungarian invasion. ...**March 23:** Henry of Trastámara secures Castile by Peter the Cruel's defeat at Montiel.

1371. September 26: Turks defeat Serbs at Cirnomen and Bulgarians at Samakow.

Africa, Asia & Pacific

1358–1389. Sikandar Shah (c. 1340–1389) rules as king of Bengal.

1360. Firuz Shah Tughluq founds city of Jaunpur in India.

1362–1363. Firuz Shah Tughluq's invasion of Sind is repulsed.

1363. Timur begins conquest of Asia.

1365. Rule of the Il-Khans dissolves in Persia.

1368. Mongol Yüan dynasty in China is overthrown by the Ming dynasty.

1368–1398. Chu Yüan-chang reigns as first Ming emperor.

1369–1405. Timur rules the Mongols.

1371. Timur subdues territories of Khwarazm (in central Asia). ...Chu Yüan-chang drives Mongols out of Szechwan.

Americas

1364. Aztec capital of Tenochitlán, in Mexico, is the largest city in present-day Central America.

1367. Aztecs become mercenaries for the Tepenec.

Science, Invention & Technology

c. 1358. Windlass, or cranequin, a type of crossbow with steel bow and locking device, is developed in Europe.

1360. Arab physician Ibn al-Khatib (c. 1313–1375) writes about the virtues of wine and recommends its consumption to non-Muslims.

1362. Portland stone, a limestone cement from the Isle of Portland that sets in water, is used in the reconstruction of Westminster Abbey in England.

1364. Italian Giovanni Dondi (1318–1389) designs the astrarium, a sophisticated astronomical clock that can plot the movements of the sun, moon and known planets.

1367. Florence's Ponte Vecchio over the Arno River in Italy is completed.

Religion, Culture & Arts

1362. William Langland (c. 1332–1400) completes *Piers Plowman.*

1362–1370. Urban V (c. 1300–1370) is pope.

1364. University of Krakow in Poland is established.

1366. English Parliament refuses to pay feudal tribute to the pope.

1368. Edward III deposes Simon Langham (1310–1376) as Archbishop of Canterbury.

1369. Geoffrey Chaucer (1340–1400) completes *Boke of the Buchesse.*

1370. Pope Urban V returns to Avignon.

1370–1378. Gregory XI (c. 1310–1378) is pope.

▲***Drawing of a knight and his squire, based on the Ellesmere manuscript of Chaucer's* Canterbury Tales *(1380–1400).***

British Isles & Western Europe

1372. September: French take Angoulême and La Rochelle. ...**June 23:** French and Castilians defeat English off La Rochelle. ...**August 7:** French take Poitiers.

1373. John (1340–1399) of Gaunt invades France from Calais to Bordeaux.

1375. June 27: Anglo-French truce of Bruges confines English to Bordeaux, Bayonne and Calais.

1377. French attack English coast. ...**June 21:** Edward III (b. 1312) dies and is succeeded as king of England by his grandson, Richard II (1367–1400).

1380. Dmitri Donskoi (1350–1389) of Muscovy (Moscow) defeats Mongols at Kulikov. ...**September 16:** Charles V (b. 1338) of France dies and is succeeded by Charles VI (1368–1422).

1381. French and English declare a truce.

1382. September 11: Louis I (b. 1326) of Hungary and Poland dies.

1384. Jadwiga (1374–1399), daughter of Louis I, is crowned queen of Poland. ...Anglo-Scottish war is renewed.

1385. Anglo-French war is renewed.

1388. April 9: Swiss defeat Leopold IV (fl. 14th century) of Austria at Näfels. ...**August 19:** Scots defeat English at Otterburn (Chevy Chase).

1389. February 24: Danes defeat Albert of Sweden at Falköping, establishing union of Sweden, Denmark, and Norway.

1390–1406. Robert III (1340–1406) is king of Scotland.

1392. Charles VI of France goes mad. ...England bars foreigners from retail trade.

Mediterranean Basin

1372. Venice and Genoa are at war. ...**August 27:** Sicily, under Frederick III (1341–1371), separates from Naples.

1373–1374. Turks subdue western Thrace (in Greece).

1375. Mamelukes take Sis, capital of Armenia Minor, ending Armenian independence.

1376–1379. Andronicus IV Palaeologus (?–1385) is Byzantine emperor.

1378–1381. Venice defeats Genoa in War of Chioggia.

1379–1390. John I (1358–1390) is king of Castile and León.

1379–1391. John V Palaenlogus of Byzantine is restored.

1380–1381. Charles III of Durazzo (1345–1386) rebels and captures Naples, seizing the crown in 1381.

1382–1402. Company of Navarre rules in the Morea (in Greece).

1382. Turks capture Sofia. ...**June 27:** Joan I of Naples dies (b. 1326).

1383–1433. John I (1357–1433), illegitimate son of Peter I, is regent and (from 1385) king of Portugal.

1385. John I of Portugal defeats John I of Castile and León at Aljubarotta.

1386. Charles III (b. 1345) of Naples dies, starting war of succession.

1389. Turks defeat Serbs at Kosovo.

1389–1402. Bajazet I (c. 1360–1403) is the fourth Ottoman sultan.

1390–1406. Henry III (1379–1406) is king of Castile.

1391–1425. Manuel II Palaeologus (c. 1370–1425) is Byzantine emperor.

Africa, Asia & Pacific

1380–1383. Timur campaigns in Afghanistan, Persia and Kurdistan.

1381. Timur conquers Herat.

1382–1411. David I (c. 1360–1411) reigns in Ethiopia.

1386. Timur subdues western Persia, Georgia, Armenia and Azerbaijan.

c. 1390–1400. Tutsi move into present-day Rwanda and Burundi.

1392. The warlord I Songgy (fl. 14th and 15th centuries) establishes Korean ruling dynasty, with capital at Seoul.

Americas

1375. Pecos produces glaze ware and imports pottery from the west and the north. ...Aztecs elect a ruler for the first time.

c. 1390. Chalchihuites culture in northwestern Mexico declines. ...Quiché dominate the Guatemalan highlands.

Science, Invention & Technology

1372. First eyeless iron needles are produced in Nuremberg and Schwabach, Germany.

c. 1375. Willem Beuckelszoon's herring salting and cleaning techniques are adapted to ship-board processing.

1377. Flemish develop carded wool for the manufacture of coarse cloth and hats.

▲ ***This 14th-century manuscript illumination shows Charles V of France seated in his study. An astrological sphere placed above his desk is indicative of his strong interest in astrology.***

1385. Elaborate silk mills, with as many as 120 spindles working at one time, are used in the Lucca region of Tuscany, Italy.

1388. English enact sanitation measures in the aftermath of the Black Death (bubonic plague).

Religion, Culture & Arts

1374. July 18: Petrarch (b. 1304) dies.

1375. The character of Robin Hood appears in English popular literature. ...**December 21:** Giovanni Boccaccio (b. 1313) dies.

1378. Great Schism begins: Urban VI (c. 1318–1389) is elected pope at Rome (**April 8**); Clement VII (c. 1342–1394) at Fondi (**September 20**). England, Italy, Austria, Bohemia, Hungary recognize Urban VI; France, Spain Sicily, Scotland, Cyprus recognize Clement VII.

1380–1400. Geoffrey Chaucer (c. 1340–1400) writes *The Canterbury Tales*.

1381. Simon Sudbury (b. c.1310), archbishop of Canterbury, is beheaded by insurgents.

1382. John Wycliffe (c. 1330–1384) is expelled from Oxford University, and his doctrines are condemned by London Synod.

1384. December 31: John Wycliffe (b. c. 1330) dies.

1385. Wang Meng (fl. 14th century), one of the four great masters of Chinese landscape painting, dies.

1387. Work begins on Milan Cathedral.

1388. Lollards are severely persecuted in England.

1389. Boniface IX (c. 1340–1404) is elected pope at Rome.

1390. John Wycliffe's writings begin to circulate in Bohemia.

1391. University of Ferrara in Italy is established.

British Isles & Western Europe

1394. May 8: Wenceslas (1361–1419), king of Germany and Bohemia, is taken prisoner by rebellious Bohemian barons.

1396. November 4: Richard II of England marries Isabella of France at Calais.

1397. Union of Kalmar joins Sweden, Denmark and Norway.

1399. September 29–30: Richard II is deposed and Henry IV (1367–1413) of Lancaster succeeds to throne of England. ...**October 15:** Acts of last Parliament of Richard II are annulled.

1400. February 14: Richard II (b. 1367) is murdered. ...**August 20:** Rhenish electors depose Wenceslas and (August 21) elect Rupert (1352–1410) of the Palatinate German king.

1401. January 18: Poland and Lithuania formally unite.

1402. June 22: English defeat Scots at Nesbit Moor.

1403. July 21: Henry IV defeats rebellious Percies at Shrewsbury and subdues Northumberland.

1404. April 21: Philip II (b. 1342) of Burgundy dies, and is succeeded by his son, John the Fearless (1371–1419).

1406. Treaty of Aberdaron between Percies, Mortimer and Glyndwr partitions England. ...James I (1394–1437) of Scotland is held prisoner in England. ...Robert III (b. 1340) of Scotland dies. ...Long Parliament reorganizes finances, reforms county elections, regulates succession to crown, controls Privy Council.

1410. Civil war in France between followers of the duke of Orléans and the duke of Burgundy breaks out. ...King Rupert (b. 1352) of Germany dies. Sigismund (1368–1437), king of Hungary from 1387, is elected king of the Romans.

1413. March 20: Henry IV (b. 1367) dies. ...**April 9:** Henry V (1387–1422) is coronated king of England.

Mediterranean Basin

1395–1410. Martin I (1356–1410) is king of Aragon.

1396. September 27: Bajazet I defeats Christian army at Nicopolis. ...**October 25:** Charles VI of France becomes overlord of Genoa.

1396–1397. Turks invade Greece and the Morea.

1399. Milan conquers Pisa.

1400. Emperor Manuel II Palaeologus visits France and England to obtain aid against Turks. ...The Medici begin their rise to power in Florence. ...Timur lays waste to Georgia and advances into Asia Minor.

1401. March 24: Timur conquers Damascus. ...**July 22:** Timur conquers Baghdad.

1402. Timur defeats the Ottoman sultan Bajazet I at Ankara and takes him prisoner. ...Mehmed I (?–1421) becomes Ottoman sultan.

1404–1405. Venice absorbs Verona and Vicenza.

1406. Venice acquires Padua. ...Florentines subdue Pisa.

1406–1454. John II (1405–1454) is king of Castile and León.

1408. April 21: Ladislaus (1377–1414) of Naples seizes Rome.

1410. May 31: Martin I (b. 1374), king of Sicily, dies.

1411. May 19: Louis of Anjou (1377–1417) defeats Ladislaus of Naples at Rocca Secca. ...**October 31:** Peace between Castile and Portugal is declared.

1412–1416. Ferdinand I (c. 1379–1416) is king of Aragon.

1414–1435. Joan II (1371–1435) is queen of Naples.

Africa, Asia & Pacific

1395. Timur's campaigns in Astrakhan close trade routes between Russia and China.

1398–1402. Chien-Wen (c. 1377–1440) reigns as second Ming emperor of China.

1399–1414. Delhi is without regular government after being conquered by Timur.

c. 1400–1410. Nguni settlers move into Natal (in southern Africa). ...Great Enclosure is built at present-day Zimbabwe.

1401. Siam extends control over entire Malay Peninsula.

1402–1424. Yung-lo (1360–1424) reigns as third Ming emperor of China.

1405. February 18: Timur (b. 1336) dies and is succeeded by his son Shah Rokh (1377–1447).

1405–1407. Chinese armada raids coast of Sumatra.

1408. Chinese fleet raids Ceylon (present-day Sri Lanka).

1411–1443. Ahmad Shah (fl. 15th century) reigns as king of Gujarat and founds Ahmadabad.

1414–1431. Jalal al-Din (c. 1390–1414) rules in Bengal, which gradually converts to Islam.

Americas

c. 1395. Incan Temple of the Sun in Cuzco, the southern capital, is built using dry masonry technique.

c. 1400. Quecha language (Incan) dominates southern Peru. ...Hohokam culture in present-day southern Arizona disappears. ...Norse explorations of America end. ...Younge culture in present-day southeastern Michigan establishes villages, hunts, gathers and engages in some agriculture. ...Whittlesey culture in present-day northwestern Ohio establishes villages and develops farming corn, beans, squash, and sunflowers. ...Middle Mississippi culture in the present-day Ohio Valley builds log houses and manufactures painted pottery. ...Fort Ancient culture in present-day southern Ohio, southern Indiana, northern Kentucky and western West Virginia establishes villages and farms corn. ...Mille Lacs culture in present-day central Minnesota establishes camps and dome-shaped houses, hunting and gathering and possibly some farming. ...Oneota culture in present-day northern Illinois, eastern Minnesota, Iowa, Nebraska, Kansas and southwestern Missouri occupies rock shelters and earth lodges and engages in farming and hunting. ...Nebraska culture builds underground houses, farms several crops and manufactures differerent kinds of pottery. ...Etowah culture in present-day middle Mississippi region constructs mounds and uses materials of Southern Death cult. ...Key Marco culture on southern Gulf coast of present-day Florida builds thatch-covered houses and produces pottery for cooking.

Science, Invention & Technology

1396. Koreans use bronze type.

c. 1400. Irish whiskey and Scotch whisky are made from barley and other grains. ...Germans make cannonballs that tightly fit the bore of the cannon to maximize force. ...Egyptians make playing cards. ...Tatars catapult plague victims over the walls of enemy cities, an early form of biological warfare. ...Europeans use blown glass to make bottles. ...Arabs and Italians use substitution ciphers to make coded messages. ...Cotton is introduced to England. ...Screw jacks are used to lift wagons for wheel repair. ...First needles with eyes are made in Holland and Belgium. ...First examples of porcelain reach Europe from the Orient. ...Binnacle is invented in Europe; it consists of a glass case that protects a ship's compass from the elements and allows it to remain level with the ship's movements. ...Dutch begin to use windmills to drain polders in their land reclamation schemes. ...Chinese develop two-stage rocket that time-releases a swarm of arrows upon reaching its target. ...Peoples of the Kagera region of present-day western Tanzania are known for their iron smithing. ...Germans develop a four-heddle loom. ...Swiss invent the halberd, an eight-foot spear with hook and ax blade near its tip. ...Chinese develop a solar year of 365 ¼ days.

1411. Cesarean sections are performed at Frankfurt-am-Main in Germany.

Religion, Culture & Arts

1394. Benedict XIII (c. 1340–1424) is elected pope at Avignon.

1396–1414. Thomas Arundel (c. 1350–1414) is Archbishop of Canterbury.

1398–1399. Archbishop Arundel is banished by Richard II of England.

1400. First known manuscript of *Sir Gawain and the Green Knight*, a Middle English poem on the Arthurian theme, appears. ...**October 25:** Geoffrey Chaucer (b. c. 1304) dies.

c. 1400–1500. The English Morris dance, with six men, a fool, a man dressed as a woman and a hobby-horse, is developed.

1403. Wycliffism, preached by John Huss (1369–1415), spreads in Bohemia.

1404. University of Turin in Italy is established.

1406–1415. Gregory XII (c. 1360–1415) is pope.

1408. June 29: Thirteen cardinals of both parties summon council to end schism.

1409. Council of Pisa meets: Benedict XIII and Gregory XII are deposed. ...**June 26:** Alexander V (c. 1350–1410) is elected antipope, producing rivalry of three popes.

1411. John XXIII (?–1419) who succeeded Alexander V as antipope, excommunicates John Huss, who had refused to obey his summons. ...University of St. Andrews, Scotland, is established.

1412. John Huss writes *Adversus indulgentias: Contra bullam pape.*

1413. February 8: John XXIII condemns Wycliffe's writings.

1414–1443. Henry Chicheley (c. 1370–1443) is Archbishop of Canterbury.

British Isles & Western Europe

1415. Henry V defeats French at Agincourt.

1416. October 8: Treaty of Calais between Henry V, Emperor Manuel II Palaeologus, and John of Burgundy is signed.

1417. September 20. Henry V takes Caen.

1419. Rouen capitulates to Henry V. ...John (b. 1371) of Burgundy is murdered by agents of the dauphin at Montereau. John's son, Philip III (1396–1467), succeeds him as duke of Burgundy.

1420. June 2: Henry V marries Catherine (1401–1437) of France. ...**December 1:** Henry V enters Paris.

1422. Hussites defeat Sigismund at Deutschbrod. ...Henry V (b. 1387) of England dies and is succeeded by Henry VI (1421–1471). ...Charles VI (b. 1368) dies and is succeeded as king of France by Charles VII (1403–1461).

1423. James I of Scotland is released from prison in England.

1424. August 17: English defeat French and Scots at Verneuil.

1425. August 2: English take Le Mans.

1425–1462. Vasily II (1415–1462) is grand duke of Muscovy (Moscow).

1427. September 5: French defeat English at Montargis.

1428. July 3. By the Treaty of Delft, Philip III, the Good, acquires Holland, Zeeland and Hainaut.

1429. May 1–3: Joan of Arc (1412–1431) raises siege of Orléans.

1430. May 23: Joan of Arc is captured by Burgundians at Compiègne.

1431. Joan of Arc (b. 1412) is burnt at the stake in Rouen. ...English king Henry VI is crowned king of France at Paris.

1431–1433. First German peasant revolt takes place near Worms.

1433. January 9: Władysław II (1351–1434) grants Polish noblemen habeas corpus in constitution of Krakow.

1435. In Peace of Arras between Charles VII of France and Philip III, the Good, of Burgundy, Philip obtains Macon, Auxerre, and part of Picardy.

Mediterranean Basin

1415. August 21: Portuguese conquer Ceuta (in North Africa).

1416. Venetians defeat Turks off Gallipoli.

1416–1458. Alfonso V (1396–1458) is king of Aragon and Sicily and (from 1442) of Naples.

1418. Portuguese occupy Madeira Islands off northwest Africa.

1420. Venice acquires Friuli and Belluno.

1421. Florence acquires Livorno.

1421–1451. Ottoman sultan Murad II (1404–1451), son of Mehmed I, is emir of Turks.

1423. Venice buys Salonika.

1424–1427. Ottoman sultan Murad II extends reconquest of Anatolia.

1425–1448. John VIII Palaeologus (c. 1400–1448) is Byzantine emperor.

1427–1550. Wattasid dynasty rules in Fez (in Morocco).

1428. April 19: In Peace of Ferrara, Milan cedes Brescia and Bergamo to Venice.

1429. March: Turks take Salonika.

1431. Portuguese discover the Azores.

1434–1464. Cosimo de' Medici (1389–1464) begins Medicean rule over Florence.

1435–1442. René I (1409–1480), duke of Anjou, is titular king of Naples.

Africa, Asia & Pacific

1417–1419. Chinese naval expedition makes contact with Mogadishu, Barawa and Malindi (in East Africa).

1421. Beijing is made capital of China.

1424–1425. Hung-hsi (1378–1425) is fourth Ming emperor of China.

1425–1435. Hsüan-te (1398–1435) is fifth Ming emperor of China.

1428. Famine touches off strikes and riots in Japan.

1431–1432. Chinese fleet visits Red Sea port of Jeddah, on the coast of present-day Saudi Arabia.

1433. Portuguese explorer Gil Eames (fl. 15th century) becomes the first European to round Cape Bojador, West Africa.

1435. Portuguese caravel carries first West African slaves to Europe.

Americas

▲*An Aztec tribute list from the* **Codex Mendoza.**

1426. Maxtlatzin succeeds his father Tezozomoc, Tepenec conquerer of central Mexico.

1427. Tezozomoc dies.

1428. Aztecs begin collecting imperial tribute.

Science, Invention & Technology

1416. Dutch fishermen introduce the drift net.

c. 1420. Italian monasteries and nunneries become centers of cotton cloth production. ...Brace and bit is invented in Flanders. ...French monk Dom Pinchon (fl. early 15th century) experiments with fertilization of fish eggs. ...Count Jan Zizka (c. 1376–1424) of Bohemia constructs a fortified battle wagon.

c. 1425. Venetian Giovanni di Fontana builds a gunpowder-fueled rocket car. ...Europeans discover the explosive advantage of granulated gunpowder over fine gunpowder.

1428. Arabs establish an observatory at Samarkand, Uzbekistan.

1429. Joan of Arc's forces use rockets in the battle of Orleáns.

c. 1430. First spring-driven clocks are made in Europe. ...Porcelain Tower is completed in Nanking, China, after 19 years of construction. It will be destroyed in 1853.

1435. Nuremberg, Germany, becomes a center for the manufacture of gunpowder.

Religion, Culture & Arts

1415. Dutch mystic Thomas à Kempis (1380–1471) writes *De Imitatione Christi* in poetic prose. ...**July 6:** John Huss (b. 1369) is burned as a heretic.

1417. Benedict XIII, Gregory XII, and John XXIII are deposed. ...Martin V (1368–1431) is elected pope.

1418. February 22: Martin V condemns doctrines of John Wycliffe and John Huss (*Inter cunctas*).

1420. Great Temple of the Dragon is built in Beijing.

1422. University of Besançon in France is established. ...Andrei Rublyov (c. 1360–1430), considered among the greatest Russian painters of religious themes, decorates Cathedral of the Trinity at Troitsky-Sergieva.

1424–1429. Clement VIII (c. 1390–1446) is antipope.

1428. Masaccio (Tommaso di Giovanni di Simone Guidi, b. c. 1401), considered the most influential Italian painter of his time, dies.

1430–1443. Florentine architect Filippo Brunelleschi (1377–1446) completes Pazzi Chapel near Santa Croce in Florence.

1431–1447. Eugenius IV (1383–1447) is pope.

1432. May 6: Jan van Eyck (1390–1441) finishes altarpiece of St. John's in Ghent.

1433. Earliest documented painting by Fra Angelico (Guido di Pietro; 1387–1455).

1434. May 29: During a revolt in Rome, Pope Eugenius IV flees to Florence.

British Isles & Western Europe

1436. April 13. French recover Paris.

1437. James I (b. 1394) is murdered at Perth, Scotland, and is succeeded by James II (1430–1460). ...Sigismund (b. 1368) dies.

1438. Diet of Nuremberg begins to reform the Holy Roman Empire.

1440. February 1: Frederick III (1415–1493) is elected German king (as Frederick IV) and Holy Roman Emperor.

1444. November 10: Władysław III (b. 1424) of Poland and Hungary is killed in battle of Varna against Turks.

1445. April 22: Henry VI marries Margaret of Anjou (1430–1482).

1447–1492. Casimir IV (1427–1492) is king of Poland and Lithuania.

1448. Frederick II (1413–1471) of Brandenburg subdues Berlin and makes it his capital. ...Anglo-Scottish war is renewed. ...French recover Maine and Anjou.

1449. March 24: English break truce, capturing Fougères. French recover Normandy.

1449–1453. War between towns and princes in south Germany.

1450. August 1: Christian I (1426–1481) of Denmark becomes king of Norway. ...**August 12:** French recover Cherbourg.

1451. French conquer Guienne.

1452. October 23: English recapture Bordeaux.

1453. July 17: French defeat English at Castillon. ...**October 19:** Bordeaux surrenders to the French. English hold only Calais and Channel Islands.

Mediterranean Basin

1437. October 16: Portuguese abandon North African foothold at Ceuta.

1441. Venice acquires Ravenna. ...Turks renew the siege of Constantinople.

1443. Hungarian János Hunyadi (1387–1456) defeats Turks at Nish. ...**February 26:** Alfonso V of Aragon, Sicily, and Naples transfers his court to Naples.

1445. Portugal settles the Azores.

1447. Filippo Maria Visconti dies; Alfonso V of Naples and house of Orléans claim Milan. ...Skanderbeg (1403–1468) of Albania defeats Murad II.

1448. October 19: Murad II defeats János Hunyadi at Kosovo.

1449–1453. Constantine XI (c. 1400–1453) reigns as the last Byzantine emperor.

1450. February 26: Francesco Sforza (1401–1466) enters Milan and assumes title of duke.

1451–1481. Mehmed II (1432–1481), son of Murad II, reigns as Ottoman sultan.

1452. Frederick II (1411–1464) of Saxony creates Borso, marquis of Este, duke of Modena and Reggio.

1453. April 20: Genoese defeat Turks off Constantinople. ...**May 29:** Turks capture Constantinople.

Africa, Asia & Pacific

1436. Mahmud Khan founds dynasty in Malwa (in India).

1436–1449. Cheng-t'ung (c. 1420–1464) reigns as sixth Ming emperor of China.

1443–1469. Narapati (fl. 15th century) rules as king of Ava (in Burma).

1444. Portuguese explorer Nino Tristram (?–1447) reaches the Senegal River in West Africa. ...Portuguese explorer Dinís Dias (fl. 15th century) discovers Cape Verde.

1447. Timur's son and successor Shah Rokh (b. 1377) dies in Samarkand. ...India, Persia, and Afghanistan gain independence after break-up of Timur's empire.

1448. Dinís Dias reaches Sierra Leone on the coast of West Africa.

1449–1450. Ming emperor Cheng-t'ung is captured by the Mongols and held prisoner for one year.

1449–1457. Ching-t'ai (1428–1457) reigns as seventh Ming emperor of China.

1450. Mocha in southwest Arabia emerges as main export center of coffee.

1451–1489. Bahlol Lodi (?–1489) reigns as first Afghan king of Delhi.

Americas

1438. Inca embark on a course of expansion from present-day northern Ecuador to present-day central Chile.

1448. Inca invade Araucanias in present-day southern Chile.

c. 1450. Inca begin building Cuzco, their capital, using massive irregularly shaped stone blocks closely fitted together with mortar. ...Inca begin a massive expansion of their culture. ...Mayapan becomes the capital of Yucatán. ...Pawnee move northeastward near the Missouri River. ...Southern Death cult religion spreads through present-day Mississippi Valley. ...Lamar culture builds palisaded villages and makes pottery in many different styles.

Science, Invention & Technology

1436. Buckwheat from central Asia is introduced to Europe in the Mecklenburg region of Germany. It will later become the staple crop of northern France.

c. 1440. Peruvian Inca use Inca stone, composed of highly polished volcanic rock (obsidian), for mirrors. ...Ruprecht Rust (? – 1447) of Germany invents copper-plated engraving.

1449. Ulagh-Beg (1394–1449), a Muslim, catalogs more than 1,000 stars and develops a method of calculating their positions.

c. 1450. First printing inks are developed in Europe from varnish and linseed oil. ...Cannonballs made of cast iron gain widespread use in Europe. ...Spanish invent the harquebus, a shoulder-mounted predecessor of the musket. ...The fusee, a device that allows clocks to function at a more constant rate, is added to timepieces.

1451. Nicholas of Cusa (1401–1464) invents eyeglasses with concave lenses for correcting nearsightedness.

1453. Ottomans develop large guns, which are deployed in the siege of Constantinople.

Religion, Culture & Arts

1436. July 5: Iglau Compact establishes peace with Hussites.

1438. July 7: Pragmatic Sanction of Bourges asserts French liberties against papacy.

c. 1440. Composer Josquin des Prés (d. 1521) is born.

1443–1452. John Stafford (?–1452) is archbishop of Canterbury.

1444. Leonardo Bruni (b. c. 1370), humanist, dies.

1445. Rome Council is dissolved.

1446. Florentine architect Filippo Brunelleschi (b. 1377) dies.

1448. February 17: Vienna concordat with Emperor Frederick III marks final failure of conciliar movement. ...**July:** Basel Council moves to Lausanne.

1449. April 7: Felix V (c. 1390–1451), the last antipope, resigns. ...**April 25:** Lausanne Council is dissolved.

1450. Pope Nicholas V (1397–1455) establishes Vatican Library. ...University of Barcelona in Spain is established. ...University of Trier in Germany, is established. ...The pavane, a stately dance of gliding steps to a 32-bar tune, is first performed. ...The *Neidhartspiel*, one of the best-known German carnival plays, is performed for the first time. ...Development of the Japanese puppet play.

1451. University of Glasgow, Scotland, is established.

1452–1454. John Kemp (1380–1454) is archbishop of Canterbury.

British Isles & Europe

1454. Under Peace of Lodi between Venice and Milan, Venice secures Brescia, Bergamo, Crema and Treviglio.

1454–1474. Henry IV (1425–1474) reigns in Castile.

1455. Richard (1411–1460), third duke of York, defeats royal forces at St. Albans, beginning the Wars of the Roses.

1456. Turks conquer Athens, but the Acropolis holds out. ...**February 25:** Duke of York is removed from English protectorship.

1457. July 2: Christian I of Denmark and Norway is crowned king of Sweden. ...**November 23:** Skanderbeg of Albania defeats Turks at Alessio.

1458. January 24: Matthias Corvinus (1443–1490) is elected king of Hungary. ...**June:** Turks take Acropolis in Athens.

1459. Turks conquer Serbia. ...Henry VI quells Yorkist uprising at Blore Heath.

1460. Turks conquer Morea in Greece. ...Richard, third duke of York, defeats Henry VI at Northampton and takes him prisoner. ...**August 3:** James II (b. 1430) of Scotland is killed at Roxburgh and is succeeded by James III (1452–1488). ...**December 30:** Queen Margaret of Anjou, wife of Henry VI, defeats and kills Richard of York (b. 1411) at Wakefield.

1461. War breaks out between Frederick III and his brother, Albert VI, who dies. ...**February 2:** Edward of York (1442–1483) wins battle of Mortimer's Cross. ...**February 17:** Queen Margaret defeats Richard Neville, earl of Warwick (1428–1471) at St. Albans. ...**March 4:** Henry VI is deposed. ...**March 29:** Edward of York defeats Henry VI at Towton; Henry VI flees to Scotland. ...**June 28:** Edward of York is crowned king of England, becoming Edward IV. ...**July 22:** Charles VII (b. 1403) of France dies and is succeeded by Louis XI (1423–1483).

1462. September–December: Richard Neville, earl of Warwick, defeats Queen Margaret and the French.

1463: Turks conquer Bosnia. ...**October 8:** Truce of Hesdin between Edward IV and Louis XI is enacted.

Africa & Middle East

1455. May 15: Crusade against Turks proclaimed (*Ad summi apostolatus apicem*).

1459–1460. Congress of Mantua, presided over by Pope Pius II (1405–1464), decides on Crusade against Turks.

c. 1460–1480. Matope reigns on the Zimbabwe plateau south of the Zambezi River.

c. 1460–1500. Mossi raiders reach Walata on the edge of the Sahara.

1461. Turks conquer Trebizond on Black Sea coast of Anatolia. ...Persians expand northward into Georgia.

1463–1479. Venetians and Turks wage intermittent warfare over Venice's trade interests in the Levant.

Asia & Pacific

1456. Moluccas (Spice Islands) repel invasion from Siam.

1456–1466. Bhre Vengker (c. 1440–1466) reigns in Majapahit (in Java).

c. 1456–1477. Mansur Shah (c. 1440–1477) reigns as sultan of Malacca (in Malaya).

1457. Timurid leader Abu Said (1426–1469) captures Herat (in Afghanistan).

1457–1464. Ming emperor Cheng-t'ung is restored to his throne in China and assumes the name T'ien-shun.

1459–1474. Rukin al-Din Barbak (c. 1435–1474), a once-enslaved Ethiopian, rules in Bengal (India).

1459–1511. Mahmud Shah Bigarha (c. 1440–1511) reigns as king of Gujarat (in India).

1461. Plague and famine touch off uprisings in Japan.

1461–1463. Nizam (c. 1453–1463) is sultan of Bahmani.

1463–1482. Muhammad III (c. 1440–1482) reigns as sultan of Bahmani.

Americas

c. 1454. Inca begin a massive expansion of their culture.

▲ ***This early 16th-century drawing portrays a troopship with seafaring Chinese soldiers of the Ming period.***

c. 1460. Mayapan becomes the capital of Yucatán.

1460–1470. Inca conquer the Chimús in Peru.

Science, Invention & Technology

1454. Johannes Gutenberg (c. 1397–1468) prints 300 copies of the Bible in Latin with a moveable-type printing press of his own invention at Mainz, Germany.

c. 1460. Printing dies are invented and put into use in Europe. ...Europeans use smokejacks, a form of barbecue pits built into the bases of chimneys. ...Portuguese explorers bring hand-held folding fans back from China. ...Advent of larger and more seaworthy vessels, especially in England and Portugal, makes it possible to sail beyond the European coastlines and into the open waters of the ocean. ...Ethiopians invent the first known water pipe, which is used for the smoking of hashish. ...Silk screening, another innovation developed by the Chinese, makes its debut in Europe. ...Sugar is introduced to England. ...Johann Regiomontanus (1436–1476) of Germany develops a decimal system.

Religion, Culture & Arts

1454–1486. Thomas Bourchier (1404–1486) is archbishop of canterbury.

1455–1458. Calixtus III (1378–1458) is pope.

1457. Johannes Gutenberg prints the *Pergation Calendar*, first medical publication printed in Europe. ...**August 1:** Lorenzo Valla (b. 1407), Italian humanist, dies.

1458. Ausias March (b. 1397), regarded as greatest Catalan poet of his time, dies.

1458–1464. Pius II (1405–1464) is pope.

1459. November 12: University of Basel in Switzerland is established.

1460. Andrea Mantegna (1431–1506) is appointed court painter to the Gonzaga family at Mantua.

1460–1483. St. George's Chapel at Windsor Castle is built.

1461. François Villon (1431–1463), French lyrical poet, writes, *Le Testament*. ...**November 27:** Louis XI temporarily annuls Pragmatic Sanction of Bourges.

1462. March 31: Pope Pius II annuls Prague Compact and forbids chalice to the laity.

1463. University of Nantes in France is established. ...French poet François Villon (b. 1431) dies.

British Isles & Europe

1464. June 1: Edward IV of England and Scots make peace. ...**June 19:** Louis XI establishes French royal mail.

1465. July 16: Burgundy and rebels defeat Louis XI at Montlhéry.

1465–1470. Henry VI of England is imprisoned.

1466. October 19: At second Peace of Thorn, Teutonic Order cedes Pomerellen, Ermland and Kulmerland to Poland, and East Prussia is made a Polish fief.

1467. Turks conquer Herzegovina. ...Philip III (b. 1396) of Burgundy dies.

1468. Turks conquer Albania. ...**October 9:** Louis XI of France and Charles the Bold (1433–1477), duke of Burgandy, meet at Péronne.

1469. Sigmund of Tyrol (1427–1496) pawns Upper Alsace to Charles the Bold in Treaty of St. Omer. ...Richard Neville, earl of Warwick, defeats Edward IV at Edgecote. ...Charles the Bold acquires Alsace, Breisgau and Ghent.

1469–1492. Lorenzo de' Medici (1449–1492), the Magnificent, rules Florence.

1470. October 3: Edward IV of England flees to Flanders. Richard Neville, earl of Warwick, restores Henry VI.

c. 1471. Louis XI takes Amiens from Charles the Bold. ...Richard Neville (b. 1428), earl of Warwick, is defeated and killed by Edward IV at Barnet. ...Edward IV defeats Queen Margaret and kills Edward, Prince of Wales (b. 1453), at Tewkesbury. ...Edward IV enters London; Henry VI (b. 1421) is murdered. ...Swedes under Sten Sture (c. 1440–1503) defeat Christian I of Denmark, Norway and Sweden at Brunkeberg.

1474. July 27: Edward IV and Charles the Bold agree on a treaty.

1474–1479. Rival claimants fight war of succession in Aragon.

1474–1504. Isabella (1451–1504) reigns as queen of Castile, jointly from 1479 with Ferdinand II (1452–1516) of Aragon.

Africa & Middle East

1464–1492. Sonni Ali the Great (?–1492) reigns as king of Songhai.

1465. Sonni Ali makes war on Songhai's Central African neighbors.

1466. June 12: Portuguese establish government in Cape Verde Islands and Guinea on the West African mainland.

1467–1468. Al-Zahir Timurbugha (fl. 15th century) rules as Mamaluke sultan of Egypt.

1468. Sonni Ali evicts the Tuareg from Timbuktu in the Sahara.

1468–1478. Baeda Mariam (c. 1450–1478) rules in Ethiopia.

1468–1495. Al-Ashraf Sayf al-Din Quait Bey (c. 1450–1495) reigns as Mameluke sultan of Egypt.

1469–1478. Uzun Hasan (c. 1420–1478) reigns in Persia.

1469. Persians control Armenia, Kurdistan, Azerbaijan, and Iran.

c. 1470. Ngazargarmu is established as capital of Bornu (present-day Nigeria).

1471. Portuguese expedition explores the Niger River estuary. ...Portuguese trade in gold along the Guinea coast. ...**August.** Portuguese conquer Tangier.

1472. Portuguese navigator Lopo Gonçalves (fl. 15th century) crosses the Equator. ...Portugal's Fernando Po (fl. 15th century) discovers the offshore West African island that will bear his name.

1472–1504. Ali Ghadji (c. 1460–1504) reigns as king of Kanem.

1473. Songhai achieves independence from the empire of Mali. ...Ottoman Turks defeat Persians at Erzinjan.

c. 1473. Sonni Ali of Songhai takes Jenné on the Niger River.

Asia & Pacific

1464–1487. Ch'eng-hua (1447–1487) reigns as Ming emperor of China.

1467–1477. Civil war over successor to the shogunate devastates Kyoto, Japan.

1469–1481. Thihathura (c. 1450–1481) reigns as king of Ava (in Burma).

1469–1501. Ghiyas al-Din (?–1501) is sultan of Malwa (in India).

1470–1474. Russian merchant expedition visits Bahmani in search of trade.

1471. Annam (Vietnam) annexes its neighbor Champa (southern Vietnam).

1472–1492. Dammazedi (fl. 15th century) rules as king of Hanthawaddy and Pegu (in Burma).

1473–1474. Famine devastates the Deccan (in southern India).

Americas

1468. First period of Aztec conquest of Mexico ends.

▲ *Isabella of Castile (right) and Ferdinand of Aragon (left) kneel before the Madonna in this painting by an anonymous artist.*

1472. Dietrich Pining (fl. 15th century), Danish admiral, sights Newfoundland.

Science, Invention & Technology

1465. German printers set up a printing press at Subiaco, Italy. ...Printing and typography spread from Germany to Venice, Rome, Paris, Lyon, Rouen and Utrecht.

1466. A three-masted sailing carrack is built in France.

1470. First printshop in France is established in Paris. ...Nicolas Jenson (1420–1480), working in Venice, adapts Roman script to typography. ...Italian Leon Alberti (1404–1472) describes a cipher wheel for decoding messages. ...Aztecs invent accordion-fold books. ...Paper manufacturing becomes an important industry among the Aztecs of Mexico.

1474. First Spanish printing press is set up in Valencia. ...First book in Poland is printed.

Religion, Culture & Arts

1464–1471. Paul II (1417–1471) is pope.

1465. The University of Bruges in Belgium is established. ...Venetian painter Giovanni Bellini (c. 1430–1516) paints his *Agony in the Garden*.

1466. December 13: Florentine sculptor Donatello (b. 1386) dies.

1468. Pope Paul II abolishes Roman Academy. ...Johannes Gutenberg (b. c. 1397) dies.

1469. Fra Filippo Lippi (b. 1406), Italian painter, dies.

1470–1480. Sandro Botticelli (1445–1510) paints the *Primavera* (*Spring*) for Lorenzo de Medici.

1471. The University of Genoa, Italy, is established.

1471–1484. Sixtus IV (1414–1484) is pope.

1472. Leonardo da Vinci (1452–1519) registers in the painter's guild in Florence. ...The University of Munich is established.

1474. Andrea Mantegna (1431–1506) paints frescoes in Camera degli Sposi, Palazzo Ducale, Mantua. ...Antwerp Cathedral is completed. ...**November 27:** Guillaume Dufay (b. 1400), French composer, dies.

British Isles & Europe

1475. July: Edward IV of England invades France. ...**August 29:** Peace of Picquigny between Edward IV and Louis XI. ...**November:** Charles the Bold conquers Lorraine.

1477. Charles the Bold (b. 1433) is killed at Nancy. ...Louis XI seizes Burgundy and Artois; René I, father of Queen Margaret, recovers Lorraine.

1477–1513. Gerald Fitzgerald (?–1513), lord of Kildare, rules in Ireland.

1478. England establishes the Court of the Star Chamber. ...**May 2:** Giuliano de' Medici is assassinated.

1479. Aragon and Castile are united under Ferdinand II and Isabella, forming the basis of modern Spain. ...Maximilian (1459–1519) defeats French at Guinegate.

1480. March 6: In Treaty of Toledo, Spain recognizes conquest of Morocco by Portugal, which cedes claims to the Canary Islands.

1481. Louis XI of France subdues Franche-Comté, Provence and Maine. ...John II (1455–1495) of Portugal curbs power of the nobles and executes 80. ...**April:** War breaks out between England and Scotland.

1482. December 23: Peace of Arras divides Burgundy; Maximilian obtains Netherlands, Luxembourg, and Franche-Comté.

1483. April 9: Edward IV (b. 1442) dies and is succeeded as king of England by Edward V. ...**June 26:** Richard of Gloucester (1452–1485) usurps the throne. ...**July:** Edward V (b. 1470) and his brother are murdered. ...**August 30:** Louis XI (b. 1423) dies and is succeeded as king of France by Charles VIII (1470–1498).

1483–1501. Hans (1455–1513) reigns as king of Denmark, Norway, and Sweden.

1485. Brittany revolts against Charles VIII. ...**August 22:** Richard III (b. 1452) is defeated and killed at Bosworth. ...**November 7:** Henry VII (1457–1509) is crowned king of England.

1485–1508. Muscovites build the walls of the Kremlin.

Africa & Middle East

c. 1475. African state of Warri is established.

1475. December 21: Portuguese explorers reach present-day Sáo Tomé.

1476. Spanish occupy the Canary Islands.

1476–1507. Mai Ali (c. 1460–1507) rules Bornu (present-day Nigeria).

1478–1490. Yakub (fl. 15th century) reigns as shah of Persia.

1479–1480. Mossi states subdue Walata (in West Central Africa).

c. 1479. Changa breaks free of Monotmotapa control (in Central Africa).

1481. First Englishmen reach the West African coast.

1481–1512. Bajazet II (1446–1512) reigns as sultan of the Ottoman Empire.

1482. Portuguese settle on Gold Coast, West Africa. ...Mouth of the Congo River is discovered by Portuguese explorer Diego Cão (fl. 15th century).

1483. Sonni Ali of Songhai evicts Mossi invaders from Walata.

1484–1491. Turks make inconclusive war on Mameluke Egypt.

1485. Portuguese colonize present-day Sáo Tomé.

1485–1486. Portuguese expedition reaches West African state of Benin; trade links are established.

Asia & Pacific

1475–1541. Gedon Gyafso? (fl. 15 and 16th centuries) rules as Dalai Lama in Tibet.

1477–1488. Sultan Ala al-Din Shah (c. 1450–1488) is ruler of Malacca (Malay Peninsula).

1481–1502. Minkhaung (c. 1460–1502) reigns as king of Ava (in Burma).

1482. End of Bahmani kingdom in the Deccan (in India).

1482–1518. Bahmani dominions break up into independent states.

1484–1508. Parakrama Bahu VIII (c. 1460–1508) reigns as king of Kotte (in present-day Sri Lanka).

1485–1491. Bloody dynastic struggles devastate Vijayanagar (in India).

Americas

1476–1520. One of the last Aztec temples is built at Malinalco.

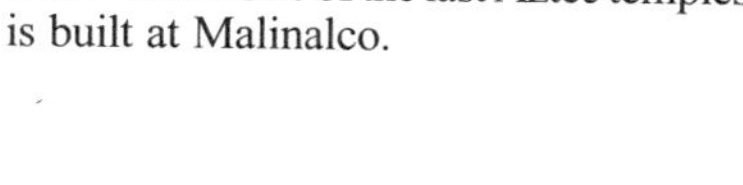

▲ *This 15th-century Flemish miniature depicts Charles the Bold overseeing a meeting with a chapter of the Order of the Golden Fleece.*

c. 1485. Pawnee move northeastward near the Missouri River.

Science, Invention & Technology

1476. William Caxton sets up the first English printing press in Westminster. ...First plainsong books with music are printed in Rome.

1478. Tapestry industry is centered in Brussels. ...European publishers first use copper engravings.

c. 1480. Cloth parachutes are developed in Italy.

1481. A tooth-extraction forceps called a pelican is invented by German Johann Schrenk (fl. 15th century).

1484. Giovanni d'Arcoli (Arculanus) (fl. 15th century) suggests use of gold leaf for dental fillings.

Religion, Culture & Arts

1475. *Rules of Chess*, first book printed in English, is written by William Caxton (c. 1421–1491) in Cologne, Germany. ...Michelangelo Buonarroti (d. 1564) is born .

c. 1476. Andrea del Verrocchio (c. 1435–1488) sculpts the bronze statue *David*.

1477. The University of Uppsala in Sweden is established. ...*The Dictes or Sayengis of the Philosophres* is printed by Caxton. ...Universities of Mainz and Tubingen in Germany are established.

1478. Ferdinand II establishes the Spanish Inquisition.

1479. Copenhagen University is founded.

1481–1483. Frescoes in the Vatican's Sistine Chapel are painted.

1483. October 17: Spanish Inquisition comes under joint direction of state and church. ...**November 10:** Martin Luther (d. 1546) is born.

1484. Hieronymus Bosch (c. 1450-1516) paints the *Garden of Earthly Delights*.

1484–1492. Innocent VIII (1432–1492) is pope.

1485. Diet of Kuttenberg grants equal rights to Roman Catholics and Utraquists in Bohemia. ...*Le Morte d'Arthur* by Sir Thomas Malory (?–1471) is printed by Caxton. ...Venetian printer strikes off the first copies of the Koran in Arabic....**September 15:** Pedro de Arbues (b. 1442), Spanish inquisitor, is murdered.

British Isles & Europe

1486. February 16: Maximilian I is elected king of Germany.

1487. Ivan III (1440–1505) of Muscovy (Moscow) subdues Kazan. ...**April 17:** Commercial treaty of Novgorod between Russians and Hanseatic League. ...**May 5:** Yorkists rebel against Tudor rule. ...**June 16:** Rebel Yorkists defeated at Stoke-on-Trent.

1488. France defeats rebel dukes of Brittany and Orléans at St. Auban du Cormier, ending the "Foolish War." ...**February 14:** Swabian League is formed in southern Germany. ...**June 11:** James III is murdered and is succeeded as king of Scotland by James IV (1473–1513). ...**July 28:** Bretons are defeated at St. Aubin. ...**October 5:** England and Scotland begin two-year truce.

1489. Soldiers returning to Aragon from eastern Mediterranean cause first recorded epidemic of typhus in Europe. ...**February 10:** England and Brittany form the Alliance of Redon. ...**February 14:** Holy Roman Emperor and England enter into the Treaty of Dordrecht. ...**March 27:** England and Spain enter into a commercial treaty. ...**April 6:** Hans Waldmann (b. 1435), Burgomaster of Zurich, is executed for his dictatorial tendencies.

1490. January 20: England and Denmark agree to peace.

1490–1516. Ulászló II (1456–1516), king of Bohemia from 1471, reigns as king of Hungary.

1491. November 7: Under Treaty of Pressburg, Ulászló II of Bohemia and Hungary acknowledges Habsburgs' right of succession. ...**December 21:** England and Scotland agree to five-year truce of Coldstream.

1492. January 2: Spaniards conquer Granada. ...**April 8:** Lorenzo de' Medici dies. ...**October 2:** Henry VII of England lands in France. ...**November 3:** In Peace of Étaples between France and England, France abandons Perkin Warbeck (1474–1499), the pretender to the English throne.

1493. England and Flanders wage commercial war. ...**January 19:** In Peace of Barcelona between France and Spain, France cedes Roussillon and Cerdagne. ...**May 23:** In Peace of Senlis between France and Holy Roman Emperor, France renounces Netherlands and Burgundy. ...**August 19:** Frederick III (b. 1415) dies and is succeeded as Holy Roman Emperor by Maximilian I.

Africa & Middle East

1487. Bartolomeu Dias (c. 1450–1500) sails around Cape of Good Hope, becoming first European to enter Indian Ocean.

1488. Portuguese expedition under Pero da Covilhão (1450–1545) explores Red Sea coast of East Africa. Covilhão expedition touches at Aden and Hormuz.

1490. Portuguese establish sugarcane plantations on island of present-day Sáo Tomé and import slaves from Benin to work them. ...**June 3–July 30:** Congress in Rome decides upon Crusade against Turks.

1491. Portuguese explorers travel 200 miles up the Congo River.

1492. Sonni Ali the Great of Songhai dies.

1492–1542. Muhammadu Koran (?–1542) reigns as the first Muslim king of Katsina (in Central Africa).

1493–1535. Askia Muhammad (c. 1480–1535) reigns in Songhai and reorganizes the Songhai empire.

Asia & Pacific

1486–1531. Minkyinyo reigns as king of Ava (in Burma).

1487–1505. Hung-chi (1470–1505) reigns as Ming emperor of China.

1488. The popular Ikko sect (the True Pure Land sect) launches its first uprising in Japan.

1488–1511. Mahmud Shah (?–1528) is sultan of Malacca (Malay Peninsula).

1489. Yusuf establishes the independent sultanate of Bijapur in the Deccan (in India).

1489–1517. Sikandar Lodi (?–1517), the son of Bahlol Lodi, reigns as king of Delhi.

1490. Sultanate of Ahmednagar is established (in southern India).

1491. Construction of the planned city of Hyderabad in India is completed.

1492–1526. Binnya Ran (c. 1470–1526) is king of Hanthawaddy.

1493–1494. Rebel strongman Hosokawa Masamoto establishes a puppet shogunate in Kyoto.

1493–1519. Husan Shah (?–1519) reigns as king of Bengal, India.

Americas

Science, Invention & Technology

Religion, Culture & Arts

1486–1495. Kamul Ud-Din Bihzad (c. 1460–1535), Persian artist, paints series of 32 miniatures.

1487. Spanish use horse-drawn ambulances during the siege of Malaga.

1487. One of the earliest printed books on the theory of music is published at Bologna.

▲ ***This engraving from Theodore Bry's* Les Grands Voyages *(Vol. II, 1528–98) shows Christopher Columbus in a peaceful, friendly encounter with the natives of the New World.***

1488. Giovanni Bellini paints *Madonna with Saints* in the church of St. Maria dei Frari, Venice. ...Andrea del Verrocchio sculpts equestrian statue of the condottieri Bartolomeo Colleoni.

1489. Angelo Poliziano (1454–1494), humanist and poet writes *Miscellanea.*

c. 1490. Chinese invent the toothbrush. ...Leonardo da Vinci builds a hygrometer for measuring atmospheric humidity.

1491. Leonardo da Vinci describes a camera obscura, prototype of the camera. ...A globe made by German Martin Behaim (c. 1436–1506) is believed to have influenced Christopher Columbus' (1451–1506) decision to sail west.

1491. William Caxton (b. c. 1421), English writer and printer, dies.

1492. August 3: Christopher Columbus (1451–1506) sails from Palos, Spain. ...**October 12:** Columbus discovers San Salvador (in the Bahamas). ...**October 27:** Columbus discovers Cuba. ...**December 6:** Columbus discovers Haiti and Dominican Republic. ...**December 25:** *Santa Maria*, Columbus' flagship, is wrecked off Haiti.

1493. Columbus sights Antigua and Dominica and discovers Jamaica. ...**November 28:** Columbus anchors off the coast of Puerto Rico.

1492. Columbus discovers magnetic declination on his compass. Columbus, while in America, becomes first European to encounter the use of tobacco. Columbus returns to Europe with strands of popcorn. ...**April:** Earliest known blood transfusion is performed on Pope Innocent VIII.

1493. Christopher Columbus introduces pineapples, capsicums, sweet potatoes and other commodities from the Americas to Europe.

1492 Humanist Elio Antonio de Lebrija (c. 1444–1532) publishes a Spanish grammar, the first of a European language vernacular. ...**March 31:** Jews are expelled from Spain.

1492–1503. Alexander VI (c. 1431–1503) is pope.

1493. Italians are first Europeans since the ancient Romans to adopt city planning. ...**July 12 and December 23:** Latin and German versions of Hartmann Schedel's (1440–1514) *World Chronicle* are published.

British Isles & Europe

1494. Poynings's Laws make Irish legislature dependent on England. ...Maxmilian I recognizes Perkin Warbeck as king of England. ...Charles VIII invades Italy. ...**November 6:** Ivan III closes Hanseatic trade center at Novgorod. ...**November 17:** Charles VIII enters Florence and expels Medicis.

1495. February 22: Charles VIII enters Naples. ...**March 31:** Maxmilian I, Pope Alexander VI, Spain, Venice, and Milan unite to force Charles VIII to leave Italy.

1495–1521. Emmanuel the Fortunate (1469–1521) reigns in Portugal.

1496. With Edward Poynings's departure, home rule is restored in Ireland. ...*Magnus Intercursus* ends trade war between England and Flanders. ...**September:** Scots invade England.

1497. July–September: Perkin Warbeck leads rebellion in England. ...**September 30:** England and Scotland agree on truce. ...**October 28:** John II of Denmark (1455–1513) defeats Swedes at Brunkeberg and revives Scandinavian union.

1498. Maximilian I establishes Imperial Council, Chancery and Chamber. ...Charles VIII (b. 1470) dies and is succeeded as king of France by Louis XII (1462–1515). ...Niccolò Machiavelli (1469–1527) is appointed Florentine secretary. ...Peace of Étaples is renewed at Paris.

1499. Maximilian I wages "Swabian War" against Swiss League. ...**September 22:** Peace of Basel establishes Swiss independence from Holy Roman Empire. ...**November 23 and 28:** Perkin Warbeck (b. 1474) and Edward, earl of Warwick (b. 1475), are beheaded as pretenders.

Africa & Middle East

1494–1498. Naod (c. 1470–1498) reigns as emperor of Ethiopia.

1496. Spain conquers Melilla on the North African coast.

1497. November 22: Vasco da Gama's four-ship expedition rounds the Cape of Good Hope en route to India.

Asia & Pacific

1494. Babur succeeds to throne of Ferghana in Central Asia. ...Sultan Sikandar Lodi of Delhi moves to suppress rebellion in Jaunpur.

1496. A merchant from Genoa, Italy becomes the first European to reach Pegu (in Burma).

1498. May 20: Vasco da Gama's (1469–1524) expedition reaches Calicut.

This miniature by an anonymous artist of the late 15th-century shows the sovereigns of Europe praying in front of St. George. ➤

Americas

1494. Christopher Columbus visits Jamaica. ...**June 7:** In the Treaty of Tordesillas, Spain and Portugal divide New World.

1496. August 4: The city of Santo Domingo (in present-day Dominican Republic) is founded.

1497. John Cabot (c. 1450–c. 1499) and his son Sebastian Cabot (c. 1476–1557) discover the North American coast on their first voyage. ...Cabots sight land (probably Newfoundland). ...**July:** Cabots reach perhaps as far south as present-day Maine before sailing for England.

1498. Christopher Columbus explores Orinoco River in Venezuela. ...John Cabot discovers Labrador. ...Columbus visits Grenada, discovers Trinidad, and sights mainland of South America. ...**August 31:** Columbus finds the colony of Santo Domingo in rebellion.

1499. Amerigo Vespucci (1454–1512) and Alonso Hojeda (1473–1540) discover Guiana and Venezuela. ...**September:** Immunity is granted to rebel leaders in Santo Domingo. ...**September 19:** Vespucci passes Camocim, Brazil.

Science, Invention & Technology

1494. Intensive banana cultivation is discovered by the Spanish on Tenerife in the Canary Islands.

1495. Christopher Columbus introduces tomatoes to Europe. ...Mercury is first used for the treatment of syphilis, in Europe.

1497. Sebastian Cabot sails to within 20 degrees of the North Pole in search of the Northwest Passage. ...A quicksilver deposit is discovered at Illyria, Austria.

1498. An Italian man attempts to glide with wings attached to his body.

1499. Leonardo da Vinci envisions a futuristic city with two levels of traffic.

▲ ***A romanticized depiction of an encounter in the New World between Amerigo Vespucci and a native woman from Theodore Bry's*** **Histoire de l' Amérique.**

Religion, Culture & Arts

1494. Sebastian Brant (1457–1521) writes *Ship of Fools*. ...**August 11:** Hans Memling (b. 1430), Dutch painter, dies.

1495. Jews are expelled from Portugal. ...**February 10:** Aberdeen University is founded.

1495–1497. Leonardo da Vinci paints *Last Supper* in Santa Maria delle Grazie in Milan.

1497. Michelangelo Buonarroti is commissioned to carve his first *Pietà*, considered the culmination of the Florentine tradition in sculpture. ...Jesus College, Cambridge, is founded.

1498. Erasmus (c. 1466–1536) settles in Oxford. ...Albrecht Dürer (1471–1528) completes his series of large woodcuts called *The Apocalypse*. ...**May 23:** Religious reformer Girolamo Savonarola (b. 1452) is burned at the stake in Florence.

1499. Alcalá University is founded in Spain. ...Spain decrees that Muslims must convert to Christianity. ...*La Celestina*, the first great Spanish novel, is written from classical and medieval sources. ...University of Oxford institutes degrees in music.

1499–1504. Luca Signorelli (c. 1441–1523) paints *End of the World* and *Last Judgment* frescoes in Orvieto Cathedral.

British Isles & Europe

1500. February 17: Dithmarschen peasants defeat Danes at Hemmingstedt and maintain their independence. ...**July 2:** Diet of Augsburg establishes Council of Regency to administer Holy Roman Empire. ...**November 11:** Treaty of Granada between France and Spain partitions Italy.

1501. Alexander of Lithuania (1461–1506) succeeds to the Polish throne. ...Turks take Durazzo (in Albania) from Venice. ...**July–August:** Louis XII of France and Ferdinand II of Spain conquer Naples. ...**October 13:** Peace of Trento between France and Maximilian I recognizes French conquests in Upper Italy.

1502. War breaks out between France and Spain. ...Peasants in bishopric of Spires, Germany rebel. ...**August 8:** James IV of Scotland marries Margaret Tudor (1489–1541), daughter of Henry VII.

1503. Spaniards expel French from Naples. ...Spain establishes board of trade at Seville for dealings with the Americas. ...**December 29:** French and Spanish fight the battle of River Garigliano.

1504. Albert IV of Bavaria (1447?–1508) defeats Rupert (1481–1504), count Palatine, and re-unites the Bavarian duchies. ...**January 31 and May 31:** In Treaty of Lyons, France cedes Naples to Spain. ...**November 26:** Queen Isabella (b. 1451) of Castile dies.

1505. Francis of Taxis (1450–1517) establishes first regular mail (between Vienna and Brussels). ...Workers' uprising disrupts economic life in Lyons, France.

1505–1533. Vasily III (1479–1533) reigns as grand duke of Muscovy (Moscow).

1506. May 21: Christopher Columbus (b. 1451) dies. ...**December 6:** Niccolò Machiavelli creates Florentine militia, first national Italian troops.

1506–1548. Sigismund I (1467–1548) reigns as king of Poland.

Africa & Middle East

1500. Portuguese navigator Pedro Álvares Cabral (c. 1467–1520) explores Mozambique (in East Africa). ...**June 1:** Pope Alexander VI imposes a general tithe and proclaims Crusade against Turks.

1500–1516. Al-Ashraf Quansah al-Ghawri (?–1576) reigns as sultan of Egypt.

1500–1600. Small Akan Ashanti states emerge in West African forests. ...Shona kingdoms flourish in interior regions of southeast Africa between the Zambezi and Limpopo Rivers.

1502. Ismail (1486–1524) establishes Safavid dynasty in Persia. ...Sultanate of Kilwa (in East Africa) agrees to pay tribute to Portugal.

Shah Ismail (on left horse), founder of the Safavid dynasty in Persia.

1505. Portuguese soldier Francisco de Almeida (c. 1450–1510) sacks Kilwa and Mombasa in East Africa. ...Portuguese take trading center of Sofala in southeast Africa. ...Spanish take Mers-el-Kebir (in North Africa).

1505–1507. Portuguese establish factories on east coast of Africa.

1506. Portuguese explore Madagascar.

1506–1543. Nzinga Mvemba Afonso I (c. 1480–1543), a Christianized African, reigns in Kongo.

Asia & Pacific

c. 1500. Portuguese navigator Bartolomeu Dias (b. c. 1450) drowns near Cape of Good Hope. ...Population of China exceeds 15 million. ...Ceylonese capital is established at Kotte near present-day Colombo. ...Tamil kingdom emerges in northeast Ceylon.

1503. Portuguese flotilla sails home from East Indies with a cargo of 1,300 tons of pepper.

1504. Babur occupies Kabul (in Afghanistan). ...Portuguese appoint a viceroy for Cochin (in southern India).

1505. Portuguese navigator Lourenço de Almeida (?–1508), the son of Francisco de Almeida, reaches Colombo in Ceylon (present-day Sri Lanka). ...Damaging earthquake rocks India.

1505–1509. Francisco de Almeida is first Portuguese viceroy of India.

1505–1521. Cheng-te (1491–1521) reigns as Ming emperor of China.

Americas

1500. The Amazon River is discovered. ...Pedro Álvares Cabral discovers Brazil and claims it for Portugal. ...**January:** Vicente Yáñez Pinzón (fl. 1492–1509) reaches the coast of Brazil.

1501. Anglo-Portuguese Syndicate makes its first voyage to North America. ...Rodrigo de Bastidas (1460–1526) sights Panama. ...Juan de la Cosa (c. 1460–1510) explores northern coast of South America, including Gulf of Darién and Atrato River, and finds traces of gold.

1502. Second period of Aztec conquest of Mexico ends. ...Christopher Columbus embarks on his fourth voyage. ...Anglo-Portuguese Syndicate makes its second voyage to Newfoundland. Amerigo Vespucci voyages to the Americas. ...Europeans first arrive in Argentina. ...Columbus drops anchor off Portobelo, Panama. ...Bay of Rio de Janeiro is discovered. ...Columbus sights Surinam. ...**February:** Vespucci lands at Puerto San Julian, Argentina.

1503. Anglo-Portuguese make their third expedition to Newfoundland. ...**June 25:** Christopher Columbus is shipwrecked on Jamaica.

1504. French fishing vessels explore Newfoundland coast seeking a passage to the Indies through North America. ...**January:** Binot Paulmier de Gonneville (fl. 16th century), a Norman merchant, is blown off course from the West Indies and arrives on the coast of Brazil. He stays six months.

1505. Anglo-Portuguese make their fifth expedition to Newfoundland.

Science, Invention & Technology

c. 1500. Marseilles, France, becomes the center for the popular glass-printing industry. ...Leonardo da Vinci designs and creates models of flying machines but fails to experiment with them. He also invents a device attached to a wheel for measuring distance traveled. ...First portable clocks with coiled mainsprings are made by German Peter Henlein (fl. 16th century).

c. 1500. Early baby bottles in Europe have a distinctive duck-bill nipple. ...A chain-and-bucket system for lifting water is used in Europe. ...Metal grenades are first used in European combat; grenadiers in the British army specialize in handling them. ...Conquistadors introduce waterwheels to Panamanian mines. ...Conquistadors add sugar to chocolate to create first sweetened chocolate drink. ...Dished wheels, some with spokes, are added to wagons to accommodate heavier loads. ...Paper sizing, the treatment of paper with starch to make it whiter and firmer, is developed in Europe. ...Roads with wooden rails are used to haul ore from mines. ...First jib sails are mounted at the front of European ships. ...Among the early attempts to cushion the ride in vehicles, carriages are suspended with leather straps, which only cause them to sway radically. ...Aztecs use sharp-edged volcanic rock as razors. ...Vaulting, the ability to build greater structures with suspended ceilings, reaches the height of its technological limits. ...A lead-weighted triangular chip, released on a line from the rear of a ship, is used to measure distance traveled at sea. ...Art of making stained glass declines, and the technologically new art of oil painting gains favor among European artists. ...Turn screws are used in European gun manufacturing. ...Italians and Flemish develop sheep shears. ...Sailing masts mounted on oared galleys are used in the Mediterranean. ...Inhabitants of Crete and the Aegean Islands build the first jib-sail windmills. ...Tanbark and woad (for blue dye) are processed in European grinding mills. ...Aztec women use ochre, crushed insects and other natural substances as makeup. ...Cholera is first identified in Europe. ...Portuguese introduce peanuts (groundnuts) from Brazil to West Africa. ...English develop the first full-masted ships.

Religion, Culture & Arts

c. 1500. Andrea Amati (d. c. 1575), the earliest recorded member of the famous family of violin makers in Cremona, is born.

c. 1500–1600. Italian merchants begin importing Chinese porcelain.

1501. Erasmus writes *Enchiridion Militis Christiani*. ...Gawain Douglas (c. 1474–1530) writes *Palace of Honour*. University of Valencia, Spain, is established.

1501–1504. Michelangelo sculpts *David*, a larger than life-size marble sculpture. It will be considered the embodiment of Renaissance heroic spirit.

1502. Wittenberg University in Germany is founded. ...First book of masses by Josquin des Prés (c. 1450–1521) is published. ...Spain introduces book censorship and requires a license to print or sell books. ...Lucas Cranach (1472–1553) paints *St. Jerome*.

1503. William Dunbar (*c.* 1460-*c.* 1515), Scottish court poet to James IV: *The Thrissil and the Ros*. ...Leonardo da Vinci: *Mona Lisa*.

1503–1513. Julius II (1443–1513) is pope.

1504. Giorgione (c. 1478–1510) paints *Madonna* at Castelfranco. ...Lucas Cranach paints *Rest on the Flight into Egypt*.

1505. Christ's College at Cambridge is founded. ...Raphael Santi (1485–1520) paints *The Madonna and Child Enthroned with Saints*. ...Jacobi Wimpfeling (1450–1528) writes the first German history, *Epitome Rerum Germanicarum*. ...University of Seville in Spain is established. ...**July 17:** Martin Luther enters Augustinian friary at Erfurt.

1506. Donato Bramante (1444–1514) begins to rebuild St. Peter's in Rome. ...Johann Reuchlin (1455–1522): *Hebrew Grammar* and *Dictionary*. ...Frankfurt-on-the-Oder University founded. ...The sculpture group, *Laocoon*, believed to be Hellenistic, is discovered in Rome. ...Sesshu (b. 1420), considered the greatest 15th-century Japanese ink painter, dies.

British Isles & Europe	Africa & Middle East	Asia & Pacific
1507. April–May: Diet of Constance establishes Imperial Chamber and territorial taxation according to a fixed roll. ...**May 11:** France annexes Genoa.		**1507.** Maw Shans invade Ava (in Burma).
1508. February 6: Maximilian I joins League of Cambrai in opposition to Venice.	**1508.** Portuguese begin colonization of Mozambique. ...Ismail I (1487–1524), Shah of Persia occupies Baghdad. **1508–1540.** Lebna Dengel (c. 1490–1540) reigns in Ethiopia.	**1508. January:** Egyptian-Indian fleet defeats the Portuguese off Chaul.
1509. March 23: Pope Julius II joins League of Cambrai. ...**April 21:** Henry VII (b. 1457) dies and is succeeded as king of England by Henry VIII (1491–1547).	**1509. May:** Spaniards conquer Oran in North Africa.	**1509. February 2:** Portuguese defeat Egypt and Gujarat fleets off Diu (in India). **1509–1529.** Krishnadevaraya (c. 1580–1529) reigns as raja of Hindu Vijayanagar.
	1510. Spain takes Tunis and Tripoli in North Africa. ...Dynasty of the sharifs of the Banu Saad rule in Morocco. ...Ismail I, shah of Persia, subdues the Uzbeks at Marv.	**1510.** Afonso de Albuquerque (1453–1515) annexes Goa (in India) for Portugal. **1510–1515.** Afonso de Albuquerque is Portuguese viceroy of India. **1510–1524.** Ismail I, shah of Persia, reigns as sultan of Bijapur.
	1511. Babur and Persian allies conquer Samarkand.	**1511. March 4:** Afonso de Albuquerque annexes Malacca in Malaya for Portugal.
1512. April 11: After the battle of Ravenna, French are expelled from Italy. ...Spaniards invade Navarre. ...**September 6:** Medicis are restored as Florentine constitution is altered. **1512–1522.** Poland and Russia wage war.	**1512.** Askia Muhammad the Great of Songhai occupies Katsina, Kano and Zaria (in West Central Africa) **1512–1520.** Selim I (1467–1520), son of Bajazet II, reigns as sultan of Ottoman Empire.	**1512.** Golconda (in southwestern India) becomes independent. **1512–1531.** Mahmud II (?– 1531) reigns in Malwa (in India).
1513. French invade Milan, Italy. ...French are defeated at Novara, Italy. ...Maximilian I and Henry VIII defeat French at Guinegate (battle of Spurs). ...Scots, allied with French, are defeated at Flodden; James IV (b. 1473) is killed and is succeeded as king of Scotland by James V (1512–1542).	**1513.** Selim I takes Armenia for the Ottomans. ...Portuguese explorers ascend the Zambezi and establish outposts at Sena and Tefe. ...Moroccan chronicler Leo Africanus (1485–c. 1552) visits Timbuktu.	**1513.** Portuguese factory established at Diu.
1514. Princedom of Moldavia comes under Turkish sovereignty. ...A royal charter issued by King Henry VIII of England establishes Trinity House, an international shipping organization. ...**August 6:** England and France reach peace accord.	**1514.** Pope Leo X (1475–1521) issues a bull against trading in African slaves. ...Portuguese penetrate the interior of Sofala (in Mozambique). ...Afonso I (?–c. 1550) the king of Kongo, protests the growing Portuguese slave trade. ...**August:** Selim I defeats Persians and takes Tabriz and Mesopotamia for the Ottomans. **1514–1516.** Turks wage war against Persia. ...Selim I settles Kurds in Armenia.	

Americas

1507. Cartographer Martin Waldseemüller (c. 1470–1522) names New World *America* after Amerigo Vespucci.

1508. Sebastian de Ocampo (1465– c. 1508) circumnavigates Cuba, proving it is not part of a mainland.

1508–1509. Vicente Yáñez Pinzón (c. 1470–c. 1523) and Juan Díaz de Solís (c. 1470–1516) explore Honduran and Yucatán coasts. ...Spanish conquer Puerto Rico.

1509. John Cabot and Sebastian Cabot search for Northwest Passage along Hudson Bay. ...Spanish conquer and settle Jamaica. ...Slave trade in the Americas begins in Chiapas in Mexico.

1510. American east coast as far north as present-day Charleston is explored. ...San Juan, Puerto Rico, is founded.

1511. Diego Velázquez de Cuéllar (c. 1465–1522) occupies Cuba.

1512. Spanish colony of Santo Domingo begins sending $1 million in gold each year to Spain.

1513. Juan Ponce de León (1460–1521) discovers Florida and introduces citrus trees to Florida from Spain. ...**September 25:** Vasco Núñez de Balboa (1475–1519) crosses Isthmus of Panama and discovers the Pacific Ocean.

1514. Pedro Arias Dávila (c. 1440–1530) colonizes Isthmus of Panama. ...Santiago and Havana, Cuba, are founded by Diego Velázquez de Cuéllar. ...Construction begins on the Santo Domingo Cathedral, the oldest in the Western Hemisphere.

Science, Invention & Technology

▲ ***Pope Leo X in a painting by Raphael.***

1510. Sunflowers from America are introduced to Europe. ...Use of popcorn in Aztec religious fetes is observed by Hernando Cortés (1485–1547). ...Potatoes are brought from present-day Virginia and planted in Spain. ...Newfoundland fish are offered for sale at market in Rouen (France).

1512. Nutmeg is discovered by the Portuguese in the Moluccas (Spice Islands), an island group in the Indian Ocean.

1514. Green peas are introduced to England. ...Gunshot wounds, a relatively recent phenomenon, are first described in medical journals. ...The + and – signs for addition and subtraction are introduced to mathematical equations in Europe.

Religion, Culture & Arts

1508. Andrea Palladio (d. 1580), one of most influential Italian architects, is born. ...Martin Luther becomes professor of divinity at Wittenberg. ...Italian poet Lódovico Ariosto (1474–1533) stages his play *Cassaria*.

1508–1512. Michelangelo paints ceiling frescoes in Sistine Chapel.

c. 1509. Matthias Grünewald (c.1475–1528) paints *Isenheim Triptych*.

1510. Erasmus: *Institutio Christiani Principis* (*The Education of a Catholic Prince*). ...Titian (c. 1490–1576) paints *The Gypsy Madonna*.

1510–1514. Erasmus teaches Greek at Cambridge University.

1511. Venetian painter Giorgione (b. c. 1477) dies.

1512. Raphael (1483–1520) paints *Sistine Madonna*. ...Martin Luther lectures on Epistles to Romans and Galatians.

1513. Niccolò Machiavelli, historian and political theorist, writes *The Prince* (*Il Principe*). ...Marx Treizsaurwein von Ehrentreitz (c. 1450–1527): *Weisskunig*, with woodcuts by H. Burgkmair (1473–1531). ...Chartres Cathedral is completed.

1514. Albrecht Dürer (1471–1528) completes the engraving *Melancholia I*.

1514–1536. Hampton Court Palace is built.

British Isles & Europe

1515. Navarre is incorporated into Castile. ...**January 1:** Louis XII (b. 1462) of France dies and is succeeded by Francis I (1494–1547). ...**July–August:** Vienna treaties between Maximilian I, Sigismund I of Poland and Ulászló II of Bohemia and Hungary link succession of Habsburgs and Jagellons. ...**September 13–14:** Francis I defeats Swiss mercenaries at Marigano and conquers Milan. ...**December 11–14:** In Treaty of Bologna, Pope Leo X surrenders Parma and Piacenza to France. ...**December 24:** Thomas Wolsey (1473–1530) becomes Lord Chancellor.

1516. Mongols raid Poland and withdraw with stolen riches and 50,000 captives. ...**January 23:** Ferdinand I (b. 1452) of Aragon dies and is succeeded by Charles (1500–1558), grandson of Maximilian I and of Ferdinand II and Isabella. Charles reigns as king of Spain (until 1556) as Charles I. ...**March 13:** Ulászló II (b. 1456) of Bohemia and Hungary dies. ...**August 13:** Peace of Noyon between France and Spain.

1517. English merchants obtain commercial privileges in Andalusia, Spain. ...**May 1:** Thomas Wolsey suppresses May Day disturbances in London and orders 60 rioters hanged.

1518. October 2: Peace of London between England, the Holy Roman Empire, France, and Spain is a diplomatic triumph for Thomas Wolsey.

1519. January 12: Maximilian I (b. 1459) dies. **June 28:** Charles I of Spain is elected Holy Roman Emperor as Charles V.

1520. Christian II (1481–1559) of Denmark invades Sweden, massacres the nobility and seizes the throne. ...**July 14:** Henry VIII and Charles V agree on secret treaty at Calais.

Africa & Middle East

1515. Portuguese export nearly 1,500 slaves from Guinea. ...Portugal takes Hormuz on the Persian Gulf and builds a fort there. ...Turks subdue eastern Anatolia and Kurdistan.

c. 1515–1561. Muhammad Kantu (c. 1510–1561) becomes king of Kebbi and rebels against Songhai.

1516. Ottomans campaign in Syria. ...**August 24:** Ottoman forces take Aleppo. ...**September 26:** Ottomans capture Damascus.

1516–1517. Al-Ashraf Tuman-bey (?–1517) is the last Mameluke sultan of Egypt.

1517. Turks conquer Egypt and intercept traffic en route to India. ...First Ottoman governor takes office in Damascus. ...Sharif of Mecca capitulates to Ottomans. ...Portuguese burn Zaila in Adan (northeast Africa). ...Hausa Confederation defeats Songhai to become the dominant power east of the Niger River (in West Africa). ...**January 22:** Ottoman Turks sack Cairo. ...**April 14:** Ottomans hang Sultan Tuman-bey.

1518. Barbary States in North Africa founded. ...Barbarossa is killed in battle; his successors offer Barbary Algiers to the Ottomans.

1520–1566. Süleyman I (1494–1566), the Magnificent, son of Selim I, reigns as sultan of Ottoman Empire.

Asia & Pacific

c. 1515–1530. Sultanate of Atjeh is established in north Sumatra.

1516. Portuguese begin to trade with China and introduce corn to Chinese.

1517–1526. Ibrahim Lodi (1494–1536), son of Sikandar Lodi, reigns as king of Delhi.

1517. Babur raids southward into India.

1518. Chinese forces quell uprising in Kiangsi province.

1518–1532. Nasrat Shah (?–1532) reigns as king of Bengal.

1519. Great Golden Mosque is built at Delhi. ...Portuguese introduce firearms to the Chinese. ...Portuguese conclude trade treaty with Martaban in Burma.

1520. Javanese state of Majapahit passes out of existence.

1520–1521. Portuguese send trade and diplomatic mission to Beijing.

Americas

1515. Juan Díaz de Solís reaches mouth of River Plate (between present-day Argentina and Uruguay).

1516. Juan Díaz de Solís searches for a southwest passage to Orient and discovers Rio de la Plata in Argentina and explores Paraguay. ...Spanish establish vice royalty of New Spain in Mexico.

1517. September: Francisco Fernández de Córdoba (c. 1475–1525) and Antonio Alaminos (fl. 1493–1520) explore the Yucatán.

1518. Juan de Grijalava (c. 1489–1527) explores east coast of Mexico and names the region New Spain. ...French establish a settlement in Canada.

1519. Hernando Cortés conquers Cuba. ...Panama City is founded. ...Alonso Álvarez de Pineda (?–1520) explores Gulf of Mexico from Florida to Veracruz. ...**March 25:** Cortés defeats Tabascan Indians in Mexico. ...**September 5:** Cortés defeats Tlascala Indians in Mexico. ...**November 8.** Montezuma (c. 1480–1520) cordially receives Cortés at the Aztec court.

1520. Ferdinand Magellan (c. 1480–1521) enters estuary of Parana and Paraguay Rivers in Argentina. ...Magellan discovers Tierra del Fuego, at extreme southern point of South America. ...Atahualpa (c. 1502–1533) inherits Inca kingdom of Quito (in Peru) from his father. ...Cumana, Spanish settlement on coast of Venezuela, is founded. ...**June 30:** Held in captivity by Cortés, Montezuma (b. c. 1480) is killed. ...**July 7:** Cortés crushes Aztec revolt at Otumba.

Science, Invention & Technology

1515. Quarrying of peat in areas of land reclaimed from the North Sea in the Netherlands is banned when it is learned that it raises the water table and destabilizes the dike system. ...A metal rolling machine is invented in Tyrol, Austria.

A watercolor of Hernando Cortés by Christopher Weiditz painted in 1542.

1518. Augsburg, Germany, has world's first fire engines.

1519. The Joachinsthaler (origin of the word *dollar*) coin is minted in Bohemia, ...Cortés becomes first European to encounter chocolate and peanuts, in Mexico. ...**September 20:** Ferdinand Magellan (c. 1480–1521) sails from Spain on the first circumnavigation of the world.

1520. August Kotter (fl. 16th century), a German gunsmith, invents the rifle. ...Chocolate is introduced to Spain from Mexico but remains a secret for almost 100 years. ...Lyons, France, becomes a major center for the European silk industry.

c. 1520. Germans invent the wheel lock, a device that allows for the internal ignition of firearms.

Religion, Culture & Arts

1515. Correggio (1494–1534) paints *Virgin with St. Francis*. ...*Sophonisba* is written by Giovanni Giorgio Trissino (1478–1550). Not performed until 1524, it will be regarded as first Italian tragedy. ...English cleric and politician Thomas Wolsey is made a cardinal.

1515–1516. Michelangelo sculpts the statue of *Moses*.

1516. Hieronymus Bosch (b. c. 1450), a Dutch painter from northern Braban, dies. ...Thomas More (1478–1535) writes *Utopia*, an allegorical account of an ideal society. ...Corpus Christi College at Oxford is founded. ...Machiavelli: *Discorsi* and *La Mandragola*.

1516–1518. Titian paints *Assumption of the Virgin* for Santa Maria dei Frari, Venice.

1517. Seville Cathedral is completed. ...**October 31:** Martin Luther nails his 95 Theses against sale of indulgences to door of Wittenberg Palace Church.

1518. Albrecht Altdorfer (c. 1485–1538) paints the altarpiece of St. Florian Church, near Linz, Germany. ...Martin Luther, interrogated by cardinal legate Cajetanus at Augsburg, refuses to recant.

1519. Hans Holbein (c. 1497–1543) paints portrait of Bonifacius Amerbach. ...Ulrich Zwingli (1484–1531) begins Protestant preaching in Zürich. ...**May 2:** Leonardo da Vinci (b. 1452) dies at St. Cloud (in France). ...**June 27–July 16:** Martin Luther and Johann Maier von Eck (1486–1543) engage in disputation at Leipzig.

1520. Martin Luther's reform pamphlets, *To the Christian Nobility; De Captivitate Babylonica Ecclesiae; On the Freedom of a Christian*, are published. ...**April 6:** Raphael (b. 1483) dies. ...**June 15:** Pope Leo X declares Luther a heretic. ...**December 10:** Luther burns bull of excommunication.

1520–1534. Michelangelo paints the tomb Chapel of Medici, Florence.

British Isles & Europe

1521. April 28: Ferdinand (1503–1564), brother of Charles V, obtains Austrian dominions of the Habsburgs. ...**August 25:** Charles V and Thomas Wolsey agree at Bruges on secret treaty against France. ...**November 19:** Tatar raiders burn the suburbs of Muscovy (Moscow).

1521–1557. John III (1502–1557) reigns as king of Portugal.

1522. France and Scotland agree on alliance. ...**January 30–February 7:** Treaties of Brussels between Charles V and Ferdinand partition Habsburg territories. ...**May:** England declares war on France. ...**April 27:** Spaniards and Germans defeat French and Swiss at Bicocca.

1523. Charles of Bourbon, constable of France, joins Charles V; allies invade France from all sides. ...**June 15:** Gustavus Vasa (1496–1560) is proclaimed king of Sweden, ending Scandinavian union.

1524. July–August: Germans and Spaniards besiege Marseilles. ...**August:** Peasants' rebellion begins in south Germany.

1525. Great Peasants' War in south Germany, Thuringia and Alsace is violently suppressed, marking the end of free peasantry in Germany. ...**February 24:** Germans and Spaniards defeat French and Swiss at Pavia; Francis I is taken prisoner. ...**August 30:** England and France agree to a peace.

1526. Charles V and Francis I agree to a peace at Madrid. ...**August 29:** Louis II (b. 1506) of Bohemia and Hungary is defeated and killed by Turks at Mohacs. ...**October 23:** Ferdinand of Austria is elected king of Bohemia. ...**November 11:** John Zápolya (?–1571) is elected king of Hungary, but his election is contested by Ferdinand.

1527. Poles rout Mongols at Kaniow and free 80,000 Polish prisoners. ...**May 6:** Germans and Spaniards sack Rome under Charles of Bourbon, who is killed. ...**May 16:** Republic is restored at Florence. ...**August:** Ferdinand defeats Zapolya at Tokay (in Hungary).

Africa & Middle East

***A portrait of Niccolò Machiavelli, a noted Florentine politician during the Renaissance and author of* The Prince.**

1524. Ottomans quell uprising in Egypt and solidify their control of the country.

1524–1576. Tahmasp (1514–1576) reigns as shah of Persia.

1525. Banu Saad sharifs take Marrakesh in Morocco.

1526. Afonso I of Kongo renews his protests against Portuguese slave trade.

1526–1546. Muhammad Idris (c. 1500–1546) reigns as sultan of Bornu (present-day Nigeria).

1527. Somali Muslim warlord Ahmad Gran (c. 1506–1543) invades Ethiopia.

Asia & Pacific

1521. Portuguese reach Moluccas (Spice Islands).

1521–1566. Chai-ching (1507–1566) reigns as Ming emperor of China.

c. 1522. Chinese introduce reforms to simplify tax system, which brings era of economic expansion.

1523. Europeans are expelled from China. ...Japanese pirates raid in China. ...Babur invades the Punjab from Ferghana.

1524. Maw Shans seize frontier outposts of Ava (in Burma).

1525. Babur conquers the Punjab in northern India. ...Portuguese build fort at Ternate in the Moluccas (Spice Islands).

1525–1527. Spanish expedition fails to take Mindanao in the Philippines.

1526. Portuguese capture fortress of Johore (Malay Peninsula); Mahmud Shah flees to Sumatra. ...**April 21:** Babar defeats and kills Ibrahim at Panipat, establishing the Mogul dynasty at Delhi.

1527. Maw Shans sack Ava, ending Burmese dynasty of Ava. ...Portuguese ships bound for Moluccas (Spice Islands) touch on northwest coast of Australia. ...**March 16.** Babur defeats Hindu Confederacy at Kanwaha.

1527–1555 Shan chiefs rule Burma.

1527–1592. Mac dynasty rules in Annam (present-day Vietnam).

Americas

1521. Cuauhetemoc (?–1525) succeeds Montezuma as Aztec emperor and is taken prisoner by Hernando Cortés and later executed. ...Francisco de Gordillo (fl. 16th century) explores Atlantic coast from Florida to South Carolina. ...Cortés ends Aztec resistance, destroys the city of Tenochtitlán and seizes treasure of Mexico for Spain. Mexico City is built upon the ruins of Tenochtitlán.

1522. Spanish forces conquer present-day Guatemala. ...Pascuel de Andagoya (?–1548) leads land expedition from Panama and discovers Peru. ...Francisco Montano (fl. 16th century) ascends Mount Popocatepetl in Mexico.

1524. Francisco Pizarro's (1476–1541) first expedition up the San Juan River (near the present-day boundary of Ecuador and Colombia). ...**March 19:** Giovanni Verrazano (1480–1527) explores present-day North Carolina coast. ...**April 17:** Verrazano reaches New York Harbor. ...**April 21–May 6.** Verrazano explores East Coast as far as Nova Scotia.

1525. Spanish begin conquest of New Granada (in Colombia). ...Spanish gain control of Colombian coast at Santa Marta.

1526–1528. Francisco Pizarro explores swampy coast of South America below Ecuador and Colombia.

1526. Spanish conquer El Salvador. ...Lucas Vasquez de Ayllon fails to establish a settlement in present-day South Carolina.

1527. John Rut (fl. 1512–1528) sets out on a voyage to find Northwest Passage. ...Sebastian Cabot explores Paraguay River for an access route to Peru. ...Cabot constructs fortifications of Santa Espiritu in Paraguay. ...Coro, Spanish settlement on the coast of Venezuela, is founded. ...**June 10:** English Crown dispatches two ships to explore North Atlantic coast from Labrador south. ...**November 19–26:** *Mary Guildford*, an English ship, arrives in the West Indies.

Science, Invention & Technology

1521. Swedish military first uses ski patrols. ...Cesare Cesariano (1483–1543) publishes a review of the findings of his mentor Leonardo da Vinci. ...Ferdinand Magellan reaches the Mariana Islands. ...**March 15:** Magellan reaches the Philippine Islands. ...**April 27:** Magellan (b. c. 1480) is killed in a skirmish in Cebu (Philippine Islands).

1523. Sugarcane is first introduced to Cuba by the Spanish. ...Turkeys are introduced to Spain from America.

1524. German Peter Bonnewitz (fl. 16th century) proposes a standard system of time.

1525. Portuguese bring chili peppers to India from America. ...Christoff Rudolf (1494–1545) introduces the square root symbol to mathematics.

1526. Moorish geographer Leo Africanus (fl. 16th century) publishes a description of Africa, specifically of the Sudan.

Religion, Culture & Arts

1521. Melanchthon (Philipp Schwarzerd) (1497–1560) writes *Loci Communes*; systematizes Martin Luther's doctrine. ...**April 17–18:** Luther is cross-examined by Papal Nuncio at Diet of Worms. ...**May 20:** Ignatius of Loyola (1491–1556) is wounded and converted. ...**May 26:** Edict of Worms outlaws Luther and his followers.

1522. Titian paints *The Resurrection Altar*. ...**September:** First edition of Luther's New Testament is published.

1522–1523. Hadrian VI (1459–1523) is pope.

1523. At the Diet of Nuremberg, the pope promises to remove abuses.

1523–1534. Clement VII (1475–1534) is pope.

1524. Erasmus writes *Diatribede Libero Arbitrio*. ...Thomas Müntzer (1489–1525) libels Luther. ...Diet of Nuremberg orders Edict of Worms to be carried out "as far as possible."

1525. Hans Holbein: *St. Mary with Burgomaster Meier*. ...Niccolò Machiavelli: *Florentine Histories*. ...Giovanni Pierluigi da Palestrina (d. 1594) is born. He will become a composer noted for his liturgical music. ...Tosa Mitsunobu (b. 1434), considered founder of the Tosa School of Japanese Painting, dies.

1526. University of Granada in Spain is established. ...Anabaptists spread throughout southern Germany. ...Luther writes *German Mass and Order of Service* and *De Servo Arbitrio*, which challenges Erasmus. ...Albrecht Dürer paints *The Four Apostles*.

1527. Sweden, Denmark and Luneburg undergo reformation. ...**June 22:** Machiavelli (b. 1469) dies.

British Isles & Europe

1528. January 21: England declares war on Charles V. ...**February 24:** Zápolya makes treaty with Turks under Süleyman I. ...**August 30:** English defeat French at Avers. ...**September 12:** Genoa becomes a republic under Spanish protection.

1529. Jurisdiction of Star Chamber is confirmed. ...Catholics are defeated in first civil war between Protestant and Catholic Swiss Cantons. ...Treaty of Barcelona reconciles Charles V and Pope Clement VII. ...In Peace of Cambrai with Charles V, Francis I renounces claims in Italy; Charles V in Burgundy. ...**August 27:** Henry VIII accedes to Treaty of Cambrai. ...**September 21–October 14:** Turks lay siege to Vienna. ...**October 17:** English Lord Chancellor Thomas Wolsey falls and is succeeded by Thomas More (1478–1535).

1530. August 12: Imperial troops restore Medici rule in Florence. ...**November 29:** Thomas Wolsey (b. c. 1473) dies.

1531. Second civil war breaks out in Switzerland. ...English poor law makes it illegal for the able-bodied to beg. ...**January 31:** Truce between Ferdinand of Bohemia and Zápolya is declared in Hungary. ...**October 24:** Bavaria, although Roman Catholic, joins League of Schmalkalden at Saalfeld. ...**December 17:** Inquisition begins in Portugal.

1532. Christian II of Denmark fails to conquer Norway and is taken prisoner. League of Schmalkalden adopts "defensive organization." ...**May 16:** Thomas More resigns as lord chancellor. ...**May 26:** Francis I, Bavaria, Saxony and Hesse agree on alliance of Scheyern against Ferdinand of Bohemia. ...**June:** Süleyman I invades Hungary, but his invasion fails before reaching Güns.

1533. Henry VIII secretly marries Anne Boleyn (1507–1536). **April 12:** Thomas Cromwell (1485–1540) is appointed privy councillor and secretary of state in England. **April 23:** Henry VIII's marriage to Catherine of Aragon is declared void. ...**June 22:** Ferdinand of Bohemia and Ottoman sultan Süleyman I agree on peace. ...Ivan IV the Terrible (1530–1584) of Russia begins rule.

1534. March 23: Papal decree declares Henry VIII's marriage to Catherine of Aragon valid.

1534–1535. Lübeck and Holstein wage war against Denmark and Sweden.

Africa & Middle East

1528. Portuguese crush tribal resistance in East Africa and sack Mombasa.

1529–1542. Adal and Ethiopia wage intermittent war in northeast Africa.

1529. Turks begin cultivating maize (corn) in Anatolia.

1530. English open trade along West African coast. ...The number of slaves shipped annually from Kongo approaches 5,000.

1531. Ahmad Grañ takes Dawaro and Shoa in Ethiopia. ...Portuguese traders push beyond Sena in the interior of Mozambique.

1533. Ahmad Grañ captures Amhara and Lasta in Ethiopia. ...Turkish corsair Khaireddin Pasha (fl. 16th century) takes Tunis.

1534–1551. Nail (c. 1500–1551) reigns as king of the Fundj (in the upper Nile Valley).

1534. Ottoman sultan Süleyman I invades Persia and takes Tabriz and Baghdad.

Asia & Pacific

1528–1564. Ala al-Din Riayat (c. 1500–1564) reigns as sultan of Johore.

1529. Treaty of Saragossa defines Spanish-Portuguese frontier in Pacific. ...Spain gives up Moluccas. ...**May 6:** Babur defeats Hindus on the Gogra (in India).

1530. First French expedition reaches Sumatra.

1530–1531. Uzbek Turks lay siege to Herat.

1531–1550. Tabinshwehti (1512–1550) of the Toungoo dynasty reigns as king of Burma.

▲***Henry VIII, king of England.***

1534. Humayun conquers Gujarat and Malwa.

1534–1536. Forces of Pegu repel Burmese invasion.

Americas

1528. German merchants of Augsburg attempt to colonize Venezuela. ...Álvar Núñez Cabeza de Vaca (1490–1557) reaches present-day Florida. ...The first Audenicia (Spanish royal court) is set up in Mexico. ...Cabeza de Vaca visits present-day Alabama. ...**April 14:** Pánfilo de Narváez (c. 1470–1528) lands near present-day Tampa Bay, Florida, with a group of 400 colonists. ...**June 25:** Narváez reaches Apalachee Bay (near present-day Tallahassee), and fails to find gold.

1530. Fugger family of Germany attempts to colonize Sunda Islands (in East Indies) and the west coast of South America. ...Portuguese begin colonization of Brazil.

1531. Francisco Pizarro captures Inca capital of Cuzco. ...Portuguese found the city of São Vicente, Brazil.

1532. Spanish introduce horses to Peru. ...City of Cartagena, Colombia, is founded. ...Incan leader Atahualpa defeats and imprisons his brother, Huascar, uniting the Inca empire in Peru. ...Francisco Pizarro ascends the Andes. ...Sugarcane first cultivated in Brazil. ...**November 16.** Pizarro meets Atahualpa (b. c. 1502), the Inca leader, and later imprisons and executes him.

1534. Jacques Cartier (1491–1557) sights the coast of Labrador on his first voyage to North America and explores Gulf of St. Lawrence for France. He also claims Quebec for France. ...Fur trading begins between French and Indians in Canada.

Science, Invention & Technology

1528. Large-caliber muskets are in use in Spain. ...Spanish introduce wheat to Mexico. ...Hernando Cortés brings beans and sweet potatoes to Spain.

1530. Spanish conquistador Gonzalo Jiménez de Quesada (c. 1495–1579) finds potatoes being grown by the Inca of South America. ...Gemma Frisius (fl. 16th century) proposes the existence of the prime meridian of longitude. ...The first book on dentistry is published.

1531. Spanish are the first to grow tobacco commercially, at Santo Domingo in the West Indies.

1533. Gemma Frisius introduces the ground surveying method of triangulation and suggests use of timepieces (chronometers) as navigation aids.

1534. Tomatoes from America are introduced to Italy.

Religion, Culture & Arts

1528. Baldassare Castiglione (1478–1529), courtier, diplomat and writer, writes *Il Libro del Cortegiano* (*The Birth of Caution*). ...Jacob Hutter (c. 1500–1536) founds the Hutterites, a Protestant "community of love."

1529. Martin Luther publishes his hymn "A Mighty Fortress Is Our God."

1530. Earliest known contract of *commedia dell' arte* players in France. ...Catholic missionaries translate native Central American languages to Spanish and chronicle Mayan history. ...**June 25:** *Confessio Augustana* read before Diet of Augsburg.

1531. February: Henry VIII is recognized as supreme head of the Church of England. ...Charles V prohibits Reformation doctrines in Netherlands.

1532. John Calvin (1509–1564) begins work for Reformation in Paris. ...François Rabelais (1490–1553), French scholar, physician and writer, publishes *Pantagruel*. ...First edition of Geoffrey Chaucer's complete works is published. ...Ludovico Ariosto (1474–1533) publishes his epic poem *Orlando Furioso*. ...Religious peace proclaimed at Nuremberg to counter Turkish invasion.

1533. March 30: Thomas Cranmer (1489–1556) becomes Archbishop of Canterbury. ...**July 6:** Ariosto (b. 1474), Italian poet, dies. ...**July 11:** Pope Clement VII excommunicates Henry VIII.

1534. Act of Supremacy severs Church of England from Rome. ...**March 5:** Correggio (b. c. 1494) dies. ...**August 15:** Jesuit Order is founded at Paris.

British Isles & Europe

1535. Charles V occupies Milan. ...Geneva (in Switzerland) declares itself a republic. ...**February:** Defensive and offensive alliance is established between France and Turkey. ...**June:** Lübeck's navy is defeated by Danes and Swedes, ending the Hanseatic League as a great power.

1536. English and Welsh systems of government are unified. ...English parishes take on responsibility for the poor. ...**February–April:** French conquer Savoy and Piedmont. ...**July:** Charles V invades Provence. ...**September:** Charles V retreats from the siege of Marseilles. ...**May 19:** Anne Boleyn (b. 1507) is beheaded. ...**May 30:** Henry VIII marries Jane Seymour (1509–1537).

1537. Francis I and Süleyman I act in concert against Charles V in Italy and the Mediterranean. ...**October 24:** Jane Seymour (b. 1509) dies.

1538. February 24: Peace of Grosswardein between Ferdinand and Zápolya. ...**June 10:** Catholic German princes establish League of Nuremberg. ...**June 18:** Truce of Nice between Charles V and Francis I is signed. ...**September:** Venetians defeat Turkish fleet off Prevesa (in Greece).

1539–1541. Printers in Paris and Lyons go on strike.

1539. Potatoes from Ecuador are introduced to Spain. ...**February 1:** Treaty of Toledo between Charles V and Francis I is signed. ...**April 19:** Truce of Frankfurt between Charles V and Protestants.

1540. January 6: Henry VIII marries Anne of Cleves (1515–1557). ...**July 6:** Henry's marriage is declared void. ...**July 22:** John Zápolya (b. 1487) dies and is succeeded by his son John Sigismund (1540–1571). ...**July 28:** Henry marries Catherine Howard (1521–1542).

Africa & Middle East

1535. June: Charles V leads a successful expedition against Tunis.

c. 1536. Town of Zaria (in Central Africa) is established.

1538. Turks capture Aden.

1538–1540. Turks push southeastward along the coast of East Africa.

1540–1559. Galawdewos (c. 1520–1559) reigns as emperor of Ethiopia.

c. 1540–1575. Andriamanelo (?–1575) is first Merina ruler of Madagascar.

Asia & Pacific

1536. Gujarat and Malwa regain their independence.

1537. Anarchy follows abortive Mogul attempt to annex Gujarat.

1538. Forces of Tabinshwehti subdue Pegu.

1539. Afghans defeat Humayun at Chausa.

1539–1545. Sher Shah (c. 1486–1545) rules in Afghanistan and northwest India.

1539–1550. Hanthawaddy state rules Burma.

1540. Malay traders establish outpost in Makasar (in East Indies). ...**May 17:** Humayun is defeated at Kanauj and driven out of India by Sher Shah.

A portrait of Jacques Cartier, the French explorer of the Gulf of St. Lawrence.

Americas

1535. Sebastián de Benalcázar (1479–1551) founds Guayaquil (in western Ecuador). ...Antonio de Mendoza (c. 1495–1552) establishes viceroyalty of New Spain in Mexico. ...Puebla, Mexico, is founded as a link between Mexico City and the coast.

1536. Sebastian Cabot ascends Parana and Paraguay Rivers in Argentina. ...Cabeza de Vaca reaches present-day Texas, New Mexico, Arizona and possibly California. ...Inca leader Manco Inca Yupanqui (?–1545) escapes Spanish captivity and conducts a siege against Cuzco (in Peru). ...Gonzalo Jiménez de Quesada ascends Magdalena River and Andes to subdue the Chibchas, (an advanced Indian culture).

1537. Spanish arrive in Chile. ...Spanish arrive in Paraguay.

1537–1538. War between Spanish and indigenous population in Honduras.

1538. Gonzalo Pizarro (c. 1502–1558) defeats the indigenous inhabitants of Bolivia. ...Gonzalo Jiménez de Quesada founds Bogotá (in Colombia). ...Spanish conquer the Inca Culture.

1539. Spain annexes Cuba. ...Indian attacks force settlers to evacuate Asunción (Paraguay). ...Spanish explore present-day Arizona. ...**May 28:** Hernando de Soto (c. 1500–1542) arrives on coast of present-day Florida with 600 men. ...**November 17:** De Soto reaches present-day Mobile, Alabama, near Gulf of Mexico.

1540. Spanish discover gold in the mountains of Venezuela. ...Gonzalo Pizarro heads a disastrous expedition on Amazon River in search of El Dorado. ...García López de Cárdenas (fl. 16th century) discovers Grand Canyon in present-day Arizona. ...Hernando de Soto visits the Cherokee in the southeast. ...**February 23:** Francisco Coronado (1510–1554) departs from Compstelo, Mexico to conquer the fabled Seven Cities of Cíbola (in New Mexico). ...**July 7:** Coronado captures Hawikuh, renames it Granada-Cíbola and makes it his base of operations in his search of a mythical kingdom of gold. ...**August 25:** Hernando de Alarcón (fl. 16th century) sails up the Gulf of California and into Colorado River. ...**November:** Christopher Columbus's remains are sent to Santo Domingo.

Science, Invention & Technology

1535. Wild horses descended from horses introduced to the Andes of Peru only three years earlier roam the Argentine Pampas. ...Italians use a glass diving bell to search Lake Nemi for sunken boats. ...Arab alchemists isolate sulfuric acid. ...Antonio de Mendoza introduces the printing press to the New World.

1536. Frenchman Ambroise Paré (c. 1500–1590) develops procedure to cauterize wounds and improves methods of amputating human limbs.

1537. Niccolò Tartaglia (1499–1557) discusses trajectories and motions of heavenly bodies in *Nova Scientia.*

1538. Turkey is served in France for the first time.

1540. Italians develop reverberating furnaces for the manufacture of cannons and church bells.

c. 1540. Cast-iron cannons are produced in England. ...German botanist Valerius Cordus (fl. 16th century) is the first to use the term *pollen*. ...Italian Caminelleo Vitelli (fl. 16th century) of Pistoria designs first handgun (pistol).

Religion, Culture & Arts

1535. January: English bishops reject papal authority. ...**June 22:** Bishop Fisher (b. 1469) of Rochester is beheaded. ...**July 6:** Sir Thomas More (b. 1478) is beheaded.

1536. John Calvin writes *Institutio Religionis Christianae* and goes to Geneva. ...Anabaptist Jacob Hutter (b. c. 1500) is burned at the stake. ...Parliament dissolves 400 small monasteries in England. ...**July 12:** Erasmus (b. c. 1466) dies at Basel (in Switzerland). ...**July 18:** Authority of Bishop of Rome is declared void in England.

1537. Pope Paul III (1468–1549) excommunicates Catholics involved in the African slave trade. ...First Roman Catholic hymn book is published.

1538. Thomas à Becket's shrine at Canterbury as well as other shrines and relics are destroyed. ...Titian paints *The Venus of Urbino*. ...Britain bans printing of books deemed indecent.

1538–1541. John Calvin is exiled from Geneva and lives at Strasbourg.

1539. Saxon duchy and Brandenburg become Protestant. ...**April:** Greater English monasteries are dissolved. ...**May:** Henry VIII issues Six Articles. ...**July 29:** Thomas Cromwell (b. 1485) is beheaded.

1540. Francesco Guicciardini (b. 1483), Italian statesman, historian and political writer, dies. ...Pietro Aretino (1492–1556) writes the comedy *Orazia*. ...Court painters of Mewar in Rajasthan, India, illustrate story of Rana Ratan Singh and his Rani Padmini. ...Hans Holbein paints portrait of Henry VIII.

1540–1545. Benvenuto Cellini (1500–1571), Italian goldsmith and sculptor, makes gold and enamel saltcellar. It will be considered the most important surviving piece of Renaissance goldsmith's work.

British Isles & Europe

1541. Wales obtains parliamentary representation. ...**June:** Henry VIII assumes titles of king of Ireland and head of the Irish Church. ...**August 26:** Turks conquer Buda and Hungary becomes Turkish province. ...**December 29:** In Treaty of Gyalu, John Zápolya's widow cedes Hungary to Ferdinand of Bohemia.

1542. Wars are fought between Charles V and Francis I, and between England and Scotland. ...**February 13:** Catherine Howard (b. 1521) is beheaded. ...**July 12:** Henry VIII marries Catherine Parr (1512–1548). ...**November 24:** Scots are defeated at Solway Moss. ...**December 8:** Mary (d. 1587), Queen of Scots, is born. ...**December 14:** James V dies and is succeeded by his daughter Mary, Queen of Scots.

1543. Henry VIII allies with Charles V against Francis I. ...In Peace of Greenwich between England and Scotland, Prince Edward (1537–1553) is to marry Mary, Queen of Scots. ...Scottish parliament repudiates Greenwich Treaty.

1544. At Diet of Spires, Holy Roman Empire assists Charles V against France and Turkey. ...**May:** English invade Scotland, take Leith and Edinburgh. ...**July:** Charles V and Henry VIII take St. Dizier and threaten Paris. ...**September 14:** Henry VIII takes Boulogne. ...**September 18:** Peace of Crépy between Charles V and Francis I.

1545. February 25: Scots defeat English at Ancrum Moor. ...**September:** English again invade Scotland. ...**November:** Truce of Adrianople between Charles V and Süleyman I.

1546. June 7: Under Peace of Ardres, England and France agree that Boulogne will remain English for eight years.

1547. Ivan IV is crowned first Russian tsar at Muscovy (Moscow). ...Henry VIII (b. 1491) dies and is succeeded by Edward VI as king of England. ...Francis I of France dies and is succeeded by Henry II (1519–1559). ...League of Schmalkalden is defeated by Charles V at Mühlberg; John Frederick I (1503–1554) of Saxony and Philip (1504–1567) of Hesse are taken prisoner.

1548. Chantries Act abolishes religious guilds and chantries in England. ...Catherine Parr (b. 1512) dies. ...Sigismund II Augustus (1520–1572) becomes king of Poland.

Africa & Middle East

1541. Expedition of Charles V to Algeria fails. ...Portuguese forces arrive in Ethiopia.

1542. Ethiopians and Portuguese allies campaign to expel Somali invaders under Ahmad Grañ.

1543. February 21: Ahmad Grañ (b. c. 1506) is killed in battle.

1544. Portuguese establish a factory at Quelimane on southeast coast of Africa.

A portrait of Russian tsar Ivan IV, also known as Ivan the Terrible.

1548. Ottomans renew campaign in Persia and recapture Tabriz.

Asia & Pacific

1541. Portuguese reach Timor. ...Ordos (East Mongol) raiding parties ransack Shansi province in China. ...Spanish expedition from Mexico reaches the Philippines. ...Spanish navigators discover the Caroline and Palau Islands in the Pacific. ...Tabinshwehti is crowned king of lower Burma.

1542–1543. Ruy López de Villalobos (c. 1500–1544) leads Spanish expedition to the Philippines; names the islands after Philip II (1527–1598) of Spain.

1542 or 1543. First Portuguese explorers reach Japan, landing at Kyushu.

1543. Tabinshwehti fails to subdue Arakan. ...Portuguese introduce baked bread to the Japanese.

1545. Humayun captures Kandahar (in Afghanistan). ...Portuguese negotiate trade treaty with Brunei. ...Spanish explorers land on the north coast of New Guinea.

1546. Tabinshwehti extends his power north to Pagan and becomes king of all Burma.

1547. Humayun captures Kabul (in Afghanistan). ...Atjeh (in north Sumatra) naval forces attack Portuguese ships in Straits of Malacca.

1548. Burmese invade Siam.

Americas

1541. Francisco de Orellana (1490–1546) descends Amazon River. ...**May:** Hernando de Soto discovers and crosses the Mississippi River south of present-day Memphis, Tennessee. ...**May 26:** Francisco Coronado marches to upper Brazos River. ...**June 29:** Coronado crosses Arkansas River near present-day Ford, Kansas.

1542. Spanish colonies in America abolish Indian slavery. ...De Soto penetrates Ozarks and reaches present-day eastern Oklahoma before returning to the Mississippi. ...**June 27:** Juan Rodriguez Cabrillo (?–1543) sails up California coast to what will become known as Drake's Bay and claims California for Spain. ...**October:** Coronado returns to Mexico City, having failed in his search for gold.

1543. Jacques Cartier makes his fourth voyage to Canada. ...**July:** De Soto's men sail down the Mississippi. ...**September 10:** De Soto's men reach Panuco (in central Mexico).

1545. Silver deposits are discovered at Potosí, Bolivia. ...Manco Inca Yupanqui, last of Inca rulers, dies.

1546. Efforts to find El Dorado in Venezuela are aborted.

1548. Silver mines are discovered at Zacatecas, Mexico.

Science, Invention & Technology

1543. Small paddle-wheel tugboats are built for use in Barcelona's harbor.

1545. Ambroise Paré discusses his treatments for battle wounds in his treatise *Methods of Treating Wounds.* ...Italian mathematician Geronimo Cardano (1501–1576) publishes the first cubic equations.

1546. German mineralist Georg Baver (1494–1555), also known as Georgius Agricola, suggests use of chalk as form of fuller's earth for fulling fabric.

Religion, Culture & Arts

1541. Michelangelo completes *The Last Judgment* in the Sistine Chapel. ...John Knox (1513–1572) begins Reformation in Scotland. ...**April 4:** Ignatius (1491–1556) of Loyola elected first general of Jesuit Order. ...**November 20:** John Calvin organizes church at Geneva.

1542. Hermann von Wied (1477–1552), archbishop of Cologne, tries to introduce Reformation at Cologne and is deposed. ...Magdalene College at Cambridge is founded.

1543. Polish astronomer Nicolaus Copernicus (1473–1543) publishes his *On the Revolution of the Celestial Spheres*.

1544–1554. Benvenuto Cellini sculpts *Perseus* in bronze. It will be considered his masterpiece.

1545. Palatinate becomes Protestant. ...First complete edition of Martin Luther's writings is published. ...**December 13:** Council of Trent opens.

1546. Trinity College at Cambridge and Christ Church at Oxford are founded. ...The Louvre in Paris is rebuilt to the design of Pierre Lescot (1510–1578). ...Lucas Cranach (1472–1553) paints *Martin Luther*. ...**February 18:** Martin Luther (b. 1483) dies.

1547. Council of Trent moves to Bologna. ...Six Articles are repealed in England. ...John Knox is exiled to France. ...**January 1:** Michelangelo is appointed chief architect of St. Peter's.

1548. Religious drama is suppressed in France. ...Jesuit College of St. Paul is established in Moluccas (Spice Islands). ...Tintoretto (Jacopo Robusti) (1518–1594) paints *The Miracle of St. Mark*.

British Isles & Europe

1549. England forms commission to investigate the effects of common land enclosures. ...Social and religious risings occur in Devon, Cornwall, Norfolk, and Yorkshire. ...**August 9:** England declares war on France.

1550. City of Helsinki, Finland, is founded. ...**March 24:** England cedes Boulogne with Peace of Boulogne between England and France, and England and Scotland.

1551. Population of Lisbon reaches 100,000. ...**March 9:** Habsburg family treaty makes Philip II of Spain sole heir of his father, Charles V.

1552. May: Maurice of Saxony (1521–1553) secedes from Charles V, takes Augsburg and almost captures Charles V at Innsbruck.

1553. French take Corsica. ...**July 6:** Edward VI (b. 1537) dies and is succeeded by Mary I (1516–1558).

1554. Henry II of France invades Netherlands. ...**January 26:** Sir Thomas Wyatt (1520–1554) leads uprising at Rochester in England. ...**April 11:** Wyatt is beheaded. ...**July 25:** Mary I marries Philip II.

1555. Muscovy Company is chartered in London for trade with Russia. ...**October 25:** Charles V gives up Italy and Netherlands to Philip II of Spain, who renounces his claim to the German crown in favor of Maximilian II (1527–1576).

1556. Charles V gives up Spain to Philip II, who also rules in Milan, Naples, Sicily and the Netherlands. ...**February 5:** Henry II and Philip II agree on Truce of Vaucelles. ...**September 7:** Charles V abdicates in favor of his brother, Ferdinand I (1503–1564). ...**November 17:** Ferdinand I forms military council for German possessions of Habsburgs.

1557. June 7: England declares war on France. ...**August 10:** English and Spaniards defeat French at St. Quentin.

1557–1578. Sebastian (1554–1578) reigns as king of Portugal.

Africa & Middle East

1550. Ottoman Turks campaign southward down the Nile from Egypt. ...Guinea exports 1,500 slaves annually to Portugal.

c. 1550–1578. Orhogbua (c. 1540–1578), a Portuguese-educated Christian, reigns as Oba of Benin.

1551. First English traders settle in Morocco. ...Ottoman Turks occupy Tripoli in North Africa. ...Ottoman Turks capture Muscat on the Arabian Peninsula.

Philip II of Spain and his wife, Queen Mary I, are depicted in this illustration from a 1556 manuscript. ➤

1554. Katsina turns back invasion of Songhai forces. ...Sharifs of Morocco occupy Fez.

1554–1556. Arab corsairs drive Spanish from coast of North Africa.

1555. Turks and Persians conclude peace treaty; Turks retain Mesopotamia. ...Kongo ruler sends emissaries to Portugal with a request for missionaries. ...Portuguese Jesuits establish missions in Ethiopia.

1557. Ottoman Turks raid Massawa and Arkiko in northeast Africa. ...Portuguese take Zaila in northeast Africa.

Asia & Pacific

1550. Portuguese introduce peanuts and sweet potatoes to China. ...Ordos (Mongol) raiders threaten Chinese capital of Beijing. ...Burmese king Tabinshwehti (b. 1512) is murdered.

1551. Johore sultanate (Malay Peninsula) attacks Portuguese at Malacca.

1551–1581. Bayinn Naung (c. 1530–1581) reigns as king of Burma.

1555. Humayun regains his Indian empire. ...Japanese pirates attack Nanking and Hangchow in China. ...Bayinn Naung subdues Ava.

1555–1556. Famine spreads throughout northern India.

1556. January 24: Earthquake strikes Shansi province in China; an estimated 830,000 are killed. ...**February 14:** Akbar the Great (1542–1605) is formally enthroned at Kalanaur. ...**November 5:** Akbar defeats Hindus at Panipat.

1557. Portuguese establish settlement at Macao (in China).

1557–1580. Dharmapala (1551–1598) reigns as king of Kotte (Ceylon; present-day Sri Lanka) under Portuguese sponsorship.

Americas

1549. Portuguese discover gold deposits in Bahia state, Brazil. ...First Jesuit missionaries arrive in South America. ...Spanish establish a civil government in New Granada (Colombia, Panama and Venezuela). ...Tomé de Sousa (c. 1502–1579) founds Sáo Salvador and becomes Portugal's first governor general of its colony, Brazil.

1552. In Puebla, Mexico, work begins on a cathedral that will become one of the country's finest.

1553. Spanish complete their first cathedral in Mexico on site of an Aztec temple. ...Santiago del Estero, one of oldest cities in northern Argentina, is founded.

1554. January 25: Jesuits found Sáo Paulo (in Brazil) on site of an old Indian village.

1555. French settle at Guanabara Bay, Brazil.

1556. Portuguese and Spanish fishermen begin working in Newfoundland waters.

Science, Invention & Technology

1550. German Georg Rhaticus (1514–1574) publishes his trigonometry tables. ...Spanish army adopts the musket. ...Frenchman Bernard Palissy (c. 1510–1589) conducts research into use of fertilizers.

c. 1550. Frenchman Philibert de l'Orme (c. 1510–1570) introduces new standards in timber roof construction, which allow for greater spans. ...Scandinavians develop the snaphaunce, a flintlock device used for firing guns. ...Filtration and distillation techniques are used in Europe to purify water. ...Englishmen Leonard Digges (?–1571) and John Dee (1527–1608) investigate the use of lenses for magnification. ...Italians develop the trompe, a device used to blow air on forge fires.

1553. French mathematician Oronce Fine (1494–1555) invents a planetary clock.

1554. Frenchman Jean Fernel (1497–1558) (Fernelius) writes a treatise on medicine and functions of the human body. ...Flemish introduce hop growing to the Netherlands. ...Brewing industry in Britain has its beginnings in Kent.

1555. Tobacco is brought to Spain and Portugal from the Americas.

1556. Georg Baver innovates new mining methods and tools, including wheelbarrows and windlasses.

1557. The equal sign (=) is first used.

Religion, Culture & Arts

1549. Thomas Cranmer, archbishop of Canterbury, issues the first Book of Common Prayer. ...Francis Xavier (1506–1552) proselytizes in Japan and claims 300,000 Catholic converts.

1550. Italians invent the game of billiards. ...Japanese develop *ukiyoe* painting.

1550–1555. Julius III (1487–1589) is pope.

1551. Robert Estienne (c. 1498–1559) issues first Bible divided into verses. ...Giovanni Pierluigi da Palestrina (1525–1594) becomes choirmaster at St. Peter's in Rome. ...**January:** Second session of Council of Trent opens.

1552. Cranmer issues the 42 Articles, later reduced to 39 articles, the basis of Protestant Anglicanism. ...**August 2:** Treaty of Passau grants Lutherans free exercise of religion.

1553. August–September: Protestant bishops are arrested, and Roman Catholic bishops are restored in England. ...**October 16:** Lucas Cranach (b. 1472) dies.

1554. Trinity College at Oxford and Dillingen University are founded. ...**November 30:** England is reconciled with Rome, and Roman Catholicism is restored.

1555. September 25: Religious Peace of Augsburg permits Lutheran states and divides Imperial Chamber equally between Protestants and Catholics.

1555–1559. Paul IV (1476–1559) is pope.

1556. March 21: Cranmer (b. 1489) is burned at the stake. ...**March 22:** Cardinal Pole (1500–1558) becomes Archbishop of Canterbury. ...**July 31:** Ignatius (b. 1491) of Loyola dies.

1557. September 11–November 28: Disputation at Worms is held in a last attempt at reconciliation within Holy Roman Empire. ...**December 3:** First Covenant is signed in Scotland.

British Isles & Europe

1558. Upon Charles V's abdication, Ferdinand I assumes title of Holy Roman Emperor without being crowned by the pope. ...**April 24:** Mary, Queen of Scots, marries Francis (1544–1560), the French dauphin. He will become Francis II, king of France, in 1559. ...**July 13:** Count Lamoral Egmont (1522–1568) defeats French at Gravelines. ...**September 21:** Charles V (b. 1500) dies. ...**November 17:** Mary I (b. 1516) dies and is succeeded by Elizabeth I (1533–1603).

1559. April 3: In Peace of Câteau-Cambrésis between Philip II and Henry II, France restores Savoy and Piedmont, keeps Saluzzo. ...**July 10:** Henry II (b. 1519) is killed in a tournament and the Guises seize government for Francis II.

1559–1568. Frederick II (1534–1588) reigns as king of Denmark.

1560. February 27: Treaty of Berwick between Scots lords and Elizabeth I. ...**June 10:** Mary (b. 1515), Dowager Queen of Scotland, dies. ...**July 6:** Treaty of Edinburgh between England and Scotland establishes Council of Regents. French troops are evacuated. The treaty is refused by Francis II and Mary. ...**December 5:** Francis II (b. 1544) dies and is succeeded as king of France by Charles IX (1550–1574), his brother.

1561. Baltic States of Teutonic Order are secularized. Courland becomes duchy; Estonia, Swedish; and Livonia, Polish. ...Philip II makes Madrid the Spanish capital. ...**August 19:** Mary, Queen of Scots, lands in Scotland.

1561–1568. Denmark and Sweden are at war.

1562. March 1: French Protestants are massacred at Vassy, starting the Huguenot Wars (1562–1598). ...**June 1:** Ferdinand I and Turks begin eight-year truce. ...**September 20:** Maximilian II (1527–1576), son of Ferdinand I, is crowned as king of Bohemia. ...Treaty of Hampton Court between Elizabeth I and Huguenots.

1563. England's Statute of Apprentices reforms the Poor Law. ...**March 19:** Peace of Amboise ends first Huguenot war. ...**September 8:** Maximilian II is elected king of Hungary.

1564. Trade war is waged between England and Spain. Philip II confiscates English ships, instituting a mutual embargo. ...**April 11:** Anglo-French peace at Troyes. ...**July 25:** Ferdinand I (b. 1503) dies and is succeeded as Holy Roman Emperor by Maximilian II.

Africa & Middle East

1558. Barbary pirates raid Mediterranean shipping from Algiers. ...Portuguese establish East African colonial capital at Mozambique.

1559. Turks repel Spanish invasion of Algiers. ...Harar invades Ethiopia; Emperor Galawdewos (b. c. 1520) is killed in battle.

1559–1560. Russians send trading embassy to Bokhara and Persia.

c. 1560. Jesuits establish first missions in Mozambique.

c. 1560–1605. Farima (c. 1540–1605) reigns as first Mani king of Loko (in West Africa).

1561–1563. England's Muscovy Company establishes trade links with Persia.

1562. English navigator John Hawkins (1532–1595) captures 300 African slaves from a Portuguese vessel and sells them in England's first venture in the slave trade.

1563. Galla forces seize and subdue one-third of Ethiopia.

1563–1597. Sarsa Dengel (c. 1550–1597) reigns as emperor of Ethiopia.

1564. French establish a consulate at Algiers.

Asia & Pacific

1558. Akbar conquers Gwalior. ...Burma conquers the Siamese city of Chiang Mai and forces last of Shan chiefs to submit.

1559. Laos and Siam combine to check Burmese expansion.

▲ ***A portrait of Frederick II, king of Denmark.***

1562. Rajah of Jaipur submits to Akbar.

1563. Burma attacks Siam and takes Siamese king prisoner. ...Japanese riot to protest rice shortages and tax increases.

1564. Akbar annexes Malwa. ...South Indian states form alliance to resist expansion of Vijayanagar.

Americas

▲ ***Mary, Queen of Scots, with her young son, the future James VI.***

1562. Jean Ribaut (1520–1565) founds a Huguenot (French Protestant) community in present-day South Carolina. …**May:** Ribaut discovers St. Johns River in Florida.

1563. John Hawkins sells Africans as slaves in Hispaniola. …First permanent settlement is established in Costa Rica.

1564. René de Laudonnière (fl. 1562–1582) builds Fort Caroline at mouth of St. Johns River in Florida.

1564–1565. Hawkins makes his second voyage to South America.

Science, Invention & Technology

1558. Italian natural philosopher Giambattista della Porta (c. 1535–1615) writes *Natural Magic*, the first published account of the use of camera obscura as an aid to artists.

1559. Italian Realdo Columbo (c. 1516–1559) advances knowledge of human blood circulation.

1560. Brussels Canal, connecting city of Brussels, Belgium, with the Rupel River, is open. …The Academy of the Mysteries of Nature, a scientific association founded by Giambattista della Porta, is the first such organization designed to facilitate the exchange of information.

1561. Tobacco is introduced to France from Portugal by the French ambassador to Lisbon, Jean Nicot (1530–1600), whose name will be the origin of the word *nicotine*.

1564. A large graphite deposit is discovered at Cumberland, England. Mistaken for lead, its usefulness is not immediately realized. …Ambroise Paré discusses ligature of blood vessels.

Religion, Culture & Arts

1558. Spain decrees death penalty for importers or printers of unlicensed books. …**November 17:** Archbishop of Canterbury Reginald Pole (b. 1500) dies.

1559. Geneva University is founded. …Matthew Parker (1504–1575) is named Archbishop of Canterbury. …Wen Cheng-ming (b. 1470), calligrapher, printer and scholar of the revolutionary Wu school of Suchouin, dies.

1559–1565. Pius IV (1499–1565) is pope.

1560. Pieter Brueghel the Elder (c. 1525–1569) paints *Children's Games*. …**August:** Scottish parliament abolishes papal jurisdiction and adopts Calvinistic Confession.

c. 1560. School of painting is established at Cuzco (in Peru), which influences the whole of central Andean art.

1561. J. J. Scaliger (1540–1609) writes *Poetics*, which establishes modern literary criticism. …Basilica of St. Basil in Moscow is completed.

1562. University of Lille in France is established. …Tintoretto paints *The Finding of the Body of St. Mark*. …Anglican Church adopts the 39 Articles of faith. …Edict of St. Germain formally recognizes French Protestantism. …**January 18:** Council of Trent re-opens.

1563. Counter-Reformation begins in Bavaria. …**December:** Council of Trent ends. …**March 19:** Edict of Amboise grants Huguenots (French Protestants) some toleration.

1564. Puritan opposition to Anglicanism begins. …Counter-Reformation begins in Poland. …Pope Pius IV publishes the *Index of Forbidden Books*. …**February 18:** Michelangelo (b. 1475) dies. …**April 26:** William Shakespeare (d. 1616) is born. …**May 27:** John Calvin (b. 1509) dies.

British Isles & Europe

1565. May–September: Jean Parisot de La Valette (1494–1568) defends Malta successfully against Turks. ...**July 29:** Mary, Queen of Scots, marries Henry Stuart Darnley (1545–1567).

1566. Unrest begins in Netherlands. ...Süleyman I takes Chios from Genoa and invades Hungary but is stopped before Sziget. ...**March 9:** Nobles murder David Rizzio (b. 1533), secretary of French affairs and favorite of Mary, Queen of Scots, in Edinburgh, Scotland.

1567. Philip II bars foreigners and heretics from trading in Spanish dominions. ...**February 10:** Darnley (b. 1545), second husband of Mary, Queen of Scots, is murdered. ...**May 15:** Mary, Queen of Scots, marries James Bothwell (1536–1578). ...**July 24:** Mary, Queen of Scots, is forced to abdicate. ...**September 29:** Huguenot conspiracy of Meaux leads to a second civil war of religion in France.

1568. Maximilian II yields parts of Hungary to Ottoman sultan Selim II (1524–1574). ...Treaty of Longjumeau confirms Edict of Amboise. ...Mary, Queen of Scots, is defeated at Langside. ...Mary, Queen of Scots, flees to England. ...**August:** Third Huguenot War breaks out in France. ...**September:** Swedish estates dethrone Eric XIV (1533–1577).

1569. July 1: Union of Lublin establishes political unity of Poland.

1570. Ivan the Terrible sacks Nizhny Novgorod (known as Gorky between 1932 and 1991). ...**August 16:** In Treaty of Speyer, John Sigismund renounces Hungary but keeps Transylvania. ...**December 13:** Peace of Stettin between Sweden and Denmark.

1571. March 14: John Sigismund (b. 1540) of Transylvania dies and Stephen Báthory (1533–1586) is elected prince. ...**July 30:** Treaty of mutual succession between Brandenburg and Pomerania is agreed to. ...**October 7:** Austria defeats Turkish fleet off Lepanto, Greece, ending Turkish naval power.

1572. Sigismund II Augustus of Poland dies, ending Jagellon dynasty. ...Fourth Huguenot War begins with the St. Bartholomew's Day massacre of French Protestants.

Africa & Middle East

1566. September 6: Ottoman Sultan Süleyman I dies and is succeeded by Selim II (1524–1574).

1567. Galla invaders lay waste to Harar (in northeast Africa).

c. 1567–1568. Jaga warriors invade Kongo.

1568. Ottoman Turks occupy Yemen. ...Ottoman Turks conclude peace agreement with Spain. ...Jaga sack Portuguese Kongo outpost of San Salvador.

1569. English establish a consulate at Algiers. ...Talha (fl. 16th century) is elected sultan of Harar (in northeast Africa). ...Ottoman Turks besiege Astrakhan (in central Asia).

1569–1586. Dakin (c. 1550–1586) reigns as king of the Fundj (in northeast Africa).

1570. Portuguese inaugurate large-scale slave traffic between Sierra Leone and Brazil. ...Zimba raiding parties lay waste to Zambezi Basin.

c. 1570–1606. Katsina and Kano wage intermittent war for control of Sahara trade.

1571–1576. Portuguese expeditions subdue Jaga forces in Kongo.

1571–1603. Idris Alooma (c. 1550–1603) reigns as Mai of Bornu at zenith of Kanem-Bornu empire.

1572. Epidemic kills one-third of the population of Algiers. ...Holy League captures Tunis.

Asia & Pacific

1565. Work begins on fortress of Agra in India. ...Spanish occupy various islands in the Philippines. ...Portuguese raze Kotte in Ceylon (present-day Sri Lanka). ...**January 23:** Golconda and three allied states defeat army of Hindu Vijayanagar at Talikota, assuring triumph of Islam in the Deccan. ...**April 27:** Spanish establish colony at Cebu in the Philippines.

1565–1571. Spanish explorer Miguel López de Legazpi (c. 1510–1572) leads expedition to subdue the Philippines.

1567. Akbar conquers Chitor. ...Nobunaga (fl. 16th century) becomes supreme in Japan, deposes the shogun and centralizes the government. ...Spanish seafarers discover the Solomon, Marshall and Ellice Islands in South Pacific.

1568. Burma renews invasion of Siam and subdues Siamese capital in a ten-month campaign. ...Spanish explore Solomon Islands.

1568–1573. Yoshiaki (?–1573) is puppet shogun in Japan.

1569. Akbar takes Rajputana. ...Spain claims sovereignty in the Philippines.

c. 1569–1570. Abd al-Jalil (?–1570) reigns as sultan of Johore.

1570. Nagasaki in Japan opens its port to foreign traders. ...Sultanates of Bijapur and Ahmadnagar (in southwest India) combine to resist Portuguese expansion. ...**June 6:** Spanish capture Luzon in the Philippines.

c. 1570–1597. Ali Jalla Riayat (c. 1550–1597) reigns as sultan of Johore.

1571. June 3: Spain founds city of Manila in the Philippines.

1571–1580. Nobunaga crushes military power of Enryakuji monastery and moves against other Buddhist political and military forces.

1572–1620. Wan-li (1563–1620) reigns as Ming emperor of China. His is the longest reign of the dynasty.

Americas

1565. Spanish mariner Pedro Menéndez de Avilés (1519–1574) founds St. Augustine, Florida, and massacres Huguenot colony on the St. Johns River in the Franco–Spanish War.

1567. Portuguese destroy French colony at Guanabara Bay and establish the city of Rio de Janeiro. ...Diego de Losada (fl. 17th century) founds Caracas (Venezuela).

1567–1568. Slave trader John Hawkins makes his third voyage to Guinea and West Indies.

c. 1570. Hiawatha (c. 1525–1575) founds Iroquois Confederacy.

1572. English explorer Francis Drake (c. 1540–1596) begins attacking Spanish harbors in America.

Science, Invention & Technology

1565. German Konrad von Gesler (fl. 16th century) invents the "lead" pencil by inserting graphite into a wooden holder. ...Ambroise Paré invents device for cataract removal.

1568. A gold soldering process is invented by Italian sculptor Benvenuto Cellini.

1569. The French invent the wood lathe. ...Europeans use semicircular scythes for gathering stalks.

c. 1570. English develop a removable topmast for their sailing ships. ...English manufacture the first sulfur-tipped matches. ...Maize (corn) from the Americas is introduced to Africa. ...Toothpicks are developed in Europe. ...Flemish cartographer Abraham Ortelius (1527–1598) publishes the first modern atlas, *Theatre of the World.*

1571. English mathematician Leonard Digges invents a theodolite surveying instrument.

1572. Dutch use pigeons to relay messages from the besieged city of Haarlem.

Religion, Culture & Arts

1566. Christianized Moors in Spain rebel and are suppressed. ...Jean Bodin (c. 1530–1596) writes *Methodus ad Facilem Historiarum Cognitionem*, a positivistic methodology of history.

1566–1572. Pius V (1504–1572) is pope.

1567. Claudio Monteverdi (d. 1643), the first great operatic composer, is born.

1568. Czech translation of Bible is published. ...**August 18 and December 7:** Maximilian II grants religious concessions to Austrian Protestant nobility.

1568–1584: Il Gesù, mother church of Jesuit Order, is built in Rome by Giacomoda Vignola (1507–1573) and Giacomo della Porta (1537–1602).

1569. Flemish instrument maker Gerhardus Mercator (1512–1594) publishes his eponymous projection map of the world. ...**September 5:** Pieter Breughel the Elder (b. c. 1525) dies.

1570. *Quattro libri dell' architettura* by Andrea Palladio (1508–1580) is published. The ideas and designs contained in this treatise prove highly influential. ...Luís Vaz de Camões (c. 1524–1580) writes *Os Lusiadas*, an epic on Vasco da Gama's discovery of a sea route to India. ...Papal bull *Regnans in Excelsis* excommunicates Elizabeth I.

1571. April–May: Parliament forbids importation of Papal Bulls into England.

1572–1585. Gregory XIII (1502–1585) is pope. ...John Knox (b. 1513) dies.

British Isles & Europe

1573. May 9: Henry of Anjou (1551–1589) is elected king of Poland. ...**July 6:** Pacification of Boulogne ends fourth Huguenot War.

1574. Fifth Huguenot War in France begins. ...**May 30:** Charles IX (b. 1550) dies and is succeeded by his brother Henry of Poland, who becomes Henry III of France.

1575. December 14: Stephen Báthory is elected king of Poland.

1576. Maximilian II dies and is succeeded as Holy Roman Emperor by his brother, Rudolf II (1552–1612), king of Hungary and Bohemia. ...Spaniards sack Antwerp. ...Pacification of Ghent unites all Dutch provinces against Spain.

1577. February 12: Don John (1547–1578) issues Perpetual Edict to settle Dutch War, but it is refused by William of Orange (1533–1584). ...**March–September:** Sixth Huguenot War is fought in France. ...**September 17:** Peace of Bergerac confirms Peace of Beaulieu.

1578. October 1: Don John (b. 1547) of Austria dies and is succeeded by Alessandro Farnese (1545–1592), duke of Parma, as governor of the Netherlands.

1579. English Eastland Company is formed to trade with Scandinavia. ...**May 17:** In the Peace of Arras, southern Netherlands recognize Philip II of Spain.

1580. Philip II of Spain conquers Portugal.

1581. July 26: Federal Republic of the United Provinces (Holland) renounces allegiance to Spain.

1582. January 15: Russia and Poland agree on the Peace of Jam-Zapoloski. Russia is cut off from the Baltics.

Africa & Middle East

1574–1576. Portuguese colonize Angola. ...Turks expel the Spanish from Tunis. ...Indigenous forces sack Portuguese colonial capital at Mozambique.

1574–1595. Murad III (1546–1595) reigns as sultan of Ottoman Empire.

1575–1610. Ralamba (?–1610) reigns as ruler of Merina (Madagascar).

1576. Portuguese establish Luanda as capital of Angola.

1576–1577. Ismail II (1551–1577) reigns as shah of Persia.

1577. Ethiopians conquer Harar and dismantle the sultanate.

1578. Sebastian of Portugal (b. 1554) invades Morocco and is defeated and slain at Ksar el Kebir. ...Ethiopians defeat Turks and capture the fortress of Dabarwa.

1578–1587. Muhammad Khudabanda (c. 1550–1587) reigns as shah of Persia.

1578-1603. Abu al-Abbas Ahmad I (c. 1540–1603) reigns as sharif of Morocco.

1580. Spanish occupy port of Ceuta opposite Gibraltar. ...Portuguese, using many African troops, attack Ngola.

1581. Moroccans capture Tuat and begin infiltration of the Sahara from the west.

Asia & Pacific

c. 1573–1585. Venkata I (c. 1550–1585) reigns as raja of Vijayanagar.

1574. November 29: Chinese pirates attack Spanish shipping in Manila Bay.

1575. Akbar conquers Bengal.

1575–1576. Akbar reforms government administration of Delhi.

1576. Work begins on Azuchi Castle in Japan.

1577–1582. Nobunaga's military forces subdue western Japan.

1578. Population of China is estimated at 60 million. ...Spanish expedition from the Philippines takes Brunei. ...Francis Drake becomes the first Englishman to navigate the Pacific from east to west.

1579. Portuguese establish trading station in Bengal.

1580–1591. Kingdom of Kandy expands in Ceylon (present-day Sri Lanka).

1580–1611. Muhammad Quli (c. 1560–1611) rules Golconda (in southwest India).

1581. Akbar subdues Afghanistan. ...Burmese empire reaches its zenith.

1581–1599. Nanda Bayin (fl. 16th century) reigns as king of Burma.

1582. Hideyoshi (1536–1598) succeeds Nobunaga as supreme ruler in Japan.

Americas

1573. Juan de Garay (1528–1583) founds present-day Santa Fe, New Mexico.

1574. First auto-da-fé in Mexico occurs. ...Pedro Menéndez de Avilés visits Chesapeake region of present-day Maryland.

1576. Spanish discover Mayan ruins in Copán (in Honduras). ...**July:** Martin Frobisher (c. 1535–1594) annexes what will become Frobisher Bay (off Greenland) and discovers what will soon become known as Baffin Island.

1577. Frobisher makes his second voyage. ...**November:** Francis Drake embarks on voyage around the world via Cape Horn.

1578. Frobisher makes his third voyage. ...**September 6:** Drake reaches Pacific. ...**December 5:** Drake reaches Valparaiso, Chile.

1579. Sir Humphrey Gilbert's (1530–1583) expedition to West Indies fails. ...**February 5:** Drake reaches Tarapaca and Arica (in Peru). ...**June 17:** Drake proclaims English sovereignty over New Albion (in present-day California).

1580. Garay rebuilds Buenos Aires, Argentina, 39 years after the settlement was burned and abandoned.

Science, Invention & Technology

1574. German Lazarus Ercker (1530–1594) writes a treatise on minerals.

1575. Hieronymus Fabricius (1537–1619) uses forceps in the extraction of teeth. ...Wire straight pins are manufactured in Europe. ...Englishman William Gilbert (1544–1603) experiments with static electricity. ...Ambroise Paré invents an artificial leg with movable joints.

1578. Italian astronomer Egnation Dante (fl. 16th century) is first to add a directional indicator to a wind vane.

1579. First glass artificial eyes are manufactured in Europe.

c. 1580. The manufacture of wrought iron becomes a major industry in northern Europe. ...Germany develops large saltpeter works.

1581. Galileo Galilei (1564–1642) experiments with pendulums at Pisa. ...Englishman Robert Norman (fl. 16th century) discovers "dip" in compass readings caused by angle of the earth's surface.

Religion, Culture & Arts

1573. Jesuits begin Counter-Reformation in Fulda. ...Work begins on Mexico City Cathedral.

1575. Torquato Tasso (1544–1595) writes *Gerusalemme Liberata*, an epic poem in the classical style about the First Crusade. ...William Byrd (1543–1623), composer, and Thomas Tallis (1505–1585), composer and organist, jointly publish *Cantiones Sacrae*.

1576. Jean Bodin's (1530–1596) *De la République* discusses theory of absolutism, advocates religious tolerance. ...First permanent playhouse opens in London. ...Edict of Beaulieu allows reformed religion in France, except in Paris.

1577. The first volume of the *Chronicles of England, Scotland and Ireland*, by Raphael Holinshed (?–1580), English chronicler, is published. ...El Greco (1541–1614) settles in Toledo, Spain.

1578. Protestant preachers are expelled from Vienna. ...Paolo Veronese (1528–1588) begins decorating the Palace of the Doges in Venice.

1579. Edmund Spenser (c. 1552–1599) writes *The Shepheardes Calender*, a landmark in English poetry.

1580. Sir Philip Sidney (1554–1586), courtier, soldier, critic, poet and prose writer, writes *Astrophel and Stella*. ...Michel de Montaigne (1533–1592) writes Books I and II of *Essais*.

1581. Protestants are banned in the Habsburg dominions. ...University of Edinburgh, Scotland, is established.

1581–1582. Pope Gregory XIII tries in vain to reconcile Russian Church.

1582. English geographer Richard Hakluyt (c. 1552–1616) publishes *Voyages*. ...Jesuit mission in China begins.

British Isles & Europe

1584. Don Cossacks defeat Mongols near Tobol. Russia adds Siberia to its dominions. ...**July 10:** William I of Orange (b. 1533) is assassinated.

1584–1598. Fyodor I (1557–1598), last of Rurik dynasty, reigns as tsar of Russia.

1585. Henry III of France refuses sovereignty of Netherlands. ...**August 17:** Alessandro Farnese of Parma, governor of Netherlands takes Antwerp and regains Flanders and Brabant. Antwerp, sacked by Spaniards, loses its importance in international trade to Amsterdam.

1586. War of the three Henrys, Henry III, Henry of Navarre (1553–1610) and Henry of Guise. ...**October 14–15:** Mary, Queen of Scots, is tried for treason.

1587. February 8: Mary, Queen of Scots (b. 1542), is beheaded at Fotheringhay. ...**April 19:** English expedition under Sir Francis Drake attacks Cádiz. ...**August 19:** Sigismund III Vasa (1566–1632) is elected king of Poland.

1588. May 12: Barricade fighting breaks out in Paris. Henry III is forced to flee and calls Estates General to Blois. ...**July 31–August 8:** English defeat Spanish Armada, leading to the decline of the Spanish empire.

1588–1598. Boris Godunov (1551–1605) rules as regent of Russia.

1588–1648. Christian IV (1577–1648) reigns as king of Denmark.

1589. April 3: Peace is declared between Henry III and Henry of Navarre. ...**August 2:** Henry III (b. 1551) is murdered. With the house of Valois extinct, Henry of Navarre claims the crown.

1590. March 14: Henry IV defeats League at Ivry. ...**September:** Alessandro Farnese of Parma attacks Henry IV of France.

1591. May 15: Dmitri, son of Ivan the Terrible, dies. Three imposters, each known as False Dmitri, will claim to be Ivan the Terrible's son in unsuccessful efforts to rule Russia. ...Philip II of Spain suppresses liberties of Aragon.

Africa & Middle East

1585. Ngolans repel Portuguese invasion. ...Turkish corsair Amir Ali Bey (fl. 16th century) foments rebellion against Portuguese in East Africa.

1586–1628. Abbas the Great (1557–1629) reigns as shah of Persia.

1587. Zimba forces sack Kilwa (in East Africa) and cannibalize their captives. ...Turks defeat Persians near Baghdad. ...Portuguese warships quell Turk-inspired uprising along East Africa coast.

1588. English merchants found the Guinea Company to trade in African slaves. ...Zimba forces sack Mombasa; Portuguese defeat the Zimba at Malindi.

c. 1588. Portuguese establish trading centers at Lagos, Warri and on the Cameroons River (in West Africa).

1589. Ahmad al-Mansur (1560–?) of Morocco invades Songhai.

1590. Morocco annexes Timbuktu and Upper Niger. ...Shah Abbas of Persia makes peace with Ottomans, ceding Tabriz and other possessions.

c. 1590. Portuguese establish trading center at Zanzibar off East African coast.

1590–1591. Allied tribes of Jaga, Kongo, Matamba and Ndongo resist Portuguese advance into interior Central Africa.

1590–1635. Fakir al-Din al-Mani II (c. 1570–1635) is prince of Lebanon.

Asia & Pacific

1583. Akbar builds fortress of Allahabad on the River Ganges. ...Philippines are made subordinate to the colonial government of New Spain.

1584. Hideyoshi consolidates his rule over central Japan.

1587. Akbar annexes Kashmir. ...Japanese peasants are disarmed. ...Hideyoshi completes his conquest of western Japan.

1589. Golconda establishes capital at Bhagnagar and renames it Hyderabad.

1590. Akbar conquers Orissa. ...Hideyoshi completes political unification of Japan.

1590–1593. Spanish fortify Manila in the Philippines.

Americas

1583. Sir Humphrey Gilbert (c. 1539–1583) establishes first English colony in North America at Newfoundland.

1584. July: Sir Walter Raleigh (1554–1618), half-brother of Sir Humphrey Gilbert, lands on Roanoke Island off North Carolina coast.

1585. Raleigh begins colony at Roanoke Island.

1585–1587. John Davis (c. 1550–1605) tries to find Northwest Passage and discovers what will become known as Davis Straits.

1586. June: Roanoke colony is abandoned; the colonists return to England.

1587. July 22: John White (fl. 1585–1593) arrives at Roanoke Island with a second group of colonists. ...**August 18:** Virginia Dare, White's grandchild, is born. She is the first English child born in America. ...**August 25:** White leaves a group of colonists on Roanoke Island and sails to England for supplies.

1590. August 17: White returns to Roanoke Island and finds no trace of colonists, except for cryptic letters, *CRO*, carved into a tree and the word *CROATOAN* carved on a doorpost.

Science, Invention & Technology

1583. Italian Andrea Cesalpino (1519–1603) is the first to attempt to classify plants in his *De Plantis Libri.*

1585. Galileo invents hydrostatic balance, which is used to measure the density of an object.

1586. Eggplant is introduced to England and parts of Europe from northern India via the Near East. ...Simon Stevin (1548–1620) writes on several basic physical laws, including the law of the plane and hydrostatics.

1588. Italian Agostino Ramelli (c. 1531–1610) designs a cylindrical bolter for grain milling and an upright rotary desk that resembles a wooden waterwheel.

1589. William Lee (c. 1570–1610) of England invents a knitting machine.

1590. John Harington (fl. 16th century), godson of Queen Elizabeth, builds a water closet in his home, complete with a flush toilet. ...Frenchman Pierre Chamberlin (fl. 16th century) invents obstetrical forceps.

1591. Frenchman François Viète (1540–1603) introduces an algebraic lettering system.

Religion, Culture & Arts

1583–1584. "Cologne War" between Catholics and Calvinists for possession of the city's archbishopric ends with Roman Catholic victory.

1584–1585. Giordano Bruno (1548–1600): *Spaccio della Bestia Trionfante*; *Della Causa*, *Principio ed Uno; Degli Eroici Furori* (published in England).

1585. Heinrich Schütz (d. 1672), German composer, is born.

1585–1590. Sixtus V (1521–1590) is pope.

1586–1593. Cesar Baronius (1538–1607): *Annales Ecclesiastici*; standard work of Roman Catholic history.

1587. Christopher Marlowe (1564–1593) writes *Tamburlaine the Great*, the first English blank-verse tragedy for the public theatre. ...Recatholicization of bishopric of Würzburg is completed.

1588. T'ang Hsien Tsu (1550–1616): *The Peony Pavilion*; Chinese romantic drama that is still popular. ...Palace of Udaipur (India) is built. ...Palestrina publishes *Lamentations,* a collection of sacred music.

1588–1590. Domenico Fontana (1543–1607) finishes the cupola and lantern of St. Peter's in Rome.

1589. Metropolitan of Moscow becomes patriarch and independent of Constantinople. ...**December:** Sixtus V clears way for reconciliation of Henry IV of France.

1590. Edmund Spenser: *Faerie Queene.* ...Philip Sidney (1554–1586): *Arcadia.* ...Great Mosque at Isfahan is built.

c. 1590–1592. William Shakespeare composes *Henry VI, Parts I–III.*

1591. Trinity College in Dublin is founded.

British Isles & Europe

1592. November 27: John III (b. 1537) of Sweden dies and is succeeded by Sigismund III Vasa of Poland. ...**December 3:** Alessandro Farnese (b. 1545) of Parma dies.

1593. War with Turks in Hungary is renewed. ...Michael the Brave (1558–1601) becomes prince of Wallachia and wins independence from Turks.

1594. Philip II of Spain closes Lisbon to Dutch traders, spurring Dutch interest in the East Indies. ...**March 22:** Henry IV enters Paris.

1595. January 17: Henry IV declares war on Spain. ...**October 28:** Sigismund Báthory (1572–1613), prince of Transylvania defeats Turks at Giurgevo (in Bulgaria) and subdues Wallachia.

1596. England, France and Netherlands ally against Spain. ...Turks conquer Erlau (in present-day Czech Republic). ...**January:** The French League ends.

1597. English Parliament orders construction of workhouses for the poor. ...Tea drinking becomes part of English society. ...**December:** Báthory cedes Translyvania to Rudolf II.

1598. Treaty of Vervins between France and Spain ends the Huguenot Wars. ...Philip II (b. 1527) of Spain dies and is succeeded by Philip III (1578–1621). ...Charles IX (1550–1611) of Sweden defeats Sigismund III Vasa of Poland at Stangebro.

Africa & Middle East

1592. Portuguese settle at Mombasa on Africa's East Coast.

1593. Zimba warriors rout Portuguese army in southeast Africa.

1593–1596. Portuguese build Fort Jesus at Mombasa.

1595. Dutch establish first trading outposts on West Africa's Gold Coast.

1595–1603. Muhammad III (1566–1603) reigns as sultan of Ottoman Empire.

1597. Persians defeat Uzbek Turks, stopping Uzbeki raids on Persian frontiers.

1597–1603. Yakub (?–1603) reigns as emperor of Ethiopia.

1598. Dutch expand trading presence in West Africa.

Asia & Pacific

1592. Japanese invade Korea. ...English seafarer Sir James Lancaster (fl. 16th century) rounds the Malay Peninsula. ...Akbar conquers Sind. ...Le dynasty regains power in Annam (present-day Vietnam) and makes Tonkin (present-day Hanoi) the capital.

1593. Akbar sends Mogul armies into South India. ...Chinese army forces Japanese invaders to withdraw to Korea's south coast.

1594–1604. Chinese armies campaign in Annam (present-day Vietnam), Siam and Burma.

1595. Dutch begin to colonize East Indies and Sunda Islands. ...Spanish explorers discover Marquesas and Santa Cruz Islands.

1596. June 5: First Dutch ships reach Sumatra.

1597. Philip II of Spain is declared king of Ceylon (present-day Sri Lanka). ...Japan banishes Christian missionaries.

1597–1613. Ala al-Din Riayat II (?–1613) rules as sultan of Johore.

1598. Hideyoshi dies, and Tokugawa Ieyasu (1543–1616) restores shogunate in Japan. ...Five Dutch seaborne expeditions reach East Indies. Dutch take the island of Mauritius in the Indian Ocean.

1599. Mogul leader Akbar begins conquest of the Deccan. ...Moro pirates attack Spanish trade in the Philippines.

In 1595, the same year that Walter Raleigh traveled up the Orinoco River into Guiana, he took control of St. Joseph, Trinidad. In this engraving, Raleigh is guiding Spanish prisoners from St. Joseph into boats.

Americas

1592. Juan de Fuca (1536–1602) discovers present-day British Columbia.

1594. Central University at Quito, Ecuador, is established.

1595. English sack Caracas, Venezuela. ...John Hawkins (b. 1532) dies at sea near Puerto Rico. ...Sir Walter Raleigh explores 300 miles up Orinoco River into the interior of the Guiana.

1597–1598. Dutch explore Surinam (in northeast South America).

1597. Spanish found Portobelo, Panama.

1598. Spanish begin full-scale missionary work in Indian pueblos of present-day New Mexico. ...Arizona becomes part of New Spain. ...Araucanian Indians destroy most Spanish settlements in southern Chile. ...Spanish found their first regular colony at San Juan (in present-day New Mexico). ...Marquis de la Roche (1540–1606) transports two shiploads of convicts to Sable Island off the coast of Nova Scotia, but the settlement is abandoned after an uprising.

Science, Invention & Technology

1592. Cornelis Cornelisz (fl. 16th century) builds a wind-powered sawmill at Uitgeest, Holland. ...Galileo conducts his famous experiments with falling objects as professor at Padua University, Pisa, Italy. ...Venetian Prosperus Alpini (1553–1617) experiments with date palm fertilization in Egypt.

1593. Galileo invents a water-filled thermometer that has an expanding and contracting bulb.

1594. Tibi Dam at Alicante, on Spain's Mediterranean coast, is built for irrigation.

1595. An iron chain bridge, forerunner of the suspension bridge, is first described.

1598. Dutchman Cornelis Drebbel (1572–1633) attempts to construct an atmosphere-driven perpetual-motion machine.

1599. Englishman Richard Hakluyt compiles first map with recognizable representation of North America.

Religion, Culture & Arts

1592. Rialto Bridge at Venice is completed. ...Presbyterian system is established in Scotland. ...Site of Pompeii is rediscovered. ...Tintoretto paints *The Last Supper*.

1593. William Shakespeare composes *Richard III*, *The Comedy of Errors* and *Venus and Adonis*. ...English Parliament passes act against "seditious sectaries and disloyal persons." ...**May 30:** Christopher Marlowe (b. 1564) is murdered.

1594. Shakespeare composes *Titus Andronicus*, *The Taming of the Shrew*.

1595. Shakespeare composes *The Two Gentlemen of Verona*, *Love's Labour's Lost*. ...**September 17:** Pope Clement VIII absolves Henry IV.

1596. Shakespeare composes *A Midsummer Night's Dream*.

1597. Shakespeare composes *King John*, *The Merchant of Venice*, *Richard II*, *Romeo and Juliet*. ...Francis Bacon (1561–1626), statesman, lawyer, philosopher and essayist, publishes his first essays.

1598. Shakespeare composes *Henry IV, Parts I–II*, *Henry V*, *Much Ado About Nothing*. ...Ben Jonson (1573–1637): *Every Man in His Humour*. ...Spanish poet Lope de Vega (1562–1635) publishes his *Arcadia*. ...Cuzco Cathedral in Peru is completed. ...Construction begins on Globe Theatre in London. ...**January 12:** Pope Clement VIII seizes Duchy of Ferrara. ...**April 13:** Edict of Nantes grants toleration to Huguenots.

1599. James VI (1566–1625), in *Basilikon Doron*, condemns Presbyterianism and asserts divine right of kings. ...Shakespeare composes *Julius Caesar*, *Twelfth Night*, *As You Like It*.

British Isles & Europe

1600. Population of France, Europe's most populous country, reaches 16 million. ...Spain creates Chamber of the Indies to govern its American possessions. ...**January:** Hugh O'Neill (c. 1540–1616) second earl of Tyrone, leads a new uprising in Ireland. ...**February:** Charles IX of Sweden has leaders of pro-Polish party beheaded at Linköping. ...**December 31:** British East India Company is established.

1601. Severe famine strikes Russia. ...**January 17:** In Treaty of Lyons between France and Savoy, France gains Bresse, Bugey, Valromey and Gex. ...**August 19:** Michael (b. 1558) of Wallachia is murdered by Hungarians. ...**September 23:** Spanish forces land in Ireland to aid rebellion of O'Neill and Hugh Roe O'Donnell (1572–1602). ...**December 24:** English forces rout Spanish and Irish in the battle of Kinsale.

1602. January 2: Spaniards capitulate at Kinsale. ...**March 20:** Dutch East India Company is established.

1603. O'Neill submits, ending the Tyrone outbreak in Ireland. ...Queen Elizabeth I (b. 1533) dies and is succeeded by James VI of Scotland, who is proclaimed king of England, Scotland, France and Ireland as James I.

1604. Hungarian Protestants, led by István Bocskay (1557–1606), revolt against Emperor Rudolf II. ...**March 20:** Charles IX assumes title of king of Sweden. ...**August 19:** Peace between England and Spain is established. ...**September 25:** Spaniards capture Ostend.

1605. István Bocskay is elected prince of Transylvania. ...**April 23:** Russian tsar Boris Godunov dies ...**June 20:** Fyodor II (b. 1589), son of Boris Godunov and tsar for two months, is murdered. ...**November 5:** Gunpowder Plot, the conspiracy to blow up the English Parliament and King James I, is discovered.

1606. Henry IV occupies Sedan, capital of the rebellious duke of Bouillon. ...**April:** Archdukes rebel against Rudolf II, who resigns his possessions, except Bohemia and Tyrol, to Matthias (1557–1606). ...**June 23:** In Peace of Vienna between Habsburgs and Hungary, religious toleration is granted and Bocskay is acknowledged as prince of Transylvania.

Africa & Middle East

1600. Benin in West Africa flourishes as a trading center for pepper, ivory and slaves.

c. 1600. Some 30 small independent kingdoms flourish along the Gold Coast of West Africa. ...Rozwi people migrate to Zimbabwe. ...Kingdom of Bornu (present-day Nigeria) is at its zenith. ...Muslim holy men penetrate Central African interior south of Lake Chad. ...Nguni peoples (Xosa, Zulu and others) migrate to the east coast of southern Africa.

1600–1700. Lozi kingdom becomes established.

1600–1625. Galla people migrate south toward coast of present-day Kenya.

1602. French expedition reaches Madagascar.

1602–1627. Turks and Persians engage in intermittent warfare.

1603–1617. Ahmed I (c. 1580–1617) reigns as sultan of Ottoman Empire.

1603. Persians retake Erivan, Kars and Baghdad from the Ottoman Turks. ...**October 21:** Persians recapture Tabriz from Ottoman Turks.

1604–1632. Susenyos (?–1632) reigns as emperor of Ethiopia.

1606–1611. Adlan (?–1611) reigns as king of the Fundj.

A depiction of a Lutheran minister delivering a sermon during the Reformation.

Asia & Pacific

1600. Ieyasu's victory at the battle of Sekigahara establishes his rule over unified Japan. ...Japanese capital moves from Kyoto to Edo. ...Pegu is destroyed; Burma breaks up into small states. ...**April:** William Adams (1564–1620) is first Englishman to visit Japan. ...**December 14:** Spanish destroy Dutch fleet off Manila.

c. 1600. Population of India is estimated at 100 million.

1601. Akbar annexes Khandesh (in India). ...Chinese textile workers strike. ...**February 13:** Sir James Lancaster (c. 1551–1618) leads first voyage of East India Company ships. ...**December 25:** Dutch fleet defeats Portuguese off Bantam (in northwest Java).

c. 1602. Manchu forces attack Chinese cities in Manchuria.

1602–1607. Portuguese explorer Benito de Goes (1562–1607) journeys inland from Agra, India, and reaches China by crossing the Himalayas.

1603. With the accession of Ieyasu to the throne, Tokugawa family obtains shogunate. ...John Mildenhall (fl. 17th century) of the British East India Company reaches Agra, India. ...**October 2:** Spanish and Filipinos crush revolt of 25,000 Chinese living in Manila.

1604. Sir Henry Middleton (1570–1613) leads second voyage of British East India Company to Java and Moluccas.

1605. October: Jehangir (c. 1564–1627) succeeds Akbar as Mogul ruler.

1605–1623. Ieyasu's son Hidetada (1579–1632) rules as shogun of Japan.

1605–1628. Anankpetlun (c. 1580–1628) reigns as king of Burma.

1606. Spain sends expedition from Philippines to the Moluccas. ...Dutch establish trading post in Borneo. ...Dutch expedition explores north coast of New Guinea. ...Portuguese forces break six-month Dutch siege of Malacca (in Malaya). ...Spanish discover Tahiti and Hebrides Islands. ...Dutch sailors sight the west coast of the York Peninsula in Australia.

Americas

c. 1600. Cheyenne abandon their settlements in present-day Minnesota to the hostile Sioux and Ojibwa.

1601. Spaniard Juan de Oñate (c. 1550–1630) explores present-day Kansas, introducing horses to the region.

1602. Spaniard Sebastián Vizcaíno (c. 1550–1628) explores California coast and Monterey Bay. ...Englishman Bartholomew Gosnold (?–1607) sails the coast of New England and names several features, including Cape Cod and Martha's Vineyard.

1603–1604. Samuel de Champlain (1567–1635) leads expedition to Canada.

1603. Martin Pring (1580–1626) explores present-day New Hampshire. ...**March 15:** Champlain reaches Tadoussac on the St. Lawrence.

1604. French settlement established in Acadia (present-day Nova Scotia).

1605. Champlain explores present-day New Hampshire. ...**July 20:** Champlain reaches Cape Cod.

1606. John Knight (?–1606) explores shores of Newfoundland and Labrador for the East India and Muscovy Companies. ...**April 10:** First Charter of Virginia is issued to London and Plymouth Companies. ...**October 20.** Champlain reaches Vineyard Sound.

Science, Invention & Technology

c. 1600. Basil Valentine (fl. 17th century) discovers the elements bismuth and antimony. ...Italians invent leather sedan chairs. ...Holland's canal system uses inclined planes to transfer boats to different levels. This method is practical only with small craft and minor variations in canal levels. ...The Plains Indians of North America develop the tepee as a temporary shelter. ...Ice cream, or "cream ices," become popular in Europe.

c. 1601. Swedes have the first paper money in Europe.

1603. Hieronymus Fabricius discovers arterial valves in the human body.

1604. The appearance of a supernova leads Galileo to refute Aristotle's view of a steady-state universe.

1605. Italian Vittorio Zonca (fl. early 17th century) invents the gig mill, a machine with teasels used for raising the nap in cloth.

1606. Chocolate, brought earlier to Spain from America and kept a secret by the Spanish, is introduced to Italy and Belgium.

Religion, Culture & Arts

1600. William Shakespeare composes *Hamlet, The Merry Wives of Windsor*. ...**February 17:** Giordano Bruno (b. 1548) is burned at the stake in Rome.

c. 1600. The Academy of Arts is established at Bologna, Italy. ...Sculpture in Indian temple buildings begins to take form of elaborate groups of figures incorporated in piers.

1601. John Donne (1572–1631), English poet in the metaphysical tradition, publishes *On the Progresse of the Soule*. ...Shakespeare composes *Troilus and Cressida*.

1602. Persecution of Protestants in Bohemia and Hungary begins. ...Shakespeare composes *All's Well That Ends Well*. ...Bodleian Library at Oxford opens.

1602–1603. Violent recatholicization of Lower Austria takes place.

1603–1604. O-kuni (fl. 1600–1607), founder of the Japanese kabuki theater, performs before imperial court.

1604. Shakespeare composes *Othello* and *Measure for Measure*. ...The *Granth*, sacred text of the Sikhs, is compiled.

1604–1608. Peter Paul Rubens (1577–1640) works in Italy, studying and copying the work of Michelangelo, Titian, Tintoretto and Correggio.

1605. Shakespeare composes *Macbeth, King Lear*. ...Francis Bacon: *Advancement of Learning*. ...The world's first newspaper is printed in Antwerp, Belgium. ...Miguel de Cervantes Saavedra (1547–1616), Spanish novelist, playwright and poet: *Don Quixote, Part I*.

1606. Ben Jonson (c. 1572–1637): *Volpone*. ...Shakespeare composes *Antony and Cleopatra*. ...**November:** John Lyly (b. 1554), dramatist and writer, dies.

British Isles & Europe

1607. English Parliament rejects real union with Scotland.

1608. June 25: Rudolf II cedes Hungary, Austria, and Moravia to his brother Matthias.

1609. British take Londonderry. ...**September 22:** Moors are expelled from Spain.

1610. Poles invade Moscow. ...Tea is first imported into Netherlands. ...**May 14:** Henry IV (b. 1553) of France is assassinated and is succeeded by Louis XIII (1601–1643). ...**September 1:** Archduke Leopold (1586–1632) is driven out of Jülich by Brandenburg, Neuburg, England and Netherlands.

1611. Denmark declares war on Sweden. ...**May 23:** Matthias becomes king of Bohemia. ...**October 30:** Charles IX (b. 1550) of Sweden dies and is succeeded by Gustavus II Adolphus (1594–1632).

1612. January 20: Rudolf II (b. 1552) dies and is succeeded as Holy Roman Emperor by Matthias.

1613. Amsterdam Exchange is built. ...Scottish and British immigrants to Londonderry County are granted a charter. ...**January 20:** Peace of Knaeroed between Sweden and Denmark is signed. ...**February 14:** Elizabeth (1596–1662), daughter of James I of England, marries Frederick V (1596–1632), elector of the Palatinate. ...**February 21:** Mikhail (1596–1645), the first of the Romanov house, is elected Russian tsar, ending the so called Time of Trouble in Russia.

Africa & Middle East

1607. Portuguese form an alliance with Matupa in southern Zambezia. ...Dutch ships blockade Mozambique; sickness forces them to withdraw.

1609. Eleven years of sporadic revolts against the Ottomans in Egypt end.

1610. Portuguese settle the Cape Coast of Ghana.

1611. Dutch build port of Nassau in Moree on the Gold Coast.

1611–1612. Fundj in Sudan inflict a crushing defeat on Abdallabi clan.

1613. Portuguese sign a treaty with the rulers along western littoral of Madagascar.

Asia & Pacific

1607. Dutch gain supremacy in Celebes Islands.

1607–1636. Powerful sultanate of Achin rules northwest Sumatra (in Indonesia).

▲ ***Captain John Smith, one of the earliest settlers in Virginia.***

1610. Dutch stadtholder tells Japanese that the Catholics intend to foment political dissension and civil strife in Japan.

1611. Japanese begin trading with Dutch.

1612. November 29: Portuguese attack English fleet in Gulf of Khambhat (in India) and are defeated. ...**December:** English found a trading post at Surat on the Gulf of Khambhat.

1613. Jehangir permits English settlement at Surat. ...Dutch land on Timor. Japan grants English the right to trade.

1613–1614. Pegu is made the capital of the united Burmese kingdom.

Americas

1607. May 13: Jamestown is founded. ...**December 10:** Powhatan (c. 1550–1618) captures John Smith (1580–1631), and the legend of Pocahontas's (1595–1617) intervention ensues.

1608. John Smith institutes a compulsory work program in Jamestown. ...**July:** Samuel de Champlain founds city of Quebec. ...**July 24–September 7:** Smith ascends Chickahominy River and explores Chesapeake Bay.

1609. July 3: Henry Hudson (1550–1611) passes Newfoundland and continues to the Carolina coast. ...**August 28:** Hudson enters Delaware Bay. ...**September 13:** Hudson travels up what will be known as the Hudson River. ...**September 19:** Hudson sails as far as present-day Albany, New York. ...**October 5:** Smith refuses to yield his authority but leaves Jamestown.

1610–1611. Hudson explores what will be named Hudson Bay. ...Champlain devotes himself to fur trading and Indian relations in French Canada.

1610–1612. Étienne Brûlé (c. 1592–1632) explores southern Ontario.

1611. May 23: Sir Thomas Dale (?–1619), marshal of Virginia, assumes authority at Jamestown.

1611–1614. Dale completes construction of a fort at Henrico and a system of stockades.

1612. Bermudas colonized from Virginia. ...Dale's Code in Jamestown imposes severe penalties on those who create disorder. ...John Rolfe (1585–1622) introduces tobacco into Virginia.

1613. Adriaen Block (fl. 1610–1624) sails to present-day Manhattan, discovers Housatonic River, Connecticut River, Rhode Island and Block Island. ...An English raid destroys French settlements on either side of Bay of Fundy. ...**March 6–September 26:** Champlain explores the Ottawa River in search of Hudson Bay.

1613–1614. Virginia sets up a system of tenant farming.

Science, Invention & Technology

1608. First glass factory in the New World is built in Virginia. ...Danish optician Hans Lippershey (c. 1570–1619) invents a crude telescope which inspires Galileo to invent an improved version. ...Dutch use windmills to drain polders, reclaimed areas of the North Sea.

1609. Galileo invents the refracting telescope and is the first to use the instrument to make astronomical observations.

1610. Galileo discovers four of Jupiter's moons and the phases of Venus. ...First authenticated caesarean sections are performed in Europe; the women survive 25 days.

1611. European brick-building techniques are introduced to North America in Virginia Colony.

1612–1621. Jacques Callot (c. 1592–1635), French engraver, invents a new medium for engraving (linseed oil and mastic) at the Florentine court of the Medici.

1613. Salvagers use a diving bell in Stockholm's harbor.

Religion, Culture & Arts

1607. William Shakespeare composes *Timon of Athens*. ...Claudio Monteverdi's (1567–1643) first opera, *La Favola d'Orfeo*, is produced in Mantua, Italy. ...Lancelot Andrews (1555–1626) and nine other theologians are authorized to translate the first 12 books of the Bible for the King James Version.

1608. Jesuits begin translating Christian works into Chinese. ...Michelangelo Merisi (1573–1610), known as Caravaggio, paints *Burial of Saint Lucy*. ...Shakespeare composes *Pericles*. ...George Chapman (1559–1634) writes *The Conspiracy and Tragedy of Charles, Duke of Byron*.

1609. First regular weekly newspapers are printed in Germany, at Strasbourg, Augsburg and Wolfenbüttel. ...Himeja Castle is built in Japan. ...Jesuit missionaries arrive in Paraguay. ...Caravaggio: *Raising of Lazarus*. ...Shakespeare composes *Cymbeline*. ...**July 10:** Catholic League under Bavarian leadership is formed at Munich.

1610. Episcopacy in Scotland is fully restored. ...Shakespeare composes *The Winter's Tale*. ...Mateo Alemán (b. 1547), credited with reviving Spanish picaresque novel, dies. ...Jan Brueghel (1568–1625) paints *The Battle of Arbela*. ...Thomas Dekker (1572–1632), English dramatist: *If It Be Not Good, the Devil Is in It*.

1611. Authorized (King James) Version of English-language Bible is issued. ...Shakespeare composes *The Tempest*. ...George Chapman's translation of Homer's *Iliad* is completed. ...Masjid-i-Shah, the Royal Mosque at Isfahan, Persia, is erected.

1612. Jacob Böhme (1575–1624): *Aurora*; mystical philosophy. ...Peter Paul Rubens paints *Descent from the Cross*. ...Rules of the Congregation of the Oratory, a Roman Catholic religious association, are approved by Pope Paul V (1552–1621).

1613. Miguel de Cervantes writes *Novelas Ejemplares*. ...Russian tsar Mikhail orders construction of the first theater in Russia. ...Thomas Campion (1567–1620), English poet: *The Lord's Masque*. ...William Brown (1591–1645), English poet: *Britania's Pastorals* (Book 1). ...**April 7:** El Greco (b. 1541) dies.

1613–1614. John Webster (c. 1518–1625), writer of "revenge" tragedies: *The Duchess of Malfi*.

British Isles & Europe

1614. Civil war in France, begun (February 19) by Henry II (1588–1646), third prince of Condé, ends by Peace of St. Menehould (May 15). ...War breaks out between Spain and Savoy. ...**October:** Last session of French Estates General until 1789.

1615. In Peace of Tyrnau, Matthias acknowledges Gábor Bethlen (1580–1629), prince of Transylvania and future king of Hungary (1620–1621). ...**August 9:** Civil war resumes in France.

1616. Denmark fails to get a share of the East India trade. ...**November 25:** Armand-Jean du Plessis (1585–1642), who will become known as Cardinal Richelieu (1622), becomes French secretary of state.

1617. War breaks out between Sweden and Poland. ...**February 27:** In Peace of Stolbova with Russia, Sweden obtains Karelia and Ingria. ...**April:** Richelieu is dismissed. ...**October 9:** Peace between Spain and Savoy is reached.

1618. January 7: Francis Bacon is appointed Lord Chancellor. ...**May 23:** Protestants of Prague invade royal palace, starting the Thirty Years War. ...**December 24:** Poland makes truce with Sweden and Turkey. Brandenburg obtains Prussia as Polish fief.

1619. March 20: Emperor Matthias (b. 1557) dies. ...**August 26:** Bohemians depose Ferdinand II (1578–1637) and elect Frederick V (1596–1632) of the Palatinate king. ...**August 28:** Ferdinand II is elected Holy Roman Emperor.

1620. May–August: Rising of French nobles and Huguenots is suppressed; Béarn and Navarre are united with France. ...**September 20:** Turks defeat Poles at Jassy. ...**November 8:** League under Flemish general Graf von Tilly (1559–1632) defeats Frederick of Bohemia at the White Hill near Prague.

1621. Dutch West India Company is incorporated in Holland. ...**April–May:** Bacon is impeached and deprived of Great Seal. ...**January 22:** Frederick of Bohemia is banished. ...**March 31:** Philip III (b. 1578) of Spain dies and is succeeded by Philip IV (1605–1665) who renews war with the Netherlands.

Africa & Middle East

1614. Taking advantage of Moroccan weakness, Spanish occupy al-Mahdiyya.

1616. Willem Schouten (1567–1625) accomplishes the first rounding of Cape Horn.

1617. Dutch settle on the island of Gorée (in West Africa).

1618. English West Africa Company is founded; it occupies Gambia and Gold Coast.

1618–1691. Border clashes occur between Fundj in Sudan and monarch in Ethiopia.

1619. Dutch vessel with 20 slaves leaves Gold Coast of Africa bound for Jamestown.

Asia & Pacific

1614–1640. Between 5,000 and 6,000 Christians are executed in Japan.

1615. Dutch seize Moluccas in East Indies from Portuguese. ...Japanese send a spy to the southern regions to report on the activities of Europeans. ...Burmese regain Chiang Mai from the Siamese.

1616. Ieyasu (b. 1543), founder of the Tokugawan dynasty in Japan, dies. ...Dutch reach New Ireland (island near northeast Papua New Guinea). ...Siddis, largest Muslim group on the island of Janjira, form an alliance with Malik Ambar, a Habshi king, in the Deccan.

1618. Nurhachi (1559–1626) completes unification of Juchen tribes into a Manchu state and declares war on China.

1619. Dutch found Batavia, Java. ...Hoping to monopolize trade with China, British and Dutch East India Companies sign a treaty forming Dutch United East India Company. ...**May 30:** Dutch United East India Company conquers and occupies Jakarta.

1620. Siam and Annam vie for control of Khmer Kingdom. ...Wan-li (b. 1563), the longest reigning emperor of the Ming dynasty, dies. He is succeeded by T'ai-ch'ang (1582–1620) who reigns for one month. He, in turn, is succeeded by T'ien-ch'i (1605–1627).

◄ ***William Shakespeare in 1623.***

Americas

1614. Virginia colonists prevent French settlements in present-day Maine and Nova Scotia. ...United New Netherland Company establishes colony at mouth of Hudson River. ...Cornelius Jacobsen Mey (fl. 17th century) explores Lower Delaware River. ...First shipment of Virginia tobacco is sent to England. ...**April 14:** John Rolfe marries Pocahontas.

1615. Recollect friars arrive in Canada and forge a link between the French and the Indians. ...**September–October:** Étienne Brûlé travels down Susquehanna River as far as Chesapeake Bay.

1616. Dutch found the South American colony of Surinam. ...English settle Trinidad.

1617. Sir Walter Raleigh embarks on his last expedition to Guiana. ...Buenos Aires achieves partial independence under the vice-royalty of Peru. ...Administrations of Argentina and Paraguay are separated.

1618. Brûlé becomes the first European to visit present-day Sault Ste. Marie, twin ports in Michigan and Ontario.

1619. Virginia's harsh legal code is repealed. ...**July 30:** First American parliament meets in Jamestown, Virginia.

1620. African slaves are first sold in North America (in Jamestown). ...**September 17:** Pilgrims leave Plymouth, England, on the *Mayflower*. While still on board, the colonists sign the Mayflower Compact. ...**December 22:** Mayflower lands; pilgrims establish colony at Plymouth, Massachusetts.

1621. Scottish settlement in Acadia (Nova Scotia and other areas of French Canada) fails. ...Disease kills half the Plymouth settlers. ...Governor Francis Wyatt (1588–1644) establishes new regulations (council of state, elected assembly) for Virginia.

Science, Invention & Technology

1614. Scottish mathematician John Napier (1550–1617) publishes his logarithmic tables.

1616. Napier invents a calculating device, which he calls a promptuary of multiplication.

1617. German Christoph Scheiner (1579–1650) combines a refracting telescope with a camera obscura to make observations of the sun.

1619. A process for the manufacture of bricks is patented in England. ...Cornelis Drebbel invents a compound microscope.

1620. Drebbel invents a shallow-running submarine, the *James I*, and demonstrates it in the Thames River.

1621. Englishman William Oughtred (1575–1660) invents the slide rule.

Religion, Culture & Arts

1614. Mosque of Sultan Ahmed I is built in Constantinople. ...**January 27:** Ieyasu issues edict banning Christianity in Japan.

1614–1620. Michael Praetorius (1571–1621), German composer, theorist, and music publisher: *Syntagma Musicum*.

1615. Miguel de Cervantes: *Don Quixote, Part II* ...Momoyama period, which produced Japanese architectural sculpture of high quality, ends. ...Samuel Daniel (1562–1619) writes the tragicomedy *Hymen's Triumph*.

1616. Protestant churches at Posen, Poland, are demolished. ...Salomon de Brosse (c. 1565–1626), French architect, designs the facade of Saint Gervais in Paris. ...Théodore-Agrippa d' Aubigné (1552–1630) writes *Les tragiques*. ...**April 23:** Shakespeare (b. 1564) dies at Stratford.

1617. Gerbrand Adriaenszoon Bradero (1585–1618), Dutch playwright and poet: *Spaansche Brabander*.

1618. Lope de Vega begins work on the preparation of his plays for publication. ...Guillen de Castro y Bellvis (1569–1631), Spanish dramatist: *The Youthful Deeds of the Cid*. ...Vicente Martínez de Espinel (c. 1551–1624), Spanish poet, novelist and musician: *Relaciones de la vida del Escudero Marcos de Obregon*.

1619. Francis Beaumont (c. 1584–1616) and John Fletcher (1579–1625): *A King and No King*. ...Diego Rodríguez de Silva Velázquez (1599–1660) paints *The Immaculate Conception* and *The Adoration of the Magi*.

1620. Bohemia, Palatinate and Béarn are recatholicized by force. ...Francis Bacon (1561–1626): *Novum Organum Scientiarum*. ...Jacques Callot (c. 1592–1636): *Fair at Impruneta*. ...**June 19:** Massacre of Protestants in Valtellina (Italy).

1621. John Barclay (1582–1621) writes *Argenis*. ...Robert Burton (c. 1576–1640) writes *The Anatomy of Melancholy*. ...**November 16:** Gregory XV (1554–1623) settles papal election (*Aeterni Patris*).

British Isles & Europe

1622. January: Richelieu reenters Royal Council and becomes cardinal. ...**February 8:** James I dissolves English Parliament after two meetings. ...**April:** Protestants defeat Catholic League army at Wiesloch, Germany. ...**October 18:** Treaty of Montpellier confirms Edict of Nantes, leaving La Rochelle and Montauban to Huguenots.

1623. February 25: Maximilian I (1573–1651), duke of Bavaria, obtains electorate of Palatinate.

1624. Henrietta Maria (1609 – 1669), sister of Louis XIII of France, marries Charles I (1600–1649) of England. ...**March 10:** England declares war on France. ...**August 13:** Richelieu becomes chief of Royal Council.

1625. Christian IV (1577–1648), king of Denmark and Norway, invades Saxony. ...**March 27:** James I (b. 1566) dies and is succeeded by Charles I. ...**June 13:** General Albrecht Wallenstein (1583–1634) is named duke of Friedland. ...**September 15:** Huguenots are defeated under Gen. Benjamin Soubise (1583–1642), who flees to England.

1626. February 6: Peace of La Rochelle ends Huguenot revolt. ...**February 6-June 15:** At second Parliament, King Charles continues to levy tonnage and poundage and collects forced loan. ...**August 27:** Graf von Tilly defeats Christian IV of Denmark at Lutter.

1627. Huguenots revolt again. ...**August 10:** Richelieu begins siege of La Rochelle, which the English fail to relieve.

1628. The monarchy captures the Huguenot stronghold at La Rochelle. ...Richelieu becomes first minister of France and directs both foreign and domestic policy. ...**January 26:** Wallenstein obtains duchy of Mecklenburg. ...**June 7:** Under the Petition of Right, no taxes may be levied without permission of English Parliament, no one can be imprisoned without cause, martial law may not be used in times of peace.

Africa & Middle East

1622. First English ambassador to Turkey is appointed.

1623. Shah Abbas I (1571–1629) of Persia conquers Baghdad.

1623–1640. Murad IV (1612–1640) reigns as Ottoman sultan.

▲ ***The ban on foreign ships in Japanese ports did not bar Dutch traders. Pictured above is a Dutch trading vessel anchored off the coast of Nagasaki, Japan, during the 17th century.***

Asia & Pacific

1622. Jehangir loses Kandahar to Persia. ...The Hidetata shogun discovers a Spanish plan to invade Japan.

1623. Dutch massacre English colonists at Amboina in the Moluccas.

1624. First English settlement in East India is established. ...Dutch traders visit Formosa (present-day Taiwan) and build several forts on the south end. ...Spanish establish bases on the north end of Formosa. ...Spanish are denied the right to trade in Japan. ...English abandon their efforts to trade in Japan.

1625. Chinese lose control of Shenyang in northwestern China.

1626. Increasing Manchu power extending to the Liaotung Peninsula, threatens Chinese empire. ...Nurhachi (b. 1559) dies after securing allegiance of many Juchen tribes. ...Portuguese build a fort and the Chapel of Our Lady of Gua on Macao.

1627. Korea becomes tributary of China. ... Shah Jahan (1592–1666) succeeds his father as Great Mogul of India.

1627–1644. Ch'ung-chen (1611–1644) reigns as the last Ming emperor of China.

1628. Dutch conquer Java and Malacca. ...Only Chinese and Dutch traders are allowed into Japan. ...Krasnoyarsk (Siberian Russia) is founded as a Cossack fortress.

Americas

1622. March 22: Indians massacre Jamestown inhabitants, and the survivors retaliate.

1623. English and French establish settlements in St. Kitts. ...David Thomson (1592–1628) and Christopher Levett (1586–1630) establish colonies in present-day Maine and New Hampshire. ...**November 17:** John Mason (1586–1635) and Sir Ferdinando Gorges (1566–1647) are given a trading grant covering an area extending to Lake Champlain and the St. Lawrence River.

1624. Dutch found New Amsterdam (present-day Manhattan) in their newly established colony of New Netherland. ...Charter of London Company is revoked; Virginia is made a Crown colony. ...Spanish found their first permanent settlement in southwest Uruguay.

1625. French occupy Antilles and Cayenne.

1626. English occupy French area of St. Kitts. ...Roger Conant (1593–1679) sets up a trading post in Salem, Massachusetts. ...New Amsterdam becomes the capital of New Netherland.

1627. English occupy present-day Nova Scotia.

1628. England acquires Nevis. ...Eastern Canada is colonized by the French.

Science, Invention & Technology

▲ ***A portrait of Charles I of England by Daniel Mytens (1631).***

1625. John Tilsby (c. 1590–1640) opens first sizable pin factory in Gloucester, England. ...Cornelis Drebbel invents an egg incubator.

1628. Italian Giovanni Branca (fl. 17th century) conceives a vaned wheel turned by jets of steam. It will become the basis for the steam turbine.

Religion, Culture & Arts

1622. Francis Bacon: *History of Henry VII*. ...**September:** Fifty-five Japanese Christians are burned or decapitated in Nagasaki.

1622–1624. Giovanni Lorenzo Bernini (1598–1680): *Apollo and Daphne*, Galleria Borghese, Rome.

1623. First Folio edition of Shakespeare's plays is published. ...Phillip Massinger (1583–1640), English dramatist: *Duke of Milan*. ...Right of sanctuary is abolished in England. ...Tommaso Campenella (1568–1639), Italian philosopher, publishes *City of the Sun*, written during 27 years in prison for heresy.

1623–1644. Urban VIII (c. 1580–1644) is pope.

1624. Herbert of Cherbury (1583–1648): *De Veritate*; standard work on deism. ...First Japanese theater is established in Tokyo.

1625. St. Vincent de Paul (c. 1581–1660) founds Order of Sisters of Mercy. ...Jesuits arrive in Canada.

1626. John Aubrey (d. 1697), English antiquarian and biographer, is born.

1626–1656. Gol Gumbaz, Islamic mausoleum, is constructed at Bijapur (in southern India).

1627. Bacon: *New Atlantis*. ...Rome establishes the Congregation for the Propagation of the Faith in the Holy Land.

1628. David Blondel (1591–1655) proves *Decretals of Isidore* is a forgery. ...Taj Mahal is built at Agra (in India). ...First Dutch church organization is established in New Amsterdam (present-day Manhattan).

1628–1631. John Amos Comenius (1592–1670): *Informatorium der Mutterschul*, principles of primary education.

British Isles & Europe

1629. Dutch West India Company grants tracts of land to members willing to establish colonies of 50 or more persons within four years. ...**April 14:** Peace of Susa ends war between England and France. ...**June 28:** Peace of Alais destroys the political power of the Huguenots. ...**September 25:** In Truce of Altmark between Sweden and Poland, Sweden obtains Livonia and parts of Prussia.

1630. Gustav II (1594–1632) of Sweden lands an army in Pomerania. ...Weakened Hanseatic League is reduced in membership to Lübeck, Bremen and Hamburg. ...**November 5:** Treaty of Madrid ends war between England and Spain.

1631. May 20: Graf von Tilly sacks Magdeburg. ...**September 17:** Gustav II defeats Tilly at Breitenfeld. ...**November 15:** Saxons take Prague.

1632. Cardinal Richelieu suppresses insurrection headed by Gaston of Orléans, heir presumptive to the throne, and marshal Henri Montmorency. ...**April 13:** Albrecht Wallenstein, reinstated in command, drives Saxons out of Bohemia. ...**April 14:** Tilly (b. 1559) is defeated and mortally wounded at the Lech River. ...**September 3–4:** Gustav II and Wallenstein engage in the battle of Nuremberg. ...**November 16:** Wallenstein is defeated and Gustav II (b. 1594) dies at Lützen. Gustav II is succeeded by Christina (?–1654).

1633. French occupy Lorraine. ...Wallenstein attacks Swedish strongholds in Silesia. ...Wallenstein initiates peace movement and is removed by Ferdinand II on suspicion of treason. ...**June 18:** Charles I is crowned king of Scotland at Edinburgh.

1634. Denmark fails to get a share of the East India trade. ...**February 25:** Wallenstein (b. 1583) is murdered at Eger.

1635. May 19: France declares war on Spain. ...**May 30:** Saxony obtains Lusatia in Peace of Prague with emperor.

Africa & Middle East

1629. Portuguese take island of Gorée away from the Dutch.

c. 1630. Mameluke households hold predominant power in Egypt. ...Jieng invade southern region of Fundj in the Sudan. ...The bey, or commander of territorial forces, becomes a power in Morocco.

1631. In a political coup, the Sandjak beys remove vice-regent Musa Pasha of Egypt. ...Fasilados (?–1667) becomes emperor of Ethiopia.

1633. Portuguese establish a custom house in Mombasa.

1635. Persians take Erivan from Turks. ...Fakir al-Din al-Ma ni II (fl. 17th century) dies after mounting challenge to Ottoman power in North Africa. ...The Lundu aid Portuguese in crushing an uprising of Swahili chieftans north of Zambezi delta.

Asia & Pacific

1629. Dutch clash with Malacca islanders.

▲ ***The oldest known portrait of Galileo was created by Santo di Tito when Galileo was 38 years old.***

1632. Portuguese are expelled from Bengal in India. ...Russians establish a fort a Yakutsk.

1633. First English factory is established in Bengal. ...English secure a foothold in Orissa in India. ...A new Japanese daimyo mercilessly taxes the impoverished peasants.

1635. Dutch occupy Formosa (present-day Taiwan). ...Spanish establish military base in Lanboanga, Philippines, for campaigns against Muslims.

Americas

1629. English settlements established at Massachusetts Bay Colony. ...England claims the area of present-day South Carolina. ...**June 7:** Dutch establish patroonships (feudal rights) in New Amsterdam (present-day Manhattan) to promote farming and self-sufficiency and to supply colonies in Brazil and West Indies. ...**July 20:** English capture Quebec.

1630–1634. Civil government is established in Massachusetts but is restricted to church members.

1630–1640. More than 20,000 settlers immigrate to New England.

1631. English colonize Leeward Islands. ...The first American sawmill is created on the Salmon Hills River in present-day New Hampshire. ...Dutch West India Company founds settlement on the Delaware River. ...Roger Williams (1603–1683) arrives in New England and becomes pastor of the Salem church.

1632. English colonies are established in Antigua. ...Edward Winslow (1595–1655) explores Connecticut River valley. ...**March 29:** By treaty, English restore Acadia and St. Lawrence River to French.

1633. Dutch send a ship up Connecticut River and erect a small fort and trading post at Fort Good Hope (present-day Hartford). ...**May 22:** Samuel de Champlain becomes royal governor of Canada.

1634. Lord Cecil Calvert Baltimore (1605 – 1675) founds Maryland for Roman Catholic settlers. ...Dutch take island of Curaçao.

1635. English colonize Virgin Islands. ...English colonize Connecticut. ...Council of New England is dissolved. ...**September 12:** Massachusetts General Court expels Salem deputies, seating them only when they repudiate Williams, who has attacked the civil authorities for legislating matters of conscience. ...**September 13:** General Court banishes Williams but permits him to stay in the colony over the winter.

Science, Invention & Technology

1630. John Winthrop (1588–1649) introduces the eating fork to America in Massachusetts Bay Colony.

1631. The multiplication symbol (x) is introduced to mathematics. ...Frenchman Pierre Vernier (1580–1637) invents what will become known as the vernier, a measuring scale used to calculate angles and lengths in small increments.

1633. First book on first aid is published in Europe.

1633–1642. While under house arrest and until his death, Galileo devotes his time to theories on motion and trajectories.

c. 1635. Englishman John Sibthorpe (fl. 17th century) invents a coal-burning stove.

Religion, Culture & Arts

1629. Onna kabuki drama troupes, consisting of women and men dressed as women, are suppressed as immoral in Japan. ...Portuguese send missionaries to Movene Mutopu (in Zimbabwe). ...Heinrich Schütz (1585–1672), begins composing *Symphoniae Sacrae* (completed 1647–1650). ...**March 6:** Edict of Restitution orders all Church property secularized since 1552 to be restored to the Roman Church and excludes Calvinists from religious peace.

c. 1630. Nicolas Poussin (1594–1665) paints subjects from classical mythology. ...The High Baroque in Rome is developed. ...Victor Amadeus (c. 1606–1663), duke of Savoy, exiles the Waldenses, Christian dissenters.

1631–1641. Domenichino (Domenico Zampieri; 1581–1641), paints the frescoes of Gennaro Chapel in Naples Cathedral.

1631–1687. Santa Maria della Salute, a church, is built based on designs of Baldassare Longhena (1598–1682) in Venice.

1632. Dutch artist Rembrandt (1606–1669): *The Lesson in Anatomy*. ...Anthony Van Dyck (1599–1641) settles in England as court painter. ...Jean-Baptiste Lully (d. 1687), skilled musician, choreographer and composer of many ballets, operas and incidental music for the stage, is born. ...English architect Christopher Wren is born (d. 1723).

1633. William Prynne (1600–1669): *Histriomastix*; tract against stage-plays. ...John Donne's *Poems* is published posthumously. ...Sir William Davenant (1606–1668), English dramatist: *The Wits*. ...William Laud (1573–1645) becomes Archbishop of Canterbury.

1634. John Milton (1608–1674) writes *Comus*. ...Giambattista Basile's (c.1575–1632) *The Tale of Tales* is published posthumously. ...Claude Lorrain (1600–1682), French painter: *Harbor Scene*.

1635. Sir Thomas Browne (1605–1682), English physician and essayist: *Religio Medici*. ...Pedro Calderón de la Barca y Henao (1600–1681), Spanish dramatist and Poet: *Life Is a Dream*.

British Isles & Europe

1636. July: Ottavio Piccolomini (1599–1656), Italian general for the Holy Roman Empire, invades France. ...**October 4:** Swedes defeat Saxons at Wittstock.

1637. Speculation in tulips collapses in Holland. ...**February 15:** Ferdinand II (b. 1578) dies and is succeeded by Ferdinand III (1608–1657).

1638. Convenanters renew their aim to make Presbyterianism the state religion of Scotland. ...**November:** Charles I, fearing a revolution, convenes the General Assembly of Scotland, but the assembly denies royal authority and abolishes the Anglican Episcopacy.

1639. French begin to occupy Alsace. ...A second Scottish assembly reaffirms decisions of the first, including limitations on British royal authority. ...**January 24:** George Jenatsch (b. 1596), leader of Grisons, is murdered. ...**May 24:** Skirmish of Turriff marks first bloodshed in Scottish Civil War. ...**October 21:** Dutch defeat Spaniards in English Channel.

1640. Scottish army invades England and defeats forces of Charles I at Newburn. ...**May 12:** Revolts in Catalonia and (December 1) Portugal occur. Portugal becomes independent under dynasty of Braganza. ...**November 3:** Charles I calls the Long Parliament to raise money for his war against the Scots.

1641. Sir Thomas Wentworth (b. 1593) earl of Strafford, is beheaded on charge of treason. ...Star Chamber and High Commission Court are abolished in England. ...France and Portugal ally against Spain. ...Outbreak of Irish rebellion.

1642. August 22: Royal standard is raised at Nottingham, marking beginning of English Civil War. ...**October 23:** First indecisive battle of the English revolution is fought at Edgehill. ...**December 4:** Richelieu (b. 1585) dies, and Cardinal Jules Mazarin (1602–1661) becomes first minister.

1643. English Parliament secures the support of the Scottish army against Charles I. ...Louis XIII (b. 1601) dies and is succeeded as king of France by Louis XIV (1638–1715). ...**June 24:** John Hampden (b. 1594) is defeated and killed at Chalgrove Field. ...**September 15:** "First Cessation" ends Irish rebellion.

Africa & Middle East

1637. Dutch expel Portuguese from Gold Coast. ...Yohannes I (fl. 17th century) succeeds to Ethiopian throne.

1638. French take Réunion, east of Madagascar. ...Turks take Baghdad back from Persia. ...Ottoman army conquers the Caucasus.

1639. Moroccan troops install a king in the Songhai capital of Lulami (Sudan), but the king is deposed as soon as the troops leave.

c. 1639–1677. Bornu becomes dominant power in Sudan.

1640–1649. Ibrahim (1615–1649) reigns as Ottoman sultan.

1640–1650. A series of defeats compels Portuguese to abandon their fortresses and evacuate Muscat in East Africa.

1641. Garcia II (fl. 17th century), king of Kongo, forms an alliance with Dutch. ...Portuguese annex western Madagascar.

1641–1648. Dutch occupy Angola.

1642. Portuguese cede the Gold Coast to Dutch. ...French occupy parts of Madagascar. ...Fort Orange is built in southwest Ghana. ...**March:** Dutch East India Company negotiates treaty in Madagascar for guaranteeing a steady supply of slaves.

1643. French establish Fort Dauphin in Antanosy (in Madagascar).

Asia & Pacific

1636. Dutch occupy Ceylon (present-day Sri Lanka). ...Bijapur becomes tributary to Delhi. ...Last Mongol emperor of Mongolia dies, and Mongolia becomes a Chinese client state.

1637. English establish trading post at Canton. ...Portuguese are expelled from Japan. ...Japanese are prohibited from fraternizing with Europeans. ...Souligna-Vongsa (1613–1694) accedes to the throne of Laos.

1638. Cossacks reach Okhotsk Sea and establish a fort and prison. ...The shogun of Japan sends a special commission to report on artillery produced by Dutch East India Company.

1639. English establish a factory at Madras. ...Russians reach the Pacific coast of Siberia. ...Kingdom of Balambangan in East Java falls to the attack of the sultan of Mataram.

1640. Final English settlement is established in Bengal. ...Dutch monopolize trade in Japan. ...Dutch destroy Malacca.

1641. Dutch settle at Masulipatam. ...Dutch expel the Spanish from Formosa (present-day Taiwan). ...Portuguese traders are resticted to De-Jina, an island in Nagasaki harbor. ...Portuguese surrender Malacca to the Dutch.

1642. November 24: Dutch navigator Abel Tasman (1603–1659) discovers Van Diemen's Land (Tasmania). ...**December 13:** Tasman discovers New Zealand.

1643. Japanese peasant land holdings are reduced, and selling and buying of land is prohibited. ...Oyrats who stay in Jungaria conquer Semirechye.

Americas

1636. Harvard College is founded. ...**June:** Roger Williams founds Providence, Rhode Island. ...**August 24:** John Endecott (1588–1665) of Massachusetts heads a punitive expedition against the Pequots.

1637. Anne Hutchinson (1591–1643) is tried for sedition and contempt and is banished from Massachusetts. ...Royal proclamation restricts emigration from England to America. ...**July 28:** Combined forces of Massachusetts and Connecticut slaughter the Pequot remnant near New London, Connecticut.

1638. Swedes settle on Delaware River, founding colony of New Sweden. ...**March 7:** Anne Hutchinson and others found the town of Portsmouth, Rhode Island. ...**April:** John Wheelwright (1592–1679), banished from Massachusetts, founds Exeter, New Hampshire.

1639. Fundamental Orders of Connecticut, first written constitution in America, is drafted. ...**May 8:** William Coddington (1601–1678) founds Newport, Rhode Island.

1640. Dutch raid Trinidad. ...Slave labor is imported to work on sugar plantations in Jamaica.

1640–1645. Dutch expand the settlements on the Tappan Zee (an expansion of the Hudson River), the Hackensack River and Staten Island, New York.

1641. Stamford, Connecticut, is founded. ...Indians raid New Amsterdam and Staten Island. ...**October 14:** Montreal is founded.

1642. August 3: The Five Nations of the Iroquois, armed by the Dutch, attack the Huron and Algonquin.

1642–1652. Sir William Berkeley (1606–1677) introduces reforms, including abolition of poll tax, in Virginia.

1643. First settlement in Pennsylvania is established near the Delaware River. ...**August or September:** Indians murder Anne Hutchinson (b. 1591) and most of her household near present-day Pelham Bay, New York. ...**October 23:** Independent settlement of Milford joins the New Haven colony.

Science, Invention & Technology

1638. Galileo publishes in *Two New Sciences* his belief that a vacuum can exist, but disregards the idea that air has weight.

1639. English astronomer William Gascoigne (1612–1644) invents a micrometer, used in conjunction with a telescope to measure positions of heavenly bodies.

1640. First cast-iron stove is manufactured in a foundry in Lynn, Massachusetts. . . .First distillery in North America opens in New Amsterdam. . . .Italian Gasparo Berti (fl. 17th century) invents a water barometer.

1642. Beriberi is first identified as a disease. ...Frenchman Blaise Pascal (1623–1662) invents the pascaline, a calculating machine used for addition and subtraction.

1643. Typhoid fever is identified as a disease.

Religion, Culture & Arts

1636. *Le Cid* by Pierre Corneille (1606–1686) is first performed. ...Tung Ch'i-ch'ang (b. 1555), leading theorist of Wen-jen (scholar-amateur) school that dominated painting during the Ming dynasty, dies.

1637. Charles I of England attempts to introduce new prayer book into Scotland. ...René Descartes (1596–1650), French philosopher: *Discours de la méthode*. ...Ben Jonson (b. c. 1572), poet, playwright and critic, dies. ...Adriaen Brouwer (c. 1605–1638), Flemish painter: *Smokers*.

1638. February 27–March 9: National Covenant of Scots protests against church policy of Charles I. ...**May 6:** Cornelius Otto Jansen (b. 1585), originator of Jansenism, dies.

1639. First printing press in the English colonies in America is set up in Massachusetts. ...Pope Urban VII prohibits slavery of indigenous people in Brazil, Paraguay and West Indies. ...Jean de Labadie (1610–1674) leaves the Jesuits and founds a new sect, the Pietists.

1640. Thomas Hobbes (1588–1679) writes Latin trilogy *Elementorum philosophiae* (published 1642, 1655 and 1658). ...Uriel Acosta (b. c. 1591), Jewish rationalist who will influence Baruch Spinoza (1632–1677), dies. ...Peter Paul Rubens (b. 1577) dies.

1641. Descartes: *Meditationes de Prima Philosophia*. ...Recollect and Jesuit missions are established ...**October:** Protestants in Ulster are massacred. ...**December 9:** Anthony Van Dyck (b. 1599) dies.

1642. Fifth Dalai Lama becomes secular ruler of Tibet. ...Buddhism becomes established in Sikkim (India). ...Hobbes: *De Cive*.

1642–1660. Francesco Borromini (1599–1677) designs Sant'Ivo della Sapienza.

1643. September 25: Assembly of Westminster adopts Presbyterianism. Bollandists (associations of Jesuits) begin publishing *Lives of the Saints of the Christian Church*.

British Isles & Europe

1644. Henrietta Maria (1609–1669), queen of Charles I, flees to France. ...**January:** Sweden declares war on Denmark. ...**July 2:** Royalists are defeated at Marston Moor. ...**August:** French inflict severe losses on Bavarian army at Freiburg. ...**September 2:** Essex's army surrenders to Charles I at Lostwithiel. ...French are driven out of Aragon.

1645. January 21: Sir Thomas Fairfax (1612–1671) is appointed commander of parliamentary army. ...**June 14:** Oliver Cromwell (1599–1658) defeats Royalists at Naseby. ...**August 3:** French commanders defeat an Austro-Bavarian army at Nordingen. ...**August 23:** In Peace of Brömsebro between Sweden and Denmark, Denmark loses its possessions in Sweden.

1646. May 5: Charles I surrenders to Scottish army at Newark. ...**June 5:** Irish Catholics are victorious at Benburh. ...**July:** French and Swedes invade Bavaria.

1647. March 14: Frederick Henry (b. 1548), Dutch stadtholder, dies and is succeeded by William II (1626–1650). **August 8:** Parliamentary army defeats Irish at Dangan Hill.

1648. Scots begin Second Civil War. ...**August 17:** Cromwell defeats Scots at Preston. ...**October 24:** In Peace of Westphalia, which ends the Thirty Years, War, France obtains Alsace; Sweden obtains mouths of Oder, Elbe and Weser Rivers; and independence is granted to Switzerland, Netherlands, and all German states. ...**December 6:** Parliamentary soldier Thomas Pride (?–1658) expels 143 members of Parliament on grounds that they are Royalist sympathizers.

1649. January 30: Charles I (b. 1600) is beheaded. ...**March:** Order is restored in France by a compromise between the monarchy and the parliament. ...**April:** Cromwell suppresses revolt of Levellers; the Diggers (an offshoot comprising religious pacifists and opponents of private property) begin to dig up uncultivated land in Surrey and are dispersed and heavily fined. ...**May 29:** England is declared Free Commonwealth.

1650. French nobles begin their struggle against the monarchy. ...**August 1:** Cromwell forms permanent economic council. ...**September 3:** Cromwell defeats Scots at Dunbar. ...**December 19:** Edinburgh Castle surrenders to Cromwell.

Africa & Middle East

1644. Dutch settle Mauritius.

1645. Puritans from England are sent to St. Augustine Bay in Madagascar to set up a colony.

1648. Arabs capture Muscat from Portuguese. ...Dutch are ousted from Angola.

1649. Ottoman sultan Ibrahim (b. 1615) is deposed and murdered. ...Persians recapture Kandahar.

c. 1650. Black population of Africa declines as slaves are exported. ...Gonja kings launch military expeditions from their capital, Yagbum (the Niger). These will continue for the next half century. ...Guns and gunpowder become the most prized import for African rulers, who buy ammunition with their gold.

Asia & Pacific

1644. Ming dynasty in China ends and Shun-chih (1638–1661) founds the Manchu dynasty. ...Manchus reincorporate Liaoning in northeast China. ...Manchus end Giulin's status as a provincial capital in southern China. ...Tientsin gains prominence as a port for Beijing. ...Jilin province is closed to Chinese settlement. ...Manchus fortify Baoding as a military center near Beijing.

1645. Spanish fail to end Malay piracy. ...Manchus decree that Chinese males must have Manchu haircuts (the front of the head is shaved close to the crown).

1648. Red Fort in Delhi is completed.

▲ ***Oliver Cromwell is depicted as the savior of England.***

1650. A Dutch mortar gunner is sent to Japan. ...A village and fort are established at Thon Buri (in Siam).

Americas

1644. March 18: An Indian uprising in Virginia is suppressed. ...**March 24:** Roger Williams is granted a charter for an assembly of freemen in Providence, Portsmouth, Newport and Warwick, Rhode Island.

This engraving depicts a group of captured West Africans being led in chains by European slave traders. ➤

1646. English occupy the Bahamas. ...**November 14:** Robert Childs (1613–1654) and others attack Massachusetts for civil and religious discrimination against non-Puritans and for not observing the laws of England.

1647. Massachusetts passes a law requiring elementary schools in towns of at least 50 families. ...**May 11:** Peter Stuyvesant (1610–1672) arrives in New Amsterdam.

1648. The Iroquois, using Dutch firearms, disrupt Huron Confederacy. ...**May, November:** Swedes twice burn Dutch settlement at mouth of Schuylkill River (present-day Philadelphia).

1649. Maryland assembly passes Toleration Act. ...Puritan exiles from Virginia settle in Providence, Maryland. ...**January 30:** Virginia announces its allegiance to the Stuart house after the execution of Charles I and gives refuge to prominent Cavaliers.

1650. Frontier between English and Dutch colonies in North America is defined. ...French begin settlement of Grenada. ...Castries is established as the capital of St. Lucia. ...Harvard College is granted a charter. ...**October:** Parliament decrees a blockade of Virginia in retaliation for Virginia's support of the Stuart line.

Science, Invention & Technology

1647. French soldiers attach pikes to their rifles, creating the first bayonets (plug bayonets).

1648. Blaise Pascal uses a barometer to measure variations of air pressure at different altitudes.

c. 1650. English physician Thomas Sydenham (1624–1689) develops concept of systematic clinical observation of patients by their physicians. ...The giant flightless elephant bird of Madagascar is hunted to extinction. ...Rickets is identified as a disease.

Religion, Culture & Arts

1644. Antonio Escobar y Mendoza (1589–1669): *Liber Theologia Moralis*; standard work of Jesuit moral theology. ...John Milton: *Areopagitica*. ...René Descartes: *Principia Philosophiae*. ...Alessandro Algardi (1595–1654) succeeds Bernini as papal court sculptor. ...John Cotton (1584–1652), Puritan clergyman: *The Keys of the Kingdom of Heaven*.

1645. Spanish dramatist Pedro Calderón de la Barca (1600–1681): *El gran teatro del mundo*. ...Cotton: *The Way of the Churches of Christ in New England*. ...**January 10.** Archbishop William Laud (b. 1573) is beheaded for treason in England.

1646. Richard Crashaw (c. 1613–1649), English poet: *Steps to the Temple*. ...English physician Sir Thomas Browne (1605–1682): *Pseudodoxia Epidemica*.

1647. Pierre Corneille (1606–1684) writes *Rodogune*. ...Abraham Cowley (1618–1667), English poet: *The Mistress*. ...**November 11:** Lutherans acknowledge Calvinists as coreligionists.

1648. Cyrano de Bergerac (1619–1655): *Histoire comique des états de la lune*. ...Claude Lorrain (1600–1682), French painter: *The Marriage of Isaac and Rebekah*. ...New England Congregationalism is codified in *A Platform of Church Discipline*. ...**November 20:** Pope Innocent X (1574 –1655) condemns Peace of Westphalia.

1648–1651. Bernini sculpts *Fountain of the Four Rivers*, Piazza Navona, Rome.

1649. Jean de Brébeuf (b. 1593) and other French Jesuit missionaries are captured and killed by the Iroquois. ...**October 6:** Milton: *Eikonoklastes*. ...**October 16:** Maine grants all Christians the right to form churches.

1650. Anne Bradstreet (1612–1672), the first American poet: *The Tenth Muse Lately Sprung Up in America*. ...Algardi completes the tomb of Leo XI and a huge bas-relief for the altar of Leo I in St. Peter's Basilica in Rome. ...Labadie formally renounces Roman Catholic Church. ...First daily newspaper is printed in Leipzig, Germany.

British Isles & Europe

1651. September 3: Oliver Cromwell defeats Charles II at Worcester. ...**October 17:** Charles II escapes to France. ...**October 27:** Limerick, Ireland, surrenders to parliamentary forces.

1652. June 30: England declares war on Holland. ...**September:** Spaniards take Dunkirk.

1653. April 20: Cromwell expels Long Parliament. ...**July 4:** Cromwell summons "Barebones" or "little" Parliament, which enacts legislation that is the foundation of the modern British legal system. ...**December 12:** Cromwell dissolves barebones Parliament. ...**December 16:** In Instrument of Government, Cromwell is made Lord Protector with a Council of State.

1654. War breaks out between Russia and Poland. ...**April 5:** Peace of Westminster between England and Holland recognizes Navigation Act. ...**April 12:** Scotland and Ireland unite with England. ...**June 6:** Christina of Sweden abdicates in favor of Charles X (1622–1660) of Zweibrücken. ...**July 10:** Treaty between England and Portugal establishes English dominance over Portugal.

1655. July: Charles X invades Poland and takes Warsaw (August 30) and Kraków (October 8). ...**August:** French gain successes in Spanish Netherlands.

1656. Hôpital Général opens in Paris, combining poorhouse and factory. ...**February:** Spain declares war on England. ...**November 20:** In Treaty of Labiau with Brandenburg, Sweden renounces sovereignty over Prussia.

1657. March 23: Treaty of Paris between England and France establishes alliance against Spain. ...**March 31:** Humble Petition and Advice offers title of king to Cromwell. ...**May 25:** New Humble Petition and Advice creates new House of Lords and increases Cromwell's power. ...**September 19:** In Treaty of Wehlau, Poland renounces sovereignty of Prussia on behalf of Brandenburg.

1658. February: British Parliament is dissolved. ...**June–August:** English and French defeat Spaniards at battle of the Dunes in France and take Dunkirk and Gravelines. ...**August 1:** Leopold I (1640–1705) is elected Holy Roman Emperor. ...**September 3:** Cromwell (b. 1599) dies and is succeeded as Lord Protector by his son Richard (1626–1712).

Africa & Middle East

1651. Dutch East India Company occupies St. Helena in South Atlantic. ...English build Fort James at mouth of the River Gambia.

1652. Dutch found Cape Town, South Africa. ...Swedes build fort at Carolusberg, Ghana. ...Portuguese commence 50 years of struggle with Omani Arabs in East African waters.

The Dutch East India Company established a settlement at Table Bay, in Cape Town, South Africa in April 1652. The expedition began in Amsterdam on December 24, 1651, under the guidance of a ship's surgeon, Jan van Riebeck (pictured above).

Asia & Pacific

1651. Yetuna (?–1680) becomes shogun of Japan and overcomes two rebellions in Edo. ...English acquire trading privileges in Bengal.

1652. Irkutsk (in easterm Siberia) is founded as a Cossack outpost.

1654. Dutch expel the Portuguese from Ceylon (present-day Sri Lanka).

1655. Russians build forts on the Amur River near Chinese border. ...Dutch diplomats visit Beijing but fail to achieve any influence. ...Timor dynasty in Asia breaks into several khanates.

1656. Dutch begin trade with China. ...Dutch take Colombo in Ceylon from Portuguese.

1657–1688. French and Siamese form an alliance. ...Siam becomes the most consequential kingdom in southeast Asia.

1658. Dutch take Jaffenapatam, last Portuguese possession in Ceylon. ...Annam begins a long series of wars against Khmer. ...**June 7:** Aurangzeb (1618–1707), son of Shah Jahan, secures his succession as Mogul emperor through his victory at Samgarh. ...**June 18:** Shah Jahan is imprisoned by Aurangzeb.

Americas

1652. **October 29:** Massachusetts declares itself an independent commonwealth in defiance of Parliament.

1653. Virginians establish first permanent settlements in Abermarle (in North Carolina). ...**November 5:** Iroquois negotiate a peace treaty with the French.

A Quaker meeting in the 17th century.

1655. New Netherland annexes what will become New Jersey. ...**September 26:** Peter Stuyvesant defeats forces of New Sweden at Fort Casimir (present-day Newcastle, Pennsylvania), ending Swedish rule in North America.

1657–1664. Periodic conflicts erupt between Dutch and Native Americans.

1658. May 29: Quaker meetings are forbidden in Massachusetts. **October.** Massachusetts imposes the death penalty on Quakers returning to the colony.

Science, Invention & Technology

c. 1655. German Gaspar Schott (fl. 17th century) develops a calculating machine capable of ten separate sets of functions.

1655–1660. Dutchman Christiaan Huygens (1629–1695) makes several astronomical discoveries, including the rings of Saturn.

1657. German Otto von Guericke (1602–1686) conducts his famous demonstration in which two draft horses are unable to pull apart a pair of copper hemispheres with the air removed from between them (a vacuum).

Religion, Culture & Arts

1651. Thomas Hobbes: *Leviathan, or the Matter, Form and Authority of Government.* ...Sansetsu (b. 1590), leader of Japanese Kano painting school, dies. ...John Eliot (1604–1690) preaches to Native Americans and settled converts at Natick and 13 other sites in New England.

1652. Opera house is established in Vienna. ...Jan Fyt (1611–1661), Flemish painter and etcher: *Wolves Attacked by Dogs.*

1653. Izaak Walton (1593–1683): *Compleate Angler.* ...Jean-Baptiste Lully (1632–1687) composes the first of more than 30 ballets. ...Pope Innocent X condemns Jansenism.

1654. John Amos Comenius (1592–1670): *Orbis Pictus*, first picture book for children. ...Cyrano de Bergerac: *Le Pédant Foué.* ...Bell Tower of Manila Cathedral is constructed. ...Alonso Cano (1601–1667), Spanish painter, sculptor and architect: *Mysteries of the Virgin,* ...Carel Fabritius (1622–1654), Dutch painter: *The Goldfinch.*

1655. Hobbes: *De corpore politics.* ...Thomas Fuller (1608–1661), English clergyman: *The Church History of Britain, from the Birth of Christ until 1648.*

1656. Baruch Spinoza (1632–1677) withdraws from his synagogue, is excommunicated by rabbis and banished from Amsterdam. ...Jean Chapelain (1595–1674), French poet: *La Pucelle.* ...Abraham Cowley: *Miscellanies.* ...Earliest dated painting by Jan Vermeer (1632–1675).

1658. *Le Dépit amoureux*, by French comic playwright Jean-Baptiste Poquelin, known as Molière (1622–1673), is performed for Louis XIV. ...Hobbes: *De homine.*

British Isles & Europe

1659. May 7: Long Parliament is restored. ...**May 25:** Richard Cromwell resigns. ...**October 12:** Army expels Long Parliament. ...**November 7:** Peace of the Pyrenees between France and Spain; France obtains Roussillon, Cerdagne, Artois and fortresses in Flanders, Luxembourg and Hainaut and Spain resigns claims to Alsace.

1660. February 3: General George Monk (1608–1670), first duke of Albemarle, enters London and proclaims a free Parliament. ...**May 3:** Peace of Oliva ends first Northern War between Brandenburg, Poland, Austria, Sweden. ...**May 29:** Charles II reenters London.

1660–1685. Charles II reigns as king of England.

1661. March 9: Cardinal Mazarin (b. 1602) dies and personal rule of Louis XIV begins.

1662. French monarchy takes over Gobelins textile factory. ...**May 19:** Press Act establishes rigid censorship in England. ...**October 27:** Charles II sells Dunkirk to France.

1663. Irish shipping is excluded from colonial trade. ...Turnpike Act introduces turnpike-tolls in England. ...**April 18:** Turkey declares war on Austria. ...**June 8:** English and Portuguese defeat Spaniards at Ameixial in Portugal.

1664. August: Jean-Baptiste Colbert (1619–1683) establishes French East India Company. ...**August 1:** Turks defeated by imperial forces at St. Gotthard-on-the-Raab in Hungary. ...**August 10:** Peace of Eisenburg reached between Holy Roman Emperor Leopold I and Turks.

1665. Navigation Act is again enforced. ...Philip IV (b. 1605) of Spain dies.

1665–1667. Second naval war between England and Holland.

1666. June 11–14: Monk is defeated by Dutch admiral Michiel Adriaanszoon de Ruyter (1607–1676) off Dunkirk. ...**August 4:** Monk defeats Ruyter off North Foreland. ...**September 2–7:** Great Fire of London occurs.

1667. January 20: Poland cedes Smolensk and Kiev to Russia in Truce of Andrussov. ...**June 9:** Oldenburg is united with Denmark. ...**July 31:** Peace of Breda between England and Holland is signed.

Africa & Middle East

1659. Dutch take Carolusberg (in Ghana) from Swedes. ...French establish Saint-Louis, northwestern city in Senegal, as a fortified trading post. ...High ranking officers of local militia seize power from pasha of Algiers.

1660. Dutch peasants (called Boers) settle in present-day South Africa. ...Royal African Company is founded. ...Omani sack Portuguese quarter in Mombasa. ...Alawite dynasty comes to power in Morocco. ...The Kasimiya take power in Cairo, driving out the Fakariya.

1661. Ahmed Köprülü (1635–1676) replaces his father as grand vizier of Turkey. ...Sublime Porte reasserts its authority in Egypt, suspending all nonmilitary personnel. ...Sultan of Oman mounts an unsuccessful attack against Mombasa.

1662. Ahmad Bey Boshnagi (fl. 17th century), leader of the Kasimiya, is assassinated on the order of the vice-regent of Egypt.

1663. June 10: British Royal African Company is granted a charter.

1664–1667. Dutch buy Swedish colonies on African Gold Coast.

1665. Kongo is defeated in war with Angola.

1667. English take island of Gorée from the Portuguese. ...**July 31:** In Peace of Breda, England obtains Cape Coast Castle (in Ghana) and Holland keeps only Guiana.

Asia & Pacific

1659. Shivaji Bhonsie (1627–1680), founder of India's Maratha kingdom, defeats an army sent against him by a Muslim sultan. ...**May 26:** Aurangzeb formally ascends to throne of Mogul empire.

1660. Dacca becomes capital of Mughal, India. ...Dutch wrest control of Cochin from Portuguese.

1660–1669. Dutch subdue Celebes (in East Indies).

1661–1723. K'ang-hsi (1654–1722) rules as emperor of China.

1662. Dutch cease attacks on the Philippines, occupying, instead, the rich Moluccas. ...A Dutch fleet fails to dislodge Portuguese from Macao. ...The Indian capitalist class in Surat mediates between English and Mogul governor. ...Dutch abandon Formosa (present-day Taiwan) when the emperor establishes an independent kingdom.

1665. Shivaji Bhonsie, founder of Maratha kingdom, is forced to make peace with Moguls. ...English take Bombay. ...Dutch diplomats in Beijing again fail to achieve political influence.

1666. Shivaji Bhonsie escapes Aurangzeb. ...Ulan-Ude is founded as winter quarters for the Cossacks. ...**January 22:** Shah Jahan dies.

1667. Anhui and Jiangsu are made separate provinces of China.

Americas

1660. French occupy St. Lucia. ...**October 18:** Rhode Island is first colony to recognize restoration of Charles II.

1661. August 6: Under English mediation, Portuguese retain Brazil and the Dutch keep Ceylon (present-day Sri Lanka).

1662. May 3: Connecticut receives a royal charter.

1664. English take Pennsylvania and New Netherland (present-day New York and New Jersey) from Dutch. English rename New Amsterdam, the capital of New Netherland, New York.

1665. English privateers capture St. Eustatius, Saba and Tobago. ...French West India Company is set up. ...**October:** British Crown establishes a government in Maine.

1666. French capture Antigua, Montserrat and St. Christopher. ...Dutch capture Surinam. ...Massachusetts refuses to send representatives to England to answer charges of noncompliance with Crown laws. ...French settle in Vermont.

Science, Invention & Technology

1659. Sir Christopher Wren of England invents the syringe.

c. 1660 Frenchman Jean Martinet (?–1672) invents the socket bayonet.

1660. Irish-born British physicist Robert Boyle (1627–1691) develops what will be known as Boyle's Law, which explains the relationship between the pressure and volume of gases. ...Englishman Robert Hooke (1635–1703) invents a spring chronometer. ...Englishman John Ray (1627–1705) publishes a systematic classification of the planets.

1662. Blaise Pascal introduces a short-lived bus service in Paris.

1664. Hooke invents a wheel barometer while employed by Boyle.

1665. Boyle creates a siphon barometer and coins the term barometer. ...Richard Lower (1631–1691) gives a dog a blood transfusion at Oxford University in England.

1666. Cheddar cheese is first made in town of Cheddar in southwest England.

1667. Frenchman Jean-Baptiste Denis (c. 1643–1704) experiments with transfusion of blood from a lamb to a human.

Religion, Culture & Arts

1659. Molière: *Les Précieuses ridicules*. ...Henry Purcell (d. 1695), English Baroque composer is born.

1660. John Dryden (1631–1700): *Astraea redux*.

c. 1660–1670. Jan Steen (c. 1626–1679), working in Haarlem, Netherlands, paints two of his best-known pictures, *St. Nicholas' Feast* and *As the Old Sing, the Young Pipe*.

1661. Rembrandt: *The Syndics of the Cloth Hall*. ...Louis XIV establishes Royal School of Dancing, with Charles Beauchamps (1636–1705) as director.

1662. Thomas Fuller: *The Worthies of England*. ...John Evelyn (1620–1706), English writer and government official, becomes a founding member of the Royal Society.

1663. Sheldonian Theater is built in Oxford by Sir Christopher Wren. ...John Davenport (1597–1670), Puritan clergyman: *Discourse About Civil Government in a New Plantation Whose Design Is Religion*.

1664. George Etherege (1635–1691): *Love in a Tub*. ...Ch'ien Ch'ien-i (b. 1582), one of most popular Chinese poets, dies.

1665. *London Gazette* and the *Journal des Savants* begin publication. ...**November 19:** Nicolas Poussin (b. 1594) dies.

1666. Antonio Stradivari (1644–1737), establishes himself as a violinmaker at Cremona, Italy. ...Basho (Matsuo Munefusa; 1644–1694) gives up his life as a samurai and becomes a master of haiku.

1667. French dramatist Jean Racine (1639–1699): *Andromaque*. ...John Milton (1608–1674): *Paradise Lost*.

British Isles & Europe

1668. In the Alliance of The Hague, England and Holland unite against France. ...**February:** France occupies Franche-Comté. ...**February 13:** Spain recognizes independence of Portugal. ...**May 2:** In the Peace of Aix-la-Chapelle, France obtains 12 Flemish fortresses. ...**September 19:** John II Casimir Vasa (1609–1672) of Poland abdicates.

1669. Hanseatic League of Lübeck, Bremen and Hamburg is terminated. ...Michael Korybut Wisniowiecki (1640–1673) is elected king of Poland. ...**September:** Turks conquer Crete.

1670. June 1: In the secret Anglo-French Treaty of Dover, France gets free hand in Holland and England receives subsidies from France. ...**August:** France occupies Lorraine.

1671. Turks declare war on Poland.

1672. March: British navy attacks Dutch ships in Atlantic. ...**April 7:** England and France declare war on Holland. ...**October 18:** In the Treaty of Buczácz, Poland cedes Podolia to Turkey.

1672–1678. Second war between France and the Netherlands is fought.

1673. Parliament passes act forbidding Catholics to hold office. ...**June 6:** In Peace of Vossem between Brandenburg and France, elector promises not to support any enemy of Louis XIV. ...**September 16:** Austrian empire declares war on France.

1674. England withdraws from war against Holland; Spain, Holy Roman Empire, and pope ally against France. ...John III Sobieski (1624–1696) is elected king of Poland. The Dutch West India Company is dissolved. ...**May 24:** German Diet votes war against France.

1675. June 25: Great elector defeats Swedes at Rathenow and (June 28) Fehrbellin. ...**July 27:** General Henri Turenne (b. 1611) is killed at battle of Sassbach.

Africa & Middle East

1668. Ar-Rashid Muhammad ibn Ali (fl. 17th century) liberates Marrakesh, Morocco.

1669. Omani raids strike as far south as Mozambique.

1670. Portuguese defeat the Muscat Arabs in Diu. ...Vice-regent of Egypt carries out a fiscal reform with the help of the army. ...Angolans are driven out of Kongo.

1671. Senegal Company is founded. ...Dey (ruler) of Algiers is chosen by local civilian, military and pirate leaders to govern independent of Ottoman Empire.

1672. English Guinea Company merges Royal African Company and obtains monopoly of slave trade that lasts until 1698. ...Legalization of the extant holding of benefices significantly strengthens the position of the Janissaries and Arabs.

1674. Natives expel French from Madagascar.

1675. Meknes becomes capital of Meknes province in northern Morocco.

Asia & Pacific

1668. Fort William near Calcutta is founded. ...First French trading station in India is established. ...Spanish Jesuits colonize Northern Mariana Island.

1669. Dutch conquer Makasar in Celebes (Indonesia). ...Aurangzeb bans Hindu religion in India.

1670. Shivaji Bhonsie resumes war against Aurangzeb. ...**March.** French send a fleet to Ceylon (present-day Sri Lanka), but Dutch prevent a French settlement there.

1672. French occupy Pondicherry and Coromandel Coast (in India).

1673. French take Chandarnagar on Ganges River. ...French send an expedition against Ceylon. ...Mitsui family's trading and banking house is founded in Japan.

1674. Shivaji Bhonsie declares himself independent of Aurangzeb. ...English arrange commercial treaty with Shivaji Bhonsie.

Americas

1668. September 24: English replace Dutch as allies of the Five Nations.

1669. Robert Cavelier, Sieur de La Salle (1643–1687) begins his explorations of the Ohio Valley.

1670. Charles Town (present-day Charleston, South Carolina), is founded at Albermarle Point and becomes the region's first permanent settlement. ...Hudson's Bay Company is formed by Prince Rupert (1619–1682).

1671. Danes take St. Thomas. ...English West Indies (Barbados, Leeward and Windward Islands) is organized. ...English settlers defeat the Coosa Indians near Charles Town. ...**January:** Buccaneers attack Panama.

1672–1673. Cattle epidemic severely damages Virginia's economy. ...Poll tax is reintroduced in Virginia and contributes to indentured servant uprisings.

1673. Louis de Buade Frontenac (1620–1698), governor of Canada, makes peace with Iroquois. ...Panama City, the capital of Panama, is founded. ...**July 17:** French travel down the Mississippi River, reaching Arkansas.

1674. French Guiana is organized. ...**February 9:** In Peace of Westminster between England and Holland, New Netherland and New Sweden are confirmed as English possessions.

1675. June 20–25: King Philip (c. 1642–1676), chief of the Wampanoag, attacks Swansea, Massachusetts, in reprisal for the execution of three Wampanoag, beginning what will become known as King Philip's War. ...**July–September:** King Philip's attacks extend to the entire southern frontier of Massachusetts. ...**December 19:** Colonists slaughter 300 Narragansett women and children at present-day South Kingston, Rhode Island, but the Narragansett warriors escape.

Science, Invention & Technology

1668. Robert Hooke invents the camera lucida, which projects images from a mirror through a convex lens.

1669. English mathematician and physicist Sir Isaac Newton (1642–1727) writes an account of calculus in *De analysi per aequationes numero terminorum infinitas*, which will be published in 1711.

1670. Englishman William Clement (fl. 17th century) adds a minute hand to the clock.

1673. German philosopher and mathematician Gottfried Wilhelm Leibniz (1646–1716) develops the foundations of calculus. His work is conducted independently of Newton's.

1674. Christiaan Huygens invents a balance spring watch and patents a spring-driven chronometer. ...Englishman George Ravenscroft (fl. 17th century) invents lead crystal (glassware).

1675. Scarlet fever is identified as a disease. ...Clement invents a weight-driven pendulum clock with an anchor escapement. It is the most precise timepiece invented to date.

Religion, Culture & Arts

1668. Jean de La Fontaine (1621–1695): *Fables*. ...François Couperin (d. 1733), French organist, harpsichordist, teacher and composer, is born. ...Dietrich Buxtehude (1637–1707), Dutch composer and organist, begins his pre-Christmas concerts.

1669. William Penn (1644–1718) writes *No Cross, No Crown*. ...**October 4:** Rembrandt (b. 1608) dies.

1670. Rebuilding of London begins under the control of Christopher Wren, following the fire of 1666. ...Islamic teaching of the Naqshbandi brotherhood is brought to the eastern Islamic world. ...Jean de Labadie is excommunicated.

1671. John Milton: *Samson Agonistes*. ...Margaret Mary Alacoque (1647–1690) enters convent at Paray-le-Monial. She has visions of Christ's compassion that will inspire modern-day Roman Catholic devotion to the Sacred Heart.

1672. William Wycherley (1640–1716): *The Gentleman Dancing Master*. ...Richard Cumberland (1631–1718), English philosopher and theologian: *A Philosophical Inquiry into the Laws of Nature*.

1673. Molière (b. 1622) dies during rehearsal of his *Le Malade Imaginaire*.

1673–1681. Manchu emperor issues edicts of toleration for Jesuits.

1674. Wycherley: *The Country Wife*; *The Plain Dealer*. ...Nicolas Malebranche (1638–1715), French philosopher: *Recherche de la verite*. ...Nicolas Boileau-Despreaux (1636–1711), French poet and critic: *Le Lutrin*. ...Quakers purchase land in New Jersey.

1675. John Dryden: *Aurangzeb*. ...Baruch Spinoza: *Ethica Ordine Geometrico Demonstrata*. ...German theologian Philipp Jacob Spener (1635–1705): *Pious Desires*. ...Miguel de Molinos (1628–1696), Spanish Roman Catholic priest, mystic and founder of quietism: *Guidea Spirituale*.

c. 1675. Antonio Vivaldi (d. 1741), virtuoso Italian violinist, composer and priest, is born.

British Isles & Europe

1676. October 27: In the Peace of Zurawna, Turkey and Poland divide Podolia.

1676–1682. Fyodor III (1661–1682) reigns as tsar of Russia.

1677. April 11: William of Orange (1650–1702), the future William III, is defeated at Cassel by the French. ...**November 15:** William of Orange marries Mary (1662–1694), daughter of duke of York, later James II of England.

1678. August 10: In treaty of Nijmegen between France and Holland, the Dutch receive Maastricht. ...**September 17:** In another treaty of Nijmegen Spain cedes Franche-Comté and 16 Flemish towns to France.

1679. In a third Treaty of Nijmegen, Freiburg and Breisach are ceded by the Holy Roman Empire to France. ...English Habeas Corpus Act is passed. ...**June 22:** At battle of Bothwell Bridge, James Scott (1649–1685), duke of Monmouth, subdues insurrection of Scottish Covenanters. ...**June 29:** In Peace of St. Germain between Brandenburg and Sweden, Brandenburg loses all its conquests. ...**September 2:** In Peace of Fontainebleau between Denmark and Sweden, Denmark gives up all its conquests.

1680–1682. Charles XI (1655–1697) transforms Sweden into absolute monarchy.

1681. Cameronians secede from Scottish Church and form the Reformed Presbyterian Church. ...**September 30:** French take Strasbourg and Cassale.

1682. Turks proclaim Imre Tököly (1656–1705) king of Hungary.

1682–1689. Sophia (1657–1704) rules as regent of Russia.

Africa & Middle East

1676. October: Ahmad Köprülü (b. 1635), Turkish grand vizier, dies and is succeeded by Kara Mustafa (1634–1683).

1677. Holy war in Waalo, Tua Toro, Kayor and Jolof spurs slave hunts in northwest Africa (present-day Senegal, the Gambia and Mali).

1678. Holland cedes island of Gorée in West Africa to France. ...Riots caused by continuous inflation and rising corn prices break out in Egypt.

1679. Dutch settlers found Stellenbosch, South Africa. ...Director general of Dutch West India Company on Gold Coast introduces firearms to protect slave trade.

1680. First Brandenburgian expedition to West Africa takes place. ...Bashodabashi Kuchuk Mehmed IV (1642–1693) is expelled from Egypt because of his opposition to the Janissaries.

1682. Danes settle on Gold Coast (in Africa). ...Iyasus the Great(fl. 17th century) of Ethiopia champions the arts and military preparedness.

c. 1682. Kayra sultanate expands into the north and northwest part of the Sudan.

Asia & Pacific

1677. Jiangan is made a separate province of China.

1678. Mataram cedes the Preanger regions of West Java to the Dutch.

1680. Tsunayoshi (1646–1709) becomes shogun of Japan.

c. 1680. Manchu eliminate southern Chinese army commands and improve remittance of tax money to the north. ...Russian and Chinese troops clash in Manchuria.

1680–1718. Khan Teuke (c. 1660–1718) rules over reunited Kazakh hordes.

1682–1690. Sir John Child (c. 1638–1690) is governor of Bombay.

Americas

1676. Nathaniel Bacon (1647–1676) heads rebellion of Virginians against governor. ...**January:** Indian attacks kill 36 Virginians in one day. ...**February 10:** King Philip's forces sack Lancaster, Massachusetts and take captives, among them Mary Rowlandson (1635–1678). ...**May 2:** Rowlandson, who will describe her captivity in *True History*, is ransomed. ...**August 12:** King Philip (b. 1642) is killed by an Indian fighting for the colonists.

1677. Order is restored in Virginia after Bacon's Rebellion. ...French raid Trinidad. ...Massachusetts buys part of Maine.

1678. Robert Cavelier, Sieur de La Salle, explores Great Lakes region. ...**December:** French pass Niagara Falls, and Father Louis Hennepin (1640–1710) is the first to describe the falls.

1679. La Salle explores the region of present-day Indiana. ...**September 18:** New Hampshire becomes a province separate from Massachusetts.

1680. In the Westo War, the Spanish pull back from their northern settlements in the Carolinas. ...Charles Town (present-day Charleston, South Carolina) moves across the river from Albermarle Point to Oyster Point. ...Pueblos conduct a fierce revolt against Spanish in present-day southwestern United States. ...**January 15:** Hennepin builds Fort Crèvecoeur on Illinois River.

1682. William Penn (1644–1718) signs a peace treaty with the Indians. ...Pennsylvania Assembly issues constitution (Great Charter). ...La Salle builds Fort Prudhomme (near present-day Memphis). ...**April 9:** La Salle reaches mouth of the Mississippi River and names the entire region Louisiana. ...**May 5:** Penn's Frame of Government includes a governor, council and assembly elected by freeholders. ...**August 13:** Welsh settle north and west of Philadelphia.

Science, Invention & Technology

1676. Dutchman Antoni van Leeuwenhoek (1632–1723) discovers bacteria and protozoa in rainwater using a single-lens microscope.

▲ ***Sir Isaac Newton lived in this house just off Leicester Square in London, England.***

1679. Frenchman Denis Papin (1647–1712) invents a pressure cooker with a safety valve, called a steam digester.

1680. Sir Isaac Newton invents a toy horseless carriage. ...Robert Boyle invents the phosphorous match.

1682. Englishman Nehemiah Grew (1641–1712) speculates about the role of sexuality in plant reproduction. ...English astronomer Edmond Halley (1656–1742) observes a bright comet orbiting the sun in the opposite direction to the planets. Although the comet has been observed periodically throughout the centuries, Halley will be the first to undertake a serious study of this and other comets. The comet, the largest and brightest that reappears regularly, will later be named for Halley.

Religion, Culture & Arts

1676. Thomas Otway (1652–1685) writes *Don Carlos*. ...George Etherege writes *The Man of Mode*.

1676–1679. Giovanni Battista Gaulli (1639–1709) paints *Adoration of the Name of Jesus* on the ceiling of the Gesú Church in Rome.

1676–1689. Innocent XI (1611–1689) is pope.

1677. Henry Purcell (1659–1695) is succeeded by Matthew Locke (c. 1630–1677) as court composer. ...Aphra Behn (1640–1689), English novelist and dramatist: *The Rover* (Part 1). She is the first English female professional writer.

1678. First permanent German opera house opens at Hamburg. ...Ralph Cudworth (1617–1688): *Cambridge Platonist: The True Intellectual System of the Universe*. ...English preacher John Bunyan (1628–1688) publishes *The Pilgrim's Progress*.

1679. Sir William Petty (1623–1687): *A Treatise on Taxes and Contributions*. ...Gilbert Burnet (1643–1715): *History of the English Reformation*. ...Antoine Arnauld (1612–1694) is exiled from France to Belgium because of his Jansenism.

1680. The world's first national theater, the Théâtre Français (later the Comédie Française), is created. ...Pierre Bayle (1647–1706), French philosopher and critic: *Diverse Thoughts on the Comet of 1680*. ...Samuel Butler (b. 1612) dies. ...British painter Peter Lely (b. 1618) dies.

1681. French prelate Jacques-Bénigne Bossuet (1627–1704): *Treatise on Universal History*. ...French scholar Jean Mabillon (1633–1707): *De Re Diplomatica*.

1682. John Dryden: *The Medal*, a satire against sedition. ...French Protestants are excluded from guilds, civil service and the king's household. ...Behn: *The City Heiress*. ...**March:** French Assembly of Clergy defines liberties of Gallican Church. ...**March 13:** Dutch painter J. van Ruisdael (b. c. 1628) dies. ...**November 23:** French painter Claude Lorrain (b. 1600) dies.

British Isles & Europe

1683. Rye House Plot is discovered: James Scott, duke of Monmouth, is exiled to Holland; Lord William Russell (b. 1639) and Algernon Sidney (b. 1623) are beheaded. ...Turks besiege Vienna. ...**September 12:** Charles V (1643–1690) duke of Lorraine, defeats Turks at the Kahlenberg near Vienna.

1683–1706. Peter II (1648–1706) reigns as king of Portugal.

1684. Holy Roman Emperor, Poland and Venice form Holy League of Linz against Turks. ...**June:** French take Tréves and Luxembourg. ...**August 15:** Truce of Ratisbon establishes 20-year peace between Holy Roman Emperor and France.

1685. February 6: Charles II (b. 1630) dies and is succeeded by James II (1633–1701) as king of England. ...**May 20:** James II's Parliament meets.

1686. Russia declares war on Turkey. ...**September 2:** Charles V, duke of Lorraine takes Buda.

1687. August 18: Holy Roman Empire defeats Turks at Mohács. ...**September 26:** Venetians bombard Athens and destroy Parthenon and Propylae.

1688. James II recalls British troops from Holland. ...Frederick William (b. 1620), elector of Brandenburg, dies and is succeeded by Frederick III (1657–1713). ...**June 30:** Seven lords invite William of Orange to England. ...**September 24:** Louis XIV begins war against Holy Roman Empire. ...**September 25:** French invade Palatinate. ...**November 26:** Louis XIV declares war on Holland. ...**December 25:** James II escapes to France. ...**December 28:** William of Orange enters London at invitation of lords.

1689. William of Orange becomes king of England and reigns for 13 years as William III; rules jointly with Mary until her death in 1694. ...**March 12:** James II arrives in Ireland. ...**April 20:** James II begins siege of Londonderry. ...**May 12:** England and Holland join League of Augsburg. ...**July 27:** Scottish Jacobites are defeated at Killiecrankie.

1689–1725. Peter I (1672–1725), the Great, is tsar of Russia.

Africa & Middle East

1683. Brandenburg establishes trading ports on Gold Coast.

1684. English lose Tangier to Morocco. Famine strikes the Sudan.

1684–1695. Dombo Changamire (?–1695) rises to power in northeast Zambezia.

1686. French annex Madagascar.

1687. Brandenburg establishes Arguin, Guinea, as a colony.

1688. Dutch found Fort Vreedenburg on African Gold Coast.

1688–1692. Value of Egyptian currency plummets.

1689. Natal (in South Africa) becomes Dutch colony. ...Two hundred Huguenot refugees settle in present-day South Africa. ...Privileges of Royal African Company are curbed, and access is granted to others. ...**November:** Moroccans retake Larache from the Spanish.

Asia & Pacific

1683. Manchu conquer Formosa (present-day Taiwan). ...Dutch traders are admitted at Canton. ...Dutch occupy Buru Island (in western Indonesia).

1685. K'ang-hsi opens all Chinese ports to foreign trade. ...French embassy is sent to Siam. ...Japanese restrict the export of silver to China.

1686. Siamese embassy is sent to France. ...Aurangzeb annexes kingdom of Bijapur. ...Indigenous population of Calcutta resists English encroachment.

1688. Siam revolts against French influence. ...French are expelled from Burma. ...Manchu expel Galdan and rule in western Mongolia.

1689. Boundary convention of Nerchinsk is reached between Russia and China.

Americas

1683. Quakers and Mennonites settle in Germantown section of Philadelphia. ...First German immigrants arrive in America.

1684. Iroquois conduct raids in Huron country (around Lakes Erie and Ontario). ...Charter of Massachusetts Bay Colony and Massachusetts Bay Company is annulled, and the latter ceases to exist. ...French Mississippi Company is formed. ...Bermuda becomes a British colony.

1686. French capture three James Bay posts. ...**December 20:** Sir Edmund Andros (1637–1714) arrives in Boston to assume the governorship of all the New England colonies, except Connecticut and Rhode Island.

1687. French build Fort Niagara to protect themselves against English. ...La Salle (b. 1643) is murdered by his men on the banks of the Brazos River.

1688. James II revokes Connecticut and Rhode Island charters. ...English sack Portobelo (in central Panama). ...**March 24:** Increase Mather (1639–1723), president of Harvard sails for England, placing New England grievances before the Lords of Trade on August 10.

1689. Iroquois massacre French settlers at Lachine near Montreal. ...**April 18:** An armed uprising in Boston forces Andros to take refuge in a fort.

Science, Invention & Technology

1685. German Johann Zahn (fl. 17th century) produces illustrations by outlining images from a camera obscura.

1687. Frenchman Guillaume Amontons (1663–1705) invents the hygrometer, a mercury-filled device used to measure humidity.

1688. Amontons builds a barometer for use at sea. ...Frenchman Pierre Perignon (1638–1715) makes champagne and places it in a bottle with a wired cork to hold the effervescent wine inside.

Religion, Culture & Arts

1683. William Penn: *General Description of Pennsylvania.* ...Englishman Henry Purcell composes Sonatas of Three Parts.

1684. Alessandro Scarlatti (1660–1725) is appointed *maestro di cappella* of the royal chapel in Naples.

1685. Johann Sebastian Bach (d. 1750), organist and composer, is born at Eisenach, Germany. ...George Frideric Handel (d. 1759), English (naturalized) composer is born in Germany. ...Giuseppe Domenico Scarlatti (d. 1757), Italian harpsichordist and composer, is born. ...Menno van Coehoorn (fl. 17th Century): *Nieuwe Vestingbouw*; theory of fortification. ...Antoine Coysevox (1640–1720), French court sculptor: *Great Condé.* ...Aphra Behn: *The Luck Chance.* ...Richard Baxter (1615–1691) publishes paraphrase of the New Testament and is imprisoned for 18 months for sedition. ...Louis XIV revokes the Edict of Nantes; to escape the ensuing persecution, many French Protestants (Huguenots) flee the country.

1688. French establish a mission among the Penobscot. ...English dramatist and poet Thomas Shadwell (1642–1692): *The Squire of Alsatia.* ...Madame Guyon du Chesnoy (1648–1717) is introduced to French court. In 1695 she will be imprisoned for promulgating the doctrine of Quietism, which emphasizes religious contemplation. ...Quakers protest slavery in the colonies. ...**August 31:** John Bunyan (b. 1628) dies.

1689. Purcell's first opera, *Dido and Aeneas*, is produced in London. ...Toleration Act is passed in England.

British Isles & Europe

1690. April 18: Charles V (b. 1643), duke of Lorraine, dies. ...**July 11:** William III defeats James II at the Boyne (in Ireland). ...**August 19:** Louis George (?–1761) of Baden, Habsburg imperial general, defeats Turks at Szlankarmen; Mustafa Köprülü is killed in action. ...**October 8:** Turks reconquer Belgrade.

1691. July: Limerick capitulates; Protestant farmers settle in Ireland.

1692. Imperial troops capture Grosswardein from the Turks. ...**February 13:** Scottish Highlanders are massacred at Glencoe. ...**August 3:** William III is defeated by French troops led by Marshal François Henri de Luxembourg (1628–1695) at Steenkerque (in Belgium).

1693. March 14: William III vetoes bill for Triennial Parliaments. ...**May 22:** French again destroy Heidelberg. ...**July 29:** Marshal Luxembourg defeats William III at Neerwinden (in Belgium).

1694. July 27: Bank of England is established. ...**December 3:** Triennial Act comes into force. ...**December 28:** Queen Mary II (b. 1662) dies.

1695. Press censorship in England ends. ...**September 1:** William III takes Namur (in Belgium).

1696. English currency is restored under direction of John Locke and Isaac Newton. ...**July 29:** Peter the Great takes Azov from Turks. ...**October 6:** Savoy withdraws from Great Alliance and regains Pinerolo from France.

1697. Charles XI (b. 1655) of Sweden dies and is succeeded by Charles XII (1682–1718). ...**June 27:** Augustus II (1670–1733) of Saxony is elected king of Poland. ...**September 20:** In the Treaty of Ryswyck between France, England, Holland and Spain, France recognizes William III as king and Anne (1665–1714), daughter of James II, as his heir presumptive. ...**October 30:** In the Peace of Ryswyck between France and the Holy Roman Empire, France restores right bank of Rhine, and gives up claims to Palatinate.

Africa & Middle East

c. 1690. First Muslim theocracy is founded in northwest Africa.

1691–1695. Ahmed II (1642–1695) reigns as Ottoman sultan.

1692. Mehmed IV exerts control over Janissaries.

1693. French defeat English merchant fleet at Lagos (in Nigeria).

1695. Famine and epidemics sweep Egypt.

1695–1703. Mustafa II (1664–1703) reigns as Ottoman sultan.

1696. Several Africans are purchased in Constantinople for Peter the Great. ...**March:** Sultan of Oman lays siege to Mombasa, which falls, destroying Portuguese control of East African coast north of Cape Delgado.

1697. Major floods strike Egypt, relieving drought and famine. ...Egypt's tax system is overhauled.

1698. African trade is opened to all British subjects. ...Portuguese are expelled from East African coast.

Asia & Pacific

1690. English establish trading stations at Calcutta.

c. 1690. Qiqihan in northeastern China is founded as a walled military fortress.

1691. Princes of Khalkha lose their independence to Manchu.

1693. Dutch take Pondicherry (in India).

1694–1721. Shah Sultan Husayn (1668–1726) rules Persia.

1695. Indian textiles displace British goods in Indian marketplace.

1696. Fort William is built at Calcutta. ...Buddhist theocracy and Mongol aristocracy begin rule of Mongolia. ...K'ang-hsi leads an army of 80,000 with improved artillery of western design, defeats the Mongols and annexes Outer Mongolia.

1697. Russians add Kamchatka to their empire.

1698–1700. First French legation is sent to China.

Americas

1690. French oust the English from their Hudson Bay posts. ...**February 9:** French and Indians burn Schenectady, New York. ...**March 27:** French and Indians attack Salmon Falls, New Hampshire. ...**July 31:** French and Indians attack Falmouth (present-day Portland, Maine).

1691. Massachusetts receives new charter that makes it a royal colony. ...**June 27:** Maryland becomes a royal province.

1692. Royal authority is reestablished in New Hampshire. ...Spanish reassert their control over present-day New Mexico. ...Salem witchcraft panic results in trials and 20 executions. ...Earthquake strikes Jamaica. ...**June 21:** Abenaki raid Wells, Maine.

1693. English recapture the James Bay area from French. Kingston becomes capital of Jamaica.

1694. June 23: Abenaki raid Durham, New Hampshire.

1696. Navigation Acts establish vice-admiralty courts in the colonies.

1697. Hispaniola (present-day Haiti and the Dominican Republic) is partitioned; the western part of the island is ceded to France. ...**March 15:** Abenaki raid Haverhill, Massachusetts. ...**September 20:** In Peace of Ryswyck, Fort Albany is restored to Hudson's Bay Company; Acadia is given to France; East San Domingo (in present-day Dominican Republic), Cuba, and Puerto Rico in the West Indies remain with Spain.

1698–1741. Massachusetts and New Hampshire share a governor.

Science, Invention & Technology

1690. Tobacco is used by the French as an insecticide, mainly against lice, after its toxic properties are discovered by Frenchman Jean de la Quintinie (1626–1688). ...First American paper mill is established near Philadelphia. ...Denis Papin invents a single-piston atmospheric steam engine.

1692. Languedoc Canal, connecting the Bay of Biscay with the Mediterranean Sea, opens in France.

c. 1695. Englishman George Graham (1674–1751) invents the orrery, a mechanical model of the solar system, which simulates the motions of the known planets and moons.

1698. Thomas Savery (1650–1715) of England invents a water pump that uses steam instead of moving parts to create a vacuum. It is used in mining.

Religion, Culture & Arts

1690. John Locke (1632–1704), English philosopher, publishes *Two Treatises on Civil Government* and *An Essay Concerning Human Understanding*. ...French found their first mission in present-day Texas near the Neches. ...Poetical circle of Arcadia is formed in Rome.

1692. Church of England is established in Maryland. ...Jesuit mission is founded in Guevavi near Nogales, Arizona. ...National Palace is built in Mexico City. ...William and Mary College is founded. ...Purcell: *The Fairy Queen*.

1693. François Couperin is chosen by Louis XIV to be one of four organists of the royal chapel. ...Cotton Mather (1663–1728): *Wonders of the Invisible World*.

1694. Purcell: *Te Deum and Jubilate*.

1695. William Congreve (1670–1729): *Love for Love*.

1695–1697. Pierre Bayle: *Dictionnaire historique et critique*.

1696. Jesuit mission is founded in Tumacacori near Nogales, Arizona. ...Antoninette Bourignon (1616–1680), Flemish mystic, posthumously publishes *The Light of the World*.

1698. German preacher August Hermann Francke (1663–1772), an exponent of Pietism, founds Francke Endowments at Halle. ...John Toland (1670–1722), Irish philosopher: *Life of Milton*.

British Isles & Europe

1699. British Woolens Act, designed to prevent colonies from manufacturing goods that compete with England's economy, is passed. ...Peace of Karlowitz between Austria-Hungary, Poland, Venice and Turkey, is signed.

1700. March 25: In the Second Partition Treaty, Habsburg archduke Charles is given Spain, its colonies, Netherlands, and Sardinia and the French dauphin is given Italian territories. ...**November:** Charles II (b. 1661) of Spain dies and Philip (1683–1746), duke of Anjou, succeeds to Spanish crown and becomes Philip V. ...**November 30:** Charles XII defeats Peter the Great at Narva (in Estonia).

1701. The Grand Alliance against Louis XIV is reconstituted. ...Scotland refuses to approve Act of Settlement, which recognizes the German house of Hanover. ...James II (b. 1633) dies. ...**January 18:** Frederick III, elector of Brandenburg, is crowned king in Prussia, and becomes Frederick I. ...**February:** Philip V enters Madrid; French occupy southern Spanish Netherlands. ...**April–September:** Prince Eugene (1663–1736) defeats French in Lombardy. ...**June–July:** Charles XII of Sweden occupies Livonia and Courland and invades Poland.

1702. John Churchill (1650–1722), duke of Marlborough, leads British to victories in Netherlands. ...French Camisards (Huguenots) rebel against Louis XIV. ...**March 19:** William III (b. 1650) dies and is succeeded by Queen Anne in England. ...**May 4:** England, Holland and the Holy Roman Emperor declare war on France. ...**May 14:** Charles XII takes Warsaw. ...**July 19:** Charles XII defeats Poles at Klissow and seizes Kraków.

1703. Victor Amadeus II, (1666–1732) duke of Savoy, joins Austria in the War of the Spanish Succession. ...Charles XII of Sweden defeats Peter the Great at Pultusk. ...St. Petersburg is founded by Peter the Great.

1704. Camisards reject royal terms for a pardon. ...**July 15:** Stanisław I Leszczyński (1677–1766) is elected king of Poland at Charles XII's instigation. ...**August 4:** English take Gibraltar. ...**August 13:** Duke of Marlborough and Prince Eugene defeat French and Bavarians at Blenheim.

1705. Leopold I (b. 1640) dies and is succeeded as Holy Roman Emperor by Joseph I (1678–1711).

Africa & Middle East

c. 1700. Antsiranana (formerly Diégo-Suarez), a town in northern Madagascar, is occupied by French pirates. ...Toamasina (formerly Tamatave), a city in eastern Madagascar, becomes a European trading post. ...New groups and societies settle in northern Kenya and Tanzania. ...Overpopulation spreads in Congo. ...Pirates settle in Tunis. ...Persians besiege Kars (capital of northwestern province in Turkey).

1701. Lat Sukaabe (fl. 18th century), ruler of several kingdoms in northwest Africa, supports free trade with all European nations.

1702. Asiento Guinea Company is founded for slave trade between Africa and America.

1703. Janissaries and elements of the military revolt in Constantinople against the Ottomans.

1705. Beys of Husseinite dynasty become rulers of Tunis. ...Turkish troops from Algiers invade Tunisian countryside.

Asia & Pacific

1699. British buccaneer William Dampier (1652–1715) leads expedition to northwest coast of Australia. ...Bengal becomes a presidency (division) of British India.

1700. Mogul government appears in Madras and is bought off with an immense gift.

▲ A playing card depicting a scene of Queen Anne receiving an address from the new Parliament in November 1710.

1704. Mogul capital moves from Dacca to Murshidabad.

Americas

1699. Scottish settlement in Darien (in Panama) fails. ...French begin to settle in Louisiana.

1700. French build a fort at Mackinac. ...Iroquois defeat the Illinois.

1701. Yale College is founded in Connecticut. ...Delaware is chartered to have a government separate from that of Pennsylvania. ...French build a fort at Detroit.

1702. April 26: Proprietors of East Jersey and West Jersey surrender governmental authority to Crown. ...**September 10:** English from Carolinas burn and pillage St. Augustine, Florida.

1703. Delaware becomes a separate colony. ...**August 10:** Abenaki raid Maine settlements.

1704. English destroy 13 of 14 missions in Apalachee, Florida. ...French build Fort Miami on Lake Erie. ...**February 28–29:** Abenaki destroy Deerfield, Massachusetts. ...**July 1, 28:** New Englanders attack French villages of Minas and Beaubassin in an attempt to eliminate Abenaki and French power. ...**August 18–29:** French and Indians destroy English settlement at Bonavista, Newfoundland.

Science, Invention & Technology

c. 1700. Englishman Stephen Hales (1677–1761) uses a brass pipe inserted into a blood vessel to measure blood pressure. ...The hurdy-gurdy, or barrel organ, appears in the streets of Paris and other French cities. It is often played by disabled soldiers returned from the battlefront.

1701. Englishman Jethro Tull (1674–1741) invents a wheat drill for planting crops.

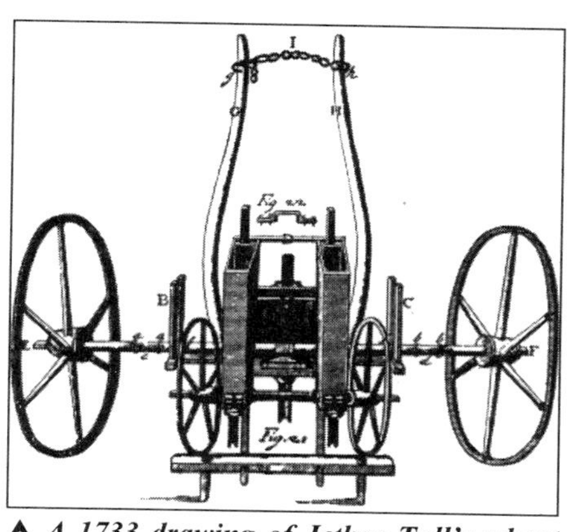

A 1733 drawing of Jethro Tull's wheat drill.

1703. Charles Newbold (fl. 18th century) of New Jersey invents an iron plow.

1705. Edmond Halley publishes *A Synopsis of the Astronomy of Comets*. In the book, Halley predicted that the large comet he observed in 1682 would reappear in 1758. When his prediction proved true, the comet was named after him.

Religion, Culture & Arts

1699. Irish dramatist George Farquhar (1678–1707): *Love and a Battle*. ...French establish a mission at Cahokia (near present-day east St. Louis). ...François Fénelon (1651–1715): *Les Adventures de Telémaque*.

1700. German Protestants finally adopt Gregorian calendar, first promulgated in 1582. ...William Congreve: *The Way of the World*, highwater mark of English Restoration theater. ...Jesuits found mission in Bac (near present-day Tucson, Arizona). ...Clement XI (1649–1721) becomes pope. ...**April 30:** John Dryden (b. 1631) dies.

c. 1700. Forty-seven Ronin (masterless samurai) commit mass suicide, sparking many legends and literary texts. ...Major architectural changes begin to occur in East Africa. ...Leatherwork begins to flourish in Nigeria.

1702. *Daily Courant*, first English daily newspaper, begins publication. ...Japanese painter Ogota Korin (1658–1716) unites the two imperial schools of Japanese painting—Kano and Yamato. ...Cotton Mather: *Magnalia Christi Americana*.

1703. *Vyedomosti*, first Russian newspaper, begins publication. ...Jesuits establish a mission at the junction of the Mississippi and the Kaskaskia Rivers. ...Madame Guyon du Chesnoy is released from prison. She will be banished to Blois.

1704. Jonathan Swift (1667–1745): *Tale of a Tub*. ...Daniel Defoe (1660–1731) starts *Weekly Review*, first American newspaper, at Boston. ...**October 28:** John Locke (b. 1632) dies. ...**October 29:** The newspaper *Vossische Zeitung* is first published at Berlin.

1705. Bernard Mandeville (1670–1733): *Fable of the Bees*; political satire. ...Moscow University is founded. ...Prosper Jolyot (pen name Crébillon,1674–1762), French poet: *Idoménée*.

British Isles & Europe

1706. February 13: Charles XII of Sweden defeats Russians and Saxons at Fraustadt (in Germany). ...**May 22:** English raise siege of Barcelona by the French. ...**May 23:** Duke of Marlborough defeats French at Ramillies and conquers Spanish Netherlands. ...**June 27:** English and Portuguese enter Madrid. ...**September 7:** Prince Eugene defeats French at Torino. ...**September 24:** In Peace of Altranstädt between Sweden and Saxony, Augustus is forced to recognize Stanisław I Leszczyński.

1707. Charles XII takes Vilna and allies with Cossacks under Ivan Stepanovich Mazepa (c. 1644–1709). ...Union formed between Castile and Aragon. ...Union formed between England and Scotland.

1708. Charles XII takes Mohilev and invades Ukraine. ...Hungarian rebels are defeated by Austrians. ...**July 11:** Duke of Marlborough and Prince Eugene defeat French at Oudenarde. ...**August:** British take Sardinia. ...**September:** British capture Minorca.

1709. Duke of Marlborough and Prince Eugene take Tournai, defeat French at Malplaquet and take Mons. ...Augustus II reassumes the throne of Poland. ...**July 8:** Peter the Great defeats Charles XII at Poltava. Charles XII flees to Turkey.

1710. French defeats lead to unsuccessful peace negotiation. ...**September 28:** Charles III enters Madrid. ...**November 30:** Turkey declares war on Russia, at Charles XII's instigation. ...**December 9:** Spanish defeat British at Brihuega (in Spain). ...**December 10:** French defeat Austrians at Villa Viciosa; Philip V reasserts control over Spain.

1711. Sir Robert Walpole (1676–1745), who will be first earl of Oxford, initiates plans for "South Sea Bubble," a scheme to exploit the riches of South America. ...**April 17:** Joseph I (b. 1678) dies and is succeeded as Holy Roman Emperor by Charles III of Spain, who becomes Charles VI. ...**April 29:** Agreement between Charles VI and Hungarian rebels. ...**July 21:** Peter the Great, surrounded by Turks at the Pruth, makes peace and restores Azov.

1712. Russians and Danes defeat Swedes in Baltic and Scandinavia. ...Last execution for witchcraft takes place in Britain. ...Peter the Great marries his mistress, who will become Catherine I (1684–1727). ...Russian capital moves from Moscow to St. Petersburg. ...Walpole, falsely convicted of corruption, is sent to the Tower of London. ...British and French declare a truce. ...Philip V of Spain renounces claims to French throne.

Africa & Middle East

1706. Iyasus the Great dies and Ethiopia enters a period of dynastic confusion and decline.

1707. In present-day South Africa, 1,780 freeholders of European descent own about 1,100 slaves.

1708–1730. Ghilzai Mir Wais (?–1730) rules Persia through the Pathans after a revolt against the Safavid dynasty.

1710. Dutch-occupied Mauritius (island in Indian Ocean) comes under French rule, and Dutch leave. ...The Shah Hussein Madrasah, a school for dervishes, is constructed. ...Prices soar in Egypt because of huge demand for coffee in Europe.

1711. Ahmad I (fl. 18th century), a Janissary, kills the Ottoman governor and rules in Tripoli. ...Janissary power begins to wane in Egypt.

1711–1714. A fierce struggle for power ensues between several political parties in Egypt.

1711–1718. Food shortages spread across the Sudan.

Asia & Pacific

1707. March 3. Aurangzeb (b. 1618) dies and is succeeded as emperor of Mogul empire by Bahadur Shah I (1643–1712). ...**November 24.** Mt. Fuji erupts.

1708. Kazan becomes capital of Volga region. ...**January 22:** Eruptions of Mt. Fuji cease.

c. 1710. Bangka (in Indonesia) becomes a main manufacturing center.

1712. War of succession between Bahadur Shah I's four sons. ...Independent state of Hyderbad (in India) is established.

Americas

1706. Charleston, South Carolina, is successfully defended against French and Spaniards. ...Spain claims Colorado but does not establish settlements.

1707. British land in Acadia (eastern Canada). ...**September 21:** Abenaki attack Winter Harbor, Maine.

1708. Deeply in debt, William Penn mortgages the province of Pennsylvania to trustees. ...**December 21:** French capture of St. Johns, Newfoundland, brings the eastern shore of Canada under French control.

1709. First mass immigration of Germans to America. They come from Palatinate to Pennsylvania.

1710. French colony in Louisiana relocates to present-day Mobile, Alabama. ...**October 16:** British significantly damage and capture Habitation Port- Royal (Annapolis Royal), the French and Abenaki stronghold in Acadia (eastern Canada).

1711. Sáo Paulo, Brazil, achieves city status. ...**May–October:** British expedition to Canada is unsuccessful. ...French capture Rio de Janeiro.

1711–1712. Indians massacre 200 settlers in the Tuscarora War, but are defeated by combined forces from South Carolina and Virginia.

1712. Slaves in New York revolt. ...North Carolina and South Carolina become separate colonies.

Science, Invention & Technology

1706. Excavations begin at Pompeii and Herculaneum.

1707. Englishman Thomas Newcomen (1663–1729) successfully demonstrates his paddle-wheel steamboat on the Fulda River in Germany.

▲ ***Hoping to westernize the Russians, Peter the Great launched many reforms, including a ban on beards. In the image above, Peter is shown attempting to cut off a nobleman's beard.***

1711. Sibilla Masters (fl. early 18th century) develops Tuscarora rice. It becomes one of the most popular patent medicines made in America.

Religion, Culture & Arts

1706. English restore religious toleration in what will become South Carolina. ...Isaac Watts (1674–1748), English theologian and author of hymn texts: *Horae Lyricae*.

1707. Francis Makemie (1658–1708), early leader of American Presbyterianism, is jailed by governor of New York for being a "strolling preacher."

1708. George Frideric Handel: *Agrippina*. ...First permanent German theater opens at Vienna. ...First Dunker congregation is established in Schwarzenau, Germany. ...Connecticut churches adopt the Saybrook Platform.

1710. Handel: *Rinaldo*. ...First Bible Society is established in Halle, Saxony, Germany. ...Irish philospher George Berkeley (1685–1753): *Treatise Concerning Principles of Human Knowledge*. ...Cotton Mather: *Essays to Do Good*. ...Gottfried Wilhelm Leibniz: *Essays in Theodicy on the Goodness of God, the Liberty of Man, and the Origin of Evil*.

1711. London Academy of Arts is opened under Sir Godfrey Kneller (1646–1723). ...Fernando Bibiena (1657–1743), Italian theater designer and architect: *Architettura civile*. ...Crébillon: *Rhadamiste et Zénobie*.

1711–1714. *Spectator*, literary periodical edited by Joseph Addison (1672–1719) and Sir Richard Steele (1672–1729), is published in London.

1712. Scottish physician and writer John Arbuthnot (1667–1735): *The History of John Bull*, which creates the character that comes to personify Britain, is first published as *Law Is a Bottomless Pit*. ...British satiric poet Alexander Pope (1688–1744) publishes mock-heroic poem *The Rape of the Lock*.

British Isles & Europe

1713. Frederick I (b. 1657) of Prussia dies and is succeeded by Frederick William I (1688–1740). ...**April 11:** In Peace of Utrecht between France and Britain, Holland, Savoy and Portugal, France recognizes Protestant succession in Britain, and France gains fortresses on northern frontier, Holland establishes barrier against France, Sicily is ceded to Savoy as kingdom. ...**June 13:** In Peace of Utrecht between Britain and Spain, Spain cedes Gibraltar and Minorca.

1714. Isabella Farnese (1692–1766) becomes queen of Spain. ...In Peace of Rastatt between France and Charles VI, France recognizes Italian possessions of Habsburgs. ...Peace of Utrecht between Spain and Holland. ...**August 1:** Queen Anne (b. 1665) dies and is succeeded by George Louis (1660–1727), elector of Hanover, who becomes George I.

1715. Sweden under Charles XII attacks Norway. ...**February 6:** Peace of Madrid between Spain and Portugal. ...**September 1:** Louis XIV (b. 1638) dies and is succeeded by Louis XV (1710–1774), his great-grandson. ...**November 15:** In Barrier Treaty between Austria and Holland, Austria obtains Spanish Netherlands and eight fortresses occupied by Dutch garrisons.

1716. April 13: Charles VI declares war on Turkey. ...**August 5:** Prince Eugene defeats Turks at Peterwardein. ...**October:** Russians occupy Mecklenburg.

1717. April 10: Sir Robert Walpole resigns as chancellor of the exchequer. ...Britain, France and Holland form Triple Alliance. ...**August 17:** Convention of Amsterdam between France, Russia and Prussia is formed to maintain treaties of Utrecht and Baden. ...**August 11:** Admiral George Byng (1663–1733) defeats Spanish off Cape Passaro. ...**August 18:** Prince Eugene captures Belgrade. ...**December 28:** Britain declares war on Spain.

1718. Britain, France, Holland and Austria form Quadruple Alliance to keep peace in Europe. ...In Peace of Passarowitz between Austria and Turkey, Austria obtains Belgrade, the Banat and part of Serbia, and Turkey keeps Morea. ...Charles XII of Sweden is killed before Frederikshall and is succeeded by his sister, Ulrika Eleonora (1688–1741).

1719. January 5: Alliance of Vienna between Charles VI, Saxony, Poland and Britain is formed against Russia and Prussia. ...**January 17:** France declares war on Spain. ...**April–June:** Spanish invasion of Scotland fails.

Africa & Middle East

1713. Smallpox outbreak kills many Europeans and most of the Khoikhoi living near present-day Cape Town, South Africa. ...Gonja kings are crushed at the battle of Tunuma (in Tuma).

1714. Tripoli becomes independent of Constantinople.

1715–1730. During the "Tulip Period," the Ottoman army is reformed.

1716. One of the warring sides of Futa Toro (in northwest Africa) calls on the Moroccans for aid.

1717. December 18: Prussia sells colonies in Africa to Dutch.

1717–1727. Competition between Dutch and British in factories on Mauritania coast results in first gum war.

1719. Populace of Timbuktu rebels against the pasha and his reign of terror, driving him out of the city.

Asia & Pacific

1713. Ietsugu (1712–1716) becomes shogun of Japan. ...Laos is split into three states: Louangphrabang, Vientiane, and Champasak.

1715. British build a permanent factory in Canton. ...Japanese restrict the export of copper to China. ...Russians make their first military expedition to Kazakh Steppe. ...Maratha dynasty founds city of Indore.

1716. Yoshimune (1684–1751) becomes shogun of Japan. ...Russians establish a fortress in southwestern Siberia. ...Omsk is founded as a Russian fortress.

1717. Mongols occupy Lhasa. ...Russians make their first military expedition to Khiva, ending in a massacre of tsarist troops.

1719. Muhammad Shah (?–1748), grandson of Bahadur Shah I, becomes Mogul emperor.

Americas

1713. April 11: In Peace of Utrecht, France cedes Newfoundland, Acadia and Hudson Bay to Britain, and Spain cedes San Sacramento to Portugal.

An image from Mark Catesby's **Natural History of Carolina** *(1731), showing "the parrot of Carolina and the Cypress of America."*

1715–1716. Yamassee attack white settlers in the Carolinas.

1716. January: Carolinians and Cherokee allies defeat Yamassee.

1717. Spanish establish the viceroyalty of New Granada, now comprising Colombia, Ecuador, Panama and Venezuela. ...Portuguese fortify a hill on the site of Montevideo.

1718. Carolinians build forts at Port Royal and Columbia to defend against French and Spanish. ...French found New Orleans. ...Scotch-Irish colonize the Cumberland Valley and push the boundaries of Pennsylvania westward.

c. 1719. French build a fort on the Wabash.

Science, Invention & Technology

1716. Edmond Halley invents a wooden diving bell that resupplies air by weighted barrels.

1717. Gabriel Daniel Fahrenheit (1686–1736) adjusts his temperature scale to 32 degrees for the freezing point and 96 degrees for the human body, from 30 and 90 degrees, respectively.

1718. J. L. Petit (1653–1730) of France invents an effective screw tourniquet.

Religion, Culture & Arts

1713. Pope Clement XI condemns Pasquier Quesnel's *Jansenist Moral Reflections* (*Bull Unigenitus*). ...George Berkeley: *The Three Dialogues Between Hylas and Philonous.*

1714. Gottfried Wilhelm Leibniz: *Principia Philosophiae.*

1715. Chikamatsu Monzaemon (1653–1724), Japan's first professional dramatist: *The Battle of Coxinga.*

1715–1720. Alexander Pope translates Homer's *Iliad.*

1716. J. B. Homann (1663–1724): *World Atlas.* ...Madame Guyon du Chesnoy (1648–1717): *Discours Chrétiens et Spirituels.*

1717. Jean-Antoine Watteau (1684–1721) paints *L'Embarquement pour l'Île de Cythère.* It will be considered his most characteristic work. ...School attendance is compulsory in Prussia.

1718. François-Marie Arouet, known as Voltaire (1694–1778): *Édipe.* ...Joseph Marie Amiot (d. 1793), Jesuit missionary to China who introduced Chinese literature and customs to Europe, is born.

1719. Daniel Defoe: *Robinson Crusoe.* ...Christian von Wolff (1679–1754), German rationalist philosopher and mathematician: *Vermunfige Gedanken.*

British Isles & Europe

1720. John Law (1671–1729) of Lauriston is appointed controller general of France. …**February 1:** In the Treaty of Stockholm between Sweden and Prussia, Prussia obtains Pomerania between Oder and Peene, including Stettin. …**February 17:** In the Peace between Quadruple Alliance and Spain, Savoy obtains Sardinia from Austria in exchange for Sicily. …**February 29:** Ulrika Eleonora, Swedish queen, abdicates in favour of her husband, Frederick I, prince of Hesse-Cassel. …**December:** National bankruptcy in France is declared.

1721. Sir Robert Walpole restores public credit. …**April 3:** Walpole is reappointed first lord of the treasury and chancellor of the exchequer. …**September 10:** In the Treaty of Nystad between Sweden and Russia, Russia obtains Livonia, Estonia, Ingria, and Eastern Karelia. …**October 22:** Peter the Great is proclaimed emperor of all the Russias.

1723. February 16: Louis XV attains majority.

1724. January: Philip V of Spain abdicates in favor of Louis. …**August 31:** Louis dies and Philip V continues to rule until 1746.

1725. February 8: Peter the Great (b. 1672) of Russia dies and is succeeded by Catherine I. …**May 1:** In the Treaty of Vienna between Austria and Spain, Spain guarantees Pragmatic Sanction and Austria agrees to aid Spain to recover Gibraltar. …**September 23:** In Treaty of Herrenhausen between Britain, France and Prussia, mutual guarantee of integrity is agreed to and Prussia's claims to Jülich-Berg are recognized.

1726. August 6: Russia and Austria enter into a treaty against Turkey.

1727. Catherine I (b. 1684) of Russia dies. …**June 12:** George I (b. 1660) dies and is succeeded by George II (1683–1760).

1727–1730. Peter II (1715–1730), grandson of Peter the Great, is tsar of Russia.

Africa & Middle East

c. 1720. Vice-regents in Egypt strengthen their authority.

1721. Holland buys last Prussian posts in Africa. …Northern Persia is damaged by an earthquake.

1722. Afghans capture Esfahan, seat of Persian government. …**September 12.** Russia takes Baku and Derbent from Persia.

1723. Turkey attacks Persia.

1724. Turks take Erivan from Persia. …French promote civil war in Futa Toro (in northwest Africa) as a way to defend their interests.

1725. Portuguese exert brief control over the East African coast. …Revolution in Futa Jallon (in western Sudan) establishes Muslim law and tradition. …Military aristocracy of Futa Toro (in northwest Africa) calls on French to help expel Moroccans.

Asia & Pacific

1720. Tibet becomes tributary to China. …Oyrats defeat Kazakh Middle Horde north of Lake Balkash.

1721. Chinese suppress revolt on Formosa (present-day Taiwan). …Bugis capture Johore and Riau.

1722. Dutch visit the Samoan Islands. …Kanoji Angria (1690–1729) defeats and puts to flight a combined attack by the British and the Portuguese.

1722–1723. Astrakhan serves as Russia's base in the campaign against Persia.

1723. Bhapol becomes the capital of the princely state of Bhopal. …Bharnagar (in western India) is founded.

1723–1735. Yung-cheng (1678–1735) reigns as emperor of China.

1724. Hyderabad becomes capital of the nizams (princes).

1725. Manchu add a fourth princedom to Mongolia.

1727. Amur frontier between Russia and China is rectified.

Americas

1720. First settlement in Vermont is established. ...The "Mississippi Bubble," John Law's push to bring more settlers into the Mississippi region, is exposed as a scheme for Law's own personal gain, and Law is forced to flee France. ...French build a fort at Kaskaskia. ...French build Fort Niagara to secure lower Great Lakes and establish a base of operations against Iroquois. ...Eastern Apache are driven from their traditional plains and are defeated by the advancing Comanche.

1721. Paraguayans stage a revolt against Spanish. They will remain independent for ten years. ...Swiss immigrants introduce rifles to America. ...**May 29:** South Carolina is incorporated as a royal colony.

1722. Dutch discover Easter Island.

1723. French build a fort on the north bank of the Missouri River. ...Araucanians in south central Chile rise up against Spanish domination. They will repeat the revolt in 1740 and 1766.

c. 1724. French in Louisiana adopt the "Code Noir," rigidly controlling the lives of blacks. ...Spanish drive Portuguese out of Uruguay. ...British build Fort Drummer near the site of Brattleboro, Vermont.

1725. British build Forts Oswego and Ontario to counteract French power in the lower Great Lakes.

1726. French build a fort at the mouth of the Illinois River. ...Montevideo is named the capital of Uruguay.

1727. Quakers demand abolition of slavery. ...Coffee is planted in Brazil.

1727–1728. Carolinians penetrate deep into Florida during Anglo-Spanish War.

Science, Invention & Technology

1720. George Graham invents a clock with a mercury-compensated pendulum for greater precision.

c. 1720. The .75 caliber Brown Bess musket is developed in Britain for the military.

Danish explorer Vitus Jonassen Bering.

1724. Gin becomes a popular drink in Britain.

1727. Automata are the rage in Europe and the term *android*, referring to a mechanized replica of a human being, is coined. ...German Johann Schulze (1687–1744) discovers that silver salts darken when exposed to sunlight. This will become an important principle in the development of photography.

Religion, Culture & Arts

1720. George Frideric Handel: *Esther*. ...Japanese shogun permits circulation of previously banned books that do not specifically propound Christianity.

1721. Lukas von Hildebrandt (1668–1745) builds Belvedere Summer Palace, Vienna. ...James Gibbs (1682–1754), an Italian architect, builds St. Martin in the Fields in London.

1722. Daniel Defoe: *Moll Flanders*. ...Jean Philippe Rameau (1683–1764), French composer: *Traité de l'harmonie*. ...Nikolaus Ludwig Graf von Zinzendorf (1700–1760), German religious reformer, grants refuge on his estate to a group of Moravians.

1723. Voltaire: *Henriade*. ...*Tu Shu Chi Ch'eng*, Chinese encyclopedia, is published. ...First Dunker church in America is established. ...**February 25:** Sir Christopher Wren (b. 1632) dies.

1724. Melchor Pérez Holguín (c. 1660–1725): *The Four Evangelists*, the last paintings by founder of the Potosí school of painting in Bolivia. ...*Boston News-Letter*, America's first regularly published newspaper, begins publication.

1725. Alexander Pope translates Homer's *Odyssey*. ...Francis Hutcheson (1694–1746), British philosopher: *Inquiry Concerning Beauty, Order, Harmony, and Design*; *Inquiry Concerning Moral, Evil and Good*. ...Giovanni Battista Vico (1668–1774), Italian philosopher of history: *Principi de scienza nuova d'intorno comune natura delle nazioni*.

1726. Allan Ramsay (c. 1685–1758) opens first circulating library, at Edinburgh. ...Jonathan Swift: *Gulliver's Travels*.

1727. American Philosophical Society is founded in Philadelphia. ...Moravian Church is established in Hermhut, Saxony, Germany.

British Isles & Europe

1728. March 6: Convention of Prado ends one-year war between Britain and Spain. ...**December 23:** In Treaty of Berlin between Charles VI and Prussia, Prussia guarantees Pragmatic Sanction and Charles VI recognizes Prussia's claims to Jülich and Berg.

1729. Corsica becomes independent of Genoa. ...King Frederick IV (1671–1730) of Denmark charters Danish East India Company.

1730. February 11: Peter II (b. 1715) of Russia dies. ...**August 4:** Frederick (1712–1786), crown prince of Prussia, tries to flee to Britain but is imprisoned by his father. ...**September 30:** Victor Amadeus II of Savoy abdicates and is succeeded by Charles Emmanuel III (1701–1773).

1731. September: French parliament declares temporal power independent of all other powers, and places clergy under jurisdiction of Crown. ...**July 22:** In Treaty of Vienna between Britain, Holland, Spain and Austria, Maritime Powers guarantee Pragmatic Sanction, and Spain obtains Parma and Piacenza.

1732. British Hat Act limits manufacturing in British colonies.

1733. Associate Presbytery withdraws from the Scottish Church.

1733–1735. During War of Polish Succession, Russia and Austria recognize Augustus III (1696–1763) of Saxony against Stanisław I Leszczyński.

1734. French, Sardinian, and Spanish troops defeat Austrians throughout Italy. ...Charles Emmanuel III of Savoy and Sardinia acquires Novara and Totona for Sardinia. ...Charles VI declares war on France. ...Russians take Danzig and expel Stanisław I Leszczyński from Poland.

1735. October 3: In Peace of Vienna, Stanisław I Leszczyński obtains Lorraine, duke of Lorraine obtains Tuscany, Austria obtains Parma and Piacenza and France guarantees Pragmatic Sanction.

1736. British statutes against witchcraft repealed. ...**May:** Turkey is at war with Austria and Russia.

Africa & Middle East

1728. Aden (in southern Yemen) is incorporated into sultanate of Lahej. ...Ali Basha (fl. 18th century), the bey's nephew, revolts. This will lead to 34 years of divided loyalties in Tunisia.

1729. Portugal loses Mombasa to the Arabs. ...Nader Shah (1688–1747) forms national army in Persia and drives out Afghans.

1730. Sultan Ahmad XII (1725–1773) of Turkey is deposed. ...The bey controls all trade with Europeans in Tunis.

1730–1754. Ottoman army is reformed, using European methods and equipment.

1731. Safavid dynasty in Persia ends.

King Augustus III, known as Russia's puppet ruler in Poland.

1734. Persians recapture Erivan from Turks. ...Yerim Mbanik (fl. 18th century), with an army of 200 to 300 horsemen and 3,000 infantry, becomes one of the most powerful kings in northwest Africa.

1735. French East India Company establishes sugar industry in Mauritius and Réunion in Indian Ocean. ...Turko-Persian War ends.

1736. Nader Shah becomes king of Persia.

Asia & Pacific

1728. Kyakhta (in southern Siberia) is founded as a trading point between Russia and China.

1729. Emperor Yung-cheng prohibits opium smoking in China.

1731. The Kazakh Lesser Horde accepts Russian protection.

1732–1733. Thousands of Japanese die in Kyoto famine.

1734–1735. Russians build a fort at Orenburg (in central Asia).

1735–1796. Chinese acquire Outer Mongolia, Tibet, Nepal and Turkistan. ...Ch'ien-lung (1711–1799) is emperor of China.

Americas

1728. Danish explorer Vitus Jonassen Bering (1681–1741) discovers what will become known as Bering Strait, between Russia and Alaska. ...**March 9:** British destroy Yamassee village near St. Augustine.

1729. Baltimore, Maryland, is founded. ...Yazoo and Natchez join Chickasaw in attacking French settlements.

c. 1730. Western Indians acquire the teepee, the horse, a form of the sun dance and deerskin clothes from Plains tribes.

1731. French fortify Crown Point on Lake Champlain. ...British factory workers are prohibited from immigrating to America.

1732. James Oglethorpe (1696–1785) founds colony of Georgia. ...Vincennes, the first fortified settlement in Indiana, is constructed.

1733. St. Thomas, St. Croix, and St. John in the West Indies become Danish. ...Molasses Act forbids American colonies to trade with French West Indies. ...**February 12:** Oglethorpe founds Savannah.

1734. Eight thousand Protestants from Salzburg, Austria, settle in Georgia. ...Charleston Neck, South Carolina, is site of first horse race in America.

1735. Peter Zenger's (1697–1746) case strengthens freedom of the press in New York. ...St. Geneviéve, French trading town, is founded near present-day St. Louis. ...Sale of alcohol is prohibited in Georgia.

1736. Guayama, Puerto Rico, is founded. ...Ojibwa move into area east of Lake Superior after fighting engagements with Iroquois.

Science, Invention & Technology

1728. Frenchman Pierre Fauchard (1678–1761) publishes his findings in dentistry. He also invents a rotary dental drill powered by catgut twisted around a cylinder.

1730. Englishman John Hadley (1682–1744) invents the quadrant, a navigating device, predecessor of the sextant. ...Anders Celsius (1701–1744) at the University of Uppsala, Sweden, observes the aurora borealis and suggests the existence of earth's magnetic field.

1732. Michael Menzies (fl. 18th century) of Scotland invents one of first mechanical threshers, which is operated by a hydraulically driven wheel.

1733. Stephen Hales publicizes his blood-pressure measuring techniques.

This medallion depicts American scientist, statesman and philosopher Benjamin Franklin.

Religion, Culture & Arts

1728. John Gay (1685–1732): *Beggar's Opera.* ...William Law (1688–1761), British clergyman: *A Serious Call to a Devout and Holy Life.* ...Jean Baptiste Siméon Chardin (1699–1779), French painter: *The Skate* and *The Buffet.*

1729. *St. Matthew Passion* by Johann Sebastian Bach is first performed. ...John Wesley (1703–1791) gathers a group of Oxford students to study and worship in a movement that becomes Methodism.

1730. Jean de Labadie's Pietist movement fails after establishing settlements in Maryland and New York.

c. 1730. William Hogarth (1697–1764) begins his sequences of narrative pictures.

1731. *Gentlemen's Magazine* appears. ...Benjamin Franklin (1706–1790) founds a subscription library. ...First operas by Giovanni Battista Pergolesi (1710–1736) are performed in Naples. ...Rameau (1683–1764): *Hippolyte et Aricie.* ...William Cowper (d. 1800), British poet, is born. ...Ralph Cudworth (1617–1688): *A Treatise Concerning Eternal and Immutable Morality*, posthumously published.

1732. Franz Joseph Haydn (d. 1809), Austrian composer, is born. ...André Charles Boulle (b. 1642), French furniture designer who developed the Buhl style of furniture inlay, dies.

1733. Pope: *Essay on Man.* ...Olof von Dalin (1708–1763), Swedish poet, founds literary journal, *Then Swänksa Argus*, modeled after the *Spectator.*

1734. Levasseur family, leading Canadian woodcarvers, carve retable of Ursuline Chapel in Quebec. ...The *Boston Weekly Post Boy* is issued. ...Voltaire: *Lettres sur les Anglais.* ...Bach: Christmas *Oratorio.*

1735. William Tennent (1673–1746) establishes the evangelical Log College in Neshaminy, Pennsylvania. ...The *Boston Evening Post* is published.

British Isles & Europe

1737. July 9: The last Medici grand dukes of Tuscany die, and Tuscany goes to Francis Stephen (fl. 18th century) of Lorraine.

1738. British Parliament debates going to war with Spain after British mariner Robert Jenkins (fl. 1731–1738) enters the House of Commons brandishing his severed ear, which Spanish coastal guards had cut off in 1731 after seizing him in the West Indies.

1739. Secret treaty between Austria and France guarantees Wittelsbach claims to Jülich-Berg. ...**September 18:** In Peace of Belgrade between Austria and Turkey, Austria cedes Orsova, Belgrade and Serbia. ...**September 23:** In Treaty of Belgrade between Russia and Turkey, Russia restores its conquests except Azov. ...**October 19:** Britain declares war on Spain.

1740. May 31: Frederick William I (b. 1688) of Prussia dies and is succeeded by Frederick II, who abolishes torture and introduces freedom of the press and worship in Prussia. ...**October 20:** Charles VI, Holy Roman Emperor, dies and is succeeded by his daughter, Maria Theresa (1717–1780), queen of Bohemia and Hungary. ...**December 16:** Frederick II enters Silesia.

1741. Elizabeth Petrovna (1709–1762), daughter of Peter the Great and Catherine I, becomes empress of Russia. ...Frederick II defeats Austrians at Mollwitz and conquers Silesia. ...**August 15:** French invade South Germany, Austria and Bohemia. ...**November 26:** French, Bavarians and Saxons conquer Prague.

1742. Charles Albert (1697–1745), elector of Bavaria, is elected Holy Roman Emperor and becomes Charles VII. ...In Peace of Berlin between Austria and Prussia, Prussia obtains Silesia and Glatz.

1743. June 27: George II of Britain defeats French at Dettingen. ...**August 17:** In Peace of Abo between Russia and Sweden, Sweden cedes southern Finland.

1744. March 15: France declares war on Britain. ...**May 25:** Prussia acquires East Friesland on death of its last prince. ...**August 15:** Frederick II invades Saxony and enters Bohemia.

1745. Madame de Pompadour (1721–1764) becomes Louis XV's mistress. ...Francis I (1708–1765) succeeds Charles VII as Holy Roman Emperor. ...**June 4:** Frederick defeats Austrians at Hohenfriedberg. ...**August 2:** Charles Edward (1720–1788) lands in Scotland and is victorious at Gladsmuir.

Africa & Middle East

1738. The Mansa of Kaabu in northwest Africa deliver some 600 slaves a year to Portuguese. ...The worst famine in its history strikes the Sudan.

1739. British sign treaty with leaders of the Gold Coast, who agree to return runaway slaves in return for rights of self-government and a tax-free existence.

1739–1741. Plague decimates 20 percent of population in eastern Mediterranean seaport of Izmir.

1740. Husseinite dynasty in Tunis ends.

c. 1740. Black resistance leads Dutch to sign a treaty of friendship with the Coromantes in Guyana. ...French and British challenge Portuguese maritime dominance in Africa.

1740–1760. Yaka kingdom is founded near Kongo kingdom.

1741. The Bu Said replaces the Yarubi ruler on East African coast. ...Iman Ahmed bin Said (?–1783) founds an independent Oman. Mosqat becomes capital of Oman. ...Famine in the Sudan leads to cannibalism.

1743. Turko-Persian War resumes. ...Kazdughliya becomes ruling party of Egypt.

1744. March: Second Ethiopian war begins, with Iyasu marching against Sennar, resulting in a Fundj victory.

1744–1745. Civil wars destroy unity of Soninki Confederacy in northwest Africa.

Asia & Pacific

1738. Eighty-four thousand peasants in Iwaki province in northern Japan demonstrate against excessive taxation.

1739. Nader Shah sacks Delhi and conquers Punjab. ...The raja of Travancore defeats a landing party of Dutch, taking more than 100 prisoners.

1740. Authority of the Indian emperor wanes in the face of European encroachment. ...Kazakh Middle Horde accepts Russian protection.

1740–1747. Nader Shah invades and dominates Transoxiana.

1741–1754. Joseph François Dupleix (1697–1763) is governor-general of French possessions in India.

1742. Legal reforms are instituted in Japan. ...Part of Kazakh Great Horde accepts Russian protection.

1743. Dutch begin a policy of direct territorial acquisition and reduction of power of sultanates in Java.

1744. British statesman Robert Clive (1725–1774) arrives at Madras (in India).

1745. Ishege (?–1761) becomes shogun of Japan. ...Dutch establish Buitenzorg (in western Indonesia).

Americas

1737. Richmond, Virginia, is founded. ...San Jose, Costa Rica, is founded.

1738. University of San Felipe in Santiago, Chile, is founded.

1739. War breaks out between British and Spanish in West Indies. ...Viceroyalty of New Granada is separated from Peru. ...James Oglethorpe erects forts at St. Simons, St. Andrews, Cumberland and Amelia Islands.

1740. University of Pennsylvania is founded. ...**January:** Oglethorpe invades Florida.

1741. Russians visit Tlingit in southeast Alaska.

1742. Spanish counterattack against English forces is crushed at St. Simons Island.

1743. First settlers arrive in present-day South Dakota.

1745. May: British conquer Louisburg (in Nova Scotia). ...Vitus Jonassen Bering discovers Aleutian Islands. ...**June:** British take Cape Breton Island.

Science, Invention & Technology

1737. Gabriel Daniel Fahrenheit's colleagues adjust the boiling point on his temperature scale. To keep the freezing and boiling points at 32 and 212 degrees, they increase the size of a degree, changing the human body temperature from 96 to 98.6 degrees.

1739. American Caspar Wister (1696–1752) opens the first glass factory in America at Salem City, New Jersey.

c. 1740. Okumara Masonobu (1691–1768) invents the Japanese "pillar print" or long vertical print.

1741. African sleeping sickness is identified as a disease.

1743. John Wyatt (fl. 18th century) invents the compound lever, which uses two or more levers working together to reduce effort.

1744. Benjamin Franklin invents the Franklin stove, which is used mainly to provide home heating.

Religion, Culture & Arts

1738. Full version of Johann Sebastian Bach's Mass in B Minor is performed. ...Aleijadinho (d. 1814), Brazilian Rococo architect and sculptor, is born.

1739. David Hume (1711–1776): *Treatise of Human Nature*. ...Voltaire: *La Pucelle*. ...Petter Dass (1647–1708), Norwegian poet: *The Trumpet of Nordland*. ...British evangelist George Whitefield (1714–1770) begins the Great Awakening in American colonies.

1740. Benedict XIV (1675–1758) becomes pope. ...Israel ben Eliezer (1699–1760), founder of Hasidism, attracts a large group of followers. ...Alexander Gottlieb Baumgarten (1714–1762): *Ethics*. ...Carl Michael Bellman (d. 1795), great Swedish lyric poet, is born.

1741. George Frideric Handel: *Messiah*. ...Voltaire: *Mahomet*.

1742. William Collins (1721–1759), English poet: *Persian Ecologues*. ...**April 13:** Handel's *Messiah* is performed for the first time in Dublin.

1743. Handel: *Samson*. ...Marie Jean Antoine Nicolas de Caritat Condorcet (d. 1794), French philosopher, political leader, and mathematician, is born.

1744. William Hogarth: *Marriage à la Mode*. ...First conference of Methodist workers is held.

1745. Julien Offroy de La Mettrie (1709–1751): *Histoire naturelle de l'âme*. ...**October 19:** Jonathan Swift (b. 1667) dies.

British Isles & Europe

1746. January 17: Charles Edward is victorious at Falkirk. ...**October 11:** French are victorious over Austrians at Rocoux; Austrians lose Netherlands.

1746–1759. Ferdinand VI (1712–1759) is king of Spain.

1747. William IV (1711–1751) is elected ruler of the Netherlands. ...**July 2:** French defeat William Augustus (1721–1765), duke of Cumberland, at Lauffeld.

1748. Charles Emmanuel III acquires Vigevaresco for Sardinia. ...**October 18:** Peace of Aix-la-Chapelle generally recognizes Pragmatic Sanction and conquest of Silesia.

1750. British Iron Act limits manufacturing in the colonies.

1751–1771. Adolphus Frederick (1710–1771) of Holstein-Gottorp, brother-in-law of Frederick II, rules as king of Sweden.

1752. Louis XV declares baptisms and marriages performed by Protestant clergymen null and void.

1755. Pasquale Paoli (1725–1807) leads Corsican uprising against Genoa. ...**November 1:** Earthquake at Lisbon kills 70,000 people.

Africa & Middle East

1747. Fundj army defeats Musabba forces in Sudan.

c. 1750. Boers in South Africa migrate into Xhosa seeking better pastures. ...Islamic reformer Muhammad ibn Abd al-Wahhab (1703–1792) urges a return to pure Islam, founding the Wahhabi movement. ...Portuguese are driven out of Mosqat (in Oman). ...Bobangi, a new ethnic group, is identified in Kongo. ...Poor climatic conditions lasting over previous 150 years in Chad and Sudan end. ...On the Cameroon coast trade enters its busiest phase. ...Slave trade booms in Lulonga Basin, in lands around the River Alima, in Boma country between the Congo and the Kwa and Lake Mai-Ndombe and in the Ubangi Basin. ...British establish a slave fort in Ghana.

1752. Internecine strife in Futa Toro (in northwest Africa) leads to domination by the Moors.

1753–1754. Biton Kulibai (fl. 18th century) destroys the capital of Sunsanna (in the Sudan) and captures its chief, Fulakora, who is put to death in Segu.

1754. Ibrahim Kahya dies, and Ridwan Kahya is killed during a Janissary revolt against a tax imposed on coffee.

1755. Severe earthquake strikes Casablanca, Morocco.

Asia & Pacific

1746. September: French conquer Madras (in India).

1747. Gurkhas invade Nepal. ...Durrani dynasty is established in Afghanistan. ...Uzbek Mangit dynasty begins to rise to power in the Khanate of Bukhara. ...Nader Shah (b. 1688) is murdered.

1748. Ahmad Shah Bahadur Mujahid-ud-din Abu Nasr (1725–1775), emir of Afghanistan, invades Punjab and becomes Mogul. French return Madras to British.

1750. Alivardi Khan (c. 1676–1756) establishes Bengal as a state virtually independent from British.

c. 1750. Port of Xiamen (in south China) is closed to foreigners. ...Georgia proclaims its independence from Ottoman Turks.

1751. Robert Clive (1725–1774), baron of Plassey, takes Arcot (in India), and defeats French. ...Ch'ien-lung, fourth emperor of the Manchu dynasty, secures control of Tibet.

1752. June 9: Trichinopoly (in India) surrenders to Clive.

1753. Dutch establish a fort at Pekalongan on the island of Javain (in southern Indonesia). ...Burma annexes Henzada.

1754. Peasants numbering 168,000 protest unfair taxation in Kurume Han in Kyushu, Japan.

1755. Alaungpaya (1714–1760) founds Rangoon, Burma (present-day Yangôn, Myanmar). ...Dutch control most of Java. ...Mataram divided into principalities of Surakarta and Yogy- akarta.

Americas

1746. An earthquake devastates Lima, Peru. ...College of New Jersey is chartered. It will open in 1747 at Elizabeth, New Jersey, and be rechartered in 1748. In 1756 it will locate to Princeton, New Jersey. In 1896, it will become Princeton University.

1748. British surrender Cape Breton to French. ...Ohio Company is founded in Virginia and Maryland.

1749. Halifax, Acadia (Nova Scotia), is founded. ...Penobscot sign peace treaty with British. ...Sugar planters found Port-au-Prince, Haiti. ...Ban on slaveholding in Georgia is lifted.

1750. Christopher Gist (1706–1759) explores the Ohio region. ...Huron settle in villages near Detroit, Michigan, and Sandusky, Ohio. ...Spanish and Portuguese sign a treaty agreeing on their South American possessions. ...**March:** Benjamin Franklin proposes a plan to unite the colonies.

1753. French troops from Canada seize the Ohio Valley.

1754. The French and Indian War begins in North America. ...Georgia becomes a royal province.

1755. June 30: British forces capture Bay of Fundy. ...**July 9:** British under General Edward Braddock (1695–1755) are defeated by French near Fort Duquesne. ...French settlers are deported from Acadia (Nova Scotia). ...**September 8:** British defeat French and Indian troops at battle of Lake George.

Science, Invention & Technology

1747. German Andreas Marggraf (1709–1782) discovers sugar in beets.

1748. Frenchman Jacques Daviel (1693–1762) makes first known extraction of a cataract from the lens of a human eye.

1749. April: Benjamin Franklin invents a barbecue spit that is automatically turned by an electric charge transmitted through a Leyden jar.

1750. Charles-Michel (1712–1789), Abbé de l'Epée, develops French Sign Language (FSL). ...Dutch develop a method of canning beef.

c. 1750. Improvements are made in the papermaking industry in the Netherlands. ...Swede Axel Fredrik Cronstedt (1722–1765) introduces the blowpipe to metallurgical experiments.

1751. Jacques du Vaucanson (1709–1782) invents the first all-metal lathe.

1752. Englishman William Hutchinson (1715–1801) invents a method of directing a beam of light from a lighthouse with a parabolic mirror.

1753. African-American Benjamin Banneker (1731–1806) completes his hand-carved wooden clock, America's first.

Religion, Culture & Arts

1746. George Frideric Handel: *Judas Maccabeus*. ...Jonathan Edwards (1703–1758): *A Treatise Concerning Religious Affections*.

1746–1784. Christians in China are persecuted.

1747. Thomas Coke (d. 1814), British clergyman and missionary for Methodist Church, is born.

1748. Scottish novelist Tobias George Smollett (1721–1771): *The Adventures of Roderick Random*. ...Jacques-Louis David (d. 1825), French painter, is born.

1749. Henry Fielding (1707–1754), English playwright and novelist: *The History of Tom Jones, a Foundling*. ...Georges Buffon (1707–1788) begins writing the 44-volume *Histoire naturelle*.

1750. Johann Sebastian Bach (b. 1685) dies at Leipzig. ...Alfonsus Liguori (1696–1787): *Le Glorie de María*. ...Baroque architecture in Europe and Americas ends. ...A council representing 10 congregations dismisses Edwards.

1750–1758. Alexander Gottlieb Baumgarten: *Esthetics* (two volumes).

1751. Thomas Gray (1716–1771) English poet: "Elegy Written in a Country Churchyard." ...Voltaire: *Siècle de Louis XIV*.

1752. Thomas Gainsborough (1727–1788) begins work as a portrait painter in Ipswich. ...Britain adopts Gregorian calendar.

1753. British Museum is founded. ...Carlo Goldoni (1707–1793), Italian playwright: *The Mistress of the Inn*.

1754. Étienne Bonnot de Condillac (1715–1780), French philosopher: *Treatise on Sensations*. ...George Crabbe (d. 1832), British poet, is born.

1755. Samuel Johnson (1709–1784), English scholar, writer, moralist and critic: *A Dictionary of the English Language*. ...Immanuel Kant (1724–1804) German philosopher: *Universal Natural History and Theory of the Heavens*. ...Jakob Frank (1726–1791), Polish mystic and theologian, becomes center of secret Jewish religious society, which is accused of immorality.

British Isles & Europe

1756. May 1: Alliance of Versailles is secured between France and Austria. ...**May 15:** Britain declares war on France. ...**June 28:** French take Minorca. ...**August 29:** Frederick II of Prussia invades Saxony; Seven Years' War begins in Europe two years after some of the combatants began fighting in North America. ...**October 1:** Frederick defeats Austrians at Lobositz. ...**October 15:** Saxon army capitulates to Frederick II at Pirna (in Germany).

1757. January 10: Holy Roman Empire declares war on Prussia. ...**June 18:** Austrians defeat Frederick II at Kolin. ...**July 26:** French defeat British at Hastenbeck. ...**August 30:** After Russian victory at Gross Jägersdorf, Russians occupy East Prussia. ...**September:** Swedes invade Pomerania. ...**September 8:** British, commanded by William Augustus, duke of Cumberland, capitulate to French at Kloster Zeven, a Benedictine abbey in Bremen, Germany. ...**November 5:** Frederick II defeats French and imperial troops at Rossbach. ...**December 5:** Frederick II defeats Austrians at Leuthen.

1758. August 25: Frederick II defeats Russians at Zorndorf.

1759. April 13: French are victorious over British at Bergen near Frankfurt. ...**August 1:** French are defeated at Minden. ...**August 10:** Ferdinand VI (b. 1712) of Spain dies and is succeeded by Charles III (1716–1788), king of Naples. ...**November 20:** British fleet defeats French off Quiberon.

1760. Tories regain power in Britain. ...**October 25:** George II (b. 1683) dies and is succeeded by George III (1738–1820), his grandson.

1761. Buckingham Palace is purchased for British royal family.

Africa & Middle East

1756. French claim Seychelles Islands (northwest of Madagascar). ...British capture French trading stations in Senegal.

1757. Sultan Sidi Muhammad (c. 1702–1790) takes power in Morocco and begins a fresh start in the Sudan, based on revival of trade.

1758. British conquer French Senegal.

1759. Earthquake devastates Roman monument in Baalbek (in Lebanon). ...British curb Siddi power in Janjira.

1761–1765. Thousands flee Hungu for Kongo after creation of Yaka state.

Asia & Pacific

1756. Ahmad Shah Bahadur Mujahid-ud-din Abu Nasr captures Delhi. ...Afghans begin 65-year rule of Jammu and Kashmir. ...Dutch conclude a treaty with sultanate of Banjermasin in the southeast corner of Borneo. ...**June 20:** Mir Qasim (?–1777) of Bengal captures Calcutta from British.

1757. Chinese defeat the Oyrats in Jungaria. ...Pegu is destroyed. ...**January 2:** Robert Clive takes Calcutta. ...**June 23:** Clive wins battle of Plassey against Bengal.

1758. Dutch capitulate to Clive at Chinsura (in India).

1758–1759. China conquers eastern Turkistan.

1759. Chinese conquer and annex Junggar Pendi (east of Mongolia). ...Chinese conquer Tarim Basin; the Khojas flee to Kokand. ...Chinese imperial edict restricts maritime trade to Guangzhou.

1760. Bijapur (in southern India) is ceded to Maratha kingdom. ...Annamese annex much of Mekong Delta from the Khmer. ...Kashi (in northwest China) comes under Chinese control. ...**September 27:** Secret treaty is signed between East India Company and Mir Qasim of Bengal.

1761. Haidar Ali (1722–1782) becomes raja of Mysore. ...**January 7:** Marathas and Sikhs defeat Ahmad Shah Bahadur Mujahid-ud-din Abu Nasr at Panipat, India. ...**January 14:** Afghans defeat Marathas at Panipat. ...**January 15:** British defeat Shah Alam II (1728–1806) at Patna. ...**January 16:** Sir Eyre Coote (1726–1783) takes Pondicherry from French.

Americas

1756. August 14: French general Louis Joseph (1712–1759), marquis de Montcalm, takes Oswego.

▲ *In* **Death of General Wolfe** *by American historical painter Benjamin West, British commander James Wolfe is portrayed dying five days before the British victory at Quebec.*

1758. July 26: British take Louisburg. ...**October:** Pennsylvania signs a treaty with the Indians agreeing not to establish settlements west of the Alleghenies. ...**November 25:** George Washington (1732–1799) takes Fort Duquesne and renames it Fort Pitt.

1759. July 25: Fort Niagara surrenders to the British. ...**September:** British win battle of Quebec; French general Montcalm, and British commander James Wolfe (b. 1727) are killed.

1760. September 8: British take Montreal, and French surrender all of their remaining holdings in Canada. ...**November 29:** Detroit surrenders to British, ending the fighting in that region; the war will not be concluded until 1763, when Europeans agree to a peace ending what they call the Seven Years' War (1756–1763).

Science, Invention & Technology

1756. Dutch discover a dilution of sulfuric acid is an efficient bleaching agent. ...Robert Bremner (fl. 18th century) invents a pendulum device for keeping the rhythm of church music, forerunner of the metronome.

1758. Englishman John Smeaton (1724–1794) develops hydraulic cement for construction of lighthouses. ...Scotsman William Cullen (1710–1790) uses ethyl ether to manufacture ice. ...**December 25:** As Edmond Halley predicted in 1682, Halley's comet reappears. It is sighted by an amateur astronomer living in Germany.

1760. Benjamin Franklin invents bifocal lenses.

1761. Englishman Nevil Maskelyne (1732–1811) develops lunar navigation tables. ...German Joseph Koelreuter (1733–1806) begins research on plant pollen and cross-pollination of tobacco plants. ...Kasper Faber (fl. 18th century) establishes a pencil factory in Nuremberg, Germany.

Religion, Culture & Arts

1756. Willem Bilderdijk (d. 1831), Dutch poet and dramatist, is born. ...Wolfgang Amadeus Mozart (d. 1791), virtuoso and composer, is born in Salzburg.

1756–1759. Alban Butler (1710–1773), British priest and hagiographer: *The Lives of the Fathers, Martyrs, and Other Principal Saints*.

1757. John Baskerville (1706–1775) publishes his edition of Virgil, which establishes him as a master of fine printing. ...William Blake (d. 1827), British poet, painter, and engraver, is born. ...Antonio Canova (d. 1822), Italian sculptor, is born. ...Sir William Chambers (1723–1796), British architect: *Designs of Chinese Buildings*.

1757–1792. Jacques Soufflot (1709–1780) begins Panthéon in Paris.

c. 1758–1773. John Singleton Copley (1738–1815) enjoys a creative period in Boston. He will be considered the most distinguished portraitist of 18th-century America.

1759. Robert Burns (d. 1796), Scottish poet, is born. ...Josiah Wedgwood (1730–1795) establishes Neoclassical style in British ceramics and is a strong force in industrialization of pottery. ...William Beckford (d. 1844), British writer and art collector, is born.

c. 1760. Francesco Guardi (1712–1793) begins to paint scenes of Venice. ...Jesuits are instrumental in expelling Jansenists from France.

1760–1778. William Boyce (1711–1779), British composer: *Cathedral Music* (three volumes).

1761. Jacques-Ange Gabriel (1698–1782) builds Petit Trianon at Versailles.

1761–1768. Robert Adam (1728–1792) serves as royal architect in London.

British Isles & Europe

1762. January 4: Britain declares war on Spain and Naples. ...**January 5:** Elizabeth (b. 1709) of Russia dies and is succeeded by Peter III (b. 1728). ...**May 5:** Peace between Russia and Prussia is declared. ...**May 22:** Peace between Prussia and Sweden is declared. ...**July 17:** Peter III is assassinated and is succeeded by Catherine II (1729–1796) the Great. ...**July 21:** Prussia defeats Austria at Burkersdorf. ...**November 1:** French capitulate at Cassel, and evacuate right bank of Rhine. ...**November 24:** Truce between Prussia, Austria, and Saxony is declared.

1763. February 10: In Treaty of Paris between Britain, France, Spain and Portugal, France retires from German war and Britain recovers Minorca. ...**February 15:** In Treaty of Hubertusburg between Prussia and Austria, Austria cedes Silesia. Together, the two treaties conclude the Seven Years' War.

1764. April 11: Russia and Prussia enter into a treaty to control Poland. ...**September 7:** Stanisław II Augustus Poniatowski (1732–1798) is elected king of Poland.

1765. August 18: Francis I (b. 1708) dies and is succeeded as Holy Roman Emperor by Joseph II (1741–1790).

1766. Caroline Matilda (1751–1775) becomes queen consort of Denmark. ...Pedro Aranda (1718–1798), Spanish statesman, puts down a revolt in Madrid. ...**February 23:** Lorraine is incorporated into France.

Africa & Middle East

▲ King Stanisław II Augustus Poniatowski of Poland.

1766. Ali Bey (1728–1773) becomes a Mameluke in Egypt. ...Ngolo Diarra (fl. 18th century) founds a new dynasty in the kingdom of Segu (in the Sudan).

1767. Dahomey begins nearly a half-century of economic depression. ...Sidi Muhammad of Morocco expels Portuguese from Mazagan.

1767–1768. Famine strikes Tripoli, Libya.

1767–1771. Kabyle insurrections in Algiers cause considerable reductions in taxes.

Asia & Pacific

1763. Uzbek Kungrat dynasty begins to rise to power in the khanate of Hivia (or Khorezm).

1764. Peasants in the Kanto region of Japan, numbering 200,000, riot to protest taxes. ...British visit Tuvalu (island in the western Pacific).

1765. British assert control over Dacca.

1765–1767. Robert Clive reforms Indian administration.

1766. Nizam Ali of Hyderabad cedes North Circars, Madras, to Britain. ...Famine strikes Bengal.

1767. Clive leaves India as it falls into chaos. ...Burmese invade Siam. ...Burmese sack Ayutthaya (in southern Siam). ...British discover Pitcairn Island. ...Shah Prithvinarayan (fl. 18th century) takes control of most of Nepal.

1767–1782. Taksin (1734–1782), a half-Chinese usurper, rules in Siam.

Americas

1762. British take St. Vincent, Grenada, Martinique, Havana and Manila. ...First British settlement at Maugerville, New Brunswick, is established.

1762–1763. Surinam is besieged by English, French and a slave insurrection.

1763. February 10: Britain, France and Spain conclude both the Seven Years' War and the French and Indian War by signing the Treaty of Paris; Britain secures St. Vincent, Tobago, Dominica, Grenada, Senegal, Canada (including Nova Scotia and Cape Breton) and Florida. Spain cedes much of Louisiana territory to France but recovers Cuba and Philippines. ...**May 9:** Pontiac's War begins when Ottawa chief Pontiac (c. 1720–1769) kills settlers outside Fort Detroit.

1764. First permanent settlement in St. Louis. ...**April:** British Parliament passes the Revenue Act, also known as the Sugar Act, which increases existing taxes on various imported goods.

1765. March 22: British Parliament passes the Stamp Act, the first direct tax on the colonists. ...**Summer:** Massachusetts legislator Samuel Adams (1722–1803) organizes the Sons of Liberty in Boston to work in secret against Stamp Act.

1766. British occupy Falkland Islands. ...French sack Caracas, Venezueula. ...**March 12:** Stamp Act is repealed and general warrants are declared illegal. Declaratory Act asserts right of British government to tax American colonies. ...**July 23:** Pontiac concludes a peace treaty with British.

1767. Hopi expel Jesuits from Arizona. ...**May:** Charles Townshend (1725–1767), chancellor of the British exchequer, pushes the Townshend Acts through Parliament; these acts tax American imports of tea, glass, paper and dyestuff.

Science, Invention & Technology

1762. John Montagu (1718–1792), fourth earl of Sandwich, serves meat between layers of bread to his gaming-table guests. The concept of the sandwich will develop from this.

1763. Scotsman Walter Hunter (1718–1783) develops methods for surgically treating wounds. ...Frenchman Pierre le Roy (fl. 18th century) invents an adjustable chronometer to compensate for temperature variations.

1765. A boring machine powered by a water-wheel is invented.

1767. John Smeaton installs a tidal pump at London Bridge.

Religion, Culture & Arts

1762. Jean-Jacques Rousseau (1712–1778), French philosopher and writer: *Du contrat social* (*The Social Contract*). ...William Lisle Bowles (d. 1850), British poet and clergyman, is born. ...André Marie de Chénier (d. 1794), French poet, is born. ...Christoph Willibald Gluck (1714–1787), German composer: *Orfeo ed Euridice*. ...John Woolman (1720–1772), American clergyman and reformer: *Some Considerations on the Keeping of Negroes (Part Two).*

1763. American painter Benjamin West (1738–1820) settles in London and becomes first American artist with international reputation. ...Charles Bulfinch (d. 1844), American architect, is born. ...William Cobbett (d. 1835), British political writer, is born. ...Chinese pagoda is built in Kew Gardens, Britain. ...Carlo Goldoni: *The Fan*. ...Jean Georges Noverre (1727–1810), French choreographer: *Medée et Jason*.

1764. Robert Adam: *Ruins of the Palace of Diocletian*. ...Jens Immanuel Baggesen (d. 1826), Danish poet, is born. ...Thomas Reid (1710–1796), founder of the common sense school of Scottish philosophy: *Inquiry into the Human Mind on the Principles of Common Sense*.

1765. Mozart (1756–1791) finishes his first symphony. ...Richard Cumberland (1732–1811), British dramatist: *Summer's Tale*.

1765–1769. William Blackstone (1723–1780): *Commentaries on the Laws of England*.

1766. George Stubbs (1724–1806), English anatomist and painter, publishes *The Anatomy of the Horse*. ...Oliver Goldsmith (1728–1774), Irish poet, novelist, essayist and playwright: *The Vicar of Wakefield*. ...First Methodist societies are established in New York, Pennsylvania, and Maryland.

1767. Moses Mendelssohn (1729–1786), German philosopher: *Phaedon*. ...The first Dutch-Japanese dictionary is compiled. ...Maria Edgeworth (d. 1849), British novelist, is born. ...Giuseppe Tartini (1692–1770), Italian composer: *The Principles of Musical Harmony*. ...Benjamin Constant (d. 1830), French writer and political figure, is born.

British Isles & Europe

1768. France buys Corsica from Genoa.

1768–1774. Russia and Turkey are at war.

1769. August 15: Napoléon Bonaparte (d. 1821) is born at Ajaccio, Corsica.

1770. January 28: Augustus (1735–1811), third duke of Grafton, resigns as prime minister of Britain and is succeeded by Frederick North (1732–1792), second earl of Guilford, known as Lord North. George III will dominate the government for the next 12 years. ...**July 5–6:** Russians defeat Turks off Tchesme (in Turkey). ...**September 14:** Censorship is abolished in Denmark.

1771. Louis XV abolishes French Estates General in an attempt to consolidate his power. ...Serfdom is abolished in Savoy.

1772. August 5: In first partition of Poland, Russia obtains the territories east of Duna and Dnieper; Austria receives Eastern Galicia and Lodomeria; Prussia receives West Prussia (except Danzig) and Ermland. ...**August 19:** French support revolution in Sweden; Gustavus III reestablishes absolutism.

1773. British East India Company becomes a semi-official agency of the British government.

1774. Cossacks revolt in Kazan against Catherine the Great; Kazan is burned by Emelan Pugachev (1726–1775), Cossack pretender to the Russian throne. ...**May 10:** Louis XV (b. 1710) dies and is succeeded by Louis XVI (1754–1793). ...**June–July:** Jean Frédéric Phélypeaux Maurepas (1701–1781) is appointed French premier. ...**August:** Louis XVI recalls Estates General.

Africa & Middle East

1768. French planters and their slaves settle in the Seychelles.

1768–1773. Ali Bey, leader of the Mamelukes, rules as sultan of Egypt.

c. 1768–1776. Babba Zaki (fl. 18th century) is first sovereign of a Hausa state to set up a corps of fusiliers as personal bodyguard.

1770. Scottish explorer James Bruce (1730–1794) discovers source of the Blue Nile. ...Tadmekket lays siege to Timbuktu, reducing the population to starvation.

1771. Ali Bey's troops seize Damascus. ...**August:** Shaykh of the Kunta makes peace in Timbuktu, reconciling warring chiefs.

1772. Shilluk power displaces the Fundj sultanate in the Sudan. ...Massive military campaigns lead to creation of two states, Mbailundu and Bihe, near Kongo kingdom.

1773. Istanbul Technical University is established.

1774. Abdul Hamid I (1725–?) becomes sultan of Turkey. ...Usuman dan Fodio (1754–1817), West African Fulani chief, begins to teach, travel and preach.

Asia & Pacific

1768. Gurkhas conquer Nepal, ending Rajput rule. ...French explorers rename the Solomon Islands the Navigators Islands. ...French visit Vanuatu (in the southwestern Pacific). ...Haidar Ali defeats British Bombay army. ...Chinese officially rename eastern Turkistan Xinjiang.

1769. Burma is made tributary to China. ...Haidar Ali of Mysore dictates peace to British at Madras. ...Thon Buri becomes capital of Siam.

1770. Marathas bring Shah Alam II, emperor of Delhi, under their control. ...Captain James Cook (1728–1779) explores Victoria on southeastern coast of Australia.

1770–1790. Japan is struck by an unprecedented 20-year cycle of disasters (volcanic eruptions, floods, epidemics, drought and famine).

1771. Some Kalmuks migrate back to Jungaria and the Ili Valley from the Volga. ...Chinese attempt to make Kazakhs vassals.

1772. Calcutta becomes capital of British India. ...French explore Australia's western coast. ...**April 13:** Warren Hastings (1732–1818) is appointed governor of Bengal.

1773. Cook sights what will become known as the Cook Islands. ...Tai Sar rebellion against Nguyen clan begins, causing civil war in Annam (present-day Vietnam). ...Hastings is appointed governor general of India; he makes the sale of opium a monopoly of British East India Company.

1774. Cook sights islands of New Caledonia (east of Australia). ...Cook visits Niue (off New Zealand). ...Cook visits Vanuatu (in the southwestern Pacific). ...Turks and Russians sign a peace treaty.

Americas

1768. Massachusetts House of Representatives approves Samuel Adams's circular letter to other colonies protesting Townshend Acts and enunciating principle of no taxation without representation.

1769. Colonial governments agree to ban most British goods in retaliation for Townshend Acts. ...Pontiac (b. c. 1720) is murdered. ...First permanent settlement in Tennessee is founded on Watuga River.

1770. American boycott of British goods fails. ...**March 5:** British soldiers open fire on rioting Boston colonists; five colonists are killed. This will become known as the Boston Massacre.

1771. Regulators riot against lack of representation in the Piedmont areas of North Carolina. ...**January:** Spain cedes Falkland Islands to Britain.

1772. Boston Assembly threatens secession from Britain unless rights of colonies are maintained. ...**June 9:** Patriots burn British revenue cutter *Gaspee* in protest against enforcement of revenue laws. ...**November 2:** First Committee of Correspondence is formed in Boston to spread news of anti-British activities.

1773. December 16: Colonists dressed as Indians board British ships in Boston harbor and throw boxes of tea overboard as a protest against the high British tax on imported tea. This will become known as the Boston Tea Party.

1774. Intolerable Acts, also known as Coercive Acts, are passed by Parliament to punish rebellious colonists; among these laws is the Quartering Act, requiring colonists to provide room and board to British soldiers. ...Quebec Act grants religious freedom to French Canadians and restores the old French form of civil law. ...Harrodsburg, first permanent settlement in Kentucky, is established. ...**September 5–October 26:** First Continental Congress meets at Philadelphia.

Science, Invention & Technology

1768. Englishman Josiah Wedgwood develops his line of unglazed stoneware.

1769. Frenchman Nicolas Cugnot (1725–1804) builds a self-propelled steam vehicle. ...Englishman Joseph Priestly (1733–1804) invents an electrostatic generator.

1770. Englishman Richard Edgeworth (1744–1817) patents the idea of caterpillar treads for vehicles but fails to develop it. ...Kentucky rifle gains in popularity. It will remain America's favored firearm for the next 100 years.

1771. American David Bushnell (1742–1824) discovers that gunpowder explodes underwater. ...A technique for fattening cattle by herding them into small rooms ("sweat boxes") is developed in Britain.

1772. James Watt (1736–1819) invents a pocket micrometer. ...Swede Johann Gahn (1745–1818) uses a blowpipe to isolate manganese. ...Swede Karl Scheele (1742–1786) discovers chlorine.

▲ *Captain James Cook in an engraving based on a picture by N. Dance.*

Religion, Culture & Arts

1768. Sir Joshua Reynolds (1723–1792) is elected president of the new Royal Academy. ...François Auguste René de Chateaubriand (d. 1848), French writer and statesman, is born. ...John Crome (d. 1821), British painter and etcher, is born. ...**June 8:** Johann Winckelmann (b. 1717), German archaeologist and historian who laid the foundation for modern scientific archaeology, is murdered at Trieste, Italy.

1769. Franciscan mission is established at San Diego. ...Clement XIV (1705–1774) becomes pope. ...Philip William Otterbein (1726–1813) and Martin Boehm (1725–1812) found United Brethren in Christ. ...John Wesley (1703–1791) sends his first missionaries to America.

1770. Ludwig van Beethoven (d. 1827), German composer of Flemish descent, is born in Bonn. ...John Murray (1741–1815) emigrates from Britain and establishes the Universalist Church in America. ...William Billings (1746–1800), American composer: *New England Psalm-Singer*. ...Johannes Ewald (1743–1781), Danish lyric poet and dramatist: *Rolf Krage*.

1771. First edition of the *Encyclopedia Britannica* is published. ...Richard Cumberland (1732–1811), British dramatist: *West Indian*. ...American novelist Charles Brockden Brown (d. 1810) is born.

1772. Friedrich Arnold Brockhaus (d. 1823), German publisher, is born. ...Domenico Cimarosa (1749–1801), Italian composer: *Le Stravaganze del conte*. ...Charles Fourier (d. 1837), French philosopher and socialist, is born. ...**November 2:** *Morning Post*, London newspaper, is published for the first time.

1773. Hirago Gennai (c. 1728–1780) introduces western painting to Japan. ...Jacques-Henri Bernardin de Saint-Pierre (1737–1814): *A Voyage to the Island of Mauritius*. ...Gottfried August Burger (1747–1794), German poet: *Lenore*. ...Robert Adam: *Works in Architecture of Robert and James Adam*.

1774. German poet Johann Wolfgang von Goethe (1749–1832) publishes *Werther*. The work will make his reputation in Europe. ...Ann Lee (1736–1784) establishes the first Shaker settlement in Watervliet, New York. ...Louise Florence d'Épinay (1726–1783), French writer: *Les Conversations d'Émilie*. ...Philip Dormer Stanhope (1694–1773), fourth earl of Chesterfield : *Letters to His Son*. ...Caspar David Friedrich (d. 1840), German Romantic painter, is born.

British Isles & Europe

An American rifleman during the American Revolution.

1776. Torture is abolished in Austria. ...**April:** In provisional Treaty of Exchange signed at Copenhagen, Russia cedes claims to Holstein.

1777. Bavaria, the Palatinate and Jülich-Berg unite. ...**February:** The Habeas Corpus Act is suspended in Britain. ...**February 24:** Joseph I (b. 1714) of Portugal dies and is succeeded by Maria I (1734–1816).

U.S. & Canada

1775. March 10: Daniel Boone (1734–1820) begins to blaze 300-mile trail from North Carolina west into Tennessee and Kentucky. ...**March 23:** In Williamsburg, Virginia., Patrick Henry (1736–1799) delivers fiery speech against British rule, ending with "Give me liberty or give me death." ...**April 14:** Benjamin Franklin and Benjamin Rush (1745–1813) start first organization promoting abolition of slavery. ...**April 19:** War for American independence begins with indecisive battles at Lexington and Concord, Massachusetts. ...**May 10:** Americans led by Ethan Allen (1738–1789) and Benedict Arnold (1741–1801) capture Fort Ticonderoga in upstate New York. ...**June 9:** Governor Guy Carleton (1724–1808) of Quebec proclaims martial law and suspends provisions of Quebec Act. ...**June 15:** Continental Congress appoints George Washington (1732–1799) commander-in-chief of American army. ...**June 17:** British win battle of Bunker Hill but suffer 1,054 casualties. ...**July 26:** Continental Congress establishes American postal system and chooses Franklin as postmaster general. ...**October 13:** Continental Congress establishes the American navy. ...**November 7:** Virginia's royal governor offers freedom to black slaves joining British army to suppress rebellion. ...**November 13:** General Richard Montgomery (1736–1775) captures Montreal for American rebels. **December 31:** Montgomery is killed while attacking Quebec.

1776. March 17: British troops under General William Howe (1729–1814) evacuate Boston. ...**July 4:** Declaration of Independence is signed at Philadelphia, Pennsylvania. ...**July 22:** Martial law ends and civil jurisdiction is reestablished in Quebec. ...**August 27:** At battle of Long Island (in New York), 20,000 British regulars led by Howe defeat 8,000 Americans led by General Israel Putnam (1718–1790). ...**September 22:** Nathan Hale (b. 1755) is hanged by British in Manhattan for espionage. ...**December 26:** Washington captures 1,000 Hessian mercenaries in dawn raid on Trenton, New Jersey.

1777. January 3: Washington wins the battle of Princeton. ...**October 4:** Washington is defeated at Germantown, Pennsylvania. ...**October 17:** British under General John Burgoyne (1722–1792) capitulate at Saratoga, New York, to American army under General Horatio Gates (1727–1806). ...**November 15:** Continental Congress adopts Articles of Confederation, America's first constitution. **December 19:** Washington leads 11,000 troops into Valley Forge, Pennsylvania. More than 3,000 will die of hunger, cold and illness.

Latin America

1775. Caguas, Puerto Rico is founded. ...Guadelupe and Martinique become separate colonies of France.

George Washington, commander-in-chief of the American army.

1776. Viceroyalty of River Plate (present-day Argentina, Bolivia, Paraguay, Uruguay) is established. ...Spanish make Buenos Aires a free port. ...Guatemala City is founded. ...American naval forces briefly hold Nassau (in the Bahamas).

1777. Spain and Portugal settle their disputes concerning South American colonies.

Africa, Asia & Pacific

1775. Muslim Fulani end 50-year holy war against pagan Susa and Mande peoples in western Sudan.

1775–1776. Shah Karim Khan (?–1779) of Persia sends expedition that occupies Basra.

1775–1776, 1778–1782. First war between Maratha Confederacy (in India) and England.

Science, Invention & Technology

1775. Englishman Richard Arkwright (1732–1792) patents his carding machine and opens a textile mill. ...American David Bushnell builds his one-man submarine, the *Turtle*.

c. 1775. Englishman Robert Bakewell (1725–1795) develops several new breeds of livestock. He will be considered the father of animal breeding. ...The Norfolk four-field crop rotation system is developed in England.

Religion, Culture & Arts

1775. French dramatist Pierre-Augustin Caron, called Beaumarchais (1732–1799): *Le Barbier de Seville* (*The Barber of Séville*). ...Katsukawa Shunsho (1726–1792): *The Hundred Poets and Their Poems in Brocade*, polychrome color prints. ...Richard Sheridan (1751–1816): *The Rivals*, a comedy of manners.

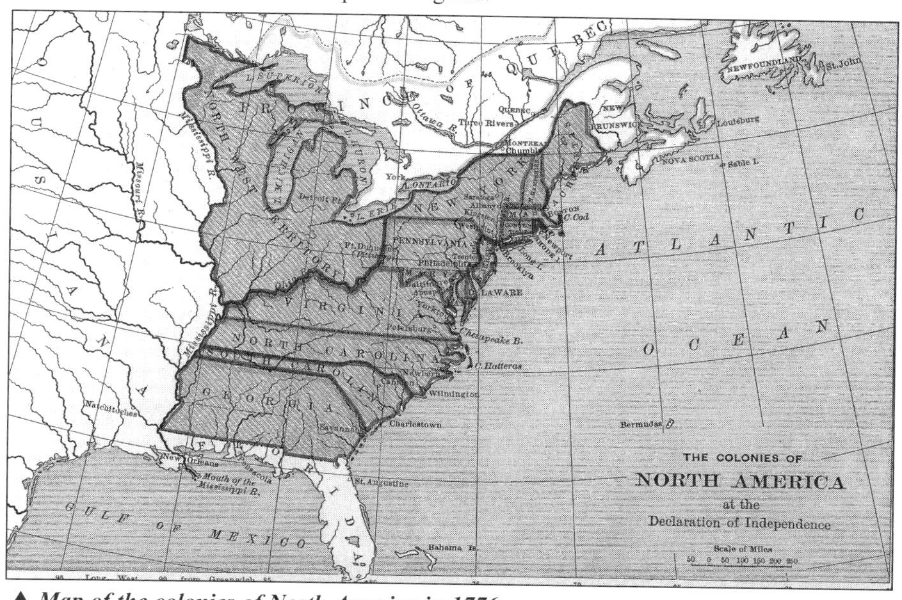

▲ Map of the colonies of North America in 1776.

1776. Boers trekking eastward from Cape Colony run into Bantu Xhosa tribe along Great Fish River. ...Tukulor power in West Africa rises.

▲ This engraving of the attack on Bunker Hill and the burning of Charles Town originally appeared in Barnard's* History of England *(1790).

1776. Thomas Paine (1737–1809), American political philosopher: *Common Sense*. ...Adam Smith (1723–1790) writes *Inquiry on the Nature and Causes of the Wealth of Nations*. ...George Romney (1734–1802) paints *Portrait of Richard Cumberland*. ...Il Teatro alla Scala (La Scala Theatre) opens in Milan. ...Friedrich Maximilian von Klinger (1752–1831), German dramatist: *Storm and Stress*.

1776–1788. Edward Gibbon (1737–1794), British historian: *Decline and Fall of the Roman Empire*.

1777. Chinese Roman Catholics introduce their religion into Korea. ...Joseph Haydn (1732–1809), composer: C Major Symphony.

British Isles & Europe

1778. January 3: Austria and Palatinate hold convention over partition of Bavaria. ...**July 3:** Prussia declares war on Austria on behalf of Bavaria.

1779. May 13: In Peace of Teschen, Austria obtains Inn district, and Prussia obtains reversionary right to Ansbach and Bayreuth. ...**June 16:** Spain declares war on Britain.

1780. March 10: Russia declares armed neutrality in the war between Britain and the United States. ...**June 2:** More than 800 die during London no-popery riots. ...**November 20:** Britain declares war on Holland.

1781–1785. Joseph II (1741–1790), king of Germany and Austria and Holy Roman Emperor, abolishes serfdom and numerous monasteries and institutes religious tolerance and freedom of the press in Austria.

1782. Ireland obtains legislative independence. ...Peter I (1747–1830) becomes prince-bishop of Montenegro. ...**December:** Russian troops commanded by Grigori Potemkin (1739–1791) invade Crimea, defeat Tatars and gain control of Black Sea.

1783. Government schools for teachers are created in Russia. ...Georgia is made a Russian protectorate. ...**September 3:** Treaty of Paris between Britain, France, Spain and the United States, Spain keeps Minorca and Britain retains Gibraltar. ...**November 10:** Charles Alexandre de Calonne (1734–1802) is appointed French controller general. ...**December 19:** William Pitt (1759–1806) takes office in Britain as chancellor of the exchequer, first lord of the treasury and prime minister.

U.S. & Canada

1778. Mary McCauley (1754–1832), one of the women whose experiences contribute to the composite legend of "Molly Pitcher," mans her husband's cannon when he collapses from heat exhaustion during battle of Monmouth, New Jersey. ...**February 6:** France and the United States agree to defensive alliance and commercial treaty. ...**May 29:** Captain James Cook lands at Nootka Sound.

1779. Montreal merchants create North West Society. ...**July 29:** General Anthony Wayne (1745–1796) captures Stony Point, New York. More than 600 British soldiers are killed or captured. ...**September 21:** Spanish governor defeats British at Baton Rouge, Louisiana, ending British drive to control Mississippi basin. ...**September 23:** Despite heavy damage to his warship *Bonhomme Richard*, John Paul Jones (1747–1792) defeats British warship *Serapis*.

1780. Pennsylvania abolishes slavery. ...**May:** British take Charles Town, South Carolina. ...**August 16:** British under Charles Cornwallis (1738–1805) defeat American Army under Horatio Gates at Camden, South Carolina. ...**September 23:** Captured British spy Major John André's (1751–1780) papers reveal that Benedict Arnold is plotting to surrender West Point.

1781. Spanish settlers in California found Los Angeles. ...**September 5:** French warships badly cripple British fleet, preventing aid to Cornwallis at Yorktown, Virginia. ...**October 19:** General Cornwallis capitulates at Yorktown, effectively ending the American Revolution. ...**November 29:** Lemuel Hayes (1753–1833) is first black minister to preach in a Congregational Church. ...**December 31:** Congress charters Bank of North America.

1782. New England discontinues use of the letter *A* ("scarlet letter") to mark adulterers. ...**June 10:** Great Seal of the United States is adopted.

1783. Massachusetts Supreme Court abolishes slavery. ...**September 3:** According to the Treaty of Paris, which formally ends the American Revolution, Britain recognizes the United States, and recovers West Indian possessions; France recovers East Indian possessions, St. Lucia and Tobago; Spain recovers Florida. ...**December 4:** British evacuate Manhattan and Staten Island. Washington takes leave of his officers at Fraunces Tavern in lower Manhattan.

Latin America

1779. France retakes Grenada from England.

1780. Peru rebels against Spanish rule. ...French build a quay in Port-au-Prince, Haiti.

1781. Georgetown is established as capital of Guyana.

1782. April 12: British defeat French fleet off Les Saintes in West Indies.

1782–1783. French occupy island of Montserrat. ...Spain occupies the Bahamas.

1783. Spanish defeat Peruvian rebels. ...France cedes Grenada and St. Kitts to England.

Africa, Asia & Pacific

1778. Annamese dynasty of the Hue-based Nguyens is overthrown. French forces drive off British troops, take back French possessions on Senegal River. ...William Paterson (1745–1806) explores southern Africa. ...James Cook explores Bering Strait seeking passage across American continent from Pacific to Atlantic. ...**January 18:** Cook discovers Hawaiian Islands.

1779. France loses Senegal and Gorée (in West Africa) to England. ...So-called Kaffir Wars, lasting until 1878, between Xhosa Bantu and Boers begin in southern Africa. ...**February 14:** Hawaiian natives kill James Cook (b. 1728) during an argument over a stolen boat.

1780. September 10: Haidar Ali, sultan of Mysore, conquers Carnatic (in India).

1781. Portugal gains Delagoa Bay (in southeastern Mozambique) from Austria. ...Chinese government suppresses Muslim insurrection in Kansu. ...British troops conquer Dutch settlements on Sumatra's western coast. ...Bodawpaya (c. 1750–1819) becomes king of Burma. ...**July 1:** British forces under Hastings defeat Haidar Ali at Porto Novo.

1782. Ali Murad (c. 1779–1785) of Zand dynasty becomes shah of Persia. ...Rama I (1782–1809) founds new dynasty in Siam. ...**December 7:** Haidar Ali (b. 1722) dies and is succeeded by his son, Tippu Sultan (c. 1749–1799), as ruler of Mysore.

1783. Persian Gulf state of Bahrain becomes independent of Persia under Sheik Ahmad al-Khalifah (fl. 18th century). ...Treaty of Paris transfers Senegal and Gorée from England to France. ...England returns Dutch colonies but secures right to trade throughout Dutch island possessions.

Science, Invention & Technology

1778. Englishman Joseph Bramah (1748–1814) invents an improved water closet flushing system and a door lock with a slotted tube key.

1779. Englishman Samuel Crompton (1753–1827) invents the spinning mule, a device used for spinning yarn that is smooth and strong.

1780. Josiah Wedgwood invents the pyrometer, a device used for measuring high temperatures. ...Lazzaro Spallanzani (1729–1799) conducts experiments with artificial insemination in dogs.

1781. The hinged bayonet is patented in England. ...German-born British astronomer William Herschel (1738–1822) discovers Uranus with a reflecting telescope he built c. 1783.

1783–1797. German astronomer Caroline Herschel (1750–1848), sister of William Herschel, discovers several nebulae and comets and creates an index to John Flamsteed's (1646–1719) star catalog.

Religion, Culture & Arts

1778. Catholic Relief Act allows Roman Catholics to swear loyalty to British Crown and repeals law mandating imprisonment of Roman Catholic priests. ...**May 30:** Voltaire (b. 1694) dies. ...**July 2:** Jean-Jacques Rousseau (b. 1712) dies.

1779. Gotthold Lessing (1729–1781), German dramatist: *Nathan the Wise*. ...Johann Wolfgang von Goethe: *Iphigenia* (in prose). ...Antonio Canova (1757–1822), leading sculptor in the Classic Revival style: *Orpheus and Eurydice, Dedalus and Icarus*. ...Richard Sheridan: *The Critic*. ...David Hume: *Dialogues Concerning Natural Religion*.

1780. Christoph Martin Wieland (1733–1813): *Oberon*. ...Bolshoi Theater of opera and ballet is founded in Moscow.

1781. Friedrich von Schiller (1759–1805): *The Robbers*. ...Immanuel Kant: *Critique of Pure Reason*. ...**January:** French financier and statesman Jacques Necker (1732–1804) publishes *Compte rendu* (*Paid Bill*).

1782. Niccolò Paganini (d. 1840), Italian composer and violinist, is born. ...William Cowper (1731–1800): *The Diverting History of John Gilpin*, a humorous ballad. ...Canova: *Theseus and the Minotaur*.

1783. Moses Mendelssohn completes translating the Torah from Hebrew into German. ...Schiller: *Fiesco*. ...Russian poet Gavril Romanovich Derzhavin (1743–1816): *Felitsa*.

British Isles & Europe

1784. Joseph II proposes to exchange Bavaria for Belgium. ...**January 6:** In Treaty of Constantinople, Ottoman Empire acknowledges that Russia has annexed Crimea. ...**March 4:** British Parliament is dissolved. Elections give William Pitt large majority. ...**May 20:** Peace of Versailles between Britain and Netherlands is signed. ...**July 4:** Joseph II abrogates constitution of Transylvania.

1785. Marie Antoinette (1755–1793) is tied to sexual and financial scandal known as the Diamond Necklace Affair. She becomes increasingly unpopular. ...Spanish Philippine Company is established. ...**June:** Warren Hastings returns to Britain. ...**November 8:** Treaty of Fontainebleau abrogates Barrier Treaty of 1715.

1786. Pitt appoints commissioners for the reduction of the national debt. ...**August 17:** Frederick II (b. 1712) of Prussia dies and is succeeded by Frederick William II (1744–1797). ...**September 26:** Commercial treaty between Britain and France lowers duties on British clothes, cotton and iron goods and on French wines, soap and olive oil.

1787. Prussia intervenes in Netherlands in favor of William V (1748–1806) against Patriot Party. ...**February 22:** French Assembly of Notables, convened to save monarchy from bankruptcy, reject Calonne's reform proposals. ...**April 17:** Calonne is banished and is replaced by Étienne Charles de Loménie de Brienne (1727–1794). ...**May:** Hastings is impeached by Edmund Burke for high crimes and misdemeanors. ...**May 25:** Assembly of Notables is dissolved without accomplishing reform.

1787–1792. Russia and Austria war against Turkey.

1788. Charles Edward (b. 1720) dies in Rome. ...**February:** Trial of Hastings begins. ...**August 8:** French Estates General is summoned for May 5, 1789. ...**August 25:** Loménie De Brienne is dismissed as French finance minister. ...**August 27:** Jacques Necker (1732–1804) is recalled as French finance minister.

U.S. & Canada

1784. *Empress of China* departs Sandy Hook, New Jersey, sails around Cape Horn and begins lucrative trade with China. ...North West Society in Canada is reorganized and becomes North West Company. British transport all Acadians remaining in Canada after expulsion order of 1755 to Maine and to Louisiana. ...**August 14:** Grigori Ivanovich Shelekhov (1747–1795), Russian trader, founds first permanent settlement in Alaska on Kodiak Island. ...**August 16:** New Brunswick is separated from Nova Scotia.

1785. May 20: Land Ordinance divides land in Old Northwest (north of Ohio River and east of Mississippi River) into townships, each containing 36 lots of 640 acres. Land is auctioned, with minimum sale of 640 acres at $1 an acre. One lot in each township is set aside to support public schools and universities. ...**September 10:** Prussia and the United States sign commercial treaty.

1786. Slavery is outlawed in New Jersey. ...**April 11:** Guy Carleton is appointed governor of all British North America, including Quebec, Nova Scotia, Prince Edward Island, Newfoundland. ...**May 20:** Prince Edward Island receives a separate government from Nova Scotia. ...**August 8:** Congress enacts decimal coinage system based on the dollar. ...**September 26:** Daniel Shays (c. 1747–1825), leading more than 1,000 men, closes state supreme court in Springfield, Massachusetts, preventing farm foreclosures.

1787. January 25: State militia beats off Shays and his followers at Springfield. ...**April 12:** Richard Allen (1760–1831) and Absalom Jones (1746–1818) organize Free African Society, a black self-help group in Philadelphia. ...**September 17:** Convention in Philadelphia adopts U.S. Constitution and sends it to states for ratification. ...**October 27:** A New York newspaper publishes the first of more than 70 essays supporting Constitution. The essays are written by James Madison (1751–1836), Alexander Hamilton (1755–1804), and John Jay (1745–1829). They will be republished as *The Federalist Papers*.

1788. June 21: U.S. Constitution comes into force when New Hampshire becomes the ninth state to ratify it. ...**September 13:** New York becomes the 11th state of the Union.

Latin America

1784. Manzanillo, Cuba is founded.

▲ ***Marie Antoinette, as a young woman, in a painting by Le Maître.***

1786. Mexico institutes significant political reforms.

1787. Bahamas become a British colony.

1787–1789. Fort Charlotte is constructed in Nassau (in the Bahamas).

Africa, Asia & Pacific

1784. Chinese government again suppresses Muslim insurrection in Kansu. ...**August 13:** British Parliament passes India Act. This introduces governmental supervision of East India Company and forbids aggressive wars and interference in native affairs by the company.

1785–1789. Jafar (?–1789) rules as shah of Persia.

1786. Annamese dynasty of the Trinh family, ruling from Tonkin (Hanoi), is overthrown. ...Raja of Kedah cedes Penang (Malaya) to England.

1786–1787. Chinese government suppresses insurrection in Formosa (present-day Taiwan).

1786–1793. Charles Cornwallis serves as governor-general of India.

1787. France intervenes in Annam (central Vietnam). ...Sierra Leone is settled as asylum for black orphans and slaves from England. ...Matsudaira Sadanobu (1759–1829), regent for child shogun Ienari (c.1780–1841), introduces administrative reforms in Japan. ...**June 28:** Treaty of Marrakesh establishes commercial relations between Morocco and the United States, which agrees to pay Morocco annual tribute of $10,000.

1788. Sir Joseph Banks (1743–1820) founds African Association to encourage exploration and trade. ...**January 26:** England establishes penal settlements near Sydney, Australia.

Science, Invention & Technology

1784. Englishman Henry Cavendish (1731–1810) produces nitric acid by using an electric charge to force nitrogen and oxygen to combine.

▲ ***German philosopher Immanuel Kant.***

1787. Joseph Eve (1760–1835) of Pennsylvania invents the cotton gin, five years before Eli Whitney's more successful model.

1788. Scottish engineer James Watt invents the centrifugal governor, a device that controls the speed of a steam engine.

Religion, Culture & Arts

1784. Jacques Louis David: *Oath of the Horatii*, painting typifying his severe Neoclassicism. ...Johann Gottfried von Herder (1744–1803), German poet and philosopher: *Ideen zur Philosophie der Geschichte der Menschheit* (*Ideas Toward a Philosophy of a History of Mankind*), completed 1791. ...Followers of Emmanuel Swedenborg (1688–1772) found New Jerusalem Church. ...**December 24:** Methodist Church is organized in America at a Maryland conference.

1785. William Cowper: *The Task*, his best-known poem. ...Wolfgang Amadeus Mozart: *Marriage of Figaro*. ...London Society for the Establishment of Sunday Schools is founded.

1786. Robert Burns: *Poems Chiefly in the Scottish Dialect*. ...Jean Dauberval (1742–1806) creates ballet *La Fille Mal Gardée* (*Useless Precautions*) for a Bordeaux theater. ...Karl Ditters von Dittersdorf (1739–1799), Austrian violinist and composer of concertos and piano works: *Dokter und Apotheker* (*Physician and Pharmacist*), his best-known opera.

1787. Friedrich von Schiller: *Don Carlos*. ...Mozart: *Don Giovanni*. ...**November 15:** German composer Christoph Willibald Gluck (b. 1714) dies.

1788. Jeremy Bentham (1748–1832): *Introduction to the Principles of Morals and Legislation*. ...Kitagawa Utamaro (1753–1806): *Ukiyo-E*, color prints based on Japanese naturalistic painting. ...Immanuel Kant: *Critique of Practical Reason*. ...**January 1:** First edition of the *Times* (London) is published.

British Isles & Europe

1789. February: Gustavus III (1746–1792) establishes absolutism in Sweden. ...**May 5:** French Estates General meets at Versailles. ...**June 17:** French Third Estate declares itself National Assembly. ...**June 27:** Three Estates in France unify. ...**July 14:** Parisians storm the Bastille, French fortress and state prison, marking the beginning of the French Revolution. ...**August 4:** Feudal system is abolished in France. ...**August 26:** French National Assembly adopts Declaration of Rights of Man, outlining rights of individuals. ...**October:** Revolution breaks out in Austrian Netherlands. ...**October 5–6:** Louis XVI is forced to move from Versailles to Paris. ...**November 12:** France is divided into 80 departments. ...**December 13:** Estates General of Austrian Netherlands deposes Joseph II and declares Austrian Netherlands republic of the United States of Belgium.

1790. Oxford-Birmingham Canal opens. ...**February 20:** Joseph II (b. 1741) dies and is succeeded as Holy Roman Emperor by Leopold II (1747–1792), grand duke of Tuscany. ...**July 14:** Louis XVI vows to uphold new French constitution at festival on Champ de Mars. ...**August 14:** By Treaty of Värälä, Sweden restores Finland to Russia. ...**September 4:** Jacques Necker resigns. ...**October:** Wolfe Tone (1763–1798) founds Society of United Irishmen, trying to unite Catholics and Protestants against British occupation. ...**December 2:** Austrians reenter Brussels and suppress Belgian revolution.

1791. Catherine the Great of Russia creates Pale of Settlement, by which Jews may reside permanently in only 25 western provinces. ...**March 2:** Allarde Law abolishes guilds and journeymen's societies in France. Henceforth, government license is required to enter a trade, business, or profession. ...**May 3:** Polish constitution modeled on French constitution, is proclaimed. ...**June 14:** Chapelier Law in France prohibits labor unions. ...**June 20:** Flight of Louis XVI is stopped at Varennes. ...**August 27:** In Declaration of Pillnitz, Austria and Prussia pledge to intervene in France if king is harmed. ...**August 30:** In Peace of Sistova, Austrians return Belgrade to Ottoman Empire in return for land in northern Bosnia. ...**September 3:** French constitution is passed. ...**October 1:** National Assembly meets at Paris.

U.S. & Canada

1789. Fort Chipewyan is built on Athabasca Lake in Alberta, Canada, and becomes headquarters for North West Company. ...**April 30:** George Washington is inaugurated president of the United States. ...**May 6:** Estevan José Martínez (1742–1798) lands at Nootka Sound to establish Spanish claims in area. ...**May 14:** Martínez seizes British ship *Iphigenia* but later releases it. ...**June 24:** Martínez takes formal possession of Nootka Port for Spain. ...**July 4:** Martínez seizes British ship *Argonaut*. ...**July 12:** Alexander Mackenzie (c. 1764–1820) reaches Arctic Ocean, and becomes first European to follow entire length of what will become known as the Mackenzie River. ...**July 14:** Martínez seizes *Princess Royal* and sends it and *Argonaut* to Mexico.

1789–1790. New York City is the capital of the United States.

1790. July 10: The site for a new capital is selected on the banks of the Potomac, and the capital of the United States moves from New York City to interim quarters in Philadelphia. The federal government will relocate to Washington, D.C., in 1800. ...**August 1:** Manuel Quimper (fl. late 18th century) claims Olympic Peninsula for Spain. ...**August 4:** The United States, under the Funding Act, guarantees federal debt and assumes responsibility for state debts. ...**October 28:** Nootka Sound Convention is signed. Spain restores British land and buildings. Spain and Britain share navigation, trade and settlement rights on America's western coast.

1791. February 25: Bank of United States is created to hold federal funds and issue paper currency. Stock in bank sells out in one hour. ...**March 3:** Congress enacts first federal tax, which is imposed on distilled spirits. The tax arouses great opposition on the frontier, where farmers distill surplus grain to make whisky. ...**March 4:** Vermont enters Union as 14th state. ...**June 10:** British Parliament passes Constitutional Act of 1791, effective December 26. Canada is divided at Ottawa River into Upper Canada (chiefly British) and Lower Canada (mainly French). Each province has an appointed government and legislative council and an elected assembly. Britain can veto colonial laws within two years of passage. One-seventh of land is to be used to support Anglican clergy, but rights of Catholic Church are reaffirmed. ...**December 15:** First ten amendments to U.S. Constitution ("Bill of Rights") are adopted by Congress after being ratified by nine states.

Latin America

1789–1794. Spain institutes several administrative reforms in Mexico.

▲ ***Empress Catherine II of Russia, also known as Catherine the Great.***

1791. August 22: African slave insurrection occurs in Santo Domingo.

Africa, Asia & Pacific

1789. Selim III (1761–1808) becomes Ottoman sultan. ...Luf Ali Khan (fl. 1783–1794) becomes last Persian shah of Zand dynasty. ...Australian government begins to allocate convicts to private employers. ...**April:** Epidemic resembling smallpox spreads throughout Australia, killing many Aborigines. ...**April 28:** Crew of HMS *Bounty* mutinies against Captain William Bligh (1754–1817) near Tonga. ...**December 29:** Tippu Sultan, ruler of Mysore, invades British Travancore (in southwestern India), beginning Third Mysore War.

1790. Mutineers from *Bounty* settle on Pitcairn Island, becoming first British settlers on the Pacific island. ...**June 1:** England forms an alliance with Marathas (in India).

1791. Charles Cornwallis takes Mangalore (Mysore). ...Jonathan Duncan (fl. late 18th century) establishes Sanskrit College at Benares. ...Spanish forces are driven from Oran on North African coast.

Science, Invention & Technology

1789. Englishman John Wilkinson (1728–1808) builds first totally iron-hulled ship. ...German Martin Klaproth (1743–1817) discovers the element uranium. ...African-American Benjamin Banneker uses mathematics to predict solar eclipse. ...Kentucky bourbon is developed from corn mash.

1790. Oliver Evans (1755–1819) receives U.S. patent on his flour-milling process. ...French Academy of Science establishes the metric system. ...First American cotton mill is built at Pawtucket, Rhode Island; it employs children between four and ten years old. ...**April 10:** Congress passes first U.S. law protecting patents. ...**May 31:** First U.S. copyright law protects plays, maps and books.

◄ ***Captain William Bligh.***

Religion, Culture & Arts

1789. Johann Wolfgang von Goethe: *Tasso*. ...William Blake (1757–1827), British mystic, painter and poet: *Songs of Innocence*. ...Jeremy Bentham: *Introduction to the Principles of Morals and Legislation*.

1790. Immanuel Kant: *Critique of Judgment*. ...National Assembly in France grants citizenship rights to Jews. ...Russian social critic Aleksandr Nikolaevich Radishchev's (1749–1802) *Journey from St. Petersburg to Moscow* leads to exile in Siberia. ...Edmund Burke (1729–1797): *Reflections on the French Revolution*. ...**July 12:** Civil Constitution of Clergy brings Catholic priests under French governmental control. ...**August 15:** John Carroll (1735–1815) is consecrated Bishop of Baltimore, becoming first Roman Catholic bishop in the United States.

1791. Donatien Alphonse François, Marquis de Sade (1740–1814): *Justine, ou les Malheurs de la Vertu* ...James Boswell (1740–1795): *The Life of Samuel Johnson*. ...Mozart: *Die Zauberflöte* (*The Magic Flute*). ...Mozart (b. 1756) dies.

1791–1792. Thomas Paine writes *The Rights of Man*, in defense of the French Revolution.

British Isles & Europe

1792. National Assembly suspends French monarchy. ...National bankruptcy is declared in France. ...In Peace of Jassy Russia obtains coast of Black Sea from Turkey. ...**March 29:** Gustavus III of Sweden is assassinated and is succeeded by Gustavus IV. ...**April 20:** France declares war on Austria. ...**May 19:** Russia invades Poland; Polish constitution is abrogated. ...**July 24:** Prussia declares war on France. ...**July 25:** Duke of Brunswick threatens destruction of Paris in *Manifesto of Coblenz*. ...**August:** Prussia and Austria invade France. ...**August 13:** French royal family is imprisoned in Temple. ...**September 2:** Massacres occur in Paris prisons. ...**September 20:** In battle of Valmy, Allies retreat. ...**September 21:** French National Convention meets to draft new constitution. ...**September 22:** French Republic is proclaimed.... **October 19:** French take Mayence and cross Rhine. ...**December 5:** Trial of Louis XVI begins.

1793. February: Britain, Austria, Prussia, Netherlands, Spain, Sardinia, Tuscany and Naples join in first coalition against France. ...**January 21:** Louis XVI (b. 1754) is executed. ...**January 23:** Russia and Prussia agree on second partition of Poland. ...**February 1:** France declares war on Britain and Netherlands. ...**March 7:** France declares war on Spain. ...**May 7:** Poland is partitioned for the second time. ...**June 2:** The Gironde falls; Reign of Terror begins in France. ...**June 24:** Second French constitution is drawn up. ...**July 13:** Jean Paul Marat (b. 1743) is murdered by Charlotte Corday (b. 1768), for which she is executed. ...**July 23:** Allies retake Mayence and drive French out of Germany. ...**Autumn:** French attack Belgium and Rhineland. ...**October 16:** Marie Antoinette (b. 1755) is executed. ...**December 26:** French defeat allies at Weissenburg.

1794. Popular uprising against Russia occurs in Poland. ...**April 4:** Russian garrisons in Warsaw are attacked. ...**April 5:** French opposition leader Georges Danton (b. 1759) and his followers are executed. ...**June 1:** General William Howe defeats French in the Channel. ...**June 15:** Russian troops occupy Kraków, Poland. ...**July 13–September 6:** Russian troops under General Aleksandr Vaslievich Suvorov (1729–1800) take Warsaw. ...**July 28:** Maximilien Robespierre (b. 1758), leading power behind the Reign of Terror, is executed. ...**October 10:** Russian and Prussian troops overwhelm Polish patriots at Maciejowice. ...**November 4:** Russians enter Warsaw. Polish revolution is crushed.

U.S. & Canada

1792. William Thornton (1759–1828) begins building Capitol in Washington, D.C. ...British navigator George Vancouver (1757–1798) explores island off Canada's west coast. The island will bear his name. ...**February 12:** Fugitive Slave Act makes it illegal to either help a slave escape or to give refuge to a runaway slave. ...**May 13:** Thomas Jefferson (1743–1826) leads formation of Democratic-Republican party to oppose Federalists. ...**May 17:** Local brokers organize New York Stock Exchange at Merchants Coffee House. ...**June 1:** Kentucky enters Union as 15th state. ...**June 4:** Vancouver takes possession of Puget Sound for Britain. ...**October 1–November 10:** Lieutenant William Broughton (1762–1821) takes *Chatham* 100 miles up Columbia River and claims area for Britain.

1793. British forces occupy St. Pierre and Miquelon Islands. ...Legislature of Upper Canada (Ontario) abolishes slavery. ...**March 4:** George Washington begins his second term as U.S. president. ...**April 22:** Washington issues Neutrality Proclamation, warning Americans to avoid aiding either side in war between Britain and France. ...**May 26–September 20:** Vancouver explores along northwest coast and claims entire area for Britain. ...**July 22:** Mackenzie, exploring for North West Company, is first European to reach Pacific by an overland route north of Mexico. ...**August:** More than 4,000 die during yellow fever epidemic in Philadelphia. ...**August 26:** Governor John Simcoe (1752–1806) establishes capital of Upper Canada at York (present-day Toronto).

1794. July: Whiskey Rebellion breaks out in western Pennsylvania. ...**August 7:** Washington calls out militias from four states to put down Whiskey Rebellion. ...**August 20:** At battle of Fallen Timbers, General Anthony Wayne routs 2,000 Indians, securing Ohio after four years of war. ...**November 19:** Jay Treaty permits United States to trade with British Isles and in British East Indies and allows Britain to seize American foodstuffs bound for France.

Latin America

1792. Mount Pelée volcano on Martinique erupts. ...Castillo del Principe (fortress) and palace of colonial governors are constructed in Havana, Cuba. ...Spanish navigators visit the San Juan Islands.

1793. Fort Fincastle is constructed in Nassau (in the Bahamas).

Louis XVI and his son in prison during the French Revolution.

1794. France repossesses Guadeloupe.

Africa, Asia & Pacific

1792. Chinese troops led by Fu-k'ang-an, (fl. late 18th century) invade Nepal, which recognizes imperial suzerainty. ...Sierra Leone Company is granted a charter. ...**February 5:** Tippu Sultan is defeated by Charles Cornwallis at Seringapatam. ...**March 19:** Tippu Sultan pays large indemnity and cedes half his territory to British East India Company.

1792–1839. Ranjit Singh (1780–1839) rules Sikhs.

1793. Ottoman emperor Selim III issues abortive "New Regulations" reforming military, tax system and commercial arrangements. ...Treaty between Burma and Siam acknowledges Siamese independence and ends Burmese invasion. ...Cornwallis's code excludes Indians from high posts and makes substantial changes in systems of taxation and justice. ...Sir John Shore (1751–1834) becomes governor general of India. ...British seize French settlements in India. ...British establish permanent settlement of Bengal. ...Zaman (fl. 18th century) becomes shah of Afghanistan. ...**February:** John MacArthur (1767–1834) becomes leader of first nonconvict settlers in Australia.

1794. Mahdoji Sindhia (fl. 18th century), ruler of central India, dies. ...Agha Muhammad (?–1797) overthrows Luf Ali Khan of Zand dynasty and founds Kajar dynasty in Persia.

Science, Invention & Technology

1792. Eli Whitney (1765–1825) invents his cotton gin, vastly increasing speed with which cotton can be cleaned.

1793. American Samuel Morey (1762–1843) develops a model steamboat with side paddle wheels. ...**January 9:** Jean-Pierre Blanchard (1753–1809) conducts America's first hot air balloon flight as Washington, Jefferson, James Madison and James Monroe (1758–1831) watch.

1794. American Robert Fulton (1765–1815) invents an inclined plane system of transferring canal boats to different levels, in place of locks, and patents it in England. ...Lancaster Turnpike, 62 miles long, opens between Philadelphia and Lancaster, Pennsylvania. It is the first macadam road in the United States. Its success will inspire many additional toll roads.

Religion, Culture & Arts

1792. Mary Wollstonecraft Godwin (1759–1797), English writer: *Vindication of the Rights of Woman*. ...The *Observer* (London newspaper) begins to appear. ...Duncan Phyfe (1768–1854) sets up as a furniture maker in New York City. ...Muhammad ibn Abd al-Wahhab (b. 1703) dies in Arabia. His Wahhabi sect teaches strict adherence to the Koran and rejects all innovations since Muhammad's death. ...**February 23:** Sir Joshua Reynolds (b. 1723), British painter, dies. ...**March 3:** Robert Adam (b. 1728), British architect, dies.

1793. Johann Gottlieb Fichte (1762–1814), German philosopher and nationalist: *Two Pamphlets, Concerning the French Revolution*. ...The Louvre is established as a public art gallery in France. ...William Blake: *Marriage of Heaven and Hell*. ...**August 25:** First services are held in first church erected in Australia. ...**October 2:** Baptist Missionary Society is founded. It is the first missionary society founded by British Protestants. ...**October 5:** Priests in France are forbidden to exercise their offices outside churches.

1794. Samuel Taylor Coleridge (1772–1834), British poet: *Fall of Robespierre*; *Ode on France*. ...Ann Radcliffe (1764–1823): *Mysteries of Udolpho*, a notable Gothic novel. ...Friedrich von Schiller: *Letters Concerning the Aesthetic Education of Mankind*. ...Fichte: *Über den Begriff der Wissenschaftslere* (*On the Science of Knowledge*). ...Blake: *Songs of Experience*.

1794–1796. Utagawa Toyokuni (1769–1825), Japanese print designer, makes a series of *Stage Representations of Actors*. It will be considered his finest work.

British Isles & Europe

1795. January 3: Russia and Austria agree to a secret treaty about final partition of Poland. ...**April 5:** In Peace of Basel between France and Prussia, Prussia grants Rhine frontier and line of demarcation secures neutrality of northern Germany. ...**April 23:** Warren Hastings is acquitted of extortion and mismanagement charges. ...**June–October:** Risings in Brittany are aided by British. ...**July 22:** Spain makes peace with France. ...**August 22:** Third French constitution is proclaimed. ...**October 24:** Third partition of Poland is agreed to. ...**November 25:** King Stanisław II Augustus Poniatowski of Poland abdicates.

1796. May 10: Napoléon defeats Austrians at Lodi. ...**August 5:** In Treaty between Prussia and France, Prussia yields possessions on left bank of Rhine in return for ecclesiastical territories. ...**October 5:** Spain declares war on Britain. ...**November 15–17:** Napoléon defeats Austrians at Arcola. ...**November 16:** Catherine the Great (b. 1729) of Russia dies and is succeeded by Paul I (1754–1801).

1797. January 14: Napoléon defeats Austrians at Rivoli. ...**January 26:** Final treaty of Polish partition is agreed to. ...**February 14:** John Jervis (1735–1823) and Horatio Nelson (1758–1805) defeat Spaniards off Cape St. Vincent. ...**July 15:** Cispadane and Cisalpine republics are united. ...**October 17:** In Peace of Campo Formio, Austria cedes Belgium and Lombardy to France and obtains Istria, Dalmatia and Venice. A secret understanding is reached concerning division of Germany. ...**November 16:** Frederick William II (b. 1744) of Prussia dies and is succeeded by Frederick William III (1770–1840). ...**December 29:** French capture Mayence.

1798. Peasants on the left bank of the Rhine are emancipated. ...Dutch government takes over assets of bankrupt Dutch East India Company. ...**February 15:** Roman Republic is proclaimed. ...**June 21:** British troops defeat Irish nationalists at Vinegar Hill in southeastern Ireland. ...**September:** Turkey declares war on France. ...**October 11:** French attempt to invade Ireland fails. British intercept French naval squadron and capture Irish leader Wolfe Tone. ...**November:** British capture Minorca. ...**November 19:** Wolfe Tone (b. 1763) commits suicide in prison while awaiting execution. ...**November 29:** Ferdinand IV (1751–1825) of Naples enters Rome. ...**December 4:** France declares war on Naples. ...**December 24:** Russia and Britain sign a treaty.

U.S. & Canada

1795. Insurance Company of North America is chartered at Philadelphia, Pennsylvania. It is first U.S. commercial firm to sell life insurance policies. ...Britain and Spain vacate Nootka Port to implement terms of Nootka Convention. ...**August 3:** In Treaty of Greenville, Indian tribes cede most of Ohio to the United States. ...**October 27:** Thomas Pinckney (1750–1828) signs treaty with Spain giving the United States free navigation of Mississippi River.

1796. June 1: Tennessee enters the Union as 16th state. ...**September 17:** In his Farewell Address, Washington criticizes political parties and "permanent alliances" with foreign nations. He declares he will not run for a third term, setting a precedent that will be respected until 1940.

1797. March 4: John Adams (1735–1826) is inaugurated second president of the United States. ...**May 15:** Adams calls first special session of Congress to debate growing crisis in Franco-American relations, which is fueled by French seizures of hundreds of American ships. ...**October 17–28:** Three agents of French government (designated X, Y and Z) refuse to allow American representatives to meet with Charles Talleyrand (1754–1838) the French foreign minister, unless they paid a bribe. This is known as the XYZ Affair.

1798. June 18: U.S. Naturalization Act increases residence requirement for citizenship from 2 to 14 years. ...**June 25:** Alien Enemies Act allows president to deport aliens suspected of being dangerous or treasonous. It is never enforced. ...**July 7:** Prompted by French seizures of American ships, undeclared war with France begins. Known as the Quasi War with France, it will continue for two years. ...**July 14:** Sedition Act punishes newspaper editors printing "false, scandalous, and malicious" statements about government officials. The act will expire in 1801. ...**November 16:** Thomas Jefferson writes Kentucky Resolution, declaring that unconstitutional acts of Congress are null and void. ...**December 24:** Virginia Resolution, written by James Madison, declares that states need not follow unconstitutional laws.

Latin America

1795. British put down revolt of Caribs on St. Vincent. ...Spanish found Melo (in Uruguay) as a military outpost. ...Venezuelans rise up against Spanish rule. ...**June:** French retake St. Lucia. ...Spain cedes its half of Santo Domingo to France.

1796. British capture Demerara, Essequibo and Berbice (Guyana).

1797. February: British take Trinidad and St. Lucia.

1798. England takes Honduras from Spain. ...British defeat Spanish at battle of St. George's Cay (in Belize). ...French Guiana becomes an overseas department of France.

Africa, Asia & Pacific

1795. Chinese troops suppress revolt by Miao tribes of Hunan and Kueichou. ...King Rama I of Siam annexes western Cambodia, including Battambang and Angkor Thom. ...**March 11:** Marathas defeat Moguls at Kurdla (in India). ...**September:** British occupy Cape of Good Hope.

1796. Agha Muhammad of Persia seizes Khorasan (in northeastern Iran). ...British discover Fanning Island and Gilbert Island. ...Ch'ien-lung, emperor of China, abdicates in favor of his son, Chia-ch'ing (1760–1820). ...**February:** Dutch surrender Ceylon (present-day Sri Lanka) to British.

1797. Richard Colley Wellesley (1760–1842) is appointed governor of India. ...British government establishes mission on Tahiti. ...British captain William Broughton (1762–1821) explores east coast of Korea. ...Fath Ali (?–1835) is shah of Persia.

1798. George Bass (1771–1803) and Matthew Flinders (1774–1814) discover what will become known as Bass Strait, separating Australia and Tasmania. ...British East India Company encourages Persian government to attack Afghanistan. ...**May 19:** French expedition to Egypt sets out. ...**July 21:** French defeat Mamelukes of Egypt at battle of Pyramids. ...**July 22:** Napoléon enters Cairo. ...**August 1:** British naval forces led by Horatio Nelson destroy French fleet during battle of the Nile. ...**September:** Ottoman Empire declares war on France.

Science, Invention & Technology

1795. Joseph Bramah (1748–1814) invents a hydraulic press. ...Jacob Perkins (1766–1849) patents a nail-cutting machine.

1796. Frenchman Joseph Montgolfier (1740–1810) invents the hydraulic ram, which lifts water to higher levels by using the force of the water.

1797. Leonardo da Vinci's manuscripts are discovered. ...Englishman Henry Maudslay (1771–1831) invents an industrial lathe for cutting screws. ...Frenchman André Garnerin (1769–1823) makes parachute jump from hot air balloon.

1798. Eli Whitney develops a milling machine for the manufacture of muskets.

Religion, Culture & Arts

1795. London Missionary Society is founded. ...William White (1748–1846) helps found the Protestant Episcopal Church of America. He serves as its first presiding bishop.

1796. Thomas Paine completes *The Age of Reason*. ...August Wilhelm von Schlegel (1767–1845) and his brother, Freidrich Schlegel (1772–1829), critics and orientalists, establish themselves in Jena, Germany. ...Haydn: *Emperor Quartet*. ...Matthew Gregory Lewis (1775–1818), diplomat and Gothic novelist, writes *The Monk*.

1797. Schlegel begins his translation of the works of Shakespeare.

1798. *Lyrical Ballads*, a collection of poems by William Wordsworth (1770–1850) and Samuel Taylor Coleridge (1772–1834), is published. ...August William Schlegel and Friedrich Schlegel establish the Romantic periodical *Athenaeum*. ...Benjamin Latrobe (1764–1820) builds Bank of Pennsylvania at Philadelphia and introduces Greek Revival style to the United States. ...Ludwig Tieck (1873–1853), German novelist and playwright, writes *Franz Sternblads Wanderungen*. It is among first German Romantic novels. ...Thomas Robert Malthus (1766–1834), English economist: *An Essay on the Principle of Population*.

British Isles & Europe

1799. William Pitt introduces income tax in Britain. ...Britain outlaws labor unions. ...**March 12:** Austria declares war on France. ...**March 25:** Austrians defeat French at Stockach. ...**June:** Britain, Russia, Austria, Turkey, Portugal and Naples join in second coalition against France. ...**August 15:** Russo-Austrian army defeats French at Novi. ...**September 19:** Anglo-Russian army defeated at Bergen (Belgium) by French. ...**September 25–27:** Russians defeated by French at Zürich. ...**November 9:** Napoléon stages coup d'état. Directory is overthrown and Napoléon becomes First Consul.

1800. Napoléon begins road over Simplon Pass. ...**January 17:** Peace of Montlucon pacifies La Vendée. ...**January 18:** Bank of France is established to finance Napoléon's wars. ...**February 17:** French administration is thoroughly centralized. ...**April:** Russian government prohibits importing of foreign books. ...**May 5:** Act of Union forms United Kingdom of Great Britain and Ireland. ...**May 14:** Government officials replace elected members of noble tribunals in Russia. ...**June 14:** Napoléon defeats Austrians at Marengo. ...**August 1:** Irish parliament is dissolved, and British Parliament accepts representatives from Irish districts. ...**December 3:** French defeat Austrians at Hohenlinden. ...**December 16:** Northern Confederacy of Russia, Prussia, Sweden and Denmark unite against Britain.

1801. Danes occupy Hamburg and Lübeck and exclude British ships from the Elbe. ...**February 9:** In Peace of Lunéville between France and Austria, France obtains left bank of Rhine and Tuscany is transformed into Kingdom of Etruria. ...**March 23:** Paul I (b. 1754) of Russia is murdered and is succeeded by Alexander I (1777–1825). ...**March 28:** Peace between France and Naples is agreed to. ...**June 5:** Anglo-Russian agreement is signed at St. Petersburg. ...**September 13:** Georgia is annexed by Russia. ...**October 9:** In peace between France and Turkey, Egypt is restored to Turkey.

1802. Russia and France agree on redistribution of Germany. ...First protective law against child labor in Britain is passed. ...**January:** Napoléon becomes president of Italian Republic. ...**March 27:** In Treaty of Amiens, Britain promises to restore its overseas conquests to France. ...**August 2:** Napoléon is appointed consul for life. ...French educational system is reorganized. ...**August–September:** Napoléon annexes Elba, Piedmont, Parma, and Piacenza.

U.S. & Canada

1799. February 1: St. John's Island is renamed Prince Edward Island, after George III's third son. ...**May 25:** Russian-American Company establishes its main trading post at Sitka. ...**November 22:** In Second Kentucky Resolution, Jefferson calls on states to nullify unconstitutional federal laws. ...**December 14:** George Washington (b. 1732) dies at Mount Vernon, Virginia.

1800. Ottawa is founded on Ottawa River in eastern Ontario. ...**May 10:** Land Act reduces minimum purchase of public land in the United States to 360 acres and allows payment over four years. ...**October 1:** United States and France mutually abrogate their treaties of 1778, ending what to Americans is known as the Quasi War with France. ...France buys Louisiana from Spain. ...United States and France mutually abrogate treaties of 1778, ending what Americans know as the Quasi War with France. ...**November 1:** John Adams becomes the first U.S. president to move into the still-unfinished Executive Mansion (later known as the White House) at 1600 Pennsylvania Avenue. ...**November 17:** Congress convenes for the first time in Washington, D.C.

1801. John Chapman (1774–1845) begins planting trees in Ohio. He will become known as "Johnny Appleseed." ...**March 4:** Thomas Jefferson is inaugurated third president of United States. ...**May 14:** Tripoli declares war on United States, hoping to gain increased tribute payments.

1802. March 16: United States Military Academy is established at West Point, New York. ...**March 27:** In Treaty of Amiens, which divides the French Revolutionary War from the Napoléonic Wars that follow, Britain restores St. Pierre and Miquelon Islands to France. ...**April 29:** Judiciary Act restores to six the number of Supreme Court justices and sets up six circuit courts, each presided over by a justice.

Latin America

1799. Turks and Caicos Islands are given representation in assembly of Bahamas. ...General Alexandre Sabès Pétion (1770–1818) joins General André Rigaud (1761–1811) in a civil war against François Dominique Toussaint L'Ouverture (c. 1743–1803), a former slave.

Courtesy: Special Collections; USMA, West Point, NY

▲The U.S. Military Academy at West Point officially opened July 4, 1802.

1801. Toussaint L'Ouverture conquers Haiti and abolishes slavery. ...Government House is constructed in Nassau. ...British occupy Virgin Islands. ...**March:** British capture Danish and Swedish islands in West Indies. ...**June 6.** In Treaty of Badajoz, Portugal cedes part of Guyana to Spain.

1802. French subdue slave rebellion initiated by Toussaint L'Ouverture in Spanish Santo Domingo. ...French under General Charles Victor Emmanuel Leclerc (1772–1802) defeat Toussaint L'Ouverture (b. c. 1743) and take him prisoner; he will die a year later in a French dungeon. ...Pétion returns to Haiti with the French and serves under Jean-Jacques Dessalines (1758–1806). ...British return St. Thomas, Virgin Islands, to Denmark.

Africa, Asia & Pacific

1799. February: Napoléon advances into Syria. ...**May 4:** British forces kill Tippu Sultan (1749–1799), military ruler of Mysore, at Seringapatam (in India) and take control of coast. ...**May 20:** Napoléon is checked at Acre (in Israel) by Turkish army. ...**July 24:** Napoléon defeats Turks at Aboukir (Egypt). ...**August 22:** Napoléon leaves Egypt.

1799–1803. Mahmud (?–1803) is shah of Afghanistan.

1800. Commercial and political treaty between Persia and British East India Company provides for military cooperation against Afghanistan and Russia. ...Russia annexes Georgia. ...**March 20:** Jean Baptiste Kléber (1753–1800) defeats Turks and Mamelukes at Heliopolis (in Egypt). ...**June 14:** Kléber is assassinated at Cairo.

1800–1834. Sungo (?–1834) is king of Korea.

1801. Rohilcund and Doab (India) are ceded to Britain. ...**May 14:** Tripoli (in present-day Libya) declares war on the United States when Captain William Bainbridge (1774–1833) refuses to pay extra tribute. ...**July 18:** Matthew Flinders begins two-year expedition to circumnavigate and map Australia. ...**September:** French evacuate Egypt.

1802. The Annamese empires of the Trinh family and the Nguyens are united to form Vietnam by Gia Long (1762–1820), originally Nguyen Phuc Anh, who declares himself emperor. He will reign until 1820. ...**December 31:** Treaty of Bassein between British East India Company and Hindu Marathas is signed.

Science, Invention & Technology

1799. First motorized air compressor used in mining is invented in England. ...France is first country to formally adopt the metric system. ...Frenchman Philippe Lebon (1769–1804) invents the thermolamp and the process of distilling its fuel from wood.

1800. Robert Fulton's submarine, *Nautilus*, is launched at Rouen, France. ...Welshman Richard Trevithick (1771–1833) builds the first locomotive.

c. 1800. German geographer Alexander von Humboldt (1769–1859) discovers ocean currents while traveling through South America.

1801. Frenchman Joseph Jacquard (1752–1834) invents programmed loom that uses punch-card patterns. ...Englishman Charles Hatchett (1765–1847) identifies element 41, niobium.

1802. DuPont de Nemours & Company begins manufacture of gunpowder at Wilmington, Delaware. ...Humboldt almost succeeds in climbing Mount Chimborazo in Ecuador.

Religion, Culture & Arts

1799. First public performance of *The Creation* by Joseph Haydn at Vienna. ...Schiller: *Wallenstein*. ...Church Missionary Society is founded. ...*Los Caprichos*, series of prints by Spanish artist Francisco de Goya (1746–1828).

1800. Library of Congress is established, with some 900 books purchased from Britain. ...Schiller: *Mary Stuart*. ...Beethoven: First Symphony. ...German Romantic poet Friedrich Leopold von Hardenberg, called Novalis (1772–1801): *Hymnen und Die Nacht*. ...**July:** Methodist camp meeting is held in Logan County, Kentucky. It is believed to be the first camp meeting held in the United States.

1800–1900. Magic lanterns, which project magnified images from transparencies or from opaque images, are equipped with limelights (cylinders of lime, or calcium oxide, heated by an oxyhydrogen flame).

1801. *New York Post* is established. ...Robert Southey (1774–1843), English poet: *Thalaba*. ...Schiller: *The Maid of Orleans*. ...Haydn: *Seasons* (oratorio). ...**July 15:** French Concordat restores Roman Catholicism.

1802. François René de Chateaubriand (1768–1848): *René*, a short autobiographical novel. ...Germaine Necker, known as Madame de Staël (1766–1817), French literary critic and novelist: *Delphine*, feminist psychological novel. ...British portrait painter George Romney (b. 1734) dies. ...Vietnamese poet Nguyen Du (1765–1820) joins the court of Gia Long.

British Isles & Europe

1803. February: By Swiss Act of Mediation, cantons regain their independence. ...**February 25:** Diet of Ratisbon reconstructs Germany. Most ecclesiastical princedoms and imperial cities are abolished and four new electorates are created. ...**April 14:** Paris banks are permitted to issue paper money. ...**May 18:** Britain declares war on France. ...**October:** Russia and Turkey make peace with France.

1804. Following Russian annexations in Georgia, Persia declares war. ...**March 21:** Code Napoléon comes into force in France. ...**August 11:** Francis II (1768–1835), the last Holy Roman Emperor, becomes Francis I of Austria additionally. ...**December 2:** Napoléon crowns himself emperor. ...**December 12:** Spain declares war on Great Britain.

1805. May 26: Napoléon becomes king of Italy. ...**October 21:** Admiral Horatio Nelson (b. 1758) destroys Franco-Spanish fleet off Trafalgar but is mortally wounded. ...**December 2:** Napoléon defeats Austrians and Russians at Austerlitz. ...**December 15:** In Franco-Prussian treaty at Schönbrunn, Prussia cedes Cleves, Neuchâtel and Ansbach in exchange for Hanover. ...**December 26:** Peace of Pressburg between France and Austria is signed.

1806. Britain declares blockade of French coasts. ...**June 5:** Louis Bonaparte (1778–1846), brother of Napoléon, is named king of Holland. ...**August 6:** Francis II renounces crown of Holy Roman Empire. ...**October 14:** Napoléon defeats Prussians and Saxons at Jena and Auerstädt. ...**November 21:** By Berlin decree, Napoléon closes continental ports against British imports. ...**December:** War breaks out between Russia and Turkey. ...**December 11:** Peace of Posen between France and Saxony is signed.

1807. Slave trade is abolished in British empire. ...**February 7–8:** Napoléon defeats Russians and Prussians at Eylau. ...**July 7:** Peace of Tilsit between France and Russia is signed. **July 9:** Peace of Tilsit between France and Prussia is signed. ...**August:** Russia invades Finland. ...**October:** France and Russia declare war on Britain. ...**December 7:** Napoléon issues the Decree of Milan against British trade.

U.S. & Canada

1803. February 24: In *Marbury v. Madison*, Chief Justice John Marshall (1755–1835) rules U.S. Supreme Court can nullify acts of Congress by declaring them unconstitutional. ...**March 1:** Ohio becomes 17th state. ...**April 30:** United States buys Louisiana from France for $15 million, extending U.S. territory to Rocky Mountains in the west, the Gulf of Mexico in the south and the border of British North America in the north.

1804. February 16: Lieutenant Stephen Decatur (1779–1820), commanding the *Intrepid*, burns captured frigate *Philadelphia*, docked at Tripoli. ...**May 14:** Captain Meriwether Lewis (1774–1809) and William Clark (1770–1830) begin 28-month expedition through western plains to Pacific Ocean. ...**July 11:** Aaron Burr (1756–1836) mortally wounds Alexander Hamilton (b. 1755) during duel at Weehawken, New Jersey. ...**September 25:** The 12th Amendment to the U.S. Constitution requires separate electoral ballots for president and vice president to prevent a tie.

1805. Simon Fraser (1776–1862) builds Rocky Mountain House at Hudson Hope, British Columbia. ...**August 9:** Zebulon M. Pike (1779–1813) sets out to explore sources of Mississippi River. ...**November 14:** Lewis and Clark expedition reaches Pacific Ocean at mouth of Columbia River.

1806. Journeymen shoemakers stage first industry-wide strike in United States. ...Fraser builds Fort St. James on Stuart Lake. ...**May 30:** Andrew Jackson (1767–1845) kills Charles Dickenson during duel. ...**August:** Pike begins to explore Arkansas River, reaching Colorado and sighting what would become known as Pike's Peak. ...**November 27:** President Thomas Jefferson warns U.S. citizens not to join Aaron Burr's expedition down Mississippi River into Spanish territory. Burr flees and is arrested.

1807. Fraser builds Fort George at Prince George, British Columbia. ...**June 30:** David Thompson (1770–1857), exploring for North West Company, is first non-Indian to cross Howse Pass in Alberta, Canada, to reach headwaters of Columbia River. ...**July:** John Colter (c. 1775–1813) explores Bighorn and Yellowstone Basins (in present-day Montana and Wyoming). ...**September 1:** Richmond, Virginia, court acquits Burr of treason because he was absent when "overt act" (start of expedition) occurred.

Latin America

1803. British acquire Trinidad. ...**June:** St. Lucia becomes permanently British. ...**September:** British take Dutch Guiana.

1804. Haiti becomes second nation in Western Hemisphere to win complete independence. Port-au-Prince becomes Haiti's capital. Jean Jacques Dessalines proclaims himself emperor of Haiti. ...Puerto Rico is opened to foreign trade.

1805. Dominica becomes a British Crown colony.

1806. Self-declared Haitian emperor Dessalines (b. c. 1758) is assassinated by Alexandre Sabès Pétion and Henri Christophe (1761–1820); Christophe becomes provisional chief of northern Haiti. ...British raids on Buenos Aires and Montevideo fail.

1807. France invades Portugal. Dethroned Portuguese royal family flees to Brazil. ...Argentine militia wards off a second attack by British. ...Pétion sets up republic in southern and western part of Haiti.

1807–1815. British reoccupy Dutch West Indies.

Africa, Asia & Pacific

1803. September 23: Richard Colley Wellesley defeats Maratha leader at Assaye (in India). ...**November 29:** Wellesley defeats Maratha armies at Argaon in Berar, ending Maratha control of Deccan. ...**December 30:** Sindhia submits to British.

1803–1805. Second Maratha War is fought.

1804. Wahhabi leaders capture Mecca and Medina. ...Hobart, Tasmania, is founded. ...Fulah dynasty launches holy war against pagan Hausa states (present-day Nigeria). ...**November 14:** British forces defeat Jaswant Rao Holkar (?–1811), Maratha ruler of Indore.

1805. Mungo Park (1771–1806) travels up Niger River. He is believed to be the first European to reach Timbuktu. ...Ottoman emperor appoints Muhammad Ali Pasha (1769–1849) governor of Egypt. ...**April 27:** William Eaton (1764–1811), commanding a mixed force of native rebels and seven U.S. marines, captures Derna during war with Tripoli. ...**June 4:** War between United States and Tripoli ends. ...**November 23:** Peace treaty between Britain and Sindhia is signed.

1806. January: British occupy Cape of Good Hope. ...Governor William Bligh (c. 1754–1817) of Australia outlaws use of rum to purchase commodities.

1807. Sierra Leone and Gambia are organized as British Crown colonies. ...**March:** British force invades Egypt and is defeated at Rosetta. ...**July:** Sultan Selim III is deposed and imprisoned by reactionary Janissaries, who oppose his efforts to modernize Ottoman Empire. ...**September:** British troops are evacuated from Alexandria, Egypt.

Science, Invention & Technology

1803. Robert Fulton is commisioned to build a steamboat by Robert R. Livingston (1746–1813), U.S. minister to France.

1804. Frenchman Nicolas Appert (1750–1841) opens world's first bottling plant south of Paris. ...Scottish engineer John Rennie (1761–1821) makes improvements on the recently invented steam dredger and uses it in construction of the London docks. Englishman George Cayley (1773–1857) builds first operational model.

1805. First mowing machine is invented in England.

1806. First covered bridge in the United States is built across Schuylkill River in Pennsylvania.

1807. Fulton navigates a steamboat on the Hudson River.

Religion, Culture & Arts

1803. First tax-supported public library is founded in Salisbury, Connecticut. ...Danish sculptor Bertel Thorwaldson (1768–1884): *Jason*. ...Sunday School Union founded in Britain.

1803–1812. Thomas Bruce (1766–1841), seventh earl of Elgin, arranges transfer of "Elgin marbles," a collection including Parthenon frieze, to British Museum.

1804. Friedrich von Schiller: *William Tell*. ...Ludwig von Beethoven's Third Symphony, a work unprecedented in its length and size of its orchestra, is first performed. ...British and Foreign Bible Society is founded. ...Jacques-Louis David (1748–1825) is appointed Napoléon's court painter. He establishes Classic Revival in French art. ...The New-York Historical Society is founded. ...St. Stephen's Catholic Church is completed. It is the only extant church in Boston designed by Charles Bulfinch (1763–1844).

1805. Sir Walter Scott (1771–1832), Scottish historian, novelist and poet: *Lay of the Last Minstrel*. ...Beethoven: *Fidelio*. ...British Institution for the Development of the Fine Arts is founded. ...Jean Auguste Ingres (1780–1867) paints *Bonaparte as First Consul*. ...**March 5:** Beethoven's Symphony no. 4 in B-flat Major is performed for first time in Vienna. ...**May 9:** Schiller (b. 1759) dies. ...**September 13:** Beethoven: Mass in C Major.

1806. Beethoven: *Appassionata*.

1807. Thomas Moore (1779–1852): *Irish Melodies*. ...Joseph Mallard William Turner (1775–1851), British painter: *Sun Rising in a Mist*. ...George Friedrich Wilhelm Hegel (1770–1832), German philosopher of the dialectical process: *Die Phänomenologie des Geistes* (*Phenomenology of the Spirit*). ...Madame de Staël: *Corinne*. ...Boston Athenaeum, a scholarly library for Boston's social elite, is formed. ...Robert Morrison (1782–1834), a Scotsman and first Protestant missionary to China, arrives in Canton.

British Isles & Europe

1808. Alexander I of Russia forbids sale of serfs at markets and fairs. ...**May 2:** Spanish insurrection against French begins. ...**May 6:** King and crown prince of Spain are forced to abdicate. ...**October:** Erfurt Congress between Napoléon, his vassals and Alexander I. ...**December 26:** Serbian rebels make Karageorge (1762–1817) country's hereditary ruler.

1809. March 29: Gustavus IV (1778–1837) of Sweden is forced to abdicate and is succeeded by Charles XIII (1748–1818). ...**May 1:** Napoléon annexes Papal States. ...**May 21–22:** Indecisive battle of Aspern between French and Austrians. ...**July 5–6:** Napoléon defeats Austrians at Wagram. ...**September 17:** In Peace of Frederikshamn with Sweden, Russia obtains Finland. ...**October 14:** In Peace of Vienna, Austria cedes Trieste and Illyrian Coast to France, Galicia to Poland and Russia, Salzburg and Inn district to Bavaria.

1810. February 10: Andreas Hofer (b. 1767), leader of Tyrolese rebellion against France and Bavaria, is executed at Mantua. ...**July 9:** Napoléon annexes Holland. ...**December 10:** Napoléon annexes Northern Hanover, Bremen, Hamburg, Lauenburg, Lübeck.

1811. February 5: Prince of Wales (the future King George IV, 1762–1830) becomes prince regent to rule in place of the insane George III. ...**February 10:** Russians take Belgrade and capture a Turkish army. ...**March:** Alexander I announces creation of Grand Duchy of Finland, with himself as grand duke. ...**April 1:** Civil Code is introduced in Austria. ...**May 8:** British defeat French at Fuentes d'Oñoro (in Spain). **May 16:** British defeat French at Albuera (in Spain). ...**December:** Russia and Britain make secret agreement aimed at breaking Napoléon's Continental System of economic warfare.

U.S. & Canada

1808. John Jacob Astor (1763–1848) of New York incorporates American Fur Company, with himself as sole stockholder. ...First U.S. temperance society is founded to agitate for outlawing alcoholic beverages. ...Louisiana court declares that marriages between slaves are illegal. ...**January 1:** Importation of slaves to the United States is prohibited.

1809. February 1: Massachusetts senator Timothy Pickering (1745–1829) proposes state nullification of 1807 Embargo Act. ...**March 1:** The Embargo Act is repealed and replaced with Nonintercourse Act, which permits trade with all countries except Britain and France. ...**March 4:** James Madison is inaugurated fourth president of the United States. ...**July 2:** Tecumseh (1768–1813), chief of Shawnee tribe, and his brother, the Prophet (c. 1775–1837), try to organize Indian Confederacy, uniting all tribes against white settlers.

1810. Population in the U.S. reaches 7,224,000, including 1,191,364 slaves. ...In *Fletcher v. Peck*, U.S. Supreme Court declares states cannot revoke contracts with private persons. ...**June 23:** Astor founds Pacific Fur Company. ...**July 12:** In New York City, court declares strike by journeyman cordwainers is illegal conspiracy. ...**October 27:** President Madison, taking advantage of a rebellion there, announces annexation of Spanish West Florida.

1811. February 2: United States renews Nonintercourse Act against British commerce. ...**April 11:** Fur traders from Astor's Pacific Fur Company set up Astoria at mouth of Columbia River. ...**June 13:** British crown grants 116,000 square miles between Lake Winnipeg and Red River headwaters (known as Red River Colony) to Thomas Douglas (1771–1820), fifth earl of Selkirk, who owns controlling stock in Hudson's Bay Company. ...**July 11:** David Thompson reaches Astoria, becoming first European to follow Columbia River from its source to Pacific Ocean. ...**November 7:** William Henry Harrison (1773–1841), governor of Indiana territory, defeats Indian forces under Shawnee chief Tecumseh at battle of Tippecanoe.

Latin America

1808. Indigenous population of West Indies revolts against French. ...Mexican officials demand that the Spanish viceroy grant them more of a role in government. ...Puerto Rico gains representation in the Spanish parliament.

1808–1821. Rio de Janeiro becomes capital of Portugal's exiled royal court.

1809. British take Martinique and Guadaloupe. ...Spanish put down uprising at Chuquisaca, Bolivia. ...People of Santo Domingo, aided by British, expel French.

1809–1824. La Paz is the center of revolutionary movement against Spanish rule.

1810. Simón Bolívar (1783–1830) becomes a major figure in South American politics. ...**May 25.** Revolutionaries take over Argentine government and establish a junta. ...**September 16.** Mexicans rebel and call for racial equality and land reform.

1810–1819. José Antonio Páez (1790–1873) leads a guerrilla war against Spanish in Venezuela.

1811. Miguel Hidalgo y Costilla (1753–1811) loses decisive battle of Calderón Bridge, thus ending his drive to reform Mexico. ...José María Morelos y Pavon (1765–1815) replaces Hidalgo as rebel leader in Mexico. ...José Gervasio Artigas (1764–1850) defeats Spanish Las Piedras (in southern Uruguay). ...Santa Cruz (in Bolivia) establishes a brief independence from Spain. ...**July:** In Caracas, Venezuela declares its independence from Spain. ...**October 12:** Paraguay declares its independence from Spain and Argentina.

1811–1820. Henri Christophe rules northern Haiti as king.

Africa, Asia & Pacific

1808. Mahmud II (1785–1839) becomes Ottoman sultan. ...First British expedition to Persia fails. ...**January 1:** British make Sierra Leone Crown colony, establish naval patrol against slave trade at Freetown, the capital. ...**January 26:** Governor William Bligh is deposed and held prisoner during Australian "Rum Rebellion."

1809. British forces capture French settlements on Senegal River. ...**April 25:** British and Sikhs agree on treaty of friendship. ...**June 17:** Afghan government promises British East India Company to oppose Persian or French attack on India.

1810. Radama I (c. 1780–1828) becomes king of Hovas, ruling much of Madagascar. ...Kamehameha I (c. 1738–1819) conquers most of Hawaiian Islands and establishes his dynasty. ...**July:** British capture Île de Bourbon and Mauritius (in Indian Ocean).

1811. March 1: Muhammad Ali Pasha of Egypt massacres Mamelukes throughout the country and begins war against Wahhabi movement in Arabia. ...**May 28:** Treaty of Bucharest ends war between Russia and Ottoman Empire, gives Russia territories along Black Sea's western coast and grants local autonomy to Serbs. ...**August:** British occupy Java.

Science, Invention & Technology

1808. Englishman Sir Humphrey Davy (1778–1829) invents the arc lamp.

1809. Jean Baptiste Lamarck (1744–1829) writes *Philosophie Zoologique.*

1810. Frenchmen Jean Delambre (1749–1822) and Pierre Méchain (1744–1805) make conclusive determination of the exact length of a meter.

c. 1810. U.S. government embarks on ambitious surveying and mapping effort, which will continue to the present day.

1811. First carpet sweeper is invented in Britain. ...Cylindrical printing press is developed in Germany.

Religion, Culture & Arts

1808. Sir Walter Scott: *Marmion.* ...Beethoven's Fifth Symphony is performed for the first time. ...Pope Pius VII (1740–1823) makes Bishop John Carrol Archbishop of Baltimore.

1808–1832. Johann Wolfgang von Goethe: *Faust.*

1809. Lord George Byron (1788–1824): *English Bards and Scotch Reviewers.* ...Washington Irving (1783–1859) writes *A History of New York*, best-selling comical history of Dutch New Amsterdam. ...*Quarterly Review* is founded in Britain. ...John Constable (1776–1837), British landscape painter: *Malvern Hall.* ...Goethe: *The Elective Affinities.*

1810. Heinrich von Kleist (1777–1811), German dramatist, novelist and poet completes *Der Prinz von Homburg*, a Romantic drama. ...Benedict Flaget (1763–1850), French-born Catholic prelate, becomes first bishop of old Northwest (Kentucky to the Great Lakes, Alleghenies to Mississippi).

1810–1814. Francisco de Goya creates his series of *Los Desastres de la Guerra* (*Disasters of War*) etchings.

1811. Thomas MacCrie (1772–1835): *Life of John Knox.* ...Jane Austen (1775–1817), British novelist: *Sense and Sensibility.* ...Friedrich Fouqué (1777–1843), German writer: *Undine*, a fairy tale. ...Two-thirds of Welsh Protestants secede from Anglican Church.

1811–1817. Scottish civil engineer Sir John Rennie (1761–1821) builds Waterloo Bridge in London.

◂***This etching is part of Francisco de Goya's series* Disasters of War.**

British Isles & Europe

1812. January 19: Arthur Wellesley (1769–1852), first duke of Wellington, recaptures Ciudad Rodrigo (in Spain) from French. ...**February 24:** Prussia allies with France. ...**March 5:** Sweden and Russia sign Treaty of Abo, promising support against France. ...**April 6:** Wellington drives French out of Badajoz (in Spain). ...**May 28:** In Treaty of Bucharest with Turkey, Russia obtains Bessarabia. ...**June 23:** Britain revokes Order in Council of 1807, which forbade American merchants to trade with France unless they first touched British ports. ...**July 22:** Wellington defeats French at Salamanca (in Spain). ...**August 12:** Wellington leads British forces into Madrid. ...**August 17:** Russians are defeated by French at Smolensk. ...**September 7:** Russians are defeated by French at Borodino. ...**September 14–October 18:** Napoléon occupies Moscow. ...**November 26–28:** Napoléon loses more than 20,000 troops crossing Berezina River (in Russia).

1813. May 2: French defeat Prussians and Russians at Lützen, Germany. ...**May 20:** Napoléon wins a costly victory over Russians and Prussians at Bautzen, Germany. ...**June 21:** Wellington defeats French at Vittoria, Spain. ...**August 12:** Austria declares war on Napoléon. ...**October:** Rhenish Confederation and kingdom of Westphalia are dissolved. ...**October 7:** Wellington crosses Bidassoa into France. ...**October 16–18:** Allies defeat Napoléon at Leipzig, Germany. ...**October 24:** Treaty of Gulistan ends Russo-Persian War. Persia recognizes Russian sovereignty over Georgia. ...**October 31:** Allied forces drive French troops from Pamplona, their last stronghold in Spain. ...**December 11:** In Treaty of Valencay, Napoléon reinstates Ferdinand VII (1784–1833) of Spain.

1814. Norway is recognized as independent kingdom, in personal union with Sweden. ...French law permits abortion to preserve mother's life. ...**January 1:** Allies cross Rhine and invade France. ...**January 5:** Joachim Murat (1767–1815), king of Naples and Napoléon's brother-in-law, joins allies. ...**January 14:** In Treaty of Kiel, Denmark cedes Norway to Sweden. ...**March 9:** In Treaty of Caumont, Austria, Prussia, Britain and Russia agree to 20-year alliance. ...**March 30:** Allies enter Paris. ...**April 11:** Napoléon abdicates and receives princedom of island of Elba. ...**May 4:** Ferdinand VIII of Spain abolishes constitution. ...**May 30:** In first Peace of Paris, France keeps frontiers of 1792 and Louis XVIII (1755–1824) is made king. ...**August 12:** Hanover becomes a kingdom.

U.S. & Canada

1812. April 30: Louisiana enters Union as 18th state. ...**June 18:** U.S. Congress declares war on Britain. ...**July:** General Isaac Brock (1769–1812), commander of British forces, prorogues Upper Canada's assembly and declares martial law. ...British defeat General William Hull (1753–1825), leader of U.S. troops invading Canada from Detroit. ...**August 15:** Indians massacre inhabitants at Fort Dearborn, Illinois. ...**August 16:** General Hull surrenders Detroit to General Brock's British forces. ...**October 5:** At battle of the Thames, forces under General Harrison defeat British troops. Chief Tecumseh (b. 1768) is killed while leading Britain's Indian allies. ...**October 13:** General Brock (b. 1769) dies at battle of Queenston Heights (on Niagara River) while repulsing Americans under General Stephen Van Rensselaer (1764–1839). **October 25:** French Canadians defeat American forces under General Wade Hampton (c. 1752–1835) on Chateauguay River. ...**December 29:** British burn Buffalo, New York.

1813. June 1: As he dies, U.S. Navy Captain James Lawrence (b.1781) cries, "Don't give up the ship!" but British warship *Shannon* captures *Chesapeake* near Boston. ...**July 24:** General Jacob J. Brown's (1775–1828) American troops fight battle of Lundy's Lane, the fiercest battle of War of 1812, without either side gaining territory. ...**August 30:** Creek War begins with massacre at Fort Mims, Alabama. Creeks murder 250 whites and take blacks as slaves. ...**September 13:** At battle of Lake Erie, U.S. Commodore Oliver Hazard Perry (1785–1819) defeats six British warships. ...**October 25:** Warship *United States* captures British frigate *Macedonian* off Madeira Islands. ...**December 29:** Winning nickname "Old Ironsides," *Constitution* destroys British warship *Java* off Brazil.

1814. April 27: Americans under General Henry Dearborn (1751–1829) burn York (Toronto), capital of Upper Canada. ...**July 5:** American forces take Fort Erie and defeat British regulars at Chippewa Plains. ...**August 19:** British troops land near Washington, D.C. ...**August 25:** British troops burn Washington, D.C. ...**September 11:** U.S. naval force captures British squadron at Battle of Plattsburgh on Lake Champlain, thwarting a British invasion from Canada. ...**September 12-15:** British troops land near Baltimore and unsuccessfully bombard Fort McHenry, inspiring Francis Scott Key (1779–1843) to write "The Star Spangled Banner." ...**September 21:** British troops invade Maine. ...**December 24:** Treaty of Ghent between Britain and the United States ends War of 1812 and restores status that existed before the war.

Latin America

1812. Argentine patriot Manuel Belgrano (1770–1820) wins a victory at Tucumán in a war against Royalists. ...Simón Bolívar's forces are defeated at Puerto Cabello, Venezuela. ...**March 26.** An earthquake destroys most of Caracas, Venezuela.

1813. Colombia breaks away from Spain. ...Bolívar becomes dictator of Venezuela. ...José María Morelos y Pavón captures Acapulco. ...Mexico declares itself independent. ...Manuel Belgrano (1770–1820) wins major victory against the Spanish at Salta, Argentina. ...Spanish defeat Belgrano in Bolivia. ...Argentina is divided into 14 provinces. ...Bernardo O'Higgins (1778–1842) is made commander of the Patriot Army in Chile. ...José Geruasio Artigas organizes an independent group of gauchos, which fails to force the Buenos Aires junta to recognize Uruguay as belonging to a federation of La Plata states. ...**August:** Bolívar enters Caracas and is given the title Liberator. ...**December:** Pavón's army is defeated in Mexico.

1814. Struggle for Uruguayan independence begins. ...British regain St. Lucia from French. ...Dutch cede Guyana to British. ...José Francisco de San Martín (1778–1850) organizes a rebel army in western Argentina. ...Spanish defeat O'Higgins at Rancugua, Chile. ...**June:** The Spanish recapture Caracas.

1814–1828. Uruguay is a province of Brazil.

Africa, Asia & Pacific

1812. Russian troops defeat Persian forces in battle of Aslanduz.

1813. November 20: George Evans (1787–1870) begins first expedition to cross the Great Dividing Range in Australia.

1813–1823. Marquess of Hastings is governor general of India.

1814. Civil courts are installed in New South Wales, Australia. ...British wage war against Gurkhas of Nepal. ...Kurozumi Munetada founds Kurozumi sect, first of modern popular Shinto sects. ...**August 13:** Cape of Good Hope becomes British colony. ...**November 25:** Persia agrees to cancel all treaties with European powers hostile to Britain in return for British subsidy of £150,000. ...**December 25:** Samuel Marsden (1764–1838), Anglican missionary, first to preach to Maori of New Zealand.

Science, Invention & Technology

1812. Marie Boivin (1773–1841), French midwife, publishes her findings in obstetrics.

1813. An iron plow with detachable pieces is invented in the United States. ...First factory combining all cotton manufacturing processes in one building opens in Waltham, Massachusetts.

1814. A two-cylinder printing press that prints both sides of paper simultaneously is invented in Germany.

Religion, Culture & Arts

1812. Lord George Byron: *Childe Harold's Pilgrimage*. ...Baptist Union of Great Britain is formed. ...First Methodist meeting in Australia is held at Sydney. ...Elizabeth Seton (1774–1821) founds the Daughters of Charity of Saint Joseph in the United States. ...**March 11:** Jews in Prussia are emancipated.

1812–1813. Brothers Jakob (1778–1865) and Wilhelm (1787–1859) Grimm: *Fairy Tales*.

◂Napoléon's victory over the Russians is depicted in this drawing of the battle of Smolensk.

1813. Baptist missionary Adoniram Judson (1788–1850) founds Karem Baptist Church at Rangoon in Burma (Yangôn). ...Percy Bysshe Shelley (1792–1822), British poet: *Queen Mab*. ...Robert Owen (1771–1858), Welsh socialist: *A New View of Society*. ...Jane Austen: *Pride and Prejudice*. ...Gioacchino Rossini (1792–1868), Italian composer of comic and bel canto operas: *L'Italiana in Algeri* (*The Italian Girl in Algiers*). ...Johann Rudolf Wyss (1781–1830), Swiss writer and philosopher: *Swiss Family Robinson*.

1814. U.S. Congress purchases Thomas Jefferson's personal book collection (some 6,500 volumes) to replace losses incurred during burning of Library of Congress. ...Sir Walter Scott: *Waverley*. ...Austen: *Mansfield Park*. ...William Wordsworth: *Excursion*. ...Byron: *Corsair*; *Lara*. ...Robert Southey, poet laureate from 1813: *Vision of Judgment*.

British Isles & Europe

1815. March 1: Napoléon lands in France. Louis XVIII flees. ...**June 1:** Napoléon issues liberal constitution. ...**June 18:** Duke of Wellington and Gebhard Blücher (1742–1819) defeat Napoléon at Waterloo. ...**June 22:** Napoléon abdicates. ...**July 7:** Allies enter Paris and Louis XVIII returns. ...**August 8:** Napoléon is banished to St. Helena. ...**September 26:** Holy Alliance is formed by Russia, Austria, Prussia, and other European countries, except Britain, Turkey and Papal States, to prevent change and disruption in Europe. ...**October 13:** Joachim Murat (b. 1767) is executed. ...**November 27:** Alexander I of Russia issues Polish constitution. ...**November 20:** In second Peace of Paris, France yields territories to Savoy and Switzerland and gives back captured land and works of art.

1816. Russian government frees serfs in Estonia. Russian businessmen are forbidden to purchase serfs for work in factories. ...Ferdinand IV of Naples begins ruling the Two Sicilies as Ferdinand I; he will hold both posts simultaneously until his death in 1825. ...**May 5:** Carl August (1757–1820) of Saxeweimar grants first German constitution.

1816–1826. John VI (1769–1826) rules as king of Portugal.

1817. Turkey grants autonomy to Serbia. ...**September 17:** Anglo-Spanish Treaty opens West Indian trade to Britain.

U.S. & Canada

1815. January 8: American forces led by Andrew Jackson defeat British at New Orleans. ...**March 3:** U.S. Congress declares war against Algiers, which had molested U.S. ships and demanded tribute. ...**May 10:** U.S. fleet, commanded by commodore Stephen Decatur (1779–1820), leaves New York for Mediterranean. ...**July:** U.S. fleet sinks Algerian warships. Algiers signs treaty giving up all claims to tribute. ...**August 13:** Thomas Douglas (1771–1820), fifth earl of Selkirk, arrives in Canada with hired soldiers and retakes forts at Red River Colony from Métis.

1816. March 20: In *Martin v. Hunter's Lessee*, U.S. Supreme Court affirms its right to review decisions of state courts. ...**April 10:** U.S. Congress authorizes a second Bank of United States to hold federal funds and to issue paper money. ...**April 27:** Tariff Act taxes iron, woolen and cotton goods to raise revenues. ...**Summer:** "Year in which there was no summer" brings snow and ice to New England, with frost as far south as Virginia. ...**June 19:** Massacre of Seven Oaks occurs near Fort Douglas in Red River Colony. Métis kill the governor of Rupert's Land. ...**December 11:** Indiana enters Union as 19th state. ...**December 28:** American Colonization Society, with John Calhoun (1782–1850) and Henry Clay (1777–1852) among sponsors, is founded to transport free blacks to Africa.

1817. February 8: U.S. Congress passes bill sponsored by Calhoun to create a permanent fund for internal improvements. ...**March 3:** President Madison vetoes internal improvements bill. ...**March 4:** James Monroe is inaugurated fifth president of the United States. ...**April 28–29:** In Rush-Bagot Treaty, United States and Britain both agree to station only one or two small vessels on Great Lakes. ...**May 1:** Acting governor of Red River colony Sir Gordon Drummond (1772–1854) orders Selkirk and North West Company to restore all goods seized during Red River colony conflict. ...**July 4:** Construction of Erie Canal begins. ...**November 20:** First Seminole Indian War begins in Florida. ...**December 10:** Mississippi enters Union as 20th state.

Latin America

1815. Congress of Vienna restores Guiana to French and awards Berbice, Demerara, and Essequibo in Guiana to British. ...José Gervasio Artigas liberates Montevideo from the Buenos Aires junta. ...Mexican revolutionaries are defeated and flee into the wilds. ...**October:** British occupy Ascension Island. ...British take Dominica. ...Spanish general Pablo Morillo (1778–1837) puts down revolution in New Grenada.

1816. Argentina declares independence. ...Bolívar, with Haitian help, invades Venezuela. ...Spanish general Pablo Morillo puts down insurrection in Bogotá. ...United Provinces of Rio de la Plata declare independence.

1817. Bolívar establishes an independent government in Venezuela. ...José Francisco de San Martín of Argentina and Bernardo O' Higgins of Chile defeat Spanish at Chacubuco, Chile. ...Bernardo O'Higgins Military School is founded in Santiago. ...Portuguese defeat Artigas and seize Montevideo. ...City of Salto (in northwestern Uruguay) is founded.

Africa, Asia & Pacific

1815. Muhammad Ali Pasha suppresses insurrection by Albanian regiments in Egypt. ...France abolishes slave trade. ...Boers revolt against British rule of Cape Colony. ...**January 16:** British declare war on king of Kandy, Ceylon. ...**March 3:** United States declares war on Algeria over pirate raids. ...**April 15–22:** Tambora volcano on Sumbawa Island, Indonesia, erupts, killing at least 10,000. ...**July 3:** Dey of Algeria signs treaty ending piracy after United States captures Algeria's main warships.

1816. Chaka (c. 1787–1816) becomes chief of a small Zulu tribe in southeastern Africa and begins to create a vast empire. ...British navy bombards Algiers, forcing bey to declare end to Christian slavery. ...**March:** War with Nepal ends. ...**March 2:** King of Kandy, Ceylon, is deposed.

1817. Radama I, Merina king, aided by British governor of Mauritius, takes control of island's main port and expels French from Madagascar.

Science, Invention & Technology

1816. Baltimore is first U.S. city to adopt a gas street lighting system. ...Thomas Drummond (1797–1840) of Scotland burns hydrogen and oxygen to produce limelight for stage sets. ...Scotsman David Brewster (1781–1868) invents the kaleidoscope. ...American Thomas Gilpin (fl. 19th century) invents machine that combines rags to make paper. This is known as the Foudrinier process.

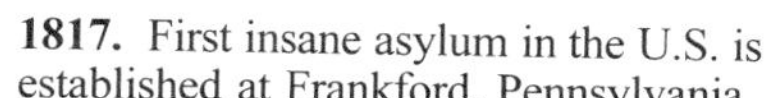

1817. First insane asylum in the U.S. is established at Frankford, Pennsylvania.

South American revolutionary leader Simón Bolívar.

Religion, Culture & Arts

1815. William Wordsworth: *White Doe of Rylstone*; *Laodamia*. ...Sir Walter Scott: *Guy Mannering*. ...Lord George Byron: *Hebrew Melodies*. ...Pierre Jean de Béranger (1780–1857): *Chansons I*. ...Antonio Canova: *Three Graces* (sculpture). ...Dugald Stewart (1753–1828): *Progress of Philosophy*. ...John Constable: *Boat Building*. ...*North American Review* is founded and will become influential among educated American readers for more than a century. ...John Nash (1752–1835) completes Brighton Pavilion for the prince of Wales. ...**September 9:** John Singleton Copley (b. 1738) dies.

1816. Percy Bysshe Shelley: *Alastor*. ...Scott: *The Antiquary*. ...Jane Austen: *Emma*. ...Johann Wolfgang von Goethe: *Journey to Italy*. ...Gioacchino Rossini composes *Il Barbiere di Siviglia* (*The Barber of Seville*). ...Pope Pius VII abolishes use of torture in heresy trials before the Inquisition. ...**April 9:** African Methodist Episcopal Church, first all-black religious denomination, is formally organized in Philadelphia. Richard Allen (1760–1831) becomes the church's first bishop.

1817. David Ricardo (1772–1823): *Principles of Political Economy and Taxation*. ...Byron: *Manfred*. ...Thomas Moore: *Lalla Rookh*. ...John Constable exhibits his landscape paintings for the first time. ...George Friedrich Wilhelm Hegel: *Encyclopedia of Philosophy*. ...Rossini composes opera *La Cenerentola* ...John Trumbull (1756–1843), painter in the grand historical style, is commissioned to decorate the U.S. Capitol. Perhaps his best known painting is *Signing of the Declaration of Independence*, painted in 1818.

British Isles & Europe

1818. British Board of Agriculture is abolished. ...**May 26:** In Bavarian constitution, Prussia is divided into ten provinces. ...**September 30–November 21:** In Congress of Aix-la-Chapelle, allied troops evacuate France.

1819. Serfdom is abolished in Mecklenburg. ...**March 23:** August von Kotzebue (b. 1761), German politician and dramatist, is assassinated by a student. ...**May 24:** Princess Alexandrina Victoria (d. 1901), the future Queen Victoria, is born. ...**September 20:** Carlsbad decrees attempt to check revolutionary and liberal movements in Germany. ...**December 7:** Constitution of Hanover takes effect.

1820. January 1–March 7: Revolution breaks out in Spain, and constitution is restored. ...**January 29:** George III (b. 1738) of Britain dies and is succeeded by George IV (1762–1830). ...**May 24:** Final act of Congress of Vienna authorizes larger German states to interfere in affairs of smaller ones. ...**July 2:** Riots against Ferdinand I, the king of the Two Sicilies, erupt in Nola, Sicily. ...**July 9:** Ferdinand I is forced to grant constitutional charter to Sicily. ...**August 24:** Revolution breaks out in Portugal. ...**October 27–December 17:** Congress of Troppau discusses policy against revolutionary tendencies in Europe.

1821. Constitutional government of Sicily is overthrown by Ferdinand I with Austria's help. ...**January 26–May 12:** Congress of Laibach resolves to take measures against revolutions in Italy and Greece. ...**March 6:** Alexander Ypsilanti (1792–1828) leads uprising at Jassy in Moldavia against Ottoman rule in Greece, beginning Greek war of independence. ...**May 5:** Napoléon (b. 1769) dies in exile on St. Helena. ...**October 5:** Greek revolutionaries take Tripolitsa, main Ottoman fort in Peloponnesian Peninsula, and massacre 10,000 of its defenders.

U.S. & Canada

1818. John Jacob Astor's fur company opens trading post at site of present-day Milwaukee, Wisconsin. ...**April 4:** Law limits stripes on U.S. flag to 13. An additional star is to be added when a new state is admitted. ...**April 18:** At battle of Suwannee, Florida, Andrew Jackson's forces crush Seminoles and their black allies. ...**May:** Fall of Pensacola, Florida, ends first Seminole War. Jackson executes two British traders suspected of inciting disorder among Indians. ...**October 20:** Convention of 1818 sets the U.S.-Canadian border at the 49th parallel from Lake of Woods, Minnesota, to the Rocky Mountains. Britain and the United States agree to jointly settle the Pacific Northwest. ...**December 3:** Illinois enters Union as 21st state.

1819. In *Trustees of Dartmouth College v. Woodward*, U.S. Supreme Court prohibits a state from revising or impairing a contract. ...**February 22:** Spain signs Adams-Onis Treaty, providing for the cession of Florida to the United States. ...**March 6:** In *McCulloch v. Maryland*, Supreme Court rules no state may tax any branch or instrument of federal government. ...**May:** Expedition under Sir William Edward Parry (1790–1855) leaves Britain, explores Lancaster Sound, Barrow Strait and Melville Sound. ...**December 14:** Alabama enters Union as 22nd state.

1820. U.S. population reaches 9,638,453, including 1,538,000 slaves. ...Indianapolis, Indiana, is founded on White River. ...**March 2:** Congress passes Missouri Compromise, allowing Missouri to enter Union as a slave state and Maine to enter as a free state and banning slavery in Louisiana territory north of Arkansas to maintain equal number of slave and free states. ...**March 14:** Maine, formerly part of Massachusetts, enters Union as 23rd state. ...**December 6:** In being reelected to a second term as U.S. president, James Monroe receives 231 electoral votes; John Quincy Adams (1767–1848) receives 1 electoral vote.

1821. Stephen Austin (1793–1836) founds Austin settlement in Texas. ...**August 10:** Missouri enters Union as 24th state. ...**August 18:** John Franklin (1786–1847) reaches Point Turnagain, Kent Peninsula, overland from York Fort. ...**September 16:** Russia claims exclusive rights in Alaska north of 51st parallel.

Latin America

1818. José Francisco de San Martín of Argentina and Bernardo O'Higgins of Chile defeat Spanish at Maipu, Chile. Chile declares its independence. Santiago becomes its capital. ...Spanish remove restrictions on trade in Cuba.

1818–1843. Jean-Pierre Boyer (1776–1850) rules as first president of Haiti.

1819. Civil war erupts in Argentina. ...**August 7:** Bolívar defeats Spanish forces at Boyacá in one of the great campaigns of military history, and Colombia thereby achieves independence. ...**December 17:** Republic of Colombia is formed under Bolívar as president and military dictator.

1820. Morillo negotiates armistice with Bolívar. ...Brazil occupies Montevideo and ends Uruguyan independence movement. ...Peace is restored to Argentina. ...**September 17:** San Martín lands an army of 6,000 men on the Peruvian coast.

1821. Costa Rica becomes independent from Spain. ...Nicaragua declares independence from Spain. ...Manuel José Arce (1787–1847) becomes head of Salvadoran army. ...Brazil annexes Banda Oriental (in Uruguay) and renames it Cisplatine Province. ...**February:** Plan of Iguala establishes an independent monarchy in Mexico and maintains the Catholic Church's privileges. ...**June 24:** Bolívar defeats Spanish army at Carabobo, ensuring Venezuelan independence. ...**September:** Spain accepts Mexico's independence.

Africa, Asia & Pacific

1818. Public flogging of convicts ends in Australia. Henceforth, floggings are to be conducted in barracks at set times. ...Muhammad Ali Pasha defeats Wahhabi movement, subjecting eastern coast of Red Sea to Egyptian rule. ...Gaspard Mollien (1796–1872) discovers the sources of the Gambia and Senegal Rivers. ...**January 6:** Peshwa's dominions are annexed by British, Rajputana states are placed under British protection.

1818–1819. Claude de Freycinet (1779–1842) explores coasts of New Guinea, Mariana Islands and Hawaii.

1819. Captain William Smith (1764–1840) discovers South Shetland Islands and claims them for Britain. ...Bagyidaw (?–1838) becomes king of Burma. ...British found Singapore.

1819–1821. Russian expedition, led by Fabian von Bellingshausen (1778–1852) and Mikhail Lazarev (c. 1778–1851), explores Antarctica.

1820. Egypt subdues Sudan and Kordofan (in Africa). ...Chinese emperor Chia-ch'ing (b. 1760) dies. ...Vietnamese emperor Minh Mang (originally Nguyen Phuoc Chi Dam) (1792–1841) begins reign, during which he persecutes Christians.

1821. Tao-kuang (1782–1850) becomes emperor of China. ...War breaks out between Ottoman Empire and Persia. ...**February 7:** American seal hunter John Davis (fl. 19th century) is first person to land on Antarctic continent near tip of Palmer Peninsula. ...**June 14:** Troops of Muhammad Ali Pasha of Egypt conquer Sennar—overthrowing Fundj sultans and establishing Ottoman rule throughout eastern Sudan. ...**December 15:** American Colonization Society buys territory on western coast of Liberia and founds Monrovia as home for repatriated slaves.

Science, Invention & Technology

1818. The two-wheeled bicycle is perfected in Germany. ...American Thomas Blanchard (1788–1864) invents gunstock lathe. ...Frenchman Louis Thenard (1777–1857) develops pure hydrogen peroxide. ...Frenchman Louis Braille (1809–1852) improves the sonography writing system for the blind developed by Charles Barbier.

1819. Packaging of foods in bottles begins in the United States. ...Englishman John Daniell (1790–1845) invents the dew-point hygrometer. ...First chocolate bar is made in Switzerland. ...**May 26:** First American steamship to cross Atlantic leaves Savannah for Liverpool.

1820. Dane Hans Christian Oersted (1777–1851) discovers magnetic field formed by coiled electric wire. ...The tedder, a haying machine that turns cut grass for drying, is invented in Britain. ...Frenchman André-Marie Ampère (1775–1836) formulates what will become known as Ampère's Law concerning the force between two electric currents. ...Arithmometer calculating machine is invented in France. ...Englishman William Sturgeon (1783–1850) creates the first electromagnet.

1821. African American Thomas Jennings (1791–1859) is first to patent dry cleaning process for clothing.

Religion, Culture & Arts

1818. Jane Austen's novels *Persuasion* and *Northanger Abbey* are published posthumously. ...London Missionary Society begins successful drive to convert Madagascar natives. ...Mary Wollstonecraft Shelley (1797–1851), British writer: *Frankenstein*. ...William Hazlitt (1778–1830), British writer: *Lectures on the English Poets*. ...John Keats (1795–1821), Romantic poet: *Endymion*. ...Nikolai Mikhailovich Karamzin (1766–1826), Russia's first major historian: *The History of the Russian Empire*. ...Katsushika Hokusai (1760–1849), Japanese painter, print designer and book illustrator, embarks on his most creative period. ...**May 3:** First Roman Catholic priests arrive in Australia.

1819. Adam Müller (1818–1884): *Necessity of a Theological Foundation of All Political Economics*. ...Victor Hugo (1802–1885), French writer: *Odes*. ...Sir Walter Scott: *Ivanhoe* and *Bride of Lammermoor*. ...Arthur Schopenhauer (1788–1860), German philosopher: *Die Welt als wille und Vorstellung* (*The World as Will and Idea*). ...Károly Kisfaludy (1788–1830), Hungarian dramatist: *A Tatárok Magyarországon* (*Tartars in Hungary*). ...Andrew Norton (1786–1853), American author and scholar known as the "Pope of Unitarianism," becomes professor of sacred literature at Harvard Divinity School.

1820. *London Magazine* begins to appear. ...Alphonse-Marie Lamartine (1790–1869), French poet: *Méditations poétiques*. ...Thomas Robert Malthus: *Principles of Political Economy*. ...Percy Bysshe Shelley: *Prometheus Unbound*. ...John Constable exhibits *The Haywain* at Royal Academy, London. ...Washington Irving: *The Sketch Book* including *Rip Van Winkle* and *The Legend of Sleepy Hollow*. ...James Savage (1779–1852): St. Luke's in Chelsea, London, is first Gothic revival church to be stone-vaulted throughout.

1821. Alessandro Manzoni (1785–1873), Italian novelist, poet: "The Fifth of May." ...Thomas De Quincey (1785–1859): *Confessions of an English Opium Eater*. ...James Fenimore Cooper (1789–1851): *The Spy*, a romance novel of the American Revolution. ...Carl Weber (1786–1826), German composer: *Der Freishütz*. ...Salvatore Vigano (b. 1769), Italian choreographer and ballet master who made La Scala greatest center of ballet in Europe, dies in Milan. ...Hegel: *Grundlinien der Philosophie des Rechts* (*The Philosophy of Right*). ...*Australian Magazine*, the first periodical in Australia, begins publication.

British Isles & Europe

1822. January 13: Assembly at Epidauros declares Greek independence. ...**February 5:** Ottoman troops take Janina in northern Greece, ending independent rule of Pasha Ali of Janina. ...**April:** Ottoman naval fleet under Kara Ali occupies Chios Island, massacring or enslaving most of the population. ...**June 19:** Greek squadrons under Admiral Constantine Kanaris (1790–1877) defeat Ottoman fleet. ...**July:** Ottoman army of 30,000 crushes Greek revolt north of Corinth. ...**September 23:** Portuguese adopt a new constitution.

1823. April 7: War between France and Spain begins. ...**August 31:** French troops storm Trocadero and reestablish Ferdinand VII as king of Spain.

1824. Anticombination laws are repealed, allowing workers in Britain to combine in harbor associations. ...**September 16:** Louis XVIII (b. 1755) dies and is succeeded by Charles X (1757–1836).

1825. Trade unions are legalized in Britain. ...**January 4:** Ferdinand IV (b. 1751) of Naples, also known as Ferdinand I of the two Sicilies, dies and is succeeded by Francis I (1777–1830). ...Ibrahim (1789–1848), son of Muhammad Ali Pasha of Egypt lands in Peloponnesian Peninsula and quickly subdues it. ...**December 13:** Nicholas I (1796–1855) succeeds Alexander I as tsar of Russia. ...**December 14:** Nicholas I ruthlessly suppresses revolt of the Decembrists, army officers demanding a less autocratic form of government.

U.S. & Canada

1822. Bank of Montreal is chartered. It is the first bank established in Canada. ...Sir William Edward Parry discovers Fury and Hecla Strait after having explored east coast of Melville Peninsula in Arctic. ...**May 30:** Slave uprising organized by Denmark Vesey (b. c. 1767) is exposed in Charleston, South Carolina, and 37 participants are executed, including Vesey.

1823. U.S. troops defeat Sauk and Fox under Chief Black Hawk (1767–1838), opening Illinois to corn farmers. ...**December 2:** President James Monroe issues Monroe Doctrine, excluding European powers from all interference in political affairs of independent republics in the Western Hemisphere.

1824. Jedediah Smith (1799–1831) discovers South Pass through Rocky Mountains. ...**March 2:** In *Gibbons v. Ogden*, U.S. Supreme Court ends monopolies on U.S. rivers, stating that federal laws regarding interstate commerce overrule state laws. ...**December 1:** Neither John Quincy Adams, Henry Clay, Andrew Jackson or William Harris Crawford (1772–1834) receives a majority of votes in electoral college.

1825. February: U.S. House of Representatives chooses John Quincy Adams as president over rivals in four-way race. ...**February 12:** Creek tribal leaders turn over their Georgia lands and promise to migrate west by September 1826. Most Creek repudiate treaty. ...**February 28:** Treaty between Britain and Russia settles boundaries between British and Russian areas of northwestern North America (Alaska). ...**March 4:** Adams is inaugurated sixth president of United States. ...**March 19:** Fort Vancouver is founded as headquarters for Canada's Columbia district. ...**March 24:** Americans are permitted to move into Mexican state of Texas-Coahuila. ...**August 19:** Chippewa, Iowa, Potawatomi, Sauk, Fox, Sioux, and Winnebago establish formal boundaries between their tribal territories in Wisconsin. ...**October 26:** Erie Canal is opened to traffic from Hudson River to Lake Erie. ...**December 6:** President Adams sends to Congress first of annual State of the Union addresses.

Latin America

1822. Simón Bolívar and José Francisco de San Martín meet in Guayaquil, Ecuador to plot total liberation of South America. ...**May:** Bolívar wins the battle of Pichincha, Ecuador, and Ecuador joins Gran Colombia, a federation of Venezuela, Panama, and Colombia that will persist until 1830. ...**July 21:** Agustín de Iturbide (1783–1824) is crowned emperor of Mexico. ...**September 7:** Brazil declares itself independent of Portugal. ...**October 12:** Dom Pedro I (1798–1834) is proclaimed emperor of Brazil.

1823. San Jose becomes the capital of Costa Rica. ...Bernardo O'Higgins is deposed in Chile and is exiled to Peru. ...Honduras becomes independent from Mexico.

1824. Bolívar is declared emperor of Peru. ...Mexico becomes a federal republic under president Guadalupe Victoria (1789–1843). ...José Fructuoso Rivera (1788–1854) becomes general commander of the forces in Uruguay. ...**February:** Royalists gain control of Lima, Peru. ...**March:** Dom Pedro I promulgates a constitution for Brazil. ...**June:** Bolívar leads his troops south to confront the Spanish in Peru. ...**August 6:** Bolívar is victorious over Spanish at Junín, Peru. ...**December 12:** Last Spanish army in South America capitulates.

1825. President Jean-Pierre Boyer of Haiti agrees to pay France large indemnity in exchange for recognition of Haiti's independence. ...Rivera and Juan Antonio Lavalleja (1784–1853) join forces to oppose Brazilian rule in Uruguay. ...Brazil and Argentina go to war over the Cisplatine Province (Uruguay). ...**August 6:** Bolivia declares independence. ...**August 29:** Portugal recognizes independence of Brazil.

1825–1829. Salvadoran soldier Manuel José Arce is first president of United Provinces of Central America (Guatemala, El Salvador, Nicaragua, Honduras and Costa Rica).

Africa, Asia & Pacific

1822. Egypt begins exporting cotton to Europe. . . .Advancing toward India, Burmese troops seize Manipur and Assam.

1822–1825. Walter Oudney (1790–c. 1825), Dixon Denham (1786–1828) and Hugh Clapperton (1788–1827) travel from Tripoli across desert to Lake Chad, then westward to Niger.

1823. Muhammad Ali Pasha of Egypt founds Khartoum in the Sudan. . . .**February 5:** James Weddell (1787–1834) reaches record southern latitude at Weddell Sea in Antarctica while searching for seals. . . .**July 19:** British provide for first Legislative Council in Australia.

1824. The name *Australia* is formally adopted. It is derived from *Terra Australis* ("South Land"). . . .**February 24:** First Burmese War with British begins. . . .**March 17:** Dutch cede Malacca to Britain in return for Bengkulen in Sumatra. . . .**May 11:** British take Yangôn (Rangoon) in Burma.

1825. War breaks out between Russia and Persia.

Science, Invention & Technology

1823. Dr. J. E. Purkinje (1787–1869), at the University of Breslau, announces his discovery that individual fingerprints are unique.

1824. Braided candlewick is introduced. . . .American Joseph Aspdin (1779–1855) patents Portland cement, which is used in underwater construction.

1825. Hans Christian Oersted isolates aluminum.

Religion, Culture & Arts

1822. Franz Schubert (1797–1828), Austrian composer: A Minor Symphony. . . .Felix Mendelssohn (1809–1847) presents his first compositions, but only to his family members. . . .Christian Johann Heinrich Heine (1797–1856): *Poems*. . . .Jean Baptiste Camille Corot (1796–1875) begins painting as a professional artist. . . .James Fenimore Cooper: *The Pilot* . . .President of Yale College prohibits football (resembling modern soccer), which has been played at Yale for some years.

1823. Friedrich Schleiermacher (1768–1834), German theologian: *Christian Dogma*. . . .Charles Lamb (1775–1834): *Essays of Elia*. . . .Vuk Stephanovic Karadzic (1787-1864), Serbian philologist and lexicographer, publishes collection of national poetry. . . . .John Constable: *Salisbury Cathedral from the Bishop's Grounds*. . . .Scottish painter Sir Henry Raeburn (b. 1756) dies.

1824. Walter Savage Landor (1775–1864), British poet: *Imaginary Conversations*. . . .Beethoven: Ninth Symphony. . . .Victor Hugo: *Ballads*. . . .Leopold von Ranke (1795–1886): *Geschichte der romanischen und germanischen Völker von 1494–1535*. . . .James Mill (1773–1836): *Essays on Government*. . . .Alexander Pushkin (1799–1837), Russian writer: *Boris Godunov*. . . .First edition of *Pepys Diary* is published. . . .John Nash (1752–1835): Buckingham Palace; Marble Arch. . . .**April 19:** Lord George Byron (b. 1788) dies at Missolonghi in Greece.

1825. January 3: Robert Owen (1771–1858) founds America's first utopian society at New Harmony, Indiana.

New York governor DeWitt Clinton pours a keg of Lake Erie water into the Atlantic Ocean when the Erie Canal opens on October 26, 1825.

British Isles & Europe

1826. March 10: John VI (b. 1769) of Portugal dies. ...**April 4:** Britain and Russia sign St. Petersburg Protocol, demanding that Greece become autonomous province within Ottoman Empire. ...**April 23:** Ottoman troops occupy fortress of Missolonghi at entrance to Gulf of Corinth after a long siege. Greek revolt is crushed. ...**April 26:** Liberal constitution is adopted in Portugal. ...**July:** Persian armies attack in Caucasus, beginning Russo-Persian War. ...**October 7:** In Russo-Turkish Convention, signed at Akkerman, merchant ships enjoy freedom of movement in Bosporus and Dardanelles straits, and Serbia, Moldavia, and Wallachia gain autonomy.

1827. Catholics become alienated when Netherlands king William I (1772–1843) gains right to veto bishops in concordat with papacy. ...To encourage religious conversion, Nicholas I of Russia orders that Jews serve in army for 25 years. ...Capo d' Istria elected president of Greek National Assembly. ...**July 6:** Treaty of London between Britain, Russia and France secures autonomy of Greece. ...**October 20:** British, French and Russian squadrons destroy Turkish-Egyptian fleet in Bay of Navarino, Greece.

1828. Test and Corporation Acts are repealed in Britain. ...**January 25:** Duke of Wellington forms Conservative ministry in Britain. ...**April 27:** Russia declares war on Turkey. ...**June 23:** Dom Miguel (1802–1866) is proclaimed king of Portugal and revokes constitution. ...**October 11:** Russians take Varna (in Bulgaria).

1829. September 14: Treaty of Adrianople ends Russo-Turkish War. Turkey recognizes independence of Danube princedoms. Russia obtains land south of Caucasus. ...**September 29:** Robert Peel (1788–1850) remodels London police.

1830. February 4: At conference in London, Greece is declared independent under protection of Britain, Russia and France. ...**June 26:** George IV (b. 1762) of England dies and is succeeded by William IV (1767–1837). ...**July 27–29:** Revolution in France. ...**August 2:** Charles X of France abdicates. ...**August 9:** Louis-Philippe (1773–1850), of the junior Bourbon-Orléans line, is crowned king of France. ...**November 16:** Duke of Wellington resigns; Charles Grey (1764–1845) forms Liberal ministry in Britain.

U.S. & Canada

1826. John Russworm (1799–1851) graduates from Bowdoin. He is believed the first black to graduate from an American college. ...**January 24:** Creek sign Treaty of Washington, nullifying February 1825 treaty and giving up less land. ...**February 13:** All-male group in Boston founds American Society for Promotion of Temperance. ...**April 8:** Secretary of State Henry Clay duels with an Andrew Jackson supporter; neither is harmed. ...**July 4:** Former presidents John Adams (b. 1735) and Thomas Jefferson (b. 1743) die. ...**August 22:** Jedediah Smith leads first expedition from Great Salt Lake, Utah, to California.

1827. Massachusetts passes first law mandating public high schools. ...Arthur Tappan (1786–1865) founds *Journal of Commerce* in New York City. ...**July 4:** New York State abolishes slavery. ...**July 27:** Fort Langley is founded on Fraser River.

1828. Women working at a mill in Dover, New Hampshire, strike over deteriorating working conditions. ...President Adams signs Tariff of Abominations, raising taxes on many imports. ...**December 19:** South Carolina legislature declares Tariff of Abominations unconstitutional. Vice President John Calhoun secretly writes *South Carolina Exposition and Protest*, which says any state may nullify federal laws within its state borders.

1829. Georgia prohibits education of slaves and free black persons. ...David Walker (fl. 19th century) appeals to blacks to revolt against slavery in widely read book *Walker's Appeal*. ...**March 4:** Andrew Jackson is inaugurated seventh president of the United States. ...**July 29:** Chippewa, Ottawa and Potawatomi cede lands in Michigan territory.

1830. May 27: President Jackson vetoes aid to Maysville (Kentucky) Road, opposing subsidies for roads and canals built in only one state. ...**May 28:** Under Indian Removal Act, all Indians are to move west of Mississippi River. ...**July 15:** At Prairie du Chien, Wisconsin, Indians, including Sioux, Sauk and Fox, sign treaty giving United States most of Iowa, Missouri and Minnesota. ...**September 15:** Chocataw exchange eight million acres east of Mississippi for land in Oklahoma.

Latin America

1826. First Pan-American Congress is convened by Simón Bolívar at Panama. ...First parliament meets in Brazil. ...Andres Santa Cruz (1792–1865) succeeds Bolívar as ruler of Peru. ...Cathedral of San Luis Potosí (in north central Mexico) is built. ...Bolivia adopts a constitution naming a president for life. ...Lima becomes capital of Peru.

1827. University of Cartagena is founded in Colombia. ...Honduran civil war begins. ...José de La Marx Cortázar (1778–1830) replaces Santa Cruz as leader of Peru. ...Argentine Unitarians help Uruguayans separate from Brazil. ...**January 26:** Peru secedes from Colombia.

1828. Uruguay becomes independent from Brazil. ...Montevideo becomes capital of Uruguay. ...After a liberal revolt in Mexico, Vicente Guerrero (1782–1831) becomes president. ...Bolivia's first president is forced to resign. ...Colombia participates in Bolívar's constitutional assembly. ...**September 24:** Bolívar barely escapes assassination by jumping from a high window.

1829. Slavery is abolished in Mexico. ...Agustín Gamarra (1785–1841) replaces de La Marx Cortázar as Peru's leader.

1830. Bolívar's Gran Colombia is divided into republics of Venezuela, Colombia and Ecuador (Panama will remain part of Colombia until 1903). ...Juan José Flores (1800–1864) becomes the first president of Ecuador. ...Venezuela is governed by an elected two-chamber national congress. ...Peace between Uruguay and Brazil is observed. ...Conservative forces defeat liberal army in Argentina. ...General Joaquîn Prieto (1786–1854) seizes control of Chilean government. ...**April 27:** Bolívar abdicates. ...**December 10:** Bolívar (b. 1783) dies.

Africa, Asia & Pacific

1826. Treaty of friendship and commerce between United States and Hawaii is signed. ...Russian troops defeat Persians at Ganja. ...British extend Cape Colony northward to Orange River. ...**February 24:** Treaty of Yandabu ends First Burmese War. British acquire Assam, Arakan, and Tenasserim coast. ...**June 15–16:** Ottoman emperor Mahmud II (1785–1839) orders Janissaries, hereditary soldiers, massacred in their barracks. ...**August 18:** Scottish explorer Alexander Gordon Laing (1793–1826) becomes first European to reach Timbuktu, in present-day Mali. ...**September 26:** Laing is murdered in Timbuktu.

1827. Russia takes Erivan and Tabriz from Persia. British settle Cocos (Keeling) Islands. ...Church Missionary Society founds Fourah Bay College in Sierra Leone. It is the first institution of higher learning in West Africa. ...British end remaining authority of Delhi emperor and remove his name from coins. ...**April 27:** Hugh Clapperton (b. 1788), first European to describe Hausa tribes, dies at Sokoto, capital of Fulah empire (present-day Nigeria).

1828. Second constitution of New South Wales takes effect. ...Radama I (b. 1779) of Madagascar dies. ...British judicial system replaces Dutch in Cape Colony. ...**February 22:** In Peace of Turkmantchai, Persia cedes provinces of Erivan and Nakhchivan to Russia and pays large indemnity.

1829. Swan River settlement is founded in Western Australia. ...**December 4:** *Suttee* (immolation of widows) is declared illegal in India, but it will persist into the 20th century.

1830. June: French conquer Algiers. ...Mysore and Cachar are annexed by British East India Company. ...**October 4:** A group of 5,000 men moves across Van Diemen's Land (in Australia), herding Aborigines into Tasman Peninsula.

Science, Invention & Technology

1826. French physicist Joseph Nicéphore Niepce (1765–1833) produces world's first photograph with light-sensitive acids on glass using a camera obscura. ...Scotsman Patrick Bell (1799–1869) invents a corn reaper with reciprocating knives.

1827. Englishman John Walker (c. 1781–1859) invents the first modern-day striking match.

1828. Frenchman Jean-Léonard-Marie Poiseuille (1799–1864) invents U-shaped glass tube filled with mercury for measuring blood pressure. ...An iron corrugating process is developed in England. ...First combine harvester is invented. ...Construction begins on Baltimore and Ohio Railroad, first public railroad in United States. ...First significant American production of china dinnerware begins in Jersey City, New Jersey.

1829. American Joseph Henry (1797–1878) invents an improved electromagnet. ...Welland Canal is opened to ships between Lake Erie and Lake Ontario in Canada. ...**August 8:** First steam-powered locomotive in America runs from Carbondale to Honesdale, Pennsylvania.

1830. American Peter Cooper (1791–1883) builds his *Tom Thumb* locomotive. ...A push lawn mower is patented in England. ...A compressed air fire fighting pump is invented. ...**December:** First passenger train service is inaugurated by the South Carolina Railroad.

c. 1830. American Sylvester Graham (1794–1851) invents the graham cracker. ...Plywood is first produced in Britain.

Religion, Culture & Arts

1826. Thomas Cole (1801–1848), American painter who will found Hudson River school, settles in Catskill, New York. ...Alfred Victor, comte de Vigny (1797–1863), French poet, playwright and novelist: *Poèmes antiques et modernes* (*Poems Ancient and Modern*) ...Benjamin Disraeli (1804–1881): *Vivian Grey*. ...Felix Mendelssohn: Overture to *Midsummer Night's Dream*. ...Franz Schubert: song cycle *Die Winterreise*. ...James Fenimore Cooper: *The Last of the Mohicans*. ...Carl Weber (b. 1786) dies. ...Society of the Sacred Heart is founded by Madeleine Sophie Baret (1779–1865). ...**December 7:** John Flaxman (b. 1755) dies.

1827. Victor Hugo: *Cromwell*. ...Cooper: *The Prairie*. ...Edgar Allan Poe's (1809–1849) first book of poetry, *Tamerlane and Other Poems*. ...*Encyclopedia Americana*'s first volume (of 13) appears. ...Schubert: *Trout Quintet*. ... Ludwig van Beethoven (b. 1770) dies at Vienna. ...**March 16:** *Freeman's Journal*, first U.S. black newspaper, begins publication in New York.

1827–1838. James Audubon (1785–1851) publishes *The Birds of America*.

1828. Adam Mickiewicz (1798–1855), Polish poet: *Konrad Wallenrod*. ...Thomas Arnold (1795–1842) is appointed headmaster of Rugby School. He will introduce major reforms to English public schools. ...Schubert (b. 1797) dies after completing String Quintet in C. ...Honoré de Balzac (1799–1850): *Les Chouans*. ...Noah Webster's (1758–1843) monumental *American Dictionary of the English Language* is published.

1829. Joseph Smith (1805–1844) publishes *The Book of Mormon*, which he claims is a translation of divine writing on golden tablets he claimed to have discovered near Palmyra, New York. ...**April 13:** Catholic Emancipation Act receives royal assent. Within three weeks, a Catholic is elected to Parliament. ...**July 29:** Wojciech Boguslawski (b. c. 1757), founder of Polish theater and author of *Cud mniemany*, dies.

1830. Alfred Tennyson (1809–1892): *Poems, Chiefly Lyrical*. ...Théophile Gautier (1811–1872): *Poésies*. ...Marie-Henri Beyle, called Stendhal (1783–1842), writes *Le Rouge et le noir* (*The Red and the Black*). ...Alexander Campbell (1788–1866) forms Disciples of Christ (often called Campbellites), claiming he has restored New Testament beliefs and practices. ...**April 6:** Smith founds Church of Jesus Christ of Latter-Day Saints, known as the Mormon Church, at Fayette, New York.

British Isles & Europe

1831. Constitutions are proclaimed in Saxony, Hesse-Cassel, Moldavia and Wallachia. ...Silk-weavers at Lyons revolt. ...**September 8:** Russians take Warsaw. ...**November 15:** Britain and France agree on separation of Belgium from Holland.

1832. The Götha Canal in Sweden opens, connecting the North Sea with the Baltic. ...**February 26:** Russians abolish Polish constitution. ...**November:** French take Antwerp to force Holland to recognize independence of Belgium.

1833. Hanover is granted a constitution. ...**June 26:** Russia and Ottoman Empire sign Treaty of Unkiar Skelessi, providing for eight-year alliance. Under secret clause, Dardanelles is closed to foreign ships on Russian demand. ...**August 29:** Parliament passes a law that abolishes slavery in all British possessions, to be achieved after six years of apprenticeship. The law goes into effect January 1, 1834. ...**September 27:** Ferdinand VII (b. 1784) of Spain dies and is succeeded by Queen Isabella II (1830–1904). ...**September 29:** Civil war breaks out in Spain. It will end in 1840 with victory of constitutional party.

U.S. & Canada

1831. January 1: William Lloyd Garrison (1805–1879) publishes first issue of militant abolitionist periodical the *Liberator*. ...**June 1:** Exploring for Britain in *Victory*, Sir James Clark Ross (1800–1862) is first to describe North Pole. ...**June 30:** Black Hawk, leader of Sauk and Fox tribes, reluctantly agrees to move west of Mississippi River. ...**August 21–22:** Nat Turner (1800–1831) murders his master and his master's family in Virginia while they sleep. Joined by more than 70 other slaves, Turner kills 60 more whites during the next two days. ...**November 11:** Nat Turner is hanged at Jerusalem, Virginia, along with 16 accomplices following America's largest slave rebellion. ...**December 5:** Former president John Quincy Adams joins House of Representatives. He will serve for 17 years.

1832. March 3: U.S. Supreme Court holds in *Worcester v. Georgia* that federal government has jurisdiction over Indians within a state. ...**April 6:** Under Chief Black Hawk, dispossessed Sauk cross Mississippi River into northern Illinois and massacre white settlers, beginning Black Hawk War. ...**May 9:** In Treaty of Payne's Landing, some Seminole chiefs agree to migrate west of Mississippi River. ...**May 21:** Democratic Party formally adopts this name at its first national convention in Baltimore. ...**July 10:** President Jackson vetoes bill to renew charter of Bank of United States. ...**July 13:** Henry Schoolcraft (1793–1864) locates source of Mississippi at Lake Itasca, Minnesota. ...**August 2:** Illinois militia massacres Black Hawk's tribe. Final removal of Sauk Indians across Mississippi River. ...**November 24:** South Carolina state convention declares tariffs of 1818 and 1832 null and void. ...**December 10:** President Jackson's Proclamation to South Carolina calls nullification absurd and threatens to use force to implement national tariffs.

1833: February 16: U.S. Supreme Court rules in *Barron v. Baltimore* that state governments are not subject to Bill of Rights. ...**March 2:** Compromise Tariff, sponsored by Henry Clay, reduces rates to 20 percent. ...Force Act authorizes president to collect tariffs, using army and navy if necessary. ...**March 3:** United States signs commercial treaty with Siam (Thailand) at Bangkok. ...**March 4:** Andrew Jackson is inaugurated for a second term.

Latin America

1831. Berbice, Demerara and Essequibo are united as British Guiana. ...From Mexico, Manuel José Arce leads an unsuccessful revolt against the United Provinces of Central America. ...Joachim Prieto becomes president of Chile. ...José Antonio Páez (1790–1873) becomes the first president of Venezuela.

1832. British sovereignty over Falkland Islands is proclaimed. ...Ecuador fails to annex part of Colombia.

German writer and dramatist Johann Wolfgang von Goethe.

1833. Constitution of Chile is promulgated. It will be in force until 1925. ...Slavery is abolished in Jamaica. ...Civil war breaks out in Ecuador. ...Antonio López de Santa Anna (1794–1876) becomes president of Mexico.

Africa, Asia & Pacific

1831. Major southern state of Mysore in India comes under British control. ...**August:** All Crown land in Australia is sold at auction for 5 shillings an acre.

Science, Invention & Technology

1831. Jane Stewart (fl. 19th century) of Scotland invents hook-and-latch fastener for clothing. ...**July:** American Cyrus McCormick (1809–1884) demonstrates his mechanical reaper.

Religion, Culture & Arts

1831. Victor Hugo: *Notre Dame de Paris*. ...Samuel Ruggles (1800–1881) creates Grammercy Park in New York City. ...John Constable: *Waterloo Bridge*. ...Vincenzo Bellini (1801–1835), Italian composer: *La Sonnambula*. ...Phi Beta Kappa becomes an honorary fraternity for students of academic distinction. ...First Jewish synagogue in Australia opens in Sydney. ...*Sydney Morning Herald*, oldest extant paper in Southern Hemisphere, is founded in Australia.

1831–1848: Honoré de Balzac (1799–1850) writes more than 50 volumes comprising *La Comédie Humaine* (*The Human Comedy*).

THE LIBERATOR.

Our Country is the World, our Countrymen are all Mankind.

BOSTON, FRIDAY, NOVEMBER 18, 1859.

PHILLIPS'S BROOKLYN LECTURE.

SELECTIONS.

EMERSON ON COURAGE.

◄ ***The first issue of the abolitionist newspaper the* Liberator *was published in 1831.***

1832. Sultan Sa'id of Oman and Muscat (1791–1856) in Arabia moves his capital to island of Zanzibar, which becomes leading trade and slaving center of East Africa. ...**April 15:** Turkey declares war on Egypt. ...**May:** Led by Abd-el-Kadar (1790–1869), emir of Mascara in northwestern Algeria, Berbers revolt against French penetration. ...**December 21:** Battle of Konya in Anatolia: Forces led by Ibrahim, son of Muhammad Ali Pasha of Egypt, devastate main Ottoman army and advance north toward Constantinople (Istanbul).

1832. French engineer Hippolyte Pixii (fl. 19th century) invents a hand-driven generator. ...Balloon frame construction is first used in design of a warehouse in Chicago. ...Rideau Canal between Bytown and Kingston, Ontario, is completed. ...**November 26:** A horse-drawn streetcar, the first in the world, begins operation in Manhattan.

1832. Polish Romantic poet and playwright Juliuzs Slowacki (1809–1849) publishes *Kordian* while in exile in France. It is first performed in Poland in 1899. ...Edward Bulwer-Lytton, first Lord Lytton (1803–1873), British novelist and statesman: *Eugene Aram*. ...Ballet dancer Maria Taglioni (1804–1884) introduces long white *tutu* of the Romantic style and dances long passages "on point." ...First concert by Polish composer Frédéric Chopin (1810–1849) in Paris. ...Horatio Greenough (1805–1852), sculptor, carves colossal figure of George Washington for Capitol. ...First meeting of Quakers in Australia is held in Hobart. ...**March 22:** Goethe (b. 1749) dies.

c. 1832. Ando Hiroshige (1797–1858) establishes a school of print design in Japan.

1833. Parliament renews charter of British East India Company, abolishing its trade in India and China and restricting it to administration of Indian territories. ...**February 20:** Russian squadron arrives in Bosporus to stop Muhammad Ali Pasha from overthrowing Ottomans. ...**May 4:** Ottoman sultan grants Syria and Adana to Muhammad Ali Pasha.

1833. American Walter Hunt (1796–1851) invents first practical sewing machine. ...American Obed Hussey (1792–1860) demonstrates his mechanical reaper.

1833. Robert Browning (1812–1889), English poet: *Pauline*. ...Scottish historian and essayist Thomas Carlyle's (1795–1837) *Sartor Resartus* first appears in *Fraser's Magazine*. It will be completed 1834. ...First public grant for education in Britain is awarded. ...Jules Michelet (1798–1874), French historian and passionate republican, begins 17-volume *Histoire de France*, which will be completed in 1867. ...Robert Mills (1781–1855) designs the Washington Monument. The actual building of the monument will not begin until 1848.

British Isles & Europe

1834. Zollverein joins Prussia and 17 other German states in customs union, providing free trade within German Confederation. ...**April 3:** Democrats riot in Frankfurt. ...**April 22:** Britain, France, Spain and Portugal form Quadruple Alliance to support governments in Spain and Portugal. ...**May 26:** Dom Miguel of Portugal surrenders and abdicates at Evoramonte.

1835. Russian government reduces Pale of Settlement, where Jews are allowed permanent residence, from 25 to 15 provinces. ...**March 2:** Francis I (b. 1768) of Austria, formerly Holy Roman Emperor Francis II, dies and is succeeded by Ferdinand I (1793–1875). ...**December 7:** First German railway opens between Nuremberg and Fürth.

1836. Chartism, workers political reform movement, is started in Britain. ...**October 29:** Louis-Napoléon's (1808–1873) military coup in Strasbourg fails, and he is exiled to the United States.

1837. Liberal constitution is adopted in Spain. ...Hanover is separated from Britain. ...**June 20:** William IV (b. 1765) of England dies and is succeeded by Queen Victoria.

U.S. & Canada

1834. York, Ontario, is renamed Toronto. ...William Sublette (c. 1799–1845) and Robert Campbell (1804–1879) found Fort Laramie in present-day Wyoming. ...**January 29:** U.S. troops end strike on Chesapeake and Ohio Canal. It is the first such federal intervention. ...**April 14:** New Whig Party is formed to oppose President Andrew Jackson's policies. ...**June 15:** N. J. Wyeth (1802–1856), a fur trader, establishes Fort Hall, the first settlement in Idaho. ...**June 30:** Congress establishes Department of Indian Affairs. ...**October 28:** Seminole Indians are ordered to evacuate Florida, by order of treaty of May 9, 1832.

1835. January: U.S. national debt is paid off. ...**June 1–5:** Fifth National Negro Convention, meeting in Philadelphia, urges blacks not to use terms *African* and *colored* when referring to Negro institutions, organizations, and themselves. ...**July 6:** Chief Justice of the United States John Marshall (b. 1755) dies. ...**July 8:** Liberty Bell cracks while tolling for death of Marshall. ...**November:** Chief Osceola (c.1800–1838) resists removal to West, setting off Second Seminole War in Florida. ...**December 28:** Seminoles massacre General Wiley Thompson (b. 1781) and his troops at Fort King. ...Seminoles massacre 100 soldiers at Fort Brooke, Florida.

1836. February 23: Mexican president Antonio López de Santa Anna, leading more than 3,000 Mexican soldiers, besieges Alamo Mission at San Antonio, Texas. ...**March 2:** Texas declares its independence, and Sam Houston (1793–1863) takes command of army. ...**March 6:** Alamo falls. All its defenders are killed. ...**April 21:** Sam Houston's Texans defeat Mexican army at battle of San Jacinto. ...**June 15:** Arkansas enters Union as 25th state.

1837. The United States suffers its first great depression. ...**January 26:** Michigan enters Union as 26th state. ...**March 3:** U.S. Congress increases Supreme Court membership from seven to nine. ...**March 4:** Martin Van Buren (1782–1862) is inaugurated eighth president. ...**December 5–7:** Government crushes rebellion led by William Lyon Mackenzie (1795–1861) in Toronto in Upper Canada. ...**December 8:** Wendell Phillips (1814–1884) delivers first of his many abolitionist tirades.

Latin America

1834. The United Provinces of Central America move their capital from Guatemala to San Salvador. ...Independence movement begins in Cuba. ...Slavery is abolished in British Guiana, Barbados and Bahamas.

1835. Peru and Bolivia unite in a federal state. ...Juan Manuel de Rosas (1793–1877) establishes dictatorship in Argentina. ...Liberal revolt fails to remove conservatives from power in Chile. ...Niterói becomes capital of Rio de Janeiro state. ...Earthquake nearly destroys Concepción, Chile. ...Vicente Rocafuerte (1783–1847) becomes the second president of Ecuador. ...Manuel Ceferino Oribe (1792–1857) becomes president of Uruguay.

1836. Mexico loses Texas territory to United States and Mexican president Antonio López de Santa Anna is captured by Americans. ...Bolivia invades Peru.

1837. Rafael Carrera (1814–1865) of Guatemala leads attack against United Provinces of Central America.

Africa, Asia & Pacific

1834. Port Philip Bay in Melbourne, Australia is settled, beginning colony of Victoria. ...British Parliament passes South Australia Colonization Act, which allows British settlement of Australia. ...Sixth Kaffir War begins when Xhosa invade British controlled territory in southeastern Cape Province. ...British annex Pitcairn Island. ...Slavery is abolished throughout British empire, with limited compensation to owners. ...**May 6:** Sikhs capture Peshawar (in present-day Pakistan) from Durrani.

1835. Sixth Kaffir War ends. Victorious British annex Adelaide province. ..."Great Trek" begins as some 12,000 Dutch settlers (Boers) flee British oppression in Cape of Good Hope. They eventually found republics of Natal, Transvaal and Orange Free State. ...Ottoman troops land in Tripoli and impose direct rule. ...Hon-jong (?–1849) becomes king of Korea. ...Muhammad (?–1849) becomes shah of Persia. ...Dost Muhammad (?–1863) becomes ruler of Afghanistan, taking title of emir and founding Barakzai dynasty. ...Queen of Madagascar outlaws Christianity and orders British missionaries to leave.

1836. Treaty of friendship and commerce between Hawaii and Britain is signed. ...**December 26:** A colony is founded in south Australia.

1837. Dutch settlers found Natal Republic (in present-day South Africa). ...Tharawaddi Min (?–1846) becomes king of Burma. ...British and regional languages replace Persian in government and law courts of India. ...**May 30:** Treaty of Tafna defines boundaries in Algeria between ports under French control and inland territories held by Abd-el-Kadar. ...**November:** Promised Russian support, Shah Muhammad of Iran besieges Afghan city of Herat.

Science, Invention & Technology

1834. Cyrus McCormick patents his mechanical reaper. ...Englishman Charles Babbage (1792–1871) creates model of an analytical engine, which works mathematical tables.

1835. German Justus von Liebig (1803–1873) develops silvering process for mirrors. ...Halley's comet returns, and its appearance is carefully recorded by observers around the world.

c. 1835. Bleaching powders are used to whiten cotton fabric.

1836. American John Daniell (1790–1845) invents an improved zinc-copper battery. ...First fiberglass-making technique is patented in France. ...**February 25:** Samuel Colt (1814–1862) secures his first patent for a revolving barrel multishot firearm.

1837. American Erastus Bigelow (1814–1879) develops a power loom for weaving lace. ...Charles Wheatstone (1802–1875) and William Cooke (1806–1879) develop and patent the telegraph in Britain. ...**July 21:** First railroad in Canada opens from La Prairie on St. Lawrence River to St. Johns on Richelieu River.

Religion, Culture & Arts

1834. Adam Mickiewicz: *Pan Tadeusz* (*Lord Thaddeus*), narrative poem about rural life in Poland's province of Lithuania. ...Zygmunt Krasinski (1812–1859), Polish Romantic poet: *Nieboska Komedia* (*Undivine Comedy*). ...Angel de Saavedra, duque de Rivas (1791–1863): narrative poem *El Moro Expósito*, first major work of the Spanish Romantic movement. ...Edward Bulwer-Lytton: *The Last Days of Pompeii*. ...**December:** First Baptist minister arrives in Australia.

1835. Robert Browning: *Paracelsus*. ...Charles Dickens (1812–1870) writes *Sketches by Boz*. ...Georg Büchner (1813–1837), German dramatist: *Danton's Death*. ...Gaetano Donizetti (1797–1848) writes his most famous opera, *Lucia di Lammermoor*, which is based on a novel by Sir Walter Scott. ...David Friedrich Strauss (1808–1874), German theologian, writes *Das Leben Jesu* (*Life of Jesus*), which holds that none of the Gospels is factually accurate.

1835–1872. Hans Christian Andersen (1805–1875) writes 168 fairy tales.

1836. Dickens: *Pickwick Papers*. ...Captain Frederick Marryat (1792–1848), British novelist: *Midshipman Easy*. ...Leopold von Ranke (1795–1886) writes *History of the Popes*. ...Alphonse de Lamartine: *Jocelyn*. ...Ralph Waldo Emerson (1803–1882), American philosopher, essayist and poet, leader of Transcendental movement: *Nature*. ...Arthur Schopenhauer: *Uber den Willen in der Natur* (*On the Will in Nature*). ...**December 9:** Opera *Ivan Susanin* (*A Life for the Tsar*) by Mikhail Ivanovich Glinka (1804–1857) opens in St. Petersburg.

1837. Struggle exists between state and Roman Catholic Church in Prussia. ...Thomas Carlyle: *French Revolution*. ...Dickens: *Oliver Twist*. ...Durham University is founded. ...Hector Berlioz (1803–1869), French composer: *Requiem, La Grande Messe des Morts*. ...Nathaniel Hawthorne (1804–1864), American novelist and short-story writer known for his themes of secret guilt and spiritual arrogance: *Twice Told Tales*. ...**March 31:** John Constable (b. 1776) dies.

British Isles & Europe

1838. November 30: France declares war on Mexico over debts.

▲A depiction of the Chinese destroying British-owned opium in Canton in July 1839.

1839. Construction begins on railroad from Warsaw to Vienna. It will be completed in 1848. ...**March 9:** First prohibition of child labor comes into force in Prussia. ...**April 19:** Treaty of London finally establishes international status of Belgium: The Scheldt is closed; Luxembourg becomes an independent grand duchy. Great powers guarantee that Belgium is "independent and perpetually neutral state."

1840. Frederick William III (b. 1770) of Prussia dies and is succeeded by Frederick William IV (1795–1861). ...**August:** Louis-Napoléon again attempts to seize power. ...**October 10:** William I of Holland resigns in favor of his son, William II (1792–1849). ...**December 15:** The remains of Napoléon I are transferred to Hôtel des Invalides, Paris.

1841. First law for the protection of workers in France is passed. ...**July 13:** At the Convention of the Straits, Britain, Russia, Austria, Prussia and France reaffirm that Bosporus and Dardanelles are closed to all foreign warships in peacetime. ...Russia loses privileged position gained by 1833 Treaty of Unkiar Skelessi. ...**August 28:** Robert Peel (1788–1850) becomes British prime minister.

U.S. & Canada

1838. Abolitionists organize Underground Railroad, assisting slaves in their escape to the North. ...More than 14,000 Cherokee in Georgia, Alabama and Tennessee are forced to travel west to Oklahoma along "Trail of Tears." ...**January 3–12:** U.S. Senate passes "Calhoun's Resolutions," which states that Congress will not interfere with slavery in states, territories or District of Columbia. ...**May 29:** John Lambton (1792–1840), earl of Durham, arrives in Canada as governor-in-chief. He is charged with investigating causes of unrest. ...**July 7:** U.S. Congress designates all railroads as postal routes. Stage coaches are used between rail lines. ...**August 18:** First U.S. maritime exploration, under Charles Wilkes (1798–1877), sets out to survey Pacific Ocean and South Seas. ...**December 3:** Joshua Giddings (1795–1864), representative from Ohio, becomes first abolitionist seated in Congress.

1839. Mississippi is first state to allow women to control their own property. ...John Sutter (1803–1880) founds Swiss settlement that becomes Sacramento, California. ...**February 4:** Lord Durham submits his report to colonial office which advocates colonial self-government and legislative union between Upper and Lower Canada. ...**February 20:** U.S. Congress forbids dueling in District of Columbia. ...**July:** Slaves take over Spanish ship *Amistad* off Cuba, kill most of crew and land in the United States.

1840. U.S. Census records a population of 17,069,453. ...**March 31:** U.S. federal employees are limited to ten-hour workday on public-works jobs. ...**July 4:** Independent Treasury Act sets up federal depositories ("sub-treasuries") independent of state banks and private businesses.

1841. First large group of Americans (48 wagons) migrates to California over Oregon Trail. ...**February 5:** Upper Canada (Ontario) and Lower Canada (Quebec) are united. ...**February 10:** Kingston is chosen as Canada's capital. ...**March 4–April 4:** President William Henry Harrison (b. 1773) dies a month after his inauguration. **April 6:** John Tyler (1790–1862) is inaugurated U.S. president. ...**March 9:** U.S. Supreme Court frees slaves who seized *Amistad*, ruling that they had been kidnapped in Africa.

Latin America

1838. Uruguay declares war on Argentina. ...Manuel Ceferino Oribe is forced to resign as president of Uruguay. ...Siege of Montevideo begins. ...Nicaragua leaves United Provinces of Central America. ...Rafael Carrera captures Guatemala City, and the United Provinces of Central America begins to disintegrate further. ...Slavery is abolished in Jamaica.

1839. American traveler John Lloyd Stephens (1805–1852) discovers and examines the antiquities of ancient Mayan civilization in Central America. ...Carrera proclaims Guatemala a sovereign republic. ...José Antonio Páez serves second term as Venezuelan president. ...Chile attacks Bolivia and Peru, dissolving union between the two countries. ...San Salvador becomes capital of an independent El Salvador.

1839–1845. Juan José Flores serves a second term as president of Ecuador.

1840. Francisco Morazán (1792–1842), president of the United Provinces of Central America, which began dissolving in 1838, resigns.

1841. Gold is discovered on boundary between Venezuela and British Guiana. ...Cathedral of Roseau is constructed in Charlotte Town, Dominica. ...Earthquake damages Cartago, Costa Rica.

Africa, Asia & Pacific

1838. Dutch settlers found the Transvaal Republic in present-day South Africa. ...Ieyoshi (?–1853) becomes shogun of Japan. ...**February**: King Dingaan (c. 1793–1843) of Zulu massacres some 60 Boer settlers and destroys Durban. ...**August 1:** Slavery is abolished in India. ...**October 1:** First Afghan War between Britain and Afghanistan begins. ...**November 1:** Prepaid postage scheme, the first in British empire, is introduced in Australia. ...**December 16:** Boers, led by Andreas Pretorius (1799–1853), defeat Zulu on Blood River, Natal.

1839. British force advances to Kabul, deposes Dost Muhammad and reinstates Shuja (?–1842) as shah. ...Boers found city of Pietermaritzburg in Republic of Natal. ...**January 1:** Australian government ends assignment of male convicts to private persons. ...Edward Wakefield (1796–1862) founds second New Zealand Company, buys out rights of earlier company and sells land to prospective colonists. ...**June 27:** Death of Ranjit Singh (b. 1780), Sikh ruler, allows British to take over Punjab. ...**July:** China seizes British-owned opium in Guangzhou (Canton), sparking first Opium War.

1840. Menen Leben Amede (?–1853) becomes empress of Ethiopia, commanding an army as regent for her son. ...Umpanda (?–1872) defeats Dingaan, and becomes king of Zulu. ...**January 22:** First British colonists land in New Zealand. ...**August 1:** Britain ends transportation of convicts to New South Wales, Australia. ...**November 27:** According to Convention of Alexandria, Muhammad Ali Pasha abandons claims to Syria and returns Ottoman navy in return for hereditary rule in Egypt.

1841. New Zealand Company founds town of Nelson on south side of Cook Strait. ...Edward Eyre (1815–1901) crosses Australia from Adelaide in east to Albany in west, exploring interior deserts. ...British companies in Niger Delta begin widespread production of palm oil. ...Sultan of Brunei in northern Borneo cedes Sarawak to Sir James Brooke (1803–1868), who rules as sultan until 1868. ...Afghans rise against British and murder British envoys.

Science, Invention & Technology

1838. Englishman Isambard K. Brunel (1806–1859) launches his *Great Western* steamship and invents the caisson for construction of London docks. ...Englishman William Grove (1811–1896) discovers process for making fuel cells. ...American inventor John Deere (1804–1886) makes his first three plows.

1839. A power loom is invented in Scotland. ...Microfilm is invented. ...American Charles Goodyear (1800–1860) discovers vulcanization, the process of hardening crude rubber. ...Joseph Whitworth (1803–1887) invents a movable planing machine (planer). ...French identify Caisson disease (the bends). ...**January 12:** Use of anthracite coal to smelt iron is introduced in Mauch Chunk, Pennsylvania.

1840. American James Bogardus (1800–1874) begins the manufacture of cast-iron beams for self-supporting building frames. ...American Samuel Morse (1791–1872) patents his telegraph signs, the dot-dash system. The system will become known as the Morse Code. ...**May 1:** First postage stamp is issued in Britain.

1841. First baby bottle is patented in United States. ...Englishman John Lawes (1814–1900) patents method of producing superphosphate fertilizer from phosphate rock. ...Englishman Frederick Moleyns (fl. 19th century) obtains patent on first incandescent lightbulb. ...American Ezra Cornell (1807–1874) purchases rights to a patented plow.

Religion, Culture & Arts

1838. Charles Dickens: *Nicholas Nickleby*. ...Hendrik Conscience (1812–1883): *De Leeuw van Vlaenderen*, immensely popular Flemish historical novel. ...Jenny Lind (1820–1887), Swedish soprano, makes her debut in Stockholm. ...Henry H. Richardson (d. 1886), architect renowned for his massive Romanesque-inspired buildings, is born. ...Victor Hugo's play *Ruy Blas* is performed for the first time; it is a triumphant success.

1839. Stendhal: *La Chartreuse de Parme* (*The Charterhouse of Parma*). ...Amandine-Aurore-Lucile Dudevant, known as George Sand (1804–1876), French novelist: *Spiridion*. ...J. M. W. Turner: *The Fighting Téméraire*. ...Frédéric Chopin publishes his 24 preludes. ...Nikolai Vasilyevich Gogol (1809–1852), Russian playwright and novelist: *Taras Bulba*. ...**November 20:** John Williams (b. 1796), English missionary to South Pacific since 1816, is eaten by cannibals in New Hebrides.

1840. Pierre-Joseph Proudhon (1809–1865), French socialist: *Qu'est-ce que la propriété? 'C'est le vol!'* (*What Is Property? It Is Theft*). ...Definitive version of *I Promessi Sposi* by Alessandro Manzoni (1785–1873), Italian poet and novelist. ...Robert Browning: *Sordello*. ...Dickens: *Old Curiosity Shop*; *Barnaby Rudge*. ...J. M. W. Turner exhibits *Rain, Steam and Speed*, a painting characteristic of his later style. ...Thomas Carlyle: *Chartism*.

1841. Ludwig Feuerbach (1804–1872), German philospher: *Essence of Christianity*. ...Arthur Schopenhauer: *Die beiden Grundprobleme der Ethik* (*The Basis of Morality*). ...Horace Greeley (1811–1872) launches *New York Tribune*. ...Carlyle: *On Heroes, Hero-Worship, and the Heroic in History*. ...Browning: *Pippa Passes*. ...New York Jesuits found St. John's College. It will become Fordham University. ...**July 17:** Humor magazine *Punch* is first published in London. ...Ralph Waldo Emerson: *Essays*.

British Isles & Europe

1842. Britain bans child and female labor underground. ...Construction begins on railroad between Moscow and St. Petersburg. It is completed in 1851. ...**August:** Chartist riots break out in British manufacturing districts.

1843. First workers cooperative society (Pioneers of Rochdale) is established in Britain. ...**November 8:** Queen Isabella II of Spain is declared of age.

1844. Factory Act regulates working hours of women and children in Britain. ...First trade union in Germany is founded. ...**June:** Nicholas I of Russia makes state visit to London. ...**August:** Potato blight in Ireland begins.

1845. Catholic cantons in Switzerland form league (Sonderbund) to protect their interests against Liberal cantons.

U.S. & Canada

1842. Massachusetts Supreme Court rules that trade unions and strikes are legal. ...In *Prigg v. Pennsylvania*, U.S. Supreme Court rules that states have no power to help or hinder slaves who attempt to escape. ...**May:** Colonel John Frémont (1813–1890) draws first expedition maps of Oregon Trail through Rocky Mountains. ...**June 25:** Members of Congress will henceforth be elected from districts. ...**August 9:** Webster-Ashburton Treaty defines frontier between Canada and Maine along 49th parallel.

1843. March 16: Hudson's Bay Company founds Fort Victoria. ...**May 2:** American settlers in Oregon set up a provisional government. ...**August 14:** Second Seminole War ends. ...**August 30–31:** National convention of abolitionist Liberty Party nominates candidates for president and vice president.

1844. February 28: U.S. secretary of state and secretary of the navy, among others, are killed when a gun explodes on board U.S.S. *Princeton*; President John Tyler, also on board, is unharmed. ...**March 6**: John Calhoun becomes secretary of state. ...**May 10:** Canada's capital is moved from Kingston to Montreal. ...**June 26:** Julia Gardiner (1820–1889) weds John Tyler. Tyler is first president to marry while in office. ...**August 13:** Revised New Jersey constitution introduces direct election of governor and ends property qualifications for voting.

1845. January 16: U.S. treaty with China opens five ports to American businessmen. ...**March 3:** Florida enters Union as 27th state. ...U.S. Congress, for first time, passes a bill over a presidential veto. ...**March 5:** James Knox Polk (1795–1849) is inaugurated 11th U.S. president. ...**May:** General Zachary Taylor (1784–1850) leads U.S. troops in advance to Corpus Christi, Texas, near Mexican border. ...**May 19:** Sir John Franklin (1786–1847) leaves London with *Erebus* and *Terror* in search of Northwest Ppassage. All expedition members will perish after the ships are abandoned in April 1848. ...**June 17:** Louis Papineau (1786–1871), former rebel, is elected to Canadian Parliament. ...**October 10:** U.S. Naval Academy opens at Annapolis, Maryland. ...**December 29:** Texas enters Union as 28th state.

Latin America

1842. Dominican University in Havana is secularized and expanded. ...Francisco Morazán invades Costa Rica in an attempt to restore United Provinces of Central America. ...José Fructuoso Rivera and Manuel Ceferino Oribe, both of Uruguay, oppose each other in nine-year civil war marked by siege of Montevideo.

1843. Slave population of Cuba grows to an estimated 436,000. ...President Jean-Pierre Boyer of Haiti is exiled. ...University of Costa Rica is founded in San Jose. ...Manuel José Arce is exiled for leading a third unsuccessful revolt in El Salvador.

1844. Mexico is shaken by military revolts. ...Revolt in Santo Domingo results in expulsion of Haitians. ...Carlos Antonio Lopez (1790–1862) becomes supreme dictator of Paraguay. ...Decisive battle for Dominica's independence is fought at Santiago de los Caballeros. ...Spanish suppress slave uprising in Cuba. ...Pedro Santana (1801–1864) is elected first president of the Dominican Republic.

1845. German immigrants found Petropolis, Brazil. ...Ramón Castilla (1797–1867) seizes the presidency of Peru, initiating a reform administration. ...Rivera is exiled from Uruguay. ...Antonio López de Santa Anna is exiled from Mexico.

1845–1849. Tomás Cipriano de Mosquera (1798–1878) becomes president of Colombia.

◄ American inventor Samuel Morse with his magnetic telegraph in 1845.

Africa, Asia & Pacific

1842. France annexes Marquesas Islands and establishes protectorate over Tahiti and Society Islands. ...British grant limited self-government to Australian colony of New South Wales. ...Troops establish British authority over Boers in Natal. ...**January:** Rebels murder the shah and massacre all 3,000 British soldiers in Afghanistan. ...**August 29:** Treaty of Nanking ends war in China, opens five ports to English merchants and cedes Hong Kong to England.

1843. Gambia in West Africa becomes a British colony. ...**May 12:** Natal is proclaimed a British colony. ...**November 28:** Britain and France recognize independence of Hawaiian Islands and promise not to annex them. ...**December 13:** British government promises Moshesh I (?–1870), king of Basutoland, protection from white settlers.

1844. March 6: Fante chiefs sign treaties known as Bond of 1844, recognizing British sovereignty over Gold Coast (present-day Ghana). ...**May 31:** British combine Natal with Cape Colony for administrative purposes. ...**August 6:** French bombard Tangier and occupy Mogador as war with Morocco begins. ...**August 14:** French troops defeat combined forces of Moroccans and Algerians led by Abd-el-Kadar at Isly in northeastern Morocco. ...**September 10:** Treaty of Tangier ends Franco-Moroccan War. Sultan of Morocco recognizes French occupation of Algeria.

1845. Anglo-French expedition against Madagascar is launched. ...**March 18:** By Convention of Lalla Maghnia, France and Morocco set boundary between Morocco and Algeria. ...**December 11:** Anglo-Sikh War begins.

English novelist Charles Dickens became famous after writing* Pickwick Papers. *"Phiz" (Hablot K. Browne) created this illustration for Dickens's serialized version, published from April 1836 to November 1837.

Science, Invention & Technology

1843. Aneroid barometer is invented in Italy. ...Isambard K. Brunel completes the Thames River tunnel. ...Englishman Charles Wheatstone invents the rheostat, electric bridge circuit. ...Ezra Cornell invents a trench-digging machine. ...First seafood cannery opens in Maine.

1844. Swede Gustav Pasch (fl. 19th century) invents the safety match.

1845. American Edmund Maynard (1813–1891) develops percussion priming system for firearms. ...Frenchmen Jean Foucault (1819–1868) and Armand Fizeau (1819–1896) produce first pictures of the sun with their clock-drive solar camera. ...Robert Thomson (1822–1873) of Scotland invents the pneumatic tire. ...George Lennox (1821–1886) of England invents an iron buoy. ...**May 24:** Samuel Morse sends first telegraph message ("What hath God wrought!") from Washington, D.C., to Baltimore.

c. 1845. Canadian Abraham Gesner (1797–1864) invents kerosene.

Religion, Culture & Arts

1842. Thomas Babington Macaulay (1800–1859), British poet, historian and statesman: *Lays of Ancient Rome*. ...Auguste Comte (1798–1857), French philosopher: *Cours de philosophie positive* (*The Course of Positive Philosophy*) ...Nikolai Gogol: *Dead Souls*. ...**October 20:** *Rienzi* by Richard Wagner (1813–1883) is first performed in Dresden, Germany. ...**December 7:** New York Philharmonic gives its first concert.

1843. Wagner: *Der Fliegende Hollander*, (*The Flying Dutchman*), first performance in Dresden. ...Macaulay: *Critical and Historical Essays*. ...Charles Dickens: *A Christmas Carol*. ...**May 18:** Scottish Church is disrupted, and Free Church of Scotland is establishment.

1844. Christian Friedrich Hebbel (1813–1863), German dramatist: *Mary Magdalen*. ...Alexandre Dumas (1802–1870), French writer: *The Three Musketeers*. ...Ludwig Tieck's (1773–1853) satiric fairy tale play *Der Gestiefelte Kater* (*Puss in Boots*) is first produced. ...**March 9:** Giuseppe Verdi's (1813–1901) opera *Ernani* opens in Venice. ...**June 27:** A mob in Carthage, Illinois, kills Mormon leader Joseph Smith (b. 1805). ...**August 8:** In Nauvoo, Illinois, Mormons name Brigham Young head of their church.

1845. Benjamin Disraeli: *Sybil*. Prosper Mérimée (1803–1870), French novelist and short-story writer: *Carmen*. ...Edgar Allan Poe: *The Raven and Other Poems*. ...Wagner: *Tannhäuser*. ...**May 1:** Methodist Church in America splits because of controversy over slavery, and Methodist Episcopal Church South is founded in Louisville, Kentucky.

British Isles & Europe

1846. March: Austrian and Russian troops suppress uprising in Kraków, Poland. ...**May 16:** Revolution in Portugal. ...**June 30:** Lord John Russell (1792–1878) becomes British prime minister. ...**July 8:** Christian VIII (1786–1848) of Denmark repudiates independence of Schleswig-Holstein. ...**November 16:** Austria annexes Kraków, Poland.

1847. Swiss create unusual military system: All men serve in standing militia, with required training every two years. ...**February 22:** Royal troops defeat Portuguese insurgents. ...**May:** Poland is made a Russian province. ...**July 20:** Swiss parliament orders dissolution of Sonderbund. Catholic cantons refuse to dissolve league and civil war begins. ...**October 21–November 29:** Catholic cantons are defeated and Sonderbund is dissolved.

1848. February 21–24: Revolution erupts in Paris. Louis-Philippe abdicates. Republic is proclaimed. ...**April 13:** Sicily declares itself independent of Naples. ...**June 23–26:** Louis Cavaignac (1802–1857) suppresses rising of Paris workers. ...**August 9:** Austro-Sardinian truce is signed at Vigevano. ...**August 26:** Truce of Malmö between Denmark and Prussia. ...**September 7:** Serfdom in Austria is abolished. ...**September 8:** Naples recovers Sicily. ...**September 12:** New Swiss constitution creates federal union, modeled on United States, increasing powers of central government while preserving cantonal autonomy in local issues. ...**October 6:** Revolution erupts in Vienna. ...**November 12:** Republican constitution is adopted in France. ...**December 2:** Ferdinand I of Austria abdicates in favor of his nephew, Francis Joseph I (1830–1916). ...**December 5:** Prussian National Assembly is dissolved; constitution is granted. ...**December 10:** Louis-Napoléon is elected president of French Republic.

U.S. & Canada

1846. March: Negotiations between United States and Mexico over purchase of California and New Mexico fail. ...**May 8.** U.S. General Zachary Taylor defeats Mexicans at Palo Alto, north of the Rio Grande. ...**May 13:** United States declares war on Mexico. ...**August 18:** Colonel Stephen Kearney (1794–1848) occupies Santa Fe, New Mexico. ...**September 14:** Santa Anna becomes commander in chief of Mexican army. ...**September 24:** Taylor's forces take Monterrey, Mexico after bloody four-day siege. ...**December 6:** Colonel Kearney defeats Mexicans at San Pasqual, California. ...**December 28:** Iowa enters Union as 29th state.

1847. January 8–10: U.S. commodore Robert F. Stockton (1795–1866) defeats Mexican troops and occupies Los Angeles, California. **February 22–23:** At battle of Buena Vista, Mexico, General Taylor's 4,800 men trounce larger force under Santa Anna. **March 9:** General Winfield Scott (1786–1866) lands 10,000 men near Veracruz, Mexico, in America's first large-scale amphibious operation. **March 27:** Veracruz surrenders to General Scott. **April 18:** Heading for Mexico City, Scott's men drive Santa Anna's larger army out of Cerro Gordo pass. ...**June 30:** Slave Dred Scott (c. 1795–1858) sues in St. Louis Circuit Court, claiming that residence in free territory had made him a free man. ...**August 19–20:** At battle of Contreras, Mexicans suffer 1,500 dead, captured or wounded. ...**September 8:** General Scott takes Molino del Rey after day-long battle.

1848. In Montreal, Tories burn parliament buildings in protest against compensation to victims of 1837 rebellion in Lower Canada. For a time, parliament meets alternately in Toronto and Quebec City. ...New York State grants women property rights equal to those of men. ...**January 24:** Gold is discovered in California at Sutter's Mill. ...**February 2:** Mexican War ends by the Treaty of Guadalupe Hidalgo: United States "purchases," for $15 million, Texas, New Mexico, California, Utah, Nevada, Colorado and parts of Arizona and Wyoming. ...**March 11:** First elected cabinet takes power in Canada. ...**May 29:** Wisconsin enters Union as 30th State. ...**July 19–20:** Elizabeth Cady Stanton (1815–1902) and Lucretia Mott (1793–1880), among others, organize first women's rights convention at Seneca Falls, New York. One hundred attendees (68 women and 32 men) sign the Declaration of Sentiments.

Latin America

1846. Colombia grants United States transit rights across Isthmus of Panama. ...Jamaica loses its imperial preference tariff.

1847. Antonio López de Santa Anna is recalled from exile and made provisional president of Mexico. ...Second Pan-American Conference is held in Lima. ...José Fructuoso Rivera is again expelled from Uruguay. ...**September 14:** U.S. troops enter Mexico City.

1847–1859. Faustin Soulouque (1785–1867) rules as Haiti's last emperor.

1848. Santa Anna is exiled from Mexico again. ...British seize San Juan del Norte (Nicaragua). ...Slavery is abolished in Guadeloupe and Virgin Islands.

1848–1849. José Antonio Páez fails in two revolutions to topple the government of Venezuela.

1848–1851. Cubans agitate for United States to annex their island.

1848–1855. Trans-Panama railroad is built.

Africa, Asia & Pacific

1846. Led by Hugh Gough (1779–1869), British forces defeat Sikhs at Sobraon in northwestern India. ...U.S. commodore James Biddle (1783–1848) visits Edo Bay, but Japanese refuse to trade. ...Pagan Min (?–1852) becomes king of Burma. ...**March 9:** British annex Kashmir by Treaty of Lahore. ...**December 16:** Peace with Sikhs brings Punjab under British control.

1847. Liberia is proclaimed as independent state. ...Vietnamese emperor Tu Duc (originally Nguyen Phuoc Hoang Nham) (1829–1883) begins reign.

1848. Algeria is proclaimed part of France and organized into departments of Algiers, Oran and Constantine. ...France ends slavery in its colonies and possessions. ...Lord Dalhousie (1812–1860) becomes governor general of India. ...**February 3:** Sir Harry Smith (1787–1860) annexes territory between the Orange and Vaal Rivers in South Africa. ...**March:** Second Sikh War breaks out. ...**August 29:** Boers, defeated at Boomplatz, retire across the Vaal. ...**November 9:** Ibrahim (b. 1789), viceroy of Egypt, dies and is succeeded by Abbas I (1813–1854).

Science, Invention & Technology

1846. American Elias Howe (1819–1867) invents a mechanical sewing machine with a bobbin. ...Italian Ascanio Sobrero (1812–1888) invents highly volatile nitroglycerin. ...American Richard Hoe (1812–1862) invents the rotary printing press.

1847. American Joseph Francis (1801–1893) invents lifeboat with corrugated iron hull. ...**July 1:** First U.S. postage stamp, the five-cent Ben Franklin, is issued.

1848. American Dr. Henry Day (1808–1890) patents first pressure-sensitive tape. ...First gutta-percha golf balls are introduced. ...Chewing gum is first manufactured for commercial sale. ...**September:** U.S. and Canadian scientists found American Association for the Advancement of Science.

▲ ***U.S. general Zachary Taylor commanding his troops at Buena Vista.***

Religion, Culture & Arts

1846. George Sand: *La mare au diable* (*The Haunted Pool*). ...Edward Lear (1812–1888), English humorist and artist: *Book of Nonsense*. ...Nathaniel Hawthorne's collection of short stories, *Mosses from an Old Manse*, is published. ...Felix Mendelssohn: first performance of *Elijah* in Birmingham, England. ...**June 16:** Pius IX (1792–1878) is elected pope. ...**June 19:** First recorded baseball game resembling modern-day sport is played in Hoboken, New Jersey.

1847–1848. William Makepeace Thackeray (1811–1863), English novelist: *Vanity Fair*.

1847. Henry Wadsworth Longfellow (1807–1882), American poet: *Evangeline*. ...Charlotte Brontë (1816–1855), English novelist: *Jane Eyre*. ...Emily Jane Brontë (1818–1848), English novelist: *Wuthering Heights*. ...Alfred Tennyson: *The Princess*. ...Peter Petrovich Njegos (1813–1851): *The Mountain Wreath*, epic poem. ...France Preseren (1800–1849): poems, among the first published in Slovenian. ...Felix Mendelssohn (b. 1809), German composer, dies. ...Greek Orthodox and Roman Catholic clergy engage in bitter and sometimes violent dispute over rights in Church of Nativity in Bethlehem. ...**September 11:** American composer Stephen Foster's (1824–1864) "Oh! Susannah," his first success, is performed in Pittsburgh. ...**December 3:** American abolitionist Frederick Douglass (c.1817–1895) begins publishing his newspaper, *North Star*.

1848. New York publishers organize Associated Press. ...Louis Blanc (1811–1882), French writer: *Droit au travail* (*The Right to Work*)....John Stuart Mill (1806–1873), English philospher and economist: *Principles of Political Economy*. ...Henri Murger (1822–1861), French poet and novelist: *Scènes de la vie de Bohème* (*Scenes from an Artist's Life*). ...Polish opera *Halka* by Stanislaw Moniuszko (1819–1872) is first performed. ...**February:** Karl Marx (1818–1883) and Friedrich Engels (1820–1895): *Communist Manifesto*. ...**July 26:** University of Wisconsin is founded at Madison. ...**November 24:** Pius IX flees to Gaeta as revolution breaks out in Rome.

British Isles & Europe

1849. February 9: Rome is proclaimed republic under Giuseppe Mazzini (1805–1872). ...**March 4:** Austrian constitution is granted. ...**March 12:** Sardinia terminates truce. ...**March 23:** Austrians are victorious in Novara. Charles Albert (1798–1849) of Sardinia abdicates in favor of Victor Emmanuel II (1820–1878) after Austrian victory at Novara. ...**March 27:** German National Assembly passes constitution. ...**March 28:** Frederick William IV of Prussia is elected "Emperor of the Germans." ...**April 3:** Frederick William IV rejects imperial crown. ...**April 14:** Hungary declares itself independent of Austria. ...**May 7:** British Navigation Laws of 1651, 1661, 1662 and 1823 are repealed, signaling the decline of British mercantilism. ...**May 11:** Giuseppe Garibaldi (1807–1882) enters Rome. ...**May 15:** Sicily submits to Naples. ...**June:** Russian troops help Austria suppress Hungarian revolutionaries. ...**June 6:** German National Assembly moves to Stuttgart. ...**June 18:** Troops disperse German National Assembly. ...**July 3:** French take Rome. ...**August 6:** Peace of Milan between Austria and Sardinia is signed. ...**August 22:** Venice submits to Austria.

1850. France and Russia dispute control of holy sites in Palestine. ...**January:** British blockade Piraeus (harbor for Athens) in response to assault on British subject (Don Pacifico). ...**March:** Special banks are established in Prussia, enabling peasants to buy land rented from landlords. During insurrection in Hesse-Cassel, Austria supports the elector; Prussia, the insurgents. ...**March 20:** Union parliament meets at Erfurt, Germany. ...**May 31:** Universal suffrage is abolished in France. ...**July 2:** Peace of Berlin is signed between Denmark and Prussia; Prussia withdraws from Schleswig-Holstein. ...**August 2:** London convention between Britain, France, Russia, Sweden and Denmark maintains integrity of Denmark. ...**September 26:** Liberty of French press is restricted.

1851. Population of England and Wales is set at 17,920,609. ...Danilo I (1826–1860) abolishes office of prince-bishop and names himself secular prince of Montenegro. ...**May 1–15:** Great Exhibition is held in London. ...**May 12:** Liberty of Prussian press is restricted. ...**August 23:** German diet appoints committee to control small states and abolishes fundamental rights. ...**December 20:** New French constitution wins plebiscite. ...**December 31:** Austrian constitution is abolished.

U.S. & Canada

1849. Elizabeth Blackwell (1821–1910) is first American woman to receive a medical degree. ...U.S. Congress establishes Department of Interior, primarily to deal with Indians in West. ...Harriet Tubman (c. 1820–1913) escapes from slavery in Maryland. She will return to Maryland and Virginia at least 20 times and will rescue more than 300 slaves. ...**March 4:** Zachary Taylor is inaugurated 12th president of the United States.

The Mormons at Winter Quarters, Nebraska, before leaving for the Great Salt Lake.

1850. Flogging is outlawed in U.S. Navy. ...Seventh U.S. Census determines population is 23,191,876. ...**July 9:** President Taylor (b. 1784) dies. ...**July 10:** Millard Fillmore (1800–1874) is inaugurated 13th president of United States. ...**September 9:** California is admitted to United States as a free state. Texas, New Mexico and Utah territories are organized. "Popular sovereignty" provision allows their residents to decide whether or not to legalize slavery. ...**September 18:** Fugitive Slave Act places runaway slaves under exclusive federal jurisdiction and provides for special U.S. commissioners, who issue arrest warrants after a summary hearing. ...**September 20:** U.S. Congress forbids slave trade in District of Columbia. ...**September 28:** Brigham Young (1801–1877), Mormon leader, is appointed first governor of Utah.

1851. Clipper ship *Flying Cloud* reaches San Francisco from New York City in 89 days, 8 hours. ...**June 2:** Maine prohibits manufacture and sale of intoxicating beverages. ...**July 23:** Sioux give up lands in Iowa and Minnesota.

Latin America

1849–1859. Juan Rafael Mora Porras (1814–1860), conservative dictator of Costa Rica, organizes the resistance against William Walker (1824–1860), an American filibuster.

1850. Colón, Panama, is founded by builders of Panama railroad. ...Rosario is established as a port of entry in Argentina. ...**April 19:** Clayton-Bulwer Treaty between Britain and the United States guarantees neutrality of proposed canal across Central America and provides that neither country will attempt to dominate or colonize territories in Central America.

1850–1853. Guatemala and El Salvador are at war.

1850–1858. José Antonio Páez is exiled from Venezuela.

1851. Liberal revolt fails to remove Conservatives from power in Chile. ...Mariano Arista (1802–1855) becomes president of Mexico. ...**August 3:** General Narcisco López (c. 1798–1851) and his American followers land in Cuba and unsuccessfully preach rebellion. ...**August 16:** Fifty American followers of López are executed in Cuba. ...**September:** Spaniards suppress Cuban revolt.

Africa, Asia & Pacific

1849. David Livingstone (1813–1873), Scottish explorer and medical missionary, discovers Lake Ngami. ...French found Libreville in Congo, using freed slaves as settlers. ...**March 30:** Britain annexes Punjab.

A Chinese print depicting the Taiping Rebellion (1850–1864)

1850. Cape Frontier War (eighth Kaffir War) begins between British and Xhosa African natives. It will last until 1853. ...Livingstone discovers Zambezi River. ...**August 5:** By Australian Constitution Act, Victoria is separated from New South Wales and South Australia and Tasmania are granted representative government. ...**August 17:** Denmark sells its possessions on Gold Coast to Britain. ...**October:** Taiping Rebellion breaks out in China. More than 20 million peasants will lose their lives before rebellion is quelled in 1864.

1851. Hsien-feng (1831–1861) becomes emperor of China. ...Gold is discovered in New South Wales and Victoria, spurring settlement of Australia. ...British government dissolves New Zealand Company and pays members £268,000. ...France establishes trading port at Cotonou (in present-day Benin), as stipulated in treaty with king of Dahomey. ...United States warns France that it will not permit European countries to annex Hawaiian Islands. ...**July 1:** Victoria is proclaimed a separate colony.

Science, Invention & Technology

1849. Austrians are first to use aerial bombing from pilotless hot-air balloons.

1850. British chemist John Mercer (1791–1866) invents the mercerization process for treating cotton fabric. ...A wooden mechanical dishwasher is invented by a man in upstate New York.

c. 1850. Levi Strauss (c. 1829–1902) designs durable coveralls for California miners.

1851. Americans Horace Smith (1808–1893) and Daniel Wesson (1825–1906) develop the breech-loading rifle. ...William Talbot (1800–1877) invents the negative-positive photographic process. ...American Gail Borden (1801–1874) develops a dried-meat biscuit. ...American William Kelly (1811–1888) develops the pneumatic conversion process for making steel but fails to patent it. ...**August 12:** Isaac Singer (1811–1875) patents a sewing machine with continuous stitching.

Religion, Culture & Arts

1849. Thomas Babington Macaulay (1800–1859) begins work on the five-volume *History of England from the Accession of James the Second.* The last volume will be published in 1861. ...Alphonse de Lamartine: *Histoire de la révolution de 1848.* ...Pierre-Joseph Proudhon: *Confessions d'un révolutionnaire.* ...Elias Lönnrot (1802–1884), Finnish linguist, publishes a revised version of *Kalevala*, the national epic poem. ...Giacomo Meyerbeer (1791–1864): *The Prophet.* ...**October 17:** Frédéric Chopin (b. 1810) dies.

1850. Charles Dickens: *David Copperfield.* ...Alfred Tennyson: *In Memoriam.* ...Gustave Courbet (1819–1877), French painter, exhibits *The Stone Breaker* and *The Burial at Ornan* in France. ...Nathaniel Hawthorne: *The Scarlet Letter.* ...Elizabeth Barrett Browning (1806–1861), British poet: *Sonnets from the Portuguese.* ...Herman Melville (1819–1891), American writer, publishes the partly autobiographical novel *White Jacket.* ...*Harper's Monthly* magazine begins publication. ...Wilhelm Kettler (1811–1877) becomes Roman Catholic Bishop of Mainz, Germany, and champions Christian Socialism. ...**April 12:** Pius IX reenters Rome. ...**April 23:** William Wordsworth (b. 1770) dies. ...**August 18:** Honoré de Balzac (b. 1799) dies. ...**September 24:** Roman Catholic Church in Britain is reorganized.

1851. Hawthorne: *The House of the Seven Gables.* ...Herman Melville: *Moby Dick.* ...Sir Joseph Paxton (1801–1865) builds the Crystal Palace in London. ...**June 5:** Harriet Beecher Stowe's (1811–1896) *Uncle Tom's Cabin* is serialized in antislavery newspapers. ...**August 22:** Yacht *America* wins international race in Britain, beginning America's Cup series of races. ...**September 18:** *New York Times* begins publication. ...**December 17:** British painter J. M. W. Turner (b. 1775) dies.

British Isles & Europe

1852. French constitution gives president monarchical powers. ...**May 8:** Treaty of London signed by Britain, France, Russia, Austria, Prussia and Sweden guarantees integrity of Denmark. ...**July 26–27:** First Congress of Cooperative Societies meets in London. ...**September 14:** Duke of Wellington (b. 1769) dies. ...**November 4:** Count Camillo Benso di Cavour (1810–1861) becomes prime minister of kingdom of Piedmont-Sardinia. ...**December 2:** Louis-Napoléon proclaims himself Emperor Napoléon III.

1853. Hanover and Oldenburg join German Zollverein. ...Prussia prohibits child labor, making it illegal to hire children under 12. ...**April 19:** Russia claims protectorate over Christians in Turkey. ...**October 16:** Turkey declares war on Russia; military operations begin in the Balkans. ...**November 21:** French plebiscite favors imperial constitution. ...**November 30:** Turkish fleet is destroyed off Sinope.

1854. March 26: Charles III (b. 1823), duke of Parma, is murdered. ...**March 27 and 28:** Britain and France declare war on Russia, commencing the Crimean War. ...**April 9:** Russia is diplomatically isolated as Britain, France, Prussia and Austria support territorial integrity of Ottoman Empire. ...**May 18:** Western powers declare blockade of Greece for having attacked Turkey. Greece promises neutrality. ...**August 8:** Russia turns down proposals by Austria, Britain, and France at Conference of Vienna. These include independence of Danubian principalities and Serbia, international protection of Christians in Ottoman Empire, free navigation on Danube and revisions to 1841 Straits Agreement. ...**September 14:** Allied armies land in Crimea. ...**September 20:** British and French defeat Russians at battle of Alma. ...**September 26:** Siege of Sebastopol begins in Crimea. ...**October 25:** British defeat Russians at battle of Balaklava but sustain heavy casualties. ...**November 5:** Allies defeat Russians at battle of Inkerman.

1855. Paris hosts world exhibition. ...**January 26:** Piedmont-Sardinia joins allies in Crimean War. ...**February 7:** Russia and Japan sign treaty, dividing Kuril Islands and confirming joint possession of Sakhalin Island. ...**March 2:** Nicholas I (b. 1796) of Russia dies and is succeeded by Alexander II (1818–1881). ...**September 11:** Sebastopol capitulates to allies. ...**November 21:** Sweden allies with Britain and France against Russia. ...**November 28:** Kars (in Turkey) surrenders to Russians.

U.S. & Canada

1852. May: Catharine E. Beecher (1800–1878) forms American Women's Education Association in New York City. ...**October 6:** American Pharmaceutical Association is founded. It is the first nationwide trade association in the United States.

1853. March 4: Franklin Pierce (1804–1869) is inaugurated 14th president of the United States. ...**March 7:** Jefferson Davis (1808–1889) becomes secretary of war. ...**July 6–8**: National Negro Convention is held in Rochester, New York. ...**July 7:** New York Central Railroad is formed through merger of ten railroads. ...**July 8:** Commodore Matthew Perry's (1794–1858) squadron reaches Tokyo Bay.

1854. Antislavery Republican Party is founded. ...Amanda Way (1828–1914) organizes Women's Temperance Army to close Indiana bars. ...Asmum Institute (present-day Lincoln University) is chartered. It is the first black college in the United States. ...**March 31:** Commodore Perry signs first commercial treaty with Japan. ...**May 30:** Kansas–Nebraska Act establishes Kansas and Nebraska as separate territories. Act nullifies Missouri Compromise, which barred slavery from region, and allows inhabitants of a territory to decide whether to allow slavery. ...**June 5:** U.S.–Canadian Reciprocal Fishing Treaty (Elgin Treaty) grants fishing rights and lowers tariffs on agricultural products. ...**June 30:** U.S. Congress ratifies Gadsden Purchase. For $10 million, Mexico cedes a rectangular strip of territory along southern borders of Arizona and New Mexico, providing ideal route for a transcontinental railroad. ...**September–December:** Canadian law distributes land previously reserved for support of Protestant clergy to counties and cities for secular purposes.

1855. Britain grants Newfoundland greater autonomy, with appointed legislative council and elected house of assembly. ...Massachusetts ends racial segregation in public schools. ...**February 10:** U.S. Congress grants citizenship to children born abroad to American parents. ...**February 24:** First U.S. Court of Claims is created, allowing citizens to present claims against federal government. ...**March 30:** Amid armed violence, a proslavery legislature is returned in Kansas's first territorial election.

Latin America

1852. Argentine dictator Juan Manuel de Rosas is overthrown, and a constituent assembly meets at Santa Fe.

1853. Argentina puts a new constitution into effect. ...Buenos Aires refuses to participate in a constitutional congress and secedes from Argentina. ...Brazil bans importation of African slaves. ...Parana becomes capital of the Argentine Confederation. ...Colombia adopts a new constitution. ...**January:** Mariano Arista is forced to resign as president of Mexico, and Antonio López de Santa Anna is made president again.

1854. San Salvador is destroyed by an earthquake, and Nueva San Salvador is founded. ...José Fructuoso Rivera (b. 1788) dies on his way to Montevideo to become part of a ruling triumvirate.

▲ ***A battle scene from the Crimean War.***

1855. Gold is discovered in French Guiana. ...A revolution ousts Santa Anna from presidency of Mexico, and he is exiled for the last time. ...Managua becomes capital of Nicaragua. ...Panama railroad is completed.

Africa, Asia & Pacific

1852. Catastrophic floods alter course of Yellow River in China. ...New Zealand is divided into six provinces and granted limited self-government. ...Boers of Transvaal raid Dimawe (in present-day Botswana), capital of Kwena tribe....Al-Hajj Umar (1797–1864), Muslim Tukulor leader (in present-day Guinea), launches holy war against pagan Mandingo and Bambara kingdoms of western Sudan. ...**December 20:** Britain annexes Pegu.

1853. Iesada (?–1858) is shogun of Japan. ...**July 1:** British introduce new constitution for Cape Colony. Parliament is elected by all British subjects (of any race) who meets certain property or salary conditions. However, governor can override wishes of Parliament....**December 11:** Britain annexes Nagpur (in India).

1854. Britain acquires Kuria Muria Islands off Arabia. ...**February 14:** By Bloemfontein Convention, Britain recognizes independence of Boers' republic of Orange Free State....**March 31:** Treaty of Kanagawa provides for diplomatic and trade relations between United States and Japan, ending Japanese policy of isolation....**April:** J. P. Hoffman (fl. 19th century) is elected first president of Orange Free State....**May 24:** First colonial parliament convenes in New Zealand. ...**July 4:** Abbas I (b. 1813), viceroy of Egypt, dies and is succeeded by Said Pasha (1822–1863). ...**November 30:** Said Pasha grants concession for construction of Suez Canal to French engineer Ferdinand de Lesseps (1805–1894).

1855. Provincial parliaments of Australia exclude Chinese immigrants, beginning policy of "white Australia." ...Self-government is achieved in all Australian colonies except in Western Australia. ...Anglo-Afghan treaty against Persia is signed.

Science, Invention & Technology

1852. Jean Foucault uses pendulum suspended inside the Panthéon to demonstrate the earth's rotation. ...American Elisha Otis (1811–1861) invents a passenger elevator with safety device that prevents the car from dropping....James Smith (1814–1870), a Scottish-Canadian, develops the cough drop. ...German Johann Heinrich Wilhelm Geissler (1815–1879) perfects vacuum tubes at University of Bonn. ...American A. B. Little (c. 1820–1870) makes improvements on the steam-powered fire engine.

1854. A pencil with a rubber eraser at one end is invented.

1854–1868. Austrian monk Gregor Mendel (1822–1884) experiments with garden peas and other plants to establish Mendel's law on genetics.

1855. Celluloid is developed in Britain. ...Joshua Stoddard (1814–1902) of Vermont invents the calliope....Germans Johann Heinrich Wilhelm Geissler and Julius Plucker (1801–1868) conduct cathode ray research.

Religion, Culture & Arts

1852. William Makepeace Thackeray: *Henry Esmond*....Alexandre Dumas: *La Dame aux Camélias*....Ivan Sergeyevich Turgenev (1818–1883), Russian novelist and short-story writer: *A Sportsman's Sketches*. ...Kuno Fischer (1824–1907): *History of Modern Philosophy*....Harriet Beecher Stowe's *Uncle Tom's Cabin* is published in book form. It evokes sympathy in the North for slaves and greatly angers Southerners.

1853. Charles Kingsley (1819–1875), British author and clergyman: *Hypatia*. ...Elizabeth Gaskell (1810–1865), British novelist: *Cranford*. ...Charlotte Yonge (1823–1901), British novelist: *The Heir of Redclyffe*. ...John Ruskin (1819–1900), art critic, publishes *The Stones of Venice*....Jean-Baptiste Lamy (1814–1888), French-born Catholic missionary, becomes archbishop of Santa Fe, New Mexico.

1854. Henry David Thoreau (1817–1862): *Walden; or Life in the Woods*. ...Auguste Comte completes *Système de politique positive*. ...Hector Berlioz: *Te Deum*. ...Theodor Mommsen (1817–1903): *Roman History*. ...**October 2:** Opulent opera house, the Academy of Music, opens in lower Manhattan....**December 8:** Pope Pius IX declares that Mary's Immaculate Conception is an article of faith for Roman Catholics....**December 9:** Alfred Tennyson: *Charge of the Light Brigade*.

1855. Walt Whitman (1819–1892): *Leaves of Grass*. ...Joseph Gobineau (1816–1882), French diplomat: *Essai sur l'inégalité des races humaines* (*Essay on the Inequality of the Races*). ...Jacob Christopher Burckhardt (1818–1897), Swiss historian: *Cicerone*. ....Anthony Trollope (1815–1882): *The Warden*. ...Bozena Nemcová (1820–1862), *The Grandmother*, realistic novel influential in developing Czech language. ...Frederick E. Church (1826–1900), American nature painter of the Hudson River school: *The Heart of the Andes*.

British Isles & Europe

1856. Britain becomes first major European country to permit corporations with limited liability. ...**February 25–March 30:** At Peace Congress of Paris, the Black Sea is declared neutral and the Danube is open to free navigation, Turkey's integrity is guaranteed, Russia cedes Bessarabia, Great Powers guarantee Danubian principalities. ...**April 15:** Britain, France and Austria guarantee integrity and independence of Turkey. ...**April 16:** Declaration of Paris abolishes privateering, defines nature of contraband and blockade, recognizes principle of free ships, free goods. ...**July 17:** Modern Swiss banking system begins, as Swiss Credit Bank (Kreditanstalt) is founded in Zürich. ...**September 3:** Prussian royalists stage unsuccessful rising in Neufchâtel, Switzerland. ...**December 2:** Franco-Spanish frontier is fixed.

1857. June 19: Prussia renounces sovereignty over Neufchâteau.

1858. January 14: Felice Orsini (1819–1858) attempts assassination of Napoléon III to bring attention to cause of Italian unification. ...**July 21:** Napoléon III and Camillo Cavour (1810–1861) meet at Plombières to prepare unification of Italy. ...**November 8:** Boundaries of Montenegro are fixed. ...**December:** Serbian diet deposes Alexander Karageorgevic (1806–1885) and declares Milan Obrenovic (1854–1901) king.

1859. April 27: Revolution breaks out in Tuscany. ...**April 28:** Revolution breaks out in Modena. ...**May:** Francis II (1836–1894) succeeds Ferdinand II as king of Two Sicilies. ...**May 1:** Revolution breaks out in Parma. ...**May 3:** France declares war on Austria. ...**June 13–15:** Insurrections erupt in Ravenna, Ferrara and Bologna against rule by papacy. ...**June 24:** In very bloody battles at Solferino and San Martino, French force Habsburg forces to withdraw. ...**July 11:** Napoléon III and Austrian emperor Francis Joseph I meet at Villafranca. Piedmont obtains Lombardy and Parma. Tuscany and Modena kingdoms are restored. ...**August 16:** France extends amnesty and political rights. ...**November 10:** Treaty of Zürich confirms Villafranca Treaty.

U.S. & Canada

1856. May 21: One man is killed when supporters of slavery sack Lawrence, Kansas, which is part of Underground Railroad. ...**May 22:** Representative Preston Brooks (1819–1857) of South Carolina severely thrashes Senator Charles Sumner (1811–1874), of Massachusetts who allegedly insulted South Carolina and its senators. ...**May 24–25:** Abolitionist John Brown (1800–1859) and six followers murder five proslavery settlers at Pottawatomie Creek, Kansas. ...**June 17–19:** Republicans nominate John Frémont for president at their first national convention. ...**June 24:** Canadian Legislative Council (upper house of parliament), hitherto appointed, will henceforth be elected. ...**August 12:** First elected assembly meets on Vancouver Island. ...**September 15:** John W. Geary (1819–1873), newly appointed governor of Kansas, uses federal troops to quell factional fighting.

1857. March 4: James Buchanan (1791–1868) is inaugurated 15th president of the United States. ...**March 6:** In the *Dred Scott* decision chief justice of the United States Roger Taney, speaking for a majority on most points, rules that blacks cannot be citizens, that Congress cannot keep slavery out of territories, and that Missouri Compromise is thus unconstitutional.

1858. Ottawa is declared capital of Canada. ...**May 11:** Minnesota enters Union as 32nd state. ...**August 21–October 15:** Series of debates for Illinois senator between Abraham Lincoln (1809–1865) and Stephen Douglas (1813–1861) are held. ...**August 24:** Parliament creates colony of British Columbia (a name chosen by Queen Victoria) carved out of Hudson's Bay Company's territories.

1859. Constock Lode, first major silver deposit in the United States, is discovered in western Nevada. ...The last slave ship to reach the United States lands at Mobile Bay, Alabama. ...**February 14:** Oregon enters Union as 33rd State. ...**March 7:** In *Ableman v. Booth* U.S. Supreme Court upholds constitutionality of Fugitive Slave Act and rules that state courts may not interfere with cases in federal courts. ...**August 27:** Edwin Drake (1819–1880) strikes oil in Pennsylvania and establishes America's first oil well. ...**October 16:** Abolitionist John Brown leads a raid on U.S. arsenal at Harper's Ferry, Virginia. ...**October 17:** A detachment of Marines led by Colonel Robert E. Lee (1802–1870) recaptures Harper's Ferry's armory and arrests Brown and his followers.

Latin America

1856. Third Pan-American Conference is held in Santiago. ...William Walker, an American who joined a revolutionary faction in Nicaragua in 1855, is elected president of that country.

1857. Costa Rica helps to defeat William Walker, conqueror of Nicaragua. ...A liberal constitution is drafted in Mexico.

1858. Brothers José Tadeo Monagas (1784–1868) and José Gregorio Monagas (1795–1858) are overthrown in Venezuela. ...Colombia establishes a new constitution.

1858–1861. Civil war rages in Mexico.

1859. President Manuel Montt (1809–1880) of Chile crushes a liberal revolt. ...**October.** After a short war, Buenos Aires agrees to join the Argentine federation.

Africa, Asia & Pacific

1856. Tasmania becomes a self-governing colony. ...**February 13:** British annex Oudh (in India). ...**February 18:** Hatt-i Hümayun reform edict by Ottoman emperor guarantees civil rights of Christians and allows foreigners to acquire property. ...**October 8:** Second Anglo-Chinese War begins when Chinese search a Chinese-owned but British-registered junk. ...**November 1:** War breaks out between Britain and Persia. ...**November 3–4:** British fleet bombards Canton (China). ...**December 16:** Boers republic of Transvaal is organized as South African Republic under Marthinus Pretorius (1819–1901), with capital at Pretoria.

1857. March 29: Sepoy (native Indian) mutiny breaks out in India. ...**May 11:** Rebel Sepoy troops capture Delhi. ...**May 25–June 1:** Chinese fleet is destroyed by British navy. ...**September 19:** Delhi is recaptured by British. ...**December 6:** Kanpur is recaptured by British. ...**December 29:** British and French take Canton. ...Britain annexes Perim (in India).

1858. Iemochi (?–1866) is shogun of Japan. ...**May 28:** In Aigun Treaty with China, Russia annexes territory north of Amur River. ...**June 26:** In Treaty of Tientsin, China opens several ports and admits European ambassadors. ...**July 8:** Governor general of India declares that Sepoy mutiny has ended. ...**December:** France begins conquest of Indochina.

1859. February 17: French troops occupy Saigon in what will soon become French colony of Cochin China (present-day southern Vietnam). ...**April 20:** Dutch and Portuguese divide Timor and neighboring islands. ...**April 25:** Ferdinand de Lesseps begins work on Suez Canal. ...**May 13:** Queensland and New South Wales are separated. ...**October 22:** Spain declares war on Morocco.

Science, Invention & Technology

1856. George Esterly (1809–1893) patents a horse-drawn row cultivator. ...Frenchman Pierre Martin (1824–1915) develops the regenerative steel making process. It will be known as the Siemens-Martin process. ...Illinois Central Railroad reaches from Chicago to Cairo in southern Illinois. It is the longest line in the United States. ...First railroad in California is built from Sacramento to Folsom. ...**April 21:** First U.S. railroad bridge is erected. It crosses Mississippi River at Rock Island, Illinois.

1857. Englishman Thomas Cochrane (1775–1860) invents compressed air rock drill for tunneling. ...Elisha Otis installs first passenger elevator in a five-story New York City department store. ...In Chicago George M. Pullman (1831–1897) begins building sleeping cars for railroads.

1858. American John Mason (fl. 19th century) invents the mason jar. ...American Ezra Warner (fl. 19th century) patents the can opener.

1859. Frenchman Jean Lenoir (1822–1900) develops the first internal combustion engine. ...Frenchman Gaston Planté (1834–1889) invents a rechargeable storage battery. ...First electric lighthouses are built in Britain. ...Charles Darwin (1809–1892), British naturalist, writes *On the Origin of Species by Means of Natural Selection.*

Religion, Culture & Arts

1856. Ralph Waldo Emerson: *English Traits.* ...James Froude (1818–1894), British historian: *History of England.* ...Gustave Flaubert (1821–1880), French novelist: *Madame Bovary.* ...**February 17:** German poet Heinrich Heine (b. 1797) dies.

1857. Anthony Trollope: *Barchester Towers.* ...Charles Dickens: *Little Dorrit.* ...National Portrait Gallery is founded in London. ...William Makepeace Thackeray: *Virginians.* ...Charles Baudelaire (1821–1867): *Les fleurs du mal.* ...Frederick E. Church (1826–1900): *Niagara Falls.* ...Elizabeth Barrett Browning: *Aurora Leigh*, best-selling novel in verse.

1858. Alfred Tennyson: *Idylls of the King.* ...Thomas Michael Madhusudna Dutt (1824–1873), poet and playwright in Bengali: *Sarmistha.* ...Thomas Carlyle: *Frederick the Great.*

1859. John Stuart Mill: *On Liberty.* ...Jacques Offenbach (1819–1880): *Orpheus in the Underworld.* ...George Sand: *Elle et lui.* ...Mary Ann Evans (1819–1880), known as George Eliot, British novelist: *Adam Bede.* ...First performance of opera *Faust* by Charles François Gounod (1818–1893). ...Mathew Brady (1823–1896) sets up photography studios in New York and Washington, D.C. ...Bahai faith is introduced to United States from Persia. ...**April 4:** "Dixie," national song of Confederacy, is first sung publicly (in New York City). ...**July 1:** In first intercollegiate baseball game, Amherst defeats Williams 73–32.

British Isles & Europe

1860. Power of Austrian Reichsrat is enlarged. ...**March 13–15:** Plebiscites in Tuscany, Parma, Modena, Romagna favor union with Piedmont. ...**April 15–22:** Plebiscites in Nice and Savoy favor union with France. ...**May 5:** Giuseppe Garibaldi and his 1,000 Redshirts sail from Genoa for Sicily. ...**May 11:** Garibaldi's forces land at Marsala in western Sicily and march inland toward Palermo. ...**May 27:** Garibaldi's forces take Palermo and set up provisional government. ...**July 20:** Garibaldi defeats Bourbon troops at Milazzo. Bourbon troops evacuate Sicily, except Messina. ...**August 22:** Garibaldi's soldiers, with connivance of British government, cross straits to Italy. ...**September 7:** Garibaldi enters Naples. ...**October 20:** New Austrian constitution is adopted.

1861. January 2: Frederick William IV (b. 1795) of Prussia dies and is succeeded by William I (1797–1888). ...**February 26:** Austrian constitution is centralized, giving more power to a central legislature. ...**March 3:** Serfs in Russia are emancipated. ...**March 17:** Victor Emmanuel II is proclaimed king of Italy. ...**April 2:** First Italian parliament meets at Turin. ...**August 21:** Hungarian diet is dissolved, resulting in government by imperial commissioners. ...**October 14:** State of siege is proclaimed in Poland.

1862. London hosts world exhibition. ...**February:** France acquires Mentone and Roquebrune from Sardinia. ...**February 5:** Moldavia and Wallachia are united under Alexandru Cuza (1820–1873) and adopt the name Romania. ...**March 29**: Commercial treaty between Prussia and France based on free-trade principles is signed. ...**June 15:** Ottoman troops bombard Belgrade after clashes between Ottoman garrison and Serbs. ...**August 29:** Garibaldi, planning to take Rome, is captured by royal troops at Aspromonte. ...**September 23:** Otto von Bismarck (1815–1898) is appointed Prussian prime minister. ...**October 7:** Prussian diet rejects increase of military credits. ...**October 13:** Bismarck governs without budget until 1866 and delivers speech in which he advocates solving German problems with "blood and iron." ...**October 26:** Revolution breaks out in Athens, and King Otho (1815–1867) abdicates.

U.S. & Canada

1860. January 1: Arkansas prohibits employment of free blacks on boats and ships navigating its rivers. ...**April 3:** First relay of Pony Express mail service leaves Saint Joseph, Missouri, for Sacramento, California. ...**November 6:** Abraham Lincoln (1809–1865) is elected 16th president of the United States. ...**December 20:** South Carolina is first state to secede from the Union, and claims all federal property within its boundaries.

1861. January 29: Kansas enters Union as 34th state. ...**February 4:** Congress of Montgomery forms a confederation of 11 Southern states under President Jefferson Davis. ...**April 12:** Confederates fire on Fort Sumter, South Carolina, marking official outbreak of American Civil War. ...**July 21:** Confederate army defeats Union army at battle of Bull Run in Manassas, Virginia. ...**September 25:** U.S. secretary of navy authorizes black enlistment.

1862. March 8: Union forces win battle of Pea Ridge, Arkansas. ...**March 9:** Confederate *Virginia* and Union *Monitor* fight first battle between ironclad warships. ...**April 6–7:** In battle of Shiloh in Tennessee, General Ulysses S. Grant's (1822–1885) forces defeat Confederates under Albert Johnston (1803–1862) and P. G. T. Beauregard (1818–1893). ...**May 1:** Captain David Farragut's (1801–1870) Union forces take New Orleans. ...**May 31:** At battles of Seven Pines and Fair Oaks, General Joseph E. Johnston's (1807–1891) Confederates stall General George McClellan's (1826–1885) advance toward Richmond, Virginia. ...**July 17:** Lincoln signs bill allowing runaway slaves from outside Union freedom within Union territory. ...**July:** Major General David Hunter (1802–1886) of Union's First Carolina Regiment enlists first black troops; many are former slaves. ...**July 12:** U.S. Congress authorizes Medal of Honor for soldiers exhibiting supreme gallantry in action. ...**September 17:** Confederate invasion of North under General Robert E. Lee is defeated by General McClellan's forces at Antietam, Maryland. ...**September 22:** Lincoln declares slaves in Confederate territory free as of January 1, 1863. ...**November 5:** General Ambrose E. Burnside (1824–1891) becomes commander of Army of the Potomac, replacing General McClellan.

Latin America

1860. William Walker (b. 1824) is captured by British and executed by Hondurans. ...**November 25:** Constitution is proclaimed in Peru.

1861. Benito Pablo Juárez (1806–1872) is elected president of Mexico. ...Moreno becomes president of Ecuador. ...José Antonio Páez returns to Venezuela to become supreme dictator. ...**March 18:** Spain annexes Santo Domingo. ...**October 31:** London Convention of Britain, France and Spain meet to try to recover Mexican investments.

1862. Bartolomé Mitre (1821–1906) is elected to six-year term as Argentine president. ...Francisco Solano López (1826–1870) becomes dictator-president of Paraguay. ...President Moreno makes Catholic Church dominant force in Ecuador. ...Belize officially becomes a British colony. ...Yucatán becomes a separate state of Mexico.

1862–1880. Three Argentine presidents institute a period of liberal reforms, building schools and public works.

1862–1884. Belize is administered by governor of Jamaica.

Africa, Asia & Pacific

1860. Turks reform their law, basing it on *Code Napoléon*. ...Vladivostok is founded on Russia's Pacific coast. ...Laborers are imported from India under three-year indentures to work on Natal sugar plantations. ...**April:** Rising of Maori on North Island in New Zealand begins Second Maori War. ...**April 26:** Peace between Spain and Morocco is established. ...**May–July:** Christians are massacred in Syria; Great Powers restore order. ...**May 17:** First Japanese ambassador to United States exchanges treaty ratifications. ...**August 21:** Anglo-French troops defeat Chinese at Palikao. ...**October 24:** In Treaty of Beijing, China ratifies Treaty of Tientsin.

1861. Britain proclaims protectorate over Bahrain Islands in Persian Gulf. ...Radama II (1830–1863), son of Ranavalona (1790–1861), becomes king of Hova and reopens Madagascar to missionaries. ...**March–September:** Russia occupies Tsushima. ...**March 19:** Maori rising in New Zealand ends. ...**August 6:** British government takes possession of Lagos coast.

1862. T'ung-chih (1856–1875) becomes emperor of China. ...Commercial treaty between Britain and Burma fixes customs duty at 5 percent and gives British right to trade anywhere in Burma. ...France purchases Obok, opposite Aden. ...King Radama II of Madagascar concludes treaties with France and Britain. ...**June 5:** In Treaty of Saigon between France and Annam (central Vietnam), Annam pays indemnity of 20 million francs and France annexes three eastern provinces of Cochin China (southern Vietnam).

Science, Invention & Technology

1860. French chemist Pierre Berthelot (1827–1907) publishes findings in synthesis of organic chemicals. ...First gas kitchen stoves become available in the United States. ...Linoleum is invented in Britain. ...African-American Elijah McCoy (1843–1929) invents a self-lubricating locomotive. ...African-American seamstress Elizabeth Keckley (c. 1818–1907) develops a dressmaking system. ...Englishman Thomas Crapper (1837–1910) invents the automatic flush toilet.

1861. American Linus Yale (1821–1868) invents first pin-tumbler locking device. ...German born American John Faber (1822–1879) opens first pencil factory in United States. ...Swedish born American John Ericsson (1803–1889) develops the ironclad warship *Monitor* for the U.S. government. ...Australians Thomas Mort (1816–1878) and James Harrison (1816–1893) open first fish-freezing plant in Australia.

1862. Englishmen Henry Coxwell (1819–1900) and James Glaisher (1809–1903) explore the upper atmosphere in manned hot air balloons. ...American Richard Gatling (1818–1903) invents the rapid-firing Gatling gun. ...**July 10:** Construction begins on Central Pacific Railway, which will open May 10, 1869.

c. 1862. Marcellin Berthelot (1827–1907) invents the calorimeter, a device that measures heat of gas combustion.

Religion, Culture & Arts

1860. George Eliot: *The Mill on the Floss*. ...Jacob Burckhardt (1818–1897): *Civilization of the Renaissance in Italy*. ...John Ruskin: *Unto This Last*. ...Nathaniel Hawthorne: *The Marble Faun* ....Wilkie Collins (1824–1889): *The Woman in White*, perhaps first true English mystery novel. ...Thomas Crawford (1813–1857) sculpts *Freedom*, armed figure for dome of U.S. Capitol. ...Franz von Suppé (1819–1895) composes *Das Pensionat*, first Viennese operetta. His later works include *Light Cavalry*, *The Beautiful Galatea*. ...Henry Poor (1812–1905) publishes *History of the Railroad and the Canals of the United States*, a volume of financial research. It will ultimately become the *Standard and Poor's Index*.

1861. Eliot: *Silas Marner*. ...Yale University confers first Ph.D. degree in United States. ...American landscape artist Frederick Bierstadt (1830–1902) completes *Laramie Peak*, first of his many vast canvases of western scenery. ...Frederick E. Church: *Icebergs*. ...Friedrich Reinhold Kreutzwald (1803–1882), Estonian author, publishes edition of *Kalevipoeg*, Estonia's national epic.

1862. Ballet master Marius Petipa (1822–1910) choreographs his first full-length ballet for the Russian Imperial Theater: *La Fille du Pharaon*. ...Henri Dunant (1828–1910): *Souvenirs de Solferino* (inspiration for Red Cross movement). ...Gustave Flaubert: *Salammbô*. ...Victor Hugo: *Les Misérables*. ...Ivan Turgenev (1818–1883), Russian novelist: *Fathers and Sons*. ...Fyodor Dostoyevsky (1821–1881), Russian novelist: *Memoirs from the House of the Dead*, the record of his experiences in a Siberian penal colony. ...Petko Slaveykov (1827–1895), in translating the Bible, creates the modern Bulgarian literary language. ...Julia Ward Howe (1819–1910), American writer: "The Battle Hymn of the Republic." ...Charles Harpur (1813–1868), Australian poet: *A Poet's Home*.

1862–1869. Lev Nikolayevich Tolstoy (1828–1910), Russian novelist: *War and Peace*.

▲ ***This Currier and Ives lithograph depicts the bombardment of Fort Sumter in 1861.***

British Isles & Europe

1863. First international postal congress is held in Paris. ...Crédit Lyonnais is founded as a deposit bank in France. ...Ferdinand Lassalle (1825–1864) founds General German Workers' Association. ...**January 22:** Polish insurrection begins. ...**February 8:** Prussia allies with Russia to suppress Polish rising. ...**March:** Poland is divided into ten provinces. ...**March 30:** William (1845–1913), prince of Denmark, is recognized as King George I of Greece. ...**August 16–September 1:** German princes meet at Frankfurt to reform Confederation, which is opposed by Prussia. ...**November 13:** Schleswig becomes Danish province. ...**November 14:** Britain cedes Ionian Islands to Greece.

1864. International Workers' Association is founded in London. ...**February 1:** Austro-Prussian troops enter Holstein. ...**March 2:** Russian government grants peasants land without payment to weaken Polish nobles. ...**April 18:** Danish are defeated at Duppel. ...**August:** Alexandru Cuza of Romania abolishes serfdom with compensation to landlords. ...**September:** Queen Maria Christina (1858–1929) returns to Spain. ...**September 15:** In Franco-Italian Treaty, Italy renounces its claims to Rome, France withdraws troops from Rome and Florence is made capital. ...**October 30:** In Peace of Vienna, Denmark cedes Schleswig, Holstein and Lauenburg to Austria. ...**November 28:** New Greek constitution introduces universal manhood suffrage and a single-chamber parliament.

1865. First women's conference in Leipzig founds *Allgemeine Deutsche Frauenverein* (General German Women's Association). ...**August 14:** At Convention of Gastein, Austria obtains Holstein, Prussia obtains Schleswig and Kiel, and Lauenburg is sold to Prussia. ...**September 20:** Austrian constitution is temporarily annulled. ...**October:** Otto von Bismarck and Napoléon III meet at Biarritz. Napoléon III acquiesces in Prussian ascendancy in Germany and a united Italy. ...**October 18:** Lord Henry Palmerston (b. 1784) dies and John Russell (1792–1878) becomes prime minister. ...**December:** Transylvania is incorporated into Hungary.

U.S. & Canada

1863. May 2–4: Confederates gain victory at Chancellorsville, Virginia. ...**June 20:** West Virginia is created from anti-slavery counties of Virginia and joins Union as free state. ...**July 1–3:** Confederates under Robert E. Lee are defeated at Gettysburg, Pennsylvania by Army of Potomac under General George Meade (1815–1872), ending second and final Southern invasion of North. ...**July 4:** Confederates surrender Vicksburg, Mississippi to Union armies led by General Ulysses S. Grant. ...**November 19:** Abraham Lincoln delivers Gettysburg Address at Gettysburg battlefield. ...**November 24–25:** Confederates are defeated at Chattanooga, Tennessee.

1864. Copper is discovered and mining operations begin in northern Newfoundland. ...**March 10:** Lincoln appoints Grant general in chief of all U.S. forces. ...**June 18:** Canadian government pledges to work for an enlarged federation, including Maritime Provinces and North West Territories. ...**September 2:** General William Tecumseh Sherman's (1820–1891) Union forces occupy Atlanta, Georgia. ...**October 10:** With Sir Étienne Taché (1795–1865) as chairman, Quebec Conference passes 72 resolutions regarding unification. Resolutions are submitted to the provinces for ratification. They will form basis for British North America Act of 1867. ...**October 31:** Nevada enters Union as 36th State. ...**December 22:** Savannah, Georgia, surrenders to Sherman's Union army.

1865. Colonial Laws Validity Act voids Canadian laws contrary to British laws. ...Physician Mary Edwards Walker (1832–1919) is awarded U. S. Medal of Honor for services to Union army. ...**April 9:** General Lee surrenders to General Grant at Appomattox Courthouse, Virginia, ensuring Union victory. ...**April 14:** President Lincoln (b. 1809) is assassinated by John Wilkes Booth (1838–1865). ...**April 15:** Andrew Johnson (1808–1875) is inaugurated 17th president of the United States. ...**April 26:** General Joseph E. Johnston surrenders last Confederate army in East at Durham, North Carolina. ...**December 18:** The 13th Amendment to Constitution abolishing slavery is ratified. ...**December 24:** Ku Klux Klan is founded in Pulaski, Tennessee.

Latin America

1863. French capture Mexico City and proclaim Archduke Maximilian (1832–1867) of Austria emperor. ...José Antonio Páez leaves Venezuela for a second exile. ...Spain seizes the guano-rich Chincha Islands from Peru. ...The Campanía Church in Santiago, Chile, burns and 2,000 perish. ...War erupts again between Guatemala and El Salvador. ...Iquitos, city in northeastern Peru and capital of Loreto Department, is founded. ...Colombia grants its provinces, including Panama, autonomy.

1864. Fourth Pan-American Conference is held in Lima. ...Brazil invades Uruguay. ...Domingo Sarmiento (1811–1888) is elected to Argentine presidency and conducts a progressive administration. ...**April 10:** Archduke Maximilian, supported by a French army, accepts Mexican crown.

1865. Spain withdraws from Santo Domingo, and the second Dominican Republic is proclaimed. ...Nueva San Salvador becomes a departmental capital of El Salvador. ...**October:** Jamaican government imposes martial law after insurrection. ...United States demands recall of French troops from Mexico.

1865–1870. Paraguay wages war against Argentina, Brazil and Uruguay.

Africa, Asia & Pacific

1863. January 30: Ismail Pasha (1830–1895) succeeds Said Pasha as viceroy of Egypt. ...**May 13:** Hova aristocrats strangle King Radama II in Madagascar, rebelling against his pro-European policies, and elect Rasoherina (?–1868) queen. ...**August 11:** French establish protectorate over Cambodia.

1864. France annexes Loyalty Islands. ...**January:** Emperor Theodore II (1818–1868) of Ethiopia imprisons British consul, European traders and missionaries. ...**July 19:** British General Charles George Gordon (1833–1885) defeats insurgent forces, ending Taiping Rebellion. Hung Hsiu-ch'üan swallows poison. ...**September 5:** American, British, Dutch and French warships jointly bombard Kagoshima (Kyushu Island) and Shimonoseki (Honshu Island) to intimidate Choshu and Satsuma daimyos, anti-Western Japanese influences.

1865. Transportation of convicts to Australia is abolished. ...Kaffraria is incorporated in Cape Colony. ...Wellington becomes capital of New Zealand. ...Ottoman emperor transfers ports of Suakin and Massawa on Red Sea to Egyptian control. ...Alfred Grandidier (1836–1921), French scientist, begins exhaustive exploration of Madagascar. It will continue through 1870. ...**September 2:** Second Maori War ends. ...**November:** Allied (British, Dutch, French and United States) naval demonstration at Osaka secures Japanese emperor's ratification of treaties.

Science, Invention & Technology

1863. Trinitrotoluene (TNT) is invented in Germany. ...Ebenezer Butterick (1826–1903) of Massachusetts markets his line of dress patterns.

1864. World's first automobile, *Kraftswagon*, is produced in Austria. ...First telegraph in Persia opens from Baghdad through Tehran to Bushire, connecting to India. ...The sulky plow is invented in the United States. ...Bicycle driving chain is patented in Britain. ...Isambard K. Brunel's Clifton Gorge supension bridge in Britain is completed five years after his death.

1865. George M. Pullman's sleeping car, designed in 1857, makes its debut. ...Karl Benz (1844–1929) builds a three-wheel car in Germany.

***This drawing of Ku Klux Klan members first appeared in the December 19, 1868, issue of* Harpers' Weekly.** ➤

Religion, Culture & Arts

1863. John Stuart Mill: *Utilitarianism.* ...Official distinction is made between soccer and rugby football in London. ...Ernest Renan (1823–1892): *Vie de Jésus* (*Life of Jesus*). ...James Whistler (1834–1903), American painter: *Symphony in White.* ...Henry Wadsworth Longfellow: *Tales of a Wayside Inn.* ...Gioacchino Rossini composes *Petite Messe Solennelle* (*Small Solemn Mass*). ...Universalist minister Olympia Brown (1835–1926) becomes first American woman to be ordained in a ministry of a regular denomination. ...Édouard Manet (1832–1883), French painter: *Le Déjeuner sur l'herbe.* ...**December 24:** William Makepeace Thackeray (b. 1811) dies.

1864. John Henry Newman (1801–1890), British Roman Catholic cardinal: *Apologia pro Vita Sua* (*Apology for My Life*). ...Samuel Crowther (c. 1809–1891) is consecrated an Anglican bishop in Nigeria. He is the first black African to hold that office. ...**August 22:** Geneva Convention for Protection of Wounded establishes the Red Cross. ...**December 8:** Pope Pius IX issues *Syllabus Errorum*, condemning liberalism, socialism and rationalism.

1865. Antonín Dvořák (1841–1904) composes his first two symphonies. ...William Booth (1829–1912) founds Salvation Army. ...Lewis Carroll (1832–1898), British writer: *Alice in Wonderland.* ...Mill: *August Comte and Positivism.* ...The *Nation*, a leading liberal magazine in U.S. politics, literature and art, is founded. ...Influential Bengali novelist Bankim Chandra Chatterji (1838–1894) publishes *Durges Nandini*, a historical romance. ...Construction begins (completed 1877) on Galleria Vittorio Emanuele in Milan. Designed by Giuseppe Mengoni (1829–1877), this cross-shaped glass and iron shopping arcade is one of the largest and finest in Europe. ...**June 10:** Richard Wagner: *Tristan and Isolde*, produced at Munich. ...**June 27:** Through treaty with Britain, Madagascar's Hova government tolerates Christians.

British Isles & Europe

1866. Vienna Women's Employment Association is founded to help women campaign for jobs as postal and telegraph workers. ...**February 22–23:** Alexandru Cuza of Romania is dethroned and is succeeded by Karl Eitel Friedrich (1839–1914), who will become Romania's first king in 1881 as Carol I. ...**June 8:** Prussia annexes Holstein. ...**June 14:** Prussia declares German Confederation dissolved. ...**June 16:** Prussians invade Saxony, Hanover and Hesse. ...**June 20:** Italy declares war on Austria. ...**June 24:** Italians are defeated at Custozza. ...**July 3:** Prussians defeat Austrians at Sadowa. ...**July 20:** Italian fleet is destroyed by Austria off Lissa. ...**July 26:** Preliminary peace between Prussia and Austria is agreed to at Nikolsburg. ...**August:** Peace treaties between Prussia and Württemberg, Baden, Bavaria and Austria are signed. Austria withdraws from Germany. ...**September 7:** Prussia annexes Hanover, Cassel, Hamburg, Nassau, Frankfurt.

1867. April: Last Ottoman soldiers leave Serbian territory under pressure from Great Powers. ...**April 17:** North German Confederation is formed, with Prussia as head. ...**May 11:** London Conference guarantees neutrality of Luxembourg. ...**June 12:** Covenant ("Ausgleich") between Austria and Hungary establishes dual monarchy with common foreign and military policies. ...**August 15:** Second Reform Bill doubles the number of voters in Britain. ...**September 23:** Serbia and Montenegro form a secret offensive and defensive alliance. ...**October 22:** Giuseppe Garibaldi marches on Rome. ...**October 28:** French troops arrive in Rome. ...**November 3:** Garibaldi is defeated by papal and French troops at Mentana.

1868. February 25: Lord Derby (1799–1869) resigns as British prime minister and is succeeded by Benjamin Disraeli (1804–1881). ...**May:** Freedom of press and assembly is granted in France. ...**September 8:** Parliamentary system is adopted in France. ...**September 17:** Marshal Juan Prim (1814–1870) leads revolution in Spain. ...**September 30:** Isabella II of Spain flees to France.

U.S. & Canada

1866. Edward Walker (1831–1901) and Charles Mitchell (1829–1912) are first blacks elected to a legislative assembly (Massachusetts House of Representatives). ...**April 9:** Civil Rights Act grants citizenship to all persons born in United States, except Indians, and punishes those who prevent free exercise of civil rights. ...**June 1:** Irish American "Fenians," raiding from Buffalo, New York, temporarily seize Fort Erie in Canada. ...**June 13:** Congress passes 14th Amendment to U.S. Constitution and sends it to states. Amendment defines citizenship for the first time and creates rights that states must protect. ...**July 16:** Overriding veto by President Andrew Johnson, Congress creates Freedmen's Bureau and authorizes military trials for those accused of infringing rights of blacks. ...**August 6:** Britain unites Vancouver Island with British Columbia.

1867. January 8: U.S. Congress gives vote to blacks in District of Columbia. ...**March 1:** Nebraska enters Union as 37th State. ...**March 9:** Congress passes first Reconstruction Act over President Johnson's veto. ...**March 28:** British North America Act becomes law. ...**March 30:** United States buys Alaska from Russia for $7.2 million. ...**July 1:** According to provisions of British North America Act, Nova Scotia, New Brunswick, Ontario and Quebec form Dominion of Canada, with its capital at Ottawa. John Alexander MacDonald (1815–1891) becomes first Canadian prime minister. ...**November:** Parliament of Dominion of Canada meets for first time.

1868. February 24: U.S. House of Representatives impeaches President Johnson under various charges, including violation of Tenure of Office and Command of the Army Acts. ...**March 13:** Senate begins impeachment trial of President Johnson. ...**April:** Treaty of Fort Laramie ends first Sioux War. ...**May 25:** Britain makes Victoria on Vancouver Island capital of British Columbia. ...**May 26:** For third time, senators vote 35–19 to convict President Johnson, one vote short of two-thirds needed. ...**May 30:** Decoration (Memorial) Day is celebrated nationally for first time. ...**July 28:** The 14th Amendment to U.S. Constitution, granting citizenship to former slaves, is ratified. ...**November 3:** Ulysses S. Grant is elected 18th U.S. president. ...**December 25:** President Johnson grants unqualified amnesty to all participants in "insurrection or rebellion" against United States.

Latin America

1866. Peru defeats Spanish at Callao with the aid of Chile, Bolivia and Ecuador. ...Dutch grant Suriname a parliament. ...Colombia resumes direct control over Panama. ...Chile and Bolivia settle boundary dispute.

1867. A cable railroad is constructed in São Paulo, Brazil. ...**March:** Last French troops evacuate Mexico. ...**June 19:** Emperor Maximilian (b. 1832) of Mexico is executed.

1868. Puerto Ricans mount unsuccessful uprising against Spanish rule.

1868–1872. President José Balta (1814–1872) conducts a vigorous program of public works in Peru.

1868–1878. Two major revolts in Cuba against Spanish mark ten-year period of resistance.

Africa, Asia & Pacific

1866. Having already imprisoned other Europeans in Ethiopia, Emperor Theodore II jails newly arrived British envoy Hormuzd Rassam (1826–1910). ...By Treaty of Thaba Bosiu, Orange Free State annexes much of Basutoland. ...**May 21:** Ottoman sultan grants right of primogeniture to Ismail Pasha of Egypt. ...**June 25:** Japan signs tariff convention with United States, Britain, France and Netherlands. It imposes a 5 percent duty on most imports and exports.

1867. France occupies three western provinces of Cochin China, which is declared a French colony. ...**April 1:** Rule by British East India Company ends and Straits Settlement in Malaya becomes British Crown colony. ...**July 26:** Russia forms governor generalship of Turkistan.

1868. King Rama IV (b. 1804) of Siam (Thailand) dies and is succeeded by his son, Rama V (1853–1910). ...**January 1:** Japan opens Kobe and Osaka to foreign trade. ...**January 3:** Emperor Mutsuhito (1852–1912) proclaims end to shoguns and reestablishes direct imperial rule. ...**March:** Japanese emperor receives French, Dutch, and British representatives. ...**April 6:** Japanese emperor takes charter oath, promising deliberative assembly. ...**April 10:** At battle of Aroge, British defeat Ethiopians. **April 13:** British storm Magdala and release European prisoners, then later withdraw from Ethiopia. Emperor Theodore II (b. 1818) commits suicide. ...**July 4** At Ueno in Edo, imperial Japanese troops defeat insurgents favoring former Tokugawa shogunate. ...**July 17:** Edo, renamed Tokyo, is made capital of Japan. ...**August 8:** French government is permitted consular jurisdiction at Tananarive after recognizing sovereignty of Merina dynasty in Madagascar.

Science, Invention & Technology

1866. The velocipede bicycle is patented in the United States. ...First steamroller is invented in Britain. ...Josephine Cochrane (?–1913) of Indiana builds first dishwashing machine in her home and later begins commercial production of it. ...New York City creates a board to cope with epidemics. ...**July 27:** Atlantic underwater cable between Britain and United States is completed.

1867. First cantilever bridge is built across River Main in Germany. ...American Joseph R. Brown invents the universal milling machine. ...Germans Nikolaus Otto (1832–1891) and Eugen Langen (1833–1895) build a two-stroke engine. ...First urban elevated railroad is built in New York City. ...Belgian Zénobe Gramme (1826–1901) invents an improved dynamo that efficiently produces an alternating current.

1868. Frenchman Georges Leclanché (1839–1882) invents the dry-cell storage battery. ...Insecticide copper acetoarsenite (Paris green) is developed. ...Norwegian Svend Foyn invents the harpoon gun.

Religion, Culture & Arts

1866. Thomas Huxley (1825–1895), British biologist and educator: *Elementary Philosophy*. ...Friedrich Albert Lange (1828–1875), German philosopher: *History of Materialism*. ...Paul Verlaine (1844–1896): *Poèmes saturniens*. ...Fyodor Dostoyevsky: *Crime and Punishment*. ...Henrik Ibsen (1828–1906), Norwegian dramatist and poet: *Brand*. ...Bedrich Smetana (1824–1884) Czech composer: *Bartered Bride*. ...George Eliot: *Felix Holt*. ...Franz Liszt (1811–1886) composes *Christus Oratorio*.

1867. Théophile Gautier (1811–1872), Paul Verlaine (1844–1896), Charles Baudelaire form Les Parnassiens (*L'art pour l'art*), a movement against Romanticism. ...Karl Marx: *Das Kapital* (first part). ...Ibsen: *Peer Gynt*. ...Johann Strauss (1825–1899) composes *Blue Danube*. ...**December 1:** Bishop Filaret (b. 1782), influential metropolitan of Moscow and author of standard Russian catechism, dies.

1868. William Morris (1834–1896), British poet and artist: *Earthly Paradise*. ...Ernst Heinrich Philipp August Haeckel (1834–1919), German biologist and philosopher: *History of Creation*. ...Johannes Brahms (1833–1897), German composer: *German Requiem*. ...Scottish architect Charles Rennie Mackintosh (d. 1929) is born. ...Louisa May Alcott (1832–1888), American novelist: *Little Women*. ...Wilkie Collins: *The Moonstone*. ...Dostoyevsky: *The Idiot*. ...**June 28:** Richard Wagner: *Meistersinger*, produced at Munich.

1868–1869. Robert Browning: *The Ring and the Book*.

British Isles & Europe

1869. German Social Democratic Party is founded. ...League for Women's Rights is founded in France. ...**January 2:** Émile Ollivier (1825–1913) becomes French premier. ...**May 10:** Alliance between France, Italy and Austria is drawn up.

1870. June 25: Isabella II of Spain abdicates in favor of Alfonso XII (1857–1885). ...**July 19:** France declares war on Prussia. ...**September 2:** Napoléon III capitulates to Prussians at Sedan, leading to his downfall. ...**September 4:** Revolution breaks out in Paris, and a republic is proclaimed. ...**September 19:** Germans begin siege of Paris. ...**October 2:** Kingdom of Italy annexes Rome and declares it Italian capital. ...**November 16:** Amadeus (1845–1890), duke of Aosta, is elected king of Spain.

1871. January 18: William I of Prussia is proclaimed German emperor at Versailles. ...**January 19:** Germans defeat French at St. Quentin. ...**January 28:** Paris capitulates to German armies. ...**February 17:** Louis Adolphe Thiers (1797–1877) is elected head of French executive. ...**May 10:** In Franco-German peace treaty at Frankfurt, France cedes Alsace and Lorraine. ...**June 20:** Trade unions are fully legalized in Britain. ...**August 31:** Thiers is elected French president. ...**December 4:** Germany adopts gold standard.

1872. July 28: France adopts general conscription.

U.S. & Canada

1869. Wyoming introduces woman suffrage. ...**March 4:** Ulysses S. Grant is inaugurated 18th president of the United States. ...**May 15:** Elizabeth Cady Stanton and Susan B. Anthony (1820–1906) found National Woman Suffrage Association. ...**September 24:** Financial manipulations by Jay Gould (1836–1892) and James Fisk (1834–1872) cause financial panic, ruining thousands of gold speculators. ...**October 11:** Métis in Red River area, in what is now Manitoba, rebel. **October 20:** Red River Métis form committee, led by Louis Riel (1844–1885). **October 30:** Métis refuse to allow William McDougall (1822–1905), lieutenant governor of Rupert's Land and North West territories to enter Minnesota. **November 2:** Riel occupies Fort Garry. **December:** Riel heads provisional government set up by Red River Métis.

1870. February 25: Mississippi senator Hiram Revels (1822–1901) takes his seat. He is first black to serve in Congress. ...**March 30:** The 15th Amendment to U.S. Constitution, granting voting rights to blacks, is ratified by states. ...**June 22:** Department of Justice is created under attorney general's direction. ...**July 15:** Britain transfers Rupert's Land to Canada and other North West Territories. Manitoba becomes Canada's fifth province. ...**August 22:** British troops end rebellion in Red River area. Riel flees to United States.

1871. March 3: Indian Appropriations Act, nullifying all Indian treaties, passes. Indians become wards of federal government. ...**May 8:** Commercial treaty between Canada and United States. ...**June 29:** British North America Act of 1871 confirms Canada's sovereignty over Rupert's Land and North West Territories. ...**July 20:** Crown colony of British Columbia becomes sixth province of Dominion of Canada. ...**October 8-October 11:** Chicago nearly burns to the ground, killing some 250 persons.

1872. Susan B. Anthony is arrested and fined $100 for leading women to cast ballots in presidential election. ...Lucy Stone (1818–1893) and her husband, Henry Brown Blackwell (1825–1909), edit *Woman's Journal*. ...**May 1:** First U.S. National Park is created at headwaters of Yellowstone River. ...**May 22:** Amnesty Act restores civil rights to most Southerners. ...**October 21:** Emperor William I of Germany awards San Juan Islands in Puget Sound to United States in arbitration with Britain. ...**December 11:** Pinckney Pinchback (1837–1921), black veteran of Union army, becomes acting governor of Louisiana.

Latin America

1869. April 20: A republican government is organized in Cuba.

1870. Kingston becomes capital of Jamaica. ...Bartolomé Mitre, former president of Argentina, founds *La Nación*, a newspaper.

1870–1882. Costa Rica, under President Tomás Guardia (1832–1882), enacts an ambitious program of public works and foreign investment.

1870–1888. President Guzman Blanco (1829–1899) dominates Venezuela.

1871. Peru signs a truce with Spanish. ...Antigua, Barbuda and Virgin Islands become part of the Leeward Islands Federation. ...Brazil emancipates children born of slave mothers. ...Limón, Costa Rica, is founded. ...Benito Juárez is again elected president of Mexico. ...Montserrat becomes part of the Leeward Islands Federation. ...Cuba ends importation of cheap Chinese laborers.

1872. Juárez (b. 1806) dies and is succeeded by Sebastián Lerdo de Tejada (1827–1889), head of the Mexican supreme court.

1872–1876. Manuel Pardo (1834–1878) becomes first civilian president of Peru and devotes himself to improving the country's financial position.

Africa, Asia & Pacific

1869. November 16: Suez Canal is opened.

American feminist Susan B. Anthony.

1870. Western Australia gains representative government. ...Diamonds are found in Orange Free State. ...Sayyid Barghash (?–1888) becomes sultan of Zanzibar. ...Sher Ali (?–1879) becomes emir of Afghanistan. ...Steamship travel is established between New Zealand and San Francisco. ...Sir Samuel Barker (fl. 19th century), commanding Egyptian troops, conquers Upper Nile region and suppresses slave trade. ...**June 21:** Chinese mob murders French consul and 20 other foreigners in Tientsin.

1871. Basutoland is united with Cape Colony. ...Japanese government establishes ministry of education. ...**August 29:** Japanese government abolishes military fiefs. ...**September 3:** China and Japan sign treaty establishing diplomatic and commercial relations. ...**October 27:** Britain grants Kimberley diamond fields, on border of Orange Free State, to state of Griqualand West. ...**October 28:** British journalist and explorer Henry Morton Stanley (1841–1904) finds and rescues Scottish missionary David Livingstone (1813–1873) at Ujiji (in Tanzania).

1872. Griqualand West is annexed to Cape Colony. ...Johannes IV (?–1889) proclaims himself emperor of Ethiopia. ...Treaty ending Maori Wars recognizes Maori rule over half of North Island of New Zealand. ...Japan enacts nationwide conscription to replace samurai. ...Egyptian troops occupy Red Sea coast and Harrar, cutting off Ethiopia from the sea. ...**February 2:** Holland cedes Gold Coast possessions to Britain. ...**February 8:** Lord Mayo (b. 1830), viceroy of India, is murdered. ...**October:** Self-government is established in Cape Colony.

Science, Invention & Technology

1869. Cleveland Abbe (1838–1916) establishes first weather forecasting service in United States. ...Massachusetts establishes first state board of health. ...American Margaret Knight (1838–1914) invents the square-bottom paper bag. ...First desalination plant begins operation in Britain. ...American George Westinghouse (1846–1914) invents a train braking system. ...Frenchman Hippolyte Mège-Mouriès (1873–1920) invents oleomargarine. ...American John Hyatt (1837–1920) develops celluloid as a substitute for ivory for billiard balls.

1870. German chemist Adolf von Baeyer (1835–1917) synthesizes indigo. ...American Luther Burbank (1849–1926) begins work on hybridization of numerous plant species. ...U.S. Weather Service is established. ...*McCall's* enters the dress pattern market in competition with *Butterick*. ...Englishman James Starley (1830–1881) invents the "penny-farthing" bicycle, so nicknamed for the disparate sizes of its wheels.

1871. First widespread use of arc lighting comes with invention of the direct current dynamo. ...Englishman Richard Maddox (1816–1902) invents the dry photographic plate.

1872. American Benjamin Hotchkiss (1826–1885) develops a five-barrel machine gun. ...Japan's first railroad connects Tokyo and Yokohama on Honshu Island.

Religion, Culture & Arts

1869. John Stuart Mill's *Subjection of Women* furthers feminist movement. ...Paul Verlaine: *Fêtes galantes*. ...Matthew Arnold (1822–1888), British poet and critic: *Culture and Anarchy*. ...Alphonse Daudet (1840–1897), French writer: *Lettres de mon moulin* (*Messages from My Windmill*). ...Piano Concerto in A Minor by Norwegian composer Edvard Grieg (1843–1907) is first performed in Copenhagen. ...College for Women (afterwards Girton College) is founded in Cambridge. ...**July 1:** Hereditary priesthood is abolished in Russia. ...**December 8:** Vatican Council meets.

1870. Dante Gabriel Rossetti (1828–1892), English poet and painter: *Dante's Dream*. ...Ballet *Coppélia* by Léo Delibes (1836–1891) is first performed in Paris. ...Claude Monet (1840–1926), French artist: *Le Pont Neuf*. ...Camille Pissarro (1830–1903), French painter: *Louveciennes Road*. ...**March 15:** Cincinnati Red Stockings, first openly professional baseball team, is organized. ...**June 6:** Charles Dickens (b. 1812) dies. ...**November 6:** Rutgers beats Princeton 6-4 in first intercollegiate football game.

1871. Michael Bakunin (1814–1876): *Dieu et l'état* (*God and the State*), an anarchist tract. ...First Impressionist exhibition at Paris. ...First production of *Aida* by Giuseppe Verdi (1813–1901) is held in Egypt to celebrate opening of Suez Canal. ...Thomas Eakins (1844–1916), American painter known for keen realism: *Max Schmitt in a Single Scull*.

1871–1893. Émile Zola (1840–1902), French novelist: *Les Rougon-Macquart*, a series of 20 novels.

1872. Englishman Walter Wingfield (1833–1912), inspired by game of poona he played while stationed in India, invents tennis. ...Samuel Langhorne Clemens (1835–1910), American writer known as Mark Twain: *Roughing It*. ...Samuel Butler (1835–1902), British author: *Erewhon*, a utopian novel. ...Friedrich Nietzsche (1844–1900), German poet and philosopher: *The Birth of Tragedy*. ...Charles Taze Russell (1860–1941) organizes Jehovah's Witnesses. ... First Baptist Church is built in Boston. ...**January 18:** First issue of *Publishers Weekly* appears. ...**May 1:** Strasbourg University opens. ...**June 19:** Jesuits are expelled from Germany.

British Isles & Europe

1873. Marie-Edme MacMahon (1808–1893) is elected French president. ...**January 9:** Napoléon III (b. 1808) dies. ...**February 11:** Amadeus of Spain abdicates, and a republic is proclaimed. ...**April 2:** Reform of Austrian franchise favors German language. ...**May 24:** Louis Adolphe Thiers resigns French presidency. ...**September 15:** Germans evacuate France.

1874. January 3: Marshal Francisco Serrano (1810–1885) becomes dictator of Spain. ...**January 13:** Russia adopts general conscription. ...**February 2:** Conservative ministry under Benjamin Disraeli takes office in Britain. ...**April 19:** Swiss constitution is revised and centralized. ...**August 30:** Factory Act in Britain limits working week to 56 ½ hours. ...France prohibits child labor and women working underground and introduces factory inspectors.

1875. German Reichsbank is founded. ...**January 9:** Alfonso XII lands at Barcelona and is recognized as king. ...**January 30:** Republican constitution is established in France. ...**May 20:** Seventeen other European nations join France in adopting metric system of measurement. ...**July 1:** Universal Postal Union is founded.

1876. January–February: French republicans win decisive victory in elections. ...**June 30:** Serbia declares war on Ottoman Empire, hoping to acquire Bulgaria. **July 2:** Montenegro joins Serbia in war with Ottoman Empire. **September 1:** Ottoman troops destroy Serbian forces at Alexinatz. Serbs appeal to Great Powers for mediation.

1877. Germany adopts uniform administration and justice procedure. ...**March 23:** Switzerland introduces factory inspection. ...**April 24:** Russia declares war on Turkey. ...**May 16:** MacMahon appoints monarchist ministry in France. **October 14:** French republicans defeat MacMahon's policy at the polls.

U.S. & Canada

1873. March 3: U.S. Congress prohibits mailing of obscene literature. ...**March 4:** Ulysses S. Grant is inaugurated for second term. ...**May 23:** North West Mounted Police are established in Canada. ...**July 1:** Prince Edward Island becomes Canada's seventh province. ...**September 18:** Failure of Jay Cooke and Company, financial house that marketed federal bonds during Civil War, sparks severe economic crisis in the United States. ...**November 8:** City of Winnipeg is incorporated. ...**November 19:** William Tweed ("Boss Tweed") (1823–1878) is convicted of fraud and sentenced to 12 years in prison in New York City.

1874. Canada introduces voting by secret ballot and holding elections on a single day. ...Marxist socialists found Workingman's Party in New York City. The name will be changed to Socialist Labor Party in 1877. ...**November 7:** Cartoonist Thomas Nast (1840–1902) is first to use elephant as symbol for Republican Party in *Harper's Weekly*. ...**November 18:** Woman's Christian Temperance Union is organized in Cleveland, Ohio.

1875. March 1: Civil Rights Act forbids racial discrimination and separation in public accommodations, and prohibits exclusion of blacks from juries. ...**March 5:** Blanche Kelso Bruce (1841–1898), Mississippi Republican, begins term in U.S. Senate. Bruce is first black to serve full Senate term. ...**December 4:** Boss Tweed escapes from New York City prison and flees to Cuba.

1876. Boss Tweed, who left Cuba for Spain, is extradited. He will die in a New York City jail two years later. ...**June 25:** Sitting Bull's (c. 1813–1890) Sioux slaughter General George Custer (1839–1876) and all 265 of his men at battle of Little Big Horn. ...**August:** Colorado enters Union as 37th state.

1877. Baltimore and Ohio Railroad workers strike against a proposed 10 percent wage cut. Strike spreads to railroad workers at other U.S. companies, becoming first great strike in U.S. history. ...**March 4:** Rutherford B. Hayes (1822–1893) is inaugurated 19th president of the United States. ...**March 18:** Hayes appoints Frederick Douglass U.S. marshal for District of Columbia. ...**September 22:** Crowfoot (c. 1836–1890), chief of Blackfoot, cedes to Canada all Blackfoot claims to land east of Rocky Mountains and west of Cypress Hills.

Latin America

1873. Turks and Caicos Islands are annexed to Jamaica. ...Slavery is abolished in Puerto Rico. ...Peru signs a secret defensive alliance with Bolivia. ...**October 18:** Ecuador is transformed into theocracy. ...**October 31:** Spanish gunboat seizes American ship *Virginius*, and 36 people (captain, crew, and passengers) are executed, bringing Spain and United States close to war.

1874. Banana cultivation is introduced in Costa Rica. ...Bartolomé Mitre is defeated in election for Argentine presidency and stages unsuccessful revolt. ...Bolivia and Chile settle boundary dispute.

1874–1880. Nicolas Avellaneda (1837–1885) is elected president of Argentina.

1875. A rebellion begins in Cuba. ...President Moreno of Ecuador is assassinated.

1876. José de la Cruz Porfirio Díaz (1830–1915) leads a successful revolt in Mexico. ...Riots erupt in Barbados when British propose uniting it to the Windward Islands. ...Marco Aurelio Soto (1846–1908) becomes liberal dictator of Honduras.

1877. Argentine congress approves amnesty for Mitre and his followers. ...Ponce, Puerto Rico, receives a royal title and becomes a city. Mayagüez, Puerto Rico, is also made a city. ...Grenada becomes a British Crown colony. ...**December 12:** Díaz becomes president of Mexico.

Africa, Asia & Pacific

1873. Severe economic crisis devastates Australia. ...Peter Egerton Warburton (1813–1889), British explorer, begins to cross Australian continent; during travels, he discovers Darling River in southeast Australia. ...**January 1:** Japan adopts Gregorian calendar in place of lunar calendar. ...**June 4:** Under British pressure, sultan of Zanzibar prohibits export of slaves and closes public slave markets. ...**July**: Japanese government sets land tax at 3 percent, regardless of size of harvest.

1874. Gold Coast is declared British Crown colony. ...General Charles George Gordon (1833–1885), as governor general of Sudan for Egyptian khedive, establishes posts on upper Nile and completes suppression of slave trade. ...**January 31:** British forces led by Viscount Garnet Wolseley (1833–1913) defeat Ashanti troops at Amoaful (present-day Ghana). ...**March 15:** France assumes protectorate over Annam (central Vietnam). ...**October 25:** Britain annexes Fiji Islands.

1875. Turkey is bankrupt. ...Japan cedes Sakhalin Island (jointly administered since 1855) to Russia, which recognizes Japanese claim to Kurile Islands. ...**January 30:** Reciprocity treaty with United States admits Hawaiian sugar free of duty. ...**October 12:** Provincial governments in New Zealand are abolished. ...**November 25:** Britain buys Suez Canal shares from Egyptian viceroy.

1876. Japan acquires Bonin Islands (in Philippine Sea) from Spain. ...First Chinese railroad is built in Shanghai. ...**June 4:** Ottoman sultan Abdul Aziz (1830–1876) is overthrown by Midhat Pasha (1822–1884). **August 31:** Abdul Hamid II (1842–1918) becomes Ottoman sultan. **December 23:** Turkish constitution is granted.

1877. March 17: First Turkish parliament meets. ...**April 12:** Britain annexes Transvaal. ...**August:** Last Cape Frontier War breaks out between British and Xhosa in southern Africa. ...**September 14:** Saigo-Takamori (b. 1828) kills himself following failure of last rebellion (on Kyushu Island) of Japanese samurai. ...**October:** Treaty of commerce between Britain and Hova government of Madagascar, proclaiming liberation of slaves.

Science, Invention & Technology

1873. Margarine is commercially introduced in the United States. ...First cable cars begin running in San Francisco. ...The first silo for feed storage is built in the United States.

1874. James Eads (1820–1887) designs first steel arch bridge in St. Louis. ...An electric dental drill is invented in the United States. ...Crystal rectifier, used to convert alternating electric current to direct current, is patented. ...**November 24:** Joseph Glidden (1813–1906) receives patent for barbed wire, which will end open range in U.S. West.

1875. The tricycle is invented in England. ...**June:** Alexander Graham Bell (1847–1922) invents an intermittent transmitter.

1876. German Karl Linde (1842–1934) builds an ammonia compressor for refrigerators. ...Englishman William Crookes (1832–1919) experiments with cathode ray tubes and discovers streams of subatomic particles flowing through them. ...Bell beats Elisha Gray (1835–1901) by a few hours with patent of telephone.

1877. German American Emile Berliner (1851–1929) invents a voice transmitter for the telephone. ...Frenchmen Louis Cailletet (1832–1913) and Raoul Pictet (1846–1929) succeed in creating liquid nitrogen and oxygen at temperatures near absolute zero. ...The refrigerated railroad boxcar is developed in the United States. ...Thomas Edison (1847–1931) invents a stencil copying machine. ...American Dr. John Harvey Kellogg (1852–1943) introduces granola and peanut butter. ...Carl Gustaf de Laval (1845–1913) of Sweden invents a centrifuge cream separator.

Religion, Culture & Arts

1873. Jules Verne (1828–1905), French author of science fiction: *Around the World in 80 Days*. ...Arthur Rimbaud (1854–1891), French poet: *Une Saison en enfer*. ...Matthew Arnold: *Literature and Dogma*. ...George Inness (1825–1894), influential American painter of sentimental landscapes: *Home of the Heron*. ...**May 13:** Mexican government decrees that religious rites may not take place outside church buildings. ...**December:** Papal nuncio is expelled from Switzerland.

1874. William Stubbs (1825–1901) writes *Constitutional History of England*. ...Paul Verlaine: *Romance sans Paroles*. ...Modest Petrovich Mussorgsky (1839–1881) composes *Pictures at an Exhibition*. ...**December 4:** Mexican government outlaws religious instruction and exercises in all federal, state and municipal schools.

1875. Helena Petrovna Blavatsky (1831–1891) founds Theosophical Society. ...Mark Twain: *Adventures of Tom Sawyer*. ...First production of *Carmen* by Georges Bizet (1838–1875) is at Opéra Comique in Paris. ...Mary Baker Eddy (1821–1910), American religious leader, publishes *Science and Health*, key text of Christian Science denomination.

1876. Brahms completes Symphony no. 1 in C Minor. ...Stéphane Mallarmé (1842–1898), chief influence on the Symbolist movement: *L'Après-midi d'un faune* (*The Afternoon of a Faun*). ...American Library Association is founded and introduces Dewey Decimal system. ...**February 2:** National League of professional baseball teams is formed.

1877. Leo Tolstoy: *Anna Karenina*. ...William Morris begins public campaign for renewal of craftsmanship and dignity of labor. ...Aleksandr Porfiryevich Borodin (1833–1887) completes his Symphony no. 2 in B Minor. ...José Echegaray (1832–1916): *O locura o santidad* (*Folly or Holiness*). ...Camille Pissarro: *Les Toites rouges*. ...**December 30:** Brahms: Symphony no. 2 in D Major is performed for the first time, in Vienna.

British Isles & Europe

1878. Workshop Act further regulates hours and conditions of employment in Britain. ...International Women's Rights Congress takes place in Paris. ...**January 9:** Victor Emmanuel II (b. 1820) of Italy dies and is succeeded by Umberto I (1844–1900). ...**January 20:** Russians take Adrianople. ...**June 4:** Ottoman Empire cedes Cyprus to Britain in return for promise of naval support against Russian attack. ...**June 13–July 13:** At the Berlin Congress, Bosnia and Herzegovina are put under Austrian administration, Russia gains Bessarabia, Romania gains Dobrudja, Montenegro gains Antivari, Romania and Serbia become independent, Eastern Rumelia becomes semi-independent of Turkey. ...**October 11:** Austria and Prussia annul clause in the Peace of Prague concerning plebiscite in Schleswig.

1879. January 30: Marie-Edme MacMahon resigns and Jules Grévy (1807–1891) is elected French president. ...**August 4:** Alsace-Lorraine is declared Reichsland (German territory) under governor general. ...**October 7:** Otto von Bismarck creates the Dual Alliance with a secret treaty between Germany and Austro-Hungarian empire. Each party promises to aid the other if it is attacked by Russia. ...**November 27:** French chamber moves from Versailles to Paris.

1881. First known birth control clinic is opened in Amsterdam. ...**March 13:** Alexander II (b. 1818) of Russia is murdered and is succeeded by Alexander III (1854–1894). ...**June 6:** Three Emperors League comprising Russia, Germany and Austria-Hungary, created in 1873, is renewed. ...**July 3:** Britain induces Turkey to cede Thessaly and Epirus to Greece. ...**August 26:** Temporary regulations place Russia under rule of martial law. They will remain in effect until 1917.

U.S. & Canada

1878. January 1: Knights of Labor, the first union to organize all workers, regardless of their craft, is founded. ...**January 10:** Senate defeats (16–34) a woman suffrage constitutional amendment. The amendment will be reintroduced in each Congress until it is finally passed after World War I. ...**February 28:** Bland-Allison Act re-introduces silver standard. ...**April 16:** In *Reynolds v. United States*, Supreme Court upholds prohibition of polygamy, practiced by Mormons. The 1st Amendment, court rules, does not require toleration of "criminal" or "immoral" acts. ...**August 21:** Lawyers meet in Saratoga, New York, to found American Bar Association. ...**October 17:** Conservatives win general election in Canada. Sir John MacDonald (1815–1891) becomes prime minister.

1879. February 15: U.S. Congress says female attorneys may argue cases before U.S. Supreme Court. ...**February 22:** Frank W. Woolworth (1852–1919) opens a 5 cent store in Utica, New York; all goods are same price. ...**May 7:** California adopts state constitutional provision forbidding employment of Chinese.

1880. U.S. Census counts 50,155,783. ...Newfoundland government loans £1 million to construct railway from St. Johns to Hall's Bay. ...**March 1:** U.S. Supreme Court supports Civil Rights Act of 1875 and rules that blacks cannot be barred from juries....**July 31:** All British possessions in North America, except for Newfoundland, are annexed to Canada.

1881. First major gold strike in Alaska leads to rapid development of Juneau. ...**February 16:** Second Canadian Pacific Railway Company is chartered. Government grants company $25 million and 25 million acres of land. ...**March 4:** James Garfield (1831–1881) is inaugurated 20th president of United States. ...**May 21:** American Red Cross Association is founded, with Clara Barton (1821–1912) as first president. ...**July 2:** Garfield is shot and severely wounded by Charles Guiteau (1844–1882), a disgruntled office seeker. ...**July 20:** Chief Sitting Bull, fugitive since battle of Little Big Horn, surrenders to U.S. troops in Dakota Territory. ...**September 19:** Garfield dies. ...**September 20:** Vice President Chester A. Arthur (1829–1886) becomes 21st U.S. president.

Latin America

1879. Chile seizes Bolivian port of Antofagasta.

1879–1883. Chile fights "saltpeter war" against Bolivia and Peru.

1879–1880. General Julio Argentino Roca (1843–1914) conquers Argentina's indigenous population, making colonization of southwestern Argentina possible.

1880. Federalism triumphs in Argentina. ...Tegucigalpa becomes capital of Honduras. ...General Roca becomes president of Argentina. ...British writer Edward Whymper (1840–1911) explores Antisana volcano in northern Ecuador.

1881–1883. Chilean soldiers loot Lima during the War of the Pacific.

1881. French begin work on the Panama Canal. ...Chile and Argentina set the boundary in Tierra del Fuego.

Africa, Asia & Pacific

1878. United States, Germany and Britain make commercial treaties with Samoa. ...Thibaw (1858–1916) becomes king of Burma. ...**March:** Britain annexes Walvis Bay. ...**June 4:** Britain acquires Cyprus from Turkey. ...**November:** Second Afghan War between Britain and Afghanistan begins.

***This drawing of the explosion that killed Russia's Alexander II appeared in the* Illustrated London News.**

1879. January 22: Zulu soldiers massacre British troops at Isandhlwana. ...**May 16:** In Treaty of Gandamak, in return for £60,000 annual subsidy, British occupy Khyber Pass, take control of Afghan foreign relations and have full trading rights throughout Afghanistan. ...**July 4:** British forces smash Zulus at battle of Ulundi ...**August 28:** British expedition captures and deposes Cetewayo (c. 1836–1884), king of Zulus.

1880. Cecil Rhodes (1853–1902) founds De Beers Mining Company. Abd ar-Rahman (1840–1901) becomes emir of Afghanistan. ...**October 13:** Transvaal declares itself independent. **October 16:** War breaks out between Britain and Transvaal. **December 30:** Oom Paul Kruger (1825–1904) proclaims a Boer republic independent of Britain's Cape Colony, but the rebellion is soon crushed.

1881. New Zealand limits immigration of Chinese and other Asians. ...Japanese government promises to convene national assembly in 1890. ...Second Afghan War ends. ...**January 28:** Boers defeat British at Laing's Neck. **February 26:** British are defeated at Majuba Hill. ...**May 12:** France assumes protectorate of Tunis. ...**July:** Muhammad Ahmad (1844–1885), member of a dervish religious order, proclaims himself Mahdi and preaches holy war against infidels. ...**August 8:** Pretoria Convention restores South African Republic under British suzerainty. ...**September 9:** Nationalists in Egypt stage an uprising.

Science, Invention & Technology

1878. Englishman Joseph Swan (1828–1914) invents the carbon filament for incandescent light bulbs. ...Cutting-wheel can opener is invented in United States.

1879. Cleveland becomes first American city to adopt arc street lighting. ...Edwin Hall (1855–1938) discovers that a magnetic field is produced when an electric current passes through a gold conductor. This will be known as the Hall effect. ...American John Browning (1855–1926) patents his single-shot rifle. ...American Herman Hollerith (1860–1929) begins work on a punch-card population tabulator. It will be used in the 1890 U.S. census.

1880. American Frederic Ives (1856–1937) develops the halftone process for printing photographs and illustrations. ...Gasoline blowtorch is patented.

1881. Lewis Latimer (1848–1928), African American inventor, patents long-lasting carbon filaments for lamps. ...American Albert Michelson (1852–1931) invents the interferometer, a device used to split and reunite a beam of light. ...Frenchman Étienne-Jules Marey (1830–1904) invents the first movie camera. ...The *Fenian Ram*, the first submarine capable of making controlled angle dive, is built by the U.S. government. ...**January 27:** Thomas Edison patents his incandescent lamp.

Religion, Culture & Arts

1878. Theodor Fontane (1819–1898), German writer: *Before the Storm*. ...Auguste Rodin (1840–1917) exhibits his first major sculpture: *The Age of Bronze*. ...**June:** William Booth (1829–1912) founds the Salvation Army, a missionary group organized along military lines, in London.

1879. George Meredith (1828–1909), English poet and novelist: *The Egoist*. ...Henry James (1843–1916), American novelist: *Daisy Miller*. ....August Strindberg (1849–1912): *The Red Room*. ...Robert Louis Stevenson (1850–1894), Scottish writer: *Travels with a Donkey in the Cévennes*. ...**May 16:** Antonín Dvořák: *Slavonic Dances* first performed in Prague. ...Fyodor Dostoyevsky: *The Brothers Karamazov*.

1880. Claude Debussy (1862–1918) composes his first piano works. ...Joaquim Maria Machado de Assis (1839–1908), Brazilian novelist: *Memória Póstumas de Bas Cubas* (*Epitaph for a Small Winner*). ...Giovanni Verga (1840–1922), Sicilian novelist of Realist (*verisme*) school: *Cavalleria rusticana*. ...Frances Xavier Cabrini (1850–1917), Italian American Roman Catholic nun, founds Missionary Sisters of the Sacred Heart of Jesus.

1881. Women are permitted to act on Japanese stage for first time. ...Revised Version of New Testament is published. ...Paul Verlaine: *Sagesse*. ...Henrik Ibsen: *Ghosts*. ...Anatole France (1844–1924), French writer: *Le Crime de Sylvestre Bonnard*. ...Leopold von Ranke: *History of the World*. ...Vatican archives are opened to historians. ...James: *Portrait of a Lady*. ...José Echegaray: *El gran Galeoto* (*The Great Galeoto*). ...John Singer Sargent (1856–1925), American portrait painter: *Portrait of a Lady*. ...Verga: *I Malavoglia* (*House by the Medlar Tree*). ...**July 4:** Booker T. Washington (1856–1915) opens Tuskegee Institute in Alabama, leading agricultural-industrial training school for African Americans.

British Isles & Europe

1882. British Parliament passes act giving married women property rights. ...**January 6:** Milan (1854–1901) of Serbia assumes title of king. ...**May 6:** Lord Frederick Cavendish (b. 1836), chief secretary for Ireland, and his secretary, Thomas Henry Burke (b. 1829), are assassinated in Phoenix Park, Dublin, by Irish nationalists in the Phoenix Park Murders. ...**May 20:** Italy joins Austro-German alliance, forming Triple Alliance. ...**June 6:** The Hague Convention fixes three-mile limit for territorial waters.

1883. Transcaucasus railroad from Baku to Batum is completed. ...**October 30:** Secret alliance between Romania and Austria is formed.

1884. Norwegian constitution incorporates democratic reforms. ...French trade unions are recognized by legislation. ...Three Emperors League, comprised of Russia, Germany and Austria-Hungary, is renewed for last time. ...Holy Synod of Russia takes control of all primary schools and favors church schools over secular schools. ...**January:** Russia abolishes poll tax, the last remnant of serfdom. ...**September 23:** Russian government eliminates autonomy of universities and restricts higher education for women.

1885. Russia prohibits night labor by women and children. ...**July 24:** Conservative ministry led by Lord Robert Salisbury (1830–1903) takes office in Britain. ...**September 18:** Revolution in Eastern Rumelia unites Rumelia with Bulgaria. ...**November 13:** Serbs invade Bulgaria. ...**November 17:** Serbs are defeated at Slivnitza. ...**December 28:** Jules Grévy is re-elected French president.

U.S. & Canada

1882. January 2: Standard Oil Company, organized with capital of $70 million, is first company in which board of trustees controls stock of many other companies. ...**March 22:** U.S. Congress suppresses polygamy in territories, including Utah. ...**April 3:** Jesse James (b. 1847) is fatally shot in back of the head by a fellow outlaw. ...**May 6:** U.S. Exclusion Act bars additional Chinese immigration for ten years. ...**June 30:** Charles Guiteau is executed for assassination of President Garfield.

1883. January 6: Pendleton Act reforms U.S. Civil Service, establishing civil service exams and hiring by merit for some federal government openings. ...**October 15:** U.S. Supreme Court rules 1875 Civil Rights Act forbids only state-sponsored discrimination, not discrimination by individuals and corporations.

1884. March 3: U.S. Supreme Court rules that Congress can make paper money ("greenbacks") legal tender, even in peacetime. ...**March 4:** Iowa prohibits sale of alcohol. ...**May 17:** Organic Act applies laws of Oregon to Alaska, ending government by war department. ...**June 27:** Bureau of Labor is created within Department of Interior. ...**August 5:** Cornerstone for Statue of Liberty's pedestal is laid at Bedloe's Island in New York. ...**October 5:** U.S. Congress establishes U.S. Naval War College.

1885. March 4: Grover Cleveland (1837–1908) is inaugurated 22nd president of United States. ...**March 18:** Louis Riel (1844–1885) leads a second rebellion of Indians and Métis in Saskatchewan. **March 25:** Riel's rebels defeat North West Mounted Police at Duck Lake. **May 15:** Riel surrenders as Canadian militia crushes rebellion. ...**July 23:** Ulysses S. Grant (b. 1822) dies. He will be buried in a mausoleum (Grant's Tomb) on Riverside Drive in New York City. ...**November 7:** Canadian Pacific Railroad, with 2905 miles of track joining Atlantic and Pacific coasts, is completed. ...**November 16:** Louis Riel (b. 1844) is hanged in Edmonton, Alberta, intensifying hostility between French Quebec and British Ontario.

Latin America

1882–1899. Dominican Republic is ruled by dictator Ulises Heureaux (1845–1899).

1883. October 20: In Peace of Ancón, Peru cedes saltpeter provinces to Chile.

1884. Belize City becomes the capital of British Honduras. ...Jamaica adopts a new constitution, partially restoring representative government. ...**April 4:** Bolivia cedes its coast to Chile. ...**November:** Britain annexes St. Lucia Bay. ...**December 10:** José de la Cruz Porfirio Díaz again becomes president of Mexico.

1885. Barbados becomes a separate colony. ...In an antifederalist revolution, Colombia adopts a conservative constitution. ...Coffee growing develops in São Paulo states of Brazil. ...Brazil liberates slaves over the age of 60. ...Liberal revolt is suppressed in Colombia.

Africa, Asia & Pacific

1882. Italy occupies Assab and establishes colony of Eritrea. ...Afrikaner Bond is formed in Cape Colony. ...France claims a protectorate over northwestern portion of Madagascar. ...Insurrection begins against French in Tonkin (northern Vietnam), Indochina. ...**June 28:** Anglo-French agreement establishes boundaries between Sierra Leone and French Guinea. ...**July 11:** In response to revolt of Arab pasha, British bombard Alexandria. ...**September 13:** British victory at Tel-el-Kebir is followed by occupation of Egypt and Sudan.

1883. Led by Joseph Gallieni (1849–1916), French forces begin conquest of upper Niger region in West Africa. Sir Evelyn Baring (1841–1917), later Lord Cromer, effectively rules over Egypt as British consul general. ...**May:** Paul Kruger becomes president of South African Republic (Transvaal). ...**September:** Boers found Stellaland Republic (South Africa). ...**November 5:** Muhammad Ahmad defeats British at El Ubbayid (Kordofan) in Sudan.

1884. February 18: Charles George Gordon is sent to Sudan to evacuate Egyptian garrison from Khartoum. ...**March 13:** British proclaim protectorate over Basutoland. ...**April–August:** Germany occupies South-West Africa, Togoland and Cameroons. ...**June 6:** Treaty of Hue gives French right to militarily occupy any place in Annam (central Vietnam), which effectively becomes French colony. ...**July 5:** Gustav Nachtigal (1834–1885) proclaims German protectorate over Togoland coast. ...**August 23:** French naval forces virtually destroy Chinese navy while it is anchored at Foochow. ...**November 6:** Southwest New Guinea and adjoining islands become British protectorates.

1885. A. O. Hume (1829–1912) founds Indian National Congress, which holds first meeting in Bombay. ...Japanese establish Western-style cabinet government, with Hirobumi Ito (1841–1909) as prime minister and nine departmental ministers responsible to him. ...**February 26:** Congo Free State under Leopold II (1835–1909) of Belgium is established. ...**October 22:** Third Burmese War begins, as British demand right to trade throughout Burma and to control Burmese foreign relations. ...**December 11:** British sign treaty regulating relations with sultan of Johore in Malaya. ...**December 17:** In treaty with Queen Ranavalona III (1861–1917), France takes control of foreign relations and occupies Tamatave until Madagascar pays indemnity. Diégo-Suarez is ceded to France.

Science, Invention & Technology

1882. Shoe-lasting machine is invented. ...American Schuyler Wheeler (1860–1923) is first to commercially produce the electric fan.

c. 1882. First home refrigerators are marketed in Germany.

1883. Washington Roebling (1837–1926) completes Brooklyn Bridge in New York. ...First functional photoelectric cell is developed. ...American Harriet Strong (1844–1929) develops system of canals and dams for irrigation and flood control. ...**November 18:** U.S. and Canadian railroads adopt system of standard time.

1884. American Lewis Waterman (1837–1901) invents a capillary action ink pen. ...The mimeograph machine is developed. ...Prime meridian of longitude is established at Royal Greenwich Observatory in Britain. ...British-born American inventor Hiram Maxim (1840–1916) invents a single-barrel automatic machine gun. ...American George Eastman (1854–1932) introduces his emulsified paper photographic film. ...German Ottmar Mergenthaler (1854–1899) invents linotype. ...**May:** First cargo of frozen meat is sent from Brisbane, Australia, to London.

1885. Austrian Karl Auer (1858–1929) invents the incandescent gas mantle. ...American William Painter (1838–1906) invents a metal bottle cap. ...Germans Wilhelm Maybach (1846–1929) and Gottlieb Daimler (1834–1900) equip a bicycle with an internal combustion engine to make the first motorcycle.

c. 1885: First iron ore cargo ships ("lakers") ply the Great Lakes.

Religion, Culture & Arts

1882. Richard Wagner: *Parsifal*. ...William Dean Howells (1837–1920), author of realistic novels of contemporary life: *A Modern Instance*. ...New and widely copied version of *La Fille mal Gardée (Useless Precautions)* opens in St. Petersburg. ...**February 7:** After winning world heavyweight bare-knuckle championship, John L. Sullivan (1858–1918) tours United States, enhancing boxing's respectability. ...**March 29:** Knights of Columbus, first national fraternal society for Catholics, is chartered.

1883. Yale wins first national college football championship. ...Robert Louis Stevenson: *Treasure Island*. ...Olive Schreiner (1855–1920), South African writer: *The Story of a South African Farm*. ...James Whitcomb Riley (1849–1916), widely popular poet in Hoosier (Indiana) dialect: *The Old Swimmin' Hole and 'Leven More Poems*. ...Metropolitan Opera House opens in New York City. ...Friedrich Nietzsche begins writing *Also sprach Zarathustra*.

1884. Commission for Sagrada Familia Church, Barcelona, is given to Antonio Gaudí Cornet (1852–1926). ...Helen Hunt Jackson (1830–1885): romantic novel *Ramona*, a popular defense of American Indians. ...John Singer Sargent moves to London, where he exhibits *Madame Gautreau* (*Madame X*). ...Winslow Homer (1836–1910) settles in Maine and begins to specialize in marine paintings ...Architect William Jenney (1832–1907) is first to use steel construction in ten-story Home Life Insurance office building in Chicago. ...Gabriele d'Annunzio (1863–1938): *Terra Vergine*. ...Henrik Ibsen: *Wild Duck*. ...**February 1:** *Oxford English Dictionary* begins to appear.

1885. Mark Twain: *The Adventures of Huckleberry Finn*. ...Scott Joplin (1868–1917) moves to St. Louis, Missouri, and begins playing ragtime, among earliest forms of jazz. ....Henri Rousseau (1844–1910), an untaught, "primitive" French artist, begins painting in retirement. ...Mary Cassatt (1846–1925), American Impressionist painter: *Lady at the Tea Table*. ...Josiah Royce (1855–1916), American metaphysician: *The Religious Aspect of Philosophy*. ...**February 21:** Washington Monument is dedicated in U.S. capital.

1885–1887. Auguste Renoir (1841–1919), French Impressionist painter, paints *Les Grandes Baigneuses*.

British Isles & Europe

1886. February 1: Liberal ministry under William Gladstone (1809–1898) takes over in Britain. ...**March 3:** Peace of Bucharest between Serbia and Bulgaria confirms status quo. ...**April 26:** Prussian law expropriates Polish landowners in western Prussia and Posen. ...**June:** Home Rule for Ireland, proposed by Gladstone, is defeated in British Parliament. ...**June 23:** Bonaparte and Orléans families are banished from France. ...**July 26:** Conservative ministry under Lord Salisbury (1830–1903) returns to office.

1887. August 1: Francesco Crispi (1819–1901) becomes Italian prime minister. ...**December 2:** French president Jules Grévy resigns owing to financial scandals. ...**December 12:** Triple Alliance between Britain, Austria and Italy is formed to maintain status quo in Near East.

1888. Members of the French government are bribed by officials of French Panama Canal Company in order to keep bankrupt company afloat. ...**March 9:** German emperor William I dies and is succeeded by Frederick III (1831–1888). ...**June 15:** German emperor Frederick III (b. 1797) dies and is succeeded by William II (1859–1941). ...**October 14–15:** Hamburg and Bremen join German Customs Union.

1889. January 30: Habsburg Crown Prince Rudolf (b. 1858) is found dead at Mayerling hunting lodge with mistress Baroness Marie Vetsera. ...Social Democratic Party is formed in Sweden. ...First congress of Socialist International (league of Socialist parties in various nations) meets in Paris. ...**February 1:** General Georges Boulanger (1837–1891) flees France. ...**July 24:** Rural districts in Russia are to be governed by appointed bureaucrats with all administrative and judicial powers. ...**August 19–September 14:** London dockers strike.

U.S. & Canada

1886. January 19: U.S. Congress provides for succession if president dies, resigns, is removed or becomes incompetent. ...**May 4:** Bomb explodes during riot at Chicago's Haymarket Square, killing seven and wounding about 60 policemen. ...**September 4:** Geronimo (c. 1829–1909), inveterate Apache raider, surrenders in Arizona. All Chiricahua Apaches are removed to Florida and later to Oklahoma. ...**October 25:** In *Wabash, St. Louis & Pacific Railway v. Illinois*, U.S. Supreme Court rules that states cannot regulate interstate commerce taking place within a state's borders. ...**October 28:** President Cleveland unveils and dedicates Statue of Liberty. ...**December 8:** American Federation of Labor is founded under the leadership of Samuel Gompers (1850–1924).

1887. February 4: Interstate Commerce Act regulates U.S. railways. ...**February 8:** Dawes Severalty Act gives land to individual Indians, which is to be held in trust by U.S. government.

1888. February: Louisville, Kentucky, first U.S. locality to use "Australian" (secret) ballot. ...**June 13:** Congress establishes Department of Labor. ...**July 29–December 7:** More than 400 die during yellow fever epidemic in Jacksonville, Florida. ...**September 5:** Labor Day is first observed as a legal holiday, in New York State.

1889. Jane Addams (1860–1935) founds Hull House to aid poor in Chicago slums. ...General Federation of Women's Clubs is founded. Unique to America, women's clubs will enjoy significant political and social power. ...**January 1:** Electrocution replaces hanging in New York State. ...**February 22:** North Dakota and South Dakota, Montana, and Washington are admitted to the Union. ...**March 4:** Benjamin Harrison (1833–1901) is inaugurated 23rd president of the United States. ...**April 22:** Government opens land in Oklahoma to non-Indian settlers.

Latin America

1886. Liberal José Manuel Balmaceda (1840–1891) is elected president of Argentina. ...Slavery is abolished in Cuba.

1886–1890. President A. A. Caceres (1836–1923) of Peru creates a foreign syndicate to bolster his country's economy.

1887. Venezuela breaks diplomatic relations with Britain over boundary dispute with British Guiana.

1888. Trinidad and Tobago are joined politically. ...A second university is established in Santiago, Chile. ...**May 13:** Serfdom is abolished in Brazil.

Courtesy: University Library Collection, University of Illinois at Chicago

American feminist Jane Addams as a young woman. Addams founded Hull House in 1889. ➤

1889. French Panama Canal Company is bankrupt. ...Rio de Janeiro becomes capital of Brazilian Republic. ...**November 15:** Dom Pedro II (1825–1891) of Brazil abdicates and a republic is proclaimed. Manuel Deodora da Fonseca (1827–1892) becomes the first president of the Brazilian Republic.

1889–1890. First modern Pan-American Conference is held in Washington, D.C.

Africa, Asia & Pacific

1886. French troops occupy entire Comoros group of islands. ...**January 1:** British annex Upper Burma. ...**January 13:** British set up colony at Lagos, on Nigeria's coast. ...**July 10**: Royal Niger Company is granted charter and given full control over British sphere of influence in Nigeria. ...**October 27:** Last rebellion in Senegal ends as French troops kill Lat Dior (b. c. 1820), Muslim Wolof king of Cayor region. ...**October 30:** British protectorate is proclaimed over Sokotra (in Yemen). ...**November 1:** Anglo-German accord recognizes Sayyid Barghash, sultan of Zanzibar, as ruler of coasts of present-day Somalia, Tanzania and Kenya. Germany annexes inland Tanzania, and Britain takes inland Kenya.

1887. France organizes Cambodia, Annam, Cochin China and Tonkin into Union of Indochina. ...Hawaii leases Pearl Harbor on Oahu to United States as naval station. ...**January 26:** Ethiopian soldiers annihilate Italian forces at battle of Dogali. ...**October 1:** Baluchistan is united with India.

1888. Paul Kruger is reelected president of South African Republic (Transvaal). ...Cecil Rhodes unites Kimberley diamond companies, creating a virtual monopoly of South African diamond mines. ...**April:** Japanese emperor creates privy council as advisory body. ...**May 12:** British protectorate is established over North Borneo, Brunei, and Sarawak. ...**September:** Arabs rise in German East Africa (present-day Tanzania, Rwanda and Burundi). ...**October:** Rhodes secures mining concessions from Lobengula (c. 1833–1894), king of Mashonaland (Zimbabwe). ...**October 29:** European powers and Ottoman Empire sign Suez Canal Convention (Treaty of Constantinople), declaring canal free and open to all merchant and military ships during wartime as well as during peacetime.

1889. January 10: France declares protectorate over Ivory Coast. ...**February 11:** Japanese emperor Matsuhito (1852–1912) accepts constitution drafted by Prince Ito Hirobumi, which establishes limited constitutional monarchy and bicameral legislature. ...**May 2:** Treaty of Uccialli implies Italian protectorate over Abyssinia (Ethiopia). ...**June 4:** Britain, United States and Germany agree on condominium control over Samoa. ...**December:** Aritomo Yamagata (1838–1922) becomes Japanese prime minister.

Science, Invention & Technology

1886. Electrolytic reduction method for mass production of aluminum is developed. ...*New York Tribune* is first newspaper publisher to use linotype. ...German Robert Bosch (1874–1940) invents the electric magneto. ...American doctor John Pemberton (1831–1888) develops Coca-Cola in Atlanta, Georgia. ...Charles Dodgson, pen name Lewis Carroll (1832–1898), designs a logic machine. ...Lee Company begins manufacturing denim jeans in Kansas.

1887. Ludovic Zamenhof (1859–1917) of Poland develops Esperanto. It will become the most widely used universal language. ...German Adolf Fick (1829–1901) makes first contact lenses. ...Gustave Eiffel (1832–1923) builds Eiffel Tower of steel for 1887 Paris Exhibition.

1888. American John Gregg (1862–1948) develops his phonetic system of shorthand. ...John Browning invents pump-action shotgun. ...Nikola Tesla (1856–1943) invents and patents electric motor. ...**November 24:** First railway in China is built.

1889. British chemist Frederick Abel (1826–1902) and Scottish-born British physicist James Dewar (1842–1923) develop Cordite, a smokeless gunpowder. ...Frenchman Édouard Branly (1844–1940) discovers coherence property of Hertzian (electromagnetic) radio waves. ...American Herbert Dow (1866–1930) begins processing bromine from brine extracted from eastern Michigan by electrolytic methods. ...Cantilever bridge is built across Firth of Forth in Scotland. ...International standard of marine channel markings is adopted.

Religion, Culture & Arts

1886. Thomas Hardy (1840–1928), English poet and novelist: *The Mayor of Casterbridge*. ...French novelist Louis-Marie-Julien Viaud (1850–1923), known as Pierre Loti: *Pêcheur d'Islande*. ...Friedrich Nietzsche: *Beyond Good and Evil*. ...Henrik Ibsen: *Rosmersholm*. ...Robert Louis Stevenson: *The Strange Case of Dr. Jekyll and Mr. Hyde*; *Kidnapped* ...Howells: *Indian Summer*. ...Henry James: *Princess Casamassima*. ...Georges Seurat (1859–1891) exhibits in Paris *Un Dimanche d'été à la Grande-Jatte*, his first painting to employ pointillism, the juxtaposition of pure colors in small dots so that they are blended by the eye. ...Edvard Munch (1863–1944), Norwegian painter: *The Sick Child*.

1887. Sir Arthur Conan Doyle (1859–1930), creator of detective Sherlock Holmes: *A Study in Scarlet*. ...August Strindberg: *The Father* and *Son of a Servant*.

1888. Austrian composer Gustav Mahler's (1860–1911) first symphony is completed. ...Dutch painter Vincent van Gogh (1853–1890) moves to Arles. ...Rudyard Kipling (1865–1936), English writer: *Plain Tales from the Hills*. ...Anatole France: *La Vie littéraire*. ...Auguste Rodin: *The Burghers of Calais*. ...Lord James Bryce (1838–1922), British historian and ambassador to United States: *The American Commonwealth*. ...Henry C. Lea (1825–1909), American historian: *The History of the Inquisition in the Middle Ages*. ...**July 12:** Quebec compensates Jesuit order for confiscated lands.

1889. Gerhart Hauptmann (1862–1946), German writer: *Before Dawn*. ...George Bernard Shaw (1856–1950), British dramatist and critic: *Fabian Essays* ...Henry Adams (1838–1918), American historian, completes nine-volume *History of the United States During the Administrations of Thomas Jefferson and James Madison*. ...Edward MacDowell (1861–1908) performs his Second Piano Concerto in D Minor in New York City. ...Richard Strauss (1864–1949), German composer and conductor: *Don Juan*. ...Paul Gauguin (1848–1903), French painter: *The Yellow Christ*. ...**July 8:** *Wall Street Journal* begins publication.

British Isles & Europe

1890. Wilhelmina (1880–1962) becomes queen of the Netherlands. ...British feminist Charlotte Despart (1844–1939) is elected a poor law guardian for Kingston upon Thames. ...**March 20:** Otto von Bismarck is dismissed, and Leo Caprivi (1831–1899) is appointed Reich chancellor. ...**March 27:** Spain adopts universal suffrage. ...**July 1:** At Anglo-German Convention, Britain exchanges Heligoland for Zanzibar and Pemba off East African coast. ...**July 2:** Antislavery congress is held in Brussels. ...**October 21:** German Social Democrats adopt new program at Congress of Erfurt. ...**November 23:** Grand Duchy of Luxembourg is separated from Netherlands.

1891. April 9: Pan-German League is founded. ...**May 31:** Work begins on trans-Siberian railway. It will be completed in 1904. ...**July:** French fleet visits Kronstadt, Russian naval base near St. Petersburg. ...**September 30:** General Georges Boulanger (b. 1837) commits suicide.

1892. Income tax is adopted in Netherlands. ...**February 1:** Gold standard is adopted in Austro-Hungarian empire. ...**August 17:** France and Russia agree on military convention. ...**August 18:** William Gladstone forms his fourth ministry. ...**September:** Count Sergei Witte (1849–1915) is appointed Russian minister of finance.

1893. Germany signs commercial treaties with Romania, Serbia and Spain. ...Customs war between France and Switzerland begins. ...**January 13:** British Independent Labor Party meets for the first time. ...**April 13:** Alexander (1876–1903) of Serbia declares himself of age. ...**October 29:** Eduard Taaffe (1833–1895), Austro-Hungarian prime minister, resigns.

U.S. & Canada

1890. May 1: Bank of America at Philadelphia fails, causing other banks to also fail. ...**July 2:** Sherman Antitrust Act outlaws contracts and conspiracies "in restraint of trade." ...**July 3:** Idaho is admitted to the Union as 43rd state. ...**July 10:** Wyoming is admitted to the Union as 44th state. ...**October 1:** U.S. Congress passes protective McKinley Tariff Act. ...**December 15:** Sitting Bull (b. c. 1830), Sioux chief, is killed in South Dakota during skirmish with Indian police. ...**December 29:** During last major battle between United States and Indians, at least 200 Indians and 25 whites die at Wounded Knee Creek, South Dakota.

1891. March 3: U.S. Congress passes Forest Preserve Act, and President Benjamin Harrison creates 13 preserves covering 21 million acres. ...**March 13:** Eleven Sicilian immigrants who had been indicted for murder of city's police chief are lynched in New Orleans. ...**September 22:** Presidential proclamation opens 900,000 acres of Indian land in Oklahoma.

1892. May 10: The 1882 Exclusion Act is extended for ten years. ...**July 1:** Workers strike at Carnegie Steel Company's factory in Homestead, Pennsylvania. **July 6:** Four men are killed, hundreds wounded at Homestead strike, as company tries to land Pinkerton agents by boat to break the strike. **July 9:** Pennsylvanian state militia restores order at Homestead strike. **November 20:** Homestead strike ends with union's total defeat.

1893. U.S. Congress creates rank of ambassador. (Previously, highest rank was minister.) ...**June 20:** Eugene V. Debs (1855–1926) founds American Railway Union, open to all workers, whatever their craft. It will gain 150,000 members within one year. ...**September 7:** United States and Canada agree to work together against illegal immigration. ...**November 1:** A special session of Congress repeals Sherman Silver Purchase Act.

Latin America

1890. The National University is founded in Asunción, Paraguay. ...Manaus, Brazil, becomes a rubber boomtown. ...Costa Rican railroad is constructed at Limón.

1891. Bartolomé Mitre loses election for presidency in Argentina. ...José Balmaceda attempts a military coup in Argentina, fails, and commits suicide. ...**April 1.** Constitution of United States of Brazil is promulgated. ...**November:** President Manuel Fonseca of Brazil dissolves congress and assumes dictatorial power.

1892. José María Reina Barrios (?–1898) is elected president of Guatemala. ...José Martí (1853–1895) founds Cuban revolutionary journal, *Patria.*

1893. Cuba proclaims equal status of blacks and whites. ...Liberal leader José Santos Zelaya (1853–1919) is brought to power in a revolution in Nicaragua.

Henry Clay Frick (seated, left), chairman of the Carnegie Steel Company. He was shot and wounded by an anarchist after bringing in 300 Pinkerton agents to help quell a strike at the company's Homestead, Pennsylvania mill. ➤

Africa, Asia & Pacific

1890. To eliminate need for extra territoriality, Japanese emperor formally approves new civil, commercial and criminal codes of law based on Western models. ...**June 14:** Britain establishes protectorate over Zanzibar. ...**July:** First general election in Japan is held. Only males over 25 years old who pay substantial taxes are allowed to vote. ...**August 5:** Anglo-French agreement on Nigeria reached. ...**October 22:** Self-government is established in Western Australia. ...**November 29:** First Japanese Diet opens. ...**December 18:** Frederick Lugard (1858-1945), British commander in East Africa, occupies Uganda for British East Africa Company.

1891. Charter of British South Africa Company is extended to north of Zambezi River. ...**January 20:** Lydia Liliuokalani (1838–1917) becomes queen of Hawaii. ...**April 15:** Belgian Katanga Company is created to exploit mineral wealth of Congo Free State province of Katanga.

1892. January 7: Abbas II (1874–1944) succeeds Tewfik Pasha (1852–1892) as viceroy of Egypt. ...**October 15:** Anglo-German agreement over Cameroons is reached. ...**December 5:** Forced labor is imposed on natives of Congo Free State.

1893. Paul Kruger is reelected president of South African Republic (Transvaal). ...War breaks out between France and Siam. ...Colony of Western Australia introduces compulsory primary education. ...Britain declares Malawi part of British Central African Protectorate. ...Women receive vote in New Zealand. ...France declares protectorate over Laos, interior region along Mekong River. ...**January 14:** Hawaiian queen Liliuokalani promulgates new constitution. American residents organize "committee of safety." **January 16:** U.S. Marines land in Hawaii. **January 17:** American residents in Hawaii organize provisional government and abolish monarchy. **February 1:** U.S. ambassador proclaims protectorate over Hawaii. ...**May 10:** Self-government is established in Natal. ...Durand Agreement fixes Afghan-Indian frontier from Chitral to Baluchistan. ...**November 17:** Dahomey is made French protectorate. ...**December 4:** Anglo-French agreement over Siam is reached. ...**December 16:** French forces defeat Tuaregs and occupy Jenné and Timbuktu.

Science, Invention & Technology

1890. Englishman Joseph Lodge (1851–1940) invents the coherer, a radio wave detector. ...American Stephen Babcock (1843–1931) develops centrifugal butter-fat test for dairy industry. ...**June 21:** U.S. Army successfully tests Maxim gun, first truly automatic machine gun.

1891. Fingerprinting for identification is first used. ...Cork-lined metal bottle cap is invented. ...American William Burroughs (1855–1898) invents the adding machine.

1892. First electric radiator is invented. ...American Frank Hall (1836–1918) invents a Braille writing machine for the blind.

1893. Nikola Tesla and Westinghouse supply World's Columbian Exposition in Chicago with alternating current (AC) lighting system. ...American George Ferris's (1859–1896) invention, the Ferris wheel, is introduced at the World's Columbian Exposition. ...African American surgeon Daniel Williams (1858–1931) performs first surgery that successfully closes an open wound to the heart of a stabbing victim. ...The modern metal-framed bicycle is invented in England. ...Karl Benz builds a four-wheeled automobile. ...First color photographs are produced in France. ...The abrasive material Carborundum is patented.

Religion, Culture & Arts

1890. Knut Hamsun (1859–1952), Norwegian novelist: *Hunger*. ...Arthur Thayer Mahan (1840–1914), American historian: *The Influence of Sea Power upon History, 1660–1783*. ...Pietro Mascagni (1863–1945) Italian composer: *Cavalleria rusticana*. ...Jacob August Riis (1849–1914), Danish-born American journalist and reformer: *How the Other Half Lives*, a photographic study of slum life. ...Emily Dickinson: *Poems*, published posthumously. ...**June 9:** Victor Herbert: (1859–1924), Irish-born conductor and composer: *Robin Hood*. ...**July 29:** Vincent van Gogh (b. 1853) commits suicide.

1891. Oscar Wilde (1854–1900), Irish dramatist and poet: *The Picture of Dorian Gray*. ...Selma Lagerlöf (1858–1940), Swedish novelist: *The Story of Gösta Berling*. ...Carnegie Hall in New York City opens. ...James Naismith (1861–1939) invents game of basketball at Springfield (Massachusetts) YMCA.

1892. Pope Leo XIII (1810–1903) orders French Catholics to accept the Republic. ...Maurice Maeterlinck (1862–1949), Belgian dramatist and poet: play *Pelléas et Mélisande*. ...**September 7:** In first boxing match using marquis of Queensberry rules—requiring gloves and three-minute rounds—James J. Corbett (1866–1933) knocks out John L. Sullivan, becoming heavyweight champion. ...**October 6:** Alfred, Lord Tennyson (b. 1809) dies.

1893. Victorien Sardou (1831–1908), French dramatist: *Mme. Sans-Gêne*. ...Henry Adams: *Mont-Saint-Michel and Chartres*. ...Stephen Crane (1871–1900), American writer: *Maggie: A Child of the Streets*. ...Pyotr Ilich Tchaikovsky: Symphony no. 6 in B Minor (*Pathétique*). ...Henryk Sienkiewicz (1846–1916), Polish novelist and patriot: *Pan Michael*. ...Giacomo Puccini (1858–1924), Italian composer: *Manon Lescaut*. ...Jean Sibelius (1865–1957), Finnish composer: *Karelia* (suite for orchestra); *The Swan of Tuonela*. ...Edvard Munch: *The Scream*. ...Antonín Dvořák (1841–1904) composes his symphony *From the New World*. ...Louis Comfort Tiffany (1848–1933) begins to make Favrile glass (sprayed with iron salt solution when hot to give it a metallic sheen). ...**July:** Frederick Jackson Turner (1861–1932), American historian, writes an influential paper, "The Significance of the Frontier in American History." ...Pope Leo XIII issues *Providentissimus Deus*, outlining norms of biblical criticism for Roman Catholics.

British Isles & Europe

1894. Federation of German Women's Associations is founded. ...Agricultural laborers riot in Sicily. ...**August:** Armenians are massacred by Ottoman Turks. ...**March 3:** William Gladstone resigns and is succeeded by Archibald Philip Primrose (1847–1929), fifth earl of Rosebery, as British prime minister. ...**June 24:** Marie François Sadi Carnot (b. 1837), French president, is assassinated by an Italian anarchist and is succeeded by Jean Paul Casimir-Périer (1847–1907). ...**October 15:** Alfred Dreyfus (1859–1935), Jewish officer in French army, is court martialed for selling military secrets to Germany. ...**October 26:** Reich chancellor Leo Caprivi (1831–1899) resigns and is succeeded by Chlodwig Karl Viktor, known as Prince Hohenlohe (1819–1901). ...**November 1:** Alexander III (b. 1845) of Russia dies and is succeeded by Nicholas II (1868–1918).

1895. January 5: Dreyfus is condemned to solitary confinement for life on Devil's Island near French Guiana. ...**January 17:** Félix Faure (1841–1899) is elected French president. ...**June 22:** Rosebery ministry is defeated and is succeeded by Conservative ministry under Lord Salisbury. ...**July 15:** Stefan Stambolov (b. 1854), Bulgarian premier who opposed Russians, is assassinated. ...**August 30:** Instruction in Catholic religion is required in all Belgian public schools.

1896. March: Ferdinand I (1861–1948) of Bulgaria is recognized by Russia. ...**June 3:** Russia and China sign mutual defense treaty against Japan. ...**January 3:** Kaiser William II invokes tension between Britain and Prussia with "Kruger telegram," in which he congratulates South African president Paul Kruger for successfully ending British risings in South Africa. ...**October 24:** Otto von Bismarck publishes Russo-German Reinsurance Treaty.

U.S. & Canada

1894. February 8: U.S. Congress repeals Enforcement Act of 1871, returning control of elections to states. ...**April 30:** Jacob Coxey (1854–1951) leads 400 persons ("Coxey's army") from Ohio to Washington, D.C., to protest unemployment. ...**May 11:** Workers at Pullman Palace Car Company in Chicago strike. ...**June 26:** To assist Pullman strikers, Eugene Debs's American Railway Union calls a strike of all railway workers. ...**July 2–3:** Courts issue injunction against railroad strikers for "interference with interstate commerce and postal service." ...**August 18:** U.S. Congress creates Bureau of Immigration. ...**November 22:** United States and Japan sign commercial treaty. ...**December 14:** Debs receives six-month sentence for failing to obey injunction in Pullman strike.

1895. January 21: In *United States v. E. C. Knight*, Supreme Court finds Sherman Antitrust Act applies only to companies directly involved in interstate commerce, not to those in manufacturing. ...**May 20:** Supreme Court invalidates graduated income tax in 1894 Tariff Act. ...**September 18:** Booker T. Washington, principal of Tuskegee Institute, delivers his controversial "Atlanta Compromise" speech. Washington asks whites to aid black economic and educational progress but plays down the need to attain political power and social equality.

1896. January 4: Utah enters Union as 45th state. Its constitution includes woman suffrage. ...**January 21:** National Association of Manufacturers holds first convention in Cincinnati, Ohio. ...**May 18:** In *Plessy v. Ferguson*, U.S. Supreme Court asserts that segregation is legal if both races are offered equal facilities. ...**May 22:** Spain declines U.S. offer to help end revolution in Cuba. ...**July 7:** At Democratic convention, William Jennings Bryan (1860–1925) calls for easy money, declaring "You shall not crucify mankind upon a cross of gold." ...**July 11:** Wilfrid Laurier (1841–1919), Liberal Party leader, becomes first French Canadian prime minister. Laurier will stress Canada's economic development and will move toward independence. ...**August 16:** Gold is discovered on Klondike River in Canada's Yukon Territory. News of strike reaches United States in June 1897, setting off gold rush. ...**October 1:** U.S. Postal Service establishes system of rural free delivery.

Latin America

1894. First railway over Andes opens. ...José Martí's revolutionary cadre is intercepted in Florida and forced to postpone landing in Cuba.

1895. Cuba fights Spain for its independence. ...**May 19:** Martí (b. 1853) is killed in skirmish with Spanish forces in Cuba. ...**June 28:** Nicaragua, Honduras and El Salvador unite.

▲ *In this illustration from the January 13, 1895, edition of* **Le Petit Journal**, *Alfred Dreyfus is humiliated when one of his soldiers breaks Dreyfus's sword in front of the troops.*

Africa, Asia & Pacific

1894. March 15: French and German governments settle boundary between Cameroons and French Congo. ...**April 11:** Uganda is declared British protectorate. ...**June 22:** Dahomey is declared a French colony. ...**July:** War breaks out between British troops and Matabele tribes of South Africa. ...**July 4:** Republic of Hawaii is proclaimed, with Stanford B. Dole (1844–1926) as president. ...**July 16:** By Aoki-Kimberley Treaty effective 1899, Britain abolishes extra-territoriality, places British subjects under Japanese courts. ...**August 7:** United States recognizes Republic of Hawaii.

1894–1895. Sino-Japanese War is fought. Japan emerges victorious and gains substantial concessions from China, including control over Formosa (Taiwan).

1895. French government establishes French West Africa federation of colonies (present-day Guinea, Mali, Ivory Coast and Senegal), with its capital at Dakar. ...**April 17:** In Peace of Shimonoseki, China recognizes independence of Korea and cedes Formosa and Liaotung to Japan. ...**September 30:** French proclaim protectorate over Madagascar. ...**December 29:** Sir Leander Jameson (1853–1917) leads unsuccessful raid into South African Republic (Transvaal), hoping to start a British rebellion against Boers.

1896. General Herbert Kitchener (1850–1916) begins British conquest of Sudan. ...Muzaffar ud-Din (1853–1907) becomes shah of Persia. ...**January 6:** Cecil Rhodes resigns premiership of Cape Colony. ...**January 20:** British forces occupy Kumasi, capital of Ashanti Kingdom, and annex it to Gold Coast (present-day Ghana). ...**March 1:** Abyssinians defeat Italians at Adowa. ...**July 1:** Treaty creates Federated Malay States—comprised of Perak, Selangor, Negri Sembilan and Pahang—under one British resident-general. ...**August 6:** Madagascar is proclaimed a French colony. ...**August 26:** Led by Emilio Aguinaldo (1869–1964), Philippine insurrection against Spanish rule begins. ...**September 1:** French military force conquers Ougadougou, capital of Mossi kingdom (present-day Burkina Faso). ...**September 21:** Kitchener's Anglo-Egyptian troops occupy Dongola in Sudan. ...**September 30:** By Franco-Italian agreement, France takes control of Tunis. ...**October 18:** By Treaty of Addis Ababa, Italian protectorate over Abyssinia is withdrawn. ...**December 30:** Spanish authorities execute José Rizal (b. 1861), prominent Filipino leader.

Science, Invention & Technology

1894. German Otto Lilienthal (1848–1896) makes first manned glider flights from an artificial hill. ...Frenchmen Louis (1864–1948) and Auguste Lumière (1862–1954) invent the Cinématographe, which serves the dual purpose of camera and projector.

1895. Russian Aleksandr Popov (1859–1906) greatly increases distance of radio wave reception by adding a wire to Lodge's coherer, making first antenna. ...American Charles Post (1854–1914) develops Postum cereal coffee substitute. ...First electric trolley cars begin operating in Moscow.

1896. American Samuel Langley's (1834–1906) unmanned aerodrome flies half mile. ...First political buttons appear during U.S. presidential campaign. ...The ice cream cone appears in the United States. ...Charles King (1868–1957) manufactures first Detroit-made automobile. ...Sphygmomanometer, device for measuring blood pressure, is invented. ...Henry Ford (1863–1947) manufactures his first automobile at Dearborn, Michigan. ...**January 24:** Crewmen from Norwegian whaler *Antarctic* are first to land on Antarctic mainland. ...**April 23:** First public showing of a motion picture takes place at Koster and Bial's Music Hall in New York City.

Religion, Culture & Arts

1894. Rudyard Kipling: *The Jungle Book*. ...Anton Chekhov (1860–1904): *In the Twilight*. ...Anthony Hope (1863–1933): *The Prisoner of Zenda*, a classic historical romance. ...Lord Halifax (1881–1959) starts Anglo-Catholic movement. ...Knut Hamsun: *Pan*. ...George Bernard Shaw: *Arms and the Man*. ...Ivan Vasov (1850–1921), Bulgarian novelist and poet: *Under the Yoke*. ...**October 29:** Hungarian government grants freedom of religious worship and recognizes Jewish religion.

1895. William Randolph Hearst (1863–1951) acquires New York *Journal*. ...William Butler Yeats (1865–1939), Irish poet and playwright: *Poems*. ...Stephen Crane: *The Red Badge of Courage*. ...Oscar Wilde: *The Importance of Being Earnest*. ...Willem Mengelberg (1871–1951), Dutch composer, becomes conductor of the Amsterdam Concertgebouw. ...Edvard Munch: *In Hell: Self-Portrait* ...**January 6:** Mother Church in Boston of the Christian Science denomination is consecrated.

1896. Gerhart Hauptmann: *Florian Geyer*; *Versunkene Glocke*. ...Elizabeth M. Gilmer (Dorothy Dix) begins column offering advice to lovelorn in *New Orleans Picayune*. ...Giacomo Puccini: *La Bohème*. ...George Santayana (1863–1962), Spanish American poet and philosopher: *The Sense of Beauty*, his first major philosophical work. ...A. E. Houseman (1859–1936), English classical scholar and poet: *A Shropshire Lad*. ...First comic strip, "The Yellow Kid," appears in the New York *World*. ...Richard Strauss: *Also sprach Zarathustra*, tone poem. ...Paul Gauguin: *Nave, Nave Mahana*. ...First modern Olympic games begin in Athens, Greece. U.S. team wins 9 of the 12 events.

British Isles & Europe

1897. First census of Russian empire sets population at 129 million, 87 percent rural. ...**March 18:** Crete proclaims union with Greece. ...**April 18:** Greece declares war on Turkey. ...**May 12:** Turks defeat Greeks in Thessaly. ...**August 6:** Employers in Britain become liable for injuries received during the course of work. ...**August 29:** Theodor Herzl (1860–1904) opens first Zionist Congress in Basel, Switzerland. ...**November:** France holds inquiry on Dreyfus case. ...**December 16:** Peace of Constantinople between Greece and Turkey is signed.

1898. Universal suffrage for men only is introduced in Norway. ...**January 13:** Émile Zola (1840–1902), French novelist, defends Alfred Dreyfus and denounces French general staff in an open letter published in newspaper. ...**April–May:** Laborers and peasants riot in Italy. ...**April 24:** Spain declares war on United States. ...**July 30:** Bismarck (b. 1815) dies. ...**August 31:** Wilhelmina, queen of Netherlands, comes of age.

1899. February 18: Émile François Loubet (1838–1929) is elected French president. ...**May 18–July 29:** First Peace Conference held at The Hague bans poison gas, expanding bullets and aerial bombing from hot air balloons. ...**June 26:** International Women's Rights Congress meets in London.

1900. Giovanni Giolitti (1842–1928) begins financial and social reforms in Italy. ...**February 27:** British Labour Party is founded. ...**July 29:** Umberto I (b. 1844) of Italy is assassinated and is succeeded by his son, Victor Emmanuel III (1869–1946). ...**October 17:** Bernhard von Bülow (1849–1929) is appointed German chancellor. ...**December 14–16:** Franco-Italian agreement over Mediterranean is reached.

U.S. & Canada

1897. Canadian parliament institutes preferential tariff, giving Britain lower rates. ...**February 17:** National Congress of Mothers is founded in Washington, D.C. It will become National Congress of Parents and Teachers in 1924. ...**March 4:** William McKinley (1843–1901) is inaugurated 25th president of United States. ...**March 31:** Dingley Bill increases U.S. protective tariff. ...**September 11:** Twenty men are killed when deputy sheriffs fire on coal miners striking in Hazelton and Latimer, Pennsylvania.

1898. Canadian Northern Railway is chartered. ...**January 1:** Five boroughs are merged to create an enlarged New York City. ...**April 25:** United States declares war on Spain.

1899. March 20: Secretary of State John Hay (1838–1905) announces "open door policy," which states that nations should allow the United States access to their spheres of influence in China. ...**October 29:** First Canadian troops leave for Boer War in South Africa.

1900. U.S. census records a population of 75,994,575. ...Eugene Debs founds Socialist Party, which has split off from Socialist Labor Party. ...**Spring:** Carry Nation (1846–1911), temperance activist, embarks on a decade of wreaking havoc with her hatchet in saloons across Kansas while her companions sing hymns. ...**June 8:** White Pass and Yukon Railway connecting Whitehorse with Skagway, Alaska, is completed. ...**August 15:** U.S. troops join international expedition that liberates Beijing, China, which is besieged by antiforeign revolutionaries known as Boxers.

Latin America

1897. Spain grants Puerto Rico limited autonomy.

1898. Manuel Estrada Cabrera (1857–1924) begins 22 years of dictatorial rule in Guatemala. ...**February 15:** U.S. battleship *Maine* is sunk in Havana harbor. ...**July 1:** U.S. forces seize heights commanding Santiago, Cuba, during battles of El Caney and San Juan Hill. ...**July 3:** U.S. ships attack and destroy Spanish fleet in Santiago harbor. ...**July 14:** Commander of Spanish forces surrenders to United States. ...**July 17:** Santiago surrenders to U.S. forces. ...**December 10:** Treaty of Paris between United States and Spain is signed. Spain cedes Cuba and Puerto Rico to United States.

1899. Argentina, Brazil and Chile agree to strive to maintain peace in South America. ...Civil war breaks out in Colombia. ...Cipriano Castro becomes dictator in Venezuela. ...Trinidad and Tobago become a joint British colony. ...**October 3.** Frontier between British Guiana and Venezuela is settled.

1900. Mexico builds a central canal. ...U.S. government establishes civil government in Puerto Rico.

Boxers attack British and French soldiers in early 1900s. ➤

Africa, Asia & Pacific

1897. January 27: French protectorate over Upper Volta is established. ...**February 28:** General Joseph Simon Gallieni (1849–1916) deposes Queen Ranavalona, putting end to Hova kingdom in Madagascar. ...**March 1:** Japan is put on gold standard. ...**June 16:** Treaty annexing Hawaii to United States is signed. ...**August 7:** Anglo-Egyptian forces take Abu Hamed in Sudan. ...**October:** King of Korea proclaims himself emperor. ...**December 14:** Rebel leader Emilio Aguinaldo (1870–1964) agrees to end insurrection and leave Philippines.

1898. February 9: Paul Kruger is re-elected president of South African Republic (Transvaal). ...**May 1:** Admiral George Dewey's (1837–1917) U.S. fleet destroys Spanish navy in Manila Bay. ...**June 20:** U.S. sailors and marines occupy Guam in western Pacific Ocean. ...**August 13:** U.S. and Filipino forces capture Manila. ...**September 2:** Lord Kitchener defeats dervishes at Omdurman (in Sudan). ...**September 19:** Anglo-Egyptian troops under Kitchener arrive at Fashoda. ...**October 11:** Boer War between Britain and Transvaal begins. ...**December 10:** By Treaty of Paris, Spain cedes Philippines to United States.

1899. January 20: Malolos constitution is proclaimed in Philippines, with Aguinaldo as president. **February 4:** Insurrection against U.S. rule begins in Philippines. ...**September:** Muhammad ben Abdullah, Somali chief (called "Mad Mullah" by European enemies) proclaims himself Mahdi and begins systematic raids on British and Italian possessions.

1900. New Zealand annexes Cook, Savage and Suvarov Islands. ...**February 27:** Boer troops led by General Piet Cronje (1835–1911) capitulate to British army at Paardeberg (in South Africa). ...**April 22:** French military expedition defeats forces of Rabah Zubayr at Kusseri (present-day Chad), joining their African colonies into one contiguous territory. ...**May 31:** British troops occupy Johannesburg. ...**June 13:** Rebellion begins against foreign influence in China as Boxers enter Beijing. ...**June 21:** Having merged Boxers into imperial army, Empress Tzu Hsi (1834–1908) orders all foreigners executed and declares war against Britain, Germany, Japan, Russian, and United States. ...**July 10:** Ethiopia and Italy define frontier between their territories. ...**July 9:** Commonwealth of Australia constitution is proclaimed. ...**August 14:** International army enters Beijing to relieve besieged Western diplomats. ...**October:** Russia completes occupation of Manchuria.

Science, Invention & Technology

1897. Joseph Thomson (1856–1940) demonstrates existence of subatomic particles. ....German Wilhelm Maybach (1846–1929) develops first practical automobile radiator. ...German Rudolf Diesel (1858–1913) develops a highly efficient engine that runs on kerosene. ...**October 1:** Boston subway opens. It is first underground system in United States.

c. 1897. Jenny coupler, a safety mechanism that automatically couples railroad cars, is developed.

1898. Bailey Carriage Company of Massachusetts builds an electric carriage. ...First flashlight, weighing more than six pounds, is introduced in New York. ...Danish physicist Valdemar Poulsen (1869–1942) invents the telegraphone, a magnetic recording device. ...Louis Renault (1843–1918) builds his first automobile in France.

1899. Renault builds first manual automobile transmission. ...African American Dr. George Grant (1835–1902) invents a wooden golf tee. ...First riding lawn mower is invented in Britain. ...Otis Elevator Company installs first escalator in a New York factory.

1900. William Burton (1865–1954), at Standard Oil Company, develops the thermal cracking method of refining gasoline. ...The paper clip is patented in Germany. ...George Eastman begins marketing the Brownie camera.

c. 1900. George Washington Carver (1864–1943) conducts experiments with peanuts, sweet potatoes and other crops to produce numerous commercial products.

Religion, Culture & Arts

1897. Edmond de Rostand (1868–1918), French poet and dramatist: *Cyrano de Bergerac.* ...*The Sorcerer's Apprentice* by Paul Dukas (1865–1935) is first performed in Paris. ...Henry Bergson (1859–1941), French philosopher: *Time and Free Will.* ...Josiah Royce (1855–1916): *The Conception of God.* ...Paul Gauguin: *Where Do We Come From? What Are We? Where Are We Going?*, large multiscene painting.

1898. Käthe Kollwitz (1867–1945) publishes a series of prints inspired by Gerhart Hauptmann's play *The Weavers.* ...Konstantin Stanislavsky (1863–1938) and Vladimir Ivanovich Nemirovich-Danchenko (1859–1943) found the Moscow Art Theatre. ...*The Seagull* by Anton Chekhov is produced at Moscow Art Theatre. ...George Bernard Shaw: *Caesar and Cleopatra.* ...Richard Strauss: *Don Quixote*, tone poem. ...**May 29:** First Orthodox Church in Australia is erected in Sydney.

1899. Ernst Haeckel (1834–1919), German biologist and philosopher: *Riddle of the Universe.* ...Jazz begins to develop in New Orleans. ...Maurice Ravel (1875–1937), French composer: *Pavane pour une infante défunte* (*Pavane for a Dead Princess*).

1900. Joseph Conrad (1857–1924) novelist: *Lord Jim.* ...L. Frank Baum (1856–1919): *The Wonderful Wizard of Oz.* ...Shaw: *Three Plays for Puritans.* ...Theodore Dreiser (1871–1945), American novelist: *Sister Carrie.* ...Beatrix Potter (1866–1943), British writer and illustrator, privately publishes *The Tale of Peter Rabbit.* ...Opera *Tosca* by Giacomo Puccini first performed in Rome. ...Jean Sibelius: symphonic poem *Finlandia.* ...Isadora Duncan (1877–1927), American dancer, makes her first successful appearance in Paris. ...**January 29:** Various professional baseball teams form American League. ...**March 29:** Isaac M. Wise (b. 1875), founder of the Reform movement in American Judaism and president of Hebrew Union College in Cincinnati, Ohio, dies.

British Isles & Europe

1901. January 22: Queen Victoria (b. 1819) dies and is succeeded by Edward VII (1841–1910). ...**December 27:** Britain breaks off negotiations on Anglo-German alliance.

1902. Vyacheslav Plehve (1846–1904) suppresses Russian peasants' revolt. ...**January 30:** Anglo-Japanese Alliance recognizes Japan's interest in Korea. If either nation goes to war with third power, its ally must remain neutral; if a fourth power attacks, ally must join the war. ...**June 28:** Triple Alliance is renewed. ...**June 30–August 11:** Second Colonial Conference is held in London to discuss defense of colonies. ...**July 12:** Conservative ministry led by Arthur Balfour (1848–1930) takes office in Britain.

1903. April 19–20: Widespread pogrom in Kishinev, Ukraine, is encouraged by local authorities and Russia's interior minister. ...**June:** Russian government intensifies policy of Russification and seizes property of Armenian clergy. ...**June 15:** Serbia assembly elects Peter Karageorgevic (1844–1921) as king and restores 1889 constitution. ...**August 29:** Sergei Witte, Russian minister of finance, is dismissed. **November:** Russian Social Democratic Party splits into Mensheviks and Bolsheviks.

1904. Finland gives women the vote. ...**April 8:** Entente cordiale between France and Britain produces agreements over Morocco, Siam, Newfoundland and Egypt. ...**June 6–20:** International Conference of Women meets in Berlin.

U.S. & Canada

1901. January 10: Oil is discovered in Spindletop area of southeastern Texas. ...**February 2:** U.S. Army establishes Army Nurse Corps. ...**February 23:** J. P. Morgan (1837–1913) founds U.S. Steel. ...**September 6:** President William McKinley (b. 1843) is shot in Buffalo, New York. **September 14:** McKinley dies and Theodore Roosevelt (1858–1919) is sworn in as president.

1902. French Canadian unions form Canadian and Catholic Confederation of Labor. ...**June 28:** United States buys rights of French Panama Company.

1903. February 23: In *Champion v. Ames*, U.S. Supreme Court rules for first time that federal police power is superior to that of states, thus permitting federal regulation of food, drugs and other substances. ...**October 20:** Alaska frontier between Canada and United States is settled.

1904. January 4: U.S. Supreme Court rules that Puerto Ricans may not be refused admission into United States. ...**March 14:** U.S. Supreme Court dissolves Northern Securities Company, a giant railroad trust. ...**November 8:** Roosevelt is elected president by a wide margin. ...**December 6:** Roosevelt announces his "corollary" to Monroe Doctrine, stating that United States has sole responsibility to police Western Hemisphere.

Latin America

1901. Cuba Convention makes Cuba a U.S. protectorate. ...Tomás Estrada Palma (1835–1908) is elected first president of the Cuban Republic. ...**November 18:** Hay-Pauncefote Treaty between United States and Britain is signed, conceding U.S. control over proposed Panama Canal.

1902. United States acquires perpetual control over Panama Canal. ...A volcanic fire on Martinique destroys town of St. Pierre. ...Boundary dispute between Argentina and Chile is settled. ...**May 20:** U.S. military rule ends in Cuba.

1903. United States acquires right to maintain a naval base at Guantánamo Bay, Cuba. ...Bolivia is forced to cede territory to Brazil. ...**November 3:** Panama makes itself independent of Colombia. U.S. naval forces assist revolt in Panama against Colombian rule. ...**November 18:** Hay-Bunau-Varilla Treaty between the United States and Panama is signed, establishing U.S. control over ten-mile-wide Panama Canal Zone.

1903–1907. José Batlle y Ordóñez (1856–1929) serves first term as Uruguayan president.

1904. Rafael Reyes (1850–1921) becomes dictator of Colombia. ...Chile grants Bolivia access to the sea at Antofagasta. ...**February 26:** U.S. Senate ratifies Hay-Bunau-Varilla Treaty, providing United States with land in Panama for cross-isthmus canal. ...**March 8:** President Roosevelt names Rear Admiral John G. Walker head of Canal Commission to supervise construction of Panama Canal. ...**May 4:** Panama Canal Zone is legally transferred to United States.

The front of the great seal of Queen Victoria.

Africa, Asia & Pacific

1901. January 1: Australian constitution is proclaimed. Former colonies become states in Commonwealth of Australia. ...**September 7:** Boxer Rebellion ends. Chinese government agrees to pay indemnity and increases concessions to foreign powers. ...**December:** Uganda Railway from Mombasa to Lake Victoria opens.

1902. Belgians suppress widespread native uprising in Angola. ...**February 6:** French government agrees to subsidize railroad between Djibouti and Addis Ababa, Ethiopia. ...**April 9:** Australia grants universal adult suffrage for federal elections. ...**May 31:** Peace of Vereeniging ends Boer War. Britain gains sovereignty over Transvaal and Orange Free State (in South Africa). ...**December 13:** Russia induces Persia to promulgate new tariff, which is favorable to Russian interests and unfavorable to British.

1903. New Zealand introduces preferential tariffs for British goods. ...**July:** Russo-Japanese negotiations over Manchuria fail.

1904. January: Herrero rising breaks out in German southwest Africa. ...**February 8:** Japanese torpedo boats make surprise night attack on Russian fleet at Port Arthur. ...**February 10:** Japan and Russia declare war on each other. ...**April 13:** Battleship *Petropavlosk* hits mine and sinks, as Russian fleet fails to break Japanese blockade at Port Arthur. ...**May 1:** Japanese army defeats Russian troops on Yalu River. ...**July 14:** Paul Kruger dies in Switzerland. ...**August:** British military forces capture Lhasa, capital of Tibet. ...**August 31:** Japanese force Russian withdrawal from Liaoyang, north of Port Arthur. ...**September 7:** Dalai Lama of Tibet signs treaty granting Britain trading posts and promising not to cede territory to a foreign nation.

Science, Invention & Technology

1901. Austrian pathologist Karl Landsteiner (1868–1943) identifies three blood types. ...Reginald Fessenden (1866–1932) invents a high-frequency alternator to produce amplitude modulation (AM) radio waves. ...Eldridge Johnson (1867–1945) makes improvements on gramophone and on recording discs. ...First powdered instant coffee is introduced at the Pan American Exhibition in Buffalo, New York.

1902. First gasoline-powered armored car is invented. ...The spark plug is invented. ...Frenchman Charles Richet (1850–1935) identifies anaphylaxis as the mechanism in allergic reactions. ...Frenchman Alexis Carrel (1873–1944) performs first blood vessel suture. ...Renault offers drum brakes on his automobiles. ...American Michael Owens (1859–1923) invents a bottle-making machine and begins manufacturing bottles. ...**October 23**: Telephone cable from Vancouver to Brisbane, Australia is completed.

1903. Dutch physiologist Willem Einthoven (1860–1927) invents the electrocardiogram. ...Italian professor Annibale Pastore (1868–1936) builds a mechanical logic machine. ...James Dewar develops the Dewar flask, a vacuum bottle that can be used to store hot or cold liquids. ...Russian Konstantin Tsiolkovsky (1857–1935) develops rocket with fuel cell containing liquid hydrogen and liquid oxygen. ...**December 17:** Orville Wright (1871–1948) and Wilbur Wright (1867–1812) make the first manned airplane flight in Kitty Hawk, North Carolina.

1904. Englishman John Fleming (1849–1945) invents the thermionic valve, or vacuum tube, while in the employ of Thomas Edison. ...American Benjamin Holt (1849–1920) invents the first caterpillar tractor. ...Frenchman Charles Pathé (1873–1957) invents a variable speed movie projector. ...**July 31:** Trans-Siberian 4,607-mile railroad is completed. ...**October 27:** New York City subway system opens. It will become the largest in the United States.

Religion, Culture & Arts

1901. Thomas Mann (1875–1955), German novelist: *Buddenbrooks*. ...Upton Sinclair (1878–1969), American writer: *The Jungle*. ...Frank Lloyd Wright (1869–1959), American architect, lectures in Chicago on "The Art and Craft of the Machine." ...The first of 12 volumes of the *Jewish Encyclopedia* is published in United States. ...Booker T. Washington: *Up from Slavery*.

1902. Maurice Utrillo (1883–1955) begins to paint Montmartre and the Paris suburbs. ...Maxim Gorky (1868–1936): *Night's Lodging*. ...André Gide (1869–1951), French author: *L'Immoraliste (The Immoralist)*. ...Owen Wister (1860–1938) writes *The Virginian*, among the most popular novels set in American West. ...Hilaire Belloc (1870–1953), British author, philosopher: *The Path to Rome* ...Benedetto Croce (1866–1952), Italian philosopher, historian and statesman: *Estetica*; first volume of *Filosofia della spirito* (*Philosophy of the Spirit*).

1903. Bertrand Russell (1872–1970), British philosopher and mathematician: *The Principles of Mathematics*. ...Jack London (1876–1916) writes *The Call of the Wild*. ...Samuel Butler: *Way of All Flesh*. ...Arthur Schnitzler (1862–1931), Austrian dramatist: *Reigen*. ...Otto Weininger (1888–1903): *Sex and Character*. ...W. E. B. Du Bois (1868–1963) African American civil rights leader: *The Souls of Black Folk*. ...Theodore Dreiser: *The Financier*. ...**March 18:** French religious orders are dissolved. ...**October:** In the first World Series, the Boston Red Sox defeat the Pittsburgh Pirates.

1904. G. K. Chesterton (1874–1936) writes *Napoleon of Notting Hill*. ...J. M. Barrie (1860–1937) writes *Peter Pan*. ...Winston Churchill (1871–1947) writes *The Crossing*. ...Romain Rolland (1866–1944), French author and pacifist: first volume (of ten) of *Jean Christophe*, possibly the longest novel ever written. ...Ida Tarbell (1857–1944) writes *The History of the Standard Oil Company*, a muckraking classic. ...Lincoln Steffens's (1866–1936) *Shame of the Cities* attacks fraud and graft. ...O. Henry (1862–1910), pen name of American short story writer William Sydney Porter, writes *Cabbages and Kings*. ...George M. Cohan (1878–1942), American showman and composer: *Little Johnny Jones*. ...London: *The Sea Wolf*. ...Jean Sibelius: *Kuolema*, incidental music, includes "Valse Triste." ...Constantin Brancusi (1876–1957), Romanian sculptor, settles in Paris. ...**March 8:** German anti-Jesuit law is revised.

British Isles & Europe

1905. January 22: On Bloody Sunday, Russian soldiers fire on crowd of peaceful protesters in St. Petersburg. ...**March 31:** German emperor Wilhelm II visits Tangier, initiating Moroccan crisis with France. ...**August 12:** Anglo-Japanese Alliance is renewed for ten years and is strengthened. ...**November 16:** Sergei Witte is appointed Russian prime minister. ...**November 18:** Prince Charles (1872–1957) of Denmark is elected King Haakon VII of Norway. ...**November 28:** Sinn Féin is founded in Dublin. ...**December 5:** Liberal ministry under Sir Henry Campbell-Bannerman (1836–1908) takes office in Britain. ...**December 6:** State and church are separated in France.

1906. May 5: Witte cabinet falls in Russia and is succeeded by cabinet led by Ivan Goremykin (1839–1917). ...**May 6:** Russian reform constitution is promulgated. ...**May 10:** First Russian Duma meets. ...**July 12:** French court of appeals exonerates Alfred Dreyfus, and he is reinstated in French army. ...**November:** Oil pipeline from Baku to Batum on the Black Sea is completed. ...**November 22:** Russian village communities are abolished.

1907. March–April: Army suppresses widespread insurrection by Moldavian peasants. Martial law is proclaimed in Romania. ...**March 19–June 16:** Second Russian Duma meets. ...**April 15–May 14:** Third Imperial (Colonial) Conference for defense of the colonies meets in London. ...**May 16:** Anglo-Spanish agreement over Mediterranean is reached. ...**June 14:** Woman suffrage is granted in Norway. ...**June 15–October 18:** Second Peace Conference at The Hague meets to discuss arms reduction. ...**November 14:** Third Russian Duma meets. ...**December 8:** King Oscar II (b. 1829) of Sweden dies and is succeeded by Gustavus V (1858–1950).

1908. Robert Baden-Powell (1857–1941) founds Boy Scouts in Britain. ...Women in London stage marches and demonstrations to demand the vote. ...Crystal Macmillan is first woman to address British House of Lords. ...**April 8:** Henry Herbert Asquith (1852–1928) takes office in Britain, with David Lloyd George (1863–1945) chancellor of exchequer. ...**September 13–18:** Revisionists defeat Marxists at German Social Democratic rally at Nuremberg. ...**October 6:** Austria annexes Bosnia and Herzegovina. ...**October 12:** Crete proclaims union with Greece. ...**December 2:** Revolt against Austrian rule in Bohemia breaks out.

U.S. & Canada

1905. Robert S. Abbott begins publishing militant black newspaper *Chicago Defender*. ...**February 20:** In *Jacobson v. Massachusetts*, U.S. Supreme Court rules that states may require vaccinations. ...**February 23:** Rotary Club is founded in Chicago. ...**April 17:** In *Lochner v. New York*, U.S. Supreme Court rules that states cannot set maximum number of hours employees may work. ...**July 8:** Debs, William Haywood (1869–1928), and others found Industrial Workers of the World (nicknamed "Wobblies") to gain union control of production. ...**September 1:** Alberta and Saskatchewan become Canada's eighth and ninth provinces. ...**October:** U.S. government anti-mosquito campaign ends yellow fever epidemic in New Orleans, after 400 persons die.

1906. April 18–21: In San Francisco, California, fires rage for three days following severe earthquake. Some 452 are killed. ...**September 22–24:** Eight die during major race riot in Atlanta, Georgia. ...**September 24:** Devil's Tower in Wyoming is first national monument under Preservation of American Antiquities Act. ...**December 10:** President Roosevelt wins Nobel Peace Prize for helping end Russo-Japanese War.

1907. January 26: In first regulation of campaign spending, U.S. Congress outlaws corporate contributions to candidates for national office. ...**March 14:** President Roosevelt negotiates "Gentlemen's Agreement" with Japanese officials that excludes Japanese laborers from entering United States. ...**November 16:** Oklahoma enters Union as 46th state. ...**December 16:** Sailing from West Coast for Australia, "Great White Fleet" of U.S. naval ships begins around-the-world cruise.

1908. Civil Service Commission is appointed in Canada to select civil officials. ...**January 21:** Sullivan Ordinance forbids women to smoke in public places in New York City. ...**October 1:** Henry Ford introduces Model T.

Latin America

1905. Dominican Republic is bankrupt.

1906. U.S. troops reoccupy Cuba. ...Dominican Republic signs 50-year treaty giving United States control over its customs department in exchange for the United States assuming the country's foreign debt. ...United States decides to build a lock canal in Panama. ...Tomás Estrada Palma is reelected president of Cuba but resigns after the opposition charges electoral fraud. ...**August:** Earthquake destroys Valparaiso and extensively damages Santiago, Chile.

1907–1911. President Eloy Alfaro's (1864–1912) administration adopts a more liberal constitution for Ecuador.

1908. U.S. forces land in Panama. ...Juan Vicente Gómez (1857–1935) becomes dictator of Venezuela. ...President Augusto Leguía y Salcedo (1863–1932) initiates economic reforms in Peru.

1908–1912. In his first term, President Augosto Leguía y Salcedo of Peru spurs economic development through a ruling oligarchy.

Africa, Asia & Pacific

1905. March 1–9: Japanese defeat Russians at Mukden. ...**March 21:** Rebuffing Russian advances, Afghan government reaffirms earlier treaties and engagements with Britain. ...**June 9:** At battle of Tsushima, Russian fleet is largely destroyed by Japanese. ...**August 20:** Sun Yat-sen (1866–1925) issues *San Min Chu I*, announcing "Three People's Principles" of nationalism, democracy and livelihood. ...**September 5:** By Treaty of Portsmouth (New Hampshire), which ends Russo-Japanese War, Russia cedes Port Arthur and Dalian to Japan. ...**November 18:** Japan establishes protectorate over Korea.

1906. Aga Khan (1877–1957) founds All-Indian Muslim League. ...**May 3:** Britain forces Ottoman Empire to renounce claims to Sinai Peninsula, which becomes Egyptian territory. ...**October 1:** Egypt, Britain and Ottoman Empire agree on boundary of Sinai Peninsula. ...**October 7:** First national assembly meets at Tehran and draws up constitution. ...**December 30:** Muzaffar ud-Din, shah of Persia, grants first constitution.

1907. Muhammad Ali (1872–1925) becomes shah of Persia. ...**February 26:** Louis Botha (1862–1919) is elected prime minister of British colony of Transvaal. ... **March 22:** Transvaal government restricts immigration from India. **June 14:** Transvaal government expels 50,000 Chinese who had been brought in as laborers. ...**August 31:** At Anglo-Russian Convention on Tibet, Russia and Britain recognize Chinese dominion over Tibet. ...**September 26:** New Zealand receives status of dominion within British empire. ...**October:** China convenes elected consultative assemblies in provinces.

1908. Congo Free State becomes colony of Belgian Congo. ...**May 26:** Large deposits of oil are discovered in southwestern Persia. ...**July 24:** Abdul Hamid II (1842–1918), Ottoman sultan, restores 1876 constitution, bowing to demands of Young Turks, nationalistic reformers. ...**October 12:** Representatives of Transvaal, Orange Free State, Cape Colony and Natal draft a constitution that will create Union of South Africa in 1910. ...**November 30:** With Root-Takahira Agreement, Japan and United States declare mutual respect for each other's Pacific possessions and acknowledge integrity of China.

Science, Invention & Technology

1905. Russian Nikolai Korotkoff suggests use of stethoscope for measuring diastolic blood pressure. ...German-born physicist Albert Einstein (1879–1955), who will become an American citizen in 1940, uses his quantum theory to demonstrate that photoelectric cells depend on intensity of light, not wave length. ...Sarah Walker (1867–1919), known as Madame C. J. Walker, develops and markets a line of cosmetics, becoming one of the most successful African Americans of her time. ...First practical milking machines are marketed in the United States. ...A fire extinguisher containing carbonic acid solution, which smothers flames, is invented. ...First cornea transplant is performed in Austria. ...African American Robert Pelham (1859–1943) creates a tabulating machine for the U.S. Census of Manufacturing.

1906. German Hermann Anschutz-Kaempfe (1872–1931) patents his gyrocompass. ...The audion radio wave detector is patented. ...Australian William L. Bragg (1890–1971) announces his findings on radioactivity. ...Reginald Fessenden makes first AM radio broadcast on East Coast of United States. It is received by owners of Fessenden radios. ...Brazilian Alberto Santos-Dumont (1873–1937) makes first airplane flight in Europe.

1907. Ernest Rutherford (1871–1937) discovers and names atom nuclei. ...American Elmer Sperry (1860–1930) improves the gyrocompass.

1908. Frenchman Henri Farman (1874–1958) sets airplane flight distance record of 17 miles (26 kilometers). ...British Antarctic expedition climbs Mount Erebus, Antarctica. ...American Hiram Percy Maxim (1869–1936), son of Hiram Maxim, invents the gun silencer. ...Paper coffee filter is invented. ...First oscillating electric fan is introduced in the United States by the Eck Company.

Religion, Culture & Arts

1905. First performance, in Vienna, of *The Merry Widow* by Franz Lehár (1870–1948). ...Choreographer Michel Fokine (1880–1942) creates *The Dying Swan* as a solo for dancer Anna Pavlova (1881–1931). ...British novelist H. G. Wells (1866–1946) writes *Modern Utopia*. ...Miguel de Unamuno (1864–1936), Spanish writer: *Vida de Don Quijote y Sancho*. ...Wilhelm Dilthey (1833–1911) writes *Experience and Poetry*. ...George Santayana: *The Life of Reason*. ...E. M. (Edward Morgan) Forster (1879–1970), British novelist: *Where Angels Fear to Tread*. ...Edith Wharton: *The House of Mirth*. ...Mary Cassatt: *Mother and Child*. ...**May 15:** Debendranath Tagore (b. 1817), Indian philosopher and leader of movement to reform Hinduism, dies.

1906: Yi Injik (1862–1916), *Tears of Blood*, first Western-style Korean novel, is published as serial. ...George M. Cohan: *Forty-five Minutes from Broadway*, featuring "You're a Grand Old Flag," is staged. ...Ruth St. Denis (1877–1968), choreographer: *Radha*. ...Aristide Maillol (1861–1944), French sculptor: *Action in Chains* ...Frank Lloyd Wright: Unity Temple. ...**October 22:** Paul Cézanne (b. 1839) dies.

1907. French painter Georges Braque (1882–1963) begins experimenting on forms which will develop into Cubism. ...Stefan George (1868–1933), German poet: *The Seventh Ring*. ...British pianist Myra Hess (1890–1965) makes her London debut. ...Frank Lloyd Wright completes Robie House in Chicago. ...Florenz Ziegfeld (1869–1932), American theatrical producer: first of the "Ziegfeld Follies," which introduced many celebrated performers. ...Pablo Picasso (1881–1973) paints *Les Demoiselles d'Avignon*.

1908. G. K. Chesterton: *The Man Who Was Thursday*. ...Arnold Bennett (1867–1931), English novelist of provincial life: *The Old Wives' Tales*. ...Vaslav Nijinsky (1890–1950) makes his debut as dancer at the Maryinsky Theatre. ....Harry Emerson Fosdick (1878–1969) becomes professor of practical theology at Union Theological Seminary. ...Mary Baker Eddy begins publication of the *Christian Science Monitor*. ...**December 26:** American Jack Johnson (1878–1946) becomes first black heavyweight boxing champion by defeating Tommy Burns of Canada.

British Isles & Europe

1909. March 31: Serbia yields in Bosnia dispute with Austria. ...**July 14:** Theobald von Bethmann-Hollweg (1856–1921) becomes German chancellor. ...**July 26–September 26:** Revolutionary uprising breaks out in Catalonia (Spain). ...**November 30:** Lords reject David Lloyd George's finance bill. Parliament is dissolved. ...**December 17:** Leopold II (b. 1835) of Belgium dies and is succeeded by Albert (1875–1934).

1910. May 6: Edward VII (b. 1841) dies and is succeeded by George V (1865–1936). ...**July 3:** Self-government in Finland is abolished. ...**October 4:** Revolution breaks out in Portugal. King Manuel II (1889–1932) flees to Britain. **October 5:** Seeking to weaken Catholic Church, new government of Portugal expels religious orders and forbids religious instruction in primary schools. ...**November 4–5:** William II of Germany and Nicholas II of Russia meet at Potsdam to discuss mutual defense.

1911. Commonwealth Copyright Act takes effect throughout British empire. ...**July 6:** Parliament Act reduces power of House of Lords in Britain. ...**August 20:** Constituent Assembly adopts Portuguese Republican constitution. ...**September 14:** Pyotr Stolypin (b. 1862), Russian prime minister, is murdered by a revolutionary terrorist. ...**September 29:** Seeking to annex Tripoli, Italy declares war on Ottoman Empire. ...**October 5:** Italian troops land at Tripoli and occupy town. Other coastal towns are rapidly occupied, but resistance continues inland. ...**December 12:** José Canalejas (b. 1854), Spanish prime minister, is murdered by Spanish anarchist.

1912. January: Portuguese troops arrest hundreds of revolutionary syndicalists during a strike in Lisbon. ...**January–February:** Italian fleet bombards cities on Red Sea and Syrian coasts. ...**February 29:** Balkan League is formed between Serbia and Bulgaria. Greece and Montenegro later join the alliance. ...**May 4–16:** Italian troops seize Rhodes and other Dodecanese Islands from Ottoman Empire. ...**October 17–December 3:** First Balkan War breaks out between Ottoman Empire and Balkan League (Bulgaria, Greece, Montenegro and Serbia). ...**October 18:** In Treaty of Lausanne between Turkey and Italy, Italy obtains Tripoli. ...**November 12:** Albanian independence is declared at Vlorë. ...**December 5:** Triple Alliance is renewed.

U.S. & Canada

1909. Boundary Waters Treaty creates joint committee to settle disputes between United States and Canada. ...**March 4:** William Howard Taft (1857–1930) is inaugurated 27th president of United States. ...**April 6:** Robert Peary (1856–1920) and a team of five men are first people to reach North Pole. ...**June 1:** W. E. B. Du Bois, Jane Addams, John Dewey (1859–1952) and others found National Association for the Advancement of Colored People.

1910. U.S. Census records population of 91,972,266. ...Luther Halsey Gulick (1865–1918) establishes Camp Fire Girls in Lake Sebago, Maine. ...**February 8:** Boy Scouts of America is chartered in Washington, D.C. ...**June 25:** Mann Act prohibits interstate transportation of women for immoral purposes. ...**September 2:** First female police officer is appointed in Los Angeles under civil service regulations. ...**November 8:** Victor L. Berger (1860–1929), is first Socialist elected to U.S. Congress.

1911. January 21: Senators Robert La Follette (1855–1925) and Jonathan Bourne (1855–1940) form National Progressive Republican League to promote direct democracy through political primaries and the initiative, referendum and recall. ...**March 25:** Some 146 garment workers, mostly young women, die during fire in Triangle Building in New York City. Disaster spurs revision of building code and labor laws. ...**December 21:** U.S. Congress abrogates treaties with Russia, which refuses to recognize U.S. passports held by Jews and Protestant clergy.

1912. Naval Bill creates Canadian navy. ...Alaska receives territorial status, with U.S. Congress reserving power to veto Alaskan legislation. ...**January 5:** New Mexico enters Union as 47th state. ...**January 22:** Florida East Coast Railroad opens line between U.S. mainland and Key West. ...**February 14:** Arizona enters Union as 48th state. ...**March 9:** Juliette Gordon Low (1860–1927) founds American version of British organization Girl Guides at Savannah, Georgia. The organization will be renamed Girl Scouts in 1913. ...**April 14–15:** Steamship *Titanic* strikes an iceberg and sinks, killing 1,502. ...**November 6:** Woodrow Wilson (1856–1924) is elected U.S. president by defeating William Howard Taft, Theodore Roosevelt and Eugene Debs.

Latin America

1909. Civil war breaks out in Honduras. ...U.S. troops leave Cuba.

1910. November 10: An armed revolt against José de la Cruz Porfirio Díaz begins in Mexico.

1910–1917. The second Mexican revolution is fought.

1911. Buenos Aires-Valparaiso railway opens. ...**May.** President Díaz is forced to resign by revolutionaries. ...**November:** Francisco Indalécio Madero (1873–1913) is elected president of Mexico. Emiliano Zapata (1879–1919) loses faith in Madero and proposes agrarian reform plan.

1911–1915. Under second term of President José Batlle y Ordóñez, social and economic progress makes Uruguay one of the more stable and prosperous countries of South America.

1912. U.S. Marines land in Nicaragua to support its president during a revolution. ...U.S. forces land in Panama. ...U.S. forces land in Cuba to quell insurrection.

Africa, Asia & Pacific

1909. February 9: France and Germany agree on division of Morocco. ...**March 10:** By treaty with Siam, Britain secures sovereignty over Kelantan, Trengganu, Kedah and Perlis, which comprise Unfederated Malay States. ...**April 27:** Nationalist Young Turks army officers overthrow Ottoman emperor Abdul Hamid II and install his younger brother Muhammad V (1844–1918). ...**July 15:** Muhammad Ali, shah of Persia, is deposed and is succeeded by Ahmed Mirza (1898–1930).

1910. Rama VI (1881–1925) succeeds Rama V as king of Siam. ...**May 31:** Union of South Africa is created with Dominion status. ...**July 4:** Russia and Japan agree over Manchuria and Korea. ...**August 24:** Japan annexes Korea. ...**September 15:** South African Party, dominated by nationalistic Boers, wins parliamentary election in South Africa. ...**October:** China convenes national assembly with half the representatives elected. ...**December 17:** Louis Botha (1862–1919) is first prime minister of South Africa.

1911. Factory Act in Japan limits women and children to 12-hour workday and sets minimum age for employment at 10 years (12 years for heavy labor). ...**April 5:** Uprising in Szechwan begins Chinese revolution against Ch'ing dynasty. By December, insurrection spreads to 14 provinces. ...**September 28:** Italy declares war on Ottoman Empire. ...**October 5:** Italian troops bombard and capture Tripoli from Ottoman Empire. ...**October 11:** At Wu-ch'ang, capital of Hukwang province, Chinese troops mutiny, capturing arsenal and mint. ...**October 26:** Wu-ch'ang revolutionaries proclaim establishment of republic. ...**November 4:** Germany gives up all claims in Morocco in return for French territory in Congo. ...**November 18:** Outer Mongolia declares its independence from China.

1912. January 1: Republic of China is proclaimed in Nanking with Sun Yat-sen as provisional president. ...**February 12:** Emperor Hsüng T'ung (1906–1967) of China abdicates, ending Ch'ing dynasty. ...**February 26:** Railroad from Dar-es-Salaam to Tabora in German East Africa is opened. ...**March 10:** Yüan Shih-k'ai (1859–1916) replaces Sun Yat-sen as provisional president of China. ...**July 12:** Mutsuhito (b. 1852), Meiji emperor of Japan, dies and is succeeded by son Yoshihito (?–1926). ...**November 5:** Sino-Russian accord recognizes autonomy of Mongolia under Russian protection.

Science, Invention & Technology

1909. German Fritz Haber (1868–1934) develops process for synthesizing ammonia. ...American William Pickering (1858–1938) publishes his calculations of the location of the planet Pluto. ...Russian-born American Igor Sikorsky (1889–1972) builds a helicopter prototype. ...**March 30:** Cantilever-style Queensboro Bridge over East River in New York City opens. ...**December 31:** Manhattan Bridge, a suspension bridge, over East River in New York City opens.

1910. American Irving Langmuir (1881–1957) invents tungsten filament. ...Neon light is invented. ...Aluminum foil is invented. ...Halley's comet returns. Its long tail and outbursts of dust jets are photographed for the first time.

c. 1910. First rubber baby bottle nipples become available. ...Norwegian Kristian Birkeland (1867–1917) succeeds in fixing atmospheric nitrogen. ...Gauge blocks for precision measurements in machining are developed.

1911. Dutch scientist Heike Onnes (1853–1926) discovers phenomenon of superconductivity. ...Sperry demonstrates his automatic pilot system on aircraft. ...Maytag Company introduces its Hired Girl electric washing machine. ...Scot Charles Wilson (1869–1959) invents the cloud chamber for tracking subatomic particles. ...In Libya, Italian soldiers are the first to use aircraft during a war.

1912. American Edwin Armstrong (1877–1963) patents his regenerative circuit, produced by linking Lee De Forest's (1873–1961) audions to amplify radio signals. ...First successful parachute jump from an airplane is made. ...John Abel (1857–1938) invents a blood dialysis machine at Johns Hopkins University. ...De Forest invents the oscillator, which generates radio signals. ...Gregorian calendar is adopted in China. ...First electric blanket is invented in United States. ...Electric starter for automobiles is invented. ...William L. Bragg (1890–1971) and William H. Bragg (1862–1942) invent the X-ray spectroscope.

Religion, Culture & Arts

1909. Sergei Diaghilev (1872–1929) founds Ballets Russes in Paris. ...Gustav Mahler completes his ninth symphony, considered to be his greatest. ...Ezra Pound (1885–1972), American poet: *Personae*; *Exultations*. ...Gertrude Stein (1874–1946), American writer: *Three Lives*. ...Ferenc Molnár (1878–1952), Hungarian dramatist: *Liliom*. ...André Gide: *La Porte étroite* (*Strait is the Gate*). ...Richard Strauss: opera *Elektra*. ...Henri Matisse (1869–1954) paints *La Danse* and *La Musique*.

1910. Sir Arthur Quiller-Couch (1863–1944), British writer: *Lady Good for Nothing*. ...Russian Anna Akhmatova (1889–1967) publishes her first book of poems. ...Edwin Arlington Robinson (1869–1935), American poet: *The Town Down the River*. ...Igor Stravinsky (1882–1971), Russian-born composer: *The Firebird*.

1911. Arnold Schoenberg completes his *Harmonielehre*, an important publication on harmony. ...Irving Berlin (1888–1989), American songwriter and composer: *Alexander's Ragtime Band*. ...Rupert Brooke (1887–1915), English poet: *Poems*. ...H. G. Wells: *The New Machiavelli*. ...John Masefield (1878–1967), English poet: *The Everlasting Mercy*. ...Richard Strauss and Hugo von Hofmannsthal (1874–1929), Austrian dramatist and poet: *Der Rosenkavalier*, opera. ...Frederick W. Taylor (1856–1915), American industrial engineer, publishes *The Principles of Scientific Management*. ...Edith Wharton: *Ethan Frome*. ...Kathleen Norris (1880–1966), American writer: *Mother*. ...**April 21:** State and church are separated in Portugal.

1912. George Bernard Shaw: *Pygmalion*. ...Zane Grey (1872–1939), American western novelist: *Riders of the Purple Sage*. ...Claude McKay (1890–1948), American poet and novelist and a leader of Harlem Renaissance: *Songs of Jamaica*. ...Jerome Kern (1885–1945), American composer: operetta *The Red Petticoat*. ...W. C. Handy (1873–1858) publishes *Memphis Blues*, bringing the blues into the mainstream of American popular music. ...Leopold Stokowski (1882–1977) becomes conductor of the Philadelphia Orchestra. ...Henrietta Szold (1860–1945) founds Hadassah, welfare organization for Jews. ...Mack Sennett (1880–1960) founds Keystone Studio to make hectic, anarchistic comedy films.

British Isles & Europe

1913. January 17: Raymond Poincaré (1860–1934) is elected French president. ...**February 3–April 23:** Second Balkan War, between Bulgaria and Serbia, breaks out. ...**May 19–August 10:** Third Balkan War between Bulgaria and Romania breaks out. ...**July 26:** Bohemian constitution is abolished. ...**August 10:** By Treaty of Bucharest, Bulgaria is stripped of most of its territory. ...**November:** Riots break out in Zabern in Alsace-Lorraine after German soldiers act improperly towards crowds. ...**December 13:** Britain and France oppose German-Turkish military convention.

1914. March 10: Suffragette riots break out in London. ...**March 10:** Antonio Salandra (1853–1931) replaces Giovanni Giolitti (1842–1928) as Italian prime minister. ...**March 30:** Herbert Asquith is appointed British secretary for war. ...**June 28:** Austrian archduke Francis Ferdinand (b. 1863) is murdered at Sarajevo by a Serbian nationalist. **July 23:** Austria issues ultimatum to Serbia, demanding the suppression of Serbian nationalist groups. **July 25:** Serbia rejects ultimatum; Austrian envoy leaves Belgrade. **July 28:** Austria-Hungary declares war on Serbia and Serbia declares war on Austria-Hungary. **August 1:** Germany declares war on Russia and Russia declares war on Germany. **August 2:** Germany issues ultimatum to Belgium, asking for right of passage through Belgium to attack France. Germans occupy Luxembourg. British fleet mobilized. **August 3:** Germany declares war on France. **August 4:** Germans invade Belgium. Britain declares war on Germany. Switzerland declares neutrality. **August 5:** Montenegro declares war on Austria-Hungary. **August 6:** Austria-Hungary declares war on Russia. Serbia declares war on Germany. **August 12:** Britain and France declare war on Austria-Hungary. ...**August 12–14:** Austria-Hungary launches offensive against Serbia. ...**August 16:** Germans take Liège. **August 20:** Germans occupy Brussels. ...**August 22:** Paul von Hindenburg (1847–1934) is appointed German commander in East Prussia, Erich Ludendorff (1865–1937) becomes chief of staff. ...**August 22–24:** Germans defeat British at battle of Mons (in Belgium). **August 25:** Germans take Namur and destroy Louvain. ...**August 27–30:** Von Hindenburg defeats Russian Second Army at battle of Tannenberg. ...**August 30:** Germans take Amiens, France. **August 31:** Germans take Givet and Montmédy and cross Oise in France. ...**September 3–4:** Germans cross Marne and advance between Aisne and Marne. ...**September 4:** In London Treaty, Britain, France and Russia agree not to make separate peace.

U.S. & Canada

1913. February 25: The 16th amendment to U.S. constitution authorizes federal government to collect income tax. ...**April 8:** U.S. president Woodrow Wilson speaks before Congress on tariff revision. He is the first president to address Congress in person since 1800. ...**April 19:** California passes law prohibiting Japanese immigrants from owning land. ...**May 30:** Canadian senate defeats navy bill, calling for contribution of three battleships to imperial navy. ...**May 31:** The 17th amendment to U.S. Constitution provides for popular election of senators. ...**December 23:** Federal Reserve System is established in United States, creating a central banking system.

1914. April 7: Canadian Grand Trunk Pacific Railway is completed. ...**May 21:** Three hundred Hindus on ship in Vancouver harbor are refused entrance to Canada and sent back to India. ...**August 1:** Marcus Garvey (1887–1940), Jamaican-born black nationalist, founds Universal Negro Improvement Association in Kingston, Jamaica. ...**August 4:** Canada automatically joins conflict when Britain declares war on Germany. Some 425,000 Canadians will serve overseas, and almost 61,000 will be killed. ...**August 18:** Special session of Canadian parliament votes war budget. ...**September 26:** Federal Trade Commission is established in United States to prevent unfair methods of competition in interstate commerce. ...**October 15:** Clayton Antitrust Act is passed in the United States, prohibiting price cutting to freeze out competitors, exclusive sales contracts and legalized peaceful strikes and picketing.

Latin America

1913. Victoriano Huerta (1854–1916), conspiring with rebel leaders, occupies Mexico City and assumes power.

1914. Colombia recognizes Panama's independence. ...Argentina, Brazil and Chile mediate dispute between the United States and Mexico. ...Huerta resigns, and Venustiano Carranza (1859–1920) becomes president of Mexico after U.S. military intervention. ...Emiliano Zapata (1879–1919) and his revolutionaries enter Mexico City. ...**April 21–22:** U.S. fleet shells and takes Veracruz, Mexico. ...**August 15:** Panama Canal is completed and opened informally. It will be officially dedicated on July 12, 1920.

1914–1918. Argentina remains neutral during World War I but is a major supplier of food stuffs to the Allies. ...Chile remains neutral during World War I.

Austrian archduke Francis Ferdinand. His assassination sparked the beginning of World War I. ➤

Africa, Asia & Pacific

1913. January 23: Headed by Enver Pasha (1881–1922), Young Turks take power in Constantinople. ...**April 8:** Although Chinese national assembly convenes, President Yüan Shih-Kai rules dictatorially without consulting assembly. ...**June 1:** English is declared official language of Philippines. ...**June 14:** Immigration Act restricts entry into and movement of Asiatics in South Africa. ...**June 20:** Union of South Africa imposes Native Land Act, which assigns three-quarters of land to whites. ...**August 6:** Sun Yat-sen flees to Japan to escape forces of Yüan Shih-k'ai. ...**October 6:** Intimidated by his troops, national assembly reelects Yüan Shih-k'ai president of China.

1914. French forces occupy Tibesti Mountains, completing occupation of Chad. ...**January 11:** Yüan Shih-k'ai dissolves Chinese national assembly and governs without parliament. ...**February 1:** Dar-es-Salaam Railroad in German East Africa is extended to shore of Lake Tanganyika. ...**May 1:** Yüan Shih-k'ai promulgates new constitution, giving himself total power for ten years. ...**May 12:** Sultan of Johore accepts a general adviser and increased British supervision and control. ...**August 15:** Japanese issue an ultimatum demanding withdrawal of German fleet from Far East and surrender of Kiaochow within one week. **August 23:** Having received no reply to its ultimatum, Japan declares war on Germany. ...**August 26:** Togoland capitulates to British and French. ...**August 29:** New Zealanders occupy Samoa. ...**September 2:** By Lomé Convention, Britain and France divide German Togoland. ...**September 9:** British take Lüderitz Bay, southwest Africa. ...**September 10:** German raiding cruiser *Emden* enters Bay of Bengal. ...**September 12:** Japanese occupy German possessions in Pacific. ...**September 17:** British take Duala, Cameroons. ...**September 21:** New Zealand expeditionary force occupies German New Guinea. ...**September 29:** *Emden* shells Madras. ...**October 7:** Japanese take island of Yap. ...**October 13–November 12:** Union of South Africa troops put down Boer rebellion in Transvaal. ...**October 30:** Ottoman Empire declares war on Britain and Russia; its fleet bombards Odessa and other Russian Black Sea ports. ...**November 3:** Russia declares war on Ottoman Empire. ...**November 5:** Britain declares war on Ottoman Empire and formally annexes Cyprus. ...**November 6:** Egypt declares war on Ottoman Empire. ...**November 7:** Japanese take Tsingtao (in China). ...**November 9:** British sink *Emden* off Sumatra. ...**November 22:** British occupy Basra (in Iraq).

Science, Invention & Technology

1913. Dutch-born American Herman Fokker (1890–1939) designs an aircraft machine gun synchronized with the propeller for the German military. ...Gyrostabilizers are installed on U.S. ships. ...Danish astronomer Ejnar Hertzsprung (1873–1967) determines distance to numerous stars and the size of the Milky Way. ...American William Coolidge (1873–1975) patents the X-ray tube. ...Stainless steel is first cast in Sheffield, England.

1914. Military tanks with Caterpillar treads are first used. ...American Ambrose Swasey (1846–1937) begins research into problem of metal fatigue. ...Flamethrowers are first used in combat by Germans. ...**March 27:** First successful human blood transfusion takes place in a Brussels hospital. ...**November:** Strapless brassiere is developed.

American poet Robert Frost.

Religion, Culture & Arts

1913. Marcel Duchamp (1887–1968), Cubist and Futurist painter: *Nude Descending a Staircase*. ...D. H. Lawrence (1885–1930), British novelist: *Sons and Lovers*. ...Willa Cather (1873–1947), American writer: *O Pioneers!* ...Charles Beard (1874–1948), American historian: *An Economic Interpretation of the Constitution*. ...Kirsten Flagstad (1895–1962), Norwegian Wagnerian soprano, makes her debut at the Oslo opera. ...Joseph Stella (1877–1946), Italian-born painter of New York City: *Battle of Lights, Coney Island* ...Led by Solomon Schecter (1847–1915), rabbis of the Conservative movement form United Synagogue of America. ...B'nai B'rith creates Anti-Defamation League.

1914. Hugh Walpole (1884–1941), English novelist: *The Duchess of Wrexe*. James Joyce (1882–1941), Irish author: *Dubliners*, short stories. ...Robert Frost (1874–1963), American poet: *North of Boston*, including "Mending Wall" and "Death of the Hired Man." ...André Gide: *Lafcadio's Adventures*. ...Edgar Rice Burroughs (1875–1950), American novelist: *Tarzan of the Apes*. ...Vachel Lindsey (1879–1931) American poet: *The Congo and Other Poems*. ...Richard Strauss: *Die Frau ohne Schatten* (*Woman without a Shadow*), opera. ...Giorgio de Chirico (1888–1978), Italian painter: *Mystery and Melancholy of a Street*. ...Paul Klee (1879–1940), Swiss artist, visits Tunis and begins to work in color for the first time. ...**April 2:** A ten-day constitutional convention opens in Hot Springs, Arkansas, to form the Assemblies of God. It will be among the largest Pentecostal sects in America.

British Isles & Europe

U.S. & Canada

Latin America

1914 (Continued). September 5–9: First battle of the Marne: German invasion of France falters when it encounters Allied forces on the Marne River (in France). ...**September 8–14:** Russian First Army is defeated by Germans at battle of Masurian Lakes. ...**September 9–15:** Germans retreat northward from the Marne and take up defensive positions on the Aisne River (in France). ...**September 28:** Germans and Austrians advance toward Warsaw-Ivangorod and River San. ...**October 9:** Germans take Antwerp. **October 17–30:** At battle of the Yser River (in Belgium), Belgians halt advancing Germans by flooding area surrounding Yser River. ...**October 27:** Germans and Austrians retreat in Poland. ...**October 30–November 18:** At first battle of Ypres, British expeditionary forces block German attempt to advance south. ...**November 1:** Paul von Hindenburg is appointed German commander in chief on Eastern front. ...**December 3–9:** Serbs defeat Austrians south of Belgrade. **December 15:** Austrians evacuate Belgrade.

▲ ***British luxury liner* Lusitania.**

1915. January 23: Austro-German offensive against Russians begins in Carpathians. ...**February 7–21:** At battle in Masuria, Russians evacuate East Prussia. ...**February 18:** Germany begins submarine warfare against merchantmen. ...**February 22:** Germany launches an air raid on Essex. ...**February 23:** Britain closes North Sea and on March 1 will declare blockade of Germany. ...**March 19–20:** Germany launches air raids on Yarmouth and King's Lynn. ...**March 24–26:** British raid Schleswig air base. ...**March 30–April 14:** Germans capture St. Mihiel (in France). ...**March 31–April 5:** Zeppelins raid southern counties of Britain. ...**April 22:** Germans use poison gas at second battle of Ypres. ...**May 1–3:** Austrian and German forces break through Allied lines at Gorlice-Tarnów. ...**May 4:** Italy leaves Triple Alliance. ...**May 7:** British luxury liner *Lusitania* is sunk as Germany begins unrestricted submarine warfare; 128 Americans are among 1,198 casualties. ...**May 23:** Italy declares war on Austria. ...**May 26:** British coalition government is formed under Herbert Asquith. ...**June 23–July 7:** Austrians and Italians fight to inconclusive outcome in first battle of Isonzo. ...**July 18–August 3:** Second battle of Isonzo results in another stalemate. ...**August 1–5:** Germans take Mitau, Cholm and Ivangorod. ...**August 19:** Germans take Warsaw. ...**August 20:** Italy declares war on Turkey. ...**August 23:** Eleuthérios Venizélos (1864–1936) is appointed Greek premier. ...**August 27:** Austria begins offensive in Eastern Galicia and Volhynia.

1915. January 25: In *Coppage v. Kansas*, U.S. Supreme Court rules that employers may refuse employment to union members. ...**January 26:** U.S. Congress establishes Rocky Mountain National Park in Colorado. ...**January 28:** Congress creates U.S. Coast Guard. ...**June:** Bethlehem Steel sends ten submarines to Britain via Canada in order to keep U.S. stance of neutrality. ...**June 7:** Secretary of State William Jennings Bryan resigns when ordered to send second note to Germany protesting the sinking of the *Lusitania*. ...**June 23:** Robert Lansing (1864–1928) is appointed secretary of state. ...**June 24:** United States makes first big loan to Allies. ...**July 2:** A bomb explodes in the U.S. Senate reception room but does not kill anyone. ...**October 5:** Germany apologizes to United States for sinking the *Lusitania* and offers reparations. ...**October 15:** Led by J. P. Morgan Company, U.S. banks loan Britain and France $500 million, largest loan ever made to that time. ...**November 26:** In Atlanta, Georgia, Colonel William J. Simmons (1888–1945) revives Ku Klux Klan.

1915. United States recognizes government of President Venustiano Carranza of Mexico. ...The dictator of Haiti is killed in a popular uprising. ...Argentina, Brazil and Chile draft but do not sign a treaty of mutual cooperation for peace in South America. ...U.S. Army occupies Haiti.

German commander-in-chief Paul von Hindenburg. ➤

Africa, Asia & Pacific

1914 (Continued). December: Russian forces defeat Ottoman troops led by Enver Pasha at Sarikanus in Russian Armenia. ...**December 9:** Turkish garrison of Kurna, Mesopotamia, surrenders to British. ...**December 17:** British protectorate is proclaimed over Egypt; Abbas II is deposed.

^ In 1915, British Bluejackets land at Mudros Bay on the island of Lemnos during the Gallipoli campaign.

1915. Britain formally annexes Gilbert and Ellice Islands. ...**January 15:** Japan submits 21 demands, calling for extensive Japanese police power and control of natural resources in China. ...**February 2–4:** At battle of Suez Canal, Turks are repulsed by British. ...**February 19–March 18:** At battle of Gallipoli, British and French troops begin unsuccessful attempt to invade Turkey via the Gallipoli Peninsula. The French will eventually abandon the attack, but the British will fight on until the beginning of 1916. ...**February 20:** Louis Botha of South Africa invades South-West Africa. ...**March 15:** British sink the *Dresden* in the Pacific. ...**Spring:** Ottoman troops begin to deport entire Armenian population from border with Russia to Syria and Mesopotamia. Ultimately, nearly one million Armenians will perish. ...**April 12–14:** British repel Turkish attack on Basra (in Iraq). ...**April 20:** Anglo-French troops take Mandera, Cameroons. ...With Russian assistance, Armenians rebel at Van on Lake Van's eastern shore. ...**April 25:** Having landed on Gallipoli Peninsula in the Dardanelles, British and French troops are joined by Australians and New Zealanders. ...**May 12:** South Africans take Windhoek, capital of South-West Africa. ...**May 16:** British fail to land at Smyrna. ...**May 25:** President Yüan Shih-k'ai accepts Japan's 21 demands. ...**June 3:** British take Amara, Mesopotamia. ...**July 9:** South-West Africa capitulates to South Africa. ...**August 5:** Ottoman troops recapture Van from Russian and Armenian forces.

Science, Invention & Technology

1915. Submarine detection system is developed. ...Frenchman Paul Langevin (1872–1946) perfects the ultrasonic wave system (sonar) developed by Russian Konstantin Chilowski (1881–1958). ...Corning Glass Works introduces Corningware, heat-resistant glass cookware. ...**September 29:** First transcontinental wireless telephone call is made.

Religion, Culture & Arts

1915. Ford Madox Ford (1873–1939) writes *The Good Soldier*. ...William Somerset Maugham (1874–1965) writes *Of Human Bondage*. ...Mohammed Iqbal (1877–1938) writes *Secrets of the Self*. ...Akutagawa Ryunosuke (1892–1927), Japanese short-story writer: *Rashomon*. ...Edgar Lee Masters (1868–1950), American poet: *The Spoon River Anthology*. ...Carl Sandburg, (1878–1967), American poet in colloquial English: *Chicago Poems*. ...Edgar Goodspeed (1971–1962), American biblical scholar, head of New Testament Department at University of Chicago, publishes translations into modern English. ...Daniel Chester French (1850–1931), American sculptor: *Alma Mater*. ...**February 8:** Epic silent film about post-Civil War South, *The Birth of a Nation*, produced and directed by D. W. Griffith (1875–1948), has its world premiere in Los Angeles. Heroine Lillian Gish (1896–1993) becomes one of America's first movie stars.

1915–1920. Italian painter Amedeo Modigliani (1884–1920) paints his major works during this period.

< This British soldier in Mesopotamia is equipped with a gas mask and dressed in shorts, a concession to the desert conditions. Wristwatches were issued as standard gear to World War I soldiers because they were easier to read than traditional pocket watches.

British Isles & Europe

1915 (Continued). September 3: Germans take Grodno. ...**September 8:** Zeppelins raid London and Britain's east counties. ...**September 16:** Germans take Pinsk. ...**September 22–October 13:** Allied offensive at Artois (in France) is inconclusive. ...**September 22–November 6:** At battle in Champagne, despite continuous influx of French troops, Allies gain only a few thousand yards. ...**October 6–9:** Austro-German offensive against Serbia begins. ...**October 14:** Serbia and other Allies declare war on Bulgaria. ...**October 18–November 4:** No gains are made in third battle of Isonzo. ...**October 29:** Aristide Briand (1862–1932) becomes French prime minister. ...**November 10–December 3:** Fourth battle of Isonzo leads to yet another stalemate. ...**November 24–29:** Bulgarians defeat Serbians at battle of Kosovo (in Serbia). ...**December 9–13:** Anglo-French offensive towards Serbia is checked on Greek frontier.

1916. January 14: Austrians take Cetinje. ...**January 23:** Austrians take Scutari in Albania. ...**February 21–December 18:** At battle of Verdun, Germans attack French forces, gaining little ground in nearly one year of fighting. Combined casualties reach 750,000. ...**February 29:** Germans resume submarine warfare. ...**April 23:** At Easter Rising in Dublin, 2,000 Dubliners unsuccessfully rebel against British rule. ...**May 15–31:** Austrians launch offensive between Adige and Brenta. ...**May 16:** France and Britain secretly agree on how to divide Ottoman Empire at conclusion of war with the signing of the Sykes-Picot agreement. ...**May 31–June 1:** At battle of Jutland, British defeat German fleet despite heavy losses. British naval supremacy is definitely established. ...**June 4–7:** Russia launches offensives toward Luck, west of Tarnopol and north of Czernowitz. ...**June 6–24:** Allies blockade Greece. ...**June 7:** Russians take Luck. ...**June 10:** Russians cross Dniester. ...**June 13:** Russia launches offensive at Baranovici. ...**June 22:** British stage air raids on Karlsruhe, Cologne, and Trier. ...**July:** Russians launch general offensive. ...**July 1–November 18:** Allied offensive at Somme results in only small gains and nearly 600,000 Allied casualties; German casualties are 450,000. ...**July 16:** Russians take Czernowitz. ...**July 28:** Russians take Brody. ...**August 7–10:** Russians break through at Zalosce. ...**August 27:** Romania declares war on Austria. ...**August 28:** Germany declares war on Romania. ...Italy declares war on Germany. ...**August 29:** Paul von Hindenburg is appointed German chief of general staff, and Erich Ludendorff is appointed quartermaster general.

U.S. & Canada

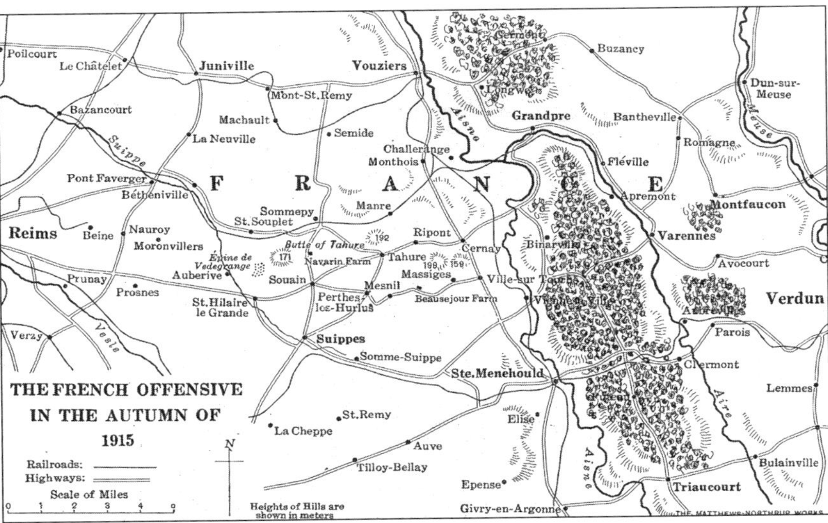

▲ *A map of the French offensive in the autumn of 1915.*

1916. Marcus Garvey brings his Universal Negro Improvement Association (UNIA) to Harlem. ...**January 24:** In *Brushaber v. Union Pacific*, U.S. Supreme Court, declares federal income tax is constitutional. ...**January 28:** President Wilson appoints Louis D. Brandeis (1856–1941) to the U.S. Supreme Court. He is the first Jew to sit on the Court. ...**February 3–4:** Fire destroys Canadian parliament buildings in Ottawa. ...**February 29:** South Carolina sets 14 as minimum age to work in mills, mines and factories. ...**March 24:** German submarine sinks French steamer *Sussex*. American passengers are aboard. ...**May 27:** President Wilson addresses the League to Enforce Peace and defends U.S. position of neutrality. ...**June 3:** U.S. Congress passes the National Defense Act, authorizing a standing army of 175,000 and a National Guard of 450,000 soldiers. ...**July 2:** Henrietta "Hetty" Green (b. 1835), the richest woman in the United States, dies, leaving an estate of some $100 million. ...**July 11:** Federal Road Aid Act provides $5 million to improve U.S. roads and establishes system of highway class- ifications. ...**July 17:** Federal Farm Loan Bank Act establishes system of 12 land banks. ...**August 25**: Office of National Parks is established in U.S. Department of Interior. It will become National Park Service in 1934. ...**August 29:** U.S. Congress passes the navy Act, a ten-year plan to enlarge the navy. ...**September 3:** Adamson Act provides eight-hour workday for most railroad workers in United States.

Latin America

1916. U.S. Marines occupy Dominican Republic. ...Nicaragua grants United States exclusive rights to a canal. ...Coastal banking interests dominate Ecuador. ...**January 10:** Followers of Francisco "Pancho" Villa (1877–1923) remove 17 U.S. mining engineers from a train in Mexico and kill 16 of them. United States responds by launching a year-long unsuccessful search for Villa in Mexico.

1916–1920. Alfredo Moreno (c. 1880–1940) is president of Ecuador.

1916–1922. Radical Party takes power in Argentina and begins to institute numerous reforms.

Africa, Asia & Pacific

1915 (Continued). September 28: British take Al-Kut, Mesopotamia. ...**November 22–24:** British are defeated at Ctesiphon (in Iraq). ...**December 7:** British are besieged in Al-Kut. ...**December 10:** British begin to evacuate troops from the beaches of Gallipoli.

Still Picture Branch, National Archives, College Park, MD

^ *Pancho Villa (fourth from left) with other Mexican revolutionaries (c. 1913).*

1916. Turkish offensive toward Persia begins. ...Yüan Shih-k'ai (b. 1859) dies in China. ...Belgian forces occupy districts of Rwanda and Urundi in German East Africa. ...Judith (Zauditu) (1876–1926), daughter of Menelik, becomes empress of Ethiopia. ...**January 1:** British enter Yaounde in the Cameroons. ...**January 9:** After bitter resistance from Ottoman forces under Kemal Mustafa (1881–1938), Allies abandon attack on Gallipoli in the Dardanelles. Approximately 250,000 Ottoman troops perish, and the Allies lose some 50,000 men. ...**February 4:** National Bank of Philippines is created and made depository for public funds. ...**February 6–15:** German troops leave Cameroons for Spanish Río Muni. ...**February 10:** Jan Smuts (1870–1950) takes over command of British troops in East Africa. ...**February 18:** Last German troops in Cameroons surrender. ...**March 5:** Joint expedition by British, Belgian, Portuguese and South African troops invades German East Africa (present-day Tanzania) but cannot overcome small German force. ...**June 7:** Hussein ibn Ali (1856-1931), grand sharif of Mecca, leads an insurrection against Ottoman rule. ...**July 1:** Turks take Kermanshah (in Iran). ...**July 3:** Russian government recognizes Japanese influence in China, and Japan recognizes Russian advance into Outer Mongolia. ...**July 7:** Smuts occupies Tanga (in Tanzania). ...**August 10:** Turks take Hamadan (in Iran). ...**August 29:** Jones Act abolishes Philippine Commission, creates elective senate, vests greater autonomy in Philippine government. ...**September 4:** British take Dar-es-Salaam. ...**September 19:** Belgian forces occupy Tabora on Lake Tanganyika.

Science, Invention & Technology

1916. American Elmer Sperry (1860–1930) invents a high-intensity searchlight ....A three-inch mortar gun is developed. ...American Clarence Birdseye (1886–1956) develops quick-freezing method of storing food. ...Japanese Kotaro Honda (1870–1954) develops a powerful magnet called the ALNICO using cobalt and tungsten steel.

< *Marcus Garvey, founder of the Back to Africa movement.*

Religion, Culture & Arts

1916. John Dewey: *Democracy and Education*. ...James Joyce: novel *Portrait of the Artist as a Young Man*. ...George Bernard Shaw: *Heartbreak House*. ...Robert Frost: *Mountain Interval*, including "The Road Not Taken" and "Birches." ...José Clemente Orozco (1883–1949) exhibits a series of wash drawings titled *Mexico in Revolution*. ...Foundation in Zürich of the Dada movement of anti-art. ...Henri Matisse: *The Piano Lesson*. ...D. W. Griffith directs mammoth silent movie *Intolerance*.

British Isles & Europe

1916 (Continued). October 15: Allies occupy Athens. ...**October 24–November 5:** French stage offensive east of Verdun. ...**November 1–7:** Italians and Austrians fight at ninth battle of Isonzo. ...**December 7:** Coalition ministry under Lloyd George takes office in Britain. ...**December 12:** Central Powers make peace offer. ...**December 15–17:** French launch offensive between Meuse and Woëvre Plain. ...**December 30:** Allies refuse peace plan proposed by Central Powers.

1917. February 1: Submarine warfare resumes with 103 German U-boats. ...**March 8–14: (February 23–March 1, Old Style)** In February revolution in Russia, workers in Petrograd (St. Petersburg) go on strike, resulting in outbreak of riots. Soldiers in Petrograd join workers in revolt. ...**March 16:** Nicholas II abdicates. Georgi Lvov (1861–1925) and Aleksandr Kerensky (1881–1970) form cabinet. ...**March 19:** Théodule Ribot (1839–1916) becomes French prime minister. ...**April 4:** British take offensive in Artois. ...**April 9:** French offensive in Champagne begins. ...**April 9–May 3:** At Battle of Arras, Canadian forces capture Vimy Ridge. ...**April 16:** Having been sent in a sealed train by German authorities, Vladimir Lenin (1870–1924) arrives at Finland Station in Petrograd, Russia. ...**May 15:** General Henri Pétain (1856–1951) is appointed French commander-in-chief. ...**June 26:** First U.S. troops arrive in France. ...**June 27:** Eleuthérios Venizélos, Greek premier, joins Allies. ...**July 1–11:** Russians break through at Zborov and on Dniester. ...**July 12–17:** Germans are first to use mustard gas at Ypres. ...**July 22:** Kerensky becomes Russian premier. ...**August 3:** Russians take Czernowitz. ...**September 15:** Kerensky proclaims Russian Republic. ...**September 20:** British offensive near Ypres resumes. ...**October 24–27:** Austro-German forces achieve breakthrough at battle of Caporetto. ...**November 1:** Georg Hertling (1843–1919) becomes German chancellor. ...**November 2:** Germans retreat beyond Aisne-Oise and Ailette Canals. ...**November 5–7:** Conference of Rapallo establishes Supreme War Council of Allies. ...**November 6 (October 24, Old Style):** Bolsheviks seize power in Petrograd (St. Petersburg). Lenin is made head of new government. ...**November 10–12:** Counterrevolution of Kerensky and Lavr Kornilov (1870–1918) fails. ...**November 17:** Georges Clemenceau (1841–1929) becomes French prime minister. ...**November 26:** Russian Soviets offer armistice to Central Powers. ...**November 28:** Estonia declares independence from Russia. ...**November 30–December 7:** Germans counterattack at Cambrai.

U.S. & Canada

1916 (Continued). September 7: Under U.S. Shipping Board Act, Congress appropriates $50 million to purchase or build new merchant ships. ...**November 7:** Woodrow Wilson is reelected president, defeating Charles Evans Hughes (1862–1948), by promising to keep United States out of war. Representative Jeannette Rankin (1880–1973) from Montana is first woman elected to U.S. Congress. ...**December 8:** President Wilson signs treaty with Canada, protecting migratory birds.

1917. Federal income tax is introduced in Canada. ...In *Buchanan v. Warley*, U.S. Supreme Court overturns Kentucky law forbidding blacks and whites from residing on same block. ...**January 17:** Denmark sells Virgin Islands to United States for $25 million. ...**January 22:** President Wilson delivers a speech to Congress in which he calls for "peace without victory" and introduces his hope for a "community of nations." ...**February 3:** President Wilson breaks diplomatic relations with Germany after Germany announces its intentions to resume unrestricted submarine warfare. ...**March 8:** U.S. Senate adopts cloture rule: two-thirds of senators present and voting may limit debate. ...**March 18–21:** Four U.S. merchant ships are sunk by German submarines. ...**April 2:** President Wilson asks Congress for a declaration of war against Germany. **April 4:** U.S. Senate votes 82 to 6 in favor of declaring war on Germany. **April 6:** With a vote of 373 to 50, U.S. House of Representatives votes to declare war on Germany. With this vote, the United States officially declares war on Germany. ...**April 24:** Liberty Loan Act authorizes bond issue. By 1919, loan drives will net 60 percent of money needed to finance war. ...**May 18:** Under Selective Service Act, all American men aged 21 through 30 must register for military service. ...**June 15:** Espionage Act provides up to 20 years in prison for hindering war effort or aiding enemy. ...**August:** U.S. Congress passes the Lever Food and Fuel Act. ...**August 23:** During quarrel with local police, black soldiers march on Houston, Texas; at least 13 die in ensuing riot. Thirteen soldiers are tried and hanged soon after. **September 3:** Another five black soldiers are hanged for participating in Houston riot. ...**September 26:** Canada passes a law conscripting men between ages of 20 and 45. ...**November 11:** New York grants women the vote. ...**December 7:** United States declares war on Austria-Hungary. ...**December 8:** Explosion aboard a French munitions ship destroys half of Halifax, Nova Scotia in Canada. ...**December 17:** Pro-war coalition government defeats Liberals in Canadian general elections.

Latin America

1917. Colombia settles boundary disputes with Ecuador. ...The elected leader of Costa Rica is overthrown. ...A new constitution is promulgated in Mexico. ...U.S. citizenship is granted to Puerto Ricans. ...**April:** Panama enters World War I on Allied side. ...**April 17:** Cuba enters World War I on Allied side. ...**August:** Brazil severs diplomatic relations with Germany. ...**October:** Brazil enters World War I on the Allied side.

1917–1918. An earthquake destroys Guatemala City.

▲ ***French commander-in-chief, General Henri Pétain.***

Africa, Asia & Pacific

1916 (Continued). November: British troops advance from Egypt into Sinai Peninsula. ...**December 13:** British offensive in Mesopotamia begins. ...**December 23:** British take El Arish, Palestine.

1917. Britain, France and Italy recognize Hussein ibn Ali of Hashimite dynasty as first king of Hejaz region near Mecca. ...**February 14:** China declares war on Germany. ...**February 24:** Turks are defeated and evacuate Al-Kut and Sanna-i-Yat. ...**March 11:** British take Baghdad. Turks retreat from Persia. ...**March 26–28:** First battle of Gaza ends in British victory. ...**April 13:** Turks retreat further in Mesopotamia. ...**April 18–19:** Second battle of Gaza ends in another British victory. ...**June 29:** Britsih field marshal Edmund Allenby (1861–1936) takes command in Palestine. ...**July 6:** T. E. Lawrence (1888–1935), known as Lawrence of Arabia, leads Arab forces seizing Aqaba from Ottoman Empire. ...**July 19:** Russians leave Mesopotamian front. ...**July 22:** In order to influence postwar peace treaties, Siam declares war on Germany and Austria-Hungary. ...**August 30:** Turks take Marivan, Persia. ...**September 28:** Anglo-Indian forces capture Ramadieh (in Mesopotamia). ...**November 2:** In Balfour Declaration, British foreign secretary Arthur Balfour (1848–1930) announces that Britain will support establishment of Jewish homeland in Palestine. ...**November 7:** British take Gaza. ...**November 17:** British take Jaffa (in Palestine). ...**December 9:** Allenby enters Jerusalem.

Science, Invention & Technology

1917. Albert Einstein develops his theory of stimulated emission, the foundation for laser technology. ...Edwin Howard Armstrong (1890–1954) develops the superheterodyne circuit. ...Mustard gas for chemical warfare is developed. ...Frenchman Georges Claude (1870–1960) develops method of synthesizing ammonia for commercial production. ...Germans develop the Paris gun, capable of firing shells up to 75 miles.

Religion, Culture & Arts

1917. Georges Braque begins concentrating on still-life paintings. ...William Butler Yeats (1865–1939), Irish playwright and poet: *The Wild Swans at Coole*. ...Knut Hamsun: *The Growth of the Soil*. ...Siegfried Sassoon (1886–1967), British novelist and poet of World War I: *The Old Huntsman*. ...Edna Saint Vincent Millay (1892–1950), American poet: *Renascence*. ...Premiere of First Symphony by Sergei Sergeyevich Prokofiev (1891–1953), Russian composer, pianist and conductor. ...Mary Pickford (1893–1979), "America's sweetheart" and perhaps most popular silent movie actress, stars in *Rebecca of Sunnybrook Farm*. ...George M. Cohan (1878–1942) writes the song "Over There." ...W. C. Handy: *Beale Street Blues*. ...Giorgio de Chirico paints *Grand Metaphysical Interior*.

Soldiers fighting for the Bolsheviks during the Russian Revolution. ➤

British Isles & Europe

1917 (Continued). December 2: Hostilities are suspended on Russian front. ...**December 3:** Austro-German offensive in Italy is definitely stopped. ...**December 5:** Germany signs armistice with Russia. ...**December 9:** Germany signs armistice with Romania.

1918. February 5: Soviet government seizes properties of Russian Orthodox Church and closes its schools and monasteries. ...**March 3:** Treaty of Brest-Litovsk between Central Powers and Russia ends war on eastern front. ...**March 7:** Germany and Finland sign peace treaty. ...**April 24–26:** British win victory at Villers-Bretonneux. ...**July 15–17:** In the last German offensive of World War I, second battle of Marne, the Germans launch an unsuccessful attack on Reims. ...**July 16:** Nicholas II (b. 1868) of Russia and his family are murdered by Soviets. ...**July 22:** Allies cross Marne. ...**August 2:** Germans evacuate Soissons and left banks of Vesle and Aisne. ...**September 4:** Germans retreat to Siegfried Line. ...**September 12–14:** Americans take St. Mihiel salient. ...**September 15:** Allies break through on Bulgarian front between Cerna and Vardar. ...**September 26:** General Allied offensive begins. ...**October 26:** Ludendorff is dismissed as German commander. ...**October 30:** Turkey surrenders unconditionally. ...**November 3:** Allies sign armistice with Austria-Hungary. ...**November 7:** French and Americans take Sedan. ...**November 9:** Revolution breaks out in Berlin. German Republic is proclaimed. Friedrich Ebert (1871–1925) becomes German chancellor. ...**November 10:** William II flees to Holland. Council of People's Delegates assumes power in Germany. ...**November 11:** Allies sign armistice with Germany at Compiègne. ...**November 14:** The union of Czech Lands and Slovakia as Czechoslavakia is proclaimed.. ...**December 8–22:** Bolsheviks take power in Estonia, Lithuania and Latvia.

1919. January 5: National Socialist (Nazi) Party is founded in Germany. ...**January 17:** Red Army seizes Kaunas, Lithuania. ...**January 18:** Allied leaders meet at Paris Peace Conference to determine peace terms for Central Powers. ...**January 21:** In Dublin, 73 Irish members of British Parliament form Dáil Éireann (Assembly of Ireland) and elect Eamon de Valera (1882–1975) president. ...**March 10:** Russian capital is moved from Petrograd to Moscow. ...**March 21–August 1:** Hungary is proclaimed a Soviet republic. ...**March 23:** In Milan, Benito Mussolini (1883–1943) forms the Fascist organization *Fascio di Combattimento*.

U.S. & Canada

1917 (Continued). December 18: Because of the war, U.S. government takes control of virtually all railroads.

1918. January 8: In an address before both houses of Congress, President Woodrow Wilson issues his Fourteen Points peace program. ...**March:** Women 21 and over are given vote in Canada. ...**March 4:** Bernard Baruch (1870–1965) is named to U.S. War Industries Board with near dictatorial powers. ...**March 19:** U.S. Congress introduces daylight saving time, from April through October. ...**May 16:** Sedition Act provides severe penalties for persons attacking U.S. war effort or using "disloyal, profane, scurrilous, or abusive language" about U.S. government. ...**September:** Worldwide influenza pandemic that will kill more than 20 million people within months begins. ...**September 14:** Eugene V. Debs, Socialist leader, is sentenced to ten years in jail for interfering with U.S. military recruiting. ...**December 18:** U.S. Congress passes and sends to the states for ratification Prohibition (18th) Amendment.

During prohibition, it was common for customs inspectors to find liquor hidden in a traveler's luggage. ➤

1919. March 10: In *Schenk v. United States*, U.S. Supreme Court upholds Espionage Act. ...**March 15:** In Paris, U.S. soldiers form American Legion. ...**June 21:** Police and troops suppress a general strike in Winnipeg, Canada. ...**July 1:** Daily airmail service begins between Chicago and New York City. ...**July 10:** President Wilson sends Treaty of Versailles and League of Nations covenant to Senate. ...**July 14:** United States resumes commercial trade with Germany. ...**July 27:** Thirty-eight are killed and more than 500 injured in Chicago race riot. ...**August 31:** Communist Party of America is founded in Chicago, Illinois.

Latin America

1918. Oil is discovered in Venezuela. ...Mayagüez, Puerto Rico, is badly damaged in an earthquake. ...U.S. forces land in Panama. ...Mexico nationalizes its oil fields. ...José Batlle Ordóñez's concept of a plural presidency is adopted in Uruguay.

1919. Gabriel Terra (1873–1942) suspends the Uruguayan constitution. ...University of Concepción (in Chile) is founded. ...Emiliano Zapata (b. c. 1879) is murdered.

1919–1930. In his second term, President Augosto Leguía y Salcedo becomes virtual dictator of Peru, increasing the country's exports in the years following the completion in 1914 of the Panama Canal.

Africa, Asia & Pacific

1918. February 21: Australians take Jericho (in Palestine). ...**April 5:** Japanese troops occupy Vladivostok. ...**May 21:** Railroad from Djibouti to Addis Ababa (begun in 1897) is completed. ...**June 16:** Turks enter Tabriz, Persia. ...**July 13:** Last Turkish offensive in Palestine attempts to recover Jericho. **July 14:** Turkish offensive on Jericho is checked by Australians. ...**August 2:** Japanese advance in Siberia begins. ...**September 19:** British break through in Palestine. ...**October 1:** Australians enter Damascus. ...**October 18:** British occupy Aleppo. French occupy Alexandretta. ...**October 30:** Allies and Ottoman Empire sign armistice. ...**November 2:** Germans invade Northern Rhodesia. **November 14:** Germans capitulate in Northern Rhodesia.

1919. January 10: British troops occupy Baghdad. ...**March 1:** Japanese brutally crush Korean insurrection. ...**March 18:** British Parliament passes Government of India Acts, instituting self-governing bodies and increasing number of Indians in bureaucracy. ...**March 30:** Mohandas Gandhi (1869–1948) begins civil disobedience against British rule in India. ...**April 13:** At Amritsar in Punjab, northern India, British troops fire on Indian insurgents, killing some 400 and wounding 1,200. ...**May:** Aziz ibn Saud (c.1888–1953), leader of Wahhabi movement of Najd, defeats forces of Hussein, king of Hejaz.

Science, Invention & Technology

1918. First airship flight across Atlantic made by British. ...Twisted filament for brighter light is invented. ...Soviets adopt the Gregorian calendar. ...Kelvinator refrigerators are marketed in United States. ...Alexander Graham Bell invents a hydrofoil craft that will break speedboat records.

1919. Frigidaire refrigerators are marketed in United States.

Religion, Culture & Arts

1918. Lytton Strachey (1880–1932), British biographer and debunker of traditional verities: *Eminent Victorians* ...Siegfried Sassoon: *Counterattack* ...Carl Sandburg: *Cornhuskers.* ...Willa Cather: *My Ántonia.* ...Ernest Ansermet (1883–1969) founds the Orchestre de la Suisse Romande in Geneva. ...Rosa Ponselle (1897–1981), American dramatic soprano, makes her debut at New York's Metropolitan Opera, where she will star until 1937. ...Joseph Stella (1877–1946), Italian-American painter: *The Gas Tank.* ...**December 14:** Premiere in New York City of Giacomo Puccini's *Il Trittico*, three one-act operas comprising *Il Tabarro, Suor Angelica* and *Gianni Schicchi.*

1918–1922. Oswald Spengler (1880–1936), German philosopher and historian: *Der Untergang des Abendlandes* (*The Decline of the West*).

1919. Karl Jaspers (1883–1969), German psychopathologist and philosopher: *Psychologie der Weltanschauungen.* ...In *Psychology from the Standpoint of a Behaviorist*, American John B. Watson (1878–1958) expounds theory (henceforth called *behaviorism*) that human behavior is totally determined by environmental factors. ...Josiah Royce: *Lectures on Modern Idealism.* ...Étienne Gilson (1913–1978), French historian and neo-Thomist philosopher: *The Philosophy of St. Thomas Aquinas* ...Hermann Hesse (1877–1962), German novelist and poet: *Demian* ...Sherwood Anderson (1876–1941): *Winesburg, Ohio.*

Alexander Graham Bell makes an early long-distance call from New York City to Chicago in 1892.

British Isles & Europe

1919 (Continued). April 11: Geneva, Switzerland, is chosen as headquarters of League of Nations. ...**April 20:** Led by Joseph Pilsudski (1867–1935), Polish forces throw Red Army out of Wilno and Kaunas in Lithuania. ...**June 9:** Red Army takes Ufa. ...**June 28:** By Treaty of Versailles, signed by Allied leaders, limitations are placed on Germany's army, war reparations are to be paid by Germany to Allied powers, Germany is forced to accept responsibility for the war. Those signing recognize Switzerland's perpetual neutrality. ...**September 10:** By Treaty of St. Germain, Austro-Hungarian monarchy is abolished, new Republic of Austria is established and limitations are placed on Austrian army. ...**October 27:** Lord Curzon (1859–1925) succeeds Arthur Balfour as foreign secretary. ...**November 27:** Bulgaria signs Treaty of Neuilly, ceding land to Serbia, Greece and Romania and limiting its army to 20,000.

1920. Britain introduces unemployment insurance for all workers except domestic servants and farm workers. ...**January 17:** Paul Deschanel (1855–1922) is elected French president. ...**February 28:** Hungarian constitution is adopted. ...**February 29:** Czechoslovakian constitution is adopted. ...**March 13–17:** Wolfgang Kapp (1858–1922), hoping to restore German monarchy, leads unsuccessful armed revolt in Berlin. ...**April 24:** Polish forces advance as Russian-Polish War begins. **July 6:** Russians mount offensive against Poland. ...**August 10:** Treaty of Sèvres is signed by Constantinople government but is later rejected by Turkish nationalists. Treaty gives Greece Smyrna, Dodecanese Islands (except Rhodes), Imbros and Tenedos and eastern Thrace. ...**August 14–16:** Poles defeat Russians at Warsaw. ...**September 16:** Deschanel resigns. ...**September 23:** Alexandre Millerand (1859–1943) is elected French president. ...**October 9:** Poland annexes Vilna. ...**November 12:** By Treaty of Rapallo between Italy and Yugoslavia, Italy obtains Zara and renounces Split and Sebenico, and Fiume is made independent. ...**November 15–December 18:** First League of Nations assembly meets. Mandates are allotted and International Court is established. ...**November 16:** Baron Pyotr Wrangel (1878–1928) is expelled from Crimea, ending Russian counterrevolution. ...**December 2:** In Treaty of Alexandropol, Armenia cedes half its territory to Turkey. ...**December 3:** Austria joins League of Nations. ...**December 15–22:** At Brussels Conference, Germany is required to pay enormous war reparations to Allies over 42 years. ...**December 19:** King Constantine (1868–1923) is restored in Greece.

U.S. & Canada

1919 (Continued). September 3: Against his doctors' advice, an exhausted President Woodrow Wilson begins a nationwide tour to promote Versailles Treaty and League of Nations. ...**September 9:** Governor Calvin Coolidge (1872–1933) replaces striking Boston policemen, declaring, "There is no right to strike against the public safety by anybody, anywhere, any time." ...**September 26:** President Wilson suffers devastating stroke and is taken back to Washington, D.C. ...**October 28:** Over President Wilson's veto, Congress passes Volstead Act, providing for enforcement of 18th Amendment. ...**October 29:** International Labor Conference meets in Washington, D.C., and adopts eight-hour workday. ...**November 19:** U.S. Senate turns down Treaty of Versailles by 55–39 vote.

1920. Prohibition comes into force in United States. ...U.S. Census records population of 105,710,620. ...Canadian government takes over Grand Trunk Railway and merges it with Canadian Northern as Canadian National Railways. ...League of Women Voters is founded in Chicago. ...Government estimates average life expectancy in United States at 54 years. ...Eva Dykes (1893–1980) and Georgiana R. Simpson (1866–1944) are first black women to receive Ph.Ds. ...**January 5:** Attorney General A. Mitchell Palmer (1872–1936) authorizes raids on suspected Communists. More than 4,000 are arrested, and 556 are deported. ...**January 16:** U.S. Senate votes against joining League of Nations. ...**February 15:** Secretary of State Robert Lansing resigns. ...**April 9:** U.S. Congress terminates state of war with Germany. ...**April 15:** Robbers murder paymaster and guard at Massachusetts shoe factory. Three weeks later, Italian anarchists Nicola Sacco (1891–1927) and Bartolomeo Vanzetti (1888–1927) are arrested and charged with the crime. ...**May 10:** As sign of its increasing independence from Britain, Canadian government announces that an ambassador will be sent to Washington, D.C. ...**August 26:** The 19th Amendment grants U.S. women suffrage. ...**November 2:** Warren G. Harding (1865–1923) is elected 29th president of United States.

Latin America

U.S. president Woodrow Wilson.

1920. Arturo Alessandri Palma is elected president of Chile. ...Peru abrogates its republican constitution. ...Liberals gain power in Chile. ...President Manuel Estrada Cabrera of Guatemala is forced to resign. ...Puerto Barios becomes a departmental capital of Guatemala. ...**May 20:** Venustiano Carranza, president of Mexico, is assassinated. ...**May 24:** Adolfo de la Huerta (1882–1955) is elected president of Mexico.

1920–1923. Bahamas becomes a station for rumrunners during American Prohibition.

At the National Suffrage Association headquarters in Washington, D.C., Alice Paul rejoices soon after the ratification of the 19th Amendment.

Africa, Asia & Pacific

1919 (Continued). May 3–August 8: War breaks out between Britain and Afghanistan. ...**May 7**: Supreme War Council assigns Samoa as mandate to New Zealand. New Zealand, Britain and Australia share mandate over phosphate-rich Nauru Island, which Australia administers. All other German colonies south of equator go to Australia. Council assigns German East Africa to Britain. ...**May 15:** Greek troops occupy Anatolian coast around city of Smyrna. ...**July:** Popular insurrection against British begins in Iraq. It will not be suppressed until December. ...**August 8:** By Treaty of Rawalpindi, Britain grants limited independence to Afghanistan. ...**August 21:** United States completes fortifications and dry dock at Pearl Harbor. ...**September 15:** China terminates war with Germany.

1920. January 10: Formal peace between Japan and Germany becomes official by exchange of ratifications. ...British mandate over German East Africa becomes effective. Colony is renamed Tanganyika. German settlers are sent home; their estates are confiscated. ...**February:** Destour (Constitution) Party is founded in Tunisia to gain greater autonomy from France. ...**March 11:** National congress proclaims Faisal I (1885–1933) king of Syria. ...**April 8:** East Africa protectorate is transformed into Kenya colony. ...**April 23:** Turkish nationalists set up provisional government at Ankara, with Kemal Atatürk (1881–1938) as president. ...**April 25:** Supreme Allied Council assigns Britain mandate over Palestine and Transjordan on terms set forth in 1917 Balfour Declaration. ...**May 5:** Britain accepts mandate over Iraq. ...**June 22:** Greek armies attack in European Turkey and in Asia Minor. ...**July–December:** Arab insurrection against British occupation of Iraq. ...**July 9:** Greek troops take Bursa in Asia Minor. ...**July 24:** French occupy Damascus, depose Faisal I as king of Syria. ...**August 10:** By Treaty of Sèvres, victorious Allies carve up Ottoman Empire. ...**September 1:** Treaty with Siam abolishes U.S. extraterritorial rights and grants Siam tariff autonomy. ...**October 21:** Turkish army takes Kars from Armenian Republic. ...**November–December:** Drought in northern China kills some 500,000 and impoverishes millions more. ...**December 2:** By Treaty of Alexandropol, Armenia cedes Kars to Turkey. ...**December 3:** What remains of Armenia is declared Soviet republic under Russian domination.

Science, Invention & Technology

American novelist Edith Wharton.

1920. Band-Aid adhesive bandages are first marketed in United States by Johnson & Johnson Company. ...Saran packaging film is produced by Dow Chemical Company. ...Ethyl gasoline additive is developed at General Motors.

This map, based on the Treaty of Versailles, shows the evacuation of Allied troops from Germany's Rhineland. The area marked 1 is to be evacuated in five years, 2 in ten years and 3 in fifteen years.

Religion, Culture & Arts

1919 (Continued). Walter Gropius (1883–1969) establishes the Bauhaus school of design in Germany, bringing all the arts together in creating a building and all its furnishings as united whole. In his work, Gropius stresses the use of glass walls. ...H. L. Mencken (1880–1956), American journalist and critic: *The American Language*. ...John Reed (1887–1920), American polemicist and poet: *Ten Days That Shook the World*, a partisan account of the Russian Revolution. ...Juilliard School of Music is founded in New York City. ...D. W. Griffith directs silent movie *Broken Blossoms*. ...Charlie Chaplin (1889–1977), Douglas Fairbanks (1883–1939), Griffith, and Mary Pickford form United Artists movie studio.

1920. Wilfred Owen (1893–1918), English poet: Posthumous publication of war poems. ...Sinclair Lewis (1885–1951), first American to win Nobel Prize for literature: *Main Street*. ...Edith Wharton: *The Age of Innocence*. ...Dutch artist Piet Mondrian (1874–1944) publishes *Le Neoplasticisme*, summarizing his theories of painting. ...Joan of Arc is canonized. ...Sidonie-Gabrielle Colette, (1873–1954), French novelist: *Chéri*. ...Eugene O'Neill (1888–1953), American playwright: *The Emperor Jones*. ...Agatha Christie (1890–1976), prolific author of mystery novels and plays, publishes *The Mysterious Affair at Styles*, which introduces the Belgian detective Hercule Poirot ...Ezra Pound: *Hugh Selwyn Mauberley*. ...Carl Sandburg: *Smoke and Steel* ...Joseph Stella: *Brooklyn Bridge*.

1920–1922. Sigrid Undset (1882–1949), Norwegian novelist: *Kristin Lavransdatter* (three volumns), tells of love and religion in medieval Norway.

1920–1923. Jaroslav Hašek (1883–1923), Czech writer: *The Good Soldier Schweik*.

1920–1930. American painter John Marin (1870–1953) becomes a formative influence in the development of abstract painting.

British Isles & Europe

1921. February 19–22: France and Poland sign treaty of mutual aid and military cooperation, aimed at Germany and Russia. ...**March 3:** Poland, Romania, and Hungary promise mutual military aid if Russia attacks any of them. ...**March 18:** Peace of Riga ends Russo-Polish War and divides Ukrainian and Belorussian (Belarus) areas between Poland and Russia. ...**March 20:** League of Nations plebiscite divides Upper Silesia between Poland and Germany. Southeastern area, with heavy industry, votes for Poland. ...**May 10:** Karl Wirth (1879–1956) becomes German chancellor. ...**August 11:** Vladimir Lenin's government decrees New Economic Policy (NEP), which permits some private enterprise and allows foreigners to set up businesses. ...**August 26:** Mathias Erzberger (b. 1875), German minister of finance, is assassinated. ...**December 6:** Irish Peace Agreement is signed in London.

1922. January 12: Raymond Poincaré (1860–1934) becomes French prime minister. ...**May 26:** Lenin suffers stroke and loses power of speech. Joseph Stalin (1879–1953) becomes principal link between Lenin and Politburo. ...**October 4:** Geneva Protocol: Austria renounces Anschluss with Germany and receives loan. ...**October 19:** David Lloyd George coalition cabinet is overthrown in Britain. ...**October 23:** Andrew Bonar Law (1858–1923) becomes British prime minister. ...**October 28:** Benito Mussolini leads Fascist march on Rome. King Victor Emmanuel III appoints Mussolini prime minister. ...**November 22:** Wilhelm Cuno (1876–1933) becomes German chancellor. ...**December 30:** Union of Soviet Socialist Republics (USSR) is created. It includes Russia, Siberia, Ukraine, Byelorussia and Transcaucasia (Georgia, Armenia, Azerbaijan).

1923. French occupy Ruhr district (January 10), Offenburg and Appenweier (February 4), Darmstadt, Mannheim, and Karlsruhe (March 3–6). ...**March 14:** Allies assign Vilna and Eastern Galicia to Poland. ...**May 22:** Stanley Baldwin (1867–1947) succeeds Bonar Law as British prime minister. ...**July 6:** New Soviet constitution comes into force. ...**September 14:** Primo de Rivera assumes Spanish dictatorship. ...**October 21–November 30:** Separatists riot in Rhineland and Palatinate. ...**November 8–9:** Coup attempt led by Adolf Hitler (1889–1945) fails in Munich. ...**November 10:** Reparations Recovery Act is suspended. ...**November 20:** German currency is stabilized after months of hyperinflation. ...**November 30:** Wilhelm Marx (1863–1946) becomes German chancellor.

U.S. & Canada

1921. Liberals win Canadian elections. ...**March 4:** Warren G. Harding is inaugurated U.S. president. ...**May 19:** President Harding signs law to restrict immigration. Only 375,000 immigrants may enter United States each year under a system that limits number from each nationality entering. ...**June 20:** Alice Robertson (1854–1931) is first woman to preside over U.S. House of Representatives. ...**August 29:** United States and Hungary agree on peace treaty. ...**November 12–February 6, 1922:** Harding presides over Disarmament Conference in Washington, D.C. ...**December 13:** In Four-Power Pacific Treaty, France, Japan, Britain and United States agree to respect each other's possessions in Pacific. ...**December 23:** Harding commutes prison sentences of Eugene V. Debs and 23 others convicted under 1917 Espionage Act. ...**December 29:** William Mackenzie King (1874–1950) becomes Canadian prime minister.

1922. February 6: Washington Naval Agreement between United States, Britain and Japan limits tonnage for each country's navy. **May 26:** U.S. Federal Narcotics Control Board is created. ...**September:** King declares that Canada will not automatically support British commitments in Europe. ...**October 3:** Rebecca Latimer Felton (1835–1930) is appointed first U.S. female senator and serves until November to fill vacancy.

1923. Texas bars blacks from voting in Democratic Party primaries. ...**January 6:** U.S. Senate recalls occupation forces from Rhineland. ...**March:** U.S.-Canadian treaty on North Pacific halibut fisheries is signed. ...**March 5:** Montana and Nevada enact old-age pensions. ...**June 19:** Anglo-American war debt convention is signed by Stanley Baldwin and Andrew Mellon (1855–1937). ...**August 2:** President Harding dies. **August 3:** Vice President Calvin Coolidge is inaugurated president. ...**September 15:** Oklahoma governor imposes martial law to curb Ku Klux Klan terrorism. ...**December 18:** Commercial treaty between United States and Germany is signed.

Latin America

1921. The United States recognizes Panama's independence. ...A U.S. Senate investigation finds that the purpose of the U.S. invasion of Haiti (to prepare the country for self-government) has been ignored. ...Provisional government of Guatemala is overthrown.

1922. Marcelo Torcuato de Alvear (1868–1942) is named president of Argentina. ...Brazil suffers an economic crisis.

1923. Pancho Villa (b. c. 1877), dies. ...A Pan-American Highway is proposed at Fifth International Conference of American States. ...**April 26.** Mexico recognizes oil concessions granted before 1917. ...**September 3:** United States resumes relations with Mexico.

Africa, Asia & Pacific

1921. February 21: Reza Khan (1877–1944) marches on Tehran and establishes a new government, with himself as commander in chief. ...**March 23–June 17:** Greek troops attack Turkish territory in Asia Minor. After bitter fighting, Greeks occupy Afiun-Karahissar and Eskişehir. ...**July:** Chinese Communist Party is founded. ...**July 21:** Led by Abd-el-Krim (1882–1963), Berbers annihilate Spanish troops at Anual on Morocco's northeastern coast. ...**July 23:** British East Africa is renamed Kenya and made a Crown colony. ...**August 18:** Turkish army begins counter offensive against Greeks invading Anatolia. ...**August 24–...September 16:** At battle of Sakarya, due to desperate Turkish defense, Greek armies fail to reach Ankara. ...**August 30:** Turkish forces drive Greeks from Afiun-Karahissar. ...**November 22:** Britain recognizes independence of Afghanistan in treaty ending Third Afghan War, fought since 1919.

1922. February 6: Anglo-Japanese Alliance lapses. Nine-Power Treaty secures independence of China and compels Japan to restore Shantung to China. ...**February 28:** Britain abolishes protectorate over Egypt. ...**March 15:** Britain recognizes independence of Egypt under Fuad I (1868–1936). ...**July 24:** League of Nations approves British mandate over Palestine and Transjordan and French mandate over Syria. ...**August 28–September 5:** Turks mount counteroffensive against Greek invaders in Asia Minor. Greek armies break and flee in confusion to coast. ...**September 9–14**: Turkish armies take Smyrna, which is largely destroyed by fire. ...**October 10:** British mandate over Iraq becomes permanent alliance. ...**November 17:** Muhammad VI (1861–1926), last Ottoman sultan, flees to Malta.

1923. February 2: Stanley Bruce (1883–1967) becomes Australian prime minister. ...**April 20:** Egyptian constitution is proclaimed. ...**May 25:** Britain proclaims independence of Transjordan under Emir Abdullah. ...**July 23:** Treaty of Lausanne is signed by Turkey, Allies, Greece, Bulgaria and Yugoslavia. It recognizes independence of Turkey. ...**September 1:** Southern Rhodesia becomes British Crown colony, with extensive local autonomy. ...**September 29:** Palestine mandate comes into force. ...**October 29:** Under Turkish Republican constitution, Kemal Atatürk becomes president. ...**December 18:** Britain, France and Spain declare that Tangier, Morocco, is permanently demilitarized and is to be governed by international commission. ...Britain declares protectorate over Egypt.

Science, Invention & Technology

1921. An Iowa farmer introduces the Eskimo Pie, a chocolate-coated ice cream bar on a stick.

1922. American Philo T. Farnsworth (1906–1921) produces crude television image using cathode ray tube. ...Massey-Harris Company of Canada introduces first motorized combine harvester.

1923. Swede Theodor Svedberg (1884–1971) builds a high-speed centrifuge which produces a force 100,000 times that of normal gravity. ...Victoria (Australia) police are first to use two-way radios between headquarters and patrol cars. ...George Eastman introduces a home movie camera and projector. ...American Lee De Forest demonstrates to movie executives his motion picture sound track. ...Austrian neurologist Sigmund Freud (1856–1939), the founder of psychoanalysis, publishes *Das Ich und das Es*.

Religion, Culture & Arts

1921. Luigi Pirandello (1867–1936), Italian playwright: *Six Characters in Search of an Author*. ...Franz Werfel (1890–1945), Austrian playwright and novelist: *Bocksgesang* (*Goat Song*). ...Aldous Huxley (1894–1963), British novelist and critic: *Crome Yellow*. ...Eugene O'Neill: *Anna Christie*. ...George Bernard Shaw: *Back to Methuselah* ...D. H. Lawrence: *Women in Love*. ...Henri Matisse: *The Moorish Screen*. ...Sigmund Romberg (1887–1951), American composer of popular operettas: *Blossom Time*. ...American blues singer Bessie Smith (1894–1937) makes her first recording. ...Alfred Stieglitz (1864–1946) gives a one-man exhibition in New York City of photographs stressing the artistic qualities inherent in the subject. ...Pablo Picasso: *Two Seated Women*; *The Three Musicians*.

1922. T. S. Eliot (1888–1965), American poet: *The Waste Land*. ...James Joyce: *Ulysses*. ...F. Scott Fitzgerald (1896–1940), American author: *The Beautiful and the Damned*. ...William Faulkner (1897–1962), American novelist: *Sanctuary*. ...DeWitt Wallace (1889–1981), American editor and publisher, founds *Reader's Digest*, which condenses material already published elsewhere. ...Louis "Satchmo" Armstrong (1900–1971), American jazz trumpet player, joins King Oliver's Creole Jazz Band in Chicago. ...Friedrich W. Murnau (1888–1931) directs the film *Nosferatu*, a retelling of the Dracula story. ...Robert Flaherty (1884–1951) directs *Nanook of the North*, a documentary film of Eskimo life. ...**September 12:** Episcopalian House of Bishops deletes the word *obey* from U.S. Episcopalian marriage vows.

1923. P. G. Wodehouse (1881–1975), British author of humorous novels, plays and musical comedies: *The Inimitable Jeeves*. ...Shaw: *Saint Joan*. ...New studios for the British Broadcasting Company open at Savoy Hill, London, and the first opera is broadcast. ...Cecil B. DeMille (1881–1959), American movie producer and director: *The Ten Commandments*. ...**May 3:** A church conclave controlled by Communists defrocks Patriarch Tikhon and expels him from Russian Orthodox Church.

British Isles & Europe

1924. January 21: Vladimir Lenin (b. 1870) dies. ...**January 24:** Non-Fascist trade unions are dissolved in Italy. ...**January 27:** With Treaty of Rome, Italy gains port of Fiume but abandons claims on Dalmatia to kingdom of Serbs, Croats and Slovenes (Yugoslavia). ...**February 1:** Britain recognizes Soviet government. ...**February 23:** British Reparation Recovery duties are reduced to 5 percent. ...**March 9:** Fiume is incorporated into Italy. ...**March 24:** Greece is proclaimed a republic. ...**April 1:** For his role in the "Beer Hall Putsch" (attempted coup) in 1923, Adolf Hitler is sentenced to five years' confinement but is released on December 20. While in jail, he will write *Mein Kampf* (*My Struggle*), expounding Nazi ideology. ...**May 4:** Nazis and Communists gain in German elections. ...**May 11:** Leftist bloc defeats rightist coalition in French elections. ...**June 10:** Giacomo Matteotti (b. 1885) is murdered by Fascist assassins. ...**June 13:** Gaston Doumergue (1863–1937) is elected French president. ...**June 15:** Édouard Herriot (1872–1957) becomes French prime minister. ...**July 16–August 16:** London Reparations Conference accepts Dawes Plan for German schedule of war reparations. ...**August 29:** Reichstag passes Dawes Acts on reparations. ...**September 1:** Dawes Plan comes into force. ...**October 2:** Geneva Protocol brands aggressive war an international crime. ...**October 25:** State of emergency ends in Germany.

1925. January 22: National Assembly declares Albania a republic, with Ahmed Bey Zogu (1895–1961) as first president. ...**March 10:** Britain refuses to support terms outlined in Geneva Protocol. ...**April 3:** British repeal Reparations Recovery Act. ...**April 10:** Paul Painlevé (1863–1933) becomes French prime minister. ...**April 26:** Hindenburg is elected president of Germany. ...**April 28:** Britain returns to the gold standard, with the pound set at prewar rate of U.S. $4.80. ...**May 4–June 17:** Geneva conference on trade in arms meets. ...**July 20:** French troops evacuate Westphalia. ...**July 31:** French troops evacuate Ruhr district. ...**August 29:** Conspirators in Kapp revolt receive amnesty from German government. ...**October 25:** Locarno (Switzerland) Conference opens, with delegates from Germany, France, Britain, Italy, Belgium, Poland and Czechoslovakia. ...**December 1:** Locarno treaties signed in London guarantee borders of Rhineland, Belgium, France and Germany. This is the first step in Germany's reentry into world affairs.

U.S. & Canada

1924. Price of Ford Model T reaches its lowest point: $190 without a self-starter. ...Miriam "Ma" Ferguson (1875–1961) receives Democratic nomination for Texas governor. ...**February 3:** Woodrow Wilson (b. 1856) dies. ...**March 21:** Canadian parliament ratifies liquor treaty between Britain and United States. ...**March 31:** In Oregon case, U.S. Supreme Court declares states may not require that all children attend public schools. ...**April 9**: Under Dawes Plan, United States will loan $200 million to Germany, so Germans can pay reparations to U.S. Allies. ...**May 19:** Passed over President Calvin Coolidge's veto, Soldiers' Bonus Act offers 20-year annuities at cost of $2 billion. ...**May 26:** New law limits annual immigration from each country to 2 percent of its nationals in U.S. in 1890, totally excludes Japanese. ...**June 15:** Congress makes all native-born Indians citizens of the United States. ...**June 30:** Teapot Dome Scandal: Federal grand jury indicts Albert Fall (1861–1944), former secretary of interior, and oil company executives Harry Sinclair (1876–1956), Edward L. Doheny (1856–1935) and Edward L. Doheny Jr. (?–1929). Allegedly, Sinclair bribed Fall to lease Teapot Dome reserve in Wyoming. Dohenys allegedly gave Fall $100,000 for leases on Elk Hills Naval Reserve in California. ...**November 4:** Calvin Coolidge, who became president on the death of Warren G. Harding, is elected to a full term.

1925. January 5: Nellie Ross (1876–1977), first female governor, in Wyoming, takes office to complete her late husband's term. ...**January 11:** Frank Billings Kellogg (1856–1937) is appointed secretary of state. ...**February 8:** Marcus Garvey begins five-year sentence for mail fraud related to his steamship line. ...**March 13:** Tennessee law makes it illegal to teach any theory denying biblical story of human creation. ...**May 8:** A. Philip Randolph (1889–1979) organizes Brotherhood of Sleeping Car Porters, trailblazing black labor union. ...**July 21:** After a sensational trial, John Scopes (1900–1970) is convicted and fined in Tennessee for teaching evolution. ...**August 8:** Some 40,000 Ku Klux Klan members march in Washington, D.C. ...**August 18:** Agreement on war debts between United States and Belgium is reached. ...**October:** Florida land boom reaches its peak. Speculation surpasses any other mania in U.S. history. ...**November 12:** Agreement on war debts between United States and Italy is reached.

Latin America

1924. Pan-American Treaty to prevent conflicts between nations is signed. ...Military takes power in Chile. ...U.S. troops evacuate Dominican Republic. ...The Alianza Popular Revolucionaria Americana, a new political party, is established in Peru. ...Representative government is introduced in St. Lucia. ...**July:** A large-scale revolt occurs in São Paulo. The rebels are defeated by the army, which supports President Artur da Silva Bernardes (1875–1955). ...**July 6:** Plutarco Elías Calles (1877–1945) is elected president of Mexico. ...**November:** Liberal Party leader Gerardo Machado y Morales (1871–1939) is elected president of Cuba.

1925. The military takes power in Ecuador. ...A second military coup takes place in Chile. ...U.S. occupation of Nicaragua ends. ...Treaty with United States confirms Cuban sovereignty over Isla de la Juventud. ...Bolivia settles boundary dispute with Argentina.

Africa, Asia & Pacific

1924. January 21: Agreement fixes boundaries between French Sudan and Anglo-Egyptian Sudan. ...**February 2:** Turkish National Assembly abolishes caliphate. ...**February 3:** German-Turkish treaty of friendship is signed. ...**February 19:** Ahmad, shah of Persia, is dethroned. Reza Khan is appointed regent. ...**March 10:** Japan gives up extraterritorial rights and grants Siam tariff autonomy. ...**June 30:** James Hertzog (1866–1942) becomes South African prime minister. ...**July 15:** Britain cedes Jubaland (in Kenya) to Italy. ...**November 5:** Civil war breaks out in China. ...**November 26:** Outer Mongolia is proclaimed Mongolian People's Republic; its capital is renamed Ulan Bator (Red Hero).

Science, Invention & Technology

1924. Frequency modulation (FM) radio broadcasting is invented. ...American Edward Appleton (1892–1965) discovers the ionosphere. He names it the Kennelly-Heaviside layer. ...DuPont Company begins to produce cellophane packaging. ...American physician George Frederick Dick (1881–1967) develops the Dick test for susceptibility to scarlet fever. ...Nonflammable celluloid safety film is made available to movie industry. ...Austrian psychoanalyst Otto Rank (1884–1939), a protégé of Sigmund Freud, writes *Das Trauma der Geburt*.

Religion, Culture & Arts

1924. E. M. Forster: *A Passage to India.* ...André Breton (1896–1966), poet and novelist, one of the founders of the Surrealist movement in literature: *Manifeste du Surréalisme*. ...Thomas Mann: *The Magic Mountain*. ...Pablo Neruda (1904–1973), Chilean poet: *Veinte poemas de amor y una canción desesperada* (*Twenty Love Poems and a Song of Despair*). ...Robinson Jeffers (1887–1962), American poet: *Tamar and Other Poems*. ...Eugene O'Neill: *All God's Chillun Got Wings*; *Desire Under the Elms*. ...George Gershwin (1898–1936), American composer: *Rhapsody in Blue*. ...Sigmund Romberg (1887–1951), Hungarian-born American composer: *The Student Prince*. ...Richard Strauss begins work on the opera *The Egyptian Helen*. It is completed 1927. ...Danish-born American Wagnerian tenor Lauritz Melchior (1890–1973) makes his London debut at Covent Garden. ...Marian Anderson (1902–1955), African American contralto, begins her concert career. ...Serge Koussevitsky (1884–1951), Russian-born American conductor, becomes conductor of the Boston Symphony Orchestra. ...Edward Elgar (1857–1934) is appointed Master of the King's Music. ...Walt Disney (1907–1966) begins making cartoon films in Hollywood with *Alice in Cartoonland*. ...Georgia O'Keeffe (1887–1986), American artist: *Dark Corn*.

Still Picture Branch, National Archives, College Park, MD

^ *George Gershwin, American popular composer during the 1920s and 1930s.*

1925. Rama VII (1893–1941) becomes king of Siam. ...**January 1:** French unite districts of Damascus and Aleppo to form state of Syria. ...**May 21:** Field Marshal Herbert Charles Plumer (1857–1932) succeeds Sir H. Samuel (1870–1963) as high commissioner for Palestine. ...**August:** Turkish government abolishes polygamy and introduces divorce. ...**August 26:** Henri Pétain assembles 150,000 French troops to attack Abd-el-Krim's forces in Morocco. ...**September 2:** Turkey suppresses religious monastic and dervish orders. ...**October 6:** Italy and Egypt reach an agreement on Cyrenaica (Libya) border. ...**October 18–20:** French bombard Damascus. ...**November:** Turkish government forbids wearing of fez by men and discourages the use of veil by women. ...**December 13:** National Assembly proclaims Reza Khan shah of Persia. ...**December 16:** League of Nations council assigns most of Mosul to Iraq. ...**December 17:** Alliance between Turkey and Soviet Union, establishing close political and economic collaboration, is signed.

1925. Thompson machine gun, or Tommy gun, which uses the delayed blowback principle for firing from moving vehicles, is developed. ...**October 2:** John L. Baird (1888–1946) makes his first television transmission.

c. 1925. Richard Drew (1894–1980) develops Scotch adhesive tape at Minnesota Mining and Manufacturing (3M) Company.

1925. Posthumous publication of *The Trial* by Franz Kafka (1883–1924). ...F. Scott Fitzgerald: *The Great Gatsby*. ...Virginia Woolf (1882–1941), English novelist: *Mrs. Dalloway*; *The Common Reader*. ...François Mauriac (1885–1970), French novelist, playwright and essayist: *Le Désert de l'amour* (*The Desert of Love*). ...John Dos Passos (1896–1970) American writer: *Manhattan Transfer*. ...Theodore Dreiser: *An American Tragedy*. ...Anita Loos (1893–1981), American humorist: *Gentlemen Prefer Blondes* ...Gertrude Stein: *The Making of Americans*. ...Paul Robeson (1898–1976), African American actor and singer, stars in Eugene O'Neill's play *Emperor Jones*. ...Jerome Kern (1885–1945): *Sunny*. ...Premiere of *Wozzeck* by Alban Berg (1885–1935) at Berlin Opera. ...Josephine Baker (1906–1975), African American entertainer, moves to Paris and becomes a long-time star of the Folies Bergère ...Russian filmmaker Sergei Eisenstein (1898–1948) directs *Battleship Potemkin*. ...American filmmaker King Vidor (1894–1982) directs *The Big Parade*.

British Isles & Europe

1926. January 3–August 22: Theodore Pangalos (1878–1952) is Greek dictator. ...**January 31:** After military coup d'état in Portugal, General Antonio Carmona (1869–1951) becomes president. ...First Rhineland zone is evacuated by Allies. ...**May 12:** Joseph Pilsudski leads coup d' état in Poland. ...**July 23:** Raymond Poincaré again becomes French prime minister. ...**September 8:** Germany joins League of Nations. ...**September 11:** Spain leaves League of Nations. ...**September 25:** Pilsudski becomes Polish prime minister. ...**November 27:** Italy and Albania sign Tirana Pact. Italy undertakes to protect political, juridical and territorial status quo in Albania.

1927. April 15: Diplomatic relations are resumed between Russia and Switzerland. ...**May 13:** On Black Friday, German economic system breaks down, beginning severe economic panic. ...**May 27:** Britain breaks off diplomatic relations with Russia. ...**June 2:** New Greek constitution is adopted. ...**July 15–16:** Socialists riot in Vienna. Palace of Justice is burned.

1928. April 22 and 29: Leftist parties win French elections. ...**May 7:** Britain reduces voting age for women to 21, same as for men. ...**May 20:** Leftist parties gain in German elections. ...**June 11:** Reparations agent demands final settlement of German liabilities. ...**August 2:** Italy and Abyssinia sign treaty of friendship. ...**September 1:** Ahmed Bey Zogu proclaims himself Zog I, king of the Albanians. ...**October 4–16:** Plebiscite against new battleships fails in Germany. ...**December 22:** Commission of experts for reparations is appointed.

1929. Kingdom of Serbs, Croats and Slovenes is renamed Yugoslavia. ...Margaret Bondfield (1873–1953) becomes minister of labor and first woman in British cabinet. ...**January 31:** Leon Trotsky (1879–1940) is expelled from Russia. ...**March 24:** In Italian elections, 99.4 percent allegedly vote for Fascist list. ...**May 26:** Soviet congress passes Five-Year Plan. ...**June 5:** Labour ministry under Ramsay MacDonald (1866–1937) takes office in Britain. ...**July 24:** Kellogg-Briand Pact comes into force. ...**July 27:** Aristide Briand (1862–1932) succeeds Poincaré as French prime minister. ...**August 6–31:** Reparations conference at The Hague settles evacuation of Rhineland. ...**October 3:** Anglo-Russian relations are resumed. ...**November 3:** André Tardieu (1876–1945) takes office as French prime minister. ...**November 13:** Bank for International Payments is founded in Basel. ...**November 24:** Georges Clemenceau (b. 1841) dies.

U.S. & Canada

1926. Britain recognizes Canada's autonomy. ...**May 20:** U.S. President Calvin Coolidge signs Civil Aviation Act to regulate air travel and license pilots and airports. ...**July 2:** U.S. Congress establishes Army Air Corps. ...**September 18:** Hurricane ravages Florida and Gulf states, killing 372 persons and ending Florida's land boom. ...**October 25:** In *Myers v. United States*, U.S. Supreme Court nullifies 1876 act, ruling president may remove executive officers without Senate's consent.

1927. February 18: United States and Canada establish diplomatic relations and exchange ambassadors. ...**March 7:** In *Nixon v. Herndon*, U.S. Supreme Court strikes down Texas law excluding blacks from voting in Democratic primaries. ...**August 23:** Nicola Sacco (b. 1891) and Bartolomeo Vanzetti (b. 1888) are executed in Massachusetts despite widespread demonstrations against the executions.

1928. March 10: U.S. Alien Property Act provides $300 million to compensate German nationals and companies for property seized in 1917. ...**May 22:** Merchant Marine Act provides subsidies to private shipping companies. ...**June 26–29:** Democrats nominate Alfred E. Smith (1873–1944) for president, the first Roman Catholic candidate. ...**November 7:** Republican Herbert Hoover (1874–1964) is elected 31st president of United States. Oscar DePriest (1871–1951) is first black elected to Congress since 1901 and first ever from a Northern state (Illinois).

1929. January 15: U.S. Senate passes, 85–1, Kellogg-Briand Pact, outlawing war and calling for arbitration of international controversies. Sixty-two nations will eventually sign pact. ...**February 2:** Federal Reserve Board forbids loans to buy stocks on margin. ...**February 14:** Al Capone's (1899–1947) mob lines up six members of rival Chicago gang against garage wall and shoots them in the "St. Valentine's Day Massacre." ...**May 17:** Capone receives one-year sentence for carrying concealed weapon. ...**May 27:** In *United States v. Schwimmer*, U.S. Supreme Court upholds denial of citizenship to avowed pacifist. ...**June 15:** Agricultural Marketing Act establishes Federal Farm Board to aid cooperatives and to help stabilize prices. ...**September 14:** United States joins International Court. ...**October 29:** On Black Tuesday, collapse of stock prices on New York Stock Exchange will be considered among factors that trigger Great Depression.

Latin America

1926. U.S. occupation of Nicaragua resumes. ...**May 24:** Mexico nationalizes minerals and oil. ...**July 2:** In response to Catholic militant uprisings, Mexico closes church-run schools and bans church services.

1926–1927. Civil war erupts in Nicaragua.

1927. Factions in Nicaragua agree to a binding election. ...**April 11:** Carlos Ibáñez (1877–1960) assumes dictatorship in Chile. ...**August:** Brazil outlaws strikes.

1928. General José Maria Moncado (1868–1948) is elected president of Nicaragua. ...**January 16:** U.S. president Calvin Coolidge opens a Pan-American Conference in Havana, Cuba. ...**April 1:** Hipólito Irigoyen (1850–1933) becomes president of Argentina. ...**July 1:** Alvaro Obregon (1880–1928) becomes president of Mexico. ...**July 17:** Obregon is assassinated. ...**September 10:** Argentina nationalizes oil industry. ...**December 6:** War breaks out between Bolivia and Paraguay.

1929. Free navigation of Amazon River is guaranteed by Colombia-Brazil Treaty. ...United Fruit Company purchases Cuyamel, Honduras. ...**May 17:** Chile and Peru settle Tacna-Arica conflict. ...**June 21:** Agreement between state and church in Mexico. ...**September 16:** Peace between Bolivia and Paraguay is reached. ...**November 17:** Pascual Ortiz Rubio (1877–1963) is elected president of Mexico.

Africa, Asia & Pacific

1926. January 8: Aziz ibn Saud becomes king of Hejaz. ...**June 5:** Anglo-Turkish agreement on independence of Mosul (Iraq) is reached. ...**July:** Chiang Kai-shek (1887–1975) begins expedition into northern China, seeking to increase area controlled by Kuomintang (Nationalist) Party. ...**September 2:** Atatürk chooses all candidates for elections in Turkey and is unanimously elected president for four years. ...**December 25:** Japanese emperor Yoshihito (b. 1879) dies and is succeeded by Hirohito (1901–1989).

1927. Chiang Kai-shek overthrows Hankow government in China. ...**March:** Kuomintang troops suppress peasant insurrection—led by Mao Zedong (1893–1976) with Chinese Communist support—against Kuomintang in Honan province. ...**April 12:** Chiang Kai-shek organizes government at Nanking and purges Communists in Kuomintang Party.

1928. April 9: Government declares Islam is no longer state religion of Turkey. ...**June 3:** Bomb blows up train carrying Chang Tso-lin (1897–1979), warlord of Manchuria, giving Japanese excuse to invade China. ...**June 8:** Chiang Kai-shek's Kuomintang armies occupy Beijing, but Chiang maintains capital at Nanking. ...**July 19:** China annuls all "unequal treaties." ...**October 6:** Chiang Kai-shek is elected president of China. ...**November 3:** Turkey introduces Latin alphabet.

1929. Unrest between Jews and Arabs in Palestine erupts. ...**January 14:** Rebels force resignation of Amanullah (1892–1960), king of Afghanistan, who has tried to curb power of Muslim leaders. ...**May 20:** Japanese evacuate Shantung. ...**August 11:** Persia recognizes legitimacy of Iraqi state.

Science, Invention & Technology

1926. First electric lawn mower is invented. ...American Robert Goddard (1882–1945) develops an efficient rocket fuel by combining gasoline with liquid oxygen. ...American George Dempster (1887–1964) introduces his Dempster-Dumpster, which can transfer materials into a truck by an automatic lift. ..."Feedback-feedforward" method of canceling radio signal distortion is discovered. ...John Baird (1888–1946) makes television transmission from London, England to Glasgow, Scotland. ...Reusable aerosol spray can is invented.

1927. American architect R. Buckminster Fuller (1895–1983) designs his futuristic Dymaxion house. ...Eugene Freyssinet (1879–1962) uses steel rods to reinforce concrete. ...**May 21:** Charles Lindbergh (1902–1974) completes first nonstop solo flight from New York City to Paris. ...**November 13:** The Holland Tunnel , America's first underwater motor vehicle tunnel, opens. It links New York and New Jersey.

1928. A radio interference detector is built by scientists at Bell Laboratories. ...Baird makes first transatlantic television transmission from London to New York City. ...Ernst Ruska (1906–1988) and Vladimir Zworykin (1889–1982), working in the United States, invent the kinescope, predecessor of the television. ...American Harry Nyquist (1889–1976), at Bell Laboratories, discovers method of maximizing accuracy of sound wave duplication.

1929. German doctor Werner Forssmann (1904–1979) develops the cardiac catheter, plastic tube inserted through arm to view arteries. ...German Herman Staudinger (1881–1965) invents synthetic rubber. ...Iron lung, an artificial respirator, is invented. It will be used to keep polio patients alive. ...First magnetic recording is made in Germany. ...Englishmen John Cockroft (1897–1967) and E. T. S. Walton (1903–1995) build a proton accelerator. ...**May 31:** First trans-Pacific flight leaves California; reaches Brisbane, Australia, on June 9.

Religion, Culture & Arts

1926. Ernest Hemingway (1899–1961), American novelist: *The Sun Also Rises*. ...Dorothy Parker (1893–1967) American writer: *Enough Rope*. ...A. A. Milne (1882–1956), British writer: *Winnie the Pooh*. ...Sigmund Romberg: *The Desert Song*. ...Russian artist Wassily Kandinsky (1866–1944) publishes *Point and Line to Plane*, a theory of drawing based on the symbolic value of signs. ...Fritz Lang (1890–1976) and his wife, scriptwriter Thea von Harbou (1888–1954), make *Metropolis*, a film of a futuristic city-state. ...Italian-born American actor Rudolph Valentino (b. 1895) dies. ...Georgia O'Keeffe: *Black Iris*.

1927. Willa Cather: *Death Comes for the Archbishop*. ...Janet Gaynor (1906–1984) wins first Academy Award for best actress for her role in the film *Sunrise*. ...**April 2:** Archbishop of Mexico and five other Catholic dignitaries are deported, charged with complicity in a Catholic riot. ...**December 27:** House of Lords accepts, but House of Commons rejects, proposed new prayer book for Church of England, first since 16th century.

1928. Radclyffe Hall (1886–1943), British novelist: *The Well of Loneliness*. ...George Gershwin: *An American in Paris*. ...George Balanchine (1904–1983), Russian-born American choreographer: *Apollo*. ...*The Last Command*, directed by Austrian-born American filmmaker Josef von Sternberg (1894–1969).

c. 1928–1938. Salvador Dali (1904–1989) becomes leading exponent of Surrealist movement.

1929. Erich Maria Remarque (1898–1970), German novelist: *All Quiet on the Western Front*. ...Thomas Clayton Wolfe (1900–1958), American novelist: *Look Homeward Angel*. ...Ivy Compton-Burnett (1892–1969), English writer: *Brothers and Sisters*. ...Edmund Wilson (1895–1972), American writer: *I Thought of Daisy*, a novel. ...François Mauriac (1885–1970): *Dieu et Mammon* (*God and Mammon*). ...Paul Claudel (1868–1955): play *Le Soulier de satin* (*The Satin Slipper*). ...Noel Coward (1899–1973), British actor, playwright, and composer: operetta *Bitter Sweet*. ...Chrysler Building in New York City, by William van Alen, is erected. ...King Vidor directs *Hallelujah*, first movie with an all-black cast. ...**February 11:** Lateran Treaty establishes Vatican City.

British Isles & Europe

1930. In France, construction begins on the Maginot Line of fortifications along border from Switzerland to Belgium. ...**January 3–20:** At Second Reparations Conference at The Hague, Germany is required to pay reparations over 59 years. ...**January 23:** Wilhelm Frick (1877–1946) becomes first Nazi minister of German state in Thuringia. ...**January 28:** Dictatorship of Primo de Rivera ends in Spain. ...**March 30:** Heinrich Brüning (1885–1970) forms cabinet without Reichstag majority. ...**April 22:** Naval pact is signed in London. United States and Britain are allowed only 15 capital ships each. Japan is limited to 9. ...**May 17:** Young Plan for German reparations goes into effect, replacing Dawes Plan. ...**September 14:** German elections result in 107 Nazis taking seats in Reichstag. ...**October 1–November 14:** At British Empire Conference, Statute of Westminster defines status of dominions.

1931. Women 23 and older gain the vote in Spain. ...**January 12:** Allied Military Control Commission is dissolved. ...**January 27:** Pierre Laval (1883–1945) becomes French prime minister. ...**March 17:** Tariff truce convention fails. ...**March 21:** Austro-German customs union is announced. France, Italy and Czechoslovakia protest. ...**April 14:** Revolution in Spain forces King Alfonso to flee abroad. ...**May 13:** Paul Doumer (1857–1932) is elected French president. ...**June 15:** Russia and Poland agree on treaty of friendship and commerce. ...**July 13:** Danatbank fails in Germany, causing other German banks to close until August 5. ...**September 7–December 1:** Second India Conference in London is attended by Mohandas Gandhi. ...**September 12:** Mexico joins League of Nations. ...**September 17:** Germany reaches standstill agreement with creditors. ...**September 21:** Britain abandons gold standard. ...**December 9:** Spanish republican constitution is adopted. Alcalá Zamora is elected president. ...**December 11:** British Parliament passes Statute of Westminster, declaring dominions of Australia, Canada, Ireland, Newfoundland, New Zealand and South Africa sovereign within their own borders.

U.S. & Canada

1930. U.S. Census records population of 122,775,046. Population center is located three miles northeast of Linton, Indiana. ...**May 15:** United Airlines and Boeing employ first flight attendants, all female. ...**June 17:** Hawley Smoot Tariff comes into force in United States. High tariffs add to economic crisis. ...**July 3:** Combining all federal agencies for former service personnel, U.S. Congress creates Veterans Administration. ...**August 7:** Conservative ministry of Richard Bennett (1870–1947) takes office in Canada. ...**December 11:** Bank of United States in New York City closes. Some 400,000 depositors are affected by nation's largest bank failure.

1931. Construction begins on Hoover Dam on Colorado River. It will be completed 1936. ...**March 25:** Nine black youths are arrested in Scottsboro, Alabama, charged with raping two white women. Their convictions will be overturned by U.S. Supreme Court (1932) because defendants were not given adequate legal representation. A second trial results in conviction which is again overturned by Supreme Court, this time because blacks had been excluded from jury. A third and final trial also results in conviction. ...**June 20:** President Hoover proposes moratorium for one year on reparations and war debts. ...**October 17:** Federal court in Chicago sentences Al Capone to 11 years imprisonment for tax evasion. ...**December 11:** Statute of Westminster becomes law, recognizing Canada's full autonomy from Britain.

Latin America

1930. Most of Santo Domingo is destroyed by a hurricane. ...A U.S. presidential commission recommends that Haiti be allowed to elect its legislature. ...Liberals return to power in Colombia. ...Lázaro Cárdenas (1895–1970) becomes head of the National Revolutionary Party in Mexico. ...President Augusto Leguía y Salcedo of Peru is overthrown, and Peru is torn between rivalries of leftists and rightists. ...**January 20:** War breaks out again between Bolivia and Paraguay. ...**September 5–8:** During revolution in Argentina, Hipolito Irigoyen is deposed. ...**October 4–November 3:** After revolution in Brazil, Getúlio Dornelles Vargas (1883–1954) becomes president.

1931. Managua, Nicaragua, is badly damaged by an earthquake. ...Harmodio Arias (1886–1962) seizes power in Panama. ...Government of Virgin Islands is transferred from U.S. Navy to Department of the Interior. ...**February:** General Jorge Ubico Castañeda (1878–1946) is elected president of Guatemala. ...**July 25:** Ibáñez, president of Chile, resigns. ...**November 8:** Agustín Justo (1876–1943) is elected Argentine president.

1931–1939. Rightists take control in Peru.

1931–1940. Several juntas and 12 presidents try to govern in unstable Ecuador.

1931–1944. El Salvador is ruled by dictator General Maximiliano Hernández Martínez (1888–1944).

In this photo taken during the third Scottsboro trial, civil rights attorney Samuel Leibowitz (left), looks at defendant Haywood Patterson, who displays a horseshoe for good luck. ➤

Africa, Asia & Pacific

1930. January 1: Extraterritoriality is abolished in China. ...**March 12:** Mohandas Gandhi opens civil disobedience campaign in India. ...**March 28:** Turkish government gives Constantinople new name of Istanbul. ...**April 3:** Ras Tafari (1891–1975) becomes Emperor Haile Selassie of Abyssinia (Ethiopia). ...**May 5:** Gandhi is arrested in India and imprisoned until January 1931. ...**May 19:** White women receive vote in South Africa. ...**June 30:** Britain recognizes independence of Iraq. ...**October 1:** Britain restores the seaport of Wei-hai-wei to China. ...**October 22:** Fuad I of Egypt suspends 1923 constitution and rules as dictator. ...**October 30:** By Treaty of Ankara, Turkey and Greece recognize territorial status quo and agree to naval equality in eastern Mediterranean. ...**December 19:** Lord Willingdon (1866–1941) becomes viceroy of India.

1931. March 4: Agreement between Gandhi and Lord Irwin ends civil disobedience campaign. ...**March 26:** Treaty of friendship between Iraq and Transjordan is signed. ...**August 22:** Ethiopian government claims to have freed some 2 million slaves. ...**September 18:** Japan begins military operations in Manchuria. ...**November:** Mao Zedong is elected chairman of the newly established Soviet Republic of China, based in Kiangsi province in southeast China. ...**December 11:** Japan abandons gold standard. ...**December 19:** Joseph Lyons's (1879–1939) United Australia Party wins parliament from Labour Party.

Science, Invention & Technology

1930. American Andre Clavier (1894–1972) builds a parabolic dish antenna for transatlantic radio transmissions. ...Swiss Auguste Picard (1884–1962) attaches a sealed gondola to a hot air balloon and ascends to 113,000 feet (34,442 meters). ...American Wallace Carothers (1896–1937) at DuPont Company develops neoprene polymer. ...Freon, the coolant used in air conditioners, is discovered. ...**May 11:** Adler Planetarium, first in United States, opens in Chicago. ...**June 6:** American Charles William Beebe (1877–1962) descends to record 800 feet (244 meters) off Bermuda in a bathysphere.

1931. The stroboscope, used in high-speed photography, is invented. ...American Frederick McKay (1874–1959) determines that fluoride in water supply prevents tooth decay. ...Edwin Land (1909–1991) invents a synthetic sheet polarizer. ...First successful electric razor is marketed in United States. ...Alka-Seltzer antacid tablet is developed in United States by Miles Laboratories. ...American doctor John Gibbon Jr. (1903–1973) begins building first heart-lung machine. ...**May 1:** Empire State Building in New York City—world's tallest until 1970s—is dedicated. ...**May 27:** Picard makes record hot air balloon ascent to 51,775 feet (15,781 meters) at Augsburg, Germany.

Religion, Culture & Arts

1930. Hart Crane (1899–1932), American poet: *The Bridge*. ...Katherine Anne Porter (1890–1980), American writer: *Flowering Judas and Other Stories*. ...Noel Coward: play, *Private Lives*. ...René Magritte (1898–1967), Belgian painter: *On the Threshold of Liberty*, one of best-known surrealist paintings. ...Adolf von Harnack (b. 1851), German theologian and historian, dies. His *History of Dogma* remains influential. ...Henry Ironside (1876–1951), American evangelist known as "Archbishop of Fundamentalism," becomes pastor (until 1948) of Moody Memorial Church, Chicago. ...Movie *Little Caesar*, starring Edward G. Robinson (1893–1973), Romanian-born American actor. ...Josef von Sternberg directs *Der Blaue Engel* (*The Blue Angel*), starring Marlene Dietrich (1901–1992). ...American movie *Morocco*, directed by Sternberg and starring Dietrich.

1931. Pearl S. Buck (1892–1973): *The Good Earth*, Pulitzer Prize–winning novel about modern China. ...Edmund Wilson: *Axel's Castle*, about symbolism and other imaginative literature. ...Karl Jaspers (1883–1969): *Die geistige Situation der Zeit* (*Man in the Modern Age*). ...Max Eastman: *The Literary Mind: Its Place in an Age of Science*. ...Dorothy Parker: *Death and Taxes* (verse). ...Coward: *Cavalcade*. ...Eugene O'Neill: *Mourning Becomes Electra*. ...Stephen Vincent Benét (1898–1943): *Ballads and Poems, 1915–1930*. ..."Star Spangled Banner" becomes official national anthem of United States. ...Lily Pons (1904–1976), French-born coloratura soprano, makes her debut at New York's Metropolitan Opera. She will sing leading roles there for 25 years. ...Georgia O'Keeffe: *Cow's Skull, Red, White, and Blue*. ...Jean Marie Villeneuve (1883–1947) becomes archbishop of Quebec. ...Film *Frankenstein*, starring Boris Karloff (1887–1969), is released. ...*Daddy Long Legs*, starring Janet Gaynor, is released. ...**September 29:** Episcopal Church convention permits remarriage.

Courtesy: Pearl S. Buck Foundation, Perkasie, PA

◀ ***King Gustav V of Sweden presents Pearl S. Buck with the 1938 Nobel Prize for literature.***

British Isles & Europe

1932. Austria again renounces Anschluss with Germany. ...**January 22:** Second Russian Five-Year Plan is issued. ...**January 25:** Russia and Poland sign nonaggression pact. ...**February 2:** Disarmament conference opens at Geneva. ...**March 9:** Republican Party leader Eamon De Valera becomes president of Irish parliament and immediately abolishes oath of allegiance to British Crown. ...**April 10:** Paul von Hindenburg is reelected president of Germany. ...**April 24:** Nazis win elections in Prussia, Bavaria, Württemberg, Hamburg. ...**May 6:** French president Paul Doumer (b. 1857) is assassinated by an insane Russian émigré. ...**May 10:** Albert Lebrun (1871–1950) is elected French president. ...**June 16–July 9:** At Reparations Conference of Lausanne, final conditional payments are accepted by Germany. ...**July 13:** Anglo-French pact of friendship is signed at Lausanne. ...**July 31:** In German elections, 230 Nazis are elected to Reichstag. ...**November 6:** In German elections, 196 Nazis are elected to Reichstag. ...**November 8–9:** Stalin's second wife commits suicide under mysterious circumstances. ...**November 19–December 24:** Third India Conference meets in London to discuss affairs in India. ...**November 27:** Russia and Poland renew nonaggression pact. ...**December 27:** Abolished during the revolution, internal passports are reintroduced in Soviet Union.

1933. January 12: Central Committee approves purge of Communist Party in Soviet Union; membership falls from 3.5 million to 2.35 million during next two years. ...**January 30:** Adolf Hitler is appointed German chancellor. ...**February 27:** Reichstag building in Berlin is destroyed by fire. ...**March 5:** In German elections, Nazis get 44 percent of vote. ...**March 7:** Englebert Dollfuss (1892–1934) suspends parliamentary government in Austria. ...**March 10:** Panayoti Tsaldaris (1884–1970) becomes Greek prime minister. ...**June 15:** Venizélos again becomes Greek prime minister. ...**July 3–5:** London Convention defining aggression is signed by Afghanistan, Estonia, Latvia, Persia, Poland, Romania, Russia, Turkey, Czechoslovakia and Yugoslavia. ...**July 14:** German parties other than Nazi Party are outlawed. ...**September 3:** Irish opposition parties form United Ireland Party. ...**October 14:** Germany leaves Disarmament Conference and League of Nations. ...**November 12:** Nazis allegedly win 95 percent of vote in German elections. ...**November 14:** Ion George Duca (1879–1933) forms liberal ministry in Romania. **December 30:** Duca is murdered by Iron Guard.

U.S. & Canada

1932. More than 13,000,000 are unemployed in United States. ...Prime Minister Richard Bedford Bennett (1870–1947) sets up Canadian Broadcasting Commission to control radio broadcasts. ...**January 22:** Reconstruction Finance Corporation (RFC) is established in United States with $2 billion available for loans to failing banks and other financial institutions. ...**February 27:** Glass-Steagall Act regulates U.S. securities industry and authorizes sale of gold to ease credit. ...**March 1:** The 20-month old son of famous aviator Charles Lindbergh is kidnapped. His body will be found on May 12, after payment of a $50,000 ransom. ...**July–August:** At Conference at Ottawa, Canada, Commonwealth members give each other trade preference. ...**July 18:** United States and Canada agree to construct St. Lawrence Seaway to connect Great Lakes with Atlantic Ocean, with costs to be split evenly between two nations. ...**July 21:** U.S. Emergency Relief Act provides $300 million in loans to states for welfare. It authorizes RFC to borrow up to $3 billion and to make loans to state and local governments for public works. ...**July 22:** U.S. Federal Home Loan Bank Act creates 12 regional banks to discount home loans for building and loan associations, savings banks and insurance companies. ...**November 8:** Franklin Delano Roosevelt (1882–1945) is elected 32nd U.S. president.

1933. January 13: U.S. Congress passes a law for Philippine independence. It will later be rejected by Philippine legislature. ...**March 4:** Roosevelt is inaugurated president. ...Frances Perkins (1882–1965) becomes secretary of labor and first female member of U.S. cabinet. ...**March 6–9:** Roosevelt closes all U.S. banks ...**March 31:** U.S. Congress establishes Civilian Conservation Corps to provide jobs to unemployed young men. ...**May 18:** U.S. Congress creates Tennessee Valley Authority. ...**June 16:** National Industrial Recovery Act is passed by U.S. Congress. It calls for fair competition in industries and collective bargaining with labor and limits production. U.S. Congress passes Banking Act, establishing Federal Bank Deposit Insurance Corporation. ...**August 5:** By executive order, Roosevelt creates National Labor Board, headed by Senator Robert Wagner (1877–1953), to protect workers seeking to establish unions. ...**November 29:** Because of debt resulting from incompetence and corruption, Newfoundland loses its status as autonomous dominion and again becomes crown colony. ...**December 5:** The 21st Amendment to U.S. Constitution is adopted, repealing 18th Amendment (Prohibition).

Latin America

1932. Tiburcio Carias (1876–1969) begins 16-year dictatorship in Honduras. ...**June 6–18:** After revolution in Chile, socialist government is established. ...**July 11–October 3:** Revolt against President Getúlio Dornelles Vargas in Brazil is put down. ...**September 1:** War breaks out between Peru and Colombia for Leticia harbor. ...**July 31:** War breaks out between Bolivia and Paraguay. ...**September 4:** Ortíz Rubio is reelected Mexican president. ...**September 14:** Military stages coup d'état in Chile.

German Nazi leader Adolf Hitler just after his release from prison in 1924.

1933. January 2: U.S. troops leave Nicaragua. ...**March 31:** Gabriel Terra (1873–1942) assumes dictatorship in Uruguay. ...**May 1:** President Sanchez Cerro (b. 1892) of Peru is assassinated. ...**May 10:** Paraguay declares war on Bolivia. ...**August:** A general uprising forces Cuban president Gerardo Machado (1871–1939) into exile. ...**October 11:** Nonaggression pact among South American countries is signed at Rio de Janeiro. ...**November 16:** Brazilian Constitutional Assembly grants dictatorial powers to Vargas.

1933–1934. Radicals stage unsuccessful uprising in Argentina.

Africa, Asia & Pacific

1932. Oil is discovered in Bahrain. ...Indian government receives special powers for six months from Britain. ...**January 2:** Manchukuo Republic, with Japanese puppet government, is proclaimed in Manchuria. ...**January 4:** Gandhi is arrested by British for civil disobedience. ...**January 28:** Japanese occupy Shanghai. ...**March 9:** Former Chinese emperor Pu Yi (1906–1967) is installed as president of Manchukuo. ...**May 16:** Ki Inukai (b. 1855), Japanese prime minister, is assassinated. ...**June 18:** Turkey joins League of Nations. ...**June 27:** Rama VII of Siam is forced to grant constitution. ...**September 15:** Japan declares protectorate over Manchukuo. ...**September 22:** Aziz ibn Saud (1888–1953), member of Wahhabi dynasty, renames kingdom of Najd and Hejaz kingdom of Saudi Arabia. ...**October 3:** British mandate over Iraq terminates. Iraq joins League of Nations. ...**November 29:** Persia cancels concession of Anglo-Persian Oil Company . ...**December 9:** Japanese invade Jehol province in China.

Science, Invention & Technology

1932. First spring-action pop-up toaster is marketed in United States. ...First automated dishwasher is marketed to an unreceptive public. ...**May 20–21:** American Amelia Earhart (1897–1937) makes first solo flight across Atlantic Ocean by a woman. She flies from Newfoundland to Ireland. ...**December:** Parking meter is patented.

***A scene from the stage version of Erskine Caldwell's* Tobacco Road.**

Religion, Culture & Arts

1932. First exhibition of mobile sculpture by Alexander Calder (1896–1976). ...Aldous Huxley: *Brave New World.* ...Christopher Isherwood (1904–1986), British novelist and playwright: *The Memorial.* ...Erskine Caldwell (1903–1987), American novelist of the rural South: *Tobacco Road.* ...Elizabeth Bowen (1899–1973), Irish novelist: *To the North.* ...François Mauriac: *Le Noeud de vipères* (*Vipers' Tangle*). ...James T. Farrell (1904–1979), American novelist: *Young Lonigan*, first of a trilogy about lower-class life in Chicago. ...Thomas Hart Benton (1889–1975), American artist portraying the Midwest in a spirited realistic style: *Cotton Pickers.* ...Grant Wood (1892–1942), American painter: *Daughters of Revolution.* ...Georgia O'Keeffe: *Jack-in-the Pulpit No. 2.* ...Reinhold Niebuhr (1892–1971), American neo-conservative theologian and social critic: *Moral Man and Immoral Society.* ...Étienne Gilson (1884–1978), French philosopher and historian: *The Spirit of Medieval Philosophy.* ...*Rasputin and the Empress*, movie starring Lionel Barrymore (1878–1954), Ethel Barrymore (1879–1959), and John Barrymore (1882–1942). ...Cary Grant (1904–1986), English-born American actor, makes his Hollywood debut in *Blond Venus.*

1933. February 3: Anglo-Persian oil conflict is settled. ...**February 23–March 12:** Japanese occupy China north of Great Wall. ...**February 24:** League of Nations adopts Lytton Report on Manchuria condemning Japan. ...**February 27:** Japan leaves League of Nations. ...**May 26:** Australia claims one third of Antarctic continent. ...**May 29:** Saudi Arabia grants Standard Oil Company of California 60-year concession to pump oil. ...**September 8:** King Faisal I of Iraq dies and is succeeded by Ghazi (1912–1939).

1933. American Wiley Post (1899–1935) becomes first person to fly around the world. ...Last Tasmanian tiger dies in Australian zoo. ...Spam canned meat product is first marketed in United States.

Amelia Earhart in a publicity photo taken shortly after her solo flight across the Atlantic Ocean.

1933. Bertolt Brecht (1898–1956), German dramatist: *Mutter Courage* (*Mother Courage*). ...First exhibition by photographer Henri Cartier-Bresson (1908–) in New York. ...Greek poet Konstantinos Kavafis, known as Cavafy, dies. ...Gertrude Stein: *The Autobiography of Alice B. Toklas.* ...André Malraux (1901–1976), French novelist and politician: *La Condition Humaine* (*Man's Faith*). ...Franz Werfel: *Die vierzig Tage des Musa Dagh* (*The Forty Days of Musa Dagh*). ...Noel Coward: *Design for Living.* ...Caldwell: *God's Little Acre.* ...Jerome Kern's musical *Roberta* includes song "Smoke Gets in Your Eyes." ...Dorothy Day (1897–1933), American Roman Catholic social activist, founds the newspaper *Catholic Worker.* ...Movie *The Private Life of Henry VIII*, starring Charles Laughton (1899–1961), is released. ...Movie *Dinner at Eight*, starring John Barrymore, is released. ...Movie *Emperor Jones*, starring Paul Robeson, is released. ...Movie *Flying Down to Rio*, starring Fred Astaire (1899–1987), American dancer, is released.

c. 1933. Paul Hindemith (1895–1963) develops music using 12-note scale.

British Isles & Europe

1934. January 26: Germany and Poland agree on ten-year nonaggression pact. ...**January 30:** Édouard Daladier (1884–1970) becomes French prime minister. ...**February 17:** King Albert of Belgium dies and is succeeded by Leopold III (1901–1983). ...**March 16–17:** Austria, Italy and Hungary sign Rome Protocols, agreeing to cooperate in foreign affairs against Czechoslovakia, Romania and Yugoslavia. ...**April 7:** Russia and Finland extend nonaggression pact for ten years. ...**May 19:** Boris III (1894–1943), tsar of Bulgaria, sets up a dictatorial regime. ...**June 15:** Germany announces suspension of all cash transfers on debts abroad. ...**July 25:** Nazis revolt in Austria. ...**August 2:** Paul von Hindenburg (b. 1847) dies. ...**August 19:** Hitler makes himself president, naming himself *Der Führer*. ...**September 18:** Russia is admitted to League of Nations. ...**October 9:** King Alexander (b. 1888) of Yugoslavia and French foreign minister Jean Louis Barthou (b. 1862) are assassinated at Marseilles by a Montenegrin nationalist. ...**December 14:** Alexander Zaïmis (1855–1936) is reelected Greek president.

1935. Germany repudiates the military clauses in Versailles Treaty and introduces compulsory military service. ...**March 1–11:** Rising in Greece, headed by Venizélos, is suppressed by Greek government. ...**April 23:** New Polish constitution comes into force. ...**May 2:** Franco-Russian treaty of mutual assistance is signed. ...**May 12:** Joseph Pilsudski (b. 1867) dies. ...**June 7:** Stanley Baldwin returns to office as British prime minister. ...**September 15:** Nuremberg Laws make swastika official flag of Germany and reinforce anti-Semitism. ...**September 17:** Kurt von Schuschnigg (1897–1977) stages coup d'état in Austria. ...**September 22:** Stalin restores military ranks in Red Army. ...**October 2:** Italians invade Abyssinia (Ethiopia). ...**October 7:** League of Nations declares Italy aggressor in Abyssinia. ...**October 28:** Greece is proclaimed a monarchy. ...**November 3:** Greek plebiscite favors King George II. ...**November 18:** League of Nations applies economic sanctions against Italy for aggressions against Abyssinia. ...**December 18:** Edvard Beneš (1884–1948) is elected Czechoslovak president.

U.S. & Canada

1934. Bank of Canada is established to control all banks in that nation. ...Five girls, first quintuplets known to survive, are born to Dionne family in Ontario. ...Florence Ellinwood Allen (1884–1966) is appointed first female judge on U.S. Circuit Court. ...**March 29:** U.S. Congress passes a second law for Philippine independence, which will be approved by Philippine legislature in 1935. ...**May 29:** Cuba abrogates U.S. right of intervention. ...**June 6:** President Franklin Roosevelt signs law creating Securities and Exchange Commission to regulate stock exchanges. ...**June 19:** U.S. Congress creates Federal Communications Commission to regulate national and international communication by telegraph, cable and radio. ...**July 22:** John Dillinger (b.1902), Public Enemy Number One, is shot and killed outside a Chicago movie theatre by FBI agents.

1935. Canadian government sets up board of grain commissioners (to control wheat sales) and a commission to prohibit monopolies harming public. ...Appeals from Canadian courts to British Privy Council are abolished in criminal cases. ...Canadian government creates unemployment insurance, imposes minimum wage, limits workweek to six eight-hour days. ...**January 7 and May 27:** U.S. Supreme Court declares parts of National Industrial Recovery Act unconstitutional. ...**July 5:** U.S. government requires management to deal collectively with unions, permits closed shop and creates National Labor Relations Board. ...**August 14:** Roosevelt signs Social Security Act. ...**August 24:** Social Credit Party, advocating more equal distribution of purchasing power, wins control of Alberta, Canada, and 17 seats in Canadian parliament. ...**September 8:** Huey Long (b. 1893), senator from and former governor of Louisiana, is assassinated while visiting Baton Rouge. ...**October 14:** Liberals win Canadian elections by landslide. ...**October 23:** Mackenzie King, Liberal leader, becomes Canadian prime minister for third time. ...**November 15:** Prime Minister King signs reciprocal trade agreement with United States. ...**December 9–13**: Conference of federal and provincial governments agrees unanimously that Canada should gain power from Britain to amend Canadian constitution.

Latin America

1934. U.S. Marines are withdrawn from Haiti. ...U.S. possession of Guantanamo Bay, Cuba, is confirmed by treaty. ...José María Velasco Ibarra (1893–1979) is elected president of Ecuador. ...The first university in São Paolo is established. ...**May 24:** Peru and Colombia settle Leticia conflict. ...**July 16:** Brazilian constitution is promulgated. ...**July 17:** Getúlio Dornelles Vargas is elected president of Brazil. ...**November 30.** Lázaro Cárdenas succeeds Rodríguez as president of Mexico.

1935. University of Panama is founded. ...Madden Dam, providing additional water for locks of Panama Canal, is completed. ...**June 12:** Armistice between Bolivia and Paraguay is signed. ...**August 20:** President Velasce Ibarra of Ecuador is deposed by army. ...**November:** Communist-led revolts in Pernambuco and Rio de Janeiro result in the declaration of martial law in Brazil.

▲ ***A Wanted poster for criminal John Dillinger.***

Africa, Asia & Pacific

1934. January: Turkey introduces Five-Year Plan for developing industry, most of which is owned by government. ...**March 1:** Pu Yi (1906–1967) assumes title of Emperor Kang Te of Manchukuo. ...**April 7:** Mohandas Gandhi suspends civil disobedience campaign. ...**June 12:** Cape parliament passes South Africa Status bill. ...**July 14:** Oil pipe line from Mosul in Iraq to Tripoli in Syria opens. ...**September 17:** United Australia Party wins Australian elections. ...**October 16:** Chinese Communist Red Army under Mao Zedong, badly beaten by Chiang Kai-shek's forces, begins Long March, traveling 6,000 miles from Kiangsi to northwestern Shensi province. ...**November 7:** Joseph Lyons (1879–1939) forms Australian coalition cabinet. ...**December 5:** Transvaal National Party and Free State South African Party fuse to become United Party.

1935. January 7: In Franco-Italian agreement at Marseilles, France cedes part of its East African possessions. ...**March 1:** Women vote for first time in Turkish national elections. Eighteen women are elected to national assembly. Atatürk is reelected president for four years. ...**March 2:** Rama VII of Siam abdicates. ...**March 21:** Persia is renamed Iran. ...**March 23:** Soviet Union sells Chinese Eastern Railway to Japan. ...**August 2:** Government of India Act is passed, calling for creation of elected provincial and federal legislatures. ...**September 17:** Manuel Quezon (1878–1944) is elected first president of Philippines Commonwealth. ...**October:** Chinese Communists complete Long March to Shensi province and establish capital at Yenan. ...**November 27:** Labor Party wins New Zealand elections for first time. ...**December 1:** Chiang Kai-shek is elected president of Chinese executive. ...**December 5:** Labor Party takes power in New Zealand and promises extensive nationalization under Marxist socialist program.

Science, Invention & Technology

1934. Italian-born American physicist Enrico Fermi (1901–1954) begins work on discovery that will earn him the 1938 Nobel Prize for physics: neutron-induced nuclear reactions. ...British company Vent-Axia introduces the first window fan. ...The modern light bulb is introduced. ...First full-service laundro- mat opens in Fort Worth, Texas. ...General Electric Company introduces first fluorescent lamp in United States. ...Citroën is the first automobile to offer front-wheel drive. ...**December 8:** Weekly airmail service between Britain and Australia is inaugurated.

1935. French doctor Alexis Carrel (1873–1944) and American aviator Charles Lindbergh invent the perfusion pump for artificial blood circulation. ...African American Julian Percy (c. 1880–1940) develops soya derivatives. ...American seismologist Charles Richter (1900–1985) develops the Richter scale for measuring the magnitude of earthquakes. ...The electric organ is invented. ...First panty girdles are marketed in United States. ...AEG corporation of Germany markets first record/playback tape recorder. ...First self-propelled combine harvester is marketed in United States. ...**January 14:** Oil pipeline opens between Mosul, Iraq and Haifa, Palestine. ...Lower Zambezi Bridge (more than 12,000 feet long) opens between Beria on south bank and Nyasaland on north bank. ...**July 16:** First parking meters in the United States are installed on one side of street in Oklahoma City. Although meters are unpopular with public, merchants realize they help increase customer turnover rate, and their use is expanded.

c. 1935. Fluid-activated hydraulic brake systems are introduced. ...American Gregory Pincus (1903–1967) begins experimentation with in-vitro fertilization (IVF). ...Pasteurized milk becomes standard in United States. ...First lie detector is developed in United States.

Religion, Culture & Arts

1934. Recognizing social influence of cinema, Legion of Decency begins to rate motion pictures for Roman Catholics. ...Lewis Mumford (1895–1990), American social critic: *Technics and Civilization*. ...Marguerite Yourcenar (1903–1987), French novelist: *Denier du rêve (A Coin in Nine Hands)*. ...Isak Dinesen (1885–1962), Danish writer who primarily wrote in English: *Seven Gothic Tales*. ...William Saroyan (1908–1981), American writer: *The Daring Young Man on the Flying Trapeze*, short stories. ...Henry Miller (1891–1980), American author: *The Tropic of Cancer* is published in Paris and banned as pornographic in the United States, where it will be published in 1962. ...Margot Fonteyn (1919–1991), British dancer, makes her debut at the Royal Ballet. She will remain a star there for decades. ...Lincoln Kirsten (1907–1989), American showman and writer, founds School of the American Ballet. ...*It Happened One Night*, directed by Frank Capra (1897–1991) and starring Clark Gable (1901–1960) and Claudette Colbert (1905–1996).

1935. Karl Jaspers: *Vernunft und Existenz (Reason and Existence)*. ...John Steinbeck (1902–1968), American novelist: *Tortilla Flat*. ...John O'Hara, American novelist: *Butterfield Eight*. ...Thomas Wolfe: *Of Time and the River*. ...Isaac Bashevis Singer (1904–1991), Polish writer in Yiddish: *Satan in Gornay*. ...Christopher Isherwood: *Mr. Norris Changes Trains*. ...Roy Harris (1898–1979), American composer of music on nationalistic themes: "When Johnny Comes Marching Home." ...Kirsten Flagstad makes her debut at Metropolitan opera in New York. ...*Porgy and Bess*, by American writer DuBose Heyward (1885–1940) with music by George Gershwin, is first performed. ...Georgia O'Keeffe: *Sunflower, New Mexico II*. ...*Mutiny on the Bounty*, starring Charles Laughton. ...*The Thirty-Nine Steps*, British movie directed by Alfred Hitchcock (1899–1980).

1935–1936. Helen Hayes (1900–1993) portrays Queen Victoria in the play *Victoria Regina*.

c. 1935–1940. Boogie-woogie, a style of jazz in the blues manner, develops.

British Isles & Europe

1936. January 20: King George V (b. 1865) of England dies and is succeeded by Edward VIII (1894–1972). ...**March 7:** Germany denounces Locarno Treaty and occupies demilitarized Rhineland zone. ...**April 10:** Spanish parliament dismisses President Niceto Alcalá Zamora y Torres (1877–1949). ...**April 13:** General John Metaxas (1871–1941) becomes Greek prime minister. ...**June 19:** Irish Republican Army is declared illegal. ...**July 11:** Germany acknowledges Austrian independence. ...**July 18:** General Francisco Franco (1892–1975) leads army insurrection in Spain. ...**September 9:** Nonintervention Committee of all European powers meets in London. ...**October 1:** Franco is appointed chief of Spanish state. ...**October 19:** German Four-Year Plan is promulgated. ...**November 1:** Mussolini proclaims Rome-Berlin Axis. ...**November 14:** Germany denounces Versailles Treaty clauses on internationalization of German waterways. ...**November 18:** Germany and Italy recognize Franco's government. ...**December 10:** Edward VIII abdicates to marry American divorcée Wallis Simpson (1896–1986). ...**December 11:** Duke of York (1895–1952) becomes King George VI .

1937. January 15: Russian congress adopts new constitution. ...**February 8:** Spanish insurgents take Malaga. ...**February 27:** French chamber passes defense plan. Schneider-Creusot factory is nationalized. Maginot Line is extended. Ministry of defense is created. ...**March 18:** Italian legions are defeated at Brihuega. Insurgent attack on Madrid is checked in Spanish Civil War. ...**April 22:** Austrian chancellor Kurt von Schuschnigg meets Mussolini in Venice. ...**April 24:** Britain and France release Belgium from Locarno Treaty obligations. ...**April 27:** Spanish insurgents destroy Guernica in air attack. ...**May 28:** Stanley Baldwin resigns as British prime minister and is succeeded by Neville Chamberlain (1869–1940). ...**June 9:** Poland, Romania, and USSR guarantee their borders against invasion by each other. ...**June 11:** Eight Russian army chiefs are executed. During the following months, Stalin executes most of Soviet army's top leadership and 35,000 of 80,000 other officers. ...**June 23:** Germany and Italy withdraw from Nonintervention Committee. ...**July 21:** New constitution declares Irish Free State completely sovereign within British Commonwealth. ...**October 17:** Riots break out in Sudeten German part of Czechoslovakia. ...**November 6:** Italy joins German-Japanese Anti-Comintern Pact.

U.S. & Canada

1936. January 6: In *United States v. Butler*, U.S. Supreme Court declares Agricultural Adjustment Act unconstitutional. ...**January 28:** Canadian high court invalidates much of social legislation passed in 1935. ...**November 3:** Franklin Roosevelt is reelected U.S. president in landslide. ...**December 8:** In *Gibbs v. Board of Education*, U.S. Supreme Court rules that black and white school teachers in Montgomery County, Maryland, must receive equal pay for equal work.

The remains of the German airship **Hindenburg** *after its crash at Lakehurst, New Jersey, on May 6, 1937.*

1937. January 28: Judicial committee of British Privy Council confirms decision of Canada's high court invalidating social legislation of 1935. ...**March 26:** William Hastie (1904–1976) is confirmed as judge of Virgin Islands District Court. He is first African American federal judge. ...**May 1:** Roosevelt signs U.S. Neutrality Act, banning shipments of war matériel to European belligerents at discretion of president. ...**May 6:** German airship *Hindenburg* crashes and is consumed by fire at Lakehurst, New Jersey. ...**May 24:** New York permits women to serve as jurors. ...**July 2:** During her around-the-world flight, Amelia Earhart suddenly vanishes, causing endless speculation and rumors. ...**August 6:** Trade pact between United States and Soviet Union is signed. ...**August 15:** Canadian prime minister Mackenzie King appoints commission to study amendment of British North America Act of 1867, especially regarding relations between federal and provincial governments.

Latin America

1936. Reformist Party takes power in Costa Rica. ...Panama and United States renegotiate Panama Canal Treaty. ...Liberals enact constitutional reforms in Colombia. ...Cuban senate impeaches President Miguel Mariano Gómez (1890–1950). ...Mexico builds longitudinal canals and passes Expropriation Act. ...**January 21:** Peace between Bolivia and Paraguay is reached. ...**May:** In response to the left-wing Popular Front, the right wing establishes the National Front in Argentina. ...**December 1–16:** Pan-American Peace Conference is held in Buenos Aires.

1937. Dominican troops massacre thousands of Haitian immigrants. ...Anastasio Somoza (1896–1956) becomes dictator of Nicaragua. ...Luís Muñoz Marín (1898–1980) founds Popular Democratic Party in Puerto Rico. ...Poor economic conditions in Barbados cause severe unrest. ...University of Brazil is established. ...**February 20:** Paraguay withdraws from League of Nations. ...**March 2:** President Lázaro Cárdenas assumes control of Mexican oil resources. ...**May 26:** Bolivia and Paraguay resume diplomatic relations. ...**July 13:** Military stages coup d'état in Bolivia. ...**October 30:** Roberto Ortíz (1886–1942) is elected president of Argentina. ...**November 10:** New constitution is promulgated in Brazil. ...**December 14:** All political parties in Brazil are dissolved.

1937–1945. Getúlio Dornelles Vargas rules as dictator of Brazil.

Africa, Asia & Pacific

1936. Five million Chinese starve to death as floods and drought wipe out crops in Honan and Szechwan provinces. ...**February 26–29:** Dissatisfied young Japanese army officers murder several ministers and generals as attempted military coup fails. ...**March 9:** Koki Hirota (1878–1948) becomes prime minister of Japan, with cabinet dominated by military. ...**April 8:** Treaty of mutual assistance between Soviet Union and Mongolia is signed. ...**April 28:** King Fuad of Egypt dies and is succeeded by King Farouk (1920–1965). ...**May 9:** Italy proclaims annexation of Abyssinia (Ethiopia). Italian king takes title of emperor of Ethiopia. ...**May 10:** Nahas Pasha (1876–1965) forms all-Wafdist cabinet in Egypt. ...**August 11:** Chiang Kai-shek enters Canton. Unity of China is almost restored. ...**August 26:** Anglo-Egyptian treaty ends British military occupation of Egypt. Treaty calls for all British troops to be out of Egypt by 1956. ...**September 9:** French-Syrian treaty is signed. France promises to end mandate within three years and to include Jebel Druse, Alouite and Alexandretta in Syrian state. Lebanon will remain separate. ...**October 12:** Palestinians end six-month general strike protesting Britain's allowing Jews to immigrate and buy land.

1937. February 20: Congress Party wins majority of seats in six Indian provinces. ...**April 1:** Indian constitution comes into force. Burma and Aden are separated from India. ...**April 30:** Japanese government loses general election. ...**May 26:** Egypt joins League of Nations. ...**June 1:** Prince Konoye (1891–1945) becomes Japanese prime minister. ...**July 7:** Plan for partition of Palestine is published. ...Incident near Beijing leads to Japanese aggression against China. ...**July 8:** Nonaggression pact between Afghanistan, Iran, Iraq, and Turkey signed at Tehran. ...**July 19:** Japanese troops occupy Beijing, initiating second Sino-Japanese War. ...**July 29:** Japanese occupy Tientsin. ...**August 11:** Japanese sailors land near Shanghai. ...**October 1:** Higher Arab Committee in Palestine is declared illegal. ...**November 3–24:** Conference of Nine Powers meets at Brussels to discuss action to take in Sino-Japanese War. ...**November 9:** Japanese capture Shanghai. ...**November 20:** Japanese take Suchow. ...**December 12–13:** Japanese take Nanking, killing approximately 350,000 civilians in so-called Rape of Nanking. ...Japanese forces sink U.S. navy gunboat *Panay* and two merchant ships near Nanking. ...**December 24:** Japanese troops occupy Hangchow.

Science, Invention & Technology

1936. Scottish physicist Sir Robert Watson-Watt (1892–1973) invents a pulse radar altimeter. ...German company BASF makes first public tape recording. ...German company IG Farben begins manufacturing Plexiglas contact lenses. ...American Ernest Lawrence (1901–1958) builds first cyclotron, proton accelerator, at the University of California at Berkeley. ...Svedberg centrifuge produces force 525,000 times normal gravity. ...Boulder Dam is completed on Colorado River, Nevada/Arizona border. It will be renamed Hoover Dam.

1937. Grote Reber (1911–) builds first radio telescope from salvaged parts in his backyard in suburban Chicago. ...American Earl Tupper (1907–1983) develops Tupperware, impervious plastic ware for domestic use. ...Trans-Pacific line establishes regular air connections from California to Manila, with stop at Hawaii.

c. 1937. Irish-born Englishman Harry Ferguson (1884–1960) develops a farm tractor system with interchangeable implements. ...American Vannevar Bush (1890–1974) invents a digital computer. ...American Marvin Camras (1916–1995) makes recording using magnetic wire instead of magnetic tape.

Religion, Culture & Arts

1936. A. J. Ayer (1910–1989), English philosopher of logical positivism: *Language, Truth, and Logic*. ...Sidney Hook (1902–1989), American political philosopher: *From Hegel to Marx*. ...François Mauriac: *La Vie de Jésus* (*The Life of Jesus*). ...Rainer Maria Rilke (1875–1926), German poet: *Sonnets to Orpheus*. ...Carl Sandburg: *The People, Yes*. ...Robert Frost: *A Further Range*. ...Daphne du Maurier, British novelist (1907–1989): *Jamaica Inn*, among her romances touched by mystery and irony. ...Margaret Mitchell's (1900–1949) *Gone with the Wind* sells 1,000,000 copies in six months. ...Elizabeth Bowen: *The House in Paris*. ...William Faulkner: *Absalom, Absalom* ...Gian Carlo Menotti (1911–), Italian-American opera composer: *Amelia Goes to the Ball*. ...Aaron Copland (1900–1990), American composer: *El Salón México*, for orchestra. ...Étienne Gilson: *Christianisme et philosophie* (*Christianity and Philosophy*). ...*Life* magazine begins publication. ...Olympic Games are held in Berlin, Germany. African American track star Jesse Owens (1913–1980) becomes the first person to win four gold medals. ...Frank Capra: *Mr. Deeds Goes to Town*.

1937. Hector de Saint Denys Garneau (1912–1943), French-Canadian poet: *Regards et jeux dans l'espace* (*Glances and Games in Space*). ...John Steinbeck: *Of Mice and Men*. ...James M. Cain (1892–1977): *Serenade*. ...J. R. R. Tolkien (1892–1973), British professor of medieval literature: *Beowulf: The Monster and His Critics*; *The Hobbit*. ...Igor Stravinsky: *Jeu des Cartes*, ballet ...Alban Berg's *Lulu*, an opera, is performed for the first time, almost two years after Berg's death. ...Zinka Milanov (1906–1989), dramatic soprano, makes her debut at New York's Metropolitan Opera. She will star until 1966. ...Pablo Picasso: *Guernica*. ...Jean Renoir (1894–1979), French movie director: *La Grande Illusion* (*The Grand Illusion*) about World War I prisoners of war. ...Museum of Modern Art, designed by American architect Edward Durell Stone (1902–1978), opens in New York City. ...Salo Wittmayer Baron (1895–1989), Polish-born American historian, publishes three-volume edition of *A Social and Religious History of the Jews*, which grows to 18 volumes by his death. ...*Stella Dallas*, starring American actress Barbara Stanwyck (1907–1990). ...*Tovarich*, starring Greta Garbo and Charles Boyer (1899–1978), French-born actor. ...**June 22:** African American Joe Louis (1914–1981) defeats James J. Braddock to become world heavyweight boxing champion.

British Isles & Europe

1938. March 11: German troops enter Austria. ...**March 12:** Austria is declared part of German Reich Anschluss. ...**May 3–9:** Adolf Hitler meets Benito Mussolini in Rome. ...**July 25:** Lord Runciman's (1870–1949) mission to Prague reports in favor of Nazi claims. **August 12:** Germany mobilizes. **September 7:** Clash between Czechs and Sudeten Germans at Moravska Ostrava. Negotiations break down. **September 15:** Chamberlain meets Hitler at Berchtesgaden to discuss Sudeten crisis. **September 18:** Anglo-French proposals on Czech question are made. **September 22–23:** Chamberlain meets Hitler at Godesberg. **September 29:** At Munich Conference, Neville Chamberlain, Édouard Daladier, Mussolini, and Hitler agree on transfer of Sudeten territory to Germany by Czechoslovakia. Chamberlain returns to London and proclaims, "Peace in our time." **October 1–10:** German troops occupy Sudeten territory. ...**October 21:** Czechs terminate pact with Soviet Union. ...**November 8–14:** Violent pogroms against Jews are conducted in Germany by Nazis. ...**November 21:** Autonomy is granted to Slovakia and Ruthenia. ...**November 26:** Soviet Union and Poland sign declaration of friendship. ...**December 22:** Italy denounces January 7, 1935, agreement with France.

1939. January 26: Spanish Nationalists capture Barcelona. **February 28:** Britain recognizes Franco government in Spain. ...**March 14:** Slovakia proclaims independence under German protection. **March 15:** German troops occupy Czechoslovakia. ...**March 16:** Bohemia and Moravia are declared German protectorates. ...**March 22:** Lithuania cedes Memel to Germany. ...Poland rejects German ultimatum, demanding return of Danzig and Polish Corridor. Hitler prepares invasion of Poland. Germany and Soviet Union begin negotiating division of Poland, as Hitler forces Romania to repudiate Polish alliance. **March 24:** British guarantee Poland's integrity. ...**March 29–30:** Franco occupies Madrid. ...**April 6:** Hitler instructs German army to prepare for Case White, invasion of Poland. ...**April 7:** Italy invades Albania. ...**April 13:** British guarantee is extended to Romania and Greece. ...**April 16:** Soviet Union proposes alliance with Britain and France. ...**April 16:** Victor Emmanuel III accepts crown of Albania. ...**April 28:** Hitler denounces nonaggression pact with Poland. ...**May 19:** France agrees to send troops and to bomb Germany if Hitler's armies invade Poland. ...**May 22:** Germany and Italy agree on alliance for ten years. ...**August 23:** Germany and Soviet Union sign nonaggression Pact. ...**August 25:** Anglo-Polish pact of mutual assistance is signed.

U.S. & Canada

1938. Democrat Crystal Bird Fauset (1893–1965) becomes first African-American woman elected to U. S. House of Representatives. ...**March 21:** U.S. Congress passes Naval Expansion Act, authorizing more than a billion dollars in new ship construction for U.S. Navy. ...**May 24:** U.S. Congress passes Labor Standards Act, establishing a minimum hourly wage of 25 cents. ...**October 24:** Labor Standards Act goes into effect. ...**November 8:** After U.S. midterm elections, the Senate is made up of 69 Democrats and 23 Republicans; the House of Representatives has 261 Democrats and 168 Republicans.

1939. March 20: U.S. ambassador to Germany is recalled. ...**April 15:** Roosevelt issues "peace plea" to Hitler. ...**April 28:** Hitler rejects peace plea. ...**May 17:** King George VI (1895–1952) and his wife, Elizabeth Bowes-Lyon (1900–), are first reigning British monarchs to visit Canada. ...**June 7–11:** George VI and Elizabeth are first reigning British monarchs to visit the United States.

Latin America

1938. Jamaicans riot against British racial policies and unemployment. ...Alexander Bustamente (1884–1977) organizes the Bustamente Industrial Trade Union in Jamaica. ...Mexican oil workers strike. ...**March 19:** Mexico expropriates British and U.S. oil properties. ...**May 11:** Pro-Nazi revolt is suppressed in Brazil. ...**July 12:** Venezuela withdraws from League of Nations. ...**September 5:** Nazi plot fails in Chile. ...**October:** Brazil and Germany break diplomatic relations. ...**October 10:** Frontier between Bolivia and Paraguay is fixed by international arbitration. ...**October 25:** Pedro Aguirre Cerda (1879–1941) is elected president of Chile. ...**December 9–26:** Eighth Pan-American Conference in Lima issues "Declaration of Lima" against "all foreign intervention or activity" in Americas and reaffirms that nations will consult with one another in the event of an outside attack.

1939. U.S. Senate ratifies new Panama Canal Treaty, which increases Panama's annuity from United States. ...Inter-American Neutrality Conference is held in Panama. ...An earthquake kills 28,000 in Chile. ...Puerto Rico becomes a key U.S. military base.

Still Picture Branch, National Archives, College Park, MD

▲ ***A German police unit enters Austria in March 1938.***

Africa, Asia & Pacific

1938. April 27: Greece and Turkey agree on treaty of friendship. ...**May 12:** Manchukuo is recognized by Germany. ...**July 3–August 11:** Soviet-Japanese hostilities break out on border of Manchukuo. ...**September 27–28:** League of Nations pronounces Japan to be aggressor and invites members to support China. ...**October 15:** France recognizes Italian conquest of Abyssinia (Ethiopia). ...**October 21:** Japanese enter Canton. **October 25:** Japanese enter Hankow. ...Libya is declared part of Italy. ...**November 2:** Japan withdraws from technical organizations of League of Nations. ...**November 10:** Kemal Atatürk (b. 1881) dies. ...**November 11:** Ismet Inönü (1884–1973) is elected Turkish president. ...**December 28:** Iran severs diplomatic relations with France.

1939. January: Trans-Iranian Railway opens from Caspian Sea to Persian Gulf. ...**February 10:** Japanese occupy Hainan Island. ...**March 14:** Robert Menzies (1894–1978) forms government in Australia. ...**April 4:** King Ghazi of Iraq dies and is succeeded by Faisal II (1935–1958). ...**May 17:** British White Paper promises Palestine independence within ten years. ...**June 23:** French agree to cede Alexandretta to Republic of Turkey.

Science, Invention & Technology

1938. Non-reflecting glass is invented. ...Britain secretly builds an extensive radar defense network on English Channel and North Sea coasts. ...U.S. government passes laws requiring testing of medicines before marketing, effectively ending the infamous patent medicine trade. ...The trampoline is invented. ...Nylon is developed. ...Englishman Alan Turing (1912–1954) develops the Universal Turing Machine, forerunner of the computer.

c. 1938. First automated car washes open in United States.

1939. First jet engine, invented by German Hans von Ohain (1911–), is tested. ...John Atanasoff and Clifford Berry develop the A-B-C (Atanasoff-Berry Computer). ...Disposable aerosol spray can is developed in the United States. ...Howard Aiken (1900–1973) begins building the Mark I computer at IBM. ...Owens-Corning Company markets fiberglass insulation. ...Russian Vladimir Zworykin (1889–1982) makes an improved electron microscope for magnification up to x2,000,000. ...At Pylos, Greece, an expedition discovers some 600 clay tablets in "Linear B," earliest form of Greek.

Religion, Culture & Arts

1938. Graham Greene (1904–1991), British novelist: *Brighton Rock*. ...Daphne du Maurier: *Rebecca*. ...John Dos Passos: *U.S.A.*, a trilogy collecting *The 42nd Parallel* (1930), *1919* (1932), and *The Big Money* (1936). ...Andre Malraux: *L'Espoir* (*Man's Hope*). ...Thornton Wilder (1897–1975): play *Our Town*. ...Cyril Lionel Robert James (1901–1989): *The Black Jacobins: Toussaint L'Ouverture and the San Domingo Revolution*. ...Ballet *Billy the Kid*, music by Aaron Copland, choreography by Eugene Loring (1914–1982). ...Eugene Ormandy (1899–1985), Hungarian-born American conductor, becomes conductor of Philadelphia Orchestra. ...World Council of Churches is founded. Dutch cleric Willem Adolph Visser't Hooft (1900–1985) is named first general secretary. ...German government imprisons Martin Niemöller (1892–1984), theologian and church leader who opposes National Socialism. ...Leni Riefenstahl makes the documentary film *Olympia*, about 1936 Olympic Games. ...Walt Disney's *Snow White and the Seven Dwarfs*, first feature-length animated film. ...*The Lady Vanishes*, directed by Alfred Hitchcock, is released.

1939. Raymond Chandler (1888–1959), American author of dark psychological mysteries: *The Big Sleep*. ...Antoine de Saint-Exupéry (1900–1944), French aviator and author: *Terre des hommes* (*Wind, Sand, and Stars*). ...Henry Miller's novel *The Tropic of Capricorn* is published in Paris; U.S. publication 1962. ...John Steinbeck: *The Grapes of Wrath*. ...Daughters of the American Revolution will not allow Marian Anderson to sing at Constitution Hall because she is black. First Lady Eleanor Roosevelt arranges concert at Lincoln Memorial. ...Religious Bodies Law gives Japanese government control over all religions in Japan. ...Film *Stagecoach*, directed by John Ford (1895–1973) and starring John Wayne (1907–1979), is released. The film establishes Wayne's career as a western star. ...Film *The Wizard of Oz*, starring Judy Garland (1922–1969), is released. ...Film *Mr. Smith Goes to Washington*, directed by Frank Capra and starring American actor Jimmy Stewart (1908–1997), is released. ...**May 10:** Methodist Episcopal Church South merges with parent church, from which it split in 1848. ...**July 8:** Havelock Ellis (b. 1859) dies. English physician and investigator of sexual habits, Ellis was the author of *Studies in the Psychology of Sex*.

International Affairs; European, African, Mideast War Zone

1939. September 1: Germany invades Poland, marking the beginning of World War II. **September 3:** Britain and France declare war on Germany. ...**September 16:** German troops surround Warsaw and demand surrender, but Poles refuse. **September 17:** Soviet Union invades Poland from East. **September 27:** Warsaw surrenders to Germany. **September 28:** Germany and Soviet Union partition Poland. **September 30:** A Polish government in exile is established in Paris. It later moves to London. ...**October 3:** I Corps of the British Expeditionary Force takes over protection of a sector of the Belgium-French border. ...**October 10:** Finland mobilizes its troops after resisting demands from the Soviet Union to make changes in their border. ...**October 19:** Germany officially incorporates parts of western Poland into the Reich. ...**November 28:** Soviet Union denounces nonaggression pact with Finland. **November 30:** Soviet Union invades Finland after Finns refuse to cede territory to Soviets. **December 2:** Soviet Union is expelled from the League of Nations after refusing to accept league mediation in the dispute with Finland.

1940. March 13: Finland signs peace treaty with Soviet Union. ...**March 20:** Paul Reynaud (1878–1966) becomes French prime minister. ...**April 9:** Germans invade Denmark and Norway. **April 30**: King Haakon VII leaves Norway for Britain, where he sets-up a government in exile. ...**May 10:** Germany invades Holland, Belgium and Luxembourg. ...Winston Churchill (1874–1965) forms coalition government in Britain. ...**May 15:** Dutch capitulate. French front is penetrated. ...**May 16:** British and French begin retreat from advanced positions in Belgium. **May 17:** German troops enter Brussels. ...**May 20:** German forces advance to the English Channel through northern France by way of Amiens and Abbeville, dividing Allied forces. ...**May 21:** British, French and Belgian forces fail in attempt to cut through German salient at Arras. ...**May 28:** Belgians capitulate. ...Germans capture Narvik, Norway. ...**May 27–June 4:** Surrounded by German troops, 200,000 British and 130,000 French soldiers are evacuated from the beaches of Dunkirk, leaving most of their supplies and equipment behind. **June 3:** Some 40,000 French troops who failed to evacuate Dunkirk are captured by the Germans. ...**June 9:** Haakon VII orders Norwegian forces to cease fire. ...**June 10:** Italy declares war on Britain and France. ...**June 11:** Paris is declared an open city; French forces retreat to the south in confusion.

U.S. & Canadian Domestic Developments

1939. September 3: In fireside chat, U.S. president Franklin Roosevelt notes he cannot expect Americans to be neutral in thought toward war in Europe. ...**September 4:** Secretary of State Cordell Hull (1871–1955) warns U.S. citizens not to travel to Europe except under extreme necessity. ...**September 5:** Roosevelt declares U.S. neutrality in European conflict. ...**September 8:** Roosevelt declares a limited national emergency. ...**September 10:** Canada declares war on Germany. ...**October 3:** Declaration of Panama specifies western Atlantic safety zones, declaring action by belligerent powers is forbidden. ...**October 11:** Letter from Albert Einstein urging U.S. development of nuclear weapon is delivered to Roosevelt. ...**October 18:** U.S. ports and territorial waters are closed to belligerent submarines. ...**November 4:** U.S. Neutrality Act repeals arms embargo, enabling Britain and France to purchase U.S. weapons on "cash and carry" basis to fight Nazis.

1940. U.S. Census sets population at 131,669,275. ...**January 4:** Frank Murphy (1890–1949) is nominated to the Supreme Court by President Roosevelt. He will be confirmed by Senate January 16. ...**January 30:** First checks are issued by U.S. Social Security Administration. ...**April 26:** Woman suffrage enacted for first time in Quebec, Canada. ...**May 16:** Roosevelt calls for the production of 50,000 aircraft. ...**May 25:** Roosevelt creates by executive order the Office of Emergency Management. ...**May 28:** Roosevelt names a National Defense Advisory Commission headed by William S. Knudsen (1879–1948) to coordinate economic aspects of defense. ...**June 2:** The national convention of the Communist Party of the United States meets in New York City to nominate national candidates for 1940 election. ...**June 3:** U.S. War Department agrees to sell millions of dollars' worth of surplus and outdated armaments and aircraft to Britain.

Asia & Pacific War Zone

1939. September 3: Australia and New Zealand declare war on Germany. ...**September 4:** South African Assembly votes down neutrality in World War II. Jan Christian Smuts (1870–1950) replaces J. B. M. Hertzog (1866–1942) as prime minister of South Africa. ...**September 6:** South Africa declares war on Germany. ...**September 16:** Soviet-Japanese armistice is reached in Manchurian-Mongolian border clashes. It is a setback for Japanese. ...**September 23:** Admiral Kichisaburo Nomura (1877–1964) is appointed Japanese foreign minister. ...**November 24:** Japanese sever China from French Indochina.

1940. Japanese control northeastern third of China, all major seaports and Hainan Island. ...Japan dissolves all political parties. ...Mohandas Gandhi begins another noncooperation campaign against Britain. ...**January 14:** Japanese cabinet resigns. Admiral Mitsumasa Yonai (1880–1948) establishes new government. ...**February 1:** More than 50 percent of budget introduced to Japanese Diet is devoted to the military.

▲ ***King Haakon VII of Norway (right) with his son, Crown Prince Olaf, in 1940, soon after Germany invaded Norway.***

Latin America

1939. September: Argentina proclaims its neutrality in World War II. . . . **December 17:** German pocket battleship *Graf Spee* is scuttled by its crew off Montevideo, Uruguay, after receiving the misinformation that the British cruiser *Renown* is in the area.

Still Picture Branch, National Archives, College Park, MD

This photo was taken near Warsaw soon after the Germans invaded Poland in 1939.

1940. Manuel Ávila Camacho (1897–1955) becomes president of Mexico. Arnulfo Arias (1901–1988) is elected president of Panama. . . . Reformist Party is reelected in Costa Rica. . . . Rural Colombians migrate to Bogotá in search of work. . . . Dominica is attached to the Windward Islands. . . . Fulgencio Batista Zaldívar (1901–1973) is elected president of Cuba. . . . United States institutes hydroelectric power program in Puerto Rico. . . . Luís Muñoz Marín's Popular Democratic Party wins control of Puerto Rican legislature and he becomes president of the senate.

Science, Invention & Technology

1940. The recoilless rifle is developed in Germany. . . . Frequency modulation (FM) wavelengths are first regulated by the U.S. Federal Communications Commission, but World War II delays their use. . . . R. Buckminster Fuller develops the Dymaxion Deployment Unit (DDU) for the U.S. military. The transportable units provide easily deployed living and working quarters. . . . Igor Sikorsky begins production of helicopters for U.S. forces. . . . Americans Edwin McMillan (1907–1991) and Philip Abelson (1913–) discover the element neptunium, the first transuranium element. . . . American Glenn T. Seaborg (1912–) discovers plutonium. . . . The highly successful Rolls Royce engine is developed by the British. . . . Frederick Jones (1892–1961) obtains a U.S. patent for a cooling unit for the transport of perishable foods. . . . American scientists develop an efficient process for making silicone compound. . . . The first commercially viable snowmobile, the B-12, is developed in Canada. . . . American chemist Linus Pauling (1901–1994) publishes his findings on the use of antibodies. . . . American Vincent du Vigneaud (1901–1978) synthesizes biotin, a coenzyme that metabolizes carbohydrates in the body. . . . Mars Candy Company develops M & M candy with melt-resistant chocolate coating for American GI's. . . . **April 20:** The electron microscope is publicly tested for the first time in Camden, New Jersey.

Religion, Culture & Arts

1939. Pope Pius XI (b. 1857) dies. Cardinal Eugenio Pacelli is elected Pope Pius XII (1876–1958). . . . Henry Moore (1898–1986) sculpts *Reclining Figure*. . . . Pablo Picasso paints *Night Fishing at Antibes*. . . . Frank Lloyd Wright's Johnson building is completed. . . . Film version of *Gone with the Wind* is released and becomes a huge hit. . . . Arna Bontemps (1902–1973): *Drums at Dusk*. . . . John Dos Passos: *Adventures of a Young Man*. . . . Lillian Hellman (1905–1984), American dramatist: *The Little Foxes*. . . . Aldous Huxley: *After Many a Summer Dies the Swan*. . . . James Joyce: *Finnegans Wake*. . . . J. P. Marquand (1893–1960) American novelist: *Wickford Point*. . . . Katherine Anne Porter: *Pale Horse, Pale Rider*. . . . Carl Van Doren (1885–1950): *Benjamin Franklin* (Pulitzer Prize, biography.) . . . Nathaniel Weinstein (1903–1940), known as Nathaniel West: *The Day of the Locust*.

1940. National survey shows that nearly 30 million American homes have radios. . . . John Ford directs film version of Steinbeck's *Grapes of Wrath*. . . . Charlie Chaplin (1889–1977): *The Great Dictator*. . . . Irving Berlin: *Louisiana Purchase*. . . . Raymond Chandler: *Farewell, My Lovely*. . . . Walter Van Tilburg Clark (1909–1971): *The Ox-Bow Incident*. . . . William Faulkner: *The Hamlet*. . . . Graham Greene: *The Power and the Glory*. . . . George S. Kaufman (1899–1961) with Moss Hart (1904–1961): *George Washington Slept Here*. . . . Arthur Koestler (1905–1983): *Darkness at Noon*, a book on Soviet purge trials. . . . Ernest Hemingway: *For Whom the Bell Tolls*. . . . Carson McCullers (1917–1967), American novelist: *The Heart Is a Lonely Hunter*. . . . Eugene O'Neill: *Long Day's Journey into Night*. . . . Carl Sandburg: *Abraham Lincoln* (Pulitzer Prize, history). . . . William Saroyan: *The Time of Your Life* (Pulitzer Prize, drama). . . . James Thurber (1894–1961), American humorist: *The Male Animal*. . . . Thomas Wolfe's *You Can't Go Home Again* is posthumously published. . . . Richard Wright (1908–1960), African American writer: *Native Son*. . . . *Rebecca*, Alfred Hitchcock's first Hollywood film, wins the Academy Award for best picture. . . . Chicago Bears defeat Washington Redskins 73–0 in the National Football League championship game. . . . Stanford defeats Nebraska in the Rose Bowl.

International Affairs; European, African, Mideast War Zone

1940 (Continued). June 12–22: Soviets occupy Lithuania, Estonia and Latvia. ...**June 14:** Germans enter Paris. ...**June 16:** British offer of Anglo-French union is rejected; Henri Pétain becomes French prime minister. ...**June 18:** General Charles de Gaulle (1890–1970) broadcasts from Britain, urging French to fight on. ...**June 22:** Armistice between Germany and France comes into force. ...**June 23:** De Gaulle starts Free French movement from exile in England. ...**June 24:** France signs armistice with Italy and relocates capital to Vichy. ...**June 28:** Britain recognizes de Gaulle as "leader of all free Frenchmen." ...**July 3:** To prevent Nazis from using French fleet at Oran and Mers-el-Kebir, British sink elements of the fleet. ...**July 13–15:** Italian forces move into British colony of Kenya. ...**July 21:** Soviet Union formally annexes Lithuania, Latvia and Estonia. ...**August 4:** Italians invade British Somaliland. ...**August 8–September 6:** At battle of Britain, German Luftwaffe suffers heavy losses in its attempt to knock out the Royal Air Force in hopes of preparing the way for a ground invasion. ...**September 7–October 31:** London blitz begins. Germans conduct nightly air raids over London. The blitz will continue into 1941. ...**September 13:** Italians invade Egypt from Libya. ...**September 25:** Germans install Vidkun Quisling (1887–1945) as leader of Norway. ...**October 18:** Anti-Semitic laws are introduced in Vichy France. ...**October 28:** Italy attacks Greece. ...**November 14:** German bombers raid British city of Coventry.

1941. January 20: Adolf Hitler announces he will intervene in Greece if British come to aid of Greeks. ...**February 9:** Germans occupy Bulgaria. ...**February 12:** German general Erwin Rommel (1891–1944) lands in North Africa with German troops to support Italians. ...**March 24–April 11:** German troops under Rommel advance through Libya, isolating British troops at Tobruk in eastern Libya. ...**April 1–3:** Pro-Axis rebels overthrow pro-Allied government in Iraq. ...**April 6:** Germans invade Yugoslavia and Greece. **April 17:** Germans accept surrender of Yugoslavia. ...**April 27–29:** Germans enter Athens, and British evacuate Greece. ...**May 4:** Rommel's forces surround the British garrison at Tobruk. ...**May 10:** Rudolph Hess (1894–1987), Hitler's deputy, lands in Scotland in an unauthorized attempt to strike a deal with the British. He is imprisoned.

U.S. & Canadian Domestic Developments

1940 (Continued). June 17: U.S. Navy requests appropriation of $4 billion to build a two-ocean navy. ...**June 20:** U.S. president Franklin Roosevelt names Henry Stimson (1867–1950) secretary of war and Frank Knox (1874–1944) secretary of the navy. ...**June 28:** Roosevelt selects Donald Nelson (1888–1959) to serve as coordinator of national defense purchases. ...**June 29:** Republicans nominate Wendell L. Willkie (1892–1944) for president. ...**July 18:** Democrats nominate Roosevelt for third term as president. ...**August 18:** Canadian prime minister Mackenzie King and President Roosevelt meet in Ogdensburg, New York, to establish Joint Board on Defense. ...**September 3:** United States and Britain agree on transfer of 50 U.S. destroyers for 99-year leases on bases in Newfoundland and in the Caribbean. ...**September 16:** United States introduces Selective Service, first peacetime compulsory military service, with draft age set from 21 to 36. ...**October 10:** In Canada, 30,000 men begin compulsory military training. ...**October 24:** Under Fair Labor Standards Act, 40-hour work week goes into effect in the United States. ...**November 5:** Roosevelt is reelected for third term, defeating Willkie (449 electoral votes to 82). ...**December 10:** Through extension of U.S. export license regulation, U.S. companies are not allowed to export iron and steel products to Japan.

1941. January 9: Japanese residents of British Columbia, Canada, are required to register with the government. ...**March 11:** Roosevelt signs Lend-Lease bill, an arrangement to sell, transfer, lend or lease war supplies to nations considered vital to U.S. defense. ...**April 9:** United States signs agreement with Danish minister for U.S. protection of Greenland. The agreement is renounced in occupied Denmark. ...**April 10:** Roosevelt announces that safety zone proclaimed by Inter-American Neutrality Conference in 1939 is to be moved eastward to 25th meridian. ...**April 14:** Secret talks between U.S. officials and Icelandic consul prepare way for agreement on U.S. occupation of Iceland. ...**April 15:** Roosevelt appoints Harry Hopkins (1890–1946) to administer Lend-Lease program. ...**April 24:** Roosevelt orders U.S. Navy to report to British operation of German ships west of Iceland. ...**May 1:** Defense savings bonds and stamps go on sale in United States.

Asia & Pacific War Zone

1940 (Continued). September: By Tripartite Pact, Japan joins the Rome-Berlin Axis. ...**October 1:** Burma road opens to supply Chiang Kai-shek's army in China. ...**November 30:** Japanese recognize Nanking Chinese government headed by Wang Ching-wei (1883–1944), who will rule as a puppet of Japanese until 1944.

Ho Chi Minh led the Vietnamese revolt against the French and went on to become president of North Vietnam.

1941. Ho Chi Minh (c. 1890–1969), born Nguyen That Thanh, forms the Vietminh to gain Vietnamese independence. ...Norodom Sihanouk (1922–) begins his reign as king of Cambodia.

Latin America

1940 (Continued). July 20–July 30: Havana Conference of United States and Latin American nations sets policies regarding exclusion of warships from territorial waters and control of subversive activities. "Act of Havana" authorizes Western Hemisphere nations to seize European possessions threatened by aggression. ...**August 20:** Leon Trotsky (b. 1879) is assassinated while in exile in Mexico. ...**September:** Higinio Morínigo (1890–1950) takes power in Paraguay. He makes improvements in education, health and public roads and suppresses several rebellions.

1941. Brazil joins Inter-American Coffee Board to control coffee production. ...U.S. Customs receivership of Dominican Republic is terminated. ...Dominican Republic declares war on the Axis. ...An avalanche of mud and water wipes out much of Huaras, Peru, and kills 6,000 people. ...President Arnulfo Arias of Panama is ousted for being pro-Fascist. ...Peru sides with Allies in World War II. ...Plutarco Calles (1877–1945), former president of Mexico, returns from six-year exile. ...Mexico allows United States to use its airfields. ...Colombia and Costa Rica join the Allies. ...Ecuador and Peru fight a war over a border dispute.

Science, Invention & Technology

1940 (Continued). June 15: B. F. Goodrich Company exhibits first tires made from synthetic rubber. ...**July:** Karl Landsteiner and Walter Weiner (1899–1981) discover Rhesus factor in blood. Deadly transfusion reactions can now be avoided. ...Rheumatoid factor in arthritis is discovered. ...**July 2:** The Lake Washington Floating Bridge in Seattle Washington, the largest floating bridge ever built, opens to traffic. ...**July 8:** TWA flies first commercial flight using pressurized cabins (from New York City to Burbank, California). ...**August:** Hungarian-born American Peter Goldmark (1906–1977) develops the field-sequential color system, the basis for color television transmission. ...**August 24:** Use of penicillin as therapeutic agent begins. ...**September:** Australian Howard Florey (1898–1968) and German Ernst Chain (1906–1979) develop penicillin as an antibiotic. ...**October:** Astatine, element 85, is artificially created by a team of scientists at the University of California, Berkeley. ...**December:** The first freeway in Los Angeles, Arroyo Seco Parkway, opens.

c. 1940. Hungarian Leo Sziland (1898–1964), while in London, realizes the effect of nuclear fission and its destructive potential. ...James Wright (1927–1980), at General Electric Company, develops a new synthetic rubber. ...H. Trendley Dean (1893–1962), at the U.S. Public Health Service, establishes a level of one part per million as the recommendation for fluoridation of public water supply.

1941. German American Fritz Lipmann (1899–1986) discovers adenosine triphosphate (ATP), which delivers energy to human body from metabolizing food. ...Claude Shannon (1916–), at Bell Laboratories, develops binary mathematical language, which uses only 1 or 0 in all its dialogue. It will be basis for computer software. ...Fortification of foods with niacin is begun in United States to eliminate pellagra, a fatal vitamin deficiency. ...Russian-born American Albert Sabin (1906–1993) determines that polio virus enters the body through digestive tract. ...Standard tuberculosis skin test is develeped in the United States. ...J. Presper Eckert, Jr. (1919–1995) and John Mauchly (1907–1980) develop the ENIAC computer at the University of Pennsylvania. ...African American Charles Drew (1904–1950) discovers method for processing and preserving blood plasma. ...A reusable aerosol spray can is patented in United States. ...Polyvinyl chloride (PVC) is first developed in France.

Religion, Culture & Arts

1940 (Continued). July: Charles Eames (1909–1978) and Eero Saarinen (1910–1961), furniture designers, win prizes at the Museum of Modern Art competition for organic design in home furnishings. **October 2–8:** The Cincinnati Reds defeat the Detroit Tigers to win the World Series.

Wisconsin Center for Film and Theater Research, Madison, WI

British film director Alfred Hitchcock.

1941. *Antioch Review* is founded in Yellow Springs, Ohio. ...National Gallery of Art opens in Washington, D.C. ...John Huston (1906–1987) writes and directs *The Maltese Falcon*. ...Orson Welles (1915–1985) co-writes, directs and stars in *Citizen Kane*. ...Ted Shawn (1891–1972) begins annual dance festival at Jacob's Pillow, Massachusetts. ...Alfred Hitchcock: *Suspicion*. ...John Ford: *How Green Was My Valley*. ...James Agee (1909–1955), American writer: *Let Us Now Praise Famous Men*. ...Ludwig Bemelmans (1898–1962), American writer: *Hotel Splendide*. ...Noel Coward: *Blithe Spirit*. ...Edna Ferber (1887–1968), American novelist: *Saratoga Trunk*. ...F. Scott Fitzgerald: *The Last Tycoon*, unfinished novel, posthumously published. ...Ellen Glasgow (1873–1945): *In This Our Life* (Pulitzer Prize, literature). ...Lillian Hellman: *Watch on the Rhine*. ...J. P. Marquand: *H. M. Pulham, Esquire*. ...Carson McCullers: *Reflections in a Golden Eye*. ...Americans Charles Bernard Nordhoff (1887–1947) and James Norman Hall (1887–1951) write *Botany Bay*.

International Affairs; European, African, Mideast War Zone

1941 (Continued). May 13: Martin Bormann (1900–1945) assumes position as Adolf Hitler's deputy. ...**May 15–19:** Germans begin bombing raids on Crete. ...**May 20–June 1:** German airborne forces complete the capture of Crete, inflicting heavy casualties on British, who evacuate nearly 20,000 men. ...**June 17:** Rommel's forces push back and defeat British Operation Battleaxe in Egypt. ...**June 22:** Germany invades Soviet Union in a three-pronged attack—north toward Leningrad, center toward Moscow and south toward Kiev. ...**July 8:** Germany, Italy and Hungary announce the partition of Yugoslavia, leaving only Croatia as nominally independent. ...**July 11:** Allies and Vichy French sign armistice in Syria. ...**July 12:** Britain and Soviet Union sign defensive alliance. ...**August:** Germans begin 900-day siege of Leningrad (St. Petersburg) that kills hundreds of thousands of citizens. ...**August 25–29:** British and Soviets secure Iran. ...**September 4:** U.S. destroyer *Greer* is attacked by German U-boat ...**September 19:** Germans take Kiev. ...**October 2–December 6:** During battle for Moscow, German troops, ill prepared for the Russian winter, reach the outskirts of Moscow by November 15, but their offensive is halted by Soviets in December. ...**November 9:** Germans seal off last rail link to Leningrad. ...**November 27:** Last Italian troops surrender at Gondar, Abyssinia (Ethiopia). ...**December 11:** Germany and Italy declare war on United States.

1942. January 10: Germany launches offensive in the Crimea. ...**January 20:** Holocaust intensifies as Hitler approves "final solution of the Jewish problem," authorizing extermination camps. ...**January 21–February 5:** Rommel launches counteroffensive in North Africa, driving from El Agheila through Benghazi and past Derna. ...**February 1–March 31:** Germans launch attacks on U.S. shipping off Atlantic coast and in Caribbean, sinking more than 50 ships in this region alone. ...**February 6:** Roosevelt and Winston Churchill appoint combined chiefs of staff.

U.S. & Canadian Domestic Developments

1941 (Continued). May 28: Franklin Roosevelt appoints Harold Ickes (1874–1952) petroleum coordinator for national defense. ...**June 25:** Fair Employment Practices Committee is established to monitor and curb racial discrimination in war production and U.S. government employment by Executive Order 8802. ...**July 2:** U.S. Federal Power Commission creates 17-state electric power pool to aid in production of aluminum. ...**July 26:** Roosevelt freezes Japanese assets in United States and closes Panama Canal to Japanese vessels. ...**August 1:** Roosevelt forbids export of oil and aviation fuel from United States except to Britain and Allies in Western Hemisphere, in a measure directed at Japan. ...**August 14:** Roosevelt and Churchill announce signing Atlantic Charter August 12 in Argentia Bay off Newfoundland. ...**November 17:** U.S. merchant vessels are authorized to be armed and allowed to carry goods to belligerent ports on U.S. ships, reflecting repeal of Neutrality Act. ...**December 8:** Following December 7 Japanese attack on Pearl Harbor, Hawaii, U.S. Congress declares war on Japan. ...**December 9:** Canada orders blackout on Pacific coast of British Columbia. ...**December 11:** United States recognizes state of war with Germany and Italy, following declarations of war by those nations against United States. ...**December 18:** Roosevelt creates Office of Defense Transportation. ...**December 19**: Draft age is extended by U.S. Congress to men aged 20–44. ...**December 23:** Several unions issue a no-strike pledge for duration of the war.

1942. January 7: U.S. Federal Loan Administration announces $4 billion program to increase synthetic rubber production. ...**January 12:** U.S. National War Labor Board is established to resolve labor disputes by arbitration and mediation, replacing National Defense Mediation Board. ...**January 15–28:** At Rio de Janeiro Conference, Latin American republics agree to break relations with Axis powers. ...**January 15:** Roosevelt appoints War Production Board to mobilize resources for the war effort, replacing several agencies and boards. ...**January 28:** Office of Civilian Defense is established with New York mayor Fiorello H. La Guardia (1882–1947) as director. ...**January 30:** Office of Price Administration is empowered to set price ceilings on commodities and to fix rents. ...**February 7:** War Shipping Administration is established. ...**February 9:** "War time" is established, setting daylight saving time for duration of the war.

Asia & Pacific War Zone

1941 (Continued). July 2: China breaks off relations with Axis powers. ...**July 30:** Japanese bombers damage U.S. gunboat *Tutiula* in Chungking, China. ...**September 6:** Japanese Imperial Conference decides on war preparations. ...**December 2:** Japanese naval forces receive coded message to proceed with planned attack. ...**December 7:** Japanese attack U.S. Navy base at Pearl Harbor, Hawaii. ...**December 8:** Japanese attack Philippines, destroying U.S. aircraft on ground. ...Japanese begin attack on Malaya. ...**December 9:** Japanese occupy Bangkok, Thailand. ...**December 10:** British movement north through Malaya is repulsed by Japanese. ...Japanese move troops into northern Luzon, Philippines. ...Japanese bomb U.S. base at Cavite, Philippines. ...Japanese aircraft sink British battleships *Prince of Wales* and *Renown* off Malaya. ...**December 11:** Japanese take Guam. ...Americans withstand first attack on Wake Island. ...**December 13:** British withdraw from mainland China to island of Hong Kong. ...British withdraw from Kra Peninsula on Burmese side of Malay Peninsula. ...**December 18–19:** Japanese begin attacks on Hong Kong. ...**December 21–22:** Japanese make major landings in Luzon, and begin advance to Manila. ...**December 23:** Japanese take Wake Island. ...Japanese attack Burma and Sarawak in Dutch East Indies. ...**December 25:** Hong Kong surrenders to Japan. ...U.S. and Filipino defenders fall back at Carmen, Luzon. ...**December 28:** Japanese take Ipoh, Malaya.

1942. January 5: Japanese take Kuala Lumpur, Malaya. ...**January 16:** Japanese take Endau, Malaya. ...**January 20–May 8:** Japanese advance through Burma against British and Chinese. ...**January 23–25:** At battle of Makasar Straits, U.S. and Dutch forces are defeated by Japanese, allowing Japanese to reach Borneo. ...**January 24:** Japanese take Balikpapan, Borneo. ...**January 25:** Japanese take Kluang, Malaya. ...**January 31:** British retreat from Malay mainland to Singapore. ...**February 3:** Japanese begin major attack on Java, Dutch East Indies. ...**February 4:** Japanese complete capture of Amboina, Dutch East Indies. ...Japanese ships damage U.S. cruisers in Makasar Straits. ...British refuse Japanese demand to surrender Singapore. ...**February 8:** Japanese forces land on island of Singapore. ...**February 11:** Allied forces pull back into city of Singapore. ...**February 14:** Japanese paratroopers land on Sumatra. ...**February 15:** British forces surrender Singapore.

Latin America

1941 (Continued). December: Cuba declares war on the Axis. ...**December 8:** Mexico severs diplomatic relations with Japan. ...**December 9:** Nicaragua enters World War II on Allied side.

1941–1942. Alexander Bustamente (1884–1977) is imprisoned in Britain for his trade union and political activities in Jamaica. ...Geronimo Mendez (1900–1954) serves as interim president of Chile.

Science, Invention & Technology

1941 (Continued). Englishmen Archer Martin (1910–) and Richard Synge (1914–) develop paper chromatography, method of detecting presence of chemical compounds. ...Englishman John Whinfield (1901–1966) develops Terylene synthetic fiber.

c. 1941. Anthrax bombs, a form of biochemical warfare, are developed by the British. ...DDT is widely used in World War II as a defoliant. ...William Shockley (1910–1989) conducts research for United States in the detection of submarines. ...Penicillin is mass produced for the first time. ...Silicon compounds become widely used during World War II as insulation material and in manufacture of small parts. ...American John van Vleck (1899–1980) discovers that oxygen and water molecules in atmosphere absorb radar signals, affecting the wavelengths.

Religion, Culture & Arts

1941 (Continued). Clifford Odets (1906–1963), American dramatist: *Clash by Night*. ...Anya Seton (1916–1990): *My Theodosia*. ...Irwin Shaw (1913–1984), American writer: *Welcome to the City*. ...William Shirer (1904–1993): *Berlin Diary*. ...Thomas Wolfe: *The Hills Beyond* (posthumously published). ...Budd Schulberg (1914–), American writer: *What Makes Sammy Run*. ...Sherwood Anderson (b. 1877) dies. ...Walt Disney receives his ninth Academy Award for a cartoon film. ...No novel is awarded the Pulitzer Prize. ...Chicago Bears defeat New York Giants to win the National Football League championship. ...The University of Minnesota wins its second straight national college football championship. ...**June 2:** New York Yankee first baseman Lou Gehrig (b. 1903) dies. ...**July 17:** Joe DiMaggio's (1914–1999) 56-game hitting streak comes to an end in Cleveland. ...**October 1–6:** New York Yankees beat crosstown rivals Brooklyn Dodgers to win the World Series.

Still Picture Branch, National Archives, College Park, MD

◀ ***Damaged U.S. warships at Pearl Harbor, Hawaii, on December 7, 1941, shortly after the Japanese aerial attack.***

1942. Conservative Party leader Ramón Castillo (1873–1944) succeeds Radical Party leader Roberto Ortíz (1885–1942) as president of Argentina. ...Ecuador cedes a large part of its territory to Peru. ...Lázaro Cárdenas is made commander of the Mexican forces on the Pacific coast. ...U.S. Operation Bootstrap increases manufacturing and living standards in Puerto Rico. ...Panama enters World War II on Allied side. ...**January:** Argentina and Chile are the only South American countries that refuse to break relations with the Axis. ...**January 12:** Mexico and United States establish a joint defense commission. ...**January 15–28:** Rio de Janeiro Conference of 21 American republics recommends breaking diplomatic relations with the Axis.

1942. United States authorizes Manhattan Project for development of the atomic bomb. ...Wernher von Braun's (1912–1977) A-4 rocket, later redesignated V-2, is successfully launched by Germans. ...Englishwoman Rosalind Franklin (1920–1958) begins research into X-ray diffraction photography. This will lead to photographs of DNA. ...Germans develop an advanced computer for developing coded messages. The machine is referred to as Fish by British intelligence. ...Frenchman Jacques Cousteau (1910–1997) invents the aqualung diving apparatus. ...Kodak develops the infrared photographic process. ...Naphthenic acid, or napalm, is developed at Harvard University. ...American astronomer Dorthea Klimpke Roberts (b. 1861), the first female director of Bureau of Measurements and first woman to receive a doctorate from the Sorbonne, dies. ...General Electric researchers make improvements in smoke screens for troops. ...Science fiction novelist Isaac Asimov (1920–1992) coins term *robotics*.

1942. Robert Motherwell's (1915–1991) paintings are exhibited for the first time at the International Surrealist Exhibition in New York City. ...Irving Berlin: "White Christmas" (song). ...Bing Crosby (1904–1977) stars in the film *Holiday Inn*. ...Bess Streeter Aldrich (1881–1954): *The Lieutenant's Lady*. ...Jean Anouilh (1910–1987): *Antigone*. ...William Rose Benét (1886–1950): *The Dust Which Is God* (Pulitzer Prize, poetry) ...Pearl S. Buck: *Dragon Seed*. ...James M. Cain: *Love's Lovely Counterfeit*. ...Albert Camus (1913–1960), French writer: *The Stranger* and *The Myth of Sisyphus*. ...Noel Coward: *Present Laughter*. ...Lloyd Douglas (1877–1951): *The Robe*. ...Isak Dinesen: *Winter's Tales*. ...William Faulkner: *Go Down Moses and Other Stories*. ...Howard Fast (1914–): *The Unvanquished*. ...C. S. Lewis (1898–1963): *The Screwtape Letters*. ...Mary McCarthy (1912–1989): *The Company She Keeps*. ...Elliot Paul (1891–1958): *The Last Time I Saw Paris*. ...J. P. Marquand: *Last Laugh, Mr. Moto*.

International Affairs; European, African, Mideast War Zone

1942 (Continued). April 16: King George VI awards George Cross to the people of Malta for their heroic defense of the island. ...**April 24:** Germans begin bombing of British towns in reprisal for March 28 British raid on Lübeck. ...**May 12–17:** Germans smash Soviet offensive on Kharkov front. ...**May 27:** Czech resistance fighters attempt to assassinate Reinhard Heydrich (b. 1904), German "Reichs protektor." He dies a week later from his wounds. ...**May 29:** Germans advance in Soviet Union, encircling more than 200,000 Soviet troops west of the Donets River. ...**June 7:** Germans launch offensive against Sebastopol. ...**June 9:** Nazis wipe out Lidice, Czechoslovakia, in retaliation for the assassination of Heydrich, killing all males over the age of 16 and sending women and children to concentration camps. ...**June 21:** British surrender Tobruk to Erwin Rommel. ...**June 23:** German troops enter Egypt. ...**June 25:** General Dwight D. Eisenhower (1890–1969) becomes commander in chief of U.S. forces in European theater. ...**June 28–September 1:** German forces advance toward the Volga River in Soviet Union, entering outskirts of Stalingrad (Volgograd) in September. ...**July 1:** German advance reaches British defenses around El Alamein (in Egypt). ...**August 7:** General Bernard Montgomery (1887–1976) takes over Eighth Army in North Africa, taking operational control at the front on August 13. ...**August 19:** Canadian and British troops raid Dieppe, France, to test German defenses. Germans repulse the attack and inflict 3,600 casualties. ...**August 30–31:** Rommel attempts to drive British forces out of Egypt, but resistance organized by Montgomery stops the drive. ...**September 1:** Germans enter Stalingrad suburbs. **September 23:** Soviet counteroffensive near Stalingrad begins. ...**October 23–November 4:** Montgomery attacks and defeats German forces at El Alamein, taking 30,000 prisoners. ...**November 8:** Allies land troops in Morocco and Algeria after negotiating for support among Vichy French forces. ...**November 11:** Vichy authorities in Morocco and Algeria sign an armistice with Allies. ...**November 11–12:** Germans occupy Vichy France. ...**November 12–15:** Germans rapidly land troops in Tunisia to repulse Allied advances from Algeria. ...**November 19–23:** Soviet army completes successful counteroffensive at Stalingrad, encircling more than 300,000 German troops. ...**November 27:** French navy is scuttled in Toulon, France, to avoid use by Germans. ...**December 13:** Germans evacuate El Agheila as British troops launch offensive.

U.S. & Canadian Domestic Developments

1942 (Continued). February 16: Executive Order 9066 begins the evacuation of Japanese Americans from U.S. West Coast. ...**February 19:** Franklin Roosevelt authorizes secretary of war to remove persons from restricted military areas. Secretary orders relocation of about 110,000 Japanese Americans living in California, Oregon, Washington and Arizona. ...**March 17:** Leaders of AFL and CIO announce a no-strike agreement for the duration of the war. ...**April 14:** Board of Economic Warfare is established under Henry Wallace (1888–1965) to stockpile strategic materials and to deny enemy access to materials. ...**May 5:** Rationing of sugar is introduced in United States. ...**May 15:** Gasoline rationing introduced in 17 states. ...**May 31:** War Production Board orders the production of 50 types of home electrical appliances to cease. ...**June 9:** United States and Britain establish Combined Production Resources Board and Combined Food Board. ...**June 13:** Office of War Information is established to control news and propaganda. ...Office of Strategic Services is established to engage in intelligence operations abroad. ...**June 27:** German submarine lands team of four saboteurs on Long Island, New York. ...**July 3:** Four German saboteurs land in Florida, and, with the earlier group, are arrested by Federal Bureau of Investigations. ...**July 30:** Women Appointed for Voluntary Emergency Service (WAVES) is established as unit of U.S. Naval Reserve. ...**August 13:** Brigadier General Leslie Groves (1896–1970) is appointed to head the Manhattan Engineer District, charged with building an atomic bomb. ...**September 15:** William Martin Jeffers (1876–1953) is appointed rubber administrator with authority over all synthetic rubber programs. ...**October 3:** James Francis Byrnes (1879–1972) is appointed director of economic stabilization. ...**October 19:** Italian alien residents in United States are no longer considered enemy aliens. ...**November:** Henry Kaiser (1882–1967) demonstrates ability to construct a Liberty ship in 4 days, 15 hours. ...**November 2:** U.S. government institutes Controlled Materials Plan, setting priorities. ...**November 3:** U.S. congressional elections result in Democrats losing 8 seats in Senate and 50 in House of Representatives, but they hold majority in both houses. ...**November 13:** Draft age in United States is lowered to 18. ...**November 28:** At the Coconut Grove night club in Boston, 487 die when fire engulfs the club. ...**November 29:** Coffee rationing is instituted. ...**December 1:** U.S. office of the petroleum administrator for war, headed by Harold Ickes, is established, supplanting earlier office of petroleum coordinator.

Asia & Pacific War Zone

1942 (Continued). February 27–March 1: At battle of Java Sea, Japanese defeat Allied naval force of 5 cruisers, 11 destroyers. ...**March 2:** Japanese take Batavia, Java. ...**March 7:** Japanese forces begin landing in New Guinea. ...**March 9:** Java surrenders to Japanese. ...**March 11:** General Douglas MacArthur (1880–1964) leaves Luzon, declaring, "I shall return." **March 17:** MacArthur takes post of supreme commander of Allied forces in western Pacific. ...**March 30:** U.S. Joint Chiefs divide Pacific theater into naval zone under Admiral Charles Nimitz (1885–1966) and southwest Pacific under MacArthur. ...**April 3:** Japanese begin final attack on U.S. defenders on Bataan. **April 8:** Americans defeated by Japanese at Bataan. **April 9:** General Edward P. King (1884–1958) surrenders U.S. forces in Luzon to Japanese. Bataan death march of 100 miles begins. ...**April 18:** Lieutenant Colonel James Doolittle (1896–1993) leads bombing raid on Tokyo, using carrier-based planes. ...**April 29:** Japanese bombard Americans and Filipinos on Corregidor. ...**May 6:** U.S. forces on Corregidor in Manila Bay capitulate to Japanese. ...**May 7–11:** Despite heavy naval losses at battle of the Coral Sea, U.S. forces prevent Japanese from taking Port Moresby. ...**May 30:** Japanese carriers move out for attack on Port Moresby (in New Guinea). ...**June 3–6:** At battle of Midway, Japanese attack island, but U.S. Navy air units inflict heavy damage on Japanese fleet, sinking four aircraft carriers. ...**August 7:** U.S. troops land on Guadalcanal, beginning battle for Solomon Islands. ...**August 9:** Japanese sink four U.S. cruisers in Savo Island battle off Guadalcanal. ...**September 12–13:** U.S. forces repel strong Japanese attack on Guadalcanal. ...**October 1:** U.S. and Australian forces advance against Japanese in New Guinea. ...**October 11–12:** At battle of Cape Esperance off Guadalcanal, Japanese and Americans both sink ships. ...**October 13–14:** Japanese battleship shells Henderson Field, Guadalcanal. ...**October 21–26:** Japanese launch unsuccessful ground offensive against U.S. forces on Guadalcanal. ...**October 26:** In battle of Santa Cruz, Japanese sink U.S. carrier *Hornet*. ...**November 13:** At battle of Guadalcanal, U.S. Navy cut Japanese supply route. ...**November 30:** At battle of Tassafaronga, U.S. Navy repels Japanese relief ships headed for Guadalcanal. ...**December 18:** Allied forces take Cape Endiadere, New Guinea. ...**December 31:** Japanese command decides to evacuate Guadalcanal, issuing orders January 4.

Latin America

1942 (Continued). March 19: Guatemala permits U.S. air bases to defend the Panama Canal. ...**March 30:** Brazil and United States agree on common defense aims at meeting between Presidents Getúlio Dornelles Vargas and Franklin Roosevelt. ...**April 11:** Chile enters World War II on the side of the Allies. ...**April 21:** A meeting between Presidents Manuel Ávila Camacho and Roosevelt reaffirms friendly relations between Mexico and United States. ...**May 22:** Mexico declares war on Axis powers. ...**August 22:** Brazil declares war on Germany and Italy after shipping losses. ...**December 21:** In clash with striking miners, Bolivian soldiers kill hundreds of miners.

1942–1946. Radical Party leader Juan Antonio Ríos Morales (1888–1946) serves as president of Chile.

Science, Invention & Technology

1942 (Continued).October 1: The first American jet plane, the XP-59, has its first test flight. ...**December 2:** Enrico Fermi, at the Chicago Metallurgical Laboratory, successfully demonstrates the first self-sustained nuclear chain reaction.

c. 1942. Flack jackets and bulletproof vests are first used. ...Egyptian-born Englishwoman Dorothy Hodgkin (1907–1994) develops methods of synthesizing penicillin. ...Freeze-drying process is first used to preserve blood plasma and penicillin.... United States develops the shoulder-held M9A1 rocket launcher, nicknamed bazooka. ...Amphibious assault craft for shore landings are developed by the Allies. ...Weather tracking radar is first used in the war effort. ...American Florence van Straten (1913–) directs incorporation of weather phenomena in planning military maneuvers. ...Germans develop the Schmeisser submachine gun, or burp gun. ...Sonar navigation systems are installed on submarines.

Religion, Culture & Arts

1942 (Continued). Mari Sandoz (1901–1966), American writer: *Crazy Horse*. ...William Saroyan: *Razzle Dazzle*. ...John Steinbeck: *The Moon Is Down*. ...William L. White (1900–1973), American writer: *They Were Expendable*. ...Thornton Wilder, American writer: *The Skin of Our Teeth* (play). ...Philip Wylie (1902–1971), American writer: *Generation of Vipers*. ...Zora Neale Hurston (1901–1960), African American writer: *Dust Tracks on the Road*. ...Japanese poet Akiko Otori Yosano (b. 1878) dies. ...Actress Carole Lombard (b. 1908) dies in an airplane crash. ...American writer Alice Hegan Rice (b. 1870) dies. ...Orson Welles directs his second film, *The Magnificent Ambersons*. ...John Huston directs *In This Our Life*. ...*Mrs. Miniver*, directed by William Wyler (1902–1981), wins Academy Award for best picture. ...Ohio State wins national college football championship. ...Georgia defeats UCLA in the Rose Bowl. ...Washington Redskins defeat Chicago Bears to win the National Football League championship. ...Edith Stein (b. 1891), a German nun, is killed in Auschwitz gas chamber. Stein, a converted Jew, will be canonized a saint in 1998. ...**September 30–October 5:** St. Louis Cardinals beat defending champion New York Yankees to win World Series.

▲ ***A U.S. carrier (left) and two destroyers (right) confront the Japanese near Guadalcanal during the battle of Santa Cruz.***

International Affairs; European, African, Mideast War Zone

1943. January 11: Siege of Leningrad (St. Petersburg) is partially broken after more than a year's isolation. ...**January 14–26:** At Casablanca Conference, Franklin Roosevelt demands Germany's "unconditional surrender." ...**January 25:** Soviets recapture Voronesh from Germans. ...**January 31:** Field Marshal F. von Paulus, (1890–1957), commander of German troops at Stalingrad (Volgograd), surrenders to Soviet Army. ...**February 2:** Last German troops at Stalingrad surrender. ...**February 4–March 31:** Soviet troops move through the Caucasus, pushing Germans back to the Sea of Azov. ...**February 22:** Germans begin a counteroffensive in Soviet Union. ...**March 9:** Erwin Rommel leaves North Africa and tries to persuade Adolf Hitler and Benito Mussolini to abandon holdings in Africa. ...**April 14:** In North Africa, Axis troops form defensive perimeters around Tunis and Bizerta. ...**April 19:** The Warsaw ghetto attempts a rising against Germans. ...**April 24:** SS troops begin final massacre of Jews in Warsaw ghetto, killing the last 70,000 of an original population of more than 100,000. ...**May 13:** Axis forces numbering 250,000 surrender in Tunisia. ...**July 5–July 12:** Largest tank battle of the war takes place at Kursk in Soviet Union, with more than 6,000 tanks on each side, resulting in severe casualties on both sides and German withdrawal. ...**July 9–August 17:** Allies invade and capture Italian island of Sicily. ...**July 25:** The king of Italy dismisses Mussolini, who is immediately imprisoned. Marshal Pietro Badoglio (1871–1956) is named new head of government. ...**August 19–September 8:** Italians negotiate surrender. ...**August 24:** Heinrich Himmler (1900–1945) is appointed German minister of the interior. ...**September 3:** Allies begin invasion of southern Italy. **September 9:** Allies land at Salerno. Italian surrender is announced. ...**September 12:** German paratroopers rescue Mussolini from imprisonment in Abruzzi mountains. ...**September 18:** German forces evacuate Sardinia. **September 23:** Mussolini proclaims foundation of Italian Social Republic, which is administered by German forces. **September 25:** Soviets take Smolensk. ...**September 29:** General Eisenhower and Marshal Bodoglio of Italy sign full armistice agreement. ...**October 7:** Soviets cross Dnieper River. ...**October 13:** Italy declares war on Germany. ...**November 6:** Soviets take Kiev. ...**November 26–December 2:** At Tehran meeting between Roosevelt, Churchill and Stalin, Allies agree on postwar occupation of Germany. ...**December 14:** Soviets take Cherkassy. ...**December 31:** Soviets take Zhitomir.

U.S. & Canadian Domestic Developments

1943. February 9: A 48-hour workweek is established for all U.S. plants engaged in war production. ...**March 16:** Canada rules resident aliens, except enemy aliens, are to be called for military service; U.S. citizens living in Canada may opt for U.S. service. ...**March 29:** Rationing of meat, fat and cheese begins in United States. ...**May 1:** Coal mines are seized by U.S. government after miners disobey order from War Labor Board to return to work. ...**May 27:** Roosevelt orders strengthening of Fair Employment Practices Committee, requiring mandatory inclusion of nondiscrimination clauses in war contracts. ...**June:** "Zoot suit" riots in Los Angeles of off-duty white servicemen against Mexican American youths takes place. ...**June 2:** Canada opens first consulate general office in New York City. ...**June 9:** U.S. Congress enacts Current Tax Payment Act, which provides for income taxes to be withheld on wages. ...**June 20–22:** Race riot in Detroit, Michigan, in which 34 people are killed and 800 injured, is quelled by federal troops. ...**June 25:** Smith-Connally Anti-strike Act, or War Labor Disputes Act, passed over Roosevelt's veto, broadens government's power to seize plants during labor conflicts and to order 30-day cooling-off periods. ...**July:** Administration announces ending of Works Projects Administration (WPA) and National Youth Administration (NYA), to be closed in September and December, respectively. ...**July 15:** Roosevelt establishes Office of Economic Warfare, which takes over functions of the Board of Economic Warfare and foreign operations of the Reconstruction Finance Corporation. ...**July 19:** The "Big Inch," oil pipeline from Texas to Pennsylvania, opens to transport petroleum more than 1,200 miles, avoiding submarine-infested sea route to East Coast. ...**July 26:** On insistence of Mackenzie King, Canadian troop participation in Sicilian and Italian campaign is publicly identified. ...**August 1:** In race riot in Harlem, New York City, 6 die and 543 are injured. ...**September 21:** House of Representatives passes Fulbright Resolution, supporting concept of a permanent United Nations (UN) in postwar era. ...**November 5:** U.S. Senate passes resolution introduced by Senator Thomas Terry Connally (1877–1963) that supports permanent UN, requiring Senate ratification of any treaty to implement organization. ...**December 17:** Chinese Exclusion Acts of 1882 and 1902 are repealed and a quota of about 100 is set for Chinese immigration. ...**December 27, 1943–January 18, 1944:** All U.S. railroads are seized by presidential order. They will be returned to owners after wage dispute with unions is settled.

Asia & Pacific War Zone

1943. January 10: U.S. forces begin major offensive in Guadalcanal. ...**January 22:** Last Japanese forces are cleared from Papua. ...**February 1:** Japanese begin evacuation of Guadalcanal. ...**February 9:** Guadalcanal is cleared of Japanese after six months of hard fighting by marines and other U.S. forces. ...**February 21:** U.S. assault on Russell Island, Solomons, begins. ...**March 1–3:** At battle of the Bismarck Sea, U.S. bombers intercept Japanese ships carrying reinforcements to New Guinea, sinking four destroyers and killing about 3,000 Japanese. ...**April 18:** Admiral Isoroku Yamamoto (1884–1943), commander of the Japanese Combined Fleet, is shot down over Bougainville, after U.S. code breakers learn of flight. ...**May 11–30:** Attu Island in Aleutians is recaptured from Japanese. ...**June 18:** Archibald Wavell (1883–1950) becomes viceroy of India. ...**June 23–26:** U.S. forces advance with landings in New Guinea. ...**July 25:** U.S. forces begin major offensive in New Georgia. ...**July 28:** Japanese evacuate Kiska, Aleutian Islands. ...**August 13:** U.S. aircraft bomb oilfields in Borneo. ...**August 25:** Lord Mountbatten (1900–1979) becomes supreme Allied commander in Southeast Asia. ...Last Japanese resistance at New Georgia is eliminated. ...**September 4–March 5, 1944:** Australian and U.S. forces take the Huon Peninsula, New Guinea. **September 16:** Australians take Lae, New Guinea **September 24:** Australians take airfield at Finschafen, New Guinea. ...**September 25:** Japanese begin evacuation of Kolombangara, Solomon Islands. ...**October 2:** Australians take town of Finschafen, Huon Peninsula, New Guinea. ...**October 20:** Japanese transfer carrier aircraft to Rabaul, New Britain. ...**November 2:** United States air attacks destroy Japanese planes at Rabaul. **November 11:** Further U.S. air attacks destroy most remaining Japanese planes at Rabaul. ...**November 13–20:** U.S. bombs Tarawa, Gilbert Islands, in preparation for attack on islands. ...**November 20–23:** U.S. Marines capture Tarawa from Japanese in bloody battle. ...**November 25:** Allies bomb Formosa (Taiwan), destroying Japanese aircraft on ground. ...Australians capture Sattelberg, New Guinea. ...Last battle against Japanese night-supply ships off Solomons is fought. ...**November 29:** Australians capture Gusika, New Guinea. ...**December 15:** Australians capture Lakona, New Guinea. ...**December 19:** U.S. forces take Arawe airstrip, New Britain. ...**December 24:** Australians take Wandokai, Huon Peninsula, New Guinea. ...**December 26:** U.S. Marines land near Cape Gloucester, New Britain. ...**December 28–30:** U.S. forces capture Japanese airfield at Cape Gloucester.

Latin America

1943. President Ramón Castillo of Argentina is overthrown by a military coup. ...Alexander Bustamente forms the Jamaica Labor Party. ...Bolivia declares war on Axis. ...National Revolutionary Movement seizes power in Bolivia. Gualberto Villaroel López (1908–1946) becomes president. ...Juan José de Amezaga (1881–1956) becomes president of Uruguay. ...Rafael Leónidas Trujillo Molina (1891–1961) resumes the presidency of Dominican Republic. ...**January 20:** Chile breaks off relations with the Axis. ...**December:** Pro-miners union stages a successful revolt in Bolivia.

1943–1944. Pedro Ramírez (1899–1950) serves as president of Argentina.

Science, Invention & Technology

1943. American George Rieveschl Jr. (1916–) discovers an antihistamine. ...German American Max Delbruck (1906–1981) and Italian American Salvador Luria (1912–1991) publish their findings on bacterial mutations. ...British develop a computer called Colossus for decoding messages by the German computer Fish. ...American Edwin Land conceives his instant photographic process. ...German Karl Ziegler (1898–1973) discovers process for making polyethylene. ...Discovery of a mold on cantaloupe makes large-scale production of penicillin possible. ...Otto Stern (1888–1969) wins the Nobel Prize in physics for his contributions to the development of the molecular ray movement. ...**January 5:** George Washington Carver (b. c. 1864), African American agricultural chemist, dies. During his lifetime, Carver developed hundreds of synthetic products from cotton, peanuts and soybeans.

c. 1943. The blow-molding method is first used in the manufacture of plastic products. ...New variations of TNT explosives are developed for warfare. ...Germans develop electronically guided torpedoes. ...First aluminum cans make their debut in the soft drink industry, among other applications. ...American Wendell Stanley (1904–1971) invents a purified influenza vaccine by using a centrifuge.

Wisconsin Center for Film and Theater Research, Madison, WI

▲ *Ethel Waters in a scene from Vincente Minnelli's movie version of* **Cabin in the Sky.**

Religion, Culture & Arts

1943. Richard Rodgers (1902–1979) and Oscar Hammerstein (1895–1960) write the musical *Oklahoma!* ...Kurt Weill (1900–1950) writes musical comedy *One Touch of Venus*. ...American painter Jackson Pollock (1912–1956) holds his first one man show. ...Aaron Copland: *A Lincoln Portrait*. ...Louis Adamic (1899–1951): *My Native Land*. ...Bertolt Brecht: *The Life of Galileo* and *The Good Woman of Setzuan*. ...Raymond Chandler: *The Lady in the Lake*. ...Noel Coward: *This Happy Breed*. ...Simone de Beauvoir (1908–1986), French writer: *She Came to Stay*. ...John Dos Passos: *Number One*. ...T. S. Eliot: *Four Quartets*. ...Howard Fast: *Citizen Tom Paine*. ...Robert Frost: "A Witness Tree" (Pulitzer Prize, poetry). ...Ayn Rand (1905–1982), Russian-born American writer: *The Fountainhead*. ...William Saroyan: *The Human Comedy*. ...Upton Sinclair: *Dragon's Teeth* (Pulitzer Prize, novel). ...Betty Smith (1904–1972), American writer: *A Tree Grows in Brooklyn*. ...James Thurber: *Men, Women, and Dogs*. ...John Van Druten (1901–1957): *The Voice of the Turtle*. ...Robert Penn Warren: *At Heaven's Gate*. ...Wendell Wilkie: *One World*. ...Simone Weil (b. 1903), French philosopher and educator, dies. ...Ethel Waters (1896–1977) heads an all African American cast in Vincente Minnelli's (1910–1986) musical *Cabin in the Sky*. ...Alfred Hitchcock directs *Shadow of a Doubt*. ...E. M. Delafield (b. 1890), British novelist, dies. ...Camille Claudel (b. 1864), French sculptor, dies. ...Beatrix Potter (b. 1866), the creator of the Peter Rabbit books, dies. ...The All-American Girls Baseball League, the first professional baseball league for women, is organized. It will last until 1954. ...Chicago Bears defeat Washington Redskins in the NFL championship game. ...*Casablanca* wins Academy Award for best picture. Jennifer Jones (1919–) wins the Academy Award for best actress. ...**June 14:** U.S. Supreme Court rules in favor of Jehovah's Witnesses, stating that children cannot be compelled to salute the flag. ...**October 5–11:** New York Yankees defeat the defending champions St. Louis Cardinals to win World Series.

International Affairs; European, African, Mideast War Zone

1944. January 11: Benito Mussolini has his son-in-law and former foreign affairs minister, Count Ciano (b. 1903), executed. ...**January 15–Febuary 21:** Soviets launch offensive from Leningrad to Pskov. ...**January 16:** General Dwight D. Eisenhower assumes position as commander in chief of the Allied Expeditionary Forces. ...**January 22:** Allied forces land at Nettuno and Anzio in Italy. However, German forces contain the Allies at the beachhead until May 23. ...**February 20:** Massive Allied bombing raids over German cities begin. ...**April 8–May 5:** Soviets begin recapture of Crimea. **April 16:** Yalta is recaptured by Soviets. **May 9:** Sebastopol falls to Soviets. ...**May 12–15:** After bitter struggle, Allies break German Gustav Line in Cassino, Italy, and begin advancing north to Rome. **June 1–3:** Germans evacuate Rome, declaring it an open city. ...**June 4:** Allies liberate Rome. ...**June 6:** Normandy invasion, D-Day, begins with Allied landings on French beaches commanded by General Eisenhower. ...**June 10:** Soviets begin offensive against Finland. ...**June 15:** Flying bomb (V-1 rocket) attacks on London begin. ...**June 27:** Cherbourg is taken, providing Allies with major port to support troops in France, but German demolitions delay its use. ...**July 13:** Vilna is captured by Soviet army. ...**July 14:** Soviets begin offensive in Poland. ...**July 27:** U.S. troops take Saint-Lô, France. ...**August 1–October 2:** Poles rise in Warsaw. Polish underground army mounts major attack on Germans but is crushed as Soviets, in offensive positions just outside the city, do nothing to aid underground army. ...**August 17:** Soviets reach East Prussia. ...**August 25:** Allies liberate Paris. ...**August 30:** Provisional government under Charles de Gaulle begins operation in Paris. ...Soviets take Ploesti, Romania. ...**September 3:** Brussels is liberated by Allies. ...**September 8:** First V-2 weapon lands in London. ...**October 3:** U.S. troops break German Siegfried defensive line north of Aachen, Germany. ...**October 6:** Soviets invade Hungary. ...**October 9–19:** At Moscow Conference between Winston Churchill and Joseph Stalin, an informal agreement is reached. Soviets will dominate Romania and Bulgaria, British will dominate Greece, and both will share equal influence in Yugoslavia and Hungary. ...**October 14:** Athens is liberated by British. ...**October 15:** Admiral Nicholas Horthy (1868–1957), prime minister of Hungary, seeks armistice with Soviets but is removed by Germans. ...**October 21:** Aachen becomes first important German city captured by Allies. ...**October 23:** De Gaulle's provisional government is recognized by Allies.

U.S. & Canadian Domestic Developments

1944. January 19: All U.S. railways are officially returned to their owners. ...**April 19:** U.S. House of Representatives extends Lend-Lease program to June 30, 1945. ...**April 24:** After refusal of Montgomery Ward Company to accept government order settling labor dispute, Franklin Roosevelt threatens seizure of the company. ...**April 26:** Montgomery Ward plant is seized by the U.S. Army. ...**May 2:** After a series of unauthorized local wildcat strikes, AFL leadership reaffirms no-strike pledge. ...**May 3:** Meat rationing ends on all but choice cuts. ...**May 20:** Communist Party of the United States dissolves. Communist Political Association is formed. ...**June 5:** In a Supreme Court ruling, insurance companies are declared subject to the Sherman Antitrust Act. ...**June 22:** Roosevelt signs the Servicemen's Readjustment Act, known as GI Bill of Rights, setting up educational and other benefits for veterans. ...**June 27:** Republican Party nominates New York governor Thomas E. Dewey (1902–1971) for president. ...**July 1–July 22:** Conference of 44 nations at Bretton Woods, New Hampshire, establishes the International Monetary Fund and the International Bank for Reconstruction and Development. ...**July 6:** A fire at the main tent of the Ringling Brothers and Barnum & Bailey Circus in Hartford, Connecticut, kills 167 people and injures 175. ...**July 19:** Democratic Party nominates Roosevelt for president and Senator Harry S. Truman (1884–1972) for vice president. ...**August 16:** United States freezes assets of Argentina for pro-Axis policies. ...**August 21–October 7, 1944:** At a conference at Dumbarton Oaks in Washington, D.C., representatives of United States, China, Soviet Union and Britain draft plans for United Nations charter. ...**September 11–16:** Roosevelt and Churchill meet in Quebec City, Canada, to discuss occupation zones and policy for postwar Germany. ...**September 15:** A major hurricane hits U.S. Atlantic coast from Cape Hatteras to Canadian border, killing 50 people. ...**October 3:** Roosevelt names James F. Byrnes to head Office of War Mobilization and Reconversion. ...**October 20:** A liquid natural-gas fire kills 131 people in Cleveland, Ohio, and destroys 29 acres of homes and stores. ...**November 7:** Roosevelt is reelected with 432 electoral votes to Dewey's 99 electoral votes, winning 36 of 48 states. ...**November 24:** Canadian defense minister announces draft call for overseas service, provoking widespread protests.

Asia & Pacific War Zone

1944. January 2: U.S. forces take Saidor, Huon Peninsula, New Guinea. ...**February 1–6:** U.S. troops capture Kwajalein Island from Japanese. ...**February 17:** U.S. forces land on Eniwetok, Marshall Islands. ...**February 17–18:** U.S. naval forces sink Japanese cruiser and two destroyers off Truk, Caroline Islands. ...**February 23:** U.S. forces attack Rota, Tinian and Saipan in the Mariana Islands. ...U.S. forces take Eniwetok as Japanese fight nearly to last man. ...**February 29:** U.S. forces land on Los Negros, Admiralty Islands, bypassing Japanese at Rabaul, New Britain. ...**March 2:** U.S. forces take airfield at Momote, Admiralty Islands. ...**March 20:** U.S. Marines take islands of St. Matthias Group, completing bypass of Rabaul. ...**March 24:** Last Japanese effort to recapture Bougainville Island fails. ...**April:** Japanese begin offensive to capture airfields in southeast China used by United States to launch attacks against Japan. ...**April 2:** Japanese cut road between Imphal and Kohima in Manipur, India. ...**April 4:** Japanese cut supply roads to Kohima in Nagaland, India. ...**April 30:** British forces turn back Japanese advance towards Imphal, India. ...**May 17:** U.S. and British aircraft bomb oilfields in Java. ...**May 22:** U.S. destroyers bombard Wake Island. ...**June 11:** U.S. carrier aircraft attack Tinian and Saipan in the Marianas. ...**June 15–August 2:** U.S. forces invade Mariana Islands, killing nearly all Japanese defenders. **June 15–July 9:** U.S. forces capture Saipan Island from Japanese. ...**June 19:** British naval forces attack Japanese positions in Nicobar Islands, Indian Ocean. ...**July 20–August 3:** Guam is reconquered by U.S. forces. ...**July 24–August 2:** U.S. forces take Tinian Island. ...**July 30:** U.S. troops take Sansapor, extreme western New Guinea. ...**August 4–5:** U.S. naval forces bombard Iwo Jima and Chichi Jima. ...**September 3:** U.S. warships bombard Japanese positions on Wake Island. ...**September 12–14:** U.S. carrier-based aircraft attack Japanese targets in Philippines. ...**September 17–October 13:** Palau Islands are captured by Allies. ...**October 5:** Japanese take Foochow, last seaport in Chinese hands. ...**October 12–14:** U.S. carrier-based aircraft attack Japanese ground-based aircraft on Formosa. ...**October 16–20:** Allies begin air bombardment and invasion of Philippines. ...**October 20–December 25:** U.S. Sixth Army encircles and defeats Japanese 35th Army on Leyte. **October 21:** First recorded kamikaze attack is directed against Australian ship in Leyte operations. **October 23–26:** At battle of Leyte Gulf, Allies destroy major remnants of Japanese fleet, paving the way for invasion of Philippines.

Latin America

1944. Argentinian army colonels take charge of Argentina. ...Pro-Axis elements of Bolivia's ruling party are removed. President Gualberto Villaroel López establishes a dictatorship. ...Carlos Alberto Arroyo del Río (1893–1969), liberal president of Ecuador, is forced from office. ...In a coup, José María Velasco Ibarra becomes president of Ecuador for second time. ...Universal adult suffrage is introduced in Jamaica. Jamaica becomes self-governing. ...Chile enters World War II on side of Allies. ...Colombia enacts a new labor code. ...Mexico agrees to pay U.S. oil companies for expropriated properties. ...Grau San Martín is elected president of Cuba. ...Dictatorial rule of General Maximiliano Hernández Martínez (1882–1966) ends in El Salvador. ...Edelmiro Farrell (c. 1890–1950) becomes president of Argentina. ...**January 26:** Argentina breaks off relations with the Axis. ...**June:** A general strike forces the resignation of President Castañeda of Guatemala.

◄ *American computer pioneer Grace Hopper.*

Science, Invention & Technology

1944. Harvard University chemists Robert Woodward (1917–1980) and William Doering (1917–) synthesize quinine, used for treatment of malaria. ...Germans develop snorkeling submarines that run immediately below water surface to avoid radar detection. ...Germans begin using the Messerschmidt jet aircraft. ...American doctor Helen Taussig (1898–1986) develops an operation to correct cyanosis, commonly known as blue-baby syndrome. ...First eye banks are established in United States for eye transplants. ...Porous filter paper replaces absorbing powder in the chromatography process. ...Howard Aiken develops the Mark II computer. American Grace Hopper (1906–1992) plays a major role in programming the Mark I and Mark II computers. ...A shortage of manpower during World War II leads to the development of combine harvesting brigades in the U.S. grain belt. ...American Jay Forrester (1918–) develops the WHIRLWIND digital computer. ...The U.S. Gloster Meteor is first jet aircraft to use Frank Whittle's (1907–1996) gas turbine engine. ...American mathematician John von Neumann (1903–1957) joins the effort to build ENIAC computer. He also writes his game theory. ...Thermography, the dry-copy method of photocopying, is developed by Carl Miller (1913–) at 3M Company in Minnesota. ...Ukrainian American Vladimir Veksler (1907–1966) solves the problem of synchronizing particles with an accelerating electrical field in a cyclotron. ...An American team of Glenn T. Seaborg, Lee Morgan (1920–), and Albert Ghiorso (1915–) produce the element americum. ...Swiss Italian Daniel Bovet (1907–1992) develops the antihistamine pyrilamine. ...American Oswald Avery (1877–1955) publishes his findings on chromosomes and pioneers knowledge of DNA. ...Element 96, curium, named for Marie Curie and Pierre Curie, is discovered at the University of Chicago. ...American Gregory Pincus (1903–1967) begins research on the human reproductive system and hormones. ...American Selman Waksman (1888–1973) develops streptomycin, the first antibiotic. It will be used to treat tuberculosis.

Religion, Culture & Arts

1944. First performance of the ballet *Fancy Free* by Jerome Robbins (1918–1998), with music by Leonard Bernstein (1918–1990). ...Aaron Copland: *Appalachian Spring* (Pulitzer Prize for music). ...Bernstein: *On the Town*, musical comedy. ...Stephen Vincent Benét (1898–1943): *Western Star* (Pulitzer Prize, poetry). ...Catherine Drinker Bowen (1897–1973), American writer: *Yankee from Olympus:Justice Holmes and His Family*. ...Van Wyck Brooks (1886–1963), American writer: *The World of Washington Irving*. ...Albert Camus: *Caligula*. ...Howard Fast: *Freedom Road*. ...John Hersey (1914–1993), American writer: *A Bell for Adano* (Pulitzer Prize, fiction). ...Charles Jackson (1903–1968): *The Lost Weekend*. ...Paul Osborn (1901–1988) adapts novel by John Hersey into play: *A Bell for Adano*. ...Somerset Maugham: *The Razor's Edge*. ...Anaïs Nin (1903–1977), American writer: *Under a Glass Bell*. ...George Santayana: *Persons and Places*. ...Jean-Paul Sartre (1905–1980), French philosopher, playwright and novelist: *No Exit*.. ...Irwin Shaw: *Sons and Soldiers*. ...Anya Seton: *Dragonwyck*. ...Rex Stout (1886–1975), American writer: *Not Quite Dead Enough*. ...John Van Druten: *I Remember Mama*. ...Kathleen Winsor (1919–), American writer: *Forever Amber*. ...Aimee Semple McPherson (b. 1890), Canadian-born evangelist, dies. ...American writer Ida Tarbell (b. 1857) dies. ...Howard Hawks (1896–1977) directs the screen version of Ernest Hemingway's novel *To Have and Have Not*. ...Leo McCarey's (1898–1969) *Going My Way* wins the Academy Award for best picture. Its star, Bing Crosby (1901–1977), wins the award for best actor. Ingrid Bergman wins the Academy Award for best actress for her performance in George Cukor's (1899–1983) *Gaslight*. ...Walter Piston (1894–1976), American composer: Second Symphony. ...Artist Charles Dana Gibson (b. 1867), creator of the Gibson Girl, dies. ...Green Bay Packers defeat New York Giants in the NFL championship game. ...**October 4–9:** St. Louis Cardinals of National League defeat the St. Louis Browns of the American League to win World Series.

International Affairs; European, African, Mideast War Zone

1944 (Continued). December 16–December 26: At Battle of the Bulge, Germans mount surprise attack on Allies, with aim of capturing Antwerp, Belgium, in last major German offensive. **December 26:** U.S. 101st Airborne units at Bastogne are relieved by U.S. Fourth Armored Division. **December 30:** Allies begin counteroffensive against German bulge in the Ardennes, with first objective of relieving surrounded U.S. units at Bastogne.

1945. January 12–14: Soviet troops begin advance through Poland. ...**January 20:** Soviets sign armistice with Hungary. ...**February 4:** Belgium is liberated by Allies. ...**February 4–11:** Winston Churchill, Joseph Stalin and Franklin Roosevelt meet at Yalta and agree to postwar Polish borders and Soviet participation in war against Japan. ...**February 13–15:** British and American planes firebomb Dresden, killing more than 70,000 civilians and refugees. ...**March 7:** U.S. forces cross Rhine at undefended bridge at Remagen. ...**March 23:** British and Canadian forces advance past the Rhine south of Wesel. ...**March 25:** U.S. forces break out of Remagen bridgehead and begin to surround German Ruhr pocket under Field Marshal Walter Model (1891–1945). ...**March 30:** Soviet forces enter Austria at Koszeg. ...**April 13:** Vienna is captured by Soviets. ...**April 16:** Soviet and U.S. troops first link up near Dresden. ...**April 20:** U.S. Seventh Army takes Nuremberg. ...**April 21:** Soviets reach Berlin. **April 24:** Soviet troops complete the encirclement of Berlin. ...**April 26:** Soviets and Americans link up near Torgau. ...**April 28:** Benito Mussolini (b. 1883) is captured and executed by Italian partisans. ...**April 29:** Germans in Italy unconditionally surrender. ...U.S. troops liberate Dachau concentration camp. ...**April 30:** Adolf Hitler (b. 1889) commits suicide in Berlin bunker as Soviets close in. **May 2:** Berlin surrenders. ...**May 4:** Admiral Karl Dönitz, successor to Hitler, negotiates surrender of German forces in Germany, Holland and Denmark. ...**May 7:** All German fighting forces unconditionally surrender. ...**May 8:** Fighting between Allies and Germans officially stops in Europe at 11:01 P.M. local time. ...**July 17:** Harry S. Truman, Stalin and Churchill meet at Potsdam. **July 26:** Clement Attlee (1883–1967) becomes British prime minister and replaces Churchill at Potsdam. ...**August 2:** By Potsdam Agreement, Nazism is outlawed, Germany's eastern provinces are transferred to Soviet Union and Poland and an agreement for trying war criminals is reached.

U.S. & Canadian Domestic Developments

1944 (Continued). December 8: Prime Minister Mackenzie King wins confidence vote in Canada, 143–70. ...**December 15:** U.S. Congress creates rank of five-star general for Dwight D. Eisenhower, Henry "Hap" Arnold (1886–1950), Douglas MacArthur and George C. Marshall (1880–1959).

1945. January 2: Relocation of Japanese Americans in United States ends. ...**January 11:** Franklin Roosevelt calls for National Service Act, requiring either military service or employment. It will be voted down by Senate April 3. ...**January 15–May 8:** A nationwide dimout, or reduction of lighting, is ordered to conserve fuel supplies. ...**January 31:** Private Eddie Slovik (b. 1920) is executed by firing squad for desertion. It is first such execution since the Civil War. ...**February 26–May 9:** A midnight entertainment curfew is established to conserve fuel. ...**April 12:** President Roosevelt (b. 1882) dies at Warm Springs, Georgia. Vice President Truman is sworn in as 33rd president of United States...**April–June:** Conference of 50 nations in San Francisco organizes United Nations. ...**May 8:** Americans celebrate V-E Day in recognition of German surrender the prior evening. ...**June 25:** United Nations Charter is signed in San Francisco. ...**July 1:** New York Commission to Prevent Racial Discrimination in Employment is established. ...**July 16:** Scientists working in the Manhattan Engineer District successfully test the first nuclear explosion at Alamogordo, New Mexico. ...**July 27:** Communist Political Association is re-established as Communist Party, U.S.A. ...**July 28:** U.S. Senate ratifies United Nations charter. ...B-25 aircraft crashes into Empire State Building at 78th floor. ...**August 14:** United States celebrates V-J Day, marking end of World War II. ...**August 15–September 30:** More than 820,000 U.S. war production plant workers are laid off. ...**August 18:** Truman orders end of controls on consumer production and on collective bargaining, ending wartime economic controls. ...**August 21:** United States terminates Lend-Lease program. ...**September 16:** Truman presents 21-point plan, a comprehensive social program, to Congress. It will be known as the Fair Deal. ...**October 4:** War Production Board is terminated and its functions transferred to the Civilian Production Administration. ...**November 8:** Revenue Act provides for reductions of $6 billion of U.S. taxes. ...**December 20:** Tire rationing ends. ...**December 31:** All U.S. rationing, except for sugar, ends.

Asia & Pacific War Zone

1944 (Continued). December 10: U.S. troops take Ormoc, main Japanese base on Leyte, Philippines. ...**December 31:** U.S. Sixth Army gains virtual control of Leyte.

1945. January 9: U.S. forces land on Luzon, Philippines. Japanese retreat to mountain areas, abandoning beachheads to U.S. forces. ...**January 20–27:** Chinese forces advance to clear Ledo Road in Burma, linking India and China. ...**January 24:** U.S. forces reduce Japanese on Mindoro, Philippines, to stragglers. ...**February 4–March 3:** At battle of Manila, Japanese lose 20,000 men. ...**February 16–26:** U.S. paratroopers recapture Corregidor Island, Philippines. ...**February 19:** U.S. invasion of Iwo Jima begins. **February 23:** U.S. Marines raise flag on Mt. Suribachi, Iwo Jima. ...**March 5–March 29:** Japanese launch counteroffensive south of Mandalay, Burma. ...**March 9–10:** Intense firestorm bombing of Tokyo kills 80,000–120,000 civilians. ...**March 20:** Allies recapture Mandalay, Burma. ...**March 23–31:** Bombardment of Okinawa begins. ...**March 26:** Japanese resistance on Iwo Jima ends. ...**April 1:** U.S. invasion of Okinawa begins. ...**May 3:** Rangoon (Yangôn) is recaptured by Allies. **May 6:** Allied forces link up north of Rangoon, completing liberation of Burma. ...**June 21:** Okinawa is captured by U.S. Marines after long bloody battle. ...**July 1–3:** Australians land at Balikpapan, Borneo, and capture the city from Japanese. ...**July 5:** Philippines are fully liberated. ...**August 6:** U.S. plane *Enola Gay* drops first atomic bomb on Hiroshima, killing an estimated 140,000 people and destroying 70,000 of the city's 76,000 buildings. ...**August 9:** United States drops second atomic bomb on Nagasaki, killing nearly 70,000 people. ...**August 10:** Japanese announce they will accept Potsdam Declaration as basis for peace. ...**August 14:** Japanese unconditionally surrender. ...**August 16:** Emperor of Japan issues cease-fire order to all troops. ...**August 18:** Harbin, Manchuria, is taken by Soviet troops. ...**August 22:** Japanese troops in Manchuria officially surrender to Soviets. ...**September 2:** General MacArthur accepts formal Japanese surrender aboard battleship *Missouri*. ...**September 8:** MacArthur enters Tokyo. ...**September 9:** Japanese surrender in China. ...**September 12:** Japanese surrender in Southeast Asia at Singapore.

Latin America

1944 (Continued). December: Juan José Arévalo (1904–1990) is elected president of Guatemala.

1944–1945. Brazilian expeditionary force participates in Allied campaign in Italy.

1945. A military coup places Rómulo Betancourt (1908–1981) in power as president of Venezuela. ...Venezuela enters World War II on side of Allies. ...Salvador Castañeda Castro becomes president of El Salvador. ...Bolivia, Colombia, Cuba, Dominican Republic, El Savador, Mexico, Nicaragua, and Chile become founding members of the United Nations. ...A coalition of liberal and leftist parties wins power in Peru. ...Miguel Alemán Valdés resigns as Mexico's minister of interior to run for the presidency and is elected the following year. ...Arnulfo Arias returns to Panama in preparation for another presidential election. He wins in 1948. ...Lázaro Cárdenas, Mexican minster of defense, retires. ...Alberto Lleras Camargo (1906–1990) becomes president designate of Colombia. ...A military junta takes power in Haiti. ...Enrique Adolfo Jiménez Brin (1888–1970) becomes president of Panama. ...**February:** Publishers force Brazilian government to relax press censorship. ...Peru declares war on the Axis. ...**February 21–March 8:** Inter-American Conference on Problems of War and Peace meets at Chapultepec Castle, Mexico City. ...**February 28:** Congressional and presidential elections are announced in Brazil. ...**March:** A new constitution is promulgated in El Salvador. ...**March 3:** Act of Chapultepec declares that an attack on one American state by another will be regarded as aggression against all. ...**March 27:** Argentina enters World War II on side of the Allies and becomes a member of the United Nations. ...A new constitution is promulgated in Guatemala. ...**April:** Brazil declares amnesty for all political prisoners, including Communists. ...**April 4:** Argentina is admitted to Pan-American Union. ...**October:** A military coup forces President Getúlio Dornelles Vargas of Brazil to resign. ...**October 9:** Juan Perón (1895–1974) is forced to resign his posts as vice president and minister of war in Argentina. He is imprisoned, which provokes a governmental crises. **October 17:** Argentina's governmental crisis is resolved when Perón's labor supporters secure his release from prison in preparation for his election to the presidency the following year.

Science, Invention & Technology

1945. A German pilot is killed in first attempt of a manned rocket launching. ...The herbicide 2,4-D is developed in the United States. ...American geologist Harry Hess (1906–1969) discovers the existence of sea mounts, submerged and partly submerged mountains rising from ocean floors. ...American Benjamin Duggar (1872–1956) develops the antibiotic oreomycin for treatment of rickettsia. ...First frozen dinners are offered on airline flights. ...Polaroid Corporation contracts with the U.S. government to produce military optics. ...Americans Felix Bloch (1905–1983) and Edward Purcell (b. 1912) develop nuclear magnetic resonance (NMR) spectroscopy. This leads to process of magnetic resonance imaging. ...Raytheon Corporation in U.S. undertakes initial research toward development of the microwave oven. ...Baron Marcel Bich (1914–1994) of Paris begins selling his inexpensive pens. They will be marketed in the United States under the Bic label. ...William Shockley at Bell Laboratories leads research team in development of semiconductors. ...Tupperware Corporation introduces its first product, a seven-ounce plastic bathroom tumbler. ...A deep-sea underwater camera used for geological observations is invented. ...German Konrad Zuse (1910–1995) develops the Z Machine, first computer with a stored program. ...Fluoride is first introduced to public water supply in Newburgh, New York, and Grand Rapids, Michigan. ...Englishman Peter Medawar (1915–1987) investigates the problem of skin graft rejections. ...Acid citrate dextrose is introduced as an agent in the preservation of donated blood supply.

Religion, Culture & Arts

1944 (Continued). December 15: Big-band leader Glenn Miller's (b. 1904) plane is reported missing in a flight from Paris to London.

1945. Simone de Beauvoir and Jean-Paul Sartre found *Les Temps Modernes*. ...Eric Blair (1903–1950), known as George Orwell, British novelist: *Animal Farm*, a fable about Communism. ...Mary Chase (1907–1981), American writer: *Harvey*. ...Norman Cousins (1912–1990): *Modern Man Is Obsolete*. ...Robert Frost: *A Masque of Reason* (play). ...Jean Giraudoux (1882–1944), French novelist: *The Madwoman of Chaillot*. ...Arthur Koestler: *The Yogi and the Commissar*. ...Carlo Levi (1902–1975), Italian writer: *Christ Stopped at Eboli*. ...Sinclair Lewis: *Cass Timberlane*. ...Henry Miller: *The Air Conditioned Nightmare* (commentary). ...John Steinbeck: *Cannery Row*. ...James Thurber: *The Thurber Carnival*. ...Mika Waltari (1908–1979), French novelist: *The Egyptian*. ...Evelyn Waugh (1903–1966), English writer: *Brideshead Revisited*. ...Jessamyn West (1907–1984), American writer: *The Friendly Persuasion*. ...E. B. White (1899–1985), American writer: *Stuart Little*. ...Tennessee Williams (1911–1983), American playwright: *The Glass Menagerie*. ...Richard Wright: *Black Boy*. ...Billy Wilder's (1906–) *The Lost Weekend* wins the Academy Award for best picture. Its star, Ray Milland (1905–1986), wins the best actor award. Joan Crawford (1906–1977) wins best actress for her performance in Michael Curtiz's (1888–1962) *Mildred Pierce*. ...Cleveland Rams defeat Washington Redskins in the NFL championship game. ...**October 3–10:** Detroit Tigers defeat Chicago Cubs to win the World Series.

International Affairs

1946. January 10: First meeting of the UN General Assembly is held in London. ...**January 24:** Atomic Energy Commission is established by the UN. ...**February 1:** Trygve Lie (1896–1968) of Norway is elected secretary general of UN. ...**March 5:** In speech at Fulton, Missouri, Winston Churchill advocates Anglo-U.S. "fraternal association" against Soviet expansion and declares Iron Curtain has fallen across Europe. ...**April 18:** League of Nations is terminated. ...**July 22:** International Health Conference in New York adopts constitution for World Health Organization (WHO). ...**July 22–October 15:** Peace Conference for World War II is held in Paris. ...**July 24:** Diplomat Bernard Baruch (1870–1965) urges the UN Atomic Energy Commission to control atomic weapons. ...**October 23:** Second meeting of the UN General Assembly is held in Flushing, New York. ...**November 4:** United States and China sign an agreement of friendship and trade.

1947. February 10: Peace treaties for World War II are signed in Paris. ...**March 1:** International Monetary Fund (IMF) begins operations. ...**April 4:** International Civil Aviation Organization (ICAO) is established as UN agency. ...**March 30:** Pakistan and Yemen are admitted to UN ...**September 2:** United States and other nations at the Inter-American Defense Conference in Brazil sign pact of mutual security. ...**September 17:** UN passes resolution calling for free elections in Korea. ...**September 22:** Marshall Plan to rebuild Europe is accepted by 16 nations. ...**October 5:** Cominform, the Communist information organization, is established in Belgrade. ...**November 30:** UN votes for the division of Palestine.

1948. March 17: Brussels Treaty for a 50-year military, economic and social alliance is signed by Britain, France, Belgium, the Netherlands and Luxembourg. ...**April 7:** World Health Organization is established by UN. ...**April 16:** Organization for European Economic Cooperation is established to strengthen Europe economically. ...**April 30:** Charter of Organization of American States is signed in Bogotá. ...**May 10:** South Korea holds first elections, but North Korea bans participation. ...**May 14:** United States is first nation to recognize Israel. ...**August 25:** Soviet Union breaks off diplomatic relations with United States, accusing it of kidnapping two Soviet teachers. ...**December 23:** Seven Japanese war criminals, including Tojo, are hanged.

Western & Eastern Europe

1946. January 2: King Zog I of Albania is deposed by Communist government. ...**January 20:** Charles de Gaulle resigns as French prime minister. ...**February 1:** Hungary is proclaimed a republic. ...**March 1:** Bank of England is nationalized by Labor government. ...**March 9:** Juho Kusti Paasikivi (1870–1956) is elected president of Finland. ...**May 9:** Victor Emmanuel III of Italy abdicates in favor of Umberto II (1904–1983). ...**May 26:** Communists win national elections in Czechoslovakia. ...**June 2:** Italian plebiscite backs republic. ...**June 10:** Italian republic is proclaimed. ...**September 1:** Greek plebiscite supports monarchy. ...**September 19:** Churchill advocates European Union in Zurich speech. ...**September 28:** George II returns to Greece. ...**October 1:** International Military Tribunal sentences Nazi leaders in Nuremberg, Germany. ...**October 13:** French plebiscite supports constitution of Fourth Republic.

1947. January 16: Vincent Auriol (1884–1966) is elected French president. ...**February 5:** Boleslaw Bierut (1892–1956) becomes president of Poland. ...**April 1:** George II of Greece dies and is succeeded by Paul I (1901–1964). ...**April 20:** Christian X (b. 1870) of Denmark dies and is succeeded by Frederick IX (1899–1972). ...**May 4:** Communists are excluded from French cabinet. ...**August 31:** Communists win national elections in Hungary. ...**October 29:** Benelux customs union is established for Belgium, Netherlands and Luxembourg. ...**December 22:** Italian constitution is passed.

1948. February 20: Communist police in Czechoslovakia put down civilian protests. ...**February 25:** Complete Communist rule is established in Czechoslovakia. ...**April 28:** Luxembourg constitution abandons unarmed neutrality. ...**May 10:** Luigi Einaudi (1874–1961) is elected president of Italy. ...**June 7:** Edvard Beneš resigns as president of Czechoslovakia. **June 14:** Klement Gottwald (1896–1953) is elected president of Czechoslovakia. ...**June 18:** Soviets begin land blockade of West Berlin. United States and Britain airlift in supplies in effort to break blockade. ...**June 28:** Yugoslavia is expelled from Cominform. ...**September 4:** Queen Wilhelmina of Netherlands abdicates. ...**November 30:** Soviet administration is set up in East Berlin.

U.S. & Canada

1946. March 25: War Assets Administration is created in United States to dispose of surplus military equipment. ...**June 3:** U.S. Supreme Court rules that interstate buses cannot use segregated seating. ...**July 15:** President Harry S. Truman extends wartime price controls for one year. ...**August 1:** U.S. Atomic Energy Commissions is established. ...**August 2:** U.S. Congress passes Legislative Reorganization Act, requiring lobbyists to register. ...**November 5:** Republicans take control of both houses of Congress. ...**December 5:** John D. Rockefeller (1874–1960) gives $8.5 million to help build UN headquarters in New York City. ...**December 7:** Fire at the Winecoff Hotel in Atlanta, Georgia, the worst hotel fire in U.S. history, kills 127. ...**December 31:** President Truman makes a formal proclamation that all World War II hostilities have ended.

1947. President Truman establishes the Central Intelligence Agency (CIA) as a successor to the wartime Office of Strategic Services. ...**April:** Freedom Rides of integrated buses tour the South. This idea will find popular support in the 1960s. ...**March 12:** President Truman proposes the Truman Doctrine to combat Communism. ...**April 16:** Presidential adviser Bernard Baruch coins the term *cold war*. ...**June 5:** U.S. Secretary of State George C. Marshall proposes the Marshall Plan. ...**June 23:** Congress overrides President Truman's veto to pass the Taft-Hartley Labor Act. ...**September 12:** James V. Forrestal (1892–1949), secretary of the navy, becomes the first secretary of defense.

1948. March 31: U.S. Congress passes the Marshall Aid Act, providing $5.3 billion for European aid. ...**June 24:** President Truman signs Selective Service Act to reinstate peacetime draft. ...**July 22:** Progressive Party is formed by dissident Democrats. They nominate Henry Wallace (1888–1969) for president. ...**July 26:** President Truman issues an executive order banning segregation in the armed forces. ...**November 2:** Truman wins reelection, defeating Republican candidate Thomas Dewey in surprise upset. Margaret Chase Smith (1897– 1995), a Republican from Maine, is first female senator to be elected. ...**December 15:** Alger Hiss (1904–1996), former State Department official, is indicted for perjury after denying he was involved in a Communist spy ring.

Asia, Africa & Latin America

1946. January 5: China recognizes independence of Mongolia. ...**February 24:** Juan Perón becomes president of Argentina. ...**March 6:** France recognizes Vietnam as a free state within the French Union. ...**March 22:** Jordan's independence is recognized by Britain. ...**May 25:** Emir Abdullah (1882–1951) of Jordan assumes title of king. ...**June:** France supports Cochin China's becoming a separate republic; Vietnamese want to incorporate it. ...**July 4:** Philippine Republic becomes independent nation. ...**November 3:** New Japanese constitution is promulgated by General Douglas MacArthur. ...**December 19:** Communist-led Vietminh forces open hostilities against French in Hanoi, launching an eight-year war for independence.

1947. January 1: Nigeria is granted partial self-government by Britain. ...**August 24:** President José María Velasco Ibarra of Ecuador is deposed. ...**March 25:** Netherlands recognizes independence of Indonesia. ...**June 3:** Partition of India and Pakistan is announced. ...**August 15:** India and Pakistan become British dominions. ...**September 24:** Constitution of Burma is passed. ...**September 26:** Britain announces withdrawal from Palestine. ...**October 17:** By Anglo-Burmese treaty, Burma leaves British Commonwealth.

1948. January 4: Burma becomes independent of Britain as the Union of Myanmar. ...**January 30:** Mohandas Gandhi (b. 1869) is assassinated by Hindu nationalists. ...**February 4:** Ceylon becomes a British dominion. ...**May 1:** North Korea is proclaimed Communist People's Republic. ...**May 14:** The State of Israel is proclaimed. ...**May 15:** Arab League invades Palestine. ...**June 3:** President Higino Morínigo of Paraguay is deposed by Juan González (1897–1966). ...**July 20:** Syngman Rhee (1875–1965) is elected president of South Korea. ...**September 17:** Count Folke Bernadotte (b. 1895) is assassinated in Israel by Jewish terrorists. ...**October 30:** General Manuel Odría (1897–1974) seizes power in Peru. ...**December 1:** Costa Rican army is dissolved.

Science, Invention & Technology

1946. American Willard Libby (1908–1980) develops his atomic clock theory. ...Hungarian American Georg von Bekesy (1899–1972) invents a pure-tone audiometer for testing human hearing. ...Citrus growers in Lake Wales, Florida, develop frozen concentrated orange juice. ...Freeze-drying is introduced to the American food industry. ...American Luis Alvarez (1911–1988) designs a linear accelerator with drift tubes surrounded by a variable magnetic field, capable of creating higher energies. ...Michelin Tire Company patents radial tires in United States. ...Florence van Straten develops rocketsonde, a weather data collection package delivered to the upper atmosphere in a rocket. ...DuPont Company patents and markets a polyester fiber known as dacronin in the United States (Fiber V in Britain). ...**November:** Ford Motor Company develops one of the first computerized automated assembly lines.

1947. DuPont Company patents Orlon, the first commercial acrylic fiber. ...American pilot Chuck Yeager (1923–) breaks the speed of sound in his X–1 aircraft at an altitude of 30,000 feet. ...A team led by American John Bardeen (1908–1991) successfully amplifies an electric current using a transistor. ...Haloid Company, later renamed Xerox Corporation, purchases rights to the copying machine invented by Chester Carlson (1906–1968). ...Hungarian American Dennis Gabor (1900–1979) creates the first three-dimensional picture with an electron microscope and refers to it as a *hologram*. ...A synthetic fiber called Vinyon is patented by Carbide and Carbon Chemicals Corporation in the United States.

1948. First tubeless automobile tires are marketed in the United States. ...American Claude Shannon at Bell Laboratories develops preliminary methods of digital data storage, which later leads to invention of the compact disc. ...Dramamine, used to prevent motion sickness, is developed. ...American Norbert Wiener (1894–1964) discusses his research into automated communications and coins the term *cybernetics*. ...Cosmologists Thomas Gold (1920–) and Hermann Bondi (1919–) announce their steady-state theory that the nature of the universe is homogeneous. ...American Robert Abplanalp (1920–) invents an efficient valve for aerosol cans. ...The binary number system is used to create the language for the EDVAC and EDSAC first-generation computers.

Religion, Culture & Arts

1946. London's Sadler's Wells Ballet, with Frederick Ashton (1906–1988) as chief choreographer, moves to Covent Garden. ...Nikos Kazantzakis (1885–1957), Greek writer: *Zorba the Greek*. ...William Carlos Williams (1883–1963), American poet: "Paterson." ...Eugene O'Neill: *The Iceman Cometh*. ...William Wyler's *The Best Years of Our Lives* wins the Academy Award for best picture. Fredric March (1897–1975), the star of the film, wins the award for best actor. Olivia de Havilland (1916–) is named best actress. ...**July 7:** Mother Cabrini (1850–1917) becomes the first American saint. ...**July 27**: Gertrude Stein (b. 1874), American writer, dies. ...**October 6–15:** St. Louis Cardinals defeat Boston Red Sox to win the World Series.

1946–1947. British sculptor Henry Moore (1850–1917) has his first one-man exhibition in United States.

1947. Robert Penn Warren's *All the King's Men* wins Pulitzer Prize for fiction. ...Malcolm Lowry (1909–1957), English novelist: *Under the Volcano*. ...Albert Camus: *La Peste* (*The Plague*). ...Tennessee Williams: *A Streetcar Named Desire*. ...Elia Kazan's (1909–) *Gentleman's Agreement* wins the Academy Award for best picture. ...Playing for the Brooklyn Dodgers, Jackie Robinson (1919–1972) becomes the first black man to play baseball in the major leagues. ...**September 30–October 6:** New York Yankees defeat Brooklyn Dodgers to win the World Series.

1948. Georges Sim (1903–1989), known as Georges Simenon, Belgian master of the psychological crime novel: *Pedigree*. ...Alan Paton (1903–1988), South African novelist: *Cry the Beloved Country*, an anti-apartheid novel. ...Norman Mailer (1923–), American writer: *The Naked and the Dead*. ...Columbia Record Company releases the first long-playing record. ...Willem de Kooning (1904–1997), Dutch-born artist, has his first one-man U.S. exhibition. It establishes him as a leading abstract artist. ...World Jewish Congress convenes in Montreux, Switzerland. World Coucil of Churches is established in Amsterdam. ...Laurence Olivier's (1907–1989) *Hamlet* wins the Academy Award for best picture. ...**October 6–11:** Cleveland Indians defeat Boston Braves to win the World Series.

International Affairs

1949. January 1: India and Pakistan sign a truce for Kashmir. ...**April 4:** North Atlantic Treaty Organization (NATO) is established to oppose Soviet expansion in Europe. ...**May 5:** European nations establish the Council of Europe and choose Strasbourg, France, as its headquarters. ...**May 11:** Israel is admitted to UN. ...**June 29:** United States withdraws troops from Korea. ...**August:** Four new Geneva Conventions are put into effect to protect prisoners of war and civilians. ...**August 29:** Soviets test their first atomic bomb. ...**October 1:** Britain and France recognize China's Communist government, but United States does not. ...**October 24:** UN headquarters in New York City are dedicated. ...**November 21:** UN General Assembly votes to make Italy's colonies independent. ...**December 15:** Marshall Plan is extended fully to West Germany.

1950. January 27: United States signs bilateral defense pacts with Britain, France, Italy, Denmark, Belgium, the Netherlands, Norway and Luxembourg. ...**March 23:** World Meteorological Organization (WMO) of the UN is established. ...**June 25:** North Korean forces invade South Korea. ...**June 27:** UN Security Council authorizes armed intervention in Korea. ...**June 30:** UN troops begin leaving for Korea. ...**September 15:** U.S. military forces land at Inchon, South Korea. ...**September 26:** UN forces recapture Seoul in South Korea. ...**October 7:** UN troops attack North Korea. ...**November 20:** UN troops reach Manchurian border. ...**November 25:** Chinese troops launch offensive, pushing UN forces south. ...**December 18:** General Dwight D. Eisenhower is appointed supreme commander of NATO.

1951. January 4: North Korean and Chinese forces retake Seoul in South Korea. ...**April 4:** Supreme Headquarters Allied Powers Europe (SHAPE) opens in Paris. ...**April 18:** European Coal and Steel Treaty is signed. European Community members pledge to pool their coal and steel resources for a unified market. ...**April 27:** Danish-U.S. agreement on defense of Greenland is signed. ...**July:** Cease-fire talks begin in Korea. ...**August 30:** United States and the Philippines sign trade agreement. ...**September 1:** United States, Australia and New Zealand sign tripartite agreement for mutual security. ...**September 8:** Japan signs peace treaty with Allies at San Francisco. ...**December 20:** Greece is voted into the UN Security Council.

Western & Eastern Europe

1949. March 4: Vyacheslav Molotov (1890–1986) is replaced as Soviet foreign minister by Andrei Vyshinsky (1883–1954). ...**April 18:** Ireland leaves Commonwealth. ...**April 27:** British monarch is recognized as head of the Commonwealth. ...**May 1:** British gas industry is nationalized. ...**May 12:** Soviet Union officially lifts Berlin blockade. ...**May 23:** Federal Republic of Germany (West Germany) comes into being. ...**August 9:** Greece and Turkey join Council of Europe. ...**September 12:** Theodor Heuss (1884–1963) is elected West German president. ...**September 15:** Konrad Adenauer (1876–1967) becomes West German chancellor. ...**October 7:** German Democratic Republic (East Germany) is established under Communist regime. ...**October 11:** Wilhelm Pieck (1876–1960) is elected president of East Germany.

1950. February 23: Labour wins six-seat majority in British elections. **February 28:** Clement Attlee continues as British prime minister after the Labour party narrowly wins in general elections. ...**March 7:** Iceland joins Council of Europe. ...**May 22:** Celâl Bayar is elected president of Turkey. ...**June 15:** West Germany joins Council of Europe. ...**July 6:** East Germany and Poland agree on frontier treaty. ...**July 22:** Leopold III (1901–1983) of Belgium returns from exile. **August 11:** Prince Baudouin (1930–1993) is appointed regent in Belgium. ...**October 29:** Gustav V (b. 1858) of Sweden dies and is succeeded by Gustav VI (1882–1973). ...**November 28:** Oder-Neisse Line is accepted by East Germany and Poland as border.

1951. May 25: British spies Guy Burgess (1910–1963) and Donald Maclean (1913–1983) escape to Soviet Union. ...**June 17:** Gaullists win elections for French National Assembly. ...**July 16:** Leopold III of Belgium abdicates in favor of Baudouin. ...**October 25:** Conservatives win 16 seat majority in British elections, returning Winston Churchill as prime minister and Anthony Eden (1897–1977) as foreign secretary.

U.S. & Canada

1949. Newfoundland joins the Canadian Confederation. ...William Levitt (1907–1994) builds Levittown, New York, a suburban community of prefabricated houses on a former potato field in Long Island. ...**January 3:** U.S. Supreme Court rules states can ban the closed shop. ...**January 21:** Dean Acheson (1893–1971) becomes U.S. secretary of state. ...**March 31:** Newfoundland becomes tenth Canadian province. ...**June 27:** U.S. Supreme Court rules that evidence gathered by illegal search and seizure may be used in court cases. ...**July 15:** President Harry S. Truman signs the Housing Act. ...**August 11:** General Omar Bradley (1893–1981) becomes chairman of the Joint Chiefs of Staff. ...**November 1:** Eastern Airlines DC-4 collides with fighter plane over Washington, D.C., killing 55 people.

1950. January 17: Robbers take $2.8 million from Brink's, Inc. in Boston. ...**January 25:** Alger Hiss is sentenced to five years in jail for perjury. ...**January 31:** Truman authorizes research and production of hydrogen bomb by the Atomic Energy Commission. ...**May 11:** Truman dedicates Grand Coulee Dam in Washington State. ...**August 25:** Truman orders army to seize railroads to avoid a general strike. ...**September 21:** George C. Marshall becomes U.S. secretary of defense. ...**September 23:** U.S. Congress passes law requiring Communists to register. ...**November 7:** Richard M. Nixon (1913–1994) is elected to the U.S. Senate, after serving in the House of Representatives from 1947.

1951. February 26: U.S. presidents are limited to two terms by the 22nd Amendment to the U.S. Constitution. ...**March 29:** Julius Rosenberg (1918–1953) and Ethel Rosenberg (1916–1953) are found guilty of selling atomic secrets to Soviets. ...**April 5:** Rosenbergs are sentenced to death. ...**April 11:** Truman removes Douglas MacArthur from his command in Korea. ...**April 19:** MacArthur gives an emotional farewell speech to Congress and the American people. ...**April 24:** University of North Carolina admits first African American student. ...**July 11:** Mississippi River floods in Illinois, Missouri, Kansas and Oklahoma cause more than $1 billion in damages. ...**August 14:** William Randolph Hearst (b. 1863), U.S. press baron, dies. ...**October 10:** Mutual Security Act, which provides $7.5 billion for foreign aid in technical, military and economic areas, is passed by U.S. Congress.

Asia, Africa & Latin America

1949. January 21: Chiang Kai-shek resigns as president of Nationalist China. ...**January 30:** Felipe López (1900–1954) seizes power in Paraguay. ...**February 16:** Chaim Weizmann (1874–1952) is elected first president of Israel. ...**March 8:** France recognizes Cochin China as part of an independent Vietnam within French Union. ...**May 11:** Siam is renamed Thailand. ...**July 19:** France grants Laos independence within French Union. ...**September 21:** People's Republic of China is proclaimed in Beijing. ...**November 8:** France grants Cambodia independence within French Union. ...**December 8:** Taipei on Formosa becomes provisional capital of China.

1950. January 20: Dutch colonies in Latin America obtain self-government. ...**January 26:** India is proclaimed a republic. Rajendra Prasad (1884–1963) becomes president. ...**March 1:** Chiang Kai-shek is proclaimed president of Nationalist China on Formosa. ...**August 14:** Unitary constitution comes into force in Indonesia. ...**October 7:** Chinese invade Tibet.

1951. January 1: Gold Coast constitution comes into force. ...**July 20:** Emir Abdullah of Jordan is assassinated. ...**October 16:** Pakistan prime minister Liaquat Ali Khan (b. 1895) is assassinated. ...**November 11:** Juan Perón is reelected president of Argentina. ...**December 24:** Kingdom of Libya is established under Idris as-Sanusi (1890–1983).

Science, Invention & Technology

1949. J. Presper Eckert Jr. and John Mauchly develop BINAC, the first computer to use magnetic storage tape. BINAC will be used in guided missiles. ...Jay Forrester invents a magnetic core memory information storage system for computers. ...Leo Esaki (1925–) develops the tunnel diode, a smaller and more efficient version of the transistor. ...German Konrad Zuse (1910–1995) builds Z4 computer in Zurich, Switzerland.

1950. The Seeburg Company introduces the first jukebox that plays 45-rpm records. ...African American Percy Julian (1899–1975) develops a low-cost method of synthesizing sterols (alcohol solids). ...**June:** Ludwig Audrieth (1901–1967) and Michael Sveda (1912–) develop sucaryl artificial sweetener.

c. 1950. Total joint arthroplasty is developed for the artificial replacement of damaged joint components in the human body. ...Seat belts, gas turbine engines and power steering become available in automobiles. ...Disc brakes become standard in automobiles. ...Saxitoxin, a poison found in marine plankton, is developed by the Central Intelligence Agency (CIA) as a biological weapon. ...The electric tuning fork is introduced in Swiss watches. ...The availability of synthetic fertilizers leads U.S. farmers to abandon crop rotation in favor of intensive farming. ...The first passenger hydrofoil is invented in West Germany.

Juan Perón ➤

Religion, Culture & Arts

1949. Arthur Miller (1915–), American playwright: *Death of a Salesman*. ...William Faulkner wins the Nobel Prize for literature. ...George Orwell: *1984*. ...Carol Reed (1906–1976) directs the film *The Third Man*. ...Robert Rossen's (1908–1966) film version of Robert Penn Warren's *All the King's Men* wins the Academy Award for best picture. Its star, Broderick Crawford (1910–1986), wins the award for best actor. Olivia de Havilland wins best actress...**February 19:** American poet Ezra Pound receives the Bollingen Prize for poetry while in a hospital for the criminally insane. ...**April 7:** The musical *South Pacific* by Richard Rodgers and Oscar Hammerstein opens in New York City. ...**July 13:** Roman Catholic Church excommunicates Communists. ...**October 5–9:** New York Yankees defeat Brooklyn Dodgers to win the World Series.

1950. Lee Strasberg (1901–1982) becomes director of the Actors' Studio, which follows the principles of Stanislavsky (the Method). ...Lever House in New York City, designed by Louis Skidmore (1897–1962), Nathaniel Owings (1903–1984) and John Merrill (1896–1975), is the first important postwar skyscraper. ...Billy Wilder directs *Sunset Boulevard*. ...Joseph L. Mankiewicz's (1909–1993) *All About Eve*, starring Bette Davis (1908–1989), wins the Academy Award for best picture. ...**October 4–7:** New York Yankees sweep Philadelphia Phillies to win the World Series. ...**November 2:** George Bernard Shaw (b. 1856), Irish author and dramatist, dies.

1951. *Amahl and the Night Visitors* by Gian Carlo Menotti becomes the first opera to be written specially for television. ...Japanese filmmaker Akira Kurosawa (1910–1998) wins Venice Grand Prix with *Rashomon*. This opens the Western market to Japanese films. ...Igor Stravinsky: *The Rake's Progress* (opera). ...American painter Jackson Pollock, the best-known "action painter," begins to paint in black and white only. ...Herman Wouk (1915–), American writer: *The Caine Mutiny*. ...J. D. Salinger (1919–), American writer: *The Catcher in the Rye*. ...Vincente Minnelli's *An American in Paris* wins the Academy Award for best picture. Humphrey Bogart (1899–1957) wins the award for best actor. Vivien Leigh (1913–1967) wins the award for best actress. ...**October 4–10:** New York Yankees defeat New York Giants to win the World Series.

International Affairs

1952. February 18: Greece and Turkey join NATO. ...**April 28:** Matthew Ridgway (1895–1993) replaces Dwight D. Eisenhower as supreme commander of NATO forces in Europe. ...**May 25:** European Defense Community is established. ...**May 26:** United States, Britain, France and West Germany sign peace agreement. ...**July–August:** U.S. Air Force begins a series of bombing raids over North Korea. ...**August 23:** Arab League Security Pact comes into force. ...**August 29:** U.S. Air Force launches a major air raid against the former North Korean capital of Pyongyang, virtually destroying the entire city. ...**September 15:** Eritrea and West Ethiopia unite. ...**October 3:** Britain explodes its first atomic weapon, on the Monte Bello Islands off Australia. ...**October 21:** British troops arrive in Kenya to put down Mau Mau terrorism. ...**November 1:** United States tests world's first hydrogen (fusion) bomb, at Eniwetok Atoll in South Pacific. ...**December 5:** President Eisenhower visits U.S. and UN troops in Korea.

1953. January 6: Socialists of Asian countries hold conference in Yangôn (Rangoon), Burma (Myanmar). ...**February 10:** Constitution for the European Political Community is approved. ...**March 28:** Libya joins Arab League. ...**April 7:** Dag Hammarskjöld (1905–1961) of Sweden is elected secretary general of UN. ...**April 11:** A prisoner exchange between UN military forces and Communist troops is arranged in Korea. ...**July 27:** Korean armistice signed at Panmunjon, Korea, ends Korean War. ...**July 29:** Soviet warplane downs U.S. B-50 bomber off the coast of Siberia. ...**August 1:** Central African Federation is established for Northern Rhodesia (present-day Zambia), Southern Rhodesia (present-day Zimbabwe) and Nyasaland (present-day Malawi). ...**September 26:** United States approves aid package to Spain in order to establish military bases there. ...**December 4:** U.S., British and French leaders meet in Bermuda to discuss the exchange of nuclear information.

Western & Eastern Europe

1952. February 6: Britain's George VI (b. 1895) dies and is succeeded by Elizabeth II (1926–). ...**July 22:** New Polish constitution is adopted. ...**August 10:** European Coal and Steel Community is inaugurated. ...**October 5:** First Congress of the Communist Party since 1939 opens in Soviet Union.

Earl Warren, chief justice (1953–1969) of the U.S. Supreme Court. ➤

1953. January 13: Constitution of People's Republic of Yugoslavia is adopted. ...**January 14:** Josip Broz Tito (1892–1980) is elected first president of Yugoslavia. ...**March 5:** Soviet leader Joseph Stalin (b. 1879) dies. ...**June 2:** Queen Elizabeth II is crowned in Britain. ...**June 5:** New constitution and law of succession are adopted in Denmark. ...**June 17:** Anti-Communist riots break out in East Germany. ...**July 5:** Imre Nagy (1895–1958) becomes prime minister of Hungary. ...**September 12:** Nikita Khrushchev (1894–1971) becomes first secretary of the Central Committee of the Communist Party in the Soviet Union. ...**December 23:** Soviet deputy premier Lavrenty Beria (b. 1899) is tried and executed on charges of conspiracy. ...**December 24:** René Coty (1882–1962) is elected French president.

U.S. & Canada

1952: January 24: Vincent Massey (1887–1967) becomes governor general of Canada. ...**March 2:** U.S. Supreme Court rules that subversives can be banned from teaching in public schools. ...**April 8:** Truman orders U.S. steel mills seized to avoid a strike. ...**April 26:** Collision in the Azores of two U.S. warships, aircraft carrier *Wasp* and destroyer *Hobson*, sinks the latter, killing 176. ...**May 23:** U.S. railroads are returned to private ownership after almost two years of government confiscation. ...**June 2:** U.S. Supreme Court rules Truman's seizure of the steel mills illegal. They are returned to owners. ...**June 27:** U.S. Senate passes Immigration and Naturalization Act, which retains 1920 immigration quotas by national origin. ...**July 16:** U.S. Congress passes the Korean GI Bill of Rights to provide benefits to veterans of Korean War. ...**September 27:** After being accused of having an extra campaign fund, Republican vice presidential candidate Richard M. Nixon, running mate of Dwight D. Eisenhower, makes his televised "Checkers speech," saying the only gift he had accepted was a dog named Checkers. ...**November 4:** Eisenhower is elected U.S. president, beating Adlai Stevenson (1900–1965) by a large margin. ...**November 10:** U.S. Supreme Court rules that segregation is illegal on interstate railway travel.

1953. January 27: Secretary of State John Foster Dulles (1888–1959) pledges U.S. support for people living "behind the Iron Curtain." ...**February 6:** Office of Price Stabilization lifts controls on wages and salaries. ...**March 17:** Office of Price Stabilization ends all price controls. ...**April 1:** U.S. Department of Health, Education and Welfare (HEW) is established. **April 11:** Oveta Culp Hobby (1905–1995) is named HEW secretary. ...**June 8:** Tornadoes kill 139 in Ohio and Michigan. ...**June 9:** Tornadoes kill 86 in Massachusetts. ...**June 19:** Julius Rosenberg (b. 1918) and Ethel Rosenberg (b. 1916), convicted spies who many believe are innocent, are electrocuted. ...**August 15:** General Matthew Ridgway becomes chief of staff of U.S. Army. ...**October 5:** Earl Warren (1891–1974) becomes chief justice of the U.S. Supreme Court. ...**November 24:** Senator Joseph McCarthy (1908–1957) accuses former president Truman of aiding suspected Communists. ...**December 8:** President Eisenhower proposes Atoms for Peace program to UN General Assembly. ...**December 23:** Robert Oppenheimer's (1904–1967) security pass is withdrawn because he is suspected of Communist sympathies.

Asia, Africa & Latin America

1952. January 1: Nigerian constitution comes into force. ...**March 1:** Pandit Nehru's (1889–1964) Congress Party wins India's first national election. ...**March 10:** General Fulgencio Batista Zaldívar seizes power in Cuba. ...**July 6:** Ruiz Cortines (1891–1973) is elected president of Mexico. ...**July 23:** General Muhammad Neguib (1901–1984) seizes power in Egypt. ...**July 25:** Commonwealth constitution of Puerto Rico comes into force. ...**July 26:** Egyptian King Farouk (1920–1965) abdicates in favor of Fuad II (1952–).

1953. June 13: General Gustavo Rojas (1900–1975) seizes power in Colombia. ...**June 18:** General Neguib proclaims republic of Egypt. ...**August 1:** Federation of Rhodesia and Nyasaland takes effect. ...**August 19:** Muhammad Mosaddeq's (1880–1967) regime is overthrown in Iran, and Muhammad Reza Pahlavi (1919–1980), shah of Iran since 1941, returns to country, having been forced to flee by Mosaddeq's supporters. ...**August 20:** Sultan Sidi Muhammad (1910–1961) of Morocco is deposed by Muhammad VI (1881–1976). ...**October 9:** Arab Liberation Movement wins Syrian election. ...**November 9:** King Abdul Aziz (b. 1880) of Saudi Arabia dies and is succeeded by King Saud (1902–1966).

Science, Invention & Technology

1952. American Donald Glaser (1926–) invents the bubble chamber for photographing cosmic particles. ...American doctor Charles Hufnagel (1916–1989) invents an artificial heart valve that prevents aortic backflow. ...The first plastic contact lens is invented in Britain. ...Forrester develops the Semiautomatic Ground Environment (SAGE) air defense system. ...Englishman Alastair Pilkington (1920–1995) develops a floating process for the manufacture of flat glass. ...American Orville Redenbacher (1907–1995) develops a hybrid popping corn. ...American doctor Virginia Apgar (1909–1974) introduces the Apgar Score, a standardized system of evaluating the health of newborn babies. ...**April 15:** U.S. Air Force's YB-52 Stratofortress bomber has its maiden flight.

1953. American James Watson (1928–) and Englishman Francis Crick (1916–) discover deoxyribonucleic acid (DNA). ...The synthetic material Vinyon is used in making artificial blood vessels. ...Remington Rand Company develops an early version of a computer line printer. ...Microtone Company introduces a transistorized hearing aid. ...A heart-lung machine is first used successfully on a human patient. ...Charles Draper (1901–1987), at the Massachusetts Institute of Technology, develops inertial guidance system (automatic pilot) for the U.S. Air Force. ...Frenchman Auguste Piccard (1884–1962) descends to 10,335 feet (3,150 meters) off Capri, in the Mediterranean Sea, in his bathyscaphe *Trieste*. ...Charles Townes (1915–) and his associates at Columbia University in New York City construct an ammonia maser, a highly accurate microwave timepiece.

Religion, Culture & Arts

1952. Amos Tutuola, Nigerian novelist: *The Palm-Wine Drinkard*. ...Ralph Ellison (1914–1994), African American novelist: *Invisible Man*. ...Samuel Beckett (1906–1989), Irish playwright: *Waiting for Godot*. ...Bishop Fulton J. Sheen (1895–1979) begins television program, *Life Is Worth Living*. ...Agatha Christie's long-running play *The Mousetrap* premiers. ...Fred Zinnemann (1907–1997) directs *High Noon*. ...Gene Kelly (1912–1996) directs and stars in the film *Singing in the Rain*. ...Cecil B. DeMille's *The Greatest Show on Earth* wins the Academy Award for best picture. Gary Cooper (1901–1961) wins the award for best actor. Shirley Booth (1907–1992) wins best actress award. ...**September 23:** Rocky Marciano (1924–1969) wins world heavyweight boxing championship. ...**October 1–7:** New York Yankees defeat Brooklyn Dodgers to win their fourth straight World Series.

1953. Willem de Kooning exhibits his first paintings of female figures in Expressionist style. ...J. Paul Getty (1892–1976) founds the J. Paul Getty Museum in Malibu, California. ...Ernest Hemingway's *The Old Man and the Sea* wins the Pulitzer Prize for fiction. ...Arthur Miller: *The Crucible*. ...Rosamond Lehmann (1903–1990), British novelist: *The Echoing Grove*. ...Nadine Gordimer (1923–), South African novelist: *The Lying Days*. ...Dmitri Shostakovich (1906–1975), Russian composer: Symphony No. 10. ...Zinneman's *From Here to Eternity* wins the Academy Award for best picture. William Holden (1918–1981) wins the award for best actor. Audrey Hepburn (1929–1993) is named Best Actress. ...**September 30–October 5:** New York Yankees defeat Brooklyn Dodgers to win their fifth straight World Series.

International Affairs

1954. March 8: United States and Japan reach agreement on defense pact. ...**June 20:** UN Security Council calls for peace in Guatemala. ...**July 21:** Armistice in Indochina, dividing Vietnam into North Vietnam and South Vietnam, is signed at Geneva. ...**August 9:** Greece, Turkey and Yugoslavia sign defensive alliance. ...**August 30:** France rejects European Defense Community. ...**September 8:** Southeast Asia Collective Defense Treaty is signed at Manila. ...**October 23:** Paris agreements establish Western European Union, a defensive, economic, social, and cultural organization consisting of Belgium, France, West Germany, Britain, Italy, Luxembourg and the Netherlands. ...**December 2:** United States and Taiwan sign mutual defense treaty.

1955. February 23: First meeting of the Southeast Asia Treaty Organization (SEATO) is held in Bangkok, Thailand. ...**February 24:** Iraq and Turkey sign the Baghdad Pact to repel Communist activities. ...**April 4:** Britain joins the Baghdad Pact. ...**May 9:** West Germany joins NATO. ...**May 14:** East European Defense Treaty (Warsaw Pact), the Soviet bloc's response to NATO, is signed in Warsaw. ...**August 8:** International Conference on the Peaceful Uses of Atomic Energy meets in Geneva.

1956. April 7: Spain ends its protectorate over Morocco. ...**April 17:** Egypt, Saudi Arabia and Yemen sign a military treaty. ...**April 18–27:** Bandung Conference of Asian and African nations meets in Java. ...**June 13:** International Criminal Police Organization (Interpol) is established. ...**July 20:** International Finance Corporation of the UN comes into force. ...**October 25:** Syria and Jordan sign pact placing their armed forces under Egyptian control. ...**October 26:** Statute of the International Atomic Energy Agency is signed in New York City by 70 countries. ...**November 15:** UN forces takeover Suez Canal Zone. ...**December 18:** Japan is admitted to UN.

Western & Eastern Europe

1954. January 17: Chairman Milovan Djilas (1911–1995) is expelled from Yugoslavian Communist Party for having liberal views. ...**February 19:** Crimea, formerly part of Russia, is incorporated into the Ukraine. ...**May 18:** European Convention on Human Rights comes into force. ...**July 3:** Food rationing in Britain ends. ...**October 5:** Italy and Yugoslavia reach an understanding on Trieste.

1955. Hungarian prime minister Imre Nagy is removed from office because of his independent minded policies. ...**February 8:** Nikolai Bulganin (1895–1975) succeeds Georgi Malenkov (1902–1988) as Soviet premier. ...**April 6:** Winston Churchill resigns. Anthony Eden becomes prime minister of Britain. ...**April 29:** Giovanni Gronchi (1887–1978) is elected president of Italy. ...**May 5:** Occupation of West Germany officially ends. ...**May 15:** Austrian state treaty is signed in Vienna. ...**May 26:** Conservatives win solid majority in British House of Commons. ...**July 13:** Ruth Ellis (b. 1926), convicted of murder, is the last woman hanged in Britain. ...**October 23:** European statute of Saar territory is rejected by referendum.

1956. January 26: Soviet Union withdraws forces from Finland. ...**February 25:** First secretary of the Communist Party Nikita Khrushchev initiates de-Stalinization programs in Soviet Union. ...**April 17:** Cominform, the information agency of Soviet satelite states, is dissolved. ...**October 21:** Wladyslaw Gomulka (1905–1982) becomes Polish premier after bloodless overthrow of Stalinist regime. ...**October 23:** Anti-Stalinist revolution breaks out in Hungary. ...**October 24:** Imre Nagy is recalled as prime minister of new neutral government of Hungary. ...**November 2:** Hungary asks for Western assistance to oppose Soviet suppression. ...**November 4–22:** Hungarian revolution is suppressed by Soviet forces.

U.S. & Canada

1954. March 1: Five U.S. congressmen are wounded by Puerto Rican separatists who fire from the spectators' gallery. ...**April 1:** President Dwight Eisenhower signs bill that establishes U.S. Air Force Academy in Colorado Springs, Colorado. ...**April 22:** Senator Joseph McCarthy begins two months of televised hearings into Communist infiltration in the U.S. Army. ...**May 17:** In landmark *Brown v. Board of Education*, U.S. Supreme Court declares racial segregation in public schools is unconstitutional. ...**September 27:** United States and Canada agree to establish a Distant Early Warning (DEW) line of radar stations in Canada. ...**November 2:** Democrats retake both houses of Congress. ...**November 23:** General Motors produces its 50 millionth car. ...**December 2:** U.S. Senate votes to condemn McCarthy.

1955. January 19: President Eisenhower conducts the first televised presidential press conference. It is filmed and broadcast later by the networks. ...**August 12:** U.S. minimum wage increases from 75 cents to $1. ...**August 19:** Hurricane kills 179 in northeastern states. ...**September 24:** President Eisenhower suffers a mild heart attack and enters a Denver hospital. ...**September 26:** New York Stock Exchange loses $44 billion in one day, a record. ...**December 1:** Rosa Parks (1913–) an African American, refuses to give up her bus seat in Montgomery, Alabama. The Reverend Martin Luther King Jr. (1929–1968), pastor of Dexter Avenue Baptist Church, supports her by leading a bus boycott. ...**December 2:** American Federation of Labor and Congress of Industrial Organizations merge into one trade union (AFL-CIO).

1956. February 6: University of Alabama enrolls its first African American student, but she is suspended following campus unrest. ...**May 23:** U.S. Congress approves $750 million in subsidies to farmers who reduce production of specific crops. ...**June 29:** U.S. interstate highway system is assured by passage of the Highway Act. ...**June 30:** TWA and United airlines planes collide over the Grand Canyon, killing 128. ...**July 26:** The Italian liner *Andrea Doria* sinks after colliding with the Swedish liner *Stockholm* 60 miles off Nantucket, Massachusetts; about 1,650 are rescued. ...**November 6:** Eisenhower easily wins reelection. Dalip Singh Saund (1899–1973) becomes first Asian American congressman elected to U.S. House of Representatives. ...**December 21:** Martin Luther King Jr. ends the Montgomery bus boycott after the city agrees to comply with law to integrate its buses.

Asia, Africa & Latin America

1954. April 18: General Abdel Nasser (1918–1970) becomes prime minister of Egypt. ...**April 21:** U.S. Air Force transports French troops to embattled Dien Bien Phu in Vietnam. ...**May 5:** Army deposes President Frederico Chaves (1878–1978) of Paraguay. ...**May 7:** French troops surrender Dien Bien Phu to Vietnamese forces. ...**June 18–27:** President Jacobo Arbenz (1913–1971) of Guatemala is overthrown by U.S. supported Castillo Armas (1914–1957). ...**August 24:** President Getúlio Dornelles Vargas (b. 1883) of Brazil commits suicide and is succeeded by Vice President João Café Filho (1899–1970). ...**October 19:** Britain and Egypt reach agreement on withdrawal of British troops from Suez Canal. ...**November 1:** National revolt against French rule in Algeria begins.

1955. February 12: United States begins to train South Vietnamese troops. ...**September 19:** Juan Perón's regime in Argentina is overthrown by army. ...**October 26:** South Vietnam is proclaimed a republic under Ngo Dinh Diem (1901–1963). ...**November 9:** South Africa quits the UN General Assembly.

1956. January 1: Sudan attains independence. ...**March 2:** France recognizes independence of Morocco. ...**March 20:** France recognizes independence of Tunisia. ...**May 1:** Argentina restores its 1853 constitution. ...**May 28:** India takes over former French colonies. ...**June 18:** Britain evacuates Suez Canal Zone. ...**June 23:** Nasser becomes president of Egypt. ...**July 26:** Egypt nationalizes Suez Canal. ...**October 29:** Israel attacks Egypt. **October 31:** British and French warplanes bomb Egyptian airfields. ...**November 5:** British paratroopers land at Port Said, Egypt. ...**December 2:** Fidel Castro (1927–) and his revolutionaries land in Cuba.

Science, Invention & Technology

1954. Wernher von Braun's Jupiter-C four-stage jet reaches an altitude of 700 miles. ...Willem Johan Kolff's dialysis machine is used as an interim step in a kidney transplant. ...Frozen dinners are first marketed in the United States. ...The hobbing machine, first numerically controlled machining tool, is used for making gears. ...Italian Giulio Natta (1903–1979) develops a highly versatile polypropylene. ...**January 21:** The *Nautilus*, the first atomic-powered submarine, is christened by First Lady Mamie Eisenhower at its launch in Groton, Connecticut.

1955. Ernst Alexanderson (1878–1975) creates a color broadcasting system for Radio Corporation of America (RCA). ...The wind feather system replaces the Beaufort wind scale in weather reporting. ...The first plastic bottle cap liners are introduced. ...International Business Machines (IBM) develops the first computer hard disk drive. ...Percy Bridgman (1882–1961) at General Electric Corporation develops the first synthetic diamonds. ...The radar range, first microwave oven, is introduced. ...**September:** The first transatlantic telephone cable is completed.

c. 1955. Gregory Pincus (1903–1967) and his colleagues develop the birth control pill.

1956. A symposium is held at Dartmouth College, New Hampshire, to discuss artificial intelligence (AI). ...John Backus (1924–) at IBM develops FORTRAN, a computer programming language. ...Proctor & Gamble adds fluoride to its Crest toothpaste. ...American Leo Fender (1909–1991) patents his Fender Stratocaster, the first electric guitar. ...The first portable electric typewriter is made available. ...Swiss Georges de Mestral (1907–1990) develops Velcro fastener. ...Patsy Sherman (1930–) and Samuel Smith (1927–) at 3M Company develop Scotchguard fabric protector.

Religion, Culture & Arts

1954. Kingsley Amis (1922–1995), English novelist: *Lucky Jim*. ...Ernest Hemingway is awarded the Nobel Prize for literature. ...William Golding (1911–1993), English novelist: *Lord of the Flies*. ...American composer Charles Edward Ives (b. 1874) dies. ...Tennessee Williams: *Cat on a Hot Tin Roof*. ...Elia Kazan directs the film *On the Waterfront*, which wins the Academy Award for best picture. Its star, Marlon Brando (1924–), wins the award for best actor. Grace Kelly (1928–1982) wins as best actress. ...Akira Kurosawa directs the film *The Seven Samurai*. ...**September 29–October 2:** New York Giants defeat Cleveland Indians to win the World Series in a four-game sweep. ...**November 3:** Henry Matisse (b. 1869), French painter and sculptor, dies.

1955. Vladimir Nabokov (1899–1977), Russian-born American writer: *Lolita*. ...Marian Anderson sings the part of Ulrica in Verdi's *Masked Ball*, becoming the first African-American singer to perform at the New York Metropolitan Opera. ...William Faulkner: *A Fable*. It wins the Pulitzer Prize in fiction. ...Nicholas Ray (1911–1979) directs *Rebel Without a Cause*, starring James Dean (1931–1955). ...Delbert Mann's (1920–) *Marty* wins the Academy Award for best picture. Its star, Ernest Borgnine (1917–) wins the award for best actor. Anna Magnani (1908–1973) is named best actress. ...**September 28–October 4:** Brooklyn Dodgers defeat New York Yankees to win their first World Series. ...**December 12:** Evangelist Billy Graham (1918–) opens a national headquarters.

1956. Allen Ginsberg (1926–1998), poet of the Beat generation: "Howl." ...MacKinley Kantor (1904–1977): *Andersonville*. It wins the Pulitzer Prize for fiction. ...The musical *My Fair Lady*, based on the play *Pygmalion* by George Bernard Shaw, opens in New York City. ...Michael Anderson's (1920–) *Around the World in 80 Days* wins the Academy Award for best picture. Yul Brynner (1915–1985) wins the Academy Award for best actor. Ingrid Bergman is named best actress. ...Satyajit Ray (1921–1992) directs the Indian film *Aparajito* (*The Unvanquished*). ...**May 2:** Methodist Church in the United States calls for racial integration in its churches. ...**August 11:** Jackson Pollock (b. 1912), Abstract Expressionist painter, dies. ...**October 3–10:** New York Yankees defeat Brooklyn Dodgers to win the World Series. In game five of the series, Don Larsen (1929–) pitches the first and only perfect game (no hits, no walks, no errors) in World Series history.

International Affairs

1957. March 18: Disarmament Subcommittee of the UN opens session in London. ...**March 25:** Treaty of Rome is signed by France, West Germany, Italy, Belgium, Luxembourg and the Netherlands to establish the European Economic Community (ECC), popularly called the Common Market. ...**June 7:** United States and Poland finalize plans for U.S. agricultural and mining loans. ...**July 29:** International Atomic Energy Agency comes into force. ...**December 16:** NATO holds summit meeting of national leaders in Paris.

1958. January 1: West Germany joins NATO. ...**January 27:** United States and Soviet Union sign agreement for educational, cultural, athletic and technology exchanges. ...**February 3:** Benelux Economic Union is created by a treaty signed by Belgium, Luxembourg and the Netherlands. ...**March 17:** International Maritime Organization (IMO) of the UN is established. ...**June 8:** U.S. helicopter makes emergency landing in East Germany; its crew is held. ...**July 15:** U.S. troops are called in by Lebanese government to secure stability. ...**July 19:** United Arab Republic breaks diplomatic relations with Jordan. ...East Germany releases U.S. helicopter crew held for 11 days. ...**August 13:** United States withdraws most of its troops from Lebanon. ...**September 28:** Guinea leaves the French Union. ...**October 25:** Last U.S. troops leave Lebanon. ...**October 26:** Chinese troops withdraw from North Korea. ...**October 31–December 19:** United States, Britain, and Soviet Union hold conference on banning nuclear weapons but find little agreement. ...**December 28:** European Payments Union is replaced by European Monetary Agreement.

Western & Eastern Europe

1957. January 1: Saar territory is incorporated into West Germany. ...**January 9:** Eden resigns as British prime minister. ...**January 10:** Harold Macmillan (1894–1986) becomes British prime minister. ...**June 6:** The Rent Act ends many rent controls in Britain. ...**September 15:** Konrad Adenauer's Christian Democratic Union party wins landslide victory in West German elections.

1958. March 27: Nikita Khrushchev becomes Soviet premier. ...**June 1:** Charles de Gaulle becomes premier of France. ...**June 17:** Imre Nagy (b. 1896), former prime minister of Hungary, is executed. ...**September 28:** Referendum in France approves constitution of Fifth Republic (36.5 million for, 5.4 million against), giving executive stronger power. ...**December 5:** First section of superhighway in Britain is opened around Preston. ...**December 21:** De Gaulle is elected president of France.

U.S. & Canada

1957. January 18: Three U.S. Air Force jets complete nonstop around-the-world flights. ...**February:** Southern Christian Leadership Conference is established by Martin Luther King Jr. to seek total integration. ...**April 22:** Ku Klux Klan opens membership to Roman Catholics. ...**May 2:** Senator Joseph McCarthy (b. 1908) dies. ...**May 20:** AFL-CIO expells Dave Beck (1894–1993) from its executive committee for misusing union funds. ...**June 10:** Conservative John Diefenbaker (1895–1975) becomes prime minister following Canadian elections. ...**June 28:** Hurricane hits Louisiana and Texas; 531 are dead or missing. ...**August 29:** U.S. Congress passes Civil Rights Act, which establishes Civil Rights Commission and guarantees African Americans the right to vote. ...**September 4:** Arkansas governor Orval Faubus (1910–1994) uses National Guard to prevent nine African American students from enrolling at Little Rock's Central High School. **September 24:** Eisenhower sends federal troops to Little Rock to enforce desegregation of public schools. ...**November 25:** President Eisenhower suffers a mild stroke.

1958. May 12: United States and Canada initiate the North American Air Defense Command (NORAD) to detect incoming missiles. ...**May 30:** Unknown soldiers of World War II and Korean War are buried at Arlington Cemetery. ...**June 16:** U.S. Supreme Court rules that passports cannot be withheld because of a citizen's political affiliations or opinions. ...**August 6:** President Eisenhower signs the Defense Reorganization Act, giving more power to the secretary of defense. ...**August 23:** U.S. Congress passes the National Defense Education Act, which provides $1 billion in loans and funds for students' college education. ...**September:** Martin Luther King Jr. is wounded by an African American woman who stabs him in Harlem. ...**September 22:** Sherman Adams (1899–1986), President Eisenhower's chief of staff, resigns after a congressional panel determines he accepted expensive gifts. ...**November 4:** Democrats win both houses of U.S. Congress in midterm elections.

◄ ***American civil rights leader Martin Luther King Jr.***

Asia, Africa & Latin America

1957. Israeli forces withdraw from Egyptian territory. ...**March 6:** Gold Coast becomes an independent nation, changing its name to Ghana. ...**March 29:** Suez Canal reopens. ...**July 25:** Tunisia is proclaimed a republic. ...**July 26:** President Carlos Castillo Armas of Guatemala is assassinated. ...**August 13:** Syria expels three U.S. diplomats accused of plotting against the government. ...**August 31:** Federation of Malaya attains independence.

1957–1960. Nobusuke Kishi (1896–1987) serves as prime minister of Japan.

1958. February 1: Egypt and Syria form the United Arab Republic. ...**February 14:** Iraq and Jordan form Arab Federation. ...**May 13:** U.S. vice president Richard M. Nixon visits Venezuela and is harassed by demonstrators in Caracas. ...**June 14:** France announces the withdrawal of its forces from Morocco. ...**July 14:** King Faisal II (b. 1935) of Iraq is assassinated. Iraq is proclaimed a republic and withdraws from Arab Federation and Baghdad Pact. ...**July 20:** United Arab Republic breaks relations with Jordan. ...**December 3:** Indonesia nationalizes Dutch companies.

1958–1962. Arturo Frondizi (1908–1995) serves as president of Argentina.

Science, Invention & Technology

1957. American William Kouwenhoven (1886–1975) implants a ventricular defibrillator in a dog's chest. ...The first electric can opener is introduced. ...The Frisbee, originally called the Li'l Abner and later the Pluto Platter, is marketed by Wham-O Toy Company. ...African American doctor Vance Marchbanks (1905–1973) indentifies physical fatigue as a major factor in military accidents. ...American Bette Graham (1924–1980) markets her Mistake Out typing correction fluid. It is later renamed Liquid Paper. ...Grace Murray Hopper develops COBOL computer language. ...**September:** The first compact car, the Rambler, is introduced by American Motors. ...**October 4:** Soviet Union launches the first artificial space satellite, the *Sputnik.* **November 3:** Soviet Union launches a second *Sputnik* satellite. This time it carries a dog into orbit. ...**December 6:** U.S. Vanguard rocket, the U.S. answer to *Sputnik*, explodes on takeoff at Cape Canaveral, Florida. ...**December 17:** U.S. Army tests first Atlas intercontinental ballistic missile (ICBM). ...**December 18:** U.S. atomic power plant at Shippingport, Pennsylvania., the nation's first, begins to generate electricity.

1958. The first bifocal contact lenses are introduced. ...Allis Chalmers farm machinery company introduces the cylindrical straw bale press. ...Wham-O Toy Company introduces the Hula Hoop, based on a bamboo exercise ring developed in Australia. ...American Wilson Greatbatch (1919–) invents the heart pacemaker. ...Mason Sones (1918–1985) develops the coronary arteriography technique of catheterization. ...R. Buckminster Fuller builds geodesic dome with a diameter of 125.9 meters in Baton Rouge, Louisiana. ...**January 31:** The first U.S. earth satellite, *Explorer*, is launched at Cape Canaveral, Florida. ...**July 29:** National Aeronautics and Space Administration (NASA) is established. ...**August 8:** *Nautilus* makes the first undersea crossing of the Arctic, traveling 1,830 miles from Point Barrow, Alaska, to Spitsbergen, Norway in four days. ...**October 26:** Pan American World Airlines begins first U.S. jet flights to Europe. ...**December 10:** National Airlines begins first jet airline passenger service within United States, between New York City and Miami.

Religion, Culture & Arts

1957. Giuseppe Tomasi de Lampedusa (1896–1957), Italian novelist: *The Leopard.* ...Rebecca West: *The Fountain Overflows.* ...Jack Kerouac (1922–1969), novelist of the Beat generation: *On the Road.* ...Boris Pasternak (1890–1960), Russian novelist: *Dr. Zhivago.* ...David Lean's (1908–1991) *The Bridge on the River Kwai* wins the Academy Awards for best picture. The star of the film, Alec Guinness (1914–), is named best actor. Joanne Woodward (1930–) is named best actress for her role in *The Three Faces of Eve.* ...**January 16:** Arturo Toscanini (b. 1867), one of the greatest musical conductors of all time, dies. ...**June 15:** The Count Basie Band becomes the first African American band to play in the Starlight Roof Room of the Waldorf-Astoria Hotel in New York City. ...**September 26:** *West Side Story*, a musical with lyrics by Stephen Sondheim (1930–) and music by Leonard Bernstein, opens in New York City. ...**October 2–10:** Milwaukee Braves defeat New York Yankees to win the World Series.

1957–1973. The Sydney Opera House by J¢rn Utzon (1918–), building with a sail-like roofscape, is constructed.

1958. Chinua Achebe (1930–), Nigerian novelist: *Things Fall Apart.* ...Rebecca West: *The Court and the Castle.* ...Barbara Pym (1913–1980), British novelist: *A Glass of Blessings.* ...Edna Ferber: *Ice Palace.* ...Ordination of women is approved by Church of the Brethren in United States ...Ludwig Mies van der Rohe (1886–1969) and Philip Johnson (1906–): Seagram Building in New York. ...First stereophonic records are produced in the United States. ...Orson Welles directs the film *Touch of Evil.* ...Vincente Minnelli's *Gigi* wins the Academy Award for best picture. David Niven (1909–1983) is named best actor. Susan Hayward (1918–1975) wins best actress. ...**March 25:** Sugar Ray Robinson (1920–1989) wins the middleweight boxing championship, becoming the first boxer to regain his crown five times. ...**May:** United Press International is formed by merger of United Press and International News Services. ...United Presbyterian Church is established in United States. ...**June:** United Church of Christ is created in United States with merger of Evangelicals and Congregationalists. ...**October 1–9:** New York Yankees defeat Milwaukee Braves to win the World Series.

International Affairs

1959. Formal charter organizing the Council for Mutual Economic Assistance (COMECON) is ratified by Albania, Bulgaria, Cuba, Czechoslovakia, East Germany, Hungary, Mongolia, Poland, Romania and the Soviet Union. ...**February 19:** Greek-Turkish-British agreement on Cyprus grants independence and constitution to Cyprus. ...**March 5:** United States signs bilateral defense agreements with Turkey, Iran and Pakistan. ...**March 9:** Yemen joins the United Arab Republic to establish the United Arab States. ...**October 9:** Baghdad Pact is renamed Central Treaty Organization (CENTO), with headquarters in Ankara. ...**November 10:** UN General Assembly condemns racial discrimination, with special censure of South Africa. ...**November 29:** European Free Trade Association (EFTA) is created by Britain, Sweden, Denmark, Norway, Switzerland, Austria and Portugal in Stockholm, Sweden.

1960. March 15–June 27: Disarmament conference begins in Geneva, but no agreement is reached. ...**May 1:** Soviet military shoots down Gary Powers in U.S. U-2 spy plane over Ural Mountains....**May 16:** Khrushchev walks out of Paris summit meeting with Eisenhower because of U-2 incident. ...**July 15:** UN intervenes in Congo to stop civil war. ...**August 10:** Treaty to preserve Antarctica for scientific purposes is signed by the United States, Britain, Japan, Norway, Belgium and South Africa. ...**August 19:** U-2 pilot Powers is sentenced to ten years for spying by Soviet Union. ...**September 14:** Organization of Petroleum Exporting Countries (OPEC) is established....**September 24:** International Development Association (IDA) of the UN is established.

1961. January 7: African charter to coordinate political policy is signed by leaders of African nations. ...**April 13:** UN General Assembly again condemns apartheid in South Africa. ...**May 28:** Amnesty International is founded. ...**May 31:** U.S. president John F. Kennedy and French president Charles de Gaulle meet in Paris. ...**June 4–5:** Kennedy and Khrushchev meet in Vienna. ...**September 15:** Summit conference on Berlin is held in Washington, D.C., by leaders of United States, Britain, Soviet Union and France. ...**September 18:** Dag Hammarskjöld (b. 1905), UN secretary general, is killed in an airplane crash in Congo. ...**September 30:** Organization for European Economic Cooperation is replaced by Organization for Economic Cooperation and Development (OECD). ...**November 3:** U Thant (1909–1974) of Burma is elected acting secretary general of UN.

Western & Eastern Europe

1959. February 1: Swiss reject woman suffrage in national elections. ...**February 23–28:** First session of European Court of Human Rights is held in Strasbourg. ...**May 24:** Britain renames Empire Day Commonwealth Day. ...**June 17:** Eamon de Valera (1882–1975) is elected president of Ireland. ...**July 1:** Heinrich Lübke (1894–1972) is elected president of West Germany. ...**October 8:** Conservatives increase their majority in British Parliament in elections, and Harold Macmillan is reelected prime minister.

1960. France becomes a nuclear power. ...**April 14:** All East German agriculture becomes collective. ...**May 8:** Leonid Brezhnev (1906–1982) becomes chairman of the Presidium of the Supreme Soviet....**May 27:** Army takes over government of Turkey. ...**August 16:** Cyprus becomes independent with Archbishop Makarios (1913–1977) as president. ...**August 25:** Soviet Communist Party condemns hard-line doctrine of China's Mao Zedong.

1961. February 27: Britain and Iceland end dispute over fishing rights....**March 26:** Christian Socialist Party loses majority in Belgian elections and forms coalition government with Socialists....**August 13:** East Germany begins constructing Berlin Wall to halt defections to the West. ...**October 25:** General Cemal Gursel (1895–1966) is elected president of Turkey. ...**October 31:** Stalin's body is removed from Lenin Mausoleum in Moscow. All cities and other places named after Stalin are renamed. ...**November 7:** Adenauer is reelected West German chancellor. ...**December 9:** Soviet Union breaks off relations with pro-Chinese Albania. Albania is expelled from COMECON.

U.S. & Canada

1959. January 3: Alaska is admitted to Union as 49th state. ...**April 18:** Christian Herter (1895–1966) becomes U.S. secretary of state. ...**April 25:** Joint U.S.-Canadian St. Lawrence Seaway opens navigation from Great Lakes to Atlantic Ocean. ...**May 20:** U.S. citizenship is restored to 5,000 Japanese Americans stripped of it during World War II. ...**May 22:** United States and Canada sign agreement for joint research and development of nuclear energy. ...**May 24:** John Foster Dulles (b. 1888) dies. ...**August 21:** Hawaii is admitted to Union as 50th state. ...**November 7:** U.S. Supreme Court orders an end to 116-day steel strike, the nation's longest. ...**November 9:** Department of Health, Education and Welfare announces that cranberries have been contaminated by a weed killer, and cranberry sales drop dramatically. ...**November 19:** Ford discontinues its Edsel model, which proved unpopular during its two years of existence.

1960. February 1: Lunch-counter sit-ins begin in the South after four African American college students are refused service in a Woolworth's in Greensboro, North Carolina. ...**February 2:** U.S. Senate passes the 23rd Amendment to the U.S. Constitution, banning the poll tax for federal elections and permitting residents of the District of Columbia to vote. ...**September 26:** Presidential candidates John F. Kennedy (1917–1963) and Richard M. Nixon hold the first of four televised debates. ...**October 25:** Martin Luther King Jr. is jailed in Atlanta on a traffic violation. ...**November 4:** Kennedy defeats Nixon in presidential election. ...**December 12:** President-elect Kennedy names Dean Rusk (1909–1994) secretary of state.

1961. January 20: John F. Kennedy is inaugurated 35th president of the United States. He advises, "Ask not what your country can do for you, ask what you can do for your country." ...**January 21:** Robert F. Kennedy (1925–1968) is sworn in as U.S. attorney general. ...**January 25:** President Kennedy holds the first presidential press conference to be televised live. ...**March 1:** President Kennedy creates the Peace Corps for international people-to-people aid programs. ...**March 29:** States ratify the 23rd Amendment to the U.S. Constitution. ...**May:** Freedom Rides begin on a large scale, with buses carrying integrated passengers into the South to protest segregated interstate transportation. ...**September 5:** United States announces it is resuming nuclear tests. ...U.S. Congress passes legislation making airplane hijacking a federal crime.

Asia, Africa & Latin America

1959. January 1–3: Fulgencio Batista Zaldívar's regime in Cuba is overthrown by Fidel Castro. **February 16:** Castro becomes premier of Cuba. ...**March:** Revolt in Tibet against Chinese fails. Dalai Lama flees to India. ...**April:** The second National People's Congress is held in China. ...**April 26:** A small detachment of Cubans unsuccessfully invades Panama. ...**June 3:** Singapore becomes a self-governing state. ...**June 4:** Cuba seizes U.S.-owned sugar plantations. ...**August 16:** United Arab Republic resumes relations with Jordan.

1960. March 21: Blacks in Sharpeville, South Africa, are massacred by police. ...**April 27:** French Togoland becomes independent. ...**June 30:** Belgian Congo becomes independent. ...**July 1:** Ghana and Somalia become republics. ...**July 8:** Belgian troops enter the Congo. ...**August 21:** Federation of Mali breaks up into Mali and Senegal. ...**September 2:** Final Belgian troops leave Congo, following UN demands. ...**October 1:** Nigeria becomes independent. ...**December 13:** Central American Common Market is established.

1961. January 1: United States breaks diplomatic relations with Cuba. ...**February 18:** Latin American Free Trade Association is established. ...**March 15:** Prime Minister Hendrik Verwoerd (1901–1966) withdraws South Africa from British Commonwealth. ...**April 27:** Sierra Leone becomes independent. ...**May 17–20:** In what is known as the Bay of Pigs Invasion, more than 1,500 Cuban exiles, organized and trained by U.S. CIA, stage an unsuccessful attempt to overthrow Castro regime in Cuba. ...**May 30:** Rafael Trujillo (b. 1891), dictator of Dominican Republic, is assassinated. ...**May 31:** Union of South Africa becomes a republic. ...**June 1:** Northern Cameroons joins Federation of Nigeria. ...**September 29:** Syria quits the United Arab Republic to form the Syrian Arab Republic. ...**December 9:** Tanganyika becomes independent.

Science, Invention & Technology

1959. American Robert Noyce (1927–1990) patents the integrated circuit (microchip). ...American researchers develop the conversation machine, capable of answering simple questions. ...American Lee De Forest patents an automatic dialing apparatus for the telephone. ...Soviet spacecraft *Luna 3* loops around the far side of the moon. ...The Ski-Doo snowmobile is introduced in the United States, popularizing snowmobiling. ...**September 16:** Xerox Corporation introduces the Xerox 914, first automated copying machine, developed by Chester Carlson.

1960. Factor VIII protein extract from human blood becomes available for hemophiliacs. ...*Tiros I* satellite is launched by the United States. ...Teflon non-stick cookware is made available in the United States. ...The M-17 gas mask is developed for the U.S. military as protection against biological and chemical warfare. ...General Electric Corporation develops cubic boron nitride (CBN), an industrial abrasive. ...Photogrammetry (aerial photography) becomes an essential part of land surveying. ...**June 21:** America's first plant to convert salt water to freshwater, owned by Dow Chemical Company, is opened by President Kennedy.

1961. The first successful artificial heart valve, the Starr-Edwards valve, is implanted in human patients. ...African American engineer Ozzie Williams (1921–) develops control rockets for the U.S. space program.... American doctor Irving Cooper (1922–1985) uses cryosurgery, a freezing technique, in eye cataract removal. ...Proctor & Gamble introduces Pampers disposable diapers. ...**April 12:** Soviet cosmonaut Yuri Gagarin (1934–1968) becomes the first person in space, orbiting the earth for 89 minutes.

c. 1961. Boots Company of Britain develops Ibuprofen pain reliever, as an aspirin substitute.

Religion, Culture & Arts

1959. Günter Grass (1927–): *The Tin Drum*. ...William Burroughs (1914–1997), American writer: *Naked Lunch*. ...Harold Pinter (1930–) writes the play *The Caretaker*. ...John Updike (1932–), American writer: *Poorhouse Fair*. ...Truman Capote (1924–1984): *Breakfast at Tiffany's*. ...Alain Resnais (1922–) directs the French film *Hiroshima, mon amour*. ...William Wyler's *Ben-Hur* wins the Academy Award for best picture. Its star, Charlton Heston (1923–) wins the award for best actor. Simone Signoret (1921–1985) is named best actress. ...**July 17:** Blues singer Billie Holiday (b. 1915) dies. ...**October:** Los Angeles Dodgers defeat Chicago White Sox to win the World Series. ...**November 16:** The musical *The Sound of Music* by Richard Rodgers and Oscar Hammerstein opens in New York City.

1960. Isaac Bashevis Singer (1904–1991): *The Magician of Lublin*. ...Federico Fellini (1920–1993) directs the Italian film *La Dolce Vita*. ...Alfred Hitchcock directs *Psycho*. ...Billy Wilder's *The Apartment*, starring Jack Lemmon (1925–) and Shirley MacLaine (1934–), wins the Academy Award for best picture. Burt Lancaster (1913–1996) is named best actor. Elizabeth Taylor (1932–) wins the award for best actress. ...Updike: *Rabbit Run*. ...Robert Bolt (1924–1995), British dramatist: *A Man for All Seasons*. ...Guggenheim Museum, designed by Frank Lloyd Wright, is completed in New York City. ...**October 5–13:** Pittsburgh Pirates defeat New York Yankees to win the World Series.

1961. Patrick White (1912–1990), Australian writer: *Riders in the Chariot*. ...Muriel Spark (1918–): *The Prime of Miss Jean Brodie*. ...François Truffaut (1932–1984) directs the French film *Jules et Jim*. ...Jerome Robbins's and Robert Wise's (1914–) *West Side Story* wins the Academy Award for best picture. ...Jean Anouilh (1910–1987), French dramatist: *Becket*. ...Soviet authorities close synagogues in Moscow. ...**January 10:** Dashiell Hammett (b. 1894), writer of detective stories, dies. ...**June 16:** Soviet ballet star Rudolf Nureyev (1939–1993) defects to the West. ...**October 1:** Roger Maris (1934–1985) hits his 61st home run of the season, breaking the record of 60 set by Babe Ruth (1895–1948) in 1927. ...**October:** New York Yankees defeat Cincinnati Reds to win the World Series. ...**November 20:** Russian Orthodox Church joins World Council of Churches.

International Affairs

1962. Group of Ten (G–10) industrialized nations agree in Paris to loan money to the International Monetary Fund. The nations are United States, Canada, Britain, West Germany, Japan, France, Italy, Sweden, Belgium and the Netherlands. ...**January 14:** European Economic Community members agree to establish a Common Agricultural Policy. ...**January 31:** Cuba is expelled from Organization of American States. **February 10:** Soviets release U-2 pilot Gary Powers after nearly two years. ...**March 23:** Scandinavian nations sign the Helsinki Convention on Nordic cooperation. ...**May 31:** After a lengthy trial, Nazi criminal Adolf Eichmann (b. 1906) is hanged by the Israelis. ...**October 22–November 20:** In what is known as the Cuban missile crisis, President Kennedy orders naval quarantine of Cuba after learning of Soviet missile sites on the island. Kennedy warns that an attack from Cuban bases will mean U.S. retaliation against Soviets. Soviet premier Khrushchev agrees to withdraw the missiles, and United States lifts its quarantine. ...**December 23:** United States and Cuba strike a deal to trade American food and medical and agricultural supplies for more than 1,000 men captured during the Bay of Pigs invasion.

1963. Zanzibar joins the UN. ...**January 22:** West Germany and France sign a treaty of cooperation. ...**January 29:** French president Charles de Gaulle vetoes Britain's entry into European Economic Community. ...**March 19:** United States and Central American nations sign agreement in San Jose, Costa Rica, to fight Communism. ...**June 20:** United States and Soviet Union agree to establish a "hot line" phone connection between their leaders. ...**June 26–July 3:** President Kennedy tours West Germany, Britain and Italy. ...**August 5:** United States, Soviet Union and Britain agree on Nuclear Test Ban Treaty. ...**August 30:** U.S.–Soviet "hot line" link becomes operational. ...**October 10:** The limited nuclear test ban takes effect. ...**December 17:** United States cedes a small area of El Paso, Texas, to Mexico.

Western & Eastern Europe

1962. April 14: Georges Pompidou (1911–1974) succeeds Michel Debré (1912–1996) as French prime minister. ...**May 6:** Antonio Segni (1891–1972) is elected president of Italy. ...**September 2:** Soviet Union sends arms to Cuba. ...**November 29:** Britain and France sign agreement to build Concorde aircraft. ...**December 11:** Coalition government is formed in West Germany by Christian Democrats, Christian Socialists and Free Democrats.

1963. January 14: French president de Gaulle turns down U.S. Polaris missile offer. ...**April 7:** New constitution is adopted in Yugoslavia. ...**June 5:** British defense minister John Profumo (1915–) resigns during the Christine Keeler (1942–) sex scandal. ...**August 8:** The "Great Train Robbery" occurs in Britain when 15 men steal 2.5 million pounds from the London-Glasgow mail train. ...**October 15:** Ludwig Erhard (1897–1977) succeeds Konrad Adenauer as West German chancellor. ...**October 18:** Macmillan resigns as British prime minister. ...**October 19:** Sir Alec Douglas Home (1903–1992) becomes prime minister of Britain. ...**December 22:** Fighting breaks out between Greeks and Turks in Cyprus. Makarios calls in British and UN forces and UN mediator.

U.S. & Canada

1962. February 14: Jacqueline Kennedy's (1929–1994) tour of the newly restored White House is broadcast to more than 46 million Americans. ...**March 1:** American Airlines Boeing 707 crashes at New York's Idlewild Airport, killing 95. ...**March 26:** U.S. Supreme Court rules that federal courts can decide on the constitutionality of apportionment of state legislatures. ...**April 10:** President Kennedy criticizes the rise in steel prices. ...**April 13:** Steel companies cancel the price hike. ...**June 19:** U.S. Supreme Court rules that evidence obtained illegally cannot be used in state court cases. ...**September:** U.S. minimum wage is raised from $1 to $1.15. ...**October 1:** James Meredith (1933–) becomes the first African American student enrolled at the University of Mississippi. ...**November 6:** Democrats retain majorities in both houses of Congress in midterm elections. Edward Kennedy (1932–), younger brother of John and Robert, is elected to the U.S. Senate.

1963. March 18: U.S. Supreme Court rules that all indigent defendants in criminal cases must have state-appointed attorneys. ...**April 12:** Martin Luther King Jr. is jailed in Birmingham, Alabama, and writes "Letter from the Birmingham Jail" about why he believes in civil disobedience. ...**April 22:** Liberal Lester Pearson (1897–1972) becomes prime minister of Canada. ...**May 5:** U.S. Air Force Academy graduates its first four African American cadets. ...**June 12:** Medgar Evers (b. 1925), a field secretary for the National Association for the Advancement of Colored People (NAACP), is murdered in Mississippi. ...**August 18:** Meredith becomes the first African American to graduate from the University of Mississippi. ...**August 28:** King gives his "I have a dream" speech before more than 200,000 civil rights demonstrators at the Lincoln Memorial. ...**September 17:** The 16th Street Baptist Church in Birmingham, Alabama is bombed, killing two African American children and injuring 17. ...**November 22:** President John F. Kennedy (b. 1917) is assassinated in Dallas, Texas, and is succeeded by Vice President Lyndon B. Johnson (1908–1973). ...**November 24:** Lee Harvey Oswald (b. 1939), Kennedy's alleged assassin, is shot while in Dallas police custody by Jack Ruby (1911–1967). ...**November 29:** President Johnson appoints a commission to investigate Kennedy's assassination.

Asia, Africa & Latin America

1962. January 1: Western Samoa becomes independent. ...**March 1:** Pakistan adopts a presidential constitution. ...**March 28:** Army seizes power in Syria. ...**March 29:** President Arturo Frondizi of Argentina is deposed by Argentine army. ...**July 1:** Burundi and Rwanda become independent. ...**July 3:** France grants full independence to Algeria. ...**July 18:** Peruvian army deposes President Manuel Prado (1889–1967). ...**August 6:** Jamaica becomes independent. ...**August 16:** Algeria joins Arab League. ...**August 31:** Trinidad and Tobago becomes an independent nation. ...**September 27:** Revolution in Yemen abolishes monarchy. ...**October 9:** Uganda becomes independent. ...**October 20–November 21:** China invades India. ...**November 5:** Saudi Arabia breaks relations with the United Arab Republic. ...**December:** Tanganyika becomes a republic within the British Commonwealth.

1963. February 1: Malawi becomes self-governing. ...**February 9:** President Abdul Karim Qasim (b. 1914) of Iraq is overthrown and executed. ...**May 25:** Organization of African Unity is set up in Addis Ababa, Ethiopia by 32 African countries. ...**September 16:** Federation of Malaysia is formed by Singapore, Sarawak and Sabah. ...**October 1:** Nigeria becomes a republic. ...**October 4–November 2:** Algerian forces are badly beaten in war with Morocco. ...**November 1:** Dissident Vietnamese generals, encouraged by U.S. government, overthrow and murder Ngo Dinh Diem (b. 1901) in South Vietnam, killing Diem. ...**December 10:** Zanzibar becomes independent. ...**December 12:** Kenya gains independence.

Science, Invention & Technology

1962. IBM introduces a typewriter with a spherical typing element and stationary carriage. ...The findings of Brian Josephson (1940–) lead to development of the Josephson junction, pairs of superconducting metals separated by a thin insulating layer, used in computers and scientific instruments. ...The first telephone call is relayed from a communications satellite. ...Western Union Company introduces the automated Telex message service in United States. ...**February 20:** John Glenn (1921–) becomes the first American to orbit the earth. ...**April 26:** The first internationally sponsored satellite, *Ariel*, is launched from Cape Canaveral, Florida. ...**August 27:** U.S. spacecraft *Mariner II* is launched from Cape Canaveral, Florida, on a 15-week trajectory toward Venus. **December 14:** *Mariner II* begins to transmit information about Venus back to earth.

1963. Philips Company of the Netherlands introduces the monophonic audiocassette. ...Arno Penzias (1933–) and Robert Wilson (1936–) discover the background noise, or "hiss," from the big bang, using a radio telescope. ...The largest radio telescope dish, 1,000 feet in diameter, is built into the mountains at Arecibo, Puerto Rico. ...The tranquilizer Valium is introduced. ...British doctor Roy Calne (1930–) performs the first kidney transplant using cyclosporin, a rejection suppressing drug. ...Communications satellites *Syncom I*, *II* and *III* are launched. ...Lincoln Laboratories introduces Sketchpad, the predecessor of computer-aided design (CAD) graphics systems, for industrial applications. ...The computer light pen is developed by I. E. Sutherland (1938–) at MIT. ...Emmet Leith (1927–) and Juris Upatnieks (1936–) produce the first holographic image at the University of Michigan. ...The first successful particle collider is constructed at the Italian National Laboratories. ...Color film is made available by Polaroid Corporation for its instant cameras. ...The felt-tipped marker is introduced by Pentel Company of Japan.

Religion, Culture & Arts

1962. Katherine Anne Porter writes *Ship of Fools*. ...John Steinbeck is awarded Nobel Prize in literature. ...Aleksander Isayevich Solzhenitsyn (1918–), Russian writer: *One Day in the Life of Ivan Denisovich*. ...Edward Albee (1928–), American playwright: *Who's Afraid of Virginia Woolf?* ...First partnership of Margot Fonteyn (1919–1991) and Rudolf Nureyev, dancing in *Giselle* at Covent Garden. ...David Lean wins his second best director Academy Award, for the film *Lawrence of Arabia*, which is also named best picture. ...Robert Rauschenberg (1925–) begins using silk-screen printing to provide repeating images. ...Roman Catholic Church retains Latin as the language for Mass. ...American singer and songwriter Bob Dylan (1941–) releases his self-titled debut album. ...**June 25:** U.S. Supreme Court rules that prayer in public schools is unconstitutional. ...**September 25:** Sonny Liston (1932–1971) defeats Floyd Patterson (1935–) to become heavyweight boxing champion. ...**October:** New York Yankees beat San Francisco Giants to win the World Series. ...**October 11:** Second Vatican Council, which will implement many reforms in the Roman Catholic Church, is opened by Pope John XXIII (1881–1963).

1963. Wole Soyinka (1934–), Nigerian playwright: *The Lion and the Jewel*. ...William Faulkner's *The Reivers* wins the Pulitzer Prize for fiction. ...Sylvia Plath (b. 1932) dies. ...The Beatles have their first hit songs in Britain. ...American film director Joseph Losey (1909–1984) directs *The Servant*. ...Luchino Visconti (1906–1976) directs film *The Leopard*. ...Ingmar Bergman (1918–) directs the film *The Silence*. ...Tony Richardson's (1928–1991) film version of Henry Fielding's 1749 novel *Tom Jones* wins the Academy Award for best picture. Sidney Poitier (1924–) is named best actor and Patricia Neal (1926–) wins best actress. ...The Guggenheim Museum in New York stages a Pop art show, featuring works by Andy Warhol (1928–1987), Roy Lichtenstein (1923–) and Claes Oldenburg (1929–). ...Vatican Council of the Roman Catholic Church approves local languages for use at Mass. ...*Pacem in Terris* encyclical issued by Pope John XXIII. ...**June 3:** Pope John XXIII (b. 1881) dies. ...**June 21:** Cardinal Giovanni Battista Montini (1897–1978) is elected Pope Paul VI. ...**October 2–6:** Los Angeles Dodgers defeat New York Yankees to win the World Series.

International Affairs

1964. Malawi, Malta and Zambia join UN. ...UN creates the Conference on Trade and Development (UNCTAD). ...**January 9:** Panama breaks diplomatic relations with United States. ...**January 28:** Soviet warplanes shoot down a U.S. Air Force plane over East Germany, killing three airmen. ...**March 23:** UN conference on trade and development in Geneva is attended by representatives of 115 countries. ...**May 19:** United States issues formal complaint to Soviets about microphones hidden in U.S. embassy in Moscow. ...**October 16:** China explodes an atomic bomb in Sinkiang province, becoming the world's fifth nuclear power.

1965. Singapore becomes an independent member of the UN. ...**January 7:** Indonesia withdraws from UN. ...**April 21:** International Disarmament Commission meets in New York City with representatives from 114 nations. ...**December 10:** UN Security Council is enlarged from 11 members to 15. ...**December 16:** UN Security Council votes mandatory sanctions against white government of Rhodesia (Zimbabwe).

Cuban revolutionary leader Fidel Castro, speaking in Washington, D.C., in 1959.

Western & Eastern Europe

1964. March 6: King Paul (b. 1901) of Greece dies and is succeeded by Constantine II (1940–). ...**April 1:** Unified Ministry of Defense is established in Britain. ...**April 4:** Archbishop Makarios cancels treaty between Greece, Turkey, and Cyprus as fighting accelerates on Cyprus. ...**July 15:** Anastas Mikoyan (1895–1978) becomes chairman of the Presidium of the Supreme Soviet. ...**September 21:** Malta becomes independent. ...**October 14:** Soviet premier Khrushchev is ousted and replaced as premier by Aleksei Kosygin (1904–1980). Leonid Brezhnev becomes first secretary of Communist Party. ...**October 15:** Labour Party wins majority in British elections (317 Labour, 304 Conservative, 9 Liberal). Harold Wilson (1916–1995) becomes prime minister. ...**November 12:** Charlotte (1896–1985) of Luxembourg abdicates and is succeeded by Grand Duke Jean (1921–). ...**November 26:** Britain borrows $3 billion from international bankers.

1965. January 24: Winston Churchill (b. 1874) dies. ...**May 12:** West Germany establishes diplomatic relations with Israel. ...**July 2:** France begins boycott of European Economic Community meetings. ...**November 9:** Britain abolishes death penalty. ...**December 9:** Nikolai Podgorny (1903–1983) becomes chairman of the presidium of the Supreme Soviet. ...**December 14:** Britain and Ireland agree on free-trade pact. ...**December 19:** Charles de Gaulle is reelected French president. ...**December 31:** Common Market Commission, Coal and Steel Authority and Euratom are merged into one authority.

U.S. & Canada

1964. January 13: Federal Trade Commission announces that all cigarette packages must carry a warning that smoking is hazardous to health. ...**March 9:** In *New York Times v. Sullivan*, U.S. Supreme Court rules that public officials must prove malice in order to sue the media about reports on their public actions. ...**March 16:** President Lyndon Johnson asks Congress for $962 million for a "war on poverty." ...**July:** Race riots in New York State lead to 6 deaths and more than 1,000 arrests. ...**July 2:** Landmark Civil Rights Act is signed by President Johnson. Act outlaws discrimination of many kinds, including racial, religious and gender-based, in public places, schools and employment. ...**August 4:** Three civil rights workers are found murdered near Philadelphia, Mississippi. ...**August 8:** U.S. Congress passes President Johnson's antipoverty bill with funding of $947 million. ...**September 27:** Warren Commission issues report saying John F. Kennedy was killed by Lee Harvey Oswald acting alone. ...**October 1:** Students begin a 32-hour sit-in on the campus of the University of California at Berkeley after political activities are banned. ...**November 3:** Johnson is reelected president in a landslide victory, defeating Barry Goldwater (1909–1998).

1965. January 4: In his State of the Union speech to Congress, President Johnson calls for the creation of a "Great Society" to eliminate poverty and racial discrimination. ...**February 21:** Malcolm X (b. 1925) is assassinated while addressing a rally in Harlem. ...**March 7:** Alabama state troopers, numbering around 200, attack civil rights protesters as they begin a march led by Martin Luther King Jr. from Selma to Montgomery. ...**March 25:** Some 25,000 civil rights marchers arrive in Montgomery after weeks of confrontation on the road from Selma. ...**July 30:** Medical Care for the Aged (Medicare) is signed by President Johnson. ...**August 6:** Johnson signs the Voting Rights Act, which allows federal supervision of voter enrollment. ...**August 11–16:** Race riots in the Watts district of Los Angeles kill 34, injure more than 800 and cause estimated property damages of $200 million. ...**September 9:** President Johnson signs the Omnibus Housing Act. It creates the Department of Housing and Urban Development, which will be headed by Robert Weaver (1907–1997), the first African American cabinet member. ...**October 3:** United States abolishes immigration quotas by national origins. ...**November 9–10:** Power failure blacks out seven northeastern states and two Canadian provinces.

Asia, Africa & Latin America

1964. March 31: President João Goulart (1918–1976) of Brazil is deposed by Brazilian military. ...**April 8:** United States sends troops to the Dominican Republic to end civil war. ...**April 15:** Goulart is succeeded by Humberto Castelo (1900–1967). ...**April 27:** Tanganyika and Zanzibar unite as Tanzania. ...**May 26:** Organization of American States (OAS) agrees to send a peacekeeping force to the Dominican Republic to replace U.S. troops. ...**May 27:** Indian prime minister Jawaharlal Nehru (b. 1889) dies and is succeeded on June 2 by Lal Bahadur Shastri (1904–1966). ...**June 15:** Last French forces leave Algeria. ...**July 6:** Malawi (Nyasaland) becomes independent nation. ...**August 2:** North Vietnamese allegedly attack U.S. warships in Tonkin Gulf. Retaliatory bombing of North Vietnam begins. ...**September 2:** Indonesian regular troops begin raids on Malaysia. ...**October 24:** Zambia (Northern Rhodesia) becomes independent. ...**November 2:** King Saud (1902–1966) of Saudi Arabia is deposed by his brother Faisal (1906–1975). ...**December 12:** Kenya becomes a republic.

1965. February 18: Gambia becomes independent. ...**March 3:** U.S. Marines begin landing in force in South Vietnam. ...**April 9–June 30:** India and Pakistan fight on Kutch-Sind border. ...**April 30:** U.S. forces protect new leadership after coup in Dominican Republic. ...**June:** United States switches status of its advisers in South Vietnam, about 23,000 military personnel, to combat readiness. ...**June 8:** U.S. troops in Vietnam are authorized to take offensive action. ...**June 19:** The president of Algeria is deposed by Colonel Houari Boumedienne (1927–1978). ...**June 30:** India and Pakistan sign a cease-fire. ...**August 9:** Singapore secedes from Malaysia. ...**September 1–22:** India and Pakistan go to war over Kashmir. ...**September 6:** Indian troops invade West Pakistan. ...**September 29:** Soviet Union announces it is supplying military aid to North Vietnam. ...**October 16:** Afghanistan becomes a parliamentary democracy.

Science, Invention & Technology

1964. Rand Corporation develops the digitizing tablet for computer-aided design systems.

Courtesy: John F. Kennedy Library, Boston, MA

U.S. president John F. Kennedy.

1965. American James Schlatter (1945–) develops aspartame artificial sweetener. ...Stephanie Kwolek (1923–) at Du Pont develops Kevlar synthetic fiber. ...The memory typewriter is introduced by IBM. ...Two amateur Japanese astronomers spot a new comet and name it Ikeya-Seki. ...**February 20:** *Ranger 8*, a satellite launched on February 17, begins to send pictures of the moon's surface back to earth. ...**March 23:** The first manned U.S. *Gemini* flight is launched from Cape Kennedy, Florida. ...**June 3:** Major Edward White (1930–1967) is the first American to walk in space. ...**July:** *Mariner 4* begins to transmit pictures of Mars back to earth. ...**December 8:** First DC-9 jet is put into service by Delta Airlines.

Religion, Culture & Arts

1964. Saul Bellow (1915–), American novelist: *Herzog*. ...*The Persecution and Assassination of Marat, as Performed by the Inmates of the Asylum of Charenton under the Direction of the Marquis de Sade* by Peter Weiss (1916–1982), playwright and director of experimental films, is produced in Germany. ...Cole Porter (b. 1893), composer of popular songs and works for the stage, dies. ...Stanley Kubrick (1928–) directs the film *Dr. Strangelove or: How I Learned to Stop Worrying and Love the Bomb*. ...George Cukor's *My Fair Lady* wins the Academy Award for best picture. ...U.S. bishops approve English for use in Mass. ...**January 5:** Pope Paul VI meets Patriarch Athenagoras I (1886–1964) of the Orthodox Church, the first meeting of a pope and patriarch in more than 500 years. ...**February:** The Beatles make their American debut on the *Ed Sullivan Show*. ...**February 25:** Cassius Clay (1942–) defeats Sonny Liston to become heavyweight boxing champion. (Clay will later change his name to Muhammad Ali.) ...**May 7:** Roman Catholic Church in England and Wales rejects approval of contraceptive pills. ...**September 22:** The musical *Fiddler on the Roof* by Sheldon Harnick (1924–) and Jerry Bock (1928–) opens in New York City. ...**October 7–15:** St. Louis Cardinals defeat New York Yankees to win the World Series.

1965. The Gateway Arch in St. Louis is completed. Designed by Finnish architect Eero Saarinen (1910–1961), it is the largest free-standing arch in the world. ...Derek Walcott (1930–), Antillean dramatist and poet: *The Castaway*. ...Neil Simon (1927–), American playwright: *The Odd Couple*. ...David Lean directs the film *Dr. Zhivago*. ...Robert Wise's *The Sound of Music* wins the Academy Award for best picture. Lee Marvin (1924–1987) is named best actor. Julie Christie (1941–) wins the award for best actress. ...Actress Clara Bow (b. 1905) dies. ...The Rolling Stones have their first big hit in the United States, "(I Can't Get No) Satisfaction." ...Second Vatican Council exonerates the Jews for the crucifixion of Christ. ...**January 4:** Poet T. S. Eliot (b. 1888) dies. ...**March:** The Boston Celtics win their seventh consecutive National Basketball Association championship. ...**August 8:** Writer Shirley Jackson (b. 1916) dies. ...**September:** Second Vatican Council adopts the Declaration on Religious Liberty written by U.S. bishops. ...**October:** Los Angeles Dodgers defeat Minnesota Twins to win the World Series. ...**October 4:** Pope Paul VI addresses the UN General Assembly and conducts Mass in Yankee Stadium. ...**December 8:** Second Vatican Council closes.

International Affairs

1966. Indonesia rejoins the UN. ...**January 15:** Treaty of friendship is signed by Soviet Union and Mongolia. ...**January 30:** France ends boycott of European Economic Community meetings. ...**April 9:** UN gives Britain permission to use force to stop oil shipments to Rhodesia (Zimbabwe). ...**July 1:** France withdraws from NATO.

Western & Eastern Europe

1966. April: Soviet Union announces new Five-Year Plan. ...**March 31:** Labour increases majority in British elections. ...**May 6:** Ian Brady (1938–) and Myra Hindley (1942–) are convicted of the "Moors murders" in Britain and receive life sentences. ...**June 2:** Eamon de Valera is reelected president of Ireland. ...**June 25–July 2:** The 23rd Communist Party Congress of Soviet Union meets in Moscow. ...**July 7:** European Nuclear Energy Agency is created at Mol. ...**July 24:** Members of the European Economic Community finalize the organization of the Common Agricultural Policy. ...**November 9:** John Lynch (1917–) becomes Irish prime minister. ...**November 22:** Spanish government passes new constitution ...**December 31:** The European Free Trade Association (EFTA) ends tariffs for industrial products.

U.S. & Canada

1966. Anti-Vietnam War protests in cities and campuses increase throughout the United States. ...**January 10:** Georgia legislature bars Julian Bond (1940–), African-American activist, from taking his seat because of his anti-Vietnam War statements. ...**June 13:** In *Miranda v. Arizona*, U.S. Supreme Court rules that suspects must be read their rights before interrogation. ...**June 26:** Large civil rights rally is held in Jackson, Mississippi. ...**July 1:** Medicare comes into operation. ...**July 12–15:** Race riots take place in Chicago. ...**July 19:** Richard Speck (1941–) is arrested in Chicago for the slayings of eight student nurses. ...**August 1:** Charles Whitman (1941–1966) kills 16 and wounds 30 by firing from the University of Texas tower. ...**September 11:** Stokely Carmichael (1941–1998), national chairman of the Student Nonviolent Coordinating Committee, is arrested for inciting race riots in Atlanta. ...**September 27:** Race riots take place in San Francisco after a young African American boy is shot. ...**October 15:** U.S. Department of Transportation is established. ...**November 3:** President Lyndon B. Johnson signs the Demonstration Cities and Metropolitan Redevelopment Act, known as the Model Cities Act, which provides $1 billion to revitalize the central areas of up to 70 cities. ...Johnson signs the Clean Waters Restoration Act to clean up U.S. rivers and lakes. ...**November 8:** Edward Brooke (1919–), Republican from Massachusetts, is elected the first African American U.S. senator in 85 years.

◀ French president Charles de Gaulle.

1967. The Association of Southeast Asian Nations (ASEAN) is established by Indonesia, Singapore, Malaysia, Thailand, and the Philippines. ...**January 27:** United States, Soviet Union and 58 other nations sign agreement banning nuclear weapons in space. ...**March 31:** NATO moves its Supreme Headquarters from France to Belgium.

1967. January: More than 13,000 electrical workers go on strike in Spain to protest the arrest of several labor leaders. ...**February 21:** French president Charles de Gaulle publicly condemns the war in Vietnam. ...**March 25:** In London, 2,000 demonstrators protest U.S. involvement in Vietnam. ...**April 4:** Spain increases government control over the press. ...**April 8:** Fighting breaks out between Greek and Turkish Cypriots. ...**April 21:** Military coup by right-wing military officers seizes power in Greece. ...**May 11:** Britain formally applies for membership in the Common Market. ...**May 16:** De Gaulle again vetoes British membership in the Common Market.

1967. February 10: The 25th Amendment to the U.S. Constitution is ratified. The vice president will become president if the chief executive is incapacitated, dies or resigns. If the post of vice president becomes vacant, the president will nominate a new vice president. ...**March 1:** Adam Clayton Powell (1908–1972), African American congressman from New York, is denied his seat because of charges that he misused government funds. ...**April 15:** Large anti-Vietnam War rallies are held in New York City and San Francisco. ...**April 27–October 29:** Canada holds Expo '67 to celebrate the centennial of Canadian confederation.

Asia, Africa & Latin America

1966. January 10: Tashkent Declaration ends confrontation between Pakistan and India. ...**January 11:** Indian prime minister Shastri (b. 1904) dies. ...**January 15:** During military coup in Nigeria, prime minister Sir Abubakar Tafawa Balewa (b. 1912) is assassinated. ...**January 24:** Indira Ghandi (1917–1984) becomes prime minister of India. ...**February 22:** President Milton Obote (1924–) suspends constitution of Uganda. ...**February 24:** Army coup deposes President Kwame Nkrumah of Ghana. ...**March 21:** Chiang Kai-shek is reelected president of Taiwan. ...**April 30:** Great Proletarian Cultural Revolution is launched in China. ...**May 2:** Tibet is made autonomous region of China. ...**May 26:** British Guiana attains independence and is renamed Guyana. ...**June 29:** President Arturo Illia of Argentina is deposed by military leaders and replaced by General Juan Onganía (1914–1995). ...Hanoi and Haiphong, North Vietnam, are bombed by U.S. forces. ...**July 1:** President Mendez Montenegro (1915–1996) returns Guatemala to democratic government. ...**July 8:** King of Burundi, Mwambutsa IV (1912–1977), is deposed. ...**August 1:** Lieutenant Colonel Yakubu Gowon (1934–) succeeds General Johnson Ironsi (1924–1966) as head of state in Nigeria. ...**August 11:** Confrontation between Indonesia and Malaysia ends. ...**August 13:** Cultural Revolution is endorsed by the Central Committee of the Chinese Communist Party. ...**September 6:** South African prime minister Hendrik Verwoerd (b. 1901) is assassinated. ...**September 13:** Balthazar Vorster (1915–1983) becomes prime minister of South Africa. ...**September 30:** Bechuanaland attains independence as republic of Botswana. ...**October 4:** Basutoland attains independence as kingdom of Lesotho. ...**October 13:** South African apartheid laws are extended to South West Africa. ...**November 28:** Burundi becomes a republic.

1967. January: U.S. troops in Vietnam number more than 400,000. ... **March 15:** Brazil gets new constitution under President Artur da Costa e Silva (1902–1969). ...**March 27:** Andrew Juxon-Smith (1933–) assumes power in Sierra Leone and suspends constitution. ...**May:** U.S. planes bomb the center of Hanoi. In Khesanh, U.S. and North Vietnamese troops clash in a long and bloody battle. ...**May 27:** Nigeria is divided into 12 states. ...**May 30:** Biafra, under Lieutenant Colonel Odumegwu Ojukwu (1933–), secedes from Nigeria triggering civil war.

Science, Invention & Technology

1966. Life-support systems become standard equipment on ambulances in United States and Canada. ...Philips Company introduces the stereo audiocassette. ...American Allan Cormack (1924–) and Englishman Godfrey Hounsfield (1919–) develop computerized axial tomography (CAT) scan for visual medical analysis. ...The Houston Astrodome, the first enclosed stadium, opens. ...Fiber optics are first used in telecommunications. ...American Mary Spaeth (1938–) invents the tunable dye laser, which can emit various colors. ...**April 3:** The Soviet spacecraft *Luna 10* is the first spacecraft to achieve lunar orbit. ...**June 2:** *Surveyor I*, launched May 30, makes the first soft landing on the moon and begins transmitting pictures to earth.

1967. German Harald Jensen (1908–1994) develops acelsufame K artificial sweetener. ...American Samuel Kountz (1930–1981) develops a machine for preserving donated kidneys. ...Dr. Rene Favalaro (1923–) at the Cleveland Clinic performs the first coronary bypass surgery. ...American astronomers Jocelyn Bell Burrell (1943–) and Antony Hewish (1924–) use a radio telescope to discover first pulsar. ...**January 27:** Three astronauts—Virgil Grissom (b. 1926), Edward White (b. 1930), and Roger Chaffee (b. 1935)—die in their *Apollo* capsule in a fire that breaks out during tests on the launchpad at Cape Kennedy, Florida.

Religion, Culture & Arts

1966. Lincoln Center in New York City is completed. The most opulent post-war entertainment center, it involved four architects: Philip Johnson, Wallace Harrison (1895–1981), Max Abramovitz (1908–) and Eero Saarinen. ...Yukio Mishima (1925–1970), Japanese writer: *The Sailor Who Fell from Grace with the Sea.* ...Truman Capote: *In Cold Blood.* ...Fred Zinnemann's *A Man for All Seasons* wins the Academy Award for best picture. ...Vatican abolishes the office of inquisitor and the *Index of Forbidden Books* that listed those books banned to Catholics. Vatican announces a liberalization of the fasting and abstinence rules. ...**June 8:** The National Football League and the American Football League announce they will merge and be known as the National Football League. ...**October:** Baltimore Orioles defeat Los Angeles Dodgers to win the World Series. ...**December 15:** Walt Disney (b. 1901), whose name became identified with animation and theme parks, dies.

▲ ***U.S. troops from the First Cavalry Division jump from a UH-1D Iroquois helicopter as part of Operation Oregon during the Vietnam War.***

1967. Gabriel García Marquez (1928–), Colombian novelist: *One Hundred Years of Solitude.* ...The Beatles release *Sgt. Pepper's Lonely Hearts Club Band*, one of the most influential rock albums ever recorded. ...*The Graduate*, directed by Mike Nichols (1931–), is released. ...*In the Heat of the Night* wins the Academy Award for best picture. The star of the film, Rod Steiger (1925–) is named best actor. Katharine Hepburn (1907–) wins as best actress. ...**January:** In the first Super Bowl, Green Bay Packers crush Kansas City Chiefs 35–10. ...**May 15:** Painter Edward Hopper (b. 1883) dies. ...**May 22:** Poet Langston Hughes (b. 1902) dies.

International Affairs

1967 (Continued). June 23 and 25: President Johnson and Soviet premier Aleksei Kosygin hold summit at Glassboro State College in New Jersey. ...**June 30:** Geneva Conference of 53 nations agrees to cut tariffs and to increase food programs to Third World countries. ...**November 30:** British forces withdraw from South Yemen.

1968. Swaziland joins UN. ...**January 19:** Colombia and Soviet Union resume diplomatic relations. ...**January 23:** North Koreans seize USS *Pueblo* and crew in Sea of Japan. ...**March 25:** Iceland joins General Agreement on Tariffs and Trade (GATT). ...**April 22:** United States, Soviet Union and Britain sign an agreement pledging cooperation in the rescue of astronauts. ...**May 10:** Vietnam peace talks begin in Paris. ...**June 12:** Nuclear Nonproliferation Treaty is adopted by UN. ...**July:** The Nuclear Nonproliferation Treaty is signed by 62 nations. ...**August 22:** UN Security Council condemns Soviet-led invasion of Czechoslovakia. ...**December 22:** North Koreans release crew of USS *Pueblo*.

Western & Eastern Europe

1967 (Continued). July 14: British House of Commons passes a law liberalizing abortion. ...**July 27:** British government decriminalizes homosexual acts between consenting adults over 21. ...**September 20:** *Queen Elizabeth II* ocean liner is launched by Queen Elizabeth II. ...**October 27–28:** Student protesters and police clash in Madrid, Spain. ...**November 26:** Heavy rains and winds kill 138 people in Portugal. ...**December 1:** Due to student protests, government officials close Madrid University. ...**December 13:** King Constantine XIII leaves Greece.

1968. Portugal grants franchise to all literate women. ...**April:** In what is known as Prague Spring, Czechoslovakian Communist Party leader Alexander Dubcek (1921–1992) institutes programs of liberalization. ...**March 8–9:** Student unrest breaks out in Poland. ...**April 27:** Britain legalizes abortion in cases when continuing the pregnancy will harm the mother or fetus. ...**May 10:** Students and police battle in Paris during the "Night of the Barricades." ...**May 14:** Czechoslovakian government introduces liberal reforms. ...**June 12:** French government bans student demonstrations. ...**June 30:** Gaullists win big victory in national elections. ...**August 20–21:** Warsaw Pact countries invade Czechoslovakia and overthrow liberal Communist government. ...**September:** Prime Minister Antonio Salazar (1889–1970) of Portugal suffers debilitating stroke and is replaced by Marcelo Caetano (1906–1980). ...**September 29:** New constitution is adopted in Greece.

Shirley Chisholm, the first African American woman elected to U.S. Congress.

U.S. & Canada

1967 (Continued). July 23–30: Race riots in Detroit, Michigan, kill 40 and injure 2,000. Blocks are burned, and some 5,000 are made homeless. ...**October 2:** Thurgood Marshall (1908–1993) becomes the first African American U.S. Supreme Court Justice. ...**October 20:** Mississippi jury convicts 11 men, including the Neshoba County deputy sheriff, for murdering three civil rights workers in August 1964. ...**November 7:** African Americans are elected mayors in major cities for the first time. They are Carl Stokes (1927–1996) in Cleveland, Ohio, and Richard Hatcher (1933–) in Gary, Indiana.

1968. January 30: U.S. Senate confirms Clark Clifford as secretary of defense. ...**February 29:** President's National Advisory Commission on Civil Disorders warns about "white racism" and the United States becoming divided by race. ...**March 16:** Senator Robert F. Kennedy announces his intention to run for president. ...**March 22:** President Lyndon Johnson names General William Westmoreland (1914–) U.S. Army chief of staff. ...**March 31:** President Johnson makes a surprise announcement that he will not run for reelection. ...**April 4:** Civil rights leader Martin Luther King Jr. (b. 1929) is assassinated by James Earl Ray (1928–1998) in Memphis, Tennessee. ...**April 11:** U.S. Congress passes Civil Rights Act of 1968, outlawing racial discrimination in selling and renting houses. ...**April 20:** Liberal Pierre Trudeau (1919–) becomes prime minister of Canada. ...**April 30:** About 630 people are arrested after some 5,000 students conduct a weeklong protest at Columbia University, occupying five buildings on campus. ...**June 6:** Robert Kennedy (b. 1925) dies after being shot the previous day in Los Angeles by Sirhan Sirhan (1944–). ...**June 23:** More than 50,000 campaigners for civil rights and against poverty march on Washington, D.C. They are led by the Reverend Ralph Abernathy (1926–1990), who succeeded Martin Luther King as leader of the Southern Christian Leadership Conference. ...**June 26:** Canada's Liberal Party wins landslide victory behind Trudeau. ...**August 26–29:** Anti-Vietnam War protests and violent police reactions mar Democractic National Convention in Chicago. Vice President Hubert Humphrey (1911–1978) is nominated presidential candidate at that convention. ...**November 5:** Richard M. Nixon wins presidential election. ...Shirley Chisholm (1924–) becomes the first African American woman elected to U.S. Congress. ...**December 11:** United States unemployment hits 3.3 percent, a 15-year low.

Asia, Africa & Latin America

1967 (Continued). June 5: In Six-Day War between Israel and Egypt, Syria and Jordan, Israel takes Sinai, West Bank, Old Jerusalem, and Golan Heights. ...**September 30:** U.S. planes bomb missile sites in North Vietnam. ...**October 9:** Che Guevara (b. 1928), Argentinian guerilla leader, is killed in Bolivia. ...**November 5:** Egypt withdraws from Yemen. President Abdulla-al-Sallal (1920–1994) of Yemen is deposed. ...**November 7:** U.S. planes bomb North Vietnamese railroad facilities near the Chinese border. ...**December 11:** An earthquake in India kills more than 200 people.

1968. Bonin Islands are returned to Japan from the United States. ...**January 31:** Pacific island of Nauru becomes an independent republic. ...**January 31–February 25:** In the Tet Offensive, the Vietcong launch the heaviest and most coordinated effort of the Vietnam War, attacking more than 30 major South Vietnamese cities. Although the attacks by the Vietcong ultimately prove unsuccessful, the offensive helps to turn the tide of American opinion against the Vietnam War. ...**February 19:** Rann of Kutch dispute between India and Pakistan is settled. ...**March:** Labor riots erupt on the island of Antigua. ...**March 12:** Mauritius gains independence. ...**March 26:** Constitutional government is restored in Sierra Leone. Siaka Stevens (1905–1988) becomes prime minister. ...**June:** Uruguay declares limited martial law due to strikes throughout the country. ...**June 20:** Brazilian students take over a building on the campus of the University of Rio de Janeiro to protest poor education facilities. ...**July–August:** Violence between student protesters and police erupts in Mexico. ...**August:** Number of U.S. troops in Vietnam reaches 500,000. ...**September 6:** Swaziland becomes independent nation. ...**September 16:** UN secretary general calls for a halt to the U.S. bombing of North Vietnam. ...**October 3:** During military coup in Peru, General J. Velasco Alvarado (1910–1977) becomes president. ...**October 31:** U.S. halts bombing of North Vietnam. ...**November 29–30:** British troops leave Aden, and People's Republic of South Yemen is proclaimed.

Science, Invention & Technology

1967 (Continued). October: Soviet space probe *Venera 4* lands on Venus. ... **November 9:** The unmanned *Apollo 4* completes a test orbit of earth. ...**December:** South African doctors perform the first human heart transplant. ...**December 14:** Biochemists at Stanford University announce they have produced synthetic DNA.

1968. A vaccine against mumps is licensed for distribution. ...English doctors Robert Edwards (1925–) and Patrick Steptoe (1913–1988) begin research on in vitro fertilization (IVF). ...The first 911 emergency phone number goes into service in New York City. ...American Marcian Hoff (1937–) develops the Intel microprocessor (computer chip). Intel Corporation is founded the same year by Robert Noyce (1927–1990). ...The Soviet Tupelov Tu-144 is world's first passenger supersonic aircraft. ...**September 19:** An unmanned Soviet lunar probe orbits the moon. ...**October 11:** *Apollo 7* begins an 11-day flight, orbiting earth and transmitting live television broadcasts. ...**December 27:** *Apollo 8* completes a five-day flight that includes ten orbits of the moon.

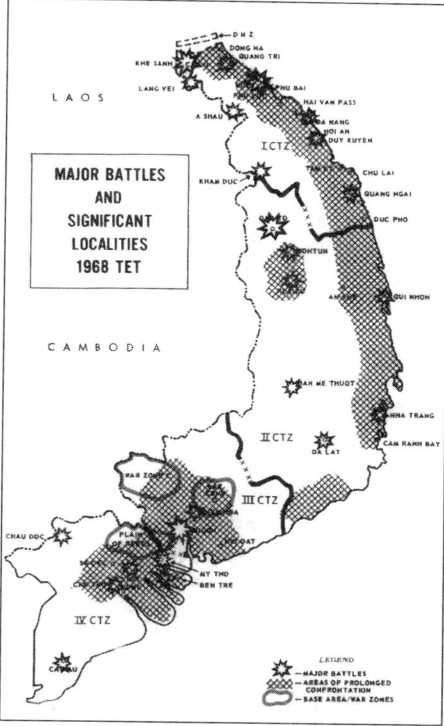

Religion, Culture & Arts

1967 (Continued). June 7: Writer Dorothy Parker (b. 1894) dies. ...**June 10:** Actor Spencer Tracy (b. 1900) dies. ...**October:** St. Louis Cardinals defeat Boston Red Sox to win the World Series. ...**October 3:** Folk singer Woody Guthrie (b. 1912) dies.

1968. James Baldwin (1924–1987), African American writer: *Tell Me How Long the Train's Been Gone*. ...Yasunari Kawabata (1899–1972) is the first Japanese to receive the Nobel Prize for literature. ...William Styron (1925–), American writer: *The Confessions of Nat Turner*, which wins the Pulitzer Prize in fiction. ...Ludwig Mies van der Rohe (1886–1969) designs the National Gallery in West Berlin. ...*2001: A Space Odyssey*, directed by Stanley Kubrick, is released. ...Roman Polanski (1933–) directs *Rosemary's Baby*. ...Carol Reed's *Oliver!* wins the Academy Award for best picture. Cliff Robertson (1925–) is named best actor. Barbra Streisand (1942–) and Katharine Hepburn tie for best actress. ...South African Council of Churches condemns apartheid. ...Albania bans all churches. ...Boston Celtics defeat Los Angeles Lakers to win the NBA championship. ...**January 14:** In the second Super Bowl, Green Bay Packers defeat Oakland Raiders 33–14. ...**April 16:** Novelist Edna Ferber dies. ...**April 29:** The rock musical *Hair*, featuring nudity, opens in New York City. It is written by Gerome Ragni (1942–), James Rado (1939–) and Galt MacDermot (1928–). ...**July 29:** *Humanae Vitae*, a papal encyclical, bans the use of artificial contraceptives by Catholics. ...**September:** Abu-Simbel Nile temples are reerected and relocated from flooded area behind Aswan Dam in Egypt. ...**October:** Detroit Tigers defeat St. Louis Cardinals to win the World Series. ...**November 25:** Upton Sinclair (b. 1878) dies. ...**December 20:** Novelist John Steinbeck (b. 1902) dies.

◄ ***The Tet Offensive was a decisive turning point during the Vietnam War. This map shows the major battles that began on January 31, 1968.***

International Affairs

1969. February 23–March 2: U.S. President Richard M. Nixon visits the leaders of Britain, France, West Germany, Belgium and Italy. ...**March 19:** British forces land on the island of Anguilla after it declares its independence, and they restore its British dependency status. ...**July 23–August 3:** President Nixon travels around the world on goodwill trip that includes a visit to Romania. ...**November 11:** China's 20th application to join the UN is rejected. ...**November 17:** Strategic Arms Limitation Talks (SALT) begin in Helsinki, Finland, between the United States and Soviet Union.

1970. Fiji joins the UN. ...**April 22:** The first international Earth Day to promote environmental improvements is observed. ...**August 12:** Soviet Union and West Germany sign treaty of friendship. ...**September 12:** Palestinian terrorists explode bombs on three hijacked planes in Jordan. ...**September 27:** Arab leaders sign agreement in Cairo to end civil war in Jordan, and the Palestine Liberation Organization (PLO) agrees to leave Jordan.

1971. United Arab Emirates, Bahrain, Qatar, Bhutan and Oman join the UN. ...**February 11:** In Moscow, 40 nations, excluding France and China, sign an agreement banning seabed atomic weapons. ...**May 27:** Egypt and Soviet Union sign treaty of friendship. ...**June 10:** United States ends its trade embargo on China. ...**August 9:** India signs friendship treaty with Soviet Union. ...**August 19:** NATO forces leave Malta. ...**October 1:** Joseph Luns succeeds Manlio Brosio as secretary general of NATO. ...**October 25:** China becomes member of UN. ...Taiwan vacates Security Council seat. ...**December 31:** U Thant resigns as secretary general of UN and is succeeded by Kurt Waldheim (1918–) of Austria.

Western & Eastern Europe

1969. January 1: New Czech constitution is adopted. ...**April 28:** French president Charles de Gaulle resigns after his French constitutional reform referendum is defeated. ...**June 15:** Georges Pompidou is elected president of France. ...**August 13:** Soviet forces violate Chinese border. ...**September 28:** Willy Brandt (1913–1992) forms social democratic government in West Germany.

1970. January 1: Age of majority is lowered to 18 in Britain. ...**March 1:** Socialists win Austrian national elections. ...**March 20:** Soviet Union and Czechoslovakia sign treaty of friendship. ...**March 21–22:** Lenin centenary celebrations are held in Moscow. ...**June 19:** West Germany lowers voting age to 18. ...**July 8:** Alexander Dubcek is expelled by Czech Communist Party. ...**July 16–29:** British dock strike provokes British government to declare state of emergency. ...**July 17–20:** Soviet-Finnish treaty of friendship and mutual assistance is extended for 20 years. ...**October 19:** Major oil deposits are found in the North Sea. ...**November 9:** Charles de Gaulle (b. 1890) dies. ...**December 7:** West Germany and Poland sign treaty recognizing Oder-Neisse Line. ...**December 14–18:** Riots erupt in Polish Baltic ports.

1971. January 31: East Berlin and West Berlin restore telephone connection after 19 years. ...**February 5:** First British soldier on duty in Northern Ireland is killed. ...**February 14:** Soviet Union announces ninth Five-Year Plan. ...**February 15:** Britain adopts decimal currency system. ...**March 23:** Brian Faulkner (1921–1977) becomes prime minister of Northern Ireland. ...**May 3:** Walter Ulbricht (1893–1973) of East Germany is succeeded by Erich Honecker (1912–1994). ...**June 17:** Dom Mintoff (1916–) becomes prime minister of Malta. ...**September 11:** Former Soviet premier Nikita Khrushchev (b. 1894) dies. ...**October 31:** Women are elected to Swiss parliament for the first time. ...**December 24:** Giovanni Leone (1908–1994) becomes sixth president of Italy.

U.S. & Canada

1969. March 28: Dwight D. Eisenhower (b. 1890) dies. ...**May 14:** U.S. Supreme Court justice Abe Fortas (1910–1982) resigns because of allegations he accepted illegal donations. ...**June 9:** Warren Burger (1907–1995) is confirmed by U.S. Senate as chief justice of the Supreme Court. ...**August 9:** Followers of cult leader Charles Manson (1934–) kill actress Sharon Tate (b. 1943), her unborn child and four others. ...**November 15:** Some 150,000 anti-Vietnam War protesters gather in Washington, D.C., in America's largest antiwar rally. ...**November 20:** Alcatraz Island in San Francisco Bay is seized by 78 Native Americans, who demand that it be given to their people. ...**December 6:** Chicago police raid Black Panther headquarters and kill two leaders of the organization.

1970. February 18: "Chicago Seven" antiwar protesters are acquitted of inciting a riot during the 1968 Democratic National Convention in Chicago. ...**May 4:** National Guard troops kill four students at Kent State University in Ohio during an antiwar demonstration. ...**June 20:** Constitutional amendment lowering U.S. voting age to 18 wins ratification. ...**August 12:** U.S. Post Office becomes independent of the government. ...**September 15:** Members of the United Auto Workers go on strike at General Motors in the United States and Canada. ...**October 16:** State of insurrection is proclaimed in Quebec. ...**October 17:** Pierre Laporte (b. 1921), minister of labor for Quebec, Canada, is found dead seven days after being kidnapped by Quebec separatists. ...**November 30:** U.S. population passes 203 million. ...**December 29:** President Nixon signs the Occupational Safety and Health Act.

1971. January 26: Manson and three followers are sentenced to death for the Sharon Tate murders. ...**March 1:** A bomb explodes in a bathroom of the U.S. Senate. No one is injured. ...**March 31:** Lieutenant William Calley Jr. (1943–) is sentenced to life imprisonment for directing the My Lai massacre in Vietnam on March 16, 1968. His sentence is reduced to 20 years on August 20. ...**April 20:** U.S. Supreme Court upholds busing as a means of integrating schools. ...**August 21:** An attempted prison escape at San Quentin, California, results in three prisoners and three guards killed. ...**September 13:** New York State troopers put down Attica prison riot of about 1,000 prisoners after four days. The confrontation leaves 31 prisoners and 9 hostages dead. ...**September 17:** U.S. Supreme Court justice Hugo Black (1886–1971) retires after 34 years.

Asia, Africa & Latin America

1969. March 17: Golda Meir (1898–1978) becomes prime minister of Israel. ...**March 24:** President Ayub Khan (1907–1974) of Pakistan resigns. ...**March 31:** President Yahya Khan (1917–1980) proclaims martial law in Pakistan. ...**May 25:** Sudan is taken over by revolutionary council. ...**July 8:** United States begins withdrawing troops from Vietnam. ...**September 1:** King Idris (1890–1983) of Libya is deposed in bloodless coup led by Muammar Qaddafi (1942–). ...**September 3:** North Vietnamese leader Ho Chi Minh (b. 1890) dies. ...**October 3:** Bhutan becomes a democratic monarchy. ...**October 21:** Somali President Abdirashid Ali Shermarke (b. 1919) is assassinated in military coup.

1970. February 23: Guyana becomes a republic in British Commonwealth. ...**March 18:** Prince Norodom Sihanouk (b. 1922) of Cambodia is deposed by General Lon Nol (1913–1985). ...**March 31:** King Moshoeshoe II (1938–) is exiled from Lesotho. ...**June 4:** Pacific island of Tonga becomes independent. ...**June 22:** President José María Velasco Ibarra assumes dictatorial powers in Ecuador. ...**June 27–July 4:** In general election in Ceylon, Sirimavo Bandaranaike (1916–) forms left-wing coalition. ...**June 29:** Last U.S. troops are withdrawn from Cambodia. ...**July 5:** Luis Echeverría Álvarez (1922–) is elected president of Mexico. ...**September 28:** Egyptian President Abdel Nasser (b. 1918) dies and is succeeded by Anwar Sadat (1918–1981). ...**October 7:** General Juan José Torres (1921–1976) of Bolivia proclaims himself president. ...**October 10:** Fiji becomes independent nation.

1971. March 10: William McMahon (1908–1988) becomes prime minister of Australia. ...**March 11:** In Indian elections, Indira Gandhi is returned to power with clear majority. ...**March 26:** Shaikh Mujibur Rahman (1920–1975) secedes from Pakistan and declares Bangladesh a republic. ...**April 21:** President François Duvalier (b. 1907) of Haiti dies and is succeeded by his son, Jean-Claude (1951–). ...**November 27:** Congo is renamed Republic of Zaire. It will become the Democratic Republic of the Congo in 1997. ...**December 3:** India mobilizes following weeks of fighting on Pakistan border. ...**December 6:** India recognizes Bangladesh's independence. ...**December 14:** Government of Pakistan resigns. ...**December 16:** Pakistan forces surrender to India. ...**December 17:** Pakistan president Khan resigns and is succeeded by Zulfikar Bhutto (1928–1979).

Science, Invention & Technology

1969. The Concorde supersonic jet, built jointly by Britain and France, makes its inaugural transatlantic flight. ...The first artificial heart implant is performed in Texas by Denton Cooley (1920–). ...Random access memory (RAM) replaces magnetic core memories in computers. ...The tilting-disc artificial heart valve is developed. ...American Alan Shugart (1930–) develops the 8-inch floppy disk for computers. ...NASA engineers Maxime Faget (1921–) and Robert Gilruth (1913–) commence work on the space shuttle. ...**July 20:** Neil Armstrong (1930–) and Edwin "Buzz" Aldrin (1930–) become the first men to walk on the surface of the moon. ...**November 14–20:** *Apollo 12* becomes the second mission to land men on the moon.

1970. U.S. government mandates catalytic converters be added to all new automobiles for more efficient fuel consumption. ...Philips Company markets the first videocassette recorder (VCR). ...The first halogen lamps are marketed. ...Chinese American An Wang (1920–1989) introduces the computerized word processor. ...The first electronic cash registers become available.

1971. Ken Thompson (1943–) and Denis Ritchie (1941–) develop UNIX computer operating system at Bell Labs. ...**January:** American astronomers announce the discoveries of two new galaxies. ...**January 31–February 9:** *Apollo 14* becomes the third manned American mission to land on the moon. ...**April:** Soviet Union's space station *Solyut 1* is placed in orbit. ...**July:** Researchers in Texas announce the isolation of a cancer-causing virus in human cells. ...**July 26–August 7:** *Apollo 15* becomes the fourth manned American mission to land on the moon.

Religion, Culture & Arts

1969. Paul Newman (1925–) and Robert Redford (1937–) star in *Butch Cassidy and the Sundance Kid.* ...Mario Puzo (1921–), American novelist: *The Godfather.* ...Kurt Vonnegut (1922–), American novelist: *Slaughterhouse Five.* ...Philip Roth (1933–), American novelist: *Portnoy's Complaint.* ...The Who releases the "rock opera" *Tommy.* ...John Schlesinger's (1926–) *Midnight Cowboy* wins Academy Award for best picture. John Wayne (1907–1979) wins best actor. Maggie Smith (1934–) wins best actress. ...**January 12:** New York Jets defeat Baltimore Colts in Super Bowl III. ...**August 15–18:** Woodstock Music and Art Fair is held in Bethel, New York. ...**October:** New York Mets defeat Baltimore Orioles to win the World Series.

1970. Athol Fugard (1932–), South African playwright: *People Are Living Here.* ...The Beatles announce they will no longer perform as a band. ...The completed New English Bible is published. ...The Church of England creates the General Synod. ...Franklin J. Schaffner's (1920–1989) *Patton* wins the Academy Award for best picture. The film's star, George C. Scott (1927–), is named best actor. Glenda Jackson (1936–) is named best actress. ...**January 11:** Kansas City Chiefs defeat Minnesota Vikings 23–7 in Super Bowl IV. ...**June:** British Methodist Church approves the ordination of women. ...**September 18:** Singer-guitarist Jimi Hendrix (b. 1942) dies. ...**October:** Baltimore Orioles defeat Cincinnati Reds to win the World Series. ...Singer Janis Joplin (b. 1943) dies.

1971. Church of England permits members of other Christian religions to take Communion in its churches. ...Dmitri Shostakovich (1906–1975), Soviet composer: Symphony no. 15. ...William Friedkin's (1939–) *The French Connection* wins the Academy Award for best picture. The film's star, Gene Hackman (1931–) is named best actor. Jane Fonda (1937–) wins best actress. ...**January 17:** Baltimore Colts defeat Dallas Cowboys 16–13 in Super Bowl V. ...**July 3:** Singer-songwriter Jim Morrison (b. 1943) of the Doors dies. ...**September 8:** The Kennedy Center in Washington, D.C., opens with Leonard Bernstein's *Mass.* ...**October:** Pittsburgh Pirates defeat Baltimore Orioles to win the World Series. ...*Look* magazine ends publication. ...**October 17:** The musical *Jesus Christ Superstar*, by Andrew Lloyd Webber (1948–), opens in New York City.

International Affairs

1972. Conference on Security and Cooperation in Europe is established. In 1995, it will be renamed Organization for Security and Cooperation in Europe. ...**April 10:** United States, Britain, Soviet Union and about 70 other nations sign agreement to outlaw biological weapons. ...**April 18:** Bangladesh is admitted to Commonwealth. ...**May 26:** United States and Soviet Union sign SALT I and ABM treaties, limiting the amount of nuclear weapons and outlining the basic principles of détente. ...**June 5–16:** First World Conference on the Human Environment meets in Stockholm. ...**July 8:** United States agrees to sell Soviet Union grain for $650 million. ...**September 5:** Arab terrorists kill 11 Israeli athletes at the Olympics in Munich. ...**October:** United States grants Soviet Union most-favored-nation trading status. ...**November 21:** United States and Soviet Union begin SALT II talks in Geneva.

1973. March 16: Fourteen countries meet in Paris and decide to create a floating exchange-rate system. ...**June 24:** Soviet leader Leonid Brezhnev, visiting the United States, becomes the first Soviet leader to speak to Americans on television. ...**August 15:** United States ends bombing of Cambodia ...**August 29:** Egypt and Libya are united. ...**September 18:** West Germany and East Germany join the UN. ...**October 21:** Arab nations impose a total ban on exporting oil to the United States. ...**December 17:** Arab terrorists hijack a German airliner at Rome airport and kill 31 people.

Western & Eastern Europe

1972. January 14: Frederick IX (b. 1899) of Denmark dies and is succeeded by his daughter Margrethe II (1940–). ...**January 22:** The European Economic Community (EEC) Treaty is signed by Britain, Ireland, Denmark, and Norway. ...**January 30:** British troops kill 13 civilians in Northern Ireland on Bloody Sunday. ...**February 9:** Coal strike causes British government to declare state of emergency. ...**March 21:** George Papadopoulos (1919–1996) becomes regent of Greece. ...**March 30:** British government suspends Stormont and assumes direct rule in Northern Ireland. ...**June 1–15:** West German police arrest Baader-Meinhof terrorists. ...**July 5:** Pierre Messmer (1916–) succeeds Jacques Chaban-Delmas (1915–) as French prime minister. ...**September 26:** Norway withdraws application from EEC treaty, following referendum. ...**December 21:** West Germany and East Germany sign a treaty to establish friendly and equal relationships.

1973. January 1: Britain, Denmark and Ireland become members of EEC ...**February:** The European Trade Union Confederation is established. ...**March 2–19:** Currency crisis forces European exchange markets to close. ...**April 28:** In Barcelona, Spain, 24,000 auto workers go on strike, crippling the Spanish automobile industry. ...**June 12:** A car bomb in Coleraine, Northern Ireland, kills 6 people and injures 33. ...**September 16:** Gustav VI (b. 1882) of Sweden dies and is succeeded by his grandson, Carl XVI Gustav (1946–). ...**October 15:** Britain and Iceland end year-long "Cod War," a dispute over fishing rights. ...**November 24:** An IRA bomb explodes in the Northern Ireland town of Newry, killing 3 people and injuring 36. ...**December 18:** IRA begins Christmas bombing campaign in London's shopping areas. ...**December 20:** Spanish prime minister Luis Carrero Blanco (b. 1903) is assassinated in Madrid.

U.S. & Canada

1972. January 20: New York Stock Exchange accepts its first female governor, Juanita Morris Kreps (1921–). ...**March 22:** U.S. Senate passes (84 to 8) the Equal Rights Amendment, which bans discrimination against women, and sends it to the states for ratification. ...**May 2:** J. Edgar Hoover (b. 1895), director of the FBI, dies. ...**May 15** Governor George Wallace of Alabama is shot and paralyzed during a presidential campaign stop in Laurel, Maryland. ...**June 4:** Angela Davis (1944–), an African American Communist and activist, is found not guilty of murder and conspiracy by a jury in San Jose, California. ...**June 17:** Five men are arrested for breaking into Democratic National Committee headquarters in the Watergate office building in Washington, D.C. They were trying to install listening devices. ...**June 29:** U.S. Supreme Court declares death penalty violates Constitution. ...**November 7:** Richard M. Nixon wins reelection in a landslide over George McGovern (1922–). ...**November 9:** Andrew Young (1932–) from Georgia becomes the first Southern African-American Congressman elected since Reconstruction.

1973. January 22: In *Roe v. Wade*, U.S. Supreme Court rules that states cannot prevent a woman from having an abortion in the first three months of her pregnancy. ...**April 30:** Watergate involvement causes the resignation of Attorney General Richard Kleindienst (1923–) and presidential aides H. R. Haldeman (1926–1993), John Ehrlichman (1925–1999) and John Dean (1938–). ...**June 25:** Dean tells U.S. Senate hearings that Nixon conspired to cover up Watergate break-in. ...**July 17:** U.S. Senate Watergate Committee asks for President Nixon's tapes, but he refuses to provide them. ...**October 10:** Vice President Spiro T. Agnew (1918–1996) resigns after being charged with tax evasion while he was governor of Maryland. ...**October 12:** U.S. Court of Appeals orders President Nixon to hand over his Watergate tapes. ...**October 20:** President Nixon orders Attorney General Elliot Richardson (1920–) to fire special prosecutor Archibald Cox, but Richardson resigns along with his assistant William Ruckelshaus (1932–). Solicitor General Robert Bork (1927–) then fires Cox. ...**November 1:** Nixon administration selects Leon Jaworski (1905–1982) as special Watergate prosecutor to replace Cox. ...**November 9:** Six Watergate defendants are sentenced. ...**December 6:** Gerald Ford (1913–) is sworn in as vice president, having been appointed to replace Agnew.

Asia, Africa & Latin America

1972. January 13: Kofi Busia (1913–1978) is deposed by military coup in Ghana. Lieutenant Colonel Ignatius Kutu Acheampong (1931–1979) takes power. ...**February 15:** President José María Velasco Ibarra of Ecuador is deposed by Brigadier General Guillermo Rodríguez Lara (1923–). ...**March 28:** First parliamentary elections are held in Gambia. ...**April 7:** President Abeid Karume (b. 1905) of Zanzibar is assassinated. ...**April 14:** United States resumes bombing of Hanoi and Haiphong in North Vietnam. ...**April 21:** Zulfikar Bhutto becomes president of Pakistan under new constitution. ...**May 15:** Pacific islands of Ryukyu and Okinawa revert to Japan. ...**May 22:** Ceylon becomes republic of Sri Lanka. ...**July 21:** King of Bhutan (b. 1929) dies and is succeeded on July 24 by Crown Prince Jigme Singhi Wangchuk (1955–). ...**August 9:** President Idi Amin of Uganda orders expulsion of Asians holding British passports. ...**December 4:** President Ramón Ernesto Cruz (1903–1985) of Honduras is overthrown in military coup and is succeeded by Oswaldo López Arellano (1922–).

1973. January 27: Peace agreement for Vietnam is signed. U.S. troops cease hostilities in Vietnam and begin withdrawal. ...**February 12:** North Vietnam releases first U.S. prisoners of war. ...**March 11:** Argentine general elections give Perónists 50 percent of vote and 45 of 69 senate seats. ...**March 29:** Last U.S. combat troops leave Vietnam. ...**July 4:** Caribbean Community and Common Market (CARICOM) is established for economic, educational, cultural and other areas of cooperation. ...**July 17:** King Zahir (b. 1914) of Afghanistan is deposed by General Mohammad Daoud (1908–1978); republic is proclaimed. ...**August 12:** Fazal Elahi is elected president of Pakistan. Bhutto becomes prime minister. **August 14:** Pakistan's new constitution comes into effect. ...**September 4:** Guinea-Bissau proclaims itself independent from Portugal. ...**September 11:** Leftist government of President Salvador Allende (1908–1973) of Chile is overthrown by armed forces. ...**September 23:** Juan Perón is elected Argentinian president. His wife, Isabel Perón (1931–), becomes vice president. ...**October 6–25:** Yom Kippur War: Egyptian and Syrian troops attack Israel during Jewish holiday. Israelis maintain positions and gain ground on east bank of the Suez Canal. ...**October 14–16:** Military regime in Thailand is overthrown by student revolt. ...**November 11:** Israel and Egypt sign a cease-fire agreement.

Science, Invention & Technology

1972. Texas Instruments introduces the electronic calculator with light-emitting diode (LED). ...Researchers discover that chlorofluorocarbons deplete the earth's upper atmosphere (ozone). ...Godfrey Hounsfield patents the CAT scanner. ...U.S. Environmental Protection Agency bans use of DDT. ...United States launches the first *LANDSAT* earth surveying satellite. ...Polaroid SX-70 color film is introduced. It makes instant ten-second photographs. ...John Charnly (1911–1982) perfects his Teflon joint replacement procedure for human patients. ...**April 20–23:** Astronauts John Young (1930–) and Charles Duke (1935–) spend a record 71 hours on the surface of the moon. ...**June 26:** U.S. Air Force introduces its F-15 jet fighter. ...**December 7–19:** *Apollo 17* becomes the last American manned mission to land on the moon.

1973. DuPont develops polyethylene-terephthalate, a plastic strong enough to hold carbonated beverages. ...Point of sale (POS) computer terminals become available to the retailing industry. ...First cochlear implant is made in the human ear. ...Typewriters with correction tape are introduced. ...**April 5:** United States launches *Pioneer 11* on an unmanned mission to explore Jupiter. ...**May 24:** The U.S. *Skylab* space station is put into orbit.

Religion, Culture & Arts

1972. *The Godfather*, directed by Francis Ford Coppola (1939–), wins the Academy Award for best picture. The star of the film, Marlon Brando, is named best actor but refuses to accept the award. Liza Minnelli (1946–) wins best actress. ...United Reform Church is created in Britain by merger of Presbyterian Church in England and Congregational Church in England and Wales. ...**January 16:** Dallas Cowboys defeat Miami Dolphins 24–3 to win Super Bowl VI. ...**October:** Oakland Athletics defeat Cincinnati Reds to win the World Series. ...**October 24:** Jackie Robinson (b. 1919) dies. ...**November 1:** Poet Ezra Pound (b. 1885) dies.

1973. Mother Teresa (1910–1997) is given the first Templeton Prize for Progress in Religion. ...Eudora Welty (1909–), American writer: *The Optimist's Daughter*. ...George Roy Hill's (1922–) *The Sting* wins the Academy Award for best picture. Jack Lemmon (1925–) is named best actor. Glenda Jackson wins as best actress. ...**January 14:** Miami Dolphins defeat Washington Redskins 14–7 in Super Bowl VII. ...**October:** Oakland Athletics defeat New York Mets to win the World Series.

Courtesy: NASA, Washington, D.C.

▲ ***An official photo of* Apollo 17 *astronauts taken in October 1972, two months before the last manned American mission to the moon. Posing on their moon rover are (l-r): Harrison Schmitt, Ron Evans and Gene Cernan.***

International Affairs

1974. Bangladesh, Grenada and Guinea-Bissau join UN. ...**March 18:** Arab nations lift total ban on oil exports to United States. ...**April 16:** UNICEF announces plans to aid areas in North Vietnam. ...**June 27:** Summit meeting between President Richard M. Nixon and Soviet leader Leonid Brezhnev begins in Moscow. ...**September 4:** United States establishes formal relations with East Germany. ...**November 24:** President Gerald Ford and Brezhnev discuss the SALT II treaty, but no progress is made. ...**December:** OPEC leaders agree to raise the price of oil and adopt a new, uniform pricing system. ...World Intellectual Property Organization (WIPO), established in 1970, becomes agency of the UN.

1975. April 29–30: Final evacuation of U.S. military personnel from Saigon as Communists enter city. ...**May 15:** U.S. Navy and Marines come to the aid of the U.S. merchant ship *Mayaguez*, captured by Cambodia, but lose 38 servicemen in the rescue of 39 seaman. ...**June 16:** Simonstown (naval) agreement between Britain and South Africa ends. ...**June 17:** Residents of the Northern Mariana Islands vote to become a U.S. territory. ...**July 15:** United States and Soviet Union cooperate in the *Apollo-Soyuz* space mission. ...**August 1:** The final act to guarantee human rights and international peace is signed by 30 European nations at the Helsinki Conference on Security.

Western & Eastern Europe

1974. January 10: British mine workers begin strike. ...**February 13:** Aleksandr Solzhenitsyn (1918–) is expelled from Soviet Union after publication of *The Gulag Archipelago*. ...**February 27:** Swedish royal family loses its powers. ...**February 28:** British general elections result in no overall majority for Conservatives or Labour. ...**March 4:** Edward Heath (1916–) resigns as British prime minister. Harold Wilson forms Labour government. ...**March 11:** British mineworkers end strike after £103 million pay settlement. ...**April 25:** Portuguese government is overthrown by military. President Américo Tomás (1894–1987) and Prime Minister Marcelo Caetano (1904–1980) are detained. Antonio Spínola (1910–1996) heads government. ...**May 6:** West German chancellor Willy Brandt resigns, and Helmut Schmidt (1918–) takes over. ...**May 19:** Valery Giscard d'Estaing (1926–) is elected French president. ...**July 15:** Archbishop Makarios of Cyprus is overthrown in military coup. ...**October 10:** Labour Party wins slim majority in British national elections. ...**November 17:** Konstantino Karamanlis (1907–) is elected prime minister of Greece. ...**November 23:** Military dictatorship ends in Greece. ...**November 28:** Britain passes prevention of terrorism bill.

1975. February 1: Norway imposes a one-year ban on immigration of foreign laborers. ...**February 13:** Turkish Cypriot state is proclaimed in northern part of island. ...**February 18:** Italy's Constitutional Court rules that abortions are legal if the physical or mental health of the mother is in danger. ...**May 29:** Gustav Husák (1913–1991) becomes president of Czechoslovakia. ...**June 5:** Britain votes to remain within EEC ...**June 7:** New Greek constitution is adopted. ...**June 18:** First North Sea oil is pumped to British mainland. ...**August 29:** Eamon de Valera (b. 1882) of Ireland dies. ...**October 7:** East Germany and Soviet Union sign 20-year treaty of friendship, cooperation and mutual assistance in Moscow. ...**October 24:** "Guildford Four" are sentenced to life imprisonment for IRA bombings of British pubs. ...**November 1:** Catalan and Basque languages are legalized in Spain. ...**November 20:** General Francisco Franco (b. 1892) of Spain dies; King Juan Carlos I (1938–) takes power.

U.S. & Canada

1974. January 31: U.S. Congress passes the Child Abuse Prevention and Treatment Act. ...**April 3:** President Nixon announces that he will pay $432,787 in back income taxes. ...**May 9:** Hearings concerning the impeachment of President Nixon begin in the House Judiciary Committee. ...**July 9:** Earl Warren (b. 1891), former chief justice of the U.S. Supreme Court, dies. ...**July 24:** U.S. Supreme Court rules President Nixon must turn over tapes to Leon Jaworski, the special Watergate prosecutor. ...**July 24–30:** House Judiciary Committee recommends three articles of impeachment against President Nixon. ...**August 9:** Nixon resigns as president as a result of Watergate scandal and is succeeded by Vice President Gerald Ford. ...**August 26:** Charles A. Lindbergh (b. 1902), who made the first transatlantic solo flight, dies. ...**September 9:** President Ford pardons Nixon. ...**September 12:** Sporadic violence begins in south Boston as busing to integrate schools begins. The troubles last three months. ...**November 5:** Ella Grasso (1919–1981) becomes Connecticut's first female governor. ...**December 19:** Nelson A. Rockefeller (1908–1979) is sworn in as U.S. vice president.

1975. February 27: Attorney General Edward Levi (1911–) tells House of Representatives subcommittee that J. Edgar Hoover, former head of the FBI, kept illegal files on politicians and political activists. ...**March 9:** Work begins on the Alaskan pipeline. ...**March 11:** Commission on Civil Rights reports that schools in the South are more integrated than those in the North. ...**June 10:** A panel headed by Vice President Rockefeller reports that the CIA illegally spied on about 30,000 political activists and infiltrated radical groups. ...**July 28:** U.S. Congress extends the Voting Rights Act of 1965 for seven more years. ...**July 31:** James Hoffa (b. 1913), former head of the Teamsters Union, is missing. He will not be found and will be presumed murdered. ...**September 5:** President Ford survives an assassination attempt in Sacramento, California. ...**September 22:** President Ford survives another assassination attempt when a radical protester in San Francisco fires a single shot. ...**November 12:** William O. Douglas (1898–1980) resigns from the U.S. Supreme Court after 36 years. ...**December 9:** President Ford signs a bill that authorizes the U.S. Treasury to loan New York City $2.3 billion each year until 1978 to avoid that city's bankruptcy.

Asia, Africa & Latin America

1974. February 7: Grenada becomes an independent nation within British Commonwealth. ...**February 22:** Pakistan recognizes Bangladesh. ...**April 11:** Golda Meir resigns, and General Yitzhak Rabin (1922–1995) becomes prime minister of Israel on April 26. ...**May 8:** India's railway workers begin a nationwide strike, demanding higher wages, shorter hours and less expensive food. **May 28:** India's railway strike is crushed by the government, resulting in 25,000 to 50,000 arrests. ...**June 13:** Military coup in Yemen Arab Republic (Northern Yemen). ...**July 1:** Juan Perón (b. 1895) dies and is succeeded by his wife, Isabel Perón, as president of Argentina. ...**July 20:** Turkey invades Cyprus. ...**September 12:** Emperor Haile Selassie (1892–1975) of Ethiopia is deposed by military coup. ...**September 26:** Guinea-Bissau is granted independence by Portugal.

1975. March 25: King Faisal (b. 1905) of Saudi Arabia is assassinated and is succeeded by King Khaled (1913–1982). ...**April 5:** Chiang Kai-shek (b. 1887), president of Taiwan, dies and is succeeded by Yen Chia-kan (1905–1993). ...**April 30:** South Vietnam surrenders to Communist forces, ending the Vietnam War. ...**May 26–28:** Economic Community of West African States (ECOWAS) is created. ...**June 5:** Suez Canal reopens to international shipping. ...**June 25:** Mozambique becomes independent. ...**July 6:** Comoros Islands declare independence from France. ...**July 29:** General Yakuba Gowan (1934–) is overthrown as Nigeria's head of state in bloodless coup. General Murtala Muhammad (1917–1976) replaces him. ...**August 15:** Shaikh Mujibur Rahman (b. 1920) of Bangladesh is assassinated by pro-Pakistani soldiers. ...**August 27:** Ethiopian emperor Haile Selassie (b. 1891) dies. ...**August 29:** President Juan Alvardo (1910–1977) of Peru is overthrown and replaced by General Francisco Morales Bermúdez (1921–). ...**September 16:** Papua New Guinea becomes independent. ...**November 11:** Angola becomes independent. ...**November 25:** Surinam becomes independent. ...**December 3:** Communist forces gain complete control of Laos. ...**December 7:** Indonesia invades Portuguese East Timor.

Science, Invention & Technology

1974. American Bill Gates (1955–) writes a BASIC software application for personal computers. ...The artificial sweetener aspartame is approved by the U.S. Food and Drug Administration (FDA). ...Ibuprofen is made available as a prescription drug under the name Motrin.

1975. Raymond Kurzweil (1948–) at MIT develops a reading machine for the blind. ...Chlorofluorocarbons are banned in the U.S. ...The axial combine harvester is developed by International Harvester and New Holland companies. ...American Joseph Harrington (1908–1986) develops *autofacturing*, first fully automated unmanned industrial work station. ...**February:** Scientists at the University of Arizona discover evidence in the atmosphere of Jupiter. ...**July 17:** A U.S. *Apollo* spacecraft and a Soviet *Soyuz* spacecraft link up in space, 140 miles above the surface of the earth. ...**October:** Two Soviet spacecraft, the *Venera 9* and the *Venera 10*, land on Mars and begin to transmit pictures back to the earth.

Religion, Culture & Arts

1974. May 24: Duke Ellington (b. 1899), African American jazz composer and band leader, dies. ...Martin Scorsese (1942–) directs *Mean Streets*. ...*The Godfather, Part II* wins the Academy Award for best picture. The director of the film, Francis Ford Coppola, is named best director. ...**January 13:** Miami Dolphins beat Minnesota Vikings 24–7 to win Super Bowl VIII. ...**October:** Oakland Athletics beat Los Angeles Dodgers to win their third consecutive World Series.

1975. *Nashville*, directed by Robert Altman (1925–), is released. ...*Jaws*, directed by Steven Spielberg (1947–), is released. ...*One Flew Over the Cuckoo's Nest* wins the Academy Award for best picture. The film's director, Milos Forman (1932–) is named best director while the two stars of the film, Jack Nicholson (1937–) and Louise Fletcher (1940–), win the awards for best actor and best actress. ...Bruce Springsteen releases the album *Born to Run*. ...**January 12:** Pittsburgh Steelers defeat Minnesota Vikings 16–6 to win Super Bowl IX. ...**June 18:** The Anglican Church of Canada votes in favor of ordaining women. ...**September 14:** Mother Elizabeth Ann Seton (1774–1821) becomes the first person born in the United States to become a saint. ...**October:** Cincinnati Reds defeat Boston Red Sox to win the World Series. ...**December 7:** Thornton Wilder (b. 1897) dies.

On August 9, 1974, Richard M. Nixon became the first U.S. president to resign from office. In this photo, Nixon departs from the lawn of the White House moments after his resignation became official. ➤

International Affairs

1976. January 13: Argentina, in a dispute over the Falkland Islands, breaks diplomatic relations with Britain ...**June 18:** International Fund for Agricultural Development (IFAD) of UN established. ...**July 3:** Israeli commandos rescue 103 hostages on hijacked plane at Entebbe, Uganda.

1977. Vietnam joins the UN. ...**June 30:** Southeast Asia Treaty Organization (SEATO) is terminated. ...**September 7:** United States and Panama sign Panama Canal Treaty dealing with defense and permanent neutrality until 1999, when U.S. jurisdiction will end. ...**November 5:** United States withdraws from International Labor Organization. ...**December:** International Fund for Agricultural Development begins operations.

1978. Dominica and Solomon Islands join UN. ...**June 29:** Vietnam is admitted to COMECON. ...**September 5–17:** At the Camp David Summit, Anwar Sadat, Menachim Begin (1913–1992) and Jimmy Carter meet to discuss peace between Egypt and Israel. ...**December 10:** Begin and Sadat receive Nobel Peace Prize for reaching Mideast accord.

Western & Eastern Europe

1976. February 19: Iceland breaks diplomatic relations with Britain over new "Cod War" fishing rights. ...**February 24–March 5:** The 25th Congress of Communist Party of the Soviet Union is held in Moscow. ...**March 5:** Britain imposes direct rule on Northern Ireland. ...**April 5:** James Callaghan (1912–) becomes British prime minister. ...**June 1:** Iceland and Britain end "Cod War." ...**June 20:** Communists make gains in Italian national elections. ...**October 13:** Charter 77 manifesto demanding reforms in human rights is published in Czechoslovakia.

1977. January 3: Britain borrows $3.9 billion from International Monetary Fund. ...**March 15:** British government nationalizes shipbuilding and aircraft industries. ...**April 9:** Communist Party is legalized in Spain. ...**May 14:** Don Juan de Borbón renounces all claims to the Spanish throne. ...**June 16:** Leonid Brezhnev is elected chairman of the Presidium of the Supreme Soviet. ...**July 1:** Free trade in industrial products is approved by the European Free Trade Association (EFTA) and the European Community (EC). ...**August 3:** Makarios (b. 1913) of Cyprus dies and is succeeded by Spyros Kyprianou (1932–). ...**September 29:** Catalonia is granted autonomy within Spanish state.

1978. European Court rules that EC law has precedence over a member nation's law. ...**January 18:** European Court of Human Rights rules that Great Britain is guilty of inhumane treatment of Northern Ireland prisoners. ...**January 23:** Sweden becomes first country to ban aerosol sprays. ...**March 16:** Red Brigade terrorists in Italy kidnap former prime minister Aldo Moro (1916–1978). ...**April 3:** First radio broadcasts of British Parliamentary sessions begin. ...**May 9:** Moro's body is found in Italy after government refuses terrorists' demands. ...**October 31:** New Spanish constitution replaces the Fundamental Laws of Franco's regime. ...**November 27:** Mikhail Gorbachev (1931–) becomes secretary of the Central Committee of the Communist Party of the Soviet Union.

U.S. & Canada

1976. July 2: U.S. Supreme Court rules that capital punishment is constitutional. ...**July 14:** Canada ends death penalty. ...**August 1:** Flash flooding in the Colorado River Canyon kills 139. ...**September 30:** California enacts "right-to-die" law, the nation's first. ...**October 4:** U.S. secretary of agriculture Earl Butz resigns after making a racist joke. ...**November 2:** Jimmy Carter (1924–) is elected president, narrowly defeating Gerald Ford. ...**November 15:** The separatist Parti Québécois wins Quebec provincial election. ...**December 3:** Carter names Cyrus Vance (1917–) secretary of state. ...**December 6:** Thomas P. "Tip" O'Neill (1912–1994) becomes Speaker of the House. ...**December 20:** Richard Daley (b. 1902), controversial mayor of Chicago, dies.

1977. January 17: Gary Gilmore (b. 1940), a convicted murderer, is executed by a Utah firing squad, the first U.S. execution in ten years. ...**January 21:** President Carter pardons most of the estimated 10,000 U.S. Vietnam War draft dodgers. ...**June 10:** James Earl Ray, convicted killer of Martin Luther King Jr., and six other convicts escape from Tennessee's Brushy Mountain State Prison. They will be captured three days later. ...**June 30:** United States cancels development of the B-1 bomber. ...**July 13:** New York City has an extensive power blackout, and some 4,000 looters are arrested. ...**August 4:** U.S. Energy Department is created. ...**September 8:** United States and Canada agree to build a pipeline from Canadian gas fields to the United States ...**November 18–21:** First National Women's Conference is held in Houston. ...**December 10:** Farmers demand increased government support by driving their tractors into 30 state capitals.

1978. June 28: U.S. Supreme Court rules that racial quotas are unconstitutional. It found that Allan Bakke (1940–), a white applicant to the University of California Medical School at Davis, suffered reverse discrimination when he was rejected. ...**October 6:** Hannah Hilborn Gray (1930–) becomes president of the University of Chicago; she is the nation's first African American university president. ...**October 20:** The Dow Jones Industrial Average drops 59.08 points. ...**October 26:** President Carter signs the Government Ethics Law, requiring financial disclosures by politicians and judges. ...**December 16:** Cleveland, Ohio, becomes the first U.S. city to default on payments since the Great Depression.

Asia, Africa & Latin America

1976. January 8: Chinese leader Chou En-lai (b. 1898) dies and is succeeded by Hua Kuo-feng (1920–) on February 8. ...**February 13:** General Murtala Muhammad (b. 1917) of Nigeria is assassinated in an attempted coup. ...**March 24:** President Isabel Perón of Argentina is overthrown by military. General Jorge Videla (1925–) becomes president on March 29. ...**June 12:** President Juan María Bordaberry Arocena (b. 1928) of Uruguay is deposed. ...**July 2:** Reunification of Vietnam is proclaimed. ...**September 9:** Chinese Communist leader Mao Zedong (b. 1893) dies. ...**November 1:** President Michel Micombero (1940–1983) of Burundi is overthrown. A 30-member Supreme Council of Revolution assumes power. ...**December 1:** José López Portillo (1920–) is elected president of Mexico.

1977. February 3: Teferi Benti (b. 1921), Ethiopian head of state, is assassinated. ...**March 18:** President Marien Ngouabi (b. 1938) of Congo is assassinated by commando squad. ...**March 22:** Indira Gandhi resigns as prime minister of India and is replaced two days later by Morarji Desai (1896–1995). ...**June 27:** Republic of Djibouti, formerly French Territory of the Afars and Issas, becomes independent. ...**July 5:** General Muhammad Zia (1924–1988) becomes president of Pakistan after military coup. ...**July 22:** Chinese Communist Party expels Gang of Four. ...**September 12:** African nationalist leader Steven Biko (b. 1946) dies in police custody in South Africa. ...**November 19:** President Anwar Sadat of Egypt arrives in Israel on peace mission. ...**December 25:** Prime Minister Menachem Begin of Israel visits Egypt on peace mission.

1978. John Vorster (1915–1983) becomes president of the Republic of South Africa. ...**April 19:** Yitshak Navon (1921–) is elected president of Israel. ...**July 7:** Solomon Islands become independent. ...**July 21:** Juan Pereda Asbón (1932–) becomes president of Bolivia and is deposed by General David Padilla Arancibia on November 24. ...**August 22:** Kenyan independence leader Jomo Kenyatta (b. 1889) dies. ...**November 3:** Dominica becomes independent. ...**December 8:** Former Israeli prime minister Golda Meir (b. 1898) dies.

Science, Invention & Technology

1976. A pivoting bileaflet artificial heart valve is introduced at St. Jude Medical Center in Fullerton, California. ...DNA analysis is first used in prenatal testing. ...Keuffel & Esser (K & E) Company donates its last slide rule to the Smithsonian Institution in Washington, D.C. ...An ultrasonic surgery device for cataract removal is developed in the United States. ...The inkjet computer printer is introduced by IBM. ...The HEARSAY-II computer speech recognition machine is developed at Carnegie-Mellon University in Pittsburgh. ...Genentech Company, first genetic engineering firm, is established in United States. ...The *Viking I* probe lands on Mars.

1977. American Gordon Gould (1920–) patents the laser, which he originally developed in the 1960s. ...Americans Steve Jobs (1955–) and Stephen Wozniak (1950–) build the Apple II, first viable personal computer. ...Polaroid Corporation introduces instant home movies on cassette. ...Hungarian Erno Rubik (1944–) patents the Rubik's Cube puzzle toy. It will become a fad in the United States. ...The United States secretly develops the F-117A stealth aircraft, built largely of materials that evade radar detection.

1978. Bell Labs introduces Advanced Mobile Phone Service in Chicago. It is the first cellular phone service. ...The computer program CHESS 4.5, developed at Northwestern University in Chicago, is capable of master-level chess competition. ...Magnavox Company introduces its videodisc player, a digital compact disc player. ...IBM markets first typewriter with rotary print wheels. ...**November 15:** Anthropologist Margaret Mead (b. 1901) dies.

Religion, Culture & Arts

1976. Saul Bellow's *Humboldt's Gift* is awarded the Nobel Prize for literature. ...Martin Scorsese directs *Taxi Driver*, starring Robert De Niro (1943–). ...John G. Avildsen's (1935–) *Rocky*, written by and starring Sylvester Stallone (1946–), wins the Academy Award for best picture. ...**January 12:** Agatha Christie (b. 1891), British writer of detective stories, dies. ...**January 18:** Pittsburgh Steelers defeat Dallas Cowboys in Super Bowl X. ...**July:** Vatican suspends Monsignor Marcel Lefebre (1905–1991) because of his opposition to Second Vatican Council. ...**September 16:** Episcopal Church approves the ordination of women. ...**October:** Cincinnati Reds defeat New York Yankees to win the World Series.

1977. Centre National d'Art et de Culture Georges Pompidou (Pompidou Center), designed by British architect Richard Rogers (1933–), opens in Paris. ...John Travolta (1954–) stars in John Badham's (1939–) *Saturday Night Fever*. The film's soundtrack, with several songs by the Bee Gees, becomes one of the best-selling albums in history. ...*Annie Hall* wins the Academy Award for best picture. The film's director, Woody Allen (1935–), is named best director, and its star, Diane Keaton (1946–), wins the best actress award. ...**January 9:** Oakland Raiders beat Minnesota Vikings 32–14 to win Super Bowl XI. ...**September 16:** Maria Callas (b. 1923), Greek American opera singer, dies. ...**October:** New York Yankees defeat Los Angeles Dodgers to win the World Series. ...**November 10:** Roman Catholic bishops in the United States announce that Pope Paul VI will no longer excommunicate divorced American Catholics who marry again.

1978. Isaac Bashevis Singer is awarded the Nobel Prize for literature. ...John Irving (1942–), American writer: *The World According to Garp*. ...Michael Cimino's (1943–) *The Deer Hunter* wins the Academy Award for best picture. Jon Voight (1938–) is named best actor. Jane Fonda wins best actress. ...**January 15:** Dallas Cowboys defeat Denver Broncos 27–10 in Super Bowl XII. ...**June 9:** Mormon Church declares African Americans can be admitted to priesthood. ...**August 6:** Pope Paul VI (b. 1897) dies. ...**August 27:** John Paul I (b. 1912) is elected pope but dies on September 28. ...**October:** New York Yankees defeat Los Angeles Dodgers to win the World Series. ...**October 16:** John Paul II (1920–) is elected pope, the first non-Italian pope in 450 years. ...**November 8:** Painter and illustrator Norman Rockwell (b. 1894) dies.

International Affairs

1979. St. Lucia joins the UN. ...**January 1:** United States and China restore diplomatic relations. ...**February 23–March 16:** Northern Yemen and Southern Yemen engage in war. **March 29:** Northern Yemen and Southern Yemen sign an agreement of unification. ...**June 18:** SALT II Treaty to limit amount of nuclear weapons is signed by U.S. president Jimmy Carter and Soviet leader Leonid Brezhnev in Geneva. ...**July 11:** Whaling is banned in Red Sea, Arabian Sea and most of the Indian Ocean. ...**October 7:** NATO reaffirms its decision to deploy long-range nuclear weapons in Europe.

1980. Zimbabwe and St. Vincent and the Grenadines join the UN. ...United States rejoins the International Labor Organization. ...**January 24:** United States agrees to sell arms to China. ...**January 29:** Canadians help six U.S. embassy aides flee Iran. ...**February 26:** Israeli and Egyptian ambassadors are exchanged for the first time. ...**April 7:** United States breaks off diplomatic relations with Iran. ...**July 19:** Olympic Games open in Moscow but are boycotted by more than 30 countries, including the United States, as protest against Soviet invasion of Afghanistan.

Western & Eastern Europe

1979. January 1: Jura is established as a new canton of the Swiss Confederation. ...**March 13:** European monetary system is inaugurated. ...**March 31:** British military presence in Malta ends. ...**May 3:** Conservative Party wins majority in British general election. Margaret Thatcher (1925–) becomes first female British prime minister. ...**June 7 and 10:** First direct elections to the European Parliament are held. ...**July 6:** West Germany abolishes statute of limitations on war crimes. ...**August 27:** Earl Mount- batten (b. 1900) of Burma is murdered by IRA terrorists.

1980. January 12–14: West German Green Party is formally constituted as a national political party. ...**March 2:** Swiss national referendum rejects separation of church and state. ...**April 10:** Spain reopens border with Gibraltar (it closed in 1969). ...**April 30:** Queen Juliana of the Netherlands abdicates in favor of her daughter, Princess Beatrix (1938–). ...**May 4:** Tito (b. 1892), leader of Yugoslavia, dies. ...**August 1:** Vigdís Finnbogadóttir (1930–) becomes president of Iceland. ...**August 14:** Polish workers strike and occupy Gdansk shipyard. ...**September 17:** Anti-Communist Solidarity movement is founded in Poland. ...**October 26:** About 50,000 people march in London for the Campaign for Nuclear Disarmament. ...**December 4:** Francisco Sá Carneiro (b. 1934), Portuguese prime minister, is killed in airplane crash. ...**December 7:** António Ramalho Eanes (1935–) is reelected president of Portugal. ...**December 18:** Soviet politician Aleksei Kosygin (b. 1904) dies.

U.S. & Canada

1979. January: William Clements (1917–) becomes first elected Republican governor of Texas since Reconstruction. ...**February 5:** Farmers drive tractors and other vehicles into Washington, D.C., to jam traffic in a protest over low price supports for agriculture. ...**March 28:** Radioactive material is released during a partial meltdown in a nuclear reactor on Three Mile Island near Harrisburg, Pennsylvania. ...**May 18:** Jury awards $10.5 million to the estate of Karen Silkwood, who sued the Kerr-McGee plutonium plant for radiation poisoning. She was killed in an automobile crash that some believe was suspicious. ...**May 22:** Progressive Conservative Party wins Canadian national elections, and Joseph Clark (1939–) becomes Canada's youngest prime minister. ...**July 25:** Paul Volcker (1927–) is appointed chairman of the Federal Reserve Board. ...**October 30:** Shirley Hufstedler (1925–) is appointed head of the new U.S. Department of Education. ...**November 1:** U.S. government announces $1.5 billion loan to the Chrysler Corporation.

1980. January 18: Gold rises to $802 on the New York financial market. ...**February 18:** Pierre Trudeau wins a second term as prime minister of Canada as his Liberal Party wins the national elections. ...**March 27:** Silver market drops $5 an ounce to $10.80, wiping out profits made by the Texas brothers Nelson and W. Herbert "Bunker" Hunt, who had manipulated the market until the price was $50 an ounce. ...**March 31:** U.S. banking industry is deregulated. ...**April 2:** President Jimmy Carter signs a law diverting high oil industry profits to the Internal Revenue Service. ...**May 18:** Mount St. Helens volcano in Washington State erupts and causes widespread destruction. Some 60 people are killed in this and subsequent eruptions May 25 and June 12. ...Race riots in Miami kill 17. ...**May 20:** Quebec votes against giving the Parti Québécois government a mandate to negotiate independence from Canada. ...**June 20:** U.S. Congress deregulates trucking industry. ...**June 27:** Peacetime draft registration is established for men aged 19 and 20. ...**November 4:** Ronald Reagan easily defeats Jimmy Carter in presidential elections. ...**November 21:** Fire at the MGM Grand Hotel in Las Vegas kills 81.

Asia, Africa & Latin America

1979. January 6–7: Vietnamese invade Cambodia and capture Phnom Penh. ...**February 1:** Ayatollah Khomeini (1900–1989) returns to Iran from exile in France. ...**March 26:** Egypt and Israel sign peace treaty, ending the state of war. ...**June 20:** President Yusuf Lule (1912–1985) of Uganda is ousted and replaced by Geoffrey Binaisa (1920–). ...**July 17:** Anastasio Somoza Debayle (1925–1980) resigns as president of Nicaragua and goes into exile. ...**September 20:** Emperor Jean-Bédel Bokassa (1921–) of the Central African Empire is deposed by French-backed coup. ...**October 15:** Military coup overthrows President Carlos Romero (1924–) of El Salvador. ...**October 26:** President Chung Hee Park (b. 1917) of South Korea is assassinated by members of Korean central intelligence agency. ...**November 1:** President Walter Guevára Arze (1911–1996) of Bolivia is overthrown in coup. ...**November 4:** U.S. embassy in Tehran is seized by Islamic revolutionary "students," who will hold 59 Americans hostage until January 20, 1981. ...**December 27:** Over 30,000 Soviet troops begin to cross the Afghanistan border to shore up pro-Soviet Afghans.

1980. March 30: President Ton Duc Thang (b. 1888) of Vietnam dies. ...**April 18:** Republic of Zimbabwe becomes independent. ...**April 25:** U.S. commandos fail to rescue American hostages in Iran, and eight commandos die. ...**June 12:** Masayoshi Ohira (b. 1910), Japanese prime minister, dies. ...**June 23:** Sanjay Gandhi (b. 1946) is killed in plane accident in India. ...**July 27:** The shah of Iran (b. 1919) dies of cancer in Cairo. ...**July 30:** Israel makes Jerusalem its capital. ...**September 7:** Zhao Ziyang becomes Chinese prime minister. ...**September 11:** New constitution takes effect in Chile. ...**September 17:** Former president Somoza (b. 1925) of Nicaragua is assassinated in Paraguay. ...**September 19:** Iraq invades and occupies 90 square miles of Iran. ...**September 22:** Conflict between Iran and Iraq escalates. ...**October 18:** Australians reelect Malcolm Fraser (b. 1930) as prime minister for second term. ...**October 26:** Julius Nyerere (1922–) is elected president of Tanzania for fifth term. ...**October 30:** Peace and border treaty is signed by El Salvador and Honduras. ...**November 20:** Trial of Gang of Four, leading Chinese radicals of the Cultural Revolution, opens in Beijing. It will be concluded on December 29. The defendants are accused of many abuses, including causing the deaths of more than 34,000 people. ...**November 24:** Trinidad and Tobago holds first parliamentary election.

Science, Invention & Technology

1979. Sony Corporation of Japan markets the first Walkman headphone sets. ...The United States bans use of polychlorinated biphenyl (PCB) because of the toxic effect of accumulated amounts in the human body.

Courtesy: Jimmy Carter Library, Atlanta, GA

Canadian prime minister Pierre Trudeau (left) visits U.S. president Jimmy Carter (right) at the White House in 1977.

1980. Frenchman Étienne-Émile Baulieu (1926–) develops the steroid RU 486. ...A trace atmosphere is discovered on the planet Pluto. ...Luis Alvarez (1911–1988) postulates that the extinction of the dinosaurs was caused by a meteor impact.... Ultrasound begins to be used for routine fetal examinations.

Courtesy: Ronald Reagan Library, Simi Valley, CA

Mother Teresa accepts the Medal of Freedom from U.S. president Ronald Reagan in 1985.

Religion, Culture & Arts

1979. Peter Shaffer (1926–), British dramatist: *Amadeus.* ...Francis Ford Coppola directs the film *Apocalypse Now.* ...Robert Benton's (1932–) *Kramer vs. Kramer* wins the Academy Award for best picture. The film's star, Dustin Hoffman (1937–), wins the award for best actor. Sally Field (1946–) wins best actress. ...**January 21:** Pittsburgh Steelers defeat Dallas Cowboys 35–31 to win Super Bowl XIII. ...**March 25:** Robert Runcie (1921–) becomes Archbishop of Canterbury for the Church of England. ...**October:** Pittsburgh Pirates defeat Baltimore Orioles to win the World Series. ...**October 17:** Nobel Peace Prize is awarded to Mother Teresa for her work with poor of India.

1980. Church of England publishes the *Alternative Service Book*, its first new prayer book since 1662. ...Philip Glass (1937–), American composer: the opera *Satyagraha.* ...Film director Alfred Hitchcock (b. 1899) dies. ...Martin Scorsese directs the film *Raging Bull.* ...Robert Redford's *Ordinary People*, starring Mary Tyler Moore (1937–), wins the Academy Award for best picture. Robert De Niro is named best actor. Sissy Spacek (1949–) wins as best actress. ...Norman Mailer's *The Executioner's Song* wins the Pulitzer Prize for nonfiction. ...U2 release their debut album, *Boy.* ...**January:** Pittsburgh Steelers defeat Los Angeles Rams 31–19 in Super Bowl XIV. ...**March 24:** Archbishop Romero (b. 1917) of El Salvador is murdered. ...**June 8:** Novelist Henry Miller (b. 1891) dies. ...**October:** Philadelphia Phillies beat Kansas City Royals to win the World Series. ...**December 8:** Former Beatle John Lennon (b. 1940) is murdered in front of his apartment complex in New York City.

International Affairs

1981. Antigua and Barbuda, Belize, and Vanuatu join the UN. ...**April 24:** United States ends its embargo on selling grain to the Soviet Union. ...**May 6:** United States expels all Libyan diplomats. ...**June 8:** Israeli warplanes bomb nuclear reactor being built in Iraq. ...**August 19:** U.S. Navy planes down two Libyan warplanes off the coast of Libya. ...**December 28:** United States imposes an embargo on high technology exports to the Soviet Union.

1982. January 1: Javier Pérez de Cuellar (1920–) of Peru becomes secretary-general of the UN. ...**April 2:** Argentina invades the Falkland Islands. ...**April 3:** UN Security Council demands Argentina withdraw forces from the Falkland Islands. ...**May 2:** Britain lands on East Falklands, and on June 15 Argentinian troops surrender the Falkland Islands. ...**June 29:** Strategic Arms Reduction Talks (START) open in Geneva.

1983. St. Kitts and Nevis joins the UN ...**January 18:** Funding of International Monetary Fund is increased for emergencies. ...**September 1:** Soviet warplane shoots down South Korean airliner, killing all 269 onboard. ...**October 28:** United States vetoes UN resolution condemning U.S. military intervention in Grenada.

Western & Eastern Europe

1981. January 1: Greece joins European Community. ...**January 29:** Adolfo González (1932–) resigns as Spanish prime minister. ...**February 4:** Gro Harlem Brundtland (1939–) is elected Norway's first female prime minister. ...**February 9:** General Wojciech Jaruzelski (1923–) becomes Polish prime minister. ...**May 10:** Giscard d'Estaing is defeated by François Mitterand (1916–1996) in French presidential election. ...**June 14:** Referendum on equal rights for women in Switzerland succeeds. ...**June 16:** Liberals and Social Democratic Party in Britain form political and electoral alliance. ...**June 21:** Socialists win landslide victory in French national elections. ...**August 3–5:** Solidarity union protesters blockade Warsaw's business district. ...**September 5–10:** Solidarity union holds first national congress in Poland. ...**September 30:** France abolishes the death penalty. ...**December 13:** Martial law is declared in Poland.

1982. January 27: Mauno Koivisto (1923–) becomes president of Finland. ...**June 30:** Spain joins NATO. ...**August 8:** France grants Corsica its own assembly. ...**September 14:** Princess Grace, the former Grace Kelly (b. 1929) of Monaco, dies. ...**October 8:** Solidarity union is banned in Poland. ...**November 10:** Soviet leader Leonid Brezhnev (b. 1906) dies. Yuri Andropov (1914–1984) succeeds him as general secretary of Communist Party. ...**December 2:** Felipe González (1942–) becomes Spanish prime minister. ...**December 12:** About 20,000 women camp around RAF base at Greenham Common to protest U.S. cruise missile deployment there.

1983. March 6: Christian Democrats win German national elections. ...**May 26:** Steingrímur Hermannsson (1928–) becomes prime minister of Iceland. ...**June 9:** Conservatives under prime minister Margaret Thatcher increase majority in British election. ...**June 16:** Yuri Andropov becomes chairman of the Presidium of the Supreme Soviet. ...**July 21:** Poland ends martial law. ...**October 5:** Lech Walesa (1943–) of Poland's Solidarity movement is awarded Nobel Peace Prize. ...**October 22:** Protests are held throughout Europe over U.S. deployment of cruise and Pershing II missiles.

U.S. & Canada

1981. March 30: President Ronald Reagan is shot and wounded in front of a Washington, D.C., hotel. ...**June 22:** U.S. naturalizes 9,700 people in Memorial Stadium in Los Angeles. It is the nation's largest naturalization ceremony ever. ...**July 18:** Two elevated walkways collapse in the Hyatt Hotel in Kansas City, Missouri, killing 111. ...**July 22:** Chrysler Corporation announces a profit after two years of record losses and government loans. ...**July 29:** U.S. Congress passes largest tax cut in nation's history. ...**August 3:** Federal air traffic controllers begin a nationwide strike. Most will be fired by President Reagan two days later. ...**September 21:** Sandra Day O'Connor (1930–) becomes the first female associate justice of the U.S. Supreme Court. ...**November 3:** George Wallace wins fourth term as Alabama governor, this time with African American support. ...**December 4:** President Reagan expands CIA power to include domestic intelligence gathering.

1982. March 25: Canada Act making Canada a fully sovereign state, passes British Parliament. ...**June 30:** After ten years, Equal Rights Amendment fails to win ratification by three states (of 38 required). ...**July 10:** A Pan American 727 airliner crashes in New Orleans, killing 156. ...**July 28:** San Francisco bans the sale and possession of handguns. It is the nation's first city ban. ...**October 5:** Johnson & Johnson recall Tylenol, the aspirin substitute, after seven people in Chicago die after taking Tylenol that was laced with cyanide. ...**October 13:** President Reagan signs the Job Training Partnership Act, which promotes cooperation between government and business.

1983. January 12: President Reagan names Elizabeth Dole (1936–) secretary of transportation. ...**March 23:** President Reagan proposes a "Star Wars" defense system. ...**April 13:** Chicago elects its first African American mayor, Harold Washington (1922–1987). ...**April 24:** Some 80,000 Canadians in many cities protest U.S. plans to test cruise missiles in Alberta. ...**May 24:** Jesse Jackson (1941–) becomes first African American to address the Alabama legislature. ...**August 27:** Some 250,000 people march on Washington, D.C., seeking "Jobs for Peace and Freedom" on the 20th anniversary of Martin Luther King Jr.'s famous Washington march. ...**November 2:** President Reagan signs law that creates Martin Luther King Day, a national holiday to be celebrated on the third Monday in January.

Asia, Africa & Latin America

1981. January 20: Iran releases U.S. hostages after 444 days. ...**January 25:** Jiang Qing (1914–1991), widow of Mao Zedong, is sentenced to death (later commuted to life imprisonment) for atrocities committed during China's Cultural Revolution. ...**May 24:** President Jaime Roldós Aguilera (b. 1940) of Ecuador is killed in an airplane crash and is succeeded by Osvaldo Hurtado Larrea (1941–). ...**June 16:** President Ferdinand Marcos (1917–1989) of the Philippines is reelected. ...**August 1:** Panamanian dictator Omar Torrijos Herrera (b. 1929) is killed in an airplane crash. ...**October 5:** Sayyed Ali Khamenei (1940–) is elected president of Iran. ...**October 6:** President Anwar Sadat (b. 1918) of Egypt is assassinated by Muslim extremists. Hosni Mubarak (1928–) becomes president on October 13. ...**December 3:** South African government gives "independence" to Ciskei Black Homeland. ...**December 14:** Israel annexes Golan Heights.

1982. January 27: Honduras ends military rule and installs President Roberto Suazo Córdova (1927–). ...**June 5:** Israeli forces invade Lebanon. ...**June 13:** King Khaled (b. 1913) of Saudi Arabia dies and is succeeded by King Fahd (1923–). ...**June 17:** President Leopoldo Galtieri (1926–) of Argentina is replaced by Reynaldo Bignone (1928–). ...**August 31:** First phase of withdrawal of PLO and Syrian forces from Beirut, Lebanon begins. ...**September 14:** President Bashir Gemayel (b. 1947) of Lebanon is assassinated in Beirut and is succeeded by Amin Gemayel (1942–) on September 23. ...**September 26:** U.S., French and Italian peacekeeping troops enter Lebanon.

1983. June 18: Li Xiannian (1905–1992) is elected president of China. ...**June 24:** Yasir Arafat (1929–), leader of the PLO, is expelled from Syria. ...**August 21:** Opposition leader Benigno Aquino (b. 1932) is assassinated on his return to Philippines from exile. ...**September 15:** Israeli prime minister Begin resigns and is replaced by Yitzhak Shamir (1915–) on October 10. ...**October 14:** Prime Minister Maurice Bishop (b. c. 1945) of Grenada is overthrown. He will be murdered on October 19. ...**October 23:** Suicide bomber kills 241 American marines and navymen in Beirut, Lebanon. ...**October 25:** U.S. and Caribbean military forces intervene in Grenada. ...**December 5:** Military junta in Argentina is dissolved. New civilian government under President Raúl Alfonsín (1927–) takes office on December 10 and announces that junta members face criminal charges.

Science, Invention & Technology

1981. U.S. Centers for Disease Control identifies Acquired Immune Deficiency Syndrome (AIDS). ...Floppy disks for computers are first marketed. ...IBM markets its first personal computer. ...Aseptic sterilized food packaging becomes commercially available. ...**April 12–14:** U.S. space shuttle *Columbia* makes its first voyage.

1982. Atari Company of Japan develops video games. ...Insulin, created from genetically altered organisms, is approved by the FDA. ...**December 2:** The first totally artificial heart, the Jarvik-7, designed by Robert Jarvik (1946–), is implanted into the chest of Barney Clark (1921–1983) by Dr. William de Vrie (1943–) at the University of Utah Medical Center.

1983. Aspartame artificial sweetener is approved by the U.S. FDA for use in carbonated beverages. ...The Cellular One mobile telephone system is introduced in the United States. ...Ashton-Tate introduces the dBASE computer database in United States. ...Apple Computer, Inc., introduces the first mouse peripheral. ...Ibuprofen is made available over the counter in the United States. ...Sony and Philips jointly introduce the prerecorded optical compact disc. ...**March 23:** Artificial heart recipient Barney Clark (b. 1921) dies after 112 days. ...**April 4–9:** The U.S. space shuttle *Challenger* makes its first voyage. ...**June 18–24:** Sally Ride (1951–) is the first American woman in space during the second flight of the space shuttle *Challenger*.

Religion, Culture & Arts

1981. Karel Reisz (1926–) directs the film *The French Lieutenant's Woman*. ...*Chariots of Fire* wins the Academy Award for best picture. Henry Fonda (1905–1983) is named best actor. Katharine Hepburn wins best actress. ...**January:** Oakland Raiders defeat Philadelphia Eagles 27–10 in Super Bowl XV. ...**May 11:** The musical *Cats* by Andrew Lloyd Webber opens in London. ...**May 13:** Pope John Paul II is wounded in an assassination attempt by Mehmet Ali Agca. ...**October:** Los Angeles Dodgers defeat New York Yankees to win the World Series. ...**November 12:** Church of England approves the ordination of women.

1982. Thomas Keneally (1935–), Australian novelist: *Schindler's Ark*. ...Richard Attenborough's (1923–) *Gandhi* wins the Academy Award for best picture. The star of the film, Ben Kingsley (1946–), is named best actor. Meryl Streep (1951–) wins as best actress. ...Michael Jackson's (1958–) *Thriller*, the best-selling album in history, is released. ...U.S. Catholic Conference begins the National Catholic Telecommunications Network. ...Vatican resumes diplomatic relations with Britain after more than 400 years. ...**January:** San Francisco 49ers defeat Cincinnati Bengals 26–21 in Super Bowl XVI. ...**October:** St. Louis Cardinals beat Milwaukee Brewers to win the World Series.

1983. African American novelist Alice Walker's (1944–) *The Color Purple* wins the Pulitzer Prize for fiction. ...William Golding (1910–1993), British novelist, is awarded Nobel Prize for literature. ...James L. Brooks's (1940–) *Terms of Endearment* wins the Academy Award for best picture. The film's star, Shirley MacLaine (1934–), is named best actress. Robert Duvall (1931–) wins as best actor. ...R.E.M. release their debut album, *Murmur*. ...**January:** Washington Redskins defeat Miami Dolphins 23–17 to win Super Bowl XVII. ...**May 28:** Pope John Paul II makes the first visit to Britain by a sitting pope. ...**October:** Baltimore Orioles defeat Philadelphia Phillies to win the World Series.

International Affairs

1984. Brunei joins UN. ...**January 1:** United States deploys missiles in northern Europe. ...**January 10:** Vatican establishes full diplomatic relations with United States. ...**February:** Libyan People's Bureau in London is taken over by "revolutionary students." ...**April 22:** Britain severs diplomatic relations with Libya. ...**April 26–May 1:** President Ronald Reagan visits China and signs agreement for cultural exchanges. ...**July 8:** Olympic Games open in Los Angeles and are boycotted by 17 countries. ...**September 26:** Joint Declaration on Hong Kong is initialized by China and Britain. It is ratified by the British Parliament on December 5 and 10 and signed in Beijing on December 19. Britain is to hand over Hong Kong to China in 1997. ...**November 26:** United States renews diplomatic relations with Iraq. ...**December 11:** UN Law of the Sea Treaty is signed by 159 nations; abstentions include Britain, United States and West Germany. ...**December 31:** United States withdraws from UNESCO over mismanagement and anti-U.S. bias.

1985. Commercial whaling is banned by the International Whaling Commission. ...**February 20:** British prime minister Margaret Thatcher addresses the U.S. Congress. ...**May 5:** President Reagan visits Germany for ceremonies in the Bergen-Belsen concentration camp and the Bitburg cemetery containing Nazi graves. ...**June 14–30:** Shiite Muslim terrorists hijack TWA airplane and kill U.S. navy man before releasing passengers and crew. ...**July 11:** French agents sink Greenpeace ship *Rainbow Warrior* in New Zealand, killing one. ...**September 9:** United States begins limited economic sanctions against South Africa. ...**September 10:** European Community (EC) imposes economic sanctions on South Africa. ...**September 22:** Group of Seven major industrial nations is established to discuss world economy. They are United States, Canada, Britain, France, West Germany, Italy and Japan. ...**October 7:** Palestinian terrorists hijack Italian cruise liner *Achille Lauro* off the coast of Egypt and kill one American. ...**November 19–20:** President Reagan and Soviet leader Mikhail Gorbachev hold a summit in Geneva, Switzerland. ...**November 25:** Egyptian troops in Malta storm airliner hijacked by terrorists in Athens; 59 die.

Western & Eastern Europe

1984. February 9: Soviet president Yuri Andropov (b. 1914) dies. ...**March 12:** British coal miners at 100 mines strike. ...**April 11:** Konstantin Chernenko (1911–1985) succeeds Yuri Andropov as Soviet leader. ...**May 26:** Danube Black Sea Canal opens. ...**October 12:** Prime Minister Thatcher and British cabinet members escape unharmed in IRA bombing at Brighton hotel. ...**October 19:** Pro-Solidarity Polish priest Jersy Popieluszko (b. 1947) is kidnapped and murdered by internal affairs police.

1985. February 1: Greenland withdraws from European Community. ...**February 4–5:** Spain reopens its border with Gibraltar. ...**March 10:** Soviet leader Chernenko (b. 1911) dies, and Mikhail Gorbachev is appointed Communist Party general secretary on March 11. ...President Konstantinos Karamanlis of Greece resigns and is succeeded on March 29 by Christos Sartzetakis (1929–). ...**April 11:** Enver Hoxha (b. 1908) of Albania dies and is succeeded on April 13 by Ramiz Alia (1925–). ...**July 2:** Andrei Gromyko (1909–1989) is elected president of the Soviet Union. ...**September 28–29:** Major riots by blacks break out in the Brixton section of London. ...**November 15:** In Anglo-Irish agreement on Northern Ireland, Ireland agrees not to contest Northern Ireland's allegiance to Britain. **December 17:** Ulster Unionist MPs resign over Anglo-Irish accord.

U.S. & Canada

1984. United States records 79 bank failures, the most since 1938. ...**February 29:** Pierre Trudeau resigns as Canadian prime minister and leader of the Liberal Party. ...**May 12:** World's Fair opens in New Orleans. Only 7 million, instead of the predicted 12 million, will attend. It will be a financial failure and close on November 11. ...**July 11:** New York passes a compulsory seat belt law, the nation's first. ...**July 12:** At the Democratic Convention, Representative Geraldine Ferraro (1935–) is chosen as the first female vice presidential candidate. ...**August:** Fires destroy 250,000 acres in Montana. ...**September 4:** Brian Mulroney (1939–), a Conservative, becomes prime minister of Canada. ...**November 6:** President Reagan is reelected in a landslide victory over Walter Mondale (1928–). ...**December 22:** Bernard Goetz (1947–) shoots and wounds four African American teenagers on a New York subway. He later claims he acted in self-defense.

1985. Canada and United States establish a team to investigate acid rain. ...**January 20:** Ronald Reagan is inaugurated and begins his second term as U.S. president. ...**February 17:** General William Westmoreland drops his $120 million libel suit against CBS for a documentary saying he lied about enemy troop strengths during the Vietnam War. ...**July 10:** Coca-Cola, which introduced a new taste in April that was rejected by customers, announces it will produce the original version as Coca-Cola Classic. ...**August 2:** Delta Airlines airplane crashes at Dallas–Fort Worth airport, killing 136. ...**August 25:** Bar Harbor Airlines plane crash in Maine kills Samantha Smith, the 13-year-old who had visited the Soviet Union a year earlier as an unofficial ambassador. ...**December 12:** Charter airplane crash off Gander, Newfoundland, kills 258 U.S. servicemen of the U.S. 101st Airborne Division.

Asia, Africa & Latin America

1984. January 3: Brunei gains independence. ...**February:** UN peacekeeping troops begin withdrawing from Lebanon. ...**April 12:** Edward Sokoine (b. 1938), president of Tanzania, is killed in accident. ...**June 5:** Indian troops attack Sikh militants in Golden Temple in Amritsar. ...**August 4:** Upper Volta is renamed Burkina Faso. ...**September 10:** Ethiopia becomes a Communist state under Mengistu Mariam (1937–). ...**September 14:** P. W. Botha (1916–) becomes president of South Africa. ...**October 27:** Famine relief to Ethiopia begins. ...**October 31:** Indian prime minister Indira Gandhi (b. 1917) is assassinated by her security guards and is succeeded by her youngest son, Rajiv (1944–1991). ...**November 4:** Leftist Sandinistas led by Daniel Ortega (1945–) win elections in Nicaragua. ...**November 25:** Uruguay returns to civilian rule. ...**November 29:** After Vatican mediation, treaty settles Beagle Channel dispute between Argentina and Chile. ...**December 3:** Union Carbide chemical plant disaster in Bhopal, India, leaves 1,745 dead and 200,000 injured.

1985. January 10: Ortega is sworn in as president of Nicaragua. ...**January 15:** Tancredo Neves (b. 1910) is elected first civilian president of Brazil since 1964, but dies on April 21 before taking office. ...**January 25:** Triracial and tricameral parliament are inaugurated in South Africa. ...**January 31:** President Botha of South Africa offers Nelson Mandela (1918–) freedom if he renounces violence. The offer is refused. ...**March 28:** President Devan Nair (1923–) of Singapore resigns. ...**April 10:** China ratifies agreement with Britain on future of Hong Kong. ...**April 22:** José Sarney (1930–) becomes president of Brazil. ...**April 24:** Israel completes second phase of withdrawal from southern Lebanon. ...**May 8–9:** Violence breaks out in New Caledonia over independence issue. ...**May 24:** Cyclone at mouth of Ganges causes 10,000 deaths in Bangladesh. ...**June 14:** South African security forces searching for members of the African National Congress raid houses in Gaborone, Botswana. ...**June 20:** North Korea and South Korea reach limited agreement on economic cooperation. ...**July 20:** State of emergency is declared in 36 areas of the Transvaal and eastern Cape provinces of South Africa following unrest in Soweto. ...**July 29:** Tito Okello (1914–1996) is sworn in as president of Uganda. ...**September 2:** Pol Pot (1926–1998) resigns as head of Khmer Rouge army. ...**September 19:** Massive earthquake destroys large areas of Mexico City, killing more than 4,000 people.

Science, Invention & Technology

1984. *European 3* satellite project discovers that solar wind sweeps through space at more than 1 million kilometers an hour. ...Apple introduces its Macintosh personal minicomputer. ...First e-mail service is offered on computer networks. ...Factor VIII, genetically engineered blood clotting agent, is proved effective. ...**August 30–September 5:** U.S. space shuttle *Discovery* makes its first voyage.

1985. Gerd Binnig (1947–) and Calvin Quate (1923–) design the first atomic force microscope (AFM). ...First affordable facsimile (fax) machines become widely available. ...British Antarctic survey discovers a hole in the ozone layer over Antarctica.

Courtesy: Ronald Reagan Library, Simi Valley, CA

◀ ***President-elect George Bush (left), President Ronald Reagan (center) and Soviet leader Mikhail Gorbachev (right) field reporters' questions during Gorbachev's December 1988 visit to New York City.***

Religion, Culture & Arts

1984. Italy ends official state link with Roman Catholic religion. ...Milan Kundera (1929–), Czech-born French novelist: *The Unbearable Lightness of Being*. ...Wim Wenders (1945–), German film director: *Paris, Texas*. ...Milos Forman's *Amadeus* wins the Academy Award for best picture. ...**January:** Los Angeles Raiders defeat Washington Redskins 38–9 to win Super Bowl XVIII. ...**April 26:** Count Basie (b. 1904), African American band leader, dies. ...**May 19:** Britain's poet laureate Sir John Betjeman (b. 1906) dies. ...**August 25:** Truman Capote (b. 1924), American novelist, dies. ...**July 9:** Lightning damages York Minister, England, three days after the controversial David Jenkins (1925–) is consecrated bishop of Durham there. ...**October:** Detroit Tigers defeat San Diego Padres to win the World Series. ...**October 7:** Twenty-four U.S. nuns place a full-page ad in the *New York Times* supporting a woman's right to have an abortion.

1985. Edward James (Ted) Hughes (1930–1998) becomes the British poet laureate. ...Christo (1935–), U.S. avant-garde artist, wraps the Pont Neuf bridge in Paris in sheeting. ...Lloyds Building, designed by British architect Richard Rogers (1933–), opens in London. ...Sydney Pollack's (1934–) *Out of Africa* wins the Academy Award for best picture. ...**January:** San Francisco 49ers defeat Miami Dolphins in Super Bowl XIX. ...**July 13:** Live Aid charity concerts, featuring several top rock and pop performers, are held in Philadelphia and London to raise money for African famine relief. ...**October:** Kansas City Royals defeat St. Louis Cardinals to win the World Series.

International Affairs

1986. UN Industrial Development Organization (UNIDO) is established as specialized agency. ...**January 7:** U.S. imposes economic sanctions on Libya. ...**March 16:** Switzerland rejects UN membership in referendum. ...**April 14–15:** United States warplanes bomb Libya in retaliation for terrorist attack on Berlin night club frequented by U.S. soldiers. ...**April 15:** European Community imposes diplomatic sanctions on Libya because of terrorist acts. ...**June 20:** UN conference of 120 countries in Paris urges sanctions against South Africa. ...**September 16:** European Community agrees to ban new investment in South Africa and ban South African imports of iron, steel and gold coins into Europe. ...**October 10:** Javier Pérez de Cuéllar is reelected secretary general of UN. ...**October 11–12:** Ronald Reagan and Mikhail Gorbachev meet at Reykjavík, Iceland. ...**October 12:** Queen Elizabeth II arrives in China, becoming the first British monarch to visit that country. ...**November 25:** France, Australia, New Zealand and United States sign a treaty to control nuclear pollution. ...**December 29:** Full diplomatic relations between Britain and Guatemala resume.

1987. April 13: China and Portugal agree on reversion of Macao to China in December 1999. ...**May 17:** A missile fired by an Iraqi warplane in the Persian Gulf hits the USS *Stark*, killing 37. ...**July 4:** France sentences Klaus Barbie (1913–1991), Nazi Gestapo chief deported from the United States, to life in prison. ...**October 19:** U.S. Navy ships attack Iranian oil terminals. ...**December 8:** United States and Soviet Union agree on treaty to eliminate intermediate-range land-based nuclear missiles within three years.

Western & Eastern Europe

1986. January 1: Spain and Portugal join the European Community. ...**February 16:** Mário Soares (1924–) is elected president of Portugal. ...**February 28:** Olaf Palme (b. 1927), prime minister of Sweden, is assassinated in front of Stockholm movie theater. ...**April 26:** Reactor at nuclear power station at Chernobyl in Soviet Union explodes and catches fire, spreading radioactivity over large areas of Ukraine and Eastern Europe. ...**May 9:** Minority Labor government takes office in Norway, with Gro Harlem Brundtland as prime minister. ...**May 16:** Branko Mikalic (1928–) replaces Milka Planinc (1924–) as prime minister of Yugoslavia. ...**May 21:** General election in the Netherlands returns ruling coalition government. ...**June 8:** Kurt Waldheim is elected president of Austria. Franz Vranitsky (1937–) is chancellor. New government is sworn in June 16. ...**June 12:** Ulster Assembly is dissolved by British government. ...**June 22:** General election in Spain returns ruling Socialist Party. ...**December 19:** Soviet government ends internal exile of Andrei Sakharov (1921–1989) for dissident activities.

1987. Boris Yeltsin (1931–), head of Moscow Communist Party, is dismissed. ...**January 25:** General elections in West Germany retain the coalition government of Helmut Kohl (1930–). ...**February 17:** Fianna Fail Party wins general election in Ireland. Charles Haughey (1925–) becomes prime minister. ...**March 3:** Prime minister Benito Craxi (1934–) of Italy resigns. ...**April 3:** Finnish government resigns, leading to a Conservative-led coalition government led by H. Holkeri (1937–). ...**June 11:** Conservatives win election in Britain. Margaret Thatcher becomes prime minister for a third term. ...**June 25:** Miklós Németh (1948–) becomes prime minister of Hungary, and Károly Grósz (1930–1996) becomes chairman of Council of Ministers. ...**July 1:** Single European Act of the European Community (EC) comes into force. ...**September 15:** Diplomatic relations between West Germany and Albania are established. ...**November 2:** Gorbachev attacks Joseph Stalin in speech. ...**December 17:** Gustáv Husák (1913–1991) resigns as head of Czech Communist Party and is replaced by Mílos Jakes (1922–).

U.S. & Canada

1986. January 28: Space shuttle *Challenger* blows up immediately after launch from Cape Canaveral, Florida, killing all seven astronauts on board. ...**February 19:** United States ratifies UN Convention on the Prevention and Punishment of Genocide. ...**April 18:** Actor Clint Eastwood (1930–) is elected mayor of Carmel, California ...**April 28:** General Motors replaces Exxon as the largest U.S. company. ...**June 6:** U.S. national debt rises above $2 trillion mark. ...**July 2:** U.S. Supreme Court upholds affirmative action as a means of promoting racial equality. ...**July 4:** Statue of Liberty is reopened after renovations. ...**September 17:** U.S. Senate confirms William Rehnquist's nomination as chief justice of the Supreme Court. ...**October 1:** Former President Jimmy Carter opens the Carter Presidential Center in Atlanta, Georgia. ...**November 4:** In mid-term elections, Democrats retain control of House and win control of Senate. ...**November 7:** President Reagan signs an immigration bill that offers amnesty to illegal migrants. ...**November 13:** United States admits sale of arms via Israel to Iran in return for Iranian help in freeing U.S. hostages in Lebanon. ...**November 14:** Ivan Boesky (1937–), New York securities trader, pleads guilty to insider trading and must return profits and pay $100 million fine. ...**November 25:** White House acknowledges money from the secret sale of arms to Iran has gone to Contra rebels in Nicaragua.

1987. January 5: President Reagan submits the first trillion-dollar national budget. ...**April 7:** Harold Washington is reelected mayor of Chicago. ...**May–August:** Hearings about the Iran-Contra affair are conducted by Senate and House committees. Colonel Oliver North (1943–) says he felt President Reagan was aware of his activities. ...**June 3:** Agreement between central and provincial governments in Canada redefines federalism and recognizes Quebec as a "distinct society" within the federation. ...**October 19:** Down 508 points, Dow Jones Industrial Average loses 23 percent of its value and causes financial markets worldwide to fall. ...**October 23:** U.S. Senate rejects Robert Bork's appointment as new associate justice of the Supreme Court. ...**October 24:** AFL-CIO readmits Teamsters Union, which had been expelled in 1957. ...**November 18:** U.S. congressional report says President Reagan is responsible for the Iran-Contra scandal. ...**November 23:** Chicago mayor Harold Washington (b. 1922) dies.

Asia, Africa & Latin America

1986. February 7: In presidential elections in the Philippines, Ferdinand Marcos and Corazon Aquino (1933–) both claim victory. Marcos goes into exile. Provisional government is installed under Aquino, with Salvador Laurel (1928–) as prime minister. ...**March 7:** State of emergency in South Africa is lifted. ...**June 27:** International Court of Justice rules U.S. involvement in Nicaraguan politics is illegal. ...**October 10:** Earthquake in El Salvador kills more than 1,200 people. ...**October 15:** President Hussain Ershad (1929–) of Bangladesh is reelected. ...**October 19:** President Samora Machel (b. 1933) of Mozambique is killed in airplane crash. ...**October 20:** Yitzhak Shamir forms new government in Israel, and shares prime ministership with Shimon Peres (1923–) of Labor Party. ...**October 23:** Marshall Islands begin new status of "free association" with the United States. ...**November 9:** Prime Minister Ali Lotfi (1935–) of Egypt is dismissed and is replaced by Atif Sidqi (1930–). ...**November 11:** Martial law in Bangladesh ends. ...**November 20:** President Babrak Karmal (1929–) of Afghanistan resigns. ...**November 27:** Philippine government and Communist rebels sign cease-fire agreement. ...**November 30:** General André Kolingba (1936–) is elected president of Central African Republic. ...**December 6:** General elections in Taiwan return ruling Kuomintang Party to power.

1987. March 5–6: Earthquake in northeastern Ecuador kills more than 4,000. ...**July 1:** United States suspends aid to Panama. ...**July 11:** Australian voters reelect prime minister Robert Hawke (1929–). ...**August 3–5:** Gaza Strip is sealed off from Israel and placed under curfew. ...**November 6:** Yasuhiro Nakasone (1917–) retires as prime minister of Japan and is succeeded by Noboru Takeshita (1924–). ...**November 10:** President Seyni Kountché (b. 1931) of Niger dies and is succeeded by Colonel Ali Saibou (1940–). ...**November 27:** State of emergency is imposed in Bangladesh. ...**November 29–30:** Elections in Haiti are canceled after widespread bloodshed. United States suspends aid. ...**November 29:** Terrorists blow up a South Korean airliner, killing 115 people. ...**December 6:** Rabuka resigns as head of state in Fiji. Ratu Mara (1920–) is appointed prime minister, and Ratu Sir Penaia Ganilau (1918–1993), former governor-general, is appointed president. ...**December 22:** Zimbabwe becomes a one-party state. ...**December 28:** Diplomatic relations between Libya and Tunisia resume.

Science, Invention & Technology

1986. Following the death of William Schroeder (b. 1932), a 620-day artificial heart transplant survivor, artificial heart transplants are virtually halted. ...Bill Gates creates MS-DOS computer operating system. ...Robert Gundlach (1926–) invents an improved snowmaking machine. ...Halley's comet returns. ...**June 12:** United States records 21,517 AIDS cases.

1987. Gates's Microsoft Corporation introduces MS/2 computer operating system. ...The 3.5 inch floppy disk becomes available. ...As concerns over hazardous waste created by petroleum-based inks grow, soy-based inks become widely used.

Religion, Culture & Arts

1986. Desmond Tutu (1931–) becomes the first black archbishop of Cape Town, South Africa. ...The Vatican rules Father Charles Curran (1934–) of the United States unfit to teach because of his views on such issues as abortion, homosexuality, and contraception. ...Oliver Stone's (1948–) *Platoon* wins the Academy Award for best picture. ...**January:** Chicago Bears defeat New England Patriots 46–10 in Super Bowl XX. ...**September:** Robert Penn Warren is named the first U.S. poet laureate. ...**October:** New York Mets defeat Boston Red Sox to win the World Series.

Courtesy: NASA, Washington, D.C.

▲ *The crew of the U.S. Space Shuttle* **Challenger** *(left to right, front row) Michael J. Smith, Francis Scobee and Ronald McNair; (rear) Ellison Onizuka, Christa McAuliffe, Gregory Jarvis and Judith Resnik. All seven died on January 28, 1986, when* **Challenger** *exploded seconds after lift-off.*

1987. Joseph Brodsky (1940–1996), Soviet-born American poet, is awarded Nobel Prize for literature. ...Tom Wolfe (1931–), American novelist: *Bonfire of the Vanities*. ...Director Bernardo Bertolucci's (1940–) *The Last Emperor* wins the Academy Award for best picture. Michael Douglas (1944–) is named best actor. Cher (1946–) wins as best actress. ...U2 release *The Joshua Tree*, which will win the Grammy for album of the year. ...**January:** New York Giants defeat Denver Broncos 39–20 in Super Bowl XXI. ...**September:** Richard Wilbur (1921–) is named U.S. poet laureate. ...**March 10:** Vatican issues document titled *Instruction on Respect for Human Life in Its Origin and on the Dignity of Procreation: Replies to Certain Questions of the Day*, which outlines the Roman Catholic Church's objections to abortion and birth control. ...**February 21:** Andy Warhol (b. 1927), pop art leader, dies. ...**March 20:** Jim Bakker (1941–) resigns as head of the religious television program *PTL Club* after admitting to an affair with a church secretary. ...**October:** Minnesota Twins defeat St. Louis Cardinals to win the World Series.

International Affairs

1988. April 14: Soviet forces agree to withdraw from Afghanistan. ...**April 18:** U.S. Navy destroys six Iranian ships. ...**June 1:** Intermediate Nuclear Forces Treaty signed in Moscow by Ronald Reagan and Mikhail Gorbachev. ...**July 3:** U.S. cruiser *Vincennes* accidentally shoots down an Iranian civilian airliner in the Persian Gulf. ...**November 30:** United States refuses visa to Yasir Arafat, leader of the Palestine Liberation Organization (PLO), to address the UN General Assembly. ...**December 21:** Pan American airliner is blown up by terrorist bomb over Lockerbie, Scotland, killing 259 passengers and 11 others on the ground. Libyan terrorists are suspected. ...**December 22:** South Africa, Angola and Cuba sign agreement to end South African administration of Namibia, to withdraw Cuban troops and to arrange future Namibian independence.

1989. February 2: Soviet Union withdraws final troops from Afghanistan. ...**February 17:** Arab Maghreb Union for economic cooperation is signed by leaders of Libya, Algeria, Morocco, Tunisia, and Mauritania. ...**March 2:** Iran severs diplomatic relations with Britain. ...**June 12:** Bonn document, giving all European nations the right to self-government, is signed by Gorbachev and West German chancellor Kohl. ...**August 27:** Iran and Britain resume diplomatic links. ...**September 25:** UN Security Council imposes air blockade of Iraq. ...**October 1:** British Commonwealth readmits Pakistan as 49th member state.

Western & Eastern Europe

1988. February 21: George Vassiliou (1931–) becomes president of Cyprus. ...**May 8:** President François Mitterand of France is reelected for second seven-year term. ...**June 29:** Brunó Ferenc Straub (1914–1996) becomes president of Hungary. ...**September 28:** Coalition government in Iceland is formed under Prime Minister Steingrímur Hermannsson (1928–). ...**October 1:** Popular Front in Estonia begins movement for increased freedom from the Soviet Union. Similar movements are launched in Latvia on October 9 and Lithuania on October 23. ...**November 24:** Miklós Németh (1948–) becomes chairman of Council of Ministers in Hungary. ...**December 1:** Soviet parliament approves constitutional reforms, establishing an executive presidency and an elected congress as the supreme body of state. ...**December 7:** Massive earthquake destroys Spitak in Armenia, Soviet Union, killing more than 55,000 people.

1989. March 26: Soviet Union holds first multi-candidate parliamentary elections. Many Communist Party hardliners lose seats. ...**April 9:** Soviet security forces suppress pro-independence demonstrations in Tbilisi, capital of Georgia. ...**April 17:** Solidarity is officially legalized in Poland. ...**May 17:** Czech dissident playwright Václav Havel (1936–) is released from jail. ...**June 18:** Solidarity wins all but one seat in new bicameral national assembly elections in Poland. ...**August 20:** Serbs stage national protest against federal government in Yugoslavia. ...**August 24:** One-party rule ends in Poland. Tadeusz Mazowiecki (1927–) becomes new premier. ...**September 10:** Hungary opens border with Austria, allowing mass exodus of East Germans to the West. ...**September 12:** Elected government dominated by Solidarity representatives takes office in Poland. ...**September 27:** Slovene parliament passes constitutional amendment giving it the right to secede from Yugoslavia. ...**October 3:** East Germany's border with Czechoslovakia is closed in an attempt to halt East German emigration. ...**October 18:** Erich Honecker retires as leader of Communist Party in East Germany and is replaced by Egon Krenz (1937–).

U.S. & Canada

1988. January 2: Canada-United States Free Trade Agreement is signed. ...**February 3:** U.S. Senate confirms Anthony Kennedy's (1936–) nomination as Supreme Court associate justice. He is sworn in February 18. ...**April 4:** Arizona governor Evan Mecham (1924–) is impeached for diverting campaign funds. ...**May 4:** U.S. deadline for illegal alien amnesty arrives; nearly 1.4 million applications have been received. ...**June 14:** Howard Baker (1925–), White House chief of staff, resigns. ...**July:** Yellowstone National Park is devastated by 12 separate wildfires that consume 88,000 acres. ...**August 10:** President Reagan signs a bill offering apologies and reparations to Japanese Americans interned during World War II. ...**November 8:** George Bush (1924–) is elected president, defeating Michael Dukakis (1933–). ...**November 21:** Brian Mulroney's Conservative Party wins Canada's elections, with a reduced majority in the lower house. ...**December 21:** Drexel Burnham Lambert, a major securities firm, pleads guilty to insider trading and stock manipulation and must pay $650 million in penalties.

1989. January 11: U.S. Surgeon General C. Everett Koop (1916–) reports cigarette smoking killed about 390,000 Americans in 1985. ...**February 10:** Ron Brown (1941–1996) becomes chairman of the Democratic National Committee. He is the first African American to lead a major American political party. ...**March 24:** *Exxon Valdez* oil tanker ruptures on reefs in Prince William Sound, Alaska, causing the worst tanker oil spill in U.S. history. ...**May 4:** Oliver North is convicted of illegal activities in the Iran-Contra affair. ...**May 31:** Jim Wright (1922–), Speaker of the U.S. House of Representatives, resigns after charges of ethical wrongdoings. ...**July 3:** U.S. Supreme Court upholds some restrictions on a woman's right to have an abortion. ...**July 6:** North is given a three-year suspended sentence, required to pay a $150,000 fine, and ordered to perform 1,200 hours of community service work. ...**August 9:** President Bush signs legislation providing $166 billion to bail out the savings and loan industry. ...**August 10:** General Colin Powell (1937–) is nominated by President Bush as the first African American chairman of the Joint Chiefs of Staff. ...**October 17:** Earthquake hits the San Francisco area, killing more than 60. It struck minutes before the World Series began there.

Asia, Africa & Latin America

1988. January 13: President Chiang Ching-kuo (b. 1909) of Taiwan dies and is succeeded by Lee Teng-hui (1923–). ...**February 8:** General Manuel Noriega (1939–), commander of the Panamanian defense forces, is charged by a U.S. federal grand jury with drug offenses. ...**February 24:** Seventeen anti-apartheid organizations are banned in South Africa. ...**March 4:** United States freezes Panamanian assets. ...**March 23:** Iraq uses toxic weapons in war against Iran. ...**May 14:** State of emergency is proclaimed in Tigre and Eritrea, Ethiopia. ...**July 6:** Carlos Salinas de Gortari (1948–) wins presidential election in Mexico. ...**July 31:** King Hussein (1935–1999) of Jordan announces severance of legal and administrative ties with Israeli-occupied West Bank. ...**August 3:** Martial law is imposed in Burma. ...**August 19:** Maung Maung (1925–1994) becomes president of Burma. ...**August 8:** Iran and Iraq begin cease-fire. ...**August 17:** President Zia-ul-Haq (b. 1924) of Pakistan is killed in an airplane crash. Ghulam Ishaq Khan (1915–) is appointed acting president. ...**August 20:** Eight-year war between Iran and Iraq ends. ...**October 3:** War between Chad and Libya ends. ...**November 12–15:** Palestine National Council in Algiers proclaims a State of Palestine, with Jerusalem as its capital.

1989. January 7: Hirohito (b. 1901), emperor of Japan, dies and is succeeded by Akihito (1933–). ...**February 3:** F. W. de Klerk (1936–) is elected head of ruling National Party in South Africa, replacing P. W. Botha. ...**April 18:** Students begin demonstrations in Beijing, China. **April 22:** Crowd of more than 100,000 stage protest in Beijing's Tiananmen Square. **May 13:** Students in Tiananmen Square begin hunger strike. **May 20:** Martial law is declared in Beijing. ...**June 2:** Sosuke Uno (b. 1922) is elected prime minister of Japan. ...**June 3:** Iranian leader Ayatollah Khomeini (b. 1900) dies. ...**June 4:** Chinese troops open fire to disperse crowds in Tiananmen Square, killing and injuring hundreds, and arrest more than 10,000 protesters. ...**June 19:** Burma adopts new name Union of Myanmar. ...**July 23:** Japan's ruling Liberal-Democratic Party loses elections and Prime Minister Uno resigns. ...**July 29:** Speaker Hashemi Rafsanjani (1934–) is elected president of Iran. ...**August 9:** Toshiki Kaifu (1931–) becomes Japanese prime minister. ...**August 15:** De Klerk becomes acting president of South Africa. ...**August 28:** Ferdinand Marcos (b. 1917) of the Philippines dies in Hawaii. ...**September 26:** Vietnamese troops officially withdraw from Cambodia.

Science, Invention & Technology

1988. U.S. FDA approves limited use of synthetic ligaments for humans. ...Minoxidil, first known remedy for baldness, is approved for use by FDA. ...American Henry Erlich (1925–) develops the highly reliable method of identification using DNA "fingerprinting." ...The world's fastest supercomputer, the Cray-3, is introduced.

c. 1988. Pocket telephones become widely available. ...Smaller floppy disks with greater storage capacities are developed.

1989. A 300-foot radio telescope at the National Radio Observatory at Green Bank, West Virginia, collapses from metal fatigue. ...American Paul Hansma (1946–) is first to use an atomic-force microscope to observe blood clotting.

▲ ***Jordan's King Hussein (left) during a White House visit with President Ronald Reagan in May 1985.***

Religion, Culture & Arts

1988. Karlheinz Stockhausen (1928–), German composer: *Montag aus Licht* (*Monday from Light*). ...African American writer Toni Morrison's (1931–) *Beloved* wins the Pulitzer Prize for fiction. ...Pedro Almodovar (1951–), Spanish film director: *Women on the Verge of a Nervous Breakdown*. ...Barry Levinson's (1942–) *Rain Man* wins the Academy Award for best picture. The film's star, Dustin Hoffman, is named best actor. Jodie Foster (1962–) wins best actress. ...Some U.S. church groups condemn the film *The Last Temptation of Christ*, directed by Martin Scorsese, for being what they consider blasphemous. ...*False Start* by Jasper Johns (1930–) sells for $17,050,000 at auction, a record for a living artist. ...**January:** Washington Redskins beat Denver Broncos 42–10 to win Super Bowl XXII. ...**May 5:** Eugene Antonio Marino (1934–) becomes the first African American archbishop of the Roman Catholic church when installed in Atlanta. ...**September:** Howard Nemerov (1920–1991) is named U.S. poet laureate. ...**October:** Los Angeles Dodgers defeat Oakland Athletics to win the World Series.

1989. British author Salman Rushdie (1947–) goes into hiding after Iran's Ayatollah Khomeini issues a *fatwa* (death order) because he considers Rushdie's book *Satanic Verses* blasphemous. ...Kazuo Ishiguro (1954–), Japanese-born British novelist: *The Remains of the Day*. ...Robert Penn Warren (b. 1905) dies. ...Amy Tan (1952–), American writer: *The Joy Luck Club*. ...Corcoran Gallery in Washington cancels an exhibition of erotic photographs by Robert Mapplethorpe (1946–1989). ...Woody Allen directs *Crimes and Misdemeanors*. ...Spike Lee (1955–) directs *Do the Right Thing*. ...Bruce Beresford's (1940–) *Driving Miss Daisy* wins the Academy Award for best picture. The film's star, Jessica Tandy (1909–1994), is named best actress. Daniel Day-Lewis (1957–) is named best actor. ...**January:** San Francisco 49ers defeat Cincinnati Bengals 20–16 to win Super Bowl XXIII. ...**February 11:** Barbara Harris (1931–) is the first female bishop ordained by the Episcopal Church. She is Suffragan Bishop of Massachusetts. ...**July 17:** Full diplomatic relations between the Vatican and Poland are restored. ...**September 22:** Irving Berlin (b. 1888), famed American composer, dies. ...**October:** San Francisco Giants defeat Oakland Athletics to win the World Series.

International Affairs

1989 (Continued). November: Asia-Pacific Economic Cooperation (APEC) is established in Singapore. ...**December 1:** Soviet leader Mikhail Gorbachev meets with Pope John Paul II at the Vatican. ...**December 2–3:** Summit meeting between U.S. President George Bush and Gorbachev is held off Malta.

1990. Liechtenstein and Namibia join the UN Group of 15 (G15), nonindustrialized nations that meet to discuss solutions to economic problems. ...**May 21:** Unification of Northern Yemen and Southern Yemen as the Yemen Republic becomes official. ...**May 31–June 3:** In Washington, D.C., Bush and Gorbachev agree to reduce the number of long-range nuclear missiles and to destroy half of their chemical weapons. ...**July 6:** Western nations propose close ties with Soviet Union and its former satellite countries. ...**August 2:** UN security council condemns Iraqi invasion of Kuwait. ...**August 6:** UN Security Council imposes oil embargo on Iraq. ...**August 7:** United States sends troops to Saudi Arabia to deter Iraqi aggression. ...**November 8:** UN Security Council sets January 15, 1991, as deadline for Iraq to withdraw from Kuwait. ...**November 19:** Conventional Forces in Europe Treaty is signed by all 22 NATO and Warsaw Pact nations. The treaty provides for mutual reductions in conventional weapons in Europe. ...**November 21:** Delegates from United States, Canada and 34 European nations sign the Charter of Paris for a New Europe. The treaty disbands the Cold War camps of Eastern Europe and Western Europe, ending the Cold War. ...**November 29:** UN Security Council authorizes force against Iraqi troops in Kuwait. ...**December 6:** Iraqi leader Saddam Hussein (1937–) announces he will free all foreign hostages, some 2,000 captives, his government holds.

Western & Eastern Europe

1989 (Continued). November 10: East Germany opens Berlin Wall. ...**December 10:** New federal government with non-Communist majority is formed in Czechoslovakia. ...**December 21:** Deportation order for Protestant pastor Father László Tokes (1952–) provokes revolution in Romania. ...**December 25:** President Nicolae Ceausescu (b. 1918) of Romania is toppled and executed. ...**December 29:** Václav Havel is elected president of Czechoslovakia.

1990. January 13: Romania outlaws Communist Party. ...**January 29:** Polish Communist Party is dissolved and reformed as Social Democratic Party. ...**February 7:** Central Committee of Communist Party ends its one-party monopoly in Soviet Union. ...**March 11:** Lithuania passes unilateral act restoring independence from Soviet Union. ...**March 15:** Mikhail Gorbachev is sworn in as first (and last) president of Soviet Union. ...**March 25:** Estonian Communist Party votes for independence from Soviet Union. ...**March 30:** Soviet troops occupy Communist government buildings in Lithuania. ...**May 4:** Latvia declares independence from Soviet Union. ...**May 8:** Estonia declares independence from Soviet Union. ...**May 27:** Free elections are held in Poland. ...**May 29:** Boris Yeltsin is elected president of Russian Soviet Federal Socialist Republic. ...**June 20:** Russian Republic declares itself a sovereign state. ...**June 21:** East Germany and West Germany approve treaty on economic union and agree on inviolability of Polish border. ...**July 3:** Slovenia secedes from Yugoslavia and declares itself a sovereign state. ...**July 16:** Ukraine declares itself a sovereign state. ...**August 3:** Árpád Gönvz (1922–) is elected president of Hungary. ...**August 21:** European Community plans a unified monetary system. ...**August 29:** State of emergency is declared in Yerevan, Armenia. ...**August 31:** East Germany and West Germany agree on reunification. ...**October 3:** East Germany reunifies with West Germany. ...**October 8:** Britain joins European exchange-rate mechanism. ...**October 15:** Gorbachev is awarded Nobel Peace Prize. ...**November 9:** Mary Robinson (1944–) becomes first female president of Ireland. ...**November 22:** Margaret Thatcher resigns as British prime minister. **November 27:** John Major (1943–) becomes British prime minister. ...**December 1:** Channel tunnel is breached as workers from Britain and France meet. ...**December 2:** Helmut Kohl becomes first chancellor of reunited Germany. ...**December 7:** Solidarity leader Lech Walesa becomes president of Poland.

U.S. & Canada

1989 (Continued). November 7: Lawrence Douglas Wilder (1931–) is elected governor of Virginia. He is the nation's first African American governor since Reconstruction.

1990. February 13: Securities firm Drexel Burnham Lambert files for bankruptcy. It was involved in scandals in 1988 and paid major fines. ...**March 22:** *Exxon Valdez* captain Joseph Hazelwood (1946–) is found guilty of negligence. On March 23, he will be fined $50,000 and sentenced to community service. ...**April 22:** Americans celebrate the 20th anniversary of Earth Day with festivals and exhibits. ...**June 4:** Jack Kevorkian (1928–) helps a terminally ill Oregon woman commit suicide. He will become known as "Doctor Death" for his development of a "suicide machine" that helps terminally ill patients end their lives. ...**June 23:** Meech Lake Accord, a set of constitutional reforms designed to induce Quebec to accept the Canada Act, fails. ...**July 20:** U.S. Supreme Court justice William Brennan (1906–) resigns due to ill health. ...**July 26:** President Bush signs the Americans with Disabilities Act, which provides equal rights for handicapped people. ...**September 27:** U.S. Senate confirms David Souter (1939–) as new Supreme Court justice. ...**November 5:** President Bush signs a bill to reduce the national debt by $500 billion over five years.

Asia, Africa & Latin America

1989 (Continued). November 24: Elias Hrawi (1930–) is elected president of Lebanon. ...**November 26:** Rajiv Gandhi's (1904–1991) party is defeated by National Front coalition in general elections in India. ...**December 19:** Panama is invaded by U.S. troops intent on capturing General Manuel Noriega.

1990. January 3: General Noriega surrenders to U.S. troops in Panama and is arrested on drug charges. ...**January 19:** Indian government assumes direct political control of Jammu and Kashmir. ...**January 26:** Daniel Ortega of Nicaragua is defeated in general elections by Violeta Chamorro (1929–). ...**February 2:** Ban on African National Congress is lifted in South Africa. ...**February 11:** Nelson Mandela is released from South African prison after 27 years. ...**February 12:** Carmen Lawrence (1948–) becomes first female prime minister in Australian history. ...**March 11:** General Prosper Avril (1937–) of Haiti resigns. ...**March 21:** Namibia becomes independent, with Sam Nujoma as president. ...**April 30:** Chinese lift martial law in Llasa, Tibet. ...**May 2:** Talks between African National Congress and South African government begin. ...**May 27:** Multiparty elections in Myanmar (Burma) are won by opposition party, but military refuses to hand over power July 2. ...**May 28:** Iraq accuses oil-producing countries of keeping prices too low. ...**June 11:** Alberto Fujimori (1938–) is elected president of Peru. ...**June 27:** Civil war in Nicaragua formally ends. ...**July 2:** Antigovernment troops led by Charles Taylor (1948–) launch an attack on Monrovia, Liberia. ...**July 30:** Liberian forces loyal to President Samuel Doe massacre 600 refugees in a church in Monrovia. ...**August 1:** Iraq invades Kuwait. ...**August 6:** Prime Minister Benazir Bhutto (1953–) and her government are dismissed by the president of Pakistan. ...**August 27:** UN Security Council agrees on plan to end civil war in Cambodia. ...**November 10:** Chandra Shekhar (1927–) is sworn in as prime minister of India. ...**November 26:** Lee Kuan Yew (1923–) resigns after 31 years as prime minister of Singapore. ...**December 13:** Oliver Tambo (1917–1993), president of the African National Congress, returns to South Africa after 30 years in exile.

Science, Invention & Technology

1990. U.S. government admits the existence of the F-117A stealth aircraft, 13 years after its development. ...Prosthetic artificial bone material is first marketed. ...Digital audio tape (DAT) recorders are made available in United States. ...General Motors introduces the Impact electric car to limited public acceptance. ...Imperial Chemical Industries of England develops Biopol biodegradable plastic. ...Japan's Industrial Research Institute develops flexible ceramic compounds. ...Organogenesis Company develops and tests its living blood vessel equivalent. ...Norplant timed-release birth control device, implanted under the skin, is introduced.

c. 1990. Farming experiences a general shift back to crop rotation after four decades of intensive farming using fertilizers, which left an accumulation of toxins in the soil and water table.

Religion, Culture & Arts

1990. Mormon Church eliminates ceremonies that might offend women and members of other churches. ...Pope John Paul II dedicates the world's largest cathedral in Yamoussoukro, Ivory Coast. ...The new Council of Churches for Britain and Ireland includes Roman Catholic and black churches. ...V. S. Naipaul (1932–), Trinidadian novelist resident in Britain: *India*. ...Vincent Van Gogh's *Portrait of Dr. Gachet* sells for a record $82.5 million. ...*GoodFellas*, directed by Martin Scorsese, is released. ...Kevin Costner's (1955–) *Dances with Wolves* wins the Academy Award for best picture. Jeremy Irons (1948–) is named best actor. Kathy Bates (1948–) wins as best actress. ...David Lynch directs the television series *Twin Peaks*. ...**January:** San Francisco 49ers defeat Denver Broncos 55–10 to win Super Bowl XXIV. ...**February 9:** Hungary restores diplomatic relations with Vatican. ...**September:** Mark Strand (1934–) is appointed U.S. poet laureate. ...**October:** Cincinnati Reds defeat Oakland Athletics to win the World Series.

Courtesy: Cincinnati Reds, MLB, Cincinnati, OH

Cincinnati Reds outfielder Billy Hatcher (above), a key player in the 1990 World Series against the Oakland Athletics. In the four-game sweep, Hatcher batted .750, going 7 for 7 in the first two games of the series.

International Affairs

1991. January 4: UN Security Council condemns Israel for its treatment of Palestinians in the occupied territories. ...**January 17:** Persian Gulf War begins with large U.S. air strikes against Iraq. **January 23–30:** Iraq spills massive amounts of oil into the Persian Gulf, creating the largest slick ever, 60 miles long and 20 miles wide. ...**March 2–3:** UN approves terms ending the Gulf War. Allies and Iraqis meet to arrange a cease-fire. **April 6:** Iraq formally accepts terms for Gulf War cease-fire. ...**April 15:** Thirty-nine countries meet in London to establish the European Bank for Reconstruction and Development. ...**April 16:** United States, Britain and France agree to establish refugee centers for Kurds in northern Iraq. ...**July 1:** Warsaw Pact, established in 1955 as military counterweight to NATO, ceases to exist. ...**July 10:** United States lifts economic sanctions against South Africa, which is moving to dismantle apartheid. ...**July 11–14:** At a Washington, D.C., summit, United States and Soviet Union agree to reduce their nuclear arsenals. ...**August 1:** Israel agrees to Middle East peace negotiations so long as the Palestine Liberation Organization is excluded. ...**August 15:** UN agrees to let Iraq, under economic sanctions, sell a limited amount of oil for food and medicine. ...**September 17:** UN admits seven new countries: Latvia, Lithuania, Estonia, North Korea, South Korea, the Marshall Islands and Micronesia; membership stands at 166. ...**October 4:** Twenty-four nations sign agreement banning oil and mineral exploration in Antarctica for 50 years. ...**October 30:** Israeli and Arab leaders, including Palestinian representatives, open peace negotiations in Madrid. ...**December 16:** UN repeals 1975 resolution equating Zionism with racism.

1992. February 28: UN warns Iraq to begin dismantling weapons plants under the 1991 cease-fire agreement. ...**April 15:** UN sanctions against Libya, which is accused of two airliner bombings that killed hundreds, come into effect. ...**May 22:** In Nairobi, Kenya, 98 countries endorse a biodiversity treaty to protect the world's plant and animal life.

Western & Eastern Europe

1991. January 7–13: Soviets send troops into two insurgent Baltic republics. Soldiers fire on crowd in Vilnius, Lithuania, killing 15. ...**January 20:** Between 100,000 and 300,000 people demonstrate in Moscow against the Baltic crackdown. ...**February 9:** Lithuanians vote to secede from the Soviet Union. ...**February 19:** Boris Yeltsin, Russian opposition leader, calls on President Gorbachev to resign. ...**March 3:** Estonians and Latvians vote to break away from the Soviet Union. **April 9:** Georgia becomes the fifth Soviet republic to secede. ...**May 15:** Edith Cresson (1934–), a Socialist, becomes France's first female prime minister. ...**June 12:** Taking 60 percent of the vote, Yeltsin becomes the first democratically elected president of Russia. ...**June 19–21:** Last Soviet troops leave Hungary and Czechoslovakia. ...**June 20:** German parliament votes to transfer capital from Bonn to Berlin. ...**August 18–21:** Soviet officials attempt to overthrow President Gorbachev fails, weakening central government. The failed coup will result in the suppression of the Communist Party and the collapse of the Soviet Union. ...**August 24:** Ukraine declares independence from Soviet Union. ...**December 8:** Leaders of three former Soviet republics, Russia, Ukraine and Belarus, agree to form the Commonwealth of Independent States. ...**December 11:** European Community approves a plan for a single currency for member states by 1999....**December 19:** Germany recognizes Croatia and Slovenia as independent, furthering the breakup of Yugoslavia. ...**December 25:** Gorbachev resigns as president of the Soviet Union. ...**December 31:** Soviet Union officially ceases to exist.

1992. January 15: European Community recognizes the independence of the breakaway Yugoslav republics of Croatia and Slovenia. ...**February 29–March 1:** Voters in the Yugoslav republic of Bosnia-Herzegovina vote overwhelmingly for independence. ...**April 9:** In Britain, Conservatives win parliamentary elections. ...**April 27:** Betty Boothroyd (1929–) becomes the first female speaker of the House of Commons in Britain. ...**May 22:** UN imposes sanctions on Yugoslavia in an effort to halt the civil war. ...**June 18–21:** Negotiations end in an agreement for a formal split of Czechoslovakia into two independent countries: the Czech Republic and Slovakia, effective January 1993.

U.S. & Canada

1991. January 18: After 62 years, bankrupt Eastern Airlines ceases flying. ...**March 3:** Amateur video cameraman records Los Angeles police officers beating Rodney King (1965–), an African American motorist stopped for a traffic violation. ...**March 19–21:** U.S. Congress approves a $78 billion bailout to pay depositers at bankrupt savings and loan associations. ...**April 17:** The Dow Jones Industrial Average of selected stocks tops 3,000 for the first time. ...**April 24:** U.S. judge rejects Exxon's offer to pay $100 million in damages for the *Exxon Valdez* oil spill on the Alaska coast, calling the amount insufficient. ...**June 27:** Thurgood Marshall (1908–1993), the first African American U.S. Supreme Court justice, announces he will retire. ...**July 1:** President Bush nominates Clarence Thomas (1948–) for Thurgood Marshall's Supreme Court seat. ...**July 10:** Bush approves an independent commission's recommendation to close 38 U.S. military bases. ...**July 22:** Milwaukee police charge Jeffrey Dahmer (1960–1997) with the murder and dismemberment of 11 men. ...**October 3:** Arkansas governor Bill Clinton (1946–) announces he will seek the Democratic nomination for president in 1992. ...**October 15:** Despite confirmation hearings that dealt with charges he sexually harassed Anita Hill (1956–), a law professor who once worked for him, Thomas wins confirmation to the U.S. Supreme Court. ...**December 4:** Pan American World Airways, a pioneer in commerical aviation, goes out of business. ...**December 18:** General Motors says it will close 21 of its 125 auto plants in the United States and Canada, thereby dropping 74,000 employees.

1992. April 9: Former Panamanian president Manuel Noriega (1938–) is convicted of racketeering and drug trafficking charges in a U.S. court in Miami. ...**April 21:** California executes its first condemned killer in 25 years, Robert Alton Harris (b. 1953), who murdered two teenage boys in 1978. ...**April 29–May 1:** Riots erupt in Los Angeles when a Simi Valley jury acquits four white police officers in the videotaped beating of Rodney King. The death toll during the riots will reach 52. ...**June 26:** U.S. Navy's Tailhook scandal leads to the resignation of navy secretary H. Lawrence Garrett III (1939–).

Asia, Africa & Latin America

1991. February 1: South African president F. W. de Klerk says he will seek repeal of the country's apartheid laws. ...Earthquake strikes Afghanistan and Pakistan, killing 1,200 people. ...**March:** Epidemic of cholera spreads in Peru; 55,000 are affected. ...**March 16:** Saddam Hussein announces his government has crushed a Shiite uprising in Iraq. ...**April 30:** Cyclone kills 150,000 in Bangladesh. ...**May 24–25:** More than 14,000 Ethiopian Jews are airlifted to Israel. ...**May 31:** Angolan government and rebel group sign peace agreement to end 16 years of war. ...**June 9–13:** Eruptions of the Philippine volcano Pinatubo kill 435 persons and force 20,000 to flee. ...**June 17:** South Africa's parliament repeals apartheid laws. ...**June 19:** Pablo Escobar (1969–1993), reputed leader of the Medellín drug cartel, surrenders to authorities in Colombia. ...**September 25:** Government of El Salvador and insurgent groups agree to a cease-fire in the country's long civil war. ...**September 30:** Coup in Haiti ousts President Jean-Bertrand Aristide (1953–). ...**November:** With the end of a long civil war, Prince Norodom Sihanouk returns from exile to become president of Cambodia.

1992. January 12: Algeria's military rulers void December 1991 election results that would have given power to Islamic fundamentalists. ...**February 16:** Palestinians reject Israeli offer of local government autonomy in the occupied territories. ...**March 17:** In a referendum, whites give President de Klerk authority to end white minority rule in South Africa. ...**April 5:** Peru's president Alberto Fujimori dissolves congress and imposes presidential rule, with press censorship and arrests of political opponents. ...**May 24:** Mass pro-democracy demonstrations force the resignation of Thailand's army-backed prime minister. ...**June 23:** Israelis give election victory to the Labor Party, which favors a land-for-peace agreement with Palestinians.

Science, Invention & Technology

1991. January 24: United States reports that 161,073 persons have contracted AIDS; of these, 100,777 have died. ...**March 29:** University of California at Los Angeles publishes 11-year study that concludes air pollution can seriously damage lung tissue and cause breathing difficulties. ...**May 9:** British scientists report finding the precise gene on the Y chromosome that determines maleness in mice. ...**June 5–14:** U.S. space shuttle *Columbia*, carrying 29 rats and 2,478 jellyfish, studies biological effects of space travel. ...**July 11:** A total eclipse of the sun is visible for nearly seven minutes, close to the maximum, in Hawaii, Mexico, Central America and Brazil. ...**August 24:** British medical journal the *Lancet* reports moderate drinking reduces risk of heart disease. ...**October 9:** U.S. National Aeronautics and Space Administration (NASA) reports the ozone in the stratosphere is at the lowest on record. ...**October 22:** DuPont, a leading maker of chlorofluorocarbons, says it will stop producing the ozone-depleting chemicals by 1997. ...**November 7:** Scientists at the Jet Propulsion Laboratory in California report that radar images suggest ice on the north pole of Mercury, the planet closest to the sun. ...**November 26:** Japan says it will stop using large fishing nets, which kill many fish, whales, birds and other creatures not used for food.

1992. February 20: Report says spending on research and development in the United States is falling for the first time in 15 years. ...**March 24–April 2:** The U.S. space shuttle *Atlantis* initiates a space-based study of the earth's threatened atmosphere. ...**April 23:** Astronomers' discovery of slight temperature variations in the most distant matter yet studied provides evidence in support of the big bang theory of creation. ...**May 7–16:** Spacewalkers from the space shuttle *Endeavor* capture and repair a malfunctioning communications satellite, the highlight of the nine-day mission. ...**May 14:** Bush administration opens Pacific Northwest habitat of the endangered spotted owl to logging.

Religion, Culture & Arts

1991. American writer Isaac Bashevis Singer (b. 1904) dies. ...British writer Graham Greene (b. 1904) dies. ...Film director David Lean (b. 1908) dies. ...Film director Frank Capra (b. 1897) dies. Oliver Stone (1946–) directs the films *JFK* and *The Doors*. ...Geena Davis (1957–) and Susan Sarandon (1946–) star in Ridley Scott's (1937–) *Thelma and Louise*. ...Jonathan Demme's (1944–) *Silence of the Lambs* wins the Academy Award for best picture. The film's two stars, Anthony Hopkins (1937–) and Jodie Foster (1962–) are honored as best actor and best actress. ...Nirvana releases the album *Nevermind*, establishing the commercial potential of "alternative" rock. ...U2 releases the album *Achting Baby*. ...**January 9:** Rembert G. Weakland (1927–), the Roman Catholic archbishop of Milwaukee, says he favors ordaining married men to ease the priest shortage in the United States. ...**January 27:** New York Giants defeat Buffalo Bills 20–19 to win Super Bowl XXV. ...**April 14:** Thieves break into an Amsterdam museum and steal 20 paintings by Vincent Van Gogh. The paintings will be found in an abandoned car. ...**May 2:** Papal encyclical warns free market nations to correct injustices in their economic systems. ...**June 10:** General Assembly of the 2.9-million member Presbyterian Church USA rejects a report urging the church to ease its prohibitions on homosexual sex and sex outside marriage. ...**September:** Huntington Library in San Marino, California, agrees to open its restricted film archive of Dead Sea Scrolls for general scholarly use. ...**October:** Minnesota Twins defeat Atlanta Braves to win the World Series.

1992. *Unforgiven*, directed by Clint Eastwood, wins the Academy Award for best picture. Eastwood is named best director. Al Pacino (1940–) is named best actor. Emma Thompson (1959–) wins best actress. ...**January:** Washington Redskins beat Buffalo Bills 37–24 to win Super Bowl XXVI. ...**April 8:** American tennis star Arthur Ashe (1943–1993), the first African American to win the U.S. Open, says he has the AIDS virus. ... **May 22:** After 29 years, Johnny Carson (1925–) hosts his last *Tonight Show* on NBC television.

International Affairs

1992 (Continued). August 12: United States, Canada and Mexico approve a draft of a free-trade treaty. ...**August 13:** UN Security Council authorizes military force to get humanitarian aid into Bosnia-Herzegovina. ...**September 14:** UN peacekeepers arrive in Somalia to oversee food shipments for famine relief. ...**October 23:** Vietnam agrees to supply all available information on the 2,265 Americans still unaccounted for after the Vietnam War. ...**December 9:** U.S.-led military force reaches Somalia to deliver food for famine relief.

1993. January: United States and Russia agree on START II arms treaty that would reduce nuclear arsenals by two-thirds. ...**January 13:** U.S., British and French warplanes attack missile batteries and radar sites in Iraq. ...In Paris, 120 nations sign a treaty banning the manufacture and use of chemical weapons. ...**February 22:** UN Security Council agrees to establish an international court to prosecute war crimes in the former Yugoslavia. ...**March 15:** A UN commission reports the United States-backed Salvadoran army committed most of the human rights violations during El Salvador's long civil war. ...**March 26:** UN approves a 28,000-strong peacekeeping force to replace U.S. peacekeepers in Somalia. ...**June 24:** Kurdish militants attack Turkish diplomatic posts and businesses in more than 20 European cities. Swiss police shoot and kill one Kurdish demonstrator. ...**July 9:** World's seven leading industrial nations offer a $3 billion loan package to boost Russia's sagging economy. ...**September 9:** Clash with U.S. peacekeepers in Mogadishu leaves 100 Somali dead. ...**October 5:** China explodes a nuclear weapon in its western desert, violating an informal international moratorium on nuclear tests. ...**November 20–22:** United States, Canada and Mexico ratify the North American Free Trade Agreement (NAFTA).

Western & Eastern Europe

1992 (Continued). September 22: UN votes to expel Yugoslavia for fomenting war in Bosnia-Herzegovina. ...**November 16:** UN Security Council authorizes a naval blockade to enforce international economic sanctions on Yugoslavia. ...**November 17:** Czech and Slovak regional parliaments adopt a joint resolution authorizing the breakup of Czechoslovakia into two independent republics. ...**December 9:** Charles (1948–), the Prince of Wales, heir to the British throne, and his wife, Diana (1960–1997), announce they will separate. ...**December 20:** Slobodan Milosevic, regarded as the chief instigator of the civil war in Bosnia-Herzegovina, is reelected president of Serbia.

1993. January 1: Czech Republic and Slovakia formally become independent nations. ...**February 9:** Netherlands parliament approves guidelines for euthanasia, or "mercy killing." Netherlands is a leader in the euthanasia movement. ...**April 8:** Newly independent former Yugoslav republic of Macedonia becomes a member of the UN. ...**April 25:** In a national referendum, 58 percent of Russian voters approve the social and economic policies of the Yeltsin government. ...**April 29:** Queen Elizabeth II of Britain announces that Buckingham Palace, her London home, will be open to admission-paying tourists. ...**May 7:** In a privatization drive, the Polish parliament transfers control of 600 state-owned firms to investment funds. ...**May 15–16:** In a referendum, Bosnian Serbs overwhelmingly reject a UN-sponsored peace plan for Bosnia-Herzegovina. ...**May 18:** Danish voters approve the Maastricht Treaty for closer European union, reversing the result of a 1992 referendum. ...**May 27:** Terrorist bomb detonates near the Uffizi Gallery in Florence, Italy, killing five. ...**July 22–August 2:** Britain completes ratification of the Maastrict European Union Treaty. ...**August 7:** Last 6,000 Russian troops leave Poland. Russian military forces have been stationed there since the end of World War II. ...**September 6:** The Swedish firm Volvo and the French concern Renault merge, creating the world's sixth-largest automaker. ...**September 23:** Russian president Boris Yeltsin announces presidential elections for June 1994. ...**November 1:** After a two-year ratification process, the Maastricht European Union Treaty takes effect. ...**December 12:** Russians narrowly approve Yeltsin's proposed draft constitution.

U.S. & Canada

1992 (Continued). July 16: Democratic Party nominates Bill Clinton for U.S. president. ...**August 24:** Hurricane Andrew strikes southern Florida, killing 30, leaving 250,000 homeless and causing $7.3 billion in damages. ...**November 3:** Clinton is elected 42nd president of the United States, defeating incumbent George Bush and independent candidate Ross Perot (1930–). ...**November 22:** Ten women accuse U.S. senator Robert Packwood (1932–) of sexual harassment. ...**December 24:** Outgoing President Bush pardons former defense secretary Caspar Weinberger (1917–) and five other former officials in the Iran-Contra affair.

1993. February 24: With his approval rating at 17 percent, Brian Mulroney announces he will resign as prime minister of Canada. ...**February 26:** Terrorist bomb explodes at the World Trade Center in New York City, killing six. ...**March 10–11:** Senate confirms Janet Reno (1938–) as first female attorney general of United States. ...**April 17:** Federal jury in Los Angeles finds two police officers guilty in the beating of Rodney King; two others are acquitted. ...**April 19:** Federal agents attack the Branch Davidian cult compound in Waco, Texas, ending a 51-day siege. Seventy-two cultists die in fire that consumes the compound. ...**April 28:** Defense Secretary Les Aspin (1938–1995) lifts the ban on female pilots in combat. ...**June 14:** President Clinton nominates Judge Ruth Bader Ginsburg (1933–) to replace retiring Justice Byron White (1917–) on the U.S. Supreme Court. ...**June 25:** Kim Campbell (1947–) becomes Canada's first female prime minister, succeeding Brian Mulroney. ...**July 19:** President Clinton announces a "don't ask, don't tell, don't pursue" policy on homosexuals in the military. ...**July 20:** Vincent Foster (b. 1945), a legal adviser to the Clinton White House, is found shot to death in a Virginia park, an apparent suicide. ...**August 25:** A federal grand jury indicts Sheikh Omar Abdel Rahman (1938–), a Muslim cleric, in an alleged conspiracy to carry out a terrorist campaign in New York City. ...**October 25:** The opposition Liberal Party wins an upset victory in Canada's general elections. ...**November 4:** Liberal Party leader Jean Chrétien (1934–) takes office as Canada's 20th prime minister. ...**November 16:** Federal Appeals Court strikes down the U.S. Defense Department's policy barring homosexuals from the military. ...**November 30:** President Clinton signs the Brady Bill gun-control measure, which requires a waiting period to buy a handgun.

Asia, Africa & Latin America

1992 (Continued). July 2: Labor Party head Yitzhak Rabin (1922–1995) becomes prime minister of Israel. ...**July 21–22:** Pablo Escobar escapes from his Colombia prison. ...**October 2:** Brazilian president Fernando Collor de Mello (1949–), facing corruption charges, says he will resign his office. ...**November 27:** For the second time in a year, rebellious military officers in Venezuela fail in a coup attempt. ...**December 6:** Hindu militants wreck a Muslim mosque in the Indian city of Ayodhya, touching off new sectarian violence in that country. ...**December 16–17:** Israel expels 415 Palestinians said to be sympathizers of the radical Muslim Hamas organization.

1993. February 12: South African government and the African National Congress agree on a plan for black majority rule of the country. ...**March 25:** Israel's Likud Party chooses a new leader, conservative Benjamin Netanyahu (1949–). ...**May 28:** President Clinton extends most-favored-nation trading status to China by one year, citing improvements in the country's human rights record. ...**June 1–6:** Army overthrows Guatemala's president Jorge Serrano (1945–). Guatemalan congress chooses the country's human rights ombudsman, Ramiro de León (1942–), to succeed Serrano. ...**June 3:** Prince Norodom Sihanouk tries to form a coalition government with Cambodia's two leading political parties. ...**June 9:** Japan's Crown Prince Naruhito (1960–) weds Masako Owada (1963–) in a traditional Shinto ceremony at the Imperial Palace in Tokyo. ...**July 3:** Haitian leaders reach accord to restore ousted president Jean-Bertrand Aristide to office by October. ...**July 25–31:** Israeli reprisal attacks on guerrillas in southern Lebanon kill 130 and wound 500, mostly civilians. ...**August 6:** Morihiro Hosokawa (1938–), head of a reform coalition, becomes prime minister of Japan. ...**August 31:** Israeli government approves in principle a proposal for interim Palestinian self-rule. ...**September 13:** At a meeting in Washington, D.C., Israel and the Palestine Liberation Organization sign agreement for interim Palestinian rule in the occupied territories. ...**September 23:** Israeli parliament approves peace agreement with Palestine Liberation Organization by a 61–50 vote. ...**September 24:** Cambodia restores Prince Sihanouk, who reigned from 1941 to 1955, to the throne as king. ...**October 12:** Indian government puts the death toll from a September earthquake in south India at 9,748 persons. ...**December 2:** Colombian police and soldiers kill fugitive cartel leader Pablo Escobar (b. 1969).

Science, Invention & Technology

1992 (Continued). July 13: Three of the world's largest electronics manufacturers—IBM, Siemens, and Toshiba—agree to collaborate on development of more powerful computer memory chips. ...**October 1–2:** U.S. scientists release the first two maps of human chromosomes, part of the international Human Genome Project. ...**October 12:** U.S. space agency NASA announces the start of a long-term search of the universe for signs of extraterrestrial life. ...**December 30:** U.S. Environmental Protection Agency removes California gray whale, once nearly extinct, from the endangered species list, saying it is fully recovered.

1993. January 7: U.S. Environmental Protection Agency warns nonsmokers they are at risk of cancer and other diseases from secondhand smoke. ...**June 7–9:** Ninth International Congress on AIDS reports the deadly HIV virus on the rise worldwide, especially in Africa and Southeast Asia. ...**August 21:** U.S. ground control loses contact with the $980 million *Mars Observer* spacecraft as it nears Mars. ...**October 21:** U.S. Congress shuts down the four-year-old superconducting supercollider, citing escalating cost estimates approaching $11 billion; the project would have allowed scientists to study high-speed collisions of atomic particles. ...**December 4–7:** Crew of the space shuttle *Endeavor*, in five spacewalks, repair flawed main mirror and other problems in the Hubble space telescope.

The Twin Towers of New York City's World Trade Center, prior to the explosion on January 26, 1993.

Religion, Culture & Arts

1992 (Continued). October: Toronto Blue Jays defeat Atlanta Braves to win the World Series. ...**October 31:** Pope John Paul II says the Catholic Church was wrong to condemn Galileo Galilei for his theories. ... **November 11:** Church of England votes to ordain women. ...**November 16:** Roman Catholic Church issues a new universal catechism to replace the version in use for the past 400 years.

1993. Steven Spielberg's *Schindler's List*, a film exploring the brutality of the Holocaust, wins the Academy Award for best picture. Tom Hanks (1956–) is named best actor. Holly Hunter (1958–) wins best actress. ...Pearl Jam release the album *Vs.*, which sells a record 950,000 copies in its first week in stores. ...**January:** University of Chicago announces the finding of a 4,300-year-old figurine of a domesticated horse in Asia Minor; it is said to be the oldest known sculpture of a horse. ...**January 31:** Iran reaffirms its 1989 death sentence against British author Salman Rushdie. ...Dallas Cowboys beat Buffalo Bills 52–17 to win Super Bowl XXVII. ...**May 12:** Two slivers of wood said to be from the cross on which Jesus Christ was crucified are sold at a Paris auction for $18,000. ...**June 11:** *Jurassic Park*, directed by Steven Spielberg, opens and sets a first-day box office earnings record of $18.2 million. ...**June 20:** Chicago Bulls, led by Michael Jordan (1964–), win their third consecutive National Basketball Association championship. ...**August 15:** Pope John Paul II, on a tour of the United States, says Mass for 400,000 near Denver, Colorado. ...**September 23:** International Olympic Committee, responding to criticism of China's human rights record, rejects Beijing as the site of the 2000 Olympics. ...**October:** Toronto Blue Jays defeat Philadelphia Phillies to win their second straight World Series. ...**October 6:** Basketball superstar Michael Jordan retires from the Chicago Bulls and decides to play professional baseball. After spending a season with a minor league baseball team, Jordon will return to the Chicago Bulls at the end of the 1994–1995 season. In January 1999 he will announce his retirement for what he claims will be the last time.

International Affairs

1994. January 10: NATO leaders approve a plan to expand the alliance by admitting some Eastern European nations of the former Soviet bloc. ...**January 14:** U.S. president Bill Clinton, Russian president Boris Yeltsin and Ukraine president Leonid Kravchuk (1934–) sign a treaty under which Ukraine agrees to give up its nuclear arsenal. ...**March 16–21:** International Atomic Energy Agency charges North Korea with obstruction and demands cooperation in its inspection of the country's nuclear facilities. ...**July 31:** UN authorizes a U.S.-led force to invade Haiti and restore Jean-Bertrand Aristide to power. ...**August 13:** United States and North Korea sign an agreement in Geneva that allows UN inspectors to tour North Korea's main nuclear laboratory. ...**September 18:** Haiti's military government agrees to relinquish power, avoiding an invasion by U.S.-led forces. **September 19:** U.S. forces arrive in Haiti to ensure a peaceful return to power for Aristide. ...**November 7:** Yugoslav war crimes tribunal at The Hague in the Netherlands indicts Serb detention camp commander for crimes against humanity.

1995. January 28: United States and Vietnam agree to exchange low-level diplomats, the first step toward resumption of full diplomatic ties. ...**January 30:** UN authorizes 6,000-strong peacekeeping contingent to take over from U.S. invasion force in Haiti. ...**February 13:** War crimes tribunal indicts 21 Serbs for crimes against humanity during the Bosnian civil war, in which Bosnian Serb forces carried out ethnic cleansing of Muslim areas. ...**March 3:** Admitting failure to establish stable government there, UN withdraws its last 2,400 peacekeepers from Somalia. ...**March 31:** UN peacekeepers replace U.S. troops in Haiti.

Western & Eastern Europe

1994. February 17: Under threat of NATO air strikes, Bosnian Serbs agree to withdraw from the commanding heights around Sarajevo. ...**April 23:** NATO air attacks force Bosnian Serbs to withdraw from the Muslim enclave of Gorazde. ...**May 11:** With the Conservative win in Italy's parliamentary elections, Silvio Berlusconi (1936–) of Forza Italia is sworn in as prime minister. ...**May 13:** United States, Russia and five European countries propose a roughly equal partition of Bosnia-Herzegovina between the Muslim-Croat federation and the Bosnian Serbs. ...**June 4:** Hungarian Socialist Party, led by former Communists, now in the majority in parliament, chooses its leader Gyula Horn (1932–) as prime minister. ...**June 8:** In Geneva, Muslims, Croats and Serbs agree to a UN-monitored cease-fire. ...**July 2:** Albanian court convicts the last Communist president, Ramiz Alia (1925–), of abuses of power and sentences him to nine years in prison. ...**August 31:** After six months of negotiations, the Irish Republican Army announces a cease-fire and says it will seek a political solution to the troubles in Northern Ireland. ...**October 16:** German chancellor Helmut Kohl retains power in national elections, but with his parliamentary majority reduced from 134 seats to 10. ...**December 9:** British government and Sinn Féin, the political wing of the Irish Republican Army, open talks aimed at ending 25 years of violence in Northern Ireland. **December 11:** Russian military forces invade the southern republic of Chechnya, which declared itself independent in 1991. ...**December 31:** Parties in the Bosnian civil war agree to another cease-fire, this one to last four months.

1995. January 13: Russian parliament urges President Boris Yeltsin to seek a political settlement in Chechnya, where at great cost Russian forces are slowly subduing the capital, Grozny. ...**January 18:** Lamberto Dini (1931–) becomes prime minister of Italy. ...**February 21:** A Russian commission estimates 25,000 civilians have perished in the two-month conflict in breakaway Chechnya. ...**May 1:** With expiration of the four-month cease-fire in the former Yugoslavia, Croats launch offensive against Serb positions in Croatia. ...**May 7:** On his third attempt, Conservative Jacques Chirac (1932–) is elected president of France.

U.S. & Canada

1994. January 17: An earthquake rocks the Los Angeles area, killing 61 and destroying or damaging 45,000 dwellings. ...**January 20:** Attorney General Janet Reno appoints a special prosecutor to investigate the Whitewater real estate deal involving President Clinton and the first lady, Hillary Rodham Clinton. ...**February 15:** Tarnished by the Tailhook scandal, Chief of Naval Operations Admiral Frank Kelso (1933–) says he will take early retirement. ...**February 21:** Central Intelligence Agency official Aldrich Ames (1941–) admits he and his wife sold secrets to the Soviet Union and, later, to Russia. ...**March 4:** U.S. federal court convicts four men accused of the 1993 bombing of the World Trade Center in New York City. ...**April 22:** Former president Richard M. Nixon (b. 1913) dies. ...**April 28:** U.S. navy expels 28 midshipmen from the U.S. Naval Academy in the biggest cheating scandal in the academy's history. ...Ames is sentenced to life in prison for spying for the Russians . ...**May 6:** In a lawsuit, former Arkansas state employee Paula Jones (1966–) accuses President Clinton, of making an unwanted sexual advance toward her in 1991 while he was governor of Arkansas. ...**May 13:** President Clinton nominates Appeals Court judge Stephen Breyer (1938–) to the U.S. Supreme Court. ...**June 17:** O. J. Simpson (1947–), former football star and actor, is arrested in the murder of his former wife, Nicole Brown Simpson (b. 1959), and her friend, Ronald Goldman (b. 1969), in Los Angeles. ...**July 22:** A federal court orders the Citadel in Charleston, South Carolina, a state-funded all-male military academy, to admit women. ...**July 29:** U.S. Senate approves the Supreme Court nomination of Breyer. ...**November 8:** In midterm elections, Republicans win control of both house of Congress for the first time since 1952. ...**December 5:** House Republicans elect Newt Gingrich (1943–) of Georgia the Speaker.

1995. January 31: Prosecution opens the double-murder case against Simpson in Los Angeles. ...**February 7:** Ramzi Ahmed Yousef (b. c. 1968–), alleged mastermind of the 1993 bombing of the World Trade Center in New York City, is arrested in Pakistan. ...**April 19:** A bomb explodes at the Alfred P. Murrah Federal Building in Oklahoma City, Oklahoma; 169 are killed and 400 are injured. ...**April 21:** Police arrest Timothy McVeigh (1968–), a Gulf War veteran, and charge him in the Oklahoma City bombing. ...**May 10:** Terry Nichols (1955–), earlier accused of conspiracy in the Oklahoma City bombing, is also charged.

Asia, Africa & Latin America

1994. January 1–4: Peasants in southern Mexican state of Chiapas launch uprising, and more than 100 are killed. Government will offer amnesty to insurgents. ...**February 25:** Israeli settler opens fire on a West Bank mosque, killing 29 worshippers (three others are trampled to death), wounding 150 and threatening the Mideast peace process. ...**April 8:** Eight months after taking office, Japanese prime minister Hosokawa resigns in wake of allegations he accepted an illegal loan. ...**April 26:** Cease-fire halts tribal conflict in Burundi and Rwanda. Estimate of civilian death toll rises to 200,000. ...**April 26–29:** South Africa conducts its first universal suffrage election, choosing a president, a 400-seat national assembly and a 90-seat senate. ...**May 2:** Nelson Mandela, who spent 27 years in prison as an opponent of apartheid, claims victory in South Africa's presidential election. ...United States pledges $15 million in humanitarian aid to Rwanda. Estimate of death toll in civil war between Hutus and Tutsis is revised upward to 500,000. ...**July 8:** Kim Il Sung (b. 1912), leader of North Korea since its founding in 1948, dies. ...**October 26:** Israel and Jordan sign a peace treaty. Jordan is the first Arab nation to make formal peace with Israel since Egypt in 1979.

Science, Invention & Technology

1994. March 10: The Centers for Disease Control announces AIDS cases in the United States doubled in 1993, to 103,500. ...**May 6:** British and French heads of state inaugurate the 31-mile Channel tunnel linking Britain to the continent of Europe. ...**July 16–22:** Fragments of the comet Shoemaker-Levy 9 strike Jupiter at speeds of up to 130,000 mph. The Hubble telescope photographs the cataclysm. ...**September 14:** U.S.-Canadian researchers say they found the gene believed responsible for about half of all hereditary breast cancer cases.

Religion, Culture & Arts

1994. Robert Zemeckis's (1952–) *Forrest Gump* wins the Academy Award for best picture. The film's star, Tom Hanks, wins his second consecutive Academy Award for best actor. Jessica Lange (1949–) is named best actress. ...**January 30:** In a rematch of the 1993 Super Bowl, Dallas Cowboys again beat Buffalo Bills, 30–13, to win Super Bowl XXVIII. ...**March 12:** Church of England admits two women to the priesthood, the first women ordained over its 460-year history. ...**April 8:** Kurt Cobain (b. 1967), singer, songwriter and guitarist with the band Nirvana, is found dead of a self-inflicted gunshot wound in his Seattle home. ...In the Sistine Chapel, Pope John Paul II unveils Michelangelo's restored fresco *The Last Judgment*. ...**August 11:** U.S. major league baseball players go out on strike, bringing the season to an abrupt halt. ...**September 14:** The acting baseball commissioner announces that, because of the players' strike, there will not be a World Series in 1994. ...**December 24:** Three explorers find ancient paintings and engravings in a cave in the Ardèche region of southern France.

Courtesy: April Pearce-Lowe

O.J. Simpson's home on Rockingham Drive in Brentwood, California, as it appeared in June 1994, soon after his ex-wife, Nicole Brown Simpson, was murdered. Police pursued Simpson in a slow-moving car chase that ended inside the gate of Simpson's house. ➤

1995. January 17: Earthquake devastates Kobe, Japan, and vicinity, killing 5,000 and injuring 26,500. ...**January 31:** U.S. president Clinton authorizes a $20 billion line of credit to avert a financial calamity in Mexico, where falling value of the peso has threatened Mexico's ability to pay its international debts. ...**March 20:** Intentional release of nerve gas in a Tokyo subway station kills 12. Members of a religious cult are blamed.

1995. May 10: Scientists affirm reappearance of the deadly Ebola virus, which has killed more than half its victims, in Zaire (Congo). ...**June 29:** The U.S. space shuttle *Atlantis* docks with the Russian space station *Mir*. Scientists from the two craft conduct joint experiments.

1995. Mel Gibson's (1956–) *Braveheart* wins the Academy Award for best picture. Nicolas Cage (1964–) is named best actor. Susan Sarandon wins best actress. ...**January 30:** San Francisco 49ers defeat San Diego Chargers to win Super Bowl XXIX. ...**March 30:** Pope John Paul II reaffirms church opposition to abortion, contraception, in vitro fertilization and euthanasia. ...**April 2:** Owners of major league baseball teams accept players' offer to return to work, ending the longest sports strike in history. ...**June 7:** French officials say testing shows the Ardèche cave paintings, discovered in December 1994, are at least 30,340 years old.

International Affairs

1995 (Continued). July 11: Twenty years after the close of the Vietnam War, the United States and Vietnam open diplomatic relations.

1996. January 29: Bowing to international protests, France ends a series of nuclear tests in the Pacific at the sixth of eight planned explosions. ...**May 20:** Agreement with UN permits Iraq to sell oil, with proceeds to be used for food and medicine. ...**September 3–4:** U.S. missiles strike targets in Iraq in retaliation for Iraqi attacks on Kurdish territory. UN suspends oil-sales agreement. ...**September 10:** UN approves a comprehensive nuclear test ban treaty. ...**December 17:** Kofi Annan (1938–) of Ghana is named secretary-general of the UN, replacing Boutros Boutros-Ghali (1922–) of Egypt.

Western & Eastern Europe

1995 (Continued). June 15: Bosnian Muslims open an offensive with the objective of lifting the 38-month siege of Sarajevo. ...**July 30:** Negotiated truce ends the fighting in Chechnya. Its status in the Russian republic will be determined later. ...**September 8:** Parties in Bosnia agree to a peace plan that will create two self-ruling states. ...**October 12:** A new cease-fire takes hold in Bosnia. ...**November 19:** Alexander Kwasniewski (1954–), a former Communist, is elected president of Poland, defeating incumbent Lech Walesa. ...**November 21–27:** Bosnian factions reach a comprehensive peace agreement, effectively splitting the country in two. United States is to enforce the treaty with 20,000 troops in place for at least a year. ...**December 17:** In Russian elections, Communists record parliamentary gains, taking 22 percent of the vote and 157 of 450 seats in the Duma; they had held only 45 seats.

1996. February 3: Bosnian Serb, Muslim and Croat withdrawals, part of the 1995 peace agreement, bring the siege of Sarajevo to an end. ...**March 13:** Gunman opens fire on a kindergarten gymnasium in Dunblane, Scotland, killing 16 children. He then shoots himself. ...**May 4:** Centrist José María Aznar (1953–) is chosen prime minister of Spain. ...**May 16:** Romano Prodi (1939–) of the center-left Oliver Tree Coalition becomes prime minister of Italy. ...**July 3:** Boris Yeltsin wins a runoff election with 54 percent of the vote to retain the presidency of Russia. ...**August 28:** A divorce decree ends the 15-year marriage of Prince Charles, heir to the throne of Britain, and Princess Diana.

U.S. & Canada

1995 (Continued). August 12: Shannon Faulkner (1975–) is the first female admitted to the Citadel. Six days later, she resigns. ...**October 1:** A U.S. federal court convicts Sheik Omar Abdel Rahman and nine other Muslims of plotting terrorist acts, including bombings and assassinations in New York City. ...**October 3:** A jury in Los Angeles acquits O. J. Simpson of the 1994 killings of his former wife, Nicole Brown Simpson, and her friend, Ronald Goldman. ...**October 30:** Quebec narrowly votes to remain a part of Canada. In a referendum, 49.4 percent support sovereignty for the province. ...**December 10:** With U.S. Congress and the White House at an impasse over the 1996 budget, many government operations are shut down; some 280,000 government workers are sent home on furlough.

1996. January 6: U.S. government shutdown ends with a tentative budget agreement between President Clinton and Congress. ...**March 8:** Jack Kevorkian is acquitted of breaking Michigan's physician-assisted suicide law. He has been present at 27 suicides since 1990. ...**April 3:** U.S. agents in Montana arrest Theodore Kaczynski (1942–), a former college professor, as a suspect in the Unabomber case. The bomber has killed 3 and wounded 23 others in series of attacks since 1978. ...**April 10:** President Clinton vetoes a bill that would ban the late-term procedure known as partial-birth abortion. ...**September 21:** President Clinton signs the Defense of Marriage Act, which allows states to disregard same-sex unions even when they are certified in another state. ...**May 28:** Two Clinton partners in the Whitewater real estate deal, James McDougal (1941–1998) and Susan McDougal (1950–), are convicted of fraud and conspiracy in Arkansas. The same jury convicts Arkansas governor Jim Guy Tucker (1943–) on similar charges. ...**July 17:** An explosion shatters a Paris-bound TWA jetliner over the Atlantic, killing all 230 on board. ...**August 22:** President Clinton signs welfare overhaul legislation, ending the 61-year federal guarantee of cash assistance to poor families with children. ...**November 5:** President Clinton wins reelection, defeating Robert Dole (1923–) and independent candidate Ross Perot. Republicans retain control of U.S. Congress.

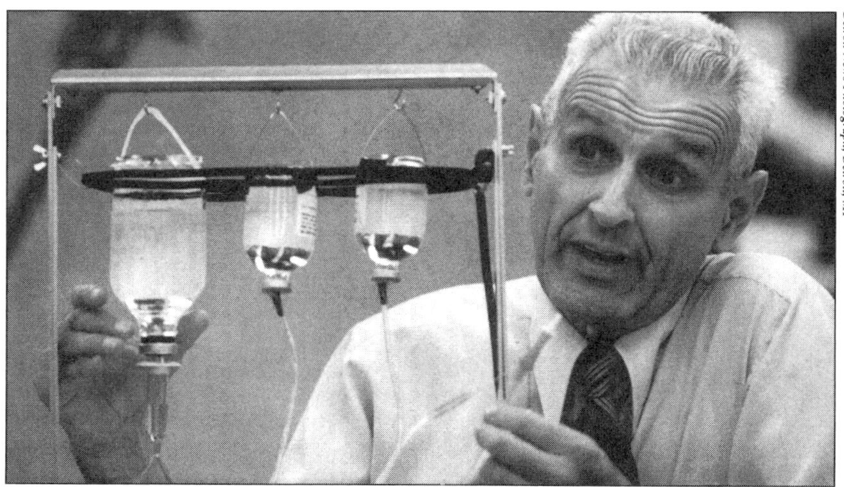

Detroit News Photograph, Detroit, MI

▲ ***Dr. Jack Kevorkian with his "suicide machine," which helped many terminally ill patients commit suicide during 1990s.***

Asia, Africa & Latin America

1995 (Continued). July 10: Military rulers in Myanmar (Burma) free political activist Daw Aung San Suu Kyi from house arrest. She is 1991Nobel Peace Prize laureate. ...**November 4:** Israeli prime minister Yitzhak Rabin (b. 1922) is shot and killed. ...**November 10:** Nigeria's military government hangs nine dissidents, including environmentalist Ken Saro-Wiwa (b. 1941); 52-member Commonwealth of Nations condemns Nigeria.

1996. January 1: Ryutaro Hashimoto (1937–) becomes prime minister of Japan, the first Socialist to hold the office since 1948. ...**January 20:** Palestine Liberation Organization (PLO) chairman Yasir Arafat is elected president of the Palestinian Authority, which is taking control of Israeli-occupied territory in the West Bank and Gaza. ...**May 29:** Benjamin Netanyahu of the conservative Likud Party, a critic of the peace accord with the PLO, is elected prime minister of Israel. ...**June 25:** Bomb explosion at a military complex near Dharan, Saudi Arabia, kills 19 U.S. service personnel. ...**October 20:** Free marketer Arnoldo Alemán (1946–) is elected president of Nicaragua. He defeats Daniel Ortega of the left-wing Sandinista movement. ...**November 12:** Two jetliners collide in midair near New Delhi, India. All 351 on board the two aircraft are killed.

Science, Invention & Technology

1995 (Continued). August 24: World Health Organization declares Ebola outbreak in Zaire (Congo) at an end; 244 of 315 known victims have died.

AP/Wide World Photos, New York, NY

Princess Diana in June 1997 at the National Museum of Women in the Arts in Washington, D.C.; she is at a benefit to support victims of land mines. ➤

1996. January 2: A Nature Conservancy survey puts one-third of 20,000 U.S. plant and animal species on the rare or imperiled list. ...**January 17:** Californian astronomers discover two planet-like bodies outside the solar system, a relatively close 35 light-years from earth. ...**January 31:** Astronomers find a new galaxy in the constellation Virgo 14 billion light-years from earth. ...**July 5:** UN reports AIDS is spreading more rapidly among women worldwide; 5.8 million are said to have died of AIDS since the beginning of the outbreak. ...**August 6:** NASA says rock samples from Mars suggest "a primitive form of microscopic life" is possible beyond earth. ...**September 26:** Shannon Lucid (1943–) lands in Florida after 188 days in space, setting the American record and women's world record for length of time in space. ...**October 17:** Texas researchers report that a chemical in tobacco damages the gene that suppresses uncontrolled growth of tumor-causing cells; they say this explains why smoking causes cancer.

Religion, Culture & Arts

1995 (Continued). September 6: Baltimore Orioles shortstop Cal Ripken Jr. (1960–) plays his 2,131st consecutive game, breaking Lou Gehrig's 1939 record. ...**October:** Atlanta Braves defeat Cleveland Indians to win the World Series. ...**October 4–8:** Pope John Paul II makes his fourth visit to the United States; he conducts Mass for 120,000 in Central Park, in New York City. ...**October 16:** As many as 600,000 African-American men turn out in Washington, D.C., for the Million Man March, a Nation of Islam rally intended to affirm family and community.

1996. *The English Patient* wins the Academy Award for best picture. Geoffrey Rush (1951–) is named best actor. Frances McDormand (1957–) wins best actress. ...**January 15:** Five leading African American church denominations form a for-profit company to boost African American consumers' buying power for health insurance, mortgage loans, durable goods and food. The churches claim 20 million members. ...**January 31:** Dallas Cowboys defeat Pittsburgh Steelers 27–17 to win Super Bowl XXX. ...**March 4:** Paul McCartney (1942–), George Harrison (1943–) and Ringo Starr (1940–) of the 1960s' rock group the Beatles reject a $225 million offer for a reunion tour of Japan, Europe and the United States. ...**October:** New York Yankees defeat Atlanta Braves to win the World Series.

International Affairs

1997. January 20: The UN issues two major reports warning of possible water shortages within the next 30 years. ...**March 20:** UN Secretary General Kofi Annan endorses a plan for an all-African military force. ...**March 21:** U.S. president Bill Clinton and Russian president Boris Yeltsin reach an agreement regarding NATO's expansion into eastern Europe. ...**March 31:** U.S. general Wesley Clark is named commander of NATO forces in Europe.

1998. January–February: Iraq's Saddam Hussein refuses to allow UN weapons inspectors into various Iraqi installations. Only after threatened air strikes does Hussein allow the inspections to take place. ...**June 24:** The UN releases a report saying that in certain areas of Africa, one in four adults has the HIV virus. ...**June 30:** The UN announces that it will begin a program to treat 30,000 pregnant women infected with the HIV virus in 11 countries. ...**August:** Hussein again refuses to allow UN weapons inspectors into some Iraqi sites. ...**August 13:** The UN Security Council condemns the August 7 terrorist bombings of U.S. embassies in Nairobi, Kenya, and Dar-es-Salaam, United Republic of Tanzania. ...**August 20:** U.S. cruise missiles strike alleged terrorist training complexes in Afghanistan and an alleged chemical weapons factory in Sudan. ...**September 1–2:** Boris Yeltsin and Bill Clinton hold a two-day summit in Moscow. ...**September 2:** The UN tribunal finds Jean-Paul Akayesu (1953–), a former mayor of Taba, Rwanda, guilty of genocide. ...**September 24:** The UN Security Council sends a warning to President Slobodan Milosevic of Serbia to stop Serbian attacks on civilians in the Kosovo region or face international intervention.

Western & Eastern Europe

1997. January 5: Greek Cypriots agree to buy surface-to-air missiles from Russia. ...Russian troop withdrawal from Chechnya is completed. ...**January 22:** A Communist attempt in parliament to oust Russian president Boris Yeltsin fails. ...**March 18:** Finland votes against joining NATO. ...**August 31:** Britain's Princess Diana (b. 1960) is killed in an automobile accident in Paris, France. ...**November 1:** Mary McAleese (1951–), born in the British province of Northern Ireland, wins the presidency of the Irish republic.

1998. February 3: A U.S. jet flying too low slices the cables of a ski gondola in Italy, plunging the gondola to the ground, killing the 20 people aboard. ...**March–April:** Ethnic Albanian rebels in the Serbian province of Kosovo begin to intensify their attacks against the Serbian government. ...**April:** Russian duma confirms Sergei Kiriyenko (1963–) as Russian prime minister. ...**May 23:** Irish voters overwhelmingly approve Irish peace plan in a referendum vote. ...**August 15:** In the deadliest paramilitary attack ever in Northern Ireland, a car bomb explodes in the town of Omagh, killing 28 and injuring over 200 people. ...**August–September:** Russian economy is in turmoil amidst widespread political disarray. ...**September 11:** Russian duma confirms Yevgeny Primakov as Russian prime minister. ...**September 27:** In German elections, Chancellor Helmut Kohl is defeated by challenger Gerhard Schroeder.

U.S. & Canada

1997. A gunman opens fire on tourists atop the Empire State Building in New York City. ...**January 16:** Six people are injured after a bomb explodes at an abortion clinic in Atlanta, Georgia. ...**January 20:** Bill Clinton is inaugurated for his second term as U.S. president. ...**February 11:** A civil jury in California finds O.J. Simpson liable for the "wrongful deaths" of his former wife, Nicole Brown Simpson, and her friend Ronald Goldman. ...**April 27:** The trial of Timothy McVeigh, accused of bombing a federal building in Oklahoma City, begins in federal court in Denver, Colorado. ...**May:** A volunteerism summit is held in Philadelphia, Pennsylvania. ...**June 3:** McVeigh is found guilty of the bombing of a federal building in Oklahoma City. ...**July 13:** The jury in the trial of McVeigh sentences him to death. ...**August 5:** President Clinton signs a balanced budget bill with the aim of balancing the federal budget by the year 2002.

1998. January 26: Accused Unabomber Theodore Kaczynski pleads guilty to sending letter bombs. ...**April 2:** A federal judge dismisses Paula Jones's sexual harassment lawsuit against President Clinton. ...**April 6:** The Dow Jones Industrial Average closes above 9,000 for the first time. ...**May 4:** Kaczynski is given four consecutive life sentences. ...**July 24:** A gunman opens fire inside the U.S. Capitol, killing two police officers and wounding one visitor. ...**August 17:** President Clinton becomes the first sitting president to testify before a federal grand jury (via closed circuit television). Later that evening, in a nationally televised address, Clinton admits to having had an "inappropriate" relationship with former White House intern Monica Lewinsky (1973–). ...**August 31:** The Dow Jones Industrial Average loses 512 points, the second largest single day loss in history. ...**September 2:** A Swissair jet crashes into the Atlantic Ocean south of Halifax, Nova Scotia, killing 227. ...**September 10:** Independent prosecutor Kenneth Starr (1946–) releases his findings to U.S. Congress regarding the relationship between President Clinton and Lewinsky. ...**September 11:** The Starr Report is publicly released over the Internet. ...**November 7:** Speaker of the House Newt Gingrich announces his resignation. ...**December 19:** Clinton becomes the first elected president in U.S. history to be impeached. (Andrew Johnson, impeached in 1868, had succeeded to the presidency after the assassination of Abraham Lincoln.)

Asia, Africa & Latin America

1997. January 2: In Singapore's parliamentary elections, the Ruling People's Action Party wins 81 out of 83 parliamentary seats. ...**January 16:** Israeli troops begin to pullout of Hebron. ...**February 26:** Israel approves construction of new Jewish homes in Arab East Jerusalem. ...**March 17:** In El Salvador, left-wing coalition makes major gains in city and congressional elections.

1998. May: Anti-government riots break out in several cities throughout Indonesia. ...Israel celebrates its 50th anniversary. ...**May 18–20:** In separate tests, India explodes five nuclear devices and declares itself a "nuclear power." ...**May 21:** Bowing to antigovernment rioting, Indonesian president Suharto (1921–) resigns. ...**May 28:** In response to India's tests of nuclear devices, Pakistan conducts its first underground test of a nuclear device, enlarging the club of confirmed nuclear powers to seven. ...**August 7:** Terrorist bombs explode at the U.S. embassies in Nairobi, Kenya and Dar-es-Salaam, United Republic of Tanzania, killing over 100 people and injuring more than 1,000. ...**September 11:** The city hall building in Jaffna, Sri Lanka, is bombed, killing the city's mayor, police chief and military commander. ...**September 27–30:** More than 1,300 Sri Lankan soldiers and Tamil rebels die in fighting near Colombo, Sri Lanka.

Science, Invention & Technology

1997. Scientists discover the three-dimensional shape of gp120, the protein structure on the surface of the HIV virus. ...**March:** English scientists announce that they have cloned an adult sheep using cells from another sheep's udder.

1998. March: Scientists announce the discovery of four newly forming solar systems, all between 25 and 220 light years away from earth. ...**March 27:** The FDA approves the impotence pill Viagra for sale in United States. ...**April 13:** "Dolly," the sheep cloned from another sheep's cells, gives birth to a lamb. ...**June:** The FDA approves the first large-scale efficacy trials of an AIDS vaccine. ...**July 21:** Astronaut Alan Shepard, Jr. (b. 1923), the first American in space, dies. ...**September 23:** A man in Lyons, France, becomes the first person to undergo a hand and forearm transplant.

Religion, Culture & Arts

1997. Poet Allen Ginsberg (b. 1926) dies. ...Helen Hunt (1963–) wins the Academy Award for best actress. Jack Nicholson is named best actor. ...**January:** Green Bay Packers defeat New England Patriots 35–21 to win Super Bowl XXXI. ...**October:** Florida Marlins defeat Cleveland Indians to win the World Series. ...**December 19:** *Titanic*, directed by James Cameron (1951–), is released. By the spring of 1998, it will become the all-time biggest money-maker in history, earning over $1.8 billion worldwide. The film will go on to win the Academy Award for best picture.

1997–1998. In a season of American political scandals, several comedies based more or less loosely on current events are released, among them Barry Levinson's *Wag the Dog,* Mike Nichols's *Primary Colors*, and Warren Beatty's (1937–) *Bulworth.*

Courtesy: United Nations, New York, NY

UN Secretary-General Kofi Annan addresses the staff of the United Nations in January 1997.

1998. The American Film Institute names *Citizen Kane*, directed by Orson Welles, the best American movie ever made. ...Bob Dylan's (1941–) *Time Out of Mind* wins the Grammy Award for album of the year. ...**January:** Denver Broncos defeat Green Bay Packers 32–25 to win Super Bowl XXXII. ...**May 14:** *Seinfeld*, one of the most popular television shows in U.S. history, airs its final episode. ...Singer and actor Frank Sinatra (b. 1915), considered the greatest popular singer of the 20th century, dies. ...**June:** Chicago Bulls defeat Utah Jazz to win their third straight NBA Championship. ...**July 24:** Steven Spielberg's *Saving Private Ryan* is released. ...**September 6:** Japanese filmmaker Akira Kurosawa (b. 1910), considered one of the world's greatest directors, dies. ...**September 8:** St. Louis Cardinals's first baseman Mark McGwire (1964–) hits his 62nd home run of the season, breaking the single-season home run total set by Roger Maris (1934–1985) in 1961. On September 13, Chicago Cubs' outfielder Sammy Sosa (1968–) also breaks Maris's record. ...**September 27:** In the last game of the season, McGwire hits two home runs, bringing his record-setting season total to 70. Sosa ends the season with 66 home runs. ...**October:** New York Yankees defeat San Diego Padres to win the World Series.

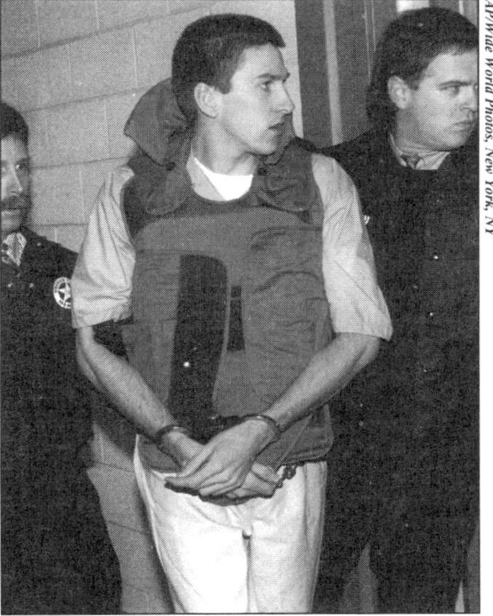
AP/Wide World Photos, New York, NY

Two U.S. marshals escort Timothy McVeigh to the federal courthouse in Oklahoma City on January 31, 1996, to attend a hearing on a change of venue for his trial.

INDEX

The letters *A*, *B* and *C* following each page number designate the first, second and third columns, respectively, on each page. Italicized numbers denote an illustration on that page.

A

A ("scarlet letter"), 224B
Aachen, 332A
Ab urb condita (Livy), 31C
abacus, 91B
Abbas I (shah of Persia), 182B
Abbas I (viceroy of Egypt), 259A, 263A
Abbas II (viceroy of Egypt), 283A, 297A
Abbas the Great (shah of Persia), 172B
Abbe, Cleveland, 273B
Abbeville, 322A
Abbott, Robert S., 290B
Abd al-Jalil (sultan of Johore), 168C
Abd ar-Rahman (emir of Afghanistan), 277A
Abd ar-Rahman II, 78B
Abd ar-Rahman III, 84B
Abd-el-Kadar (emir of Mascara), 251A, 253A, 257A
Abd-el-Krim, 307A, 309A
Abdallabi, 178B
Abdallah, 82B
Abdalmalik, 70B
Abdel Rahman, Sheikh Omar, 378C
Abdul Aziz (king of Saudi Arabia), 341A
Abdul Aziz (sultan of Ottoman Empire), 275A
Abdul Hamid I (sultan of Ottoman Empire), 220B
Abdul Hamid II (sultan of Ottoman Empire), 275A, 291A, 293A
Abdulla-al-Sallal (president of Yemen), 355A
Abdullah (emir of Transjordan), 307A
Abdullah (king of Jordan), 337A, 339A
Abel, Frederick, 281B
Abel, John, 293B
Abélard, Pierre, 101C, 103C
Abelson, Philip, 323B
Abenaki, 201A, 203A, 205A
Aberdaron, Treaty of, 134A
Aberdeen University, 149C
Abermarle, 191A
Abernathy, Ralph, 354C
Ableman v. Booth, 264B
ABM (anti-ballistic missile) Treaty, 358A
Abo
  Peace of, 212A
  Treaty of, 240A
abolitionism, abolitionists, 250B, 252B, 254B, 256B, 259C, 264B
Aborigines, 229A, 249A
abortion, 358C, 360B, 360C, 369C, 371C, 372C, 381C, 382C, 384C
Aboukir, battle of, 235A
Abplanalp, Robert, 337B
Abraham, 4B
Abraham Lincoln (Sandburg), 323C
Abramovitz, Max, 353C
abrasive, industrial, 347B
Abruzzi, 330A
Absalom, Absalom (Faulkner), 319C
Abstract Expressionism, 305C, 337C, 341C, 343C
Abu Abdollah Ja'far Rudaki, 87C
Abu al-Abbas Ahmad I (sharif of Morocco), 170B
Abu Hamed, 287A
Abu Mervan ibn Zuh, 103B
Abu Nasr, Ahmad Shah Bahadur Mujahid-ud-din (emir of Afghanistan), 214C, 216C
Abu Said, 140C
Abu-Simbel, 9C, 355C
Abyssinia, Abyssinians, 62C, 64C, 68C. *See also* Ethiopia, Ethiopians
  and India, 58C
  and Italy, 281A, 285A, 310A, 316A, 319A
  World War II, 326A
Academy of the Mysteries of Nature, 167B
Acadia, Acadians, 177A, 181A, 185A, 201A, 205A, 207A, 215A, 226B
Acapulco, 240C
accelerator, linear, 337B
acelsufame K, 353B
Achaean League, 22C, 24C, 26C
Acheampong, Ignatius Kutu (leader of Ghana), 359A
Achebe, Chinua, 345C
Acheson, Dean, 338C
Achille Lauro (Italian cruise liner), 368A
Achilleis (Statius), 39C
Achin, 178C
acid citrate dextrose, 335B
Acoma, 97A
Acosta, Uriel, 187C
Acragas, 16C
Acre, 106B, 112B, 120B, 235A
Acropolis, 16C, 19C, 140A
Acrotiri, 6C
acrylic, 337A
Action in Chains (Maillol), 291C
Actium, battle of, 30A
acupuncture, *93*
Adal, 158B
Adalbert (king of Italy), 86B
Adalwald, 66B
Adam, Robert, 217C, 219C, 221C, 231C
Adam Bede (Eliot), 265C
Adamic, Louis, 331C
Adamnan, Saint, 73C
Adams, Henry, 281C, 283C
Adams, John (president of U.S.), 232B, 234B, 246B, 248B
Adams, John Quincy (president of U.S.), 244B, 246B, 248B, 250B
Adams, Samuel, 219A, 221A
Adams, Sherman, 344C
Adams, William, 176C
Adams-Onis Treaty, 244B
Adamson Act, 298B
Adan, 154B
Adana, 251A
Addams, Jane, *280,* 292B
adding machine, 283B
Addis Ababa, 289A, 303A, 349A
  Treaty of, 285A
Addison, Joseph, 205C
Adelaide, 253A, 255A
Aden, 146B, 160B, 210B, 267A, 319A, 355A
Adena culture, 32C, 63A
Adenauer, Konrad (chancellor of West Germany), 338B, 344B, 346B, 348B
adenosine triphosphate (ATP), 325B
Adige River, 129B, 298A
Adlan (king of Fundj), 176B
Admiralty Islands, 332C
Adolf, count of Nassau (king of Germany), 120A
Adolphus Frederick (king of Sweden), 214A
Adoration of the Magi, The (Velázquez), 181C
Adoration of the Name of Jesus (Gaulli), 197C
Adowa, battle of, 285A
Adrian IV, Pope, 104A, 105C
Adrianople, 56B, 130B, 276A
  Treaty of, 248A
  Truce of, 162A
Adriatic Sea, 51C
Adulis, 24A, 34B
Advanced Mobile Phone Service, 363B
Advancement of Learning (Bacon), 177C
Adventures de Télémaque, Les (Fénelon), 203C
Adventures of a Young Man (Dos Passos), 323C
Adventures of Huckleberry Finn, The (Twain), 279C
Adventures of Roderick Random, The (Smollett), 215C
Adventures of Tom Sawyer (Twain), 275C
Adversus indulgentias: Contra bullam pape (Huss), 135C
AEG Corporation, 317B
Aegean Islands, 151B
Aegean peoples, 4C
Aegina (Greek island), 14C
Aegospotami, battle of, 20C
Aelfric the Grammarian, 89C, 93C
Aelia Capitolina, 40B
Aemilian, 46A
Aequi, 23A
aerodrome, unmanned, 285B
Aeropagitica (Milton), 189C
Aeschylus, 17C
Aesop, *13,* 13C
Aesop's Fables (Aesop), 13C
Aeterni Patris (Gregory XV), 181C
Aethelstan (king of England), 84A, 85C, 86A
Aethiopica (Heliodorus), 47C
Aëtius, Flavius, 60B
Afars and Issas, French Territory of the, 363A
Afghanistan, Afghans, 140C, 150C, 162C, 216C, 351A, 384A
  Akbar and, 170C
  Barakzai dynasty, 253A
  and Britain, 239A, 255A, 257A, 263A, 277A, 291A, 305A
  Durrani dynasty, 214C, 253A
  earthquake in, 377A
  government, 160C, 214C, 231A, 253A, 273A, 311A, 359A
  independence of, 307A
  and India, 138C, 283A
  and Iran, 253A, 319A
  and Iraq, 319A
  Kurt dynasty, 114C
  and London Convention (1933), 314A
  and Persia, 208B, 210B, 233A, 263A
  science and technology, 79B
  and Soviet Union, 364A, 365A, 372A
  Third Afghan War, 307A
  and Timur, 132C, 138C
  and Turkey, 319A
Afiun-Karahissar, 307A
AFL-CIO, 328B, 332B, 342C, 344C, 370C
Afonso de Albuquerque (viceroy of India), 152C
Afonso I (king of Kongo), 152B, 156B
Afonso I (king of Portugal), 100B, 102B
Afonso III (king of Portugal), 114B
Afonso IV (king of Portugal), 124B
Africa, Africans, 48B, 144B, 157B, 168B. *See also individual countries*
  AIDS in, 379B
  and America, 169B
  arts, 375C
  and Britain, 200B
  and Europe, 202B
  famine in, 369C
  guns in, 196B
  and Holland, 208B
  politics, 346A
  and Portugal, 170B, 212B
  pottery, 38A
  and Prussia, 206B
  and Red Sea coast, 62C
  religion, 43A
  and Romans, 46B
  settlement, 58B, 62C
  slave trade, 167A, 181A, 188B, 214B
African Association, 227A
African Methodist Episcopal Church, 243C
African National Congress, 369A, 375A, 379A
African sleeping sickness, 213B
Africanus, Leo, 152B, 157B
Afrikaners, 279A. *See also* Boers
Afrique Occidentale Française, 285A
After Many a Summer Dies the Swan (Huxley), 323C
Aga Khan, 291A
Agade, 5B
Age of Bronze, The (Rodin), 277C
Age of Innocence, The (Wharton), 305C
Age of Reason, The (Paine), 233C
Agee, James, 325C
Agenais, 118A
Agha Muhammad (shah of Persia), 231A, 233A
Agilulf (king of Langobards), 66A
Agincourt, battle of, 136A
Agis IV (king of Sparta), 24C
Agliote, St. Pietro at, 81C
Agnes of Poitou, 92A
Agnew, Spiro T., 358C
Agony in the Garden (Bellini), 143C
Agora, 61B
Agra, 168C, 176C, 183C
Agrarian Law, 19A
Agricola, Georgius. See Bauer, Georg
Agricola, Gnaeus Julius, 36A, 38A
Agricola (Tacitus), 39C
Agricultural Adjustment Act, 318B
Agricultural Marketing Act, 310B
Agrippa, Marcus Vipsanius, 30A, 31B
Agrippa I, Herod (king of Judaea and Samaria), 34B, 35A
Agrippina, 34A
Agrippina (Handel), 205C
Aguinaldo, Emilio (president of Philippines), 285A, 287A
Aguirre Cerda, Pedro (president of Chile), 320C
Aguiy-Ironsi, Johnson (ruler of Nigeria), 353A
Ahab (king of Israel), 10B
Ahmad al-Khalifah (sheik of Bahrain), 225A
Ahmad Bey Boshnagi (ruler of Kasimiya), 192B
Ahmad Grañ, 156B, 158B, 162B
Ahmad I (governor of Tripoli), 204B
Ahmad Shah (king of Gujarat), 134C
Ahmad (shah of Persia), 309A
Ahmad XII (sultan of Ottoman Empire), 210B
Ahmadabad, 134C
Ahmadnagar, 168C
Ahmed Bey Zogu (president of Albania), 308A, 310A

Ahmed I (sultan of Ottoman Empire), 176B, 181C
Ahmed II (sultan of Ottoman Empire), 200B
Ahmed Mirza (shah of Persia), 293A
Ahmednagar, 146C
Ahmose I (king of Egypt), 6A
Ahom Shans, 114C
Ahualolco colony, 40C
Aida (Verdi), 273C
AIDS (acquired immune deficiency syndrome), 371B, 377B, 377C, 381B, 383B. *See also* HIV virus
  Ninth International Congress on, 379B
  vaccine trials, 385B
Aigun Treaty, 265A
Aiken, Howard, 321B, 333B
Ailette Canal, 300A
Ain Jaluta, 116C
air compressor, 235B
Air Conditioned Nightmare, The (Miller), 335C
air force, U. S. *See* U.S. Air Force. *See also* jets
airplanes, 151B. *See also* U.S. Air Force; jets; *individual airlines*
  automatic pilot system, 293B, 341B
  domestic flights, 345B
  first manned flight, 289B
  flight attendants, 312B
  flight distance record, 291B
  flight in Europe, 291B
  frozen dinners on, 335B
  international flights, 303B, 311B, 315B, 345B
  parachuting from, 293B
  pressurized cabins, 325B
  during war, 293B
Aisne, 294A
Aisne-Oise Canal, 300A
Aisne River, 296A, 302A
Aistulf, 74A, 74B
Aix-la-Chapelle, 74A, 77C, 80A, 82A, 88A, 116A, 120A
  Congress of, 244A
  Peace of, 194A, 214A
Ajaccio, 220A
Ajanta, Temple of, 73C
Akan Ashanti, 150B
Akayesu, Jean-Paul (of Rwanda), 384A
Akbar the Great (emperor of India), 164C, 166C, 168C, 170C, 172C, 174C, 176C
Akhmatova, Anna, 293C
Akhthoes (king of Egypt), 4A
Akihito (emperor of Japan), 373A
Akiko Otori Yosano, 329C
Akira Kurosawa, 343C, 385C
Akkad, Akkadians, 4B
Akkerman, 248A
Aksum, kingdom of, 58C
Akutagawa Ryyunosuke, 297C
Al Mina, 12C
Alabama, 63A, 65A, 99A, 159A, 161A, 205A, 240B, 244B, 254B, 312B, 342C, 348C, 350C, 366C
  University of, 342C
Alacoque, Margaret Mary, 195C
Alais, Peace of, 184A
Alalia, 16C
Alam II (emperor of Delhi), 216C, 220C
Alamanni, 46A, 48A, 50A, 54A, 60A
Alaminos, Antonio, 155A
Alamo Mission, 252B
Alamogordo, 334
Alani, 58B
Alarcón, Hernando de, 161A
Alaric II (king of Visigoths), 60B
Alaric (king of Visigoths), 56A, 58B
Alaska, 36C, 38C, 63A, 107A, 213A, 270B, 278B, 288B, 346C, 372C, 376C
  Bering Strait, 211A
  gold strike in, 276B
  and Russia, 226B, 244B
  and United States, 292B
  White Pass and Yukon Railway, 286B
Alastor (Shelley), 243C
Alauddin, 126B
Alaungpaya, 214C
Alaungsithu (king of Pagan), 100C
Alawite dynasty. *See* Morocco
Alban, Saint, 51A
Albania, Albanians, 118B, 128B, 292A, 308A, 380B
  and Austria, 298A
  Communism in, 336B
  and Egypt, 243A
  government, 368B
  and Italy, 310A, 320A
  religion, 355C
  and Serbia, 384B
  and Soviet Union, 346B
  and Turkey, 140A, 142A, 150A
  and West Germany, 370B
Albany (Australia), 255A
Albany (N.Y.), 179A
Albee, Edward Franklin, 349C
Albermarle Point, 195A, 197A
Albert, Charles, 212A
Albert I, the Bear of Brandenburg, 104A
Albert I (king of Belgium), 292A, 316A
Albert I (king of Germany), 118A, 120A, 122A, 124A
Albert II (king of Germany), 138A
Albert IV (duke of Bavaria), 150A
Albert VI (duke of Styria), 140A
Albert of Mecklenburg (king of Sweden), 130A, 132A
Alberta, 228B, 236B, 290B, 366C
Alberti, Leon, 143B
Albertus Magnus, Saint, 119C
Albigensian Crusade, Albigenses, 114B
Albinus, Clodius, 42A
Albucasis, 91B
Albuera, battle of, 238A
Alcalá University, 149C
Alcalá Zamora y Torres, Niceto (president of Spain), 318A
Alcaraz, battle of, 98B
Alcatraz Island, 356C
alchemy, 59B, 73B, 81B, 123B, 161B
alcohol, 211A
  distillation, 113B
  solids, 339B
Alcott, Louisa May, 271C
Alcuin, 79C
Aldrich, Bess Streeter, 327C
Aldrin, Edwin "Buzz," 357B
Aleijadinho, 213C
Alemán, Arnoldo (president of Nicaragua), 383A
Alemán, Mateo, 179C
Alemán Valdéz, Miguel (president of Mexico), 335A
Alençon, 94A
Alentejo, battle of, 102B
Aleppo, 91B, 154B, 303A, 309A
Alesia, battle of, 29A
Alessio, battle of, 140A
Aleut culture, 65A
Aleutian Islands, 213A, 330C
Alexander I (emperor of Russia), 234A, 238A, 242A, 246A
Alexander II, Pope, 95C
Alexander II (king of Scotland), 110A, 114A
Alexander II (tsar of Russia), 262A, 276A, *277*
Alexander III, Pope, 105C, 107C
Alexander III (king of Scotland), 114A
Alexander III (tsar of Russia), 276A, 284A
Alexander IV, Pope, 116A, 116B
Alexander V (antipope), 135C
Alexander VI, Pope, 147A, 147C, 148A, 150B
Alexander culture, 63A
Alexander (king of Yugoslavia), 316A
Alexander of Lithuania (king of Poland), 150A
Alexander of Serbia, 282A
Alexander the Great (king of Egypt), 20C, 22A, 22B, 22C, 23C
Alexander's Ragtime Band (Berlin), 293C
Alexanderson, Ernst, 343B
Alexandreis (Châtillon), 123C
Alexandretta, 303A, 319A, 321A
Alexandria, 22A, 23B, 23C, 35A, 49B, 55B, 81B, 130B, 237A, 279A
  Convention of, 255A
  Library of, 57C
  School of, 23C, 45A
  Synod of, 55A
Alexandropol, Treaty of, 304A
Alexinatz, battle of, 274A
Alexius I Comnenus (emperor of Byzantium), 96B, 98B
Alexius III Angelus (emperor of Byzantium), 108B
Alfaro, Eloy (president of Ecuador), 290C
Alfonsín, Raúl (president of Argentina), 367A
Alfonso I (king of Aragon), 98B, 100B
Alfonso III (king of Aragon), 120A
Alfonso V (king of Aragon, Sicily, and Naples), 136B, 138B
Alfonso V (king of León), 88B, 92B
Alfonso VI (king of Castille and León), 94B
Alfonso VII (king of Castille and León), 100B, 102B, 104B
Alfonso VIII (king of Castile), 104B
Alfonso X (king of Castile and León), 114B, 115B, 116A, 118B, 119B
Alfonso XI (king of Castile and León), 124B, 126B, 128B
Alfonso XII (king of Spain), 272A, 274A
Alfonso XIII (king of Spain), 312A
Alfred, 92A
Alfred P. Murrah Federal Building, 380C
Alfred the Great (king of England), 80A, 82A, 83C
Algardi, Alessandro, 189C
Algarve, 114B, 116B
algebraic lettering system, 173B
Algeciras, 80B
Algeria, Algerians, 162B, 251A
  202 B.C., 25A
  and Arab League, 349A
  in Arab Maghreb Union, 372A
  and France, 249A, 253A, 257A, 259A, 343A, 349A, 351A
  government, 351A
  and Morocco, 349A
  Muslims in, 94B, 377A
  revolution in, 343A
  slave trade, 243A
  and United States, 243A
  War of 1812, 242B
  World War II, 328A
Algiceras, 128B
Algiers, 72C, 154B, 166B, 168B, 192B, 194B, 202B, 218B, 242B, 259A, 373A
Algonquin, 87A, 187A
Ali, 70B
Ali, Muhammad (Cassius Clay), 351C
Ali Agca, Mehmet, 367C
Ali Basha, 210B
Ali Bey (sultan of Egypt), 172B, 218B, 220B
Ali Jalla Riayat (sultan of Johore), 168C
Ali Murad (shah of Persia), 225A
Alia, Ramiz (president of Albania), 368B, 380B
Alianza Popular Revolucionaria Americana, 308C
Alicante, 175B
Alice in Cartoonland (Disney), 309C
Alice in Wonderland (Carroll), 269C
Alien Enemies Act, 232B
Alien Property Act, 310B
Alima River, 214B
Alivardi Khan (king of Bengal), 214C
Aljubarotta, battle of, 132B
Alka-Seltzer, 313B
All About Eve (movie), 339C
All-American Girls Baseball League, 331C
All God's Chillun Got Wings (O'Neill), 309C
All Quiet on the Western Front (Remarque), 311C
All the King's Men (movie), 339C
All the King's Men (Warren), 337C
Allahabad, 172C
Allarde Law, 228A
Allectus, 50A
Allegheny Mountains, 217A, 239C
Allen, Ethan, 222B
Allen, Florence Ellinwood, 316B
Allen, Richard, 226B, 243C
Allen, Woody, 363C, 373C
Allenby, Edmund, 301A
Allende, Salvador (president of Chile), 359A
Allgemeine Deutsche Frauenverein, 268A
Allied Expeditionary Forces, 332A
Allied Military Control Commission, 312A
Allies (Persian Gulf War), 376A
Allies (World War I), 296A, 296B, 298A, 299A, 300A, 300C, 302A, 303A, 304A, 305A, 306A, 307A, 310A
Allies (World War II), 322A, 325A, 326A, 326B, 327A, 328A, 328C, 329A, 329B, 330A, 330C, 332A, 332C, 333A, 334A, 334C, 335A, 338A
Allis Chalmers Manufacturing Company, 345B
All's Well That Ends Well (Shakespeare), 177C
Alma, battle of, 262A
Alma Mater (French), 297C
Almagest (Ptolemy), 79B
Almeida, Francisco de, 150B, 150C
Almeida, Lourenço de, 150C
Almodovar, Pedro, 373C
Almohades, 100B
Almoravids, 94B, 94C, 96B, 96C
Alnwick, 98A
Alodia, 64C
Alouite, 319A
Alp-Arslan, 94B, 96B
alphabet
  Cyrillic, 81B
  Etruscan, 15C
  Greek, 15C
  Japanese, 81C
  Phoenician, 11C
  phonetic, 7C
  Roman, 39B
Alpini, Prosperus, 175B
Alps, 103B

Alsace, 54A, 60A, 142A, 156A, 186A, 188A, 192A, 272A
Alsace-Lorraine, 276A, 294A
Also sprach Zarathustra (Nietzsche), 219C
Also sprach Zarathustra (Strauss), 285C
Altdorfer, Albrecht, 155C
alternating current (AC), 283B
Alternative Service Book, 365C
Altman, Robert, 361C
Altmark, Truce of, 184A
Alton, Treaty of, 98A
Altranstädt, Peace of, 204A
aluminum, 247B, 281B 331B, 293B, 326B
Alvarado, Juan Velasco (president of Peru), 355A
Alvarez, Luis, 337B, 365B
Amadeus, duke of Aosta (king of Spain), 272A, 274A
Amadeus, Victor, 185C
Amadeus (movie), 369C
Amadeus (Shaffer), 365C
Amahl and the Night Visitors (Menotti), 339C
Amalfi, 96B, 102B
Amalric I (king of Jerusalem), 104B
Amanullah (emir and king of Afghanistan), 311A
Amara, 297A
Amargosa culture, 65A
Amasis II (king of Egypt), 14A, 16A
Amati, Andrea, 151C
Amazon River, 9C, 10B, 151A, 161A, 163A, 310C
Amboina, 182C, 326C
Amboise
  Edict of, 167C, 168A
  Peace of, 166A
Ambrose, Saint, 57A
ambulances, 91B, 147B, 353B
Ameixial, battle of, 192A
Amelia Goes to the Ball (Menotti), 319C
Amelia Island, 213A
Amenemhet I (king of Egypt), 4A
Amenemhet III (king of Egypt), 4A
Amenhotep I (king of Egypt), 6A
Amenhotep II (king of Egypt), 8A
Amenhotep III (king of Egypt), 8A
Amenhotep IV (king of Egypt), 9C
Amerbach, Bonifacius, 155C
America, 147A, 149A, 153A, 161B. *See also* American colonies; United States
    and Africa, 169B
    agriculture, 4B, 115A, 159B
    and Columbus, 147B
    and England, 169A
America (yacht), 261C
American Airlines 1962 crash, 348C
American Association for the Advancement of Science, 259B
American Ballet, School of the, 317C
American Bar Association, 276B
American colonies, 179B
  Boston Tea Party, 221A
  and England, 187A, 189A, 202A
  and Europe, 153B
  and Germany, 199A
  and Holland, 189A
  industry, 213B
  printing in, 187C
  religion, 209C, 213C
  science and technology, 227B, 231B
  slavery, 199C, 202B, 205A, 209A, 215A, 222B
  and Spain, 163A, 176A, 177B
  Stamp Act, 219A
  taxes, 219A
  Townshend Acts, 221A
American Colonization Society, 242B, 245A
American Commonwealth, The (Bryce), 281C
American Dictionary of the English Language (Webster), 249C
American Federation of Labor, 280B, 342C
American Film Institute, 385C
American Fur Company, 238B
American in Paris, An (Gershwin), 311C
American in Paris, An (movie), 339C
American Language, The (Mencken), 305C
American Legion, 302B
American Library Association, 275C
American Motors Company, 345B
American Pharmaceutical Association, 262B
American Philosophical Society, 209C
American Railway Union, 282B, 284B
American Red Cross Association, 276B
American Revolution, 222B, 224B, 245C
American Revolution, Daughters of the, 321C
American Society for Promotion of Temperance, 248B
American Women's Education Association, 262B
Americans with Disabilities Act, 374C
America's Cup, 261C
"America's sweetheart," 301C
americum, 333B
Ames, Aldrich, 380C
Amezaga, Juan José de (president of Uruguay), 331A
Amhara, 158B
Amherst, 265C
Amida, 54B
Amiens, 142A, 294A, 322A
  Mise of, 116A
  Treaty of, 234A, 234B
Amiens Cathedral, 111C
Amin, Idi (president of Uganda), 359A
Amiot, Joseph Marie, 207C
Amis, Kingsley, 343C
Amistad (Spanish ship), 254B
Ammianus Marcellinus, 57C
Ammisaduga, 7B
ammonia
  compressor, 275B
  maser, 341B
  synthetic, 293B, 301B
ammunition, 29B
Amnesty Act, 272B
Amnesty International, 346A
Amoaful, battle of, 275A
Amoghavarsna, 78C
Amon (Egyptian god), 5C, 22A
Amontons, Guillaume, 199B
Ampère, André, 245B
amphibious assault craft, 329B
Amphipolis, battle of, 20C
Amr Mosque, 69C
Amritsar, 303A, 369A
Amsterdam, 129B, 172A, *190,* 191C, 276A
    Concertgebouw, 285C
    Convention of, 206A
    Exchange, 178A
Amur River, 190C, 208C, 265A
Amyrtaios, 20A
An American Tragedy (Dreiser), 309C
An Shigao, 39A
Anabaptists, 157C, 161C
Anacletus II, 100B
Anafesto, Paoluccio, 72B
Anagni, 107C, 123C
Anahuac Valley, 105A
Ananda Temple, 99C
Anankpetlun (king of Burma), 176C
anaphylaxis, 289B
Anasazi culture, 44C, 73A, 81A, 83A, 93A, 109A, 115A
Anastasius I (emperor of Byzantium), 60B
Anastasius II (emperor of Byzantium), 72B
Anatolia, 4C, 5A, 6C, 9B, 94B, 136B, 140B, 154B, 158B, 251A, 307A. *See also* Asia Minor; Turkey
anatomy, 3B
Anatomy of Melancholy (Burton), 181C
Anatomy of the Horse, The (Stubbs), 219C
Anaxagoras, 17B
Anaximander, 15B
Anchluss, 306A
Ancón, Peace of, 278C
Ancona, 112B
Ancrum Moor, battle of, 162A
Andagoya, Pascuel de, 157A
Andalusia, 74B, 154A
Andersen, Hans Christian, 253C
Anderson, Marian, 309C, 321C, 343C
Anderson, Michael, 343C
Anderson, Sherwood, 303C, 327C
Andersonville (Kantor), 343C
Andes Mountains, 12B, 61A, 85A, 159A, 161A, 161B, 284C
Andhra culture, 39C
Andorra, 118B
André, John, 224B
Andrea Doria (Italian ocean liner), 342C
Andrew (brother of Hungarian Louis I), 128B
Andrews, Lancelot, 179C
Andria (Terence), 27C
Andriamanelo, 160B
android, 209B
Andromaque (Racine), 193C
Andronicus I Comnenus (emperor of Byzantium), 106B
Andronicus II Palaeologus (emperor of Byzantium), 122B, 126B
Andronicus III Palaeologus (emperor of Byzantium), 126B
Andronicus IV Palaeologus (emperor of Byzantium), 132B
Andropov, Yuri (leader of Soviet Union), 366B, 368B
Andros, Sir Edmund, 199A
Andrussov, Truce of, 192A
Aneirin, 67C
Angelico, Fra, 137C
Angevins, 122B
Angkor, 77C, 80C, 83C, 106C
Angkor Thom, 233A
Angkor Wat, 99C
Angles, 60A
Anglesey, 34A
Anglican Church, 165C, 167C, 228B, 239C, 361C
Anglo-Burmese Wars, 279A
Anglo-Chinese Wars, 265A
Anglo-French War, 98A
Anglo-German Convention of 1890, 282A
Anglo-Japanese Alliance, 288A, 290A, 307A
Anglo-Persian Oil Company, 315A
Anglo-Portuguese Syndicate, 151A
Anglo-Saxon Chronicle, 83C
Anglo-Saxons, 60A, 66A, 95B, *103*
Anglo-Spanish Treaty, 242A
Anglo-Spanish War, 209A
Angola, 170B, 186B, 188B, 192B, 194B, 361A, 377A
    and Belgium, 289A
    and Cuba, 372A
    and Namibia, 372A
    and South Africa, 372A
Angoulême, 132A
Anguilla, 356A
Anhilwara, 108C
Anhui province, 192C
Ani, battle of, 114B
Animal Farm (Orwell), 335C
animals, breeding of, 223B
animals, extinct, 189B
Anjou, 102A, 104A, 108A, 110A, 138A
Ankara, 134B, 305A, 307A, 346A
  Treaty of, 313A
Anna Christie (O'Neill), 307C
Anna Karenina (Tolstoy), 275C
Annales Ecclesiastici (Baronius), 173C
Annales (Tacitus), 39C
Annam, Annamites, 34B, 60C, 88C. *See also* Vietnam
    and Champa, 142C
    and China, 72C, 82C, 174C
    civil war in, 220C
    and France, 227A, 267A, 275A, 279A, 281A
    and Khmer, 180C, 190C, 216C
    Le dynasty, 174C
    Mac dynasty, 156C
    and Mongolia, 114C, 118C
    Nguyen dynasty, 225A, 235A
    Trinh dynasty, 227A, 235A
Annan, Kofi (secretary-general of United Nations), 382A, 384A, *385*
Annapolis, 256B
Annapolis Royal, 205A
Anne (queen of England), 200A, 202A, 206A
Annie Hall (movie), 363C
Annunciation (Martini), 127C
Anouilh, Jean, 327C, 347C
Ansbach, 224A, 236A
Anschluss, 306A, 314A, 320A
Anschutz-Kaempfe, Hermann, 291B
Anselm, Saint (Archbishop of Canterbury), 99C
Ansermet, Ernest, 303C
antacid tablet, 313B
Antanosy, 186B
Antarctic (Norwegian whaler), 285B
Antarctica, 245A, 247A, 285B, 291B, 346A, 369B, 376A
Anthony, Susan B., 272B, *273*
Anthony of Thebes, 49A, 51A
anthrax bombs, 327B
Anti-Comintern Pact, 318A
Anti-Defamation League, 295C
anti-Semitism, 316A, 324A
antibodies, 323B
Antietam, battle of, 266B
Antigone (Anouilh), 327C
Antigone (Sophocles), 19C
Antigonus Doson, 24C
Antigua, 147A, 185A, 193A, 272C, 355A, 366A
Antikythera, 31B
Antilles, 183A
antimony, 177B
Antinopolis, 38B
Antinoüs, 38B
Antioch, 51B, 55C
  earthquake in, 62C, 64C, 66C, 98B, 102B
  Synod of, 49A, 53A
Antioch Review, 325C
Antipas, Herod, 33A
Antiquary, The (Scott), 243C
Antisana, 276C
Antisthenes, 21C
Antofagasta, 276C, 288C
Antoinette, Marie, *226,* 226A, 230A
Antonine Wall, 40A, 42A
Antoninus Pius (emperor of Rome), 40A
Antony, Mark, 29A, *30,* 30A, 30B
Antony and Cleopatra (Shakespeare), 177C
Antsiranana, 202B

Antwerp, 122A, 170A, 172A, 177C, 250A, 296A, 334A
Antwerp Cathedral, 143C
Anual, battle of, 307A
Anzio, 332A
Aoki-Kimberley Treaty, 285A
Aosta, 30A, 272A
Apache, 91A, 101A, 121A, 209A, 280B
Apalachee, 203A
Apalachee Bay, 159A
Aparajito (Ray), 343C
apartheid, 347A, 353A, 355C, 373A, 376A, 377A, 381A
Apartment, The (movie), 347C
Apelles, 23C
Apennines, 23A
Aper, Arrius, 48A
Apgar, Virginia, 341B
Apgar Score, 341B
Aphilas, 47C
Apicius, 35C
Apocalypse, The (Dürer), 149C
Apocalypse Now (movie), 365C
Apollinarianism, 55A
Apollinaris the Younger, 55A
Apollo, 31A, 65C
Apollo space program, 353B, 361B
  Apollo 4, 355B
  Apollo 7, 355B
  Apollo 8, 355B
  Apollo 12, 357B
  Apollo 14, 357B
  Apollo 15, 357B
  Apollo 17, 359B
Apollo and Daphne (Bernini), 183C
Apollo (Balanchine), 311C
Apollo-Soyuz Test Project (ASTP), 360A
Apollodorus of Damascus, 39C
Apollonius of Perga, 25B
Apologia pro Vita Sua (Newman), 269C
Apologies (Justin), 41A
Apology (Plato), 21C
Apology (Tertullian), 43A
Appalachian Spring (Copland), 333C
Appassionata (Beethoven), 237C
Appenweier, 306A
Appert, Nicolas, 237B
Appian, 41C
Appian Way, 23A
Apple Computer, Inc., 367B, 369B
Appleton, Edward, 309B
Appomattox Courthouse, 268B
Apprentices, Statute of, 166A
Après-Midi d'un faune, L' (Mallarmé), 275C
Apries (king of Egypt), 14A
Apuleius, Lucius, 43C
Apulia, 86B, 95C, 102B
Aqaba, 301A
Aqua Appia, 23A
Aquinas, Thomas, 117C, 119C
Aquino, Benigno, Jr., 367A
Aquino, Corazon (president of Philippines), 371A
aquired immune deficiency syndrome. *See* AIDS
Aquitaine, 85C, 93C, 106A
Ar-Rashid Muhammad ibn Ali, 194B
Arab Federation, 345A
Arab League, 337A, 349A
  Security Pact, 340A
Arab Liberation Movement, 341A
Arab Maghreb Union, 372A
Arabia, Arabs, 70B, 78C, 98B, 251A. *See also* Wahhabi
  and Afghanistan, 70C
  agriculture, 138C
  alchemy, 75B, 161B
  arts, 87C, 93C, 105B, 109C, 113C
  astronomy, 97B
  and Britain, 301A
  and Byzantium, 72C
  and China, 101B
  coinage, 106B
  and Crete, 78B, 86B
  and East Africa, 88C
  and Egypt, 86B, 239A
  Fatimids, 82B, 84C, 86B, 86C
  and France, 74A, 82B, 88B
  in German East Africa, 281A
  and Ghana, 94C
  government, 60C
  horse racing in, 73C
  and India, 77B
  and Israel, 358A
  and Italy, 80B, 84B, 88B, 90B
  and Jews, 311A
  law and society, 74C
  and Madagascar, 85B, 86C
  and Malaya, 76C
  medicine, 103B, 125B, 131B
  and Moluccas, 72C
  Muscat, 194B
  Omani, 190B
  and Persia, 68C
  and Portugal, 188B, 210B
  postal service, 119B
  and Sardinia, 94B
  science and technology, 59B, 67B, 73B, 79B, 81B, 83B, 91B, 93B, 95B, 99B, 101B, 109B, 123B, 129B, 135B, 137B
  and Sicily, 82B, 86B
  and Spain, 164B
  and Tunisia, 104B
Arabian Sea, 364A
Aradashir I, 44B
Arafat, Yasir, 367A, 372A, 383A
Aragon, 92B, 96B, 98B, 100B, 102B, 108B, 110B, 112B, 118A, 118B, 120A, 120B, 124B, 126B, 134B, 136B, 138B, 142A, 144A, 146A, 154A, 172A, 188A, 204A
Arakan, 162C, 249A
Aranda, Pedro, 218A
Araucania, Araucanians, 139A, 175A, 209A
Arausio, 33C
Arawak people, 35C, 42C
Arawe airstrip, 330C
Arbenz, Jacobo (president of Guatemala), 343A
Arbogast, 56A
Arbues, Pedro de, 145C
Arbuthnot, John, 205C
arc street lighting. *See* lamps, lighting
Arcadia (Sidney), 173C
Arcadia (Vega), 175C
Arcadius (emperor of Rome), 56B
Arce, Manuel José, 244C, 250C, 256C
Archaic Age, 12C, 65A
"Archbishop of Fundamentalism," 313C
Archimedes, 23B
architecture
  Baroque, 215C
  Gothic, 73C, 99C, 111C, 115C
  Gothic Revival, 245C
  Greek Revival, 233C
  Mesoamerican, 38C
  Rococo, 213C
  Roman, 33C, 39C
  Romanesque, 81C, 95C, 99C, 255C
  vaulted ceilings, 151B
Architettura civile (Bibiena), 205C
Arcola, battle of, 232A
Arcoli, Giovanni d', 145B
Arcot, 214C
Arctic, 3B, 10B, 85A, 91B, 127A, 246B, 345B
Arctic Ocean, 228B
Ardashir I, 44B
Ardèche, 381C
Ardennes, 334A
Ardoin, 90A
Ardour River, 101B
Ardres, Peace of, 162A
Arecibo, 349B
Aretino, Pietro, 161C
Arévalo, Juan José (president of Guatemala), 335A
Arezzo, Guido d', 91C, 93C
Argaon, battle of, 237A
Argenis (Barclay), 181C
Argentia Bay, 326B
Argentina, 151A, 155A, 165A, 171A, 260C, 272C, 286C
  Argentine Confederation, 262C
  arts, 95A
  and Axis, 327A
  and Bolivia, 308C
  and Brazil, 246C
  and Britain, 236C, 362A
  and Buenos Aires, 264C
  and Chile, 276C, 288C, 369A
  civil war in, 244C
  and Falkland Islands, 362A, 366A
  and Germany, 333A, 335A
  government, 181A, 238C, 252C, 262B, 266C, 268C, 274C, 280C, 282C, 312C, 314C, 318C, 331A, 333A, 339A, 343A, 345A, 349A, 359A, 361A, 363A, 367A
  industry, 310C
  and Italy, 333A, 335A
  and Paraguay, 268C
  and Peru, 161B, 244C
  politics, 276C, 298C, 318C, 327A
  revolution in, 312C
  River Plate, 222C
  and Royalists, 240C, 242C
  and United Nations, 335A, 366A
  and United States, 332B
  and Uruguay, 246C, 248C, 254C
  World War I, 294C
  World War II, 322C
Argives, 16C
Argonaut (British ship), 228B
Argos, 12C, 16C
Arguin, 198B
Ari the Wise, 101C
Arianism, Arians, 53A
Arias, Harmodio (president of Panama), 312C
Arias Dávila, Pedro, 153A
Arias, Arnulfo (president of Panama), 323A, 325A, 335A
Arica, 171A
Ariel, 349B
Ariminum, 25A
Ariosto, Ludovico, 153C, 159C
Arista, Mariano (president of Mexico), 260C, 262C
Aristarchus of Samos, 23B
Aristide, Jean-Bertrand, 377A, 379A, 380A
Aristonicus, 26C
Aristophanes, 21C
Aristotle, 21C, 23B, 23C, 177B
Arius, 53A
Arizona, 32C, 59A, 63A, 67A, 73A, 99A, 103A, 117A, 119A, 129A, 135A, 161A, 175A, 201C, 203C, 219A, 258B, 262B, 292B, 328B, 372C
  drought in, 101A, 119A
  University of, 361B
Arkansas, 63A, 65A, 99A, 195A, 252B, 266B, 295C, 344C, 376C, 380C, 382C
Arkansas River, 163A, 236B
Arkiko, 164B
Arkwright, Richard, 223B
Arles, 88B, 130A, 281C
  Council of, 51A
Arlington Cemetery, 344C
armed forces, U.S., 323C, *353. See also individual branches, e.g.,* U.S. Army
  1996 bomb in Dharan, 383A
  closed military bases, 376C
  homosexuals in, 378C
  military optics, 335B
  and Nassau, 222C
  and ski gondola accident, 384B
Armenia, Armenians, 32B, 40B, 49A, 50B, 51A, 54B, 58C, 61C, 96B, 102B, 108B, 142B, 306A, 374B
  and Arabs, 70B
  arts, 69C
  Bagratide dynasty, 80C
  and Byzantium, 92B
  earthquake in, 372B
  and Egypt, 132B
  government, 80C, 82C
  and Mesopotamia, 297A
  and Mongolia, 112C, 114B, 114C
  and Ottoman Empire, 152B, 284A, 297A
  and Persia, 56B
  and Russia, 288A, 297A
  and Syria, 297A
  and Timur, 132C
  and Turkey, 94B, 304A, 305A
Armenia Minor, 96B, 132B
Arminius, 32A
armor, 3B, 9B, 77B, 93B
Arms and the Man (Shaw), 285C
Armstrong, Edwin Howard, 293B, 301B
Armstrong, Louis "Satchmo," 307C
Armstrong, Neil, 357B
army, U.S. *See* U.S. Army
Arnauld, Antoine, 197C
Arno River, 131B
Arnold, Benedict, 222B, 224B
Arnold, Henry "Hap," 334B
Arnold, Matthew, 273C, 275C
Arnold, Thomas, 249C
Arnold of Brescia, 104B
Arnulf, 82A, 82B
Aroge, battle of, 271A
Around the World in 80 Days (movie), 343C
Around the World in 80 Days (Verne), 275C
Arras, 322A
  battle of (1917), 300A
  Peace of (1435), 136A
  Peace of (1482), 144A
  Peace of (1579), 170A
Arrian, 43C
arrowheads, 93B
Arroyo del Río, Carlos Alberto (president of Ecuador), 333A
Ars Amatoria (Ovid), 33C
Ars antiqua, 117C
Ars Poetica (Horace), 33C
Arsacid empire, 24B
"Art and Craft of the Machine, The" (Wright), 289C
Art of Husbandry (Virgil), 31C
Artaxerxes I (king of Persia), 18B
Artaxerxes III (king of Persia), 22C
Artemis, Temple of, 17C
arthritis, rheumatoid, 325B
Arthur, Chester A. (president of U.S.), 276B
Arthur (legendary king of Britons), 64A, 103C, 107C, 135C
Arthur of Brittany, 108A
Articles of Confederation, 222B
artificial insemination, 125B, 225B
artificial intelligence (AI), 343B
Artigas, José Gervasio, 238C, 240C, 242C
Artois, 144A, 192A, 300A
  battle of, 298A
Arundel, 102A

Arundel, Thomas (Archbishop of Canterbury), 135C
Aryans, 6B
Arzachel, 97B
As the Old Sing, the Young Pipe (Steen), 193C
As You Like It (Shakespeare), 175C
Ascalon, battle of, 98B
Ascension, The (Cynewulf), 75C
Ascension Island, 242C
Asclepiades, 27B
Asen, Ivan and Peter (joint tsars of Bulgaria), 106A
Ashanti, 150B, 275A, 285A
Ashe, Arthur, 377C
Ashmolean Museum, *80*
Ashot I (king of Armenia), 80C, 82C
Ashton, Frederick, 337C
Ashton-Tate, 367B
Ashurbanipal (king of Assyria), 13C
Asia, 4C, 59B, 82C, 90C, 113B, 116C, 118C, 130C, 148C, 168B, 208C, 210C
  agriculture, 139B
  and New Zealand, 277A
  Timor dynasty, 190C
  and United States, 300B
Asia Minor, 44A, 54B, 56B, 62C, 112B, 305A, 307A. *See also* Anatolia; Turkey
  arts, 379C
  earthquake in, 74C, 118C
  and Persians, 68B
  plague in, 42B
  and Timur, 134B
  and Turkey, 92B, 94B, 96B
Asia-Pacific Economic Cooperation (APEC), 374A
Asiento Guinea Company, 202B
Asimov, Isaac, 327B
Askia Muhammad the Great (king of Songhai), 146B, 152B
Aslanduz, battle of, 241A
Asmum Institute, 262B
Asoka (emperor of India), 25C
aspartame, 351B, 361B, 367B
Aspdin, Joseph, 247B
Aspern, battle of, 238A
Aspin, Les, 378C
aspirin, 347B, 366C
Aspromonte, battle of, 266A
Asquith, Herbert Henry, 290A, 294A, 296A
Assab, 279A
Assam, kingdom of, 114C, 247A, 249A
Assassins, 118C
Assaye, 237A
Assemblies of God, 295C
assembly line, computerized, 337B
Associated Press (AP), 259C
Association of Southeast Asian Nations (ASEAN), 352A
Assumption of the Virgin (Titian), 155C
Assyria, Assyrians, 3B, 6B, 10B, *12,* 12A, 12B, 13C, 14B
Astaire, Fred, 315C
astatine, 325B
Astor, John Jacob, 238B, 244B
Astoria, 238B
Astraea redux (Dryden), 193C
Astrakhan, 134C, 168B, 208C
astrarium, 131B
astrolabe, 59B, 81B
astrology, *133*
astronomy, 41B, 115B, 131B, 139B, 163C, 171B, 181B, 187B, 191B, 201B. *See also individual planets*
  new galaxies, 357B, 383B, 385B
  planet classification, 193B
Astrophel and Stella (Sidney), 171C
Asturias, kingdom of, 84B
Asunción, 161A, 282C
Aswan Dam, 9C, 355C
At Heaven's Gate (Warren), 331C
Atahualpa (ruler of Incas), 155A, 159A
Atanasoff, John, 321B
Atari Company, 367B
Atatürk, Kemal (president of Turkey), 299A, 305A, 307A, 311A, 317A, 321A
Athabasca, Lake, 228B
Athanaric, 54A
Athanasius, Saint, 53A, 57A
Athapascans, 109A
Athena, 16C
Athenaeum (Schlegel), 233C
Athenaeus, 45C
Athenagoras I (patriarch of the Orthodox Church), 351C
Athens, 10C, 41C, 48A, 61B, 198A. *See also* Greece
  621 B.C.–546 B.C., 12C, 14C, 16C
  485 B.C.–404 B.C., 18B, 18C, 19B, 19C, 21C
  423 B.C.–335 B.C., 20B, 20C, 22C, 23C
  Academy of, 21C, 63B
  jurors in, 18C
  law and society, 14C, 38A, 136A, 150A, 166A, 222A, 235C, 244A, 256A, 260A, 272A, 274A, 280A, 282A, 286A, 289C, 290A, 354B, 356B, 368A
  plague in, 18C, 64A, 70A, 130A
  revolution in, 266A
  silver in, 18C
  and Turkey, 140A
Athis, Treaty of, 122A
Atjeh, sultanate of, 154C, 162C
Atlanta, 268B, 296B, 310B, 346C, 352C, 370C, 381B, 384C
  race riot in, 290B
  Winecoff Hotel fire, 336C
Atlanta Braves, 377C, 379C, 383C
"Atlanta Compromise," 284B
Atlantic Charter, 326B
Atlantic Ocean, 57B, 157A, 225A, 245B, 314B, 346C, 384C
  Erie Canal and, *247*
  flight across, 303A
  U.S.-Britain cable, 271B
Atlantis, 377B, 381B
atomic weapons, 327B, 328B, 334C, 336A, 338A, 356A. *See also* nuclear weapons
atoms
  atom nuclei, 291B
  atomic clock theory, 337B
  atomic energy, 19B
  atomic power plant, 345B
  cloud chamber, 293B
  particle collider, 349B
  sub-atomic particles, 275B, 293B
  supercollider, 379B
  synchronizing particles, 333B
Atoms for Peace, 340C
Atothis (king of Egypt), 3B
Atrato River, 151A
Attar, Farid od-Din, 109C
Attenborough, Richard, 367C
Attica prison riot, 356C
Attila (ruler of Huns), 58A, 60B
Attlee, Clement (prime minister of Britain), 334A, 338B
Attu Island, 330C
Aubigné, Théodore-Agrippa d', 181C
Aubrey, John, 183C
Audaghost, 88C
Audenicia, 159A
audiometer, 337B
Audrieth, Ludwig, 339B
Audubon, James, 249C
Auer, Karl, 279B
Auerstädt, battle of, 236A
Augsburg, 86A, 91B, 109B, 155B, 155C, 159A, 164A, 179C, 313B
  Diet of, 150A, 159C
  League of, 198A
  Peace of (1555), 165C
Augsburg Cathedral, 99C
August, Carl, 242A
August Comte and Positivism (Mill), 269C
Augusta (U.S. ship), 326B
Augustine, Saint, 55A, 59C
Augustine (Archbishop of Canterbury), 67C
Augustine (Bishop of Hippo), 57A
Augustine Gospels, 59
Augustulus, Romulus (emperor of Rome), 60A
Augustus (duke of Grafton), 220A
Augustus II of Saxony (king of Poland), 200A, 204A
Augustus III, 210A
Augustus (Roman emperor), 30A, *31,* 31A, 31C, 32A, 33A, 33C
Aung San Suu Kyi, Daw, 383A
Aurangzeb (Dryden), 195C
Aurangzeb (emperor of Mogul empire), 190C, 192C, 194C, 198C, 204C
Auray, battle of, 130A
Aurelian (emperor of Rome), 48A,
Aurelius, Marcus (emperor of Rome), 40A, 41A, 42A, *43,* 43A, 43C
Auriol, Vincent (president of France), 336B
Aurora (Böhme), 179C
Aurora Leigh (Browning), 265C
Auschwitz, 329C
Ausculum, battle of, 22C
Austen, Jane, 239C, 241C, 243C, 245C
Austerlitz, battle of, 236A
Austin, Stephen, 244B
Australia, Australians, 156C, 176C, 220C, 227A, 229A, 231A, 231C, 233A, 235A, 237A, 239A, 303A, 315B. *See also* Aborigines
  3000 B.C., 2B, 3B
  and Antarctica, 315A
  arts, 345C, 367C
  Australian Constitution Act, 261A
  Australian Magazine, 245C
  and Borneo, 334C
  and Britain, 247A, 251A, 257A, 312A, 317B
  and Chinese, 263A
  convicts in, 245A, 255A, 269A
  economy, 275A
  education, 283A
  and England, 202C
  and Germany, 305A, 322C
  government, 273A, 283A, 287A, 289A, 307A, 317A, 321A, 357A, 371A
  Great Dividing Range, 241A
  and Japan, 328C
  and Nauru Island, 305A
  New South Wales, 241A
  and New Zealand, 338A
  on nuclear pollution, 370A
  politics, 313A, 317A
  postal service in, 255A
  religion, 241C, 245C, 251C, 253C, 287C
  science and technology, 267B, 291B, 325B, 345B
  settlement of, 249A, 253A, 261A
  South Australia Colonization Act, 253A
  suffrage in, 289A
  and Syria, 303A
  and Turkey, 297A
  and United States, 328C, 330C, 338A
  World War II, 322C, 330C
Austrasia, 64A, 72A
Austria, Austrians, 106A, 108A, 116A, 120A, 122A, 124A, 149B, 170A, 178A, 254A, 261B. *See also* Austro-Hungarian empire
  and Albania, 298A
  arts, 211C, 267C, 307C, 311C
  Austro-German alliance, 278A
  and Belgium, 228A
  and Bohemia, 290A
  and Bosnia, 276A, 290A, 292A
  and Brandenburg, 192A
  and Britain, 280A, 294A
  Civil Code, 238A
  and Czechoslovakia, 316A
  and Denmark, 248A, 268A
  in European Free Trade Association, 346A
  and France, 188A, 194A, 212A, 214A, 216A, 230A, 234A, 236A, 238A, 240A, 264A, 272A, 294A
  and Germany, 118A, 270A, 296A, 306A, 312A, 314A, 320A
  government, 260A, 266A, 268A, 304A, 314A
  and Habsburgs, 156A
  Hallstatt culture, 11B, 13A
  and Herzegovina, 276A, 290A
  and Hesse-Cassel, 260A
  and Holy Alliance, 242A
  and Hungary, 204A, 260A, 270A, 316A, 372B
  industry, 115B
  and Italy, 270A, 272A, 280A, 296A, 298A, 300A, 302A, 316A
  law and society, 220A, 222A, 224A, 274A
  and League of Nations, 304A
  medicine, 291B
  and Montenegro, 294A, 298A
  and Mozambique, 225A
  and Naples, 244A
  Nazis in, 316A
  and Ottoman Empire, 262A
  and Piedmont, 244A
  and Poland, 192A, 220A, 258A, 296A
  politics, 356B
  and Prussia, 218A, 224A, 268A, 270A, 276A
  Reichsrat, 266A
  religion, 133C, 169C, 177C, 211A
  restoration of sovereignty treaty, 342B
  and Romania, 278A, 298A, 316A
  and Romans, 50A
  and Russia, 232A, 258A, 260A, 294A, 296A
  and Sardinia, 258A, 260A
  and Savoy, 208A
  science and technology, 155B, 269B
  and Serbia, 292A, 294A, 296A, 298A
  and Soviet Union, 334A
  and Spain, 210A
  and Sweden, 192A
  and Switzerland, 132A
  and Turkey, 168A, 192A, 226A, 264A
  and Venice, 260A
  War of the Spanish Succession, 202A
  World War I, 296A
  and Yugoslavia, 316A
Austria-Hungary. *See* Austro-Hungarian empire
Austrian Netherlands, 228A
Austro-German alliance, 278A

Austro-Hungarian empire, 282A. *See also* Austria; Hungary
and Poland, 202A
and Russia, 298A, 302A
and Serbia, 294A
and Siam, 301A
in Three Emperors' League, 276A, 278A
and Treaty of St. Germain, 304A
and Turkey, 202A
and United States, 300B
and Venice, 202A
World War I, 294A, 302A
Authari (king of Langobards), 64A
auto-da-fé, 171A
Autobiography (Josephus), 39C
Autobiography of Alice B. Toklas, The (Stein), 315C
autofacturing, 361B
automata, 209B
automobile(s). *See also individual makes and manufacturers*
armored, 101B, 289B
Benz, 283B
brakes, 289B, 317B, 339B
catalytic converters, 357B
compact, 345B
Detroit-made, 285B
electric starter, 293B
front-wheel drive, 317B
Henry Ford's first, 285B
Impact electric car, 375B
industry, 376C
Kraftswagon, 269B
manual transmission, 287B
Model T, 290B, 308B
power steering, 339B
radiator, 287B
Renault's first, 287B
seatbelts, 339B
spark plug, 289B
three-wheeled, 269B
Autun Cathedral, 101C
Auvergne, 99C
Auxerre, 136A
Ava, kingdom of, 68B, 138C, 142C, 144C, 146C, 152C, 156C, 164C
Avantivarman, 83B
Avear, Marcelo Torcuato de (president of Argentina), 306C
Avebury, 3C
Avellaneda, Nicolas (president of Argentina), 274C
Avenzoar, 103B
Averroës, 109C
Avers, battle of, 158A
Aversa, 92B
Avery, Oswald, 333B
Avicebron, 97C
Avicenna, 93C
Avignon, 127C, 131C, 135C
Ávila Camacho, Manuel (president of Mexico), 323A, 329A
Avildsen, John G., 363C
Avril, Prosper (president of Haiti), 375A
Axel's Castle (Wilson), 313C
Axis powers, 318A, 324C, 326B, 327A, 329A, 330A, 331A, 332B, 333A, 335A
Axum, kingdom of, 34B
Ayer, A. J., 319C
Ayllon, Lucas Vasquez de, 157A
Ayodhya, 379A
Ayrshire, battle of, 122A
Ayub Khan, Mohammad (president of Pakistan), 357A
Ayutthaya, 218C
Ayyubid, 114B
Azerbaijan, 132C, 142B, 306A
Aziz ibn Saud (king of Najd and Hejaz), 303A, 311A
Aznar, José María (prime minister of Spain), 382B
Azores, 136B, 138B, 340C
Azotos, 12B
Azov, 200A, 204A, 212A
Azov, Sea of, 330A
Aztalan culture, 123A
Aztec empire, Aztecs, 32C, 40C, 105A, 109A, 123A, 125A, 127A, 129A, 131A, 133A, 137A, 143A, 143B, 145A, 151A, 151B, 153B, 155A, 157A, 165A
Azuchi Castle, 170C

B

Baader-Meinhof terrorists, 358B
Baal, 11C
Baalbek, 216B
Babba Zaki, 220B
Babbage, Charles, 253B
Babcock, Stephen, 283B
Babur, 148C, 150C, 152B, 154C, 156C, 158C
Babylon, Babylonia, Babylonians, 3B, 4B, 6B, 12B, 16B
Alexander the Great, 22B
astronomy, 5B, 7B, 13B, 21B
Hanging Gardens, 15C
Jews taken to, 14B
Bach, Johann Sebastian, 199C, 203C, 211C, 213C, 215C
Back to Africa movement, *299*
Back to Methuselah (Shaw), 307C
Backus, John, 343B
Bacon, Francis (lord chancellor of England), 175C, 177C, 180A, 181C, 183C
Bacon, Nathaniel, 197A
Bacon, Roger, 115B, 117C
Bacon's Rebellion, 197A
bacteria, 197B, 331B
Bactria, 34B
Badajoz, 234B, 240A
Baden, 200A, 206A, 270A
Baden-Powell, Robert, 290A
Badham, John, 363C
badminton, 123B
Badoglio, Pietro (prime minister of Italy), 330A
Badr, battle of, 68C
Baduila (king of Italy), 64B
Baeda Mariam (emperor of Ethiopia), 142B
Baeyer, Adolf von, 273B
Baffin Island, 171A
bag, paper, 273B
Baggesen, Jens Immanuel, 219C
Baghdad, 74C, 77C, 78C, 79C, 86B, 87B, 87C, 94B, 98B, 116B, 152B, 158B, 172B, 176B, 186B, 269B, 301A, 303A
and Mongolia, 116C
Pact, 342A, 345A, 346A
and Timur, 134B
Bagratide dynasty. *See* Armenia
Bagyidaw, 245A
Bahadur Shah I (emperor of Mogul empire), 204C, 206C
Bahai, 265C
Bahamas, 147A, 189A, 224C, 226C, 230C, 234B, 304C
slave trade, 252C
Bahia, 165A
Bahlol Lodi (king of Delhi), 146C
Bahmani, kingdom of, 140C, 142C, 144C
Bahrain, 225A, 267A, 315A, 356A
Bahram V (king of Persia), 58C
Baiae, Gulf of, 35B
Bailey Carriage Company, 287B
Bainbridge, William, 235A
Baird, John L., 309B, 311B
Bajazet I (sultan of Ottoman Empire), 132B, 134B
Bajazet II (sultan of Ottoman Empire), 144B, 152B
Baker, Howard, 372C
Baker, Josephine, 309C
bakers' marks, 117B
Bakewell, Robert, 223B
Bakke, Allan, 362C
Bakker, Jim, 371C
Baku, 81B, 208B, 278A, 290A
Bakunin, Michael, 273C
Balaklava, battle of, 262A
Balambangan, kingdom of, 186C
Balamir, 54A
Balanchine, George, 311C
Balban (sultan of Delhi), 116C, 118C
Balboa, Vasco Núñez de, 153A
baldness, 373B
Baldwin, James, 355C
Baldwin, Stanley (prime minister of Britain), 306A, 306B, 316A, 318A
Baldwin I (king of Jerusalem), 98B
Baldwin II (king of Jerusalem), 100B
Baldwin III (king of Jerusalem), 102B
Baldwin IV (king of Jerusalem), 104B
Balearic Islands, 100B, 128B
Balewa, Sir Abubakar Tafawa (prime minister of Nigeria), 353A
Balfour, Arthur (prime minister of Britain), 288A, 301A, 304A
Balfour Declaration, 301A, 305A, 310B
Bali, 88C
Balikpapan, 326C, 334C
Baliol, Edward (king of Scotland), 126A
Baliol, John (king of Scotland), 120A
Balkan League, 292A
Balkan Wars, 292A, 294A
Balkans, 5A, 44A, 53A, 96B, 262A.
ball bearings, 39B
Ballads and Poems, 1915–1930 (Benét), 313C
Ballads (Hugo), 247C
Ballamir, 56B
Ballets Russes, Les, 293C
Balliol College, 119C
ballistae, 99B
ballot, "Australian" secret, 280B
Balmaceda, José Manuel (president of Argentina), 280C, 282C
Balta, José (president of Peru), 270C
Baltic Sea, 250A
Baltics, 170A, 204A, 376B
Baltimore, 211A, 240B, 243B, 257B
Baltimore, Cecil Calvert, 185A
Baltimore and Ohio Railroad, 249B, 274B
Baltimore Colts, 357C
Baltimore Orioles, 353C, 357C, 365C, 367C, 383C
Baluchistan, 68C, 281A, 283A
Balzac, Honoré de, 249C, 251C, 261C
Bambara, 263A
Bamberg, 108A
Bamberg Apocalypse, 91C
bamboo, 53B
Ban Zhao, 39C
banana cultivation, 149B
Banat, 206A
Band-Aid bandages, 305B
Banda Oriental, 244C
Bandaranaike, Sirimavo (prime minister of Ceylon), 357A
Bandung Conference, 342A
Bangka, 204C
Bangkok, 326C, 342A
Bangladesh, 104C, 108C, 357A, 358A, 360A, 369A
cyclone in, 377A
government, 371A
and Pakistan, 361A
Banjermasin, 216C
Bank for International Payments, 310A
Bank of America, 282B
Bank of Canada, 316B
Bank of England, 200A, 336B
Bank of Montreal, 246B
Bank of North America, 224B
Bank of Pennsylvania, 233C
Bank of United States, 228B, 242B, 250B, 312B
banking system, 30A
bankruptcy, 208A
Banks, Sir Joseph, 227A
Banneker, Benjamin, 215B, 229B
Bannockburn, battle of, 124A
Bantam, 176C
Bantu, 16A, 48B, 223A
Banu Saad dynasty. *See* Morocco
Baoding, 188C
Baphaion, battle of, 122B
Baptist Church, 273C
Baptist Missionary Society, 231C
Baptist Union of Great Britain, 241C
Baptists, 253C
Bar Harbor Airlines (1985 crash), 368C
Bar Kokba, Simon, 40A
Barakzai dynasty. *See* Afghanistan
Baranovici, 298A
Barawa, 136C
Barbados, 195A, 252C, 274C, 278C, 318C
Barbarossa, 154B
Barbary pirates, 166B
Barbary States, 154B
barbecue spit, 215B
Barbégal, 51B
Barbie, Klaus, 370A
Barbier, Charles, 245B
Barbier de Séville, Le (Beaumarchais), 223C
Barbiere di Siviglia, Il (Rossini), 243C
Barbuda, 272C, 366A
Barcelona, 204A, 320A, 358B
Peace of (1493), 146A
Sagrada Familia Church, 279C
transportation, 163B
Treaty of (1529), 158A
University of, 139C
Barchester Towers (Trollope), 265C
Barclay, John, 181C
Bardeen, John, 337B
Bardstown, 239C
Baret, Madeleine Sophie, 249C
Barghash, Sayyid (sultan of Zanzibar), 273A, 281A
Bari, 96B
Baring, Sir Evelyn, 279A
Barker, Sir Samuel, 273A
Barnaby Rudge (Dickens), 255C
Barnard, *223*
Barnet, battle of, 142A
barometer, 189B, 193B, 199B
aneroid, 257B
water, 187B
Baron, Salo Wittmayer, 319C
Baronius, Cesar, 173C
Baroque archictecture, 185C
Baroque music, 193C
Barrie, J. M, 289C
Barrier, Treaty of 1715, 206A, 226A
Barrios, José María Reina (president of Guatemala), 282C
Barron v. Baltimore, 250B
Barrow Strait, 244B
Barrymore, Ethel, 315C
Barrymore, John, 315C
Barrymore, Lionel, 315C
Bartered Bride (Smetana), 271C
Barthou, Jean Louis, 316A
Barton, Clara, 276B
Barton Ramie, 79A
Baruch, Bernard, 302B, 336A, 336C
baseball, 259C. *See also individual teams*
All-American Girls Baseball League, 331C

American League, 287C, 333C
first intercollegiate game, 265C
major league strike, 381C
National League, 275C
professional, 273C
Basel, 161C, 286A, 310A
Council of, 139C
Peace of, 148A, 232A
University of, 141C
BASF, 319B
Basho, 193C
Basie, Count, 369C
Basil I (emperor of Byzantium), 80B
Basil II (emperor of Byzantium), 88B
Basil the Great (Bishop of Caesarea), 55A
Basile, Giambattista, 185C
Basilica Aemilia, 31C
Basilikon Doron (James VI), 175C
Baskerville, John, 217C
basket making, 61A, 63A
basketball, 283C
National Basketball Association (NBA), 351C, 355C, 379C, 385C
Basques, 76A
Basra, 68C, 74C, 223A, 295A, 297A
Bass, George, 233A
Bass Strait, 233A
Bassein, Treaty of, 235A
Bastidas, Rodrigo de, 151A
Bastille, 228A
Bastogne, 334A
Basutoland, 257A, 271A, 273A, 279A, 353A
Bataan province, 328C
Batavia, 36A, 180C, 328C
Bates, Kathy, 375C
Bath, 88A
Báthory, Sigismund (prince of Transylvania), 174A
Báthory, Stephen (prince of Transylvania and king of Poland), 168A, 170A
baths, 29B, 31C, 39C, 45C
of Titus, 37C
Batista Zaldívar, Fulgencio (president of Cuba), 323A, 341A, 347A
Batlle y Ordóñez, José (president of Uruguay), 288C, 292C, 302C
Baton Rouge, 316B, 345B
Baton Rouge, battle of, 224B
Battambang, 233A
battery, 255B
dry-cell storage, 271B
rechargeable storage, 265B
zinc-copper, 253B
"Battle Hymn of the Republic, The" (Howe), 267C
Battle of Arbela, The (Brueghel), 179C
Battle of Coxinga, The (Chikamatsu), 207C
Battle of Lights (Stella), 295C
Battleship Potemkin (Eisenstein), 309C
Batum, 278A, 290A
Baudelaire, Charles, 265C, 271C
Baudouin I (king of Belgium), 338B
Bauer, Georg, 163B, 165B
Bauhaus, 305C
Baulieu, Étienne-Émile, 365B
Baum, L. Frank, 287C
Baumgarten, Alexander Gottlieb, 213C, 215C
Bautzen, battle of, 240A
Bavaria, Bavarians, 74A, 81B, 84A, 88A, 150A, 158A, 167C, 179C, 182A, 188A, 202A, 212A, 222A, 224A, 226A, 238A, 244A
Nazis in, 314A
and Prussia, 270A
Baxter, Richard, 199C
Bay of Pigs invasion, 347A, 348A
Bayar, Celâl (president of Turkey), 338B
Baybars I (sultan of Egypt), 116B, 116C, 118C
Bayeux Tapestry, *95,* 97C, *103*
Bayinn Naung (king of Burma), 164C
Bayle, Pierre, 197C, 201C
Bayonne (France), 132A
Bayreuth, 224A
bazooka, 329B
Beagle Channel dispute, 369A
Beaker people, 5A, 5C
Beale Street Blues (Handy), 301C
beans, 115A, 159B
Beard, Charles, 295C
Beard-Hater (Julian), 55C
Béarn, 180A, 181C
Beat generation, 343C, 345C
Beatles, 349C, 351C, 357C, 365C, 383C
Beatrix (queen of the Netherlands), 364B
Beatty, Warren, 385C
Beaubassin, 203A
Beauchamps, Charles, 193C
Beaulieu, 170A
Edict of, 171C
Beaumarchais, Pierre-Augustin Caron de, 223C
Beaumont, Francis, 181C
Beaumont (Tex.), 288B
Beauregard, P.G.T., 266B
Beautiful and the Damned, The (Fitzgerald), 307C
Beautiful Galatea, The (Suppé), 267C
Beauvoir, Simone de, 331C, 335C
Bechuanaland, 353A
Beck, Dave, 344C
Becket, Thomas à, Saint (Archbishop of Canterbury), 105C, 161C
Becket (Anouilh), 347C
Beckett, Samuel, 341C
Beckford, William, 217C
Bede, the Venerable, Saint, 73C
Bedloe's Island, 278B
bee keeping, 2A
Bee Gees, 363C
Beebe, Charles William, 313B
Beecher, Catharine E., 262B
beer, brewing industry, 77B, 79B, 81B, 109B, 165B
Beethoven, Ludwig van, 221C, 235C, 237C, 239C, 247C, 249C
beets, 215B
Before Dawn (Hauptmann), 281C
Before the Storm (Fontane), 277C
Beggar's Opera (Gay), 211C
Begin, Menachem (prime minister of Israel), 362A, 363A
Behaim, Martin, 147B
behaviorism, behaviorists, 303C
Behn, Aphra, 197C, 199C
Beiden Grundprobleme der Ethik, Die (Schopenhauer), 255C
Beijing, 10B, 84C, 100C, 102C, 110C, 136C, 137C, 154C, 164C, 188C, 190C, 192C, 339A, 373A, 379C
Beirut, 108B, 367A
Bekesy, Georg von, 337B
Belarus, 298A, 306A
Belgium, Belgians, 54A, 123C, 135B, 143C, 167B, 177B, 177C, 197C, 200A, 226A, 228A, 230A, 232A, 234A, 254A, 312A, 334A
and Angola, 289A
and Antarctica, 346A
and Benelux Economic Union, 344A
and Britain, 336A
coal mining, 107B
and Congo, 279A, 283A
dwellings, 63B
education, 284A
and France, 308A, 318A, 336A
and France border, 322 A
and Germany, 294A, 296A, 308A, 322A, 334A
government, 292A
and Holland, 250A
industry, 59B
and International Monetary Fund, 348A
law and society, 228A
and Luxembourg, 336A
mining, 127B
and NATO, 352A
and Netherlands, 336A
politics, 346B
religion, 284A
revolution in, 127B
and Rwanda, 299A
and Tanzania, 299A
and Treaty of Rome, 344A
and United Nations, 347A
and United States, 308B, 338A,
and Urundi, 299A
in Western European Union, 342A
World War I, 294A, 296A
World War II, 322A
Belgrade, 94B, 200A, 206A, 228A, 238A, 266A, 294A, 296A, 336A
Peace of, 212A
Belgrano, Manuel, 240C
Belisarius (emperor of Byzantium), 62B, 64B, 65B
Belize, 79A, 232C, 266C, 366A
Belize City, 278C
Bell, Alexander Graham, 275B, 303B
Bell, Patrick, 249B
Bell-Burnell, Jocelyn, 353B
Bell for Adano, A (Hersey), 333C
Bell for Adano, A (Osborn), 333C
Bell Laboratories, 311B, 325B, 335B, 337B, 357B, 363B
Bellingshausen, Fabian von, 245A
Bellini, Giovanni, 143C, 147C
Bellini, Vincenzo, 251C
Bellman, Carl Michael, 213C
Belloc, Hilaire, 289C
Bellow, Saul, 351C, 363C
bellows, water-powered, 125B
bells, church, 161B
Bellum Iugurthinum (Sallust), 31C
Bellum Judaicum (Josephus), 37C
Belluno, 136B
Belorus, 376B
Belorussia. *See* Belarus
Beloved (Morrison), 373C
Belshazzar (king of Babylonia), 16B
belt drive, 31B
Belvedere Summer Palace, 209C
Bemelmans, Ludwig, 325C
Ben-Hur (movie), 347C
ben Maimon, Moses, 109C
Benadryl, 331B
Benalcázar, Sebastián de, 161A
Benares, 62C, 229A
Benburh, battle of, 188A
Benedict VII, Pope, 89C
Benedict IX, Pope, 93C
Benedict XII, Pope, 127C
Benedict XIII, Pope, 135C, 137C
Benedict XIV, Pope, 213C
Benedictines, 93C
Benelux customs union, 336B
Benelux Economic Union, 344A
Beneš, Edvard, 316A, 336B
Benét, Stephen Vincent, 313C, 333C
Benét, William Rose, 327C
Benevento, battle of, 116B
Beneventum, 76A
Bengal, 78C, 104C, 108C, 112C, 118C, 128C, 130C, 134C, 140C, 146C, 154C, 170C, 184C, 186C, 190C, 202C, 214C, 216C, 218C, 220C, 231A
Bengal, Bay of, 295A
Benghazi, 326A
Bengkulen, 247A
Benin, 82C, 144B, 146B, 164B, 176B, 261A
Benjamin Franklin (Van Doren), 323C
Bennett, Arnold, 291C
Bennett, Richard Bedford (prime minister of Canada), 312B, 314B
Bentham, Jeremy, 227C, 229C
Benti, Teferi (leader of Ethiopia), 363A
Benton, Robert, 365C
Benton, Thomas Hart, 315C
Benz, Karl, 269B, 283B
Benzaiten, *127*
Beornwulf, 78A
Beowulf: The Monster and His Critics (Tolkien), 319C
Beowulf (anon.), *72,* 73C
Béranger, Pierre Jean de, 243C
Berar, 237A
Berbers, 40B, 74C, 76C, 84B, 88C, 94C, 96B, 251A, 307A
Berbice, 232C, 242C, 250C
Berchtesgaden, 320A
Berengar I (king and emperor of Italy), 82B
Berengar II (king of Italy), 86B
Berengar IV, Raymond, 102B
Beresford, Bruce, 373C
Berezina River, 240A
Berg, 210A
Berg, Alban, 309C, 319C
Bergamo, 136B, 140A
Bergen, battles of, 216A, 234A
Bergen-Belsen, 368A
Berger, Victor L., 292B
Bergerac, Cyrano de, 189C, 191C
Bergerac, Peace of, 170A
Bergman, Ingmar, 349C
Bergman, Ingrid, 329C, 333C, 343C
Bergson, Henry, 287C
Beria, 317B
Beria, Lavrenty, 340B
beriberi, 187B
Bering, Vitus Jonassen, *209,* 211A, 213A
Bering Sea, 17C, 38C
Bering Strait, 211A, 225A
Berkeley, George, 205C, 207C
Berkeley, Sir William, 187A
Berlin, 138A, 203C, 288A, 319C, 334A, 370A, 376B
blockade, 336B, 338B
and Britain, 346A
Congress, 276A
Decree, 236A
East, 336B, 356B
and France, 346A
law and society, 302A, 304A
National Gallery, 355C
Opera, 309C
Peace of (1742), 212A
Peace of (1850), 260A
Reichstag, 314A
and Soviet Union, 338B, 346A
Treaty of (1728), 210A
and United States, 346A
Wall, 346B, 374B
West, 356B
Berlin, Irving, 293C, 323C, 327C, 373C
Berlin Diary (Shirer), 327C
Berliner, Emile, 275B
Berlioz, Hector, 253C, 263C
Berlusconi, Silvio (prime minister of Italy), 380B
Bermuda, 179A, 199A, 313B, 340A
Bernadotte, Folke, 337A
Bernard of Clairvaux, 101C, 103C, 105C

Bernardo O'Higgins Military School, 240C, 246C
Bernicia, kingdom of, 64A, 66A, 68A
Bernini, Giovanni Lorenzo, 183C, 189C
Bernstein, Leonard, 333C, 345C, 357C
Berry, 106A
Berry, Clifford, 321B
Berryman, Clifford, *318*
Berthelot, Marcellin, 267B
Berthelot, Pierre, 267B
Bertil, Gasparo, 187B
Bertolucci, Bernardo, 371C
Berwick, 106A, 124A, 126A, 130A, 166A
Besançon, University of, 137C
Bessarabia, 240A, 264A, 276A
Best Years of Our Lives, The (movie), 337C
Betancourt, Rómulo (president of Venezuela), 335A
Bethlehem, 33A, 63C, 259C
Bethlehem Steel Company, 296B
Bethlen, Gábor (prince of Transylvania), 180A
Béthune Orchies, 122A
Betjeman, Sir John, 369C
Beuckelszoon, Willem, 119B, 133B
Beyle, Marie-Henri, 249C
Beyond Good and Evil (Nietzsche), 281C
Bezabde, 54B
Bhagavad-Gita (Vyasa), 25C
Bhagnagar, 172C
Bhapol, 208C
Bharata, 59C
Bharnagar, 208C
Bhartrihari, 71C
Bhoja (king of Kanauj), 78C
Bhonsie, Shivaji, 192C, 194C
Bhopal, 208C, 369A
Bhre Vengker, 140C
Bhutan, 356A, 357A, 359A
Bhutto, Benazir (prime minister of Pakistan), 375A
Bhutto, Zulfikar (prime minister of Pakistan), 357A
Biafra, 353A
Biarritz, 268A
Bibiena, Fernando, 205C
Bible, 8A, 23C, 141B, 165C, 169C, 179C, 267C, 297C
Bible Society, 205C
Bic Corporation, 335B
Bich, Marcel, 335B
Bicocca, battle of, 156A
bicycle, 245B, 269B
  modern metal-framed, 283B
  "penny-farthing," 273B
  velocipede, 271B
Bidassoa, 240A
Biddle, James, 259A
Bierstadt, Frederick, 267C
Bierut, Boleslaw (president of Poland), 336B
big bang theory, 349B, 377B
Big Bend culture, 81A
Big Money, The (Dos Passos), 321C
Big Parade, The (movie), 309C
Big Sleep, The (Chandler), 321C,
Bigarha, Mahmud Shah (king of Gujarat), 140C
Bigelow, Erastus, 253B
Bighorn Basin, 236B
Bignone, Reynaldo (president of Argentina), 367A
Bihar, 76C
Bihe, 220B
Bijapur, 146C, 152C, 168C, 183C, 186C, 198C, 216C
Biko, Steven, 363A
Bilderdijk, Willem, 217C
Bill of Rights, 228B, 250B
billiards, 165C
Billings, William, 221C
Billy Graham, 343C
Billy the Kid (Copland and Loring), 321C
Binaisa, Geoffrey (president of Uganda), 365A
binnacle, 135B
Binnig, Gerd, 369B
Binnya Ran (king of Hanthawaddy), 146C
bio-chemical weapons, 135B, 301B, 327B, 339B, 347B, 358A, 373A, 381A, 384A
Biopol, 375B
biotin, snythetic, 323B
"Birches" (Frost), 299C
Birds of America, The (Audubon), 249C
Birdseye, Clarence, 299B
Birkeland, Kristian, 293B
Birmingham, 348C
birth control, 11B, 351C, 355C, 381C
  clinic, 276A
  pill, 343B
  timed-release device, 375B
Birth of a Nation, The (movie), 297C
Birth of Caution, The (Castiglione), 159C
Birth of Tragedy, The (Nietzsche), 273C
Biscay, Bay of, 201B
biscuit, dried-meat, 261B
Bishop, Maurice (prime minister of Grenada), 367A
Bismarck, Otto von (chancellor of German empire), 266A, 268A, 276A, 282A, 284A, 286A
Bismarck Sea, battle of the, 330C
bismuth, 177B
Bitburg, 368A
Biton Kulibai, 214B
Bitter Sweet (Coward), 311C
Bizerta, 330A
Bizet, Georges, 275C
Black, Hugo, 356C
Black Boy (Wright), 335C
Black Death, 128A, 130A, 133B
Black Forest, 54A
Black Friars, 111C
Black Hawk, 246B, 250B
Black Iris (O'Keeffe), 311C
Black Jacobins: Toussaint L'Ouverture and the San Domingo Revolution, The (James), 321C
Black Panthers, 356C
Black Sea, 40A, 42B, 44A, 56B, 123B, 140B, 264A
  700 B.C.–631 B.C., 12C
  Baku-Batum oil pipeline, 290A
  Danube-Black Sea Canal, 368B
  and Russia, 224A, 230A, 239A
  Vikings and, 72A
Black Tuesday, 310A
Blackfoot, 274B
Blackstone, William, 219C
Blackwell, Elizabeth, 260B
Blackwell, Henry Brown, 272B
Blair, Eric, 335C
Blake, William, 217C, 229C, 231C
Blanc, Louis, 259C
Blanchard, Jean-Pierre, 231B
Blanchard, Thomas, 245B
Blanco, Guzman (president of Venezuela), 272C
Bland-Allison Act, 276B
blanket, electric, 293B
Blavatsky, Helena Petrovna, 275C
bleach, bleaching, 125B, 217B, 253B
Blenheim, battle of, 202A
Bligh, William (governor of Australia), 229A, 237A, 239A
blind
  reading machine for the, 361B
  writing system for the, 245B
Blithe Spirit (Coward), 325C
blitzkrieg, 324A
Bloch, Felix, 335B
Block, Adriaen, 179A
Block Island, 179A
Bloemfontein Convention, 263A
Blois, 112A, 172A, 203C
Blond Venus (movie), 315C
Blondel, David, 183C
blood
  atomic-force microscope for, 373B
  circulation, 167B
  dialysis machine, 293B, 343B
  Factor VIII, 347B, 369B
  perfusion pump, 317B
  plasma, freeze-dried, 329B
  preservation of, 325B, 335B
  pressure, 203B, 211B, 249B, 291B
  Rhesus factor, 325B
  sphygmomanometer, 285B
  transfusion, 147B, 193B, 249B, 295B
  types, 287B, 289B
  vessels, 167B, 289B, 341B, 375B
Blood River, 255A
Bloody Sunday (Northern Ireland), 358B
Bloody Sunday (Russia), 290A
Blore Heath, 140A
Blossom Time (Romberg), 307C
blowpipe, 215B, 221B
blowtorch, gasoline, 277B
Blücher, Gebhard, 242A
Blue Angel, The (movie), 313C
blue baby syndrome, 333B
Blue Danube (Strauss), 271C
Bluetooth, Harold (king of Denmark), 84A
B'nai B'rith, 295C
Boadicea (queen of England), 34A
Board of Economic Warfare, 330B
Board of Economic Welfare, 328B
Boat Building (Constable), 243C
boat(s), 27B, 29B, 31B, 161B. *See also* ship(s)
  longboat, 50-oar, 15B
  mills, 109B
  oars, 3B
  paddle-wheel tugboat, 163B
  paddleboat, 77B, 103B
  reed, 3B
  sail-powered, 3B
  steamboats, 205B, 231B, 237B
Bobangi, 214B
Boccaccio, Giovanni, 129C, 133C
Bock, Jerry, 351C
Bocksgesang (Werfel), 307C
Bocskay, István (prince of Transylvania), 176A
Bodawpaya (king of Burma), 225A
Bodin, Jean, 169C, 171C
Bodleian Library, 177C
Boehm, Martin, 221C
Boeing Company, 312B
Boers, 192B, 259A, 265A. *See also* Afrikaners
  Boer War, 286B, 287A, 289A
  and Botswana, 263A
  and Britain, 243A, 253A, 257A, 263A, 277A, 285A, 287A
  rebellion, 295A
  in South African Party, 293A
  and Stellaland Republic, 279A
  and Xhosa, 214B, 223A, 225A
  and Zulu, 255A
Boesky, Ivan, 370C
Boethius, 63C
Bogardus, James, 255B
Bogart, Humphrey, 329C, 339C
Bogotá, 161A, 242C, 323A, 336A
Boguslawski, Wojciech, 249C
Bohème, La (Puccini), 285C
Bohemia, Bohemians, 76A, 84A, 85B, 86A, 96A, 104A, 114A, 116A, 118A, 122A, 134A, 135C, 137B, 138A, 145C, 146A, 154A, 155B, 156A, 166A, 170A, 176A, 177C, 178A, 180A, 181C, 184A, 212A, 320A
  and Austria, 290A
  coinage, 155B
  government, 294A
  Premyslid dynasty, 122A
  religion, 133C
Bohemond (prince of Antioch), 98B
Böhme, Jacob, 179C
Boileau-Despreaux, Nicolas, 195C
Boivin, Marie, 241B
Bokassa, Jean-Bédel (emperor of Central African Empire), 365A
Boke of the Buchesse (Chaucer), 131C
Bokhara, 166B
Boleslav II, 86A
Boleyn, Anne, 158A, 160A
Bolívar, Simón, 238C, 240C, 242C, *243*, 244C, 246C, 248C
  in Venezuela, 244C
Bolivia, Bolivians, 99A, 163A, 329A, 355A
  and Argentina, 308C
  arts, 209C
  and Brazil, 288C
  and Chile, 254C, 270C, 274C, 276C, 278C, 288C
  and Germany, 331A
  government, 248C, 318C, 333A, 363A, 365A
  independence of, 246C
  and Italy, 331A
  and Paraguay, 310C, 312C, 314C, 316C, 318C, 320C
  and Peru, 252C, 274C
  politics, 331A
  River Plate, 222C
  silver in, 163A
  and Spain, 161A, 238C, 270C
  in United Nations, 335A
  World War II, 331A
Bollandists, 187C
Bollingen Prize for Poetry, 339C
Bologna, 119B, 147C, 154A, 163C, 264A
Bolshevik Revolution, 300A, *301*
Bolsheviks, 288A, 302A
Bolt, Robert, 347C
bolter, cylindrical, 173B
Boma, 214B
Bombay, 192C, 196C, 279A
Bona, 92B, 104B
Bonaparte, House of, 280A
Bonaparte, Louis (king of Holland), 236A
Bonaparte, Napoléon, 220A. *See* Napoléon I
Bonaparte as First Consul (Ingres), 237C
Bonavista, 203A
Bond, Julian, 352C
Bond of 1844, 257A
Bondfield, Margaret, 310A
Bondi, Hermann, 337B
bone, artificial, 375B
Bonfire of the Vanities (Wolfe), 371C
Bonhomme Richard (U.S. ship), 224B
Boniface, Saint, 73C
Boniface VII, Pope, 89C
Boniface VIII, Pope, 123C
Boniface IX, Pope, 133C
Bonin Islands, 275A, 355A
Bonn, 221C, 372A, 376B
  University of, 263B
Bonnewitz, Peter, 157B
Bontemps, Arna, 323C
booby traps, 119B

boogie-woogie, 317C
Book of Common Prayer (Cranmer), 165C
Book of Knowledge of Ingenious Mechanical Devices (al-Jazari), 109B
Book of Mormon (Smith), 249C
Book of Nonsense (Lear), 259C
Book of Roads and Kingdoms, The (al-Bakri), 99B
bookbinding, 33C, 45A
books, 55C, 143B, 145B, 147C, 151C, 167C. *See also individual books*
Boomplatz, battle of, 259A
Boone, Daniel, 222B
Booth, John Wilkes, 268B
Booth, Shirley, 341C
Booth, William, 269C, 277C
Boothroyd, Betty, 376B
Boots Company, 347B
Bordaberry Arocena, Juan María (president of Uruguay), 363A
Bordeaux, 122A, 132A, 138A, 227C
Borden, Gail, 261B
Borgnine, Ernest, 343C
Boris Godunov (Pushkin), 247C
Boris I (prince of Bulgaria), 81C
Boris III (tsar of Bulgaria), 316A
Bork, Robert, 358C, 370C
Bormann, Martin, 326A
Borneo, 88C, 176C, 216C, 255A, 281A, 326C, 330C
Bornhöved, battle of, 112A
Bornu, kingdom of, 142B, 144B, 156B, 168B, 176B, 186B
Borobudur, 77C
Borodin, Aleksandr Porfiyevich, 275C
Borodino, battle of, 240A
Boroughbridge, battle of, 124A
Borromini, Francesco, 187C
Bosch, Hieronymus, 145C, 155C
Bosch, Robert, 281B
Bosnia, Bosnians, 380A, 382B
  and Austria, 228A, 276A, 290A, 292A
  and Serbia, 292A, 380A, 380B, 382B
  and Turkey, 140A
  and United States, 382B
Bosnia-Herzegovina, 376B, 380B. *See also* Herzegovina
    civil war, 378B, 380B, 382B
    and United Nations, 378A, 378B
Bosporus, 128B, 248A, 251A, 254A
Bosra Cathedral, 63C
Bossuet, Jacques-Bénigne, 197C
Boston, 199A, 203C, 217C, 219A, 221A, 222B, 239C, 273C, 287B, 328B
    Boston Evening Post, 211C
    Boston Massacre, 221A
    Boston News-Letter, 209C
    Boston Weekly Post Boy, 211C
    Brink's robbery in, 338C
    riots in, 360C
    St. Stephen's Catholic Church, 237C
Boston Athenaeum, 237C
Boston Braves, 337C
Boston Celtics, 351C, 355C
Boston Red Sox, 289C, 337C, 355C, 361C, 371C
Boston Symphony Orchestra, 309C
Boston Tea Party, 221A
Boswell, James, 229C
Bosworth, battle of, 144A
Botany Bay (Hall), 325C
Botha, Louis (prime minister of South Africa), 291A, 293A, 297A, 369A
Botha, P. W. (president of South Africa), 369A, 373A
Bothwell, James, 168A
Bothwell Bridge, battle of, 196A
Botswana, 353A, 369A
Botticelli, Sandro, 143C
bottling, bottles, 245B
  baby, 151B, 255B, 293B
  caps and cap liners, 283B
  manufacturing, 237B, 289B
  vacuum, 289B
Bougainville, 330C, 332C
Bouillon, duke of, 176A
Boulanger, Georges, 280A, 282A
Boulder Dam, 319B
Boulle, André Charles, 211C
Boulogne, 43B, 162A, 164A, 170A
Boumedienne, Houari, 351A
Boundary Waters Treaty, 292B
Bounty, HMS (British ship), 229A
Bourbon, House of, 266A
Bourbon, Île de, 239A
Bourchier, Thomas (Archbishop of Canterbury), 141C
Bourges, Pragmatic Sanction of, 139C
Bourgneuf, 130A
Bourignon, Antoinette, 201C
Bourne, Jonathan, 292B
Boutros-Ghali, Boutros (secretary-general of United Nations), 382A
Bouvines, battle of, 110A
Bovet, Daniel, 333B
Bow, Clara, 351C
bow and arrow, 63B
Bowdoin College, 248B
Bowen, Catherine Drinker, 333C
Bowen, Elizabeth, 315C, 319C
Bowes-Lyon, Elizabeth (Queen Mother), 320B
Bowles, William Lisle, 219C
Boxers, Boxer Rebellion, 286B, 289A
boxing, 283C, 291C
Boy Scouts of America, 292B
Boyacá, battle of, 244C
Boyce, William, 217C
Boyer, Jean-Pierre (president of Haiti), 244C, 246C, 256C
Boyle, Robert, 193B, 197B
Boyle's Law, 193B
Boyne, battle of the, 200A
Braban, 155C
Brabant, 54A, 172A
brace and bit, 137B
Braddock, Edward, 215A
Braddock, James J., 319C
Bradero, Gerbrand Adriaenszoon, 181C
Bradley, Omar (chairman of Joint Chiefs of Staff), 338C
Bradstreet, Anne, 189C
Brady, Ian, 352B
Brady, Mathew, 265C
Brady bill, 378C
Braganza dynasty. *See* Portugal
Bragg, William H., 293B
Bragg, William L., 291B, 293B
Brahms, Johannes, 271C, 275C
Braille, 283B
Braille, Louis, 245B
Bramah, Joseph, 225B, 233B
Bramante, Donato, 151C
Branca, Giovanni, 183B
Branch Davidian cult, 378C
Brancusi, Constantin, 289C
Brand (Ibsen), 271C
Brandeis, Louis D., 298B
Brandenburg, 104A, 138A, 161C, 168A, 178A, 180A, 190A, 192A, 194A, 196A, 196B, 198B, 202A
Brando, Marlon, 343C, 359C
Brandt, Willy (chancellor of West Germany), 356B, 360B
brandy, 63B, 123B
Branly, Édouard, 281B
Brant, Sebastian, 149C
Braque, Georges, 291C, 301C
Brasidas, 20C
brassiere, strapless, 295B
Brattleboro, 209A
Braun, Wernher von, 327B, 343B
Brave New World (Huxley), 315C
Braveheart (movie), 381C
Bravo Valley culture, 85A
Brazil, Brazilians, 149A, 151A, 151B, 187C, 205A, 280C, 286C, 377B
  and Argentina, 246C
  arts, 213C
  and Bolivia, 288C
  economics, 306C
  and France, 165A
  and Germany, 256C, 300C, 320C, 329A
  government, 282C, 316C, 318C, 335A, 343A, 351A, 353A, 369A
  and Holland, 185A
  industry, 209A, 278C, 282C
  and Inter-American Coffee Board, 325A
  and Italy, 329A, 335A
  law and society, 280C, 310C, 312C, 314C, 355A
  Nazis in, 320C
  and Paraguay, 268C
  and Portugal, 159A, 165A, 193A, 236C, 238C, 246C
  railroad in, 270C
  and Sierra Leone, 168B
  slave trade, 187C, 262C, 272C, 278C
  and United States, 329A
  University of, 318C
  and Uruguay, 240C, 244C, 246C, 248C, 268C
  World War I, 300C
  World War II, 329A, 335A
brazilwood, 84C
Brazos River, 163A, 199A
bread, 39B, 162C
Breakfast at Tiffany's (Capote), 347C
Brébeuf, Jean de, 189C
Brecht, Bertolt, 315C, 331C
Breda, Peace of, 192A, 192B
Breisach, 196A
Breisgau, 142A
Breitenfeld, battle of, 184A
Bremen, 113C, 184A, 194A, 216A, 238A, 280A
Bremner, Robert, 217B
Brennan, William, 374C
Brennus, 21A
Brenta River, 298A
Brescia, 104B, 136B, 140A
Breslau, University of, 247B
Bresse, 176A
Brest-Litovsk, Treaty of, 302A
Breton, André, 309C
Breton Succession, War of, 126A
Bretton Woods Conference, 332B
Brewster, David, 243B
Breyer, Stephen, 380C
Brezhnev, Leonid Ilich (leader of Soviet Union), 346B, 350B, 358A, 360A, 362B, 364A, 366B
Briand, Aristide (prime minister of France), 298A, 310A
bricks, 3B, 179B, 181B
Bride of Lammermoor (Scott), 245C
Brideshead Revisited (Waugh), 335C
Bridge, The (Crane), 313C
Bridge on the River Kwai, The (Lean), 345C
bridges, 103B, 107B. *See also individual bridges*
    cantilever, 271B, 281B
    covered, 237B
    floating, 325B
    railroad, 265B
    Roman, 35B
    steel arch, 275B
    suspension, 63A, 175B, 269B, 293B.
Bridgman, Percy, 343B
Brigantes, 40A
Brighton Pavilion, 243C
Brighton Rock (Greene), 321C
Brihuega, battle of, 204A, 318A
Brindisi, 96B, 104B
Brink's, Inc., 338C
Brisbane, 279B, 289B, 311B
Britain, British, 214A, 240A, 251C, 254A, 310A. *See also* England
  and Acadians, 226B
  Act of Union, 234A
  and Aden, 355A
  and Afghanistan, 255A, 257A, 263A, 277A, 291A, 305A, 307A
  and Algeria, 243A
  and American colonies, 221A
  American Revolution, 222B, 224A, 224B
  Anglo-American war debt (WW I), 306B
  and Anguilla, 356A
  and Antarctica, 346A, 369B
  and Arabia, 301A
  arts, 21C, 217C, 229C, 231C, 237C, 239C, 241C, 243C, 245C, 249C, 251C, 253C, 257C, 259C, 263B, 265C, 267C, 269C, 273C, 277C, 281C, 283C, 285C, 289C, 293C, 295C, 299C, 303C, 305C, 307C, 309C, 311C, 313C, 315C, 321C, 331C, 335C, 345C, 353C, 357C, 365C, 367C, 369C, 373C
  and Ashanti, 285A
  and Australia, 227A, 247A, 253A, 257A, 312A, 317B
  and Austria, 280A, 294A
  and Bahamas, 226C
  and Bahrain, 267A
  and Bangladesh, 358A
  and Barbados, 274C
  and Basutoland, 257A
  and Belgium, 318A, 336A
  and Boers, 253A, 257A, 263A, 285A
  and Borneo, 281A
  and Brittany, 232A
  and Brunei, 281A
  and Burma, 267A, 279A, 281A, 337A
  and Cameroons, 283A, 295A, 299A
  and Canada, 230B, 270B, 272B, 276B, 286B, 294B, 304B, 306B, 310B, 312A, 316B, 320B
  and Cape Colony, 243A, 249A, 257A
  and Cape of Good Hope, 233A, 241A
  and Ceylon, 243A, 337A
  and China, *254,* 255A, 257A, 265A, 267A, 313A, 338A, 368A, 369A, 370A
  in Common Market, 352B
  and Cyprus, 277A, 295A
  and Czechoslovakia, 320A
  and Denmark, 260A, 261A, 262A, 358B
  and Dutch Guiana, 236C
  and East Africa, 299A
  and East Indies, 332C
  economy, 308A, 312A, 350B, 356B
  in EEC, 360B

and Egypt, 273A, 275A, 279A, 297A, 301A, 307A, 319A, 343A
and Ellice Islands, 297A
and Ethiopia, 269A, 271A
and European Court of Human Rights, 362B
in European Free Trade Association, 346A
exploration, 157A, 250B
and Falkland Islands, 221A, 250C, 362B, 366A
and Federated Malay States, 285A
and Fiji Islands, 275A
food rationing in, 342B
and France, 206A, 215A, 216A, 230A, 234B, 236A, 238A, 238B, 248A, 250A, 260A, 279A, 288A, 294A, 298A, 300A, 302A, 306B, 307A, 308A, 314A, 324A, 328A, 336A, 340A, 348A, 348B, 352B, 357B, 374B, 376A, 381B
and French Senegal, 216B
in G-7, 368A
and Gambia, 257A
and Geneva Protocol, 308A
and German East Africa, 305A
and Germany, 288A, 294A, 296A, 298A, 304A, 322A, 324A, 326A, 328A, 334A
and Ghana, 257A
and Gilbert Islands, 297A
and Gold Coast, 257A, 261A 275A
government, 84A, 100A, 106A, 110A, 120A, 124A, 128A, 134A, 138A, 146A, 242A, 260A, 274A, 278A, 279A, 284A, 286A, 292A, 310A, 340B, 342B, 347A, 353A, 360B, 363A, 369A, 381A
and Greece, 260A, 268A, 320A, 324A, 332A, 346A, 348B
and Grenada, 224C, 274C
and Guadeloupe, 238C
and Guatemala, 370A
and Guyana, 240C
and Hawaii, 253A
and Hawaiian Islands, 257A
and Heligoland, 282A
and Holland, 247A, 273A, 322A, 334A
and Holy Alliance, 242A
and Honduras, 266C
and Hong Kong, 257A
and Hungary, 326A, 332A
and Iceland, 346B, 358B, 362B
and India, 216C, 218C, 220C, 223A, 229A, 231A, 235A, 237A, 245A, 249A, 251A, 253A, 255A, 257A, 259A, 261A, 263A, 265A, 303A, 332C, 337A
and International Monetary Fund, 348A, 362B
and IRA, 358B
and Iran, 326A, 372A
and Iraq, 295A, 299A, 301A, 303A, 305A, 307A, 313A, 315A, 342A, 378A
and Ireland, 228A, 278A, 280A, 298A, 312A, 314A, 318A, 338B, 350B, 368B
and Israel, 376A, 377A, 379A
and Italy, 102B, 104B, 124B, 143B, 266A, 280A, 298A, 300A, 302A, 304A, 308A, 309A, 318A, 320A, 324A, 326A, 330A, 334A
and Jamaica, 320C
and Japan, 269A, 271A, 285A, 288A, 290A, 295A, 305A, 306B, 312A, 318A, 326C, 332C
and Johore, 295A
and Jordan, 337A, 356A
and Kenya, 281A, 307A, 309A, 340A
and Kurds, 376A
and Lagos, 267A
law and society, 234A, 237C, 246A, 264A, 270A, 276A, 290A, 294A, 304A, 310A, 313A, 344B, 356B
and League of Nations, 314A
and Libya, 324A, 368A
and Lithuania, 320A
and Lüderitz Bay (SW Africa), 295A
and Luxembourg, 294A, 322A, 336A
and Maastricht Treaty, 378B
and Madagascar, 253A, 257A, 267A, 269C, 275A
and Malawi, 283A
and Malaya, 271A, 279A, 293A
and Malta, 364B
and Manchukuo, 321A
and Martinique, 238C
and Mecca, 301A
and the Mediterranean, 290A
and Mesopotamia, 297A, 299A, 301A
and Mexico, 266C, 320C, 329A
and Mongolia, 114A
and Morocco, 293A, 293C
and Natal, 257A
and Nauru Island, 305A
and Netherlands, 336A
and New Guinea, 279A
and New Zealand, 291A, 312A
and Newfoundland, 173A, 262B, 312A
and Nicaragua, 258C
and Nigeria, 281A, 283A, 337A
and Nonintervention Committee, 318A
and Normans, 94A, 98A
and North Africa, 324A, 330A
and North America, 149A
and North Sea oil, 360B
and Northern Ireland, 356B, 358B, 362B, 368B, 380B
and Norway, 322A
and nuclear weapons, 340A, 344A
and Orange Free State, 273A, 289A
and Ottoman Empire, 276A, 291A, 295A
and Pakistan, 337A
and Palestine, 301A, 303A, 305A, 307A, 319A, 321A, 337A
and Paris gun, 301B
and Pemba, 282A
and Persia, 239A, 263A, 265A
and Peru, 335A
and Poland, 296A, 316A
politics, 248A, 252A, 272A, 280A, 282A, 286A, 290A, 293A, 302A, 308A, 336B, 338B, 342B, 346B, 350B, 352B, 364B, 366B, 370B,
population (1851), 260A
and Portugal, 120B, 151A
pottery in, 3A
and Prussia, 232A, 284A
in Quadruple Alliance, 252A
religion, 225C, 241C, 261C, 273C, 285C, 321C, 351C, 359C
and Rhodesia, 307A
and Romans, 34A, 35B, 36A, 38A, 39B, 40A, 41C, 42A, 44A, 48A, 50A, 56A, 58A
and Russia, 246B, 248A, 262A, 294A, 296A, 298A, 300A, 302A, 310A
and Samoa, 277A, 281A
and Sarawak, 281A
science and technology, 215B, 221B, 223B, 225B, 229B, 235B, 239B, 241B, 245B, 247B, 249B, 253B, 255B, 257B, 261B, 263B, 265B, 267B, 269B, 271B, 273B, 275B, 277B, 281B, 283B, 285B, 287B, 289B, 291B, 293B, 295B, 301B, 311B, 317B, 319B, 321B, 321C, 323B, 327B, 329B, 331B, 333B, 335B, 339B, 341B, 349B, 353B, 355B, 357B, 369B, 375B, 381B, 385B
and Senegal, 225A
and Siam, 293A, 301A
and Sinai Peninsula, 291A
and Singapore, 245A, 326A, 326C
slave trade, 214B, 236A, 250A, 252A, 253A
and Somalia, 281A, 287A
and South Africa, 285A, 287A, 289A
and South Shetland Islands, 245A
and Soviet Union, 308A, 320A, 326A, 330A
and Spain, 218A, 228B, 232B, 282A, 307A, 318A, 320A
and St. Lucia, 236C, 240C
and St. Vincent, 232C
and Sudan, 279A, 285A, 287A
and Suez Canal, 275A, 343A
and Tanganyika, 305A
and Tanzania, 281A, 299A
and Tibet, 289A
and Transjordan, 305A, 307A
transportation, 117B, 141B, 252A
and Transvaal, 275A, 277A, 287A, 289A
and Trinidad, 236C
and Turkey, 264A, 276A, 294A, 297A, 299A, 303A, 309A, 311A, 342A, 346A
and Uganda, 283A, 285A, 359A
and United Nations, 332B, 343A, 346A, 352A, 370A
and United States, 177A, 260B, 287A, 288C, 296B, 312A, 314B, 318B, 320B, 326B, 330A, 338A, 340A, 346A, 348A, 352B, 354A, 356A, 368A
and Vatican City, 367C
and Venezuela, 280C
and Walvis Bay, 277A
in War of 1812, 240A, 242B
and West Germany, 340A, 346A
and West Indies, 242A
in World War I, 296A, 302A
and Xhosa, 261A, 275A
and Yemen, 281A, 354A
and Zanzibar, 275A, 281A, 282A, 283A
Britania's Pastorals (Brown), 179C
British and Foreign Bible Society, 237C
British Bluejackets, *297*
British Board of Agriculture, 244A
British Broadcast Company, 307C
British Central African Protectorate, 283A
British Columbia, 175A, 236B, 270B, 272B, 324B, 326B
British Commonwealth, 314B, 338B, 347A, 357A, 361A, 372A
British East Africa, 307A. *See also* Kenya
British East Africa Company, 283A
British East India Company, 176A, 176C, 180C, 220A, 220C, 231A, 233A, 235A, 239A, 251A, 271A
British East Indies, 230B
British Empire Conference, 312A
British Expeditionary Force, 322A
British Guiana, 250C, 254C, 280C, 353A. *See also* Guyana
slave trade, 252C
and Venezuela, 286C
British Honduras, 278C
British Institution for the Development of the Fine Arts, 237C
British Isles. *See* Britain
British Methodist Church, 357C
British Museum, 237C
British Navigation Laws, 260A
British North America Acts, 268B, 270B, 272B, 318B
British Privy Council, 316B, 318B
British Revenue Act, 219A
British Royal African Company, 192B
British Somaliland, 324A
British South Africa Company, 283A
British White Paper, 321A
British Woolens Act, 202A
Brittany, Bretons, 73C, 108A, 110A, 112A, 128A, 144A, 146A, 232A
Brixen, Synod of, 97C
Brock, Isaac, 240B
Brockhaus, Friedrich Arnold, 221C
Brodsky, Joseph, 371C
Brody, 298A
Broken Blossoms (Griffith), 305C
bromine, 281B, 283B
Brömsebro, Peace of, 188A
Brontë, Charlotte, 259C
Brontë, Emily Jane, 259C
bronze, Bronze Age, 2C, 3B, 8C, 9B, 135B, 163C
in Britain, 7A
in China, *7*
in Egypt, 5B
in Europe, 7B
Greek, 17A
in Japan, 23B
in Peru, 93A
Roman, 31B
used by Egyptians, 15B
Brooke, Edward, 352C
Brooke, Rupert, 293C
Brooke, Sir James, 255A
Brooklyn Bridge (Stella), 305C
Brooklyn Dodgers, 327C, 337C, 339C, 341C, 343C
Brooks, James L., 367C
Brooks, Preston, 264B
Brooks, Van Wyck, 333C
Brosio, Manlio (secretary-general of NATO), 356A
Brosse, Salomon de, 181C
Brotherhood of Sleeping Car Porters, 308B
Brothers and Sisters (Burnett), 311C
Brothers Karamazov, The (Dostoyevsky), 277C
Broughton, William, 230B, 233A
Brouwer, Adriaen, 187C
Brown, Charles Brockden, 221C
Brown, Jacob J., 240B
Brown, John, 264B
Brown, Joseph R., 271B
Brown, Olympia, 269C
Brown, Ron, 372C
Brown, William, 179C
Brown v. Board of Education, 342C
Browne, Hablot K., *257*
Browne, Sir Thomas, 185C, 189C
Browning, Elizabeth Barrett, 261C, 265C
Browning, John, 277B, 281B
Browning, Robert, 251C, 253C, 255C, 271C

Bruce, Blanche Kelso, 274B
Bruce, James, 220B
Bruce, Stanley (prime minister of Australia), 307A
Bruce, Thomas, 237C
Brueghel, Jan, 179C
Brueghel, Pieter (the Elder), 167C, 169C
Bruges, 122A, 132A, 156A
University of, 143C
Brûlé, Étienne, 179A, 181A
Brunanburh, battle of, 84A
Brundtland, Gro Harlem (prime minister of Norway), 366B, 370B
Brunei, 162C, 170C, 281A, 368A, 369A
Brunei, sultan of, 255A
Brunel, Isambard K., 255B, 257B, 269B
Brunelleschi, Filippo, 137C, 139C
Bruni, Leonardo, 139C
Brüning, Heinrich (chancellor of Germany), 312A
Brunkeberg, 148A
battle of, 142A
Bruno, Giordano, 173C, 177C
Bruno of Cologne, 97C
Brunswick, 106A, 108A
Brunswick, duke of, 230A
Brushaber v. Union Pacific, 298B
Brushy Mountain State Prison, 362C
Brussels, 145B, 150A, 167B, 228A, 294A, 295B, 319A, 322A
Canal, 167B
Conference, 304A
liberation of, 332A
slave trade, 282A
Treaties of (1522), 156A
Treaty of (1948), 336A
Bry, Theodor, *147, 149*
Bryan, William Jennings, 284B, 296B
Bryce, James, 281C
Bu Said, 212B
bubonic plague, 128A, 133B, 135B. *See also individual countries*
Buchanan, James (president of U.S.), 264B
Buchanan v. Warley, 300B
Bucharest
Peace of, 280A
Treaty of, 239A, 240A, 294A
Büchner, Georg, 253C
Buck, Pearl S., 313C, 327C
Bucket Chicken House, 105C
buckets, staved, 83B
buckwheat, 139B
Buczácz, Treaty of, 194A
Buda, 162A, 198A
Buddenbrooks (Mann), 289C
Buddha, 15C, 19C, 33A, 61C, 75B
Buddhism, Buddhists, 19C, 25C, 31A, 34B, 37A, 51A, 73C
in China, 39A, 57B, 63C, 65C, 79C
in India, 39A, 55C, 187C
in Japan, 65C, 94C, 100C, 107C, 123C, 168C
in Korea, 57A
in Mongolia, 200C
Tantric school, 67C
in Tibet, 78C
Buddhist University, 67C
Buena Vista, 258B, *259*
Buenos Aires, 171A, 181A, 236C, 240C, 242C, 318C
and Argentina, 262C, 264C
and Spain, 222C
to Valparaiso railway, 292C
Buffalo, 240B, 288B
"Fenians" in, 270B
Pan American Exhibition, 289B
Buffalo Bills, 377C, 379C, 381C
Buffet, The (Chardin), 211C
Buffon, Georges, 215C
Bugey, 176A
Bugis, 208C
Buhl furniture inlay, 211C
Buitenzorg, 212C
Bukhara, 70C, 82C, 110C, 214C
Bukong Temple, 83C
Bulfinch, Charles, 219C, 237C
Bulganin, Nikolai (premier of Soviet Union), 342B
Bulgaria, Bulgarians, 78A, 80A, 81C, 82A, 84A, 84B, 85C, 86A, 88B, 106A, 174A, 274A
437 B.C., 18C
and Allies, 307A
arts, 369C
in Balkan League, 292A
and Germany, 324A
government, 284A
and Greece, 304A, 307A
and Romania, 294A, 304A
and Russia, 302A
and Serbia, 278A, 280A, 294A, 298A
and Soviet Union, 332A
and Turkey, 72B, 130B, 307A
World War I, 302A
World War II, 324A
and Yugoslavia, 304A
Bulgars, 78A, 128B
Bulge, Battle of the, 334A
Bull Run, battle of, 266B
Bulwer-Lytton, Edward, 251C, 253C
Bulworth (movie), 385C
Bunker Hill, *223*
battle of, 222B
Bunyan, John, 197C, 199C
Buonarroti, Michelangelo, 145C. *See* Michelangelo
buoy, 95B, 257B
Burbank, Luther, 273B
Burckhardt, Jacob, 263C, 267C
Bureau of Measurements, 327B
Burford, battle of, 74A
Burger, Gottfried August, 221C
Burger, Warren E., 356C
Burgess, Guy, 338B
Burgh-on-Sands, 122A
Burghers of Calais, The (Rodin), 281C
Burgkmair, H., 153C
Burgoyne, John, 222B
Burgundy, Burgundians, 48A, 58A, 60B, 62A, 64A, 74A, 85C, 92A, 130A, 134A, 136A, 142A, 144A, 146A, 158A
Burgundy, duke of, 134A
Burial at Ornan, The (Courbet), 261C
Burial of Saint Lucy (Caraveggio), 179C
Burke, Edmund, 226A, 229C
Burke, Thomas Henry, 278A
Burkersdorf, battle of, 218A
Burkino Faso, 369A
Burma, Burmese, 76C, 80C, 90C, 96C, 99C, 112C, 118C, 138C, 142C, 144C, 146C, 152C, 156C, 158C, 160C, 162C, 164C, 166C, 168C, 170C, 174C, 176C, 178C, 180C, 198C, 214C, 218C, 220C, 225A, 231A, 241C, 245A, 253A, 259A, 277A, 319A, 324C, 340A, 346A, 373A, 383A. *See also* Myanmar
and Britain, 267A, 279A, 281A, 337A
Burmese War, 247A, 249A
and China, 334C
government, 104C, 114C, 116C, 337A
Hanthawaddy dynasty, 120C
and India, 247A
and Italy, 148C
and Japan, 326C, 334C
and Mongolia, 120C
and Portugal, 154C
and Thailand, 110C
Toungoo dynasty, 158C
and United States, 334C
World War II, 326C
Burnet, Gilbert, 197C
Burnett, Ivy Compton, 311C
Burns, Robert, 217C, 227C
Burns, Tommy, 291C
Burnside, Ambrose E., 266B
Burr, Aaron, 236B
Burroughs, Edgar Rice, 295C
Burroughs, William (inventor), 283B
Burroughs, William (writer), 347C
Bursa, 305A
Burton, Robert, 181C
Burton, William, 287B
Buru Island, 198C
Burundi, 132C, 349A, 353A, 363A, 381A
Bush, George (president of U.S.), *369,* 372C, 374A, 374C, 376C, 377B, 378C
Bush, Vannevar, 319B
Bushnell, David, 221B, 223B
Busia, Kofi (prime minister of Ghana, 359A
Bustamente, Alexander, 320C, 327A, 331A
Bustamente Industrial Trade Union, 320C
Butler, Alban, 217C
Butler, Samuel, 197C, 273C, 289C
butter, 59B
Butterfield Eight (O'Hara), 317C
Butterick, Ebenezer, 269B
buttons, political, 285B
Butz, Earl, 362C
Buxtehude, Dietrich, 195C
Buyides, 86B
Byelorussia. *See* Belarus
Byland, battle of, 124A
Byng, George, 206A
Byodoin, Temple of, 94C
Byrd, William, 171C
Byrnes, James Francis, 328B, 332B
Byron, George Gordon, 239C, 241C, 243C, 247C
Bytown, 251B
Byzantium, Byzantines, 52A, 55B, 61C, 64B, 69B, 74B, 75C, 77C, 82B, 86B, 88B, 93C, 94B, 102B, 104B, 106B, 108B. *See also* Constantinople; *individual leaders*
660 B.C., 12B
and Antioch, 98B
and Arabs, 70B
arts, 55B, 63C, 99C
and Crusaders, 91B
and Egypt, 118B
famine in, 84B
and Genoa, 128B
government, 138B
industry, 63B
and Italy, 96B
and Macedonia, 92B
and North Africa, 72C
and Ottoman Empire, 122B
and Patzinaks, 100B
and Persia, 64C
and Russia, 84B
science and technology, 67B
and Turkey, 134B, 158A
and Venice, 78B

C

C Major Symphony (Haydn), 223C
Cabbages and Kings (O. Henry), 289C
Cabeza de Vaca, Álvar Núñez, 159A, 161A
Cabin in the Sky (Minnelli), 331C
cable, underwater, 271B
cable cars, 275B
Cabot, John, 149A, 153A
Cabot, Sebastian, 149A, 149B, 153A, 157A, 161A
Cabral, Pedro Álvares, 150B, 151A
Cabrera, Manuel Estrada (dictator of Guatemala), 286C, 304C
Cabrillo, Juan Rodriguez, 163A
Cabrini, Saint Frances Xavier, 277C, 337C
Cacaxtla, 71A
Caceres, A. A. (president of Peru), 280C
Cachar, 249A
Cádiz, battle of, 172A
Cadsand, battle of, 126A
Caedmon, 71C
Caen, 136A
Caesar, Gaius Julius, *28,* 28A, 29A, 35C
Caesar and Cleopatra (Shaw), 287C
Caesarea, 35A, 55B
Caetano, Marcello (prime minister of Portugal), 354B, 360B
Café Filho, João, 343A
Cage, Nicolas, 381C
Cahokia, 203C
Caiaphas, 33A
Cailletet, Louis, 275B
Cain, James M., 319C, 327C
Caine Mutiny, The (Wouk), 339C
Cairo, 154B, 192B, 233A
Hassan mosque, 129C
Old Cairo, 68B, 69C, 77C, 81B
University of, 87C
Cairo (Illinois), 265B
caisson, 255B
Caisson disease, 255B
Cajetanus, 155C
Calais, 128A, 132A, 134A, 138A
Treaty of, 136A, 154A
calculating devices, 191B
arithmometer, 245B
electronic calculator, 359B
pascaline, 187B
promptuary of multiplication, 181B
slide rule, 181B
vernier, 185B
Calcutta, 194C, 198C, 200C, 216C, 220C
Calder, Alexander, 315C
Calderón Bridge, battle of, 238C
Calderón de la Barca, Pedro, 185C, 189C
Caldwell, Erskine, 315C
Caleb (king of Abyssinia), 62C
Caledonia, Caledonians, 36A, 42A
calendar(s)
Arab, 95B
Babylonian, 13B
Chinese, 7C, 19B, 135B
Egyptian, 5B
Georgian, 215C
Gregorian, 203C, 275A, 293B, 303B
Hebrew, 51B
Islamic, 69C
Japanese, 275A
Julian, 29A, 300A
lunar, 275A
Mayan, 3B, 32C, 38C, 42C, *48,* 52C, 69A
Calhoun, John C., 242B, 248B, 256B
"Calhoun's Resolutions," 254B
Calicut, 148C
California, 65A, 77A, 161A, 163A, 171A, 177A, 224B, 254B, 258A, 258B, 260B, 311B, 319B, 328B, 341C, 362C, 383B
death penalty in, 376C
Gulf of, 161A
Japanese in, 294B
University of, at Berkeley, 319B, 325B, 350C
University of, at Los Angeles

(UCLA), 329C, 377B
University of, Medical School, 362C
Caligula (Camus), 333C
Caligula (emperor of Rome), 32A, 34A, 35B, 43B
Calixtus I, Pope, 45A
Calixtus III, Pope, 141C
Call of the Wild, The (London), 289C
Callaghan, James (prime minister of Britain), 362B
Callao, battle of, 270C
Callas, Maria, 363C
Calles, Plutarco Elías (president of Mexico), 308C, 325A
Calley, William, Jr., 356C
calliope, 263
Callot, Jacques, 179B, 181C
Calne, Roy, 349B
Calonne, Charles Alexandre de, 224A, 226A
calorimeter, 267B
Calvin, John, 159C, 161C, 163C, 167C
Calvinism, Calvinists, 167C
and Catholics, 173C, 185C
and Lutherans, 189C
Cambodia, Cambodians, 77C, 78C, 99C, 100C, 106C, 118C, 233A, 281A, 324C, 379A
and France, 269A
government, 377A
and United Nations, 375A
and United States, 357A, 358A, 360A
and Vietnam, 373A
Cambrai
battle of, 300A
League of, 152A
Peace of, 158A
Cambridge, 273C
University, 109C, 151C, 153C, 163C
Cambridge Platonist: The True Intellectual System of the Universe (Cudworth), 197C
Cambyses II (king of Persia), 16A
Camden, 323B
battle of, 224B
Camera degli Sposi, 143C
camera(s). *See also* photography
Brownie, 287B
clock-drive solar, 257B
deep-sea underwater, 335B
instant, 349B
lucida, 195B
obscura, 83B, 147B, 167B, 181B, 199B, 249B
Cameron, James, 385C
Cameroons, 214B, 279A, 295A
and Britain, 283A, 297A, 299A
and France, 297A
and French Congo, 285A
and Germany, 283A, 299A
and Nigeria, 347A
Cameroons River, 172B
Camillus, Marcus Furius, 21A
Camisards, 202A
Camlan, battle of, 64A
Camocim, 149A
Camões, Luís Vaz de, 169C
Camp David summit, 362A
camp meeting, 235C
Campaign for Nuclear Disarmament, 364B
Campanía Church, 268C
Campbell, Alexander, 249C
Campbell, Kim (prime minister of Canada), 378C
Campbell, Robert, 252B
Campbel-Bannerman, Henry, 290A
Campbellites, 249C
Campenella, Tommaso, 183C
Campfire Girls, 292B
camphor, 84C
Campion, Thomas, 179C
Campo Formio, Peace of, 232A
Camras, Marvin, 319B
Camus, Albert, 327C, 333C, 337C
can opener, 265B, 277B, 345B
Canaan, Canaanites, 4B, 7C, 8A
Canada, Canadians, 85A, 177A, 211C, 246B, 254B, 256B, 258B, 264B, 270B, 290B, 298B, 353B
2000 B.C., 5B
and Acadians, 226B
Act of Union, 254B
and American Indians, 159A, 181A, 195A, 274B
automobile industry, 376C
blackout in, 326B, 350C
and Britain, 205A, 219A, 272B, 276B, 286B, 294B, 304B, 306B, 308B, 310B, 312A, 316B, 320B
British North America Acts, 268B, 270B, 272B
Canada Act, 366C, 374C
Canada-U.S. Free Trade Agreement, 372C
Canadian Confederation, 338C
Canadian-U.S. Free Trade Agreement, 372C
Civil Service Commission, 290B
Colonial Laws Validity Act, 268B
conscription in, 300B, 302B, 324B, 330B, 332B
division of, 228B
exploration of, 163A, 236B
Expo '67, 352C
and France, 155A, 159A, 183A, 185A, 215A, 217A, 328A
French Canada, 179A, 221A, 240B, 284B, 288B
in G-7, 368A
and Germany, 294B, 322B, 334A
government, 258B, 264B, 268B, 284B, 316B, 344C, 368C
and India, 294B
and International Monetary Fund, 348A
Inuit people, 127A
and Italy, 330B
and Japan, 324B
law and society, 230B, 240B, 252B, 262B, 268B, 274B, 302B, 318B, 322B, 362C
and League of Nations, 302B
Levasseur family, 211C
and Mexico, 378A
and NAFTA, 378A
Naval Bill, 292B
navy of, 294B
North West Mounted Police, 274B
politics, 276B, 300B, 306B, 312B, 316B, 354C, 364C, 370C, 372C, 378C
religion, 183C, 294B, 361C
Riel Rebellion, 278B
science and technology, 257B, 259B, 381B
Separatists in, 356C, 362C, 382C
and Sicily, 330B
and South Africa, 286B
and Statute of Westminster, 312B
taxes, 300B
transportation, 253B, 276B, 279B
and United States, 244B, 256B, 272B, 282B, 288B, 292B, 300B, 306B, 308B, 310B, 314B, 316B, 318B, 324B, 330B, 342C, 344C, 346C, 362C, 364A, 366C, 368C, 372C, 378A
U.S.–Canadian Reciprocal Fishing Treaty, 262B
World War I, 294B, 296B, 300A
World War II, 326B, 328A
Canadian and Catholic Confederation of Labor, 288B
Canadian Broadcasting Commission, 314B
Canadian Grand Trunk Pacific Railway, 294B
Canadian National Railways, 304B
Canadian Northern Railway, 286B, 304B
Canadian Pacific Railroad, 278B
Canal Commission, 288C
Canalejas, José (prime minister of Spain), 292A
Canary Islands, 124B, 144A, 144B, 149B
cancer
breast, 381B
and smoking, 383B
virus, 357B
Candia, 110B
candles, 55B, 66A, 81B
candlewick, 247B
Candy Creek culture, 73A
Cannae, 25A
battle of, 92B
cannery, seafood, 257B
Cannery Row (Steinbeck), 335C
cannibalism, 212B
canning, 215B
cannons, cannonballs, 123B, 125B, 129B, 135B, 139B, 161B
Cano, Alonso, 191C
Canosa, *96*
Canova, Antonio, 217C, 225C, 243C
Canterbury, 80A, 90A, 102A, 161C
Canterbury Cathedral, 103B, 105C
Canterbury Tales, The (Chaucer), *131,* 133C
Cantilène de Sainte Eulalie, 83C
Cantiones Sacrae (Byrd & Tallis), 171C
Canton province, 80C, 186C, 198C, 206C, 237C, *254,* 255A, 265A, 319A, 321A
Canute VI (king of Denmark), 106A
Cão, Diego, 144B
Cape Bojador, 136C
Cape Bon, 60B
Cape Breton Island, 213A, 215A, 219A
Cape Canaveral, 345B, 349B, 370C. *See also* Cape Kennedy
Cape Coast Castle, 192B
Cape Cod, 177A
Cape Colony, 223A, 243A, 249A, 261A, 263A, 269A, 273A, 277A, 279A, 285A
and Britain, 257A
and South Africa, 291A
Cape Delgado, 200B
Cape Endiadere, 328C
Cape Esperance, battle of, 328C
Cape Frontier War, 261A, 275A
Cape Gloucester, 330C
Cape Horn, 171A, 180B, 226B
Cape Kennedy, 351B, 353B. *See also* Cape Canaveral
Cape of Good Hope, 146B, 148B, 150C, 233A, 237A, 241A, 253A
Cape Passaro, 206A
Cape Province, 253A
Cape St. Vincent, 232A
Cape Town, *190,* 190B, 206B, 371C
Cape Verde, 138C, 142B
Capet, Hugh (king of France), 88A
Capetian dynasty. *See* France
Capitoline Wolf, *11*
Capone, Al, 310B, 312B
Caporetto, battle of, 300A
Capote, Truman, 347C, 353C, 369C
Capra, Frank, 317C, 319C, 321C, 377C
Capreae, 32A, 35B
Caprichos, Los (Goya), 235C
Caprivi, Leo (chancellor of Germany), 282A, 284A
Capua, 23A
car wash, automated, 321B
Carabobo, battle of, 244C
Caracalla, Edict of, 44B
Caracalla (emperor of Rome), 42A, 44A, 44B, 45A, 45C
Caracas, 169A, 175A, 219A, 238C, 240C, 345A
Caractacus, 34A
Carausius, Marcus Aurelius (king of England), 48A, 50A
Caravaggio, 179C
Carbide and Carbon Chemicals Corporation, 337B
Carbondale, 249B
Carborundum, 283B
Carcassonne, 99C
Carchemish, 14B
Cardano, Geronimo, 163B
Cárdenas, García López, 161A
Cárdenas, Lázaro (president and minister of defense of Mexico), 312C, 316C, 318C, 327A, 335A
carding machine, 223B
cards, playing, 135B
Caretaker, The (Pinter), 347C
Caria, 20C
Carias, Tiburcio (dictator of Honduras), 314C
Caribbean, 324B, 326A
Caribbean Community and Common Market (CARICOM), 359A
Caribs, 232C
Carinthia, 88A
Carinus (emperor of Rome), 48A
Carl XVI Gustaf (king of Sweden), 358B
Carleton, Guy (governor of British North America), 222B, 226B
Carloman (king of southern France), 80A
Carlsbad, 244A
Carlson, Chester, 337B, 347B
Carlyle, Thomas, 251C, 253C, 255C, 265C
Carmel, 370C
Carmen (Bizet), 275C
Carmen (Mérimée), 257C
Carmen Seculare (Horace), 31C
Carmichael, Stokely, 352C
Carmona, Antonio (president of Portugal), 310A
Carnatic, 225A
Carnegie-Mellon University, 363B
Carnegie Steel Company, 282B
Carniola, 118A
Carnot, Marie François Sadi (president of France), 284A
Carolinas, Carolinians, 179A, 197A, 203A, 207A, 209A
Caroline Islands, 162C, 332C
Caroline Matilda (queen consort of Denmark), 218A
Carolusberg, 190B, 192B
Carothers, Wallace, 313B
Carpathian Mountains, 42A, 296A
carpentry, 111B
carpet sweeper, 239B
carpets, 65B
Carranza, Venustiano (president of Mexico), 294C, 296C, 304C
Carrel, Alexis, 289B, 317B
Carrera, Rafael, 252C, 254C
Carrero Blanco, Luis (prime minister of Spain), 358B
Carrhae, battle of, 28B
carriages, 67B, 151B, 197B, 287B

Carroll, John (Archbishop of Baltimore), 229C, 239C
Carroll, Lewis, 269C, 281B
Carson, Johnny, 377C
Cartagena, 58B, 60B, 159A
University of, 248C
Cartago, 254C
Carter, Jimmy (president of U.S.), 362A, 362C, 364A, 364C, *365,* 370C
Carter Presidential Center, 370C
Carthage, Carthaginians, 10A, 17A, 17B, 25A, 27A, 41B, 45A, 46B, 47A, 72C
Third Council of, 57A
Carthage (Ill.), 257C
Carthusian Order, 97C
Cartier, Jacques, 159A, *160,* 163A
Cartier-Bresson, Henri, 315C
carts and chariots, 137B
in Anatolia, *6*
in Egypt, 7B
in Greece, 7B
in Mesopotamia, 3B
in Mongolia, 119B
Carus, Marcus Aurelius (emperor of Rome), 48A
Carver, George Washington, 287B, 331B
Casa Grande, 73A
Casablanca, 214B
Conference, 330A
Casablanca (movie), 329C, 331C
cash register, electronic, 357B
Casimir III the Great (king of Poland), 126A, 130A
Casimir IV (king of Poland and Lithuania), 138A
Casimir-Périer, Jean Paul (president of France), 284A
Caspian Sea, 24B, 81B, 321A
Cass Timberlane (Lewis), 335C
Cassale, 196A
Cassander (king of Macedonia), 22C
Cassaria (Lodovico), 153C
Cassatt, Mary, 279C, 291C
Cassel, 270A
battles of, 96A, 196A, 218A
Cassino, 332A
cast iron, 77B
Castañeda Castro, Salvador (president of El Salvador), 335A
Castaway, The (Walcott), 351C
caste system, 14B
Castel del Monte, 115C
Castelfranco, 151C
Castelo, Humberto (president of Brazil), 351A
Castiglione, Baldassare, 159C
Castile, Castilians, 92B, 94B, 95B, 96B, 97C, 100B, 101C, 102B, 104B, 106B, 110B, 112A, 112B, 114B, 115B, 116A, 118B, 119B, 120B, 124B, 126B, 128B, 130B, 132A, 132B, 134B, 140A, 142A, 144A, 150A, 154A, 204A
Castilla, Ramón (president of Peru), 256C
Castillo, Ramón (president of Argentina), 327A, 331A
Castillo Armas, Carlos (president of Guatemala), 343A, 345A
Castillon, battle of, 138A
Castries, 189A
Castro, Cipriano (dictator of Venezuela), 286C
Castro, Fidel (premier of Cuba), 343A, 347A, *350*
Castro y Bellvis, Guillen de, 181C
casts, bone-setting, 99B
CAT (computerized axial tomography) scan, scanner, 353B, 359B
Cat on a Hot Tin Roof (Williams), 343C
Catalan, 111B, 123B, 141C
Catalonia, 102B, 110B, 186A, 292A, 362B
catapult, 17B, 29B, 91B, 95B, 99B
cataracts, 169B, 215B, 347B, 363B
Catcher in the Rye (Salinger), 339C
Câteau-Cambrésis, Peace of, 166A
Caterpillar, 221B, 289B, 295B
Catesby, Mark, *207*
cathedral, world's largest, 375C
Cathedral Music (Boyce), 217C
Cather, Willa, 295C, 303C, 311C
Catherine I (empress of Russia), 204A, 208A, 212A
Catherine II the Great (empress of Russia), 218A, 220A, *228,* 228A, 232A
Catherine of Aragon, 158A
Catherine of France, 136A
cathode ray, 263B, 275B
Catholic Conference, U.S., 367C
Catholic League, 179C, 182A
Catholic Relief Act, 225C
Catholic Worker, 315C
Catholicism, Catholics, 67C, 181C, 189C, 225C. *See also* Christianity, Christians; Jesuits; Vatican City; *individual leaders*
on abortion, 371C
Anglo-Catholic movement, 285C
in Austria, 177C
on birth control, 351C, 355C
in Britain, 261C
and Calvinists, 173C, 185C
in Canada, 228B
catechism of, 379C
Catholic Emancipation Act, 249C
in China, 223C
on Church of Nativity, 259C
and Communism, 339C
Congregation of the Oratory, 179C
in Council of Churches for Britain and Ireland, 375C
on divorce, 363C
ecclesiastics, 93C, 97C, 99C, 101C, 121C, 377B, 377C, 379C
in Ecuador, 266C
Edict of Restitution, 185C
in England, 165C
in France, 229C, 231C, 235C, 283C
on free economies, 377C
on Galileo, 379C
in Germany, 160A
holding office, 194A
hymn book of, 161C
and Immaculate Conception, 263C
in Ireland, 188A
in Italy, 369C
in Japan, 165C, 178C
Knights of Columbus, 279C
in Ku Klux Klan, 344C
and Maryland, 185A
Mass, 349C, 351C
in Mexico, 310C, 311C
and motion picture rating, 317C
in Netherlands, 248A
and Protestants, 158A, 228A
in Prussia, 253C
reforms in, 349C
in Russia, 273C
and Sacred Heart, 195C
and slave trade, 161C
in Switzerland, 256A, 258A, 275C
and Ultraquists, 145C
and umbrellas, 99B
in United States, 229C
Cato the Elder, 25A
cats, 2A
Cats (Lloyd Webber), 367C
cattle, fattening, 221B
Catullus, Gaius Valerius, 29C
Catuvellauni, 32A
Cauac Sky, 75A
Caucasus, 116C, 186B, 248A, 330A
Caumont, Treaty of, 240A
Cavafy, 315C
Cavaignac, Louis, 258A
Cavalcade (Coward), 313C
Cavaliers, 189A
Cavalleria rusticana (Mascagni), 283C
Cavalleria rusticana (Verga), 277C
Cavendish, Frederick, 278A
Cavendish, Henry, 227B
Cavite, 326C
Cavour, Camillo Benso di (prime minister of Piedmont-Sardinia), 262A, 264A
Caxton, William, 145B, 147C
Cayenne, 183A
Cayley, George, 237B
Cayor, 281A
CBS Inc., 368C
Ceausescu, Nicolae (president of Romania), 374B
Cebu, 157B, 168C
Celebes, 178C, 192C, 194C
Celestina, La (Rojas), 149C
Celestine I, Pope, 59C
Cellini, Benvenuto, 161C, 163C, 169B
cells, photoelectric, 291B
Cellular One, 367B
celluloid, 263B, 273B, 309B
Celsius, Anders, 211B
Celsus, 43A, 47A
Celsus, Aulus Cornelius, 33B
Celts, Celtics, 7A, 7B, 9A, 24C, 31B, 66A, 77B, 84A, 105C
coinage, 25A
and Etruscans, 17A
Hallstat culture, 11B, 13A
iron tools and weapons, 17B
La Tène culture, 21A
migrations of, 19A
cement, 131B, 217B, 247B
Cenerentola, La (Rossini), 243C
censorship, 151C, 209C, 220A
census, 19A, 30A, 32A. *See also* U.S. Census
Centers for Disease Control, 381B
Central Africa, 122C, 142B, 146B
Central African Federation, 340A
Central America, 131A, 260B, 348A, 377B. *See also individual countries*
Central America, Federation of, 254C
Central American Common Market, 347A
Central American Republics, Union of, 258C
Central Intelligence Agency (CIA), 336C, 339B, 360C
Central Pacific Railway, 267B
Central Powers, 300A, 302A
Central Treaty Organization (CENTO), 346A
Central University, 175A
Centre National d'Art et de Culture Georges Pompidou, 363C
centrifuge
butterfat test, 283B
cream separator, 275B
governor, 227B
high-speed, 307B
and influenza vaccine, 331B
Svedberg, 319B
Cenwulf (king of Mercia), 76A, 78A
Ceolwulf (king of Northumbria), 74A
ceramics, 217C
Cerdagne, 146A, 192A
Cerna, 302A
Cernan, Gene, *359*
Cerro, Sanchez (president of Peru), 314C
Cerro Gordo, 258B
Cerros, 50C
Cerularius, Michael, 95C
Cervantes, Miguel de, 177C, 179C, 181C
Cesalpino, Andrea, 173B
Cesarean sections, 135B, 179B
Cesariano, Cesare, 157B
Cetewayo (king of Zulus), 277A
Cetinje, 298A
Ceuta, 84B, 136B, 138B, 170B
Ceylon, 60C, 63B, 76C, 88C, 90C, 94C, 104C, 110C, 116C, 134C, 150C, 164C, 168C, 170C, 174C, 186C, 190C, 193A, 194C, 233A, 243A, 337A, 357A, 359A. *See also* Sri Lanka
Cézanne, Paul, 291C
Chaban-Delmas, Jacques (prime minister of France), 358B
Chacubuco, battle of, 242C
Chad, 41B, 214B
and France, 287A, 295A
and Libya, 373A
Chaeronea, battle of, 22C
Chaffee, Roger, 353B
Chai-ching (emperor of China), 156C
Chain, Ernst, 325B
Chaka, 243A
Chalchihuites, Chalchihuites culture, 44C, 133A
Chalcis, 12C
Chalgrove Field, battle of, 186A
chalk, 163
Challenger, 367B, 370C, *371*
Châlons, 60B
Chalukya dynasty. *See* India, Indians
Chamberlain, Neville (prime minister of Britain), 318A, 320A
Chamberlin, Pierre, 173B
Chambers, Sir William, 217C
Chamorro, Violeta Barrios de (president of Nicaragua), 375A
Champ de Mars, 228A
Champa, 90C, 106C, 112C, 142C
champagne (beverage), 199B
Champagne (France), 112A, 130A, 298A, 300A
Champasak, 206C
Champion v. Ames, 288B
Champlain, Samuel de, 177A, 179A, 185A
Chan-Bahlum, Lord, 71A
Chan Chan, 91A, 109A
Chancellorsville, 268B
Chand Bardai, 109C
Chandarnagar, 194C
Chanderi, 122C
Chandler, Raymond, 321C, 323C, 331C
Chandragupta I (emperor of India), 52B
Chandragupta II (emperor of India), 56B
Chang Hing, 39B
Chang Ssu-Hsun, 89B
Chang Tao-ling, 34B
Chang Tso-lin, 311A
Changa, 144B
Changan, 52B, 69C, 72C, 82C
Changsu (king of Koguryo), 58C
Channel Islands, 126A, 138A
channel markings, 281B
Chanson de Roland, 91C
Chansons I (Béranger), 243C
Chantries Act, 162A
Chapelain, Jean, 191C
Chapelier Law, 228A
Chaplin, Charlie, 305C, 323C
Chapman, George, 179C

Chapman, John, 234B
Chapultepec, Act of, 335A
Chapultepec Castle, 335A
Chardin, Jean Baptiste Siméon, 211C
Charge of the Light Brigade (Tennyson), 263C
chariots. *See* carts and chariots
Chariots of Fire (movie), 367C
Charlemagne (king of Franks), 74A, *75,* 76A, 77B, 78A, 79C, 91C, 105C
Charles I (king of England and Scotland), 182A, *183,* 184A, 186A, 187C, 188A, 189A
Charles I (king of Spain), 154A
Charles II , the Bad (king of Navarre), 128B, 130B
Charles II (emperor of Rome), 80A
Charles II (England), 190A, 192A, 192C, 193A, 198A
Charles II (king of Spain), 202A
Charles III, duke of Parma, 262A
Charles III, the Fat (emperor of Rome and king of Swabia), 80A, 82A
Charles III, the Simple (king of France), 82A
Charles III (king of Spain and Naples), 216A
Charles III of Durazzo (king of Naples), 132B
Charles IV (king of France), 124A, 126A
Charles IV (king of Germany and Burgundy and Holy Roman Emperor), 128A, 130A
Charles V (duke of Lorraine), 198A, 200A
Charles V (king of France), 130A, 132A, *133*
Charles V (king of Spain and Holy Roman Emperor), 154A, 156A, 158A, 159C, 160A, 160B, 162A, 162B, 164A, 166A
Charles VI (Habsburg), 202A
Charles VI (Holy Roman Emperor), 204A, 206A, 210A, 212A
Charles VI (king of France), 132A, 134B, 136A
Charles VII (Holy Roman Emperor), 212A
Charles VII (king of France), 136A, 140A
Charles VIII (king of France), 144A, 148A
Charles IX (king of France), 166A, 170A
Charles IX (Sweden), 174A, 176A, 178A
Charles X (king of France), 246A, 248A
Charles X of Zweibrücken (king of Sweden), 190A
Charles XI (king of Sweden), 196A, 200A
Charles XII (king of Sweden), 200A, 202A, 204A, 206A
Charles XIII (king of Sweden), 238A
Charles Albert (king of Sardinia), 260A
Charles and Diana, 378B, 382B
Charles Emmanuel III (duke of Savoy and Sardinia), 210A, 214A
Charles-Michel, 215B
Charles of Anjou, 116B, 118B
Charles of Blois, 126A, 128A, 130A
Charles of Bourbon (constable of France), 156A
Charles of Luxembourg, 128A
Charles (prince of Denmark), 290A
Charles (prince of Romania), 270A
Charles (prince of Wales), 378B, 382B
Charles the Bold (duke of Burgundy), 142A, 144A, *145*
Charles the Good, 100A
Charles Town, 195A, 197A, *223,* 224B
Charleston, 153A, 195A, 197A, 205A, 246B, 380C
Charleston Neck, 211A
Charlotte (grand duchess of Luxembourg), 350B
Charlotte Town, 254C
Charnly, John, 359B
Charter of Paris for a New Europe, 374A
Chartism, Chartists, 252A, 256A
Chartres, 111C, 112A
Chartres Cathedral, 109C, *117,* 153C
Chartreuse de Parme, La (Stendhal), 255C
Chase, Mary, 335C
Château Gaillard, 109C
Chateaubriand, François René de, 221C, 235C
Chateauguay River, 240B
Chatham (British ship), 230B
Châtillon, Walter, 123C
Chattanooga, 268B
Chatterji, Bankim Chamdra, 269C
Chaucer, Geoffrey, 131C, 133C, 135C, 159C
Chaul, 152C
Chausa, battle of, 160C
Chaves, Frederico (president of Paraguay), 343A
Chavin culture, 12B
Chechnya, 380B, 382B, 384B
Cheddar, 193B
cheese
  cheddar, 193B
  rationing, 330B, 334B
Chefren. *See* Khafra
Chekhov, Anton, 285C, 287C
Chekiang province, 80C, 82C
chemicals, organic, 267B
Chen dynasty. *See* China, Chinese
Ch'eng-hua (emperor of China), 142C
Cheng-te (emperor of China), 150C
Cheng-t'ung (emperor of China), 138C, 140C
Chénier, André Marie de, 219C
Cheops. *See* Khufu
Cher, 371C
Cherbourg, 138A, 332A
Chéri (Colette), 305C
Cherkassy, 330A
Chernobyl. *See* Soviet Union
Chernenko, Konstantin (leader of Soviet Union), 368B
Cherokee, 161A, 207A, 254B
Chesapeake, 171A
Chesapeake and Ohio Canal, 252B
Chesapeake Bay, 179A, 181A
Chesapeake (U.S. warship), 240B
chess, 363B
Chester, 88A, 111B
  battle of, 66A
Chester Cycle, 123C
Chesterton, G. K., 289C, 291C
Chevy Chase, 132A
Cheyenne, 177A
Chi-chou pottery, 83C
Chia-ch'ing (emperor of China), 233A, 254A
Chia Tun, 79B
Chiang Ching-kuo (president of Taiwan), 373A
Chiang Kai-shek (leader of Nationalist China), 311A, 317A, 319A, 324C, 339A, 353A, 361A
Chiang Mai, 120C, 166C, 180C
Chiapas, 50C, 153A
Chibchas, 161A
Chicago, 265B, 272B, 304B, 315C, 316B, 352C, 370C
  Adler Planetarium, 313B
  African-American mayor of, 366C
  Black Panthers, 356C
  Columbian Exposition, 283B
  Haymarket Riot, 280B
  Hull House, 280B
  Moody Memorial Church, 313C
  Northwestern University, 363B
  politics, 302B
  Pullman Palace Car Company, 284B
  race riot in, 302B
  Robey House, 291C
  Unity Temple, 289C
  University of, 297C, 333B, 362C, 379C
  Vietnam War protests in, 354C
Chicago Bears, 323C, 327C, 329C, 331C, 371C
Chicago Bulls, 379C, 385C
Chicago Cubs, 335C, 385C
Chicago Defender, 290B
Chicago Metallurgical Laboratory, 329B
Chicago Poems (Sandburg), 297C
"Chicago Seven," 356C
Chicago White Sox, 347C
Chicasaw, 211A
Chicheley, Henry (Archbishop of Canterbury), 135C
Chichén Itzá, 61A, 71A, 87A, 91A, 111A
Chichi Jima, 332C
Chichimecs, 109A
Chickahominy River, 179A
chicle, 91A
Ch'ien Ch'ien-i, 193C
Ch'ien-lung (emperor of China), 210C, 214C, 233A
Chien-Wen (emperor of China), 134C
Chihli, 120C
Chihuahua, 129A
Chikamatsu Monzaemon, 207C
Child, Sir John (governor of Bombay), 196C
Child Abuse Prevention and Treatment Act, 360C
Childe Harold's Pilgrimage (Byron), 241C
Childebert I (king of Franks), 62A, 62B
Childeric II, 70A
Childeric III, 74A
Children's Games (Brueghel), 167C
Childs, Robert, 189A
Chile, 139A, 161A, 171A, 175A, 209A, 240C, 268C, 286C, 302C
  and Argentina, 276C, 288C, 369A
  arts, 309C
  and Bolivia, 254C, 270C, 274C, 276C, 278C, 288C
  earthquake in, 252C, 320C
  education, 213A
  and Germany, 327A, 331A
  government, 246C, 248C, 250C, 260C, 304C, 308C, 314C, 320C, 327A, 365A
  and Italy, 327A, 331A
  law and society, 264C
  Nazis in, 320C
  and Peru, 254C, 276C, 278C, 310C
  politics, 329A
  and Spain, 244C, 270C
  in United Nations, 335A
  World War I, 294C
  World War II, 327A, 329A, 333A
Chilowski, Konstantin, 297B
Chimic, 61A
Chimú, Chimú culture, 91A, 107A, 109A, 123B, 141A
China, Chinese, 5B, 33B, 33C, 34B, 39C, 42B, 44B, 50B, 90C, 92C, 105C, 200C, 307A
  3000 B.C.–2200 B.C., 2B, 3B, 4B, 5B, 5C
  1766 B.C.–1020 B.C., 6B, 7C, 8B, 10B, 11C
  687 B.C.–500 B.C., 12B, 13B, 13C, 15C, 16B, 17B
  479 B.C.–360 B.C., 19B, 19C, 20B, 21B
  240 B.C.–20 B.C., 24B, 25B, 25C, 26B, 29B, 31B
  agriculture, 53B, 95B
  and Annam, 72C, 88C, 174C
  and Arabs, 101B
  arts, 5C, 7C, 11C, 13C, 19C, 25C, 27C, 33C, 37C, 39C, *45,* 45A, 45C, 53C, 55C, 63C, 67C, 69B, 71C, 73C, 83C, 85B, 87C, 89C, 97C, 115C, 129C, 133C, 173C, 187C, 193C, 209C
  and Australia, 263A
  and Axis powers, 326C
  Boxers, Boxer Rebellion, 286B, 287A, 289A
  and Britain, 186B, 219C, 251A, 255A, 257A, 265A, 267A, 287A, 313A, 338A, 368A, 369A, 370A
  and Burma, 334C
  and Ceylon, 134C
  Chen dynasty, 64C
  Chi dynasty, 60C, 64C
  Chin ("gold") dynasty, 100C
  Chin (Jin) dynasty, 48B, 52B, 53C, 58C
  Ch'in (Qin) dynasty, 24B, 25C
  Ch'ing dynasty, 293A
  Chou dynasty, 8B, 9C
  Chu dynasty, 64C, 65C
  Communism in, 317A, 338A, 363A
  Confucius and, 43A
  and Cuba, 272C
  Cultural Revolution, 353A, 365A, 367A
  and East Africa, 136C
  economy, 76C, 90C, 94C, 156C, 187A
  education, 32B, 63B
  and Europe, 116C, 156C
  extraterritoriality in, 313A
  and France, 200C, 267A, 279A, 338A
  Gang of Four, 363A, 365A
  and Germany, 287A, 301A, 305A
  government, 48B, 140C, 142C, 156C, 180C, 192C, 291A, 293A, 295A, 299A, 319A, 324C, 339A, 363A, 367A
  Han dynasty, 24B, 26B, 32B, 36B, *38,* 38B, *42,* 42B, 44B
  and Holland, 192A, 198C
  horses in, 25B
  Hou-Chou dynasty, 84C, 86C
  Hou-Tang dynasty, 84C
  Hsin dynasty, 32B
  Imperial Library, 67B
  and India, 67B, 80C, 349A
  and Indochina, 322C
  industry, 41B, 43B, 64B, 91B, 99B, 115B, 123C, 125B
  and Italy, 151C
  and Japan, 46B, 66C, 106C, 111B, 113B, 156C, 174C, 182C, 198C, 206C, 273A, 284A, 285A, 287A, 295A, 297A, 299A, 307A, 311A, 315A, 317A, 319A, 321A,

322C, 326C, 332C, 334C
and Korea, 40B, 66C, 68C, 70C, 182C, 223C, 285A, 338A
Kuomintang, 311A
law and society, 84C, 98C, 103B, 104C, 135B, 150C, 170C, 176C, 214C, 233A, 273A, 293A, 293B, 309A
and League of Nations, 321A
Liao dynasty, 100C
Liap (Khitan) dynasty, 84C
Manchu dynasty, 188C, 214C
and Manchuria, 176C, 180C, 182C, 196C
Ming dynasty, 130C, 134C, 136C, 138C, 140C, *141,* 142C, 150C, 156C, 168C, 180C, 182C, 187C, 188C
and Mongolia, 38B, 102C, 110C, *111,* 112C, 114C, 116C, 118C, 119B, 124C, 128C, 130C, 138C, 162C, 186C, 293A, 337A
National Academy of China, 49B
National Assembly, 293A, 295A
National People's Congress, 347A
natural disasters in, 80C, 120C, 126C, 164C, 263A, 305A, 319A
and Nepal, 231A
and New Zealand, 277A
and North Korea, 344A
and nuclear weapons, 378A
and Olympic Games, 379C
opium, Opium War, *254,* 255A
Pearl S. Buck and, 313C
and Philippines, 176C
plague in, 42B
politics, 311A, 339A
and Portugal, 141B, 154C, 164C, 176C, 370A
religion, 37A, 39A, 51A, 57A, 57B, 61C, 63C, 69C, 77C, 79C, 81C, 121C, 123B, 134B, 171C, 179C, 207C, 215C, 225A, 227A, 237C
and Russia, 134C, 190C, 196C, 198C, 208C, 210C, 265A, 284A, 287A, 293A, 317A
science and technology, 5B, 32B, 39B, 45B, 49B, 55B, 59B, 61B 63B, 65B, 67B, 73B, 75B, 79B, 81B, 83B, 85B, 89B, 93B, 95B, 97B, 99B, 103B, 105B, 107B, 109B, 121B, 127B, 135B, 137B, 141B, 147B, 281B
Shang dynasty, 6B, 7C
and Soviet Union, 313A, 346B, 356B
and Spain, 170C
Sui dynasty, 64C, 66C
and Sumatra, 134C
Sung dynasty, 58C, 60C, 86C, 88C, 108C, 112C, 116C
Taiping Rebellion, 261A, 263A, 269A
Tang dynasty, 66C, 68C, 69C, 70C, 71C, 75C, 80C, 82C
and Tarim Basin, 216C
and Tartars, 101B
Tiananmen Square Massacre, 373A
and Tibet, 72C, 74C, 76C, 208C, 291A, 339A, 347A, 353A, 375A
transportation and infrastructure, 29B, 66C, 67B, 77B, 79B, *141,* 275A, 281B
and Transvaal, 291A
and Turkey, 66C
and Turkistan, 68C, 216C, 220C
and United Nations, 332B, 356A
and United States, 226B, 256B, 276B, 286B, 287A, 336A, 338A, 356A, 364A, 368A, 379A
and Vietnam, 60C, 82C, 96C
Wei dynasty, 44B, 56B, 62C
World War II, 326C
Wu dynasty, 44B
Yüan dynasty, 116C, 118C, 130C
china (dinnerware), 249B
Chincha Islands, 268C
Chindaswinth (king of Visigoths), 68A
Chinese Communist Party, 307A, 311A, 353A, 374B
Chinese Eastern Railway, 317A
Chinese Exclusion Acts, 278B, 330B
Ch'ing-pai, 123C
Ching-t'ai (emperor of China), 138C
Ching-teo Chen, 91B
Chinsura, 216C
Chioggia, War of, 132B
Chios, 168A, 246A
Chippewa, 246B, 248B
Chippewa Plains, battle of, 240B
Chirac, Jacques (president of France), 380B
Chirico, Giorgio de, 295C, 301C
Chisolm, Shirley, 354C
Chitimecs, 99A
Chitor, 168C
Chitral, 283A
chlorine, 221B
chlorofluorocarbons, 359B, 361B, 377B
Cho Wen-chun, 27C
Choans, Les (Balzac), 249C
Chocataw, 248B
chocolate, 151B, 155B, 177B, 245B
Chola empire, 88C, 90C, 92C
cholera, 151B, 377A
Cholm, 296A
Cholula, 63C, 71A
Chopin, Frédéric, 251C, 255C, 261C
Choshu, 269A
Chosroes I (king of Persia), 62C
Chou dynasty. *See* China, Chinese
Chou En-lai (premier of China), 363A
Chremonidean War, 24C
Chrétien, Jean, 378C
Christ Church, 163C
Christ Stopped at Eboli (Levi), 335C
Christian Dogma (Schleiermacher), 247C
Christian I (king of Denmark, Norway, and Sweden), 138A, 140A, 142A
Christian II (king of Denmark), 154A, 158A
Christian IV (king of Denmark and Norway), 172A, 182A
Christian Science, 275C, 285C
Christian Science Monitor, 291C
Christian Socialism, 261C
Christian VIII (king of Denmark), 258A
Christian X (king of Denmark), 336B
Christianisme et philosophie (Gilson), 319C
Christianity, Christians, 59C, 61C, 63B. *See also* Crusades; *individual denominations*
in Africa, 43A
in ancient Rome, 55A, 55C, 67C
in Bulgaria, 81C
in China, 77C, 121C, 179C
Christian Council, 43A
in England, 43A, 71C
in Germany, 73C, 91C
in Hungary, 87C
in Japan, 174C, 181C, 209C
in Jerusalem, 33A
and Lebanon, 100B
in Madagascar, 269C
in Norway, 88A, 89C
in Palestine, 33A, 39A
persecutions by Chinese, 215C
persecutions by Japanese, 180C, 183C
persecutions by Jews, 62C
persecutions by Persians, 58C
persecutions by Romans, 35A, 43A, 45A, 47A, 51A
persecutions by Seleucians, 53A
persecutions by Turks, 41A
persecutions by Vandals, 60B
persecutions by Visigoths, 53A
persecutions of heretics, 57A
in Persia, 61B
in Spain, 82B, 149C, 169C
in United States, 189C
in Wales, 65C
Christie, Agatha, 305C, 341C, 363C
Christie, Julie, 351C
Christina (queen of Sweden), 184A, 190A
Christmas Carol (Dickens), 257C
Christo, 369C
Christophe, Henri (king of Haiti), 236C, 238C
Christ's College, 151C
Christus Oratorio (Liszt), 271C
chromatography, paper, 327B, 333B
chromosomes, 333B, 377B, 379B
Chronicles of England, Scotland and Ireland (Holinshed), 171C
Chronicon (Eusebius), 53C
chrotta, 66A
Chrysler Corporation, 364C, 366C
Chu dynasty. *See* China, Chinese
Chu Yüan-chang, 128C, 130C
Chuguji, 71C
Ch'ung-chen (emperor of China), 182C
Chungking, 326C
Chuquisaca, 238C
Church, Frederick E., 263C, 265C, 267C
Church History of Britain, from the Birth of Christ until 1648, The (Fuller), 191C
Church Missionary Society, 235C, 249A
Church of England, 311C, 357C, 365C, 367C, 379C
General Synod of, 357C
ordination of women, 381C
Church of the Brethren, 345C
Churchill, John (duke of Marlborough), 202A
Churchill, Winston (American novelist), 289C
Churchill, Sir Winston (prime minister of Britain), 322A, 326A, 326B, 330A, 332A, 332B, 334A, 336A, 336B, 338B, 342B, 350B
CIA (Central Intelligence Agency), 347A, 366C, 380C
Cimino, Michael, 363C
Ciano, Galeazzo, 332A
Cicero, Marcus Tullius, *29,* 29A, 29C, 31C
Cicerone (Burckhardt), 263C
Cid, El, 98B
Cid, Le (Corneille), 187C
cider, 59B
Cilicia, Cilicians, 12C, 96B, 106A, 118C
Cimarosa, Domenico, 221C
Cimbri, 27A
Cincinnati, 284B, 287C
Cincinnati Bengals, 367C, 373C
Cincinnati Red Stockings, 273C, 325C, 347C, 357C, 359C, 361C, 363C, 375C
Cinema. *See* movie(s)
Cinématographe, 285B
circuit
integrated, 347B
regenerative, 293B
superheterodyne, 301B
Circus Maximus, 15C
Cirnomen, 130B
Cirrha, 14C
Cisalpine, 232A
Cispadane, 232A
Cisplatine Province, 244C, 246C
Cistercian order, 105C
Citadel, The, 380C, 382C
Citium, 23C
Citizen Kane (Welles), 325C, 385C
Citizen Tom Paine (Fast), 331C
citizenship, U.S., 270B, 308B
Citroën, 317B
citrus, 153A
City Heiress, The (Behn), 197C
City of the Sun (Campenella), 183C
city planning, 147C, 149B
Ciudad Rodrigo, 240A
Civil Aviation Act, 310B
Civil Rights, 342C, 346C, 348C, 352C
Acts, 274B, 278B, 350C
Commission, 344C
demonstration, 354C
civil service, 30A
Civil War, American, 266B, 274B, 297C, 334B
Civilian Production Administration, 334B
Civilis, Claudius, 36A
Civilization of the Renaissance in Italy (Burckhardt), 267C
Civitas Dei (Augustine), 59C
Civitate, 94A
Clapperton, Hugh, 247A, 249A
Clark, Barney, 367B
Clark, Joseph (prime minister of Canada), 364C
Clark, Walter Van Tilburg, 323C
Clark, Wesley, 384A
Clark, William, 236B
Clash by Night (Odets), 327C
Classe, 65C
Classic Revival art, 237C
Classic Revival sculpture, 225C
Claude, Georges, 301B
Claudel, Camille, 331C
Claudel, Paul, 311C
Claudius I (emperor of Rome), 34A
Claudius II, Marcus Aurelius (emperor of Rome), 48A
Clavier, Andre, 313B
Clay, Cassius. *See* Muhammad Ali
Clay, Henry, 242B, 246B, 248B, 250B
Clayton Antitrust Act, 294B
Clayton-Bulwer Treaty, 260C
Clean Waters Restoration Act, 352C
Cleisthenes, 14C, 16C
Clemenceau, Georges (prime minister of France), 300A, 310A
Clemens, Samuel Langhorne. *See* Mark Twain
Clement, William, 195B
Clement II, Pope, 95C
Clement III (antipope), 97C
Clement IV, Pope, 116B
Clement of Alexandria, 45A
Clement V, Pope, 123C, 125C
Clement VI, Pope, 129C
Clement VII, Pope, 157C, 158A, 159C
Clement VII (antipope), 133C
Clement VIII, Pope, 175C

Clement VIII (antipope), 137C
Clement XI, Pope, 203C, 207B
Clement XIV, Pope, 221C
Clements, William, 364C
Cleomenes I (king of Sparta), 16C, 18C
Cleomenes III (king of Sparta), 24C
Cleon, 20C
Cleopatra VII (queen of Egypt), 28A, 30B
Clericis laicos (papal bull), 121C
Clermont, Council of, 98B
Clermont-Ferrand, 99C
Cleveland, Grover (president of U.S.), 277B, 278B, 280B
Cleveland Clinic, 353B
Cleveland Indians, 337C, 343C, 383C, 385C
Cleveland (Ohio), 327C, 332B, 354C, 362C
Cleveland Rams, 335C
Cleves, 236A
Cleves, Anne of, 160A
Cliff Palace, 99A
Clifford, Clark, 354C
Clifton Gorge, 269B
Clinton, DeWitt, *247*
Clinton, Bill (president of U.S.), 376C, 378C, 379A, 380A, 380C, 381A, 382C, 384A, 384C
  impeached, 384C
Clinton, Hillary Rodham, 380C
Clive, Robert (baron of Plassey), 212C, 214C, 216C, 218C
Cloaca Maxima, 15A
clocks, 77B, 87B, 89B, 109B, 119B, 123B, 127B, 129B, 131B, 137B
  hand-carved wooden, 215B
  minute hand, 195B
  pendulum, 195B, 209B
  planetary, 165B
  portable, 151B
  water, 77B
Clodius, 29A
Clodomir (king of Franks), 62A
cloisonné, 91C
cloning, 385B
Clontarf, battle of, 90A
Clotaire I (king of Franks), 62A
Clouds, The (Aristophanes), 21C
Clovis I (king of Franks), 60A, 62A
Cluny, 95C
  Abbey of, 85C, 97C, 99C
  Abbot of, 103C
Clyde, 36A, 40A
Cnut (king of Denmark), 90A, 92A
coal
  mining, 31B, 91B, 107B, 113B, 127B, 286B, 330B
  stove, 185B
  strikes, 286B, 358B, 368B
Coal and Steel Authority, 350B
Coastal culture, 73A
Cobain, Kurt, 381C
Cobbett, William, 219C
Coblenz, 126A
Coca-Cola, 281B
Coca-Cola Company, The, 368C
Cocherel, battle of, 130B
Cochin, 150C, 192C
Cochin China, 265A, 267A, 271A, 281A, 337A
Cochrane, Josephine, 271B
Cochrane, Thomas, 265B
Cockroft, John, 311B
Coconut Grove, 328B
Cocos Islands, 249A
"Cod War," 358B, 362B
Coddington, William, 187A
Code Napoléon, 236A, 267A
"Code Noir," 209A
Code of Hammurabi, 6B
Codex Bezae, 63C
Codex Mendoza, 137
Codex Theodosianus, 58B
Coehoorn, Menno, van, 199C
Coercive Acts, 221A
coffee, 204B, 209A, 278C
  instant, 289B
  Inter-American Coffee Board, 325A
  Merchants Coffee House, 230B
  Mocha, 138C
  paper filter, 291B
  rationing, 328B, 334B
Cohan, George M., 289C, 301C
Cohan, Robert M., 291C
Coimbra, 125C
Coimbra, University of, 121C
Coke, Thomas, 215C
Colbert, Claudette, 317A
Colbert, Jean-Baptiste, 192A
Cold War, 374A
cold war, 336C
Coldstream, 146A
Coleridge, Samuel Taylor, 231C, 233C
Coles Creek culture, 123A
Colette (Sidonie Gabrielle Colette), 305C
College for Women, 273C
Colleoni, Bartolomeo, 147C
Collins, Wilkie, 267C, 271C
Collins, William, 213C
Collor de Mello, Fernando (president of Brazil), 379A
Cologne, 60A, 77C, 80A, 82A, 97C, 107C, 145C, 163C, 298A
Cologne Cathedral, 115C
"Cologne War," 173C
Colombia, 157A, 159A, 266C, 288C, 377A, 379A
  arts, 353C
  and Ecuador, 300C
  education, 248C
  government, 244C, 262C, 264C, 341A
  law and society, 268C, 278C, 286C, 333A
  in New Granada, 207A
  and Panama, 254C, 256C, 270C, 288C, 294C
  and Peru, 248C, 314C, 316C
  politics, 278C, 312C, 318C
  and Soviet Union, 354A
  and Spain, 161A, 165A, 240C
  and Union of 1819, 250C
  in United Nations, 335A
  and United States, 258C
  World War II, 325A
Colombo, 150C, 190C, 385A
Colón, 260C
Colonial Conference, 288A, 290A
Color Purple, The (Walker), 367C
Colorado, 97A, 99A, 115A, 205A, 236B, 258B, 274B, 296B
Colorado River, 77A, 161A, 312B, 319B
Colorado River Canyon, 362C
Colorado Springs, 342C
Colosseum, 37C, 58B
Colossus of Rhodes, 23C
Colt, Samuel, 253B
Colter, John, 236B
Columba, Saint, 65C
Columbia, 207A
Columbia, 367B, 377B
Columbia-Brazil Treaty, 310C
Columbia Record Company, 337C
Columbia River, 230B, 236B, 238B
Columbo, Realdo, 167B
Columbus, Christopher, 147A, 147B, 149A, 149B, 150A, 151A, 161A
Columbus (N.M.), 298B
Comanche, 209A
Combined Food Board, 328B
Combined Production Resources Board, 328B
Comédie Française, 197C
Comédie Humaine, La (Balzac), 251C
Comedy of Errors, The (Shakespeare), 175C
Comenius, John Amos, 183C, 191C
comets, 25B, 351B, 371B, 381B
  Halley's, 25B, 371B
  Ikeya-Seki, 351B
  Shoemaker-Levy 9, 381B
comic strip, 285C
Command of the Army Act, 270B
commedia dell-arte, 159C
Commentaries on the Laws of England (Blackstone), 219C
Commission on Civil Rights, 360C
Committees of Correspondence, 221A
Commodus, Lucius Aurelius, 42A
Common Agricultural Policy, 348A, 352B
Common Market, 344A, 352B
Common Market Commission, 350B
Common Reader, The (Woolf), 309C
Common Sense (Paine), 223C
Commonwealth Copyright Act, 292A
Commonwealth Day, 346B
Commonwealth of Independent States, 376B
Commonwealth of Nations, 383A
communications, automated, 337B
Communion, 357C
Communism, Communists, 304B, 316C, 348A, 360A, 361A. *See also individual countries*
  Animal Farm on, 335C
  Cominform, 336A
  in Roman Catholic Church, 339C
  and Russian Orthodox Church, 307C
Communist Manifesto, The (Marx and Engels), 259C
Communist Party of America, 302B
Communist Party of the United States of America, 322B, 334B
Communist People's Republic, 337A
Communist Political Association, 332B, 334B
Comoros, 281A, 361A
compact disc (CD), 337B, 367B
compact disc player, 363B
Company She Keeps, The (McCarthy), 327C
compass, 33B, 67B, 77B, 97B, 99B, 103B, 107B, 119B, 135B, 147B, 171B, 291B
Compiègne, 136A, 302A
Compleate Angler (Walton), 191C
compounds, flexible ceramic, 375B
Compromise Tariff, 250B
Compstelo, 161A
Compte rendu (Necker), 225C
computer(s)
  A-B-C (Atanasoff-Berry Computer), 321B
  Apple II, 363B
  BASIC software, 361B
  BINAC, 339B
  binary language, 325B, 337B
  CHESS 4.5, 363B
  COBOL, 345B
  Colossus, 331B
  computer-aided design (CAD), 349B, 351B
  Cray-3, 373B
  dBASE, 367B
  digital, 319B
  digitizing tablet for graphics systems, 351B
  E-mail service, 369B
  EDSAC, 337B
  EDVAC, 337B
  ENIAC, 325B, 333B
  Fish, 327B
  floppy disks, 357B, 367B, 371B, 373B
  FORTRAN, 343B
  hard disk drive, 343B
  HEARSAY-II speech recognition, 363B
  inkjet computer printer, 363B
  Intel microprocessor, 355B
  light pen, 349B
  line printer, 341B
  Macintosh personal minicomputer, 369B
  magnetic storage, 339B
  Mark I, 321B, 333B
  Mark II, 333B
  microchip, 347B
  mouse peripheral, 367B
  MS/2 operating system, 371B
  MS-DOS operating system, 371B
  personal, 363B, 367B
  powerful memory chips, 379B
  RAM (random access memory), 357B
  in retail industry, 359B
  supercomputer, 373B
  Universal Turing Machine, 321B
  UNIX, 357B
  WHIRLWIND digital, 333B
  word processor, 357B
  Z Machine, 335B
  Z4, 339B
Comstock Lode, 264B
Comte, Auguste, 257C, 263C
Comus (Milton), 185C
Conant, Roger, 183A
Concepción, 252C
  University of, 302C
Conception of God, The (Royce), 287C
Concord, battle of, 222B
Concordat of 1801, 235C
Concorde, 348B, 357B
concrete, 27B, 39B
  poured, 289C
  reinforced, 311B
Condé, 180A
Condillac, Étienne Bonnet de, 215C
Condition Humaine, La (Malraux), 315C
Condorcet, Marie Jean Antoine Nicolas de Caritat, 213C
Coney Island (Stella), 295C
Confederacy, Confederates, 265C, 266B, 268B
Conference on Security and Cooperation in Europe, 358A
Confesio Augustana, 159C
Confessions d'un révolutionnaire (Proudhon), 261C
Confessions of an English Opium Eater (Quincey), 245C
Confessions of Nat Turner, The (Styron), 355C
Confucianism, 43A, 49A
Confucius, 11C, *15,* 15C, 19C
Congo and Other Poems, The (Lindsey), 295C
Congo (Belgian Congo, Congo Free State), 202B, 214B, 261A, 279A, 291A, 347A, 357A. *See also* Zaire
  and Belgium, 283A
  and Germany, 293A
  Hammarskjöld in, 346A
  and United Nations, 346A, 347A
Congo River, 144B, 146B
Congregation for the Propagation of the Faith, 183C
Congregation of the Oratory, 179C
Congregational Church, 224B, 345C, 359C
Congregationalism, Congregationalists, 189C

Congress, U.S., 224B, 228B, 229B, 234B, 382C. *See also individual legislation*
African-Americans in, 272B, 310B, 320B, 352C, 354C, 358C
on Alaska, 292B
and Army Air Corps, 310B
and Banking Act, 314B
on campaign spending, 290B
on child abuse, 360C
on citizenship, 262B
on civil rights, 344C
during the Civil War, 266B
and Civilian Conservation Corps, 314B
and Coast Guard, 296B
on coinage system, 226B
on Communists, 338C
creates ambassadorship, 282B
on currency, 242B
on daylight saving time, 302B
declares war on Britain, 240B
and Department of Indian Affairs, 252B
and Department of Interior, 260B
on dueling, 254B
on education, 344C
election of, 256B
on elections, 284B
on farm subsidies, 342C
first federal tax, 228
on foreign aid, 338C
on funding for "war on poverty," 350C
on Gadsden Purchase, 262B
on Indians, 308B
on Iran-Contra Affair, 370C
Library of, 235C, 241C
on lobbyists, 336C
on minimum wage, 320B
and National Guard, 298B
and National Industrial Recovery Act, 314B
on navy, 298B, 320B
on new merchant ships, 300B
on obscene literature, 274B
on Philippines, 314B
politics, 292B, 336C, 342C
on polygamy, 278B
on postwar aid, 336C
on presidential succession, 280B
and presidential veto, 256B
on prohibition, 302B
on racial discrimination, 354C
and rank of five-star general, 334B
on regulating communications, 316B
and Rocky Mountain National Park, 296B
on savings and loan associations, 376C
on slave trade, 254B
and Starr report, 384C
on supercollider, 379B
on Taft-Hartley Labor Act, 336C
on taxes, 366C
and Tennessee Valley Authority, 314B
and Thatcher, Margaret, 368A
on treaties with Russia, 292B
unconstitutional acts of, 232B
and U.S. Department of Labor, 280B
and U.S. Naval War College, 278B
and U.S. Supreme Court, 236B, 252B
on veterans' benefits, 312B, 340C
on war against Algiers, 242B
on war with Japan, 326B
on women as attorneys, 276B
women in, 300B
and Woodrow Wilson, 294B
Congress of Cooperative Societies, 262A
Congress of Industrial Organizations (CIO), 342C
Congreve, William, 201C, 203C
Connally, Thomas Terry, 330B
Connecticut, 185A, 187A, 193A, 199A, 203A, 205C, 237C, 360C
Connecticut River, 179A, 185A
Conrad, Joseph, 287C
Conrad I (king of Germany), 84A
Conrad II (Holy Roman Emperor and king of Germany), 92A, 92B
Conrad III (king of Germany), 102A, 102B
Conrad IV (king of Germany), 112A, 114A
Conrad (king of Italy), 100B
Conrad of Montferrat (king of Jerusalem), 106B
Conradin, 118B
Conscience, Hendrik, 255C
Conspiracy and Tragedy of Charles, Duke of Byron (Chapman), 179C
Constable, John, 239C, 243C, 245C, 247C, 251C, 253C
Constance, 106A
Diet of, 152A
Treaty of, 104B
Constans (emperor of Rome), 52A, 54A
Constans II (emperor of Byzantium), 68B
Constant, Benjamin, 219C
Constantia, 55C
Constantine I, Pope, 72B
Constantine I (king of Greece), 304A
Constantine I (king of Scots), 76A
Constantine II (emperor of Byzantium), 52A
Constantine II (king of Greece), 350B
Constantine III (king of Scots), 82A
Constantine IV (emperor of Byzantium), 70B
Constantine V (emperor of Byzantium), 74B
Constantine VI (emperor of Byzantium), 76B
Constantine VII (emperor of Byzantium), 84B
Constantine VIII (emperor of Byzantium), 92B
Constantine IX (emperor of Byzantium), 92B
Constantine X (emperor of Byzantium), 94B
Constantine XI (emperor of Byzantium), 138B
Constantine XIII (king of Greece), 354B
Constantine (Algeria), 259A
Constantine the Great (emperor of Byzantium), 50A, 51A, 52A, 53A, 53C, 54A, 55C
Constantine's arch, 53C
Constantinople, 52A, 57A, 62B, 63C, 64B, 65B, 66B, 68B, 69B, 70B, 72B, 80B, 82B, 84B, 85C, 95C, 108B, 122B, 138B, 173C, 181C, 200B, 202B, 206B, 251A, 285A, 304A, 313A. *See also* Istanbul
Fifth Council of, 65C
Peace of (1897), 286A
Treaty of (1784), 226A
Treaty of (1888), 281A
and Turkey, 139B
Constantius I (emperor of Rome), 50A
Constantius II (emperor of Rome), 52A, 53A, 54A
Constitutio de feudis, 92B
Constitution, U.S., 222B, 226B, 228B
1st Amendment, 276B
12th Amendment, 236B
13th Amendment, 268B
14th Amendment, 270B
15th Amendment, 272B
16th amendment, 294B
17th amendment, 294B
18th Amendment, 302B, 304B, 314B
19th Amendment, 304B
21st Amendment, 314B
22nd Amendment, 338C
23rd Amendment, 346C
25th Amendment, 352C
26th Amendment, 356C
and death penalty, 358C
Constitution Hall, 321C
Constitution of 17 articles, 66C
Constitution (U.S. warship), 240B
Constitutional Act of 1971, 228B
Constitutional Convention, 226B
Constitutional History of England (Stubbs), 275C
contact lenses, 281B
bifocal, 217B, 345B
plastic, 341B
Plexiglas, 319B
Continental Congress, 221A, 222B
Continental System, 238A
Contra Celsum (Origen), 47A
contraception. *See* birth control
Contreras, battle of, 258B
Controlled Materials Plan, 328B
Convention on the Prevention and Punishment of Genicide, 370C
Conventional Forces in Europe (CFE) Treaty, 374A
conversation machine, 347B
Conversations d'Émilie (Épinay), 221C
Conway
battle of, 120A
Treaty of, 118A
Cook, James, 220C, *221,* 224B, 225A
Cook Inlet, 36C
Cook Islands, 80C, 220C, 287A
Cook Strait, 255A
Cooke, Jay, and Company, 274B
Cooke, William, 253B
Cooley, Denton, 357B
Coolidge, Calvin (president of U.S.), 304B, 306B, 308B, 310B, 310C
Coolidge, William, 295A
Cooper, Gary, 341C
Cooper, Irving, 347B
Cooper, James Fenimore, 245C, 247C, 249C
Cooper, Peter, 249B
Coosa, 195A
Coote, Sir Eyre, 216C
Copán, 67A, *71,* 71A, 75A, 83A, 171A
Copán River, *71*
Copell culture, 65A
Copenhagen, 222A
Copenhagen University, 145C
Copernicus, Nicolaus, 163C
Copland, Aaron, 319C, 321C, 331C, 333C
Copley, John Singleton, 217C, 243C
Coppage v. Kansas, 296B
Coppélia (Delibes), 273C
copper, copper culture, 73A, 87B, 91B, 139B, 145B,
in Africa, 7B, 13B
coins, 72C
in Japan, 206C
in Newfoundland, 268B
in North America, 3B
in Sinai Peninsula, 6A
Coppola, Francis Ford, 359C, 361C, 365C
Coptic art, 63C, 81C
Coptic Church, 45A
copy machine, 337B
automated, 347B
mimeograph, 279B
stencil, 275B
thermography, 333B
copyright, 229B
Corbeil, Treaty of, 116B
Corbett, James J., 283C
Corday, Charlotte, 230A
Cordite, 281B
Córdoba, 72B, 76B, 78B, 80B, 82B, 84B, 85B, 86B, 88B, 89B, 90B, 92B, 94B, 112B
Cordus, Cremutius, 33C
Cordus, Valerius, 161B
Corfe, 88A
Corfu, 102B
Corinne (Staël), 237C
Corinth, Corinthians, 12C, 14C, 15B, 26C, 28C, 48A, 91B, 103B, 246A
Corinth, Gulf of, 248A
Corinth Isthmus, 31B
Corinthian War, 20C
Cormack, Allan, 353B
corn
in Africa, 169B, 196B
in Anatolia, 158B
in China, 154C
mill, 75B
in Persia, 15B
popping, 341B
reaper, 35B, 249B
in Rome, 38A, 40A
in United States, 4B, 103A, 115A, 123A, 229B, 246B
Corneille, Pierre, 187C, 189C
Cornelisz, Cornelis, 175B
Cornell, Ezra, 255B, 257B
Cornhuskers (Sandburg), 303C
Corning Glass Works, 297B
Corningware, 297B
Cornwall, 114B, 116A, 164A
Cornwallis, Charles, 224B, 227A, 229A, 231A
Coro, 157A
Coromandel Coast, 194C
Coromantes, 212B
Coronado, Francisco, 161A, 163A
Corot, Jean Baptiste Camille, 247C
corpore politics, De (Hobbes), 191C
Corpus Christi, 256B
Festival of, 125C
Corpus Christi College, 129C, 155C
Corral phase, 77A
Correggio, 155C, 159C, 177C
Corregidor Island, 328C, 334C
Corsair (Byron), 241C
Corsica, Corsicans, 100B, 104B, 164A, 210A, 214A, 220A, 366B
Cortázar, José de la Marx, 248C
Cortenuova, 112B
Cortes, 110B
Cortés, Hernando, 153B, 155A, 155B, 157A, 159B
Cortines, Ruiz (president of Mexico), 341A
Corvey, 87C
Abbey of, 77B
Corvinus, Matthias (king of Hungary), 140A
Cosa, Juan de la, 151A
Cosmas Indicopleustes, 63B,
cosmetics, 151B
in Egypt, 4A
in Rome, 35B
Cossacks, 172A, 182C, 186C, 190C, 192C, 204A, 220A

Costa e Silva, Artur da (president of Brazil), 353A
Costa Rica, Costa Ricans, 65A, 167A, 213A, 246C, 260C, 264C, 272C, 300C
  agriculture, 274C
  earthquake in, 254C
  government, 337A
  politics, 318C, 323A
  and Spain, 244C
  transportation, 282C
  University of, 256C
  World War II, 325A
Costner, Kevin, 375C
Cotonou, 261A
cotton, cotton industry, 2B, 91B, 99B, 113B, 123B, 137B, 229B, 241B, 247A
  bleaching, 253B
  and Carver, 331B
  in England, 135B
  gin, 227B, 231B
  mercerization of, 261B
  mill, 229B
  in paper, 71B
  tax on goods made of, 242B
Cotton, John, 189C
Cotton Pickers (Benton), 315C
Coty, René (president of France), 340B
Cotzumalhualpa culture, 44C
Council for Mutual Assistance (COMECON), 346A, 362A
Council of Churches for Britain and Ireland, 375C
Council of Europe, 338A, 338B
Council of People's Delegates, 302A
Count Basie Band, 345C
Count of Monte Cristo, The (Dumas), 257C
Counter-Reformation, 167C, 171C
Counterattack (Sassoon), 303C
Country Wife, The (Wycherley), 195C
Couperin, François, 195C, 201C
Courbet, Gustave, 261C
Courland, 166A, 202A
Cours de philosophie positive (Comte), 257C
Court and the Castle, The (West), 345C
Cousins, Norman, 335C
Cousteau, Jacques, 327B
Covandonga, battle of, 72B
Covenant, First, 165C
Coventry, 324A
coveralls, 261B
Covilhão, Pero da, 146B
Coward, Sir Noel, 311C, 313C, 315C, 325C, 327C, 331C
Cowley, Abraham, 189C, 191C
Cowper, William, 211C, 225C, 227C
Cow's Skull, Red, White, and Blue (O'Keeffe), 313C
Cox, Archibald, 358C
Coxey, Jacob, 284B
Coxwell, Henry, 267B
Coysevox, Antoine, 199C
Crabbe, George, 215C
Cranach, Lucas, 151C, 163C, 165C
Crane, Hart, 313C
Crane, Stephen, 283C, 285C
Cranford (Gaskell), 263C
crank, compound, 127B
Cranmer, Thomas (Archbishop of Canterbury), 159C, 165C
Crapper, Thomas, 267B
Crashaw, Richard, 189C
Crassus, 29A
Crawford, Broderick, 339C
Crawford, Joan, 335C
Crawford, Thomas, 267C
Crawford, William Harris, 246B
Craxi, Benito (prime minister of Italy), 370B
Crayford, 60A
Crazy Horse (Sandoz), 329C
Creation, The (Haydn), 235C
Crébillon, 203C, 205C
Crécy, battle of, 128A, 129B
Crédit Lyonnais, 268A
Creek, 240B, 246B, 248B
Crema, 104B, 140A
cremation, 9C
Cremona, 66B, 151C, 193C
Crépy, Peace of, 162A
crescent rolls, 111B
Cresson, Edith (prime minister of France), 376B
Crete, Cretans, 2C, 4A, 4C, 5C, 6C, *7*, 9C, 10C, 31B, 110B, 130B, 151B, 194A, 290A, 326A
  and Arabs, 78B
  arts, 5C, 9C
  and Byzantium, 84B, 86B
  and Greece, 286A
Crick, Francis, 341B
Crime and Punishment (Dostoyevsky), 271C
Crime de Sylvestre Bonnard, Le (France), 277C
Crimea, 224A, 226A, 262A, 326A, 332A
  and Russia, 342B
  and Ukraine, 342B
Crimean Peninsula, 42B
Crimean War, 262A
Crimes and Misdemeanors (Allen), 373C
Crispi, Francesco (prime minister of Italy), 280A
Crispus (son of Constantine the Great), 52A
Critic, The (Sheridan), 225C
Critical and Historical Essays (Macaulay), 257C
Critique of Judgment (Kant), 229C
Critique of Practical Reason (Kant), 227C
Critique of Pure Reason (Kant), 225C
Croatia, Croatians, 98B, 308A, 310A, 326A, 376B, 380B, 382B
Croce, Benedetto, 289C
Croissenbrunn, battle of, 116A
Crome, John, 221C
Crome Yellow (Huxley), 307C
Cromer, 279A
Crompton, Samuel, 225B
Cromwell, Oliver, 188A, 190A
Cromwell, Richard, 190A, 192A
Cromwell, Thomas, 158A, 161C
Cromwell (Hugo), 249C
Cronje, Piet, 287A
Cronstedt, Axel Fredrik, 215B
Crookes, William, 275B
crop rotation, 75B, 223B, 339B, 375B
Crosby, Bing, 327C, 333C
crossbow, 21B, 65B, 91B, 95B, 99B, 103B, 125B, 131B
crosses, 71B
Crossing, The (Churchill), 289C
Croton, 17B
crowd (stringed instrument), 66A
Crowfoot, 274B
Crown Point, 211A
Crowther, Samuel, 269C
Crucero culture, 50C
Crucible, The (Miller), 341C
Crusades, Crusaders, 91B, 97C, 99B, 103B, 108B, 111B, 115B
  First Crusade, 98B, 171C
  Second Crusade, 102A
  Third Crusade, 106B
  Fourth Crusade, 108B
  Seventh Crusade, 118B
  Albigensian Crusade, 106B, 110B
  in Germany, 113C
  and Jerusalem, 114B
  and Syria, 120B, 122B
  and Turkey, 140B, 146B, 150B
Cruz, Ramón Ernesto (president of Honduras), 359A
crwth, 66A
Cry the Beloved Country (Paton), 337C
cryosurgery, 347B
crystal rectifier, 275B
Crystal River culture, 109A
Ctesibius, 23B
Ctesiphon, battle of, 299A
Cuauhetemoc (emperor of Aztecs), 157A
Cuba, Cubans, 147A, 153A, 155A, 226C, 230C, 286C
  and Angola, 372A
  and Castro, 343A
  and China, 272C
  Cuba Convention, 288C
  government, 272C, 282C, 290C, 318C, 341A, 347A
  independence of, 252C
  law and society, 260C, 274C
  and Namibia, 372A
  and Organization of American States, 348A
  and Panama, 347A
  slave trade, 256C, 280C
  and South Africa, 372A
  and Soviet Union, 348A, 348B
  and Spain, 157B, 161A, 201A, 219A, 244C, 260C, 270C, 284B, 286C
  in United Nations, 335A
  and United States, 258C, 286C, 288C, 290C, 292C, 308C, 316B, 316C, 347A, 348A
  William "Boss" Tweed in, 274B
  World War I, 300C
  World War II, 327A
Cuban missile crisis, 348A
cubic boron nitride (CBN), 347B
Cubism, Cubists, 291C, 295C
Cud mniemany (Boguslawski), 249C
Cudworth, Ralph, 197C, 211C
Cugnot, Nicolas, 221B
Cuilean (king of Scots), 86A
Cukor, George, 333C, 351C
Cullen, William, 217B
Cult of the Dead, 83A
Cultural Revolution. *See* China, Chinese
Culture and Anarchy (Arnold), 273C
Cum inter nonnullos (papal bull), 125C
Cumae, 12C, 16C
Cumana, 155A
Cumberland, Richard, 195C, 219C, 221C
Cumberland (England), 86A, 90A, 98A, 104A, 167B, 214A, 216A
Cumberland Island, 213A
Cumberland Valley, 207A
cuneiform script. *See* writing
Cuno, Wilhelm (chancellor of Germany), 306A
Cunobelinus (king of the Catuvellauni), 32A, 34A
Cura Pastoralis (Gregory), 83C
Curaçao, 185A
curfew, 334B
Curie, Marie and Pierre, 333B
curium, 333B
Curl Nose, 56C, 59A
Curran, Charles, 371C
Current Tax Payment Act, 330B
Currier and Ives, *267*
Curtiz, Michael, 335C
Curzola, 120B
Curzon, Lord, 304A
Custer, George, 274B
Customs, U.S., 325A
customs duties, 14C, 108B, 184B, 267A
Custozza, battle of, 270A
Cuthred (king of Wessex), 74A
Cuyamel, 310C
Cuza, Alexandru (prince of Romania), 266A, 268A, 270A
Cuzco, 99A, 135A, 139A, 159A, 161A, 167C
Cuzco Cathedral, 175C
cyanosis, 333B
cybernetics, 337B
cyclosporin, 349B
cyclotron, proton accelerator, 319B
Cymbeline (Shakespeare), 179C
Cynewulf, 75C
Cynicism, 21C
Cypress Hills, 274B
Cyprian (Bishop of Carthage), 47A
Cyprus, Cypriots, 70B, 91B, 103B, 106B, 108B, 133C, 276A, 277A, 346A, 348B, 352B, 362B
  and Britain, 295A
  government, 360B, 372B
  and Greece, 350B
  independence of, 346B
  and Russia, 384B
  and Turkey, 350B, 361A
Cyrano de Bergerac (Rostand), 287C
Cyrenaica, 309A
Cyrene, 12A
Cyril, Saint, 81B, 81C
Cyrus the Great (king of Persia), 16B
Cyselus (king of Corinth), 12C
Czechoslovakia, 174A, 304A, 376B, 378B
  arts, 369C
  and Austria, 312A
  and Britain, 320A
  Charter 77 manifesto, 362B
  Communism in, 336B, 354B, 356B
  and East Germany, 372B
  and France, 308A, 320A
  and Germany, 312A, 320A, 328A
  government, 316A, 356B, 374B
  and London Convention of 1933, 314A
  Prague Spring, 354B
  riots in, 318A
  and Russia, 320A
  and Soviet Union, 354A, 356B, 376B
  and Sudetenland, 320A
  and United Nations, 354A
  and Warsaw Pact, 354B
  World War II, 328A
Czernowitz, 298A, 300A

D

D-Day, 332A
da Vinci, Leonardo. *See* Leonardo da Vinci
Dabarwa, 170B
Dacca, 192C, 202C, 218C
Dachau, 334A
Dacia, 38A, 39C, 46A, 48A
dacronin, 337B
Dada movement, 299C
Daddy Long Legs (movie), 313C
Dagobert I (king of Franks), 68A
Dahmer, Jeffrey, 376C
Dahomey, 218B, 261A, 283A, 285A
Dai Viet, 100C
Dáil Éireann, 302A
Daily Courant, 203C
Daimler, Gottlieb, 279B
Daisy Miller (James), 277C
Dakar, 285A
Dakin (king of Fundj), 168B
Dakota Territory, 276B
Daladier, Édouard (prime minister of France), 316A, 320A
Dalai Lama, 187C, 289A, 347A

Dale, Sir Thomas, 179A
Dale's Code, 179A
Daley, Richard, 362C
Dalhousie, James Andrew (governor-general of India), 259A
Dalin, Olof von, 211C
Dalip Singh Saund, 342C
Dallas, 348C
Dallas Cowboys, 357C, 359C, 363C, 365C, 379C, 381C, 383C
Dalmatia, 90B, 98B, 130B, 232A, 308A
Dalry, battle of, 122A
Damascus, 12B, 35A, 39C, 66B, 67B, 68B, 70B, 72C, 73C, 74C, 96B, 104B, 122C, 134B, 154B, 220B, 305A, 309A
Damasus I, Pope, 55A, 57A
Damasus II, Pope, 95C
Damdam, 110C
Dame aux Camélias, La (Dumas), 263C
Damietta, 114B
Dammazedi (king of Hanthawaddy and Pegu), 142C
Dampier, William, 202C
dams, 3B, 4A, 87B, 91B, 175B, 279B. *See also individual dams*
Danatbank, 312A
Dance, N., *221*
Dances with Wolves (movie), 375C
Danegeld, 90A
Dangan Hill, battle of, 188A
Daniel, Samuel, 181C
Daniell, John, 245B, 253B
Danilo I (prince of Montenegro), 260A
Danish East India Company, 210A
d'Annunzio, Gabriele, 279C
Danse, La (Matisse), 293C
Dante, Egnation, 171B
Dante Alighieri, 121C, 123C, *125*, 125C
Dante's Dream (Rossetti), 273C
Danton, Georges, 230A
Danton's Death (Büchner), 253C
Danube River, 44A, 48A, 56A, 96B, 103B, 262A, 264A
Danzig, 210A, 220A, 320A
Daoud Khan, Mohammad (president of Afghanistan), 359A
Dar-es-Salaam, 293A, 295A, 299A, 384A, 385A
Dardanelles, 248A, 250A, 254A, 297A, 299A
Dare, Virginia, 173A
Darién, Gulf of, 151A, 203A
Daring Young Man on the Flying Trapeze, The (Saroyan), 317C
Darius II (king of Persia), 20B
Darius III, 22B
Darius the Great (king of Persia), 16A, 16B, 16C, 17B
Dark Ages, 63B, 67B
Dark Corn (O'Keeffe), 309C
Darkness at Noon (Koestler), 323C
Darling River, 275A
Darmstadt, 306A
Darnley, Henry Stuart, 168A
d'Arras, Gautier, 105C
Dartmouth College, 343B
Darwin, Charles, 265B
Das Ich und das Es (Freud), 307B
Das Kapital (Marx), 271C
Das Pensionat (Suppé), 267C
Das Trauma der Geburt (Rank), 309B
Dass, Petter, 213C
Dauberval, Jean, 227C
Daudet, Alphonse, 273C
Daughters of Charity of St. Joseph, 241C
Daughters of Revolution (Wood), 315C
Daughters of the American Revolution, 321C
Daura, 82C
Davenant, Sir William, 185C
Davenport, John, 193C
David, Jacques-Louis, 215C, 227C, 237C
David, Saint, 65C
David Copperfield (Dickens), 261C
David I (emperor of Ethiopia), 132C
David I (king of Scotland), 102A, 104A
David II (king of Scotland), 126A, 130A
David III of Georgia, 98B
David (king of Israel), 10B
David (Michaelangelo), 151C
David (Verrochio), 145C
Daviel, Jacques, 215B
Davis, Angela, 358C
Davis, Bette, 339C
Davis, Geena, 377C
Davis, Jefferson, 262B, 266B
Davis, John, 173A, 245A
Davis Straits, 173A
Davy, Sir Humphrey, 239B
Dawaro, 158B
Day, Dorothy, 315C
Day, Henry, 259B
Day-Lewis, Daniel, 373C
Day of the Locust, The (West), 323C
daylight saving time, 302B, 326B
DDT, 327B, 359B
De Abstinentia (Porphyry), 51C
De analysi per aequationes numero terminorum infinitas (Newton), 195B
De Architectura (Vitruvius), 33C
De Beers Mining Company, 277A
De Bello Gallico (Caesar), 29C
De Captivitate Babylonica Ecclesiae (Luther), 155C
De Catholicae Ecclesia Unitate (Cyprian), 47A
De Cive (Hobbes), 187C
De Forest, Lee, 293B, 307B, 347B
de Gaulle, Charles (president of France), 324A, 332A, 336B, 344B, 346A, 348A, 348B, 350B, 352B, 356B
de Havilland, Olivia, 337C, 339C
De Imitatione Christi (Thomas à Kempis), 137C
De-Jina, 186C
de Klerk, F. W. (president of South Africa), 373A, 377A
de Kooning, Willem, 337C, 341C
De la République (Bodin), 171C
de la Roche, Marquis, 175A
De Leeuw van Vlaenderen (Conscience), 255C
De Lesseps, 265A
De Masteria Medica (Dioscordius), 35B
De Plantis Libri (Cesalpino), 173B
De Principiis (Origen), 45A
De Re Diplomatica (Mabillon), 197C
De Republica (Cicero), 29C
De Servo Arbitrio (Luther), 157C
de Soto, Hernando, 161A, 163A
De Temporum Ratione (Bede), 73C
de Valera, Eamon (president of Ireland), 314A, 346B, 352B, 360B
De Veritate (Herbert of Cherbury), 183C
De Vita Constantini (Eusebius), 53C
de Vrie, William, 367B
Dead, Street of the, 54C
Dead Sea Scrolls, 27C, 37A, 377C
Dead Souls (Gogol), 257C
Dean, H. Trendley, 325B
Dean, James, 343C
Dean, John, 358C
Dearborn, Henry, 240B
Death and Taxes (Parker), 313C
Death Comes for the Archbishop (Cather), 311C
Death of a Salesman (Miller), 339C
Death of General Wolfe (West), *217*
"Death of the Hired Man" (Frost), 295C
Debré, Michel (prime minister of France), 348B
Debs, Eugene V., 282B, 284B, 286B, 290B, 292B, 302B, 306B
Debussy, Claude, 277C
Decameron (Boccaccio), 129C
Decatur, Stephen, 236B, 242B
Deccan, 38B, 66C, 74C, 78C, 89C, 124C, 128C, 142C, 144C, 146C, 168C, 174C, 180C, 237A
Decebalus of Dacia, 36A
decimal numbers, 77B, 141B
Decius, Trajanus (emperor of Rome), 46A, 47A
Declaration of Independence, 222B
Declaration of Rights of Man, 228A
Declaration on Religious Liberty, 351C
Declaratory Act, 219A
declination, magnetic, 147B
Decline and Fall of the Roman Empire (Gibbon), 223C
Decline of the West, The (Spengler), 303C
Decoration Day, 270B
Decretals of Isidore, 183C
Dedalus and Icarus (Canova), 225C
Dee, John, 165B
Deer Hunter, The (Cimino), 363C
Deere, John, 255B
Deerfield, 203A
Defense of Marriage Act, 382C
Defense Reorganization Act, 344C
Defoe, Daniel, 203C, 207C, 209C
Degli Eroici Furori (Bruno), 173C
Deipnosophistae (Athenaeus), 45C
Deir el-Bahri, 9C
Deir el-Medina, 6A
Déjeuner sur l'herbe, Le (Manet), 269C
Dekker, Thomas, 179C
Delafield, E. M., 331C
Delagoa Bay, 225A
Delambre, Jean, 239B
Delaware, 203A
Delaware Bay, 179A
Delaware River, 181A, 185A, 187A
Delbruck, Max, 331B
Delft, Treaty of, 136A
Delhi, 88C, 110C, 114C, 116C, 118C, 120C, 122C, 124C, 126C, 128C, 134C, 138C, 146C, 148C, 154C, 156C, 170C, 186C, 188C, 212C, 216C, 220C, 249A, 265A
Delian League, 18C
Delibes, Léo, 273C
Della Causa, Principio ed Uno (Bruno), 173C
Delos (Greek island), 18C, 26C
Delphi, 14C, 24C
Delphine (Staël), 235C
Delta Airlines, 351B, 368C
Demerara, 232C, 242C, 250C
Demetrius, 41C
Demian (Hesse), 303C
DeMille, Cecil B., 307C, 341C
Demme, Jonathan, 377C
Democracy and Education (Dewey), 299C
Democratic Convention (1896), 284B
Democratic Convention (1984), 368C
Democratic National Committee, 358C, 372C
Democratic National Convention (1968), 354C, 356C
Democratic Party, 250B, 308B, 310B, 320B, 332B, 336C, 342C, 344C, 348C, 370C, 376C, 378C
Democratic-Republican Party, 230B
Demoiselles d'Avignon, Les (Picasso), 291C
Demonstration Cities and Metropolitan Redevelopment Act, 352C
Demosthenes, 20C, 22C
Dempster, George, 311B
Denham, Dixon, 247A
Denia, 90B
Denier du rêve (Yourcenar), 317C
De Niro, Robert, 363C, 365C
Denis, Jean-Baptiste, 193B
Denis (monk), *96*
Denmark, Danes, 80A, 82A, 84A, 88A, 90A, 92A, 96A, 106A, 132A, 134A, 138A, 140A, 142A, 143A, 144A, 146A, 148A, 150A, 154A, 157C, 158A, 160A, 166A, 168A, 172A, 178A, 179B, 180A, 182A, 184A, 188A, 192A, 195A, 196A, 196B, 204A, *209*, 211A, 218A, 234A, 234B, 240A, 258A, 268A, 290A, 300B, 378B
  and Austria, 268A
  and Britain, 261A, 358B
  in European Free Trade Association, 346A
  and Germany, 334A
  and Gold Coast, 261A
  government, 340B
  and Ireland, 358B
  London Convention, 260A
  and Prussia, 258A, 260A
  and United States, 324B, 338A
  World War II, 322A, 324B
dentistry, 91B, 145B, 159B, 171B
  electric drill, 275B
  fluoride, fluoridation, 313B, 325B, 335B, 343B
  rotary drill, 211B
Denver, 379C, 384C
Denver Broncos, 363C, 371C, 373C, 375C, 385C
Deorham, 64A
Dépit Amoureux, Le (Poquelin), 191C
DePriest, Oscar, 310B
Der Blaue Engel (movie), 313C
Der Prinz von Homburg (Kleist), 239C
Derbent, 208B
Derby, 111B
Derby, Lord (prime minister of England), 270A
Derna, 237A, 326A
dervishes, 105C, 119C, 204B, 277A, 287A, 309A
Derzhavin, Gavril Romanovich, 225C
Desai, Morarji (prime minister of India), 363A
Desastres de la Guerra, Los (Goya), 239C
Descartes, René, 187C, 189C
Descent from the Cross (Rubens), 179C
Deschanel, Paul (president of France), 304A
Désert de l'Amour, Le (Mauriac), 309C
Desert Song, The (Romberg), 311C
desertion, execution for, 334B
Desiderius (king of Langobards), 74B
Design for Living (Coward), 315C
Designs of Chinese Buildings (Chambers), 217C
Desire Under the Elms (O'Neill), 309C
desk, rotary upright, 173B
Despart, Charlotte, 282A

Dessalines, Jean Jacques, 234B, 236C
détente, 358A
Detroit, 203A, 215A, 217A, 240B, 370C
race riots in, 330B, 354C
Tigers, 325C, 335C, 355C, 369C
Dettingen, battle of, 212A
Deutschbrod, battle of, 136A
Deutsches Requiem, Ein (Brahms), 271C
Devan Nair (president of Singapore), 369A
Devil's Island, 284A
Devil's Tower, 290B
Devon, 164A
Devonshire, 88A, 121B
Dewar, James, 281B, 289B
Dewar flask, 289B
Dewey, George, 287A
Dewey, John, 292B, 299C
Dewey, Thomas E., 332B, 336C
Dewey Decimal system, 275C
Dhar, 122C
Dharan, 383A
Dharmapala (king of Bengal), 78C
Dharmapala (king of Kotte), 164C
di Rienzo, Cola, 128B
Diaghilev, Sergei, 293C
Dialogues Concerning Natural Religion (Hume), 225C
Diamond Necklace Affair, 226A
Diamond Sutra, The, 81, 81C
diamonds
mining, 281A
synethetic, 343B
Diana, Princess, 378B, 382B, *383,* 384B
diapers, disposable, 347B
Diarmait (king of Ireland), 64A
Dias, Bartolomeu, 146B, 150C
Dias, Dinís, 138C
Diatribede Libero Arbitrio (Erasmus), 157C
Díaz, José de la Cruz Porfirio (president of Mexico), 274C, 278C, 292C
Díaz de Solís, Juan, 155A
Díaz de Vivar, Rodrigo, 98B
Dick test, 309B
Dickens, Charles, 253C, 255C, 257C, 261C, 265C, 273C
Dickenson, Charles, 236B
Dickinson, Emily, 283C
Dickson Mounds, 87A
dictionary, 11C, 219C
Dictionary of the English Language, A (Johnson), 215C
Dictionnaire historique et critique (Bayle), 201C
Didius Julianus, Marcus (emperor of Rome), 42A
Dido and Aeneas (Purcell), 199C
Die Phänomenologie des Geistes (Hegel), 237C
Die Vierzig Tage des Musa Dagh (Werfel), 315C
Die Welt als wille und Verstellung (Schopenhauer), 245C
Diefenbaker, John (prime minister of Canada), 344C
Diégo-Suarez, 202B, 279A
Diem, Ngo Dinh. *See* Ngo Dinh Diem.
Dien Bien Phu, 343A
Dieppe, 328A
die(s), 73B, 141B
Die Winterreise (Schubert), 249C
Die Zauberflöte (Mozart), 229C
Diesel, Rudolf, 287B
Dietrich, Marlene, 313C
Dieu et l'état (Bakunin), 273C
Dieu et Mammon (Mauriac), 311C
Diggers, 188A
Digges, Leonard, 165B, 169B
digital data storage, 337B
dikes, 5B, 76A, 155B
Dillingen University, 165C
Dillinger, John, 316B
Dilthey, Wilhelm, 291C
DiMaggio, Joe, 327C
Dimanche d'été à la Grande-Jatte, Un (Seurat), 281C
Dimawe, 263A
Din, Ghiyas al- (sultan of Malwa), 142C
Din, Jalalal al- (king of Bengal), 134C
Din al-Mani II, Fakir al- (prince of Lebanon), 172B, 184B
Din Barbak, Rukin al- (king of Bengal), 140C
Din Quait Bey, al-Ashraf Sayf al- (sultan of Egypt), 142B
Din Riayat, Ala al- (sultan of Johore), 158C
Din Riayat II, Ala al- (sultan of Johore), 174C
Din Shah, Sultan Ala al- (sultan of Malacca), 144C
Dinan, *95*
Dinesen, Isak, 317C, 327C
Dingaan (king of Zulu), 255A
Dingley Tariff Act, 286B
Dini, Lamberto (prime minister of Italy), 380B
Diniz the Husbandman (king of Portugal), 118B
Dinner at Eight (movie), 315C
dinosaurs, extinction of, 365B
Diocletian (emperor of Rome), 48A, 49A, 50A, 50B, 51A, 51B, 51C
Diogenes, 21C
Dionne quintuplets, 316B
Dionysius, Pope, 49A
Dionysius of Alexandria, 39B
Dionysius of Halicarnassus, 31C
Dionysius the Areopagite, 63C
Dioscordius, Pedanius, 35B
Directory, 234A
Disarmament Conferences, 306B, 346A
Disasters of War (Goya), 239C
Disciples of Christ, 249C
Discorsi (Machiavelli), 155C
Discours de la méthode (Descartes), 187C
Discourse About Civil Government in a New Plantation Whose Design Is Religion (Davenport), 193C
Discovery, 369B
discrimination, 350C, 362C
Discus Thrower (Myron), 19C
dishwashing machines, 261B, 271B, 315B
Disney, Walt, 309C, 321C, 327C, 353C
Disraeli, Benjamin, 249C, 257C, 270A, 274A
distant early warning radar network (DEW line), 342C
District of Columbia, 254B, 260B, 270B, 274B, 346C. *See also* Washington, D.C.
Dithmarschen, 150A
Dittersdorf, Karl Ditters von, 227C
Diu, 152C, 194B
Diverse Thoughts on the Comet of 1680 (Bayle), 197C
Diverting History of John Gilpin, The (Cowper), 225C
Divine Comedy, The (Dante), 123C, *125,* 125C
diving, divers. *See also* submarines
aqualung apparatus, 327B
bathysphere, 313B
diving bells, 161B, 179B, 207B
Dix, Dorothy, 285C
"Dixie," 265C
Djebe Djougar, 41B
Djelaleddin Rumi, 119C
Djibouti, 289A, 303A, 363A
Djilas, Milovan, 342B
Dmitri, 172A
DNA (deoxyribonucleic acid), 327B, 333B, 341B, 373B
in prenatal testing, 363B
synthetic, 355B
Dnieper, 220A
Dnieper River, 330A
Dniester River, 298A, 300A
Do the Right Thing (movie), 373C
Doab, 235A
Dodecanese Islands, 292A, 304A
Dodgson, Charles, 281B
Doe, Samuel (president of Liberia), 375A
Doering, William, 333B
Dogali, battle of, 281A
Doges, Palace of the, 123C, 171C
dogs, 2A
Doheny, Edward L., 308B
Doheny, Edward L., Jr., 308B
Dokter und Apotheker (Dittersdorf), 227C
Dolce Vita, La (Fellini), 347C
Dole, Elizabeth, 366C
Dole, Robert, 382C
Dole, Stanford B., 285A
Dollfuss, Englebert, 314A
"Dolly," 385B
Dombo Changamire, 198B
Dome of the Rock, 69C
Domenichino, 185C
Domesday Book, 96A
Domfront, 94A
Dominica, 147A, 219A, 236C, 242C, 254C, 256C, 323A, 362A, 363A
Dominican Republic, 147A, 149A, 201A, 256C, 268C, 278C
and Haiti, 318C
in United Nations, 335A
and United States, 290C, 298C, 308C, 351A
World War II, 325A
Dominicans (mendicant order), 111C, 119C
Domitian (emperor of Rome), 36A, 37C, 38A
Domna, Julia, 45C
Don Carlos (Otway), 197C
Don Carlos (Schiller), 227C
Don Giovanni (Mozart), 227C
Don Juan (Strauss), 281C
Don Pacifico Affair, 260A
Don Quixote (Cervantes), 177C, 181C
Don Quixote (Strauss), 287C
Donald I (king of Scots), 82A
Donatello, 143C
Dondi, Giovanni, 131B
Donets River, 328A
Dong Zhuo, 42B
Dongola, 285A
Dönitz, Karl, 334A
Donizetti, Gaetano, 253C
Donne, John, 177C, 185C
Donskoi, Dmitri, 130A, 132A
"don't ask, don't tell, don't pursue" policy, 378C
Doolittle, James, 328C
Doors (rock group), 357C
Doors, The (movie), 377C
Dordrecht, Treaty of, 146A
Dorians, 10C
Dornelles, Getúlio (dictator of Brazil), 312C
Dorset culture, 38C
Dorset (England), 85C, 88A
Dos Passos, John, 309C, 321C, 323C, 331C
Dost Muhammad (emir of Afghanistan), 253A, 255A
Dostoyevsky, Fyodor, 267C, 271C, 277C
Douai, 122A
Douglas, Gawain, 151C
Douglas, Lloyd, 327C
Douglas, Michael, 371C
Douglas, Stephen, 264B
Douglas, Thomas, fifth earl of Selkirk, 238B, 242B
Douglas, William O., 360C
Douglass, Frederick, 259C, 274B
Doumer, Paul (president of France), 312A, 314A
Doumergue, Gaston (president of France), 308A
Douro Valley, 29B
Dover, 39B, 75B, 248B
Treaty of, 194A
Dow, Herbert, 281B
Dow Chemical Company, 305B, 347B
Dow Jones Industrial Average, 362C, 370C, 376C, 384C
Doyle, Sir Arthur Conan, 281C
Dr. Strangelove (movie), 351C
Dr. Zhivago (movie), 351C
Dr. Zhivago (Pasternak), 345C
Draco, 12C
Dracula, 307C
Dragon, Great Temple of the, 137C
Dragon Seed (Buck), 327C
Dragon's Teeth (Sinclair), 331C
Dragonwyck (Seton), 333C
drainage system, 103B
Drake, Edwin, 264B
Drake, Sir Francis, 169A, 170C, 171A, 172A
Drake's Bay, 163A
dramamine, 337B
Draper, Charles, 341B
Drebbel, Cornelis, 175B, 181B, 183B
Dred Scott decision, 264B
dredger, 237B
Dreiser, Theodore, 287C, 289C, 309C
Dresden, battle of, 334A
Dresden (German ship), 297A
dressmaking, 267B, 269B
Drew, Charles, 325B
Drew, Richard, 309B
Drexel Burnham Lambert, 372C, 374C
Dreyfus, Alfred, 284A, 286A, 290A
Driving Miss Daisy (movie), 373C
Droit au travail (Blanc), 259C
drugs, hallucinogenic, 32C, 42C
Druids, 35A
Drummond, Sir Gordon, 242B
Drummond, Thomas, 243B
drums, 87C
Drums at Dusk (Bontemps), 323C
Drusus, 32A
Druten, John Van, 331C, 333C
dry cleaning, 245B
Dryden, John, 193C, 195C, 197C, 203C
Du Bois, W.E.B., 289C, 292B
Du contrat social (Rousseau), 219C
du Maurier, Dame Daphne, 319C, 321C
Dual Alliance, 276A
Duala, 295A
Dubcek, Alexander, 354B, 356B
Dublin, Dubliners, 173C, 213C, 278A, 290A, 298A, 302A
Dubliners (Joyce), 295C
Duca, Ion George (prime minister of Romania), 314A
Duchamp, Marcel, 295C
Duchess of Malfi, The (Webster), 179C
Duchess of Wrexe, The (Walpole), 295C
Duck Lake, 278B
Dudevant, Amandine-Aurore-Lucile. *See* George Sand
Dufay, Guillaume, 143C

Duggar, Benjamin, 335B
Dukakis, Michael, 372C
Dukas, Paul, 287C
Duke, Charles, 359B
Duke of Milan (Massinger), 183C
Dulles, John Foster, 340C, 346C
Dulwich Gallery, 241C
Duma, 290A
Dumas, Alexandre, 257C, 263C
Dumbarton Oaks Conference, 332B
Duna, 220A
Dunant, Henri, 267C
Dunbar, battle of, 120A, 188A
Dunbar, William, 151C
Dunblane, 382B
Duncan, Isadora, 287C
Duncan, Jonathan, 229A
Duncan (king of Scotland), 92A
Dunes, battle of, 190A
Dunker, 205C, 209C
Dunkirk, 192A, 322A
  battle of, 190A
Dunstan (Archbishop of Canterbury), 87C
Dupleix, Joseph François (governor-general of India), 212C
Duplin Moor, battle of, 126A
DuPont de Nemours & Company, 235B, 309B, 313B, 337B, 351B, 359B, 377B
Duppel, battle of, 268A
Durand Agreement, 283A
Durazzo, 132B, 150A
Durban, 255A
Dürer, Albrecht, 149C, 153C, 157C
Durges Nandini (Chatterji), 269C
Durham, 201A, 268B
  Agreement of, 102A
Durham, Lord, 254B
Durham University, 253C
Dürnkrut, battle of, 118A
Durrani dynasty. *See* Afghanistan
Dušan, Stephen (king of Serbia), 128B
Dust Tracks on the Road (Hurston), 329C
Dust Which Is God, The (Benét), 327C
Dutch East India Company, 176A, 180C, 186B, 190B, 232A
Dutch East Indies. *See* Indonesia
Dutch United East India Company, 180C
Dutch War, 170A
Dutch West India Company, 180A, 184A, 185A, 194A, 196B
Dutt, Michael Madhusudna, 265C
Duvalier, François (president of Haiti), 357A
Duvalier, Jean-Claude (president of Haiti), 357A
Duvall, Robert, 367C
Dvořák, Antonín, 269C, 277C, 283C
Dwarasamudra, 124C
dwellings
  balloon frame construction, 251B
  cast-iron frame, 255B
  cliff-side, 109A
  log, 38C
  pueblos, 97A
  rectangular, 63A
  on refuse mounds, 63B
  teepees, 211A
  underground, 38C
dyes, dyeing, 35C, 109B, 151B, 273B
Dying Swan, The (Fokine), 291C
Dykes, Eva, 304B
Dylan, Bob, 349C, 385C
Dymaxion Deployment Unit (DDU), 323B
Dymaxion house, 311B
Dzibilichaltun, 46C, 67A, 73A, 79A

E

Eads, James, 275B
Eakins, Thomas, 273C
Eames, Charles, 325C
Eames, Gil, 136C
Eanes, António Ramalho (president of Portugal), 364B
Eanred, 78A
Earhart, Amelia, 315B, 318B
earth
  Earth Day, 356A, 374C
  fuller's, 163B
  magnetic field of, 211B
  rotation of, 263B
Earthly Paradise (Morris), 271C
East Africa, 5B, 108C, 120C, 305A
  and Arabs, 72B, 88C
  arts, 203C
  and Britain, 299A
  and China, 136C
  and France, 317A
  government, 212B
  and Italy, 317A
  and Persia, 88C
  and Portugal, 146B, 150B, 158B, 166B, 172B, 174B, 186B, 190B, 208B
  slave trade, 251A
  and Turkey, 160B
East Anglia, 69C, 76A, 80A, 84A
East Friesland, 212A
East Germany, 346B, 350A
  and Berlin Wall, 346B, 374B
  Communism in, 338B, 372B
  and Czechoslovakia, 372B
  and Poland, 338B
  on reunification, 374B
  riots in, 340B
  and Soviet Union, 360B
  treaty of equal relationships, 358B
  in United Nations, 358A
  and United States, 344A, 360A
East India Company, 176C, 177A, 180A, 216C, 227A, 249A
East Indies, 70C, 74C, 88C, 150C, 159A, 174C, 180C, 184A, 192C, 224B. *See also* Indonesia
  and Holland, 174A
  and Malaya, 160C
  Sanjaya dynasty, 74C, 76C, 78C
East Java, 84C, 88C, 90C, 186C
East San Domingo, 201A
Easter Island, 58C, 209A
Easter Rising, 298A
Eastern Airlines, 338C, 376C
Eastern Galicia, 306A
Eastern Karelia, 208A
Eastern Roman Empire. *See* Byzantium, Byzantines
Eastern Slavs, 86A
Eastland Company, 170A
Eastman, George, 279B, 287B, 307B
Eastman, Max, 313C
Eastwood, Clint, 370C, 377C
Eaton, William, 237A
Ebert, Friedrich (chancellor of Germany), 302A
Ebola virus, 381B, 383B
ebony, 84C
Ebro River, 102B
Echegaray, José, 275C, 277C
Echeverría Álvarez, Luis (president of Mexico), 357A
Echoing Grove, The (Lehmann), 341C
Eck, Johann Maier von, 155C
Eck Company, 291B
Eckert, J. Presper, Jr., 325B, 339B
eclipses, 17B
Ecloga, 74C
Economic Community of West African States (ECOWAS), 361A
Economic Interpretation of the Constitution (Beard), 295C
Ecuador, 61A, 139A, 157A, 161A, 175A, 235B, 298C
  Artisana volcano, 276C
  arts, 77A
  civil war in, 250C
  and Colombia, 248C, 250C, 300C
  earthquake in, 371A
  government, 252C, 254C, 266C, 274C, 290C, 298C, 308C, 312C, 357A, 359A, 367A
  in New Granada, 207A
  and Peru, 325A, 327A
  religion, 266C
  and Spain, 160A, 238C, 246C, 270C
  and Union of 1819, 250C
Ed Sullivan Show, 351C
Eddy, Mary Baker, 275C, 291C
Eden, Anthony (prime minister of Britain), 338B, 342B, 344B
Edgar the Peaceable (king of England), 86A, 88A
Edgecote, battle of, 142A
Edgehill, battle of, 186A
Edgeworth, Maria, 219C
Edgeworth, Richard, 221B
Edictum Chlotacharii II, 67C
Edinburgh, 162A, 168A, 184A, 209C
  Treaty of, 166A
  University of, 171C
Edinburgh Castle, 188A
Edington, 80A
Édipe (Voltaire), 207C
Edirne, 130B
Edison, Thomas, 275B, 277B, 289B
Edmonton, 278B
Edmund, Prince, 116B
Edmund I (king of England), 86A
Edo, 176C, 190C, 271A
Edo Bay, 259A
Edred (king of England), 86A
Edsel, 346C
Edward I (king of England), 116A
Edward I (king of England), 118A, 120A, 121C, *122,* 122A
Edward II (king of England), 122A, 124A
Edward III (king of England and France), 124A, 126A, 128A, 130A, 131C, 132A
Edward IV (king of England), 140A, 142A, 144A
Edward V (king of England), 144A
Edward VI (king of England), 162A, 164A
Edward VII (king of England), 288A, 292A
Edward VIII (king of England), 318A
Edward (earl of Warwick), 148A
Edward of York, 140A
Edward (prince of Wales), 142A
Edward the Black Prince, 128A, 130A, 130B
Edward the Confessor (king of England), 92A, 94A
Edward the Elder (king of England), 82A, 84A
Edward the Martyr, Saint, 88A
Edwards, Jonathan, 215C
Edwards, Robert, 355B
Edwy (king of England), 86A
Egbert (king of England), 78A
Eger, 184A
egg incubator, 183B
eggplant, 173B
Egica (king of Visigoths), 70A
Egmont, Lamoral, 166A
Egoist, The (Meredith), 277C
Egypt, Egyptians, 38B, 45A, 48B, 55B, 116C, 192B, 288A
  3500 B.C.–2000 B.C., 2A, 3B, 3C, 4A, 4B, 5B, 5C
  1750 B.C.–1250 B.C., 6A, 6B, 6C, 7B, 7C, 8A, 8B, 9B, 9C
  1100 B.C.–605 B.C., 10A, 10B, 11B, 11C, 12A, 12B, 13B, 13C
  600 B.C.–270 B.C., 14A, 14B, 14C, 15B, 16A, 18A, 22A, 22B, 23C
  222 B.C.–25 B.C., 24A, 25C, 26A, 30B
  agriculture, 40A, 40B, 73B, 123B
  and Albania, 243A
  arts, 3C, 5C, 9C, 11C, 23C, 25C, 63C, 67B
  and Britain, 273A, 275A, 279A, 297A, 301A, 307A, 319A, 343A
  and Byzantium, 118B
  and Crusaders, 98B, 110B
  and Damascus, 220B
  economy, 198B, 200B, 204B
  education, 87C
  and Ethiopia, 273A
  and Fatamids, 82B, 86B
  and France, 114B, 233A, 235A, 343A
  and Germany, 112B, 324A, 328A
  government, 80B, 94B, 116B, 142B, 150B, 184B, 192B, 194B, 208B, 212B, 218B, 269A, 283A, 307A, 319A, 341A, 357A
  Hyksos dynasty, 6A, 7B
  and India, 34B, 58C
  industry, 247A
  and Israel, 343A, 345A, 355A, 359A, 362A, 363A, 364A, 365A, 381A
  and Italy, 88B, 309A, 324A
  and Jordan, 342A, 355A
  law and society, 196B, 277A
  in League of Nations, 319A
  and Libya, 358A
  and Malta, 368A
  Mamelukes, 114B, 116B, 116C, 118C, 120B, 132B, 142B, 144B, 154B, 184B, 218B, 220B, 233A, 235A, 239A
  and Mongolia, 120B
  natural disasters in, 200B
  and Ottoman Empire, 156B, 164B, 178B, 237A, 245A, 269A, 271A, 295A
  and Peloponnesian Peninsula, 246A
  and Persians, 66B
  plague in, 42B, 64B, 128B
  and Portugal, 152C
  and Red Sea, 245A
  religion, 3C, 47A, 49A, 53A, 68B, 69C, 81C
  and Romans, 40B, 44B, 50B
  and Saudi Arabia, 342A
  science and technology, 49B, 83B, 135B, 175B
  and Sinai Peninsula, 291A
  Six-Day War, 355A
  and Soviet Union, 356A
  and Sudan, 245A, 279A, 285A, 287A
  and Suez Canal, 343A
  and Syria, 104B, 255A, 342A, 345A, 359A
  Tulunid dynasty, 80B, 81C
  and Turkey, 144B, 154B, 234A, 248A, 251A
  and United States, 362A
  and Venice, 122B
  and Wahhabi, 239A
  World War II, 324A, 326A, 328A
  and Yemen, 342A, 355A
  Yom Kippur War, 359A

Egyptian, The (Waltari), 335C
Egyptian Helen, The (Strauss), 309C
Ehrlichman, John, 358C
Eichmann, Adolf, 348A
Eiffel, Gustave, 281B
1818, Convention of, 244B
Eikonoklastes (Milton), 189C
Einaudi, Luigi (president of Italy), 336B
Einhard, 79C
Einstein, Albert, 291B, 301B, 322B
Einthoven, Willem, 289B
Eisenach, 199C
Eisenburg, Peace of, 192A
Eisenhower, Dwight D. (president of U.S.), 328A, 330A, 332A, 334B, 338A, 340A, 340C, 342C, 344C, 346A, 356C
Eisenhower, Mamie, 343B
Eisenstein, Sergei, 309C
Ekkehart, 85C
El Agheila, 326A, 328A
El Alamein, 328A
El Arish, 301A
El Caney, battle of, 286C
El Dorado, 161A, 163A
El Mirador, 50C
El Paso, 348A
El Salvador, 42C, 50C, 157A, 254C, 256C, 312C
  civil war in, 377A, 378A
  earthquake in, 371A
  government, 335A, 365A, 385A
  and Guatemala, 260C, 268C
  and Honduras, 284C, 365A
  independence of, 254C
  and Nicaragua, 284C
  pyramids in, 40C
  and United Nations, 335A, 378A
El Trapiche, 42C
El Ubbayid, battle of, 279A
Elagabalus (emperor of Rome), 44A, 45A, 45B
Elahi, Fazal (president of Pakistan), 359A
Elba, 234A, 240A
Elbe River, 58A, 78A, 188A, 234A
elderly, the, 98C, 290A
Eleanor of Aquitaine, 102A, 104A
elections, U.S.
  of 1904, 288B
  of 1912, 292B
  of 1916, 300B
  of 1920, 304B
  of 1924, 308B
  of 1928, 310B
  of 1932, 314B
  of 1936, 318B
  of 1940, 324B
  of 1942, 328B
  of 1944, 332B
  of 1948, 336C
  of 1952, 340C
  of 1956, 342C
  of 1958, 344C
  of 1960, 346C
  of 1962, 348C
  of 1964, 350C
  of 1968, 354C
  of 1972, 358C
  of 1976, 362C
  of 1980, 364C
  of 1984, 368C
  of 1988, 372C
  of 1992, 378C
  of 1996, 382C
Elective Affinities, The (Goethe), 239C
Electra (Euripides), 21C
electricity, static, 171B
"Elegy Written in a Country Churchyard" (Gray), 215C
Elektra (Strauss), 293C
Elementary Philosophy (Huxley), 271C
Elementorum philosophiae (Hobbes), 187C
Elements (Euclid), 23B, 75C
Elene (Cynewulf), 75C
elevator, passenger, 263B, 265B
Elfheah, Saint (Archbishop of Canterbury), 90A
Elgar, Edward, 309C
Elgin marbles, 237C
Elgin Treaty, 262B
Elijah (Hebrew prophet), 11C
Elijah (Mendelssohn), 259C
Eliot, George, 265C, 267C, 271C
Eliot, John, 191C
Eliot, T. S., 307C, 331C, 351C
Elizabeth (empress of Russia), 212A, 218A
Elizabeth I (queen of England), 166A, 169C, 173B, 176A
Elizabeth II (queen of England), 340B, 354B, 370A, 378B
Elizabeth (N.J.), 215A
Elizabeth (queen of Frederick V of Bohemia), 178A
Elk Hills Naval Reserve, 308B
Elle et lui (Sand), 265C
Ellendun, battle of, 78A
Ellesmere, *131*
Ellice Islands, 168C, 297A
Ellington, Duke, 361C
Ellis, Havelock, 321C
Ellis, Ruth, 342B
Ellison, Ralph, 341C
Ellora, 33A, 75C
Embargo Act, 238B
Embarquement pour l'Île de Cythère, L' (Watteau), 207C
Emden (German cruiser), 295A
Emergency Relief Act, 314B
Emerson, Ralph Waldo, 253C, 255C, 265C
Eminent Victorians (Strachey), 303C
emission, stimulated, 301B
Emma (Austen), 243C
Emmanuel the Fortunate (king of Portugal), 148A
Emperor Jones, The (O'Neill), 305C, 309C
Emperor Jones (movie), 315C
Emperor Quartet (Haydn), 233C
Empire Day, 346B
Empire State Building, 313B, 334B, 384C
Empress of China (U.S. ship), 226B
Enchiridion Militis Christiani (Erasmus), 151C
Encyclopedia of Philosophy (Hegel), 243C
encyclopedias, 89B, 89C, *93*
  Americana, 249C
  Britannica, 221C
End of the World (Signorelli), 149C
Endau, 326C
Endeavor, 377B, 379B
Endecott, John, 187A
Endymion (Keats), 245C
Enforcement Act of 1871, 284B
Engels, Friedrich, 259C
engine(s)
  centrifugal governor steam, 227B
  gas turbine, 333B, 339B
  internal combustion, 265B
  jet, 321B
  kerosine, 287B
  programmable analytical, 253B
  Rolls Royce, 323B
  steam engine, 201B
  two-stroke, 271B
England, Church of, 159C, 201C
England, English, 54A, 57A, 64A, 72A, 96A, 113B, 121B, 153B, 168A, 171B, 171C. *See also* Britain
  2300 B.C.–700 B.C., 5A, 5C, 7A, 9A, 10B, 13A, 13B
  550 B.C.–54 B.C., 17A, 22C, 25A, 29A
  and Africa, 200B
  agriculture, 75B, 79C, 101B
  and Algeria, 168B
  and America, 169A, 171A, 181A, 185A, 187A, 202A, 203A, 209A, 211A, 214A
  Anglo-Spanish War, 209A
  arts, 71C, 83C, 93C, 99B, 99C, 115C, 123B, 123C, 133C, 147C, 177C, 185C, 195C, 197C, 199C, 201C, 203C, 209C, 211C
  and Australia, 202C
  and Bahamas, 189A
  and Bermuda, 199A
  and Canada, 205A
  Catuvellauni in, 32A
  censorship in, 161C
  and China, 186C, 206C
  and Danes, 90A, 92A, 96A
  Domesday Book, 96A
  education, 117C, 119C, 121C, 129C, 165C
  English Civil War, 186A
  exploration, 157A, 170C, 174C
  and Five Nations, 195A
  and France, 97C, 100A, 106A, 110A, 112A, 114A, 120A, 122A, 124A, 128A, 129B, 130A, 132A, 134A, 136A, 140A, 144A, 152A, 156A, 158A, 164B, 166A, 179A, 182B, 184A, 194A, 200A, 200B, 201A, 202A, 204A, 207A, 215A
  and Germany, 79C
  government, 78A, 80A, 82A, 84A, 88A, 102A, 111C, 192A
  and Holland, 182C, 190A, 192A, 194A, 198A, 200A, 206A, 206B
  and Holy Roman Empire, 154A
  and India, 109B, 173B, 178C, 182C, 184C, 186C, 190C, 192C, 198C, 200C, 214C
  industry, 109B, 113B, 115B, 123B, 161B, 165B, 183B
  and Ireland, 104A, 130A
  and Japan, 176C
  law and society, 92A, 158A, 163C, 164A, 200A, 211A
  and Madagascar, 188B
  and Morocco, 164B, 198B
  and Portugal, 178C, 190A, 192B, 192C, 193A, 206A, 208C
  rebellion in, 148A
  religion, 43A, 69C, 71C, 73C, 77C, 91C, 97C, 121C, 129C, 131C, 133C, 157C, 160A, 161C, 162A, 165C, 166A, 169C, 182A, 189C, 191C, 195C, 201C, 203C, 205C, 209C, 213C, 215C
  and Savoy, 206A
  and Scandinavia, 170A
  science and technology, 73B, 81B, 95B, 103B, 107B, 109B, 123B, 125B, 129B, 133B, 135B, 141B, 145B, 147B, 151B, 155B, 157B, 161B, 165B, 169B, 171B, 173B, 175B, 179C, 181B, 185B, 187B, 189B, 189C, 191B, 193B, 195B, 197B, 199B, 201B, 203B, 205B, 207B, 209B, 211B, 227B, 237B
  and Scotland, 126A, 138A, 142A, 146A, 162A, 166A, 186A, 187C, 188A
  slave trade, 158B, 166B, 167A, 169A, 172B, 194B, 204B, 212B
  soccer in, 111B
  and Spain, 116A, 128A, 145A, 154A, 156A, 158A, 166A, 172A, 174A, 176A, 184A, 192A, 204A, 206A, 208A, 210A, 212A, 213A
  and St. Kitts, 183A
  taxes, 90A, 187A, 234A
  and Turkey, 182B
  and Venezuela, 175A
  and Vikings, 76A
  and Wales, 86A, 109C, 118A, 160A
  and West Africa, 144B, 158B, 190B
Engleburg, 105B
English Bards and Scotch Reviewers (Byron), 239C
English Channel, 34A, 39B, 186A, 230A, 321B, 322A, 374B, 381B
English Channel tunnel, 381B
English Guinea Company, 194B
English Morris dance, 135C
English Patient, The (movie), 383C
English Restoration theatre, 203C
English Traits (Emerson), 265C
English West Africa Company, 180B
English West Indies, 195A
engraving, 179B
Enheduanna, 5C
Eniwetok, 332C, 340A
Enola Gay (U.S. plane), 334C
Enough Rope (Parker), 311C
Enryaku-ji, 168C
Entebbe, 362A
Enver Pasha, 295A
Enzio (king of Sardinia), 114B
Epaminondas, 20C
Ephesus, 17C, 32B, 59C
Epic of Gilgamesh (anon.), 5C
Epictetus, 41C
Epicureanism, 23C
Epicurus, 23C
Epidauros, Assembly at, 246A
Epigrams (Martial), 37C
Épinay, Louise Florence d', 221C
Epiphania, 91B
Epirus, 23A, 98B, 276A
Episcopal Church, 307C, 313C, 363C, 373C
Episcopalian House of Bishops, 307C
Epitaph for a Small Winner (Machado de Assis), 277C
Epitome Rerum Germanicarum (Wimpfeling), 151C
Epodes (Horace), 31C
Equal Rights Amendment (ERA), 358C, 366C
Eracle (d'Arras), 105C
Erasistratus, 25B
Erasmus, Desiderius, 149C, 151C, 153C, 157C, 161C
Eratosthenes, 25B
Ercker, Lazarus, 171B
Erebus (British ship), 256B
Eretria, 12C
Erewhom (Butler), 273C
Erfurt, 151C, 260A
  Congress of, 238A, 282A
Erhard, Ludwig (chancellor of Germany), 348B
Eric the Red, 89A, 91A
Eric XIV (king of Sweden), 168A
Ericsson, John, 267B
Ericsson, Leif, 91A
Erie Canal, 242B, 246B, *247*
Erik II Magnusson (king of Norway), 118A
Eritrea, 279A, 340A, 373A
Erivan, 176B, 184B, 208B, 210B, 249A

Erlau, 174A
Erlich, Henry, 373B
Ermland, 142A, 220A
Ernani (Verdi), 257C
Ershad, Hussain (president of Bangladesh), 371A
Erthogrul (sultan of Ottoman Empire), 112B, 120B
Erzberger, Mathias, 306A
Erzinjan, battles of, 114C, 142B
Esaki, Leo, 339B
Escobar, Pablo, 377A, 379A
Escobar y Mendoza, Antonio, 189C
Esfahan, 208B
Eskimo Pie, 307B
Eskimos, 5B, 17C, 50C, 91B, 127A, 307C. *See also* Inuit people
Eskişehir, 307A
Esonians, 77B
Esperanto, 281B
Espinel, Vicente Martínez de, 181C
Espionage Act, 300B, 306B
Espoir, L' (Malraux), 321C
Essai sur l'inégalité des races humaines (Gobineau), 263C
Essais (Montaigne), 171C
Essay Concerning Human Understanding, An (Locke), 201C
Essay on Man (Pope), 211C
Essays (Emerson), 255C
Essays inTheodicy on the Goodness of God, the Liberty of Man, and the Origin (Leibniz), 205C
Essays of Elia (Lamb), 247C
Essays on Government (Mill), 247C
Essays to Do Good (Mather), 205C
Essence of Christianity (Feuerbach), 255C
Essenes, 27C
Essequibo, 232C, 242C, 250C
Essex, 80A, 88A, 188A, 296A
Este, Borso d', 138B
Esterly, George, 265B
Estetica (Croce), 289C
Esther (Handel), 209C
Esthetics (Baumgarten), 215C
Estienne, Robert I, 165C
Estonia, 166A, 202A, 208A, 242A, 300A, 374B, 376A, 376B
  Bolsheviks in, 302A
  and London Convention (1933), 314A
  and Soviet Union, 324A, 372B
  World War II, 324A
Estrada Palma, Tomás (president of Cuba), 288C, 290C
Étaples, Peace of, 146A, 148A
Ethan Frome (Wharton), 293C
Ethelbald (king of Mercia), 72A, 74A
Ethelbald of Wessex, 80A
Ethelbert (king of England), 64A, 80A
Ethelfrith (king of Bernicia), 66A
Ethelred I (king of England), 80A
Ethelred II (king of England), 88A, 90A
Ethelwulf (king of England), 78A, 80A
Etherege, George, 193C, 197C
Ethica Ordine Geometrico Demonstrata (Spinoza), 195C
Ethics (Baumgarten), 213C
Ethiopia, Ethiopians, 34B, 45A, 52B, 54B, 110C, 166B, 316A 340A, 373A. *See also* Abyssinia, Abyssinians
  264 B.C.–25 B.C., 24A, 30B
  and Adal, 158B
  arts, 47C
  and Britain, 269A, 271A
  Communism in, 369A
  decline of, 204B
  and Egypt, 273A
  famine in, 369A
  government, 128C, 132C, 142B, 148B, 152B, 160B, 170B, 174B, 176B, 184B, 186B, 196B, 255A, 273A, 299A, 361A
  infrastructure, 289A
  and Israel, 377A
  and Italy, 281A, 287A
  and Portugal, 162B
  religion, 55A, 156B, 164B
  science and technology, 141B
  Second Ethiopian War, 212B
  slave trade, 313A
  and Sudan, 180B
Etowa culture, 135A
Etruria, kingdom of, 234A
Etruscans, 11A, 12C, 13A, 13C, 15C, 16C, 25A
  arch devised by, 15B
  Etruscan Caere, 21A
  and Greece, 15A
  and Rome, 17A
Euboea, 12C
Eucharist, 117C
Euclid, 23B, 75C
Eudoxus, 21B
Eugene Aram (Bulwer-Lytton), 251C
Eugene (prince of Savoy), 202A, 204A, 206A
Eugenius, 56A, 57A
Eugenius III, Pope, 103C, 104B
Eugenius IV, Pope, 137C
Eupalinus of Megara, 17B
Euphrates River, 2B, 5B, 38A, 83B, 84B, 116B
Euratom, 350B
Euric, 60B
Euripides, *19,* 19C, 21C
Europe, Europeans, 6B, 54A, 60A, 74A, 78A, 83B, 149B, 177B. *See also individual countries*
  3000 B.C.–400 B.C., 3A, 13A
  agriculture, 59B, 67B, 75B, 127B, 139B
  and America, 153B, 181A
  and Arabs, 87C
  and Argentina, 151A
  and Chernobyl disaster, 370B
  and China, 116C, 156C, 207C
  cholera in, 151B
  economy, 358B, 364B
  and India, 173B, 212C
  and Indian Ocean, 146B
  industry, 59C, 65B, 77B, 119B, 123B, 135B, 171B
  and Japan, 180C, 186C
  medicine, 141C, 179B
  and Mongolia, 113B
  and North Africa, 202B, 210B
  plague in, 64B, 70A, 74B, 128A
  science and technology, 63B, 73B, 77B, 91B, 99B, 107B, 109B, 115B, 121B, 123B, 125B, 129B, 131B, 137B, 141B, 145B, 151B, 165B, 169B, 171B, 209B, 369B
  Seven Years' War, 216A, 217A, 218A, 219A
  slave trade, 136C, *189,* 204B
  space program, 369B
  and Turkey, 128B
  typhus in, 146A
  and United States, 368A
  and West Africa, 136C
European 3, 369B
European Bank for Reconstruction and Development, 376A
European Coal and Steel Community, 340B
European Coal and Steel Treaty, 338A
European Community (EC), 338A, 362B, 366B, 368A
  and Greenland, 368B
  and Libya, 370A
  Portugal in, 370B
  a single currency, 376B
  and South Africa, 370A
  Spain in, 370B
  unified currency, 374B
European Convention on Human Rights, 342B
European Court of Human Rights, 346B, 362B
European Defense Community, 340A, 342A
European Economic Community (EEC), 344A, 348A, 350B, 352A, 352B, 360B
  treaty, 358B
European Free Trade Association (EFTA), 346A, 352B, 362B
European Monetary Agreement, 344A
European Nuclear Energy Agency, 352B
European Parliament, 364B
European Payments Union, 344A
European Political Community, 340A
European Trade Union Confederation, 358B
European Union, 336B
Eusebius of Caesarea, 51A, 53C
Eusebius of Nicomedia, 53A
euthanasia, 381C
Evangelical Church, 345C
Evangeline (Longfellow), 259C
Evans, George, 241A
Evans, Oliver, 229B
Evans, Ron, *359*
Eve, Joseph, 227B
Evelyn, John, 193C
Ever Pasha, 297A
Everlasting Mercy, The (Masefield), 293C
Evers, Medgar, 348C
Every Man in His Humour (Jonson), 175C
Evesham, battle of, 116A
evolution theory, 308B
Evoramonte, 252A
Ewald, Johannes, 221C
Ex Semine Abrahae, 99C
Exchange, Treaty of, 222A
exchange rate system, floating, 358A
Excursion (Wordsworth), 241C
Executioner's Song, The (Mailer), 365C
Exeter, 34A, 187A
Exit qui seminat (papal bull), 121C
Experience and Poetry (Dilthey), 291C
Explorer, 345B
explosives, 102C, 105B, 109B, 115B, 137B
  bombs, 93B, 95B
  flamethrowers, 91B, 295B
  Greek "fire missiles," 70B, 83B
  grenades, 91B, 101B, 123B, 151B
  mustard gas, 301B
  TNT, 331B
  torpedoes, 331B
Expo '67, 352C
Expropriation Act, 318C
extermination camps, 326A
Exultations (Pound), 293C
Exxon Corporation, 370C, 376C
Exxon Valdez (U.S. oil tanker), 372C, 374C, 376C
Eyck, Jan van, 137C
eye(s). *See also* contact lenses
  artificial, 171B
  banks, 333B
  cataracts, 215B
  cornea transplant, 291B
  glasses, 129B, 139B
Eylau, battle of, 236A
Eynsham, 89C
Eyre, Edward, 255A
Ezra the Scribe, *18,* 18B

F

Faber, John, 267B
Faber, Kasper, 217B
Fabian, Pope, 45A, 47A
Fabian Essays (Shaw), 281C
Fabius Pictor, Quintus, 25C
Fable, A (Faulkner), 343C
Fable of the Bees (Mandeville), 203C
Fables (La Fontaine), 195C
fabric protector, 343B
Fabricius, Hieronymus, 171B, 177B
Fabritius, Carel, 191C
factories, 206B, 206C
Factory Acts, 256A, 274A
Factory and Workshop Act, 276A
Faerie Queene (Spenser), 173C
Faget, Maxine, 357B
Fahd (king of Saudi Arabia), 367A
Fahrenheit, Gabriel Daniel, 207B, 213B
Fair at Impruneta (Callot), 181C
Fair Deal, 334B
Fair Employment Practices Committee, 326B, 330B
Fair Labor Standards Act, 324B
Fair Oaks, battle of, 266B
Fairbanks, Douglas, 305C
Fairfax, Sir Thomas, 188A
Fairy Queen, The (Purcell), 201C
Fairy Tales (Grimm), 241C
Faisal I (king of Iraq), 315A
Faisal I (king of Syria), 305A
Faisal II (king of Iraq), 321A, 345A
Faisal (king of Saudi Arabia), 351A, 361A
Fakariya, 192B
falconry, *113*
Falieri, Marino, 128B
Falkirk, battle of, 120A, 214A
Falkland Islands, 219A, 221A, 250C, 362A, 366A
Falköping, battle of, 132A
Fall, Albert, 308B
Fall of Robespierre (Coleridge), 231C
Fallen Timbers, battle of, 230B
Falmouth, 201A
"False Start" (Johns), 373C
false teeth, 67B
fan, 73B, 141B
  electric, 279B, 291B
  window, 317B
Fan, The (Goldoni), 219C
Fancy Free (Robbins and Bernstein), 333C
Fanning Island, 233A
Fante, 257A
Farewell, My Lovely (Chandler), 323C
Farid, Umar ibn, al- 109C, 113C
Farima (king of Loko), 166B
farm machinery
  bale press, 345B
  Caterpillar tractor, 289B
  combine harvesters, 249B, 307B, 317B, 361B
  combine harvesting brigades, 333B
  corn reaper, 249B
  Dempster-Dumpster, 311B
  horse-drawn grain reaper, 253B
  mechanical reaper, 251B
  milking machines, 291B
  row cultivator, 265B
  tedder, 245B
  tractor, 319B
Farman, Henri, 291B
Farnese, Alessandro of Parma (governor of the Netherlands), 170A, 172A, 174A

Farnese, Isabella (queen of Spain), 206A
Farnsworth, Philo T., 307B
Faroe Islands, 76A
Farouk (king of Egypt), 319A, 341A
Farquhar, George, 203C
Farragut, David, 266B
Farrell, Edelmiro (president of Argentina), 333A
Farrell, James T., 315C
Fars province, 87B
Fascio di Combattimento, 302A
Fascism, Fascists, 302A, 306A, 308A, 310A, 325A
Fashoda, 287A
Fasilados (emperor of Ethiopia), 184B
Fast, Howard, 327C, 331C, 333C
fat rationing, 330B, 334B
Fates of the Apostles (Cynewulf), 75C
Fath Ali (shah of Persia), 233A
Father, The (Strindberg), 281C
Fathers and Sons (Turgenev), 267C
fatigue, physical, 345B
Fatimids, 82B, 84B, 86B,
Faubus, Orval, 344C
Fauchard, Pierre, 211B
Faulkner, Brian (prime minister of Northern Ireland), 356B
Faulkner, Shannon, 382C
Faulkner, William, 307C, 319C, 323C, 327C, 339C, 343C, 349C
Faulkner culture, 65A
Faure, Félix (president of France), 284A
Fauset, Crystal Bird, 320B
Faust (Goethe), 239C,
Faust (Gounod), 265C
Fausta, *51,* 52A
Favalaro, Rene, 353B
Favola d'Orfeo, La (Monteverdi), 179C
Favrile glass, 283C
fax (facsimile) machine, 369B
Fayette, 249C
"Feast of Love," 41A
Federal Bank Deposit Insurance Corporation, 314B
Federal Bureau of Investigation (FBI), 328B, 358C, 360C
Federal Communications Commission, 316B, 323B
Federal Farm Board, 310B
Federal Farm Loan Bank Act, 298B
Federal Home Loan Bank Act, 314B
Federal Loan Administration, 326B
Federal Power Commission, 326B
Federal Republic of Germany. *See* West Germany
Federal Republic of the United Provinces. *See* Holland, Dutch
Federal Reserve Board, 310B, 364C
Federal Reserve System, 294B
Federal Road Aid Act, 298B
Federal Trade Commission, 294B, 350C
Federalism, Federalists, 230B
Federalist Papers, The, 226B
Fehrbellin, battle of, 194A
Felitsa (Derzhavin), 225C
Felix Holt (Eliot), 271C
Felix V, 139C
Fellini, Federico, 347C
Felton, Rebecca Latimer, 306B
Fender, Leo, 343B
Fender Stratocaster, 343B
Fénelon, François, 203C
Fenian Ram (submarine), 277B
"Fenians," 270B
Ferber, Edna, 325C, 345C, 355C
Ferdinand I (emperor of Austria), 252A, 258A
Ferdinand I (Holy Roman Emperor and king of Bohemia and Hungary), 156A, 158A, 160A, 162A, 164A, 166A
Ferdinand I (king of Aragon), 134B
Ferdinand I (king of Castile), 92B
Ferdinand I (king of Naples), 246A
Ferdinand I (king Two Sicilies), 242A, 244A, 246A
Ferdinand II (Holy Roman Emperor and king of Bohemia and Hungary), 180A, 184A, 186A
Ferdinand II (king of Aragon), 142A, *143,* 144A, 145C, 150A, 154A
Ferdinand II (king of Two Sicilies), 264A
Ferdinand III (Holy Roman Emperor), 186A
Ferdinand III (king of Castile and León), 110B, 112A, 112B, 114B
Ferdinand IV (king of Castile and Léon), 120B
Ferdinand IV (Naples), 232A, 242A, 246A
Ferdinand VI (king of Spain), 214A, 216A
Ferdinand VII (king of Spain), 240A, 250A
Ferdinand (king of Bulgaria), 284A
Ferghana, kingdom of, 148C, 156C
Ferguson, Harry, 319B
Ferguson, Miriam "Ma," 308B
Fermi, Enrico, 317B, 329B
Fernel, Jean, 165B
Ferrara, 175C, 264A
Peace of, 136B
University of, 133C
Ferraro, Geraldine, 368C
Ferris, George, 283B
Ferris wheel, 283B
fertility tests, 9B
fertilization. *See also* reproductive system
artificial insemination, 125B
of date palms, 175B
of fish eggs, 137B
in-vitro (IVF), 317B, 355B
fertilizers, 165B
superphosphate, 255B
synthetic, 339B
Fessenden, Reginald, 289B, 291B
Festus, 35A
Fêtes galantes (Verlaine), 273C
Feuerbach, Ludwig, 255C
Fez, 136B, 164B
fiber optics, 353B
Fiber V, 337B
fiberglass, 253B, 321B
Fichte, Johann Gottlieb, 231C
Fick, Adolf, 281B
Fiddler on the Roof (Harnick and Bock), 351C
Fidelio (Beethoven), 237C
Field, Sally, 365C
Fielding, Henry, 215C, 349C
Fiesco (Schiller), 225C
Fiesole, 58B
Fifth of May, The (Manzoni), 245C
Fifth Symphony (Beethoven), 239C
Fighting Téméraire, The (Turner), 255C
Fiji, 275A, 356A, 357A, 371A
Filaret (Bishop of Moscow), 271C
Fille du Pharaon, La (Petipa), 267C
Fille Mal Gardée, La (Dauberval), 227C, 279C
Fillmore, Millard (president of U.S.), 260B
film. *See* movie(s)
Filosofia della spirito, Vol. I (Croce), 289C
Financier, The (Dreiser), 289C
Finding of the Body of St. Mark, The (Tintoretto), 167C
Fine, Oronce, 165B
fingerprints, fingerprinting, 247B, 283B, 373B
Finland, 164A, 212A, 228A, 236A, 238A, 292A, 384B
and Germany, 302A
government, 366B
politics, 370B
and Soviet Union, 316A, 322A, 332A, 342B, 356B
suffrage in, 288A
Finland Station, 300A
Finlandia (Sibelius), 287C
Finnbogadóttir, Vigdis (president of Iceland), 364B
Finnegans Wake (Joyce), 323C
Finschafen, 330C
fire
drill, 3B
engine, 155B, 263B
fighting equipment, 249B, 291B
safety, 111B, 121B
firearms. *See* guns
Firebird, The (Stravinsky), 293C
first aid, 185B
First Symphony (Beethoven), 235C
First Symphony (Prokofiev), 301C
Firth of Forth, 36A, 40A, 281B
Firuz (king of Persia), 60C
Firuz Shah Tughluq (sultan of Delhi), 128C, 130C
Fischer, Kuno, 263C
Fish, 327B, 331B
fish, fishing, 137B, 153B
"Cod War," 358B, 362B
fertilization of eggs, 137B
fish farming, 31B, 35B
fish-freezing plant, 267B
by Japan, 377B
in Newfoundland, 165A
North Pacific halibut fisheries, 306B
U.S.-Canadian Reciprocal Fishing Treaty, 262B
Fisher (Bishop of Rochester), 161C
Fisher culture, 123A
Fisk, James, 272B
Fitzgerald, F. Scott, 307C, 309C, 325C
Fitzgerald, Gerald (leader of Ireland), 144A
Fiume, 304A, 308A
Five Nations, 195A
Fizeau, Armand, 257B
Flagellants, 117C, 129C
Flaget, Benedict, 239C
Flagstad, Kirsten, 295C, 317C
Flagstaff, 103A
Flaherty, Robert, 307C
Flamininus, Titus Quinctius, 24C
Flamsteed, John, 225B
Flanders, Flemish, 87B, 96A, 100A, 123B, 123C, 126A, 133B, 137B, 142A, 146A, 148A, 151B, 165B, 169B, 169C, 172A, 180A, 187C, 191C, 192A, 194A, 201C
Flaubert, Gustave, 265C, 267C
flax, 123B, 129B
Flaxman, John, 249C
Fleming, John, 289B
Flemish, 122A, 130A, 133A
Fletcher, John, 181C
Fletcher, Louise, 361C
Fletcher v. Peck, 238B
Fleurs du mal, Les (Baudelaire), 265C
Fliegende Hollander, Der (Wagner), 257C
Flinders, Matthew, 233A, 235A
flint, 5B
Flodden, battle of, 152A
Floral Park, 46C
Florence, 100B, 106B, 115B, 116B, 119C, 121C, 122B, 127C, 129B, 131B, 134B, 136B, 137C, 139C, 142A, 143C, 148A, 149C, 152A, 155C, 156A, 158A, 268A, 378B
Florence, University of, 125C
Florentine Histories (Machiavelli), 157C
Flores, Juan José (president of Ecuador), 248C, 254C
Florey, Howard, 325B
Florian Geyer (Hauptmann), 285C
Florida, 83A, 85A, 99A, 135A, 153A, 157A, 159A, 161A, 167A, 169A, 203A, 209A, 219A, 224B, 242B, 244B, 252B, 256B, 280B, 308B, 310B, 328B, 378C, 2313A
East Coast Railroad, 292B
Seminole, Seminole Wars, 242B, 244B, 250B, 252B, 256B
Florida Marlins, 385C
Florus, 36B
Flowering Judas and Other Stories (Porter), 313C
fluoride, fluoridation, 313B, 325B, 335B, 343B
Flushing, 336A
Flying Cloud (clipper ship), 260B
Flying Down to Rio (movie), 315C
Flying Dutchman, The (Wagner), 257C
Foggia, battle of, 116B
Foix, 118B
Fokine, Michel, 291C
Fokker, Herman, 295A
Folies Bergère, 309C
Folly or Holiness (Echegaray), 275C
Folsom, 265B
Fonda, Henry, 367C
Fonda, Jane, 357C, 363C
Fondi, 133C
Fonseca, Manuel Deodora da (president of Brazil), 280C, 282C
Fontainebleau
Peace of (1679), 196A
Treaty of (1785), 226A
Fontana, Domenico, 173C
Fontana, Giovanni di, 137B
Fontane, Theodor, 277C
Fontenoy, battle of, 78A
Fonteyn, Dame Margot, 317C, 349C
Foochow, 279A, 332C
food
cooling unit for perishable, 323B
freeze-dried, 337B
frozen, 299B, 343B
packaging, 245B, 367B
Food and Drug Administration (FDA), 367B
"Foolish War," 146A
football
American Football League (AFL), 353C
intercollegiate, 247C, 273C. *See also individual teams*
National Football League (NFL), 323C, 327C, 329C, 331C, 333C, 335C, 353C
For Whom the Bell Tolls (Hemingway), 323C
Force Act, 250B
Ford, Ford Madox, 297C
Ford, Gerald R. (president of U.S.), 358C, 360A, 360C, 362C
Ford, Henry, 285B, 290B
Ford, John, 321C, 323C, 325C
Ford (Kans.), 163A
Ford Motor Company, 308B, 337B, 346C
Fordham University, 255C
Forest Preserve Act, 282B
Forever Amber (Winsor), 333C
forge, 73B, 99B, 107B
Forman, Milos, 361C, 369C
Formosa, 182C, 184C, 186C, 192C, 198C, 208C, 227A, 285A, 330C, 332C, 339A, 342A

Forrest Gump (movie), 381C
Forrestal, James V., 336C
Forrester, Jay, 333B, 339B, 341B
Forssmann, Werner, 311B
Forster, E. M., 291C, 309C
Fortas, Abe, 356C
forts
  Albany, 201A
  Ancient culture, 135A
  Brooke, 252B
  Caroline, 167A
  Casimir, 191A
  Charlotte, 226C
  Chipewyan, 228B
  Crèvecoeur, 197A
  Dauphin, 186B
  Dearborn, 240B
  Detroit, 219A
  Douglas, 242B
  Drummer, 209A
  Duquesne, 215A, 217A
  Erie, 240B, 270B
  Fincastle, 230C
  Garry, 272B
  George, 236B
  Good Hope, 185A
  Hall, 252B
  James, 190B
  Jesus, 174B
  King, 252B
  Langley, 248B
  Laramie, 252B, 270B
  McHenry, 240B
  Miami, 203A
  Mims, 240B
  Niagara, 199A, 209A, 217A
  Ontario, 209A
  Orange, 186B
  Oswego, 209A
  Pitt, 217A
  Prudhomme, 197A
  St. James, 236B
  Sumter, 266B, *267*
  Ticonderoga, 222B
  Vancouver, 246B
  Victoria, 256B
  Vreedenburg, 198B
  William, 194C, 200C
  Worth, 317B
  York, 244B
Forty-Five Minutes from Broadway (Cohan), 291C
42nd Parallel, The (Dos Passos), 321C
42 Articles of Faith, 165C
Forum, 39C
Fosdick, Harry Emerson, 291C
Fosse Way, 34A
fossils, 97B
Foster, Jodie, 373C, 377C
Foster, Stephen, 259C
Foster, Vincent, 378C
Fotheringhay, 172A
Foucault, Jean, 257B, 263B
Foudrinier process, 243B
Fougères, 138A
Fountain of the Four Rivers (Bernini), 189C
Fountain Overflows, The (West), 345C
Fountainhead, The (Rand), 331C
Fouqué, Friedrich, 239C
Four Apostles, The (Dürer), 157C
Four Evangelists, The (Holguín), 209C
Four Heavenly Kings, Temple of the, 67C
Four-Power Pacific Treaty, 306B
Four Quartets (Eliot), 331C
Fourah Bay College, 249A
Fourier, Charles, 221C
Fourteen Points, 302B
Fox, 246B, 248B, 250B
Foyn, Svend, 271B
Fraga, battle of, 100B
France, Anatole, 277C, 281C
France, French, 7C, 31C, 33C, 35B, 99B, 138A, 146A, 165B, 185B, 203A, 254A, 300B, 381C. *See also* Franks; Gaul; *individual cities*
  Academy of Science, 229B
  and Acadia, 185A
  agriculture, 139B
  Albigensian Crusade in, 110B
  and Algeria, 166B, 249A, 253A, 257A, 259A, 343A, 349A, 351A
  and America, 205A, 209A
  and American Indians, 159A, 181A, 191A, 211A
  and Andorra, 118B
  and Annam, 227A, 235A, 275A, 279A
  and Arabs, 74A, 82B, 88B
  arts, 83C, 99B, 101C, 109C, 117C, 141C, 143C, 159C, 181C, 185C, 187C, 193C, 195C, 211C, 215C, 229C, 231C, 237C, 243C, 245C, 247C, 249C, 251C, 257C, 259C, 263C, 265C, 267C, 269C, 273C, 275C, 277C, 281C, 285C, 287C, 289C, 295C, 299C, 307C, 309C, 313C, 315C, 321C, 331C, 335C, 347C, 381C
  Assembly of Clergy, 197C
  Assembly of Notables, 226A
  on atomic weapons, 356A
  and Australia, 220C
  and Austria, 188A, 194A, 212A, 214A, 216A, 234A, 264A, 272A, 294A, 312A
  Bank of France, 234A
  and Belgium, 308A, 318A, 336A
  and Benin, 261A
  and Berbers, 251A
  and Berlin, 346A
  and Brazil, 165A
  and Britain, 100A, 104A, 106A, 108A, 110A, 112A, 114A, 120A, 122A, 124A, 128A, 129B, 130A, 132A, 134A, 136A, 140A, 144A, 146A, 156A, 158A, 164A, 166A, 179A, 182A, 184A, 190A, 194A, 200A, 200B, 201A, 204A, 206A, 207A, 215A, 216A, 224A, 226A, 230B, 236A, 238B, 248A, 250A, 262A, 279A, 288A, 294A, 298A, 300A, 302A, 306B, 307A, 308A, 314A, 324A, 328A, 336A, 340A, 348A, 348B, 352B, 357B, 374B, 376A, 381B
  and Cambodia, 269A
  and Canada, 155A, 199A, 328A
  Capetian dynasty, 126A
  and Chad, 287A, 295A
  and China, 200C, 265A, 267A, 279A, 338A
  Civil Code, 236A
  Civil Constitution of Clergy, 229C
  and Cochin China, 271A
  Communism in, 336B
  and Comoros, 281A, 361A
  and Congo, 261A
  conscription in, 272A
  and Corsica, 220A, 366B
  Crimean War, 262A
  and Czechoslovakia, 308A, 320A
  and Dahomey, 285A
  on death penalty, 366B
  and Denmark, 248A, 260A
  and East Africa, 317A
  economy, 230A
  education, 113C, 121C, 123B, 123C, 137C, 167C, 234A
  and Egypt, 114B, 233A, 343A
  Estates General, 122A, 172A, 180A, 220A, 226A, 228A
  on European Defense Community, 342A
  and European Economic Community, 350B, 352A
  exploration, 159A, 195A
  Franco-German War, 272A
  Franco-Italian Treaty, 268A
  Franco-Moroccan War, 257A
  Franco-Prussian Treaty, 236A
  Franco-Spanish War, 169A
  French and Indian War, 215A, 217A, 219A
  French Concordat, 235C
  French Revolution, 228A, 229C
  French Revolutionary War, 234B
  in G-7, 368A
  and Genoa, 134B, 152A
  and Germany, 80A, 88A, 136A, 156A, 218A, 274A, 285A, 293A, 294A, 296A, 298A, 300A, 302A, 304A, 306A, 308A, 312A, 320A, 322A, 324A, 332A
  government, 82A, 86A, 118A, *133,* 166A, 208A, 230A, 258A, 260A, 262A, 270A, 272A, 274A, 276A, 278A, 304A, 308A, 310A, 318A, 332A, 336B, 344B, 366B
  and Greenpeace, 368A
  and Grenada, 189A, 224C
  and Guadeloupe, 230C
  and Guinea, 285A, 344A
  and Haiti, 246C
  and Hawaiian Islands, 257A, 261A
  and Holland, 194A, 196A, 196B, 200A, 204B, 206A
  and Holy Roman Empire, 146A, 154A, 186A, 198A, 200A
  Huguenots, 166A, 168A, 170A, 174A, 175C, 180A
  and India, 194C, 214C, 216C, 217A, 231A, 343A
  and Indochina, 265A, 281A
  industry, 125B, 151B, 155B, 237B, 250A, 289B
  and International Monetary Fund, 348A
  and Iran, 321A
  and Iraq, 378A
  and Italy, 43B, 148A, 154A, 158A, 202A, 260A, 264A, 268A, 270A, 272A, 286A, 308A, 317A, 320A, 321A
  and Ivory Coast, 281A, 285A
  and Japan, 269A, 271A, 306B
  and Kurds, 376A
  and Laos, 283A, 339A
  law and society, 171C, 180A, 190A, 228A, 229C, 240A, 254A, 260A, 270A, 274A, 278A, 290A, 354B
  and Lebanon, 367A
  and Loyalty Islands, 269A
  and Luxembourg, 198A, 336A
  and Madagascar, 176B, 194B, 198B, 202B, 243A, 247A, 257A, 267A, 269A, 271A, 279A, 285A
  and Mali, 285A
  and Marquesas Islands, 257A
  and Mecca, 301A
  medicine, 119B, 161B, 163B, 165B, 167A, 169B, 171B, 173B, 211B, 215B, 255B, 289B, 317B
  and Mexico, 254A, 266C, 268C, 270C
  Moors in, 72B
  and Morocco, 257A, 290A, 293A, 309A, 343A, 345A
  Napoleonic Wars, 232A, 234A, 235A, 236A, 238A, 240A, 242A
  National Assembly, 228A, 229C, 230A, 338B
  National Convention, 230A
  and NATO, 352A
  and Nazis, 370A
  and Netherlands, 164A, 336A
  and Newfoundland, 151A, 153B
  and Niger, 279A
  and Nigeria, 283A
  and Northwest Africa, 208B
  and Nova Scotia, 177A
  on nuclear pollution, 370A
  and nuclear weapons, 346B, 382A
  and Obok, 267A
  and Ottoman Empire, 160A
  in Pacific, 220C
  and Panama Canal, 276C, 280A
  and Poland, 306A, 308A, 320A, 322A
  politics, 274A, 338B, 354B, 366B
  population, 176A
  and Portugal, 167B, 169A, 206A, 212B, 236C
  postal service, 142A
  and Pragmatic Sanction, 210A
  and Prussia, 232A, 240A, 266A, 272A
  in Quadruple Alliance, 252A
  Quasi War, 232B
  religion, 55A, 85C, 89C, 103C, 107C, 111C, 133C, 139C, 163C, 166A, 167C, 197C, 201C, 203C, 217C, 283C, 289C
  and Réunion, 186B
  revolutions, 130A, 248A, 258A
  and Russia, 248A, 260A, 262A, 282A, 294A, 306A
  and Sardinia, 266A
  and Savoy, 206A, 242A, 266A
  science and technology, 87B, 101B, 107B, 109B, 115B, 119B, 127B, 137B, 165B, 169B, 179B, 189B, 193B, 197B, 199B, 201B, 207B, 221B, 233B, 235B, 237B, 239B, 241B, 245B, 249B, 251B, 257B, 263A, 265B, 267B, 271B, 273B, 275B, 277B, 281B, 285B, 287B, 289B, 291B, 297B, 301B, 327B, 335B, 341B, 357B, 365B, 381B, 385B
  and Senegal, 192B, 225A, 281A, 285A
  settlement of, 58A
  Seven Years' War, 219A
  and Seychelles, 216B, 220B
  and Siam, 190C, 198C, 283A
  slave trade, 243A
  and Society Islands, 257A
  and Soviet Union, 316A
  and Spain, 130B, 150A, 154A, 156A, 174A, 192A, 200A, 238A, 246A, 264A, 307A
  and Spanish Netherlands, 190A
  and St. Kitts, 183A
  and St. Lucia, 193A, 232C, 240C
  and Strasbourg, 196A
  and Sudan, 302A
  and Sumatra, 158C
  and Switzerland, 242A, 282A
  and Syria, 305A, 307A, 309A, 319A
  and Tahiti, 257A

and Togoland, 295A
transportation, 107B, 143B
and Treaty of Rome, 344A
and Trinidad, 197A
and Tunis, 277A, 285A
and Tunisia, 305A, 343A
and Turkey, 160A, 232A, 264A, 294A, 297A, 303A, 321A
and United States, 224B, 232B, 234B, 236B, 288B, 296B, 300A, 302A, 306B, 338A, 340A, 346A, 348B, 352B, 356A, 376A
and Upper Volta, 285A
and Vichy government, 324A, 326A, 328A
and Vietnam, 337A, 339A, 343A
War of Breton Succession, 126A
and West Germany, 340A, 348A
and West Indies, 238C
in Western European Union, 342A
World War I, 294A, 296A, 298A, 300A
World War II, 322A, 324A, 328A, 332A
Franche-Comté, 144A, 194A
Francis, Joseph, 259B
Francis I (Holy Roman Emperor), 212A, 218A
Francis I (emperor of Austria), 236A
Francis I (king of France), 154A, 156A, 158A, 160A, 162A
Francis I (king of Naples), 246A
Francis II (king of France), 166A
Francis II (king of Two Sicilies), 264A
Francis II (Holy Roman Emperor and emperor of Austria), 236A, 252A
Francis Ferdinand (archduke of Austria), 294A
Francis Joseph (emperor of Austria and king of Hungary), 258A, 264A
Francis of Assisi, Saint, 107C, 111C, 113C
Francis of Taxis, 150A
Francis Stephen (duke of Tuscany), 212A
Franciscans, 125C
Francke, August Hermann, 201C
Francke Endowments, 201C
Francken, Frans, *14*
Franco, Francisco (dictator of Spain), 318A, 320A, 360B, 362B
François, Donatien Alphonse, 229C
François-Marie Arouet, 207C
Franconia, 84A
Frank, Jakob, 215C
Frankenstein (movie), 313C
Frankenstein (Shelley), 245C
Frankford, 243B
Frankfurt-am-Main, 135B, 216A, 252A, 268A, 270A
Treaty of (1871), 272A
Truce of (1539), 160A
Frankfurt-on-the-Oder University, 151C
Franklin, Benjamin, *211,* 213B, 215A, 215B, 217B, 222B, 259B
Franklin, Rosalind, 327B
Franklin, Sir John, 244B, 256B
Franks, 46A, 48A, 50A, 54A, 58A, 60A, 62A, 62B, 64A, 68A, *69,* 70A, 74A, 76A. *See also* France; Gaul
Franz Sternblads Wanderungen (Tieck), 233C
Fraser, Malcolm (prime minister of Australia), 365A
Fraser, Simon, 236B
Fraser River, 248B
Fraser's Magazine, 251C
Frau ohne Schatten, Die (Strauss), 295C
Fraunces Tavern, 224B
Fraustadt, battle of, 204A
Frederick I Barbarossa (Holy Roman Emperor and king of Germany), 102A, 104A, 104B, 106A, 106B, 107C
Frederick I (king of Prussia), 202A, 206A
Frederick I of Hesse-Cassel (king of Sweden), 208A
Frederick II (Holy Roman Emperor and king of Sicily, Germany, Jerusalem), 108B, 110A, 110B, 112A, 112B, 113C, 114A, 114B,
Frederick II (king of Denmark), 166A
Frederick II (king of Prussia), 212A, 214A, 216A, 226A
Frederick II (king of Sicily), 120B
Frederick II of Brandenburg, 138A, 138B
Frederick III (elector of Brandenburg), 198A, 202A
Frederick III (emperor of Germany), 280A
Frederick III (king of Germany and Holy Roman Emperor), 138A, 139C, 140A, 146A
Frederick III (king of Sicily), 132B
Frederick IV (king of Denmark), 210A
Frederick IV (king of Germany and Holy Roman emperor), 138A
Frederick IV of Naples, 232A
Frederick V (elector of the Palatinate and king of Bohemia), 178A, 180A
Frederick IX (king of Denmark), 336B, 358B
Frederick (crown prince of Prussia), 210A
Frederick Henry (stadtholder of the Netherlands), 188A
Frederick of Austria (king of Germany), 124A, 126A
Frederick the Great (Carlyle), 265C
Frederick William (elector of Brandenburg), 194A, 198A
Frederick William I (king of Prussia), 206A, 212A
Frederick William II (king of Prussia), 226A, 232A
Frederick William III (king of Prussia), 232A, 254A
Frederick William IV (king of Prussia), 254A, 260A, 266A
Frederikshall, 206A
Frederikshamn, Peace of, 238A
Free African Society, 226B
Freedmen's Bureau, 270B
Freedom (Crawford), 267C
Freedom Rides, 336C, 346C
Freedom Road (Fast), 333C
Freetown, 239A
freeway, 325B
Freiburg, 103B, 196A
battle of, 188A
Freischütz (Weber), 245C
Frémont, John, 256B
French, Daniel Chester, 297C
French Congo, 285A
French Connection, The (movie), 357C
French East India Company, 192A, 210B
French Guiana, 195A, 232C, 262C, 284A
French League, 174A
French Lieutenant's Woman, The (Reisz), 367C
French Mississippi Company, 199A
French Revolution (Carlyle), 253C
French Sign Language (FSL), 215B
French Togoland, 347A
French Union, 337A, 339A, 344A
French West Africa, 285A
French West India Company, 193A
French West Indies, 211A
freon, 313B
Fréteval, 108A
Freud, Sigmund, 307B, 309B
Freycinet, Claude de, 245A
Freydis, 91A
Freysinet, Eugene, 311B
Frick, Henry Clay, *282*
Frick, Wilhelm, 312A
Friedrich, Caspar David, 221C
Friedrich, Karl Eitel, 270A
Friedkin, William, 357C
Friendly Persuasion, The (West), 335C
Frisbee, 345B
Frisia, Frisians, 116A, 128A
Frisius, Gemma, 159B
Friuli, 136B
Frobisher, Martin, 171A
Frobisher Bay, 171A
From Hegel to Marx (Hook), 319C
From Here to Eternity (movie), 341C
From the New World (Dvorák), 283C
Frondizi, Arturo (president of Argentina), 345A, 349A
Frontenac, Louis de Buade (governor of Canda), 195A
Frontenac culture, 50C
Frontinus, Sextius Julius, 39C
Fronto, Marcus Cornelius, 43C
Frost, Robert, 295C, 299C, 319C, 331C, 335C
Froude, James, 265C
frozen dinners, 335B, 343B
Fruit Garden, The (Saadi), 117C
fruit tree cultivation, 59B
Fu-k'ang-an, 231A
Fuad I (king of Egypt), 307A, 313A, 319A
Fuad II (king of Egypt), 341A
Fuca, Juan de, 175A
fuel
cells, 255B
from wood, 235B
Fuentes d'Oñoro, battle of, 238A
Fugard, Athol, 357C
Fugger, 159A
Fugitive Slave Act, 230B, 256B, 260B, 264B
Fujimori, Alberto (president of Peru), 375A, 377A
Fujiwara family. *See* Japan
Fulah dynasty. *See* Nigeria
Fulakora, 214B
Fulani, 220B, 223A
Fulbright Resolution, 330B
Fulda, 75C, 77C, 171C
Fulda River, 205B
Fuliana (Cynewulf), 75C
Fulk of Anjou (king of Jerusalem), 100B
Fuller, R. Buckminster, 311B, 323B, 345B
Fuller, Thomas, 191C, 193C
Fulton, 336A
Fulton, Robert, 231B, 235B, 237B
Fumomadi the Great (sultan of Pate), 120C
Funan, 46B
Fundamental Laws, 362B
Funding Act, 228B
Fundj, 158B, 168B, 176B, 178B, 180B, 184B, 212B, 214B, 220B, 245A
Fundy, Bay of, 179A, 215A
fur trading, 159A
furnaces
blast, 77B, 109B, 123B, 127B
reverberating, 161B
furniture making, 83B, 91C, 123B, 211C, 231C
Fürth, 252A
Further Range, A (Frost), 319C
Fury and Hecla Strait, 246B
fusee, 139B
Fustat, 68B, 81B
Futa Jallon, 208B
Futa Toro, 206B, 208B, 214B
Futurism, Futurists, 295C
Fyodor I (tsar of Russia), 172A
Fyodor II (tsar of Russia), 176A
Fyodor III (tsar of Russia), 196A
Fyt, Jan, 191C

G

G-7 (Group of Seven), 368A, 378A
G-10 (Group of Ten), 348A
G15 (Group of Fifteen), 374A
Gable, Clark, 317C
Gabor, Dennis, 337B
Gaborone, 369A
Gabriel, Jacques-Ange, 217C
Gadir, 11A
Gadsden Purchase, 262B
Gaeta, 259C
Gagarin, Yuri, 347B
Gahn, Johann, 221B
Gainsborough, Thomas, 215C
Gaius, 41C
Galawdewos (emperor of Ethiopia), 160B, 166B
Galba, Servius Sulpicius (emperor of Rome), 36A
Galdan, 198C
Galen, 45C
Galerius (emperor of Rome), 50A, 50B, 51A
Galicia, 220A, 238A, 296A
Galileo Galilei, 171B, 173B, 175B, 177B, 179B, *184,* 185B, 187B, 379C
Galla people, 166B, 168B, 176B
Gallia Transalpina, 27A
Gallic Wars, The (Caesar), 29C
Gallican Church, 197C
Gallieni, Joseph Simon, 279A, 287A
Gallienus (emperor of Rome), 46A, 48A, 49C
Gallipoli, 128B, 136B
battle of, 297A, 299A
Gallipoli Peninsula, 297A
Gallus, Cornelius, 31C
Gallus (emperor of Rome), 46A
Galtieri, Leopoldo (president of Argentina), 367A
galvanometer, 245B
Gama, Vasco da, 148B, 148C, 169C
Gamarra, Agustín, 248C
Gambia, 180B, 237A, 257A, 351A, 359A
Gambia River, 190B, 245A
game theory, 333B
Gandamak, Treaty of, 277A
Gandersheim, 87C
Gandhara, 33A
Gandhi, Indira (prime minister of India), 353A, 357A, 363A, 369A
Gandhi, Mohandas, 303A, 312A, 313A, 315A, 317A, 322C, 337A
Gandhi, Rajiv (prime minister of India), 369A, 375A
Gandhi, Sanjay, 365B
Gandhi (movie), 367C
Ganges River, 92C, 106C, 172C, 194C, 369A
Ganilau, Ratu Sir Penaia (president), 371A
Ganja, battle of, 249A
Gao, 82C, 90C
Garay, Juan de, 171A
Garbo, Greta, 319C
Garcia II (king of Kongo), 186B
Garde-Freinet, 82B, 88B
Garden of Earthly Delights (Bosch), 145C

gardening, landscape, 83C
Gardiner, Julia, 256B
Garfield, James (president of U.S.), 276B, 278B
gargoyles, 109C
Garibaldi, Giuseppe, 260A, 266A, 270A
Garigliano River, battle of, 150A
Garland, Judy, 321C
Garneau, Hector de Saint Denys, 319C
Garnerin, André, 233B
Garrett, H. Lawrence III, 376C
Garrison, William Lloyd, 250B
Garvey, Marcus, 294B, 298B, *299*, 308B
Gary (Ind.), 354C
gas
  industry, 338B
  liquefaction of, 275B
  M-17 mask, 347B
  mustard, 300A, 301B
  natural, 39B, 51B, 53B, 55B
  poison, 296A
Gas Tank, The (Stella), 303C
Gascoigne, William, 187B
Gascony, 108A, 110A, 112A, 114A, 120A, 122A
Gaskell, Elizabeth, 263C
Gaslight (movie), 333C
gasoline
  ethyl, 305B
  rationing, 328B, 334B
  refining, 287B
Gaspee (British ship), 221A
Gastein, Convention of, 268A
Gaston of Orléans, 184A
Gates, Horatio, 222B, 224B
Gates, Bill, 361B, 371B
Gatling, Richard, 267B
Gaudí (i Cornet), Antonio, 279C
gauge blocks, 293B
Gauguin, Paul, 281C, 285C, 287C
Gaul, Gauls, 13A, 21A, 25A, 27A, 29A, 35C, 36A, 46A, 50A, 54A, 56A, 64A, 72A
Gaulli, Giovanni Battista, 197C
Gautier, Théophile, 249C, 271C
Gay, John, 211C
Gaynor, Janet, 311C, 313C
Gaza, 383A
  battle of, 301A
Gaza Strip, 371A
Gdansk, 364B
gears, 343B
Geary, John W., 264B
Gedimin, 124A
Gedon Gyafso (Dalai Lama of Tibet), 144C
Gehrig, Lou, 327C, 383C
Geissler, Heinrich, 263B
Geissler, Johann Heinrich Wilhelm, 263B
Geistige Situation der Zeit, Die (Jaspers), 313C
Geler, Konrad von, 169B
Gelimer (king of Vandals), 62B
Gemayel, Amin (president of Lebanon), 367A
Gemayel, Bashir (president of Lebanon), 367A
Gemini, 351B
gemstones, 33B
Genentech Company, 363B
General Agreement on Tariffs and Trade (GATT), 354A
General Assembly, 336A
General Council of the Church, Second, 57A
General Description of Pennsylvania (Penn), 199C
General Electric Company, 317B, 325B, 327B, 343B, 347B
General Motors Corporation, 305B, 342C, 356C, 370C, 375B, 376C
Generation of Vipers (Wylie), 329C
generator, 221B, 251B, 271B, 273B
Genesis, Book of, 11C
genetics engineering, 363B
Geneva, 122A, 160A, 161C, 163C, 303C, 342A
  Conference (1967), 354A
  conference on trade in arms (1925), 308A
  Convention for Protection of Wounded (1864), 269C
  Conventions (1949), 338A
  Disarmament Conference (1932), 314A
  Disarmament Conference (1960), 346A
  and League of Nations, 304A
  Protocol, 306A, 308A
  University, 167C
Genghis Khan (emperor of the Mongols), 104C, 106C, *107,* 108C, 110C, 112C
Gengzhi Tu, *99*
Gennai, Hirago, 221C
Gennaro Chapel, 185C
Genoa, 88B, 90B, 92B, 100B, 114B, 116B, 118B, 120B, 124B, 128B, 130B, 132B, 134B, 138B, 148C, 152A, 158A, 168A, 210A, 214A, 220A, 266A
  University of, 143C
Genseric (king of Vandals), 58B, 60B
Gentleman Dancing Master, The (Wycherley), 195C
Gentleman's Agreement (movie), 337C
Gentlemen Prefer Blonds (Loos), 309C
"Gentlemen's Agreement," 290B
Gentlemen's Magazine, 211C
geodesic dome, 345B
Geoffrey Martel of Anjou, 94A
Geoffrey of Monmouth, 103C
Geoffrey Plantagenet of Anjou, 102A
Geographica (Strabo), 31C
Geography, Guide to (Ptolemy), 45B
geometry, 13B, 23B
George, David Lloyd (prime minister of Britain), 290A, 292A, 300A, 306A
George, Louis, 200A
George, Stefan, 291C
George I (king of England), 206A, 208A
George I (king of Greece), 268A
George II (king of England), 208A, 212A, 216A
George II (king of Greece), 316A
George II (president of Greece), 336B
George III (king of England), 216A, 220A, 234B, 238A, 244A
George IV (king of England), 238A, 244A, 248A
George V (king of England), 292A, 318A
George V (king of Georgia), 124B
George VI (king of England), 318A, 320B, 328A, 340B
George VII, Pope, 97C
George Cross, 328A
George (prince of Wales), 238A, 243C
George Washington Slept Here (Kaufman and Hart), 323C
Georgetown, 224C
Georgia, Republic of, 91A, 98B, 106C, 114B, 123A, 124B, 132C, 134B, 140B, 211A, 214C, 224A, 234A, 235A, 236A, 240A, 306A, 352C, 372B, 376B
Georgia (U.S.), 211A, 215A, 246B, 248B, 254B, 268B, 380C
Georgia State University, 329C
Georgics (Virgil), 31C
German Confederation, 252A, 270A
German Democratic Republic. *See* East Germany
German East Africa, 281A, 293A, 295A, 299A
  and Britain, 305A
  and Mozambique, 301A
German (language), 83C
German Mass and Order of Service (Luther), 157C
German New Guinea, 295A
German Republic, 302A
German-Soviet Union Nonaggression Pact, 320A
German Women's Associations, Federation of, 268A, 284A
German Workers' Association, 268A
Germania (Tacitus), 39C
Germanicus, 32A, 32B
Germantown, 199A
  battle of, 222B
Germany, Germans, 46A, 50A, 86A, 103B, 112A, 151B, 164A. *See also* East Germany *and* West Germany
  12 B.C., 32A
  agriculture, 78A, 139B
  and Alsace-Lorraine, 276A
  and America, 199A, 205A
  and Argentina, 333A, 335A
  arts, 87C, 91B, 91C, 115C, 119C, 135B, 145C, 155C, 173C, 181C, 197C, 199C, 205C, 207C, 221C, 229C, 231C, 237C, 239C, 241C, 247C, 249C, 251C, 253C, 257C, 259C, 269C, 273C, 281C, 283C, 285C, 287C, 289C, 293C, 295C, 303C, 305C, 307C, 309C, 311C, 313C, 331C, 369C, 373C
  and Australia, 305A
  and Austria, 270A, 278A, 296A, 306A, 312A, 314A, 318A, 320A
  Bauhaus in, 305C
  and Belarus, 298A
  and Belgium, 294A, 296A, 308A, 322A, 334A
  and Bohemia, 118A
  and Bolivia, 331A
  and Brazil, 256C, 300C, 320C, 329A
  and Britain, 288A, 294A, 296A, 297A, 298A, 304A, 308A, 324A, 326A, 328A, 334A
  and Bulgaria, 324A
  and Cameroons, 279A, 283A, 299A
  and Canada, 294B, 334A
  and the Caribbean, 326A
  Carlsbad decrees, 244A
  and Chile, 327A, 331A
  and China, 301A, 305A
  Communism in, 308A
  and Congo, 293A
  conscription in, 316A
  and Crete, 326A
  and Crimea, 326A
  and Crusades, 113C
  Customs Union, 280A
  and Czechoslovakia, 320A, 328A
  Dawes Plan, 308A, 308B
  and Denmark, 322A, 334A
  Diet of Ratisbon, 236A
  and Dreyfus Affair, 284A
  economy, 272A, 306A, 310A, 312A
  education, 139C, 151C
  and Egypt, 324A, 328A
  and England, 79C
  and Finland, 302A
  Flagellants in, 117C
  Four-Year Plan, 318A
  and France, 80A, 88A, 136A, 156A, 194A, 212A, 218A, 230A, 234A, 240A, 272A, 274A, 285A, 293A, 294A, 296A, 298A, 298B, 300A, 302A, 304A, 306A, 308A, 324A, 332A
  and Greece, 324A
  industry, 41B, 77B, 113B, 125B, 137B, 171B, 217B, 249B, 273B, 295B, 319B, 321B, 327B, 362B
  Jews in, 81C
  in League of Nations, 310A
  Magyars and, 82A
  Nazis in, 308A, 314A
  and Poland, 320A, 322A, 330A, 332A, 334A
  and reparations, 314A
  reunified, 376B, 380B, 384B
  in Rhineland, 318A
  and Rhodesia, 303A
  and Romania, 282A, 298A, 302A, 320A
  Romans and, 40A, 52A
  and Samoa, 277A, 281A
  and Serbia, 282A, 294A, 298A
  and Somalia, 281A
  and South Africa, 279A, 289A, 293A, 297A, 312A, 347A, 360A
  and Soviet Union, 320A 326A, 328A, 330A, 332A, 334A, 336B, 338B, 348A, 354A, 358A
  and Spain, 156A
  St. Vitus's Dance in, 74A, 92A
  and Switzerland, 156A
  and Tanganyika, 305A
  and Tanzania, 281A, 299A
  in Three Emperors' League, 276A, 278A
  and Togoland, 279A, 295A
  and Treaty of Versailles, 304A, 316A, 318A
  and Tunisia, 328A
  and Turkey, 294A
  and United States, 296B, 300B, 302B, 304A, 306B, 308B, 320B, 324B, 326A, 326B, 328B, 330A, 332A, 336A, 336B, 338A, 368A, 376A
  and Upper Silesia, 306A
  and Venezuela, 159A
  on war debt, 316A
  and Yugoslavia, 307A, 324A, 326A, 332A
  and Zanzibar, 281A, 282A
Geronimo, 280B
Gershwin, George, 309C, 311C, 317C
Gertrude (queen of Hungary), 110A
Gerusalemme Liberata (Tasso), 171C
Geschichte der romanischen und germanischen Völker von 1494–1535 (Ranke), 247C
Gesner, Abraham, 257B
Gesta Pontificum Anglorum (Wm. of Malmesbury), 103C
Gesta Regum Anglorum (Wm. of Malmesbury), 103C
Gestiefelte Kater, Der (Tieck), 257C
Geta (emperor of Rome), 44A
Getty, J. Paul, 341C
Getty Museum, J. Paul, 341C
Gettysburg, battle of, 268B
Gettysburg Address, 268B
Gex, 176A
Ghadji, Ali (king of Kanem), 142B
Ghana, 44B, 74C, 84C, 88C, 94C, 96C, 108C, 114C, 178B, 186B, 190B, 192B, 214B, 275A, 285A,

345A, 347A, 382A. *See also* Gold Coast
and Britain, 257A
government, 353A, 359A
Soninke dynasty, 96C
Ghassan, 62C
Ghawri, al-Ashraf Quansah al- (sultan of Egypt), 150B
Ghazi (king of Iraq), 315A, 321A
Ghazna, Ghazni, 88C, 90C, 92C, 102C
Ghent, 126A, 142A
Pacification of, 170A
Treaty of, 240B
Ghent Altarpiece (van Eyck), 137C
Ghibellines, 116B, 118B
Ghilzai Mir Wais (shah of Persia), 204B
Ghiorso, Albert, 333B
Ghor, 102C, 108C
Ghosts (Ibsen), 277C
Ghulam Ishaq Khan (president of Pakistan), 373A
GI Bill of Rights, 332B, 340C
Gia Long, 235A
Gianni Schicchi (Puccini), 303C
Gibbon, Edward, 223C
Gibbon, John, Jr., 313B
Gibbons v. Ogden, 246B
Gibbs, James, 209C
Gibbs v. Board of Education, 318B
Gibraltar, 126B, 170B, 202A, 206A, 208A, 224A, 364B, 368B
Gibson, Charles Dana, 333C
Gibson, Mel, 381C
Gibson Girl, 333C
Giddings, Joshua, 254B
Gide, André, 289C, 293C, 295C
Gigi (movie), 345C
Gijimasu, 98C
Gilbert, Abbé, 87B
Gilbert, Sir Humphrey, 171A, 173A
Gilbert, William, 171B
Gilbert Islands, 233A, 297A, 330C
Gilmer, Elizabeth M., 285C
Gilmore, Gary, 362C
Gilpin, Thomas, 243B
Gilruth, Robert, 357B
Gilson, Étienne, 303C, 315C, 319C
gin, 209B
ginger, 59B
Gingrich, Newt, 380C, 384C
Ginsberg, Allen, 343C, 385C
Ginsburg, Ruth Bader, 378C
Giolitti, Giovanni (prime minister of Italy), 286A, 294A
Giorgione, 151C, 153C
Giraudoux, Jean, 335C
Girl Scouts, 292B
Gironde, 230A
Girton College, 273C
Giscard d'Estaing, Valéry (president of France), 360B, 366B
Giselle (ballet), 349C
Gish, Lillian, 297C
Gislebertus, 101C
Gist, Christopher, 215A
Gitagovinda, 99C
Giulin, 188C
Giurgevo, battle of, 174A
Givet, 294A
Giza, 3C
Glacial Kame culture, 77A
Gladsmuir, battle of, 212A
Gladstone, William (prime minister of Britain), 280A, 282A, 284A
Glaisher, James, 267B
Glaser, Donald, 341B
Glasgow, 311B
Glasgow, Ellen, 325C
Glasgow, University of, 139C
glass, glassware, 5B, 29B, 45B, 59B, 67B, 71B, 77B, 91B, 103B, 109B, 115B, 121B, 135B, 151B, 213B. *See also* stained glass
in Africa, 5B
in America, 213B
Favrile, 283C
floating process for, 341B
German, 41B
glass walls, 305C
lead crystal, 195B
Merovingian, 59C
non-reflecting, 321B
painting on, 91B
Roman, 33C
in Virginia, 179B
Glass, Philip, 365C
Glass Menagerie, The (Williams), 335C
Glass of Blessings, A (Pym), 345C
Glass-Steagall Act, 314B
Glassboro State College, 354A
Glatz, 212A
Glencoe, battle of, 200A
Glenn, John, 349B
Glidden, Joseph, 275B
glider(s), 149B, 285B
Glinka, Mikhail Ivanovich, 253C
globe, 35B, 147B
Glorie de María, Le (Liguori), 215C
Glossary (Aelfric), 89C
Glostershire, 64A
Gloucester, 102A, 110A, 183B
Gloucester Cathedral, 97C
Gluck, Christoph Willibald, 219C, 227C
Glyndwr, 134A
Go Down Moses and Other Stories (Faulkner), 327C
Goa, 152C
Goat Song (Werfel), 307C
Gobelins, 192A
Gobineau, Joseph, 263C
God, 53A
Truce of, 93C
God and Mammon (Mauriac), 311C
Godaigo (emperor of Japan), 126C
Goddard, Robert, 311B
Godesberg, 320A
Godfather, Part II, The (movie), 361C
Godfather, The (movie), 359C
Godfather, The (Puzo), 357C
Godfrey of Lorraine, 94B
Gododdin, The (Aneirin), 67C
Godomar II (king of Burgundy), 62A
God's Little Acre (Caldwell), 315C
Godunov, Boris (tsar of Russia), 172A, 176A
Godwin, 94A
Goes, Benito de, 176C
Goethe, Johann Wolfgang von, 221C, 225C, 229C, 239C, 243C, *250*,
Goetz, Bernard, 368C
Gogol, Nikolai Vasilyevich, 255C, 257C
Gogra River, 158C
Going My Way (movie), 333C
Gokomere culture, 62C
Gol Gumbaz, 183C
Golan Heights, 355A, 367A
Golconda, 152C, 168C, 170C, 172C
gold, 91B, 93A, 103B, 142B, 163A
in Africa, 188B
in Brazil, 165A
for dental fillings, 145B
in Mesoamerica, 77A
in Peru, 5C
price of, 364C
Renaissance, 161C
rush, 258B, 284B
in Santo Domingo, 153A
soldering, 169B
in South America, 151A, 254C
standard in Germany, 272A
Gold, Thomas, 337B
Gold Coast, 144B, 178B, 186B, 192B, 196B, 198B, 212B, 261A, 273A, 285A, 339A, 345A. *See also* Ghana
and Britain, 180B, 257A, 275A
and Holland, 174B
Golden Fleece, Order of the, *145*
Golden Horde, 120C
Golden House, 37C
Goldfinch, The (Fabritius), 191C
Golding, William, 343C, 367C
Goldman, Ronald, 380C, 382C, 384C
Goldmark, Peter, 325B
Goldoni, Carlo, 215C, 219C
Goldsmith, Oliver, 219C
Goldwater, Barry, 350C
golf, 85B, 99C
balls, 259B
wooden tee, 287B
Gomez, Juan Vicente (dictator of Venezuela), 290C
Gómez, Miguel Mariano, 318C
Gompers, Samuel, 280B
Gomulka, Wladyslaw (premier of Poland), 342B
Gonçalves, Lopo, 142B
Göncz, Árpád (president of Hungary), 374B
Gondar, 326A
Gone with the Wind (Mitchell), 319C
Gone with the Wind (movie), 323C
Gongo Musa, 122C
Gonja, 188B, 206B
Gonneville, Binot Paulmier, 151A
Gonzaga, House of, 141C
Gonzaga, Louis, 126B
González, Adolfo (prime minister of Spain), 366B
González, Felipe (prime minister of Spain), 366B
González, Juan (president of Paraguay), 337A
Good Earth, The (Buck), 313C
Good Soldier, The (Ford), 297C
Good Soldier Schweik, The (Hašek), 305C
Good Woman of Setzuan, The (Brecht), 331C
GoodFellas (movie), 375C
Goodrich Company, B. F., 325B
Goodspeed, Edgar, 297C
Gorazde, 380A
Gorbachev, Mikhail (president of Soviet Union), 362B, 368A, 368B, *369*, 370A, 370B, 372A, 374A, 374B, 376B
Gordian knot, 22C
Gordianus I (emperor of African Roman Empire), 46B
Gordianus II (emperor of African Roman Empire), 46B
Gordianus III (emperor of Rome), 44A, 46A
Gordillo, Francisco de, 157A
Gordimer, Nadine, 341C
Gordon, Charles George (governor-general of Sudan), 269A, 275A, 279A
Gorée, 180B, 184B, 192B, 196B, 225A
Goremykin, Ivan (premier of Russia), 290A
Gorges, Sir Ferdinando, 183A
Gorky, 168A
Gorky, Maxim, 289C
Gorlice-Tarnów, 296A
Gorm (king of Denmark), 82A
Goslar, 87B
Synod of, 93C
Gosnold, Bartholomew, 177A
Gospels, 91C, 253C
Got, Bertrand de, 123C
Gotamiputa Sri Satakani, 38B
Götha Canal, 250A
Goths, 40A, 42B, 44A, 46A, 48A, 52A, *53*, 56B, 64B
Gotoba, 109C
Gottwald, Klement (president of Czechoslovakia), 336B
Gough, Hugh, 259A
Goulart, João, 351A
Gould, Gordon, 363B
Gould, Jay, 272B
Gounod, Charles François, 265C
Government Ethics Law, 362C
Government of India Acts, 303A, 317A
Gowan, Yakubu (leader of Nigeria), 353A, 361A
Goya, Francisco de, 235C, 239C
gp120, 385B
Grace (princess of Monaco). *See* Grace Kelly.
Graduate, The (movie), 353C
Graf Spee (German battleship), 323A
Graham, Bette, 345B
Graham, George, 201B, 209B
Graham, Sylvester, 249B
graham cracker, 249B
Gramme, Zénobe, 271B
gramophone, 289B
Gran Colombia, 246C, 248C
Gran Galeoto, El (Echegaray), 277C
Gran teatro del mundo, El (Calderón de la Barca), 189C
Granada, 74B, 112B, 114B, 124B, 126B, 146A
Treaty of, 150A
University of, 157C
Granada-Cíbola, 161A
Grand Alliance, 202A
Grand Canal, 66C, 89B
Grand Canyon, 161A, 342C
Grand Catalan Company, 122B
Grand Coulee Dam, 338C
Grand Metaphysical Interior (Chirico), 301C
Grand Rapids, 335B
Grand Trunk Railway, 304B
Grande Illusion, La (Renoir), 319C
Grandes Baigneuses, Les (Renoir), 279C
Grandidier, Alfred, 269A
Grandmother, The (Nemcová), 263C
Grands Voyages, Les (Bry), *147*
Granicus, battle of, 22C
granola, 275B
Grant, Cary, 315C
Grant, George, 287B
Grant, Ulysses S. (president of U.S.), 266B, 268B, 270B, 272B, 274B, 278B
Granth, 177C
Grapes of Wrath, The (Steinbeck), 321C
Grapes of Wrath, The (movie), 323C
graphite, 167B, 169B
Grass, Günter, 347C
Grasso, Ella, 360C
Gratian (emperor of Rome), 56A, 57A
Gravelines, battles of, 166A, 190A
gravity, 101B
Gray, Elisha, 275B
Gray, Hannah Hilborn, 362C
Gray, Thomas, 215C
Great Alliance, 200A
Great Awakening, 213C
Great Britain. *See* Britain; England
Great Condé, 199C
Great Depression, 310B, 362C
Great Dictator, The (Chaplin), 323C
great elector. *See* Frederick William
Great Enclosure, 134C
Great Fish River, 223A
Great Gatsby, The (Fitzgerald), 309C

Great Golden Mosque, 154C
Great Hallelujah, 113C
Great Lakes, 87A, 197A, 209A, 239C, 314B, 346C
3000 B.C.–1000 B.C., 3B, 11C
arts, 11C
iron ore cargo ships on, 279B
pottery in region, 11C
Rush-Bagot Treaty, 242B
Great Powers, 267A, 270A, 274A, 284A
Great Proletarian Cultural Revolution, 353A
Great Salt Lake, 248B, *260*
Great Schism, 133C
"Great Society," 350C
Great Stupa, 39A
"Great Train Robbery," 348B
"Great Trek," 253A
Great Wall of China, 24B, 33B, 315A
Great Western (British steamship), 255B
"Great White Fleet," 290B
Greatbatch, Wilson, 345B
Greatest Show on Earth, The (movie), 341C
Greco, El, 171C, 179C
Greece, ancient
3000 B.C.–1175 B.C., 2C, 4C, 7B, 7C, 8A, 8C
1100 B.C.–620 B.C., 10C, 11B, 11C, 12A, 12C, 13A, 13B, 13C
600 B.C.–428 B.C., 14C, 16A, 16C, 17A, 17B, 17C, 18A, 18C, 19B, 19C
414 B.C.–190 B.C., 20C, 21B, 21C, 22C, 23B, 23C, 24C, 25B
171 B.C.–30 B.C., 26C, 27B, 28C, 31B, 31C
Greece, Greeks, 19C, 96B, 122B, 296A, 321B, "fire missiles." *See also* Athens
and Allies, 307A
arts, 7C, 11C, 13C, 15C, 17C, 19C, 21C, 23C, 31C, 33C, 39C, 41C, 43C, 45C, 47C, 63C, 315C
and Asia Minor, 305A
in Balkan League, 292A
and Britain, 260A, 268A, 332A, 346A, 348B
and Bulgaria, 84B, 88B, 304A, 307A
in Council of Europe, 338B
and Crete, 286A, 290A
and Cyprus, 350B
and European Community, 366B
and Genoa, 114B
and Germany, 324A
government, 268A, 308A, 310A, 314A, 336B, 352B, 354B, 360B, 368B
independence of, 246A, 248A
industry, 91B
and Italy, 324A
law and society, 14C, 16C, 244A
National Assembly, 248A
in NATO, 340A
and Normandy, 102B
and Ottoman Empire, 244A, 248A
religion, 87C
and Romans, 49B
and Saracens, 82B
science and technology, 15B, 35B, 51B, 61B, 71B, 77B, 83B, 109B
slave trade, 20C, 26C
and Smyrna, 305A
and Turkey, 128B, 132B, 134B, 140A, 160A, 262A, 276A, 286A, 304A, 305A, 307A, 313A, 321A, 342A, 346A, 348B, 350B, 352B
and United Nations, 338A, 348B
and Venice, 97B
World War I, 298A, 300A
World War II, 324A
and Yugoslavia, 342A
Greek Orthodox Church, 259C
Greeley, Horace, 255C
Green, Henrietta "Hetty," 298B
Green Bay Packers, 333C, 353C, 355C, 385C
Greene, Graham, 321C, 323C, 377C
Greenham Common, 366B
Greenland, 89A, 101B, 127A, 171A, 324B, 338A, 368B
Greenough, Horatio, 251C
Greenpeace, 368A
Greensboro, 346C
Greenville, Treaty of, 232B
Greenwich, Treaty of, 162A
Greer (U.S. destroyer), 326A
Gregg, John, 281B
Gregory II , Pope, 73C
Gregory III , Pope, 75C
Gregory IV , Pope, 79C
Gregory VII , Pope, *96*
Gregory IX , Pope, 112B, 113C
Gregory X , Pope, 119C
Gregory XI , Pope, 131C
Gregory XII , Pope, 135C, 137C
Gregory XIII , Pope, 169C, 171C
Gregory XV , 181C
Gregory of Nyssa, 55A
Gregory of Tours, Saint, 67C
Gregory the Illuminator, 51A
Grenada, 149A, 189A, 219A, 224C, 274C, 360A, 361A, 366A, 367A
Grenadines, 364A
Grévy, Jules (president of France), 276A, 278A, 280A
Grew, Nehemiah, 197B
Grey, Charles, 248A
Grey, Zane, 293C
Grieg, Edvard, 273C
Griffith, D. W., 297C, 299C, 305C
Grijalava, Juan de, 155A
Grimm, Jakob and Wilhelm, 241C
grindstone, 79B, 81B
Griqualand West, 273A
Grisons, 186A
Grissom, Virgil, 353B
Grodno, 298A
Gromyko, Andrei (president of Soviet Union), 368B
Gronchi, Giovanni (president of Italy), 342B
Gropius, Walter, 305C
Gross Jägersdorf, battle of, 216A
Grosswardein, 200A
Peace of, 160A
Grósz, Károly
Groton, 343B
Grove, William, 255B
Groves, Leslie, 328B
Growth of the Soil, The (Hamsun), 301C
Grozny, 380B
Grundlinien der Philosophie des Rechts (Hegel), 245C
Grünewald, Matthias, 153C
Guadalcanal, *329*, 330C
battle of, 328C
Guadalupe Hidalgo, Treaty of, 258B
Guadeloupe, 230C, 238C, 258C
Guam, 286C, 287A, 326C, 332C
Guanabara Bay, 165A, 169A
Guang Wudi (emperor of China), 34B
Guangzhou, 216C, 255A
Guantánamo Bay, 288C, 316C
Guardi, Francesco, 217C
Guardia, Tomás (president of Costa Rica), 272C
Guatemala, 32C, 50C, 52C, 56C, 59A, 113A, 133A, 157A, 246C, 254C, 282C, 304C
and Britain, 370A
and Chile, 312C
and El Salvador, 260C, 268C
government, 286C, 306C, 335A, 343A, 379A
and United Provinces, 252C
and United States, 329A
Guatemala City, 222C, 254C
earthquake in, 300C
Guayama, 211A
Guayaquil, 161A, 246C
Guelph VI, 104B
Guelphs, 116B, 122B
Guericke, Otto von, 191B
Guernica, 318A
Guernica (Picasso), 319C
Guerrero, Vicente (president of Mexico), 248C
Guevara, Che, 355A
Guevara Arze, Walter (president of Bolivia), 365A
Guevavi, 201C
Guiana, 149A, *174*, 175A, 181A, 192B, 242C
Guicciardini, Francesco, 161C
Guidea Spirituale (Molinos), 195C
Guienne, 110A, 126A, 138A
"Guildford Four," 360B
guilds, 66A, 228A
Guilford, Earl of, 220A
Guinea, 142B, 154B, 164B, 169A, 198B, 263A, 279A, 285A
and France, 344A
and Portugal, 142B
slave trade, 164B
Guinea-Bissau, 359A, 360A, 361A
Guinea Company, 172B
Guinegate, battles of, 144A, 152A
Guinness, Alec, 345C
Guiscard, Robert, 94B, 95C
Guise, House of, 166A
guitar, electric, 343B
Guiteau, Charles, 276B, 278B
Gujara, 62C
Gujarat, 86C, 92C, 108C, 134C, 140C, 152C, 158C, 160C
Gulag Archipelago, The (Solzhenitsyn), 360B
Gulf Coast cultures, 61A
Gulick, Mrs. Luther Halsey, 292B
Gulistan, Treaty of, 240A, 241A
Gulliver's Travels (Swift), 209C
gum, 91A
chewing, 259B
war, 206B
Gunderic (king of Vandals), 58B
Gundlach, Robert, 371B
Gunpowder Plot, 176A
gun(s), 101B, 121B, 123B, 139B, 154C, 155B, 188B, 189A. *See also* machine gun(s); rifle
bayonets, 189B, 193B, 225B
Brady bill, 378C
Gatling, 267B
gunpowder, 91B, 109B, 123B, 137B, 188B, 221B, 235B, 281B
gunshot wounds, 153B
gunstock lathe, 245B
harpoon, 271B
mortar gun, 299B
mounted on ships, 129B
muskets, 159B, 165B, 209B, 233B
Paris gun, 301B
percussion priming system, 257B
pistol, 161B
pump-action shot-, 281B
revolving barrel multishot, 253B
San Francisco ban on, 366C
silencer, 291B
snaphaunce, 165B
Güns, 158A
Gupta dynasty. *See* India, Indians
Gurkhas, 214C, 220C, 241A
Gursel, Cemal (president of Turkey), 346B
Gusika, 330C
Gustav (king of Sweden), *313*
Gustav V (king of Sweden), 338B
Gustav VI Adolf (king of Sweden), 338B, 358B
Gustav Line, 332A
Gustavus II Adolphus (king of Sweden), 178A, 184A
Gustavus III (king of Sweden), 220A, 228A, 230A
Gustavus IV (king of Sweden), 230A, 238A
Gustavus V (king of Sweden), 290A
Gutenberg, Johannes, 141B, 141C, 143C
Guthrie, Woody, 355C
Guy Mannering (Scott), 243C
Guy of Lusignan (king of Jerusalem), 106B
Guyana, 212B, 224C, 232C, 234B, 240C, 353A, 357A. *See also* British Guiana
Guyon du Chesnoy, Madame, 199C, 203C, 207C
Guyuk Khan (emperor of Mongols), 114C
Gwalior, 108C, 166C
Gwynedd, 86A
Gyalu, Treaty of, 162A
Gypsy Madonna, The (Titian), 153C
gyrocompass, 291B

H

H. M. Pulham, Esquire (Marquand), 325C
H-bomb, 338C
Haakon IV (king of Norway), 116A
Haakon VII (king of Norway), 290A, 322A, *322*
Haarlem, 169B, 193C
Habe, 98C
Habeas Corpus Act, 196A, 222A
Haber, Fritz, 293B
Habitation Port-Royal, 205A
Habsburg, House of, 118A, 146A, 154A, 156A, 164A, 171C, 176A, 200A, 202A, 206A, 264A, 280A
Hackensack River, 187A
Hackman, Gene, 357C
Hadassah, 293C
Hadley, John, 211B
Hadrian (emperor of Rome), 36A, 38A, 39A, 39B, 39C, 40A, 41C
Hadrian I, Pope, 75C
Hadrian VI, Pope, 157C
Hadrian's Wall, *36*, 39B, 44A, 54A
Haeckel, Ernst Heinrich Philipp August, 271C, 287C
Hague, The, 286A, 310A, 312A,380A
Alliance of, 194A
Convention (1882), 278A
Peace Conference (1899), 286A
Peace Conference (1907), 290A
Haidar Ali (sultan of Mysore), 216C, 220C, 225A
Haifa l, 317B
haiku, 193C
Haile Selassie I, 313A
Hainan Island, 321A, 322C
Hainaut, 128A, 136A, 192A
Haiphong, 353A, 359A
Hair (Ragni, Rado, MacDermot), 355C
Haiti, 147A, 201A, 215A, 224C, 234B, 236C, 238C, 242C, 244C, 256C, 258C, 296C, 379A
and Dominican Republic, 318C
and France, 246C
government, 335A, 375A, 377A

and Santo Domingo, 256C
and United Nations, 380A
and United States, 296C, 306C, 312C, 316C, 371A
Hajj Umar, al-, 263A
Hakam I, 76B
Hakam II, 86B
Hakluyt, Richard, 171C, 175B
halberd, 135B
Haldeman, H. R., 358C
Hale, Nathan, 222B
Hales, Stephen, 203B, 211B
Halidon Hill, battle of, 126A
Halifax (Nova Scotia), 215A, 300B, 384C
Halifax, Lord, 285C
Halka (Moniuszko), 259C
Hall, Edwin, 277B
Hall, Frank, 283B
Hall, James Norman, 325C
Hall, Radclyffe, 311C
Hall effect, 277B
Halle (Germany), 201C, 205C
Hallelujah (movie), 311C
Halley, Edmund, 197B, 203B, 207B
Halley's comet, 25B, 197B, 203B, 217B, 253B, 293B, 371B
Hall's Bay, 276B
Hallstatt culture, 11B, 13A
Haloid Company, 337B
Hamadan, 299A
Hamas, 379A
Hamasa, 79C
Hamburg (Germany), 78A, 184A, 194A, 197C, 234A, 238A, 270A, 280A, 314A
Hamilton, Alexander, 226B, 236B
Hamilton culture, 91A
Hamlet, The (Faulkner), 323C
Hamlet (movie), 337C
Hamlet (Shakespeare), 177C
Hammarskjöld, Dag (secretary-general of United Nations), 340A, 346A
Hammerstein, Oscar, 331C, 347C
Hammett, Dashiell, 347C
Hammurabi (king of Babylonia), 4B, 6B
Hampden, John, 186A
Hampshire, 88A
Hampton, Wade, 240B
Hampton Court, Treaty of, 166A
Hampton Court Palace, 153C
Hamsun, Knut, 283C, 285C, 301C
Han dynasty. *See* China, Chinese
Handel, George Frideric, 199C, 205C, 209C, 213C, 215C
Handy, W. C., 293C, 301C
Hangchow, 118C, 164C, 319A
Hanging Gardens, 15C
Hankow, 311A, 321A
Hanks, Tom, 379C, 381C
Hannibal, *25*, 25A, 27A
Hanno of Carthage, 16A
Hanoi, 116C, 120C, 174C, 227A, 353A, 359A
Hanover, House of, 202A
Hanover (German state), 206A, 236A, 238A, 240A, 244A, 250A, 252A, 262A, 270A
Hans (king of Denmark, Norway, and Sweden), 144A
Hanseatic League, 115B, 120A, 146A, 148A, 160A, 184A, 194A
Hansma, Paul, 373B
Hanthawaddy, kingdom of, 142C, 146C, 160C
Hanthawaddy dynasty. *See* Burma, Burmese
Harapala, 124C
Harar, 166B, 168B, 170B
Harbin, 334C
Harbor Scene (Lorrain), 185C
Hardacnut (king of England), 92A
Hardenberg, Friedrich Leopold von, 235C
Harding, Warren G. (president of U.S.), 304B, 306B
Hardy, Thomas, 281C
Harith II, al- 62C
Harlem, 298B, 330B, 344C, 350C
Harlem Brundtland, Gro (prime minister of Norway), 370B
Harlem Renaissance, 293C
Harmonielehre (Schoenberg), 293C
harnesses, 85B
Harnick, Sheldon, 351C
Harold I (king of England), 92A
Harold II, 94A
Harper's Ferry, 264B
Harper's Monthly magazine, 261C
Harper's Weekly, *269*, 274B
Harpur, Charles, 267C
harquebus, 139B
Harrar, 273A
Harrington, John, 173B
Harrington, Joseph, 361B
Harris, Barbara (Suffragen Bishop of Massachusetts), 373C
Harris, Robert Alton, 376C
Harris, Roy, 317C
Harrison, Benjamin (president of U.S.), 280B, 282B
Harrison, George, 383C
Harrison, James, 267B
Harrison, Wallace, 353C
Harrison, William Henry (president of U.S.), 238B, 240B, 254B
Harrodsburg, 221A
Harrowing of Hell, The, 115C
Harsha, 66C, 68C, 70C
Hart, Moss, 323C
Hartford, 185A, 332B
Harud, Saifa (emperor of Ethiopia), 128C
Harvard College, 187A, 189A, 199A
Harvard Divinity School, 245C
Harvard University, 327B, 333B
Harvey (Chase), 335C
Harz Mountains, 87B, 109B
Hasan Bahmani (king of Kulbarga), 128C
Hašek, Jaroslav, 305C
Hashimite dynasty. *See* Saudi Arabia
Hashimoto Ryutaro (prime minister of Japan), 383A
Hasidism, Hasids, 213C
Hastenbeck, battle of, 216A
Hastie, William, 318B
Hastings, battle of, 94A
Hastings, Warren (governor-general of India), 220C, 225A, 226A, 232A
Hat Act, 210A
Hatcher, Billy, *375*
Hatcher, Richard, 354C
Hatchett, Charles, 235B
Hatshepsut (queen of Egypt), 8A
Hatt-i Hümayun, 265A
Hattusas, 6C
Haughey, Charles (prime minister of Ireland), 370B
Hauptmann, Gerhart, 281C, 285C, 287C
Hausa Confederation, 154B
Hausa dynasty. *See* Nigeria
Hausaland, 94C
Havana, 153A, 219A, 286C, 310C
"Act of Havana," 325A
Castillo del Principe, 230C
Dominican University, 256C
Havana Conference, 325A
Havel, Václav (president of Czech Republic), 372B, 374B
Havel River, 84A
Haverhill, 201A
Hawaii, Hawaiians, 32B, 225A, 239A, 245A, 261A, 283A, 319B, 326C, 346C, 377B
and Britain, 253A, 257A
and France, 257A
government, 283A, 285A
and Japan, 326B
and Polynesians, 108C
settlement of, 60C, 76C
and United States, 249A, 275A, 281A, 283A, 287A
Hawaii-Loa, 60C
Hawikuh, 161A
Hawke, Robert (prime minister), 371A
Hawkins, John, 166B, 167A, 169A, 175A
Hawks, Howard, 333C
Hawley-Smoot Tariff, 312B
Hawthorne, Nathaniel, 253C, 259C, 261C, 267C
Hay, John, 286B
Hay-Bunau-Varilla Treaty, 288C
Hay-Pauncefote Treaty, 288C
Haydn, Franz Joseph, 211C, 223C, 233C, 235C
Hayes, Helen, 317C
Hayes, Lemuel, 224B
Hayes, Rutherford B. (president of U.S.), 274B
Haymarket Riot, 280B
Haytham, Ibn al-, 83B, 93B
Haywain, The (Constable), 245C
Hayward, Susan, 345C
Haywood, William, 290B
Hazelton (Pa.), 286B
Hazelwood, Joseph, 374C
Hazlitt, William, 245C
health, board of, 273B
health care, 98C
hearing, 337B
cochlear implant, 359B
transistorized hearing aid, 341B
Hearst, William Randolph, 285C, 338C
heart
arterial valves, 177B
artificial implant, 357B, 367B
artificial valve, 341B, 347B, 363B
cardiac catheter, 311B
catheterization, 345B
coronary bypass, 353B
effects of drinking on, 377B
electro-cardiogram, 289B
heart-lung machine, 313B, 341B
open-heart surgery, 283B
pacemaker, 345B
tilting-disc artificial valve, 357B
transplants, 355B, 371B
ventricular defibrillator, 345B
Heart Is a Lonely Hunter, The (McCullers), 323C
Heart of the Andes, The (Church), 263C
Heartbreak House (Shaw), 299C
heat, heating, 31B, 67B, 73B
Heath, Edward, 360B
Hebbel, Christian Friedrich, 257C
Hebrew Grammar and Dictionary (Reuchlin), 151C
Hebrew Melodies (Byron), 243C
Hebrew Union College, 287C
Hebrews. *See* Israel, Israelites
Hebrides Islands, 3A, 116A, 176C
Hebron, 385A
Hegel, George Friedrich Wilhelm, 237C, 243C, 245C
Hegira, 69C
Heian, 76C
Heidelberg, 200A
Heine, Christian Johann Heinrich, 247C, 265C
Heir of Redclyffe, The (Yonge), 263C
Helei province, 93B
Helena (mother of Constantine the Great), 51A
Helge River, 92A
helicopter, 293B, 323B
UH-ID Iroquois, *353*
Heliodorus of Emesa, 47C
Heliogabalus (emperor of Rome), 44A
Heliopolis, battle of, 235A
Hellespont, 66B
Hellman, Lillian, 323C, 325C
Héloïse, 103C
Helots, 20C, 24C
Helsinki, 164A, 356A
Conference on Security, 360A
Convention, 348A
Hemingway, Ernest, 311C, 323C, 333C, 341C, 343C
Hemmingstedt, battle of, 150A
Henderson Field, 328C
Hendrix, Jimi, 357C
Henlein, Peter, 151B
Hennepin, Louis, 197A
Henreid, Paul, 319C
Henriade (Voltaire), 209C
Henrico, 179A
Henricus (Bishop of Greenland), 101A
Henrietta Maria (queen of England), 182A, 188A
Henry, Joseph, 249B
Henry, O., 289C
Henry, Patrick, 222B
Henry, Prince, 106A
Henry I (king of England), 98A, 99B, 100A, 102A
Henry I (king of France), 92A, 94A
Henry I (king of Germany), 84A
Henry II (Castile), 130B
Henry II (king of England), 104A, 105C, 106A, 106B
Henry II (king of France), 162A, 164A, 166A
Henry II (king of Germany and Lombardy), 90A
Henry II (king of Jerusalem), 114A, 118B
Henry II (prince of Condé), 180A
Henry III (Holy Roman Emperor and king of Germany), 92A, 94A, 95C
Henry III (king of Castile), 132B
Henry III (king of England), 110A, 112A, 114A, 116A, 118A
Henry III (king of France), 170A, 172A
Henry IV (Holy Roman Emperor and king of Germany), 94A, 96A, 96B, 97C, 98A
Henry IV (king of Castile), 140A
Henry IV (king of France), 172A, 173C, 174A, 175C, 176A, 178A
Henry IV of Lancaster (king of England), 134A
Henry IV (Shakespeare), 175C
Henry V (Holy Roman Emperor and king of Germany), 98A, 98B, 100A, 100B, 101C, 136A
Henry V (king of England), 134A
Henry V (Shakespeare), 175C
Henry VI (Holy Roman Emperor, king of Germany, king of Sicily), 106A, 108A, 108B
Henry VI (king of England and France), 136A, 138A, 140A, 142A
Henry VI (Shakespeare), 173C
Henry VII (king of England), 144A, 146A, 150A, 152A
Henry VII (king of Germany and Holy Roman Emperor), 124A, 124B
Henry VII (king of the Romans), 112A
Henry VIII (king of England and Ireland), 152A, 154A, 158A, 159C, 160A, 161C, 162A
Henry Esmond (Thackeray), 263C
Henry of Anjou (king of England), 104A

Henry of Anjou (king of Poland), 170A
Henry of Carinthia (king of Bohemia), 122A
Henry of Guise, 172A
Henry of Navarre, 172A
Henry the Illustrious, 110A
Henry the Lion (of Saxony), 104A, 106A, 108A
Henzada, 214C
Hepburn, Audrey, 341C
Hepburn, Katharine, 353C, 355C, 367C
Heraclea, 22C
Heracleides Ponticus, 23B
Heraclitus, 17C
Heraclius (emperor of Byzantium), 68B
Herat, 114C, 116C, 132C, 140C, 158C, 253A
Herault, 107B
herb cultivation, 78A
Herbert, Victor, 283C
Herbert of Cherbury, 183C
herbicide 2,4-D, 335B
Herculaneum, 36A, 205B
Herder, Johann Gottfried von, 227C
Herihor, 10A
Hermannsson, Steingrímur (prime minister of Iceland), 366B, 372B
Hermhut, 209C
Hernández de Córdoba, Francisco, 155A
Hernández Martínez, Maximiliano (dictator of El Salvador), 312C, 333A
Herod the Great, 31A, 32B
Herodes, 41C
Herodian, 47C
Herodotus, 19C
Herophilus, 25B
Herrenhausen, Treaty of, 208A
Herrero, 289A
herring salting, 119B, 133B
Herriot, Édouard (prime minister of France), 308A
Herschel, Caroline, 225B
Herschel, William, 225B
Hersey, John, 333C
Herter, Christian, 346C
Hertling, Georg (chancellor of Germany), 300A
Hertzog, James M. (prime minister of South Africa), 309A, 322C
Hertzsprung, Ejnar, 295A
Herzegovina, 142A. *See also* Bosnia-Herzegovina
  and Austria, 276A, 290A
  and Russia, 380B
  and United States, 380B
Herzl, Theodor, 286A
Herzog (Bellow), 351C
Hesdin, Truce of, 140A
Hesiod, 13C
Hess, Harry, 335B
Hess, Myra, 291C
Hess, Rudolph, 324A
Hesse, Hermann, 303C
Hesse, Hessians, 158A, 222B, 270A
Hesse-Cassel, 208A, 250A, 260A
Heston, Charlton, 347C
Heureaux, Ulises (dictator of Dominican Republic), 278C
Heuss, Theodor (president of West Germany), 338B
Hewish, Antony, 353B
Heydrich, Reinhard, 328A
Heyward, DuBose, 317C
Hi-Khio, 87C
Hiawatha, 169A
Hidalgo y Costilla, Miguel, 238C
Hidetata, 182C
Hideyoshi, Toyotomi (emperor of Japan), 170C, 172C, 174C
hieroglyphics, 3C, 5C, 9C, 25C, 51B
Hieronymus, 59C
High Noon (Zinnemann), 341C
Higher Arab Committee, 319A
Highway Act, 342C
hijackings, 346C, 358A, 362A, 368A
Hijaz, 301A, 303A, 315A
Hildebrandt, Lukas von, 209C
Hilderic (king of Vandals), 62B
Hill, Anita, 376C
Hill, George Roy, 359C
Hillel, 33A
Hills Beyond, The (Wolfe), 327C
Himalayas, 176C
Himeja Castle, 179C
Himiko (empress of Japan), 46B
Himmler, Heinrich, 330A
Hindemith, Paul, 315C
Hindenburg, Paul von (president of Germany), 294A, 296A, 298A, 308A, 314A, 316A
Hindenburg (German airship), 318B
Hindley, Myra, 352B
Hinduism, Hindus, 11B, 51A, 53A, 168C, 194C, 337A, 379A
  and Akbar, 164C
  arts, 91C, 109C
  and Babur, 158C
  in Canada, 294B
  Hindu league, 90C
  in India, 92C, 291C
  medicine, 31B
  in Sumatra, 70C
Hipparchus, 25B, 27B
Hippias, 16C
Hippocrates, 19B
Hippolyte et Aricie (Rameau), 211C
Hippolytus (antipope), 45A, 47A
Hiragana, 81C
Hirohito (emperor of Japan), 311A, 373A
Hiroshige, 251C
Hiroshima, 334C
Hiroshima mon amour (Resnais), 347C
Hisham, 72B
Hisham I, 76B
Hisham III, 92B
Hispaniola, 167A, 201A
Hiss, Alger, 336C, 338C
Histoire comique des états de la lune (Bergerac), 189C
Histoire de France (Michelet), 251C
Histoire de la révolution de 1848 (Lamartine), 261C
Histoire de l'Amérique, 149
Histoire naturelle (Buffon), 215C
Histoire naturelle de l'âme (La Mettrie), 213C
Historia calamitatum mearum (Abélard), 103C
Historia Francorum (Gregory), 67C
Historia naturalis (Pliny), 37B
Historia regum Britanniae (Geoffrey of Monmouth), 103C
Historiae Romanae (Paterculus), 33C
Historiae (Tacitus), 39C
Historical Studies (Strabo), 33C
History of Creation (Haeckel), 271C
History of Dogma (von Harnack), 313C
History of England (Barnard), *223*
History of England from the Accession of James II (Macaulay), 261C
History of England (Froude), 265C
History of Henry VII (Bacon), 183C
History of John Bull, The (Arbuthnot), 205C
History of Materialism (Lange), 271C
History of Modern Philosophy (Fischer), 263C
History of New York, A (Irving), 239C
History of the English Reformation (Burnet), 197C
History of the Inquisition in the Middle Ages, The (Lea), 281C
History of the Jewish War (Josephus), 37C
History of the Popes (Ranke), 253C
History of the Railroad and the Canals of the U.S. (Poor), 267C
History of the Roman Empire, The (Karamzin), 245C
History of the Standard Oil Company, The (Tarbell), 289C
History of the U.S. During the Administrations of Thomas Jefferson and James Madison (Adams), 281C
History of the World (Ranke), 277C
History of Tom Jones, a Foundling, The (Fielding), 215C
Histriomastix (Prynne), 185C
Hitchcock, Alfred, 321C, 323C, 325C, 331C, 347C, 365C
Hitler, Adolf (chancellor of Germany), 306A, 308A, 314A, 316A, 324A, 326A, 330A, 334A
  and Chamberlain, 320A
  and Mussolini, 320A
  on Sudetenland, 320A
  and United States, 320B
Hittin, 106B
Hittite empire, 4C, *6*, 6B, 6C, 8B, 8C, 9B. *See also* Anatolia
HIV virus, 384A, 385B. *See also* AIDS
Hivia, 218C
Ho Chi Minh, 324C, 357A
Hobart, 237A, 251C
Hobbes, Thomas, 187C, 191C
Hobbit, The (Tolkien), 319C
Hobby, Oveta Culp, 340C
Hobson (U.S. destroyer), 340C
Hodgkin, Dorothy, 329B
Hoe, Richard, 259B
Hofer, Andreas, 238A
Hoff, Marcian, 355B
Hoffa, James, 360C
Hoffman, Dustin, 365C, 373C
Hoffman, J. P. (president of Orange Free State), 263A
Hofmannsthal, Hugo von, 293C
Hogarth, William, 211C, 213C
Hohenfriedberg, battle of, 212A
Hohenlinden, battle of, 234A
Hohenlohe, Prince (chancellor of Germany), 284A
Hohokam culture, 32C, 59A, 67A, 123A, 135A
Hojeda, Alonso, 149A
Hojo family. *See* Japan
Hokusai, 245C
Holbein, Hans, 155C, 157C, 161C
Holden, William, 341C
Holguín, Melchor Pérez, 209C
Holiday, Billie, 347C
Holiday Inn (movie), 327C
Holinshed, Raphael, 171C
Holkeri, Harri (prime minister of Finland), 370B
Holland, Dutch, 63B, 116A, 119B, 128A, 136A, 170A, 174C, 188A, 198B. *See also* Boers; Netherlands
  and America, 183A, 183C, 185A
  and American Indians, 191A
  arts, 149C, 155C, 181C, 185C, 191C, 195C, 197C, 285C
  and Austria, 206A
  and Belgium, 250A
  and Bering Strait, 211A
  and Britain, 224A, 233A, 247A, 273A
  and Cape Colony, 249A
  and Ceylon, 186C, 193A
  and China, 192A, 198C
  Dutch East India Company, 232A
  and East Indies, 174A, 194C, 196C, 216C
  and Easter Island, 209A
  and England, 182C, 190A, 192A, 192B, 194A, 200A, 206A, 210A
  Federal Republic of the United Provinces, 170A
  and Five Nations, 195A
  and France, 194A, 196A, 196B, 198A, 200A, 202A, 204B, 206A, 236A, 238A
  and Germany, 334A
  and Gold Coast, 174B, 178B, 198B
  gum war, 206B
  and Guyana, 212B, 240C
  and India, 200C
  and Indonesia, 178C, 214C
  industry, 59B, 186A, 215B
  and Japan, *182*, 186C, 188C, 269A, 326C
  and Malacca, 184C
  and Mauritius, 188B
  and Mozambique, 178B
  and Philippines, 192C
  and Portugal, 176C, 180C, 184B, 186B, 186C, 190C, 192C, 206A
  postal service, 169B
  and Prussia, 206B, 208B
  and Samoan Islands, 208C
  and Savoy, 206A
  science and technology, 79B, 81B, 99B, 129B, 135B, 137B, 175B, 179B, 191B, 197B, 217B, 293B
  slave trade, 186B
  and South Africa, 192B
  and Spain, 176C, 186A, 186C, 200A
  and Sumatra, 174C, 225A
  and Surinam, 175A, 181A, 270C
  and Taiwan, 184C
  and Timor, 265A
  transportation, 177B
  and Trinidad, 187A
  and West Africa, 180B
  and William II, 302A
  World War II, 322A, 326C
Holland Tunnel, 311B
Hollar, Wenzel, *97*
Hollerith, Herman, 277B
Holmes, Sherlock, 281C
Holocaust, 326A, 379C
hologram, 337B
holographic image, 349B
Holstein, 158A, 222A, 268A, 270A
Holstein-Gottorp, 214A
Holt, Benjamin, 289B
Holy Alliance, 242A
Holy Apostles, Church of the, 107C
Holy Land, 91B, 99B, 115C
Holy League, 128B, 168B
Holy Roman Empire, 86A, 88A, 90A, 92A, 95C, 98A, 100A, 102A, 106A, 108A, 110A, *113*, 118A, 124A, 128A, 138A, 148A, 150A, 165C, 166A, 178A, 190A
  and England, 154A
  and France, 146A, 154A, 186A, 194A, 196A, 198A, 200A, 202A
  government, 170A, 204A, 212A, 218A, 236A
  and Prussia, 216A
  and Spain, 154A
  and Turkey, 166A, 192A, 198A
Holy See, 88A, 125C, 129C
Holy Sepulchre, 90B
Homann, J. B., 207C

Home, Sir Alec Douglas (prime minister of Britain), 348B
Home Life Insurance, 279C
Home of the Heron (Inness), 275C
Homer, 11C, 207C, 209C
Homer, Winslow, 279C
Homestead strike, 282B
Homilies (Aelfric), 89C
homine, De (Hobbes), 191C
homosexuality
  Defense of Marriage Act, 382C
  Presbyterian Church on, 377C
  in U.S. armed forces, 378C
Homs, battle of, 120B
Hon-jong (king of Korea), 253A
Honan province, 63C, 311A, 319A
Honduras, Hondurans, 50C, 153A, 171A, 232C, 246C, 266C, 276C, 310C
  civil war in, 248C, 292C
  and El Salvador, 284C, 365A
  government, 274C, 314C, 359A, 367A
  and Mexico, 246C
  and Nicaragua, 284C
  and Spain, 161A
Honecker, Erich (leader of East Germany), 356B, 372B
Honesdale, 249B
Hong Kong, 257A, 326C, 369A
  Joint Declaration on, 368A
Honorius I, Pope, 69C
Honorius III, Pope, 111C, 112A
Honshu Island, 269A, 273B
Hook, Sidney, 319C
hook-and-latch fastener, 251B
Hooke, Robert, 193B, 195B
Hoover, Herbert (president of U.S.), 310B, 312B
Hoover, J. Edgar, 358C, 360C
Hoover Dam, 312B, 319B
Hope, Anthony, 285C
Hopewell culture, 33B, 46C, 59A, 83A, 99A
Hopi, 101A, 103A, 109A, 115A, 119A, 123A, 219A
Hopkins, Anthony, 377C
Hopkins, Harry, 324B
Hopper, Edward, 353C
Hopper, Grace, 333B
Hopper, Grace Murray, 345B
Horace, 31C, 33C
Horae Lyricae (Watts), 205C
Horikawa (emperor of Japan), 98C
hormones, 333B
Hormuz, 126C, 146B, 154B
Hormuzd (king of Persia), 64C
Horn, Gyula (premier of Hungary), 380B
Hornet (U.S. carrier), 328C
horses, 25B, 39B, 47B, 73C, 159A, 161B, 177A, 211A, 379C
Horthy, Nicholas (prime minister of Hungary), 332A
horticulture, 33B
Hosha, Enver (president of Albania), 368B
Hosokawa Masamoto, 146C
Hosokawa Morihiro (prime minister of Japan), 379A, 381A
hospitals, 103B
hostages, 370C, 374A
hot air balloon(s), 231B, 233B, 286A
  atmosphere exploration in, 267B
  bombing from, 261B
  manned, 313B
Hot Springs, 295C
Hotchkiss, Benjamin, 273B
Hotel Splendide (Bemelmans), 325C
Hou-Chou dynasty. *See* China, Chinese
Hou-Tang dynasty. *See* China, Chinese
Hounsfield, Godfrey, 353B, 359B
hourglasses, 123B
Housatonic River, 179A
Housatonic (U.S. ship), 300B
House by the Medlar Tree (Verga), 277C
House in Paris, The (Bowen), 319C
House of Commons, 212A, 311C, 376B
House of Hanover, 202A
House of Lords, 190A, 290A, 311C
House of Mirth, The (Wharton), 291C
House of Representatives, U.S., 380C
  African-Americans in, 320B
  Asian-Americans in, 342C
  on Fulbright Resolution, 330B
  impeachment of Johnson, 270B
  and Iran-Contra, 370C
  and J. Edgar Hoover, 360C
  Jim Wright in, 372C
  and John Quincy Adams, 246B, 250B
  on Lend-Lease program, 332B
  Nixon impeachment hearings in, 360C
  women in, 306B, 320B
House of the Seven Gables, The (Hawthorne), 261C
Houseman, A. E., 285C
Housing Act, 338C
Houston, Sam, 252B
Houston Astrodome, 353B
Houston (Tex.), 300B
Hova, 267A, 269A, 269C, 275A, 287A
How Green Was My Valley (Ford), 325C
How the Other Half Lives (Riis), 283C
Howard, Catherine, 160A, 162A
Howe, Elias, 259B
Howe, Julia Ward, 267C
Howe, William, 222B, 230A
Howells, William Dean, 279C, 281C
Howl (Ginsberg), 343C
Howse Pass, 236B
Höxter, 77B
Hoysala dynasty. *See* India
Hrawi, Elias (president of Lebanon), 375A
Hrosvitha, 87C
Hsi-Hsia, 92C, 112C
Hsien-feng (emperor of China), 261A
Hsien Ti (emperor of China), 42B, 44B
Hsin dynasty. *See* China, Chinese
Hsüan-te (emperor of China), 136C
Hsüng T'ung (emperor of China), 293A
Hua Kuo-feng (premier of China), 363A
Hua T'o, 45B
Huang Chao (emperor of China), 80C, 82C
Huang Ti (emperor of China), 2B, 3B
Huaras, 325A
Huascar, 159A
Huastec cultures, 83A
Hubble telescope, 379B, 381B
Hubertusburg, Treaty of, 218A
Hucbald of Belgium, 85C
Hudson, Henry, 179A
Hudson Bay, 38C, 85A, 153A, 179A, 201A, 207A
Hudson Hope, 236B
Hudson River, 179A, 181A, 187A, 237B
Hudson's Bay Company, 195A, 201A, 238B, 256B, 264B
Hue, 225A
  Treaty of, 279A
Huerta, Adolfo de la (president of Mexico), 304C
Huerta, Victoriano (president of Mexico), 294C
Hufnagel, Charles, 341B
Hufstedler, Shirley, 364C
Hugh (Abbot of Cluny), 95
Hugh of Vienne (king of Italy), 84B
Hugh Selwyn Mauberley (Pound), 305C
Hughes, Charles Evans, 300B
Hughes, Edward James, 369C
Hughes, Langston, 353C
Hugo, Victor, 245C, 247C, 249C, 251C, 255C, 267C
Huguenot Wars, 166A, 168A, 170A, 174A
Huguenots, 166A, 167A, 167C, 168A, 169A, 175C, 180A, 182A, 184A, 198B, 199C, 202A
Hukwang, 293A
Hula Hoop, 345B
Hulagu Khan (emperor of Mongols), 116C
Hull, Cordell, 322B
Hull, William, 240B
Hull House, 280B
Human Comedy, The (Balzac), 251C
Human Comedy, The (Saroyan), 331C
Human Genome Project, 379B
Humanae Vitae (papal encyclical), 355C
Humayun, 158C, 160C, 162C, 164C
Humboldt, Alexander von, 235B
Humboldt's Gift (Bellow), 363C
Hume, A. O., 279A
Hume, David, 213C, 225C
Humphrey, Hubert, 354C
Hunan province, 233A
Hundred Poets and Their Poems in Brocade, The (Shunsho), 223C
Hundred Years' War, 126A
Hung-chi (emperor of China), 146C
Hung-hsi (emperor of China), 136C
Hung Hsiu-ch'üan (emperor of China), 269A
Hungary, Hungarians, 77B, 176A, 178A, 212A. *See also* Austro-Hungarian empire
  arts, 245C, 293C
  and Austria, 204A, 260A, 270A, 316A, 372B
  and Bohemia, 116A
  and Britain, 332A
  and Byzantium, 94B, 104B
  Communism in, 336B
  and Croatia and Dalmatia, 98B
  and Czechoslovakia, 316A
  and Germany, 326A
  government, 122A, 134A, 138A, 140A, 166A, 170A, 180A, 266A, 304A, 336B, 372B, 374B
  and Habsburgs, 146A, 154A
  industry, 77B
  and Italy, 84B, 316A
  and Magyars, 110A
  and Mongolia, 114A
  and Ottoman Empire, 158A, 168A
  and Poland, 130A, 306A
  politics, 380B
  religion, 87C, 99C, 133C, 176A, 177C, 285C
  revolution in, 342B
  and Romania, 306A, 316A
  and Romans, 50A
  and Russia, 260A, 306A
  science and technology, 325B, 363B
  and Soviet Union, 302A, 332A, 334A, 342B, 376B
  and Transylvania, 268A
  and Turkey, 138B, 156A, 162A, 196A
  and United States, 306B
  and Vatican City, 375C
  and Venice, 130B
  World War II, 326A, 334A
  and Yugoslavia, 316A, 326A
Hunger (Hamsun), 283C
Hungu, 216B
Hunneric (king of Vandals), 60B
Huns, 38B, 50B, 54A, 54B, 56A, 56B, 58A, 58C, 59C, 60A, 60B, 64B
Hunt, Helen, 385C
Hunt, Nelson, 364C
Hunt, W. Herbert "Bunker," 364C
Hunt, Walter, 251B
Hunter, David, 266B
Hunter, Holly, 379C
Hunter, Walter, 219B
Huntington Library, 377C
Hunyadi, János, 138B
Huon Peninsula, 330C, 332C
hurdy-gurdy, 203B
Huron Confederacy, 187A, 189A, 199A, 215A
Hurricane Andrew, 378C
Hurston, Zora Neale, 329C
Husain, 70B
Husain, Alauddin (sultan of Ghor), 102C
Husák, Gustáv (president of Czechoslovakia), 360B, 370B
Husan Shah (king of Bengal), 146C
Husayn, Shah Sultan (king of Persia), 200C
Huss, John, 135C, 137C
Hussein, Saddam (leader of Iraq), 374A, 377A, 384A
Hussein ibn Ali (grand sharif of Mecca and king of Hejaz), 299A, 301A, 303A
Hussein ibn Talal (king of Jordan), 373A
Hussein (king of Jordan), 373A, *373*
Husseinite dynasty. *See* Tunisia
Hussey, Obed, 251B
Hussites, 136A, 139C
Huston, John, 325C, 329C
Hutcheson, Francis, 209C
Hutchinson, Anne, 187A
Hutchinson, William, 215B
Hutter, Jacob, 159C, 161C
Hutterites, 159C
Huxley, Aldous, 307C, 315C, 323C
Huxley, Thomas, 271C
Huygens, Christiaan, 191B, 195B
Hyatt, John, 273B
Hyatt Hotel accident, 366C
Hyderabad, 90C, 146C, 172C, 204C, 208C, 218C
hydraulic press, 233B
hydraulic ram, 233B
hydrofoil, 303B, 339B
hydrogen peroxide, 245B
hydrometer, 59B
hydrostatics, 173B
hygrometer, 147B, 199B, 245B
Hyksos dynasty. *See* Egypt, Egyptians
Hymen's Triumph (Daniel), 181C
Hymn (Caedmon), 71C
Hymnen und Die Nacht (Novalis), 235C
Hypatia, 55B, 59B
Hypatia (Kingsley), 263C
Hysiae, battle of, 12C

I

I Ching (Book of Changes), 19C
I-Hsing, 73B
I Remember Mama (Druten), 333C

I Thought of Daisy (Wilson), 311C
Ibáñez, Carlos (president of Chile), 310C, 312C
Iberian Peninsula, 72C, 84B
Ibn al-Hind, 64C
ibn Burd, Bashshar, 77C
ibn Hayyan, Jabir, 75B
Ibn Saud, 315A
Ibo, 122C
Ibrahim, 156C
Ibrahim Lodi (king of Delhi), 154C
Ibrahim Pasha (viceroy of Egypt), 246A, 251A, 259A
Ibrahim (sultan of Ottoman Empire), 186B, 188B
Ibsen, Henrik, 271C, 277C, 279C, 281C
Ibuprofen, 347B, 361B, 367B
ice, 217B
ice cream, 177B
  cone, 285B
  Eskimo Pie, 307B
Ice Palace (Ferber), 345C
Icebergs (Church), 267C
Iceland, Icelandics, 22C, 77B, 80A, 91A, 101C, 111C, 338B, 354A, 372B
  and Britain, 346B, 358B, 362B
  government, 364B, 366B
  and United States, 324B
  World War II, 324B
Iceman Cometh, The (O'Neill), 337C
Ickes, Harold, 326B, 328B
Idaho, 252B, 282B
Ideas Toward a Philosophy of a History of Mankind (Herder), 227C
Ideen zur Philosophie der Geschichte der Menschheit (Herder), 227C
Idiot, The (Dostoyevsky), 271C
Idoménée (Crébillon), 203C
Idris Alooma, 168B
Idris I, 76B
Idris II, 76B
Idris I (king of Libya), 339A, 357A
Idrisi, 84B
Idrisi, al-, 105B
Idylls of the King (Tennyson), 265C
Iemochi, 265A
Ienari, 227A
Iesada, 263A
Ietsugu, 206C
Ieyoshi, 255A
If It Be Not Good, the Devil Is in It (Dekker), 179C
Ife, 91C
IG Farben, 319B
Iglau Compact, 139C
Ignatius (Bishop of Antioch), 37A, 39A
Ignatius of Loyola, 157C, 163C, 165C
Iguala, Plan of, 244C
Ikhnaton (king of Egypt), 9C
Ikko sect, 146C
Il-Khans, 116C, 130C
Ili Valley, 220C
Iliad (Homer), 11C, 179C, 207C
Illia, Arturo (president of Argentina), 353A
Illinois Central Railroad, 265B
Illinois (Indians), 203A
Illinois River, 197A, 209A
Illinois (U.S.), 65A, 73A, 77A, 83A, 87A, 99A, 109A, 123A, 135A, 240B, 244B, 246B, 250B, 264B, 310B, 338C
Illyria, 149B
Illyrian Coast, 238A
Iltutmish (sultan of Delhi), 110C, 112C
Imadeddin Zengi, 100B
Imaginary Conversations (Landor), 247C
Imagines (Vargo), 31C
Iman Ahmed bin Said (sultan of Oman), 212B
Imbros, 304A
Imix Dog, 77A
Immaculate Conception, 263C
Immaculate Conception, The (Velázquez), 181C
immigration, illegal, 282B
Immigration Act, 295A
Immigration and Naturalization Act, 340C
Immoraliste, L' (Gide), 289C
Imperial Chamber, 152A, 165C
Imperial Chemical Industries (ICI), 375B
Imperial University (China), 63B
Imphal, 332C
Importance of Being Earnest, The (Wilde), 285C
Impressionism, Impressionists, 273C, 279C
In Cold Blood (Capote), 353C
In Hell, Self-Portrait (Munch), 285C
In Memoriam (Tennyson), 261C
In the Heat of the Night (movie), 353C
In the Twilight (Chekhov), 285C
In This Our Life (Glasgow), 325C
In This Our Life (movie), 329C
in-vitro fertilization, 381C
Inca empire, Inca, 91B, 99A, 135A, 139A, 139B, 141A, 155A, 159A, 159B, 161A, 163A
Inchon, 338A
Independent Treasury Act, 254B
Index of Forbidden Books, 167C, 353C
India, Indians, 5B, 33B, 38B, 44B, 54B, 68C, 76C, 84C, 98C, 104C, 106C, 130C, 138C, 144C, 146C, 166C, 168C, 194C, 204C, 208C, 225A, 269B, 313A
  2000 B.C.–30 B.C., 5B, 6B, 7C, 9B, 14B, 17C, 22B, 23C, 31B
  and Abyssinia, 58C
  and Afghanistan, 239A, 283A
  agriculture, 63B, 69B
  and Akbar, 172C
  and ancient Rome, 34B
  and Arabs, 72B, 77B
  arts, 7C, 23C, 25C, 39C, 45C, 55C, 59C, 67C, 71C, 77C, 89C, 91C, 99C, 109C, 161C, 173C, 177C
  and Babur, 154C, 156C
  and Baluchistan, 281A
  and Bangladesh, 357A
  and Britain, 109B, 178C, 182C, 186C, 192C, 198C, 200C, 202C, 216C, 218C, 220C, 223A, 227A, 229A, 235A, 237A, 245A, 249A, 251A, 255A, 257A, 259A, 261A, 265A, 303A, 315A, 322C, 332C, 337A
  and Burma, 247A
  and Canada, 294B
  and Ceylon, 110C, 116C
  Chalukya dynasty, 68C, 88C, 90C
  chemical plant disaster, 369A
  and China, 67B, 80C, 349A
  and Egypt, 34B, 58C
  and Europe, 173B, 212C
  and France, 214C, 343A
  government, 56B, 60C, 64C, 70C, 78C, 86C, 140C, 142C, 170C, 192C, 227A, 241A, 279A, 317A, 330C, 339A, 353A, 357A, 363A
  Government of India Acts, 303A
  Gupta dynasty, 52B, 53A, 60C, 64C, 71C
  and Holland, 200C
  Hoysala dynasty, 98C
  and Humayun, 164C
  and Jammu, 375A
  and Japan, 332C
  and Kashmir, 375A
  Khalji dynasty, 124C
  law and society, 231A, 249A, 265A, 361A, 369A, 379A
  Maratha dynasty, 206C, 220C, 229A, 233A, 235A
  Mauryan dynasty, 22B
  and Mesopotamia, 301A
  Mogul dynasty, 156C, 160C, 174C, 176C, 190C, 192C, 202C, 204C, 206C, 214C, 233A
  and Mongolia, 112C, 114C
  and Natal, 267A
  natural disasters in, 142C, 150C, 164C, 192C, 218C, 355A, 379A
  nuclear testing by, 385A
  and Pakistan, 337A, 338A, 351A, 353A, 355A, 357A
  Pala dynasty, 108C
  politics, 319A, 341A, 375A
  population, 176C
  and Portugal, 148B, 152C, 157B, 169C, 184C
  religion, 11B, 17C, 33A, 39A, 53A, 62C, 72C, 73C, 75C, 90C, 92C, 93C, 122C, 124C, 128C, 134C, 183C, 187C, 194C
  science and technology, 66C
  slave trade, 255A
  and Soviet Union, 356A
  and Tibet, 74C, 347A
  and Timur, 138C
  and Transvaal, 291A
  and Turkey, 154B
India Act, 227A
India Conferences, 312A, 314A
India (Naipaul), 375C
Indian Knoll culture, 65A
Indian Ocean, 63B, 77B, 116C, 146B, 153B, 174C, 204B, 210B, 239A, 332C, 364A
Indian Summer (Howells), 281C
Indiana, 63A, 77A, 135A, 197A, 211A, 238B, 242B, 247C, 312B
Indianapolis, 244B
Indians, North American, 63A, 65A, 77A, 83A, 87A, 99A, 115C, 123A, 175A. *See also individual tribes*
  Alcatraz seized by, 356C
  battle of Fallen Timbers, 230B
  battle of Little Big Horn, 274B
  Black Hawk War, 250B
  and Canada, 179A, 274B, 278B
  and colonists, 183A, 238B
  Dawes Severalty Act, 280B
  Fort Dearborn massacre, 240B
  and France, 159A, 181A, 201A, 211A
  French and Indian War, 215A, 217A
  Indian Appropriations Act, 272B
  Indian Removal Act, 248B
  land proclamation, 282B
  Ramona and, 279C
  as slaves, 163A
  in Virginia, 197A
Indians, South American, 155A. *See also individual tribes*
Indies, Chamber of the, 176A
indigo, 109B, 273B
Indochina, 265A, 281A, 337A, 342A
Indonesia, Indonesians, 44B, 77C, 194C, 198C, 204C, 212C, 214C, 231A, 350A, 351A, 385A. *See also* East Indies
  3000 B.C.–2000 B.C., 2B, 4B
  and ASEAN, 352A
  and East Timor, 361A
  government, 339A
  and Holland, 178C
  independence of, 337A
  and Japan, 326C
  and Malaysia, 353A
  and Netherlands, 339A, 345A
  in United Nations, 352A
  volcanic eruptions, 243A
  World War II, 326C
Indore, 206C, 237A
Indra III, 84C
Indraditya, 110C
Indus River, 5B, 74C
Indus Valley, 2B, 3B, 4B, 5B
Industrial Development Organization (UNIDO), 370A
Industrial Research Institute, 375B
Industrial Workers of the World, 290B
Influence of Sea Power Upon History, The (Mahan), 283C
influenza vaccine, 331B
Informatorium der Mutterschul (Comenius), 183C
infrastructure, 257B, 344B
Ingo I (king of Sweden), 96A
Ingres, Jean Auguste, 237C
Ingria, 180A, 208A
Inimitable Jeeves, The (Wodehouse), 307C
Inkerman, battle of, 262A
inks, soy-based, 371B
Inn district, 224A, 238A
Inness, George, 275C
Innocent II, Pope, 100B, 101C, 103C
Innocent III, Pope, 108B, 109C, 110A, 111C
Innocent IV, Pope, 114A, 114B, 115C
Innocent VIII, Pope, 145C, 147B
Innocent X, Pope, 189C, 191C
Innocent XI, Pope, 197C
Innsbruck, 164A
Inönü, Ismet (president of Turkey), 321A
Inquiry Concerning Beauty, Order, Harmony, and Design (Hutcheson), 209C
Inquiry Concerning Moral, Evil and Good (Hutcheson), 209C
Inquiry into the Human Mind on the Principles of Common Sense (Reid), 219C
Inquiry on the Nature and Causes of the Wealth of Nations (Smith), 223C
Inquisition, 243C
insane asylum, 243B
insecticide, 31B, 53B, 201B, 271B
Institutio Christiani Principis (Erasmus), 153C
Institutio Religionis Christianae (Calvin), 161C
Institutiones (Gaius), 41C
Instrument of Government, 190A
insulation, 321B, 327B
insulin, 367B
Insurance Company of North America, 232B
Intel Corporation, 355B
Inter-American Conference, 268C, 335A
Inter-American Defense Conference, 336A
Inter-American Neutrality Conference, 320C, 324C
Inter cunctas, 137C
intermarriage, 19A, 130A
Intermediate-Range Nuclear Forces (INF) Treaty, 372A
Internal Revenue Service, 364C

International Atomic Energy Agency, 342A, 344A, 380A
International Bank for Reconstruction and Development, 332B
International Business Machines (IBM), 321B, 343B, 349B, 351B, 363B, 367B, 379B
International Civil Aviation Organization (ICAO), 336A
International Conference of American States, 306C, 310C
International Conference on the Peaceful Uses of Atomic Energy, 342A
International Court of Justice, 304A, 310B, 371A
International Development Association (IDA), 346A
International Disarmament Commission, 350A
International Finance Corporation, 342A
International Fund for Agricultural Development (IFAD), 362A
International Harvester Company, 361B
International Health Conference, 336A
International Labor Conference, 304B
International Labor Organization, 362A, 364A
International Maritime Organization (IMO), 344A
International Military Tribunal, 336B
International Monetary Fund (IMF), 332B, 336A, 348A, 362B, 366A
International News Service, 345C
International Olympic Committee, 379C
International Surrealist Exhibition, 327C
International Whaling Commission, 368A
International Women's Rights Congress, 286A
International Workers' Association, 268A
Internet, 384C
Interpol (International Criminal Police Organization), 342A
Interstate Commerce Act, 280B
interstate highway system, 342C
Into This Last (Ruskin), 267C
Intolerable Acts, 221A
Intolerance (Griffith), 299C
Intrepid (U.S. ship), 236B
Introduction to the Principles of Morals and Legislation (Bentham), 227C, 229C
Intrusive Mount culture, 99A
Inuit people, 91B, 127A. *See also* Eskimos
Invisible Man (Ellison), 341C
Ionia, 10C, 16C, 268A
ionosphere, 309B
Iowa (Indians), 246B
Iowa (U.S.), 135A, 248B, 258B, 260B, 278B, 307B
Iphigenia (British ship), 228B
Iphigenia (Goethe), 225C
Ipiutak culture, 38C
Ipoh, 326C
Ipswich, 215C
Iquitos, 268C
IRA (Irish Republican Army), 358B, 360B
Iran, Iranians, 38B, 317A, 373C. *See also* Persia, Persians
- 550 B.C., 16B
- and Afghanistan, 253A, 319A
- and Britain, 326A
- and France, 321A
- government, 291A, 341A, 365A, 367A
- and Iraq, 319A, 365A, 367A, 373A
- and Russia, 253A, 326A
- and Salman Rushdie, 379C
- transportation, 321A
- and Turkey, 299A, 319A
- and United States, 346A, 364A, 365A, 367A, 370C
- World War II, 326A

Iran-Contra affair, 371A, 372C, 378C
Iran-Iraq War, 365A
Iraq, Iraqi, 100B. *See also* Persia
- and Afghanistan, 319A
- and Britain, 295A, 299A, 303A, 305A, 307A, 313A, 315A, 342A, 378A
- and France, 378A
- government, 311A, 345A, 349A
- and Iran, 319A, 365A, 367A, 373A
- and Israel, 366A
- and Jordan, 345A
- and Kurds, 382A
- and Kuwait, 374A, 375A
- and League of Nations, 315A
- and Mongolia, 112C
- Mosul-Tripoli oil pipeline, 309A, 317A
- and OPEC, 375A
- Persian Gulf War, 374A
- Shiites in, 377A
- and Soviet Union, 342A
- and Transjordan, 313A
- and Turkey, 297A, 319A, 342A
- and United Nations, 372A, 374A, 376A, 382A, 384A
- and United States, 368A, 370A, 376A, 378A, 382A
- World War II, 324A

Ireland, Irish, 54A, 61B, 83B, 90A, 98A, 200A, 290A, 315B, 374B
- Act of Union, 234A
- and America, 192A, 207A
- arts, 71C, 201C, 203C, 205C, 295C
- and Britain, 104A, 130A, 148A, 188A, 190A, 232A, 278A, 298A, 312A, 314A, 318A, 338B, 350B, 358B, 368B
- and Denmark, 84A, 358B
- education, 173C
- government, 106A, 111C, 144A, 162A, 302A, 318A, 346B, 352B
- Home Rule, 280A
- and Iceland, 77B
- independence of, 224A
- Irish Peace Agreement, 306A
- Irish Republican Army (IRA), 318A, 364B, 368B, 380B
- law and society, 176A, 186A, 384B
- Northern, 356B, 358B, 362B, 368B, 380B, 384B
- Peace Agreement in, 306A
- "Phoenix Park Murders," 278A
- politics, 314A, 370B
- potato blight in, 256A
- religion, 73C
- science and technology, 125B, 319B
- and Scotland, 190A

Irene (empress of Byzantium), 76B
Irigoyen, Hipólito (president of Argentina), 310C, 312C
Irish Church, 73C, 162A
Irish Melodies (Moore), 237C
Irkutsk, 190C
iron, Iron Age, 5B, 9B, 37C, 44B, 67B, 77B, 93B, 113B, 133B, 139B, 203B, 229B
- in Africa, 13B, 17B, 135B
- in Austria, 11B
- buoy of, 257B
- cast iron, 255B
- in China, 13B, 17B, 19B, 101B, 125B
- corrugated, 249B, 259B
- in Egypt, 15B
- in England, 13B, 17A
- in Europe, 73B
- in Greece, 11B
- in Japan, 23B
- production of, 123B
- in Rome, 31B, 33B, 35B, 39B, 47B
- smelting, 255B
- tax on, 242B
- used by Dorians, 10C
- wrought, 171B

Iron Act, 214A
Iron Curtain, 336A, 340C
iron lung, 311B
irons, ironing, 91B
Irons, Jeremy, 375C
Ironside, Edmund, 90A
Ironside, Henry, 313C
Iroquois Confederacy, 91A, 129A, 169A, 187A, 189A, 189C, 191A, 195A, 199A, 203A, 209A, 211A
irrigation, 39B, 67A, 67B, 73A, 83B, 107B, 175B
Irving, John, 363C
Irving, Washington, 239C, 245C
Irwin, Lord, 313A
Isaac I Comnenus (emperor of Byzantine), 94B
Isaac II Angelus (emperor of Byzantium), 106B
Isabella I (queen of Castile), 142A, *143,* 144A, 150A, 154A,
Isabella II (queen of Spain), 250A, 256A, 270A, 272A
Isabella (queen of France), 124A, 134A
Isandhlwana, battle of, 277A
Ise shrine, 69C
Isenheim Triptych (Grünewald), 153C
Isfahan, 112C, 173C, 179C
Ishege, 212C
Isherwood, Christopher, 315C, 317C
Ishiguro, Kazuo, 373C
Isis, 41A
Isla de la Juventud, 308C
Islam, Islamics, 68B, 72B, 74B, 80B, 81C, 109C, 112B, 168C. *See also* Muslims; Wahhabi
- arts, 67B
- in India, 122C, 134C, 183C
- Naqshbandi, 195C
- Nation of Islam, 383C
- in Turkey, 311A
- in West Africa, 94C

Islandinbók (Ari the Wise), 101C
Isle of Man, 90A
Isle of Portland, 131B
Isly, battle of, 257A
Ismail I (shah of Persia and sultan of Bijapur), 150B, 152C
Ismail II (shah of Persiia), 170B
Ismail Pasha (viceroy of Egypt), 269A, 271A
Iso-No-Zenji, 99C
Isonzo
- battles of, 296A, 298A, 300A

Isonzo River, 60B
Israel, Israelis, 235A, politics. *See also* Judaea, kingdom of; Palestine
- 50th anniversary of, 385A
- 1500 B.C.–150 B.C., 6A, 8A, 8B, 10B, 11C, 12B, 15C, 27C
- and Arab East Jerusalem, 385A
- and Arab terrorists, 358A
- and Egypt, 343A, 345A, 355A, 359A, 362A, 363A, 364A, 365A, 381A
- Entebbe hostage rescue, 362A
- and Ethiopia, 377A
- famine in, 6A
- and Gaza strip, 371A, 383A
- and Golan Heights, 367A
- government, 339A, 361A, 371A
- and Hebron, 385A
- independence of, 337A
- and Iraq, 366A
- Jerusalem as capital of, 365A
- and Jordan, 355A, 381A
- and Lebanon, 367A, 369A, 379A
- and Nazis, 348A
- and Palestine, 376A, 377A, 379A
- politics, 371A, 379A, 383A
- Six-Day War, 355A
- and Syria, 355A, 359A
- and United Nations, 338A, 376A
- and United States, 336A, 362A, 370C
- and West Bank, 373A, 381A, 383A
- and West Germany, 350B
- Yom Kippur War, 359A

Israel ben Eliezer, 213C
Istanbul, 313A. *See also* Constantinople
Istanbul Technical University, 220B
Istria, Capo d', 232A, 248A
It Happened One Night (movie), 317C
Italian Girl in Algiers, The (Rossini), 241C
Italian National Laboratories, 349B
Italian Social Republic, 330A
Italiana in Algeri, L' (Rossini), 241C
Italy, Italians, 46A, 50A, 56A, 96B, 150A, 159B, 164A. *See also* Rome, Romans
- 1100 B.C.–216 B.C., 11A, 12C, 13C, 21A, 25A
- on abortion, 360B
- and Abyssinia, 281A, 285A, 310A, 316A, 319A, 321A
- and Albania, 310A, 320A
- and Arabs, 78B, 80B, 84B, 88B, 90B
- and Argentina, 333A, 335A
- arts, 17A, 63C, 121C, 141C, 143C, 147C, 153C, 155C, 161C, 165C, 179C, 183C, 193C, 195C, 199C, 205C, 209C, 215C, 241C, 243C, 245C, 253C, 269C, 273C, 277C, 283C, 285C, 289C, 295C, 307C, 339C, 345C, 347C, 349C, 381C
- and Austria, 270A, 272A, 280A, 296A, 298A, 300A, 302A, 312A, 316A
- and Bolivia, 331A
- and Brazil, 329A, 335A
- and Britain, 266A, 280A, 308A, 309A, 322A, 324A
- and British Somaliland, 324A
- and Burma, 148C
- and Byzantium, 65C, 74B
- and Canada, 330B
- and Chile, 327A, 331A
- and China, 151C
- Communism in, 362B
- and Czechoslovakia, 316A
- and Dalmatia, 308A
- and East Africa, 317A
- economy, 114B
- education, 81C, 113C, 115C, 125C, 135C
- and Egypt, 88B, 309A, 324A
- and Eritrea, 279A
- and Ethiopia, 281A, 287A
- Fascism in, 310A
- Flagellants in, 117C
- and France, 148A, 152A, 154A, 158A, 160A, 236A, 264A, 268A, 272A, 286A, 308A, 317A, 320A, 322A

in G-7, 368A
and Germany, 102B, 104B, 112B, 124B, 143B, 298A, 300A, 302A, 304A, 308A, 312A, 318A, 320A, 324A, 326A, 330A, 334A
government, 82B, 86B, 100B, 126B, 234A, 276A, 280A, 302A, 336B
and Greece, 324A
and Habsburgs, 206A
and Hungary, 84B, 316A
industry, 91C, 99B, 103B, 117B, 119B, 125B, 129B, 133B, 137B, 145B
and International Monetary Fund, 348A
and Japan, 318A
and Kenya, 324A
law and society, 244A, 259C, 286A
and League of Nations, 316A, 317A
and Lebanon, 367A
and Libya, 293B, 321A, 324A
and Magyars, 82A
and Mecca, 301A
and Mexico, 329A
and Nonintervention Committee, 318A
and Normandy, 94B, 104B
and North Africa, 330A
Oliver Tree Coalition, 382B
and Ottoman Empire, 292A, 293A
and Peru, 335A
plague in, 40A
politics, 362B, 380B
and Red Sea, 292A
religion, 78A, *101,* 133C, 181C, 369C
and Rhodes, 292A
and Romania, 316A
and Rome, 272A
science and technology, 59B, 91B, 109B, 127B, 131B, 135B, 149B, 151B, 161B, 163B, 165B, 167B, 169B, 171B, 173B, 175B, 177B, 183B, 187B, 233B, 257B, 259B, 289B, 317B, 343B
settlement of, 58A, 58B, 60B, 64B
and Somalia, 287A
and Spain, 318A
and Syria, 292A
and Treaty of Rome, 344A
in Triple Alliance, 278A, 296A
and Tripoli, 292A
and Tunis, 285A
and Turkey, 292A, 296A
and United Nations, 338A
and United States, 308B, 326A, 326B, 328B, 330A, 338A, 348A, 356A
volcanic eruption in, 62B
in Western European Union, 342A
World War II, 324A, 326A, 328B, 329A, 330A, 332A, 334A
and Yugoslavia, 304A, 316A, 326A, 342B
Ith-tawi, 4A
Ito Hirobumi (prime minister of Japan), 279A, 281A
Iturbide, Agustin de, 246C
Itzas, 87A
Ivan I, 126A
Ivan III, 146A, 148A
Ivan IV the Terrible (tsar of Russia), 158A, 162A, 168A, 172A
Ivan Susanin (Glinka), 253C
Ivangorod, 296A
Ivanhoe (Scott), 245C
Ives, Charles Edward, 343C
Ives, Frederic, 277B
ivory, 4A, 84C, 176B
Ivory Coast, 281A, 285A, 375C
Ivry
League at, 172A
Treaty of, 106A
Iwaki province, 212C
Iwo Jima, 332C, 334C
Iyasu, 212B
Iyasus the Great (emperor of Ethiopia), 196B, 204B
Iyo (empress of Japan), 46B
Izapa culture, 44C
Izmir, 212B

J

J. P. Morgan Company. *See* Morgan Company
J. Paul Getty Museum. *See* Getty Museum
Jabneh, 37A
Jack-in-the Pulpit No. 2 (O'Keeffe), 315C
jackets, flack, 329B
jacks, 135B
Jackson, Andrew (president of U.S.), 236B, 242B, 244B, 246B, 248B, 250B, 252B
Jackson, Charles, 333C
Jackson, Glenda, 357C, 359C
Jackson, Helen Hunt, 279C
Jackson, Jesse, 366C
Jackson, Michael, 367C
Jackson, Shirley, 351C
Jacksonville, 280B
Jacobites, 198A
Jacob's Pillow Dance Festival, 325C
Jacobsen, Cornelius, 181A
Jacobson v. Massachusetts, 290B
Jacquerie, 130A
Jade Sky, 79A
Jadwiga (queen of Poland), 132A
Jaen, battle of, 114B
Jafar (shah of Persia), 227A
Jaffa, 301A
Jaffenapatam, 190C
Jaffna, 385A
Jaga, 168B, 172B
Jagellon dynasty. *See* Poland
Jaguar, Shield, 71A
Jaguar Paw dynasty. *See* Mayan civilization, Maya
Jain, Jainism, 17C, 93C
Jaipal, 90C
Jaipur, 166C
Jakarta, 180C
Jakes, Mílos, 370B
Jalal ad-Din ar-Rumi, 119C
Jalaluddin (sultan of Delhi), 120C
Jam-Zapoloski, Peace of, 170A
Jamaica, Jamaicans, 147A, 149A, 151A, 153A, 201A, 258C, 266C, 268C, 272C, 274C, 278C, 327A, 349A
and Britain, 320C
earthquake in, 201A
politics, 331A
slave trade, 187A, 250C, 254C
suffrage in, 333A
Jamaica Inn (du Maurier), 319C
James, Cyril Lionel Robert, 321C
James, Epistle of, 57A
James, Henry, 277C, 281C
James, Jesse, 278B
James, Saint, 35A
James Bay, 199A, 201A
James I (king of Aragon), 110B, 112B, 116B
James I (king of England, Scotland, France, and Ireland), 176A
James I (king of England), 178A, 182A
James I (king of Scotland), 134A, 136A, 138A
James I (submarine), 181B
James II (king of Aragon), 120B, 124B
James II (king of England), 196A, 198A, 199A, 200A, 202A
James II (king of Scotland), 138A, 140A
James III (king of Scotland), 140A, 146A
James IV (king of Scotland), 146A, 150A, 151C, 152A
James V (king of Scotland), 152A, 162A
James VI (king of Scotland), *167,* 175C, 176A
Jameson, Sir Leander, 285A
Jamestown, 179A, 180B, 181A, 183A
Jammu, 375A
Jamnia, Synod of, 39A
Jane Eyre (Brontë), 259C
Janina, battle of, 246A
Janissaries, 194B, 196B, 200B, 202B, 204B, 214B, 237A, 249A
Janjira, 180C, 216B
Jannu, 216C
Jansen, Cornelius Otto, 187C
Jansenism, Jansenists, 187C, 191C, 197C, 217C
Jansenist Moral Reflections (Quesnel), 207B
Japan, Japanese, 49B, 66C, 76C, 99C, *127,* 210C, 359A, 379A
300 B.C.–250 B.C., 23B, 24B
Anglo-Japanese Alliance, 307A
and Antarctica, 346A
arts, 63C, 65C, 67C, 71C, 72C, 73C, 83C, 99C, 123C, 139C, 151C, 157C, 165C, 177C, 179C, 185C, 191C, 203C, 207C, 221C, 227C, 231C, 245C, 251C, 277C, 329C, 339C, 353C, 373C, 385C
and Australia, 328C
and Axis, 324C
and Britain, 269A, 271A, 285A, 288A, 290A, 306B, 312A, 326C, 332C
and Burma, 326C, 334C
calendar, 275A
and Canada, 324B
and China, 34B, 46B, 66C, 106C, 111B, 113B, 156C, 164C, 174C, 182C, 198C, 206C, 273A, 284A, 295A, 297A, 299A, 307A, 311A, 315A, 317A, 319A, 321A, 322C, 326C, 332C, 334C
conscription in, 273A
and Dutch East Indies, 326C
economy, 287A, 313A, 322C
education, 273A
and Europe, 180C, 186C
Factory Act, 293A
and France, 269A, 271A, 306B
Fujiwara family, 82C, 86C
in G-7, 368A
and Germany, 295A, 305A, 318A
government, 82C, 98C, 168C, 170C, 172C, 176C, 190C, 196C, 227A, 255A, 263A, 265A, 271A, 277A, 279A, 281A, 283A, 293A, 319A, 322C, 337A, 345A
and Guam, 326C
Hiroshige school, 251C
Hojo family, 110C
and Holland, *182,* 186C, 188C, 269A
and Hong Kong, 326C
and India, 332C
and Indochina, 322C
industry, 63B, 113B, 375B, 377B
and International Monetary Fund, 348A
and Italy, 318A
Kamakura period, 107C
and Korea, 44B, 54B, 56B, 64C, 174C, 288A, 291A, 293A, 303A
law and society, 72C, 126C, 142C, 146C, 186C, 209C, 212C, 275A, 277C, 283A, 321C
and League of Nations, 315A, 321A
and Liaotung, 285A
and Malaya, 326C
and Manchukuo, 321A
and Manchuria, 293A, 313A, 315A
and Mexico, 327A
Minamoto family, 106C
Mitsui family, 194C
and Mongolia, 118C
natural disasters in, 68C, 136C, 140C, 210C, 220C, 381A
and Netherlands, 271A
and Philippines, 326C, 328C
plague in, 140C
politics, 373A, 383A
and Portugal, 162C, 186C
religion, 49A, 65C, 69C, 94C, 100C, 109C, 117C, 165C, 174C, 178C, 179C, 180C, 181C, 183C, 209C
and Russia, 262A, 275A, 284A, 289A, 290B, 291A, 293A, 299A, 303A, 317A
Russo-Japanese War, 290B, 291A
science and technology, 51B, 73B, 75B, 79B, 81C, 115B, 213B, 273B, 299B, 351B, 365B, 367B, 375B
and Siam, 309A
silver in, 198C
Sino-Japanese War, 285A, 319A
and Soviet Union, 321A, 322C, 334A
and Spain, 182C, 275A
Taira family, 104C, 106C
and Taiwan, 285A
taxes, 166C, 184C, 212C, 214C, 218B, 218C, 275A
and Thailand, 326C
transportation, 273B
in United Nations, 342A
and United States, 259A, 263A, 267A, 269A, 271A, 284B, 290B, 291A, 294B, 306B, 308B, 312A, 319A, 324B, 326B, 326C, 328B, 328C, 330C, 332C, 334C, 336A, 338A, 342A, 346C, 355A, 372C
World War I, 295A
World War II, 324B, 324C, 326B, 326C, 328B, 328C, 332C
and Yap Island, 295A
Japanese Combined Fleet, 330C
Japanese Imperial Conference, 326C
Jaruzelski, Wojciech (prime minister of Poland), 366B
Jarvik, Robert, 367B
Jason (Thorwaldson), 237C
Jaspers, Karl, 303C, 313C, 317C
Jassy, 244A
battle of, 180A
Peace of, 230A
Jaswant Rao Holkar (ruler of Indore), 237A
Jaunpur, 130C, 148C
Java, Javanese, 74C, 76C, 77C, 78C, 83C, 114C, 120C, 128C,

140C, 154C, 176C, 180C, 182C, 212C, 214C, 239A, 326C, 328C, 332C, 342A
Java (British warship), 240B
Java Sea, battle of, 328C
Javain, 214C
Jawa, 3B
Jaworski, Leon, 358C, 360C
Jaws (movie), 361C
Jay, John, 226B
Jay Treaty, 230B
Jaya Paramesvaravarman (king of Champa), 112C
Jayavarman III (king of Khmer), 80C
Jazari, Ismaeel al-, 99B, 109B
jazz, 279C
Jean Christophe, Vol. I (Rollland), 289C
Jean (grand duke of Luxembourg), 350B
jeans, denim, 281B
Jebel Druse, 319A
Jebusites, 10B
Jeddah, 136C
Jeffers, Robinson, 309C
Jeffers, William Martin, 328B
Jefferson, Thomas (president of U.S.), 230B, 231B, 232B, 234B, 236B, 241C, 248B
Jehangir (emperor of Moguls), 176C, 178C, 182C
Jehol province, 315A
Jehovah's Witnesses, 273C, 331C
Jena, battle of, 236A
Jenatsch, George, 186A
Jenkins, David (Bishop of Durham), 369C
Jenkins, Robert, 212A
Jenkins's Ear, War of, 212A
Jenné, 142B, 283A
Jenne empire, 92C
Jenney, William, 279C
Jennings, Thomas, 245B
Jensen, Harald, 353B
Jenson, Nicolas, 143B
Jeremiah, 13C
Jericho, 8B, 303A
Jerome, Saint, 57A
Jersey City, 249B
Jerusalem, 35A, 69C, 112B
  1000 B.C.–63 B.C., 10B, 13C, 14B, 18B, 26B, 28B
  and Britain, 301A
  and Byzantium, 68B
  as capital of Palestine, 373A
  and Crusaders, 98B
  government, 100B, 102B, 104B, 106B, 118B
  and Israel, 365A, 385A
  and Kwarazm Turks, 114B
  and Muhammadans, 90B
  and Muslims, 68B
  Old Jerusalem, 355A
  and Persians, 66B
  and Roman Empire, 36B, 40B
  Temple of, 11C, 31A, 33A, 37A
  and Turkey, 96B
Jerusalem (Va.), 250B
Jervis, John, 232A
Jesuit Order, Jesuits, 159C, 163C, 164B, 166B, 169C, 171C, 187C, 189C
  in Arizona, 201C, 203C, 219A
  in Canada, 183C
  in China, 195C, 207C
  in Germany, 273C, 289C
  and Jansenists, 217C
  and Northern Mariana Island, 194C
  in Paraguay, 179C
  in Quebec, 281C
  in South America, 165A
  in United States, 255C
Jesus Christ, *32,* 33A, 53A, 55A, 63C, 77C, *101,* 125C, 195C, 351C, 379C
Jesus Christ Superstar (Lloyd Webber), 357C
Jesus College, Cambridge, 149C
Jet Propulsion Laboratory, 377B
jets. *See also* U.S. Air Force
  B-1 bomber, 362C
  B-25 1945 crash, 334B
  Concorde, 357B
  DC-9, 351B
  F-15 fighter, 359B
  F-117A stealth, 363B, 375B
  Gloster Meteor, 333B
  jet engine, 321B
  Jupiter-C four-stage, 343B
  Messerschmidt, 333B
  Tupelov Tu-144, 355B
  U-2 spy plane, 346A
  X-1, 337B
  XP-59, 329B
  YB-52 Stratofortress bomber, 341B
Jeu des Cartes (Stravinsky), 319C
Jewish Encyclopedia, 289C
Jewish terrorists in, 337A
JFK (movie), 377C
Jiang Qing, 367A
Jiangan province, 196C
Jiangsu province, 192C
Jieng, 184B
Jilin, 188C
Jiménez Brin, Enrique Adolf (president of Panama), 335A
Jiménez de Quesada, Gonzalo, 159B, 161A
Jimmu (emperor of Japan), 12B
Joachinsthaler, 155B
Joan I (queen of Naples), 128B, 132B
Joan II (queen of Naples), 134B
Joan of Arc, 136A, 137B, 305C
Job Training Partnership Act, 366C
Jobs, Steve, 363B
"Jobs for Peace and Freedom" march, 366C
Jocelyn (Lamartine), 253C
Johannes IV (emperor of Ethiopia), 273A
Johannesburg, 287A
John, Don of Austria, 170A
John, Gospel of, 39A
John I (king of Castile and León), 132B
John I (king of Portugal), 132B
John I Tzimisces (emperor of Byzantium), 86A, 86B
John II Casimir Vasa (king of Poland), 194A
John II Comnenus (emperor of Byzantium), 100B, 102B
John II (king of Castile and León), 134B
John II (king of Denmark), 148A
John II (king of France), 128A,
John II (king of Portugal), 144A
John III, Pope, 65C
John III (Brittany), 126A
John III (king of Portugal), 156A
John III (king of Sweden), 174A
John III Sobieski (king of Poland), 194A
John III Vatatzes (emperor of Byzantium), 112B, 114B
John IV Lascaris (emperor of Byzantium), 116B
John V Palaeologus (emperor of Byzantium), 126B, 132B
John VI Cantacuzenus (emperor of Byzantium), 128B
John VI (king of Portugal), 242A, 242C, 248A
John VIII, Pope, 81C
John VIII Palaeologus (emperor of Byzantium), 136B
John XII, Pope, 87C
John XIII, Pope, 87C
John XIX, Pope, 93C
John XV, Pope, 89C
John XXII, Pope, 125C, 127C
John XXIII, Pope, 135C, 137C, 349C
John Frederick I, 162A
John (king of England), 108A, 110A
John of Burgundy, 136A
John of Gaunt, 132A
John Paul I, Pope, 363C
John Paul II, Pope, 363C, 367C, 374A, 375C, 379C, 381C, 383C
John (prince of Ireland), 106A, 110A, 111C
John the Baptist, 33A
John the Fearless (duke of Burgundy), 134A
"Johnny Appleseed," 234B
Johns, Jasper, 373C
Johns Hopkins University, 293B
Johnson, Andrew (president of U.S.), 268B, 270B, 384C
Johnson, Eldridge, 289B
Johnson, Jack, 291C
Johnson, Lyndon B. (president of U.S.), 348C, 350C, 352C, 354A,
Johnson, Philip, 345C, 353C
Johnson, Samuel, 215C
Johnson & Johnson Company, 305B, 366C
Johnson building, 323C
Johnston, Albert, 266B
Johnston, Joseph E., 266B, 268B
Johore, 156C, 158C, 164C, 168C, 174C, 208C, 279A, 295A
joint
  arthroplasty, 339B
  replacement, 359B
Joint Board on Defense, 324B
Joinville, Jean de, 125C
Jolof, 196B
Jolyot, Prosper, 203C
Jones, Absalom, 226B
Jones, Frederick, 323B
Jones, Jennifer, 331C
Jones, John Paul, 224B
Jones, Paula, 380C, 384C
Jones Act, 299A
Jonson, Ben, 175C, 177C, 187C
Jonsson, Karl, 111C
Joplin, Janis, 357C
Joplin, Scott, 279C
Jordan, 339A. *See also* Transjordan
  and Britain, 337A
  civil war in, 356A
  and Egypt, 342A, 355A
  and Iraq, 345A
  and Israel, 355A, 381A
  Six-Day War, 355A
  and Syria, 342A
  and United Arab Republic, 344A, 345A, 347A
  and West Bank, 373A
Jordan, Michael, 379C
Joseph I (Holy Roman Emperor), 202A, 204A
Joseph I (king of Portugal), 222A
Joseph II (Holy Roman Emperor and king of Germany and Austria), 218A, 224A, 226A, 228A
Josephson, Brian, 349B
Josephson junction, 349B
Josephus, Flavius, 37C, 39C
Joshua, 8B
Josiah (king of Judah), 14B
Josquin des Prés, 139C
Journal des Savants, 193C
Journey from St. Petersburg to Moscow (Radischev), 229C
Journey to Italy (Goethe), 243C
Jovian (emperor of Byzantium), 54A, 54B
Joy Luck Club, The (Tan), 373C
Joyce, James, 295C, 299C, 307C, 323C
Juan Carlos (king of Spain), 360B
Juan de Borbón, 362B
Juárez, Benito Pablo (president of Mexico), 266C, 272C
Jubaland, 309A
Juchen, 180C, 182C
Judaea, kingdom of, 30B, 32A, 32B, 34B, 35A, 36B. *See also* Israel; Israelites
Judaeus, Philo, 35A, 35C
Judah, kingdom of, 10B, 13C, 14B
Judaism, Jews, 4B, 215C. *See also* Israel; Palestine
  587 B.C.–430 B.C., 14B, 16B, 18B
  and Arabs, 311A
  arts, 109C, 187C
  in Australia, 251C
  banking system, 78A
  and Christians, 62C
  Conservative movement, 295C
  in England, 121C
  in Ethiopia, 377A
  in France, 107C, 229C
  in Germany, 81C
  Hadassah, 293C
  in Hungary, 285C
  Jesus and, 3A
  law and society, 18B
  and Pale of Settlement, 228A
  in Palestine, 319A
  persecutions of, 35A, 73C, 129C, 320A
  in Portugal, 149C
  in Prussia, 241C
  Reform movement, 287C
  and Romans, 38B, 40A, 40B
  in Russia, 248A, 252A
  and Second Vatican Council, 351C
  in Soviet Union, 347C
  in Spain, 147C
  terrorists in Palestine, 337A
  in Warsaw, 330A
Judas Maccabeus (Handel), 215C
Judiciary Act, 234B
Judson, Adoniram, 241C
Jugurtha (king of Numidia), 27A
Jugurthine War, 31C
Juilliard School of Music, 305C
jukebox, 339B
Jules et Jim (Truffaut), 347C
Julia (daughter of Augustus), 32A
Julia (daughter of Caesar), 29A
Julian, Percy, 339B
Julian the Apostate (emperor of Byzantium), 52A, *54,* 54A, 55C
Juliana (queen of the Netherlands), 364B
Jülich-Berg, 178A, 208A, 210A, 212A, 222A
Julius Caesar (Shakespeare), 175C
Julius I, Pope, 53A, 55A
Julius II, Pope, 151C, 152A
Julius III, Pope, 165C
Juneau, 276B
Jungaria, 186C, 216C, 220C
Junggar Pendi, 216C
Jungle, The (Sinclair), 289C
Jungle Book (Kipling), 285C
Junín, 246C
Jupiter (planet), 21B, 179B, 359B, 361B, 381B
Jupiter (Roman god), 17C
Jura, 364B
Jurassic Park (Spielberg), 379C
Jurchen, 100C
Justin of Samaria, 39A, 41A
Justin I (emperor of Byzantium), 62B
Justin II (emperor of Byzantium), 64B

Justine, ou les Malheurs de la Vertu (Sade), 229C
Justinian I (emperor of Byzantium), *62*, 62B, 63B, 63C
Justinian II (emperor of Byzantium), 70B, 72B
Justo, Agustín (president of Argentina), 312C
Jutes, 60A
Jutland, 11A
battle of, 298A
Juvenal, 39C
Juxon-Smith, Andrew (prime minister of Sierra Leone), 353A

K

Kaabu, 212B
kabuki, 185C
Kabul, 70C, 150C, 162C, 255A
Kabyle, 218B
Kachemak Bay culture, 36C, 63A, 91B
Kaczynski, Theodore, 382C, 384C
Kadphises, Kujula, 34B
Kaffir Wars, 225A, 253A, 261A
Kaffraria, 269A
Kafur, Malik, 122C, 124C
Kagera, 135B
Kagoshima, 269A
Kahlenberg, battle of, 198A
Kahya, Ibrahim, 214B
Kahya, Ridwan, 214B
Kaifeng, 105C
Kaifu Toshiki (prime minister of Japan), 373A
Kaikobad (sultan of Delhi), 120C
Kailasanatha Temple, 75C
Kairouan, mosque of, 71C
Kaiser, Henry, 328B
Kajar dynasty. *See* Persia
Kalambo Falls, 58C
Kalanaur, 164C
kaleidoscope, 243B
Kalevala (Lönnrot), 261C
Kalevipoeg (Kreutzwald), 267C
Kalmar Union, 134A
Kalmuks, 208C, 220C
Kalomo culture, 82C
Kama Sutra (Mallagana), 55C
Kamakura, 107C, 126C, *127*
Kamchatka, 200C
Kamehameha I (king of Hawaiian Islands), 239A
kamikaze, 332C
Kamul ud-Din Bihzad, 147C
Kana Uj, 76C, 108C
Kanagawa, Treaty of, 263A
Kanaris, Constantine, 246A
Kanauj, 78C, 84C, 92C
battle of, 160C
Kandahar, 162C, 182C, 188B
Kandinsky, Wassily, 311C
Kandy, kingdom of, 170C, 243A
Kanem, kingdom of, 94C, 106C, 112C, 142B, 168B
K'ang-hsi (emperor of China), 192C, 198C, 200C
Kang Te (emperor of Manchukuo), 317A
Kangra, 90C, 92C
Kaniaga, kingdom of, 96C
Kaniow, 156A
Kanishka, 37A
Kano
fortress of, 102C
kingdom of, 98C, 152B, 168B
painting school, 191C, 203C
Kanoji Angria, 208C
Kanpur, 265A
Kansas, 123A, 135A, 163A, 177A, 262B, 266B, 281B, 338C
Kansas City, 366C
Kansas City Chiefs, 353C, 357C
Kansas City Royals, 365C, 369C
Kansas-Nebraska Act, 262B
Kansu, 225A, 227A
Kant, Immanuel, 215C, 225C, *227*, 227C, 229C
Kanto, 218C
Kantor, MacKinley, 343C
Kanwaha, battle of, 156C
Kao Yang (emperor of China), 64C
Kapp, Wolfgang, 304A
Kapp revolt, 308A
Kara Ali, 246A
Karadzic, Vuk Stephanovic, 247C
Karageorge (ruler of Serbia), 238A
Karageorgevic, Alexander (king of Serbia), 264A
Karageorgevic, Peter (king of Serbia), 288A
Karak, kingdom of, 34B
Karakorum, 112C
Karamanlis, Konstantinos (prime minister of Greece), 360B, 368B
Karamzin, Nikolai Mikailovich, 245C
Karelia, 180A
Karelia (Sibelius), 283C
Karem Baptist Church, 241C
Karim Khan (shah of Persia), 223A
Karloff, Boris, 313C
Karlowitz, Peace of, 202A
Karlsevni, Thorfinn, 91A
Karlsruhe, 298A, 306A
Karmal, Babrak (president of Afghanistan), 371A
Karnak, Temple of, *5*, 5C
Kars, 94B, 176B, 202B, 262A, 305A
Karume, Abeid (president of Zanzibar), 359A
Kashi, 216C
Kashmir, 37A, 74C, 83B, 122C, 172C, 216C, 259A, 338A, 351A, 375A
Kasimiya, 192B
Kaskaskia Fort, 209A
Kaskaskia River, 203C
Katanga Company, 283A
Katib, Yunus ibn Sulaiman al-, 75C
Al-Kut, battles of, 299A, 301A
Katsina, kingdom of, 146B, 152B, 168B
Katsina dynasty. *See* West Africa
Katsukawa Shunsho, 223C
Kaufman, George S., 323C
Kaunas, 302A, 304A
Kavafis, Konstantinos, 315C
Kawabata Yasunari, 355C
Kayor, 196B
Kayra, 196B
Kazakh hordes, 196C, 208C, 210C, 212C, 220C
Kazakh Steppe, 206C
Kazan, 146A, 204C, 220A
Kazan, Elia, 337C, 343C
Kazantzakis, Nikos, 337C
Kazdughliya, 212B
Kearney, Stephen, 258B
Keaton, Diane, 363C
Keats, John, 245C
Kebbi, 154B
Keckley, Elizabeth, 267B
Kedah, 76C, 84C, 227A, 293A
Keeler, Christine (sex scandal), 348B
Keeling Islands, 249A
Kelantan, 293A
Kellogg, Frank Billings, 308B
Kellogg, John Harvey, 275B
Kellogg-Briand Peace Pact, 310B
Kelly, Gene, 341C
Kelly, Grace, 343C, 366B
Kelly, William, 261B
Kelso, Frank, 380C
Kelso Abbey, 99C
Kelvinator, 303B
Kemp, John (Archbishop of Canterbury), 139C
Keneally, Thomas, 367C
Kennedy, Anthony, 372C
Kennedy, Edward, 348C
Kennedy, Jacqueline, 348C
Kennedy, John F. (president of U.S.), 346A, 346C, 347B, 348A, 348C, 350C, *351*
Kennedy, Robert F., 346C, 348C, 354C
Kennelly-Heaviside layer, 309B
Kenneth II (king of Scots), 86A
Kent, kingdom of, 64A, 70A, 74A, 78A, 88A, 165B
Kent Peninsula, 244B
Kent State University, 356C
Kentucky, 63A, 65A, 135A, 221A, 222B, 230B, 235C, 239C, 248B
Kentucky bourbon, 229B
Kentucky Resolutions, 232B, 234B
Kenya, 176B, 202B, 281A, 305A, 307A, 349A, 351A. *See also* British East Africa
and Britain, 309A, 340A
and Italy, 324A
Kenyatta, Jomo (president of Kenya), 363A
Kerala, 88C, 90C
Kerensky, Aleksandr (premier of Russia), 300A
Kermanshah, 299A
Kern, Jerome, 293C, 309C, 315C
kerosene, 257B
Kerouac, Jack, 345C
Kerr-McGee Company, 364C
Kesh, 126C
Kettler, Wilhelm, 261C
Keuffel & Esser (K & E) Company, 363B
Kevlar, 351B
Kevorkian, Jack, 374C, 382C
Kew Gardens, 219C
Key, Francis Scott, 240B
Key Marco culture, 135A
Key West, 292B
Keys of the Kingdom of Heaven, The (Cotton), 189C
Keystone Studio, 293C
Khafra (king of Egypt), 3B
Khaireddin Pasha, 158B
Khaled (king of Saudi Arabia), 361A, 367A
Khalifah, Ahmad al-, 225A
Khalji, Alauddin Muhammad (sultan of Delhi), 120C, 122C, 124C
Khalji dynasty. *See* India, Indians
Khalkha, 200C
Khambhat, Gulf of, 178C
Khamenei, Sayyed Ali (president of Iran), 367A
Khandesh, 176C
Kharkov, 328A
Khartoum, 14A, 247A, 279A
Khatib, Ibn al-, 131B
Khayyam, Omar. *See* Omar Khayyam
Khazini, al- 101B
Khesanh, battle of, 353A
Khitans, 90C, 110C
Khiva, 206C
Khmer (nation), 58C, 72C, 77C, 78C, 80C, 83C, 99C, 106C, 114C, 118C, 120C, 180C, 190C
Khmer (people), 100C, 216C
Khmer Rouge, 369A
Khoikhoi, 206B
Khojas, 216C
Khomeini, Ayatollah (leader of Iran), 365A, 373A, 373C
Khorasan, 233A
Khorezm, 218C
Khri Srong Ide Tsan (king of Tibet), 74C
Khrushchev, Nikita (premier of Soviet Union), 340B, 342B, 344B, 346A, 348A, 350B, 356B
Khudabanda, Muhammad (shah of Persia), 170B
Khufu (king of Egypt), 3C
Khwarazm Turks, 110C, 112C, 114B
and Timur, 130C
Khyber Pass, 277A
Ki Inukai (prime minister of Japan), 315A
Kiangsi province, 154C, 313A, 317A
Kiaochow, 295A
Kichisaburo Nomura, 322C
Kidinnu, 21B
Kidnapped (Stevenson), 281C
kidney
machine, 353B
transplant, 349B
Kiel, Treaty of, 240A
Kiev, 81C, 88A, 89C, 96A, 124A, 192A, 326A, 330A
Kija dynasty. *See* Korea, Koreans
Kildare, Lord of, 144A
Kilkenny, Statute of, 130A
Killiecrankie, battle of, 198A
Kilwa, 150B, 172B
Kim Il Sung, 381A
Kimberly, 273A, 281A
Kindah, al-, 60C
kinescope, 311B
King, Charles, 285B
King, Edward P., 328C
King, Martin Luther, Jr., 342C, 344C, 346C, 348C, 350C, 354C, 362C, 366C
King, Rodney, 376C, 378C
King, William Mackenzie (prime minister of Canada), 306B, 316B, 318B, 324B, 330B, 334B
King and No King, A (Beaumont and Fletcher), 181C
King John (Shakespeare), 175C
King Lear (Shakespeare), 177C
King Oliver's Creole Jazz Band, 307C
King Philip's War, 195A
King's Lynn, 296A
Kingsley, Ben, 367C
Kingsley, Charles, 263C
Kingston (Jamaica), 201A, 272C, 294B
Kingston (Ontario), 251B, 254B, 256B
Kingston upon Thames, 88A, 282A
Kinsale, battle of, 176A
Kintyre, 78A
Kipling, Rudyard, 281C, 285C
Kiriyenko, Sergei (prime minister of Russia), 384B
Kirsten, Lincoln, 317C
Kisfaludy, Károly, 245C
Kishinev, 288A
Kiska, 330C
Kitagawa Utamaro, 227C
Kitchener, Herbert, 285A, 287A
Kitty Hawk, 289B
Klaproth, Martin, 229B
Kléber, Jean Baptiste, 235A
Klee, Paul, 295C
Kleindienst, Richard, 358C
Kleist, Heinrich von, 239C
Klinger, Friedrich Maximilian von, 223C
Klismos chair, 51B
Klissow, battle of, 202A
Klondike River, 284B
Kloster Zeven, 216A
Kluang, 326C
Knaeroed, Peace of, 178A
Kneller, Sir Godfrey, 205C
Knight, John, 177A
Knight, Margaret, 273B

Knights Hospitalers of St. John, Order of, 100B
Knights of Columbus, 279C
Knights of Labor, 276B
Knights Templar, 116C
knitting machine, 173B
Knossos, 4C, 6C, 8C
Knox, Frank, 324B
Knox, John, 163C, 169C
Knudsen, William S., 322B
Ko Fuang, Temple of, 81C
Kobe, 271A, 381A
Kodak, 327B
Kodiak Island, 63A, 226B
Koestler, Arthur, 323C, 335C
Koguryo, kingdom of, 30B, 50B, 58C, 66C, 70C
Kohima, 332C
Kohl, Helmut (chancellor of Germany), 370B, 372A, 380B, 384B
Koivisto, Mauno (president of Finland), 366B
Kojiki, 73C
Kokand, 216C
Koki Hirota (prime minister of Japan), 319A
Kolff, Willem John, 343B
Kolin, battle of, 216A
Kolingba, André (president of Central African Republic), 371A
Kollwitz, Käthe, 287C
Kolombangara, 330C
Kongo, kingdom of, 122C, 150B, 152B, 156B, 158B, 164B, 168B, 172B, 186B, 192B, 194B, 212B, 214B, 216B, 220B. *See also* Congo
Koniag culture, 95A
Konoye (prime minister of Japan), 319A
Konrad Wallenrod (Micklewecz), 249C
Konya, battle of, 251A
Koop, C. Everett, 372C
Köprülü, Ahmed (grand vizier of Turkey), 192B, 196B
Köprülü, Mustafa, 200A
Koran, 69C, 71C, 103C, 145C, 231C
Koran, Muhammadu (king of Katsina), 146B
Kordian (Slowacki), 251C
Kordofan, 245A
  battle of, 279A
Korea, Koreans, 34B, 58C, 90C, 132C, 336A, 337A
  3000 B.C.–18 B.C., 2B, 4B, 28B, 30B
  arts, 85C
  and Britain, 233A
  and China, 40B, 50B, 66C, 68C, 70C, 100C, 182C, 223C, 285A, 338A
  elections in, 336A
  government, 84C, 235A, 253A, 287A, 337A
  and Japan, 44B, 54B, 56B, 64C, 65C, 174C, 291A, 293A, 303A
  Kija dynasty, 8B
  and Mongolia, 110C, 128C
  North Korea, 344A, 354A, 369A, 376A, 380A, 381A
  religion, 57A
  and Russia, 293A
  science and technology, 109B, 123B, 135B
  South Korea, 365A, 366A, 369A, 376A
  Tangun dynasty, 4B
  and United Nations, 338A, 340A
  and United States, 338A, 340A
Korean Airlines (1987 crash), 371A
Korean War, 338A, 340A, 340C, 344C
Korin, Ogota, 203C
Kornilov, Lavr, 300A
Korotkoff, Nikolai, 291B
Koryo, 84C, 85C, 128C
Kosovo, 384A, 384B
  battles of, 132B, 138B, 298A
Koster and Bial's Music Hall, 285B
Kosygin, Alexei (premier of Soviet Union), 350B, 354A, 364B
Koszeg, 334A
Kotaro Honda, 299B
Kotte, kingdom of, 144C, 150C, 164C, 168C
Kotter, August, 155B
Kotuz (sultan of Egypt), 116B
Kotzebue, August von, 244A
Koungai, 118C
Kountché, Seyni (president of Niger), 371A
Kountz, Samuel, 353B
Kouwenhoven, William, 345B
Kra Peninsula, 326C
Kraftswagon, 269B
Kraków, 136A, 190A, 202A, 230A, 258A
  University of, 131C
Kramer vs. Kramer (movie), 365C
Krasinski, Zygmunt, 253C
Krasnoyarsk, 182C
Kravchuk, Leonid (president of Ukraine), 380A
Kreditanstalt, 264A
Kremlin, 144A
Krenz, Egon (leader of East Germany), 372B
Kreps, Juanita Morris, 358C
Kreutzwald, Friedrich Reinhold, 267C
Krishna I, 74C
Krishnadevaraya (raja of Vijayanagar), 152C
Kristin Lavransdatter (Undset), 305C
Kroelreuter, Joseph, 217B
Kronstadt, 282A
Kroussevitsky, Serge, 309C
Kruger, Oom Paul (president of South African Republic and Transvaal), 277A, 279A, 281A, 283A, 287A, 289A
"Kruger telegram," 284A
Ksar el Kebir, battle of, 170B
Ku K'ai-chih, 53C
Ku Klux Klan, 268B, *269,* 296B, 306B, 308B, 344C
Kuala Lumpur, 326C
Kublai Khan (emperor of Mongols), 114C, *115,* 116C, 118C, 120C
Kubrick, Stanley, 351C, 355C
Kueichou province, 233A
Kukia, 82C
Kukulcan, 89A
Kulbarga, kingdom of, 128C
Kulikov, battle of, 132A
Kulmerland, 142A
Kumaragupta, 58C
Kumasi, 285A
Kumbi, 96C
Kunchow, 112C
Kundera, Milan, 369C
Kung-Liang, 93B
Kunta, 220B
Kuolema (Sibelius), 289C
Kuomintang, 371A
Kur River, 87B
Kurdistan, 132C, 142B, 154B
Kurdla, battle of, 233A
Kurds, 152B, 378A
  and Iraq, 382A
Kuria Muria Islands, 263A
Kurile Islands, 262A, 275A
Kurna, 297A
Kurosawa Akira, 339C, 385C
Kurozumi Munetada, 241A
Kursk, 330A
Kurt dynasty. *See* Afghanistan
Kurt Waldheim, 356A
Kurume Han, 214C
Kurzweil, Raymond, 361B
Kush, kingdom of, 6A, 12A, 33C, 54B
Kusseri, battle of, 287A
Kutch-Sind border, 351A
Kuttenberg, Diet of, 145C
Kuwait, 374A, 375A
Kwa, 214B
Kwajalein Island, 332C
Kwasniewski, Alexander (president of Poland), 382B
Kwena, 263A
Kwolek, Stephanie, 351B
Kyakhta, 210C
Kyansittha (king of Pagan), 96C
Kyaswan (king of Pagan), 112C
Kyawswar (puppet king of Pagan), 120C
Kyoto, 76C, 106C, 117C, 142C, 146C, 176C, 210C
Kyprianou, Spyros, 362B
Kyushu Island, 162C, 214C, 269A, 275A

L

La Follette, Robert, 292B
La Fontaine, Jean de, 195C
La Guardia, Fiorello H., 326B
La Mettrie, Julien Offroy de, 213C
La Nación, 272C
La Paz, 238C
La Peste (Camus), 337C
La Prairie, 253B
La Roche, battle of, 128A
La Rochelle, 132A, 182A
  Peace of, 182A
La Salle, Cavelier, Robert, Sieur de, 195A, 197A, 199A
La Scala, 245C
La Tène culture, 21A
La Valette, Jean Parisot de, 168A
Labadie, Jean de, 187C, 189C, 195C, 211C
Labiau, Treaty of, 190A
Labor Day, 280B
Labor Standards Act, 320B
Labrador, 149A, 157A, 159A, 177A
Lachine, 199A
Lade, battle of, 16C
Ladislaus II, 104A
Ladislaus of Naples, 134B
Lady at the Tea Table (Cassatt), 279C
Lady Good for Nothing (Quiller-Couch), 293C
Lady in the Lake, The (Chandler), 331C
Lady Vanishes, The (movie), 321C
Lafcadio's Adventures (Gide), 295C
Lagash, 2B
Lagerlöf, Selma, 283C
Lagobards, 66B
Lagos, 172B, 200B, 267A, 281A
Lahej, 210B
Lahore, 114C
  Treaty of, 259A
Laibach, Congress of, 244A
Laing, Alexander Gordon, 249A
Laing's Neck, battle of, 277A
Lake Baikal, 69B
Lake Balkash, 208C
Lake Chad, 176B, 247A
Lake Champlain, 183A, 211A, 240B
Lake Erie, 199A, 203A, *247,* 249B
  battle of, 240B
Lake George, battle of, 215A
Lake Itasca, 250B
Lake Mai-Ndombe, 214B
Lake Nemi, 161B
Lake Ngami, 261A
Lake of Woods, 244B
Lake Ontario, 199A, 249B
Lake Regillus, battle of, 17A
Lake Sebago, 292B
Lake Superior, 211A
Lake Tanganyika, 295A, 299A
Lake Van, 297A
Lake Victoria, 289A
Lake Wales, 337B
Lake Washington Floating Bridge, 325B
Lake Winnipeg, 238B
Lakehurst, 318B
Lakhmid, kingdom of, 64C
Lakona, 330C
Lalla Maghnia, Convention of, 257A
Lalla Rookh (Moore), 243C
Lamar culture, 139A
Lamarck, Jean Baptiste, 239B
Lamartine, Alphonse Marie de, 245C, 253C, 261C
Lamb, Charles, 247C
Lambert of Spoleto, 82A
Lambeth, Treaty of, 110A
Lambityeco, 73A
Lambton, John, 254B
Lamentations (Palestrina), 173C
Lamoka culture, 65A
lamps, lighting, 51B, 55B, 77B
  arc lamp, 239B
  arc lighting, 273B
  arc street lighting, 275B, 277B
  carbon filament, 277B
  flashlight, 287B
  fluorescent lamp, 317B
  gas street lighting, 243B
  halogen, 357B
  incandescent gas mantle, 279B
  incandescent lightbulb, 255B, 277B
  interferometer, 277B
  lightbulb, 317B
  limelights, 235C
  nationwide dimout, 334B
  neon light, 293B
  searchlight, 299B
  twisted filament, 303B
Lamy, Jean Baptiste (Archbishop of Santa Fe), 263C
Lan Chang, kingdom of, 128C
Lan Na, kingdom of, 120C
Lanboanga, 184C
Lancaster, Burt, 347C
Lancaster, Sir James, 174C, 176C
Lancaster, Thomas, 124A
Lancaster (England), 134A
Lancaster (Mass.), 197A
Lancaster Sound, 244B
Lancaster Turnpike, 231B
Lancet, 377B
Land, Edwin, 313B, 331B
land, landholding, 92B, 96A
Land Act, 234B
land mines, 119B
Land Ordinance, 226B
Landini, Francesco, 125C
Landor, Walter Savage, 247C
LANDSAT, 359B
Landsteiner, Karl, 289B, 325B
Lanfranc, 95C
Lang, Fritz, 311C
Lange, Friedrich Albert, 271C
Lange, Jessica, 381C
Langen, Eugen, 271B
Langevin, Paul, 297B
Langham, Simon (Archbishop of Canterbury), 131C
Langland, William, 131C
Langley, Samuel, 285B
Langmuir, Irving, 293B
Langobards, 64A, 64B, 66A, 68A, 74A, 74B, 76A

Langside, battle of, 168A
Langton, Stephen (Archbishop of Canterbury), 109C
Language, Truth, and Logic (Ayer), 319C
language(s)
Arabic, 145C
Aramaic, 10B
Bulgarian, 267C
Esperanto, 281B
French, 123C
German, 147C
Greek, 153C
Hebrew, 83C
Indian, 31A
Latin, 72A, 103C, 141B, 147C, 349C
"Linear B" (early Greek), 321B
pictograph, 7C
Quecha, 135A
Siouan, 73A, 91A
Slovenian, 259C
Tamil, 75C
Languedoc, 110A
Languedoc Canal, 201B
Lansing, Robert, 296B, 304B
Lao-tzu, 11C, 15C
Laocoon, 151C
Laodamia (Wordworth), 243C
Laos, Laotians, 128C, 166C, 186C, 206C, 283A, 361A
Lapidaris (Alfonso X), 119B
Lapita people, 6B
Laporte, Pierre, 356C
Lara, Guillermo Rodríguez (leader of Ecuador), 359A
Lara (Byron), 241C
Lara Jonggrang, 83C
Larache, 198B
Laramie Peak (Bierstadt), 267C
Largs, battle of, 116A
Larissa, battle of, 96B
Larrea, Osvaldo Hurtado (president of Ecuador), 367A
Larsen, Don, 343C
Las Piedras, 238C
Las Vegas, 364C
laser, 363B
technology, 301B
tunable dye, 353B
Lassalle, Ferdinand, 268A
Last Command, The (von Sternberg), 311C
Last Days of Pompeii, The (Bulwer-Lytton), 253C
Last Emperor, The (Bertolucci), 371C
Last Judgment, The (Michelangelo), 163C, 381C
Last Judgment (Signorelli), 149C
Last Laugh, Mr. Moto (Marquand), 327C
Last of the Mohicans, The (Cooper), 249C
Last Supper, The (Leonardo da Vinci), 149C
Last Supper, The (Tintoretto), 175C
Last Temptation of Christ, The (movie), 373C
Last Time I Saw Paris, The (Paul), 327C
Last Tycoon, The (Fitzgerald), 325C
Lasta, 158B
Lat Dior, 281A
Lat Sukaabe, 202B
Late Woodland, 87A
Lateran
Councils, 101C, 103C, 107C, 111C
Treaty, 311C
lathe, 67B, 169B, 215B, 233B, 245B
Latimer, Lewis, 277B
Latimer (Pa.), 286B
Latin America, 325A
Latin American Free Trade Association, 347A
Latin empire, 108B
Latin Grammar (Aelfric), 89C
Latin League, 17A
Latin literature, Golden Age of, 27C
Latini, Brunetto, 117C
Latins, 112B
latitude and longitude, 101B
Latium, 23A
Latrobe, Benjamin, 233C
Latter-Day Saints, Church of Jesus Christ of, 249C
Latvia, 302A, 314A, 324A, 372B, 374B, 376A, 376B
Laud, William (Archbishop of Canterbury), 185C, 189C
Lauderdale culture, 65A
Laudonnière, René de, 167A
Lauenburg, 238A, 268A
Lauffeld, battle of, 214A
Laughton, Charles, 315C, 317C
laundromat, 317B
Laurel culture, 99A
Laurentian culture, 50C, 63A
Laurier, Wilfrid (prime minister of Canada), 284B
Lauriston, 208A
Laurium, 18C
Lausanne, 314A
Council, 139C
Treaty of, 292A, 307A
Laval, Carl Gustaf de, 275B
Laval, Pierre (prime minister of France), 312A
Lavalleja, Juan Antonio, 246C
Law, Andrew Bonar (prime minister of England), 306A
Law, John, 208A, 209A
Law, William, 211C
Law Is a Bottomless Pit (Arbuthnot), 205C
Law of the Sea treaty, 368A
Lawes, John, 255B
lawn mower, 237B, 249B, 287B, 311B
Lawrence, Carmen, 375A
Lawrence, D. H., 295C, 307C
Lawrence, Ernest, 319B
Lawrence, James, 240B
Lawrence, T. E. (Lawrence of Arabia), 301A
Lawrence (Kans.), 264B
Lawrence of Arabia (movie), 349C
law(s)
Buddhist, 100C
Code Napoléon, 267A
Draconian, 12C
first written, 4B. *See also individual laws*
Lay of the Last Minstrel (Scott), 237C
Lays of Ancient Rome (Macaulay), 257C
Lazarev, Mikhail, 245A
Le Coq, Robert, 130A
Le dynasty. *See* Annam, Annamites
Le Goulet, Treaty of, 108A
Le Maître, *226*
Le Mans, 136A
Le Neoplasticism (Mondrian), 305C
Le Petit Supplément Illustré, 284
Le Pont Neuf (Monet), 273C
le Roy, Pierre, 219B
Le Soulier de satin (Claudel), 311C
Lea, Henry C., 281C
lead, 35B
League of Nations, 302B, 304B, 306A, 307A, 309A, 310A, 312A, 314A, 336A
and China, 321A
Egypt in, 319A
Iraq in, 315A
and Italy, 316A, 317A
Japan in, 315A, 321A
and Paraguay, 318C
Russia in, 316A
and Soviet Union, 322A
Turkey in, 315A
and Venezuela, 320C
League to Enforce Peace, 298B
Lean, David, 345C, 349C, 351C, 377C
Lear, Edward, 259C
leatherwork, 203C
Leaves of Grass (Whitman), 263C
Lebanon, 100B, 172B, 216B, 319A, 344A, 370C, 375A
earthquake in, 216B
and France, 367A
and Israel, 367A, 369A, 379A
and Italy, 367A
and Syria, 367A
and United Nations, 369A
and United States, 367A, 370C
Leben Jesu, Das (Strauss), 253C
Lebna Dengel (emperor of Ethiopia), 152B
Lebon, Philippe, 235B
Lebrija, Elio Antonio de, 147C
Lebrun, Albert (president of France), 314A
Lech River, 91B, 184A
Leclanché, Georges, 271B
Leclerc, Charles-Victor-Emmanuel, 234B
Lectures on Modern Idealism (Royce), 303C
Lectures on the English Poets (Hazlitt), 245C
LED (light-emitting diode), 359B
Lee, Ann, 221C
Lee, Robert E., 264B, 266B, 268B
Lee, Spike, 373C
Lee, William, 173B
Lee Company, 281B
Lee Kuan Yew (prime minister of Singapore), 375A
Lee Teng-hui (president of Taiwan), 373A
Leek, Treaty of, 124A
Leeuwenhoek, Antoni van, 197B
Leeward Islands, 185A, 195A
Leeward Islands Federation, 272C
Lefebre, Marcel, 363C
Legazpi, Miguel López de, 168C
Legend of Sleepy Hollow, The (Irving), 245C
Legion of Decency, 317C
Legislative Reorganization Act, 336C
Legnano, 106A
Leguía y Salcedo, Augusto (president of Peru), 290C, 302C, 312C
Lehár, Franz, 291C
Lehmann, Rosamond, 341C
Leibniz, Gottfried Wilhelm, 195B, 205C, 207C
Leibowitz, Samuel, *312*
Leicester, 114A
Leicester Square, *197*
Leigh, Vivien, 339C
Leipzig, 155C, 189C, 215C, 268A
battle of, 240A
Leith, 162A
Leith, Emmet, 349B
Lely, Peter, 197C
Lemmon, Jack, 347C, 359C
Lemnos, *297*
Lend-Lease Act, 324B
Lend-Lease program, 332B, 334B
Lenin, Vladimir (leader of Soviet Union), 300A, 306A, 308A, 356B
Lenin Mausoleum, 346B
Leningrad, 332A. *See also* St. Petersburg
siege of, 326A, 330A
Lennon, John, 365C
Lennox, George, 257B
Lenoir, Jean, 265B
Lenore (Burger), 221C
lenses, 83B, 165B
Leo I, Pope, 59C, 189C
Leo I (emperor of Byzantium), 60B
Leo III, Pope, 76A, 77C
Leo III (emperor of Byzantium), 72B, 75C
Leo IV (emperor of Byzantium), 76B
Leo IV, Pope, *79*, 79C
Leo V the Armenian (emperor of Byzantium), 78B
Leo VI, the Wise (emperor of Byzantium), 82B
Leo VIII, Pope, 87C
Leo IX, Pope, 94A, 95C
Leo X, Pope, 152B, *153*, 154A, 155C
Leo XI, Pope, 189C
Leo XIII, Pope, 283C
Leo of Tripoli, 84B
León, 84B, 88B, 92B, 94B, 100B, 104B, 112A, 112B, 114B, 115B, 116A, 118B, 119B, 120B, 124B, 126B, 128B, 132B, 134B
León, Ramiro de (president of Guatemala), 379A
Leonardo da Vinci, 143C, 147B, 149B, 149C, 151B, 151C, 155C, 157B, 233B
Leone, Giovanni (president of Italy), 356B
Leontius (emperor of Byzantium), 72B
Leopard, The (Tomasi de Lampedusa), 345C
Leopard, The (Visconti), 349C
Leopold (archduke), 178A
Leopold I (Holy Roman Emperor), 190A, 192A, 202A
Leopold II, grand duke of Tuscany (Holy Roman Emperor), 228A
Leopold II (king of Belgium), 279A, 292A
Leopold III (king of Belgium), 316A, 338B
Leopold IV, 132A
Leopold V, 106A
Leovigild (king of Visigoths), 64B
Lepanto, battle of, 168A
lepers, 95B
Lepidus (ruler of African Roman Empire), 30B
Lerdo de Tejada, Sebastián (president of Mexico), 272C
Lerida, 102B
Lerida Cathedral, 109C
Les Andelys, 109C
Les Précieuses ridicules (Moliére), 193C
Les Saintes, battles of, 114A, 224C
Lesbos (Greek island), 15C, 20C
Lescot, Pierre, 163C
Lesotho, kingdom of, 353A
Lesseps, Ferdinand de, 263A
Lessing, Gotthold, 225C
Lesson in Anatomy, The (Rembrandt), 185C
Lessons for Women (Ban Zhao), 39C
Let Us Now Praise Famous Men (Agee), 325C
Leticia harbor conflict, 314C, 316C
Letters Concerning the Aesthetic Education of Mankind (Schiller), 231C
Letters to His Son (Stanhope), 221C
Lettres de mon moulin (Daudet), 273C
Lettres sur les Anglais (Voltaire), 211C
Leuthen, battle of, 216A
Levant, 6A, 140B
Levasseur family. *See* Canada

Levellers, 188A
lever, compound, 213B
Lever Food and Fuel Act, 300B
Levett, Christopher, 183A
Levi, Carlo, 335C
Levi, Edward, 360C
Leviathan, or the Matter, Form and Authority of Government (Hobbes), 191C
Levinson, Barry, 373C, 385C
Levitt, William, 338C
Levittown, 338C
Lewes, battle of, 116A
Lewinsky, Monica, 384C
Lewis, C. S., 327C
Lewis, Matthew Gregory, 233C
Lewis, Meriwether, 236B
Lewis, Sinclair, 305C, 335C
Lewis culture, 83A
Lex Canuleia, 19A
Lex Publilia, 19A
Lexington, battle of, 222B
Leyden Plate, 52C
Leyte, 332C, 334C
Leyte Gulf, battle of, 332C
Lhasa, 68C, 206C, 289A
Li Chhun, 67B
Li Kao, 77B
Li Po, 75C
Li Shih-min, *67,* 71C
Li Ssu-Hsun, 73C
Li Xiannian (president of China), 367A
Li Yu, 87C
Liaoning, 188C
Liaotung, 285A
Liaotung Peninsula, 182C
Liaoyang, 289A
Liap (Khitan) dynasty. *See* China; Manchuria
Liaquat Ali Khan (prime minister of Pakistan), 339A
Libby, Willard, 337B
Liber Theologia Moralis (Escobar y Mendoza), 189C
Liberalism, Liberals, 269C
Liberator, The, 250B, *251*
Liberia, 245A, 259A
Liberius, Pope, 55A
Liberty Bell, 252B
Liberty Loan Act, 300B
Liberty Party, 256B
libraries
  in Alexandria, 57C
  in Assyria, 13C
  Hadrian's, 39C
  in Mesopotamia, 5C
  in Rome, 37C
  in Syria, 13C
  in United States, 237C
Libreville, 261A
Libro des Cortegiano, Il (Castiglione), 159C
Libya, 8A, 10A, 235A, 309A, 339A, 376A
  in Arab League, 340A
  in Arab Maghreb Union, 372A
  and Britain, 368A
  and Chad, 373A
  and Egypt, 358A
  and European Community, 370A
  famine in, 218B
  and Germany, 324A
  and Greece, 12A
  and Italy, 293B, 321A, 324A
  terrorists, 372A
  and Tunisia, 371A
  and United States, 366A, 370A
  World War II, 324A
Lichtenstein, 374A
Lichtenstein, Roy, 349C
Licinius (emperor of Rome), 50A, 51A, 52A
Lidice, 328A
Lie, Trygve (secretary-general of United Nations), 336A
lie detector, 317B
Liebig, Justus von, 253B
Liège, 107B, 294A
Liegnitz, battle of, 114A
Lieutenant's Lady, The (Aldrich), 327C
life
  average expectancy, 304B
  extraterrestrial, 379B, 383B
  insurance, 232B
Life Is a Dream (Calderón de la Barca), 185C
"Life Is Worth Living" (TV program), 341C
Life magazine, 319C, 359C
Life of Galileo, The (Brecht), 331C
Life of John Knox (MacCrie), 239C
Life of Milton (Toland), 201C
Life of Reason, The (Santayana), 291C
Life of Samuel Johnson, The (Boswell), 229C
life-support systems, 353B
ligaments, synthetic, 373B
Light Cavalry (Suppé), 267C
Light of the World, The (Bourignon), 201C
lighthouses, 35B, 39B, 43B, 57B, 77B, 99B, 265B
lighting. *See* lamps, lighting
Liguori, St. Alfonsus, 215C
L'il Abner, 345B
Lilienthal, Otto, 285B
Liliom (Molnár), 293C
Liliuokalani, Lydia (queen of Hawaii), 283A
Lille, 122A
  University of, 167C
Lima, 215A, 246C, 248C, 258C, 268C, 276C, 320C
limbs, artificial, 171B
Limerick, 190A, 200A
Limes, 38A
Limoges, 83C, 130A
Limón, 272C, 282C
Limpopo River, 150B
Lincoln, 34A, 122A
  battles of, 102A, 110A
Lincoln, Abraham (president of U.S.), 264B, 266B, 268B
Lincoln Laboratories, 349B
Lincoln Memorial, 348C
Lincoln Portrait, A (Copland), 331C
Lincoln University, 262B
Lind, Jenny, 255C
Lindbergh, Charles A., 311B, 314B, 317B, 360C
Linde, Karl, 275B
Lindsey, Vachel, 295C
linen, 87B, 115B
Linköping, 176A
linoleum, 267B
Linton, 312B
Linz, 155C
  Holy League of, 198A
Lion and the Jewel, The (Soyinka), 349C
Lipmann, Fritz, 325B
Lippershey, Hans, 179B
Lippi, Fra Filippo, 143C
Lippinus, Fulvius, 31B
Liquid Paper, 345B
Lisbon, 72B, 102B, 164A, 167B, 174A, 214A
  University of, 121C, 125C
Lissa, 270A
Liston, Sonny, 349C, 351C
Liszt, Franz, 271C
  literary criticism, 167C
Literary Mind, The (Eastman), 313C
Literature and Dogma (Arnold), 275C
Lithuania, Lithuanians, 124A, 130A, 134A, 138A, 253C, 376A, 376B
  and Bolsheviks, 302A
  and Germany, 320A
  and Soviet Union, 304A, 324A, 372B, 374B
  World War II, 324A
Little, A. B., 263B
Little Big Horn, battle of, 274B, 276B
Little Caesar (movie), 313C
Little Colorado Valley, 115C
Little Dorrit (Dickens), 265C
Little Foxes, The (Hellman), 323C
Little Johnny Jones (Cohan), 289C
Little Rock, 344C
Little Women (Alcott), 271C
Liu Pang, 24B
Liu Sung, 60C
Liu Yu, 58C
Live Aid concerts, 369C
Liverpool, 245B
Lives of the Fathers, Martyrs, and Other Principal Saints, The (Butler), 217C
Lives of the First Twelve Caesars, The (Suetonius), 39C
Lives of the Saints of the Christian Church, 187C
Lives of the Sophists (Philostratus), 47C
Livia, 32A
Livingston, Robert R., 237B
Livingstone, David, 261A, 273A
Livius Andronicus, 25C
Livonia, 166A, 184A, 202A, 208A
Livorno, 136B
Livy (Titus Livius), 29C, 31C, 33C
Llasa, 375A
Lleras Camargo, Alberto (president of Colombia), 335A
Lloyd Webber, Andrew, 357C, 367C
Llywelyn (prince of Wales), 108A, 110A, 116A, 118A
Lobengula (king of Mashonaland), 281A
Lobositz, battle of, 216A
Locarno
  Conference, 308A
  Treaty of, 318A
Lochner v. New York, 290B
Loci Communes (Melanchthon), 157C
Locke, John, 200A, 201C, 203C
Locke, Matthew, 197C
Lockerbie, 372A
locks
  door, 225B
  pad-, 33B
  pin-tumbler, 267B
  wheel, 155B
locomotive. *See* trains
Lodge, Sir Joseph, 283B, 285B
Lodi
  battle of, 232A
  Peace of, 140A
Lodi, Bahlol, 138C
Lodomeria, 220A
Log College, 211C
logic machines, 281B, 289B
Lohengrin, 119C
Loko, kingdom of, 166B
Lolita (Nabokov), 343C
Lollards, 133C
Lombard, Carole, 329C
Lombard League, 112B
Lombardy, Lombards, 50A, 67B, 67C, 90A, 92B, 106A, 114B, 202A, 232A, 264A
Lomé Convention, 295A
Loménie de Brienne, Étienne Charles de, 226A
Lon Nol (prime minister of Cambodia), 357A
London, 34A, 44A, 88A, 100A, 110A, 111B, 142A, *197,* 198A, 217C, 294A, 311B, 332A, 336A
  Academy of Arts, 205C
  Barbican Theatre, 367C
  Billingsgate Wharf, 89B
  blitzkrieg in, 324A
  British Broadcast Company, 307C
  British Museum, 215C, 243C
  Buckingham Palace, 216A, 247C, 378B
  Conference (1867), 270A
  Convention (1840), 254A
  Convention (1850), 260A
  Convention (1861), 266C
  Convention (1933), 314A
  Covent Garden, 309C, 337C, 349C
  Crystal Palace, 261C
  Danes in, 80A, 90A
  docks, 237B, 255B, 280A
  Globe Theatre, 175C
  Great Exhibition (1851), 260A
  Great Fire (1666), 192A, 195C
  Illustrated London News, 277
  IRA bombing in, 358B
  Libyan People's Bureau, 368A
  Lloyds Building, 369C
  London Bridge, 87B, 107B, 219B
  London Magazine, 245C
  National Portrait Gallery, 265C
  Naval Conference (1930), 312A
  Newgate Prison, 110A
  Observer, 231C
  Peace of (1518), 154A
  rebuilt, 82A
  riots in, 154A, 224A, 368B
  Royal Academy, 245C
  St. Luke's Church, 245C
  St. Martin in the Fields, 209C
  St. Paul's Church, 67C, 87C
  Synod of, 133C
  television transmission in, 311B
  theatre in, 171C
  Tower of, 97C, 204A
  Treaty of (1827), 248A
  Treaty of (1839), 254A
  Treaty of (1852), 262A
  Treaty of (1914), 294A
  and Vietnam War, 352B
  Waterloo Bridge, 239C
  Westminster Abbey, 95C, 131B
  Westminster Hall, 99C
  world exhibitions (1862), 266A
  in World War I, 298A
  in World War II, 332A
London, Jack, 289C
London Company, 177A, 183A
London Gazette, 193C
London Missionary Society, 233C, 245C
London Society for the Establishment of Sunday Schools, 227C
Londonderry, 178A, 198A
Londonderry County, 178A
Long, Huey, 316B
Long Day's Journey into Night (O'Neill), 323C
Long Island, 328B, 338C
  battle of, 222B
Long March, 317A
longbow, 127B, 129B
Longfellow, Henry Wadsworth, 259C, 269C
Longhena, Baldassare, 185C
longhouse, 109A
longitude, 159B, 279B
Longjumeau, Treaty of, 168A
Lönnrot, Elias, 261C
Look Homeward Angel (Wolfe), 311C
Look magazine, 357C

Loos, Anita, 309C
López, Felipe (president of Paraguay), 339A
López, Carlos Antonio (dictator of Paraguay), 256C, 266C
López, Narcisco, 260C
López Arellano, Oswaldo (president of Honduras), 359A
López de Villalobos, Ruy, 162C
López Portillo, José (president of Mexico), 363A
Lord Jim (Conrad), 287C
Lord of the Flies (Golding), 343C
Lord Ordainers, 124A
Lord's Masque, The (Campion), 179C
Lords of Trade, 199A
Lorenzetti, Ambrogio, 125C
Loring, Eugene, 321C
l'Orme, Philibert de, 165B
Lorrain, Claude, 185C, 189C, 197C
Lorraine, 84A, 94B, 144A, 184A, 194A, 200A, 210A, 212A, 218A, 272A
Lorris, Guillaume de, 113C
Los Angeles, 224B, 258B, 292B, 297C, 354C, 378C, 380C, 382C
  Arroyo Seco Parkway, 325B
  earthquake in, 380C
  Memorial Stadium, 366C
  riots in, 330B, 350C, 376C
Los Angeles Dodgers, 347C, 349C, 351C, 353C, 361C, 363C, 367C, 373C
Los Angeles Lakers, 355C
Los Angeles Raiders, 369C
Los Angeles Rams, 365C
Los Negros, 332C
Losada, Diego de, 169A
Losey, Joseph, 349C
Lost Weekend, The (Jackson), 333C
Lost Weekend, The (movie), 335C
Lostwithiel, battle of, 188A
Lotfi, Ali (prime minister of Egypt), 371A
Lothair I (emperor of Rome), 78A
Lothair II (Holy Roman Emperor and king of Germany), 100A, 101C, 102B
Lothair III (king of Italy), 86B
Lothair (king of France), 86A, 88A
Lotharingia, 80A
Loti, Pierre, 281C
Louangphrabang, 206C
Loubet, Émile François (president of France), 286A
Louis, George (elector of Hanover), 206A
Louis, Joe, 319C
Louis I (king of Hungary and Poland), 128B, 130A, 132A
Louis I (emperor of Rome), 78A
Louis II (king of Bohemia and Hungary), 156A
Louis II (king of France), 80A
Louis II (king of Italy and Holy Roman Emperor), 80A
Louis III (king of northern France), 80A, 82A
Louis IV (king of France), 86A
Louis IV (king of Germany and Holy Roman Emperor), 124A, 126A, 127C, 128A, 129C
Louis V (king of France), 88A
Louis VI (king of France), 98A, 102A
Louis VII (king of France), 102A, 104A, 106A, 106B
Louis VIII (king of France), 110A, 112A
Louis IX (king of France), 112A, 114B, 116A, 116B, 118A, 118B
Louis X (king of France), 124A
Louis XI (king of France), 140A, 141C, 142A, 144A
Louis XII (king of France), 148A, 150A, 154A
Louis XIII (king of France), 178A, 182A, 186A
Louis XIV (king of France), 186A, 191C, 192A, 193C, 194A, 198A, 199C, 201C, 202A, 206A
Louis XV (king of France), 206A, 208A, 212A, 214A, 220A
Louis XVI (king of France), 220A, 228A, 230A
Louis XVIII (king of France), 240A, 242A, 246A
Louis of Anjou, 134B
Louis of Bavaria, 83C
Louis-Napoléon (president of French Republic), 252A, 254A, 258A, 262A. *See also* Napoléon III
Louis-Philippe (king of France), 248A, 258A
Louisburg, 213A, 217A
Louisiana, 63A, 123A, 197A, 203A, 205A, 209A, 219A, 226B, 234B, 236B, 238B, 240B, 244B, 272B, 344C, 345B
Louisiana Purchase (Berlin), 323C
Louisville, 257C, 280B
Louvain, 82A, 294A
Louveciennes Road (Pissarro), 273C
Love and a Battle (Farquhar), 203C
Love for Love (Congreve), 201C
Love in a Tub (Etherege), 193C
Love's Labour's Lost (Shakespeare), 175C
Love's Lovely Counterfeit (Cain), 327C
Low, Juliette Gordon, 292B
Lower, Richard, 193B
Lowry, Malcolm, 337C
Loyalty Islands, 269A
Loyang, 32B, 50B, 62C, 63B, 66C
Lozi, kingdom of, 176B
Lu Daolong, 93B
Luan, 65B
Luanda, 170B
Lubaantun, 79A
Lübeck, 120A, 158A, 160A, 184A, 194A, 234A, 238A, 328A
Lübke, Heinrich (president of West Germany), 346B
Lublin, Union of, 168A
Lucan, 35C, 37C
Lucca, 96B, 113B, 117B, 133B
Lucia di Lammermoor (Donizetti), 253C
Lucian, 41C
Lucid, Shannon, 383B
Lucius III, Pope, 107C
Luck, battle of, 298A
Luck Chance, The (Behn), 199C
Lucky Jim (Amis), 343C
Ludendorff, Erich, 294A, 298A, 302A
Lüderitz Bay, 295A
Ludi Saeculares, 31C
Ludwigslied, 83C
Luf Ali Khan (shah of Persia), 229A, 231A
Luftwaffe, 324A
Lugard, Frederick, 283A
Luke, Gospel of, 37A
Lulami, 186B
Lule, Yusuf (president of Uganda), 365A
Lully, Jean-Baptiste, 185C, 191C
Lulonga Basin, 214B
Lulu (Berg), 319C
Lumière, Auguste and Louis, 285B
Luna 3, 347B
Luna 10, 353B
Lundu, 184B
Lundy's Lane, battle of, 240B
Luneburg, 157C
Lunéville, Peace of, 234A
Luns, Joseph (secretary-general of NATO), 356A
Luria, Salvador, 331B
Lusatia, 184A
Lusitania (British ship), 296A, 296B
luster-painting, 67B
Luther, Martin, 145C, 151C, 153C, 155C, 157C, 159C, 163C
Lutheran Church, Lutherans, 165C, *176,* 189C
Lutrin, Le (Boileau-Despreaux), 195C
Lutter, battle of, 182A
Lützen, battles of, 184A, 240A
Luxembourg, 124A, 144A, 192A, 198A, 254A, 270A
  and Belgium, 336A
  and Benelux Economic Union, 344A
  and Britain, 336A
  and France, 336A
  and Germany, 294A
  government, 336B
  and Netherlands, 282A, 336A
  and Treaty of Rome, 344A
  and United States, 338A
  in Western European Union, 342A
  World War I, 294A
  World War II, 322A
Luxembourg, François Henri de, 200A
Luzon, 168C, 326C, 328C, 334C
Lvov, Georgi, 300A
Lyceum, 23C
Lycia, 70B
Lydia, 11A, 14C, 16C
Lying Days, The (Gordimer), 341C
Lyly, John, 177C
Lynch, David, 375C
Lynch, John (prime minister of Ireland), 352B
Lynn, 187B
Lyons, 122A, 125B, 143B, 155B, 160A, 250A, 385B
  battle of, 42A
  Council of, 114A
  Second Council of, 119C
  Treaty of, 150A, 176A
Lyons, Joseph (prime minister of Australia), 313A, 317A
lyre, 66C
Lyrical Ballads (Wordsworth), 233C
Lytton Report, 315A

M

Ma Yuan, 34B
Maarcomanni, 46A
Maastricht European Union Treaty, 378B
Mabillon, Jean, 197C
Mabinogion, The, 95C
Mac dynasty. *See* Annam, Annamites
MacAlpin, Kenneth (king of Kintyre), 78A
Macao, 164C, 182C, 192C, 370A
MacArthur, Douglas, 328C, 334B, 334C, 337A, 338C
MacArthur, John, 231A
Macaulay, Thomas Babington, 257C, 261C
Macbeth (king of Scots), 92A, 94A
Macbeth (Shakespeare), 177C
Maccabeans, 26B
Maccabeus, Judas, *26,* 26B
MacCrie, Thomas, 239C
MacDermot, Galt, 355C
MacDonald, Ramsay, 310A
MacDonald, Sir John Alexander (prime minister of Britain), 270B, 276B
MacDowell, Edward, 281C
Macedonia, 5A, 22A, 22C, 24C, 26C, 43C, 70B, 92B, 378B
Macedonian (British frigate), 240B
Macedonian Wars, 24C, 26C
Machad, Gerardo (president of Cuba), 314C
Machado de Assis, Joaquim Maria, 277C
Machado y Morales, Gerardo (president of Cuba), 308C
Machel, Samora (president of Mozambique), 371A
Machiavelli, Niccolò, 148A, 150A, 155C, *156,* 157C
machine gun(s). *See also* guns
  aircraft, 295B
  five-barrel, 273B
  Maxim, 283B
  Schmeisser sub-, 329B
  single-barrel automatic, 279B
  Thompson, 309B
machining tools
  boring machine, 219B
  compressed air rock drill, 265B
  drill bits, 67B
  hobbing machine, 343B
  nail-cutting machine, 233B
  universal milling machine, 271B
Maciejowice, 230A
Mackenzie, Alexander, 228B, 230B
Mackenzie, William Lyon, 252B
Mackenzie River, 228B
Mackinac, 203A
Mackintosh, Charles Rennie, 271C
MacLaine, Shirley, 347C, 367C
Maclean, Donald, 338B
MacMahon, Marie Edmé (president of France), 274A, 276A
Macmillan, Crystal, 290A
Macmillan, Harold (prime minister of Britain), 344B, 346B, 348B
Macon, 136A
Macon culture, 65A
Macon Plateau culture, 123A
Macrinus (emperor of Rome), 44A
Madagascar, 44B, 85B, 86C, 150B, 160B, 170B, 176B, 178B, 186B, 188B, 189B, 194B, 198B, 202B, 216B, 239A, 243A, 245C, 249A, 253A, 267A, 269A, 285A, 287A
  and Britain, 257A, 267A, 269C, 275A
  and France, 247A, 257A, 267A, 269A, 271A, 279A
  Merina dynasty, 160B, 243A, 271A
  religion, 253A, 269C
Madame Bovary (Flaubert), 265C
Madame Gautreau (Sargent), 279C
Madame Sans-Gêne (Sardou), 283C
Madden Dam, 316C
Maddox, Richard, 273B
Madeira Islands, 136B, 240B
Madero, Francisco Indalécio (president of Mexico), 292C
Madison, James (president of U.S.), 226B, 231B, 232B, 238B, 242B
Madonna and Child Enthroned with Saints, The (Raphael), 151C
Madonna (anon.), *143*
Madonna (Giorgione), 151C
Madonna with Saints (Bellini), 147C
Madras, 186C, 202C, 212C, 214C, 218C, 220C
  battle of, 295A
Madrid, 156A, 166A, 202A, 204A, 218A, 240A, 320A
  Peace of (1715), 206A
  student protests in, 354B
  Treaty of (1630), 184A
  University, 354B
madrigals, 123C
Madwoman of Chaillot, The (Giraudoux), 335C

Maeandrius, 16C
Maeterlinck, Maurice, 283C
Magadha, 16B, 22B
Magaritone, 119B
Magdala, 271A
Magdalena River, 161A
Magdalene College, 163C
Magdeburg, 184A
Magellan, Ferdinand, 155A, 155B, 157B
Maggie: A Child of the Streets (Crane), 283C
Magic Flute, The (Mozart), 229C
Magic Mountain, The (Mann), 309C
Magician of Lublin, The (Singer), 347C
Maginot Line, 312A, 318A
Magna Carta, 110A, 112A
Magnalia Christi Americana (Mather), 203C
Magnani, Anna, 343C
Magnavox Company, 363B
Magnentius (emperor of Rome), 54
magnet, 119B
  electric magneto, 281B
  electromagnet, 245B, 249B
magnetic field, 245B, 299B
magnetic resonance imaging (MRI), 335B
magnification, magnifier, 39B, 165B
Magnificent Ambersons, The (Welles), 329C
Magnus II (king of Sweden), 130A
Magnus III (king of Norway), 98A
Magnus Intercursus, 148A
Magritte, René, 313C
Magyars, 82A, 86A, 110A
Mahabharata (Vyasa), 25C, 77C
Mahan, Arthur Thayer, 283C
Mahavira, 17C
Mahdi, 76B, 277A, 287A
Mahdi, Ibrahim Ibn al-, 77C
Mahdiyya, al-, 180B
Mahdoji Sindhia (ruler of central India), 231A
Mahinda (king of Ceylon), 88C
Mahler, Gustav, 281C, 293C
Mahmud II (sultan of Malwa), 152C
Mahmud II (sultan of Ottoman Empire), 239A, 249A
Mahmud Khan, 138C
Mahmud (shah of Afghanistan), 235A
Mahmud Shah (sultan of Malacca), 146C, 156C
Mahmud (sultan of Ghazna), 88C, 90C, 92C
Mahomet I, 80B
Mahomet (Voltaire), 213C
Mahrattas, 216C
Mai Ali, 144B
Mai of Bornu, 168B
Maid of Orleans, The (Schiller), 235C
mail. *See* postal service
mail (armor), 47B, 99B
Mailer, Norman, 337C, 365C
Maillol, Aristide, 291C
Maimonides, 109C
Main River, 271B
Main Street (Lewis), 305C
Maine, 94A, 96A, 108A, 138A, 144A, 149A, 181A, 183A, 189C, 193A, 197A, 201A, 203A, 205A, 226B, 240B, 244B, 260B, 292B, 336C
Maine (U.S. battleship), 286C
Mainz, 79C, 125B, 141B, 261C
  University of, 145C
Maipo, battle of, 244C
Majapahit, 140C, 154C
Majdoji Sindhia, 231A
Major, John (prime minister of Britain), 374B
Majuba Hill, battle of, 277A
Makarios III (president of Cyprus), 346B, 348B, 350B, 360B, 362B
Makasar, 160C, 194C
Makasar Straits, battle of, 326C
Makemie, Francis, 205C
Making of Americans, The (Stein), 309C
Malacca, 140C, 144C, 146C, 152C, 164C, 176C, 182C, 184C, 186C, 247A
  Straits of, 162C
Malade Imaginaire, Le (Molière), 195C
Malaga, 318A
  siege of, 147B
malaria, 333B
Malavoglia, I (Verga), 277C
Malawi, 47B, 114C, 283A, 340A, 349A, 350A, 351A
Malay Peninsula, 118C, 134C, 144C, 146C, 156C, 164C, 174C, 326C
Malay States, Federated, 285A
Malaya, Malays, 76C, 84C, 152C, 176C, 188C, 227A, 271A, 279A, 326C
  and East Indies, 160C
  independence of, 345A
  Malaysia, Malaysians, 349A, 351A
  and ASEAN, 352A
  and Indonesia, 353A
Malcolm I (king of Scots), 86A
Malcolm II (king of Scotland), 90A, 92A
Malcolm III (king of Scots), 94A, 96A, 98A
Malcolm IV (king of Scotland), 104A
Malcolm X, 350C
Maldive Islands, 88C, 90C
Maldon, battle of, 88A
Male Animal, The (Thurber), 323C
Malebranche, Nicolas, 195C
Malek Shah (sultan of Seljuk Turks), 98B
Malenkov, Georgi (premier of Soviet Union), 342B
Malestroit, Truce of, 128A
Mali, 112C, 114C, 122C, 126C, 142B, 285A, 347A
Malibu, 341C
Malik Ambar (king of Habshi), 180C
Malinalco, 145A
Malindi, 136C
  battle of, 172B
Malinke, 112C
Mallarmé, Stéphane, 275C
Malmö, Truce of, 258A
Malolos, 287A
Malory, Sir Thomas, 145C
Malplaquet, battle of, 204A
Malraux, André, 315C, 321C
Malta, 62B, 80B, 168A, 307A, 328A, 350A, 350B, 356A
  and Britain, 364B
  and Egypt, 368A
  summit, 374A
Maltese Falcon, The (Huston), 325C
Malthus, Thomas Robert, 233C, 245C
Malventum, 23A
Malvern Hall (Constable), 239C
Malwa, 112C, 124C, 138C, 142C, 152C, 158C, 160C, 166C
Mamallapuram, 71C
Mamun, al-, 78C
Mamelukes. *See* Egypt, Egyptians
Mamun, 79C
Man, Isle of, 116A
Man for All Seasons, A (Bolt), 347C
Man for All Seasons, A (movie), 353C
Man of Mode, The (Etherege), 197C
Man Who Was Thursday, The (Chesterton), 291C
Managua, 262C, 312C
Manassas, 266B
Manaus, 282C
Manchu, 176C, 180C, 182C, 195C, 196C, 198C, 208C
Manchu dynasty. *See* China, Chinese
Manchukuo, 315A, 317A, 321A
Manchuria, 84C, 110C, 196C, 287A, 289A, 311A, 322C
  and Formosa, 198C
  and Japan, 313A, 315A
  Liap (Khitan) dynasty, 84C
  and Mongolia, 198C
  and Soviet Union, 334C
Manco Inca Yupanqui, 161A, 163A
Mandalay, 334C
Mande people, 223A
Mandela, Nelson (president of South Africa), 369A, 375A, 381A
Mandera, 297A
Mandeville, Bernard, 203C
Mandingo, kingdom of, 40B, 92C, 263A
Mandingo people, 112C
Mandragola, La (Machiavelli), 155C
Mandu, 122C
Manet, Édouard, 269C,
Manetho, 23C
Manfred (Byron), 243C
Manfred (king of Sicily), 116B, 117B
Mangalore, 229A
Mangray, 120C
Manhattan, 179A, 183A, 183C, 185A, 224B. *See also* New York City
Manhattan Engineer District, 328B
Manhattan Project, 327B, 334B
Manhattan Transfer (Dos Passos), 309C
Mani, 166B
Maniakes, George, 92B
Manichaeism, 47A, 49A
Manichaeus, 47A, 49A
Manifeste du Surréalisme (Breton), 309C
Manifesto of Coblenz (Brunswick), 230A
Manila, 168C, 172C, 176C, 219A, 319B, 326C, 342A
Manila Bay, 170C, 328C
  battles of, 287A, 334C
Manila Cathedral, 191C
Manipur, 247A, 332C
Manitoba, 272B
Mankiewicz, Joseph L., 339C
Mann, Delbert, 343C
Mann, Thomas, 289C, 309C
Mann Act, 292B
Mannheim, 306A
Manon Lescaut (Puccini), 283C
Mansa, 212B
Mansfield Park (Austen), 241C
Manshevists, 288A
Manson, Charles, 356C
Mansur, al-, 88B
Mansur, Abu Jafar al-, 74B
Mansur, Ahmad al-, 172B
Mansur Shah (sultan of Malacca), 140C
Mantegna, Andrea, 141C, 143C
Mantinea, battle of, 20C
Mantua, 66B, 126B, 141C, 143C, 179C, 238A
  Congress of, 140B
Manuel I Comnenus (emperor of Byzantium), 102B, 104B
Manuel II Palaeologus (emperor of Byzantium), 132B, 134B, 136A
Manuel II (king of Portugal), 292A
Manyakheta, 78C
Manzanillo, 226C
Manzikert, battle of, 96B
Manzoni, Alessandro, 245C, 255C
Mao Zedong (president of China), 311A, 313A, 317A, 346B, 363A, 367A
Maori, Maori Wars, 38B, 84C, 125B, 241A, 267A, 269A, 273A
Map, Walter, 107C
Mapplethorpe, Robert, 373C
map(s), 101B, 169C
  in ancient Rome, *27,* 31B
  in China, 39B, 49B, 79B, 103B
  in Greece, 15B
  of North America, 175B
  Ptolemy's, *40*
  topographical, 9B
  in United States, 239B
Mara, Ratu (prime minister of Fiji), 371A
Marat, Jean Paul, 230A
Maratha, kingdom of, 192C, 216C
  Confederacy, 223A
  Second War, 237A
Maratha dynasty. *See* India, Indians
Marathon, battle of, 18C
Maravi empire, 114C
Marble Arch, 247C
Marble Faun, The (Hawthorne), 267C
marbles, 235C
Marbury v. Madison, 236B
Marcel, Étienne, 130A
Marcellinus, Pope, 51A
Marcellus I, Pope, 51A
March, Ausias, 141C
March, Fredric, 337C
Marchbanks, Vance, 345B
Marche-les-Dames, 127B
Marchfeld, 118A
Marcian (emperor of Byzantium), 60B
Marciano, Rocky, 341C
Marcomanni, 42A
Marcos, Ferdinand (president of Philippines), 367A, 371A, 373A
Mare au diable, La (Sand), 259C
Marengo, battle of, 234A
Marey, Étienne-Jules, 277B
Margaret, "Maid of Norway" (queen of Scots), 118A, 120A
Margaret of Anjou (queen of England), 138A, 140A, 142A, 144A
margarine, 273B, 275B
Marggraf, Andreas, 215B
Margrethe II (queen of Denmark), 358B
Maria Christina (queen of Spain), 268A
Maria I (queen of Portugal), 222A
Maria Theresa (Holy Roman Emperor and queen of Bohemia and Hungary), 212A
Mariana Islands, 157B, 194C, 245A, 332C, 360A
Marigano, battle of, 154A
Marin, John, 305C
Mariner 4, 351B
Mariner II, 349B
marines, U.S. *See* U.S. Marines
Marino, Eugene Antonio (Archbishop of Atlanta), 373C
Marinus I, Pope, 83C
Maris, Roger, 347C, 385C
Maritime Powers, 210A
Marius, Gaius, 27A
Marivan, 301A
Mark, Gospel of, 37A
marker, felt-tipped, 349B
Marlborough, duke of, 202A, 204A
Marlowe, Christopher, 173C, 175C
Marmion (Scott), 239C

Marne, battles of the, 296A, 302A
Marne River, 294A
Marquand, J. P., 323C, 325C, 327C
Marquesas Islands, 50B, 58C, 76C, 108C, 174C, 257A
Marquess of Hastings (governor-general of India), 241A
Marrakesh, 96B, 156B, 194B
 Treaty of, 227A
Marriage à la Mode (Hogarth), 213C
Marriage of Figaro (Mozart), 227C
Marriage of Heaven and Hell (Blake), 231C
Marriage of Isaac and Rebekah,The (Lorrain), 189C
Marryat, Frederick, 253C
Mars, 351B, 361B, 363B, 383B
Mars Candy Company, 323B
Mars Observer, 379B
Marsala, 266A
Marsden, Samuel, 241A
Marseilles, 78B, 151B, 156A, 160A, 316A, 317A
Marshall, George C., 334B, 336C, 338C
Marshall, John, 236B, 252B
Marshall, Thurgood, 354C, 376C
Marshall Aid Act, 336C
Marshall Islands, 168C, 332C, 371A, 376A
Marshall Plan, 336A, 336C, 338A
Marston Moor, battle of, 188A
Martaban, 154C
Martel, Charles, 72A, 74A
Martha's Vineyard, 177A
Martí, José, 282C, 284C
Martial, 37C
Martin, Archer, 327B
Martin, Pierre, 265B
Martin, Saint, 55A
Martin I , Pope, 71C
Martin I (king of Aragon), 134B
Martin I (king of Sicily), 134B
Martin V , Pope, 137C
Martin Luther (Cranach), 163C
Martin Luther King Day, 366C
Martin v. Hunter's Lessee, 242B
Martinet, Jean, 193B
Martínez, Estevan José, 228B
Martini, Simone, 125C, 127C
Martinique, 219A, 230C, 238C, 288C
Marty (movie), 343C
Marv, 152B
Marvin, Lee, 351C
Marx, Karl, 259C, 271C
Marx, Wilhelm (chancellor of Germany), 306A
Marxism, Marxists, 274B, 290A, 317A
Mary, Virgin, 35A, 263C
Mary Guildford, 157A
Mary I (queen of England), 164A, 166A
Mary II (queen of England), 196A, 198A, 200A
Mary Magdalen (Hebbel), 257C
Mary (queen of Scots), 162A, 166A, *167,* 168A, 172A
Mary Stuart (Schiller), 235C
Maryinsky Theatre, 291C
Maryland, 171A, 185A, 189A, 201A, 201C, 211A, 211C, 215A, 219C, 227C, 260B, 266B, 318B
Masaccio, 137C
Masada, 36B
Mascagni, Pietro, 283C
Mascara, 251A
Masefield, John, 293C
Mashonaland, 62C, 281A
Masjid-i-Shah, 179C
Masked Ball (Verdi), 343C
Maskelyne, Nevil, 217B
Mason, John, 183A, 265B
mason jar, 265B
Masque of Reason, A (Frost), 335C
Mass (Bernstein), 357C
Mass in B Minor (Bach), 213C
Mass in C Major (Beethoven), 237C
Massachusetts, 181A, 183A, 185A, 187A, 187B, 187C, 189A, 191A, 193A, 195A, 197A, 201A, 203A, 219A, 221A, 224B, 226B, 238B, 241B, 244B, 248B, 256B, 262B, 270B, 287B, 373C
 Sacco-Vanzetti case, 304B, 310B
 tornadoes in, 340C
Massachusetts Bay Colony, 185A, 185B, 199A
Massachusetts Bay Company, 199A
Massachusetts General Court, 185A
Massachusetts Institute of Technology (MIT), 341B, 349B, 361B
Massawa, 164B, 269A
Massey, Vincent (governor-general of Canada), 340C
Massey-Harris Company, 307B
Massinger, Phillip, 183C
Massys, Quentin, *32*
Masters, Edgar Lee, 297C
Masters, Sibilla, 205B
Masts, battle of the, 70B
Masudi, al-, 85B
Masulipatam, 186C
Masuria, battle of, 296A
Matabele, 285A
Matamba, 172B
Mataram, 186C, 196C, 214C
matches, 65B, 91B, 169B, 197B, 249B, 257B
Maternus, Julius, 41B
Mathematical Collection (Pappus), 49B
mathematics
 algebraic lettering system, 173B
 (*See also* calculating devices)
  binary language, 325B
  calculus, 195B
  cubic equations, 163B
  Difference Engine, 247B
  equal sign, 165B
  logarithmic tables, 181B
  multiplication symbol, 185B
  plus and minus signs, 153B
  slide rule, 363B
  and solar eclipse, 229B
  square root symbol, 157B
  square roots, 5B
Mather, Cotton, 201C, 203C, 205C
Mather, Increase, 199A
Matilda of Tuscany, 94B, *96*
Matilda (queen of England), 100A, 102A
Matisse, Henri, 293C, 299C, 307C, 343C
Matlazincas, 111A
Matope, 140B
Matsudaira Sadanobu, 227A
Matsuhito (emperor of Japan), 281A
Matteotti, Giacomo, 308A
Matthew, Gospel of, 37A
Matthias (Holy Roman Emperor), 176A, 178A, 180A
Matupa, 178B
Mau Mau, 340A
Mauch Chunk, 255B
Mauchly, John W., 325B, 339B
Maudslay, Henry, 233B
Maugerville, 219A
Maugham, William Somerset, 297C, 333C
Maung Maung (president of Burma), 373A
Maupertuis, battle of, 128A
Mauran dynasty. *See* India, Indians
Maurepas, Jean Frédéric Phélipeaux, 220A
Mauretania, 34B
Mauriac, François, 309C, 311C, 315C, 319C
Mauriac Plains, battle of, 60B
Maurice (emperor of Byzantium), 64B
Maurice of Saxony, 164A
Mauritania, 206B, 372A
Mauritius, 174C, 188B, 204B, 210B, 239A, 243A, 355A
Mausolus (king of Caria), 20C
Maw Shans, 152C, 156C
Max Schmitt in a Single Scull (Eakins), 273C
Maxentius (emperor of Rome), 50A
Maxim, Hiram Percy, 279B, 291B
Maximian (emperor of Rome), 48A, *49,* 50A
Maximilian (archduke of Austria and emperor of Mexico), 268C, 270C
Maximilian I, duke of Bavaria (elector of Palatinate), 182A
Maximilian I (king of Germany and Holy Roman Emperor), 144A, 146A, 148A, 150A, 152A, 154A
Maximilian II (Holy Roman Emperor), 164A, 166A, 168A, 169C, 170A
Maximinus (emperor of Rome), 46A
Maximus, Magnus, 56A
Maxtlatzin, 137A
May Day riot, 154A
Mayagüez, 274C, 302C
Mayan civilization, Maya, 10B, 32C, 40C, 42C, 46C, 65A, 67A, 89A, 159C
 arts, 44C, 48C, 81A
 astronomy, 69A
 calendar, 3B, *48*
 cities, 52C, 61A, 63A, 75A, 77A, 79A, 83A, 91A, 109A, 113A
 Classic period, 50C, 85A
 Jaguar Paw dynasty, 56C, 75A
 monuments, 54C, 67C, 71A
 Post Classic period, 87A
 ruins, 171A, 254C
 science and technology, 67B, 69A, 83B
Mayapan, 99A, 113A, 139A, 141A
Maybach, Wilhelm, 279B, 287B
Mayence, 230A, 232A
Mayerling, 280A
Mayflower, 181A
Mayflower Compact, 181A
Maynard, Edmund, 257B
Mayo, Lord (viceroy of India), 273A
Mayor of Casterbridge, The (Hardy), 281C
Maytag Company, 293B
Mazagan, 218B
Mazarin, Jules, 186A, 192A
Mazepa, Ivan Stepanovich, 204A
Mazowiecki, Tadeusz, 372B
Mazzini, Giuseppe, 260A
Mbailundu, 220B
McAleese, Mary (president of Ireland), 384B
McCall's, 273B
McCarey, Leo, 333C
McCarthy, Joseph, 340C, 342C, 344C
McCarthy, Mary, 327C
McCartney, Paul, 383C
McCauley, Mary, 224B
McClellan, George, 266B
McCormick, Cyrus, 251B, 253B
McCoy, Elijah, 267B
McCullers, Carson, 323C, 325C
McCulloch v. Maryland, 244B
McDormand, Frances, 383C
McDougal, James, 382C
McDougal, Susan, 382C
McDougall, William, 272B
McGovern, George, 358C
McGwire, Mark, 385C
McKay, Claude, 293C
McKay, Frederick, 313B
McKinley, William (president of U.S.), 286B, 288B
McKinley Tariff Act, 282B
McMahon, William (prime minister of Australia), 357A
McMillan, Edwin, 323B
McPherson, Aimee Semple, 333C
McVeigh, Timothy, 380C, 384C, *385*
Mead, Margaret, 363B
Meade, George, 268B
measles, 83B
Measure for Measure (Shakespeare), 177C
measuring devices, 93B, 225B
meat
 canned, 315B
 frozen, 279B
 rationing, 330B, 332B, 334B
Meaux, 168A
 Treaty of, 112A
Mecca, 68C, 69C, 154B, 237A, 299A, 301A
Méchain, Pierre, 239B
Mecham, Evan, 372C
Mecklenburg, 139B, 182A, 206A, 244A, 244B
Medal, The (Dryden), 197C
Medal of Freedom, U.S., *365*
Medal of Honor, U.S., 266B, 268B
Medawar, Peter, 335B
Medea (Euripides), 19C
Medée et Jason (Noverre), 219C
Medellín drug cartel, 377A
Medes, 14B
Media, 14C
Mediation, Act of, 236A
Medical Care for the Aged (Medicare), 350C, 352C
Medici, Cosimo de', 136B
Medici, Giuliano de', 144A
Medici, House of, 134B, 148A, 152A, 158A, 179B, 212A
Medici, Lorenzo de' (the Magnificent), 142A, 146A
Medici, Piero di Lorenzo de', 143C
Medici Chapel, 155C
Medina, 69C, 237A
Meditationes de Prima Philosophia (Descartes), 187C
Meditations (Aurelius), 43C
Méditations poétiques (Lamartine), 245C
Mediterranean Sea, 2A, 2B, 8C, 57B, 99B, 115B, 123B, 151B, 160A, 166B, 175B, 201B, 212B, 290A, 341B
Medway, battle of, 34A
Meech Lake Accord, 374C
Megara, 12C
Mège-Mouriès, Hippolyte, 273B
Megiddo, battle of, 14B
Mehmed I (sultan of Ottoman empire), 134B, 136B
Mehmed II (sultan of Ottoman empire), 138B
Mehmed IV (sultan of Ottoman empire), 196B, 200B
Mein Kampf (Hitler), 308A
Meir, Golda (prime minister of Israel), 357A, 361A, 363A
Meissen, 110A
Meistersinger (Wagner), 271C
Meknes, 194B
Mekong Delta, 216C
Mekong River, 283A
Melancholia I (Dürer), 153C
Melanchthon, 157C
Melanesia, Melanesians, 2B, 4B, 6B
Melbourne, 253A

Melchior, Lauritz, 309C
Melilla, 148B
Mellon, Andrew, 306B
Melo, 232C
Meloria, 118B
Melville, Herman, 261C
Melville Peninsula, 246B
Melville Sound, 244B
Memel, 320A
Memling, Hans, 149C
Memoirs from the House of the Dead (Dostoyevsky), 267C
Memória Póstumas de Bras Cubas (Machado de Assis), 277C
Memorial, The (Isherwood), 315C
Memorial Day, 270B
Memphis, 197A, 354C
Memphis Blues (Handy), 293C
Memphis (Egypt), 2A, 4A, 6A, 12A, 22A
Memphis (Tenn.), 163A
Men, Women, and Dogs (Thurber), 331C
Menam Basin, 120C
Mencken, H. L., 305C
Mendel, Gregor, 263B
Mendel's law, 263B
Mendelssohn, Felix, 247C, 249C, 259C
Mendelssohn, Moses, 219C, 225C
Mendez, Geronimo (president of Chile), 327A
"Mending Wall" (Frost), 295C
Mendip Hills, 35B
Mendoza, Antonio de, 161A, 161B
Menelik II, 299A
Menen Leben Amede (empress of Ethiopia), 255A
Menéndez de Avilés, Pedro, 169A, 171A
Menes, 2A
Menevia, 65C
Mengelberg, Willem, 285C
Mengistu Mariam (leader of Ethiopia), 369A
Mengoni, Giuseppe, 269C
Mennonites, 199A
Menotti, Gian Carlo, 319C, 339C
Mentana, battle of, 270A
Mentone, 266A
Mentuhotep, Nebhepetre (king of Egypt), 4A
Menzies, Michael, 211B
Menzies, Sir Robert Gordon (prime minister of Australia), 321A
Mercator, Gerhardus, 169C
Mercer, John, 261B
mercerization, 261B
Merchant Marine Act, 310B
Merchant of Venice, The (Shakespeare), 175C
Mercia, kingdom of, 64A, 70A, 74A, 76A, 78A, 80A
mercury (element), 149B
Mercury (planet), 377B
Meredith, George, 277C
Meredith, James, 348C
Mergenthaler, Ottmar, 279B
Mérimée, Prosper, 257C
Merina, kingdom of, 170B, 239A
Merina dynasty. *See* Madagascar
Merisi, Michelangelo, 179C
Meroe, 14A, 54
Merovingians, 73C, 74A
Merrill, John, 339C
Merry Widow, The (Lehár), 291C
Merry Wives of Windsor (Shakespeare), 177C
Mers-el-Kebir, 150B, 324A
Mersen, Treaty of, 80A
Merton, 110A
Merton College, 117C
Mervan II, 74B
Mesa Verde, 97A, 99A, 115A, 123A
Mesoamerica, 8B, 34C, 35C, 40C, 44C, 50C, 59A, 71B
  agriculture in, 30C, 32C, 36C
  arts, 9C, 35C, 61A, 77A
  Classical period, 85A
  metalwork in, 77A, 91A
  pottery, 42C
  science and technology, 91C
  transportation, 36C
Mesopotamia, Mesopotamians, 2B, 3B, 4B, 5B, 5C, 6B, 22B, 42A, 48B, 50B, 53A, 77B, 152B, 164B
  and Armenia, 297A
  and Britain, 297A, 299A, 301A
  and India, 301A
  and Muslims, 68B, 68C
  and Russia, 301A
  and Turkey, 301A
messages, 169B
  coded, 135B, 143B, 327B
  decoding, 331B
Messalina, 34A
Messenia, 12C
Messiah (Handel), 213C
Messina, 94B, 106B, 266A
Messmer, Pierre (prime minister of France), 358B
Mestral, Georges de, 343B
metal fatigue, 295B, 373B
metalwork, 7B, 91A
  in China, 33B
  in Egypt, 3C
  in Mesoamerica, 77A
Metamorphoses (Golden Ass) (Apuleius), 43C
Metaxas, John (prime minister of Greece), 318A
Metellus, Caecilius, 26C
Methodism, Methodists, 211C, 213C
Methodist Church, 215C, 227C, 235C, 241C, 257C, 343C
Methodist Episcopal Church South, 257C, 321C
Methodist Society, 219C
Methodius, Saint, 79C, 81B, 81C
Methods of Treating Wounds (Paré), 163B
Methodus ad Facilem Historiarum Cognitionem (Bodin), 169C
Methuen, battle of, 122A
Métis, 242B, 272B, 278B
metric system, 229B, 235B, 239B, 274A
Metrodorus, 43C
metronome, 217B
Metropolis (movie), 311C
Metz, 77C
Meuse, 300A
Mewar, 161C
Mexican-Americans, 330B
Mexico, Gulf of, 83A
Mexico, Mexicans, 44C, 50C, 59A, 129A, 137A, 163A, 171A, 228B, 294C, 304C, 325A, 377B. *See also* Mayan civilization, Maya; Tenanyecac culture; Teotihuacán culture
  300 B.C.–40 B.C., 22B, 23B, 30C
  arts, 44C, 46C, 61A, 63A, 63C, 67A, 67C, 83C
  Aztec empire, 32C, 105A, 127A, 131A, 143A
  and Britain, 320C
  Chalchihuites culture, 133A
  early history, 75A, 77A, 79A, 83A
  economy, 115A
  and France, 254A, 268C, 270C
  and Germany, 329A
  government, 246C, 260C, 266C, 272C, 278C, 300C, 304C, 316C, 323A, 341A, 373A
  Gulf of, 155A, 161A
  and Honduras, 246C
  independence of, 240C, 244C
  industry, 73A, 79A, 109A, 143B, 155B, 302C, 310C
  and Italy, 329A
  and Japan, 327A
  law and society, 256C, 264C, 274C, 292C, 320C, 355A, 381A
  in League of Nations, 312A
  Mexican War, 258B
  Mixtecs, 91A
  and NAFTA, 378A
  Ogiso dynasty, 82C
  Olmeca-Xicalanca dynasty, 71A, 75A
  Pancho Villa and, 298B
  peanuts in, 155B
  politics, 226C, 312C
  religion, 165A, 244C, 275C, 310C, 311C
  science and technology, 44C, 59B
  slave trade, 153A, 248C
  and Spain, 155A, 157A, 159A, 159B, 161A, 162C, 228C, 238C
  transportation, 286C
  in United Nations, 335A
  and United States, 252B, 252C, 258B, 262B, 268C, 294C, 296C, 298C, 306C, 320C, 325A, 327A, 329A, 333A, 348A, 378A, 381A
  World War II, 325A, 329A
  Zapotecs in, 73A
Mexico City, 123A, 125A, 157A, 161A, 163A, 258C, 268C, 294C
  earthquake in, 369A
  National Palace, 201C
Mexico City Cathedral, 171C
Mexico in Revolution (Orozco), 299C
Meyerbeer, Giacomo, 261C
MGM Grand Hotel, 364C
Miami, 345B, 364C
Miami Dolphins, 359C, 361C, 369C
Miao, 233A
Michael I Rhangabe (emperor of Byzantium), 78B
Michael II (emperor of Byzantium), 78B
Michael III (emperor of Byzantium), 78B
Michael VII (emperor of Byzantium), 94B
Michael VIII Palaeologus (emperor of Byzantium), 116B
Michael of Wallachia, 176A
Michael the Brave (prince of Wallachia), 174A
Michelangelo, 151C, 153C, 155C, 163B, 167C, 177C, 381C
Michelet, Jules, 251C
Michelin Tire Company, 337B
Michelino, Domenico de, *125*
Michelson, Albert, 277B
Michigan, 73A, 77A, 135A, 181A, 215A, 248B, 252B, 382C
  tornadoes in, 340C
  University of, 349B
Mickiewicz, Adam, 249C, 253C
Micombero, Michel (president of Burundi), 363A
microfilm, 255B
micrometer, 221B
Micronesia, 376A
microscope, 181B
  atomic force (AFM), 369B
  electron, 321B, 323B
Microsoft Corporation, 371B
Microtone Company, 341B
microwave, 335B
  ammonia maser, 341B
  radar range, 343B
Middle East, 5B, 10B. *See also individual countries*
Middle Kingdom (Egypt), 4A
Middle Mississippi culture, 99A, 123A
Middleton, Sir Henry, 176C
Mideast peace process, 376A, 381A
Midhat Pasha (sultan of Ottoman Empire), 275A
Midnight Cowboy (movie), 357C
Midshipman Easy (Marryat), 253C
Midsummer Night's Dream, A (Shakespeare), 175C
Midway Island, battle of, 328C
Mies van der Rohe, Ludwig, 345C, 355C
Miguel, Dom (king of Portugal), 248A, 252A
Mikalic, Branko (prime minister of Yugoslavia), 370B
Mikhail (tsar of Russia), 178A, 179C
Mikoyan, Anastas, 350B
Milan, 48A, 103B, 104B, 127B, 134B, 136B, 138B, 140A, 148A, 149C, 152A, 154A, 160A, 164A, 223C, 302A
    Decree of, 236A
    Edict of, 51A
    Galleria Vittorio Emanuele, 269C
    Peace of, 260A
Milan Cathedral, 133C
Milan (king of Serbia), 278A
Milanov, Zinka, 319C
Milazzo, 266A
Mildenhall, John, 176C
Mildred Pierce (Curtiz), 335C
Miles Laboratories, 313B
Milesians, 10C, 12C
Miletus, 13B, 23C, 41C
Milford, 187A
milk
  pasteurized, 317B
  wooden churns for, 83B
Milky Way, 295A
Mill, James, 247C
Mill, John Stuart, 259C, 265C, 269C, 273C
Mill on the Floss, The (Eliot), 267C
Milland, Ray, 335C
Millay, Edna Saint Vincent, 301C
Mille Lacs culture, 135A
Miller, Arthur, 339C, 341C
Miller, Carl, 333B
Miller, Glenn, 335C
Miller, Henry, 317C, 321C, 335C, 365C
Millerand, Alexandre (president of France), 304A
millet, 109B
Million Man March, 383C
mills, 51B. *See also* sawmills
  flour, 229B
  fulling, 89B
  gig, 177B
  grain, 59B, 83B, 173B
  paper, 83B, 107B, 201B
  textile, 223B
  tidal, 97B, 101B
  twisting, 119B
Mills, Robert, 251C
Milne, A. A., 311C
Milosevic, Slobodan (president of Serbia), 378B, 384A
Miltiades, Pope, 51A
Milton, John, 185C, 189C, 193C, 195C
Milton Abbey, 85C
Milvian Bridge, battle of, 50A, 51A
Milwaukee, 244B, 376C
Milwaukee Braves, 345C
Milwaukee Brewers, 367C
Mimbres, 91C

mime theaters, 63C
mimeograph machine, 279B
Minamoto family. *See* Japan
Minas, 203A
Mindanao, 156C
Minden, battle of, 216A
Mindoro, 334C
mines, mining, 87B, 165B, 235B, 358B, 360B, 368B. *See also* substances mined
roads with rails, 151B
Roman, 39C
treatise on minerals, 171B
water pump for, 201B
Ming dynasty. *See* China, Chinese
Ming Ti (emperor of China), 34B
Minh Mang, 245A
Minkhaung (king of Ava), 144C
Minkyinyo, 146C
Minnelli, Liza, 359C
Minnelli, Vincente, 331C, 339C
Minnesota, 73A, 99A, 135A, 177A, 244B, 248B, 260B, 264B
University of, 327C
Minnesota Mining and Manufacturing (3M) Company, 309B, 333B, 343B
Minnesota Twins, 351C, 371C, 377C
Minnesota Vikings, 357C, 361C, 363C
Minoan civilization, 2C, 5C, 8C, 10C
Minorca, 204A, 206A, 216A, 218A, 224A, 232A
Minoxidil, 373B
Mintoff, Dom (prime minister of Malta), 356B
Miquelon Island, 230B, 234B
Mir, 381B
Mir Qasim, 216C
Miracle of St. Mark, The (Tintoretto), 163C
Miranda v. Arizona, 352C
Miriam, 45B
mirrors, 31B, 45B, 67B, 93B, 115B, 139B, 215B, 253B
Celtic, 31B
Gallic, 51B
Roman, 35B
Miscellanea (Poliziano), 147C
Miscellanies (Cowley), 191C
Misérables, Les (Hugo), 267C
Mishima Yukio, 353C
Mishnah, 45A
Mishongnovi, 115A
missiles
cruise, 366B
intercontinental ballistic missile (ICBM), 345B
Pershing II, 366B
Polaris, 348B
U.S. deployment in Britain, 366B
missions, missionaries, 159C, 221C, 237C
Mississippi, 63A, 99A, 123A, 242B, 254B, 268B, 348C, 354C
University of, 348C
Mississippi Basin, 224B
"Mississippi Bubble," 209A
Mississippi culture, 109A, 135A
Mississippi River, 30C, 54C, 73A, 91A, 109A, 163A, 195A, 197A, 203C, 226B, 232B, 236B, 239C, 248B, 250B, 265B, 338C
Mississippi Valley culture, 61A
Missolonghi, 247C, 248A
Missouri, 63A, 65A, 123A, 135A, 244B, 248B, 338C
Missouri Compromise, 244B, 262B, 264B
Missouri River, 139A, 145A, 209A
Missouri (U.S. battleship), 334C
Mistake Out, 345B
Mistress, The (Cowley), 189C
Mistress of the Inn, The (Goldoni), 215C
Mitau, 296A
Mitchell, Charles, 270B
Mitchell, Margaret, 319C
Mithraism, 39A, 41A
Mitla, 50C, 91A
Mitre, Bartolomé (president of Argentina), 266C, 272C, 274C, 282C
Mitsui family. *See* Japan
Mitsumasa Yonai (prime minister of Japan), 322C
Mitterand, François (president of France), 366B, 372B
Mixtec culture, 77A, 85A, 91A
Mleszko I (king of Poland), 86A
M&Ms, 323B
moa bird, 125B
Moawiya, 70B
Mobile, 161A, 205A
Mobile Bay, 264B
Moby Dick (Melville), 261C
Mocha, 138C
Moche, 77C
Mochica culture, 24B, 40C, 69A, 77A
Model, Walter, 334A
Model Cities Act, 352C
Modena, 138B, 264A, 266A
Modern Instance, A (Howells), 279C
Modern Man Is Obsolete (Cousins), 335C
Modern Utopia (Wells), 291C
Modigliani, Amedeo, 297C
Mogadishu, 82C, 86C, 114C, 120C, 136C, 378A
Mogaung, kingdom of, 110C
Mogodor, 257A
Mogollon culture, 24B, 51C, 63A, 73A
Mogul dynasty. *See* India, Indians
Mohács, battles of, 156A, 198A
Mohammad Musaddiq (shah of Iran), 341A
Mohammed Iqbal, 297C
Mohenjo-Daro, 2B, 3B
Mohilev, 204A
Moimir (prince of Slavs), 78A
Mol, 352B
Molasses Act, 211A
Molay, Jacques de, 125C
Moldavia, 152A, 244A, 248A, 250A, 266A, 290A
molecular ray movement, 331B
Moleyns, Frederick, 255B
Molière, 191C, 193C, 195C
Molino el Rey, 258B
Molinos, Miguel de, 195C
Moll Flanders (Defoe), 209C
Mollien, Gaspard, 245A
Mollwitz, battle of, 212A
"Molly Pitcher," 224B
Molnár, Ferenc, 293C
Molotov,Vyacheslav, 338B
Moluccas, 72C, 128C, 140C, 153B, 156C, 158C, 163C, 176C, 180C, 182C, 192C
Mombasa, 150B, 158B, 172B, 174B, 184B, 192B, 200B, 210B, 289A
Mommsen, Theodor, 263C
Momote, 332C
Momoyama, 181C
Mona Lisa (Leonardo da Vinci), 151C
Monagas, José Tadeo, 264C
Monagas, José Gregorio, 264C
Monarchianism, 43A
Moncado, José Maria (president of Nicaragua), 310C
Mondale, Walter, 368C
Mondrian, Piet, 305C
Monet, Claude, 273C
money, 99B, 125B, 177B, 278B
Mongke Khan (emperor of Mongols), 114C
Mongolia, Mongols, 32B, 34B, 38B, 106C, 206C, 208C, 309A, 322C
and Armenia, 114B, 114C
and Baghdad, 116B
and China, 101B, 102C, *111,* 112C, 116C, 118C, 119B, 124C, 128C, 130C, 138C, 162C, 164C, 186C, 337A
and Cossacks, 172A
and Egypt, 120B
and Europe, 113B
and Germany, 114A
government, 108C
and Hungary, 114A
and Korea, 128C
and Manchuria, 198C
and Persia, 121B
and Poland, 114A, 154A, 156A
religion, 200C
and Russia, 112A, 132A, 293A, 319A
science and technology, 119B
and Soviet Union, 352A
and Syria, 122C
and Tibet, 70C, 114C
and Timur, 130C
and Vietnam, 120C
Monitor (U.S. warship), 266B, 267B
Moniuszko, Stanislaw, 259C
Monk, George (duke of Albemarte), 192A
Monk, The (Lewis), 233C
monkeys, 2A
monks, 101B
Monmouth, 103C, 196A
battle of, 224B
Monotmotapa, 144B
Monroe, James (president of U.S.), 231B, 242B, 244B, 246B
Monroe Doctrine, 246B, 288B
Monrovia, 245A, 375A
Mons, 204A
battle of, 294A
Mons Graupius, battle of, 36A
Mont-Saint-Michel and Chartres (Adams), 283C
Mont-St.-Michel, Abbey of, 73C
Montag aus Licht (Stockhausen), 373C
Montagu, John, 219B
Montaigne, Michel de, 171C
Montana, 236B, 280B, 300B, 306B, 368C, 382C
Montanists, 45A
Montano, Francisco, 157A
Montanus of Phrygia, 41A
Montaperti, battle of, 116B
Montargis, battle of, 136A
Montauban, 182A
Montcalm, Louis Joseph de, 217A
Monte Albán, 46C, 50C, 61A, 73A, 85A, 129A
Monte Bello Islands, 340A
Montenegro, 224A, 260A, 264A, 276A, 316A
and Austria, 294A, 298A
in Balkan League, 292A
and Ottoman Empire, 274A
and Serbia, 270A
World War I, 294A
Montenegro, Mendez (president of Guatemala), 353A
Montereau, 136A
Monterey Bay, 177A
Monterrey (Mexico), 258B
Monteverdi, Claudio, 169C, 179C
Montevideo, 207A, 209A, 236C, 242C, 244C, 248C, 254C, 256C, 262C, 323A
Montezuma (emperor of Aztecs), 155A, 157A
Montfort, John de, 126A, 128A
Montfort, Simon de, Earl of Leicester, 114A, 116A, *117*
Montfort-l'Amaury, Simon IV de, 110A, 114A
Montgolfier, Joseph, 233B
Montgomery, Bernard, 328A
Montgomery, Richard, 222B
Montgomery (Ala.), 342C, 350C
Congress of, 266B
Montgomery (England), Treaty of, 116A
Montgomery Ward Company, 332B
Montiel, battle of, 130B
Montini, Giovanni Battista, 349C
Montlhéry, battle of, 142A
Montlucon, Peace of, 234A
Montmédy, 294A
Montmorency, Henri, 184A
Montpellier
Council of, 110A
Medical School, 123B
Treaty of, 182A
University of, 121C
Montreal, 187A, 199A, 217A, 222B, 224B, 256B, 258B
Montreuil, 120A
Montreux, 337C
Montserrat, 193A, 224C, 272C
Montt, Manuel (president of Chile), 264C
moon, manned missions to, 357B, 359B
Moon Is Down, The (Steinbeck), 329C
Moonstone, The (Collins), 271C
Moore, Henry, 323C, 337C
Moore, Thomas, 237C, 243C
Moorish Screen, The (Matisse), 307C
Moors, 72B, 74B, 86B, 87C
arts, 157B
and Gibraltar, 126B
in North Africa, 118B, 214B
in Portugal, 102B, 114B
in Spain, 94B, 98B, 99B, 100B, 110B, 169C, 178A
"Moors murders," 352B
Moral Man and Immoral Society (Niebuhr), 315C
Morales Bermúdez, Francisco (president of Peru), 361A
Moravia, Moravians, 81C, 82A, 118A, 178A, 209C, 320A
Moravian Church, 209C
Moravska Ostrava, 320A
Morazán, Francisco (president of United Provinces), 254C, 256C
More, Sir Thomas (lord chancellor of England), 155C, 158A, 161C
Morea, 122B, 132B, 134B, 140A, 206A
Moree, 178B
Morelos y Pavón, José María, 238C, 240C
Moreno, Alfredo (president of Ecuador), 298C
Moreno, Gabriel García (president of Ecuador), 266C, 274C
Morey, Samuel, 231B
Morgan, J. Pierpont, 288B
Morgan, Lee, 333B
Morgan Company, J. P., 296B
Morillo, Pablo, 242C, 244C
Morínigo, Higinio (president of Paraguay), 325A, 337A
Morlaix, battle of, 128A
Mormon Church, 249C, 363C, 375C
Mormons, 257C, 260B, 276B
Morning Post, 221C
Moro, Aldo (prime minister of Italy), 362B
Moro Expósito, El (Saavedia y Ramirez), 253C

Moro pirates, 174C
Morocco, Moroccans, 34B, 74B, 84B, 86B, 96B, 100B, 136B, 144A, 152B, 156B, 164B, 186B, 194B, 288A, 307A
  Alawite dynasty, 192B
  and Algeria, 349A
  in Arab Maghreb Union, 372A
  Banu Saad dynasty, 152B
  earthquake in, 214B
  and England, 198B
  and France, 208B, 257A, 290A, 293A, 309A, 343A, 345A
  Franco-Moroccan War, 257A
  and Germany, 293A
  government, 170B, 172B, 184B, 192B, 341A
  independence of, 343A
  and Northwest Africa, 206B
  and Portugal, 218B
  religion, 94B
  and Shiites, 76B
  and Spain, 180B, 265A, 267A, 342A
  and Sudan, 216B
  and United States, 227A
  Wattasid dynasty, 136B
  World War II, 328A
Morocco (movie), 313C
Morris, William, 271C, 275C
Morrison, Jim, 357C
Morrison, Robert, 237C
Morrison, Toni, 373C
Morse, Samuel, 255B, *256,* 257B
Morse Code, 255B
Mort, Thomas, 267B
Morte d'Arthur, Le (Malory), 145C
Mortemer, 94A
Mortimer, 134A
Mortimer, Roger de, 124A
Mortimer's Cross, battle of, 140A
Morton culture, 77A
Mosaddeq, Muhammad, 341A
mosaics, 99C, 101A
Moscow, 112A, 126A, 130A, 132A, 136A, 144A, 146A, 162A, 178A, 204A, 302A, 326A, 346B, 350A, 352B
  administration, 150A
  Basilica of St. Basil, 167C
  battle of, 326A
  Bolshoi Theater, 225C
  Conference, 332A
  electric trolley cars in, 285B
  Metropolitan of, 173C
  Moscow Art Theatre, 287C
  Napoléon in, 240A
  and Poland, *210*
  railroad to St. Petersburg, 256A
  summit in, 384A
  synagogues in, 347C
  and Tatars, 156A
  University, 203C
Moses, 8A, 37A
Moses (Michelangelo), 155C
Moshesh I, 257A
Moshica culture, 61A
Moshoeshoe II (king of Lesotho), 357A
Mosqat, 212B, 214B
Mosquera, Tomás Cipriano de (president of Colombia), 256C
Mosses from an Old Manse (Hawthorne), 259C
Mossi, 124C, 140B, 144B
Mossi Kingdom, 285A
most-favored-nation treatment, 379A
Mosul, 100B, 309A, 311A, 317A, 317B
  battle of, 68C
motet, 99C
Mother and Child (Cassatt), 291C
Mother Church, 285C
Mother (Norris), 293C
Motherwell, Robert, 327C
motion sickness, 337B
motor, electric, 281B
motorcycle, 279B
Motrin, 361B
Mott, Lucretia, 258B
Motul de San Jose, 83A
Mount Abu, 93C
Mount Athos, 87C
Mount Chimborao, 235B
Mount Erebus, 291B
Mount Fuji, 204C
Mount Pelée, 230C
Mount Pinatubo, 377A
Mount Popocatepetl, 157A
Mount Sinai, 8A
Mount St. Helens, 364C
Mount Suribachi, 334C
Mount Vernon, 234B
Mount Vesuvius, 36A, 62B
Mountain Interval (Frost), 299C
Mountain Wreath, The (Njegos), 259C
Mountbatten, Lord, 330C, 364B
Mourning Becomes Electra (O'Neill), 313C
Mousetrap, The (Christie), 341C
Movene Mutopu, 185C
movie(s), 285B. *See also individual movies*
  camera, 277B, 307B
  home movies on cassette, 363B
  projector, 307B
  rating of, 317C
  silent, 297C, 299C, 301C, 305C
  sound track, 307B
  variable-speed projector, 289B
Mozambique, 37C, 150B, 152B, 158B, 166B, 170B, 178B, 194B, 225A, 301A, 361A
Mozart, Wolfgang Amadeus, 217C, 219C, 227C, 229C
Mr. Deeds Goes to Town (movie), 319C
Mr. Norris Changes Trains (Isherwood), 317C
Mr. Smith Goes to Washington (movie), 321C
Mrs. Dalloway (Woolf), 309C
Mrs. Miniver (movie), 329C
Mu Ch'i, 115C
Mubarak, Hosni (president of Egypt), 367A
Mubarak (India), 124C
Much Ado About Nothing (Shakespeare), 175C
Mudros Bay, *297*
Mughal, 192C
Muhammad, 68C, 69C, 231C
Muhammad, Murtala (leader of Nigeria), 361A, 363A
Muhammad, Sidi (sultan of Morocco; c. 1702–1790), 216B, 218B
Muhammad, Sidi (sultan of Morocco; c. 1910–1961), 341A
Muhammad Adil (sultan of Delhi), 124C
Muhammad Ahmad, 277A, 279A
Muhammad Ali Pasha (of Egypt), 237A, 239A, 243A, 245A, 246A, 247A, 251A, 255A
Muhammad Ali (shah of Persia), 291A, 293A
Muhammad ben Abdullah, 287A
Muhammad I (Nasrid ruler), 112B
Muhammad Idris (sultan of Bornu), 156B
Muhammad III (sultan of Bahmani), 140C
Muhammad III (sultan of Ottoman Empire), 174B
Muhammad (Iran), 253A
Muhammad Kantu (king of Kebbi), 154B
Muhammad of Ghor, 106C, 108C
Muhammad Shah (emperor of Moguls), 206C
Muhammad (shah of Persia), 253A
Muhammad V (sultan of Ottoman Empire), 293A
Muhammad VI (sultan of Morocco), 341A
Muhammad VI (sultan of Ottoman empire), 307A
Muhammadans, 90B, 90C, 96B, 124C
Mühlberg, battle of, 162A
Mühldorf, 124A
Mujahid of Denia, 90B
Mu'jam ul-Buldam, 113C
Mukden, battle of, 291A
Mukurra, 64C
Mularaja (king of Gujarat), 86C
Müller, Adam, 245C
Mulroney, Brian (prime minister of Canada), 368C, 372C, 378C
Mumford, Lewis, 317C
mummies, 3B
mumps, 355B
Munch, Edvard, 281C, 283C, 285C
Munefusa, Matsuo, 193C
Munich, 124A, 179C, 306A
  Conference, 320A
  Olympics, 358A
  University of, 143C
Muñoz Marín, Luis, 318C, 323A
Müntzer, Thomas, 157C
Muong Nai, kingdom of, 112C
Murad I (sultan of Ottoman empire), 130B
Murad II (sultan of Ottoman Empire), 136B, 138B
Murad III (sultan of Ottoman Empire), 170B
Murad IV (sultan of Ottoman Empire), 182B
Murai, Hujr Akil al-, 60C
Murano (Venetian island), 121B
Murat, Joachim, 240A, 242A
Murcia, 112B
Muret, battle of, 110B
Murger, Henry, 259C
Murnau, Friedrich W., 307C
Muromachi, 126C
Murphy, Frank, 322B
Murray, John, 221C
Mursa Major, battle of, 54A
Murshidabad, 202C
Mursilis (king of Hittite empire), 6B
Musa Pasha (vice-regent of Egypt), 184B
Musabba, 214B
Muscat, 164B, 186B, 188B
Muscat (sultan of Arabia), 251A
Muscovy. *See* Moscow
Muscovy Company, 164A, 166B, 177A
Museum of Modern Art, 325C
music
  blues, 347C
  early, 33C, 39B, 85C, 87C, 91C
  jazz, 287C
  ragtime, 279C
  rock, 357C, 377C, 383C
  scale, 12-note, 315C
Musique, La (Matisse), 293C
Muslim League, 291A
Muslims, 69B, 70C, 76C, 91B, 176B, 379A, 382C. *See also* Islam, Islamics
  in Afghanistan, 311A
  and alchemy, 73B
  and Algeria, 94B
  in Bosnia-Herzegovina, 380A, 380B, 382B
  in Central Africa, 146B
  in China, 123B, 225A, 227A
  in Ethiopia, 156B
  and Ghana, 96C
  in India, 72C, 90C, 124C, 128C, 180C, 192C
  and Meccans, 68C
  and Morocco, 94B
  in Northwest Africa, 200B
  science and technology, 109B, 139B
  Siddis, 180C, 216B
  in Spain, 72B, 80B, 99B, 149C, 184C
  in Sudan, 208B, 223A, 263A
  and Tripoli, 68B
Mussolini, Benito (prime minister of Italy), 302A, 306A, 318A, 330A, 332A, 334A
  and Hitler, 320A
  on Sudetenland, 320A
Mussorgsky, Petrovich, 275C
Mustafa, Kara (grand vizier of Turkey), 196B
Mustafa, Kemal. *See* Atatürk, Kemal
Mustafa II (sultan of Ottoman Empire), 200B
mustard gas. *See* gas
Mutamid, al-, 80B
Mutannabi, al-, 87C
Mutawakkil, al- 80B
Mutiny on the Bounty (movie), 317C
Mutsuhito (emperor of Japan), 271A, 293A
Mutter Courage (Brecht), 315C
Mutual Security Act, 338C
Muzaffar, 90B
Muzaffar ud-Din (shah of Persia), 285A, 291A
Mwambutsa IV (king of Burundi), 353A
My Antonio (Cather), 303C
My Fair Lady (movie), 351C
My Fair Lady (play), 343C
My Lai massacre, 356C
My Left Foot (movie), 373C
My Native Land (Adamic), 331C
My Theodosia (Seton), 327C
Myanmar, 337A, 340A, 373A, 375A, 383A. *See also* Burma
Mycenaean civilization, 2C, 6C, 9C, 10C
Myers v. U.S., 310B
Myron, 19C
Mysore, Mysore Wars, 98C, 124C, 216C, 220C, 225A, 229A, 235A, 249A, 251A
Mysteries of the Virgin (Cano), 191C
Mysteries of Udolpho (Radcliffe), 231C
Mysterious Affair at Styles, The (Christie), 305C
Mystery and Melancholy of a Street (Chirico), 295C
Mytens, Daniel, *183*
Myth of Sisyphus, The (Camus), 327C

N

Nabokov, Vladmir Vladimirovich, 343C
Nachtigal, Gustav, 279A
Nacolea, battle of, 54B
Nader Shah (king of Persia), 210B, 212C, 214C
Nadoungmya (king of Pagan), 110C
Näfels, battle of, 132A
NAFTA (North American Free Trade Agreement), 378A
Nagasaki, 168C, *182,* 183C, 186C, 334C
Nagpur, 263A
Nagy, Imre (prime minister of Hungary), 340B, 342B, 344B

Nahas Pasha, 319A
Nail (king of Fundj), 158B
Naipaul, V. S., 375C
Nairobi, 376A, 384A, 385A
Naismith, James, 283C
Najara, battle of, 130B
Najd, kingdom of, 303A, 315A
Nakasone Yasuhiro (prime minister of Japan), 371A
Naked and the Dead, The (Mailer), 337C
Naked Lunch, (Burroughs), 347C
nakedness, 63B
Nakhchivan, 249A
Nalanda, 67C
Namibia, 372A, 374A, 375A
Namur, 200A, 294A
Nancy, 144A
Nanda Bayin (king of Burma), 170C
Nanking, 58C, 137B, 164C, 293A, 311A, 324C
  Academy of Painting, 87C
  Rape of, 319A
  Treaty of, 257A
Nanook of the North (movie), 307C
Nantes
  Edict of, 175C, 182A, 199C
  University of, 141C
Nantucket, 342C
Naod (emperor of Ethiopia), 148B
napalm (naphthenic acid), 327B
Napier, John, 181B
Naples, 23A, 92B, 116B, 118B, 122B, 124A, 124B, 128B, 132B, 134B, 136B, 138B, 148A, 150A, 164A, 199C, 211C, 216A, 218A, 230A, 232A, 234A, 260A, 266A
  and Sicily, 258A
Naples Cathedral, 185C
Napoléon I (emperor of France and king of Italy), 232A, 233A, 234A, 235A, 236A, 237C, 238A, 240A, *241,* 242A, 244A, 254A
Napoléon III (emperor of France), 262A, 264A, 268A, 272A, 274A
Napoleon of Notting Hill (Chesterton), 289C
Napoléonic Wars, 234B
Naqshbandi, 195C
Nara, 72C, 107C
Narapati (king of Ava), 138C
Narapatisithu (king of Pagan), 104C
Narathihapat (king of Pagan), 116C
Narbonne, 112A
narcotics, 113B
Narragansett, 195A
Narses (general), 64B
Narses (king of Persia), 50B
Naruhito (crown prince of Japan), 379A
Narva, battle of, 202A
Narváez, Pánfilo de, 159A
Narvik, 322A
NASA, 383B
Nasca, 67A
Naseby, battle of, 188A
Nash, John, 243C, 247C
Nashville (movie), 361C
Nasiruddin Mahmud (sultan of Delhi), 114C
Nasrat Shah (king of Bengal), 154C
Nasrid dynasty. *See* Spain
Nassau, 222C, 226C, 230C, 234B, 1178B
Nassau (Germany), 270A
Nasser, Gamal Abdel (president of Egypt), 343A, 357A
Nast, Thomas, 274B
Natakamani (king of Kush), 33C
Natal, 134C, 198B, 253A, 255A, 257A, 267A, 283A, 291A
Natanyahu, Benjamin (prime minister of Israel), 383A
Natchez, 211A
Nathan the Wise (Lessing), 225C
Natick, 191C
Nation, 269C
Nation, Carry, 286B
National Advisory Commission on Civil Disorders, 354C
National Aeronautics and Space Administration (NASA), 345B, 377B, 379B
National Airlines, 345B
National Association for the Advancement of Colored People (NAACP), 292B, 348C
National Association of Manufacturers, 284B
National Catholic Telecommunications Network, 367C
National Congress of Mothers, 286B
National Congress of Parents and Teachers, 286B
National Defense Act, 298B
National Defense Advisory Commission, 322B
National Defense Mediation Board, 326B
National Guard, 344C, 356C
National Industrial Recovery Act, 316B
National Labor Board, 314B
National Labor Relations Board, 316B
National Negro Convention, 252B, 262B
National Park Service, 298B
National Progressive Republican League, 292B
National Radio Observatory, 373B
National Service Act, 334B
National Socialism, 321C
National Suffrage Association, *304*
National War Labor Board, 326B
National Woman Suffrage Association, 272B
National Women's Conference, 362C
National Youth Administration, 330B
Native Americans. *See* Indians, North American
Native Land Act, 295A
Native Son (Wright), 323C
Nativity, Church of the, 63C, 259C
Natta, Giulio, 343B
Natural History of Carolina (Catesby), *207*
Natural Magic (Porta), 167B
Naturalization Act, 232B
naturalization ceremony, U.S., 366C
Nature Conservancy, 383B
Nature (Emerson), 253C
Natya Sastra, 59C
Naucratis, 12A
Nauru Island, 305A, 355A
Nautilus (Fulton's submarine), 235B
Nautilus (U.S. submarine), 343B, 345B
Nauvoo, 257C
Navajo, 91A,
Naval Expansion Act, 320B
Navarino, Bay of, 248A
Navarre, 82B, 84B, 92B, 96B, 97C, 100B, 102B, 106B, 110B, 128B, 130B, 152A, 154A, 180A
Navarre, Company of, 132B
Navas de Tolosa, battle of, 110B
Nave, Nave Mahana (Gauguin), 285C
navies, ancient
  Athenian, 20C
  Greek, 18C
  Phocaean, 17A
  William the Conqueror's, 95A
Navigation Acts, 190A, 192A, 201A
navigational aids, 123B, 159B
  lunar tables, 217B
  quadrant, 211B
Navigators Islands, 220C
Naviglio Grand Canal, 107B
Navon, Yitshak (president of Israel), 363A
navy, U.S. *See* U.S. Navy
Naxos (Greek island), 18C
Nazca culture, 63C, 75A
Nazism, Nazis, 308A, 312A, 314A, 320A, 324A, 328A, 334A, 336B, 368A, 370A. *See also individual leaders*
  in Austria, 316A
  pogroms in Germany, 320A
NBC (National Broadcasting Company), 377C
Ndongo, 172B
Neal, Patricia, 349C
Near East, 38B, 63B, 123B, 173B. *See also individual countries*
Nebraska, 63A, 65A, 123A, 262B, 270B
  University of, 323C
Nebraska culture, 135A
Nebuchadnezzar II (king of Babylonia), 14B
Necessity of a Theological Foundation of All Political Economics (Müller), 245C
Neches River, 201C
Necho II (king of Egypt), 14B
Nechtansmere, battle of, 70A
Neckam, Alexander, 107B
Necker, Germaine, 235C
Necker, Jacques, 225C, 226A, 228A
needles, 133B, 135B
Neerwinden, battle of, 200A
Nefertiti (queen of Egypt), 8A, 9C
Negi Sembilan, 285A
Neguib, Muhammad (president of Egypt), 341A
Nehemiah, 18B
Nehru, Jawaharlal (prime minister of India), 341A, 351A
Neidhartspiel, 139C
Nelson, 255A
Nelson, Donald, 324B
Nelson, Horatio, 232A, 233A, 236A
Nemausus, 31C, 33C
Nemcová, Bozena, 263C
Nemerov, Howard, 373C
Németh, Miklós (prime minister of Hungary), 370B, 372B
Nemirovich-Danchenko, Vladimir Ivanovich, 287C
Nemorarius, Jordanus, 113B
Neo-Thomism, 303C
Neoclassicism, 217C, 227C, 237C
Neolithic culture, 2C, 3A
Neoplatonism, 47C, 51C, 53A, 63C
neoprene polymer, 313B
Nepal, 15C, 80C, 210C, 214C, 218C, 220C, 231A, 241A, 243A
Nepherites, 20A
neptunium, 323B
Nerchinsk, 198C
Nero (emperor of Rome), 34A, 35A, 35B, 35C, 36A, 37C
Nerses III, 69C
Neruda, Pablo, 309C
Nerva, Marcus Cocceius (emperor of Rome), 38A
Nesbit Moor, battle of, 134A
Neshaminy, 211C
Nestorians, 77C
Netanyahu, Benjamin, 379A
Netherlands, 168A, 178A, 202A. *See also* Holland, Dutch
  and Antwerp, 172A
  arts, 193C, 375C, 377C
  and Austria, 144A, 214A
  and Belgium, 226A, 336A
  and Benelux Economic Union, 344A
  and Britain, 336A
  dike system, 155B
  and euthanasia, 378B
  and France, 146A, 164A, 230A, 336A
  government, 282A, 286A, 370B
  independence of, 188A
  and Indonesia, 337A, 339A, 345A
  industry, 165B, 215B
  and International Monetary Fund, 348A
  and Japan, 271A
  and Latin America, 339A
  and Luxembourg, 282A, 336A
  and Reformation, 159C
  religion, 248A
  science and technology, 349B, 357B
  and Spain, 170A, 174A, 180A
  taxes, 282A
  transportation, 129B
  and Treaty of Rome, 344A
  and United States, 338A
  in Western European Union, 342A
Nettuno, 332A
Neuburg, 178A
Neuchâtel, 236A
Neufchâteau, 264A
Neuilly, Treaty of, 304A
Neumann, John von, 333B,
Neustria, 64A
Neutrality Act, 318B, 322B, 326B
Neutrality Proclamation, 230B
Nevada, 258B, 264B, 268B, 306B
Nevermind (Nirvana), 377C
Neves, Tancredo (president of Brazil), 369A
Neville, Richard (earl of Warwick), 140A, 142A
Nevis, 183A, 366A
Nevsky, Alexander, 112A
New Albion, 171A
New Amsterdam, 183A, 183C, 185A, 187A, 187B, 189A, 193A, 239C. *See also* New York City
New Atlantis (Bacon), 183C
New Britain, 330C, 332C
New Brunswick, 219A, 226B, 270B
New Caledonia, 220C, 369A
New Deal, 318B
New Delhi, 1996 plane crash over, 383A
New Economic Policy (NEP), 306A
New England, 50C, 63A, 177A, 185A, 189C, 191C, 199A, 203A, 224B, 242B
  Council of, 185A
New England Patriots, 371C, 385C
New England Psalm-Singer (Billings), 221C
New English Bible, 357C
New Forest, 98A
New Georgia Islands, 330C
New Granada, 157A, 165A, 207A, 213A, 242C, 244C, 248C, 266C
New Guinea, 80C, 162C, 176C, 180C, 245A, 279A, 328C, 330C, 332C
New Hampshire, 177A, 183A, 185A, 187A, 197A, 201A, 226B, 248B
New Harmony, 247C
New Haven, 187A
New Hebrides Islands, 255C
New Holland Company, 361B
New Ireland, 180C
New Jersey, 115A, 191A, 193A, 195C, 203A, 203B, 213B, 256B, 318B

College of, 215A
early culture, 73A
Holland Tunnel, 311B
New Jerusalem Church, 227C
New London, 187A
New Machiavelli, The (Wells), 293C
New Mexico, 63A, 93A, 97A, 123A, 161A, 171A, 175A, 201A, 258B, 260B, 262B, 292B, 298B, 298C
200 B.C., 24B
New Netherland, 183A, 191A, 193A, 195A
New Orleans, 207A, 282B, 287C, 290B, 366C
battle of, 242B, 266B
New Orleans Picayune, 285C
New South Wales, 249A, 255A, 257A, 261A, 265A
New Spain, 155A, 161A, 172C, 175A
New Sweden, 187A, 191A, 195A
New Testament, 63C, 157C, 199C, 249C, 277C
New View of Society, A (Owen), 241C
New World. *See* America
New York Central Railroad, 262B
New York City, 193A, 205A, 239C, 286B, 311B, 312B, 322B, 345B, 354C, 355B. *See also* Manhattan
Actors' Studio, 339C
in American Revolution, 222B
Brooklyn Bridge, 279B
Canadian Consulate, 330B
as capital of U.S., 228B
Carnegie Hall, 283C
Central Park, 383C
Chrysler Building, 311C
Columbia University, 341B, 354C
Empire State Building, 313B, 334C, 384C
epidemics in, 271B
federal loan to, 360C
Freeman's Journal, 249C
Giovanni Verrazano in, 157A
Grammercy Park, 251C
Guggenheim Museum, 347C, 349C
Henri Cartier-Bresson and, 315C
Holland Tunnel, 311B, 311C
Idlewild Airport, 348C
Journal of Commerce, 248B
Juilliard School of Music, 305C
Koster and Bial's Music Hall, 285B
Lever House, 339C
Lincoln Center, 353C
Manhattan Academy of Music, 263C
Manhattan Bridge, 293B
Metropolitan Opera Association, 279C, 303C, 313C, 317C, 319C, 343C
Museum of Modern Art, 319C
New York *Journal,* 285C
New York Post, 235C
New York Times, 261C, 369C
New York Tribune, 255C, 281B
New York *World,* 285C
power blackout, 362C
Queensboro Bridge, 293B
religion, 211C, 219C
Seagram Building, 345C
subway in, 289B
Sullivan Ordinance, 290B
Triangle Building fire, 292B
Ulysses S. Grant in, 278B
Waldorf-Astoria Hotel, 345C
Wall Street Journal, 281C
during War of 1812, 242B
World Trade Center, 378C, 380C
New York Commission to Prevent Racial Discrimination in Employment, 334B
New York Giants (baseball), 327C, 333C, 339C, 343C
New York Giants (football), 371C, 377C
New-York Historical Society, 237C
New York Jets, 357C
New York Mets, 357C, 359C, 371C
New York Philharmonic, 257C
New York State, 50C, 63A, 65A, 91A, 99A, 103A, 115A, 187A, 193A, 226B
during American Revolution, 222B
early culture, 73A
electrocution in, 280B
freedom of the press in, 211A
race riots in, 350C
religion, 205C
seatbelt law, 368C
on slave trade, 248B
and suffrage, 300B
women's property rights, 258B
New York Stock Exchange, 230B, 310B, 342C, 358C
New York Times v. Sullivan, 350C
New York Yankees, 327C, 329C, 331C, 337C, 339C, 341C, 343C, 345C, 347C, 349C, 351C, 363C, 367C, 383C, 385C
New Zealand, New Zealanders, 38B, 80C, 84C, 125B, 186C, 241A, 255A, 263A, 267A, 269A, 273A, 275A, 277A, 287A, 289A
and Australia, 338A
and Britain, 291A, 312A
and German New Guinea, 295A
and Germany, 322C
and Nauru Island, 305A
on nuclear pollution, 370A
politics, 317A
and Samoa, 295A, 305A
suffrage in, 283A
and Turkey, 297A
World War II, 322C
New Zealand Company, 255A, 261A
Newark (England), 110A
battle of, 188A
Newbold, Charles, 203B
Newburgh, 335B
Newburn, battle of, 186A
Newcastle (England)
Treaty of, 126A
Newcastle (Pa.), 191A
Newcastle-upon-Tyne, 96A, 113B
Newcomen, Thomas, 205B
Newfoundland, 143A, 149A, 151A, 153B, 173A, 177A, 179A, 203A, 205A, 207A, 226B, 262B, 276B, 288A, 314B, 315B, 324B, 326B, 338C, 368C
1985 plane crash, 368C
and Britain, 312A
Newman, John Henry, 269C
Newman, Paul, 357C
Newport, 187A, 189A
news service, 70B
newspapers, 74C, 177C, 179C, 189C, 203C, 209C, 221C. *See also individual newspapers*
Newton, Sir Isaac, 195B, 197B, 200A
Ngazargarmu, 142B
Ngo Dinh Diem (president of South Vietnam), 343A, 349A
Ngola, Ngolans, 170B, 172B
Ngolo Diarra (king of Segu), 218B
Ngouabi, Marien (president of Congo), 363A
Nguni people, 134C, 176B
Nguyen Du, 235C
Nguyen dynasty, 220C. *See* Annam, Annamites
Nguyen Phuc Anh. *See* Gia Long.
Nguyen Phuc Chi Dam. *See* Minh Mang.
Nguyen That Thanh. *See* Ho Chi Minh.
niacin, 325B
Niagara Falls, 197A
Niagara Falls (Church), 265C
Niagara River, 240B
Nibelungenlied, 107C
Nicaea, 112B, 114B, 116B, 126B
empire of, 108B
Seventh Council of, 77C
Nicaragua, Nicaraguans, 246C, 262C, 264C
and Britain, 258C
earthquake in, 312C
and Federation of Central America, 254C
government, 310C, 318C, 365A, 375A
and Honduras, 284C
law and society, 282C, 292C, 310C, 369A, 370C
and Salvador, 284C
and Spain, 244C
in United Nations, 335A
and United States, 292C, 298C, 308C, 310C, 314C, 371A
World War II, 327A
Nice, 160A, 266A
Nicephorus I (emperor of Byzantium), 78B
Nicephorus II Phocas (emperor of Byzantium), 86B
Nicephorus III (emperor of Byzantium), 96B
Nicholas, Saint, 53A
Nicholas I (tsar of Russia), 246A, 248A, 256A, 262A
Nicholas II (tsar of Russia), 284A, 292A, 300A, 302A
Nicholas III, Pope, 119C
Nicholas V, Pope, 139C
Nicholas Nickleby (Dickens), 255C
Nicholas of Cusa, 139B
Nichols, Mike, 353C
Nichols, Terry, 380C
Nicholson, Jack, 361C, 385C
Nicobar Islands, 332C
Nicomedia, 48A, 126B
Nicopolis, battle of, 134B
Nicot, Jean, 167B
Nieboska Komedia (Krasinski), 253C
Niebuhr, Reinhold, 315C
Niemöller, Martin, 321C
Niépce, Joseph, 249B
Nietzsche, Friedrich, 273C, 279C, 281C
Nieuwe Vestingbouw (Coehoorn), 199C
Niger, 7B, 40B, 47A, 188B, 279A
Delta, 255A
River, 82C, 94C, 142B, 154B, 237A
Valley, 92C
Nigeria, Nigerians, 41C, 44B, 82C, 91C, 122C, 142B, 144B, 156B, 176B, 200B, 203C, 237A, 249A, 283A, 341A, 349A, 353A
900 B.C., 11C
arts, 11C
and Britain, 281A, 337A
Fulah dynasty, 237A, 249A
government, 337A, 353A, 361A, 383A
Hausa dynasty, 82C, 220B, 237A, 249A
independence of, 347A
and Northern Cameroons, 347A
pottery in, 11C
Night Fishing at Antibes (Picasso), 323C
Night's Lodging (Gorky), 289C
Nijinsky, Vaslav, 291C
Nijmegen, Treaties of, 196A
Nika, 62B
Nikolayevich, Lev, 267C
Nikolsburg, 270A
Nile River, 34B, 63B, 63C, 73B, 164B, 220B, 273A, 275A
battle of, 233A
Delta, 6A, 12A, 81B
transportation, 17B
Valley, 158B
nilometer, 73B, 81B
Nîmes, 31C, 33C, 35B
Nimitz, Charles, 328C
Nin, Anaïs, 333C
Nine-Power Treaty, 307A
Nine Powers, Conference of, 319A
911 emergency phone number, 355B
1919 (Dos Passos), 321C
1984 (Orwell), 339C
Nineveh, 14B, 68B
Ninian, Saint, 57A
Ninth Symphony (Beethoven), 47C
Nintoku (emperor of Japan), 50B
niobium, 235B
Nirvana (Rock Group), 377C, 381C
Nish, 48A
battle of, 138B
Niterói, 252C
nitric acid, 75B, 227B
nitrogen
atmospheric, 293B
liquid, 275B
nitroglycerin, 259B
Niue, 220C
Niven, David, 345C
Nixon, Richard M. (president of U.S.), 338C, 345A, 346C, 354C, 356A, 358C, 360A, 360C, 380C
"Checkers speech," 340C
Nixon v. Herndon, 310B
Nizam Ali, 218C
Nizam (sultan of Bahmani), 140C
Nizhny Novgorod, 168A
Njegos, Peter Petrovich, 259C
Njoro River, 5B
Nkrumah, Kwame (president of Ghana), 353A
No Cross, No Crown (Penn), 195C
No Exit (Sartre), 333C
No theater, 123C
Nobatia, 64C
Nobel Peace Prize, 290B, 362A, 365C, 366B, 374B, 383A
Nobunaga, Oda, 168C, 170C
Nobusuke Kishi (prime minister of Japan), 345A
Nochixtlan Valley, 48C
Noeud de vipères (Mauriac), 315C
Nogales, 201C
Nok culture, 11C, 41C, 44B
Nola, 244A
Nonintercourse Act, 238B
Nonintervention Committee, 318A
Nootka Convention, 232B
Nootka Port, 232B
Nootka Sound, 224B, 228B
Nootka Sound Convention, 228B
Nordhoff, Charles Bernard, 325C
Nordingen, battle of, 188A
Norfolk, 164A
Noriega, Manuel, 373A, 375A, 376C
Norman, Robert, 171B
Normandy, Normans, 82A, 84A, 90A, 90B, 92B, 93C, 94A, 94B, 96A, 96B, 98A, 98B, 100A, 102A, 102B, 103B, 103C, 104A, 104B, 105C, 106B, 107B, 108A, 138A, 151A, 332A
Normans and, 95C
Norodom Sihanouk (king of Cambodia), 324C

Norplant, 375B
Norris, Kathleen, 293C
Norse, Norsemen, 72A, 76A, 78A, 80A, 90A, 109B, 135A
North, Frederick (earl of Guilford), 220A
North, Oliver, 370C, 372C
North Africa, 102B, 106C
  and Arabs, 70B, 72B
  and Europe, 202B
  and Germany, 324A, 326A, 330A
  government, 84B
  and Italy, 330A
  and Moors, 72B, 118B, 214B
  and Morocco, 206B
  and Normandy, 104B
  and Ottoman Empire, 164B, 184B
  and Portugal, 136B, 138B, 154B
  religion, 200B
  settlement of, 64B, 64C
  slave trade, 196B, 210B, 212B
  and Spain, 148B, 150B, 152B, 229A
  and West Africa, 66C
  World War II, 326A, 328A, 330A
North America, 2B, 4B, 39B, 59A, 91A, 101B, 149A, 187B. *See also individual countries*
  3000 B.C.–1500 B.C., 3B, 7B
  agriculture, 121A
  and England, 173A
  and Europe, 179B
  exploration of, 151A, 159A
  map of, 175B
  and Norsemen, 135A
  science and technology, 63B, 91B
  settlement of, 61A, 63A, 109A
  slave trade, 181A
  and Sweden, 191A
North American Air Defense Command (NORAD), 344C
North American Review, 243C
North Atlantic Treaty Organization (NATO), 338A, 340A, 344A, 364A, 374A, 380A
  and CFE Treaty, 374A
  and Eastern Europe, 384A
  and Finland, 384B
  headquarters, 352A
  and Malta, 356A
  and Spain, 366B
  and United States, 338A
  and Warsaw Pact, 376A
North Carolina, 157A, 173A, 191A, 205A, 221A, 222B, 268B, 289B, 346C
  University of, 338C
North Circars, 218C
North Dakota, 280B
North Foreland, 192A
North German Confederation, 270A
North Island, 267A, 273A\
North Korea. *See* Korea
North of Boston (Frost), 295C
North Pacific halibut fisheries, 306B
North Pole, 149B, 250B, 292B
North Sea, 155B, 179B, 321B
  and Britain, 360B
  and Götha Canal, 250A
  oil deposits in, 356B
  World War I, 296A
North Star (Douglass), 259C
North Vietnam. *See* Vietnam
North West Company, 226B, 228B, 230B, 236B, 242B
North West Mounted Police, 278B
North West Society, 224B, 226B
North West Territories, 272B
Northampton, 140A
  Treaty of, 126A
Northanger Abbey (Austen), 245C
Northern Securities Company, 288B
Northern War, 192A
Northern Yemen. *See* Yemen
Northumberland, 104A, 134A
Northumbria, Northumbrians, 66A, 68A, 70A, 71C, 72A, 74A, 78A, 90A
Northwest, Old, 226B, 239C
Northwest Passage, 149B, 153A, 157A, 173A, 256B
Norton, Andrew, 245C
Norway, Norwegians, 88A, 92A, 96A, 98A, 109B, 116A, 118A, 120A, 132A, 134A, 138A, 140A, 142A, 144A, 158A, 182A, 206A, 240A, 278A, 290A, 305C
  and Antarctica, 346A
  arts, 77C
  and Britain, 322A, 358B
  in European Free Trade Association, 346A
  immigration policy, 360B
  politics, 370B
  religion, 88A
  suffrage in, 286A, 290A
  and United States, 338A
  World War II, 322A, 324A
Nosferatu (Murnau), 307C
Not Quite Dead Enough (Stout), 333C
Notre Dame de Paris (Hugo), 251C
Notre Dame du Port, 99C
Nottingham, 186A
Nova Scientia (Tartaglia), 161B
Nova Scotia, 91A, 157A, 175A, 177A, 181A, 183A, 213A, 215A, 219A, 226B, 270B
Novalis, 235C
Novara, 210A
  battles of, 152A, 260A
Novelas Ejemplares (Cervantes), 179C
Noverre, Jean Georges, 219C
Novgorod, 112A, 146A, 148A
Novi, battle of, 234A
Novum Organum Scientiarum (Bacon), 181C
Noyce, Robert, 347B, 355B
Noyon, Peace of, 154A
Nubia, 4A, 6A, 8A, 10A, 14A, 52B, 64C, 110C
nuclear
  chain reaction, 317B, 329B
  fission, 325B
  Nonproliferation Treaty, 354A
  test ban in space, 352A
  Test Ban Treaty (1963), 348A
  Test Ban Treaty (1996), 382A
  weapons, 344A, 358A, 364A, 380A. *See also* atomic weapons
Nude Descending a Staircase (Duchamp), 295C
Nueva San Salvador, 262C, 268C
Nujoma, Sam (president of Namibia), 375A
Nukleet culture, 107A
Numantia, 27A
Number One (Dos Passos), 331C
numerals, Arabic, 109B
Numerian (emperor of Rome), 48A
Numidia, 27A, 55A
Nureddin (sultan of Syria), 102B, 104B
Nuremberg, 103B, 133B, 137B, 159C, 217B, 252A, 290A, 334A, 336B
  battle of, 184A
  Diet of, 138A, 157C
  Laws, 316A
  League of, 160A
Nureyev, Rudolf, 347C, 349C
Nurhachi, 180C, 182C
nutmeg, 153B
Nuwas, Abu, 77C
Nyasaland, 317B, 340A, 341A, 351A
Nyere, Julius (president of Tanzania), 365A
nylon, 321B
Nyquist, Harry, 311B
Nystad, Treaty of, 208A
Nzinga Mvemba Afonso I (king of Kongo), 150B

O

O locura o santidad (Echegaray), 275C
O Pioneers! (Cather), 295C
Oahu, 281A
Oakland Athletics, 359C, 361C, 373C, 375C
Oakland Raiders, 355C, 363C, 367C
Oakley, 80A
Oath of the Horatii (David), 227C
oatmeal, 109B
Oaxaca culture, 36C, 44C, 48C
Oaxaca Valley, 40C
obelisks, 9C, 47C
Oberon (Wieland), 225C
Obok, 267A
Obote, Milton (president of Uganda), 353A
Obregon, Alvaro (president of Mexico), 310C
Obrenovic, Milan (king of Serbia), 264A
obsidian, 139B
obstetrics, 241B
Ocampo, Sebastian de, 153A
ocean currents, 235B
O'Connor, Rory, 104A
O'Connor, Sandra Day, 366C
Octavian. *See* Augustus
Odd Couple, The (Simon), 351C
Ode on France (Coleridge), 231C
Odenathus (king of Palmyra), 46B, 48B
Oder, 109B
Oder-Neisse Line, 338B, 356B, 374B
Oder River, 188A, 208A
Odes (Horace), 31C
Odes (Hugo), 245C
Odessa, 295A
Odets, Clifford, 327C
Odo of Metz, 77C
odometer, 51B
O'Donnell, Hugh Roe, 176A
Odovacar, 60A, 60B, 62B
Odría, Manuel (president of Peru), 337A
Odyssey (Homer), 11C, 209C
Oedipus Rex (Sophocles), 19C
Oersted, Hans Christian, 245B, 247B
Of Human Bondage (Maugham), 297C
Of Mice and Men (Steinbeck), 319C
Of Time and the River (Wolfe), 317C
Offa (king of Mercia), 74A, 76A, 77C
Offa's Dyke, 76A
Offenbach, Jacques, 265C
Offenburg, 306A
Office of Civilian Defense, 326B
Office of Defense Transportation, 326B
Office of Economic Warfare, 330B
Office of Emergency Management, 322B
Office of National Parks, 298B
Office of Price Administration, 326B
Office of Price Stabilization, 340C
Office of Strategic Services, 328B, 336C
Office of the Petroleum Administrator for War, 328B
Office of War Information, 328B
Office of War Mobilization and Reconversion, 332B
Ogdensburg, 324B
Oghuz Turks, 96B
Ogiso dynasty. *See* Mexico
Oglethorpe, James, 211A, 213A
"Oh! Susannah" (Foster), 259C
Ohain, Hans von, 321B
O'Hara, John, 317C
Ohio, 63A, 77A, 83A, 109A, 135A, 215A, 230B, 232B, 234B, 284B, 340C
  River, 226B
  State University, 329C
  Valley, 46C, 195A, 215A
Ohio Company, 215A
Ohira Masayoshi (prime minister of Japan), 365A
oil, 81B
  Alaskan pipeline, 360C
  in Antarctica, 376A
  Baku-Batum pipeline, 290A
  "Big Inch" pipeline (Texas-Pennsylvania), 330B
  Canadian pipeline, 362C
  Iranian, 370A
  Iraq-Palestine pipeline, 317B
  and IRS, 364C
  OPEC embargo, 360A, 374A
  spill by *Exxon Valdez,* 372C, 374C
  spill by Iraq, 376A
  used by Romans, 37B
  in Venezuela, 302C
Oise River, 294A
Ojibwa, 177A, 211A
Ojin, 49B
Ojukwu, Odumegwu, 353A
O'Keeffe, Georgia, 309C, 313C, 315C, 317C
Okello, Tito (president of Uganda), 369A
Okhotsk Sea, 186C
Okinawa, 334C, 359A
Oklahoma, 163A, 248B, 280B, 282B, 290B, 306B, 338C
Oklahoma City, 317B, 380C, 384C, *385*
Oklahoma! (Rodgers and Hammerstein), 331C
Okumara Masonobu, 213B
O'kuni, 177C
Okvik culture, 38C
Olaf (crown prince of Norway), *322*
Olaf Tryggvason (king of Norway), 88A, 90A
Old Curiosity Shop (Dickens), 255C
Old Huntsman, The (Sassoon), 301C
"Old Ironsides," 240B
Old Man and the Sea, The (Hemingway), 341C
Old Signal Butte culture, 65A
Old Swimmin' Hole and 'Leven More Poems (Riley), 279C
Old Testament, 15C, 39A, 83C
Old Wives' Tales, The (Bennett), 291C
Oldenburg, 192A, 262A
Oldenburg, Claes, 349C
Oléron, Treaty of, 120A
Oliva, Peace of, 192A
olive oil, 44B
Oliver! (movie), 355C
Oliver Twist (Dickens), 253C
Olivier, Lawrence, 337C
Ollivier, Émile, 272A
Olmec culture, 8B, 9C, 48C
Olmeca-Xicalanca dynasty. *See* Mexico
Olympia, 19C
Olympia (Riefenstahl), 321C
Olympias of Thebes, 28C
Olympic Games, 11C, 319C, 321C, 364A, 368A
Olympic Peninsula, 228B
Omagh, 384B
Oman, 212B, 214B, 251A, 356A
Oman, sultan of, 192B, 200B
Omani Turks, 192B, 194B
Omar, 68B

Omar II, 72C
Omar Khayyam, 99C
Omayyad dynasty. *See* Syria
Omdurman, battle of, 287A
Omni (king of Israel), 10B
Omnibus Housing Act, 350C
Omsk, 206C
On Heroes, Hero-Worship, and the Heroic in History (Carlyle), 255C
On Liberty (Mill), 265C
On the Freedom of a Christian (Luther), 155C
On the Love of God (Bernard of Clairvaux), 101C
On the Origin of Species by Means of Natural Selection (Darwin), 265B
On the Progresse of the Soule (Donne), 177C
On the Revolution of the Celestial Spheres (Copernicus), 163C
On the Road (Kerouac), 345C
On the Science of Knowledge (Fichte), 231C
On the Threshold of Liberty (Magritte), 313C
On the Town (Bernstein), 333C
On the Waterfront (movie), 343C
onager (catapult), 51B
Oñate, Juan de, 177A
One Flew Over the Cuckoo's Nest (movie), 361C
One Touch of Venus (Weill), 331C
One World (Wilkie), 331C
O'Neill, Eugene, 305C, 307C, 309C, 313C, 323C, 337C
O'Neill, Hugh (earl of Tyrone), 176A
O'Neill, Thomas P. "Tip," 362C
Oneota culture, 135A
Onganía, Juan (president of Argentina), 353A
Onnes, Heike, 293B
Ontario, 50C, 63A, 103A, 179A, 181A, 230B, 251B, 270B, 278B, 316B
"open door policy," 286B
Operation Battleaxe, 326A
Operation Bootstrap, 327A
Operation Oregon, *353*
opium, Opium War, 210C, 220C, *254,* 255A
Oppenheimer, Robert, 340C
Optimist's Daughter, The (Welty), 359C
Opus Maius (Bacon), 117C
Oraibi, 103A
Oran, 152B, 229A, 259A, 324A
Orange Free State, 253A, 259A, 263A, 271A, 289A
  diamonds in, 273A
  and South Africa, 291A
orange juice, 337B
Orange River, 249A
Oratorio (Bach), 211C
Orazia (Aretino), 161C
Orbis Pictus (Comenius), 191C
Orchestre de la Suisse Romande, 303C
Order in Council of 1807, 240A
Ordinary People (movie), 365C
Ordos, 162C, 164C
Oregon, 264B, 278B, 308B, 328B, 374C
Oregon Trail, 254B, 256B
Orellana, Francisco de, 163A
Orenburg, 210C
oreomycin, 335B
Orfeo ed Euridice (Gluck), 219C
organ
  barrel, 203B
  electric, 317B
Organic Act, 278B
Organic Design in Home Furnishings competition, 325C
Organization for Economic Cooperation and Development (OECD), 346A
Organization for European Economic Cooperation, 336A, 346A
Organization for Security and Cooperation in Europe, 358A
Organization of African Unity, 349A
Organization of American States (OAS), 336A, 348A, 351A
Organization of Petroleum Exporting Countries (OPEC), 346A, 360A, 375A
Organogenesis Company, 375B
Orhogbua, 164B
Oribe, Manuel Ceferino (president of Uruguay), 252C, 254C, 256C
Orient, 155A
Origen, 45A, 47A
Orinoco River, 149A, *174,* 175A
Orissa, 172C, 184C
Orkhan (sultan of Ottoman Empire), 124B, 126B, 130B
Orlando Furioso (Ariosto), 159C
Orléans, 136A, 138B, 146A
  battle of, 137B
  duke of, 134A
  House of, 280A
  University of, 123C
Orlon, 337B
Ormandy, Eugene, 321C
Ormoc, 334C
Orodes II (king of Parthia), 28B
Orozco, José Clemente, 299C
Orpheus and Eurydice (Canova), 225C
Orpheus in the Underworld (Offenbach), 265C
Orsini, Felice, 264A
Orsova, 212A
Ortega Saavedra, Daniel (president of Nicaragua), 369A, 375A, 383A
Ortelius, Abraham, 169B
Orthodox Church, 119C, 287C
Ortíz, Roberto (president of Argentina), 318C, 327A
Ortíz Rubio, Pascual (president of Mexico), 310C
Orvieto Cathedral, 149C
Orwell, George, 335C, 339C
Os Lusiadas (Camões), 169C
Osaka, 65C, 67C, 269A, 271A
Osborn, Paul, 333C
Oscar II (king of Sweden), 290A
Osceola, 252B
Oslo, 295C
Osman I (sultan of Ottoman Empire), 120B, 122B
Ostend, 176A
Ostia, 35B
ostracism, 18C
Ostrogoths, 56A, 56B, 58B, 60B, 62B, 64B
Oswald, Lee Harvey, 348C, 350C
Oswald (king of Northumbria and Bernicia), 68A
Oswego, 217A
Oswiu (king of Northumbria and Bernicia), 68A, 70A, 71C
Otakar II (king of Bohemia), 114A, 116A, 118A
Otfrid of Weissenburg, 81C
Othello (Shakespeare), 177C
Othman, 68B, 70B, 71C
Otho, 266A
Otho, Marcus Salvius, 36A
Otis, Elisha, 263B, 265B
Otis Elevator Company, 287B
Ottawa, 219A, 234B, 248B, 264B, 270B, 298B
  Conference, 314B
  River, 179A, 228B, 234B
Otterbein, Philip William, 221C
Otterburn, battle of, 132A
Otto, Nikolaus, 271B
Otto I the Great (Holy Roman Emperor), 84A, 86A, 86B, *87*
Otto II (Holy Roman Emperor), 88A, 88B
Otto III (Holy Roman Emperor), 88A, 88B
Otto IV (Holy Roman Emperor), 108A, 110A, 111C
Ottoman Empire, Ottomans, 112B, 120B, 126B, 194B, 226A, 233A, 298A. *See also* Turkey
  and Africa, 164B
  and Anatolia, 136B
  and Armenia, 152B, 284A, 297A
  army of, 210B
  and Balkan League, 292A
  and Belgrade, 228A
  and Britain, 276A, 291A, 295A, 298A, 301A
  and the Caucasus, 186B
  and Egypt, 156B, 178B, 237A, 251A, 255A, 269A, 271A, 295A
  and France, 160A, 298A
  and Georgia, 214C
  government, 130B, 132B, 138B, 144B, 168B, 170B, 174B, 182B, 188B, 200B, 229A, 239A, 291A
  and Greece, 244A, 246A, 248A
  and Hungary, 168A
  and Italy, 292A, 293A
  and Janissaries, 202B, 204B, 249A
  law and society, 231A, 265A
  and Montenegro, 274A
  and North Africa, 164B, 184B
  and Persia, 142B, 158B, 162B, 172B, 176B, 245A
  religion, 262A
  and Russia, 250A, 295A, 297A, 302A
  science and technology, 139B
  and Serbia, 266A, 270A, 274A
  and Sinai Peninsula, 291A
  and Sudan, 245A
  and Suez Canal Convention, 281A
  and Syria, 154B
  and Timur, 134B
  and Tripoli, 253A
  "Tulip Period," 206B
  World War I, 299A, 303A
  and Yemen, 168B
  and Young Turks, 293A
Otumba, 155A
Otway, Thomas, 197C
Oudenarde, battle of, 204A
Oudney, Walter, 247A
Ougadougou, 285A
Oughtred, William, 181B
Our Lady of Gua, Chapel of, 182C
Our Town (Wilder), 321C
Ourbri, kingdom of, 124C
Out of Africa (movie), 369C
Outer Mongolia, 200C, 210C, 293A, 299A, 309A
"Over There" (Cohan), 301C
Overture to Midsummer Night's Dream (Mendelssohn), 249C
Ovid, 33C
Owada Masako, 379A
Owain, 104A
Owasco culture, 115A
Owen, Robert, 241C, 247C
Owen, Wilfred, 305C
Owens, Jesse, 319C
Owens, Michael, 289B
Owens-Corning Company, 321B
Owings, Nathaniel, 339C
owl, spotted, 377B
Ox-Bow Incident, The (Clark), 323C
Oxford, 193C, 204A
  -Birmingham Canal, 228A
  Assembly of, 92A
  Provisions of, 116A
  University, 105C, 117C, 119C, 121C, 127C, 129C, 133C, 149C, 155C, 163C, 165C, 177C, 193B, 211C
Oxford English Dictionary, 279C
Oxkintok, 77A
oxygen, liquid, 275B
Oyrats, 186C, 208C, 216C
oyster farming, 41B
Oyster Point, 197A
Ozark Mountains, 123A, 163A
Ozark Plateau, 63A, 65A
ozone layer, 359B, 369B, 377B

P

Paardeberg, 287A
Paasikivi, Juho Kusti (president of Finland), 336B
Pacal, 67A, 71A
Pacelli, Eugenio, 323C
Pacem in Terris (Pope John XXIII), 349C
Pachomius, Saint, 53A
Pacific Fur Company, 238B
Pacific Ocean, 58C, 153A, 158C, 162C, 170C, 171A, 218C, 225A, 229A, 230B, 236B, 238B, 340C
  exploration of, 254B
  Four Powers Pacific Treaty, 306B
Pacino, Al, 377C
packaging
  cellophane, 309B
  food, 245B
  Saran film, 305B
Packwood, Robert, 378C
Pactum Hludovicianum, 79C
Padilla Arancibia, David (president of Bolivia), 363A
Padua, 134B
  University, 113C, 175B
Paekche, kingdom of, 30B, 84C
Páez, José Antonio (president of Venezuela), 238C, 250C, 254C, 258C, 260C, 266C, 268C
Pagan, 96C, 100C, 104C, 110C, 112C, 116C, 118C, 120C, 162C
Pagan Min (king of Burma), 259A
Paganica, 99C
Paganini, Niccolò, 225C
Pahang, 285A
Paid Bill (Necker), 225C
Paine, Thomas, 223C, 229C, 233C
Painlevé, Paul (prime minister of France), 308A
Painter, William, 279B
painting, 113C, 123C
  Chinese, 39C
  on glass, 91B
  Kano school of, 191C
  luster-, 67B
  miniature, 91C
  Nanking Academy of, 87C
  oil painting, 151B
  Tosa School of, 157C
  ukiyoe, 165C
Pakistan, 357A, 380C
  and Bangladesh, 361A
  and Britain, 337A
  earthquake in, 377A
  government, 349A, 359A, 363A
  and India, 337A, 338A, 351A, 353A, 355A, 357A
  nuclear testing by, 385A
  in United Nations, 336A
  and United States, 346A
Pala dynasty. *See* India, Indians
Palace of Honour (Douglas), 151C
Palace of the Popes, 127C
Palatinate, 134A, 163C, 178A,

180A, 181C, 182A, 198A, 200A, 205A, 222A, 224A, 306A
Palatine Chapel, 77C
Palatine Hill, 37C
Palau Islands, 162C, 332C
Palazzo Ducale, 143C
Palazzo Vecchio, 121C
Pale Horse, Pale Rider (Porter), 323C
Pale of Settlement, 228A, 252A
Palembang, 70C, 92C
Palenque, 67A, 67C, 83A
Palermo, 80B, 96B, 116B, 266A
Palestine, Palestinians, 4B, 39A, 96B, 311A, 319A, 373A
1552 B.C.–141 B.C., 6A, 8A, 13C, 22B, 26B
and Arab League, 337A
and Australia, 303A
and Britain, 301A, 303A, 305A, 307A, 319A, 321A, 337A
partition of, 319A
United Nations on, 336A
Palestine Liberation Organization (PLO), 356A, 367A, 372A, 376A, 379A, 383A
and *Achille Lauro,* 368A
Palestine National Council, 373A
Palestinian Authority, 383A
Palestrina, Giovanni Pierluigi da, 157C, 165C, 173C
Pali, 31A
Palikao, battle of, 267A
Palissy, Bernard, 165B
Palladio, Andrea, 153C, 169C
Palm Wine Drinkard (Tutuola), 341C
Palma, Arturo Alessandri (president of Chile), 304C
Palme, Olaf (prime minister of Sweden), 370B
Palmer, A. Mitchell, 304B
Palmer Peninsula, 245A
Palmerston, Henry (prime minister of England), 268A
Palmyra, kingdom of, 46B
Palmyra (N.Y.), 249C
Palo Alto, 258B
Palo Blanco, 75A
Palos, 147A
Pampers, 347B
Pamplona, 84B, 240A
Pan-American
Conferences, 248C, 258C, 264C, 268C, 280C, 310C, 318C, 320C
Exhibition, 289B
Highway, 306C
Treaty (1924), 308C
Union, 335A
Pan American World Airlines, 345B, 366C, 376C
1988 crash over Lockerbie, 372A
Pan-Andean empire, 67A
Pan Chao, 36B
Pan-German League, 282A
Pan (Hamsun), 285C
Pan Michael (Sienkiewicz), 283C
Pan Tadeusz (Mickiewicz), 253C
Panama, 65A, 151A, 151B, 153A, 157A, 195A, 260C
and Colombia, 254C, 256C, 268C, 270C, 288C, 294C
and Cuba, 347A
Declaration of, 322B
and England, 199A
Fascism in, 325A
government, 312C
independence of, 306C
Isthmus of, 153A, 258C
in New Granada, 207A
and Scotland, 203A
and Spain, 165A, 175A
transportation, 258C, 262C
and United States, 288C, 290C, 292C, 302C, 318C, 320C, 350A, 362A, 371A, 373A, 375A
University of, 316C
World War I, 300C
World War II, 327A
Panama Canal, 288C, 290C, 294C, 302C, 316C, 326B, 328C
and France, 276C
Panama Canal Company, 280A, 280C
Panama Canal Treaty, 320C, 362A
Panama City, 155A, 195A
Panay (U.S. gunboat), 319A
Pandyans, 76C, 116C, 126C
Pangalos, Theodore (dictator of Greece), 310C
Panipat, battles of, 156C, 164C, 216C
Panmunjon, 340A
Pannonia, 50A, 54A, 56A
Pantagruel (Rabelais), 159C
Pantheon, 31A, 39A, 41C
Panthéon, 263B
panty girdles, 317B
Panuco, 163A
Panungulan, 76C
Paoli, Pasquale, 214A
Papal Nuncio, 157C
Papal States, 238A, 242A
paper. *See also* writing, early
in Arabia, 73B
bag, 273B
in China, 39B, 39C, 67B
in Egypt, 5B, 83B
in Germany, 125B
in Greece, 71B
made from rags, 243B
in Mesoamerica, 59B, 91C
in Mexico, 143B
in Netherlands, 215B
sizing, 151B
in Spain, 99B, 103B
in Turkey, 27B
paper clip, 287B
Papin, Denis, 197B, 201B
Papineau, Louis, 256B
Pappus of Alexandria, 49B
Papua, 180C, 330C
Papua New Guinea, 361A
Paracas people, 13C
Paracelsus (Browning), 253C
parachute, 107B, 145B
Paradise Lost (Milton), 193C
Paraguay, Paraguayans, 155A, 157A, 325A
and Argentina, 238C, 268C
and Bolivia, 310C, 312C, 314C, 316C, 318C
and Brazil, 268C, 320C
education, 282C
government, 181A, 256C, 266C, 343A
and League of Nations, 318C
religion, 179C
River Plate, 222C
slave trade, 187C
and Spain, 161A, 209A, 238C
and Uruguay, 268C
Paraguay River, 155A, 157A, 161A
Parakrama Bahu I (king of Ceylon), 104C
Parakrama Bahu VIII (king of Kotte), 144C
Parallel Lives (Plutarch), 39C
Paramonga, 109A
Parana, 262C
Parana River, 155A, 161A
Paray-le-Monial, 195C
Pardo, Manuel (president of Peru), 272C
Paré, Ambroise, 161B, 163B, 167B, 169B, 171B
Pariegesis (Itinerary) (Pausanias), 43C
Paris, 86A, 103C, 107B, 138A, 162A, 171C, 276A, 302B, 311B, 317C, 321C, 342A, 346A
arts, 77C, 113C, 117C
Bastille, 228A
Declaration of, 264A
Eiffel Tower, 281B
Exhibition of 1887, 281B
French Revolution in, 230A
and Germany, 88A, 136A, 272A, 324A
Hôpital Général, 190A
Hôtel-Dieu, 67B
hurdy-gurdy in, 203B
Impressionists exhibition, 273C
Invalides, 254A
Josephine Baker in, 309C
law and society, 130A, 172A, 258A
liberation of, 332A
Louvre, 163C, 231C
Montmartre, 289C
"Night of the Barricades," 354B
Normans in, 82A
Norsemen in, 80A
Opéra Comique, 275C
Panthéon, 217C
paper money in, 236A
Peace Conference, 302A, 336A
Peace Congress, 264A
Peace of (1814), 240A
Peace of (1815), 242A
Pompidou Center, 363C
Pont Neuf, 369C
religion, 125C, 159C
Saint Gervais, 181C
science and technology, 107B, 119B, 143B
settlement of, 60A
Sorbonne, 115C
St. Chapelle, 115C
St. Germain des Près, 99C
Supreme Headquarters Allied Powers Europe, 338A
transportation, 193B
Treaty of (1303), 122A
Treaty of (1657), 190A
Treaty of (1763), 218A, 219A
Treaty of (1783), 224A, 224B, 225A
Treaty of (1898), 286C
University of, 115C
world exhibition in, 262A
World War II, 322A
Paris, Matthew, 117C
Paris, Texas (movie), 369C
Paris Chartres Cathedral, 117C
Paris Notre Dame Cathedral, 111C
Park, Mungo, 237A
Park Chung Hee (president of South Korea), 365A
Parker, Dorothy, 311C, 313C, 355C
Parker, Matthew (Archbishop of Canterbury), 167C
parking meters, 315B, 317B
Parks, Rosa, 342C
Parliament (British), 110A, 116A, 134A, 174A, *202*
Act of 1911, 292A
on Australia, 253A
"barebones," 190A
and Canada, 228B, 264B, 366C
and Catholics, 131C, 194A, 249C
Charles I and, 186A
Cromwell and, 190A
dissolution of, 226A
on East India Company, 227B
on Home Rule, 280A
on Hong Kong, 368A
Humble Petition and Advice, 190A
on India, 227A, 251A, 303A
and Ireland, 234A, 302A
James I and, 182A
Long, 186A, 190A, 192A
on papal bulls, 169C
on Scotland, 178A
on slave trade, 250A
on status of dominions, 312A
two houses of, 126A
on women, 278A
Parma, 154A, 210A, 234A, 264A, 266A
battle of, 114B
Parnassiens, Les, 271C
Parr, Catherine, 162A
Parry, Sir William Edward, 244B, 246B
Parsifal (Wagner), 279C
Parthenon, 19C, 198A, 243C
Parthia, Parthians, 10B, 24B, 28B, 29A, 30B, 32B, 38B, 40B, 44B
Parti Québécois, 362C
Partition, Second Treaty of, 202A
Pascal, Blaise, 187B, 189B, 193B
Pasch, Gustav, 257B
Paschal II, Pope, 99C, 101C
Pasha Ali of Janina, 246A
Passage to India, A (Forster), 309C
Passarowitz, Peace of, 206A
Passau, 87C, 103B
Treaty of, 165C
Pasternak, Boris, 345C
Pastore, Annibale, 289B
Pate, sultanate of, 108C, 120C
patents, 229B, 321B
Paterson, William, 225A
Paterson (Williams), 337C
Path to Rome, The (Belloc), 289C
Pathans, 204B
Pathé, Charles, 289B
Pathetique (Tchaikovsky) *See* Symphony no. 6 in B Minor
Patna, battle of, 216C
Paton, Alan, 337C
Patria, 282C
Patrick, Saint, 59C, 61B
pattens, 109B
pattern making, 273B
Patterson, Floyd, 349C
Patterson, Haywood, *312*
Patton (Schaffner), 357C
Patzinaks, 96B, 100B
Paul, Alice, *304*
Paul, Elliot, 327C
Paul, Saint, 35A, *37,* 37A
Paul (bishop of Antioch), 49A
Paul I, Pope, 75C
Paul I (emperor of Russia), 232A, 234A
Paul I (president of Greece), 336B, 350B
Paul II, Pope, 143C
Paul III, Pope, 161C
Paul IV, Pope, 165C
Paul V, Pope, 179C
Paul VI, Pope, 349C, 351C, 363C
Pauline (Browning), 251C
Pauling, Linus, 323B
Paulinus, Suetonius, 34A
Paulus, F. von, 330A
Pausanias (Greek historian and geographer), 43C
pavane, 139C
Pavane pour une Infante Défunte (Ravel), 287C
Pavia, 90A
battle of, 156A
Synod of, 93C
Pavlova, Anna, 291C
Pavón, 240C
Pawnee, 139A, 145A
Pawtucket, 229B
Pax Romana, 38B
Paxton, Sir Joseph, 261C
Payne's Landing, Treaty of, 250B
Pazzi Chapel, 137C
PCB (polychlorinated biphenyl), 365B
Pea Ridge, battle of, 266B
Peace Corps, 346C

peanut butter, 275B
peanuts, 151B, 155B, 164C, 331B
Pearl Harbor, 281A, 305A, 326B, 326C, *327*
pearls, 31B
Pearson, Lester (prime minister of Canada), 348C
Peary, Robert, 292B
peas, 153B
Pêcheur d'Islande, 281C
Pecos, 123A, 133A
Pedigree (Simenon), 337C
Pedro, Dom (emperor of Brazil), 246C
Pedro II (emperor of Brazil), 280C
Peel, Robert, 248A, 254A
Peene, 208A
Peer Gynt (Ibsen), 271C
Pegau, 96A
Pegu, 120C, 142C, 148C, 158C, 160C, 176C, 178C, 216C, 263A
Pekalongan, 214C
Peking. *See* Beijing
Pelagianism, 59C
Pelagius (theologian), 59C
Pelagius I, Pope, 65C
Pelekanon, battle of, 126B
Pelham, Robert, 291B
Pelham Bay, 187A
Pella, 20C
pellagra, 325B
Pelléas et Mélisande (Maeterlinck), 283C
Peloponnesian League, 16C, 18C
Peloponnesian Peninsula, 244A, 246A
Peloponnesian War, 18C, *20*
Pemberton, John, 281B
Penang, 227A
pencils, 169B, 217B, 263B, 267B
Penda (king of Mercia), 70A
Pendleton Act, 278B
pendulums, 171B
penicillin, 325B
  freeze-dried, 329B
  mass production of, 327B, 331B
  synthetic, 329B
Penn, William, 195C, 197A, 199C, 205A
Pennsylvania, 115A, 187A, 191A, 193A, 203A, 205A, 207A, 211C, 217A, 219C, 224B, 230B, 243B, 255B
  Assembly, 197A
  early culture, 73A
  industry, 264B, 268B, 282B, 286B, 345B
  University of, 213A, 325B
Penobscot, 199C, 215A
pens, 279B, 335B
Pensacola, battle of, 244B
Pentecostalism, Pentecostals, 295C
Pentel Company, 349B
Penzias, Arno, 349B
Peony Pavilion, The (T'ang Hsien Tsu), 173C
People, Yes, The (Sandburg), 319C
People Are Living Here (Fugard), 357C
People's Republic of China, 339A
Pepi II (king of Egypt), 4A
Pepin III, 74A
Pepin of Aquitaine, *75*
pepper (spice), 74A, 150C, 176B
peppers, 147B, 157B
Pepys Diary, 247C
Pequots, 187A
Perak, 285A
Percies, 134A
Percy, Julian, 317B
Pereda Asbón, Juan (president of Bolivia), 363A
Peregrinus de Maricourt, Petrus, 119B
Peres, Shimon (prime minister of Israel), 371A
Pérez de Cuellar, Javier (secretary-general of United Nations), 366A, 370A
Pergamum, 26C, 27B, 27C
Pergation Calendar, 141C
Pergolesi, Giovanni Battista, 211C
Pericles, *18,* 18C
Pericles (Shakespeare), 179C
Perignon, Pierre, 199B
Perim, 265A
Peripatetic School, 23B
Perkins, Frances, 314B
Perkins, Jacob, 233B
Perlis, 293A
Pernambuco, 316C
Perón, Isabel (president of Argentina), 359A, 361A, 363A
Perón, Juan (president of Argentina), 335A, 337A, 339A, 343A, 359A, 361A
Péronne, 142A
Perot, Ross, 378C, 382C
Perpetua of Carthage, 45A
Perpetual Edict of 1577, 170A
perpetual-motion machine, 175B
perry, 59B
Perry, Matthew, 262B
Perry, Oliver Hazard, 240B
Persecution and Assassination of Marat (Weiss), 351C
Perseus, 26C
Perseus (Cellini), 163C
Persia, Persians, 39A, 39B, 44B, 48B, 54B, 62C, 116C, 142B, 152C, 182C, 233A, 317A. *See also* Iran
  525 B.C.–334 B.C., 16A–16B, 16C, 18A, 18B, 18C, 19C, 20C, 22C
  and Afghanistan, 188B, 208B, 210B, 263A
  and Armenia, 56B, 142B
  arts, 99C, 117C, 121C, 147C
  and Azerbaijan, 142B
  and Baghdad, 152B, 182B
  and Bahrain, 225A
  and Basra, 223A
  and Britain, 235A, 239A, 263A, 265A
  and Byzantium, 64C, 68B
  earthquake in, 208B
  and East Africa, 88C
  education, 85B
  and Egypt, 66B
  and Georgia, 114B, 140B
  government, 80C, 144B, 156B, 170B, 172B, 200C, 204B, 227A, 229A, 231A, 253A, 285A, 291A, 293A, 311A
  and Il-Khans, 130C
  and India, 253A
  industry, 315A
  and Jerusalem, 66B
  Kajar dynasty, 231A
  and Khwarazm, 112C
  and Kurdistan, 142B
  law and society, 16B, 16C, 314A
  and Moluccas, 72C
  and Mongolia, 110C, 121B
  oil deposits, 291A
  and Ottoman Empire, 158B, 162B, 172B, 245A
  postal system, 67B, 69B, 95B, 222B
  religion, 47A, 61B, 68C, 179C, 265C
  and Romans, 46B, 52B, 54A, 58C
  and Russia, 166B, 236A, 240A, 241A, 247A, 248A, 249A, 289A
  Safavid dynasty, 150B, 204B, 210B
  Samanid dynasty, 80C, 82C, 90C
  Sassanid dynasty, 44B
  science and technology, 59B, 67B, 87B, 89B, 99B, 113B, 269B
  and Sicily, 79B
  and Syria, 66C
  taxes, 16B
  and Timur, 132C, 138C
  and Turkey, 152B, 164B, 176B, 184B, 186B, 202B, 299A, 301A, 303A
  and United States, 265C
  and Uzbeks, 174B
  Zand dynasty, 225A, 229A, 231A
Persian Ecologues (Collins), 213C
Persian Gulf, 126C, 154B, 267A, 321A, 370A
Persian Gulf War, 375A, 376A
Personae (Pound), 293C
Persons and Places (Santayana), 333C
Persuasion (Austen), 245C
Perth, 138A
  Treaty of, 116A
Pertinax (emperor of Rome), 42A
Peru, 5C, 40C, 75A, 77C, 93A, 97A, 123B, 157A, 171A, 325A, 377A
  200 B.C., 24B
  700 B.C.–690 B.C., 12B, 13C
  and Argentina, 161B, 244C
  arts, 13C, 63C, 67A, 69A, 77A, 167C, 175C
  and Bolivia, 252C, 274C
  and Chile, 254C, 276C, 278C, 310C
  Chimú in, 107A, 109A, 123B, 141A
  and Colombia, 248C, 314C, 316C
  earthquake in, 215A
  economy, 280C, 290C
  and Ecuador, 325A, 327A
  and Germany, 335A
  government, 181A, 248C, 256C, 266C, 302C, 304C, 312C, 335A, 349A, 355A, 377A
  Inca in, 99A, 135A, 139B, 141A, 155A, 161A
  and Italy, 335A
  Mochica culture, 24B
  and New Granada, 213A
  politics, 246C, 308C
  science and technology, 67B, 91B
  settlement of, 61A
  and Spain, 159A, 224C, 268C, 270C, 272C
  Tiahuanaco culture, 91A
  transportation, 123B
  World War II, 325A
Perugia, University of, 125C
Peshawar, 90C, 253A
Peshwa, 245A
pest control, 31B, 53B, 201B, 271B
Pétain, Henri (chief of state of France), 300A, 309A, 324A
Peter, Saint, 35A, *79, 87*
Peter I (Cyprus), 130B
Peter I (king of Portugal), 130B
Peter I of Aragon, 98B, 132B
Peter I (prince-bishop of Montenegro), 224A
Peter I the Great (tsar and emperor of Russia), 198A, 200A, 200B, 202A, 204A, *205,* 208A, 212A
Peter II (king of Aragon), 108B, 110B
Peter II (king of Portugal), 198A
Peter II (tsar of Russia), 208A, 210A
Peter III (tsar of Russia), 218A
Peter III (king of Aragon), 118B
Peter IV the Ceremonious (king of Aragon), 126B, 128B
Peter Pan (Barrie), 289C
Peter Rabbit, 331C
Peter the Cruel (king of Castile and León), 128B, 130B
Peter (tsar of Bulgaria), 84A
Peterwardein, battle of, 206A
Pétion, Alexandre Sabès, 234B, 236C
Petipa, Marius, 267C
Petit, J. L., 207B
Petit Trianon, 217C
Petite Messe Solennelle (Rossini), 269C
Petition of Right, 182A
Petrarch, 127C, 133C
Petrograd, 300A, 302A
petroleum. *See* oil
Petroleum Coordinator for National Defense, 326B
Petropavlosk (Russian battleship), 289A
Petropolis, 256C
Petty, Sir William, 197C
Pevensey, 94A
Phaedo (Plato), 21C
Phaedon (Mendelssohn), 219C
Phalaris, 16C
Pharnaces II, 29A
Pharos of Alexandria, 23C
Pharsalia (Lucan), 35C
Pharsalus, battle of, 29A
Ph.D. degree, 267C, 304B
Phenomenology of the Spirit (Hegel), 237C
Phi Beta Kappa, 251C
Philadelphia, 189A, 197A, 199A, 201B, 209C, 221A, 222B, 226B, 228B, 230B, 231B, 232B, 233C, 239C, 243C, 252B
  Eagles, 367C
  Orchestra, 293C, 321C
  Phillies, 339C, 365C, 367C, 379C
Philadelphia (U.S. frigate), 236B
Philip, King (chief of Wampanoag), 195A, 197A
Philip I (king of France), 94A, 96A, 98A
Philip II (duke of Burgundy), 134A
Philip II (king of France), 106A, 106B, 108A, 110A, 111C, 112A
Philip II (king of Macedonia), 20C, 22C
Philip II (king of Spain, Naples, Sicily, and Portugal), 162C, 164A, 166A, 168A, 170A, 172A, 174A, 174C
Philip III (king of France), 118A, *119,* 136A
Philip III (king of Spain), 174A, 180A
Philip IV (king of France), 118A, 121C, 122A, 123C, 124A
Philip IV (king of Spain), 180A, 192A
Philip V (king of France), 124A
Philip V (king of Macedonia), 24C
Philip V (king of Spain), 202A, 204A, 208A
Philip VI (king of France), 126A, 128A
Philip (duke of Anjou), 202A
Philip of Hesse, 162A
Philip of Swabia, 108A, 110A
Philip the Arabian (emperor of Rome), 46A, 46B
Philip III (duke of Burgundy), 136A, 142A
Philippi, battle of, 30A
Philippicus (emperor of Byzantium), 72B

Philippine Commission, 299A
Philippine Company, 226A
Philippine Sea, 275A
Philippines, Filipinos, 157B, 192C, 287A, 332C, 334C
and ASEAN, 352A
and China, 176C
Communism in, 371A
government, 299A, 371A
independence of, 337A
and Japan, 326C, 328C
law and society, 295A
Mount Pinatubo eruption, 377A
and Spain, 156C, 162C, 168C, 170C, 172C, 174C, 184C, 219A, 285A
Philippines, National Bank of, 299A
Philippopolis, 130B
Philips Company, 349B, 353B, 357B, 367B
Phillips, Wendell, 252B
Philo of Byzantium, 27B
Philosophical Inquiry into the Laws of Nature, A (Cumberland), 195C
Philosophy of Right, The (Hegel), 245C
Philosophy of St. Thomas Aquinas, The (Étienne), 303C
Philostratus, Flavius, 47C
Phnom Penh, 365A
Phocaeans, 16C, 17A
Phocas (emperor of Byzantium), 66B
Phoenicia, Phoenicians, 2B, 7C, 8B, 9B, 10A, 10B, 11A, 11C, 13B, 14C, 16C, 17A, 22B
Phoenix Park, 278A
photocopying. *See* copy machine
photoelectric cells, 291B
photography, 209B, 249B. *See also* camera
aerial, 347B
bubble chamber, 341B
color film, 283B, 349B, 359B
dry photographic plate, 273B
emulsified paper photographic film, 279B
halftone process, 277B
infrared process, 327B
instant, 331B
negative-positive process, 261B
photoelectric cell, 279B
stroboscope, 313B
X-ray diffraction, 327B
Phrygia, 41A, 54B
Phyfe, Duncan, 231C
physical therapy, 67B, 83B
Physician and Pharmacist (Dittersdorf), 227C
Piacenza, 154A, 210A, 234A
University of, 115C
Piano Concerto in A Minor (Grieg), 273C
Piano Lesson, The (Matisse), 299C
Picard, Auguste, 313B
Picardy, 136A
Picasso, Pablo, 291C, 307C, 319C, 323C
Piccard, Auguste, 341B
Piccolomini, Ottavio, 186A
Pichincha, battle of, 246C
Pickering, Timothy, 238B
Pickering, William, 293B
Pickford, Mary, 301C, 305C
Pickwick Papers (Dickens), 253C, 257
Picquigny, Treaty of, 144A
Pictet, Raoul, 275B
Picts, 50A, 52A, 54A, 56A, 57A, 65C, 70A
Pictures at an Exhibition (Mussorgsky), 275C
Pictures of Tilling and Weaving, 99
Pieck, Wilhelm (president of East Germany), 338B
Piedmont, 118B, 160A, 166A, 234A, 264A, 266A
Piedmont-Sardinia, kingdom of, 262A
Piedras Negras, 75A
Pierce, Franklin (president of U.S.), 262B
Piers Plowman (Langland), 131C
Pietà (Michelangelo), 149C
Pietermaritzburg, 255A
Pietism, Pietists, 187C, 201C, 211C
Pietro, Guido di, 137C
Pikatan, 78C
Pike, Zebulon M., 236B
Pike's Peak, 236B
Pilate, Pontius, *32*, 32A, 33A
Pilgrim (Bishop of Passau), 87C
Pilgrims, 181A
Pilgrim's Progress (Bunyan), 197C
Pilkington, Alistair, 341B
Pillnitz, Declaration of, 228A
Pilot, The (Cooper), 247C
Pilsudski, Joseph (premier of Poland), 304A, 310A, 316A
Pinchback, Pinckney, 272B
Pinchon, Dom, 137B
Pinckney, Thomas, 232B
Pincus, Gregory, 317B, 333B, 343B
pineapples, 147B
Pineda, Alonso Álvarez de, 155A
Pinerolo, 200A
Pining, Dietrich, 143A
Pinkerton National Detective Agency, *282*
pins, 171B, 183B
Pinsk, 298A
Pinter, Harold, 347C
Pinzón, Vicente Yáñez, 151A, 153A
Pioneer II, 359B
Pious Desires (Spener), 195C
pipe smoking, 63A
pipes, lead, 113B
Pippa Passes (Browning), 255C
Piraeus, 16C, 18C, 260A
Pirandello, Luigi, 307C
Pirna, battle of, 216A
Pisa, 90B, 92B, 94B, 98B, 100B, 102B, 103C, 105C, 116B, 118B, 124B, 134B, 171B, 175B
Council of, 103C, 135C
Pisa Cathedral, 95C, 105C
Pisano, Andrea, 127C
Pisano, Giovanni, 119C
Pisistratus, 16C
Piso, Calpurnius, 32B
Pissarro, Camille, 273C, 275C
Piston, Walter, 333C
Pistoria, 161B
Pitard, Jean, 119B
Pitcairn Island, 218C, 229A, 253A
Pitt, William, 224A, 226A, 234A
Pittsburgh, 259C
Pittsburgh Pirates, 289C, 347C, 357C, 365C
Pittsburgh Steelers, 361C, 363C, 365C, 383C
Pius II, Pope, 140B, 141C
Pius IV, Pope, 167C
Pius V, Pope, 169C
Pius VII, Pope, 239C, 243C
Pius IX, Pope, 259C, 261C, 263C, 269C
Pius XI, Pope, 323C
Pius XII, Pope, 323C
Pixii, Hippolyte, 251B
Pizarro, Francisco, 157A, 159A
Pizarro, Gonzalo, 161A
Plain Dealer, The (Wycherley), 195C
Plain Tales from the Hills (Kipling), 281C
Plains Indians, 117A, 177B, 211A
plainsong, 145B
planer, 255B
planets, 97B. *See also individual planets*
Planinc, Milka (prime minister of Yugoslavia), 370B
plant
cross-pollination, 217B
hybridization, 273B
pollen, 217B
reproduction, 175B, 197B
species, 383B
Planté, Gaston, 265B
Plassey, battle of, 216C
plastic
biodegradable, 375B
blow-molded, 331B
Tupperware, 319B
Plate River, 155A
Plateau, 32C
Platform of Church Discipline, A, 189C
Plath, Sylvia, 349C
Plato, 19C, 21B, 21C, 35A
"Platonopolis," 49C
Platoon (movie), 371C
Plattsburgh, battle of, 240B
Plautianus, 44A
Plautus, Titus Maccius, 25C
plays
mystery, 125C
shadow, 77C
Plehve, Vyacheslav, 288A
Plessis, Armand-Jean du, 180A
Plessy v. Ferguson, 284B
Pliny the Elder, 37B
Pliny the Younger, 37C, 39C
Ploesti, 332A
Plombières, 264A
Plotinus, 47C, 49C
plows, plowing, *2*, 3B, 31B, 39B, 67B, 85B, 127B, 203B, 255B
iron, 241B
sulky, 269B
Plucker, Julius, 263B
plumbing codes, 57B
Plumer, Herbert Charles (high commissioner for Palestine), 309A
Plutarch, 39C
Pluto, 293B, 365B
Pluto Platter, 345B
plutonium, 323B
Plymouth Company, 177A
Plymouth (England), 181A
Plymouth (Mass.), 181A
plywood, 249B
Po, Fernando, 142B
Po Valley, 21A
Pocahontas, 179A, 181A
Podgorny, Nikolai (president of Soviet Union), 350B
Podolia, 194A, 196A
Poe, Edgar Allan, 249C, 257C,
Poèmes antiques et modernes (Victor), 249C
Poèmes saturniens (Verlaine), 271C
Poems, Chiefly Lyrical (Tennyson), 249C
Poems (Brooke), 293C
Poems Chiefly in the Scottish Dialect (Burns), 227C
Poems (Dickinson), 283C
Poems (Donne), 185C
Poems (Heine), 247C
Poems (Yeats), 285C
Poésies (Gautier), 249C
Poetics (Scaliger), 167C
Poet's Home, A (Harpur), 267C
Poincaré, Raymond (president of France), 294A, 306A, 310A
Point and Line to Plane (Kandinsky), 311C
Point Barrow, 345B
Point Peninsula culture, 103A
Point Turnagain, 244B
pointillism, 281C
Poirot, Hercule, 305C
Poiseuille, Jean Léonard Marie, 249B
Poitier, Sidney, 349C
Poitiers, 55A, 73C, 74A, 132A
Poitou, 92A, 108A, 110A, 112A, 114A, 118A
Pol Pot (leader of Cambodia), 369A
Poland, Poles, 166A, *323*
arts, 249C, 251C, 253C, 259C, 283C
and Austria-Hungary, 130A, 192A, 202A, 258A, 296A, 306A
and Brandenburg, 192A
and Britain, 320A, 322A
Communism in, 304A, 374B
and East Germany, 338B
and Eastern Galicia, 306A
education, 131C
and France, 306A, 308A, 322A
and Germany, 142A, 296A, 306A, 316A, 320A, 322A, 330A, 332A, 334A
government, 86A, 122A, 126A, 132A, 136A, 162A, 168A, 170A, 172A, 194A, 200A, 204A, 228A, 242A, 310A, 316A, 340B, 366B, 382B
independence of, 374B
Jagellon dynasty, 154A, 168A
law and society, 230A, 266A, 268A, 314A, 354B, 356B, 378B
and Lithuania, 134A, 150A
and Lorraine, 210A
and Mongolia, 114A, 154A, 156A
Polish Corridor, 320A
politics, 374B
and Prussia, 190A, 280A
religion, 88A, 167C, 181C, 215C
and Romania, 306A, 318A, 320A
and Russia, 152A, 170A, 178A, 190A, 192A, 206A, 218A, 220A, 230A, 232A, 238A, 250A, 268A, 298A, 304A, 306A, 312A, 314A, 378B
science and technology, 143B, 163C, 281B
Solidarity, 364B, 366B, 368B, 372B
and Soviet Union, 318A, 320A, 332A, 334A
and Sweden, 176A, 180A, 184A, 190A, 192A, 202A
and Turkey, 138A, 196A, 198A, 202A
and Ukraine, 306A
and United States, 344A
and Upper Silesia, 306A
and Vatican City, 373C
and Venice, 202A
and Vilna, 304A, 306A
War of Polish Succession, 210A
and West Germany, 356B
World War I, 296A
World War II, 322A, 330A, 332A, 334A
Polanski, Roman, 355C
Polaroid Corporation, 335B, 349B, 359B, 363B
Pole, Reginald (Archbishop of Canterbury), 165C, 167C
polio, 311B, 325B
Politburo, 306A
Poliziano, Angelo, 147C
Polk, James Knox (president of U.S.), 256B
Pollack, Sydney, 369C
Pollock, Jackson, 331C, 339C, 343C
Polo, Maffeo, 116C
Polo, Marco, 116C, 118C, 120C, *121*
Polo, Niccolò, 116C
Poltava, 204A

Polycarp (Bishop of Smyrna), 41A
polyester, 337B
polyethylene, 331B
polyethylene-terephthalate, 359B
polygamy, 276B
Polynesia, Polynesians, 32B, 50B, 58C, 60C, 76C, 108C
polypropylene, 343B
Pomerania, 168A, 184A, 208A, 216A
Pomerellen, 142A
Pompadour, Madame de, 212A
Pompeii, 29B, 36A, 62B, 175C, 205B
Pompeius, Sextus, 30A
Pompey the Great, 29A, 35C
Pompidou, Georges (president of France), 348B, 356B
Ponce, 274C
Ponce de León, Juan, 153A
Pondicherry, 194C, 200C, 216C
Pons, Lily, 313C
Ponselle, Rosa, 303C
Pont d'Avignon, 107B
Pont du Gard, 35B
Pont St. Bénézet, 107B
Ponte del Castelvecchio, 129B
Ponte Vecchio, 129B, 131B
Ponthieu, 118A
Pontiac, Pontiac's War, 219A, 221A
Pontifical University, 101C
Pony Express, 266B
poona, 273C
Poor, Henry, 267C
poor, the, 104C, 174A, 190A
Poor Law, 158A, 166A, 282A
Poorhouse Fair (Updike), 347C
Pop art, 349C, 371C
Popadopoulos, George (president of Greece), 358B
popcorn, 147B, 153B
Pope, Alexander, 205C, 207C, 209C, 211C
Pope John Paul II in, 367C
Popieluszko, Jerzy, 368B
Popov, Aleksandr, 285B
"popular sovereignty," 260B
Poquelin, Jean-Baptiste, 191C
porcelain, *42*, 43B, 67C, 69B, 77B, 83C, 91B, 113B, 135B, 151C
  Korean, 85C
Porcelain Tower, 137B
Porgy and Bess (Heyward and Gershwin), 317C
Porphyry, 51C
Porras, Juan Rafael Mora (dictator of Costa Rica), 260C
Port Arthur, 291A
  battle of, 289A
Port-au-Prince, 215A, 224C, 236C
Port Moresby, 328C
Port Philip Bay, 253A
Port Royal, 207A
Port Said, 343A
Porta, Giacomo della, 169C
Porta, Giambattista della, 167B
Porte étroite (Gide), 293C
Porter, Cole, 351C
Porter, Katherine Anne, 313C, 323C, 349C
Porter, William Sydney, 289C
Portland, 201A
Portland stone, 131B
Portnoy's Complaint (Roth), 357C
Porto Novo, battle of, 225A
Portobelo, 151A, 175A, 199A
Portrait of a Lady (James), 277C
Portrait of a Lady (Sargent), 277C
Portrait of Dr. Gachet (Van Gogh), 375C
Portrait of Richard Cumberland (Romney), 223C
Portrait of the Artist as a Young Man (Joyce), 299C
Portrait of Zola (Manet), 271C
Portsmouth, Treaty of, 291A
Portsmouth (R.I.), 187A, 189A
Portugal, Portuguese, 92B, 100B, 102B, 112B, 114B, 116B, 118B, 120B, 121C, 124B, 130B, 132B, 134B, 136B, 138C, 144A, 144B, 146B, 147A, 148A, 149A, 149C, 151B, 153B, 154B, 156A, 156B, 168C, 190C, 208B, 292A, 354B
  and America, 165B
  and Angola, 170B
  and Arabs, 188B, 210B
  and Argentina, 238C
  and Bengal, 170C
  Braganza dynasty, 186A, 236A
  Brazil, Brazilians, 246C
  and Brazil, 151B, 159A, 165A, 193A, 246C
  and Brunei, 162C
  and China, 141B, 154C, 164C, 176C, 370A
  and East Africa, 158B, 172B, 174B, 190B, 200B
  and East Indies, 150C
  and Egypt, 152C
  and England, 151A, 178C, 190A, 192B, 192C, 206A
  and Ethiopia, 162B
  and European Community, 370B
  in European Free Trade Association, 346A
  and France, 167B, 169A, 186A, 206A, 234A, 236A, 236C
  government, 164A, 198A, 246A, 248A, 360B, 364B, 370B
  and Guinea, 142B
  and Guinea-Bissau, 359A, 361A
  and Holland, 176C, 180C, 184B, 186B, 186C, 192C, 206A
  and India, 148B, 152C, 157B, 184C
  industry, 146B, 152C, 162B
  and Japan, 162C, 186C
  and Kongo, 164C, 168B
  and Kotte, 164C
  law and society, 244A, 258A, 292A, 293C
  and Macao, 164C, 182C
  and Madagascar, 178B
  and Moluccas, 156C
  and Morocco, 218B
  and Mozambique, 150B, 152B, 166B, 225A
  and Muscat Arabs, 194B
  and Newfoundland, 165A
  and North Africa, 138B, 212B
  and Oman, 192B, 214B
  in Quadruple Alliance, 252A
  religion, 158A, 292A
  and Savoy, 206A
  slave trade, 136C, 146B, 152B, 154B, 156B, 164B, 168B, 212B
  and South Africa, 162B
  and Spain, 158C, 170A, 186A, 192A, 194A, 204A, 207A, 209A, 215A, 218A, 222C, 234B
  and Tanzania, 299A
  and Timor, 265A
  and West Africa, 142B, 144B, 151B
  and Zambezia, 178B
  and Zimbabwe, 185C
Porus (king of India), 22B
Posen, 181C, 280A
  Peace of, 236A
positivism, 319C
Post, Charles, 285B
Post, Wiley, 315B
postal service, 69B, 119B
  airmail, 302B, 317B
  in Australia, 255A
  in France, 142A
  international postal congress, 268A
  railroads and, 254B
  stamps, 255B, 259B
  Universal Postal Union, 274A
  U.S. rural free delivery, 284B
  between Vienna and Brussels, 150A
Postum, 285B
Postumus (emperor of Rome), 46A, 48A
potatoes, 153B, 159B, 160A
Potawatomi, 246B, 248B
Potemkin, Grigori, 224A
Pothinus (Bishop of Lyons), 43A
Potomac, army of the, 266B, 268B
Potomac River, 228B
Potosí, 163A, 209C
Potsdam, 292A
  Conference, 334A
  Declaration, 334C
Pottawatomie Creek, 264B
Potter, Beatrix, 287C, 331C
pottery, 4A, 5C, 63A, 77C, 79B, 83A, 83B, 83C, 91A, 91C, 99A, 99B, 109A, 115C, 123A, 133A, 135A, 139A, 217C. *See also individual countries and regions*
  in Argentina, 95A
  in Europe, 109B
  Mogollon, 51C
  in Spain, 87C
Poulsen, Valdemar, 287B
Pound, Ezra, 293C, 305C, 339C, 359C
Poussin, Nicolas, 185C, 193C
Poverty Point culture, 63A
powder, black, 115B
Powell, Adam Clayton, 352C
Powell, Colin, 372C
Power and the Glory, The (Greene), 323C
Powers, Gary, 346A, 348A
Powhatan, 179A
Powys, 108A
Poynings, Edward, 148A
Poynings's Laws, 148A
Prado, 73A
  Convention of, 210A
Prado, Manuel (president of Peru), 349A
Praemunire, 129C
Praetorian Guard, 32A, 36A, 42A, 44A, 48A
Praetorius, Michael, 181C
Pragmatic Sanction, 208A, 210A, 214A
  of Bourges, 141C
Prague, *97*, 180A, 184A, 212A, 320A
  Compact, 141C
  Peace of, 184A, 276A
Prairie, The (Cooper), 249C
Prairie du Chien, 248B
Prambanam, 83C
Prasad, Rajendra (president of India), 339A
Praxeas, 43A
Praxedis (Adelaide), 96A
prayer book, 365C
Pre-Inca culture, 61A
Pre-Koniag culture, 63A
Preanger, 196C
Précieuses ridicules, Les (Molière), 193C
predators, natural, 53B
Premyslid dynasty. *See* Bohemia
Prés, Josquin des, 151C
Presbyterian Church, 359C, 377C
Presbyterianism, Presbyterians, 175C, 186A, 187C, 205C
Present Laughter (Coward), 327C
Preseren, France, 259C
Preservation of American Antiquities Act, 290B
Press Act, 192A
Pressburg
  Peace of (1805), 236A
  Treaty of (1491), 146A
pressure cooker, 197B
Preston, battle of, 188A
Pretoria, 265A
  Convention, 277A
Pretorius, Andreas, 255A
Pretorius, Marthinus (president of South African Republic), 265A
Prevesa, 160A
Prices, Edict of, 51C
Pride, Thomas, 188A
Pride and Prejudice (Austen), 241C
Priestly, Joseph, 221B
Prieto, Joaquín (president of Chile), 248C, 250C
Prigg v. Pennsylvania, 256B
Prim, Juan, 270A
Primakov, Yevgeny (prime minister of Russia), 384B
Primary Colors (movie), 385C
Primavera (Botticelli), 143C
Prime of Miss Jean Brodie, The (Spark), 347C
Primrose, Archibald Philip, 284A
Prince, The (Machiavelli), 153C, *156*
Prince Edward Island, 226B, 234B, 274B
Prince George, 236B
Prince of Wales (British battleship), 326C
Prince William Sound, 372C
Princess, The (Tennyson), 259C
Princess Casamassima (James), 281C
Princess Royal (British ship), 228B
Princeton
  battle of, 222B
  University, 215A
Princeton (U.S. ship), 256B
Principe, Il (Machiavelli), 153C
Principi de scienza nuova d'intorno comune natura delle nazioni (Vico), 209C
Principia Philosophiae (Descartes), 189C
Principia Philosophiae (Leibniz), 207C
Principles of Mathematics, The (Russell), 289C
Principles of Musical Harmony, The (Tartini), 219C
Principles of Political Economy and Taxation (Ricardo), 243C
Principles of Political Economy (Malthus), 245C
Principles of Political Economy (Mill), 259C
Principles of Scientific Management, The (Taylor), 293C
Pring, Martin, 177A
printing, 105B, 121B, 135B, 161B
  in American colonies, 187C
  color, 99B
  early, 74C, 75B, 93B, 109B, 123B, 127B, 139B, 143B, 145B
  linotype, 279B, 281B
  strike, 160A
printing press, 141B, 187C
  cylindrical, 239B
  rotary, 259B
  two-cylinder, 241B
Priscillian, 57A
Prisoner of Zenda, The (Hope), 285C
Prithi Raj, 109C
Prithi Raj Raso (Chand Bardai), 109C
Prithvinarayan, Shah, 218C

Private Life of Henry VIII, The (movie), 315C
Private Lives (Coward), 313C
Probus, Marcus Aurelius (emperor of Rome), 44A, 48A, 48B
Proclamation to South Carolina (Jackson), 250B
Procopius, 54A, 54B
Proctor & Gamble, 343B, 347B
Prodi, Romano (prime minister of Italy), 382B
Profumo, John, 348B
Progress of Philosophy (Stewart), 243C
Progressive Party, 336C
Prohibition, 302B, 304B, 304C, 314B
Prokofiev, Sergei Sergeyevich, 301C
Promessi Sposi, I (Manzoni), 255C
Prometheus Unbound (Shelley), 245C
Promontory Indians, 109A
Prophet, the, 238B
Prophet, The (Meyerbeer), 261C
Propylae, 198A
Protestant Episcopal Church, 233C
Protestantism, Protestants, 155C, 159C
in Austria, 169C
in Brandenburg, 161C
in Britain, 165C, 206A, 231C
in Canada, 262B
and Catholics, 158A, 182A, 228A
in China, 237C
in Czechoslovakia, 180A
in France, 166A, 167C, 197C, 206A, 214A
in Georgia, 211A
in Germany, 203C
and Holy Roman Emperor, 160A
in Hungary, 176A
in Ireland, 200A
in Palatinate, 163C
persecution of, 177C, 181C, 187C
in Poland, 181C
in Saxony, 161C
in Vienna, 171C
in Wales, 239C
Proto-Bluff Dwellers, 65A
proton accelerator, 311B
protozoa, 197B
Proudhon, Pierre Joseph, 255C, 261C
Provence, 62B, 144A, 160A
Proverbs, Book of, 23C
Providence (Md.), 189A
Providence (R.I.), 187A, 189A
Providentissimus Deus (Pope Leo XIII), 283C
Prüm, 82A
Prussia, Prussians, 202A, 207C, 220A, 254A
and Austria, 224A, 268A, 270A, 276A
and Baden, 270A
and Bavaria, 270A
and Brandenburg, 180A
and Britain, 234A, 284A
and Cassel, 270A
and Denmark, 248A, 258A, 260A
and East Friesland, 212A
education, 207C
and France, 228A, 230A, 232A, 236A, 240A, 266A, 272A
and Frankfort, 270A
and Germany, 268A
government, 206A, 244A, 260A, 266A
and Hamburg, 270A
and Hanover, 270A
and Hesse, 270A
and Hesse-Cassel, 260A
and Holland, 206B, 208B
and Holstein, 270A
and Holy Alliance, 242A
and Holy Roman Empire, 210A
law and society, 212A, 254A, 262A
and Nassau, 270A
Nazism in, 314A
and Netherlands, 226A
and Ottoman Empire, 262A
and Poland, 142A, 190A, 280A
religion, 241C, 253C
and Russia, 218A, 268A
and Saxony, 216A, 270A
and Sweden, 184A, 190A, 208A
and Switzerland, 264A
and Teutonic Order, 112A, 118A
and United States, 226B
World War I, 294A, 296A
and Württemberg, 270A
and Zollverein, 252A
Pruth, the, 204A
Prynne, William, 185C
Psalms, 73C
Psamtek I (king of Egypt), 12A
Pseudodoxia Epidemica (Browne), 189C
Pskov, 332A
Psycho (movie), 347C
Psychologie der Weltanschauungen (Jaspers), 303C
Psychology from the Standpoint of a Behaviorist (Watson), 303C
PTL Club, 371C
Ptolemy (astronomer and geographer), 41B, 45B, 79B
Ptolemy I (king of Egypt), 22A
Ptolemy II (king of Egypt), 22A
Ptolemy IV (king of Egypt), 24A
Ptolemy VI (king of Egypt), 26A
Pu Yi (emperor of China), 315A, 317A
Publishers Weekly, 273C
Puccini, Giacomo, 283C, 285C, 287C, 303C
Pucelle, La (Chapelain), 191C
Pucelle, La (Voltaire), 213C
Puebla, 161A, 165A
Puebla Valley, 71A, 75A
Pueblo culture, 65A, 75A, 85A, 99A, 101A, 117A, 119A
Pueblo (Indians), 91C, 197A
Pueblo (U.S. ship), 354A
Puerto Barios, 304C
Puerto Cabello, battle of, 240C
Puerto Rico, Puerto Ricans, 42C, 147A, 175A, 201A, 211A, 236C, 238C, 288B, 327A, 342C, 349B
earthquake in, 302C
government, 341A
hydroelectric power in, 323A
politics, 318C
slave trade, 274C
and Spain, 153A, 270C, 286C
and United States, 286C, 300C, 320C
Puerto San Julian, 151A
Pugachev, Emelyan, 220A
Puget Sound, 230B, 272B
Pulakeshin II, 66C
Pulaski, 268B
Pullman, George M., 265B, 269B
pulsar, 353B
Pultusk, battle of, 202A
pump
tidal, 219B
water, 31B, 201B
Punch, 255C
punch-card population tabulator, 277B
Punic Wars, 25A, 27A
Punjab, 70B, 88C, 90C, 106C, 112C, 156C, 212C, 214C, 255A, 259A, 261A, 303A
Punjab Rig-Veda, 7C
Punt, 6A
Purcell, Edward, 335B
Purcell, Henry, 193C, 197C, 199C, 201C
Puritanism, Puritans, 167C, 188B, 189A, 189C, 193C
Purkinje, J. E., 247B
Pushkin, Alexander, 247C
Putnam, Israel, 222B
Puzo, Mario, 357C
PVC (polyvinyl choride), 325B
Pygmalion (Shaw), 293C, 343C
Pylos, 321B
Pym, Barbara, 345C
Pyongyang, 58C, 340A
pyramids
in Egypt, 3C, 4A, 8A
in Khmer, 83C
in Mexico, 63C, 67C
Pyramid of the Inscriptions, *83*
Pyramid of the Sun, *52*
Pyramids, battle of, 233A
Pyrenees, 116B
Peace of the, 192A
pyrilamine, 333B
pyrometer, 225B
Pyrrhus (king of Epirus), 22C, 23A
Pythagoras, 15B, 17B
Pythagorean theorem, 15B
Pytheas, 22C
Pyu, kingdom of, 76C

Q

Qaddafi, Muammar (leader of Libya), 357A
Qadesh, battle of, 8B
Qasim, Abdul Karim (president of Iraq), 349A
Qasim Firdowsi, Abu-l, 89C
Qatar, 356A
Qiqihan, 200C
Quadi, 42A
Quadruple Alliance, 206A, 208A, 252A
Quakers, 191A, 195C, 199A, 199C, 209A, 251C
Quartering Act, 221A
Quarterly Review, 239C
Quasi War, 232B
Quate, Calvin, 369B
Quattro libri dell'architettura (Palladio), 169C
Quebec, 159A, 179A, 185A, 211C, *217,* 226B, 270B, 278B, 281C, 302B, 332B, 362C, 364C, 370C, 374C, 382C
in American Revolution, 222B
battle of, 217A
Conference, 268B
Separatists in, 356C
Quebec Act, 221A, 222B
Quebec City, 258B
Quecha language, 135A
Queen Elizabeth II (British ocean liner), 354B
Queen Mab (Shelley), 241C
Queen's College, 127C
Queensland, 265A
Queenston Heights, battle of, 240B
Quelimane, 162B
Quesnel, Pasquier, 207B
Qu'est-ce que la propriété? (Proudhon), 255C
Quetzacoatl, Temple of, 50C
Quetzalpapalotl Palace, 34C
Quezon, Manuel (president of Philippines Commonwealth), 317A
Qui celum, 117C
Quiberon, 216A
Quiché, 113A, 133A
quicksilver, 149B
quietism, 199C
Quiller-Couch, Sir Arthur, 293C
Quimper, Manuel, 228B
Quincey, Thomas De, 245C
quinine, 333B
Quintilian, 39C
Quintinie, Jean de la, 201B
quintuplets, 316B
Quirigua, 75A, 77A, 79A
Quisling, Vidkun (leader of Norway), 324A
Quito, 155A, 175A,
Quli, Muhammad (ruler of Golconda), 170C
Qumran, 37A

R

Rabah Zubayr, 287A
Rabaul, 330C, 332C
Rabbit Run (Updike), 347C
Rabelais, François, 159C
Rabin, Yitzhak (prime minister of Israel), 361A, 379A, 383A
Rabuka, Sitiveni (prime minister of Fiji), 371A
racial discrimination, 22B, 262B, 343B, 346C
Racine, Jean, 193C
Radama I (king of Madagascar), 239A, 243A, 247A, 249A
Radama II (king of Madagascar), 267A, 269A
radar
defense network, 321B
detection, 363B
Distant Early Warning radar network (DEW line), 342C
microwave range, 343B
pulse altimeter, 319B
weather tracking, 329B
Radcliffe, Ann, 231C
Radha (St. Denis), 291C
radiator, 283B
radio, 323C
AM broadcasting, 291B
broadcasts, 362B
Fessenden, 291B
FM broadcasting, 309B
parabolic dish antenna, 313B
telescope, 349B, 353B, 373B
two-way, 307B
radio waves
antenna, 285B
audion detector, 291B
coherer, 283B
Hertzian, 281B
high-frequency alternator, 289B
interference detector, 311B
oscillator, 293B
signal distortion, 311B
radioactivity, 291B
Radischev, Aleksandr Nikolaevich, 229C
Rado, James, 355C
Raeburn, Sir Henry, 247C
Rafsanjani, Hashemi (president of Iran), 373A
Raging Bull (movie), 365C
Ragni, Gerome, 355C
ragtime, 279C
Rahman, Mujibur (president of Bangladesh), 357A, 361
Rahman, Sheik Omar Abdel, 382C
railroad(s), 31B
in Canada, 253B
Djibouti-Addis Ababa, 289A
elevated, 271B
first in California, 265B
Moscow-St. Petersburg, 256A
over Andes Mountains, 284C
sleeping cars, 265B, 269B
Trans-Caucasus, 278A
Trans-Siberian, 289B
Uganda Railway, 289A
Rain, Steam and Speed (Turner), 255C

Rain Man (movie), 373C
Rainbow Warrior (Greenpeace ship), 368A
Raising of Lazarus (Caravaggio), 179C
Rajaraja I, 88C, 90C
Rajasthan, 161C
Rajendra Choladeva, 90C
Rajputana, 168C, 245A
Rajputs, 76C, 106C, 109C, 220C
Rake's Progress, The (Stravinsky), 339C
Ralamba (ruler of Merina), 170B
Raleigh, Sir Walter, 173A, *174*, 175A, 181A
Rama I (king of Siam), 225A, 233A
Rama IV (king of Siam), 271A
Rama VI (king of Siam), 293A
Rama Kambeng, 120C
Rama V (king of Siam), 271A
Rama VII (king of Siam), 309A, 315A, 317A
Ramadieh, 301A
Ramaya (Valmiki), 23C
Ramayana (anon.), 77C
Rambler, 345B
Rameau, Jean Philippe, 209C, 211C
Ramelli, Agostino, 173B
Ramillies, battle of, 204A
Ramírez, Pedro (president of Argentina), 331A
Ramona (Jackson), 279C
Ramsay, Allan, 209C
Ramses II (king of Egypt), 8A
Ramses III (king of Egypt), 8A
Rana Ratan Singh, 161C
Ranavalona, 267A
Ranavalona III (queen of Madagascar), 279A, 287A
Rancugua, battle of, 240C
Rand, Ayn, 331C
Rand Corporation, 351B
Randolph, A. Philip, 308B
Ranger 8, 351B
Rangoon, 214C, 241C, 247A, 334C, 340A
Rani Padmini, 161C
Ranjit Singh, 231A, 255A
Rank, Otto, 309B
Ranke, Leopold von, 247C, 253C, 277C
Rankin, Jeannette, 300B
Rann of Kutch, 355A
Rapallo
  Conference of, 300A
  Treaty of, 304A
Rape of the Lock, The (Pope), 205C
Raphael, 151C, *153*, 153C, 155C
Ras Tafari, 313A
Rashid, Harun al-, 76C
Rashomon (Akutagawa), 297C
Rashomon (movie), 339C
Rasoherina (queen of Madagascar), 269A
Rasputin and the Empress (movie), 315C
Rassam, Hormuzd, 271A
Rastatt, Peace of, 206A
Rastrakuta, 74C, 78C, 88C
Rathenow, battle of, 194A
Rationalism, 269C
Ratisbon, 103B
  Diet of, 236A
  Truce of, 198A
Rauschenberg, Robert, 349C
Ravel, Maurice, 287C
Raven and Other Poems, The (Poe), 257C
Ravenna, 58B, *61*, *62*, 63C, 74B, 77C, 121B, 138B, 264A
  battle of, 152A
Ravenna Cosmography, 71C
Ravenscroft, George, 195B
ravioli, 119B
Rawalpindi, Treaty of, 305A
Ray, James Earl, 354C, 362C
Ray, John, 193B
Ray, Nicholas, 343C
Ray, Satyajit, 343C
Raymond of Antioch, 102B
Raytheon Corporation, 335B
razors, 151B, 313B
Razor's Edge, The (Maugham), 333C
Razzle Dazzle (Saroyan), 329C
RCA (Radio Corporation of America), 343B
Readers Digest, 307C
Reagan, Ronald (president of U.S.), 364C, *365*, 366C, 368A, 368C, *369*, 370A, 370C, 372A, 372C, *373*
Realism (literature), 277C
Realism (painting), 273C
Rebecca (du Maurier), 321C
Rebecca (Hitchcock), 323C
Rebecca of Sunnybrook Farm (movie), 301C
Rebel Without a Cause (movie), 343C
Reber, Grote, 319B
Recceswinth (king of Visigoths), 70A
Recherche de la verité (Malebranche), 195C
Reclining Figure (Moore), 323C
Recollects, Augustinian, 187C
Reconstruction Act, 270B
Reconstruction Finance Corporation (RFC), 314B, 330B
recording
  45-rpm records, 339B
  digital audiotape (DAT) recorders, 375B
  discs, 289B
  long-playing (LP) record, 337C
  magnetic, 311B, 319B
  monophonic audiocassette, 349B
  public tape recording, 319B
  record/playback tape recorder, 317B
  stereo audiocassette, 353B
  stereophonic records, 345C
  videocassette recorder (VCR), 357B
Red Army, 302A, 304A, 316A
Red Badge of Courage, The (Crane), 285C
Red Cross, 267C, 269C
Red Fort, 188C
Red Ocher culture, 73A
Red Petticoat, The (Kern), 293C
Red River, 272B
Red River Colony, 238B, 242B
Red Room, The (Strindberg), 277C
Red Sea, 58C, 136C, 146B, 245A, 269A, 273A, 364A
  264 B.C., 24A
  and Africa, 62C
  and Italy, 292A
  transportation on, 17B
Redenbacher, Orville, 341B
Redford, Robert, 357C, 365C
Redon, Alliance of, 146A
Redshirts, 266A
Reed, Carol, 339C, 355C
Reed, John, 305C
Reflections in a Golden Eye (McCullers), 325C
Reflections on the French Revolution (Burke), 229C
Reformation, 159C, 163C, *176*
Reformed Presbyterian Church, 196A
refrigerators, 279B, 303B
Regards et jeux dans l'espace (Garneau), 319C
Regency, Council of, 150A
Regents, Council of, 166A
Reggio, 138B
Regiomontanus, Johann, 141B
Regnans in Excelsis (papal bull), 169C
Rehnquist, William H., 370C
Reichenau school of illumination, 91C
Reichsbank, 274A
Reichsland, 276A
Reichstag, 308A, 312A, 314A
Reid, Thomas, 219C
Reigen (Schnitzler), 289C
Reign of Terror, 230A
Reims, battle of, 302A
Reisz, Karel, 367C
Reivers, The (Faulkner), 349C
Relaciones de la vida del Escudero Marcos de Obregon (Espinel), 181C
Religio Medici (Browne), 185C
Religious Aspect of Philosophy, The (Royce), 279C
Religious Bodies Law, 321C
R.E.M. (rock group), 367C
Remagen, 334A
Remains of the Day, The (Ishiguro), 373C
Remarque, Erich Maria, 311C
Rembrandt, 185C, 193C, 195C
Remington Rand Company, 341B
Remus, *11*
Renaissance, 151C, *156*, 161C
Renan, Ernest, 269C
Renascence (Millay), 301C
Renault, Louis, 287B, 289B, 378B
René (Chateaubriand), 235C
René I (titular king of Naples), 136B, 144A
Rennie, Sir John, 237B, 239C
Reno, Janet, 378C, 380C
Renoir, Auguste, 279C
Renoir, Jean, 319C
Renown (British cruiser), 323A, 326C
Rense, Diet of, 127C
Rensselaer, Stephen Van, 240B
Rent Act, 344B
reparations, 312A
  Conference, 310A, 312A, 314A
Recovery Act, 306A, 308A
reproductive system, 333B. *See also* fertilization
Republic, The (Cicero), 29C
Republic, The (Plato), 21C, 49C
Republican Party, Republicans, 262B, 264B, 274B, 320B, 332B, 336C, 380C, 382C
Requiem, La Grande Messe des Morts (Berlioz), 253C
Resaena, battle of, 46B
Resnais, Alain, 347C
respirator, artificial, 311B
Rest on the Flight into Egypt (Cranach), 151C
restaurants, 45C
Restitution, Edict of, 185C
Resurrection Altar, The (Titian), 157C
Reuchlin, Johann, 151C
Réunion, 186B, 210B
Revelation, Book of, 39A
Revels, Hiram, 272B
Revenue Act, 334B
Revisionism, Revisionists, 290A
Revolutionary War. *See* American Revolution
Reyes, Rafael (dictator of Colombia), 288C
Reykjvík summit, 370A
Reynaud, Paul (prime minister of France), 322A
Reynolds, Sir Joshua, 221C, 231C
Reynolds v. U.S., 276B
Reza Pahlavi Muhammad (shah of Iran), 341A, 365A
Reza Shah Pahlavi (shah of Persia), 307A, 309A,
Rhadamiste et Zénobie (Crébillon), 205C
Rhapsody in Blue (Gershwin), 309C
Rhaticus, Georg, 165B
Rhazes of Baghdad, 83B
Rhé, Isle of, 114A
Rheims Cathedral, 111C
Rhenish Confederation, 240A
rheostat, 257B
Rhine River, 11A, 29A, 36A, 48A, 54A, 58A, 60A, 77B, 200A, 218A, 230A, 232A, 234A, 240A, 334A
Rhineland, 230A, *305*, 306A, 306B, 308A, 310A, 318A
Rhoda Island (Egypt), 73B
Rhode Island, 179A, 187A, 189A, 193A, 195A, 199A, 229B
Rhodes, 23C, 27B, 114B
Rhodes, Cecil (prime minister of Cape Colony), 277A, 281A, 285A, 292A, 304A
Rhodesia, 341A, 350A, 352A
  and Germany, 303A
  Northern, 340A, 351A
  Southern, 307A, 340A
Rhone, 112A
Rhuddlan, 118A
Rialto Bridge, 175C
Riau, 208C
Ribaut, Jean, 167A
Ribot, Théodule (prime minister of France), 300A
Ricardo, David, 243C
rice, 24B, 72B, 90C
  Tuscarora, 205B
Rice, Alice Hegan, 329C
Richard (duke of York), 140A
Richard I (king of England), 106A, 106B, 108A
Richard II (king of England), 132A, 134A, 135C
Richard II (Shakespeare), 175C
Richard III, 144A
Richard III (Shakespeare), 175C
Richard of Aversa, 95C
Richard of Cornwall (king of the Romans), 114B, 116A
Richard of Gloucester, 144A
Richardson, Elliot, 358C
Richardson, Henry H., 255C
Richardson, Tony, 349C
Richelieu, Cardinal, 180A, 182A, 184A, 186A
Richelieu River, 253B
Richet, Charles, 289B
Richmond, 213A, 236B, 266B
Richter, Charles, 317B
Richter scale, 317B
Ricimer, 60A
rickets, 189B
rickettsia, 335B
Riddle of the Universe (Haeckel), 287C
Ride, Sally, 367B
Rideau Canal, 251B
Riders in the Chariot (White), 347C
Riders of the Purple Sage (Grey), 293C
Ridgway, Matthew, 340A, 340C
Riebeck, Jan van, *190*
Riefenstahl, Leni, 321C
Riel, Louis, 272B, 278B
Rienzi (Wagner), 257C
Rieveschl, George, Jr., 331B
Rifai, Ahmad al-, 105C
rifle, 209A. *See also* gun(s)
  breech-loading, 261B
  invention of, 155B
  Kentucky, 221B
  recoilless, 323B
  single-shot, 277B

Riga, Peace of, 306A
Rigaud, André, 234B
"right-to-die" law, 362C
rights, equal, 16C. *See also* civil rights; racial discrimination; women's rights
Rights of Man, The (Paine), 229C
Riis, Jacob August, 283C
Riley, James Whitcomb, 279C
Rilke, Rainer Maria, 319C
Rimini, 25A
Rinaldo (Handel), 205C
Ring and the Book, The (Browning), 271C
Ringling Brothers and Barnum & Bailey Circus, 332B
Rio de Janeiro, 151A, 169A, 205A, 238C, 280C, 314C, 316C, 355A
  Conference, 326B, 327A
Rio de Janeiro (state), 252C
Rio de la Plata, United Provinces of, 155A, 242C
Río Muni, 299A
Ríos Morales, Juan Antonio (president of Chile), 329A
Rip Van Winkle (Irving), 245C
Ripken, Cal, Jr., 383C
Ritchie, Denis, 357B
Rivals, The (Sheridan), 223C
Rivas, Angel de Saavedra, duque de, 253C
River Plate, 222C
Rivera, Diego, *123*
Rivera, José Fructuoso, 246C, 256C, 258C, 262C
Rivera, Primo de (dictator of Spain), 306A, 312A
Rivoli, battle of, 232A
Rizal, José, 285A
Rizzio, David, 168A
"Road Not Taken, The" (Frost), 299C
Roanoke Island, 173A
Robbers, The (Schiller), 225C
Robbins, Jerome, 333C, 347C
Robe, The (Douglas), 327C
Robert I, the Bruce (king of Scotland), 122A, 124A, 126A
Robert I (Count of Flanders), 96A
Robert II (king of France), 88A, 96A, 98A
Robert II (king of Scotland), 130A
Robert III (king of Scotland), 132A, 134A
Robert of Anjou (king of Naples), 124B, 125C
Robert of Belesme, 100A
Robert of Gloucester, 102A
Roberta (Kern), 315C
Roberts, Dorthea Klimpke, 327B
Robertson, Alice, 306B
Robertson, Cliff, 355C
Robeson, Paul, 309C
Robespierre, Maximilien, 230A
Robin Hood, 133C
Robin Hood (Herbert), 283C
Robinson, Edward G., 313C
Robinson, Edwin Arlington, 293C
Robinson, Jackie, 337C, 359C
Robinson, Mary (president of Ireland), 374B
Robinson, Sugar Ray, 345C
Robinson Crusoe (Defoe), 207C
robots
  autofacturing, 361B
  robotics, 327B
Robusti, Jacopo, 163C
Roca, Julio Argentino (president of Argentina), 276C
Rocafuerte, Vicente (president of Ecuador), 252C
Rocca Secca, 134B
Rochdale, Pioneers of, 256A
Rochester (England), 164A
Rochester (N.Y.), 262B
Rock Island, 265B
Rockefeller, John D., 336C
Rockefeller, Nelson A., 360C
rockets, 107B, 109B, 135B, 137B
  A-4 (V-2), 327B
  control, 347B
  early, 109B
  fuel, 311B
  with liquid hydrogen and oxygen fuel cell, 289B
  M9A1 launcher, 329B
  manned launching, 335B
  V-1, 332A
  V-2, 332A
  Vanguard, 345B
Rockwell, Norman, 363C
Rocky Mountain House, 236B
Rocky Mountain National Park, 296B
Rocky Mountains, 244B, 246B, 256B, 274B
Rocky (movie), 363C
Rocoux, battle of, 214A
Rodgers, Richard, 331C, 347C
Rodin, Auguste, 277C, 281C
Rodogune (Corneille), 189C
Rodríguez, Abelardo L. (president of Mexico), 316C
Roe v. Wade, 358C
Roebling, Washington, 279B
Roger II (king of Sicily), 100B, *101,* 101C, 102B, 104B
Rogers, Richard, 363C, 369C
Rohilcund, 235A
Rojas, Gustavo (dictator of Colombia), 341A
Roldós Aguilera, Jaime (president of Ecuador), 367A
Rolf Krage (Ewald), 221C
Rolfe, John, 179A, 181A
Rolland, Romain, 289C
rolling machine, 155B
Rolling Stones, 351C
Romagna, 266A
Roman Academy, 143C
Roman Catholic Church. *See* Catholicism, Catholics
Roman de la Rose (Loris), 113C
Roman de Troie (Sainte Maure), 105C
Roman Empire, 32A, 32B, 33A–33B, 33C, 34A, 34B, 35A–35C, 36A–36B, 37A, 37B–37C, 38A, 38B, 39A–39B, 39C, 40A–40B, 41A, 41B, 41C, 42A, 43A, 43B, 44A, 44B, 45A, 45B, 47A, 47B, 48A, 48B, 50A, 50B, 52A, 56A, 56B, 58B, 76A, 78A. *See also individual leaders*
  43 B.C.–16 B.C., 30A–30B, 31A, 31B, 31C
  aqueducts, 23A, 33C, 35B, 39B, 39C, 41B
  and Arabs, 78B
  and Armenia, 61C
  arts, 31C, 33C, 35C, 37C, 39C, 43C, 45C, 47C, 49C, 51C, 53C, 55C, 59C
  and Bulgaria, 85C
  coinage, 45B, 49B, 51B, 55A
  decline of, 46A, 46B
  and England, 58A, 58B
  government, 60A, 64B, 88B
  horses in, 39B
  industry, 39B, 59B
  medicine, 29B, 37B, 41B
  and Parthia, 38B
  and Persia, 54B, 58C
  plague in, 66B
  religion, 31A, 33A, 35A, 38B, 41A, 43A, 47A, 51A, 53A, 101C
  schism, 76A
  science and technology, 51B, 57B, 65B
  slave trade, 37B, 40A
  taxes, 30A, 40B
  transportation, 38A, 55B
Roman Empire, Eastern. *See* Byzantium, Byzantines
Roman History (Mommsen), 263C
Romance sans Paroles (Verlaine), 275C
Romania, 36A, 39C, 266A, 270A, 276A, 278A, 282A, 290A
  and Austria, 298A
  and Bulgaria, 294A, 304A
  Communism in, 374B
  and Germany, 298A, 302A, 320A
  government, 314A
  and Hungary, 306A
  Iron Guard, 314A
  law and society, 268A, 314A, 374B
  and Poland, 306A, 318A, 320A
  and Russia, 306A
  and Soviet Union, 318A, 332A
Romanov dynasty. *See* Russia
Romanticism, 221C, 233C, 235C, 239C, 245C, 251C, 253C, 263C, 271C
Romanus I Lecapenus (emperor of Byzantium), 84B
Romanus II (emperor of Byzantium), 86B
Romanus III (emperor of Byzantium), 92B
Romanus IV (emperor of Byzantium), 96B
Romberg, Sigmund, 307C, 309C, 311C
Rome, ancient
  753 B.C.–443 B.C., 11A, 15A, 15C, 17A, 17C, 19A
  409 B.C.–184 B.C., 21A, 23A, 23C, 24C, 25A, 25C
  171B.C.–82 B.C., 26C, 27A, 27B,
  75 B.C.–44 B.C., 28A, 28B, 29A, 29B, 29C
  law and society, 19A, 40A
Rome, Romans, 96B, 97C, 104B, 105C, 116A, 147C, 260A, 266A, 270A, 306A, 320A
  Academy of Arcadia, 201C
  arts, 41C, 127C, 185C
  and Church of England, 159C
  Council, 139C
  and Crusades, 146B
  earthquake in, 80B
  and France, 260A
  Galleria Borghese, 183C
  and Germany, 156A
  Gesù Church, 169C, 197C
  government, 128B, 133C, 134A, 232A, 260A
  and Italy, 268A, 272A
  and Naples, 134B, 232A
  Pantheon, 67C
  Piazza Navona, 189C
  Protocols, 316A
  revolutions in, 137C, 259C
  science and technology, 143B, 145B
  and Spain, 156A
  St. Peter's Church, 151C, 165C, 173C, 189C
  Synods of, 63C, 87C, 95C
  Treaty of, 308A, 344
  World War II, 332A
Rome-Berlin Axis. *See* Axis powers
Romeo and Juliet (Shakespeare), 175C
Romero, Carlos (president of El Salvador), 365A, 365C
Rommel, Erwin, 324A, 326A, 328A, 330A
Romney, George, 223C, 235C
Romulus, *11*
Roncesvalles, 76A
Ronin, 203C
roof
  tile, 111B
  timber, 165B
Roosevelt, Eleanor, 321C
Roosevelt, Franklin D. (president of U.S.), 314B, 316B, 318B, 320B, 322B, 324B, 326A, 326B, 328B, 329A, 330A, 330B, 332B, 334A, 334B
Roosevelt, Theodore (president of U.S.), 288B, 288C, 290B, 292B
Root-Takahira Agreement, 291A
ropes, 3B
Roquebrune, 266A
Roquefort cheese, 97B
Rosario, 260C
Rosas, Juan Manuel de (dictator of Argentina), 252C, 262C
Rose Bowl, 323C, 329C
Roseau Cathedral, 254C
Rosemary's Baby (movie), 355C
Rosenberg, Julius and Ethel, 338C, 340C
Rosenkavalier (Strauss and Hofmannsthal), 293C
roses, 79C
Rosetta, battle of, 237A
Rosetta Stone, 25C
Rosmersholm (Ibsen), 281C
Ross, James Clark, 250B
Rossbach, battle of, 216A
Rossetti, Dante Gabriel, 273C
Rossini, Gioacchino, 241C, 243C, 269C
Rostand, Edmond de, 287C
Rota, 332C
Rotary Club, 290B
rotary desk, upright, 173B
Roth, Philip, 357C
Rothari (king of Langobards), 68A
Rouen, 86A, 95C, 136A, 143B, 153B, 235B
Rouge et le Noir, Le (Stendhal), 249C
Roughing It (Twain), 273C
Rougon-Macquart, Les (Zola), 273C
Rousseau, Henri, 279C
Rousseau, Jean-Jacques, 219C, 225C
Roussillon, 128B, 146A, 192A
Rover, The (Behn), 197C
Rowlandson, Mary, 197A
Roxburgh, 106A, 140A
  Treaty of, 126A
Royal Academy, 221C
Royal African Company, 192B, 194B, 198B
Royal Air Force (RAF), 324A, 334A, 366B
Royal Ballet, 317C
Royal Council, 182A
Royal Greenwich Observatory, 279B
Royal Niger Company, 281A
Royal School of Dancing, 193C
Royal Shakespeare Company, 367C
Royal Society, 193C
Royalists, 188A
Royce, Josiah, 279C, 287C, 303C
Rozwi people, 176B
RU 486 steroid, 365B
Rubáiyát (Omar Khayyam), 99C
rubber
  synthetic, 311B, 325B, 326B, 328B
  vulcanization, 257B
Rubens, Peter Paul, *26,* 177C, 179C, 187C
Rubicon River, 29A
Rubik, Erno, 363B
Rubik's Cube, 363B
Rublyov, Andrei, 137C

Ruby, Jack, 348C
Ruckelshaus, William, 358C
Rudau, 130A
Rudolf, archduke and crown prince of Austria, 280A
Rudolf, Christoff, 157B
Rudolf I, count of Habsburg (king of Germany and Holy Roman Emperor), 118A, 120A
Rudolf II (Holy Roman Emperor), 170A, 174A, 176A, 178A
Rudolf III (king of Burgundy), 92A
Rudolf (king of Germany), 96A
Rudolf of Nuremberg, 129B
rugby football, 269C
Rugby School, 249C
Ruggles, Samuel, 251C
Ruhr district, 308A
Ruhr River, 306A, 334A
Ruins of the Palace of Diocletian (Adam), 219C
Ruisdael, J. van, 197C
Rules of Chess (Caxton), 145C
"Rum Rebellion," 239A
Rumelia, 276A, 278A
Runcie, Robert (Archbishop of Canterbury), 365C
Runciman, Lord, 320A
Runnymede, 110A
Rupel River, 167B
Rupert, count Palatine, 150A
Rupert, Prince, 195A
Rupert (king of Germany), 134A
Rupert's Land, 242B, 272B
Rurik dynasty. *See* Russia
Rush, Benjamin, 222B
Rush, Geoffrey, 383C
Rush-Bagot Treaty, 242B
Rushdie, Salman, 373C, 379C
Rusk, Dean, 346C
Ruska, Ernst, 311B
Ruskin, John, 263C, 267C
Russell, Bertrand, 289C
Russell, Charles Taze, 273C
Russell, John (prime minister of England), 258A, 268A
Russell, William, 198A
Russell Island, 330C
Russia, Russians, 54B, 162A, 182C, 184C, 200C, *205,* 206A, 254A, 267A, 374B, 376B. *See also* Soviet Union, Soviets
  and Alaska, 213A, 226B, 244B
  and Aldrich Ames, 380C
  on American Revolution, 224A
  and Antarctica, 245A
  and Armenia, 288A, 297A, 305A
  arts, 137C, 179C, 203C, 245C, 263C, 267C, 275C, 283C, 287C, 293C, 309C, 311C, 345C
  and Austria, 232A, 260A, 294A, 296A
  and Austria-Hungary, 276A, 298A, 302A
  and Bahmani, 142C
  and Baltic crackdown, 376B
  and Belarus, 306A
  and Bering Strait, 211A
  and Bessarabia, 240A, 264A, 276A
  Bloody Sunday, 290A
  and Bosnia-Herzegovina, 380B
  and Britain, 164A, 246B, 248A, 262A, 294A, 310A
  and Bulgaria, 248A, 302A
  and Burma, 249A
  and Byzantium, 84B, 86A
  and Chechnya, 380B, 382B, 384B
  and China, 134C, 190C, 196C, 198C, 208C, 210C, 265A, 284A, 293A, 317A
  Communism in, 382B, 384B
  conscription in, 274A
  and Crimea, 226A, 262A, 342B
  and Cyprus, Cypriots, 384B
  and Czech, 320A
  and Denmark, 248A, 260A
  and East Prussia, 216A
  education, 278A
  and Estonia, 300A
  famine in, 176A
  and Finland, 228A, 316A
  Five-Year Plan, 314A
  and France, 234A, 236A, *241,* 248A, 260A, 282A, 294A
  G-7 loan to, 378A
  and Georgia, 224A, 234A, 235A, 236A, 240A
  and Germany, 276A, 294A, 296A, 298A, 300A, 302A
  government, 126A, 158A, 178A, 196A, 198A, 210A, 280A, 290A, 300A, 318A, 378B, 384B
  and Hanseatic League, 146A
  and Holstein, 222A
  and Holy Alliance, 242A
  and Hungary, 260A
  and Iran, 253A, 326A
  and Japan, 262A, 275A, 284A, 289A, 290B, 291A, 293A, 299A, 303A, 317A
  and Kazakhs, 212C
  and Korea, 293A
  law and society, 238A, 242A, 246A, 266A, 276A, 278A, 288A, 292A, 314A
  in League of Nations, 316A
  and Leon Trotsky, 310A
  and Manchuria, 287A, 293A
  and Mesopotamia, 301A
  and Mongolia, 112A, 319A
  and Moscow, 132A
  Norsemen and, 72A
  and Ottoman Empire, 250A, 251A, 295A, 297A, 302A
  and Outer Mongolia, 299A
  Pale of Settlement in, 252A
  and Persia, 166B, 208B, 208C, 235A, 240A, 241A, 247A, 248A, 249A, 289A
  and Poland, 152A, 170A, 178A, 190A, 192A, 220A, 230A, 250A, 258A, 268A, 298A, 304A, 306A, 312A, 314A, 378B
  politics, 288A
  population (1897), 286A
  and Prussia, 218A, 268A
  religion, 273C
  Revolution (1917), 300A, *301,* 305C
  Romanov dynasty, 178A
  Rurik dynasty, 172A
  science and technology, 81B, 285B, 289B, 291B, 321B
  and Siberia, 172A, 186C, 206C
  in Soviet Union, 306A
  space program, 381B
  and Sweden, 180A, 204A, 208A, 240A
  and Switzerland, 310A
  Synod of, 278A
  in Three Emperors' League, 276A, 278A
  and Turkey, 80B, 82B, 90C, 198A, 212A, 220A, 220C, 262A, 274A, 276A
  and Turkistan, 271A
  and Ukraine, 300A, 306A
  and United States, 246B, 270B, 292B, 374A, 376A, 378A
  World War I, 294A, 296A, 302A
Russian-American Company, 234B
Russian Church, 171C
Russian Imperial Theater, 267C
Russian Orthodox Church, 302A, 307C, 347C
Russification, 288A
Russo-German Reinsurance Treaty, 284A
Russo-Japanese War, 290B, 291A
Russo-Persian War, 240A, 248A
Russo-Polish War, 304A, 306A
Russo-Turkish Convention, 248A
Russo-Turkish War, 248A
Russworm, John, 248B
Rust, Ruprecht, 139B
Rut, John, 157A
Ruth, Babe, 347C
Ruthenia, 320A
Rutherford, Ernest, 291B
Ruy Blas (Hugo), 255C
Ruyter, Michiel Adriaanszoon de, 192A
Rwanda, 132C, 299A, 349A, 381A, 384A
Rye House Plot, 198A
Ryswyck
  Peace of, 200A, 201A
  Treaty of, 200A
Ryukyu, 359A

S

Sá Carneiro, Francisco (prime minister of Portugal), 364B
Saadi, 117C, 121C
Saalfeld, 158A
Saar, 342B, 344B
Saarinen, Eero, 325C, 351C, 353C
Saba, 193A
Sabah, 349A
Sabin, Albert, 325B
Sable Island, 175A
Sabuktagin (emir of Ghazna), 88C
Sacco, Nicola, 304B, 310B
Sacramento, 254B, 265B, 266B, 360C
Sacred Heart, 195C
Sacred Heart, Society of the, 249C
Sacred Heart of Jesus, Missionary Sisters of the, 277C
Sacred War, 14C
Sadat, Anwar (president of Egypt), 357A, 362A, 363A, 367A
saddle, 67B
Sade, Marquis de, 229C
Sadler's Wells Ballet, 337C
Sadowa, battle of, 270A
Safad, 116C
Safavid dynasty. *See* Persia
saffron, 72B
Sagesse (Verlaine), 277C
Sahara Desert, 4A, 26A, 41B, 76C, 106C, 140B, 142B, 168B, 170B, 249A
Saibou, Ali (president of Niger), 371A
Said Pasha (viceroy of Egypt), 263A, 269A
Sa'id (sultan of Oman), 251A
Saidor, 332C
Saigo-Takamori, 275A
Saigon, 265A, 354A, 360A
  Treaty of, 267A
Sailor Who Fell from Grace with the Sea, The (Mishima), 353C
Saint-Denis, Abbey of, 103C
Saint-Exupéry, Antoine de, 321C
Saint Joan (Shaw), 307C
Saint Joseph (Mo.), 266B
Saint-Lô, 332A
Saint-Louis, 192B
Saint-Pierre, Jacques -Henri Bernardin de, 221C
Saint Vincent, 364A
Sainte Maure, Benoît de, 105C
Saipan Island, 332C
Saison en enfer, Une (Rimbaud), 275C
Sakarya, battle of, 307A
Sakhalin Island, 262A, 275A
Sakharov, Andrei, 370B
Saladero culture, 30C
Saladin (sultan of Syria), 104B, 108B, 112B
Salado culture, 73A, 109A, 123A, 129A
Salado River, battle of, 126B
Salamanca, 101C
  battle of, 240A
  University of, 111C
Salamis (Greek island), 18C
Salammbô (Flaubert), 267C
Salandra, Antonio (prime minister of Italy), 294A
Salazar, Antonio (prime minister of Portugal), 354B
Salem City (N.J.), 213B
Salem (Mass.), 183A, 185A, 201A
Saleph River, 106A
Salerno, 96B, 97C, 330A
  Medical School, 99B, 113B
  University of, 81C
Salic Law, 124A
Salinas de Gortari, Carlos (president of Mexico), 373A
Salinger, J. D., 339C
Salisbury, Lord Robert (prime minister of England), 278A, 280A, 284A
Salisbury, Treaty of, 120A
Salisbury Cathedral from the Bishop's Grounds (Constable), 247C
Salisbury (Conn.), 237C
Salish people, 83A
Sallust, 31C
Salmon Falls, 201A
Salmon Hills River, 185A
Salón México, El (Copland), 319C
Salonika, 82B, 114B, 128B, 136B
salt, salting, 73A, 79A, 109A, 119B, 133B
    desalination plant, 273B
  salt water conversion, 347B
SALT I (Strategic Arms Limitation Talks) treaty, 356A, 358A
SALT II, 358A, 360A, 364A
Salt River Basin, 117A
Salta, battle of, 240C
Salto, 242C
saltpeter, 171B
Saluzzo, 166A
Salvation Army, 269C, 277C
Salzburg, 211A, 217C, 238A
Samakow, 130B
Samanid dynasty. *See* Persia
Samaria, 10B, 34B, 41A
Samarkand, 72C, 73B, 74C, 110C, 137B, 138C, 152B
Samgarh, 190C
Samnite Wars, 23A
Samoa, Samoans, 50B, 208C, 277A, 295A, 305A
Samos (Greek island), 17B, 23B
Samosata, 49A
Samson Agonistes (Milton), 195C
Samson (Handel), 213C
Samudragupta (emperor of India), 52B, 56B
Samuel, Sir H., 309A
San Antonio, 252B
San Diego, 221C
San Diego Chargers, 381C
San Diego Padres, 369C, 385C
San Felipe, University of, 213A
San Francisco, 260B, 273A, 275B, 334B, 338A, 352C, 366C
    49ers, 367C, 369C, 373C, 375C, 381C
    anti-Vietnam War rallies in, 352C
    earthquake in, 290B, 372C
    Giants, 349C, 373C

San Germano, 112B
San Gimignano, 99C
San Jacinto, battle of, 252B
San Jose, 213A, 246C, 256C
San Juan, 153A, 175A
San Juan del Norte, 258C
San Juan Hill, battle of, 286C
San Juan Islands, 230C, 272B
San Juan River, 157A
San Luis Potosí, Cathedral of, 248C
San Marino, 377C
San Martín, Grau (president of Cuba), 333A
San Martín, José de, 240C, 242C, 244C, 246C
San Martino, battle of, 264A
San Min Chu I (Sun Yat-sen), 291A
San Pascual, 258B
San Quentin, 356C
San River, 296A
San Sacramento, 207A
San Salvador, 147A, 168B, 244C, 246C, 254C, 310C
earthquake in, 262C
and United Provinces, 252C
San Vitale, Church of, *62*, 63C, 77C
Sancerre, 112A
Sanchi, shrine of, 39A
Sancho II (king of Castile), 94B
Sancho II (king of Portugal), 112B, 114B
Sancho III (king of Spain), 92B
Sancho IV (king of Castile and León), 118B, 120B
Sand, George, 255C, 259C, 265C
Sandburg, Carl, 297C, 303C, 305C, 319C, 323C
Sandinista movement, 383A
Sandjak, 184B
Sandoz, Mari, 329C
Sandusky, 215A
sandwich, 219B
Sandwich (England), 110A
Sandy Hook, 226B
Sanhedrin, 37A
Sanjaya dynasty. *See* East Indies
Sanjusangendo Temple, 117C
Sanna-i-Yat, 301A
Sansapor, 332C
Sansetsu, 191C
Sanskrit College, 229A
Santa Anna, Antonio López de (president of Mexico), 250C, 252B, 252C, 256C, 258B, 262C
Santa Croce, 137C
Santa Cruz, Andres, 238C, 248C
Santa Cruz, battle of, 328C, *329*
Santa Cruz Islands, 174C
Santa Espiritu, 157A
Santa Fe (Argentina), 262C
Santa Fe (N.M.), 171A, 258B
Santa Maria, 75A
Santa Maria, 147A
Santa Maria dei Frari, 155C
Santa Maria della Salute, 185C
Santa Maria delle Grazie, 149C
Santa Marta, 157A
Santa Sophia, Basilica of, 63C
Santana, Pedro (president of Dominican Republic), 256C
Santayana, George, 285C, 291C, 333C
Santiago (Chile), 161A, 213A, 242C, 244C, 264C, 268C, 280C, 290C
Santiago (Cuba), 153A, 286C
Santiago de Compostela, Cathedral of, 97C
Santiago de los Caballeros, battle of, 256C
Santiago del Estero, 165A
Sant'Ivo della Sapienza, 187C
Santo Domingo, 149A, 153A, 159B, 161A, 228C, 232C, 234B, 238C, 256C, 312C
and Haiti, 256C
slave insurrection, 228C
and Spain, 266C, 268C
Santo Domingo Cathedral, 153A
Santorini, 6C
Santos-Dumont, Alberto, 291B
Santuary (Faulkner), 307C
São Paulo, 165A, 205A, 270C, 278C, 308C, 316C
São Salvador, 165A
São Tomé, 144B, 146B
São Vicente, 159A
Sapienza, 130B
Sappho, 15C
Saqqara, 3C
Saracens, 82B, 88B, 114B
Saragossa, 100B
Treaty of, 158C
Sarajevo, 294A, 380A, 382B
Saran packaging film, 305B
Sarandon, Susan, 377C, 381C
Saratoga, 222B, 276B
Saratoga Trunk (Ferber), 325C
Sarawak, 255A, 281A, 326C, 349A
Sardica, Synod of, 53A
Sardinia, Sardinians, 17A, 25A, 47A, 90B, 94B, 100B, 104B, 114B, 124B, 202A, 204A, 208A, 210A, 214A, 230A, 330A
and Austria, 258A, 260A
and France, 266A
Sardou, Victorien, 283C
Sargent, John Singer, 277C, 279C
Sargon (king of Akkad), 4B
Sarikanus, battle of, 297A
Sarmiento, Domingo (president of Argentina), 268C
Sarmistha (Dutt), 265C
Sarnath Stupa, 62C
Sarney, José (president of Brazil), 369A
Saro-Wiwa, Ken, 383A
Saroyan, William, 317C, 323C, 329C, 331C
Sarsa Dengel, 166B
Sartor Resartus (Carlyle), 251C
Sartre, Jean-Paul, 333C, 335C
Sartzetakis, Christos, 368B
Saskatchewan, 278B, 290B
Sassanid dynasty. *See* Persia
Sassbach, battle of, 194A
Sassoon, Siegfried, 301C, 303C
Satan in Gornay (Singer), 317C
Satanic Verses (Rushdie), 373C
satellites, communications, 349B, 377B. *See also individual satellites*
Satsuma, 275A
Sattelberg, 330C
Saturn, 191B
Satyagraha (Glass), 365C
Saucourt, 82A
Saud (king of Saudi Arabia), 341A, 351A
Saudi Arabia, 136C, 315A
and Egypt, 342A
government, 341A, 367A
Hashimite dynasty, 301A
industry, 315A
and United Arab Republic, 349A
and United States, 374A
and Yemen, 342A
Sauk, 246B, 248B, 250B
Saul (king of Israel), 10B
Saul of Tarsus. *See* Paul, Saint
Sault Ste. Marie, 181A
Savage, James, 245C
Savage Island, 287A
Savannah, 211A, 245B, 268B
Savannah culture, 123A
Savannah River culture, 73A
Savery, Thomas, 201B
Saving Private Ryan (movie), 385C
Savo Island, battle of, 328C
Savonarola, Girolamo, 149C
Savoy, 160A, 166A, 176A, 180A, 185C, 200A, 202A, 206A, 208A, 210A, 220A, 266A
sawmills, 127B, 175B, 185A
saws, sawing, 115B
Saxeweimar, 242A
Saxitoxin, 339B
Saxon History (Widukind), 87C
Saxony, Saxons, 54A, 56A, 60A, 71B, 74A, 77C, 78A, 96A, 103B, 104A, 138B, 158A, 161C, 162A, 182A, 184A, 186A, 204A, 205C, 206A, 209C, 210A, 212A, 216A, 218A, 236A, 250A, 270A
Saybrook Platform, 205C
Sayil, 77A
Scala Theatre, La, 223C
scale, 12-note, 315C
Scaliger, J. J., 167C
Scandinavia, Scandinavians, 77B, 89A, 99B, 115C, 148A, 156A, 165B, 170A, 204A. *See also individual countries*
Scarlatti, Alessandro, 199C
Scarlatti, Giuseppe Domenico, 199C
scarlet fever, 195B, 309B
Scarlet Letter, The (Hawthorne), 261C
Scènes de la vie de Bohème (Murger), 259C
Schaffner, Franklin J., 357C
Schecter, Solomon, 295C
Schedel, Hartmann, 147C
Scheele, Karl, 221B
Scheiner, Christoph, 181B
Scheldt, 254A
Schenectady, 201A
Schenk v. U.S., 302B
Scheyern, alliance of, 158A
Schiller, Friedrich von, 225C, 227C, 231C, 235C, 237C
Schindler's Ark (Keneally), 367C
Schindler's List (Spielberg), 379C
Schism, 61C, 95C, 103C
Schlatter, James, 351B
Schlegel, August Wilhelm von, 233C
Schlegel, Freidrich von, 233C
Schleiermacher, Friedrich, 247C
Schlesinger, John, 357C
Schleswig, 268A, 276A, 296A
Schleswig-Holstein, 258A, 260A
Schmalkalden, League of, 158A, 162A
Schmidt, Helmut (chancellor of West Germany), 360B
Schmitt, Harrison, *359*
Schneider-Creusot, 318A
Schnitzler, Arthur, 289C
Schoenberg, Arnold, 293C
Schola Cantorum, 77C
Scholasticism, 99C, 119C
Schönbrunn, 236A
Schoolcraft, Henry, 250B
Schopenhauer, Arthur, 245C, 253C, 255C
Schott, Gaspar, 191A
Schouten, Willem, 180B
Schreiner, Olive, 279C
Schrenk, Johann, 145B
Schroeder, Gerhard (chancellor of Germany), 384B
Schroeder, William, 371B
Schubert, Franz, 247C, 249C
Schulberg, Budd, 327C
Schulze, Johann, 209B
Schuschnigg, Kurt von (chancellor of Austria), 316A, 318A
Schütz, Heinrich, 173C, 185C
Schuylkill River, 189A, 237B
Schwabach, 133B
Schwarz, Berthold, 129B
Schwarzenau, 205C
Schwarzerd, Philipp, 157C
Science and Health (Eddy), 275C
Scillium, 43A
scissors, shears, 151B
Scone, 124A
Scopes, John, 308B
Scorsese, Martin, 363C, 365C, 375C
Scotchguard fabric protector, 343B
Scotland, Scots, 3A, 52A, 54A, 56A, 57A, 76A, 78A, 82A, 86A, 90A, 92A, 94A, 96A, 99C, 101B, 104A, 106A, 110A, 114A, 116A, 118A, 120A, 122A, 124A, 125B, 126A, 130A, 132A, 133C, 134A, 135C, 136A, 138A, 139C, 140A, 142A, 144A, 146A, 148A, 150A, 151C, 152A, 156A, 162A, 165C, 166A, 206A, 212A, 324A
and America, 207A
arts, 99C, 205C, 215C, 251C
"Black Parliament," 124A
Cameronians, 196A
and Canada, 181A
coinage, 101B
education, 171C
and England, 164A, 178A, 186A, 187C, 188A, 204A
and Germany, 202A
government, 176A
Highlanders, 200A
and Ireland, 190A
Jacobites, 198A
law and society, 186A, 382B
and Panama, 203A
religion, 163C, 167C, 175C, 179C, 186A, 187C, 196A, 257C
science and technology, 181B, 211B, 219B, 227B, 243B, 251B, 255B, 257B, 319B
Stuart dynasty, 130A, 189A
Scots, National Covenant of, 187C
Scott, Dred, 258B
Scott, George C., 357C
Scott, James (duke of Monmouth), 196A, 198A
Scott, Ridley, 377C
Scott, Sir Walter, 237C, 239C, 241C, 243C, 245C, 253C
Scott, Winfield, 258B
Scottish Church, 196A, 210A
Scottish Civil War, 186A
Scottsboro Case, 312B
Scream, The (Munch), 283C
screw press, 109B
screw tourniquet, 207B
Screwtape Letters, The (Lewis), 327C
Scroll Sky, 77A
Scutari, 298A
scythe, 115B, 123B, 169B
Scythians, 14B
sea mounts, 335B
Sea of Japan, 354A
Sea Wolf, The (London), 289C
Seaborg, Glenn T., 328B, 333B
seafood cannery, 257B
Seagull, The (Chekhov), 287C
Seasons (Haydn), 235C
Seattle, 325B
Sebastian (king of Portugal), 164A, 170B
Sebastopol, 262A, 328A, 332A
Sebenico, 304A
Second Canadian Pacific Railway Company, 276B
Second Piano Concerto in D Minor (MacDowell), 281C
Second Reform Bill, 270A
Secrets of the Self (Iqbal), 297C
Securities and Exchange Commission, 316B

Sedan, 176A
battle of, 272A
Sedition Act, 232B, 302B
Seeburg Company, The, 339B
Segni, Antonio (president of Italy), 348B
Segu, kingdom of, 214B, 218B
Seibal, 75A, 79A, 83A, 85A
Seigfried Line, 332A
Seinfeld, 385C
seismograph, 41B
Sejanus, 32A
Sekigahara, battle of, 176C
Selangor, 285A
Selassie, Haile (emperor of Ethiopia), 361A
Selective Service Act, 300B, 324B, 336C
Seleucia, 53A
Seleucid empire, 22B, 26B, 28B
Seleucus I (Seleucid king), 22B
Selim I (sultan of Ottoman Empire), 152B, 154B
Selim II (sultan of Ottoman Empire), 168A, 168B
Selim III (sultan of Ottoman Empire), 229A, 231A, 237A
Seljuk Turks, 92B, 92C, 94B, 96B, 98B, 112C, 114C
Selma, 350C
Semiautomatic Ground Environment (SAGE) air defense system, 341B
semiconductors, 335B
Seminole, Seminole Wars. *See* Florida
Semirechye, 186C
Semur, 95C
Sena, 152B, 158B
Senate, U.S., 320B, 374C
African-Americans in, 274B, 352C
and armed forces, 306B
bomb in, 296B, 356C
on "Calhoun's Resolutions," 254B
and cloture rule, 300B
Edward Kennedy in, 348C
on Equal Rights Amendment, 358C
on Fulbright Resolution, 330B
on Haiti, 306C
on immigration, 340C
impeachment of Johnson, 270B
and Iran-Contra, 370C
on Joseph McCarthy, 342C
on League of Nations, 304B
Nixon in, 338C
and Panama Canal, 288C
on poll tax, 346C
on Robert Bork, 370C
on Treaty of Versailles, 304B
on United Nations, 334B
on war, 310B
Watergate Committee, 358C
on woman suffrage, 276B
women in, 306B, 336C
Seneca the Elder, 35C
Senegal, 192B, 216B, 219A, 225A, 285A, 347A
and France, 281A
and Mali, 346A
and Sudan, 346A
Senegal Company, 194B
Senegal River, 138C, 225A, 239A, 245A
Senlis, Peace of, 146A
Sennar, kingdom of, 212B, 245A
Sennett, Mack, 293C
Sense and Sensibility (Austen), 239C
Sense of Beauty, The (Santayana), 285C
Seoul, 132C, 338A
Sepoy mutiny, 265A
Septimen Pass, 127B
Serapis (British ship), 224B
Serbia, Serbs, 50A, 206A, 262A, 308A, 310A
and Albania, 384B
arts, 247C
and Austria, 212A, 292A, 294A, 296A, 298A
in Balkan League, 292A
and Bosnia, 292A
and Britain, 298A
and Bulgaria, 278A, 280A, 294A, 298A
and Germany, 282A, 294A, 298A
government, 128B, 238A, 264A, 276A, 278A, 288A
independence, 239A, 248A
law and society, 128B
and Montenegro, 270A
and Ottoman Empire, 266A, 270A, 274A
and Turkey, 132B, 140A, 242A
and United Nations, 384A
World War I, 294A
and Yugoslavia, 372B, 380A
Serchio River, 89B
Serenade (Cain), 319C
Sergius (patriarch of Constantinople), 66B
sericulture. *See* silk, silk industry
Seringapatam, battles of, 231A, 235A
Serious Call to a Devout and Holy Life, A (Law), 211C
Serrano, Francisco (dictator of Spain), 274A
Serrano, Jorge (president of Guatemala), 379A
Servant, The (Losey), 349C
Servicemen's Readjustment Act, 332B
Servius Tullius (king of Rome), 15A
Sesostris I (king of Egypt), 4A
Sesostris III (king of Egypt), 4A
Sesshu, 151C
Seti I (king of Egypt), 8A
Seton, Anya, 327C, 333C
Seton, Mother Elizabeth Ann, 241C, 361C
Settlement, Act of, 202A
Seurat, Georges, 281C
Seven Golden Cities of Cíbola, 161A
Seven Gothic Tales (Dinesen), 317C
Seven Oaks, Massacre of, 242B
Seven Pines, battle of, 266B
Seven Samurai, The (Kurosawa), 343C
Seven Wonders of the World (Philo), 27B
Seven Years' War, 216A, 217A, 2 18A, 219A
Seventh Ring, The (George), 291C
Severus, Alexander (emperor of Rome), 44A, 44B, 45A, 45C, 46A
Severus, Lucius Septimius (emperor of Rome), 40A, 42A, 45A, 45C
Seville, 58B, 94B, 114B, 150A
University of, 151C
Seville Cathedral, 155C
Sèvres, Treaty of, 304A, 305A
sewing machine, 251B, 259B, 261B
Sex and Character (Weininger), 289C
sexual harassment, 380C
Seychelles, 216B
Seymour, Jane, 160A
Sforza, Francesco, 138B
Sgt. Pepper's Lonely Hearts Club Band (Beatles), 353C
Shadow of a Doubt (movie), 331C
shaduf, 123B
Shadwell, Thomas, 199C
Shaffer, Peter, 365C
Shah Hussein Madrasah, The, 204B
Shah Jahan (emperor of Moguls), 182C, 190C, 192C
Shah-Nameh (Qasim Firdowsi), 89C
Shah Rokh, 134C, 138C
Shakas, 56B
Shakers, 221C
Shakespeare, William, 167C, 173C, 175C, 177C, 179C, *180,* 181C, 183C, 233C
Shame of the Cities (Steffen), 289C
Shamir, Yitzhak (prime minister of Israel), 367A, 371A
Shan, 166C
Shang dynasty. *See* China, Chinese
Shanghai, 275A, 315A, 319A
Shangsi province, 164C
Shannon, Claude, 325B, 337B
Shannon (British warship), 240B
Shans, 120C
Shansi province, 81C, 162C
Shantung, 307A, 311A
Shapur I (king of Persia), 46B, 48B
Shapur II (king of Persia), 50B, 52B, 54B
Shapur III (king of Persia), 56B
Sharpeville, 347A
Shastri, Lal Bahadur (prime minister of India), 351A, 353A
shaving, 27C
Shaw, George Bernard, 281C, 285C, 287C, 293C, 299C, 307C, 339C, 343C
Shaw, Irwin, 327C, 333C
Shawn, Ted, 325C
Shawnee, 238B
Shaykh, 220B
Shays, Daniel, 226B
She Came to Stay (Beauvoir), 331C
Sheba, queen of, 10B
Sheen, Fulton J. (Auxiliary Bishop of New York and Bishop of Rochester), 341C
sheet polarizer, synthetic, 313B
Sheffield, 295A
Shekkhar, Chandra (prime minister of India), 375A
Sheldonian Theater, 193C
Shelekhov, Grigori Ivanovich, 226B
Shelley, Mary Wollstonecraft, 243C, 245C
Shelley, Percy Bysshe, 241C, 245C
Shen Kua, 97B
Shen Tsung (emperor of China), 94C
Shensi province, 103B, 317A
Shenyang, 182C
Shepard, Alan B., Jr., 385B
Shepheardes Calender, The (Spenser), 171C
Sher Ali (emir of Afghanistan), 273A
Sher Shah, 160C
Sheridan, Richard, 223C, 225C
Sherman, Patsy, 343B
Sherman, William Tecumseh, 268B
Sherman Antitrust Act, 282B, 284B, 332B
Sherman Silver Purchase Act, 282B
Shermarke, Abdirashid Ali (president of Somalia), 357A
Sheshonk (king of Egypt), 10A
Shi Ching (Book of Songs), 13C
Shih Huang Ti (emperor of China), 24B, 25B
Shiite Muslim terrorists, 368A
Shiites, 76B
Shilluk, 220B
Shiloh, battle of, 266B
Shimonoseki, 269A
Peace of, 285A
Shinkokinshu, 109C
Shinto, 241A
Ship of Fools (Brant), 149C
Ship of Fools (Porter), 349C
Shipping Board Act, U.S., 300B
Shippingport, 345B
ship(s), 141B, 143B. *See also* boat(s); *individual ships*
bowsprits, 115B
Corinthian, 15B
galleys, 109B
Greek, 13B
gun-mounted, 129B
gyrostabilizers on, 295A
iron-hulled, 229B
iron ore cargo, 279B
Japanese, 49B
jib sails, 151B
longships, 77B
masts, 151B, 169B
measure of distance travelled, 151B
in the Mediterranean, 121B
paddle-wheel, 55B
Phoenician, 9B, 13B
rudders, 109B, 115B
steamship, 245B, 273A
Shiraz, 112C
Shirer, William, 327C
Shitennoji, 65C
Shoa, 158B
Shockley, William, 327B, 335B
shoe-lasting machine, 279B
Shonas, 90C, 109B, 150B
Shore, Sir John (governor-general of India), 231A
shorthand, 281B
Shoshonean people, 83A
Shostakovich, Dmitri, 341C, 357C
Shotoku, Prince, *65*
Shrewsbury
battle of, 134A
Treaty of, 116A
Shrivijaya, Shrivijayans, 70C, 72C, 76C, 88C, 90C, 92C
Shropshire, battle of, 34A
Shropshire Lad, A (Houseman), 285C
Shugart, Alan, 357B
Shuja (shah of Afghanistan), 255A
Shungopovi, 115A
Shushtar, 61B
shuttlecock, 123B
Siam, Siamese, 83B, 110C, 114C, 134C, 140C, 162C, 166C, 168C, 174C, 180C, 188C, 190C, 198C, 218C, 220C, 225A, 231A, 233A, 271A, 288A, 339A. *See also* Thailand
and Austria-Hungary, 301A
and Britain, 293A
and France, 283A
and Germany, 301A
government, 315A
and Japan, 309A
Sukhotai dynasty, 110C
and United States, 250B, 305A
Sian, 73C, 103B
Sibelius, Jean, 283C, 287C, 289C
Siberia, 69B, 172A, 182C, 186C, 190C, 206C, 210C, 282A, 303A, 306A, 340A
Sibthorpe, John, 185B
Sibylline Books, 31A
Sicily, Sicilians, 8A, 12C, 13A, *20,* 25A, 27A, 98B, 100B, 103B, 103C, 104B, 106A, 106B, 108B, 114B, 116B, 117B, 120B, 132B, 134B, 136B, 138B, 164A, 206A, 208A, 244A, 266A, 282B, 330A, 330B
and Arabs, 78B, 80B, 82B, 86B
medicine, 41B
and Naples, 258A, 260A
and Normans, 94B
and Persia, 79B
religion, 133C
riot in, 284A
slave trade, 27A

Sick Child, The (Munch), 281C
Sicyon, 14C
Siddhartha Gautama, 15C, 19C
Siddis, 180C, 216B
Sidney, Algernon, 198A
Sidney, Sir Philip, 171C, 173C
Sidqi, Atif (prime minister of Egypt), 371A
Siècle de Louis XIV (Voltaire), 215C
Siegfried Line, 302A
Siemens AG, 379B
Siemens-Martin process, 265B
Siena, 125C, 127C
  University, 115C
Siena Cathedral, 119C
Sienkiewicz, Henryk, 283C
Sierra Leone, 16A, 138C, 227A, 237A, 239A, 249A, 279A, 347A, 353A
  and Brazil, 168B
  government, 355A
Sierra Leone Company, 231A
Siete Partidas, 129C
Sigismund, John (king of Hungary), 160A, 168A
Sigismund I (king of Poland), 150A, 154A
Sigismund II Augustus (king of Poland), 162A, 168A
Sigismund IV Vasa (king of Poland and Sweden), 172A, 174A
Sigismund (king of the Romans), 134A, 136A, 138A
Sigmund of Tyrol, 142A
Significance of the Frontier in American History, The (Turner), 283C
Signing of the Declaration of Independence (Trumbull), 243C
Signorelli, Luca, 149C
Signoret, Simone, 347C
Sihanouk, Norodom (king of Cambodia), 357A, 377A, 379A
Sijilmassa, 74B
Sijistan province, 87B
Sikandar Lodi (king of Delhi), 146C, 148C, 154C
Sikandar Shah (king of Bengal), 130C
Sikhs, Sikh Wars, 177C, 216C, 231A, 239A, 253A, 255A, 257A, 259A
Sikkim, 187C
Sikorsky, Igor, 293B, 323B
Silas Marner (Eliot), 267C
Silence, The (movie), 349C
Silence of the Lambs (movie), 377C
Silesia, 114A, 184A, 212A, 214A, 218A
silicone compound, 323B, 327B
Silistria, battle of, 46A
silk, silk industry, 10B, 34B, 57B, 63B, 65B, 115B, 117B, 133B, 155B
  in France, 125B
  in Japan, 99B
  in Lyons, 250A
  silk-screening, 63B, 141B, 349C
  in Spain, 83B
Silkwood, Karen, 364C
Silla, kingdom of, 64C, 70C, 84C
silo, 275B
Silva Bernardes, Artur da (president of Brazil), 308C
Silvae (Statius), 39C
silver, 4B, 87B, 93B, 103B, 121B
  Bland-Allison Act, 276B
  price of, 364C
Sherman Silver Purchase Act, 282B
Silvester I, Pope, 51A, 53A
Silvester III (antipope), 93C, 95C
Sim, Georges, 337C
Simcoe, John, 230B
Simenon, Georges, 337C
Simeon I (tsar of Bulgaria), 82A
Simmons, William J., 296B
Simon, Neil, 351C
Simone Guidi, Tommaso di Giovanni di, 137C
Simonstown Agreement, 360A
Simplon Pass, 234A
Simpson, Georgiana R., 304B
Simpson, Nicole Brown, 380C, *381,* 382C, 384C
Simpson, O. J., 380C, *381,* 382C, 384C
Simpson, Wallis, 318A
Sinagua, 59A, 99A
Sinai Peninsula, 8A, 291A, 301A, 355A
  1570 B.C., 6A
Sinatra, Frank, 385C
Sinchi Roca culture, 97A
Sinclair, Harry, 308B
Sinclair, Upton, 289C, 331C, 355C
Sind, 112C, 114C, 130C, 174C
Sindhia, 237A
Sindok (king of East Java), 84C
Singapore, 245A, 326C, 334C, 347A, 349A, 350A, 351A, 374A, 385A
  and ASEAN, 352A
  government, 369A
Singara, 52B, 54B
Singer, Isaac Bashevis, 317C, 347C, 363C, 377C
Singing in the Rain (Kelly), 341C
Single European Act, 370B
Sinhalese, 60C
Sinkiang province, 351A
Sinn Féin, 290A, 380B
Sino-Japanese War, 285A
Sinope, 10C, 12C, 262A
Siouan language, 73A, 91A
Sioux, Sioux War, 177A, 246B, 248B, 260B, 270B, 274B, 282B
Sir Gawain and the Green Knight, 135C
Sirhan, Sirhan, 354C
Siricius, Pope, 57A
Sis, 132B
Sister Carrie (Dreiser), 287C
Sisters of Mercy, Order of, 183C
Sistine Chapel, 145C, 153C, 163C
Sistine Madonna (Raphael), 153C
Sistova, Peace of, 228A
Sitka, 234B
Sittannavasal, 67C
Sitting Bull, 274B, 276B
Siwah, 22A
Six Articles, 161C, 163C
Six Characters in Search of an Author (Pirandello), 307C
Six-Day War, 355A
Sixteen Kingdoms, 50B
16th Street Baptist Church, 348C
Sixtus II, Pope, 47A
Sixtus IV, Pope, 143C
Sixtus V, Pope, 173C
"Sixty Years of Living Architecture" (Wright), 341C
Skagway, 286B
Skandagupta (emperor of India), 60C
Skanderbeg, 138B, 140A
Skate, The (Chardin), 211C
Sketch Book, The (Irving), 245C
Sketches by Boz (Dickens), 253C
Sketchpad, 349B
Ski-Doo snowmobile, 347B
ski patrols, 157B
Skidmore, Louis, 339C
skiing, 69B
skin grafts, 335B
Skin of Our Teeth, The (Wilder), 329C
Sky Xul, 77A
Skylab, 359B
skylights, 95A
Slaughterhouse Five (Vonnegut), 357C
slavery. *See names of individual countries involved*
Slaveykov, Petko, 267C
Slavs, 70B, 78A, 81B, 81C, 84A
Slivnitza, battle of, 278A
Slovakia, 320A, 378B
Slovenes, 308A, 310A
Slovenia, 372B, 374B, 376B
Slovik, Eddie, 334B
Slowacki, Juliuzs, 251C
Sluys, 126A
smallpox, 64C, 83B, 206B, 229A
Smeaton, John, 217B, 219B
Smetana, Bedrich, 271C
Smith, Adam, 223C
Smith, Alfred E., 310B
Smith, Bessie, 307C
Smith, Betty, 331C
Smith, Horace, 261B
Smith, James, 263B
Smith, Jedediah S., 246B, 248B
Smith, John, *178,* 179A
Smith, Joseph, 249C, 257C
Smith, Maggie, 357C
Smith, Margaret Chase, 336C
Smith, Samantha, 368C
Smith, Samuel, 343B
Smith, Sir Harry, 259A
Smith, William, 245A
Smith-Connally Anti-Strike Act, 330B
Smithfield, 122A
Smoke and Steel (Sandburg), 305C
"Smoke Gets in Your Eyes" (Kern), 315C
smoke screens, 327B
Smokers (Brouwer), 187C
smoking, 167B, 350C, 372C. *See also* tobacco
  and cancer, 383B
  secondhand smoke, 379B
Smolensk, 192A, 330A
  battle of, 240A, *241*
Smollett, Tobias George, 215C
Smuts, Jan Christian (prime minister of South Africa), 299A, 322C
Smyrna, 10C, 41A, 297A, 304A, 305A, 307A
snails, 31B
Snow White and the Seven Dwarfs (Disney), 321C
snowmaking machine, 371B
snowmobile, 323B, 347B
soap, 37B, 75B, 91B, 99B
Soares, Mário (president of Portugal), 370B
Sobraon, battle of, 259A
Sobrero, Ascanio, 259B
soccer, 111B, 269C
Social Contract, The (Rousseau), 219C
Social and Religious History of the Jews, A (Baron), 319C
Social Security Act, 316B
Social War, 27A
Socialism, Socialists, 269C, 302B, 310A
Socialist International Congress, 280A
Socialist Labor Party, 274B
Society Islands, 257A
Socrates, 19C, 21C
Sofala, 150B, 152B
Sofia, 78A, 132B
soft drink industry, 331B
Sogdiana, 34B
Soissons, 77C
  battle of, 302A
Synod of, 101C
Sokoine, Edward (president of Tanzania), 369A
Sokoto, 249A
Sokotra, 281A
soldering, 169B
Soldiers' Bonus Act, 308B
Solferino, battle of, 264A
Solis, Juan Díaz de, 153A
Solomon, Temple of, 14B
Solomon Islands, 168C, 220C, 328C, 330C
  independence of, 363A
  in United Nations, 362A
Solomon (king of Israel), 10B, 11C
Solon, 14C
Solway Moss, battle of, 162A
Solyut 1, 357B
Solzhenitsyn, Aleksandr Isayevich, 349C, 360B
Somalia, Somali, 82C, 86C, 114C, 156B, 162B, 347A, 357A
  and Britain, 281A, 287A
  famine in, 378A
  and Germany, 281A
  and Italy, 287A
  and United Nations, 378A, 380A
  and United States, 378A
Some Considerations on the Keeping of Negroes (Woolman), 219C
Somme, battle of, 298A
Somme le Roy, La, 119
Somoza Debayle, Anastasio (president of Nicaragua), 365A
Somoza García, Anastasio (dictator of Nicaragua), 318C
Son of a Servant (Strindberg), 281C
sonar, 297B
Sonatas of Three Parts (Purcell), 199C
Sonderbund, 256A, 258A
Sondheim, Stephen, 345C
Sones, Mason, 345B
Songgy I, 132C
Songhai empire, 82C, 90C, 126C, 142B, 144B, 146B, 152B, 154B, 164B, 172B, 186B
Songs of Experience (Blake), 231C
Songs of Innocence (Blake), 229C
Songs of Jamaica (McKay), 293C
Soninke Confederacy, 212B
Soninke dynasty. *See* Ghana
Sonnambula, La (Bellini), 251C
Sonnets from the Portuguese (Browning), 261C
Sonnets to Orpheus (Rilke), 319C
Sonni Ali the Great (king of Songhai), 142B, 144B, 146B
Sons and Lovers (Lawrence), 295C
Sons and Soldiers (Shaw), 333C
Sons of Liberty, 219A
Sony Corporation, 365B, 367B
Sopatrus, 53A
Sophia (empress of Russia), 196A
Sophistic movement, 41C
Sophocles, 19C
Sophonisba (Trissino), 155C
Sorbonne, 327B
Sorcerer's Apprentice (Dukas), 287C
Sordello (Browning), 255C
Sosa, Sammy, 385C
Sossos, 96C
Soto, Marco Aurelio (dictator of Honduras), 274C
Soubise, Benjamin, 182A
Soufflot, Jacques, 217C
Souligna-Vongsa (king of Laos), 186C
Soulouque, Faustin (emperor of Haiti), 258C
Souls of Black Folk, The (Du Bois), 289C
Soumangouroun, 108C
sound, speed of, 337B

Sound of Music, The (Rodgers and Hammerstein), 347C
Sound of Music, The (movie), 351C
sound wave duplication, 311B
Sousa, Tomé de, 165A
Souter, David, 374C
South Africa, South Africans, 109B, 114C, 253A, 297A. *See also* Boers
1000 B.C., 10A
and African National Congress, 375A, 379A
and Angola, 372A
and Antarctica, 346A
apartheid in, 347A, 353A, 355C, 373A, 376A, 377A, 381A
and Britain, 275A, 277A, 285A, 287A, 289A, 297A, 312A, 347A, 360A
and Canada, 286B
and Ciskei Black Homeland, 367A
and Cuba, 372A
and European Community, 368A, 370A
exploration of, 225A
and Germany, 279A, 284A, 322C
government, 293A
and Holland, 190B, 192B, 196B
and Myanmar, 263A
and Namibia, 372A
Steven Biko in, 363A
Union of, 291A, 293A
universal suffrage in, 381A
and Windhoek, 297A
South Africa Status bill, 317A
South African Council of Churches, 355C
South America, 149A, 151A, 155A, 157A, 159A, 159B, 215A, 222C. *See also individual countries*
Communism in, 316C
Jesuits in, 165A
nonaggression pact, 314C
slave trade, 167A
"South Sea Bubble," 204A
Spain and, 246C
South Carolina, 157A, 167A, 185A, 195A, 197A, 205A, 209A, 211A, 248B, 250B, 264B, 266B, 298B
South Carolina Exposition and Protest (Calhoun), 248B
South Carolina Railroad, 249B
South Dakota, 213A, 280B, 282B
South Kingston, 195A
South Korea. *See* Korea
South Pacific, 50B, 168C
South Pacific (Rodgers and Hammerstein), 339C
"South Sea Bubble," 204A
South Seas, 254B
South Shetland Islands, 245A
South Vietnam. *See* Vietnam
South Wales, 88A, 90A
Southampton, 88A
Southeast Asia, 379B
Southeast Asia Collective Defense Treaty, 342A
Southeast Asia Treaty Organization (SEATO), 342A, 362A
Southern Christian Leadership Conference, 344C
Southern Death cult, 135A, 139A
Southern Irish church, 69C
Southern Leadership Conference, 354C
Southern Yemen. *See* Yemen
Southey, Robert, 235C, 241C
Souvenirs de Solferino (Dunant), 267C
Soviet Union, Soviets, 306A. *See also* Russia, Russians
and Afghanistan, 364A, 365A, 372A
and Albania, 346B
and Aldrich Ames, 380C
arts, 349C, 357C
and Austria, 334A
and Baltics, 376B
and Berlin, 336B, 338B, 346A
and Britain, 308A, 320A, 326A, 330A, 336B, 338B, 348A, 354A, 358A
and Bulgaria, 332A
and Central Powers, 300A
Chernobyl disaster, 370B
and China, 313A, 346B, 356B
Churchill on, 336A
collapse of, 376B
and Colombia, 354A
Cominform, 336A, 342B
Communism in, 314A, 318A, 340B, 346B, 350B, 352B, 362B, 366B, 370B, 372B, 374B, 376B
and Crimea, 332A
and Cuba, 348A, 348B
and Czechoslovakia, 356B, 376B
earthquake in, 372B
and East Germany, 360B
and Egypt, 356A
and Estonia, 324A, 372B
and Finland, 322A, 332A, 342B, 356B
Five-Year Plans, 310A, 352B, 356B
and France, 316A, 320A
and Germany, 320A, 326A, 328A, 330A, 332A, 334A
government, 302A, 306A, 314A, 338B, 340B, 344B, 362B, 364B, 368B, 372B
and Gregorian calendar, 303B
and Hungary, 302A, 332A, 334A, 342B, 376B
and India, 356A
and Japan, 321A, 322C, 334A
and Latvia, 324A, 372B
and League of Nations, 322A
and Lithuania, 302A, 324A, 372B, 374B
and Manchukuo, 321A
and Manchuria, 334C
and Mongolia, 352A
and NATO, 338A
and Nicholas II, 302A
and North Vietnam, 351A
and nuclear weapons, 338A, 344A, 352A
and Poland, 318A, 320A, 322A, 332A, 334A
and Prussia, 332A
religion, 347C
and Romania, 318A, 332A
and Rosenbergs, 338C
and Russian Orthodox Church, 302A
and Sakharov, 370B
science and technology, 339B, 347B, 353B, 355B, 357B, 361B
and South Korea, 366A
space program, 345B, 347B, 353B, 354A, 355B, 357B, 361B
and Turkey, 309A
and United Nations, 332B, 354A
and United States, 318B, 330A, 334A, 336A, 336B, 340A, 344A, 346A, 348A, 350A, 354A, 356A, 358A, 360A, 361B, 366A, 368A, 370A, 374A, 384A
and Vatican City, 374A
in Warsaw Pact, 342A
and West Berlin, 336B
and West Germany, 356A, 372A
World War II, 322A, 324A, 326A, 328A, 330A, 332A, 334A
and Yugoslavia, 332A
Soweto, 369A
soya derivatives, 317B
soybeans, 331B
Soyinka, Wole, 349C
Soyuz, 361B
Spaansche Brabander (Bradero), 181C
Spaccio della Bestia Trionfante (Bruno), 173C
Spacek, Sissy, 365C
spade, double-bladed, 95B
Spaeth, Mary, 353B
Spain, Spaniards, 102B, 144A, 146A, 149A, 152A, 164A, 166A, 177A, 177B, 202A, 224B, 268A, 320A
2500 B.C.–206 B.C., 4C, 5A, 5C, 11A, 17A, 25A
agriculture, 153B
and America, 147A, 159B, 163A, 165B, 176A, 177B, 205A
Anglo-Spanish War, 209A
and Antwerp, 172A
and Aragon, 110B
and Argentina, 244C
arts, 5C, 87C, 97C, 99B, 109C, 129C, 171C, 175C, 185C, 189C, 239C, 253C, 373C
and Belgium, 170A
and Berbers, 307A
and Bolivia, 161A, 270C
and Britain, 128A, 146A, 154A, 156A, 158A, 166A, 172A, 184A, 192A, 204A, 206A, 208A, 210A, 212A, 213A, 218A, 224A, 232A, 232B, 236A, 307A
bullfights in, 95C
and Byzantines, 68B
and Canary Islands, 144B, 149B
Catalan and Basque languages, 360B
and Chile, 161A, 244C, 270C
and China, 170C
and Colombia, 161A, 240C
Communism in, 362B
and Costa Rica, 244C
and Cuba, 157B, 161A, 244C, 260C, 270C, 284B, 286C
and Ecuador, 160A, 246C, 270C
education, 85B, 101C, 111C, 139C, 149C, 151C, 157C
and European Community, 370B
exploration, 155B
and Falkland Islands, 221A
and Florida, 169A
and France, 130B, 148A, 150A, 154A, 156A, 174A, 190A, 192A, 194A, 200A, 230A, 234B, 238A, 240A, 246A, 264A, 307A
and Genoa, 158A
and Germany, 156A, 282A
and Gibraltar, 364B, 368B
government, 64B, 84B, 92B, 214A, 216A, 252A, 256A, 272A, 274A, 292A, 306A, 312A, 318A, 352B, 358B, 362B, 366B
and Guam, 287A
and Holland, 176C, 186A, 186C, 200A
and Holy Roman Empire, 154A
and Honduras, 161A, 171A
and Inca, 161A
industry, 34A, 83B, 103B, 113B, 358B
and Ireland, 176A
and Japan, 182C, 275A
law and society, 159B, 165B, 167C, 192A, 244A, 250A, 270A, 282A, 292A, 312A, 352B
and League of Nations, 310A
lepers in, 95B
and Malaga, 318A
and Malaya, 188C
and Marquesas Islands, 174C
and the Mediterranean, 290A
and Mexico, 155A, 157A, 159A, 228C, 238C, 244C, 266C
mines, mining, 119B
and Moors, 72B, 74B, 86B, 98B, 169C, 178A
and Morocco, 180B, 265A, 267A, 342A
Nasrid dynasty, 112B
and NATO, 366B
and Netherlands, 180A
and New Granada, 165A
and New Mexico, 201A
and Newfoundland, 165A
and Nootka Sound, 228B
and North Africa, 148B, 150B, 152B, 164B, 229A
and Ottoman Empire, 168B
and Panama, 175A
and Paraguay, 161A, 209A
and Peru, 159A, 224C, 268C, 270C, 272C
and Philippines, 156C, 162C, 168C, 170C, 172C, 174C, 184C, 226A, 285A
politics, 370B
and Portugal, 158C, 170A, 192A, 194A, 204A, 207A, 215A, 222C, 234C
and Puerto Rico, 153A, 270C, 286C
and Quadruple Alliance, 208A, 252A
religion, 73C, 82B, 90B, 96B, 114B, 133C, 147C, 149C, 169C, 195C
and Romans, 36A, 38A, 54A
and San Juan Islands, 230C
and Santo Domingo, 266C, 268C
and Savoy, 180A
science and technology, 89B, 91B, 105B, 139B, 143B, 151B, 175B
settlement of, 58B, 60B, 62B
Seven Years' War, 219A
and South America, 246C
Spanish-American War, 286A, 286B, 286C, 287A
and Switzerland, 156A
transportation, 147B
and Turkey, 166B, 170B
and United States, 244B, 274C, 284B, 286B, 340A
and Uruguay, 183A, 232C
and Venezuela, 161A, 244C
Westo War, 197A
Spallanzani, Lazzaro, 225B
Spam, 315B
Spanish-American War, 286A, 287A
Spanish Armada, 172A
Spanish Civil War, 318A
Spanish Inquisition, 145C, 158A
Spanish language, 147C
Spanish Netherlands, 190A, 202A, 204A, 206A
Spanish West Florida, 238B
Spark, Muriel, 347C
Sparta, 12C, 14C, 16C, 20B, 20C, 24C, 48A
earthquake in, 18C
slave trade, 18C, 24C
Spartacus, 29A

species, plant and animal, 383B
Speck, Richard, 352C
Spectator, 205C, 211C
spectroscope, X-ray, 293B
spectroscopy, nuclear magnetic resonance (NMR), 335B
Spener, Philipp Jacob, 195C
Spengler, Oswald, 303C
Spenser, Edmund, 171C, 173C
Sperry, Elmer, 291B, 293B, 299B
Speyer, Treaty of, 168A
Sphinx, Great, *3,* 3C
Spice Islands, 72C, 128C, 140C, 153B, 156C, 163C
spices, 34B, 84C
Spielberg, Steven, 361C, 379C, 385C
spinach, 79B
Spindletop, 288B
spinning mule, 225B
Spínola, António (president of Portugal), 360B
Spinoza, Baruch, 187C, 191C, 195C
Spires, 150A
  Diet of, 162A
Spiridion (Sand), 255C
Spirit of Medieval Philosophy, The (Gilson), 315C
Spitak, 372B
Spitsbergen, 109B, 345B
Split, 304A
spoke reel, 83B
Spoleto, 104B, 112B
spool winder, 83B
Spoon River Anthology, The (Masters), 297C
Sportsman's Sketches, A (Turgenev), 263C
Spring and Autumn Annals of Mr. Lu, The, 25C
Spring (Botticelli), 143C
Springfield, 226B, 283C
Spurs, battle of, 152A
Sputnik, 345B
Spy, The (Cooper), 245C
Squire of Alsatia, The (Shadwell), 199C
Sri Lanka, 60C, 76C, 88C, 90C, 104C, 110C, 116C, 134C, 144C, 150C, 164C, 168C, 170C, 174C, 186C, 190C, 193A, 194C, 359A, 385A. *See also* Ceylon
Ssu-ma Kuang, 97C
St. Agnese Fuori Le Mura, Church of, 69C
St. Albans, 110A
  Abbey of, *76,* 77C
  battle of, 140A
St. Andrews, University of, 135C
St. Andrews Island, 213A
St. Apollinaire, Church of, 65C
St. Auban du Cormier, battle of, 146A
St. Aubin, battle of, 146A
St. Augustine, 169A, 203A, 211A
St. Augustine Bay, 188B
St. Bartholomew's Day, Massacre of, 168A
St. Boniface, Church of, 77C
St. Brice, Massacre of, 90A
St. Christopher, 193A
St. Clair-sur-Epte, Treaty of, 84A
St. Cloud, 155C
St. Croix, 211A
St. Denis, Abbey of, 69C
St. Denis, Ruth, 291C
St. Dizier, 162A
St. Edmunds Bury Abbey, 93C
St. Eustatius, 193A
St. Florian Church, 155C
St. George, *148*
St. George's Cay, battle of, 232C
St. George's Chapel, 141C
St. Germain
  Edict of, 167C
  Peace of (1679), 196A
  Treaty of (1919), 304A
St. Gotthard, Church of, 127B
St. Gotthard-on-the-Raab, battle of, 192A
St. Gotthard Pass, 103B
St. Helena, 190B, 242A, 244A
St. Jean's Church, 73C
St. Jerome (Cranach), 151C
St. John, 211A
St. Johns, 205A, 253B, 276B
St. John's Church (Ghent), 137C
St. John's College, 255C
St. John's Island, 234B
St. Johns River, 167A, 169A
St. Joseph, *174*
St. Jude Medical Center, 363B
St. Kitts, 183A, 224C, 366A
St. Lawrence River, 159A, *160,* 177A, 183A, 185A, 253B
St. Lawrence Seaway, 314B, 346C
St. Louis, 203C, 211A, 219A, 275B, 279C, 351C
St. Louis Browns, 333C
St. Louis Cardinals, 329C, 331C, 333C, 337C, 351C, 355C, 367C, 369C, 371C, 385C
St. Louis Circuit Court, 258B
St. Lucia, 189A, 193A, 224B, 232C, 236C, 240C, 308C, 364A
St. Lucia Bay, 278C
St. Maria dei Frari, 147C
St. Maria Novella, 119C
St. Mark's Cathedral, 93C
St. Martial school, 83C
St. Martin's Church, 89C
St. Mary with Burgomaster Meier (Holbein), 157C
St. Matthew Passion (Bach), 211C
St. Matthias Islands, 332C
St. Mihiel, 296A
  battle of, 302A
St. Nicholas' Feast (Steen), 193C
St. Omer, Treaty of, 142A
St. Paul, Jesuit College of, 163C
St. Peter's Church, 53A, 163C
St. Petersburg, 202A, 204A, 234A, 253C, 256A, 282A, 290A, 300A. *See also Leningrad*
St. Petersburg Protocol, 248A
St. Pierre Island, 230B, 234B
St. Pierre (Martinique), 288C
St. Quentin, battles of, 164A, 272A
St. Sauvière de Vicomte Normandy, Abbey of, 107B
St. Simons Island, 213A
St. Thomas, 195A, 211A, 234B
St. Vincent, 219A, 232C
St. Vincent de Paul, 183C
St. Vitus's Dance, 74A, 92A
"St. Valentine's Day Massacre," 310B
stadiums, enclosed, 353B
Staël, Madame de, 235C, 237C
Stafford, John (Archbishop of Canterbury), 139C
Stage Representations of Actors (Toyokuni), 231C
Stagecoach (movie), 321C
stained glass, 99C, 103C, 109C, 151B
Stalin, Joseph (leader of Soviet Union), 306A, 314A, 316A, 318A, 330A, 332A, 334A, 340B, 370B
Stalingrad, 328A, 330A. *See also* Volgograd
Stallone, Sylvester, 363C
Stambolov, Stefan (premier of Bulgaria), 284A
Stamford, 187A
Stamford Bridge, 94A
Stamp Act, 219A
stamps, wooden, 63B
Standard, battle of the, 102A
Standard and Poor's Index, 267C
Standard Oil Company, 278B, 287B, 315A, 317A
Stanford University, 323C, 355B
Stangebro, 174A
Stanhope, Philip Dormer, 221C
Stanislavsky, Konstantin, 287C
Stanislavsky Method, 339C
Stanisław I Leszczynski (king of Poland), 202A, 204A, 210A
Stanisław II Augustus Poniatowski (king of Poland), 218A, *218,* 232A
Stanley, Henry Morton, 273A
Stanley, Wendell, 331B
Stanlin, Joseph, 346B
Stanton, Elizabeth Cady, 258B, 272B
Stanwyck, Barbara, 319C
Star Chamber, 144A, 158A, 186A
"Star Spangled Banner, The" (Key), 240B, 313C
"Star Wars" defense system, 366C
Stark (US ship), 370A
Starley, James, 273B
Starr, Kenneth, 384C
Starr, Ringo, 383C
Starr-Edwards valve, 347B
START II arms treaty, 378A
START (Strategic Arms Reduction Talks), 366A
Stasuma, 269A
State of the Union speeches, 246B, 350C
Staten Island, 187A, 224B
Statius, 39C
Statue of Liberty, 278B, 280B, 370C
Staub, Bruno Ference (president of Hungary), 372B
Staudinger, Herman, 311B
Ste. Geneviève, 211A
Ste. Menehould, Treaty of, 180A
steady-state theory, 337B
steam power, 23B
steamroller, 271B
Stedingen, 113C
steel, 67B, 261B
  in construction, 279C
  manufacturing, 265B
  stainless, 295A
Steele, Sir Richard, 205C
Steen, Jan, 193C
Steenkerque, battle of, 200A
Steffen, Lincoln, 289C
Steiger, Rod, 353C
Stein, Edith, 329C
Stein, Gertrude, 293C, 309C, 315C, 337C
Steinbeck, John, 317C, 319C, 321C, 323C, 329C, 335C, 349C, 355C
Stela cult, 59A
Stella, Joseph, 295C, 303C, 305C
Stella Dallas (movie), 319C
Stellaland Republic, 279A
Stellenbosch, 196B
stencil machine, 275B
Stendhal, 249C, 255C
Stephen, Saint, 33A
Stephen I, Pope, 47A
Stephen III, Pope, 75C
Stephen (king of England), 104A
Stephen of Blois (king of England), 102A
Stephens, John Lloyd, 254C
Steps to the Temple (Crashaw), 189C
Steptoe, Patrick, 355B
Stern, Otto, 331B
Sternberg, Josef von, 313C
Sterns Creek culture, 63A
sterols, synthetic, 339B
stethoscope, 291B
Stettin, 208A
  Peace of, 168A
Stevens, Siaka (prime minister of Sierra Leone), 355A
Stevenson, Adlai, 340C
Stevenson, Robert Louis, 277C, 279C, 281C
Stevin, Simon, 173B
Stewart, Dugald, 243C
Stewart, Jane, 251B
Stieglitz, Alfred, 307C
Stilicho, Flavius, 58B
Stimson, Henry, 324B
Sting, The (movie), 359C
Stirling Bridge, 120A
Stirling Castle, 120A, 122A
stirrup, 67B
Stobaios, Johannes, 63C
Stockach, battle of, 234A
Stockhausen, Karlheinz, 373C
Stockholm, 179B, 255C, 346A, 370B
  Treaty of, 208A
Stockholm (Swedish ocean liner), 342C
Stockton, Robert F., 258B
Stoddard, Joshua, 263B
Stoicism, 23C
Stoke-on-Trent, battle of, 146A
Stokes, Carl, 354C
Stokowski, Leopold, 293C
Stolbova, Peace of, 180A
Stolypin, Piotr (premier of Russia), 292A
Stone, Edward Durell, 319C
Stone, Lucy, 272B
Stone, Oliver, 371C, 377C
stone, stoneware, 77B, 83C, 103B
  churches, 71B
  circles, 3A, 3C
  monuments, 7C
  tools, 3B, 91B
  unglazed, 221B
  used by Inca, 139A, 139B
Stone Breaker, The (Courbet), 261C
Stonehenge, 3C, 5C
Stones of Venice, The (Ruskin), 263C
Stony Point, 224B
Storm and Stress (Klinger), 223C
Stormont House, 358B
Stormy Sky, 59A, 61A
Story of a South African Farm, The (Schreiner), 279C
Story of Gösta Berling, The (Lagerlöf), 283C
Story of the Bamboo Gatherer, The, 83C
Stout, Rex, 333C
stove
  cast-iron, 187B
  coal-burning, 185B
  Franklin, 213B
  gas kitchen, 267B
Stowe, Harriet Beecher, 261C, 263C
Strabo, 31C, 33C
Strachey, Lytton, 303C
Stradivari, Antonio, 193C
Straits
  Convention, 254A
  Settlement, 271A
Straits of Gibraltar, 120B
Strand, Mark, 375C
Stranger, The (Camus), 327C
Strange Case of Dr. Jekyll and Mr. Hyde (Stevenson), 281C
Strasberg, Lee, 339C
Strasbourg, 54A, 161C, 179C, 196A, 252A, 338A, 346B
  University, 273C
Strategematica (Frontinus), 39C
Straten, Florence van, 329B, 337B
Stratford, 181C
Stratford, John (Archbishop of Canterbury), 127C
Strato, 23B
Strauss, David Friedrich, 253C
Strauss, Johann, 271C

Strauss, Levi, 261B
Strauss, Richard, 281C, 285C, 287C, 293C, 295C, 309C
Stravaganze del conte, Le (Cimarosa), 221C
Stravinsky, Igor, 293C, 319C, 339C
Streep, Meryl, 367C
streetcar, horse-drawn, 251B
Streetcar Named Desire, A (Williams), 337C
Streisand, Barbra, 355C
streptomycin, 333B
strikes, 8A, 355A
 air traffic controllers, 366C
 coal, 286B, 286B (U.S.), 358B, 360B, 368B
 cordwainers, 238B
 electrical workers, 352B
 printers, 160A
 railway, 361A
 shoemakers, 236B
 textile workers, 176C
Strindberg, August, 277C, 281C
String Quintet in C (Schubert), 249C
Strong, Harriet, 279B
Stuart, Charles Edward, 212A, 214A, 226A
Stuart dynasty. *See* Scotland
Stuart Lake, 236B
Stuart Little (White), 335C
Stubbs, George, 219C
Stubbs, William, 275C
stucco, 119B
Student Nonviolent Coordinating Committee, 352C
Student Prince, The (Romberg), 309C
Studies in the Psychology of Sex (Ellis), 321C
Study in Scarlet, A (Doyle), 281C
Sture, Sten, 142A
Sturgeon, William, 245B
Stuttgart, 260A
Stuyvesant, Peter, 189A, 191A
Styria, 115B, 116A, 118A
Styron, William, 355C
Su Sung, 97B
Suakin, 269A
Suazo Córdova, Roberto (president of Honduras), 367A
Subiaco, 143B
Subjection of Women (Mill), 273C
Sublette, William, 252B
Sublime Porte, 192B
submarine(s), 181B. *See also individual submarines*
 atomic-powered, 343B
 detection of, 297B, 327B
 one-man, 223B
 snorkeling, 333B
 sonar navigation on, 329B
 in World War I, 296A, 296B, 298A, 298B, 300A, 300B
 in World War II, 322B, 328B, 330B
subway, 287B, 289B
sucaryl, 339B
Suchouin, 167C
Suchow, 319A
Sudan, 157B, 178B, 184B, 186B, 196B, 218B, 247A, 309A, 384A
 arts, 33C
 and Britain, 279A, 285A, 287A
 and Egypt, 245A, 279A, 285A, 287A
 and Ethiopia, 180B
 famine in, 198B, 204B, 212B
 and France, 302A
 Fundj, 214B
 government, 220B, 275A, 357A
 independence of, 343A
 and Mali, 346A
 and Morocco, 216B
 and Ottoman Empire, 245A
 religion, 208B, 223A, 263A
 and Senegal, 346A
 and United States, 302A
Sudbury, Simon (Archbishop of Canterbury), 133C
Sudetenland, 318A, 320A
Suetonius, Gaius, 39C
Suevi, 58B
Suez Canal, 263A, 265A, 273A, 273C, 275A, 345A, 361A
 battle of, 297A
 and Britain, 343A
 Convention, 281A
 in Yom Kippur War, 359A
 Zone, 342A
suffrage *See also* voting rights, Voting Rights Act
 universal, 260A, 268A, 282A, 286A, 289A, 356B, 381A
 woman, 272B, 276B, 284B, 288A, 290A, 300B, 302B, 304B, 310B, 312A, 322B, 346B
Sufi, 109C
sugar, 151B, 210B, 215A, 215B
 Byzantines and, 69B
 Egyptians and, 73B
 England and, 141B
 Jamaica and, 187A
 Moors and, 72B
 Portugal and, 146B
 rationing, 328B
Sugar Act, 219A
sugarcane, 63B, 99B, 103B, 157B, 159A
Suger, Abbé, 103C
Suharto (president of Indonesia), 385A
Sui dynasty. *See* China, Chinese
suiboko, 123C
Suiko (empress of Japan), 66C
Sujin (emperor of Japan), 44B
Sukhotai, kingdom of, 114C
Sukhotai dynasty. *See* Siam
Süleyman I the Magnificent (sultan of Ottoman Empire), 154B, 158A, 158B, 160A, 162A, 168A, 168B
sulfuric acid, 161B
Sulieman (king of Mali), 126C
Sulla, Lucius Cornelius, 27A
Sullivan, John L., 279C, 283C
Sullivan Ordinance, 290B
Sultan Tepe, 13C
Sumatra, 70C, 120C, 134C, 154C, 156C, 158C, 162C, 174C, 178C, 225A, 247A, 295A, 326A
Sumbawa Island, 243A
Sumer, Sumerians, 2B, 3C, 4B, 5B, 5C
Summer's Tale (Cumberland), 219C
Sumner, Charles, 264B
sun
 eclipse of, 14C, 377B
 Temple of the, 77C, 115A, 123A, 135A
 worship of, 9C
Sun Also Rises, The (Hemingway), 311C
Sun Rising in a Mist (Turner), 237C
Sun Yat-sen (provisional president of Republic of China), 291A, 293A, 295A
Sunda Islands, 159A, 174C
Sunday School Union, 237C
Sundiata, 112C
Sunflower, New Mexico II (O'Keeffe), 317C
sunflowers, 153B
Sung dynasty. *See* China, Chinese
Sung Yüeh pagoda, 63C
Sungo (king of Korea), 235A
Sunny (Kern), 309C
Sunrise (movie), 311C
Sunsanna, 214B
Sunset Boulevard (movie), 339C
Suor Angelica (Puccini), 303C
Super Bowl I, 353C
Super Bowl II, 355C
Super Bowl III, 357C
Super Bowl IV, 357C
Super Bowl V, 357C
Super Bowl VI, 359C
Super Bowl VII, 359C
Super Bowl VIII, 361C
Super Bowl IX, 361C
Super Bowl X, 362C
Super Bowl XI, 363C
Super Bowl XII, 363C
Super Bowl XIII, 365C
Super Bowl XIV, 365C
Super Bowl XV, 367C
Super Bowl XVI, 367C
Super Bowl XVII, 367C
Super Bowl XVIII, 369C
Super Bowl XIX, 369C
Super Bowl XX, 371C
Super Bowl XXI, 371C
Super Bowl XXII, 373C
Super Bowl XXIII, 373C
Super Bowl XXIV, 375C
Super Bowl XXV, 377C
Super Bowl XXVI, 377C
Super Bowl XXVII, 379C
Super Bowl XXVIII, 381C
Super Bowl XXIX, 381C
Super Bowl XXX, 383C
Super Bowl XXXI, 385C
Super Bowl XXXII, 385C
superconductivity, 293B
Suppé, Franz von, 267C
Supremacy, Act of, 159C
Supreme Allied Council, 305A
Supreme Court, U.S., 234B, 316B, 340C, 356C, 372C, 374C, 376C, 380C. *See also individual cases*
 on abortion, 358C, 372C
 on acts of Congress, 236B
 on affirmative action, 370C
 and African-Americans, 310B, 354C, 376C
 on Agricultural Adjustment Act, 318B
 on busing, 356C
 on capital punishment, 362C
 on Civil Rights Act (1875), 276B
 on death penalty, 358C
 on discrimination, 278B
 on education, 308B
 on equal pay, 318B
 on Espionage Act, 302B
 on evidence in state cases, 348C
 on federal police power, 288B
 on income tax, 284B, 298B
 and Indians, 250B
 on insurance companies, 332B
 on interstate commerce, 246B, 280B
 Jews on, 298B
 membership of, 252B
 on National Industrial Recovery Act, 316B
 on Northern Securities Company, 288B
 on pacifists, 310B
 on paper money, 278B
 on passport detainment, 344C
 on polygamy, 276B
 on prayer in public schools, 349C
 on presidential powers, 310B
 on public officials and the media, 350C
 on Puerto Ricans, 288B
 on racial quotas, 362C
 on racial segregation, 284B, 300B, 336C, 340C, 342C
 on rights of suspects, 352C
 Robert Bork and, 370C
 on saluting the flag, 331C
 on search and seizure, 338C
 on seizure of steel mills, 340C
 on slavery and slave trade, 254B, 256B
 on state-appointed attorneys, 348C
 on state contracts, 238B, 244B
 and state courts, 242B, 264B
 on state legislatures, 348C
 and steel industry, 346C
 on subversives, 340C
 on union members, 296B
 on vaccinations, 290B
 on Watergate tapes, 360C
 women on, 366C, 378C
 on work hours, 290B
Supreme Headquarters Allied Powers Europe (SHAPE), 338A
Supreme War Council, 300A, 305A
Surakarta, 214C
Surat, 178C, 192C
Surinam, 151A, 175A, 181A, 193A, 219A, 244C, 270C, 361A
Surrealism, Surrealists, 309C, 311C, 313C
Surrey, 188A
surveying, surveys, 45B, 159B, 239B
 photogrammetry, 347B
 theodolite surveying instrument, 169B
Surveyor I, 353B
Suryavarman II (king of Khmer), 99C, 100C
Susa, 16C
 Peace of, 184A
 people, 223A
Susenyos (emperor of Ethiopia), 176B
Suspicion (movie), 325C
Susquehanna River, 181A
Sussex, kingdom of, 60A, 71C, 88A
Sussex (French ship), 298B
Sutherland, I. E., 349B
Sutlej River, 76C
Sutri, Synod of, 95C
Sutter, John, 254B
Sutter's Mill, 258B
Suvarov Island, 287A
Suvorov, Aleksandr Vaslievich, 230A
Suwanne, battle of, 244B
Sveda, Michael, 339B
Svedberg, Theodor, 307B
Svein (king of Denmark), 88A, 90A
Sverris saga (Jonsson), 111C
Sviatoslav, 86A
Svinthila, 68B
Svold, battle of, 90A
Swabia, 108A, 110A
Swabian League, 146A
"Swabian War," 148A
Swahili, 184B
swamp reclamation, 101B
Swan, Joseph, 277B
Swan of Tuonela, The (Sibelius), 283C
Swan River, 249A
Swansea, 195A
Swasey, Ambrose, 295B
Swaziland, 354A, 355A
sweat houses, 67B
Sweden, Swedes, 88A, 92A, 96A, 100A, 130A, 132A, 134A, 140A, 142A, 144A, 145C, 148A, 154A, 156A, 157B, 157C, 158A, 160A, 166A, 168A, 176A, 177B, 178A, 180A, 184A, 186A, 187A, 188A, 189A, 190A, 190B, 191A, 192B, 194A, 196A, 202A, 204A, 206A, 208A, 211B, 211C, 213C, 214A, 215B, 216A, 220A, 228A, 230A,

234A, 234B, 238A, 240A, 250A, 255C, 340A, 360B, 362B
and Austria, 192A
and Brandenburg, 192A
and Britain, 262A
and Denmark, 248A, 260A
in European Free Trade Association, 346A
and France, 262A
government, 290A, 370B
and International Monetary Fund, 348A
and Poland, 190A, 192A
politics, 280A
and Russia, 262A
Swedenborg, Emmanuel, 227C
sweet potatoes, 147B, 159B, 164C
Swerker I (king of Sweden), 100A
Swift, Jonathan, 203C, 209C, 213C
Swift Creek culture, 83A
Swiss Alps, 127B
Swiss Confederation, 364B
Swiss Credit Bank, 264A
Swiss Family Robinson (Wyss), 241C
Swiss League, 124A, 148A
Swissair 1998 crash, 384C
Switzerland, Swiss, 103B, 105B, 132A, 135B, 141C, 148A, 154A, 158A, 160A, 161C, 188A, 209A, 236A, 245B, 254B, 274A, 304A, 312A, 356B, 364B, 366B
400 B.C.–15 B.C., 21A
in European Free Trade Association, 346A
and France, 282A
and Germany, 156A
law and society, 258A, 274A, 346B
and Prussia, 264A
religion, 256A, 275C
and Russia, 310A
science and technology, 313B
and Spain, 156A
and United Nations, 370A
World War I, 294A, 304A
Zionist Congress, 286A
swords, 91B, 103B
Sybil (Disraeli), 257C
Sydenham, Thomas, 189B
Sydney, 227A, 241C, 251C, 287C, 321A, 379C
Sydney Morning Herald, 251C
Sydney Opera House, 345C
Sykes-Picot Agreement, 298A
Syllabus Errorum (Pope Pius IX), 269C
Symbolism, Symbolists, 275C
Symphoniae Sacrae (Schütz), 185C
Symphony in A Minor (Schubert), 247C
Symphony in White (Whistler), 269C
Symphony no. 1 in C Minor (Brahms), 275C
Symphony no. 2 in B Minor (Borodin), 275C
Symphony no. 2 in D Major (Brahms), 275C
Symphony no. 2 (Piston), 333C
Symphony no. 4 in B flat Major (Beethoven), 237C
Symphony no. 6 in B Minor (*Pathétique*) (Tchaikovsky), 283C
Symphony no. 9 (Mahler), 293C
Symphony no. 10 (Shostakovich), 341C
Symphony no. 15 (Shostakovich), 357C
Symposium (Plato), 21C
Syncom I, II and III, 349B
Syndics of the Cloth Hall, The (Rembrandt), 193C
Synge, Richard, 327B
Syngman, Rhee, 337A
Syntagma Musicum (Praetorius), 181C
syphilis, 149B
Syracuse, 13A, *20,* 20C, 25A, 70B
Syria, Syrians, 12B, 32B, 45A, 48B, 62C, 106B, 317A
1475 B.C.–64 B.C., 6A, 8A, 8B, 28B
agriculture, 91B, 103B
and Arabia, 68B
and Arafat, 367A
and Armenia, 297A
arts, 13C, 87C
and Australia, 303A
and Britain, 303A
and China, 42B
and Crusades, 120B, 122B
and Egypt, 251A, 255A, 342A, 345A, 359A
and France, 235A, 305A, 307A, 309A, 319A
government, 80B, 102B, 305A, 347A, 349A
and Israel, 355A, 359A
and Italy, 292A
and Jordan, 342A
and Lebanon, 367A
medicine, 13C
and Mongolia, 116C, 122C
Omayyad dynasty, 70B, 74B, 84B
and Ottoman Empire, 154B
and Persia, 66C
plague in, 64B
politics, 341A
religion, 267A
Six-Day War, 355A
and United Arab Republic, 347A
and United States, 345A
World War II, 326A
Yom Kippur War, 359A
syringe, 193B
Système de politique positive (Comte), 263C
Système des animaux sans vertèbres (Lamarck), 239B
Szechwan province, 82C, 114C, 130C, 293A, 319A
Sziget, 168A
Sziland, Leo, 325B
Szlankarmen (battle of), 200A
Szold, Henrietta, 293C

T

Taaffe, Edouard (premier of Austria-Hungary), 282A
Tabarro, Il (Puccini), 303C
Tabascan, 155A
Tabinshwehti (king of Burma), 158C, 160C, 162C, 164C
Table Bay, *190*
Tabora, 293A, 299A
Tabriz, 116C, 152B, 158B, 162B, 172B, 176B, 249A, 303A
tabulating machine, 291B
Taché, Étienne, 268B
Tacitus, Gaius Cornelius, 39C
Tacitus, Marcus Claudius (emperor of Rome), 48A
Tacna-Arica conflict, 310C
Tadmekket, 220B
Tadoussac, 177A
Tafna, Treaty of, 253A
Taft, William Howard (president of U.S.), 292B
Taft-Hartley Labor Act, 336C
Tagaste, 55A
Taginae, 64B
Tagliacozzo (battle of), 118B
Taglioni, Maria, 251C
Tagore, Debendranath, 291C
Tahiti, 108C, 176C, 233A, 257A
Tahmasp (shah of Persia), 156B
T'ai-ch'ang (emperor of China), 180C
Tai Sar, 220C
T'ai Tsung, *67,* 71C
Tailhook affair, 380C
Taillebourg, battle of, 114A
Taipei, 339A
Taiping Rebellion, 261A, 263A, 269A
Taira family. *See* Japan
Taiwan, 182C, 186C, 192C, 198C, 208C, 227A
government, 373A
and Holland, 184C
and Japan, 285A
politics, 371A
and United Nations, 356A
Taj Mahal, 183C
Takatoki, 126C
Takeshita Noboru (prime minister of Japan), 371A
Taksin (king of Siam), 218C
Talbot, William, 261B
Tale of a Tub (Swift), 203C
Tale of Peter Rabbit, The (Potter), 287C
Tale of Tales, The (Basile), 185C
Tales of a Wayside Inn (Longfellow), 269C
Talha (sultan of Harar), 168B
Talienwan, 291A
Talikota, battle of, 168C
Tallahassee, 159A
Talleyrand, Charles, 232B
Tallis, Thomas, 171C
Talmud, 45A
Tamar and Other Poems (Jeffers), 309C
Tamara, queen of Georgia, 106C
Tamatave, 279A
Tambo, Oliver, 375A
Tambora volcano, 243A
Tamburlaine the Great (Marlowe), 173C
Tamerlane. *See* Timur
Tamerlane and Other Poems (Poe), 249C
Tamil, kingdom of, 150C
Tamil language, 75C
Tamil Nadu, 67C
Tamils, 60C, 385A
Taming of the Shrew, The (Shakespeare), 175C
Tampa Bay, 159A
Tampico people, 123A
Tamworth, 81B
Tan, Amy, 373C
Tananarive, 271A
Tandy, Jessica, 373C
Taney, Roger, 264B
Tang dynasty. *See* China, Chinese
T'ang Hsien Tsu, 173C
Tanga, 299A
Tanganyika, 305A, 347A, 349A, 351A. *See also* Tanzania
Tangier, 142B, 192C, 198B, 257A, 290A, 307A
Treaty of, 257A
Tangun dynasty. *See* Korea
Tanjore, Temple of, 91C
tanks, military
Tannenberg, battle of, 294A
Tannhäuser (Wagner), 257C
Tanzania, 135B, 202B, 273A, 281A, 299A, 351A. *See also* Tanganyika; Zanzibar
Taoism, 15C, 34B
Taormina, 82B
tape
pressure-sensitive, 259B
Scotch adhesive, 309B
tapestry industry, 145B
Tappan, Arthur, 248B
Tappan Zee, 187A
Tarapaca, 171A
Taras Bulba (Gogol), 255C
Tarawa, 330C
Tarbell, Ida, 289C, 333C
Tardieu, André (prime minister of France), 310A
Tarifa, fortress of, 120B
Tariff Act (1816), 242B
Tariff Act (1894), 284B
Tariff of Abominations, 248B
Tariff truce convention, 312A
Tarim Basin, 216C
Tarnatave, 202B
Tarnopol, 298A
Tarquinius Priscus, Lucius (king of Rome), 15A
Tarsus, 35A, 78C
Tartaglia, Niccolò, 161B
Tartini, Giuseppe, 219C
Tarzan of the Apes (Burroughs), 295C
Tashkent Declaration, 353A
Tasrif, al- 89B
Task, The (Cowper), 227C
Tasman, Abel, 186C
Tasman Peninsula, 249A
Tasmania, 186C, 233A, 237A, 261A, 265A
Tassafaronga, battle of, 328C
Tassilo, 74A
Tasso, Torquato, 171C
Tasso (Goethe), 229C
Tatar empire, 92C, 135B, 156A, 224A
Tatárok Magyarországon, A (Kisfaludy), 245C
Tate, Sharon, 356C
tattooing, 51B
Taurus, 95B
Taussig, Helen, 333B
Taxi Driver (movie), 363C
Taylor, Charles, 375A
Taylor, Elizabeth, 347C
Taylor, Frederick W., 293C
Taylor, Zachary (president of U.S.), 256B, 258B, *259,* 260B
Tbilisi, 372B
Tchaikovsky, Pyotr Ilich, 283C
Tchesme, 220A
Te Deum and Jubilate (Purcell), 201C
Te Deum (Berlioz), 263C
tea, 76C, 79B, 106C, 174A, 178A
Boston Tea Party, 221A
in China, 72C
teachers, 224A
Teamsters Union, 360C, 370C
Teapot Dome Scandal, 308B
Tears of Blood (Yi Injik), 291C
Teatro alla Scala, Il, 223C
Technics and Civilization (Mumford), 317C
Tecumseh, 238B, 240B
teepee, 211A
teeth, false, 13A
Tefe, 152B
Teflon, 347B
joint replacement, 359B
Tegucigalpa, 276C
Tehran, 269B, 291A, 307A, 319A, 330A, 365A
Teia (king of Ostrogoths), 64B
Tel-el-Kebir, battle of, 279A
Telamon, battle of, 25A
telegraph, 253B, 255B, *256,* 257B, 269B
telegraphone, 287B
telephone
automatic dialing apparatus, 347B
cellular service, 363B
and communications satellite, 349B
mobile system, 367B
pocket, 373B
telephone cable, 289B
trans-continental call, 297B
transatlantic cable, 343B
voice transmitter, 275B

telescope, 179B, 181B, 225B
Hubble, 381B
micrometer, 187B
radio, 319B
television
Brezhnev on, 358A
cathode ray tube, 307B
color broadcasting, 325B, 343B
first transmission, 309B
live broadcasts from space, 355B
opera for, 339C
presidential debates on, 346C
press conferences on, 342C, 346C
transmission, 311B
Telex, 349B
Tell Me How Long the Train's Been Gone (Baldwin), 355C
Temperance Society, 238B
temperature scale, 207B
Tempest, The (Shakespeare), 179C
Templars, Order of, 106B, 123C,125C
Templeton Prize for Progress in Religion, 359C
Temps Modernes, Les, 335C
Ten, Council of, 124B
Ten Commandments, 8A
Ten Commandments, The (DeMille), 307C
Ten Days That Shook the World (Reed), 305C
Tenanyecac culture, 38C, 71A
Tenasserim, 249A
Tenedos, 304A
Tenerife, 149B
Tennent, William, 211C
Tennessee, 63A, 65A, 73A, 91A, 109A, 163A, 221A, 222B, 232B, 254B, 266B, 268B, 308B
tennis, 45C, 273C
Tennyson, Alfred, 249C, 259C, 261C, 263C, 265C, 283C
Tenochtitlán, 123A, 125A, 129A, 131A, 157A
Tenth Muse Lately Sprung Up in America, The (Bradstreet), 189C
Tenure of Office Act, 270B
Teotenango, 105A, 111A
Teotihuacán culture, 22B, 23B, 27B, 30C, 34C, 38C, 40C, 46C, 48C, 50C, 52C, 54C, 59A, 59B, 67A, 71A, 75A
agriculture, 32C
arts, 44C, 63A
Tepenec, 131A, 137A
Terence, 27C, 87C
Teresa, Mother, 359C, 365C
Terms of Endearment (movie), 367C
Ternate, 156C
Terra, Gabriel (dictator of Uruguay), 302C, 314C
Terra Australis, 247A
Terra Vergine (d'Annunzio), 279C
Terre des hommes (Saint-Exupéry), 321C
Terror (British ship), 256B
Tertullian, 43A, 45A
Terylene, 327B
Teschen, Peace of, 224A
Tesla, Nikola, 281B, 283B
Tesoretto (Latini), 117C
Test and Corporation Acts, 248A
Testament, Le (Villon), 141C
Tet Offensive. *See* Vietnam War
Tettenhall, 84A
Teuke, Kahn (ruler of Kazakhs), 196C
Teutoburg Forest, 32A
Teutones, 11A, 27A
Teutonic Order, 112A, 118A, 130A, 142A, 166A
Tewa, 115A
Tewfik Pasha (viceroy of Egypt), 283A
Tewkesbury, battle of, 142A
Texas, 81A, 85A, 99A, 161A, 201C, 252B, 252C, 256B, 258B, 260B, 288B, 306B, 308B, 310B, 344C, 357B, 364C, 383B
University of, 352C
Texas-Coahuila, 246B
Texas Instruments, 359B
Texcalac culture, 71A
textiles, 123C
Tezcatlipoca, 85A
Tezoquipan culture, 38C
Tezozomoc, 137A
Thaba Bosiu, Treaty of, 271A
Thackeray, William Makepeace, 259C, 263C, 265C, 269C
Thailand, Thai, 112C, 114C, 118C, 339A, 359A, 377A. *See also* Siam
3500 B.C., 3B
and ASEAN, 352A
and Burma, 110C
government, 120C
World War II, 326C
Thales, 13B, 15B
Thames, battle of the, 240B
Thames River, 107B, 181B, 257B
Thanet, 88A
Thant, U, 346A, 356A
Tharawaddi Min (king of Burma), 253A
Thatcher, Margaret (prime minister of Britain), 364B, 366B, 368A, 368B, 370B, 374B
Thaton, 90C
Theaetetus, 21B
Theagenes, 12C
Theano, 17C
theatre, 173C, 175C, 179C, 183C, 203C
Théâtre Français, 197C
Theatre of the World (Ortelius), 169B
Thebais (Statius), 39C
Thebes (Egypt), 4A, 5C, 6A, 8A, 9C, 12A
Thebes (Greece), 20C, 22C, 77B
Theisir (al-Taysir), 103B
Thelaba (Southey), 235C
Themistocles, 16C, 18C
Then Swänska Argus (Dalin), 211C
Thenard, Louis, 245B
Theobald (Archbishop of Canterbury), 103C
Theobald of Champagne, 112A
Theodora (empress of Byzantium), 92B
Theodore I Lascaris (emperor of Byzantium), 108B
Theodore II Lascaris (emperor of Byzantium), 116B
Theodore II (emperor of Ethiopia), 269A, 271A
Theodoric, Friar, 113B
Theodoric I (king of Visigoths), 58B
Theodoric II (king of Visigoths), 60B
Theodoric the Great (king of Ostrogoths), 60B, *61,* 62B, 63C
Theodosius I (emperor of Byzantium), 52A, 54A, 56A, 56B, 57A
Theodosius II (emperor of Byzantium), 58B
Theodosius III (emperor of Byzantine), 72B
Theodulf of Orleans, 79C
Theophano, 88B
Theophilus (emperor of Byzantium), 78B
Theophrastus, *21,* 21B
Theosophical Society, 275C
Thera, 4C, 6C
thermionic valve, 289B
thermolamp, 235B
thermometer, 175B
Theseus and the Minotaur (Canova), 225C
Thessalians, Cavalry of, 12C
Thessalonica, 56A, 57A
Thessaly, 276A
battle of, 286A
Theuderic I (king of Franks), 62A
They Were Expendable (White), 329C
Thibaw (king of Burma), 277A
Thiers, Louis Adolphe (president of France), 272A, 274A
Thihathura (king of Ava), 142C
thimbles, 91B
Things Fall Apart (Achebe), 345C
Third Man, The (Reed), 339C
Third Reich, 316A, 320A
Third Symphony (Beethoven), 237C
Thirty-Nine Steps, The (Hitchcock), 317C
39 Articles of Faith, 165C, 167C
"Thirty Tyrants," 20C
Thirty Years' War, 180A, 188A
This Happy Breed (Coward), 331C
Thomas, Clarence, 376C
Thomas à Kempis, 137C
Thompson, David, 236B, 238B
Thompson, Emma, 377C
Thompson, Ken, 357B
Thompson, Wiley, 252B
Thomson, David, 183A
Thomson, Joseph, 287B
Thomson, Robert, 257B
Thon Buri, 188C, 220C
Thoreau, Henry David, 263C
Thorn, Treaty of, 142A
Thornton, William, 230B
Thorwaldson, Bertel, 237C
Thrace, 18C, 50A, 56A, 132B, 304A
Thrasamund (king of Vandals), 62B
thread, 119B
Three Dialogues Between Hylas and Philonous, The (Berkeley), 207C
Three Emperors' League, 276A, 278A
Three Graces (Canova), 243C
Three Kingdoms, Period of the, 28B, 44B
Three Lives (Stein), 293C
Three-Mile Island, 364C
Three Musicians, The (Picasso), 307C
"Three People's Principles," 291A
Three Plays for Puritans (Shaw), 287C
3M Company, 309B, 333B, 343B
thresher, 211B
Thrissil and the Ros, The (Dunbar), 151C
Thucydides, 21C
Thule culture, 22C, 85A
Thurber, James, 323C, 331C, 335C
Thurber Carnival, The (Thurber), 335C
Thuringia, kingdom of, 62A, 156A, 312A
Thutmose I (king of Egypt), 6A
Thutmose III (king of Egypt), 6A, 8A, 9C
Tiahuanaco culture, 42C, 61A, 91A, 99A
Tiber River, 65B
Tiberius II (emperor of Byzantium), 64B
Tiberius (Roman emperor), 30A, 32A, 33C, 34A
Tiberius Sempronius Gracchus, 27A
Tibesti Mountains, 295A
Tibet, Tibetans, 68C, 187C
Anglo-Russian Convention on, 291A
and Britain, 289A
Buddhism in, 78C
and China, 74C, 76C, 208C, 210C, 214C, 291A, 339A, 347A, 353A, 375A
government, 118C, 144C
and India, 347A
and Mongolia, 70C, 114C
and Nepal, 80C
Tibi Dam, 175B
Tibullus, 31C
Tick Island culture, 65A
Tieck, Ludwig, 233C, 257C
T'ien-ch'i (emperor of China), 180C
T'ien Shun (emperor of China), 140C
Tientsin, 188C, 273A, 319A
Treaty of, 265A, 267A
Tierra del Fuego, 155A, 276C
al-Tifashi, 105B
Tiffany, Louis Comfort, 283C
Tiflis, 98B
tiger, Tasmanian, 315B
Tiglath-Pileser III (king of Assyria), 12B
Tigre, 373A
Tigris River, 2B, 68C, 83B, 84B
Tikal, 32C, 46C, 50C, 54C, 56C, 59A, 61A, 67C, 75A
Tikhon (patriarch of Russian Orthodox Church), 307C
Tilly, Graf von, 180A, 182A, 184A
Tiloutane, 76C
Tilsby, John, 183B
Tilsit, Peace of, 236A
timber, 2A, 71B, 95, 165B
Timbuktu, 98C, 124C, 142B, 152B, 172B, 206B, 220B, 237A, 249A, 283A
time, standard, 157B
Time and Free Will (Bergson), 287C
Time of Your Life, The (Saroyan), 323C
Time Out of Mind (Dylan), 385C
timepieces, 97B, 159B. *See also* clocks
ammonia maser, 341B
chronometer, 193B, 195B, 219B
watches, 99B
Times (London), 227C
Timon of Athens (Shakespeare), 179C
Timor, 162C, 178C, 265A, 361A
Timor dynasty. *See* Asia
Timotheus of Miletus, 23C
Timur, 126C, 130C, 132C, 134B, 134C, 138C
tin, 7B, 76C, 79B, 84C
Tin Drum, The (Grass), 347C
Tinian Island, 332C
Tintoretto, 163C, 167C, 175C, 177C
Tippecanoe, battle of, 238B
Tippu Sultan (sultan of Mysore), 225A, 229A, 231A, 235A
Tirana Pact, 310A
tires
pneumatic, 257B
radial, 337B
rationing, 334B
synthetic rubber, 325B
tubeless, 337B
Tiridates III (king of Armenia), 50B, 51A
Tiros I, 347B
Titanic, 292B
Titanic (movie), 385C
Titian, 153C, 155C, 157C, 161C, 177C
Tito, Josip Broz (president of Yugoslavia), 340B, 364B
Tito, Santo di, *184*
Titus, baths of, 37C
Titus Andronicus (Shakespeare), 175C
Titus (emperor of Rome), 36B, 37C
Tivoli, 41C
Tlascala, 155A
Tlaxcalan, 81A

Tlingit, 213A
TNT (trinitrotoluene), 269B
To Have and Have Not (Hemingway), 333C
To the Christian Nobility (Luther), 155C
To the North (Bowen), 315C
Toamasina, 202B
toaster, 315B
Toba (emperor of Japan), 60C, 92C, 98C
tobacco, 147B, 159B, 165B, 167B, 179A, 181A, 201B, 217B. *See also* smoking
Tobacco Road (Caldwell), 315C
Tobago, 193A, 219A, 224B
Tobol River, 172A
Tobruk, 324A, 328A
tofu, 111B
toga, 59C
Togoland, 279A, 295A
toilet, 173B, 225B, 267B
toilet paper, 65B
Tojo, 336A
Tokay, battle of, 156A
Tokes, László, 374B
Tököly, Imre (king of Hungary), 196A
Tokugawa, 271A
Tokugawa, Hidetada, 176C
Tokugawa, Ieyasu (emperor of Japan), 174C, 176C, 180C, 181C
Tokyo, 183C, 271A, 273B, 328C, 334C, 379A, 381A
Tokyo Bay, 262B
Toland, John, 201C
Toledo, *56,* 64B, 84B, 105B, 171C
  Treaty of, 144A, 160A
Toleration Act, 189A, 199C
Toleration Edict, 51A
Tolkien, J. R. R., 319C
Tolstoy, Leo, 267C, 275C
Toltecs, 71B, 83B, 83C, 85A, 89A, *91,* 91A, 99A, 105A, 109A, 111A
Tom Jones (movie), 349C
Tomás, Américo (president of Portugal), 360B
Tomasi de Lampedusa, Giuseppe, 345C
tomatoes, 149B, 159B
Tomis, 33C
Tommy (The Who), 357C
Ton Duc Thang (president of Vietnam), 365A
Tone, Wolfe, 228A, 232A
Tonga, 229A, 357A
Tonight Show, 377C
Tonkin Gulf, 74C, 96C, 116C, 174C, 227A, 235A, 279A, 281A, 351A
Tonto Basin, 117A
toothbrush, 147B
toothpaste, 91B
toothpicks, 169B
Top Layer culture, 123A
Topitzin, 85A
Topograhica Christiane (Indicopleustes), 63C
Toqtai (khan of Mongols), 120C
Torah, 37A, 225C
Tordesillas, Treaty of, 149A
Torgau, 334A
Tories, 216A, 258B
Torino, battle of, 204A
Toronto, 230B, 252B, 258B
  battle of, 252B
Toronto Blue Jays, 379C
Torres, Juan José (president of Bolivia), 357A
Torrijos Herrera, Omar (dictator of Panama), 367A
Tortilla Flat (Steinbeck), 317C
Tortosa, 102B
torture, 222A
Tosa Mitsunobu, 157C
Tosa School of Japanese Painting, 157C
Tosca (Puccini), 287C
Toscanini, Arturo, 345C
Toshiba Corporation, 379B
Totona, 210A
Touch of Evil (movie), 345C
Toulon, 328A
Toulouse, 58A, 118A
  University, 113C
Toulouse, Count of, 98B
Toungoo dynasty. *See* Burma
Touraine, 102A, 104A, 108A
Tournai, 120A, 204A
Tours, 89C
  Council of, 105B
Toussaint L' Ouverture, 234B
Tovarich (movie), 319C
Town Down the River, The (Robinson), 293C
Townes, Charles, 341B
Townshend, Charles, 219A
Townshend Acts, 219A
Towton, battle of, 140A
Tracy, Spencer, 355C
trade, trade routes, 103B, 106C, 109A, 122A, 132A, 148A
  in Africa, 150B
  board of trade, 150A
  between Egypt and Crete, 4A
  between Italy and Egypt, 88B
  between Spanish and Aegean peoples, 4C
  in the Swiss Alps, 127B
trademarks, 117B
Trafalgar, 236A
Tragiques, Les (Aubigné), 181C
"Trail of Tears," 254B
train(s)
  braking system, 273B
  first, 235B
  Jenny coupler, 287B
  passenger, 249B
  refrigerated boxcar, 275B
  self-lubricating, 267B
  steam-powered, 249B
"Tom Thumb," 249B
Traité de l'Harmonie (Rameau), 209C
Trajan (emperor of Rome), 38A, 39C
trampoline, 321B
Trans-Iranian Railway, 321A
Trans-Pacific airline, 319B
Trans World Airlines (TWA), 325B
  1956 crash over Grand Canyon, 342C
  1966 crash over Atlantic, 382C
  terrorist hijacking, 368A
Transcaucasia, 306A
Transcendentalism, 253C
transistor, 337B
tunnel diode, 339B
Transjordan, 305A, 307A. *See also* Jordan
  independence of, 307A
  and Iraq, 313A
transmitter, intermittent, 275B
Transoxiana, 110C, 126C, 208C, 212C
transplants
  cornea, 291B
  hand and forearm, 385B
  heart, 355B, 371B
  kidney, 349B
transubstantiation, 111C
Transvaal, 253A, 255A, 265A, 275A, 277A, 281A, 283A, 285A, 287A, 289A
  Boer rebellion in, 295A
  and Britain, 287A
  and China, 291A
  government, 291A
  and India, 291A
  and South Africa, 291A
  state of emergency in, 369A
Transylvania, 56A, 168A, 174A, 176A, 180A, 226A, 268A
Trapani, 116B
Trastámara, Henry (king of Castile and León), 130B
Travolta, John, 363C
Travancore, 212C, 229A
Travels with a Donkey in the Cevennes (Stevenson), 277C
Treasure Island (Stevenson), 279C
Treatise Concerning Eternal and Immutable Morality, A (Cudworth), 211C
Treatise Concerning Religious Affections, A (Edwards), 215C
Treatise of Human Nature (Hume), 213C
Treatise on Sensations (Condillac), 215C
Treatise on Taxes and Contributions, A (Petty), 197C
Treatise on the Stomach, 93
Treatise on Universal History (Bossuet), 197C
Treaty Concerning Principles of Human Knowledge, A (Berkeley), 205C
Trebizond, 140B
trebuchet, 99B
Tree Grows in Brooklyn, A (Smith), 331C
trench-digging machine, 257B
Trengganu, 293A
Trent, Council of, 163C, 165C, 167C
Trento, Peace of, 150A
Trenton, 222B
trepanation, 41B
Trésor (Latini), 117C
Trèves, 198A
Treviglio, 140A
Treviso, 126B, 129B
Trevithick, Richard, 235B
Tri-partite Pact, 324C
Trial, The (Kafka), 309C
Tribigild, 56B
Trichinopoly, 214C
tricycle, 275B
Triennial Act, 200A
Trier, 298A
  University of, 139C
Trieste, 221C, 238A, 342B
Trieste (bathyscaphe), 341B
Trifels, 108A
trigonometry, 25B, 165B
Trinh. *See* Annam, Annamites
Trinidad, 149A, *174,* 181A, 187A, 197A, 232C, 236C
Trinidad and Tobago, 280C, 286C, 349A, 365A
Trinity, Cathedral of the, 137C
Trinity College, 163C, 165C, 173C
Trinity House, 152A
Triple Alliance, 206A, 278A, 280A, 288A, 292A, 296A
Tripoli, 70B, 98B, 102B, 152B, 164B, 204B, 206B, 218B, 234B, 235A, 236B, 237A, 247A, 292A, 317A
Tripolitsa, 244A
Trissino, Giovanni Giorgio, 155C
Tristan and Isolde (Wagner), 269C
Tristan et Iseult (anon.), 105C
Tristram, Nino, 138C
Trittico, Il (Puccini), 303C
Triumvirates, 29A, 30A
Troilus and Cressida (Shakespeare), 177C
Trois Mousquetaires, Les (Dumas), 257C
Troitsky-Sergieva, 137C
trolley cars, 285B
Trollope, Anthony, 263C, 265C
trompe, 165B
Trondheim, 103C
Tropic of Cancer, The (Miller), 317C
Tropic of Capricorn, The (Miller), 321C
Troppau, Congress of, 244A
Trotsky, Leon, 310A, 325A
trousers, 59C
Troy, 8C
Troyes, 166A
Troyville culture, 99A
Trudeau, Pierre (prime minister of Canada), 354C, 364C, *365,* 368C
True Discourse (Celsus), 43A, 47A
True History (Rowlandson), 197A
True Pure Land sect, 146C
Truffaut, François, 347C
Trujillo Molina, Rafael Leónidas (president of Dominican Republic), 331A, 347A
Truk, 332C
Truman, Harry S. (president of U.S.), 332B, 334A, 334B, 336C, 338C, 340C
Truman Doctrine, 336C
Trumbull, John, 243C
Trumpet of Nordland, The (Dass), 213C
trumpets, 87C
Trustees of Dartmouth College v. Woodward, 244B
Tryggveson, Olaf, 88A
Tsai Lun, 39B, 39C
Tsaldaris, Panayoti (prime minister of Greece), 314A
Tsingtao, 295A
Tsiolkovsky, Konstantin, 289B
Tsu-an Temple, Pagoda of, 73C
Tsunayoshi, 196C
Tsurugaoka Hachiman shrine, *127*
Tsushima, 267A
  battle of, 291A
Tu Duc (Vietnamese emperor), 259A
Tu Shih, 33B
Tu Shu Chi Ch'eng, 209C
Tua Toro, 196B
Tuaregs, 98C, 142B, 283A
Tuat, 170B
tuberculosis test, 325B
Tubingen, University of, 145C
Tubman, Harriet, 260B
Tucker, Jim Gary, 382C
Tucson, 203C
Tucumán, battle of, 240C
Tudor, Margaret, 150A
Tudors, 146A
Tukulor empire, 223A, 263A
Tula, 99A, 109A
Tula de Allende, 89A
"Tulip Period," 206B
Tull, Jethro, 203B
Tulunid dynasty. *See* Egypt
Tuma, 206B
Tumacacori, 201C
Tuman-bey, Al-Ashraf (sultan of Egypt), 154B
Tun-huang, 57B
Tung Ch'i-ch'ang, 187C
T'ung-chih, 267C
tungsten filament, 293B
Tungus, 90C
tuning fork, electric, 339B
Tunis, 92B, 102B, 104B, 112C, 116B, 118B, 152B, 158B, 160B, 168B, 170B, 202B, 210B, 212B, 277A, 295C, 330A
  and France, 285A
  and Italy, 285A
Tunisia, Tunisians, 41B, 82B, 104B, 210B, 330A
  in Arab Maghreb Union, 372A
  and France, 305A, 343A
  and Germany, 328A
  government, 345A

Husseinite dynasty, 202B, 212B
independence of, 343A
and Libya, 371A
World War II, 328A
tunnels, 5B
in ancient Greece, 17B
compressed air rock drill for, 265B
English Channel, 374B, 381B
in India, 33B
Thames River tunnel, 257B
Tunuma, battle of, 206B
Tupper, Earl, 319B
Tupperware, 319B
Tupperware Corporation, 335B
turbine, steam, 183B
Turenne, Henri, 194A
Turgenev, Ivan Sergeyevich, 263C, 267C
Turin, 266A
University of, 135C
Turing, Alan, 321B
Turkey, Turks, 48A, 64C, 106A, 164B, 264A. *See also* Anatolia; Ottoman Empire
1900 B.C.–53 B.C., 4C, 10C, 14C, 20C, 26C, 27C, 28B
and Adrianople, 130B
and Afghanistan, 319A
agriculture, 158B
and Allies, 307A
ancient, 32B, 41A
and Armenia, 304A, 305A
arts, 27C
and Athens, 140A
and Australia, 297A
and Austria, 168A, 192A, 208A, 212A, 226A
and Austria-Hungary, 202A
and Belgrade, 200A
and Bosnia, 140A
and Britain, 182B, 276A, 297A, 299A, 311A, 342A, 346A
and Bulgaria, 72B, 130B, 307A
and Byzantium, 122B, 134B, 158A
and China, 66C
and Constantinople, 138B
in Council of Europe, 338B
and Crete, 194A
and Crusade, 140B, 146B, 150B
and Cyprus, 277A, 350B, 361A
divorce in, 309A
and East Africa, 160B
economy, 275A
and Egypt, 144B, 248, 251A
and Europe, 128B
and France, 160A, 232A, 234A, 235A, 236A, 297A, 303A, 321A
and Georgia, 214C
and Germany, 294A, 309A
government, 192B, 196B, 220B, 275A, 305A, 307A, 309A, 311A, 313A, 317A, 346B
and Greece, 128B, 132B, 134B, 159C, 262A, 276A, 286A, 304A, 305A, 307A, 313A, 321A, 342A, 346A, 348B, 350B, 352B
and Herzegovina, 142A
and Holy Alliance, 242A
and Holy Roman Empire, 166A, 192A, 206A
and Hungary, 138B, 156A, 162A, 174A, 196A
industry, 317A
and Iran, 299A, 319A
and Iraq, 297A, 319A, 342A
and Italy, 292A, 296A
and Jerusalem, 96B
and Kurdistan, 154B
and Kurds, 378A
Latin alphabet, 311A
law and society, 200B, 267A, 309A, 314A, 317A
in League of Nations, 315A
and Malta, 168A
and Mesopotamia, 301A
and Moldavia, 152A
in NATO, 340A
and New Zealand, 297A
and Palestine, 303A
and Persia, 152B, 164B, 176B, 184B, 186B, 202B, 208B, 210B, 299A, 301A, 303A
and Philippopolis, 130B
plague in, 212B
and Poland, 138A, 180A, 196A, 202A
polygamy in, 309A
and Portugal, 172B
postal service, 119B
religion, 262A, 265A, 309A, 311A
and Rumelia, 276A
and Russia, 80B, 82B, 90C, 198A, 204A, 208A, 210A, 220A, 220C, 230A, 238A, 240A, 248A, 262A, 274A, 276A
Russo-Turkish Convention, 248A
and Serbia, 130B, 242A
Sha-to, 82C
and Sofia, 132B
and Soviet Union, 309A, 342A
and Spain, 166B, 170B
and Tunisia, 202B
Turko-Persian War, 210B, 212B
and United States, 346A
and Venice, 120B, 136B, 140B, 150A, 202A
and Vienna, 198A
in World War I, 301A, 302A
and Yugoslavia, 307A, 342A
turkey (animal), 157B, 161B
Turkish Federated State of Cyprus, 360B
Turkistan, 36B, 68C, 75B, 210C, 216C, 220C, 271A
Turkmantchai, Peace of, 249A
Turks and Caicos Islands, 234B, 274C
Turner, Frederick Jackson, 283C
Turner, Joseph Mallard William, 237C, 255C, 261C
Turner, Nat, 250B
Turnpike Act, 192A
Turriff, battle of, 186A
Turtle (American submarine), 223B
Tuscany, 89B, 94B, 100B, 104B, 107B, 133B, 210A, 212A, 230A, 234A, 264A, 266A
Tuscany, Matilda of, 98B
Tuscarora War, 205A
Tuskegee Institute, 275C, 284B
Tutankhamen (king of Egypt), 6A, 8A
Tutiula (U.S. gunboat), 326C
Tutsis, 132C, 381A
tutu, 251C
Tutu, Desmond (Archbishop of Cape Town), 371C
Tutuola, Amos, 341C
Tuvalu, 218C
Tuxtla, 40C
TWA. *See* Trans World Airlines
Twain, Mark, 273C, 275C, 279C
Tweed, William "Boss," 274B
Twelfth Night (Shakespeare), 175C
Twelve Tables, 19A
Twenty Love Poems and a Song of Despair (Neruda), 309C
Twenty Thousand Leagues Under the Sea (Verne), 275C
Twice Told Tales (Hawthorne), 253C
Twin Peaks (Lynch), 375C
Two Gentlemen of Verona, The (Shakespeare), 175C
Two New Sciences (Galileo), 187B
Two Pamphlets, Concerning the French Revolution (Fichte), 231C
Two Seated Women (Picasso), 307C
Two Sicilies, kingdom of, 244A, 264A
2001: A Space Odyssey (movie), 355C
Two Treatises on Civil Government (Locke), 201C
Tylenol, 366C
Tyler, John (president of U.S.), 254B, 256B
typewriter
correction fluid, 345B
correction tape, 359B
memory, 351B
portable electric, 343B
with rotary print wheel, 363B
Selectric, 349B
typhoid fever, 187B
typhus, 146A
typography, 143B
Tyre, 100B
siege of, 14B, 22B
Synod of, 53A
Tyrnau, Peace of, 180A
Tyrol, 155B, 176A, 238A
Tzu Hsi (empress of China), 287A
Tzympe, 128B

U

U2 (rock group), 365C, 371C, 377C
Uaxactún, 52C, 75A
Ubangi Basin, 214B
Über den Begriff der Wissenschaftslere (Fichte), 231C
Über den Willen in der Natur (Schopenhauer), 253C
Ubico Castañeda, Jorge (president of Guatemala), 312C, 333A
Uccialli, Treaty of, 281A
Udaipur, Palace of, 173C
Ueno, 271A
Ufa, 304A
Uffizi Gallery, 378B
Uganda, 283A, 285A, 349A, 353A, 359A, 362A, 365A
Uganda Railway, 289A
Ughetai Khan (emperor of Mongols), 112C, 114C
Uitgeest, 175B
Uji, 94C
Ujiji, 273A
Ujjain, 56B, 122C
UK. *See* Britain
Ukiyo-E (Utamaro), 227C
Ukraine, 56B, 91C, 204A, 288A, 306A, 376B
and Chernobyl disaster, 370B
and Crimea, 342B
independence of, 374B
Ulagh-Beg, 139B
Ulan Bator, 309A
Ulan-Ude, 192C
Ulászló II (king of Bohemia and Hungary), 146A, 154A
Ulbricht, Walter (leader of East Germany), 356B
Ulpianus, 45C
Ulrika Eleonora (queen of Sweden), 206A, 208A
Ulster, 187C
ultrasound, 365B
Ulundi, battle of, 277A
Ulysses (Joyce), 307C
Umayyad, 67B
Umberto I (king of Italy), 276A, 286A
Umberto II (king of Italy), 336B
umbrellas, 59B, 99B
Ummayad mosque, 73C
Umpanda (king of Zulu), 255A
UN Atomic Energy Commission, 336A
Unabomber, 382C, 384C
Unamuno, Miguel de, 291C
Unbearable Lightness of Being, The (Kundera), 369C
Uncle Tom's Cabin (Stowe), 261C, 263C
Under a Glass Bell (Nin), 333C
Under the Volcano (Lowry), 337C
Under the Yoke (Vasov), 285C
Underground Railroad, 254B, 264B
Underwood Tariff Act, 294B
Undine (Fouqué), 239C
Undset, Sigrid, 305C
UNESCO (United Nations Educational, Scientific and Cultural Organization), 368A
Unforgiven (Eastwood), 377C
UNICEF, 360A
Unified Ministry of Defense, 350B
Union Carbide Corporation, 369A
Union of 1819, 250C
Union of Soviet Socialist Republics (USSR). *See* Soviet Union
Union Theological Seminary, 291C
"Unitarianism, Pope of," 245C
United Airlines, 312B
1956 crash over Grand Canyon, 342C
United Arab Emirates, 356A
United Arab Republic (UAR), 344A, 345A, 346A, 347A, 349A
United Arab States, 346A
United Artists Corporation, 305C
United Auto Workers, 356C
United Brethren in Christ, 221C
United Church of Christ, 345C
United Fruit Company, 310C
United Irishmen, Society of, 228A
United Kingdom. *See* Britain; England
United Nations, 330B, 334B, 335A, 338A, 342A, 343A, 348A, 350A, 352A, 354A, 356A, 364A, 368A, 376A
administration, 336A, 340A, 346A, 356A, 366A, 370A, 382A, *385*
on African military force, 384A
on AIDS, 383B
and Argentina, 366A
and Atoms for Peace, 340C
and Belgium, 347A
and Bosnia-Herzegovina, 378A, 378B
and Britain, 352A
and Cambodia, 375A
Charter of, 334B
and China, 356A
Conference on Trade and Development (UNCTAD), 350A
and Congo, 346A, 347A
and Czechoslovakia, 354A
Disarmament Subcommittee, 344A
and Figi, 356A
on Guatemala, 342A
and Iraq, 372A, 374A, 376A, 382A, 384A
and Israel, 376A
and Italy, 338A
and Korea, 338A, 340A
and Kuwait, 374A
and Lebanon, 369A
and Libya, 376A
and North Korea, 380A
and North Vietnam, 355A, 360A
and Nuclear Nonproliferation Treaty, 354A

and Persian Gulf War, 376A
and Pope Paul VI, 351C
and Rockefeller, 336C
Security Council, 350A
and Serbia, 384A
and Somalia, 378A, 380A
and South Africa, 346A, 370A
and Soviet Union, 354A
and Suez Canal Zone, 342A
and Taiwan, 356A
on terrorism, 384A
and United States, 355A, 366A, 378A, 380A
on water shortages, 384A
on Zionism, 376A
United New Netherland Company, 181A
United Presbyterian Church, 345C
United Press, 345C
United Press International, 345C
United Provinces of Central America, 246C, 250C, 252C, 254C
United Reform Church, 359C
United States, 226B. *See also* America, Americans
agriculture, 229B, 246B, 364C, 375B
AIDS in, 381B
Alaska purchase, 270B
and Algeria, 243A
American Revolution, 222B, 224A, 224B
Anglo-American war debt (WW I), 306B
and Antarctica, 346A
Arab oil embargo, 358A, 360A
and Argentina, 332B
arts, 40C, 231C, 239C, 243C, 245C, 249C, 251C, 253C, 259C, 263C, 265C, 267C, 273C, 275C, 281C, 283C, 287C, 289C, 293C, 295C, 299C, 303C, 305C, 307C, 309C, 311C, 313C, 315C, 321C, 325C, 329C, 331C, 335C, 339C, 345C, 347C, 349C, 353C, 357C, 365C, 367C, 369C, 373C, 375C, 377C, 379C, 381C, 385C
and Australia, 328C, 330C, 338A
and Austria-Hungary, 300B
and Belgium, 308B, 338A, 356A
and Berlin, 346A
blackout in, 350C
and Bosnia-Herzegovina, 380B, 382B
and Brazil, 329A
and Britain, 230B, 240A, 242B, 260B, 288C, 296B, 306B, 308B, 312A, 320B, 322B, 324B, 326B, 328B, 330A, 336A, 336B, 338A, 340A, 346A, 348A, 352B, 354A, 356A, 368A, 376A
and Burma, 334C
and Cambodia, 357A, 358A, 360A
and Canada, 244B, 256B, 272B, 282B, 288B, 292B, 300B, 306B, 310B, 314B, 316B, 324B, 330B, 342C, 344C, 346C, 362C, 364A, 366C, 368C, 372C, 378A
and China, 256B, 286B, 336A, 338A, 356A, 364A, 368A, 379A
civil rights movement, 342C, 344C, 346C, 348C, 350C, 352C, 354C
Civil War, 266B, 268B
and Colombia, 258C
Communism in, 332B, 336C, 340C, 342C
conscription in, 300B, 324B, 326B, 328B, 330B, 336C, 338C, 364C
and Cuba, 258C, 286C, 288C, 290C, 292C, 308C, 316B, 316C, 347A, 348A
and Denmark, 300B, 324B, 338A
and Dominican Republic, 290C, 298C, 308C, 351A
and East Germany, 344A, 360A
and East Indies, 332C
economy, 226B, 252B, 274B, 294B, 310B, 312B, 314B, 324B, 362C, 370C, 374C, 382C, 384C
and economy, 228B, 294B
education, 226B, 255C, 344C
and Egypt, 362A
and El Salvador, 378A
embassy bombings, 384A, 385A
and Europe, 368A
food rationing in, 334B 342B
and Formosa, 342A
and France, 232B, 234B, 236B, 296B, 300A, 302A, 306B, 338A, 340A, 346A, 348B, 352B, 356A, 376A
and French Panama Company, 288B
in G-7, 368A
and Germany, 296B, 300B, 302B, 304A, 306B, 308B, 310B, 320B, 326A, 326B, 330A, 332A, 368A
gold rush, 258B, 284B
government, 350C
Great Seal of, 224B
and Grenada, 366A, 367A
and Guam, 287A
and Guatemala, 329A
and Haiti, 296C, 306C, 312C, 316C, 371A, 380A
and Hawaii, 249A, 261A, 275A, 281A, 283A, 285A, 287A
and Hungary, 306B
hurricanes in, 332B, 342C, 344C
and Iceland, 324B
immigration, 278B, 282B, 300B, 306B, 308B, 350C, 370C, 372C
industry, 231B, 233B, 241B, 243B, 244B, 245B, 248B, 249B, 253B, 257B, 265B, 267B, 269B, 271B, 273B, 275B, 281B, 283B, 286B, 289B, 297B, 305B, 307B, 309B, 315B, 323B, 325B, 326B, 329B, 330B, 337B, 340C, 343B, 346C, 348C, 349B, 351B, 364C, 367B, 368C, 372C, 373B, 376C, 377B
on International Court, 310B
and International Labor Organization, 362A, 364A
and International Monetary Fund, 348A
and Iran, 346A, 364A, 365A, 367A, 370C
Iran-Contra Affair, 370C, 371A
and Iraq, 368A, 370A, 376A, 378A, 382A
and Iron Curtain, 340C
and Israel, 336A, 362A, 370C
and Italy, 308B, 326A, 326B, 328B, 330A, 338A, 348A, 356A
and Japan, 259A, 263A, 267A, 269A, 271A, 284B, 290B, 291A, 306B, 308B, 312A, 319A, 324B, 326B, 326C, 328B, 328C, 330C, 332C, 334B, 334C, 336A, 338A, 342A, 346C, 355A, 372C
and Korea, 338A, 340A
and Kurds, 376A
and Latin America, 325A
law and society, 226B, 236B, 238B, 244B, 248B, 254B, 256B, 274B, 276B, 282B, 284B, 286B, 290B, 300B, 304B, 306B, 314B, 320B, 321B, 324B, 330B, 342C, 344C, 348C, 350C, 354C, 356C, 360C, 362C, 366C, 368A, 382C
and Lebanon, 344A, 367A, 370C
and Libya, 366A, 370A
loan to Chrysler, 364C
and Luxembourg, 338A
and Marshall Islands, 371A
Mexican War, 258B
and Mexico, 258B, 268C, 294C, 296C, 298C, 306C, 320C, 325A, 327A, 329A, 333A, 348A, 378A, 381A
and Morocco, 227A
and NAFTA, 378A
and Netherlands, 338A
and New Zealand, 338A
and Nicaragua, 292C, 298C, 308C, 310C, 314C, 371A
and North Korea, 354A, 380A
and North Vietnam, 351A, 353A, 355A, 359A
and Norway, 338A
and nuclear weapons, 339B, 340A, 344A, 346C, 352A, 370A
and Pakistan, 346A
and Palestine, 372A
and Panama, 288C, 290C, 292C, 302C, 306C, 318C, 320C, 350A, 362A, 371A, 373A, 375A
and Pearl Harbor, 305A
and Persia, 265C
Persian Gulf War, 374A
and Philippines, 287A, 338A
and Poland, 344A
politics, 230B, 256B, 274B, 286B, 306B, 332B, 334B, 336C, 344C, 348C, 370C, 376C, 378C, 380C, 382C
population (1800), 234B
population (1810), 238B
population (1820), 244B
population (1840), 254B
population (1850), 260B
population (1880), 276B
population (1900), 286B
population (1910), 292B
population (1920), 304B
population (1930), 312B
population (1940), 322B
and Prussia, 226B
public libraries, 237C
and Puerto Rico, 286C, 300C, 320C
Quasi War with France, 232B
R & D in, 377B
religion, 189C, 227C, 265C, 343C, 345C, 368A
and Romania, 356A
and Russia, 246B, 374A, 376A, 378A
and Rwanda, 381A
and Samoa, 277A, 281A
and San Juan Islands, 272B
and Saudi Arabia, 374A
science and technology, 229B, 233B, 235B, 237B, 241B, 247B, 249B, 251B, 253B, 255B, 257B, 259B, 261B, 263A, 265B, 267B, 269B, 271A, 273B, 275B, 277B, 281B, 283B, 285B, 287B, 289A, 291B, 293B, 295B, 297B, 299B, 303B, 307B, 309B, 311B, 313B, 315B, 317B, 319B, 321B, 323B, 327B, 329B, 331B, 333B, 335B, 337B, 339B, 341B, 343B, 345B, 347B, 349B, 351B, 353B, 355B, 357B, 359B, 361B, 363B, 365B, 367B, 369B, 371B, 373B, 375B, 379B, 381B, 383B, 385B
and Siam, 250B, 305A
slavery, 224B, 226B, 238B, 240B, 244B, 245A, 246B, 250B, 254B, 264B, 268B
and Somalia, 378A
and South Africa, 368A, 376A
and South Vietnam, 343A, 349A, 360A
southwestern, 63A, 75A, 83A, 85A, 91A, 91C, 101A, 103A, 109A, 121A, 123A
and Soviet Union, 318B, 330A, 334A, 336A, 336B, 340A, 344A, 346A, 348A, 350A, 354A, 356A, 358A, 360A, 361B, 366A, 368A, 370A, 374A, 384A
space program, 345B, 347B, 349B, 351B, 353B, 354A, 355B, 357B, 359B, 361B, 363B, 367B, 369B, 370C, 377B, 379B, 381B, 383B
and Spain, 232B, 274C, 284B, 286A, 286B, 286C, 287A, 340A
and Sudan, 302A
and Syria, 345A
transportation and infrastructure, 231B, 237B, 267B, 273A, 274B, 279B, 298B, 302B, 330B, 332B, 338C
and Tripoli, 235A, 237A
and Turkey, 346A
and UNESCO, 368A
and United Nations, 332B, 355A, 366A, 370C, 378A, 380A
and Venezuela, 345A
and Vietnam, 343A, 352B, 352C, 353A, 355A, 357A, 378A, 380A, 382A
and Virgin Islands, 300B
War of 1812, 240B, 242B
and West Germany, 340A, 346A, 348A, 356A
World War I, 298B, 302A
World War II, 322B, 326A, 326B, 326C, 328A, 328B, 328C, 329A, 330A, 330B, 330C, 332A, 332C, 334A–334C, 334C
United Synagogue of America, 295C
Unity Temple (Wright), 291C
Universal Natural History and Theories of the Heavens (Kant), 215C
Universal Negro Improvement Association (UNIA), 294B, 298B
Universalism, Universalists, 269C
Universalist Church, 221C
universe, steady-state, 177B
Unkiar Skelessi, Treaty of, 250A, 254A
Uno Sosuke (prime minister of Japan), 373A
Untergang des Abendlanes, Der (Spengler), 303C
Untertan, Der (Mann), 295C
Unvanquished, The (Fast), 327C
Up from Slavery (Washington), 289C

Upanishads, 11B
Upatnieks, Juris, 349B
Updike, John, 347C
Upper Alsace, 142A
Upper Niger, 172B
Upper Republican culture, 123A
Upper Silesia, 306A
Upper Volta, 285A, 287A, 369A
Uppsala, University of, 145C, 211B
Ur, 2B, 4B, 22B
Ur-Nammu (king of Ur), 4B
Ural Mountains, 346A
uranium, 229B
Uranus, 225B
Urban I, Pope, 45
Urban II, Pope, 97C, 98B, 99C
Urban IV, Pope, 117C
Urban V, Pope, 131C
Urban VI, 133C
Urban VII, Pope, 187C
Urban VIII, Pope, 183C
Ursuline Chapel, 211C
Uruguay, 155A, 246C, 258C
  and Argentina, 246C, 254C
  and Brazil, 240C, 244C, 246C, 248C, 268C
  economy, 292C
  government, 252C, 256C, 288C, 302C, 331A, 369A
  law and society, 355A
  and Paraguay, 268C
  River Plate, 222C
  and Spain, 183A, 209A, 232C, 238C
Urundi, 299A
U.S. Air Force, 359B, 362C, 363B, 375B
  inertial guidance system, 341B
  in Korean War, 340A
  non-stop around-the-world flights, 344C
  and Soviet warplanes, 350A
  in Vietnam, 343A
  air pollution, 377B
U.S. Air Force Academy, 342C, 348C
U.S. Army, 283B, 332C, 334A, 334C, 340C, 342C, 345B
  Army Air Corps, 310B
  Army Nurse Corps, 288B
U.S. Atomic Energy Commission, 336C, 338C
U.S. Bureau of Immigration, 284B
U.S. Bureau of Labor, 278B
U.S.-Canadian Reciprocal Fishing Treaty, 262B
U.S. Census, 234B, 254B, 260B, 276B, 286B, 292B, 304B, 312B, 322B
U.S. Centers for Disease Control, 367B
U.S. Circuit Court, 316B
U.S. Civil Service, 278B
U.S. Coast Guard, 296B
U.S. Court of Appeals, 358C, 378C
U.S. Court of Claims, 262B
U.S. Department of Defense, 336C, 378C
U.S. Department of Education, 364C
U.S. Department of Energy, 362C
U.S. Department of Health, Education, and Welfare, 340C, 346C
U.S. Department of Housing and Urban Development, 350C
U.S. Department of Indian Affairs, 252B
U.S. Department of Interior, 260B, 278B, 298B, 312C
U.S. Department of Justice, 272B
U.S. Department of Labor, 280B
U.S. Department of State, 336C
U.S. Department of Transportation, 352C
U.S. Environmental Protection Agency, 359B, 379B
U.S. Food and Drug Administration (FDA), 361B, 373B, 385B
U.S. Marines
  in Dominican Republic, 298C
  in Haiti, 316C
  in Hawaii, 283A
  in Nicaragua, 292C
  in Spanish-American War, 287A
  in Vietnam War, 351A, 360A
  in World War II, 330C, 332C, 334C
U.S. Military Academy, 234B
U.S. Narcotics Control Board, 306B
U.S. National Guard, 298B
U.S. Naval Academy, 256B, 380C
U.S. Naval Reserve, 328B
U.S. Naval War College, 278B
U.S. Navy
  cheating in, 380C
  and hijacked TWA plane, 368A
  and Libyan warplanes, 366A
  and *Mayaguez,* 360A
  Naval Expansion Act, 320B
  Navy Act, 298B
  in Persian Gulf, 370A, 372A
  in Spanish-American War, 287A
  Tailhook affair, 376C
  and Virgin Islands, 312C
  Washington Naval Agreement, 306B
  in World War II, 324B, 326C, 328C, 332C
U.S. Open, 377C
U.S. Post Office, 284B, 356C
U.S. Public Health Service, 325B
U.S. Social Security Administration, 322B
U.S. Steel Corporation, 288B
U.S. Treasury Department, 360C, 364C
U.S. Veterans Administration, 312B
U.S. War Department, 322B
U.S. Weather Service, 273B
U.S. v. Butler, 318B
U.S. v. E. C. Knight, 284B
U.S. v. Schwimmer, 310B
U.S.A. (Dos Passos), 321C
Usuman dan Fodio, 220B
Utagawa Toyokuni, 231C
Utah, 65A, 109A, 258B, 260B, 278B, 284B, 362C
Utah, University of, 367B
Utah Jazz, 385C
Utica, 276B
Utilitarianism (Mill), 269C
utopia, secular, 247C
Utopia (More), 155C
Utraquists, 145C
Utrecht, 143B
  Peace of, 206A, 207A
Utrillo, Maurice, 289C
Utzon, Jørn, 345C
Uxmal, 77A, *91*
Uzana (king of Pagan), 114C
Uzbek Kungrat dynasty, 218C
Uzbek Mangit dynasty, 214C
Uzbek Turks, 174B
Uzbekistan, 73B, 137B
Uzbeks, 152B, 158C
Uzun Hasan (king of Persia), 142B

V

V-E Day, 334B
V-J Day, 334B
Vaal River, 259A
vacuum tube, 263B, 289B
Vaghbata, 66C
Val-des-Dunes, battle of, 94A
Valarshapat, 40B
Valdemar, 112A
Valencay, Treaty of, 240A
Valencia, 98B, 112B, 124B, 143B
  University of, 151C
Valencia County, 97A
Valens (emperor of Byzantium), 52A, 54A, 54B, 56B
Valentine, Basil, 177B
Valentine, Saint, 49A
Valentinian I (emperor of Rome), 52A, 54A, 56A
Valentinian II (emperor of Rome), 56A
Valentinian III (emperor of Rome), 58B
Valentino, Rudolph, 311C
Valera, Eamon de (president of Ireland), 302A
Valerian, Publius Licinius (emperor of Rome), 46A, 48B
Valium, 349B
Valla, Lorenzo, 141C
Valley Forge, 222B
Valley of the Kings, 6A
vallus, 35B
Valmiki, 23C
Valmy, battle of, 230A
Valois, House of, 172A
Valparaiso, 171A, 290C, 292C
Valromey, 176A
Valtellina, 181C
Van, 297A
van Alen, William, 311C
Van Buren, Martin (president of U.S.), 252B
Van Diemen's Land, 186C, 249A
Van Doren, Carl, 323C
Van Dyck, Anthony, 185C, 187C
Van Gogh, Vincent, 281C, 283C, 375C, 377C
Vance, Cyrus, 362C
Vancouver, 264B, 270B, 289B, 294B
Vancouver, George, 230B
Vandals, 48A, 58B, 59B, 60B, 62B, 64B
Vanity Fair (Thackeray), 259C
Vanuatu, 220C, 366A
Vanzetti, Bartolomeo, 304B, 310B
Värälä, Treaty of, 228A
Varaville, battle of, 94A
Vardar, 302A
Varennes, 228A
Vargas, Getúlio Dornelles (president of Brazil), 312C, 314C, 316C, 318C, 329A, 335A, 343A
Vargo, 31C
Varman, Mahendra, 67C
Varna, 248A
  battle of, 138A
Varro, Marcus Terentius, 31B
Vasa, Gustavus (king of Sweden), 156A
vases, Greek, 13C
Vasily II (grand duke of Muscovy), 136A
Vasily III (grand duke of Muscovy), 150A
Vasov, Ivan, 285C
Vassilou, George (president of Cyprus), 372B
Vassy, massacre of, 166A
Vatican
  Councils, 273C, 349C, 351C, 363C
Vatican City, 63C, 145C, 311C
  on abortion and birth control, 371C
  archives of, 277C
  on Beagle Channel dispute, 369A
  on birth control, 371C
  and Britain, 367C
  on fasting and abstinence, 353C
  on Fr. Curran, 371C
  and Hungary, 375C
  on *Index of Forbidden Books,* 353C
  Library, 139C
  on office of inquisitor, 353C
  and Poland, 373C
  Sistine Chapel, 381C
  and Soviet Union, 374A
  and United States, 368A
Vatsayana Mallagana, 55C
Vaucanson, Jacques du, 215B
Vaucelles, Truce of, 164A
Vega, Lope de, 175C, 181C
vehicle, steam, 221B
Veii, 21A
veil, 309A
Veinte poemas de amor y una canción desesperada (Neruda), 309C
Veksler, Vladimir, 333B
Velasco Ibarra, José María (president of Ecuador), 316C, 333A, 337A, 359A
Velázquez, Diego Rodríguez de Silva, 181C
Velázquez de Cuéllar, Diego, 153A
Velcro fastener, 343B
Velleius Paterculus, 33C
Vendée, La, 234A
Venera
  4, 355B
  9, 361B
  10, 361B
Venetial Lagoon, 120B
Venezuela, Venezuelans, 149A, 155A, 157A, 169A, 219A, 260C, 268C, 379A
  20 B.C.–A.D. 300, 30C
  and Britain, 175A, 280C
  and British Guiana, 286C
  and Colombia, 244C
  and El Dorado, 163A
  and Germany, 159A
  gold in, 161A
  government, 240C, 242C, 254C, 258C, 266C, 272C, 286C, 290C
  independence of, 248C
  industry, 302C
  and League of Nations, 320C
  in New Granada, 207A
  and Spain, 165A, 232C, 238C, 244C
  and Union of 1819, 250C
  and United States, 345A
  World War II, 335A
Venice, Venetians, 60B, 72B, 78B, 79C, 88B, 90B, 93C, 97B, 104B, 106B, 108B, 110B, 116B, 120B, 121B, 122B, 123C, 124B, 126B, 128B, 130B, 132B, 134B, 136B, 137B, 138B, 140A, 140B, 143B, 143C, 145C, 147C, 148A, 150A, 152A, 153C, 155C, 160A, 171C, 175B, 175C, 185C, 198A, 217C, 232A, 318A
  and Austria, 260A
  and Austria-Hungary, 202A
  and Byzantium, 100B
  Great Council of, 120B
  and Poland, 202A
  St. Mark's Cathedral, 99C
  and Turkey, 198A, 202A
Venizélos, Eleuthérios (prime minister of Greece), 296A, 300A, 314A, 316A
Venkata I (raja of Vijayanagar), 170C
Vent-Axia, 317B
Venus and Adonis (Shakespeare), 175C
Venus (goddess), 179B, 349B, 355B
Venus of Urbino, The (Titian), 161C
Venus (planet), 7B
Veracruz, 155A, 258B, 294C
Veracruz culture, 44C, 83A
Vercingetorix, 29A

Verde Valley, 117A
Verdi, Giuseppe, 257C, 273C, 343C
Verdun
battle of, 298A, 300A
Treaty of, 78A
Vereeniging, Peace of, 289A
Verga, Giovanni, 277C
Verlaine, Paul, 271C, 273C, 275C, 277C
Vermeer, Jan, 191C
Vermont, 115A, 193A, 209A, 228B
Vermunfige Gedanken (Wolff), 207C
Verne, Jules, 275C
Verneuil, battle of, 136A
Vernier, Pierre, 185B
Vernunft und Existenz (Jaspers), 317C
Verona, 46A, 60B, 107C, 129B, 134B
Veronese, Paolo, 171C
Verrazano, Giovanni, 157A
Verrocchio, Andrea del, 145C, 147C
Versailles, 217C, 228A, 272A, 276A
Alliance of, 216A
Peace of (1784), 226A
Treaty of (1919), 302B, 304A, 304B, *305*, 316A, 318A
Versunkkene Glocke (Hauptmann), 285C
Verulamium, 41C
Verus, Lucius Aurelius (emperor of Rome), 38A, 40A, 42A
Vervins, Treaty of, 174A
Verwoerd, Hendrik (prime minister of South Africa), 347A, 353A
Vesey, Denmark, 246B
Vesle River, 302A
Vespasian (emperor of Rome), 36A, 37C
Vespucci, Amerigo, 149A, 151A, 153A
vests, bulletproof, 329B
Vetsera, Marie, 280A
Via Flaminia, 25A
Viagra, 385B
Vicar of Wakefield, The (Goldsmith), 219C
Vicenza, 134B
Vichy, 324A, 326A, 328A
Vicksburg, battle of, 268B
Vico, Giovanni Battista, 209C
Victor, Alfred, 249C
Victor, Flavius (emperor of Rome), 56A
Victor Amadeus II (duke of Savoy), 202A, 210A
Victor Emmanuel II (king of Sardinia and Italy), 260A, 266A, 276A
Victor Emmanuel III (king of Italy), 286A, 306A, 319A, 320A, 330A, 336B
Victoria, Alexandrina (queen of England), 244A, 252A, 264B, 288A
Victoria (Australia), 220C, 261A, 307B
Victoria (Canada), 270B
Victoria Regina, 317C
Victory (Ross), 250B
Vida de Don Quijote y Sancho (Unamuno), 291C
Videla, Jorge (president of Argentina), 363A
video games, 367B
videodisc player, 363B
Vidor, King (Wallis), 309C, 311C
Vie de Jésus, La (Mauriac), 319C
Vie de Jésus (Renan), 269C
Vie littéraire, La (France), 281C
Vienna, 108A, 111B, 139C, 150A, 154A, 158A, 171C, 198A, 205C, 209C, 237C
Alliance of, 206A
Conference of (1854), 262A
Congress of (1814), 242C,
Congress of (1820), 244A
Opera House, 191C
Peace of (1606), 176A
Peace of (1735), 210A
Peace of (1809), 238A
Peace of (1864), 268A
revolution in, 258A
Socialism in, 310A, 334A, 346A
transportation, 254A
Treaty of (1725), 208A
Treaty of (1731), 210A
Women's Employment Association, 270A
Vienne, Synod of, 101C
Vientiane, 206C
Viète, François, 173B
Vietnam, Vietnamese, 74C, 88C, 90C, 112C, 118C, 142C, 174C, 235A, 265A, 324C, 342A. *See also* Annam
ancient, 34B
and Cambodia, 365A, 373A
and China, 60C, 72C, 82C, 96C
in COMECON, 362A
and France, 227A, 337A, 339A, 343A
and Mongolia, 116C
North Vietnam, 342A, 351A, 353A, 355A, 359A, 360A
reunification, 363A
South Vietnam, 342A, 343A, 349A, 355A, 360A
and United Nations, 362A
and United States, 343A, 353A, 355A, 357A, 378A, 380A, 382A
Vietcong, 354A, 355A
Vietminh, 324C, 337A
Vietnam War, 352B, *353*, 353A, 354A, 355A, 359A, 361A, 378A, 382A
My Lai massacre, 356C
protests against, 352C, 354C, 356C, 362C
Tet Offensive, 355A, *355*
Westmoreland and, 368C
Vigano, Salvatore, 245C
Vigevano, 258A
Vigevaresco, 214A
Vigilius, Pope, 65C
Vigneaud, Vincent du, 323B
Vignola, Giacomoda, 169C
Vijayabahu (king of Ceylon), 94C
Vijayanagar, 144C, 152C, 166C, 168C, 170C
Viking I, 363B
Vikings, 72A, 73B, 76A, 77B, 80B, 84A, 88A, 90A, 91A, 91B
Villa, Francisco "Pancho," 298C, *299*, 306C
Villa Viciosa, battle of, 204A
Villafranca, 264A
Treaty, 264A
Villanova, 11A
Villanova, Arnau de, 123B
Villaroel López, Gualberto (president of Bolivia), 331A, 333A
Villeneuve, Jean Marie (Archbishop of Quebec), 313C
Villers-Bretonneux, battle of, 302A
Villon, François, 141C
Vilna, 204A, 304A, 306A, 332A
Vilnius, 376B
Vimy Ridge, 300A
Vincennes, 211A
Vincennes (U.S. cruiser), 372A
Vinegar Hill, battle of, 232A
Vineyard Sound, 177A
Vinland, 101B
Vinyon, 337B, 341B
violin, 151C
Virgil, 31C, 217C
Virgin in Majesty (Martini), 125C
Virgin Islands, 185A, 234B, 258C, 272C, 300B, 312C, 318B
Virgin with St. Francis (Correggio), 155C
Virginia, Virginians, 153B, *178*, 179A, 179B, 181A, 183A, 187A, 189A, 191A, 197A, 205A, 213A, 215A, 222B, 250B, 260B, 266B, 268B, 374C
Charter of, 177A
Resolution, 232B
taxes in, 195A
Virginia (Confederate ship), 266B
Virginian, The (Wister), 289C
Virginians, The (Thackeray), 265C
Virginius (U.S. ship), 274C
Virgo (constellation), 383B
Viscellinus, Cassius, 17A, 19A
Visconti, Filippo Maria, 138B
Visconti, Luchino, 349C
Visigoths, 53A, 54A, *56*, 56A, 56B, 58A, 58B, 60B, 62B, 64B, 68A, 68B, 70A
Vision of Judgment (Southey), 241C
Visnuvardhana, 114C
Visser't Hooft, Willem Adolph, 321C
Vistula, 32A
Vita Caroli Magni (Einhard), 79C
Vita Mathildis, 96
Vita Nuova (Dante), 121C
Vitalian, Pope, 71C
Vitelli, Caminelleo, 161B
Vitellius, Aulus (emperor of Rome), 36A
Vitruvius, 31B, 33C
Vittoria, 240A
Vivaldi, Antonio, 195C
Vivian Grey (Disraeli), 249C
Vizcaíno, Sebastián, 177A
Vladimir the Great (prince of Kiev), 88A, 89C
Vladislav, 99C
Vladivostok, 267A, 303A
Vleck, John van, 327B
Vlorë, 292A
Voice of the Turtle, The (Druten), 331C
Voight, Jon, 363C
Volcker, Paul, 364C
Volga River, 80A, 204C, 220C, 328A
Volgograd. *See* Stalingrad.
Volhynia, 296A
Vologeses III (king of Parthia), 40B
Volpone (Jonson), 177C
Volsci tribe, 19A
Volstead Act, 304B
Volta River Basin, 124C
Voltaire, 207C, 209C, 211C, 213C, 215C, 225C
volunteerism, 384C
Volvo, 378B
von Bethman-Hollweg, Theobald (chancellor of Germany), 292A
von Bülow, Bernhard (chancellor of Germany), 286A
von Ehrentreitz, Marx Treizsaurwein, 153C
von Harbou, Thea, 311C
von Harnack, Adolf, 313C
von Sternberg, Josef, 311C
Vonnegut, Kurt, 357C
Voronesh, 330A
Vorster, Balthazar (prime minister of South Africa), 353A
Vorster, John (president of South Africa), 363A
Vossem, Peace of, 194A
Vossische Zeitung, 203C
voting rights *See also* suffrage, 270B, 272B, 288B, 300B, 302B, 306B, 310B
Voting Rights Act, 350C, 360C
Voyage to the Island of Mauritius, A (Saint-Pierre), 221C
Voyages (Hakluyt), 171C
Vranitsky, Franz (chancellor of Austria), 370B
Vratislav II (king of Bohemia), 96A
vulcanization, 255B
Vumba, sultanate of, 108C
Vyasa, 25C
Vyedomosti, 203C
Vyshinsky, Andrei, 338B

W

Waalo, 196B
Wabash, St. Louis & Pacific Railway v. Illinois, 280B
Wabash River, 207A
Waco, 378C
Wag the Dog (movie), 385C
Wagner, Richard, 257C, 269C, 271C, 279C
Wagner, Robert, 314B
Wagram, battle of, 238A
Wagudu, 74C
Wahhab, Muhammad ibn Abd al-, 231C
Wahhabi, 214B, 231C, 237A, 239A, 245A, 303A, 315A
Wahhat, Muhammad ibn al-, 214B
Waiting for Godot (Beckett), 341C
Wake Island, 326C, 332C
Wakefield, battle of, 140A
Wakefield, Edward, 255A
Waksman, Selman, 333B
Walata, 112C, 140B, 144B
Walcott, Derek, 351C
Walden; or Life in the Woods (Thoreau), 263C
Waldenses, 185C
Waldheim, Kurt (president of Austria), 356A, 370B
Waldmann, Hans, 146A
Waldseemüller, Martin, 153A
Wales, Welsh, 34A, 64A, 65C, 76A, 86A, 95C, 104A, 108A, 109C, 110A, 118A, 120A, 127B, 162A, 197A, 239C, 260A, 351C, 359C
and England, 160A
Statute of, 118A
Welsh Wars, 118A
Walesa, Lech (president of Poland), 366B, 374B, 382B
Walker, Alice, 367C
Walker, David, 248B
Walker, Edward, 270B
Walker, John, 249B
Walker, John G., 288C
Walker, Mary Edwards, 268B
Walker, Sarah (Madame C. J. Walker), 291B
Walker, William, 260C, 264C, 266C
Walker's Appeal (Walker), 248B
Walkman, 365B
Wallace, De Witt, 307C
Wallace, George, 358C, 366C
Wallace, Henry, 328B, 336C
Wallace, William, 120A, 122A
Wallachia, 174A, 248A, 250A, 266A
Wallenstein, Albrecht (duke of Friedland and Mecklenburg), 182A, 184A
Wallenstein (Schiller), 235C
Wallia, 58A
Wallingford, Treaty of, 104A
Walpi, 123A
Walpole, Hugh, 295C
Walpole, Sir Robert (earl of Oxford), 204A, 206A, 208A
Waltari, Mika, 335C
Walter of Aquitaine (Ekkehart), 85C

Waltham, 241B
Walton, E. T. S., 311B
Walton, Izaak, 191C
Walvis Bay, 277A
Wamba (king of Visigoths), 70A
Wampanoag, 195A
Wan-li (emperor of China), 168C, 180C
Wandokai, 330C
Wang, An, 357B
Wang Chi, 69C
Wang Chien (emperor of China), 84C
Wang Ching-wei, 324C
Wang Mang (emperor of China), 32B, 33C
Wang Meng, 133C
Wang Po, 71C
Wang Wei-I, 93B
Wangchuk, Jigme Dorji (king of Bhutan), 359A
Wangchuk, Jigme Singhi (king of Bhutan), 359A
Wangfu, 41C
War and Peace (Tolstoy), 267C
War Assets Administration, 336C
War for American Independence. *See* American Revolution
War Industries Board, 302B
War Labor Board, 330B
War Labor Disputes Act, 330B
War of 1812, 240B, 242B
War of the Pacific, 276C
War of the Spanish Succession, 202A
"war on poverty," 350C
War Production Board, 326B, 328B, 334B
War Shipping Administration, 326B
Warbeck, Perkin (king of England), 146A, 148A
Warburton, Peter Egerton, 275A
Warden, The (Trollope), 263C
warfare, bio-chemical. *See* bio-chemical weapons
Warhol, Andy, 349C, 371C
Warm Springs, 334B
Warner, Ezra, 265B
Warren, Earl, 340C, 360C
Warren, Robert Penn, 331C, 337C, 371C, 373C
Warren Commission, 350C
Warri, 144B, 172B
Warring States, Age of, 20B
Wars of the Roses, 140A
Warsaw, 190A, 202A, 230A, 250A, 254A, 296A, 322A, *323*
  battle of, 304A
  Jews massacred in, 330A, 332A, 366B
  Pact, 354B, 374A, 376A
  Pact (East European Defense Treaty), 342A
Warsaw-Invangorod, 296A
Warwick, 189A
washing machine, 293B
Washington, Booker T., 277C, 284B, 289C
Washington, D.C., 228B, 257B, 284B, 308B, 346A, 364C. *See also* District of Columbia
  burned by British, 240B
  Corcoran Gallery, 373C
  Kennedy Center, 357C
  Lincoln Memorial, 321C
  National Gallery of Art, 325C
  National Museum of Women in the Arts, *383*
  Smithsonian Institute, 363B
  U.S. Capitol building, 230B, 243C, 251C, 267C, 384C
  Washington Monument, 251C, 279C
Washington, George (president of U.S.), 217A, 222B, 224B, 228B, 230B, 231B, 232B, 234B, 251C
Washington, Harold, 366C, 370C
Washington, Treaty of, 248B
Washington Naval Agreement, 306B
Washington Redskins, 323C, 329C, 331C, 335C, 359C, 367C, 369C, 373C, 377C
Washington state, 328B, 338C
Wasp (U.S. aircraft carrier), 340C
Wassenberg, 108A
Waste Land, The (Eliot), 307C
Watch on the Rhine (Hellman), 325C
water
  chain-and-bucket system, 151B
  fluoridation of, 313B, 325B, 335B, 343B
  mills, 31B, 81B, 85B
  municipal system, 107B
  pipe, 141B
  pump, 31B, 201B
  purification, 165B
  supply, 113B
Watergate Scandal, 358C, 360C
Waterloo, battle of, 242A
Waterloo Bridge (Constable), 251C
Waterman, Lewis, 279B
Waters, Ethel, 331C, *331*
Watervliet, 221C
Watling Island, 310C
Watson, James, 341B
Watson, John B., 303C
Watson-Watt, Sir Robert, 319B
Watt, James, 221B, 227B
Wattasid dynasty. *See* Morocco
Watteau, Jean-Antoine, 207C
Watts, Isaac, 205C
Watts race riots, 350C
Watuga River, 221A
Waugh, Evelyn, 335C
wavelengths, 327B
Wavell, Archibald (viceroy of India), 330C
Waverley (Scott), 241C
WAVES (Women Appointed for Voluntary Emergency Services), 328B
Way, Amanda, 262B
Way of All Flesh, The (Butler), 289C
Way of the Churches of Christ in New England, The (Cotton), 189C
Way of the World, The (Congreve), 203C
Wayne, Anthony, 224B, 230B
Wayne, John, 321C, 357C
We (Zamyatin), 305C
Weakland, Rembert G. (Archbishop of Milwaukee), 377C
weather
  Beaufort wind scale, 343B
  forecasting service, 273B
  and military maneuvers, 329B
  rocketsonde, 337B
  tracking radar, 329B
  vane, 171B
  wind feather system, 343B
Weaver, Robert, 350C
Weavers, The (Hauptmann), 287C
weaving
  by Chinese and Muslims, 123B
  four-heddle loom, 135B
  power loom, 253B, 255B
  punch-card loom, 235B
  by Toltecs, 71B
Webber, Andrew Lloyd. *See* Lloyd Webber, Andrew
Weber, Carl Maria von, 245C, 249C
Webster, John, 179C
Webster, Noah, 249C
Webster-Ashburton Treaty, 256B
Weddell, James, 247A
Weddell Sea, 247A
Wedgwood, Josiah, 217C, 221B, 225B
Wedmore, Treaty of, 80A
Weedon Island culture, 85A
Weehawken, 236B
Weekly Review, 203C
Wehlau, Treaty of, 190A
Wei Chung, *93*
Wei dynasty. *See* China, Chinese
Wei Furen, 55C
Wei-hai-wei, 313A
Weiditz, Christopher, *155*
Weil, Simone, 331C
Weill, Kurt, 331C
Weinberger, Caspar, 378C
Weiner, Walter, 325B
Weininger, Otto, 289C
Weinstein, Nathaniel, 323C
Weiss, Peter, 351C
Weissenburg, 81C, 230A
Weisskunig (von Ehrentreitz), 153C
Weizmann, Chaim (president of Israel), 339A
Welcome to the City (Shaw), 327C
Well of Loneliness, The (Hall), 311C
Welland Canal, 249B
Welles, Orson, 325C, 329C, 345C, 385C
Wellesley, Arthur, first duke of Wellington, 240A, 242A, 262A
Wellesley, Richard Colley (governor of India), 233A, 237A
Wellington (New Zealand), 269A.
Wellington, duke of. *See* Arthur Wellesley, first duke of Wellington
Wells, 201A
Wells, H. G., 291C, 293C
Welty, Eudora, 359C
Wen Chen-ming, 167C
Wen-jen, 187C
Wen Ti (emperor of China), 60C
Wenceslas, Saint, 84A
Wenceslas II (king of Bohemia), 122A
Wenceslas III (king of Bohemia), 122A
Wenceslas IV (king of Germany and Bohemia), 134A
Wenders, Wim, 369C
Wentworth, Sir Thomas, 186A
Werfel, Franz, 307C, 315C
Werther (Goethe), 221C
Wesel, 334A
Weser River, 188A
Wesley, John, 211C, 221C
Wessex, kingdom of, 62A, 64A, 69C, 74A, 76A, 78A, 84A, 90A, 94A
Wesson, 261B
West, Benjamin, *217,* 219C
West, Jessamyn, 335C
West, Nathaniel, 323C
West, Rebecca, 345C
West Africa, 82C, 98C, 102C, 108C, 112C, 124C, 151B, 176B, 220B, 225A. *See also individual countries*
  and Berbers, 88C
  education, 249A
  empire of Jenne, 92C
  and England, 144B, 158B
  and Europe, 136C
  and France, 196B
  and Holland, 174B, 180B
  and Islam, 94C
  Katsina dynasty, 98C, 164B
  and North Africa, 66C
  and Portugal, 138C, 142B, 144B
  slave trade, 176B, *189*
West Bank, 355A, 381A, 383A
West Germany, 344A
  1972 treaty of equal relationships, 358B
  and Albania, 370B
  and Arabs, 358A
  and Baader-Meinhof terrorists, 358B
  Basic Law, 338B
  and Berlin Wall, 346B
  and Britain, 340A
  in Council of Europe, 338B
  and France, 340A, 348A
  in G-7, 368A
  government, 346B, 348B, 360B, 370B
  and International Monetary Fund, 348A
  and Israel, 350B
  law and society, 356B, 368A
  and Marshall Plan, 338A
  in NATO, 242A, 344A
  occupation of, 342A, 342B
  and Poland, 356B
  politics, 344B, 348B, 364B, 366B
  on reunification, 374B
  and Saar, 344B
  and Soviet Union, 356A, 372A
  in United Nations, 358A
  and United States, 340A, 346A, 348A, 356A
  on war crimes, 364B
  in Western European Union, 342A
West Indian (Cumberland), 221C
West Indies, 30C, 151A, 157A, 159B, 169A, 171A, 185A, 201A, 211A, 212A, 213A, 224B, 224C, 234B, 238C
  and Britain, 242A
  slave trade, 187C
West Java, 196C
West Point, 224B, 234B
West Side Story (movie), 347C
West Side Story (musical, Sondheim andBernstein), 345C
West Virginia, 63A, 135A, 268B
Western European Union, 342A
Western Hemisphere, 288B
Western Samoa, 349A
Western Star (Benét), 333C
Western Union, 349B
Westinghouse, George, 273B, 283B
Westminster, 145B
  Assembly of, 187C
  Peace of, 190A, 195A
  Provisions of, 116A
  Statute of, 312A
Westmoreland, William, 354C, 368C
Westmorland, 86A, 98A, 104A
Westo War, 197A
Westphalia, kingdom of, 113B, 240A, 308A
  Peace of (1648), 188A, 189C
whales, whaling, 364A, 379B
Wham-O Toy Company, 345B
Wharton, Edith, 291C, 293C, 305C
What Makes Sammy Run (Schulberg), 327C
wheat, 159B
wheat drill, 203B
Wheatstone, Charles, 253B, 257B
wheel, 3B, 39B, 151B
  cipher, 143B
  kick-, 109B
  prayer, 59B
  spinning, 115B
  water-, 51B, 61B, 73B, 97B, 105B, 151B, 173B, 219B
wheelbarrows, 61B, 165B
Wheeler, Schuyler, 279B
Wheelwright, John, 187A
"When Johnny Comes Marching Home" (Harris), 317C
Where Angels Fear to Tread (Morgan), 291C
Where Do We Come From? What Are We? Where Are We Going? (Gauguin), 287C

Whinfield, John, 327B
whiskey, 61B, 135B
Whiskey Rebellion, 230B
Whistler, James, 269C
White, Byron, 378C
White, E. B., 335C
White, Edward, 351B, 353B
White, John, 173A
White, Patrick, 347C
White, William, 233C
White, William L., 329C
"White Christmas" (Berlin), 327C
White Doe of Rylstone (Wordsworth), 243C
White Hill, battle of, 180A
White House, 234B, 348C
White Huns, 60C, 62C
White Jacket (Melville), 261C
White Pass and Yukon Railway, 286B
White River, 244B
Whitefield, George, 213C
Whitehorse, 286B
Whitewater, 380C, 382C
Whitman, Charles, 352C
Whitman, Walt, 263C
Whitney, Eli, 227B, 231B, 233B
Whittle, Frank, 333B
Whittlesey culture, 135A
Whitworth, Joseph, 255B
Who, the (rock group), 357C
Who's Afraid of Virginia Woolf? (Albee), 349C
Whymper, Edward, 276C
Wickford Point (Marquand), 323C
Wido of Spoleto, 82B
Widukind, 77C, 87C
Wied, Hermann von (Archbishop of Cologne), 163C
Wieland, Christoph Martin, 225C
Wiener, Norbert, 337B
Wiesloch, battle of, 182A
Wight, Isle of, 126A
Wihtred (king of Kent), 70A, 72A
Wihtred's code, 72A
Wilbur, Richard, 371C
Wild Duck (Ibsen), 279C
Wild Swans at Coole, The (Yeats), 301C
Wilde, Oscar, 283C, 285C
Wilder, Billy, 335C, 339C, 347C
Wilder, Lawrence Douglas, 374C
Wilder, Thornton, 321C, 329C, 361C
Wilhelm II (emperor of Germany), 290A
Wilhelmina (queen of the Netherlands), 282A, 286A, 336B
Wilkes, Charles, 254B
Wilkie, Wendell L., 324B, 331C
Wilkinson, John, 229B
William, Count of Arles, 88B
William I. *See* William of Normandy
William I (emperor of Germany), 272A, 272B, 280A
William I (king of Netherlands), 248A, 254A
William I (king of Prussia), 266A
William II (emperor of Germany), 280A, 284A
William II (king of Sicily), 98A, 104B, 106B, 292A, 302A
William II (king of the Netherlands), 254A
William II (stadtholder of the Netherlands), 188A
William III (king of England), 196A, 198A, 200A, 202A
William IV (king of England), 248A, 252A
William IV (king of the Netherlands), 214A
William V (stadholder of Netherlands), 226A
William and Mary College, 201C
William Augustus (duke of Cumberland), 214A, 216A
William of Aquitaine, Count, 85C
William of Holland, 116A
William of Malmesbury, 103C
William of Nogaret, 123C
William of Normandy (king of England), 94A, 95, *95*, 95C, 96A, 97C, 104B
William of Occam, 129C
William of Orange, 170A, 172A
William (prince of Denmark), 268A
William Rufus (king of England), 96A
William Tell (Schiller), 237C
William the Conqueror. *See* William of Normandy
William the Lion (king of Scotland), 104A, 106A, 110A
Williams, Daniel, 283B
Williams, John, 255C, 265C
Williams, Ozzie, 347B
Williams, Roger, 185A, 187A, 189A
Williams, Tennessee, 335C, 337C, 343C
Williams, William Carlos, 337C
Williamsburg, 222B
Willingdon, Lord (viceroy of India), 313A
Wilmington, 235B
Wilmington culture, 91A
Wilno, 304A
Wilson, Edmund, 311C, 313C
Wilson, Harold (prime minister of Britain), 350B, 360B
Wilson, Robert, 349B
Wilson, Scot Charles, 293B
Wilson, Woodrow (president of U.S.), 292B, 294B, 298B, 300B, 302B, 304B, 308B
Wimpfeling, Jacobi, 151C
winch press, 109B
Winchelsea, battle of, 128A
Winchester, 102A
Winckelmann, Johann, 221C
Windhoek, 297A
windlasses, 165B
windmills, 15B, 59B, 79B, 83B, 87B, 103B, 107B, 135B, 151B, 179B
windows, 71B
Windsor, Grand Assize of, 106A
Windsor, Treaty of, 104A
Windsor Castle, 141C
Windward Islands, 195A, 274C, 323A
wine, wine industry, 109B, 123B, 131B, 199B
Winesburg, Ohio (Anderson), 303C
Wingfield, Walter, 273C
Winnebago, 246B
Winnie the Pooh (Milne), 311C
Winnipeg, 274B, 302B
Winslow, Edward, 185A
Winsor, Kathleen, 333C
Winter Harbor, 205A
Winter's Tale, The (Shakespeare), 179C
Winter's Tales (Dinesen), 327C
Winthrop, John, 185B
wire, barbed, 275B
wire drawing, 91B, 129B
Wirth, Karl, 306A
Wisconsin, 73A, 91A, 123A, 244B, 246B, 258B
  University of, 259C
Wise, Isaac M., 287C
Wise, Robert, 347C, 351C
Wisniowiecki, Michael Korybut (king of Poland), 194A
Wister, Caspar, 213B
Wister, Owen, 289C
Witan, 88A
witchcraft, 204A, 210A
Witness Tree, A (Frost), 331C
Wits, The (Davenant), 185C
Witte, Sergei Yulyevich (premier of Russia), 282A, 288A, 290A
Wittelsbachs, 110B, 212A
Wittenberg, 153C
  University, 151C
Wittenberg Palace Church, 155C
Wittstock, battle of, 186A
Wizard of Oz, The (movie), 321C
Władysław II (king of Poland), 136A
Władysław III (king of Poland and Hungary), 138A
"Wobblies," 290B
Wodehouse, P. G., 307C
Woëvre Plain, 300A
Wolfe, James, *217*, 217A
Wolfe, Thomas Clayton, 311C, 317C, 323C, 327C
Wolfe, Tom, 371C
Wolfenbüttel, 179C
Wolff, Christian von, 207C
Wolof, 281A
Wolseley, Garnet, 275A
Wolsey, Thomas (lord chancellor of England), 154A, 155C, 156A, 158A
Wolves Attacked by Dogs (Fyt), 191C
Woman in White, The (Collins), 267C
Woman without a Shadow (Strauss), 295C
Woman's Journal, 272B
Women, International Conference of, 288A
Women in Love (Lawrence), 307C
Women on the Verge of a Nervous Breakdown (Almodovar), 373C
Women Voters, League of, 304B
Women's Christian Temperance Union, 274B
Women's Clubs, General Federation of, 280B
women's rights, 369C, 372C. *See also* abortion; suffrage; *individual organizations; individual women*
  as attorneys, 287B
  in Britain, 278A, 354B
  in Church of England, 379C, 381C
  Civil Rights Act, 350C
  employment, 270A
  in Episcopal Church, 363C
  and Equal Rights Amendment, 358C
  first conference, 258B
  in France, 274A
  in India, 249A
  International Women's Rights Congress, 276A
  as jurors, 318B
  marriage, 307C, 313C
  as ministers, 269C
  in Mormon Church, 375C
  National Women's Conference, 362C
  in Norway, 290A
  property, 258, 278A
  Roman, 27A
  in Roman Catholic Church, 363C
  strike in Dover, N.H., 248B
  succession to throne, 124A
  in United States, 318B, 382C
  and wearing of veils, 6B
  Woman's Journal, 272B
  working hours, 256A
  working underground, 256A
Women's Rights, League for, 272A
Women's Temperance Army, 262B
Wonderful Wizard of Oz, The (Baum), 287C
Wonders of the Invisible World (Mather), 201C
wood
  brazil, 109B
  petrified, 77B
Wood, Grant, 315C
Woodstock (England), 99B
Woodstock Music and Art Fair, 357C
Woodward, Joanne, 345C
Woodward, Robert, 333B
wool, wool industry, 35B, 87B, 133B
  British Woolens Act, 202A
  tax on goods made of, 242B
Woolf, Virginia, 309C
Woolman, John, 219C
Woolworth, Frank W., 276B
Woolworth Co., 346C
Worcester
  battle of, 190A
  Peace of, 110A
Worcester College, 121C
Worcester v. Georgia, 250B
Wordsworth, William, 233C, 241C, 243C, 261C
Workingman's Party, 274B
Works and Days (Hesiod), 13C
Works in Architecture of Robert and James Adam (Adam), 221C
World According to Garp, The (Irving), 363C
World Atlas (Homann), 207C
World Bank. *See* International Bank for Reconstruction and Development
World Chronicle (Schedel), 147C
World Conference on the Human Environment, 358A
World Council of Churches, 321C, 347C
World Health Organization, 336A, 383B
World Intellectual Property Organization, 360A
World Jewish Congress, 337C
World Meteorological Organization, 338A
World of Washington Irving, The (Brooks), 333C
World Series, 289C, 325C, 327C, 329C, 331C, 333C, 335C, 337C, 339C, 341C, 343C, 345C, 347C, 349C, 351C, 353C, 355C, 357C, 359C, 361C, 363C, 365C, 367C, 369C, 371C, 372C, 373C, 375C, 377C, 379C, 381C, 383C, 385C
World War I, 294A, 295A, 295B, 296A, 296B, 297A, 298A, 298B, 299A, 300A, 300B, 301A, 302A, 305A, 312B
World War II, 22A, 322A, 322C, 323A–323B, 324A, 325A, 326A, 326C, 327A, 327B, 328A, 328B, 328C, 329A–329B, 329B, 330A, 331A, 332A, 333A, 333B, 334A, 334B, 335A, 336A, 336C, 344C, 372C, 378B
World's Fair (1984), 368C
Worms, 58A, 80A, 136A, 165C
  Concordat, 101C
  Diet of, 157C
  Edict of, 157C
Worthies of England, The (Fuller), 193C
Wouk, Herman, 339C
Wounded Knee Creek, battle of, 282B
wounds
  gunshot, 153B
  treatment of, 219B
Wozniak, Stephen, 363B
Wozzeck (Berg), 309C
WPA (Works Projects Administration), 330B

Wrangel, Piotr, 304A
Wren, Sir Christopher, 185C, 193B, 193C, 195C, 209C
Wright, Frank Lloyd, 289C, 291C, 323C, 347C
Wright, James, 325B
Wright, Jim, 372C
Wright, Orville and Wilbur, 289B
Wright, Richard, 323C, 335C
writing, early, 5C, 13C, 115B. *See also* hieroglyphics; paper
  Chinese, 39C, 55C
  cuneiform script, 3C
  Egyptian, 5B
  Greek, 10C
  Latin, 15C
  Mycenaean script, 9C
  Roman, 33B
  Siamese, 119C
  Sumerian, 2B, 5B
Wu-ch'ang, 293A
Wu Chen, 129C
Wu Ching (Five Classics), 19C
Wu dynasty. *See* China, Chinese
Wu school, 167C
Wu Tao-Tzu, 75C
Wu Ti (emperor of China), 48B, 62C, 63C
Wulfhere (king of Mercia), 70A
Wulfred (Archbishop of Canterbury), 79C
Württemberg, 270A, 314A
Würzburg, 173C
Wuthering Heights (Brontë), 259C
Wyatt, Francis, 181A
Wyatt, John, 213B
Wyatt, Sir Thomas, 164A
Wycherley, William, 195C
Wycliffe, John, 133C, 135C, 137C
Wycliffism, 135C
Wyeth, N. J., 252B
Wyler, William, 329C, 337C, 347C
Wylie, Philip, 329C
Wyoming, 236B, 252B, 258B, 272B, 282B, 290B, 308B
Wyss, Johann Rudolf, 241C

X

X-ray tube, 295A
Xavier, Francis, 165C
Xerox 914, 347B
Xerox Corporation, 337B, 347B
Xerxes I (king of Persia), 18B
Xhosa Bantu, 214B, 223A, 225A, 253A, 261A, 275A
Xiamen, 214C
Xianbei, 38B
Xinjiang, 220C
Xiongnu, 38B, 50B, 52B
Xolalpan, 50C
Xosa, 176B
XYZ Affair, 232B

Y

Yagbum, 188B
Yahya Khan, Agha Mohammad, 357A
Yaka, kingdom of, 212B, 216B
Yakub (emperor of Ethiopia), 174B
Yakub (shah of Persia), 144B
Yakutsk, 184C
Yale, Linus, 267B
Yale University, 203A, 247C, 267C, 279C
Yalta, 332A
  Conference, 334A
Yalu River, battle on, 289A
Yamagata, Aritomo, 281A
Yamassee, 207A, 211A
Yamamoto, Isoroku, 330C
Yamato, 203C
Yamoussoukro, 375C
Yandabu, Treaty of, 249A
Yang Kuang, 67B
Yangôn, 214C, 241C, 247C, 340A
Yankee from Olympus: Justice Holmes and His Family (Bowen), 333C
Yankee Stadium, 351C
Yaounde, 299A
Yap, 295A
Yarmouth, 296A
Yarmuk, battle of, 68B
Yarubi, 212B
Yarumela, 65A
Yaxchilan, 65A, 71A, 75A
Yazdagird II (king of Persia), 58C
Yazoo, 211A
Yeager, Chuck, 337B
Yeats, William Butler, 285C, 301C
Yellow Christ, The (Gauguin), 281C
Yellow Emperor, 2B
yellow fever, 230B, 280B, 290B
"Yellow Kid, The," 285C
Yellow River, 14B, 263A
Yellow Springs, 325C
"Yellow Turbans," 42B
Yellowstone Basin, 236B
Yellowstone National Park, 272B, 372C
Yeltsin, Boris (president of Russia), 370B, 374B, 376B, 378B, 380A, 380B, 382B, 384A, 384B
Yemen, 62C, 64C, 210B, 265A, 345A, 346A, 349A, 354A, 364A, 374A
  and Britain, 281A
  and Egypt, 342A, 355A
  government, 355A, 361A
  and Ottoman Empire, 168B
  and Saudi Arabia, 342A
  in United Nations, 336A
Yen Chia-kan (president of Taiwan), 361A
Yen Li Pen, 71C
Yenan, 317A
Yerevan, 374B
Yerim Mbanik, 210B
Yetuna, 190C
Yezid I, 70B
Yi Injik, 291C
Yiddish, 81C
Yogi and the Commisar, The (Koestler), 335C
Yogy- akarta, 214C
Yohannes I (emperor of Ethiopia), 186B
Yokohama, 273B
Yonge, Charlotte, 263C
York, Richard, third duke of, 140A
York (England), 44A, 50A, 140A, 146A
York Minister, 369C
York (Ontario), 230B, 240B, 252B
York Peninsula, 176C
Yorkshire, 164A
Yorktown, battle of, 224B
Yoshiaki, 168C
Yoshihito (emperor of Japan), 293A, 311A
Yoshimune, 206C
You Can't Go Home Again (Wolfe), 323C
Young, Andrew, 358C
Young, Brigham, 257C, 260B
Young, John, 359B
Young Lonigan (Farrell), 315C
Young Plan, 312A
Young Turks, 291A, 293A, 295A
Younge culture, 135A
Yourcenar, Marguerite, 317C
"You're a Grand Old Flag," 291C
Yousef, Ramzi Ahmed, 380C
Youthful Deeds of the Cid, The (Castro y Bellvis), 181C
Ypres, 300A
  battles of, 296A
Ypres Cloth Hall, 123C
Ypsilanti, Alexander, 244A
Yser River, battle of, 296A
Yu-chow, 84C
Yu-wen (emperor of China), 64C
Yüan dynasty. *See* China, Chinese
Yüan Shih-k'ai (provisional president of Republic of China), 293A, 295A, 297A, 299A
Yucatán Peninsula, 46C, 50C, 61A, 65A, 69A, 73A, 85A, 91A, 99A, 109A, 113A, 139A, 141A, 153A, 155A, 266C
  1000 B.C., 10B
Yucuita, 48C
Yugoslavia, 308A, 310A, 380B
  and Allies, 307A
  and Britain, 307A, 332A
  civil war in, 376B
  and Cominform, 336B
  Communism in, 342B
  and Germany, 324A, 326A
  government, 348B, 364B, 370B
  and Greece, 342A
  and Hungary, 326A
  and Italy, 304A, 326A, 342B
  and London Convention (1933), 314A
  and Serbia, 372B, 380A
  and Slovenia, 372B, 374B
  and Soviet Union, 332A
  and Turkey, 307A, 342A
  and United Nations, 376B, 378A, 378B
  World War II, 324A, 326A
Yukon Territory, 284B
Yun-Kang, 61C
Yung-cheng (emperor of China), 210C
Yunnan province, 114C, 116C
Yusa, 102C
Yussuf, 126B
Yusuf (sultan of Bijapur), 146C

Z

Zabern, 294A
Zacatecas, 163A
Zacharias, Pope, 75C
Zaghouan Springs, 41B
Zahir Shah, Mohammad (king of Afghanistan), 359A
Zahir Timurbugha al- (sultan of Egypt), 142B
Zahn, Johann, 199B
Zaila, 154B, 164B
Zaïmis, Alexander (president of Greece), 316A
Zaire, 357A, 381B, 383B. *See also* Congo
Zakkai, Johanan ben, 37A
Zalosce, 298A
Zama, 25A
Zaman (shah of Afghanistan), 231A
Zambezi Basin, 82C, 168B
Zambezi Bridge, 317B
Zambezi River, 140B, 150B, 152B, 184B, 261A, 283A
Zambezia, 178B, 198B
Zambia, 340A, 350A, 351A
Zamenhof, Ludovic, 281B
Zamora, Alcalá (president of Spain), 312A
Zampieri, Domenico, 185C
Zand dynasty. *See* Persia
Zanzibar, 172B, 251A, 273A, 281A, 283A, 349A, 351A. *See also* Tanzania
  and Britain, 283A
  government, 359A
  slave trade, 275A
  and United Nations, 348A
Zapata, Emiliano, 292C, 294C, 302C
Zápolya, John (king of Hungary), 156A, 158A, 160A, 162A
Zapotec culture, 36C, 48C, 50C, 61A, 73A
Zapotec Valley, 85A
Zara, 304A
Zaria, 152B, 160B
Zauditu (empress of Ethiopia), 299A
Zborov, 300A
Zealots, 36B, 128B
Zedekiah (king of Judah), 14B
Zeeland, 128A, 136A
Zelaya, José Santos, 282C
Zemeckis, Robert, 381C
Zen order, 109C
Zenger, Peter, 211A
Zeno (emperor of Byzantium), 60B
Zeno of Citium, 23C
Zenobia (queen of Palmyra), 48B
zeppelins, 296A, 298A
Zeus, 19C, 22A, 27C
Zhang Zhongjing, 45B
Zhao Ziyang (prime minister of China), 365A
Zhitomir, 330A
Zia-ul-Haq, Muhammad (president of Pakistan), 363A, 373A
Ziegfeld, Florenz, 291C
"Ziegfeld Follies," 291C
Ziegler, Karl, 331B
Zimba, 168B, 172B, 174B
Zimbabwe, 81C, 90C, 109B, 134C, 140B, 176B, 185C, 281A, 340A, 364A, 365A, 371A
Zinnemann, Fred, 341C, 353C
Zinzendorf, Nikolaus Ludwig, Graf von, 209C
Zizka, Jan, 137B
Zobeide, tomb of, 77C
Zöe (empress of Byzantium), 92B
Zog I (king of Albania), 310A, 336B
Zola, Émile, 273C, 286A
Zollverein, 252A, 262A
Zonca, Vittorio, 177B
zoo, 47B
zoological gardens, 99B
Zorba the Greek (Kazantzakis), 337C
Zorndorf, battle of, 216A
Zoroaster, 15C
Zoroastrianism, Zoroastrians, 15C, 49A
Zoser (king of Egypt), 3C
Zulu, 176B, 243A, 255A, 277A
Zuni, 109A
Zurawna, Peace of, 196A
Zurich, 146A, 155C, 264A
  battle of, 234A
  Churchill in, 336B
  Dada art in, 299C
  Treaty of, 264A
Zuse, Konrad, 335B, 339B
Zwingli, Ulrich, 155C
Zworykin, Vladimir, 311B, 321B

ATE DUE
from the room.
reference